CASES AND MATERIALS ON
AMERICAN PROPERTY LAW

Sixth Edition

■ ■ ■

By

Sheldon F. Kurtz
Percy Bordwell Professor of Law
University of Iowa Law School

Herbert Hovenkamp
Ben V. & Dorothy Willie Professor of Law
University of Iowa Law School

Carol Necole Brown
Professor of Law
University of North Carolina Law School

AMERICAN CASEBOOK SERIES®

WEST®
A Thomson Reuters business

Mat #41035114

COPYRIGHT © 1987, 1993 WEST PUBLISHING CO.
© West, a Thomson Business, 1999, 2003, 2007
© 2012 Thomson Reuters
    610 Opperman Drive
    St. Paul, MN 55123
    1–800–313–9378
Printed in the United States of America

ISBN: 978–0–314–26535–7

To our late parents
(Abraham Kurtz and Rosalyn Stern,
Bert Hovenkamp and Henrietta Hovenkamp,
Allen S. Brown, Jr. and Valerie J. Brown),
our spouses (Alice Kurtz, Christina Bohannan,
and Paul Clinton Harris, Sr.) and to all of our
children and grandchildren.

PREFACE

Property law is a product of scarcity and politics. Without scarcity, property law would be unnecessary. Without politics it would be impossible. Judges, legislators, administrators and constitutional conventions respond to scarcity by making political judgments that some individual or group should be granted or denied a "property right." The sum of these judgments is our American law of property.

Political judgments can be either good or bad. Thus to say that authoritative judgments creating property rights are political is not to impeach their authority, practicability, or even their virtue. Rather, it serves to underscore the fact that the creation of every property right is attended by controversy over scarce resources. Every outcome produces both winners and losers. A decision of a judge or legislator may be based on natural law, morality, economic efficiency, perceived utility, or even corruption; but invariably it gives someone wealth at the expense of someone else. No area of law is more exciting than the law allocating property rights.

This casebook combines a set of traditional legal materials drawn from state and federal court decisions and statutes, with historical, economic and social science materials designed to add important perspective to the law students' appreciation of property rights in the American legal system. These added materials—particularly the economic notes—are presented in such a way that the instructor can safely ignore them without substantial loss of integrity to the course. However, this book makes no presumptions about prior training. Even the materials on the economics of property rights can be read with confidence by the careful student untrained in economics.

This book is designed to satisfy the needs of property curricula containing from three to six semester units of property law. Chapters one through eight treat the traditional "private," or common law of property. Notable here are greater amounts of jurisprudential materials than many property casebooks contain, a variety of materials in chapters one and two to develop tools of legal methodology and analysis, additional materials on the interrelationship of laws relating to persons and property, a greater emphasis on both history and recent judicial decisions in chapter four on the law of estates and future interests, an emphasis in chapter six on nonmarital or "extramarital" alternatives to the law of marital estates, and an economically-oriented section on rent control in chapter seven, designed to give the students a brief exposure to the many conflicts between price regulation and private property rights.

Chapter eight examines the law of servitudes as a privately created and market driven set of land use control devices. Chapters nine through thirteen then examine more explicitly "regulatory" areas of property law—nuisance, eminent domain and regulatory takings, zoning and other forms of land-use

planning, the problem of housing discrimination, and regulation of cooperatives and condominiums. This edition features a revised and somewhat
streamlined approach to the law of servitudes, a nuisance chapter more
oriented toward the Second Restatement of Torts, and significant attention to
the public law problems of regulatory takings and the expanded range of
housing discrimination law.

Finally, chapters fourteen through sixteen are an overview of the law of
conveyancing, focusing on the contracting process, deeds and delivery, and
title assurance devices. We treat the market for real property for what it is: a
market, although a rather complex one.

The authors are indebted to our many students and research assistants
whose comments and suggestions have contributed to refinements of this
book over the years. We salute the most recent crop of them, namely, Hassan
Beydoun, Nicole Burgmeier, Christina Diane Cress, Bryce Dalton, Emily
Ironside, Andrew Roff, and Jon Scott. We would also like to express our
appreciation for the institutional support of the University of Iowa College of
Law and the University of Iowa Law School Foundation.

S.F.K
H.H
C.N.B

May, 2012

SUMMARY OF CONTENTS

———

TABLE OF CONTENTS

TABLE OF CASES

The principal cases are in bold type. Cases cited or discussed in the text are in roman type. References are to pages. Cases cited in principal cases and within other quoted materials are not included.

CASES AND MATERIALS ON
AMERICAN
PROPERTY LAW

Sixth Edition

CHAPTER 1

ACQUISITION OF PROPERTY RIGHTS: A FIRST LOOK

■ ■ ■

"That is property to which the following label can be attached: To the world: Keep off, unless you have my permission, which I may grant or withhold.

Signed: Private Citizen

Endorsed: The State"[1]

§ 1.1 INTRODUCTION

Imagine the isolated world of Robinson Crusoe, who lives alone on a deserted island. In order to provide shelter, Robinson builds a tree house. Who owns the tree house? If Robinson owns the tree house, certain attributes of ownership should follow. Can you state what all or some of these attributes are? If you cannot state them, why can't you? If you can't state them, does that suggest that your initial conclusion that Robinson owns the tree house may have been wrong?

Many months after Robinson lands on the deserted island, Friday comes to the island. Friday also seeks shelter on the island, finds the tree house built by Robinson, and attempts to exclude Robinson from any further use of the tree house even though Robinson claims that he owns the tree house. If they are unable to agree voluntarily which of them owns the tree house, how, in all likelihood, will their ownership dispute be resolved?

Suppose several months after Friday lands on the island you arrive on the island and Robinson and Friday who have been unable to resolve their dispute agree that you should decide who owns the tree house. How would you decide the dispute?

Suppose you decide that Robinson owns the tree house. Under what circumstances, if any, will Friday abide by your decision? If Friday refuses to abide by your decision, what do you propose to do to him?

---

1. F. Cohen, Dialogue on Private Property, 9 Rutgers L. Rev. 357, 374 (1954).

1

If you decide that Robinson owns the tree house, what are the consequences, other than that Robinson can exclude Friday from the tree house? For example, could Robinson use the tree house in a manner that would cause harm to Friday? Could Robinson refuse to permit Friday to build a tree house in an adjacent tree or require that any tree house Friday builds in the adjacent tree be aesthetically complementary to Robinson's tree house? Could Robinson refuse to sell his tree house to Friday for no reason other than that Friday was black?

If, as we suspect, you assumed your only choice was to decide that either Robinson or Friday "owned" the tree house, why is that? For example, you could have decided they both had an equal interest in the tree house. If you opted against shared ownership, does that suggest some prejudice on your part about how property rights should be allocated when conflicts over the ownership and use of property arise?

Of course, you realize that Robinson, Friday and yourself are merely fictional representatives of a much larger society where conflicts continuously arise among persons concerning "ownership" of things. You represent the state while the Robinsons might be finders of lost watches or the owners of factories; the Fridays may be persons who have borrowed goods or neighbors of a factory upon whose land the smoke and soot from the factory are deposited. The determination of the conflicting claims of persons in things is often rationalized on the basis of one or more theories that purport to explain why property rights are or should be recognized. An introduction to these theories follows.

§ 1.2 WHAT IS PROPERTY?

FRIEDMAN, THE LAW OF THE LIVING, THE LAW OF THE DEAD; PROPERTY, SUCCESSION, AND SOCIETY, 1966 WIS.L.REV. 340–349

"Property" is ... a difficult concept; a great variety of definitions have been advanced. According to Wilbert E. Moore, property consists of "institutionally defined and regulated rights of persons (or other social units) in scarce values." Willard Hurst has defined property as the "legitimate power to initiate decisions on the use of economic assets." These definitions (and others) emphasize two aspects of the meaning of property: first, what actions can be lawfully taken by the holder of rights (the "owner" of property); and second, what are the objects ("scarce values" or "economic assets") with respect to which such actions can be taken. Grave problems arise if we try to stretch these or similar definitions to include all cultures and laws of every place and every time conceivable. But for our own legal system we may regard these as adequate working definitions. They say that for us property is something of value, an asset. It is something, in other words, which can be bought, sold, or given away. The legal system defines what it is that can legitimately be treated by private persons as an economic asset—for instance, a house, a horse, or a stock certificate. It also defines what is *not* property to be bought and sold, such as the Brooklyn Bridge or a judgeship. The legal system also describes what kinds of decisions can be made with regard to economic assets, and how these decisions must or may be carried out. It defines markets, and the formalities of markets. Land can be sold, but the instrument of sale must be in writing. Stock in public corporations is traded through stock exchanges. Liquor may be sold, but in some towns not on Sunday, or only in bottles and not by the drink, or in authorized liquor stores only.

A basic fact of our social and legal system is that assets may be individually owned, and indeed usually are. Property rights, in other words, are generally held by individuals. Two or more persons may hold "undivided" interests in a piece of property, but the legal system insists for the most part on analyzing these interests as divisible though not currently divided. True joint ownership is the exception, not the rule. Ownership by a social collective—the "family" or the "clan"—is virtually unknown. By way of exception, some . . . [s]tates recognize the institution of community property. Under this system, income received and property acquired by a husband and wife during marriage belong to the marital "community." As long as the marriage lasts, "the spouses are the joint owners, or partners, with respect to gains and losses." In the rest of the country, husband and wife can and do live together in one house, eat out of the same dishes, drive in the same car, and sleep in the same bed, while "title" to each of these objects theoretically resides in one or the other, but not both unless special arrangements have been made to assume joint ownership. And the locus of title will be placed in one or the other, legally speaking, regardless of whether one or the other or both have ever given a moment's thought to who holds "title" to the assets.

Ownership by social collectives (such as the "family" or the "clan") is common in other societies. Collective ownership can be used as a device to ensure automatic succession to property rights, in contrast to an individual-property system with free transfer of property during lifetime and at death. A collectivity can be immortal though the members are not. An extended family need never die; its property can serve new masters in each generation without any formal transfer from individual owner to individual owner.

Though our society does not permit ownership of property by extended families, it does recognize ownership by aggregates akin to collectives. The government, business corporations, or churches may own property since they are "legal entities" (treated for some purposes as if individuals). And since these entities are or can be immortal, they may dispense with the need to be governed by some rules of succession which bind individuals. For example, cities and businesses never execute wills.

There are, of course, rules of property succession for collectives just as there are for individuals—but they are different rules. The right to sell corporate assets is vested in officers of the corporation, and they in turn are chosen through definite procedures, partly determined by law, partly by custom. The presidency of the corporation itself, though an "asset" of tremendous value, is not "property," which is simply a way of saying that the mode of succession applicable to the office is different than the mode of succession for houses, cows, and debentures. The same thing is true of the Presidency of the United States—a position of awesome power which, in addition, carries with it an income of more than 100,000 dollars a year. The Presidency is not "property," however, because it is not (conventionally) bought, sold, or given away; rather, succession to this office proceeds through the votes of the people. And, if the President dies in office, his successor is not named in the President's will; the Vice–President automatically assumes the role.

In other words, in our legal system a distinction can be made between valuable assets which are and those which are not within the system of the law of property. The law of property is only one—admittedly a very important one—of the various sets of rights which govern succession, and hence social continuity. It is perfectly clear that the distinction between assets which are within and those which are without the property system cannot be drawn in terms of inherent characteristics of the assets themselves. Many offices and positions in our society (the Presidency, for example) are not property. They are not capable of being bought, sold, given away, or inherited. This is not because these offices are incapable of market treatment. Some municipal positions do change hands illegally in a secret market. Hereditary offices were and are known to many societies. In some societies, wives are bought and sold, that is, treated in the same manner as our society treats "property." Land in ... [some countries] has been totally nationalized; it belongs to the state and may not (overtly) be bought and sold; in our country, there is a vigorous market in land. And so it goes. Clearly, the line between property and not-property is a social line, and just as clearly, it is drawn for social reasons. The proper functioning of our system of government depends, we think, on removing the right to vote from the property system and forbidding the purchase of votes. Otherwise economic and political power would coincide in a way thought to be extremely dangerous to democracy.

The line between property and not-property is not the only significant legal boundary from the standpoint of social continuity. Other lines are also important. There are not two principles of succession in our legal system—the property principle and the not-property principle—but many. Succession to the Presidency is governed by election, and this is characteristic of many other offices as well, although many of course are appointive. Still another principle of succession, the hereditary principle, is not formally used in our society to determine succession to offices and jobs, though informal examples can be found in craft unions and small business firms. In general, rules of succession to *office* stand outside of the property system. This does not mean that there are no "rights" to an office; the legitimately selected officeholder does not have a property right in the market sense, but he can enforce his rights by recourse to the courts if necessary. In general, office passes from the living to the living (though provision is made for succession in the event of death).

In public offices, rules of succession are laid down by positive law (that is, by statute and judicial rule). Office is not to be bought, sold, or inherited. Life tenure is a rarity, though federal judges do have it. Private positions, offices, and jobs have their own rules of succession. These rules are far too diverse for a summary statement. Consider, for example, the complexity of succession to jobs in a factory, an office, a university, a hospital; consider the various retirement provisions (mandatory and permissive) in institutions, the rules of seniority and of severance; consider the different modes of succession to executive offices in large corporations, small shops, and charitable foundations. Mostly, rules of succession to positions in private organizations are provided for by contract or by custom, rather than by positive law. But there have been important legal interventions. Through law, the power of unions has been solidified or at least ratified, and this means that for many workers a principle of seniority has replaced a principle of succession in which full discretion is in the hands of the employer.

The seniority system in industrial jobs is one of many recent changes in the direction of regularizing and standardizing job succession and hence job tenure. The right to a particular job is increasingly under legal protection, or the protection of strong occupational groups. Job tenure seems closely related, historically, to the permanence and stability of the employing institution. Extremely stable organizations may even be able and willing to guarantee life rights and security to some of their employees. The Roman Catholic Church, for example, does this for priests and members of religious orders. The civil service, the armed forces, and the tenured staffs of universities (public and private) provide examples of similar commitments, somewhat less sweeping. Business corporations have resisted the notion of granting tenure to industrial workers, but they have made more and more concessions to the unions which tend in this direction. The major corporate employers are profitable, vast, and economically stable. They approach, in other words, the permanence of a government or a church. Tenure within such bureaucratic organizations is feasible, though small, shaky businesses would find it impossible to grant firm rights of tenure and succession.

Job tenure is like a property right in that it is legally secured from adverse action. But in other senses it is not property. Our legal system closely associates the concept of property with economic risk. Maximum freedom to "initiate economic decision" with regard to a valuable right means the power to make economic gambles on the basis of that right; tenure in a job usually means a limitation on both risk and opportunity. Job tenure rights are nontransferable, are at most life interests, and give rise to no conventional problems of succession at death because they cannot be inherited.

There are, however, certain perquisites of office and job which more closely resemble transferable assets, in the sense that they are money claims that arise out of the employment contract and, like bank accounts, draw interest and increase with the passage of time. Pension rights, both public and private, are among the most valuable fringe benefits in many jobs. We need not concern ourselves with the question whether and under what circumstances pension rights are "property" in the sense that they cannot be taken away from their holder without his consent, or at least without compensation. Pension rights, by and large, are *not* property in the sense of marketable assets. They are nontransferable. Though many pension plans include death benefits for the worker's survivors, they reject the principle of freedom of testation and limit inheritance to the immediate family circle of the deceased.... We may, if we wish, call this a program of "social insurance," but it is proper to bear in mind how different it is from ordinary insurance. Ordinary insurance, for example, is an economic asset; it is property in every sense of the word. Social insurance has been boldly and frankly removed from the property system.

In fact, social security rights, like some private pension rights, are not "property" even in the sense that the rights of contributors are safe from the risk of government encroachment. In theory, Congress retains the right to abolish the whole social security system and use the amounts contributed to build rockets. In practice, even the mention of such a possibility is political suicide. In 1964 Senator Goldwater did his cause grievous harm merely by suggesting a change in the nature of the program....

Some assets stand outside the property system because they are permanently vested in the commonwealth. Not all property is of this type merely because it is publicly owned. The typewriters in the local office of Internal Revenue are "public" only in the sense that the government holds title. These machines were bought in the market and can be declared surplus and sold there. Since Internal Revenue (or at least its parent) will never die, the typewriters are not subject to a last will nor is the government likely to give them away. Acquisition, price, and disposal are befuddled with red tape, but this could also be true of business bureaucracy. And there is nothing public about access to these typewriters—an ordinary citizen cannot come in off the street and type on "his" machine.

City streets, national parks, zoos, and museums are public property of a different sort, and access to these is truly open to all. Anyone may go to the zoo (though the giraffes and lions, like the government's typewriters, are not to be used by the multitudes). A park bench illustrates what might be called common property. It is open to everyone, but obviously only one or two can sit on it at any given moment. Access is by priority in time. A man may sit on a park bench and admire the view as long as he likes; the law will enforce this use-right (if necessary) against an intruder who would force the man off. But there are no rights in a park bench apart from physical possession; the bench cannot be reserved. Succession, then, is purely a matter of one physical occupation following another physical occupation in orderly sequence, and each member of the public has a potential, limited use-right—limited to the length of time he retains physical possession. Rights to common property differ subtly from instance to instance, but the average citizen knows them almost instinctively. He learns his rights to streets, parks, and other public places as he grows up in civil society. His use-rights are completely outside of the property system, and have been so adjusted and articulated as to maximize the ease of transportation and circulation on which economic and social order depend. Homely rights to occupy a park bench and to walk the streets are functionally similar to the common-law duties of the innkeeper and the common carrier of freight, both of whom were obligated to serve the public. These positive duties of the common carrier and the innkeeper could just as easily have been analyzed as positive rights held in common by the members of the public. They were rights that guaranteed free access to use-rights necessary to ensure a workable transportation and communication network. The innkeeper and the carrier had to be paid, of course; their services were not free. But there is no essential difference between public facilities which are free and those which charge admission. When a common facility is not free, the price may be fixed or the supply rationed. In any event, one cannot buy up all available facilities. In the case of the park bench, the rationing of access is automatic—a consequence of the rule that limits the user to so much of the bench as he can physically occupy. Indeed, all common property embodies a system of rationing of access and succession: this is what makes such property common.

Historically, fields and pastures held in common were of great economic significance—for example, in medieval England or in colonial New England. The New England commons, where it survives, is no longer used to graze cattle or grow crops. It may be just another city park, treasured for its central location and antiquated charm. Historically, the commons depended upon a particular mode of agriculture and a particular style of land tenure. But recent generations have seen a tremendous expansion of common property for purposes of recreation, conservation, and aesthetics. To a great extent this trend comes from doubt in the public mind as to the fallibility of the market system. Uncontrolled, the free market might sell Mount Vernon to real-estate promoters and Yellowstone to the oil companies; the redwoods would follow the path of the heath hen and the auk. To prevent the destruction of irreplaceable assets, they have been removed from the property system (the system of markets and inheritances) and vested in the public. In place of market rules of succession, there are rules of limited physical use-rights. Title is in the government as "trustee" for the common good.

* * *

NOTES AND QUESTIONS

Professor Friedman appears to be saying two quite different things: First, something is property if it is scarce (if there was as much of it as anybody wanted, nothing would have any value, and property rights would be unnecessary); Second, something is property if the legal system identifies it as such by permitting it to be exchanged on the market.

Are both of these statements "definitions" of property? If so, aren't they inconsistent? For example, human organs for transplant are scarce and therefore quite expensive, so they are "property" under the first definition. However, federal law prohibits the sale of human organs, so they are not "property" under the second definition. Are human organs property? Perhaps Friedman is saying that *both* of these things must be true if something is to be called "property."

§ 1.3 ACQUISITION OF PROPERTY RIGHTS BY CAPTURE

PIERSON v. POST

Supreme Court of New York (1805).
3 Caines 175.

This was an action of trespass on the case commenced in a justice's court, by the present defendant against the now plaintiff.

The declaration stated that Post, being in possession of certain dogs and hounds under his command, did, "upon a certain wild and uninhabited, unpossessed and waste land, called the beach, find and start one of those noxious beasts called a fox," and whilst there hunting, chasing and pursuing the same with his dogs and hounds, and when in view thereof, Pierson, well knowing the fox was so hunted and pursued, did, in the sight of Post, to prevent his catching the same, kill and carry it off. A verdict having been rendered for the plaintiff below, the defendant there sued out a *certiorari,* and now assigned for error, that the declaration and the matters therein contained were not sufficient in law to maintain an action.

* * *

TOMPKINS, J. delivered the opinion of the court. This cause comes before us on a return to a *certiorari* directed to one of the justices of Queens county.

The question submitted by the counsel in this cause for our determination is, whether Lodowick Post, by the pursuit with his hounds in the manner alleged in his declaration, acquired such a right to, or property in, the fox as will sustain an action against Pierson for killing and taking him away?

The cause was argued with much ability by the counsel on both sides, and presents for our decision a novel and nice question. It is admitted that a fox is an animal *feræ naturæ*, and that property in such animals is acquired by occupancy only. These admissions narrow the discussion to the simple question of what acts amount to occupancy, applied to acquiring right to wild animals.

If we have recourse to the ancient writers upon general principles of law, the judgment below is obviously erroneous. Justinians Institutes, [citation omitted] and Fleta, [citation omitted] adopt the principle, that pursuit alone vests no property or right in the huntsman; and that even pursuit, accompanied with wounding, is equally ineffectual for that purpose, unless the animal be actually taken. The same principle is recognised by Bracton, [citation omitted].

Puffendorf, lib, [citation omitted] defines occupancy of beasts *feræ naturæ*, to be the actual corporal possession of them, and Bynkershock is cited as coinciding in this definition. It is indeed with hesitation that Puffendorf affirms that a wild beast mortally wounded, or greatly maimed, cannot be fairly intercepted by another, whilst the pursuit of the person inflicting the wound continues. The foregoing authorities are decisive to show that mere pursuit gave Post no legal right to the fox, but that he became the property of Pierson, who intercepted and killed him.

It therefore only remains to inquire whether there are any contrary principles, or authorities, to be found in other books, which ought to induce a different decision. Most of the cases which have occurred in England, relating to property in wild animals, have either been discussed and decided upon the principles of their positive statute regulations, or have arisen between the huntsman and the owner of the land upon which beasts *feræ naturæ* have been apprehended; the former claiming them by title of occupancy, and the latter *ratione soli*. Little satisfactory aid can, therefore, be derived from the English reporters.

Barbeyrac, in his notes on Puffendorf, does not accede to the definition of occupancy by the latter, but on the contrary, affirms, that actual bodily seizure is not, in all cases, necessary to constitute possession of wild animals. He does not, however, describe the acts which, according to his ideas, will amount to an appropriation of such animals to private use, so as to exclude the claims of all other persons, by title of occupancy, to the same animals; and he is far from averring that pursuit alone is sufficient for that purpose. To a certain extent, and as far as Barbeyrac appears to me to go, his objections to Puffendorf's definition of occupancy are reasonable and correct. That is to say, that actual bodily seizure is not indispensable to acquire right to, or possession of, wild beasts; but that, on the contrary, the mortal wounding of such beasts, by one not abandoning his pursuit, may, with the utmost propriety, be deemed possession of him; since, thereby, the pursuer manifests an unequivocal intention of appropriating the animal to his individual use, has deprived him of his natural liberty, and brought him within his certain control. So also, encompassing and securing such animals with nets and toils, or otherwise intercepting them in such a manner as to deprive them of their natural liberty, and render escape impossible, may justly be deemed to give possession of them to those persons who, by their industry and labor, have used such means of apprehending them.

. . . The case now under consideration is one of mere pursuit, and presents no circumstances or acts which can bring it within the definition of occupancy by Puffendorf, . . . or the ideas of Barbeyrac upon that subject. . . .

We are the more readily inclined to confine possession or occupancy of beasts *feræ naturæ*, within the limits prescribed by the learned authors above cited, for the sake of certainty, and preserving peace and order in society. If the first seeing, starting, or pursuing such animals, without having so wounded, circumvented or ensnared them, so as to deprive them of their natural liberty, and subject them to the control of their pursuer, should afford the basis of actions against others for intercepting and killing them, it would prove a fertile source of quarrels and litigation.

However uncourteous or unkind the conduct of Pierson towards Post, in this instance, may have been, yet his act was productive of no injury or damage for which a legal remedy can be applied. We are of opinion the judgment below was erroneous, and ought to be reversed.

LIVINGSTON, J. My opinion differs from that of the court. Of six exceptions, taken to the proceedings below, all are abandoned except the third, which reduces the controversy to a single question.

Whether a person who, with his own hounds, starts and hunts a fox on waste and uninhabited ground, and is on the point of seizing his prey, acquires such an interest in the animal, as to have a right of action against another, who in view of the huntsman and his dogs in full pursuit, and with knowledge of the chase, shall kill and carry him away?

This is a knotty point, and should have been submitted to the arbitration of sportsmen, without poring over Justinian, Fleta, Bracton, Puffendorf, Locke, Barbeyrac, or Blackstone, all of whom have been cited; they would have had no difficulty in coming to a prompt and correct conclusion. In a court thus constituted, the skin and carcass of poor reynard would have been properly disposed of, and a precedent set, interfering with no usage or custom which the experience of ages has sanctioned, and which must be so well known to every votary of Diana. But the parties have referred the question to our judgment, and we must dispose of it as well as we can, from the partial lights we possess, leaving to a higher tribunal, the correction of any mistake which we may be so unfortunate as to make. By the pleadings it is admitted that a fox is a "wild and noxious beast." Both parties have regarded him, as the law of nations does a pirate, *"hostem humani generis,"* and although *"de mortuis nil nisi bonum,"* be a maxim of our profession, the memory of the deceased has not been spared. His depredations on farmers and on barn yards, have not been forgotten; and to put him to death wherever found, is allowed to be meritorious, and of public benefit. Hence it follows, that our decision should have in view the greatest possible encouragement to the destruction of an animal, so cunning and ruthless in his career. But who would keep a pack of hounds; or what gentleman, at the sound of the horn, and at peep of day, would mount his steed, and for hours together, ... pursue the windings of this wily quadruped, if, just as night came on, and his stratagems and strength were nearly exhausted, a saucy intruder, who had not shared in the honors or labors of the chase, were permitted to come in at the death, and bear away in triumph the object of pursuit? Whatever Justinian may have thought of the matter, it must be recollected that his code was compiled many hundred years ago, and it would be very hard indeed, at the distance of so many centuries, not to have a right to establish a rule for ourselves. In his day, we read of no order of men who made it a business, in the language of the declaration in this cause, "with hounds and dogs to find, start, pursue, hunt, and chase," these animals, and that, too, without any other motive than the preservation of Roman poultry; if this diversion had been then in fashion, the lawyers who composed his institutes, would have taken care not to pass it by, without suitable encouragement. If any thing, therefore, in the digests or pandects shall appear to militate against the defendant in error, who, on this occasion, was the fox hunter, we have only to say *tempora mutantur;* and if men themselves change with the times, why should not laws also undergo an alteration?

It may be expected, however, by the learned counsel, that more particular notice be taken of their authorities. I have examined them all, and feel great difficulty in determining, whether to acquire dominion over a thing, before in common, it be sufficient that we barely see it, or know where it is, or wish for it, or make a declaration of our will respecting it; or whether, in the case of wild beasts, setting a trap, or lying in wait, or starting, or pursuing, be enough; or if an actual wounding, or killing, or bodily tact and occupation be necessary. Writers on general law, who have favored us with their speculations on these points, differ on them all; but, great as is the diversity of sentiment among them, some conclusion must be adopted on the question immediately before us. After mature deliberation, I embrace that of Barbeyrac, as the most rational, and least liable to objection. If at liberty, we might imitate the courtesy of a certain emperor, who, to avoid giving offence to the advocates of any of these different doctrines, adopted a middle course, and by ingenious distinctions, rendered it difficult to say (as often happens after a fierce and angry contest) to whom the palm of victory belonged. He ordained, that if a beast be followed with large dogs and hounds, he shall belong to the hunter, not to the chance occupant; and in like manner, if he be killed or wounded with a lance or sword; but if chased with beagles only, then he passed to the captor, not to the first pursuer. If slain with a dart, a sling, or a bow, he fell to the hunter, if still in chase, and not to him who might afterwards find and seize him.

Now, as we are without any municipal regulations of our own, and the pursuit here, for aught that appears on the case, being with dogs and hounds of imperial stature, we are at liberty to adopt one of the provisions

Dissenter's
holding

just cited, which comports also with the learned conclusion of Barbeyrac, that property in animals *feræ naturæ* may be acquired without bodily touch or manucaption, provided the pursuer be within reach, or have a reasonable prospect (which certainly existed here) of taking, what he has thus discovered an intention of converting to his own use.

When we reflect also that the interest of our husbandmen, the most useful of men in any community, will be advanced by the destruction of a beast so pernicious and incorrigible, we cannot greatly err, in saying, that a pursuit like the present, through waste and unoccupied lands, and which must inevitably and speedily have terminated in corporal possession, or bodily seisin, confers such a right to the object of it, as to make any one a wrongdoer, who shall interfere and shoulder the spoil. The justice's judgment ought therefore, in my opinion, to be affirmed.

Judgment of reversal.

NOTE ON BRIEFING CASES

Pierson v. Post is likely to be one of the first judicial opinions you will read. At this stage of your career it is important that you "brief" this case. Your brief will help you prepare and review for class. It will also help you prepare for your final examination.

A case "brief" is a synopsis of a case. While your professors may differ (and differ widely) regarding what should be in the brief, ultimately what is included is what *you* find most helpful to serve the two primary goals of the brief. Most professors would say that at a minimum the brief should include the following: (1) A statement of the **facts** of the case that bear on the ultimate outcome of the case, (2) a statement of the **issue or question** or the multiple **issues or questions** that the parties seek to have the court resolve, (3) the **holding or rule of law** adopted by the court to resolve each issue, and (4) the **rationale** used by the court to support its holding.

Your brief could easily include much more information such as: (1) the procedural history of the case, including which party won at the trial level and all of the appellate courts that heard the case, (2) the type of remedy sought such as damages, injunction or declaratory relief, (3) the respective arguments of the litigants, (4) a discussion of the precedents and governing statutes, if any, relied upon by the court, and (5) a discussion of the policy arguments made by the litigants or relied on by the court. It is often helpful to conclude the brief with your personal assessment of the rule adopted and the rationale for it, as well as a list of questions you might have about the case that you hope might be resolved in or out of class. Incidentally, the skills of issue spotting, argument development, and rationale articulation also come into play when taking a final exam.

Of course, to do all this, and to do it correctly, takes much time and effort, like the great abstract painter who must first learn to "paint fruit." But, given that the skill of briefing cases is important to both law students and practicing lawyers, your time briefing cases will be time well spent in laying the foundations for your successful study and practice of the law.

NOTES AND QUESTIONS

1. This is your first Property law case. Behind the facts stated in the court's opinion lies a greater drama than is reflected in the court's dry recitation of the events preceding the lawsuit. Immediately following the events on the beach, what is likely to have happened? Did Post simply walk from the beach to the courthouse and file a suit against Pierson? Did some judge simply hold in Post's favor without giving Pierson an opportunity to defend himself? Is the opinion you have just read the opinion of the court in which Post initially filed his suit? If not, how did the suit get to the Supreme Court of New York?

2. Have you taken care to investigate the meaning of all the words and phrases used in the court's opinion that are new to your vocabulary? For example, what does the phrase "trespass on the case" mean? Precisely what is a "writ of certiorari?" Immediately below the title of the case appears "3 Caines 175 (1805)." What is this?

3. At common law there were numerous procedural cubbyholes within which a lawsuit had to fit for the lawsuit to be properly brought before the court. The principal common law forms of action were:

(a) "trespass quare clausum fregit" (an action for money damages for defendant's direct interference with the plaintiff's actual possession of plaintiff's lands);

(b) "trespass de bonis asportatis" (an action for money damages for defendant's injury to plaintiff's personal property resulting from a "carrying away" of goods);

(c) "trespass on the case" (an action for money damages for defendant's indirect or consequential injury to plaintiff's chattels or land resulting from the defendant's wrongful act);

(d) "trover" (action to recover the value of chattel wrongfully taken or retained by the defendant);

(e) "replevin" and "detinue" (actions to recover the possession of chattels wrongfully taken from the plaintiff's possession by the defendant), and;

(f) "ejectment" (action to recover the possession of the plaintiff's real property). This action did not necessarily require the plaintiff to prove an "absolute" title. Therefore, this action was unlike the action "trespass to try title" where plaintiff's title had to be proved.[1]

Each common law form of action had its nuances that if not strictly adhered to could have resulted in the dismissal of the plaintiff's suit. See generally W. Stoebuck & D. Whitman, The Law of Property, § 1.3 at 7–10, 3d ed. (2000).

While modern forms of procedure have happily eliminated the technicalities of the common law forms, the underlying theories of an action continue to

---

1. In England, the action of ejectment required plaintiff to prove title; in America, proof of title was not always necessary. See Tapscott v. Cobbs, 52 Va. 172, 11 Gratt. 172 (1854); *supra* ch. 3.

have vitality. As a lawyer representing a client, it is imperative that you be able to formulate a theory that should entitle your client to win. For example, if W wrongfully takes a watch from O and O sues to recover the watch, O's theory would be that O had prior possession of the watch and W took it from O without O's permission. What legal authority, if any, supports the notion that O could win if O established prior possession of the watch?

Consider the form of action brought by Post. What was it? In what important respect did Post's action fail in theory?

4. Procedurally, Pierson is challenging the action in the lower court by claiming that "the declarations and the matters therein contained were not sufficient in law to maintain an action." In modern parlance, this type of challenge might take the form of a motion to dismiss (demurrer), a summary judgment, a directed verdict or a judgment notwithstanding the verdict (i.e., judgment n.o.v.) depending upon when the challenge was made. In other words, Pierson claims that even if all of the facts alleged by Post are true, Post does not have a recognizable legal claim against him. In deciding the case in this context the appellate court assumes that all of the facts alleged in the declaration are true. Therefore, the appellate court answers the question: If all of Post's allegations are true (and the court assumes they are), is Post entitled to any relief against Pierson?

5. An initial difficulty in the development of American law resulted from the historical fact of the American Revolution. To what extent, if at all, were statutes of Parliament and decisions of the English judges to be regarded as authoritative by the courts of the states? States enacted so-called "reception statutes" limiting those laws of England that were authoritative within the state. For example, Virginia provided that: "the common law of England, all statutes or acts of Parliament made in aid of the common law prior to the fourth year of the reign of King James the first, and which are of a general nature, not local to that kingdom ... shall be considered as in full force and effect." Hennings, Virginia Stats. at Large, vol. 9 (1821) pg. 127. In a similar vein Article VII, § 13 of the New York State Constitution of 1821 provided that: "Such parts of the common law, and the acts of the legislature of the colony of New York, as together did form the law of the said colony" on April 19, 1775, "and of the convention of the State of New York," in force on April 20, 1777, would continue to be the law, unless altered or repealed or deemed repugnant. See generally Friedman, A History of American Law ch. 1 (2d ed. 1985).

The doctrine of *stare decisis* lies at the heart of the development of American case law.[2] Under this doctrine, once the highest court of the state has established a legal principle, that court and all lower courts of the state will adhere to that principle in deciding *similar* cases in the future unless the

---

2. "Case law" refers to law made by judges in the context of cases presented to them for decision by adverse parties seeking a settlement of a dispute. First year law school courses focused on traditional common law subjects like property, contract and torts, often leave law students with the erroneous impression that cases are the predominant source of law in this country. In fact, however, much of our state and federal law is reflected in legislative enactments of the federal Congress, state legislatures, and municipal governing bodies. Experienced attorneys invariably seek a solution to a problem by resort to statutes and ordinances before looking to the decisions of the courts.

principle is overturned by the highest court of the state in a later case or perhaps by a statute enacted by the appropriate legislative body. If the highest court of the state has spoken on a legal issue, it is said that its opinion is binding on the lower courts of that state and consequently controls the outcome of future similar cases. In the absence of a prior controlling decision from a higher court of the state, all courts of a state may look to the laws of other jurisdictions. However, the decisions of other jurisdictions are merely persuasive. In other words, the authorities in one state are not binding on the courts of other states.

Unfortunately, it is not always clear whether an earlier articulated legal principle from a state's higher court is controlling on the court in which a legal issue is being decided. Lawyers involved in the litigation process spend a good part of their time attempting to persuade the courts that what appears at first blush to be a binding precedent is in reality a legal principle established in a distinguishable case.

In certain cases the outcome of a legal question presented to a state court for decision may be affected by federal law. To the extent federal law applies to the facts of a case, it, rather than state law, controls because of the so-called "supremacy clause" in the United States Constitution. U.S. Const. Art. VI provides that "This Constitution, and the Laws of the United States which shall be made in Pursuance thereof ... shall be the Supreme Law of the Land. ..."

The court in Pierson v. Post relied upon no prior decisions of the courts of the State of New York and counsel for neither party apparently was able to discover any controlling legal precedent. What is the basis for this assumption? The court, however, appears to give some precedential weight to certain Roman and English text writers and at best distinguished one English case. See also Blackstone's Commentaries, vol. 1, book 2, pp. 388–395: Cooley's Edition (4th) vol. 1, p. 742; Kent's Commentaries (14th Ed. O.W. Holmes ed.) vol. 2, p. 348.

Given that there appeared to be no binding authority to support Post's argument, on what basis did Post's counsel advise him to litigate? What alternative means of settling the dispute might you have suggested? Judge Livingston suggested one form of alternative dispute resolution. Why didn't the parties resort to the procedure he recommended?

6.　The dissenting judge in *Pierson* cited Blackstone as one of a number of authors who had written on the law as applied to wild animals. Blackstone wrote:

> A qualified property may subsist in wild animals "by a man's reclaiming and making them tame by art, industry and education; or by so confining them within his own immediate power, that they cannot escape and use their natural liberty. ... These are no longer the property of a man, than while they continue in his keeping or actual possession; but if at any time they regain their natural liberty, his property instantly ceases; unless they have animum revertendi (the intention of returning), which is only to be known by their usual custom of returning. ... The deer that is chased out of my park or forest, and is instantly pursued by the keeper or forester, remains still in my possession, and I still preserve my qualified

Ferea Nature

property in them. But if they stray without my knowledge, and do not return in the usual manner, it is then lawful for any stranger to take them. But if a deer, or any wild animal reclaimed, hath a collar or other mark put upon him, and goes and returns at his pleasure; ... the owner's property in him still continues, and it is not lawful for any one else to take him; but otherwise, if the deer has been long absent without returning. . . .

In all these creatures, reclaimed from the wildness of their nature, the property is not absolute but defeasible; a property, that may be destroyed if they resume their ancient wildness and are found at large. . . . But while they thus continue my qualified or defeasible property, they are as much under the protection of the law, as if they were absolutely and indefeasibly mine; and an action will lie against any man that detains them from me, or unlawfully destroys them. It is also as much felony by common law to steal such of them as are fit for food, as it is to steal tame animals; but not so, if they are only kept for pleasure, curiosity, or whim, . . . because their value is not intrinsic. . . .'' Blackstone's Commentaries, vol. 1, book 2, pp. 388–395: Cooley's Edition (4th) vol. 1, p. 742; Kent's Commentaries (14th ed.) vol. 2, p. 348.

Blackstone's *Commentaries on the Laws of England* [1765–1769] was probably the single most important book on the common law ever written. Sir William Blackstone (1723–1780) wrote the *Commentaries* as a series of lectures for laymen on the English common law. At the time only Roman Law, civil law and ecclesiastical law were approved legal subjects at Oxford University, where Blackstone lectured. The *Commentaries'* genius was their simplicity and rationalization—more than any other book, they made the common law a respectable legal institution worthy of academic study.

Blackstone's *Commentaries* was even more influential in America than in England for two reasons. First, they were a compact (four volumes, generally published in the United States as two double-sized volumes) survey of all of the common law. Second, under the reception statutes American states typically adopted English common law decisions as precedential up to the time of the revolution, but then followed American decisions thereafter. Nearly all American editions were based on the Ninth English edition of Blackstone, published in 1783. An American editor then added notes of American cases since the Revolution. As a result, a lawyer could have a handy compendium of pre-Revolutionary English cases and post-Revolutionary American cases— precisely the mixture of precedent that the reception statutes mandated. The American edition, prepared by Thomas M. Cooley, is one of the most influential of the American editions. A judge who wanted to sound erudite could read Blackstone and then cite all the sources—including Justinian, Pufendorf, and Bracton—that Blackstone himself had cited. Indeed, the entire discussion of ancient authorities in Pierson v. Post is lifted right out of 2 Blackstone, *Commentaries* 389–90.

7.   In all likelihood, was the value of what Post sought to recover from Pierson greater or less than Post's cost in bringing the lawsuit? If you think the lawsuit cost more than any possible recovery, why did Post proceed? In such case, would you have advised Post to proceed with the suit?

8. The judges who heard Pierson v. Post disagreed on the result and wrote separate opinions. Judge Tompkins delivered the opinion of the majority. Over a period of time beginning roughly before the founding of the Republic, American courts, unlike their English counterparts, began to issue opinions of the court rather than seriatim opinions of each judge. Apparently, it was thought that a single opinion expressing the reasoning of the majority and not reflecting minor differences among the judges would be more persuasive.

The practice of writing opinions for the majority was not without its critics. Thomas Jefferson, in a letter to William Johnson dated June 12, 1823, stated: "I rejoice in the example you set of *seriatim* opinions.... Why should not every judge be asked his opinion and give it from the bench, if only by yea or nea. Besides ascertaining the fact of his opinion, which the public have a right to know in order to judge whether it is impeachable or not, it would show whether the opinions were unanimous or not and thus settle more exactly the weight of their authority." Dumbauld, Political Writings of Thomas Jefferson 148–49 (1955).

[margin note: Jefferson believed more value in]

9. The judges who decided Pierson v. Post were an illustrious lot. Judge Tompkins (1774–1825), who wrote the majority opinion, served as Governor of the State of New York from 1807 to 1817 and as Vice President of the United States under President Monroe from 1817 to 1825. Judge Livingston, the dissenter, was the brother-in-law of John Jay, the first Chief Justice of the United States. Livingston was appointed an Associate Justice of the United States Supreme Court by President Jefferson and served on the Court from 1807 to 1823.

10. Having read the majority and dissenting opinions, state precisely what the holding (i.e., the rule of law) of the majority was and the rationale that supported the majority decision. What rule of law would the dissenting judge have adopted and what rationale supports that rule? Do either or both opinions rationalize the rules they would adopt by resort to so-called "public policy" arguments? If so, what are they, and to what extent do you find them convincing?

*[margin note: *see case brief*]*

11. To what extent is the legal principle decided in Pierson v. Post applicable in the following cases:

(a) Suppose NewPost, a remote descendant of her ancestor immortalized for all law students in the case of Pierson v. Post, hunts a fox on *her family's lands*. Prior to her killing the fox, NewPierson comes upon the land, kills the fox and takes it away. If NewPost sues NewPierson, in your judgment who should win?

If you conclude NewPost should win, you obviously must conclude that Pierson v. Post is inapplicable or that it was wrongly decided, in which case it should be overruled. Our hunch is that you have decided it is not applicable. Why?

If you concluded that it would be inappropriate to apply Pierson v. Post in this case because in this case NewPierson trespassed on the NewPost family lands in order to kill the fox, what does that tell you about the importance of the location of the killing to the Pierson v. Post holding? What does this tell

by the
[past]
facts

you about how we can determine whether separate cases are "like" cases or "unlike" cases?

(b) Suppose NewPost was hunting a *bear* on the public beach and before she caught it NewPierson intercepted the bear and took it away. Would these facts be controlled by Pierson v. Post?

(c) Now let's make it tougher. Suppose in the case of Pierson v. Post, the facts were as stated by the court but the events did not take place on a public beach. Rather, Post started the fox and Pierson killed the fox on land owned by one Morton who is not related to either Post or Pierson and who gave neither of them permission to be on his land. Same result? Explain. Suppose Post was hunting on Morton's land with Morton's permission. Same result? Suppose Pierson was hunting on Morton's land with Morton's permission. Same result? Suppose both Pierson and Post were hunting on Morton's land with Morton's permission. Same result? See, e.g., Rexroth v. Coon, 15 R.I. 35, 23 A. 37 (1885).

(d) Suppose Post had wounded the fox, captured it, brought it home and put it in a cage. Pierson entered Post's land, released the fox from the cage and when it returned to the beach killed it. Post sues Pierson for the value of the fox. What result? See Haywood v. State, 41 Ark. 479 (1883); State v. House, 65 N.C. 315 (1871). But see Sollers v. Sollers, 77 Md. 148, 26 A. 188 (1893) (captured fish placed in contained inlet can be taken by another fisherman).

12. A, a professional fox hunter, shot and wounded a fox. After chasing the fox until nightfall A decided to abandon the chase until the next morning. During the night B shot and killed the fox. In a suit between A and B, to what extent, if any, could either of them appropriately rely on Pierson v. Post? See Buster v. Newkirk, 20 Johns (N.Y.) 75 (1822); Liesner v. Wanie, 156 Wis. 16, 145 N.W. 374 (1914).

13. O attracted wild geese to a pond on her land. The geese that were attracted to the pond would then eat the crops on land adjoining O's land that was owned by P. If P sues O for the value of P's lost crops, can P prevail? See Andrews v. Andrews, 242 N.C. 382, 88 S.E.2d 88 (1955).

Suppose wild geese congregated on O's land. O hired a pest control company to chase the birds away. The company successfully drove the birds off O's land. In doing so, however, the birds congregated on P's land causing him to contract histoplasmosis, a fungal infection. P sues O for damages. What result? See Glave v. Michigan Terminix Company, 159 Mich.App. 537, 407 N.W.2d 36 (1987).

14. It is often said that an acquired property right in a wild animal is lost if the wild animal escapes and returns to its native habitat. Suppose A imports a rare male grey fox which she uses to breed other foxes for their pelts. A lives in an area where red foxes, not grey foxes, are commonly found. One day A's male grey fox escapes and although A tried to recapture it, she was unsuccessful. The fox was shot and killed by B, a local farmer, to protect her chickens that were being stalked by the fox. B, in turn, sells the fox's pelt to C, a local trader.

(a) If A sues C to recover the pelt or its value, who should win? See E.A. Stephens & Co. v. Albers, 81 Colo. 488, 256 P. 15 (1927) (plaintiff entitled to value of pelt from buyer where pelt had been tattooed by plaintiff).

(b) If A sues B to recover the value of the pelt, who should win?

(c) Suppose A's fox had been fleeing across state owned land when B killed it. A sues B for the return of the pelt (or its value) and for lost profits resulting from the killing of the grey fox. What result and why? See Hughes v. Reese, 144 Miss. 304, 109 So. 731 (1926); Manning v. Mitcherson, 69 Ga. 447 (1883); Conti v. ASPCA, 77 Misc.2d 61, 353 N.Y.S.2d 288 (Civ.Ct.1974).

15. A operates a fishing boat in the Atlantic Ocean. A steers the boat in a circle, pulling a large net behind the boat for the purpose of enclosing a large school of fish. When A has 30' to go to complete the circle, B, another fisherman, powers his boat through the enclosure, drops his nets and completely encircles the fish. A sues B to recover the value of the fish. Did A acquire possession of the fish? Compare Young v. Hichens, 1 Dav. & Mer. 592, 6 Q.B. 606 (1844) (a substantial enclosure of a net around a school of fish did not give the fisherman possession because escape through the opening was possible) with State v. Shaw, 67 Ohio St. 157, 65 N.E. 875 (1902) (substantial enclosure sufficient to establish possession). If you conclude that A had possession notwithstanding the 30' opening, suppose B had been chasing a school of fish and unknowingly chased them through that opening and then removed them with his own nets. Same result?

16. Shelly's Scottish terrier, Sophie, runs away from home and is caught by a neighbor the same day. Shelly immediately requests Sophie's return but the neighbor refuses. Shelly sues to recover Sophie from the neighbor who claims to own Sophie by right of occupation. The neighbor claims that Shelly's rights were terminated when Sophie ran away from home. Do you agree? Cf., Morgan v. Kroupa, 167 Vt. 99, 702 A.2d 630 (1997) (public's interest in encouraging finders to care for and shelter lost pets can override title of prior possessor where the finder diligently but unsuccessfully sought for over one year to find the prior owner).

Suppose that the local dog pound captured Sophie and demanded that Shelly pay it $25 if he wanted the dog back. Can Shelly refuse to pay this fine because Sophie is his? If Shelly were liable to pay the pound, would he also be liable to pay the neighbor who caught Sophie if he wants Sophie back?

POPOV v. HAYASHI

Superior Court, San Francisco County, California (2002).
2002 WL 31833731.

McCarthy, J.

In 1927, Babe Ruth hit sixty home runs. That record stood for thirty four years until Roger Maris broke it in 1961 with sixty one home runs. Mark McGwire hit seventy in 1998. On October 7, 2001, at PacBell Park in San Francisco, Barry Bonds hit number seventy three. That accomplishment set a record which, in all probability, will remain unbroken for years into the future.

The event was widely anticipated and received a great deal of attention.

The ball that found itself at the receiving end of Mr. Bond's bat garnered some of that attention. Baseball fans in general, and especially people at the game, understood the importance of the ball. It was worth a great deal of money[2] and whoever caught it would bask, for a brief period of time, in the reflected fame of Mr. Bonds.

With that in mind, many people who attended the game came prepared for the possibility that a record setting ball would be hit in their direction. Among this group were plaintiff Alex Popov and defendant Patrick Hayashi. They were unacquainted at the time. Both men brought baseball gloves, which they anticipated using if the ball came within their reach.

They, along with a number of others, positioned themselves in the arcade section of the ballpark. This is a standing room only area located near right field. It is in this general area that Barry Bonds hits the greatest number of home runs.[3] The area was crowded with people on October 7, 2001 and access was restricted to those who held tickets for that section.

Barry Bonds came to bat in the first inning. With nobody on base and a full count, Bonds swung at a slow knuckleball. He connected. The ball sailed over the right-field fence and into the arcade.

Josh Keppel, a cameraman who was positioned in the arcade, captured the event on videotape. Keppel filmed much of what occurred from the time Bonds hit the ball until the commotion in the arcade had subsided. He was standing very near the spot where the ball landed and he recorded a significant amount of information critical to the disposition of this case.

In addition to the Keppel tape, seventeen percipient witnesses testified as to what they saw after the ball came into the stands. The testimony of these witnesses varied on many important points. Some of the witnesses had a good vantage point and some did not. Some appeared disinterested in the outcome of the litigation and others had a clear bias. Some remembered the events well and others did not. . . .

The factual findings in this case are the result of an analysis of the testimony of all the witnesses as well as a detailed review of the Keppel tape. Those findings are as follows:

When the seventy-third home run ball went into the arcade, it landed in the upper portion of the webbing of a softball glove worn by Alex Popov. While the glove stopped the trajectory of the ball, it is not at all

---

2. It has been suggested that the ball might sell for something in excess of $1,000,000.

3. The Giants' website contains a page which shows where each of Bonds' home runs landed in 2001. This page was introduced into evidence and is part of the record. It shows that most of the balls are clustered in the arcade area.

clear that the ball was secure. Popov had to reach for the ball and in doing so, may have lost his balance.

Even as the ball was going into his glove, a crowd of people began to engulf Mr. Popov.[4] He was tackled and thrown to the ground while still in the process of attempting to complete the catch. Some people intentionally descended on him for the purpose of taking the ball away, while others were involuntarily forced to the ground by the momentum of the crowd.

Eventually, Mr. Popov was buried face down on the ground under several layers of people. At one point he had trouble breathing. Mr. Popov was grabbed, hit and kicked. People reached underneath him in the area of his glove. Neither the tape nor the testimony is sufficient to establish which individual members of the crowd were responsible for the assaults on Mr. Popov.

The videotape clearly establishes that this was an out of control mob, engaged in violent, illegal behavior. . . .

Mr. Popov intended at all times to establish and maintain possession of the ball. At some point the ball left his glove and ended up on the ground. It is impossible to establish the exact point in time that this occurred or what caused it to occur.

Mr. Hayashi was standing near Mr. Popov when the ball came into the stands. He, like Mr. Popov, was involuntarily forced to the ground. He committed no wrongful act.[5] While on the ground he saw the loose ball. He picked it up, rose to his feet and put it in his pocket.

Although the crowd was still on top of Mr. Popov, security guards had begun the process of physically pulling people off. Some people resisted those efforts. One person argued with an official and another had to be pulled off by his hair.

Mr. Hayashi kept the ball hidden. He asked Mr. Keppel to point the camera at him. At first, Mr. Keppel did not comply and Mr. Hayashi continued to hide the ball. Finally after someone else in the crowd asked Mr. Keppel to point the camera at Mr. Hayashi, Mr. Keppel complied. It was only at that point that Mr. Hayashi held the ball in the air for others to see. Someone made a motion for the ball and Mr. Hayashi put it back in his glove. It is clear that Mr. Hayashi was concerned that someone would take the ball away from him and that he was unwilling to show it until he

---

4.   Ted Kobayashi, a defense expert, testified that there was insufficient reaction time for the crowd to descend on Mr. Popov. This opinion is completely unconvincing. It is premised on the assumption that people did not begin to react until the ball hit Mr. Popov's glove. A number of witnesses testified that they began reacting while the ball was in the air. People rushed to the area where they thought the ball would land. If people were unable to anticipate where a ball will land while it is still in the air, no outfielder would ever catch a ball unless it was hit directly to him or her. Moreover, the tape itself shows people descending on Mr. Popov even as he was attempting to catch the ball.

5.   Plaintiff argues that the Keppel tape shows Mr. Hayashi biting the leg of Brian Shepard. The tape does not support such a conclusion. The testimony which suggests that a bite occurred is equally unconvincing. In addition, there is insufficient evidence that Mr. Hayashi assaulted or attempted to take the ball away from Mr. Popov.

was on videotape. Although he testified to the contrary, that portion of his testimony is unconvincing.

Mr. Popov eventually got up from the ground. He made several statements while he was on the ground and shortly after he got up which are consistent with his claim that he had achieved some level of control over the ball and that he intended to keep it. Those statements can be heard on the audio portion of the tape. When he saw that Mr. Hayashi had the ball he expressed relief and grabbed for it. Mr. Hayashi pulled the ball away.[6] Security guards then took Mr. Hayashi to a secure area of the stadium.[7]

It is important to point out what the evidence did not and could not show. Neither the camera nor the percipient witnesses were able to establish whether Mr. Popov retained control of the ball as he descended into the crowd. Mr. Popov's testimony on this question is inconsistent on several important points, ambiguous on others and, on the whole, unconvincing. We do not know when or how Mr. Popov lost the ball.

Perhaps the most critical factual finding of all is one that cannot be made. We will never know if Mr. Popov would have been able to retain control of the ball had the crowd not interfered with his efforts to do so. Resolution of that question is the work of a psychic, not a judge ...

Conversion is the wrongful exercise of dominion over the personal property of another. There must be actual interference with the plaintiff's dominion. Wrongful withholding of property can constitute actual interference even where the defendant lawfully acquired the property. If a person entitled to possession of personal property demands its return, the unjustified refusal to give the property back is conversion.

The act constituting conversion must be intentionally done. There is no requirement, however, that the defendant knows that the property belongs to another or that the defendant intends to dispossess the true owner of its use and enjoyment. Wrongful purpose is not a component of conversion. ...

Conversion does not exist, however, unless the baseball rightfully belongs to Mr. Popov. One who has neither title nor possession, nor any right to possession, cannot sue for conversion. The deciding question in this case then, is whether Mr. Popov achieved possession or the right to possession as he attempted to catch and hold on to the ball.

The parties have agreed to a starting point for the legal analysis. Prior to the time the ball was hit, it was possessed and owned by Major League Baseball. At the time it was hit it became intentionally abandoned

6. Defense counsel has attempted to characterize this encounter as one in which Mr. Popov congratulates Mr. Hayashi for getting the ball and offers him a high five. This is an argument that only a true advocate could embrace.

7. Testimony was also received about events which occurred after baseball officials escorted Mr. Hayashi to a secure area. This evidence was admitted to allow counsel to explore the possibility that Major League Baseball retained constructive possession of the ball after it landed in the stands and later gifted it to Mr. Hayashi. Defense counsel has properly abandoned this theory. There is no evidence to support it.

property. The first person who came in possession of the ball became its new owner.

The parties fundamentally disagree about the definition of possession. In order to assist the court in resolving this disagreement, four distinguished law professors participated in a forum to discuss the legal definition of possession. The professors also disagreed.

The disagreement is understandable. Although the term possession appears repeatedly throughout the law, its definition varies depending on the context in which it is used. Various courts have condemned the term as vague and meaningless.

This level of criticism is probably unwarranted.

While there is a degree of ambiguity built into the term possession, that ambiguity exists for a purpose. Courts are often called upon to resolve conflicting claims of possession in the context of commercial disputes. A stable economic environment requires rules of conduct which are understandable and consistent with the fundamental customs and practices of the industry they regulate. Without that, rules will be difficult to enforce and economic instability will result. Because each industry has different customs and practices, a single definition of possession cannot be applied to different industries without creating havoc.

This does not mean that there are no central principles governing the law of possession. It is possible to identify certain fundamental concepts that are common to every definition of possession.

Professor Roger Bernhardt[8] has recognized that "[p]ossession requires both physical control over the item and an intent to control it or exclude others from it. But these generalizations function more as guidelines than as direct determinants of possession issues. Possession is a blurred question of law and fact."[9]

Professor Brown argues that "[t]he orthodox view of possession regards it as a union of the two elements of the physical relation of the possessor to the thing, and of intent. This physical relation is the actual power over the thing in question, the ability to hold and make use of it. But a mere physical relation of the possessor to the thing in question is not enough. There must also be manifested an intent to control it."[10]

The task of this court is to use these principles as a starting point to craft a definition of possession that applies to the unique circumstances of this case.

We start with the observation that possession is a process which culminates in an event. The event is the moment in time that possession

---

8. Professor Bernhardt is the author of the textbook *Property, Cases and Statutes,* published by the West Group as well as the co-author of *Real Property in a Nutshell* with Professor Ann M. Burkhart.

9. Real Property in a Nutshell, Roger Bernhardt and Ann M. Burkhart, chapter one, page 3.

10. Brown, *The Law on Personal Property* (Callaghan and Company, 3rd Edition, 1975) § 2.6.

is achieved. The process includes the acts and thoughts of the would be possessor which lead up to the moment of possession.

The focus of the analysis in this case is not on the thoughts or intent of the actor. Mr. Popov has clearly evidenced an intent to possess the baseball and has communicated that intent to the world.[11] The question is whether he did enough to reduce the ball to his exclusive dominion and control. Were his acts sufficient to create a legally cognizable interest in the ball?

Mr. Hayashi argues that possession does not occur until the fan has complete control of the ball. Professor Brian Gray, suggests the following definition "A person who catches a baseball that enters the stands is its owner. A ball is caught if the person has achieved complete control of the ball at the point in time that the momentum of the ball and the momentum of the fan while attempting to catch the ball ceases. A baseball, which is dislodged by incidental contact with an inanimate object or another person, before momentum has ceased, is not possessed. Incidental contact with another person is contact that is not intended by the other person. The first person to pick up a loose ball and secure it becomes its possessor."[12]

Mr. Popov argues that this definition requires that a person seeking to establish possession must show unequivocal dominion and control, a standard rejected by several leading cases.[13] Instead, he offers the perspectives of Professor Bernhardt and Professor Paul Finkelman[14] who suggest that possession occurs when an individual intends to take control of a ball and manifests that intent by stopping the forward momentum of the ball whether or not complete control is achieved.

Professors Finkelman and Bernhardt have correctly pointed out that some cases recognize possession even before absolute dominion and control is achieved. Those cases require the actor to be actively and ably engaged in efforts to establish complete control.[15] Moreover, such efforts must be significant and they must be reasonably calculated to result in unequivocal dominion and control at some point in the near future.

---

11. Literally.

12. This definition is hereinafter referred to as Gray's Rule.

13. *Pierson v. Post* 3 Caines R. (N.Y.1805); *Young v. Hitchens* 6 Q.B. 606 (1844); *State v. Shaw* (1902) 67 Ohio St. 157, 65 N.E. 875.

14. Professor Finkelman is the author of the definitive law review article on the central issue in this case, *Fugitive Baseballs and Abandoned Property: Who Owns the Home Run Ball?;* Cardozo Law Review, May 2002, Paul Finkelman, (Chapman Distinguished Professor of Law).

15. The degree of control necessary to establish possession varies from circumstance to circumstance. "The law ... does not always require that one who discovers lost or abandoned property must actually have it in hand before he is vested with a legally protected interest. The law protects not only the title acquired by one who finds lost or abandoned property but also the right of the person who discovers such property, and is actively and ably engaged in reducing it to possession, to complete this process without interference from another. The courts have recognized that in order to acquire a legally cognizable interest in lost or abandoned property a finder need not always have manual possession of the thing. Rather, a finder may be protected by taking such constructive possession of the property as its nature and situation permit." *Treasure Salvors Inc. v. The Unidentified Wrecked and Abandoned Sailing Vessel*, 640 F.2d 560, 571 (1981). (emphasis added)

This rule is applied in cases involving the hunting or fishing of wild animals[16] or the salvage of sunken vessels.[17] The hunting and fishing cases recognize that a mortally wounded animal may run for a distance before falling. The hunter acquires possession upon the act of wounding the animal not the eventual capture. Similarly, whalers acquire possession by landing a harpoon, not by subduing the animal. . . .[18]

These rules are contextual in nature. They are crafted in response to the unique nature of the conduct they seek to regulate. Moreover, they are influenced by the custom and practice of each industry. The reason that absolute dominion and control is not required to establish possession in the cases cited by Mr. Popov is that such a rule would be unworkable and unreasonable. The "nature and situation" of the property at issue does not immediately lend itself to unequivocal dominion and control. It is impossible to wrap ones arms around a whale, a fleeing fox or a sunken ship.

The opposite is true of a baseball hit into the stands of a stadium. Not only is it physically possible for a person to acquire unequivocal dominion and control of an abandoned baseball, but fans generally expect a claimant to have accomplished as much. The custom and practice of the stands creates a reasonable expectation that a person will achieve full control of a ball before claiming possession. There is no reason for the legal rule to be inconsistent with that expectation. Therefore Gray's Rule is adopted as the definition of possession in this case.

The central tenant of Gray's Rule is that the actor must retain control of the ball after incidental contact with people and things. Mr. Popov has not established by a preponderance of the evidence that he would have retained control of the ball after all momentum ceased and after any incidental contact with people or objects. Consequently, he did not achieve full possession.

That finding, however, does not resolve the case. The reason we do not know whether Mr. Popov would have retained control of the ball is not because of incidental contact. It is because he was attacked. His efforts to establish possession were interrupted by the collective assault of a band of wrongdoers.[19]

---

16. *Liesner v. Wanie* (1914) 156 Wis. 16, 145 N.W. 374; *Ghen v. Rich* 8 F. 159 (D.Mass.1881); *Pierson v. Post* 3 Caines R. (N.Y.1805); *Young v. Hitchens* 6 Q.B. 606 (1844); *State v. Shaw* (1902) 67 Ohio St. 157, 65 N.E. 875. See also Herbert Hovenkamp and Sheldon Kurtz, *The Law of Property* (5th ed. West Group 2001) § 1.2.

17. *Indian River Recovery Company v. The China* 645 F.Supp. 141, 144 (D.Del.1986); *Treasure Salvors Inc. v. The Unidentified Wrecked and Abandoned Sailing Vessel* 640 F.2d 560 (1981); *Richard v. Pringle*, 293 F.Supp. 981 (S.D.N.Y.1968).

18. *Swift v. Gifford* 23 F. Cas. 558 (D.Mass.1872).

19. Professor Gray has suggested that the way to deal with this problem is to demand that Mr. Popov sue the people who assaulted him. This suggestion is unworkable for a number of reasons. First, it was an attack by a large group of people. It is impossible to separate out the people who were acting unlawfully from the people who were involuntarily pulled into the mix. Second, in order to prove damages related to the loss of the ball, Mr. Popov would have to prove that but for the actions of the crowd he would have achieved possession of the ball. As noted earlier, this is impossible.

A decision which ignored that fact would endorse the actions of the crowd by not repudiating them. Judicial rulings, particularly in cases that receive media attention, affect the way people conduct themselves. This case demands vindication of an important principle. We are a nation governed by law, not by brute force.[20]

As a matter of fundamental fairness, Mr. Popov should have had the opportunity to try to complete his catch unimpeded by unlawful activity. To hold otherwise would be to allow the result in this case to be dictated by violence. That will not happen.

For these reasons, the analysis cannot stop with the valid observation that Mr. Popov has not proved full possession.[21]

The legal question presented at this point is whether an action for conversion can proceed where the plaintiff has failed to establish possession or title. It can. An action for conversion may be brought where the plaintiff has title, possession or the right to possession. . . .[22]

[T]he court adopts the following rule. Where an actor undertakes significant but incomplete steps to achieve possession of a piece of abandoned personal property and the effort is interrupted by the unlawful acts of others, the actor has a legally cognizable pre-possessory interest in the property. That pre-possessory interest constitutes a qualified right to possession which can support a cause of action for conversion.

Possession can be likened to a journey down a path. Mr. Popov began his journey unimpeded. He was fast approaching a fork in the road. A turn in one direction would lead to possession of the ball—he would complete the catch. A turn in the other direction would result in a failure to achieve possession—he would drop the ball. Our problem is that before Mr. Popov got to the point where the road forked, he was set upon by a gang of bandits, who dislodged the ball from his grasp.

Recognition of a legally protected pre-possessory interest, vests Mr. Popov with a qualified right to possession and enables him to advance a legitimate claim to the baseball based on a conversion theory. Moreover it addresses the harm done by the unlawful actions of the crowd.

It does not, however, address the interests of Mr. Hayashi. The court is required to balance the interests of all parties.

Mr. Hayashi was not a wrongdoer. He was a victim of the same bandits that attacked Mr. Popov. The difference is that he was able to extract himself from their assault and move to the side of the road. It was there that he discovered the loose ball. When he picked up and put it in his pocket he attained unequivocal dominion and control.

---

20. There are a number of ways courts can enforce the rule of law. Major League Baseball, as well as each individual team has a duty to provide security against foreseeable violence in the stands. The failure to provide that security, or worse, the tacit acceptance of some level of violence, will inevitable lead to lawsuits against the teams and the parent organization.

21. The court is indebted to Professor Jan Stiglitz of California Western School of Law for his valuable insights and suggestions on this issue.

22. See note 14.

If Mr. Popov had achieved complete possession before Mr. Hayashi got the ball, those actions would not have divested Mr. Popov of any rights, nor would they have created any rights to which Mr. Hayashi could lay claim. Mr. Popov, however, was able to establish only a qualified pre-possessory interest in the ball. That interest does not establish a full right to possession that is protected from a subsequent legitimate claim.

On the other hand, while Mr. Hayashi appears on the surface to have done everything necessary to claim full possession of the ball, the ball itself is encumbered by the qualified pre-possessory interest of Mr. Popov. At the time Mr. Hayashi came into possession of the ball, it had, in effect, a cloud on its title.

An award of the ball to Mr. Popov would be unfair to Mr. Hayashi. It would be premised on the assumption that Mr. Popov would have caught the ball. That assumption is not supported by the facts. An award of the ball to Mr. Hayashi would unfairly penalize Mr. Popov. It would be based on the assumption that Mr. Popov would have dropped the ball. That conclusion is also unsupported by the facts.

Both men have a superior claim to the ball as against all the world. Each man has a claim of equal dignity as to the other. We are, therefore, left with something of a dilemma.

Thankfully, there is a middle ground.

The concept of equitable division was fully explored in a law review article authored by Professor R.H. Helmholz in the December 1983 edition of the Fordham Law Review.[23] Professor Helmholz addressed the problems associated with rules governing finders of lost and mislaid property. For a variety of reasons not directly relevant to the issues raised in this case, Helmholz suggested employing the equitable remedy of division to resolve competing claims between finders of lost or mislaid property and the owners of land on which the property was found.

There is no reason, however, that the same remedy cannot be applied in a case such as this, where issues of property, tort and equity intersect.

The concept of equitable division has its roots in ancient Roman law.[24] As Helmholz points out, it is useful in that it "provides an equitable way to resolve competing claims which are equally strong." Moreover, "[i]t comports with what one instinctively feels to be fair".[25]

Although there is no California case directly on point, *Arnold v. Producers Fruit Company* (1900) 128 Cal. 637, 61 P. 283 provides some insight. There, a number of different prune growers contracted with Producer's Fruit Company to dry and market their product. Producers did

---

23. *Equitable Division and the Law of Finders,* (1983) Fordham Law Review, Professor R.H. Helmholz, University of Chicago School of Law. This article built on a student comment published in 1939. *Lost, Mislaid and Abandoned Property* (1939) 8 Fordham Law Review 222.

24. Helmholz at fn. 14.

25. Id. at 315.

a bad job. They mixed fruit from many different growers together in a single bin and much of the fruit rotted because it was improperly treated.

When one of the plaintiffs offered proof that the fruit in general was rotten, Producers objected on the theory that the plaintiff could not prove that the prunes he contributed to the mix were the same prunes that rotted. The court concluded that it did not matter. After the mixing was done, each grower had an undivided interest in the whole, in proportion to the amount of fruit each had originally contributed.

The principle at work here is that where more than one party has a valid claim to a single piece of property, the court will recognize an undivided interest in the property in proportion to the strength of the claim.

Application of the principle of equitable division is illustrated in the case of *Keron v. Cashman* (1896) 33 A. 1055. In that case, five boys were walking home along a railroad track in the city of Elizabeth New Jersey. The youngest of the boys came upon an old sock that was tied shut and contained something heavy. He picked it up and swung it. The oldest boy took it away from him and beat the others with it. The sock passes from boy to boy. Each controlled it for a short time. At some point in the course of play, the sock broke open and out spilled $775 as well as some rags, cloths and ribbons.

The court noted that possession requires both physical control and the intent to reduce the property to one's possession. Control and intent must be concurrent. None of the boys intended to take possession until it became apparent that the sock contained money. Each boy had physical control of the sock at some point before that discovery was made.

Because none could present a superior claim of concurrent control and intent, the court held that each boy was entitled to an equal share of the money. Their legal claims to the property were of equal quality, therefore their entitlement to the property was also equal.

Here, the issue is not intent, or concurrence. Both men intended to possess the ball at the time they were in physical contact with it. The issue, instead, is the legal quality of the claim. With respect to that, neither can present a superior argument as against the other.

Mr. Hayashi's claim is compromised by Mr. Popov's pre-possessory interest. Mr. Popov cannot demonstrate full control. Albeit for different reasons, they stand before the court in exactly the same legal position as did the five boys. Their legal claims are of equal quality and they are equally entitled to the ball.

The court therefore declares that both plaintiff and defendant have an equal and undivided interest in the ball. Plaintiff's cause of action for conversion is sustained only as to his equal and undivided interest. In order to effectuate this ruling, the ball must be sold and the proceeds divided equally between the parties ...

NOTES AND QUESTIONS

1.   Although the Popov court relies heavily on the concepts of possession theorized in Pierson and its later progeny, Popov v. Hayashi is not strictly a case in the same vein as Pierson v. Post. Do you see why? Do you think the Pierson court would have decided the case the same way?

2.   The Popov court appears to be heavily influenced by the belief that Popov was the subject of "brute force." The court fails to take into account that such force (the crush of the crowd) could have been anticipated by Mr. Popov before he went to the ballgame. Assuming that is so, should that affect the outcome of the case?

3.   The *Popov* court adopts the concept of equitable division to "split the baby" or more precisely the ball between two innocent parties. As the court notes, that concept has been suggested as appropriate in adjudicating the rights of finders and the owners of the *locus in quo*. Should that doctrine also apply to adjudicate the rights of finders and true owners to the effect that the finder and true owner become equal owners of the found property?

4.   Judge McCarthy's estimate that the Barry Bond's record setting home run baseball would sell for something in excess of $1,000,000 was wide of the mark. In fact, when auctioned off, it was purchased by the comic book creator and avid baseball fan, Todd McFarlane, for only $450,000. Earlier Todd McFarlane had purchased Mark McGuire's 70th home run ball for about $3,000,000. McFarlane also owns Sammy Sosa's 33rd, 61st and 66th home run balls and McGuire's 63rd, 67th, 68th, and 69th home run balls.

NOTES ON THE OCCUPATION THEORY OF PROPERTY

L. BECKER, PROPERTY RIGHTS: PHILOSOPHIC FOUNDATIONS 24–25 (1977)

When the question arises as to why some people, rather than others, should own things, one of the issues which comes to mind is the question, "Who had it first?" The notion that being there first somehow justifies ownership rights is a venerable and persistent one. A close analysis will show that it does not provide a sound basis for claims to ownership, and thus contributes nothing to a theory of the general justification of property rights. But it is important to consider none the less. The reasons for its failure are illuminating.

A Priori Restrictions on First Occupancy Claims

There are times when "I was here first" *seems* to make some sense as a rationale for the claim "It's mine," but those times are special in character, and the limitations on the property claims which can plausibly be made are severe. First occupancy obviously cannot justify title to property unless (1) the object occupied is unowned; *and* (2) occupation is in some relevant sense actual as opposed to intentional or declaratory; *and*

(3) the concept of actual occupation defines with reasonable clarity how much one can occupy; *and* (4) the occupier claims no more than a share as defined by (3). The first requirement comes simply from the fact that if the thing is already owned by someone, mere occupation will not change that fact, and presumably *first* occupation is by definition impossible. The second requirement (as will be shown) is necessary to avoid making the concept of occupation altogether absurd and self-defeating. The third and fourth requirements arise, not because one needs, in justice, to put a limit on what a person can rightfully appropriate in this way (though that may also be true), but because one has to be able to specify how much an occupier occupies in order to make sense of the notion of occupation to begin with, and once such limits are specified, they define the maximum an occupier could ever rightfully claim merely on the basis of occupation. Whether an occupier *can* rightfully claim this maximum—or indeed any amount at all—is a separate issue. . . .

The Thing Occupied Must Belong to No One

First occupancy is put forward as a mode of "original" acquisition. As such it cannot operate where the thing occupied is already owned. But what about things which are not owned by anyone? Property theorists have typically said that such things are common property, or belong to everyone in common, and as such can (or cannot) be appropriated by individuals. Cicero invites readers to think of unappropriated things as seats in a public theater where one can take whatever seat is vacant (but no more than one). Others have not been convinced by the metaphor.

A distinction of some importance for this issue was urged by Pufendorf, and is incorporated in the first requirement stated here. Pufendorf sharply distinguished cases in which things were held in common "positively"—that is, were jointly owned, everyone having a well-defined share—and cases in which things were held in common only "negatively"—that is, were owned by no one but were equally available to everyone. The importance of the distinction for the theory of first occupancy may be made clear in the following way.

Where a thing is jointly owned and one's share is therefore well defined, there is no room for first occupancy claims. It is clear that first occupancy can never create a justifiable title independent of the consent of the joint owners. When a thing is jointly owned in the full liberal sense, for example, any disposition of the thing by one person without the consent of the others is a violation of their rights of ownership—even if one has taken no more than one's share. Joint ownership means joint management, and more fundamentally, joint right to the capital. And though there may be cases in which adherence to the first occupier rule (among the joint owners) is the only rational method for allocating specific shares among the owners, still the decision to allocate specific shares at all must be a joint decision. Indeed, there is a decision of considerable import to be made in defining what ownership rights will be allocated, even if an allocation has been decided on. Will the group give up joint ownership altogether? Or merely possessory and use rights? If use rights, then rights to income as well? And so forth.

* * *

RICHARD A. EPSTEIN, POSSESSION AS THE ROOT OF TITLE, 13 GA. L. REV. 1221–22, 1238–43 (1979)

A beautiful sea shell is washed ashore after a storm. A man picks it up and puts it in his pocket. A second man comes along and takes it away from him by force. The first man sues to recover the shell, and he is met with the argument that he never owned it at all. How does the legal system respond to this claim? How should it respond?

The same man finds the same shell, only now the state, through its public processes, comes along and insists that the shell belongs to the common fund. It offers the man nothing for it, claiming that the shell was found by luck and coincidence and not by planned and systematic labor. How does the legal system respond to this claim? How should it respond?

The questions just put can recur in a thousand different forms in any organized legal system. The system itself presupposes that there are rights over given things that are vested in certain individuals within that system. And the system knows full well that these property rights in things are defined not against the thing, but over the thing and against the rest of the world; that property rights normally entail (roughly) exclusive possession and use of one thing in question and the right to transfer it voluntarily to another. The exact contours of these rights, however important to basic theory, are not central to the main concern here. The more insistent question is: What principles decide *which* individuals have ownership rights (whatever they precisely entail) over *what* things.

The question must be distinguished from the related issue which simply asks what are the social or public functions of the institution of ownership. It could be decided that ownership is necessary to create effective incentives for the development and improvement of property or to reduce or eliminate conflicts between private persons. Yet even if these points are true, such broad justifications for ownership do not solve the more particular question of how given bits of property are matched with given individuals. It is to this question that the common and civil law (both of which accept the desirability of private ownership) have responded with the proposition that the taking possession of unowned things is the only possible way to acquire ownership of them. As stated, the proposition assumes a central role in the development of any legal system, because it supplies the link between assertions of act and those of right. Yet the importance of the rule making original possession the source of ownership is matched by the absence of any systematic analysis of it. . . .

* * *

At the outset I noted that it was my intention to give a qualified defense of the rule that possession is the root of title. The evidence of the qualifications are everywhere. The structure of the defense is as follows: We begin with the given that some system of property rights is necessary, if only to organize the world in ways that all individuals know the boundaries of their own conduct. The possible systems that might be used seem to number two. There are first those first possession systems (including the analogous rules for water, oil and gas, etc.); and there are systems that create original common ownership in all the citizens of the jurisdiction. Given the original necessity for some system, the real question is *not* how can any system of property rights be justified in the abstract, but *which* of these two systems has, when all is said and done, the better claim for allegiance. On balance the case tilts strongly for the first possession theories, whatever their infirmities.

There is first the question of the kind of state that is required by each of these theories. The rules of first possession, even their complicated water rights variants, require in effect a minimal sort of state which parcels out the rights between the various contenders in accordance with set rules, indifferent as to their personal characteristics, histories, or wealth. True, there will be some question of who took possession first, but the types of issues should not by any stretch of the imagination strain the institutional capacities of the judicial system. The theory of common ownership requires much more extensive public control, for someone must decide how the rights in question are to be packaged and divided amongst individuals. The exact magnitude of the control is of course somewhat hard to determine. The state could, to facilitate market transactions, simply package the resources in question—*e.g.*, do we sell land in big lots or little ones—and then put the packages out to bid, while remaining indifferent to the way in which they are used in private hands. Or the state could assume a much more aggressive role, one which requires it to condition sale, or even lease, upon complicated conditions, or which contemplates the state operation of the system as a whole. Indeed in the current political climate, it is quite possible that state ownership would lead to extensive and continuous state control. And as I tend to fear such control, I am very cautious about a system of original property rights that tends to invite its operation and expansion. Better to begin with a system that places wealth in private hands.

There is of course a related fear. The discussion has thus far been directed to the ways in which individuals acquire rights in external things. Yet there is nothing in principle which says that the theory could not be extended as well to govern the way in which individuals acquire rights in themselves. Here the theory of common ownership clearly seems to lend itself to totalitarian uses and abuses. Each individual person's talents and gifts can be treated as unearned items, much like the shell found by chance along the beach. The state therefore in its plenary capacity can allow to each individual blessed with such talents the right to use them only on terms that it sees fit. Systems of high taxation of individual income or, in more extreme circumstances, forced labor, need not be seen as impermissible exactions from the individuals for the public at large. They can be viewed as the terms on which individual talents are leased back to their natural holders, who by assumption have no original rights in them. One might argue that this extension of basic theory is not fully warranted. There is, for example, no danger of overconsumption of natural talents as there is of natural things. And the argument could be strengthened by the observation that collective ownership of external things is needed in order to prevent one person from cornering the market, while such problems do not arise with individual labor. But surely this contrast is overdrawn. On the one side, certain individuals have unique talents and on the other, it is most unlikely that any individual could claim possession of all unowned things while all others, indifferent to their welfare, sit idly by. The difference between ownership of person and ownership of things is at best a matter of degree. The system that speaks of collective ownership over things provides a less solid bulwark against public control over individual talents than a system which rests upon the first possession rules.

There is a third point which in the end comes closest to being the "ultimate point." The fundamental objection against both theories of first possession and theories of original common ownership is that neither is powerful enough to bind non-consenting individuals. The objection to both theories is analogous therefore to the objection that Hume raised a long time ago to *all* ethical propositions: it is simply not possible to move from a non-ethical premise to an ethical conclusion without there being a logical gap in the argument. Put in the context of the first possession rule, Hume's insight points to an unbridgeable logical gap between the *fact* of possession and the *right* to possession. Yet the power of Hume's general proposition is the source of its very undoing. The proposition is so strong that it undercuts any and all substantive ethical positions because it does not permit the selection of ethical theories on grounds of relative virtue. That same point applies with respect to theories of original ownership. The standard objection is *too* powerful because it destroys all possible theories when one is by necessity required; what is needed is an argument that works less like a club and more like a scalpel, one which permits a ranking amongst theories, while recognizing the imperfection of all rival contenders. Whatever the philosophy of the matter, we need some system of property rights that does bind the world, even for those who do not share in its substantive premises.

There must be some way to break a philosophical impasse, and it is in this connection that we should return again to both the institutional constraints and past practices that characterize the common law mode of adjudication. It is not that our philosophical inquiry has taken place in an intellectual vacuum. It is that the inquiry has taken place on the assumption that we can begin structuring entitlements as if we wrote upon a blank slate, indifferent to all events and practices that have developed over time. The common law courts, which always began in medias res and which always announced principles that governed particular disputes, never had the luxury of philosophical purity in some original position. If we accept these constraints upon the judiciary as unfortunate features of the legal system alone, then perhaps there is no great reason to attach any weight to them. Yet if we regard them as fair reflections of some larger social requirements, as indeed they are, then they can offer some limited criterion of relative virtue that allows us to choose between the two alternative systems of original property entitlements. The point is simply that some weight should be attached to the rules under which a society in the past has organized its property institutions. Where those rules are respected there is no need, at great expense, to reshuffle entitlements amongst different individuals, even in the absence of any clear principle that dictates how that reshuffling should take place. There is no need, moreover, to attack the interests of those who have expended their labor and taken their risks on the expectation, reasonable to all concerned, that the rules under which they entered the game will be the rules under which that game will be played until its conclusion. These rules and these alone have the status of legal rules. . . .

Within this viewpoint it is possible to show the unique place of first possession. It enjoyed in all past times the status of a legal rule, not only for the stock examples of wild animals and sea shells, but also for unoccupied land. In essence the first possession rule has been the organizing principle of most social institutions, and the heavy burden of persuasion lies upon those who wish to displace it.

The size of the burden is, moreover, very considerable. A repudiation of the first possession rule as a matter of philosophical principle calls into question all titles. It calls into question those which exist in the hands of the original possessors; it calls into question those of their heirs; it calls into question the rights of those who have purchased the titles in question for good consideration, and those who have made improvements upon land acquired on the faith of the public representation that they could keep it for their own. It may be an unresolved intellectual mystery of how a mere assertion of right can, if often repeated and acknowledged, be sufficient to generate the right in question. As an institutional matter, however, it is difficult in the extreme to conceive of any other system. As between two systems, both of which are philosophically exposed to the same objection, the choice must go to that which has the sanction of past practices. The first possession rule represents the most general principle of this sort. The particular customs and practices in certain locales represent yet another expression of the same basic point.

The institutional justification shows the limits of the basic position in connection with those things [that] have yet to be exploited by any individuals or nations. With respect to these things the first possession rule has much weaker claims because it cannot draw upon the full strength of this reliance interest. The exploitation of the ocean bed or the Antarctic regions need not rest upon the first possession rules because these have not yet embedded themselves into the institutional fiber of the social system. In these cases we have both the luxury and necessity of beginning at the beginning. First possession rules might in the end be adopted, but it is now quite possible to entertain alternative systems of property rights that depart significantly from the first possession principle. It is at this level that we can consider the question of whether all individuals are entitled to, if not the thing, then at least the wealth derived from it, and the question of what institutions and what packages of rights will tend to promote the effective use of the thing in question. For such cases, the arguments will be more congruent with the modern concerns about economic efficiency and distributional equity, and arguments about the nature and desirability of political intervention, always relevant, can assume greater force. Yet with respect to property rights that are already assigned, the first principles of thought are constrained from without, as the past has a power to bind the future. Vested rights have acquired, as it were, a life of their own.

Notes and Questions

1. Does Becker neglect the distinction between property that is unowned and property whose ownership is unknown or uncertain? Granted, very little property is absolutely unowned, in the sense that no one has ever laid claim to it. More frequently, however, the court must resolve a dispute between two persons, *neither* of whom is likely the first possessor, but one of whom must prevail. (Is that true? Can't they both prevail?) In that case, possession, or first possession, is likely to be far more important. Often the court responds to this problem of uncertainty by making clear that it is determining only who has a *better* property right as between two claimants; it is not determining who has the best title against all the world.

2. Assuming that possession is the root of title, how is it to be determined whether a person who claims title because of possession has possession? See Rose, Possession As the Origin of Property, 52 Chi. L. Rev. 73, 76 (1985) ("Possession thus means a clear act, whereby all the world understands that the pursuer has 'an unequivocal intention of appropriating the [thing] to his individual use'").

3. Epstein notes that even the simple principle "first in time is first in right"—or that property belongs to the first known possessor—makes an enormous presumption about the relationship between the state and the individual. The "first possession" theory, which is generally followed in modern capitalist societies, is very much a *private* theory about property rights. Furthermore, once this principle is admitted it spills over into all areas of the law. For example, a great deal of tort and contract law concerns remedies for the wrongful deprivation of private property rights. Likewise, much of constitutional law concerns the question whether a particular person has a private "property interest" in something that the state is trying to take away from him.

4. Is Epstein correct in his argument that a first possession theory of property rights suggests a very small state, while a theory that the state owns everything suggests a very large state? Many governments that accept the

principle of first private possession have nevertheless managed to become quite large—for example, the United States. Likewise, a state that began with the principle that the sovereign owns everything could as its first sovereign act auction everything off to the highest bidder and then evaporate. Even Marx believed that the state should own all property, but that eventually the state would become unnecessary and would "whither away and die." Perhaps Epstein is merely predicting that, Marx's view notwithstanding, Marxist societies will always have a very large state.

5.   It seems that the government itself is exempt from the prior possession rule: it has the power to assert dominion over objects not within its control, and to forbid others from claiming ownership over them. See the Endangered Species Act, 16 U.S.C.A. § 1531 et seq., especially at § 1538, which forbids any person from taking an endangered animal even on the high seas, which are outside the jurisdiction of the United States.

6.   As Epstein notes, in the final analysis *no* system of property rights may be ethically defensible on theoretical grounds. However, philosophers have an enormous luxury that judges do not. They can debate propositions forever. The judge, however, must decide cases, and she must decide them relatively quickly. Even the principle that people are entitled to a quick, nonarbitrary resolution of their disputes deserves great ethical weight.

7.   To what extent do the theories developed by Becker and Epstein find early judicial expression in Pierson v. Post?

8.   O owns land under which there is a pool of natural gas. After O removes the gas from the earth, he refills the resulting cavity with gas purchased elsewhere. Some of the gas spills out from under O's land and settles under the land of O's neighbor, O–2, who drills under his land and removes the gas. O sues O–2 to recover the value of the gas that escaped from his land. What result? Compare Hammonds v. Central Kentucky Natural Gas Co., 255 Ky. 685, 75 S.W.2d 204 (1934) (owner of escaped gas not liable in trespass to neighbor under whose land the gas settled) with Lone Star Gas Co. v. Murchison, 353 S.W.2d 870 (Tex.Civ.App.1962) and Humble Oil & Refining Co. v. West, 508 S.W.2d 812 (Tex.1974) (person who stores gas under his land does not lose title to the gas when it spills onto land of another).

Fugitive Minerals and the Rule of Capture: An Economic Note on Market Failure and the Common Law of Property Rights

Fugitive minerals are natural resources, such as oil and natural gas, that do not stay in one place, even when they are still under the ground. Such minerals not only move around, but they pay no attention to property lines. Suppose that A, B, C and D are landowners who have property over the same "pool" of oil. (A pool is a natural pocket in the earth, within which the oil can move freely. However, the pocket itself is generally sealed off from outside until someone drills into it.)

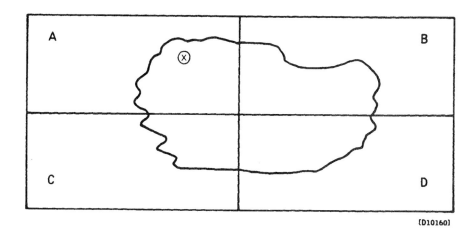

[D10160]

Suppose that A drills an oil well at point X, and oil begins flowing out of the well. Liquids and gasses flow to the point of lowest pressure. The instant A's oil well begins producing oil, B, C and D will face "drainage"— that is, oil that was initially in the pool under their land will flow toward the opening in A's land. Of course, once the oil comes out through A's well, there is no way of telling where in the pool it originated. Largely for that reason, fugitive minerals historically were governed by the rule of capture: A was entitled to have all the oil that came up through the well which she dug on her property. See Barnard v. Monongahela Natural Gas Co., 216 Pa. 362, 65 A. 801 (1906).

Under the rule of capture, B, C, and D will either have to drill wells of their own immediately, or else A will end up with all the valuable oil. Furthermore, once each of them has drilled a well, each will want to produce as fast as possible, for anything not taken out by one of the landowners today is likely to be taken out by a different landowner tomorrow. The four landowners will drill more and more wells in order to acquire as large a share as possible of the oil in their shared pool.

Think of the results that the rule of capture might produce in a country whose economy is fast becoming dependent on large scale oil production. The result of the rule of capture in the United States at the beginning of the twentieth century was a massive glut of oil on the market—so much that at one point gasoline sold for 1.5 cents per gallon. Each owner of oil producing land who suspected that his oil pool extended under someone else's land pumped as fast as possible, even when too much oil was already being produced. It was either pump today or have nothing to pump tomorrow. The problem was aggravated by the fact that most people did not know the precise boundaries of the oil pools under their land. If someone merely *suspected* that he shared an oil pool with a neighbor, he would have to pump as fast as he could.

The oil glut in the United States in the early 1900s is an example of a "market failure." A market failure occurs when the unregulated market and the common law (which is all that governs unregulated markets) is not capable of devising a solution that will make a market perform efficiently. In this particular case, the market for oil would operate efficiently—that is, supply and demand would be in balance—only if (1) all the landowners above a particular oil pool agreed to share the oil produced out of the pool; or (2) someone with the power to control oil production limited the amount of oil that each land owner produced and constantly supervised production. However, the parties may be unable to achieve the first solution, and the second is not easily available to the common law judge, who obtains jurisdiction only when someone asks for it, and who generally does not have the power or expertise to regulate an ongoing market relationship. For this reason, the production of fugitive minerals is no longer left to the rule of capture. Rather, it is regulated by state and federal agencies who control the amount of production and make sure that all owners of mineral rights over a particular pool obtain their *pro rata* share. The result is that the property of each landowner over the oil pool becomes more valuable.

Today, many markets for property rights are legislatively regulated because someone with political authority has decided that a particular market is subject to market failure, so the common law system of allocating property rights will not work. Price regulation for electric utilities and taxicabs is based on this premise. So is rent control (see chapter 7). Even the laws against race and gender discrimination in housing (see chapter 12) are based, at least in part, on society's perception that there is a "market failure" in this part of the economy—that is, that the common law is not capable of producing the optimal allocation of property rights.

NOTE ON THE LABOR THEORY OF PROPERTY

J. LOCKE, SECOND TREATISE OF GOVERNMENT, § 27, IN TWO TREATISES OF GOVERNMENT 305–06 (P. LASLETT REV.ED. 1970) (1ST ED. LONDON 1690)

Through the earth, and all inferior Creatures, be common to all Men, yet every Man has a *Property* in his own *Person*. This no Body has any right to but himself. The *Labour* of his Body, and the *Work* of his Hands, we may say, are properly his. Whatsoever then he removes out of the State that Nature hath provided, and left it is, he hath mixed his *Labour* with, and joyned to it something that is his own, and thereby makes it his *Property*. It being by him removed from the common state nature hath placed it in, it hath by this *labour* something annexed to it, that excludes the common right of other Men. For this *Labour* being the unquestionable Property of the Labourer, no Man but he can have a right to what that is once joyned to, at least where there is enough, and as good, left in common for others.

NOTES AND QUESTIONS

1. Locke's argument goes something like this:

(a) Each person has a property right in herself.

(b) It follows from (a) that each person has a property right in her own *labor*.

(c) It follows from (b) that any time someone uses her own labor on an object to increase its value she acquires a property right in it.

Does (b) in fact follow from (a)? Does (c) follow from (b)? Does (c) mean that the laborer becomes the *exclusive* owner of the object in question, or merely that the laborer acquires some property right—perhaps in common with others—in the object?

2. Admitting property rights are acquired by one's labor, to what extent does Locke's analysis define the quality and quantity of such rights? Suppose a lumberman cuts down a tree and turns it into boards. The lumberman gives the boards to A, who pays no value for them and does nothing to improve them. B finds the boards and, not knowing who the owner is, builds a table with them. A then sues B for (1) the return of the boards, (2) the value of the boards, or (3) the value of the table. B argues that A has no property right in the boards. How would Locke resolve the dispute?

3. Robert Nozick observes the following about Locke's labor theory:[26]

Before we turn to consider other theories of justice in detail, we must introduce an additional bit of complexity into the structure of the entitlement theory. This is best approached by considering Locke's attempt to specify a principle of justice in acquisition. Locke views property rights in an unowned object as originating through someone's mixing his labor with it. This gives rise to many questions. What are the boundaries of what labor is mixed with? If a private astronaut clears a place on Mars, has he mixed his labor with (so that he comes to own) the whole planet, the whole uninhabited universe, or just a particular plot? Which plot does an act bring under ownership? The minimal (possibly disconnected) area, such that an act decreases entropy in that area, and not elsewhere? Can virgin land (for the purposes of ecological investigation by high-flying airplane) come under ownership by a Lockean process? Building a fence around a territory presumably would make one the owner of only the fence (and the land immediately underneath it).

Why does mixing one's labor with something make one the owner of it? Perhaps because one owns one's labor, and so one comes to own a previously unowned thing that becomes permeated with what one owns. Ownership seeps over into the rest. But why isn't mixing what I own with what I don't own a way of losing what I own rather than a way of gaining what I don't? If I own a can of tomato juice and spill it in the sea so that its molecules (made radioactive, so I can check this) mingle evenly throughout the sea, do I thereby come to own the sea, or have I foolishly

---

26. R. Nozick, Anarchy, State and Utopia 174–175 (1974).

dissipated my tomato juice? Perhaps the idea, instead, is that laboring on something improves it and makes it more valuable; and anyone is entitled to own a thing whose value he has created. (Reinforcing this, perhaps, is the view that laboring is unpleasant. If some people made things effort-lessly, as the cartoon characters in *The Yellow Submarine* trail flowers in their wake, would they have lesser claim to their own products whose making didn't *cost* them anything?) Ignore the fact that laboring on something may make it less valuable (spraying pink enamel paint on a piece of driftwood that you have found). Why should one's entitlement extend to the whole object rather than just to the *added value* one's labor has produced? (Such reference to value might also serve to delimit the extent of ownership; for example, substitute "increases the value of" for "decreases entropy in" in the above entropy criterion.) No workable or coherent value-added property scheme has yet been devised, and any such scheme presumably would fall to objections (similar to those) that fell the theory of Henry George.

It will be implausible to view improving an object as giving full ownership to it, if the stock of unowned objects that might be improved is limited. For an object's coming under one person's ownership changes the situa-tion of all others. Whereas previously they were at liberty (in Hohfeld's sense) to use the object, they now no longer are. This change in the situation of others (by removing their liberty to act on a previously unowned object) need not worsen their situation. If I appropriate a grain of sand from Coney Island, no one else may now do as they will with *that* grain of sand. But there are plenty of other grains of sand left for them to do the same with. Or if not grains of sand, then other things. Alternative-ly, the things I do with the grain of sand I appropriate might improve the position of others, counterbalancing their loss of the liberty to use that grain. The crucial point is whether appropriation of an unowned object worsens the situation of others.

4.   One evening plaintiff raked horse manure deposited on a public street into piles to be collected by him the following day. Before the plaintiff could return to collect the manure piles, the defendant, who found them on the street, loaded them into his carts and carried them away. Plaintiff sued defendant to recover the value of the manure. In deciding the case in favor of the plaintiff the court stated:[27]

> The manure originally belonged to the travelers whose animals dropped it, but it being worthless to them was immediately abandoned; and whether it then became the property of the borough of Stamford which owned the fee of the land on which the manure lay, it is unnecessary to determine; for, if it did, the case finds that the removal of the filth would be an improvement to the borough, and no objection was made by any one to the use that the plaintiff attempted to make of it. Considering the character of such accumulations upon highways in cities and villages, and the light in which they are everywhere regarded in closely settled commu-nities, we cannot believe that the borough in this instance would have had any objection to the act of the plaintiff in removing a nuisance that

---

27.   Haslem v. Lockwood, 37 Conn. 500, 506–07 (1871).

affected the public health and the appearance of the streets. At all events, we think the facts of the case show a sufficient right in the plaintiff to the immediate possession of the property as against a mere wrong doer.

The defendant appears before the court in no enviable light. He does not pretend that he had a right to the manure, even when scattered upon the highway, superior to that of the plaintiff; but after the plaintiff had changed its original condition and greatly enhanced its value by his labor, he seized and appropriated to his own use the fruits of the plaintiff's outlay, and now seeks immunity from responsibility on the ground that the plaintiff was a wrong doer as well as himself. The conduct of the defendant is in keeping with his claim, and neither commends itself to the favorable consideration of the court. The plaintiff had the peaceable and quiet possession of the property; and we deem this sufficient until the borough of Stamford shall make complaint.

It is further claimed that if the plaintiff had a right to the property by virtue of occupancy, he lost the right when he ceased to retain the actual possession of the manure after scraping it into heaps.

We do not question the general doctrine, that where the right by occupancy exists, it exists no longer than the party retains the actual possession of the property, or till he appropriates it to his own use by removing it to some other place. If he leaves the property at the place where it was discovered, and does nothing whatsoever to enhance its value or change its nature, his right by occupancy is unquestionably gone. But the question is, if a party finds property comparatively worthless, as the plaintiff found the property in question, owing to its scattered condition upon the highway, and greatly increases its value by his labor and expense, does he lose his right if he leaves it a reasonable time to procure the means to take it away, when such means are necessary for its removal?

* * *

NOTE ON THE ECONOMIC THEORY OF PROPERTY

R. POSNER, ECONOMIC ANALYSIS OF LAW 40–42 (8TH ED. 2010)

* * * Imagine a society in which all property rights have been abolished. A farmer plants corn, fertilizes it, and erects scarecrows, but when the corn is ripe his neighbor reaps it and takes it away for his own use. The farmer has no legal remedy against his neighbor's conduct because, although ownership implies the legal right to exclude others from taking or using your property without your consent, he owns neither the land that he sowed nor the crop. Unless defensive measures are feasible (and let us assume for the moment that they are not), after a few such incidents of unauthorized taking the cultivation of land will be abandoned and society will shift to methods of subsistence (such as hunting) that involve less preparatory investment.

Although the value of the crop in our example, as measured by consumers' willingness to pay, may have greatly exceeded its cost in labor, materials, and forgone alternative uses of the land, without property rights there is no incentive to incur these costs because there is no reasonably assured reward for incurring them. The proper incentives are created by parceling out mutually exclusive rights to the use of particular resources among the members of society. If every piece of land is owned by someone—if there is always someone who can exclude all others from access to any given area—then individuals will endeavor by cultivation or other improvements to maximize the value of land. Land is just an example. The principle applies to all valuable resources.

All this has been well known for hundreds of years. In contrast, the static analysis of property rights is only 86 years old. Imagine that a number of farmers own a pasture in common, meaning that none has the right to exclude any of the others and hence none can charge the others for the use of the pasture. We can abstract from the dynamic aspects of the problem by assuming that the pasture is a natural (uncultivated) one, so that there is no question of improving it by investment. Even so, pasturing additional cows will impose a cost on all of the farmers: The cows will have to graze more in order to eat the same amount of grass, and this will reduce their weight. But because none of the farmers pays for the use of the pasture, none will take this cost into account in deciding how many additional cows to pasture, with the result that more cows will be pastured than would be efficient. (Can you see an analogy to highway congestion?)

The problem would disappear if someone owned the pasture and charged each farmer for its use. The charge to each farmer would include the cost he imposes on the other farmers by pasturing additional cows, because that cost reduces the value of the pasture to the other farmers and hence the price they are willing to pay the owner for the right to graze. (Notice the analogy to a toll road).

The creation of individual (as distinct from collective ownership rights is a necessary, rather than sufficient condition, for efficient use of resources. Suppose the farmer in our first example owns the land that he sows but is a bad farmer; his land would be more productive in someone else's hands. Efficiency requires a mechanism by which the farmer can be induced to transfer the property to someone else. A transferable property right is such a mechanism. Suppose Farmer A expects that his farm will yield him $1,000 a year above his labor and other costs, indefinitely. Just as the price of common stock is equal to the present value of the anticipated earnings to which the shareholder will be entitled, so the present value of a parcel of land that is expected to yield an annual net income of $1,000 can be calculated and is the minimum price that A will accept in exchange for his property right. Suppose that present value if $20,000. If B believes that he can use A's land more productively than A, the resent value of B's expected earnings stream will exceed that calculated by A. Suppose it is $30,000. Then at any between $20,000 and $30,000, both A and B will be made better off by a sale, and so here are strong incentives for a voluntary exchange of A's land for B's money.

This discussion to this point may seem to imply that if every valuable (meaning scarce as well as desired) resource were owned by someone (the criterion of universality), if ownership connoted the unqualified power to exclude everybody else from using the resource (exclusivity) as well as to use it oneself, and if ownership rights were freely transferable or, as lawyers say, alienable (transferability), value would be maximized. This leaves out of account, however, the costs of a property-rights system, both the obvious and the subtle ones.

Suppose a farmer thinks he can raise a hog with a market value of $1,000 at a cost of only $500 in labor and materials, for a net of $500, and that no alternative use of the land occupied by the hog would yield a greater net value—in the next best use, his income from the land would be only $200. He will want to raise the hog. But now suppose his property right is qualified in two respects: He has no right to prevent an adjacent railroad from accidentally emitting engine sparks that may set fire to the hog's pen, killing the hog prematurely; and a court may decide that his raising a hog on this land is a nuisance, in which event he will have to sell the hog on disadvantageous (why disadvantageous?) terms before it is grown. In light of these contingencies, he must reevaluate the yield of his land: He must discount his original $1,000 estimate to reflect the probability that the yield may be much less, perhaps zero. Suppose that, after this discounting, the expected revenue from raising the hog (market value times the probability that it will reach the market) is only $600. He will not raise the hog. The anticipated profit from raising the hog is now only $100, since the farmer's costs remain at $500. The next best use, we said would yield a profit of $200. He will put the land to that use even though it is a less valuable use ($200 versus $500) and so the value of the land will fall.

But the analysis is incomplete. Removing the hog may increase the value of surrounding residential land by more than the fall in value of the farmer's parcel. Alternatively, the cost of preventing the emission of engine sparks may exceed the reduction in the value of the farmer's land when he switches from raising hogs to growing, say, fireproof radishes. But, the alert reader may wish to interject, if the increase in value to others from a different use of the farmer's land exceeds the decrease in value to him, let them buy his right. The railroad can purchase an easement to emit sparks; the surrounding homeowners can purchase a covenant from the farmer not to raise hogs; there is no need to limit the farmer's property right. But ... the costs of effecting a transfer of rights—transaction costs—are often prohibitive, and when this is so, giving someone the exclusive right to a resource may reduce rather than increase efficiency.

NOTES AND QUESTIONS

1. Compare Posner with Blackstone's argument made more than 200 years earlier,

> [N]o man would be at the trouble to provide [such valued goods as shelter and clothing] so long as he had only an usufructuary property in them, which was to cease the instant he quited possession; if, as soon as he walked out of his tent, or pulled off his garment, the next stranger who came by would have a right to inhabit the one, and to wear the other.

As long as real property was held in common, argued Blackstone, primitive people squatted on it, exhausted its resources, and moved on to the next parcel. However, the growth of population and the declining availability of untouched land made such uses inefficient.

> As the world by degrees grew more populous, it daily became more difficult to find out new spots to inhabit, without encroaching upon former occupants; and, by constantly occupying the same individual spot, the fruits of the earth were consumed, and its spontaneous produce destroyed, without any provision for future supply or succession. It therefore became necessary to pursue some regular method of providing a constant subsistence.... It was clear that the earth would not produce her fruits in sufficient quantities without the assistance of tillage; but who would be at the pains of tilling it, if another might watch an opportunity to seize upon and enjoy the product of his industry, art, and labor? Had not, therefore, a separate property in lands, as well as movables, been vested in some individuals, the world must have continued a forest....[28]

2. Both Blackstone and Posner argue that rights in private property are economically efficient—that is, that society as a whole is wealthier because rights in private property are recognized. From this premise it is easy to develop arguments that more private property is better than less—in other words, that society as a whole is wealthier if public control of private property is minimized. For an extended argument supporting this proposition, see R. Epstein, Takings: Private Property and The Power of Eminent Domain (1985).

However, a number of other people have argued that this powerful argument for private property is really a subterfuge—designed principally to enable the rich to avoid giving up too much of their property to the poor. That is, expansive protection of private property rights may or may not make society as a whole better off, but it clearly improves the lot of those who happen to own a great deal of private property. See Kennedy, The Structure of Blackstone's Commentaries, 28 Buffalo L.Rev. 205 (1979); Kennedy & Michelman, Are Property and Contract Efficient?, 8 Hofstra L.Rev. 711 (1980).

3. The seminal work on the relationship between economics and the law of property is Coase, The Problem of Social Cost, 3 J.L. & Econ. 1 (1960). The

---

28. 2 W. Blackstone, Commentaries on the Laws of England 3–7 (1766).

"Coase Theorem," for which Professor Ronald Coase won a Nobel Prize for economics in 1992, is discussed more fully in chapter 9. Also important are Calabresi & Melamed, Property Rules, Liability Rules, and Inalienability: One View of the Cathedral, 85 Harv. L. Rev. 1089 (1972); Demsetz, When Does the Rule of Liability Matter?, 1 J. Legal Stud. 13 (1972). For a historical perspective on the relationship between economics and the American law of property rights, see Hovenkamp, The Economics of Legal History, 67 Minn. L. Rev. 645 (1983).

NOTE ON PROPERTY AND PERSONHOOD

MARGARET RADIN, PROPERTY AND PERSONHOOD, 34 STAN. L. REV. 957–61 (1982)

This article explores the relationship between property and person-hood, a relationship that has commonly been both ignored and taken for granted in legal thought. The premise underlying the personhood perspective is that to achieve proper self-development—to be a person—an individual needs some control over resources in the external environment. The necessary assurances of control take the form of property rights. Although explicit elaboration of this perspective is wanting in modern writing on property, the personhood perspective is often implicit in the connections that courts and commentators find between property and privacy or between property and liberty. In addition to its power to explain certain aspects of existing schemes of property entitlement, the personhood perspective can also serve as an explicit source of values for making moral distinctions in property disputes, and hence for either justifying or criticizing current law.

Almost any theory of private property rights can be referred to some notion of personhood. The theory must address the rights accruing to individual persons, and therefore necessarily implicates the nature of the entity to which they accrue. It is not surprising that personhood has played a part in property theories all along the political spectrum. Conservatives rely on an absolute conception of property as sacred to personal autonomy. Communitarians believe that changing conceptions of property reflect and shape the changing nature of persons and communities. Welfare rights liberals find entitlement to a minimal level of resources necessary to the dignity of persons even when the entitlement must curtail the property rights of others. This article does not emphasize how the notion of personhood might figure in the most prevalent traditional lines of liberal property theory: the Lockean labor-desert theory, which focuses on individual autonomy, or the utilitarian theory, which focuses on welfare maximization. It rather attempts to clarify a third strand of liberal property theory that focuses on personal embodiment or self-constitution in terms of "things." This "personhood perspective" corresponds to, or is the dominant premise of, the so-called personality theory of property. Two

main functions of any property theory are the general justification of
property rights and their delineation. . . .

Most people possess certain objects they feel are almost part of
themselves. These objects are closely bound up with personhood because
they are part of the way we constitute ourselves as continuing personal
entities in the world. They may be as different as people are different, but
some common examples might be a wedding ring, a portrait, an heirloom,
or a house.

One may gauge the strength or significance of someone's relationship
with an object by the kind of pain that would be occasioned by its loss. On
this view, an object is closely related to one's personhood if its loss causes
pain that cannot be relieved by the object's replacement. If so, that
particular object is bound up with the holder. For instance, if a wedding
ring is stolen from a jeweler, insurance proceeds can reimburse the
jeweler, but if a wedding ring is stolen from a loving wearer, the price of a
replacement will not restore the status quo—perhaps no amount of money
can do so.

The opposite of holding an object that has become a part of oneself is
holding an object that is perfectly replaceable with other goods of equal
market value. One holds such an object for purely instrumental reasons.
The archetype of such a good is, of course, money, which is almost always
held only to buy other things. A dollar is worth no more than what one
chooses to buy with it, and one dollar bill is as good as another. Other
examples are the wedding ring in the hands of the jeweler, the automobile
in the hands of the dealer, the land in the hands of the developer, or the
apartment in the hands of the commercial landlord. I shall call these
theoretical opposites—property that is bound up with a person and
property that is held purely instrumentally—personal property and fungible property respectively. . . .

Once we admit that a person can be bound up with an external
"thing" in some constitutive sense, we can argue that by virtue of this
connection the person should be accorded broad liberty with respect to
control over that "thing." But here liberty follows from property for
personhood; personhood is the basic concept, not liberty. Of course, if
liberty is viewed not as freedom from interference, or "negative freedom,"
but rather as some positive will that by acting on the external world is
constitutive of the person, then liberty comes closer to capturing the idea
of the self being intimately bound up with things in the external world.

It intuitively appears that there is such a thing as property for
personhood because people become bound up with "things." But this
intuitive view does not compel the conclusion that property for personhood deserves moral recognition or legal protection, because arguably
there is bad as well as good in being bound up with external objects. If
there is a traditional understanding that a well-developed person must
invest herself to some extent in external objects, there is no less a
traditional understanding that one should not invest oneself in the wrong

way or to too great an extent in external objects. Property is damnation as well as salvation, object-fetishism as well as moral groundwork. In this view, the relationship between the shoe fetishist and his shoe will not be respected like that between the spouse and her wedding ring. At the extreme, anyone who lives only for material objects is considered not to be a well-developed person, but rather to be lacking some important attribute of humanity.

NOTES AND QUESTIONS

1.   Should the protection afforded rights in private property differ to the extent that the property is bound up in one's personhood rather than merely being "instrumental?" If you believe that property bound up in one's personhood is deserving of more protection than property that is merely instrumental, how should that be factored in calculating money damages?

2.   What kinds of property that you own would you consider merely instrumental rather than closely aligned with your "personhood?"

§ 1.4   ACQUISITION OF PROPERTY RIGHTS BY FIND

INTRODUCTORY NOTE

In the ancient case of Armory v. Delamirie, 1 Strange 505 (1722) a chimney sweep found a ring in which there was a valuable jewel. He took it to a local jeweler to be appraised. The sweep delivered the ring to an employee of the jeweler who removed the jewel and then returned the ring to the sweep without the jewel. The sweep sued to recover the value of the jewel. The jeweler sought to defend that suit on the grounds that the sweep was not the true owner but the court held for the sweep. In one of the most famous dicta of all property cases, the court stated that the finder had a good title against "all but the rightful owner." (Do you see why this statement is "dicta?") Such broad, sweeping language suggests a strong preference for finders. What policies justify rewarding finders?

No doubt in recognition of this precept, there are almost no suits between a finder of lost property and its true owner. A recent exception is Ganter v. Kapiloff, 69 Md.App. 97, 516 A.2d 611 (1986). In *Ganter*, the true owners of a stamp worth about $150,000 sued to recover the stamp from a finder and, of course, won. What difficulties might the Kapiloff brothers have had in establishing that they were the true owners of the stamps and how might they have surmounted those difficulties? Suppose Ganter had sold the stamps to an unsuspecting collector for $150,000. Would the buyer be required to return the stamps to the Kapiloffs? See chapter 2, *infra*. Why should the true owner prevail over the finder? But see Morgan v. Kroupa, 167 Vt. 99, 702 A.2d 630 (1997) (public's interest in encouraging finders to care for and shelter lost pets can override title of prior possessor where the finder diligently but unsuccessfully sought for over one year to find the prior owner).

The typical lawsuit involving lost property is between the finder and the owner of the *"locus in quo"* (the place where the lost property was found).

FAVORITE v. MILLER

Supreme Court of Connecticut (1978).
176 Conn. 310, 407 A.2d 974.

BOGDANSKI, ASSOCIATE JUSTICE.

On July 9, 1776, a band of patriots, hearing news of the Declaration of Independence, toppled the equestrian statue of King George III, which was located in Bowling Green Park in lower Manhattan, New York. The statue, of gilded lead, was then hacked apart and the pieces ferried over Long Island Sound and loaded onto wagons at Norwalk, Connecticut, to be hauled some fifty miles northward to Oliver Wolcott's bullet-molding foundry in Litchfield, there to be cast into bullets. On the journey to Litchfield, the wagoners halted at Wilton, Connecticut, and while the patriots were imbibing, the loyalists managed to steal back pieces of the statue. The wagonload of the pieces lifted by the Tories was scattered about in the area of the Davis Swamp in Wilton and fragments of the statue have continued to turn up in that area since that time.

Although the above events have been dramatized in the intervening years, the unquestioned historical facts are: (1) the destruction of the statue; (2) cartage of the pieces to the Wolcott Foundry; (3) the pause at Wilton where part of the load was scattered over the Wilton area by loyalists; and (4) repeated discoveries of fragments over the last century.

In 1972, the defendant, Louis Miller, determined that a part of the statue might be located within property owned by the plaintiffs. On October 16 he entered the area of the Davis Swamp owned by the plaintiffs although he knew it to be private property. With the aid of a metal detector, he discovered a statuary fragment fifteen inches square and weighing twenty pounds which was embedded ten inches below the soil. He dug up this fragment and removed it from the plaintiffs' property. The plaintiffs did not learn that a piece of the statue of King George III had been found on their property until they read about it in the newspaper, long after it had been removed.

In due course, the piece of the statue made its way back to New York City, where the defendant agreed to sell it to the Museum of the City of New York for $5500. The museum continues to hold it pending resolution of this controversy.

In March of 1973, the plaintiffs instituted this action to have the fragment returned to them and the case was submitted to the court on a stipulation of facts. The trial court found the issues for the plaintiffs, from which judgment the defendant appealed to this court. The sole issue presented on appeal is whether the claim of the defendant, as finder, is superior to that of the plaintiffs, as owners of the land upon which the historic fragment was discovered.

Traditionally, when questions have arisen concerning the rights of the finder as against the person upon whose land the property was found, the resolution has turned upon the characterization given the property. Typically, if the property was found to be "lost" or "abandoned," the finder would prevail, whereas if the property was characterized as "mislaid," the owner or occupier of the land would prevail.

Lost property has traditionally been defined as involving an involuntary parting, i.e., where there is no intent on the part of the loser to part with the ownership of the property. Foster v. Fidelity Safe Deposit Co., 264 Mo. 89, 174 S.W. 376 (1915); Kuykendall v. Fisher, 61 W.Va. 87, 56 S.E. 48 (1906). . . .

Abandonment, in turn, has been defined as the voluntary relinquishment of ownership of property without reference to any particular person or purpose . . .

[M]islaid property is defined as that which is intentionally placed by the owner where he can obtain custody of it, but afterwards forgotten. . . .

It should be noted that the classification of property as "lost," "abandoned," or "mislaid" requires that a court determine the intent or mental state of the unknown party who at some time in the past parted with the ownership or control of the property.

The trial court in this case applied the traditional approach and ruled in favor of the landowners on the ground that the piece of the statue found by Miller was "mislaid." The factual basis for that conclusion is set out in the finding, where the court found that "the loyalists did not wish to have the pieces [in their possession] during the turmoil surrounding the Revolutionary War and hid them in a place where they could resort to them [after the war], but forgot where they put them."

The defendant contends that the finding was made without evidence and that the court's conclusion "is legally impossible now after 200 years with no living claimants to the fragment and the secret of its burial having died with them." While we cannot agree that the court's conclusion was legally impossible, we do agree that any conclusion as to the mental state of persons engaged in events which occurred over two hundred years ago would be of a conjectural nature and as such does not furnish an adequate basis for determining rights of twentieth century claimants.

The defendant argues further that his rights in the statue are superior to those of anyone except the true owner (i.e., the British government). He presses this claim on the ground that the law has traditionally favored the finder as against all but the true owner, and that because his efforts brought the statue to light, he should be allowed to reap the benefits of his discovery. In his brief, he asserts: "As with archeologists forever probing and unearthing the past, to guide man for the betterment of those to follow, explorers like Miller deserve encouragement, and reward, in their selfless pursuit of the hidden, the unknown."

There are, however, some difficulties with the defendant's position. The first concerns the defendant's characterization of himself as a selfless seeker after knowledge. The facts in the record do not support such a conclusion. The defendant admitted that he was in the business of selling metal detectors and that he has used his success in finding the statue as advertising to boost his sales of such metal detectors, and that the advertising has been financially rewarding. Further, there is the fact that he signed a contract with the City Museum of New York for the sale of the statuary piece and that he stands to profit thereby.

Moreover, even if we assume his motive to be that of historical research alone, that fact will not justify his entering upon the property of another without permission. It is unquestioned that in today's world even archeologists must obtain permission from owners of property and the government of the country involved before they can conduct their explorations. Similarly, mountaineers must apply for permits, sometimes years in advance of their proposed expeditions. On a more familiar level, backpackers and hikers must often obtain permits before being allowed access to certain of our national parks and forests, even though that land is public and not private. Similarly, hunters and fishermen wishing to enter upon private property must first obtain the permission of the owner before they embark upon their respective pursuits.

Although few cases are to be found in this area of the law, one line of cases which have dealt with this issue has held that except where the trespass is trivial or merely technical, the fact that the finder is trespassing is sufficient to deprive him of his normal preference over the owner of the place where the property was found.... The basis for the rule is that a wrongdoer should not be allowed to profit by his wrongdoing.... Another line of cases holds that property, other than treasure trove[1] which is found embedded in the earth is the property of the owner of the locus in quo.... The presumption in such cases is that possession of the article found is in the owner of the land and that the finder acquires no rights to the article found....

The defendant, by his own admission, knew that he was trespassing when he entered upon the property of the plaintiffs. He admitted that he was told by Gertrude Merwyn, the librarian of the Wilton Historical Society, *before* he went into the Davis Swamp area, that the land was privately owned and that Mrs. Merwyn recommended that he call the owners, whom she named, and obtain permission before he began his explorations. He also admitted that when he later told Mrs. Merwyn about

---

1. Treasure trove has traditionally been strictly and narrowly defined as "any gold or silver in coin, plate, or bullion found concealed in the earth or in a house or other private place." 1 Am.Jur.2d 6, Abandoned, Lost, and Unclaimed Property, § 4. This strict definition is well established in American law. Ferguson v. Ray, 44 Or. 557, 77 P. 600 (1904); Danielson v. Roberts, 44 Or. 108, 74 P. 913 (1904) (gold coin); Zech v. Accola, 253 Wis. 80, 33 N.W.2d 232 (1948) (paper certificates); 1 Am.Jur.2d 6, op.cit., § 4, annot., 170 A.L.R. 707. Since the fragment of the statue recovered by the defendant was of gilded lead, he makes no claim that the fragment constituted treasure trove.

his discovery, she again suggested that he contact the owners of the property, but that he failed to do so.

In the stipulation of facts submitted to the court, the defendant admitted entering the Davis Swamp property "with the belief that part of the 'King George Statue' ... might be located within said property and with the intention of removing [the] same if located." The defendant has also admitted that the piece of the statue which he found was embedded in the ground ten inches below the surface and that it was necessary for him to excavate in order to take possession of his find.

In light of those undisputed facts the defendant's trespass was neither technical nor trivial. We conclude that the fact that the property found was embedded in the earth and the fact that the defendant was a trespasser are sufficient to defeat any claim to the property which the defendant might otherwise have had as a finder.

Where the trial court reaches a correct decision but on mistaken grounds, this court has repeatedly sustained the trial court's action if proper grounds exist to support it.

* * *

The present case falls within the ambit of that principle of law and we affirm the decision of the court below.

There is no error.

In this opinion the other Judges concurred.

More on the Story of the Statue

The story of how a piece of a statue of a king of England got from Revolutionary Manhattan to a present-day swamp in Wilton, Connecticut, has become somewhat murky, but the outline is clear enough. It started with the repeal of the Stamp Act in March 1766. The Colonists were deeply grateful to William Pitt the Elder, who had been instrumental in getting the Act repealed. New York City proposed to erect a statue of Pitt, and soon money was being raised for that purpose. But the New Yorkers were shortly reminded that it would hardly be politic to put up a statue to Pitt while neglecting their gracious sovereign, George III. So they found themselves forced also to erect *his* statue.

Both statues were made in England by Joseph Wilton, a widely known sculptor of the time, and both arrived in Manhattan on the same ship in 1770. In depicting the King, Wilton had closely copied the equestrian statue of Marcus Aurelius in Rome. George, larger than life size, bestrode his horse clad in the robes of a Roman emperor, scepter in hand, laurel wreath on head. Horse and rider were made of lead and covered with gold leaf. The statue was erected on Bowling Green near the tip of Manhattan, with the aid of toasts, band music and the firing of "32 Pieces of Cannon from the Battery." . . .

Nothing untoward seems to have happened until July 9, 1776, the day when news of the Declaration of Independence reached New York. Public reading of the Declaration set off much celebrating, and the statue of George III immediately became the target of Sons of Liberty, who hauled him down. . . .

The head was hacked off and a musket ball fired into it, the nose pounded away and the laurel wreath pried off. When the statue was at last abandoned, the patriots paraded away with the head, probably to prolong their victory celebration among the taverns. They planned to display the head on a stick as the heads of traitors were once exhibited on pikes.

The plan was never carried out. There were many Loyalist informers in New York, and so the story of the purloined head almost immediately reached the British army, where it moved Captain John Montresor to action. Montresor had lived in New York for a number of years and had his contacts. He immediately sent a spy named Corby . . . to a Tory innkeeper named Cox, and Corby and Cox, by stratagems unrecorded, stole the head of the statue and buried it while the American soldiers were still chortling over their planned triumph. The American army was forced to retreat from Manhattan in November; then, as Captain Montresor wrote, the head "was dug up on our arrival, and I rewarded the men, and sent the Head by the Lady Gage to Lord Townshend in order to convince them at home of the Infamous Disposition of the Ungrateful people of this distressed Country." . . .

As for the head of the statue, it did reach England. Thomas Hutchinson, prewar governor of Massachusetts, noted in his diary that on November 22, 1777, he had called on Lady Townshend in London (Lord Charles had been author of the Townshend Acts which had done much to push the Colonists toward rebellion). He wrote: "Lady Townshend asked me if I had a mind to see an instance of American loyalty? and going to the sopha, uncovered a large gilt head, which at once appeared to be that of the King. . . . The nose is wounded and defaced, but the gilding remains fair, and as it was well executed, it retains a striking likeness." Where the head went after it left the Townshend "sopha" remains a mystery; no one has told of seeing it since.[2]

BENJAMIN v. LINDNER AVIATION, INC.

Supreme Court of Iowa (1995).
534 N.W.2d 400.

TERNUS, JUSTICE.

Appellant, Heath Benjamin, found over $18,000 in currency inside the wing of an airplane. At the time of this discovery, appellee, State Central Bank, owned the plane and it was being serviced by appellee, Lindner Aviation, Inc. All three parties claimed the money as against the true owner. . . . [T]he district court held that the currency was mislaid property and belonged to the owner of the plane . . . Benjamin appealed . . . We . . . affirm the judgment of the district court.

I. Background Facts and Proceedings.

In April of 1992, State Central Bank became the owner of an airplane when the bank repossessed it from its prior owner who had defaulted on a loan. In August of that year, the bank took the plane to Lindner Aviation for a routine annual inspection. Benjamin worked for Lindner Aviation and did the inspection.

As part of the inspection, Benjamin removed panels from the underside of the wings. Although these panels were to be removed annually as part of the routine inspection, a couple of the screws holding the panel on the left wing were so rusty that Benjamin had to use a drill to remove them. Benjamin testified that the panel probably had not been removed for several years.

Inside the left wing Benjamin discovered two packets approximately four inches high and wrapped in aluminum foil. He removed the packets from the wing and took off the foil wrapping. Inside the foil was paper currency, tied in string and wrapped in handkerchiefs. The currency was predominately twenty-dollar bills with mint dates before the 1960s, primarily in the 1950s. The money smelled musty.

Benjamin took one packet to his jeep and then reported what he had found to his supervisor, offering to divide the money with him. However, the supervisor reported the discovery to the owner of Lindner Aviation, William Engle. Engle insisted that they contact the authorities and he

2. R. Andrist, Alas, poor George, where is your head? 5 Smithsonian Magazine 74, 74–77 (1974).

called the Department of Criminal Investigation. The money was eventually turned over to the Keokuk police department.

Two days later, Benjamin filed an affidavit with the county auditor claiming that he was the finder of the currency under the provisions of Iowa Code chapter 644 (1991). Lindner Aviation and the bank also filed claims to the money. The notices required by chapter 644 were published and posted. See Iowa Code § 644.8 (1991). No one came forward within twelve months claiming to be the true owner of the money. See id. § 644.11 (if true owner does not claim property within twelve months, the right to the property vests in the finder).

Benjamin filed this declaratory judgment action against Lindner Aviation and the bank to establish his right to the property. The parties tried the case to the court. The district court held that chapter 644 applies only to "lost" property and the money here was mislaid property. The court awarded the money to the bank, holding that it was entitled to possession of the money to the exclusion of all but the true owner. The court also held that Benjamin was a "finder" within the meaning of chapter 644 and awarded him a ten percent finder's fee. See id. § 644.13 (a finder of lost property is entitled to ten percent of the value of the lost property as a reward).

Benjamin appealed. He claims that chapter 644 governs the disposition of all found property and any common law distinctions between various types of found property are no longer valid. He asserts alternatively that even under the common law classes of found property, he is entitled to the money he discovered. He claims that the trial court should have found that the property was treasure trove or was lost or abandoned rather than mislaid, thereby entitling the finder to the property.

The bank and Lindner Aviation cross-appealed. Lindner Aviation claims that if the money is mislaid property, it is entitled to the money as the owner of the premises on which the money was found, the hangar where the plane was parked. It argues in the alternative that it is the finder, not Benjamin, because Benjamin discovered the money during his work for Lindner Aviation. The bank asserts in its cross-appeal that it owns the premises where the money was found—the airplane ...

Does Chapter 644 Supersede the Common Law Classifications of Found Property?

Benjamin argues that chapter 644 governs the rights of finders of property and abrogates the common law distinctions between types of found property. As he points out, lost property statutes are intended "to encourage and facilitate the return of property to the true owner, and then to reward a finder for his honesty if the property remains unclaimed." Paset v. Old Orchard Bank & Trust Co., 62 Ill.App.3d 534, 19 Ill.Dec. 389, 393, 378 N.E.2d 1264, 1268 (1978) (interpreting a statute similar to chapter 644); accord Flood v. City Nat'l Bank, 218 Iowa 898, 908, 253 N.W. 509, 514 (1934), cert. denied, 298 U.S. 666, 56 S.Ct. 749, 80 L.Ed. 1390 (1936) (public policy reflected in lost property statute is "to provide a reward to the finder of lost goods"); Willsmore v. Township of Oceola, 106 Mich.App. 671, 308 N.W.2d 796, 804 (1981) (lost goods act "provides protection to the finder, a reasonable method of uniting goods with their true owner, and a plan which benefits the people of the state through their local governments"). These goals, Benjamin argues, can best be achieved by applying such statutes to all types of found property ...

Although a few courts have adopted an expansive view of lost property statutes, we think Iowa law is to the contrary. In 1937, we quoted and affirmed a trial court ruling that "the old law of treasure trove is not merged in the statutory law of chapter 515, 1935 Code of Iowa." Zornes v. Bowen, 223 Iowa 1141, 1145, 274 N.W. 877, 879 (1937). Chapter 515 of the 1935 Iowa Code was eventually renumbered as chapter 644. The relevant sections of chapter 644 are unchanged since our 1937 decision. As recently as 1991, we stated that "[t]he rights of finders of property vary according to the characterization of the property found." Ritz v. Selma United Methodist Church, 467 N.W.2d 266, 268 (Iowa 1991). We went on to define and apply the common law classifications of found property in deciding the rights of the parties. Id. at 269. As our prior cases show, we have continued to use the common law distinctions between classes of found property despite the legislature's enactment of chapter 644 and its predecessors.

The legislature has had many opportunities since our decision in Zornes to amend the statute so that it clearly applies to all types of found property. However, it has not done so. When the legislature leaves a statute unchanged after the supreme court has interpreted it, we presume the legislature has acquiesced in our interpretation. State v. Sheffey, 234 N.W.2d 92, 97 (Iowa 1975). Therefore, we presume here that the legislature approves of our application of chapter 644 to lost property only. Consequently, we hold that chapter 644 does not abrogate the common law classifications of found property. We note this position is consistent with that taken by most jurisdictions. See, e.g., Bishop v. Ellsworth, 91 Ill.App.2d 386, 234 N.E.2d 49, 51 (1968) (holding lost property statute does not apply to abandoned or mislaid property); Foster v. Fidelity Safe Deposit Co., 264 Mo. 89, 174 S.W. 376, 379 (1915) (refusing to apply lost property statute to property that would not be considered lost under the common law); Sovern v. Yoran, 16 Or. 269, 20 P. 100, 105 (1888) (same); Zech v. Accola, 253 Wis. 80, 33 N.W.2d 232, 235 (1948) (concluding that if legislature had intended to include treasure trove within lost property statute, it would have specifically mentioned treasure trove).

In summary, chapter 644 applies only if the property discovered can be categorized as "lost" property as that term is defined under the common law. Thus, the trial court correctly looked to the common law classifications of found property to decide who had the right to the money discovered here.

IV.   Classification of Found Property.

Under the common law, there are four categories of found property: (1) abandoned property, (2) lost property, (3) mislaid property, and (4) treasure trove. Ritz, 467 N.W.2d at 269. The rights of a finder of property depend on how the found property is classified. Id. at 268–69.

A. Abandoned property. Property is abandoned when the owner no longer wants to possess it. Cf. Pearson v. City of Guttenberg, 245 N.W.2d 519, 529 (Iowa 1976) (considering abandonment of real estate). Abandonment is shown by proof that the owner intends to abandon the property and has voluntarily relinquished all right, title and interest in the property. Ritz, 467 N.W.2d at 269; 1 Am.Jur.2d Abandoned Property §§ 11–14, at 15–20. Abandoned property belongs to the finder of the property against all others, including the former owner. Ritz, 467 N.W.2d at 269.

B. Lost property. "Property is lost when the owner unintentionally and involuntarily parts with its possession and does not know where it is." Id. (citing Eldridge v. Herman, 291 N.W.2d 319, 323 (Iowa 1980)); accord 1 Am.Jur.2d Abandoned Property § 4, at 9–10. Stolen property found by someone who did not participate in the theft is lost property. Flood, 218 Iowa at 905, 253 N.W. at 513; 1 Am.Jur.2d Abandoned Property § 5, at 11. Under chapter 644, lost property becomes the property of the finder once the statutory procedures are followed and the owner makes no claim within twelve months. Iowa Code § 644.11 (1991).

C. Mislaid property. Mislaid property is voluntarily put in a certain place by the owner who then overlooks or forgets where the property is. Ritz, 467 N.W.2d at 269. It differs from lost property in that the owner voluntarily and intentionally places mislaid property in the location where it is eventually found by another. 1 Am.Jur.2d Abandoned Property § 10, at 14. In contrast, property is not considered lost unless the owner parts with it involuntarily. Ritz, 467 N.W.2d at 269; 1 Am.Jur.2d Abandoned Property § 10, at 14; see Hill v. Schrunk, 207 Or. 71, 292 P.2d 141, 143 (1956) (carefully concealed currency was mislaid property, not lost property).

The finder of mislaid property acquires no rights to the property. 1 Am.Jur.2d Abandoned Property § 24, at 30. The right of possession of mislaid property belongs to the owner of the premises upon which the property is found, as against all persons other than the true owner. Ritz, 467 N.W.2d at 269.

D. Treasure trove. Treasure trove consists of coins or currency concealed by the owner. Id. It includes an element of antiquity. Id. To be classified as treasure trove, the property must have been hidden or concealed for such a length of time that the owner is probably dead or undiscoverable. Id.; 1 Am.Jur.2d Abandoned Property § 8, at 13. Treasure trove belongs to the finder as against all but the true owner. Zornes, 223 Iowa at 1145, 274 N.W. at 879.

V. Is There Substantial Evidence to Support the Trial Court's
Finding That the Money Found by Benjamin Was Mislaid?

We think there was substantial evidence to find that the currency discovered by Benjamin was mislaid property. In the Eldridge case, we examined the location where the money was found as a factor in determining whether the money was lost property. Eldridge, 291 N.W.2d at 323; accord 1 Am.Jur.2d Abandoned Property § 6, at 11–12 ("The place where money or property claimed as lost is found is an important factor in the determination of the question of whether it was lost or only mislaid."). Similarly, in Ritz, we considered the manner in which the money had been secreted in deciding that it had not been abandoned. Ritz, 467 N.W.2d at 269.

The place where Benjamin found the money and the manner in which it was hidden are also important here. The bills were carefully tied and wrapped and then concealed in a location that was accessible only by removing screws and a panel. These circumstances support an inference that the money was placed there intentionally. This inference supports the conclusion that the money was mislaid. Jackson v. Steinberg, 186 Or. 129, 200 P.2d 376, 378 (1948) (fact that $800 in currency was found concealed beneath the paper lining of a dresser indicates that money was intentionally concealed with intention of reclaiming it; therefore, property was mislaid, not lost); Schley v. Couch, 155 Tex. 195, 284 S.W.2d 333, 336 (1955) (holding that money found buried under garage floor was mislaid property as a matter of law because circumstances showed that money was placed there deliberately and court presumed that owner had either forgotten where he hid the money or had died before retrieving it).

The same facts that support the trial court's conclusion that the money was mislaid prevent us from ruling as a matter of law that the property was lost. Property is not considered lost unless considering the place where and the conditions under which the property is found, there is an inference that the property was left there unintentionally. 1 Am.Jur.2d Abandoned Property § 6, at 12; see Sovern, 20 P. at 105 (holding that coins found in a jar under a wooden floor of a barn were not lost property because the circumstances showed that the money was hidden there intentionally); see Farrare v. City of Pasco, 68 Wash.App. 459, 843 P.2d 1082, 1084 (1992) (where currency was deliberately concealed, it cannot be characterized as lost property). Contrary to Benjamin's position the circumstances here do not support a conclusion that the money was placed in the wing of the airplane unintentionally. Additionally, as the trial court concluded, there was no evidence suggesting that the money was placed in the wing by someone other than the owner of the money and that its location was unknown to the owner. For these reasons, we reject Benjamin's argument that the trial court was obligated to find that the currency Benjamin discovered was lost property.

We also reject Benjamin's assertion that as a matter of law this money was abandoned property. Both logic and common sense suggest that it is unlikely someone would voluntarily part with over $18,000 with the intention of terminating his ownership. The location where this money was found is much more consistent with the conclusion that the owner of the property was placing the money there for safekeeping. See Ritz, 467 N.W.2d at 269 (property not abandoned where money was buried in jars and tin cans, indicating a desire by the owner to preserve it); Jackson, 200 P.2d at 378 (because currency was concealed intentionally and deliberately, the bills could not be regarded as abandoned property); 1 Am.Jur.2d Abandoned Property § 13, at 17 (where property is concealed in such a way that the concealment appears intentional and deliberate, there can be no abandonment). We will not presume that an owner has abandoned his property when his conduct is consistent with a continued claim to the property. Linscomb v. Goodyear Tire & Rubber Co., 199 F.2d 431, 435 (8th Cir.1952) (applying Missouri law); Hoffman Management Corp. v. S.L.C. of N. Am., Inc., 800 S.W.2d 755, 762 (Mo.Ct.App.1990); Foulke v. New York Consolidated R.R., 228 N.Y. 269, 127 N.E. 237, 238 (1920); 1 Am.Jur.2d Abandoned Property §§ 14, 42, at 20, 49; cf. Bennett, 238 Iowa at 706, 28 N.W.2d at 620 (stating that there is no presumption that real property is abandoned). Therefore, we cannot rule that the district court erred in failing to find that the currency discovered by Benjamin was abandoned property.

Finally, we also conclude that the trial court was not obligated to decide that this money was treasure trove. Based on the dates of the currency, the money was no older than thirty-five years. The mint dates, the musty odor and the rusty condition of a few of the panel screws indicate that the money may have been hidden for some time. However, there was no evidence of the age of the airplane or the date of its last inspection. These facts may have shown that the money was concealed for a much shorter period of time.

Moreover, it is also significant that the airplane had a well-documented ownership history. The record reveals that there were only two owners of the plane prior to the bank. One was the person from whom the bank repossessed the plane; the other was the original purchaser of the plane when it was manufactured. Nevertheless, there is no indication that Benjamin or any other party attempted to locate and notify the prior owners of the plane, which could very possibly have led to the identification of the true owner of the money. Under these circumstances, we cannot say as a matter of law that the money meets the antiquity requirement or that it is probable that the owner of the money is not discoverable.

We think the district court had substantial evidence to support its finding that the money found by Benjamin was mislaid. The circumstances of its concealment and the location where it was found support inferences that the owner intentionally placed the money there and intended to retain ownership. We are bound by this factual finding.

VI. Is the Airplane or the Hangar the "Premises" Where the Money Was Discovered?

Because the money discovered by Benjamin was properly found to be mislaid property, it belongs to the owner of the premises where it was found. Mislaid property is entrusted to the owner of the premises where it is found rather than the finder of the property because it is assumed that the true owner may eventually recall where he has placed his property and return there to reclaim it. Willsmore, 308 N.W.2d at 802; Foster, 174 S.W. at 378; Foulke, 127 N.E. at 238–39.

We think that the premises where the money was found is the airplane, not Lindner Aviation's hangar where the airplane happened to be parked when the money was discovered. The policy behind giving ownership of mislaid property to the owner of the premises where the property was mislaid supports this conclusion. If the true owner of the money attempts to locate it, he would initially look for the plane; it is unlikely he would begin his search by contacting businesses where the airplane might have been inspected. Therefore, we affirm the trial court's judgment that the bank, as the owner of the plane, has the right to possession of the property as against all but the true owner . . .

VIII.   Summary.

We conclude that the district court's finding that the money discovered by Benjamin was mislaid property is supported by substantial evidence. Therefore, we affirm the district court's judgment that the bank has the right to the money as against all but the true owner. This decision makes it unnecessary to decide whether Benjamin or Lindner Aviation was the finder of the property. . . .

SNELL, JUSTICE (dissenting).

I respectfully dissent.

The life of the law is logic, it has been said. See Davis v. Aiken, 111 Ga.App. 505, 142 S.E.2d 112, 119 (1965) (quoting Sir Edward Coke). If so, it should be applied here.

The majority quotes with approval the general rule that whether money found is treasure trove, mislaid, abandoned, or lost property is a fact question. 1 Am.Jur.2d Abandoned, Lost, and Unclaimed Property § 41, at 49 (2d ed. 1994). In deciding a fact question, we are to consider the facts as known and all reasonable inferences to be drawn from them. Wright v. Thompson, 254 Iowa 342, 347, 117 N.W.2d 520, 523 (1962). Thus does logic, reason, and common sense enter in.

After considering the four categories of found money, the majority decides that Benjamin found mislaid money. The result is that the bank gets all the money; Benjamin, the finder, gets nothing. Apart from the obvious unfairness in result, I believe this conclusion fails to come from logical analysis.

Mislaid property is property voluntarily put in a certain place by the owner who then overlooks or forgets where the property is. Ritz v. Selma United Methodist Church, 467 N.W.2d 266, 268 (Iowa 1991). The property here consisted of two packets of paper currency totaling $18,910, three to four inches high, wrapped in aluminum foil. Inside the foil, the paper currency, predominantly twenty dollar bills, was tied with string and wrapped in handkerchiefs. Most of the mint dates were in the 1950s with one dated 1934. These packets were found in the left wing of the Mooney airplane after Benjamin removed a panel held in by rusty screws.

These facts satisfy the requirement that the property was voluntarily put in a certain place by the owner. But the second test for determining that property is mislaid is that the owner "overlooks or forgets where the property is." See Ritz, 467 N.W.2d at 269. I do not believe that the facts, logic, or common sense lead to a finding that this requirement is met. It is not likely or reasonable to suppose that a person would secrete $18,000 in an airplane wing and then forget where it was.

Cases cited by the majority contrasting "mislaid" property and "lost" property are appropriate for a comparison of these principles but do not foreclose other considerations ...

The scenario unfolded in this case convinces me that the money found in the airplane wing was abandoned. Property is abandoned when the owner no longer wants to possess it. See Ritz, 467 N.W.2d at 269; Pearson v. City of Guttenberg, 245 N.W.2d 519, 529 (Iowa 1976). The money had been there for years, possibly thirty. No owner had claimed it in that time. No claim was made by the owner after legally prescribed notice was given that it had been found. Thereafter, logic and the law support a finding that the owner has voluntarily relinquished all right, title, and interest in the property. Whether the money was abandoned due to its connection to illegal drug trafficking or is otherwise contraband property is a matter for speculation. In any event, abandonment by the true owner has legally occurred and been established.

I would hold that Benjamin is legally entitled to the entire amount of money that he found in the airplane wing as the owner of abandoned property.

NOTES AND QUESTIONS

1.   Why should the *Benjamin* court presume that the failure of the state legislature to change a judicial holding of long standing reflects legislative assent to that holding? What assumptions underlie that presumption? Was the trial court correct in awarding Benjamin a finder's fee?

2.   The *Benjamin* court did not speculate why the money was secreted in the airplane wing. Suppose, however, evidence suggested that the money had been put there by unknown drug dealers. Might that change the result? See In re Seizure of $82,000 More or Less, 119 F.Supp.2d 1013 (W.D.Mo. 2000) (distinguishing *Benjamin* on this fact and concluding the property had been abandoned).

3.   While it is generally said that a finder has good title against all the world but the true owner, where property is found on the land of another the cases abound with apparent inconsistencies in an attempt to settle the competing claims of the finder and the owner of the *locus in quo*. At either end of the spectrum are two easily administered rules—the finder wins; the owner of the *locus in quo* wins. In fact, the matter is more complicated

because of the judicial tendency to weigh multiple factors in adjudicating whether the finder or the owner of the *locus in quo* should prevail. Thus, some courts take the view that if the goods are found in an area of private property that is open to the general public, the finder wins; if the goods are found in an area of private property that is not open to the general public, the owner of the *locus in quo* wins.

It also appears that some courts are prepared to distinguish between goods which are attached to or are under the land (owner of *locus in quo* wins) and goods that are merely lying on top of the land (finder wins). Finally, and as noted in the principal case, in adjusting the competing claims of the finder and the owner of the *locus in quo,* it can make a difference whether the goods were lost (finder wins) or mislaid (owner of *locus in quo* wins).

A number of law review articles and comments have been written on the law of finders. These include: Cohen, The Finders Cases Revisited, 48 Tex. L. Rev. 1001 (1970); Paulus, Finder vs. Locus In Quo—An Outline, 6 Hastings L.J. 180 (1955); Morton, Public Policy and the Finders Cases, 1 Wyo. L.J. 101 (1946); Riesman, Possession and the Law of Finders, 52 Harv. L. Rev. 1105 (1939); Aigler, Rights of Finders, 21 Mich. L. Rev. 664 (1923); Note, Personal Property—Finding Lost Goods—Rights of Finder and Owner of Locus in Quo in Lost and Mislaid Personal Property, 21 Minn. L. Rev. 191 (1936); Comment, Finders—Rights As Against the Owner of the Locus in Quo, 46 Mich. L. Rev. 235 (1947).

4.   In many cases a dispute arises between the finder and the owner of the land on which the property is found. Generally, where personal property is found on the land of another it is awarded to the finder if the property is characterized as lost property and the finder is not a trespasser. If the found property is characterized as "mislaid property" rather than "lost property" it is awarded to the owner of the *locus in quo* even if the finder is not a trespasser but is an invitee.

> Those who award the goods to the finder adopt without much consideration a popular conception of the "finder" as the one who discovers or brings to knowledge the lost article, and then proceed to declare that the title of the finder is good as against the whole world but the true owner, regardless of the place where found.... Those courts which hold in behalf of the owner of the locus in quo proceed upon the hypothesis that the lost articles belong to the first possessor, and therefore the owner of the property within the compass of which the goods are found, since he possesses such encompassing property and excludes the general public therefrom, must necessarily also possess whatever may be found therein, even though unaware of its presence.... Both lines of authority, however, frequently draw distinctions between goods found in private, or in public or semipublic places, on the ground that if the place is private, for example a private house, then the owner of the locus in quo has the intent to possess the place and whatever may be located therein, whereas if the place is public or semipublic, for example the lobby of a bank, then no such intent can be found....
>
> [As respects mislaid goods] [t]he principle seems to be that by voluntarily placing the article down in a place suitable for such a purpose the owner

of the article constitutes the proprietor of the place some sort of bailee thereof and places it in the "protection of his house" so that the latter and not the finder is entitled to its custody.[3]

Awarding mislaid property to the owner of the *locus in quo* has also been rationalized on the grounds that the true owner will remember where she intentionally placed the mislaid goods and will return to collect them. Thus, the argument goes, awarding the goods to the owner of the *locus in quo* better protects the rights of the true owner. Do you agree? Other factors, of course may determine whether the found property is awarded to the finder or the owner of the *locus in quo* as illustrated in the principal case.

5.   The rights of the finder may be, but are not always, superior to the claims of persons, other than the true owner, who claim an interest in the found property. In each of the following cases, consider whether the finder (F) has a superior right to the property:

(a) F is employed by a hotel to clean guest rooms. F finds $5,000 in a bureau drawer in a room recently vacated by a guest of the hotel. F claims that he is entitled to the $5,000. See Jackson v. Steinberg, 186 Or. 129, 200 P.2d 376 (1948), rehearing denied 186 Or. 129, 205 P.2d 562 (1949). But see Erickson v. Sinykin, 223 Minn. 232, 26 N.W.2d 172 (1947); Ferguson v. Ray, 44 Or. 557, 77 P. 600 (1904); Roberson v. Ellis, 58 Or. 219, 114 P. 100 (1911); Danielson v. Roberts, 44 Or. 108, 74 P. 913 (1904). For a discussion of the Oregon cases, see Comment, 48 Mich. L. Rev. 352 (1950); Comment, 21 Or. L. Rev. 85 (1941). Suppose F found the money on a chair in the hotel lobby as he was leaving for home at the end of the day. Same result?

(b) F, while shopping at her favorite local clothing store, finds a purse containing $600 on the floor of the fitting room. F claims she, and not the owner of the store, is entitled to the money. Should the success of F's claim depend on whether the purse was found on the chair in the fitting room or under the chair? See McAvoy v. Medina, 11 Allen (93 Mass.) 548 (1866). Suppose the true owner of the money advertises to pay a reward to anyone who found her "lost purse." F, in response to the advertisement, returns the purse to the true owner who refuses to pay the reward. If F sues for the reward, what result? Kincaid v. Eaton, 98 Mass. 139 (1867).

(c) O drops his wallet containing $400 in cash on a public street. F–1 finds the wallet and takes possession of it. F–1 loses it in a park on his way home. Subsequently, F–2 finds the wallet and takes possession of it. F–2 then loses it in H's home where it is found by F–3. Who has the superior right to the wallet and cash as between: (1) F–1 and F–2 (See Clark v. Maloney, 3 Harr. (Del.) 68 (1840)); (2) F–2 and H; (3) F–3 and H; and (4) F–1 and H?

(d) O owns a watch. O loses the watch and F–1 finds it. F–1 later loses the watch, and it is found by F–2. If F–1 sues F–2 to recover the possession of the watch, under what circumstances, if any, can F–2

---

3. R. Brown, The Law of Personal Property 26–29 (W. Raushenbush ed., 3d ed. 1975) (citations omitted).

successfully defend this action by showing that O owns the watch? Cf. Barwick v. Barwick, 33 N.C. 80 (1850).

(e) F finds a ring owned by O and takes it to his local jeweler, J, to be appraised. After F tells the jeweler that he found the ring, J refuses to deliver it back to F. F then successfully sues J for money damages under the authority of Armory v. Delamirie, 1 Strange 505 (K.B. 1722). Subsequently, O sues J. Can O recover anything from J? Would your answer differ if F sued J for the ring rather than its value? Can O sue F for whatever F recovered from J? Can O recover more? If O recovers from J, can J recover whatever F recovered from him in the prior suit?

If you are troubled by the possibility that both F and O might recover money damages from J, should F's recovery from J be limited to the value of the ring discounted to take into account the possibility that O might also sue J to recover the value of the ring?

(f) F, while unknowingly trespassing on O's land, finds a buried watch. If O sues F to recover the watch, can F defend on the ground that F did not intentionally trespass on O's land?

(g) F, while trespassing on O's land, finds a ring which T later steals from F. If F sues T for the ring or its value, can F recover? If F recovers the value of the ring from T but it is later determined that as between F and O, O had a better claim to the ring, can O sue T for the ring? How will the suits between F and T and between O and T affect the rights of the true owner?

(h) A was employed by Y to renovate the rooms in Y's hotel. While renovating one room A removed ceiling tiles and found a box near a heating duct with $50,000. A claims title to the money as a "finder." Is the property lost or abandoned (finder wins) or mislaid (Y wins). See Terry v. A.D. Lock, Lock Hospitality, Inc., 343 Ark. 452, 37 S.W.3d 202 (2001).

6. A bailment is the rightful possession by one person of the goods of another. The person in possession of the goods is called the bailee; the person who entrusted the goods to the bailee is called the bailor. Ordinarily a bailment arises as the result of an express contractual relationship between the bailor and bailee. Thus, the accepted characterization of a finder as a bailee is somewhat of an exception to this rule. This exception is justified, nonetheless, because of an assumption that the true owner impliedly consents to the finder taking possession of the lost property. Why is this assumption made?

Generally, two severable issues arise in the law of bailments. The first involves the extent to which the bailee is liable to the bailor for the bailee's failure to return the goods to the bailor. This matter is discussed more fully in Chapter 2.

The other issue relates to the right of the bailee to recover the bailed goods or their value from a third party who has wrongfully taken or damaged the goods. The prevailing American view is that the bailee can recover the goods from a wrongdoer and that the wrongdoer cannot defeat the bailee's claim by showing title in a third person. Thus, in Traylor v. Hyatt Corporation, 122 Ga.App. 633, 178 S.E.2d 289, 290 (1970), the court observed:

> The mere right of possession of personal property, even if the holder has no valid title to it, gives him a right to maintain a suit in trover against a wrongdoer who has deprived him of that possession.... A bailee who is entitled to the possession of the property bailed has such a special interest therein as entitled him to maintain in his own name a suit against a third party for the loss or destruction of the property. Such recovery, however, is for the use or benefit of the owner.

In Berger v. 34th Street Garage, 274 A.D. 414, 416, 84 N.Y.S.2d 348, 350 (1st Dept. 1948) the court, adopting the so-called "Winkfield doctrine," observed that "in an action against a stranger for loss of goods caused by his negligence the bailee in possession can recover the full value of the goods" even though the bailee initially would not be liable to the bailor for the loss of the goods or their damage because the bailee was not at fault. Furthermore, the court observed that the wrongdoer, having paid the bailee, would have a defense if the bailor later sued the wrongdoer to recover the goods or their value.

Should it follow that if the bailee recovers from the wrongdoer the bailor cannot also recover from the wrongdoer? See Comment: Bailment: The Winkfield Doctrine, 34 Cornell L.Q. 615, 617–619 (1949). Even if you agree that a voluntary bailor should be bound, if the bailee is a finder should the true owner be bound considering the true owner did not select the bailee?

These foregoing principles can also apply where a person wrongfully comes into the possession of the goods of another. In Anderson v. Gouldberg, 51 Minn. 294, 53 N.W. 636 (1892), the plaintiff brought an action to recover the possession of pine logs from the defendant who allegedly had taken them wrongfully from the plaintiff. The plaintiff had acquired the logs by trespassing on the land of another. The trial court instructed the jury that even though the plaintiff was a trespasser, his title was good against all the world except the true owner or one claiming from the true owner. The defendant appealed a jury verdict for the plaintiff. In affirming the decision below the court stated that "[o]ne who has acquired the possession of property, whether by finding, bailment, or by mere tort, has a right to retain that possession as against a mere wrongdoer who is a stranger to the property. Any other rule would lead to an endless series of unlawful seizures and reprisals in every case where property had once passed out of the possession of the rightful owner." Id. at 296, 53 N.W. at 637. See also 1 F. Harper & F. James, The Law of Torts 118–124 (1956) (approving the rule of Anderson v. Gouldberg). Cf. W. Keeton, D. Dobbs, R. Keeton & D. Owen, Prosser & Keeton on The Law of Torts 103 (5th ed. 1984).

The rule of Anderson v. Gouldberg has apparently been rejected in North Carolina, at least in cases where the "true owner" is known at the time the suit is brought. In Barwick v. Barwick, 33 N.C. 80, 82 (1850) the North Carolina court stated:

> There are cases in the English books, and in the reports of some of our sister states to the contrary; but we must be allowed to say, that the doctrine of our Courts is fully sustained by the reason of the thing, and is

most consonant with the peculiar principles of this action. The cases differing from our decision, are all based upon a misapprehension of the principle laid down in the leading case . . . [Armory v. Delamarie]. In that case the jewel was lost, and was found by the plaintiff, a chimney sweeper. He had a right to take it into possession, and became the owner by the title of occupancy, except in the event of the true owner becoming known. The former owner of the jewel was not known, and it was properly decided that the finder might maintain trover against the defendant, to whom he had handed it for inspection, and who refused to restore it.

But the result of that case would have been very different, if the owner had been known. The defendant could then have said to the plaintiff, you have no right to make me pay you the value, when I must forthwith deliver up the property to the owner, or else pay him the value a second time.

The distinction between that case, when the possessor was the only known owner, and the ordinary case of one, who himself has the possession wrongfully and sues another wrongdoer for interfering with his possession, the true owner being known and standing by, ready to sue for the property, is as clear as day-light.

The *Barwick* court's decision was subsequently followed in Russell v. Hill, 125 N.C. 470, 34 S.E. 640 (1899).

Does it follow that if Anderson recovers from Gouldberg the true owner could later recover from Gouldberg as well? In the case of a voluntary bailment, for example, it is generally the rule that if the bailee recovers from a wrongdoer, the true owner cannot also recover from the wrongdoer. Rather the true owner must recover from the bailee. See also W. Keeton, D. Dobbs, R. Keeton & D. Owen, Prosser & Keeton on The Law of Torts 103–05 (5th ed. 1985). Where the suit is between two wrongdoers (as appears to be the case in Anderson v. Gouldberg) it is not as clear that a second suit by the true owner against the same defendant should be barred:

> [T]he burden of double payment by the second wrongdoer seems preferable to the hardship of remitting the owner to the first of two wrongdoers. Since the owner is the only innocent one of the three, he should be protected at the expense of whichever wrongdoer he can catch, and indeed it seems not too much if his protection comes at the double expense of one of them. The only alternative to this solution is to deprive the first wrongdoer of his remedy against the second.

1 F. Harper & F. James, The Law of Torts 100, 101 (1956). How does the rationale in Harper & James cut in a case like *Barwick* where the true owner is known?

7. English law recognized a special kind of lost property known as "treasure trove." Treasure trove was generally defined as gold or silver in coin, bullion, or plate concealed in a house or in the earth and having an unknown owner. See R. Brown, The Law of Personal Property 28 (W. Raushenbush ed., 3d ed. 1975). While originally the law awarded such property to the finder, ultimately the courts awarded it to the monarch. In the

United States, no state has ever claimed title to lost property on the rationale that it is treasure trove. Rather, the American courts have merged the law of treasure trove into the law of finders. More often than not treasure trove is awarded to the finder, although some courts have awarded it to the owner of the *locus in quo.* Compare Zornes v. Bowen, 223 Iowa 1141, 274 N.W. 877 (1937) with Schley v. Couch, 155 Tex. 195, 284 S.W.2d 333 (1955). Today, treasure trove is not limited to buried gold or silver. It can include money that is hidden above the ground. See, e.g., Zech v. Accola, 253 Wis. 80, 33 N.W.2d 232 (1948). See also Salvors, Finders, Good Samaritans, and Other Rescuers: An Economic Study of Law and Altruism, 7 J. Legal Stud. 83 (1978) (discussion of the economics of the principle that "the owner of lost property can post a reward and anybody who, knowing of it, complies with its terms is legally entitled to it").

8. A great number of cases have been litigated concerning money found in the safety deposit box area of a bank. The outcome of these cases may depend upon the characterization of the found property as lost or mislaid or upon the court's view of the obligation of the bank to take custody of the money for the true owner. Compare Paset v. Old Orchard Bank & Trust Co., 62 Ill.App.3d 534, 19 Ill.Dec. 389, 378 N.E.2d 1264 (1978) (finder wins) with Pyle v. Springfield Marine Bank, 330 Ill.App. 1, 70 N.E.2d 257 (1946) (finder loses).

In Cohen v. Manufacturers Safe Deposit Company, 297 N.Y. 266, 78 N.E.2d 604 (1948), the court acknowledged that if the money had been inadvertently dropped on the floor by a customer of the bank, the bank might have a claim superior to that of the finder. However, the court was unwilling to indulge in any assumption regarding how the money got on the floor, stating that for all either party knew, the money may have been left by a stranger entering the safe deposit box area under court order. The court also refused to hold for the bank on the assumption that the property had been mislaid.

9. In Favorite v. Miller, the Museum of the City of New York is holding the statuary subject to the outcome of the lawsuit. Thus, it does not appear that it has assumed any risk that Miller did not have title. Suppose, however, it had no knowledge of the suit. Rather it had purchased the fragment from Miller believing that Miller's possession gave him a clear title to the fragment. Would its belief that Miller had good title insulate it from a suit by the landowner to recover the fragment? See Chapter 2, *infra.*

10. In In re Seizure of $82.000 More or Less v. United States of America, 119 F.Supp. 2d 1013 (WD Mo. 2000), the buyer of an automobile at a government forfeiture sale of a car confiscated as the result of a drug raid took the car to a mechanic because the car was getting less miles per gallon than it should have. When inspecting the car's fuel tank the mechanic found $82,000 in the gas tank of the vehicle. The buyer claimed the money was mislaid property and that as owners of the locus in quo they were entitled to the money. The court rejected the argument that the money was mislaid. Said the court:

> Property is mislaid if it is voluntarily put down by its owner and its owner forgets where the property is.... A purse found on a counter or the seat of a bus will generally be characterized as mislaid because it is

logical to assume that the purse was intentionally placed and then forgotten. A wallet found on the floor, however, will be characterized as lost because it is unlikely that someone would put a wallet on the floor intending to return for it. If property is lost, possession of the property is entrusted to the finder of the lost property not the owner of the premises where the property is found. . . . If the property is mislaid, then the owner of the premises where the property is found is entitled to possession, not the finder. . . .

The factual record in this case does not support the Chappells' conclusion that the $82,000 is mislaid property. While the money was almost certainly placed in the gas tank intentionally, it is equally certain that the owners of the currency knew what happened to the money and chose not to claim it. Indeed, at least one district court has concluded that it is "beyond belief" that anyone would hide a large amount of currency and then suddenly forget where it was. . . .

[The cases cited by the buyer of the car] in support of their argument that the currency was mislaid are distinguishable. In *Benjamin v. Lindner Aviation, Inc.,* 534 N.W.2d 400 (Iowa 1995), a large amount of cash was found in the wing of the airplane. The cash had been in the plane for nearly 30 years and there was no evidence as to why the money was secreted or to whom it belonged. *Id.* at 407. Similarly in *Buzard,* a large amount of cash was secreted in the wall of a building. There was no way to identify how long the money had been in the wall or who might have hidden it. In both cases, the courts characterized the money as mislaid. The courts reasoned that, but for a lapse of memory, the true owners would have returned for such valuable property. The record in this case, however, is not so skeletal. There is a good explanation for why the true owners did not seek to recover the currency even though they knew where it was. The money was owned by drug dealers and if they came to claim it, they might eventually be arrested for participating in a drug conspiracy. Because the Court finds that the owner of the $82,000 knew its location, the second prong of the mislaid property test was not satisfied.

Instead of finding the property lost or mislaid, the Court finds the property abandoned. Abandonment consists of two elements: "(1) an intent to abandon, and (2) the external act by which the intention is carried into effect." *Hoffman Management Corp. v. S.L.C. of North Am., Inc.,* 800 S.W.2d 755, 762 (Mo.App.1990) (*quoting Linscomb v. Goodyear Tire & Rubber Co.,* 199 F.2d 431, 435 (8th Cir.1952)). Although abandonment should not be presumed lightly, it may be found when the evidence clearly and decisively leads to that conclusion. *Id.* This is such a case. Drug traffickers know better than to stake claims to contraband and drug proceeds. It is far more sensible for such criminals to disclaim any interest in the property and avoid possible prosecution. *See Herron v. Whiteside,* 782 S.W.2d 414, 416 (Mo.App.1989). In this case, Lopez–Velez originally contested the forfeiture of the vehicle and the $24,000, but he never showed up to pursue his claim. It would stretch credulity to conclude that he knew about the $24,000 in the battery case and that the vehicle was transporting drug proceeds, but he and the owner of the car did not know about the $82,000. Rather, the evidence shows that the original owners of the currency intended to abandon the $82,000 after the 1995 Volkswagen Golf was seized by the DEA, and that they acted on this intent by failing to come forward and claim the funds.

Under Missouri law, those who abandon property lose title.... Therefore, under Missouri law, no one owned the $82,000 while these funds were hidden in the Volkswagen Golf after it was abandoned. *See Foster v. Fidelity Safe Deposit Co.,* 162 Mo.App. 165, 145 S.W. 139, 142 (1912). The currency went back into a state of nature analogous to wild animals. *See Pierson v. Post,* 3 Cai. R. 175 (N.Y.Sup.1805). The question is who has the right to this currency which was abandoned and for a period of time was owned by no one?

Once property has been abandoned, the first finder who acquires dominion over the property becomes its owner. *Foster,* 145 S.W. at 142; *Campbell v. Cochran,* 416 A.2d 211 (Del.Super.1980). The first person to exercise dominion over this $82,000 was the Waldo mechanic. The mechanic, however, was acting as the Chappells' agent at the moment he took possession of the currency ... He had been told that there was a fuel problem with the vehicle. It was during his investigation of the fuel problem that he found the $82,000. Under these circumstances should the agent or his principal be entitled to the currency?

Missouri has not specifically addressed this question, but other jurisdictions have held that possession by the agent is in fact possession by the principal. *South Staffordshire Water Co. v. Sharman,* 2 L.R.Q.B. Div. 44 (1886); *Goodhart, Three Cases on Possession,* 3 CAMB. L.J. 195, 205–06 (1928); *Jackson v. Steinberg,* 186 Or. 129, 200 P.2d 376, 378 (1948). In *Ray v. Flower Hosp.,* 1 Ohio App.3d 127, 439 N.E.2d 942, 945 (1981) the Ohio Court of Appeals stated: "In a long line of cases where hotel chambermaids, bank janitors, bank tellers, grocery store bagboys and other employees have found property while in their employ, virtually every case has charged the employee with the duty to turn the found property over to the employer for safekeeping." The reason for such a holding is that " '... the possession of the servant ... [is] the possession of the [employer] and that, therefore, the element is wanting which would give the title to the servant as against the master ...' " (quoting *Jackson,* 200 P.2d at 379). *Also see,* Boyer, Hovenkamp & Kurtz, *The Law of Property* at 8 (4th Ed.) ("... [T]he possession of articles found during and within the scope of one's employment is generally awarded to the employer and not to the finder.")

Not all courts have agreed on this issue, however. *See, Kalyvakis v. The Olympia,* 181 F.Supp. 32, 36–37 (S.D.N.Y.1960). *Also see,* R.H. Helmholz, *Equitable Div. and the Law of Finders,* 52 FORDHAM L. REV. 313, 319 (1983) ("As with the distinction between lost and mislaid items based on the place of finding, the distinction between finding by employees and finding by non-employees has appeared incapable of consistent application over the course of the last forty-five years.")

The Court finds the more persuasive position on this question is that abandoned property found by an agent is the property of the principal, so long as the agent is acting within the scope of his agency. This is consistent with Missouri's position that an agent must account for any profits he acquires during the agency relationship. *Groh v. Shelton,* 428 S.W.2d 911, 916 (Mo.App.1968). This case is also factually distinguishable from *Kalyvakis,* 181 F.Supp. at 36–37 where a steward on a steamship found property on the deck of the ship while walking from one place to another. In contrast, the Chappells told their mechanic to fix the fuel problem in their car and it was during the mechanic's specifically assigned task that the money was located. Finally, and most importantly, this conclusion is consistent with the reasonable expectations of a car owner. One does not expect that the mechanic to whom a car is entrusted has the right to look through it and keep things which are hidden therein.

For similar reasons, the courts have held that objects found underground belong to the land owner, not the person who found them. *Allred v. Biegel,* 240 Mo.App. 818, 219 S.W.2d 665 (1949) "In such cases it is held that the presumption is that the finder has no rights therein, the presumption being that possession is in the owner of the locus in quo." *Id.* at 666. "Because of policy concerns, courts award embedded property to the locus owner. Courts consider embedded property to be an exception to the general category of lost property. By distinguishing embedded property from other finds, courts hope to eliminate waste and spoilage of property and recognize locus owners' expectations about and constructive possession of items embedded within the land." Leanna Izuel, *Property Owners' Constructive Possession of Treasure Trove: Rethinking the Finders Keepers Rule,* 38 UCLA L. REV. 1659 (1991). For all these reasons, the Court concludes that the Chappells became the owner of the $82,000 when the mechanic first found the money. *Id.* at 1018–1021.

11.   As noted in *Benjamin,* many states have adopted "lost property" statutes in an attempt to create certainty out of judicial disorder. New York statute, N.Y. Pers. Prop. Law §§ 251 et seq. (McKinney's 1976 & Supp.1986), is one of the most comprehensive. Unlike the Iowa statute, it applies to both lost and mislaid property. In part it provides:

§ 251. Definitions

1.   The term "property" as used in this article means money, instruments payable, drawn or issued to bearer or to cash, goods, chattels and tangible personal property . . .

* * *

3.   The term "lost property" as used in this article includes lost or mislaid property. Abandoned property, waifs and treasure trove, and other property which is found, shall be presumed to be lost property and such presumption shall be conclusive unless it is established in an action or proceeding commenced within six months after the date of the finding that the property is not lost property.

4.   The term "owner" as used in this article means any person entitled to possession of the lost property as against the finder and against any other person who has made a claim.

5. The term "finder" as used in this article means the person who first takes possession of lost property.

* * *

§ 252. Found Property and Found Instruments to Be Deposited With Police; Penalty for Failure to Deliver to Police; Delivery to Persons in Possession of Premises Where Found

1. ... [A]ny person who finds lost property of the value of twenty dollars or more or comes into possession of property of the value of twenty dollars or more with knowledge that it is lost property or found property shall, within ten days after the finding or acquisition of possession thereof, either return it to the owner or report such finding or acquisition of possession and deposit such property in a police station or police headquarters of the city where the finding occurred or possession was acquired. . . .

* * *

3. Except as provided in subdivision four of this section, any person who shall refuse or wilfully neglect to comply with the provisions of subdivision one or subdivision two of this section shall be guilty of a misdemeanor and upon conviction thereof shall be punished by a fine of not more than one hundred dollars or imprisonment not exceeding six months or both.

4. A person shall not be subject to criminal prosecution for failure to report a finding or acquisition of possession of found property or of a found instrument to the police and deposit such property or instrument with the police if, in lieu thereof, he delivers the property or instrument to the person in possession of the premises where the property or instrument was found, provided he had no reason to believe that such person would not comply with subdivision one or subdivision two of this section.

A person who delivers found property or a found instrument to the person in possession of the premises where the property or instrument was found is not liable to the owner or person entitled thereto for such delivery if he had no reason to believe that such person in possession of the premises would not comply with subdivision one or subdivision two of this section.

§ 254. Disposition of Lost Property

Except as provided in section two hundred fifty-six of this chapter, lost property deposited with the police ... shall be disposed of as follows:

    1. It shall be delivered to the owner, upon his demand and upon payment of all reasonable expenses incurred in connection therewith, if no written notice of any other claim to the property has been served upon the police having custody, and the time specified in subdivision seven of section two hundred fifty-three of this chapter has not expired or, if such period has expired, no demand has been

made by the finder or a person entitled to assert the right of the finder as provided in section two hundred fifty-six of this chapter.

2.   If at the end of [one year] the owner has not claimed the property . . ., it shall be delivered to the finder, or person entitled to assert the rights of the finder as provided in section two hundred fifty-six of this chapter, upon his demand therefor, and upon payment of all reasonable expenses incurred in connection therewith.

§ 256. Exceptions

1.   If a finder takes possession of lost property while he is upon premises with respect to which his presence is a crime, the person in possession of the premises where the lost property was found shall have the rights of the finder. . . .

If, . . . the finder is an employee under a duty to deliver the lost property to his employer, the employer shall have the rights of the finder as provided in section two hundred fifty-four if, before the property is delivered to the finder by the police, he shall file with the police having custody of the property a written notice asserting such rights . . .

§ 257. Title to Lost Property

1.   The title to lost property which has been deposited with the police shall vest in the finder, or other person entitled to assert the rights of the finder as provided in section two hundred fifty-six of this chapter, when the property is delivered to him in accordance with section two hundred fifty-four of this chapter and shall vest in the buyer when the property is sold as provided in section two hundred fifty-three or two hundred fifty-four of this chapter.

NOTES AND QUESTIONS

1.   If a statute like Section 256 of the New York Pers. Prop. Law applied in Connecticut and Iowa, would the result in Favorite v. Miller or Benjamin v. Lindner Aviation have been different?

2.   A man employed a carpenter to remodel the basement in the man's home. In the course of the remodeling, the carpenter found $25,000 hidden in the wall of the basement. Initially, the carpenter did not comply with the New York statute in all respects, although ultimately the money was turned over to the police. When the money was not claimed within one year by the true owner, the man who employed the carpenter sued to compel the police to give him the money. The carpenter was joined in this action. In resolving a dispute between the man and carpenter under the New York statute: (a) should it matter that the carpenter did not fully comply with the statute; (b) would it make a difference if the money was characterized as "mislaid" rather than lost property; and (c) should it matter that the man hired the carpenter? See Hurley v. City of Niagara Falls, New York, 30 A.D.2d 89, 289 N.Y.S.2d 889 (4th Dept. 1968), aff'd, 25 N.Y.2d 687, 306 N.Y.S.2d 689, 254 N.E.2d 917 (1969).

The Good Ship Titanic

On September 1, 1985, 400 miles off the coast of Newfoundland, a joint mission of American and French scientists using sophisticated underwater cameras and other equipment discovered a massive object two miles beneath the surface resting on the ocean floor. They had discovered the long romanticized "Titanic," which sunk on April 15, 1912, on its maiden voyage after hitting an iceberg in the North Atlantic. Over 1500 people perished in the tragedy. The pictures taken revealed many well-preserved items scattered across the ocean floor. Soon after the discovery was publicized, would-be treasure hunters announced plans to salvage the ship and its contents rumored to be valued at many millions of dollars. One of them, RMS Titanic, won salvage rights in 1987 and has since recovered many items of personal property from the ship, which it exhibits internationally. It has also extensively filmed the ship. Most recently, the saga of the Titanic was memorialized in a movie by director James Cameron. This movie is one of the highest grossing money making films of all time and won 11 Oscars to tie with Ben Hur for the most Oscars ever awarded a picture.

NOTES AND QUESTIONS

1. Under common law finders law, who owns the Titanic? Before answering this question, consider who might have a claim.

2. Can the head of the team that located the Titanic prevent would-be salvors from salvaging the vessel?

3. Under the law of salvage, salvors are often rewarded generously. Three elements must be established in order to present a salvage claim: (1) a marine peril, (2) rescue voluntarily rendered (i.e., there must not have been an existing legal duty to rescue) and (3) success, either in whole or in part, of recovery of the imperiled property. A salvage claim is most often made for the rescue of a ship in distress but it can also be made for the salvage of a sunken vessel. The marine peril encountered by a long-sunken vessel is the "peril of being lost through actions of the elements." Salvors of sunken vessels are often awarded full ownership of the vessel on the theory that the true owner has no intention of returning to claim the vessel. It is also stated that the mere act of discovery does not vest ownership of the discovered vessel in the finder.

> Persons who actually reduce lost or abandoned objects to possession and persons who are actively and ably engaged in efforts to do so are legally protected against interference from others, whereas persons who simply discover or locate such property, but do not undertake to reduce it to possession, are not. This principle reflects a very simple policy—the law acts to afford protection to persons who actually endeavor to return lost or abandoned goods to society as an incentive to undertake such expensive and risky ventures; the law does not clothe mere discovery with an exclusive right to the discovered property because such a rule would provide little encouragement to the discoverer to pursue the often strenuous task of actually retrieving the property and returning it to a socially useful purpose and yet would bar others from attempting to do so.

Treasure Salvors, Inc. v. Unidentified Wrecked and Abandoned Sailing Vessel, 640 F.2d 560, 572–73 (5th Cir.1981), on remand, 546 F.Supp. 919 (S.D.Fla. 1981). See also R.M.S. Titanic, Inc. v. Wrecked and Abandoned Vessel, 742 F.Supp.2d 784 (E.D.Va. 2010); Brady v. The S.S. African Queen, 179 F.Supp. 321 (E.D.Va.1960); Rickard v. Pringle, 293 F.Supp. 981 (E.D.N.Y.1968); Eads v. Brazelton, 22 Ark. 499 (1861).

The *Treasure Salvors* case is one of several lawsuits that arose after the discovery of a Spanish galleon, the Nuestra Senora de Atocha, by Treasure Salvors, Inc. The Corporation had originally discovered scattered remnants of the wreck in 1973. The bulk of the wreck was finally discovered in July of 1985. The Atocha sunk during a hurricane in 1622 while in route from Havana to Cadiz. The ship carried 47 tons of gold and silver estimated to have a current market value of more than $400,000,000.

In Columbus–America Discovery Group v. Atlantic Mutual Insurance Company, 974 F.2d 450 (4th Cir.1992), the court refused to apply the law of finders to award title to a salvor of the S.S. Central America which was reputed to have been carrying gold bullion currently worth $1 billion at the time she sank in 1857. The salvor sought to claim title as against a host of defendants including successors to the insurers who had settled with the owners of the gold at the time the S.S. Central America sunk. After discussing at great length the difference between the law of finders and the law of salvors, the court stated that:

an abandonment of sunken cargo so as to lose possession must be shown not by the mere cessation of attempts to recover, but by the owner's positive relinquishment of his rights in the property . . .

[W]hen sunken ships or their cargo are rescued from the bottom of the ocean by those other than the owners, courts favor applying the law of salvage over the law of finds. Finds law should be applied, however, in situations where the previous owners are found to have abandoned their property. Such abandonment must be proved by clear and convincing evidence, though, such as an owner's express declaration abandoning title. Should the property encompass an ancient and long lost shipwreck, a court may infer an abandonment. Such an inference would be improper, though, should a previous owner appear and assert his ownership interest; in such a case the normal presumptions would apply and an abandonment would have to be proved by strong and convincing evidence. Id. at 464–65.

By applying the law of salvors, the salvor is entitled to "the right to compensation for service, not the right to title . . . the salvor receives a payment, depending on the value of the service rendered." Id. at 460–61. When the law of finds applies, the salvor acquires title to the recovered goods.

The law of finders should not be applied to unrecovered cargo that still remains in the sunken vessel because "success of a finder is measured solely in terms of obtaining possession of specific property." Hener v. United States, 525 F.Supp. 350, 356 (S.D.N.Y.1981). For unrecovered cargo, the salvor may have rights under the law of salvage only. See Bemis v. The RMS Lusitania, 884 F.Supp. 1042 (E.D.Va.1995).

§ 1.5 ACQUISITION OF PROPERTY RIGHTS BY CREATION

WHITE v. SAMSUNG ELECTRONICS AMERICA, INC.

United States Court of Appeals for the Ninth Circuit (1992).
971 F.2d 1395.

GOODWIN, SENIOR CIRCUIT JUDGE:

This case involves a promotional "fame and fortune" dispute. In running a particular advertisement without Vanna White's permission, defendants Samsung Electronics America, Inc. (Samsung) and David Deutsch Associates, Inc. (Deutsch) attempted to capitalize on White's fame to enhance their fortune. White sued, alleging infringement of various intellectual property rights, but the district court granted summary judgment in favor of the defendants. We affirm in part, reverse in part, and remand.

Plaintiff Vanna White is the hostess of "Wheel of Fortune," one of the most popular game shows in television history. An estimated forty million people watch the program daily. Capitalizing on the fame which her participation in the show has bestowed on her, White markets her identity to various advertisers.

The dispute in this case arose out of a series of advertisements prepared for Samsung by Deutsch. The series ran in at least half a dozen publications with widespread, and in some cases national, circulation. Each of the advertisements in the series followed the same theme. Each depicted a current item from popular culture and a Samsung electronic product. Each was set in the twenty-first century and conveyed the message that the Samsung product would still be in use by that time. By hypothesizing outrageous future outcomes for the cultural items, the ads created humorous effects. For example, one lampooned current popular notions of an unhealthy diet by depicting a raw steak with the caption: "Revealed to be health food. 2010 A.D." Another depicted irreverent "news"—show host Morton Downey Jr. in front of an American flag with the caption: "Presidential candidate. 2008 A.D."

The advertisement which prompted the current dispute was for Samsung video-cassette recorders (VCRs). The ad depicted a robot, dressed in a wig, gown, and jewelry which Deutsch consciously selected to resemble White's hair and dress. The robot was posed next to a game board which is instantly recognizable as the Wheel of Fortune game show set, in a stance for which White is famous. The caption of the ad read: "Longest-running game show. 2012 A.D." Defendants referred to the ad as the "Vanna White" ad. Unlike the other celebrities used in the campaign, White neither consented to the ads nor was she paid.

Following the circulation of the robot ad, White sued Samsung and Deutsch in federal district court under: (1) California Civil Code § 3344; (2) the California common law right of publicity; and (3) § 43(a) of the Lanham Act, 15 U.S.C. § 1125(a). The district court granted summary judgment against White on each of her claims. White now appeals. . . .

[Ed. Note: The portions of the opinion pertaining to the first and third claims are omitted]

White . . . argues that the district court erred in granting summary judgment to defendants on White's common law right of publicity claim. In Eastwood v. Superior Court, 149 Cal.App.3d 409, 198 Cal.Rptr. 342 (1983), the California court of appeal stated that the common law right of publicity cause of action "may be pleaded by alleging (1) the defendant's use of the plaintiff's identity; (2) the appropriation of plaintiff's name or likeness to defendant's advantage, commercially or otherwise; (3) lack of consent; and (4) resulting injury." Id. at 417, 198 Cal.Rptr. 342 (citing Prosser, Law of Torts (4th ed. 1971) § 117, pp. 804–807). The district court dismissed White's claim for failure to satisfy Eastwood's second prong, reasoning that defendants had not appropriated White's "name or likeness" with their robot ad. We agree that the robot ad did not make use of White's name or likeness. However, the common law right of publicity is not so confined.

The Eastwood court did not hold that the right of publicity cause of action could be pleaded only by alleging an appropriation of name or likeness. Eastwood involved an unauthorized use of photographs of Clint

Eastwood and of his name. Accordingly, the Eastwood court had no occasion to consider the extent beyond the use of name or likeness to which the right of publicity reaches. That court held only that the right of publicity cause of action "may be" pleaded by alleging, inter alia, appropriation of name or likeness, not that the action may be pleaded only in those terms.

The "name or likeness" formulation referred to in Eastwood originated not as an element of the right of publicity cause of action, but as a description of the types of cases in which the cause of action had been recognized. The source of this formulation is Prosser, Privacy, 48 Cal. L.Rev. 383, 401–07 (1960), one of the earliest and most enduring articulations of the common law right of publicity cause of action. In looking at the case law to that point, Prosser recognized that right of publicity cases involved one of two basic factual scenarios: name appropriation, and picture or other likeness appropriation. Id. at 401–02, nn. 156–57.

Even though Prosser focused on appropriations of name or likeness in discussing the right of publicity, he noted that "[i]t is not impossible that there might be appropriation of the plaintiff's identity, as by impersonation, without the use of either his name or his likeness, and that this would be an invasion of his right of privacy." Id. at 401, n. 155. At the time Prosser wrote, he noted however, that "[n]o such case appears to have arisen." Id.

Since Prosser's early formulation, the case law has borne out his insight that the right of publicity is not limited to the appropriation of name or likeness. In Motschenbacher v. R.J. Reynolds Tobacco Co., 498 F.2d 821 (9th Cir.1974), the defendant had used a photograph of the plaintiff's race car in a television commercial. Although the plaintiff appeared driving the car in the photograph, his features were not visible. Even though the defendant had not appropriated the plaintiff's name or likeness, this court held that plaintiff's California right of publicity claim should reach the jury.

In Midler,[1] this court held that, even though the defendants had not used Midler's name or likeness, Midler had stated a claim for violation of her California common law right of publicity because "the defendants . . . for their own profit in selling their product did appropriate part of her identity" by using a Midler sound-alike. Id. at 463–64.

In Carson v. Here's Johnny Portable Toilets, Inc., 698 F.2d 831 (6th Cir.1983), the defendant had marketed portable toilets under the brand name "Here's Johnny"—Johnny Carson's signature "Tonight Show" introduction—without Carson's permission. The district court had dismissed Carson's Michigan common law right of publicity claim because the defendants had not used Carson's "name or likeness." Id. at 835. In reversing the district court, the sixth circuit found "the district court's

---

1. Ed. Note: Midler v. Ford Motor Co., 849 F.2d 460 (9th Cir.1988) (successful suit by Bette Midler for use in a Ford Motor advertisement of a singer mimicking Bette Midler's performance of "Do You Want to Dance, a song Midler had made famous").

conception of the right of publicity ... too narrow" and held that the right was implicated because the defendant had appropriated Carson's identity by using, inter alia, the phrase "Here's Johnny." Id. at 835–37.

These cases teach not only that the common law right of publicity reaches means of appropriation other than name or likeness, but that the specific means of appropriation are relevant only for determining whether the defendant has in fact appropriated the plaintiff's identity. The right of publicity does not require that appropriations of identity be accomplished through particular means to be actionable. It is noteworthy that the Midler and Carson defendants not only avoided using the plaintiff's name or likeness, but they also avoided appropriating the celebrity's voice, signature, and photograph. The photograph in Motschenbacher did include the plaintiff, but because the plaintiff was not visible the driver could have been an actor or dummy and the analysis in the case would have been the same.

Although the defendants in these cases avoided the most obvious means of appropriating the plaintiffs' identities, each of their actions directly implicated the commercial interests which the right of publicity is designed to protect. As the Carson court explained:

> [t]he right of publicity has developed to protect the commercial interest of celebrities in their identities. The theory of the right is that a celebrity's identity can be valuable in the promotion of products, and the celebrity has an interest that may be protected from the unauthorized commercial exploitation of that identity.... If the celebrity's identity is commercially exploited, there has been an invasion of his right whether or not his "name or likeness" is used.

Carson, 698 F.2d at 835. It is not important how the defendant has appropriated the plaintiff's identity, but whether the defendant has done so. Motschenbacher, Midler, and Carson teach the impossibility of treating the right of publicity as guarding only against a laundry list of specific means of appropriating identity. A rule which says that the right of publicity can be infringed only through the use of nine different methods of appropriating identity merely challenges the clever advertising strategist to come up with the tenth.

Indeed, if we treated the means of appropriation as dispositive in our analysis of the right of publicity, we would not only weaken the right but effectively eviscerate it. The right would fail to protect those plaintiffs most in need of its protection. Advertisers use celebrities to promote their products. The more popular the celebrity, the greater the number of people who recognize her, and the greater the visibility for the product. The identities of the most popular celebrities are not only the most attractive for advertisers, but also the easiest to evoke without resorting to obvious means such as name, likeness, or voice.

Consider a hypothetical advertisement which depicts a mechanical robot with male features, an African–American complexion, and a bald head. The robot is wearing black hightop Air Jordan basketball sneakers, and a red basketball uniform with black trim, baggy shorts, and the number 23 (though not revealing "Bulls" or "Jordan" lettering). The ad depicts the robot dunking a basketball one-handed, stiff-armed, legs extended like open scissors, and tongue hanging out. Now envision that this ad is run on television during professional basketball games. Considered individually, the robot's physical attributes, its dress, and its stance tell us little. Taken together, they lead to the only conclusion that any sports viewer who has registered a discernible pulse in the past five years would reach: the ad is about Michael Jordan.

Viewed separately, the individual aspects of the advertisement in the present case say little. Viewed together, they leave little doubt about the celebrity the ad is meant to depict. The female-shaped robot is wearing a long gown, blond wig, and large jewelry. Vanna White dresses exactly like this at times, but so do many other women. The robot is in the process of turning a block letter on a game-board. Vanna White dresses like this while turning letters on a game-board but perhaps similarly attired Scrabble-playing women do this as well. The robot is standing on what looks to be the Wheel of Fortune game show set. Vanna White dresses like this, turns letters, and does this on the Wheel of Fortune game show. She is the only one. Indeed, defendants themselves referred to their ad as the "Vanna White" ad. We are not surprised.

Television and other media create marketable celebrity identity value. Considerable energy and ingenuity are expended by those who have achieved celebrity value to exploit it for profit. The law protects the celebrity's sole right to exploit this value whether the celebrity has achieved her fame out of rare ability, dumb luck, or a combination thereof. We decline Samsung and Deutch's invitation to permit the evisceration of the common law right of publicity through means as facile as those in this case. Because White has alleged facts showing that Samsung and Deutch had appropriated her identity, the district court erred by rejecting, on summary judgment, White's common law right of publicity claim.

ALARCON, CIRCUIT JUDGE, concurring in part, dissenting in part:

Vanna White seeks recovery from Samsung based on three theories: the right to privacy, the right to publicity, and the Lanham Act. I concur in the majority's conclusions on the right to privacy. I respectfully dissent from its holdings on the right to publicity and the Lanham Act claims ...

I must dissent from the majority's holding on Vanna White's right to publicity claim. The district court found that, since the commercial advertisement did not show a "likeness" of Vanna White, Samsung did not improperly use the plaintiff's identity. The majority asserts that the use of a likeness is not required under California common law. According to the majority, recovery is authorized if there is an appropriation of one's "identity." I cannot find any holding of a California court that supports this conclusion. Furthermore, the record does not support the majority's finding that Vanna White's "identity" was appropriated.

The district court relied on Eastwood v. Superior Court, 149 Cal. App.3d 409, 198 Cal.Rptr. 342 (1983), in holding that there was no cause of action for infringement on the right to publicity because there had been no use of a likeness. In Eastwood, the California Court of Appeal described the elements of the tort of "commercial appropriation of the right of publicity" as "(1) the defendant's use of the plaintiff's identity; (2) the appropriation of plaintiff's name or likeness to defendant's advantage, . . .; (3) lack of consent; and (4) resulting injury." Id. at 417, 198 Cal.Rptr. 342. (Emphasis added).

All of the California cases that my research has disclosed hold that a cause of action for appropriation of the right to publicity requires proof of the appropriation of a name or likeness. See, e.g., Lugosi v. Universal Pictures, 25 Cal.3d 813, 603 P.2d 425, 160 Cal.Rptr. 323 (1979) ("The so-called right of publicity means in essence that the reaction of the public to name and likeness . . . endows the name and likeness of the person involved with commercially exploitable opportunities."); Guglielmi v. Spelling–Goldberg Prods., 25 Cal.3d 860, 603 P.2d 454, 457, 160 Cal.Rptr. 352, 355 (1979) (use of name of Rudolph Valentino in fictional biography allowed); Eastwood v. Superior Court, supra (use of photo and name of actor on cover of tabloid newspaper); In re Weingand, 231 Cal.App.2d 289, 41 Cal.Rptr. 778 (1964) (aspiring actor denied court approval to change name to "Peter Lorie" when famous actor Peter Lorre objected); Fairfield v. American Photocopy Equip. Co., 138 Cal.App.2d 82, 291 P.2d 194 (1955), later app. 158 Cal.App.2d 53, 322 P.2d 93 (1958) (use of attorney's name in advertisement); Gill v. Curtis Publishing Co., 38 C.2d 273, 239 P.2d 630 (1952) (use of photograph of a couple in a magazine).

Notwithstanding the fact that California case law clearly limits the test of the right to publicity to name and likeness, the majority concludes that "the common law right of publicity is not so confined." Majority opinion at p. 1397. The majority relies on two factors to support its innovative extension of the California law. The first is that the Eastwood court's statement of the elements was permissive rather than exclusive. The second is that Dean Prosser, in describing the common law right to publicity, stated that it might be possible that the right extended beyond name or likeness. These are slender reeds to support a federal court's attempt to create new law for the state of California . . .

The majority also relies on Dean Prosser's statement that "[i]t is not impossible that there might be an appropriation of the plaintiff's identity, as by impersonation, without the use of either his name or his likeness, and that this would be an invasion of his right of privacy." Prosser, Privacy, 48 Cal.L.Rev. 383, 401 n. 155 (1960). As Dean Prosser noted, however, "[n]o such case appears to have arisen." Id.

The majority states that the case law has borne out Dean Prosser's insight that the right to publicity is not limited to name or likeness. As noted above, however, the courts of California have never found an infringement on the right to publicity without the use of the plaintiff's name or likeness. . . .

The majority has focused on federal decisions in its novel extension of California Common Law. Those decisions do not provide support for the majority's decision.

In each of the federal cases relied upon by the majority, the advertisement affirmatively represented that the person depicted therein was the plaintiff. In this case, it is clear that a metal robot and not the plaintiff, Vanna White, is depicted in the commercial advertisement. The record does not show an appropriation of Vanna White's identity.

In Motschenbacher, a picture of a well-known race driver's car, including its unique markings, was used in an advertisement. Id. at 822. Although the driver could be seen in the car, his features were not visible. Id. The distinctive markings on the car were the only information shown in the ad regarding the identity of the driver. These distinctive markings compelled the inference that Motschenbacher was the person sitting in the racing car. We concluded that "California appellate courts would . . . afford legal protection to an individual's proprietary interest in his own identity." Id. at 825. (Emphasis added). Because the distinctive markings on the racing car were sufficient to identify Motschenbacher as the driver of the car, we held that an issue of fact had been raised as to whether his identity had been appropriated. Id. at 827.

In Midler v. Ford Motor Co., 849 F.2d 460 (9th Cir.1988), a singer who had been instructed to sound as much like Bette Midler as possible, sang a song in a radio commercial made famous by Bette Midler. Id. at 461. A number of persons told Bette Midler that they thought that she had made the commercial. Id. at 462. Aside from the voice, there was no information in the commercial from which the singer could be identified. We noted that "[t]he human voice is one of the most palpable ways identity is manifested." Id. at 463. We held that, "[t]o impersonate her voice is to pirate her identity," id., and concluded that Midler had raised a question of fact as to the misappropriation of her identity.

In Carson v. Here's Johnny Portable Toilets, Inc., 698 F.2d 831 (6th Cir.1983), the Sixth Circuit was called upon to interpret Michigan's common-law right to publicity. The case involved a manufacturer who used the words, "Here's Johnny," on portable toilets. Id. at 832–33. These same words were used to introduce the star of a popular late-night television program. There was nothing to indicate that this use of the phrase on the portable toilets was not associated with Johnny Carson's television program. The court found that "[h]ere there was an appropriation of Carson's identity," which violated the right to publicity. Id. at 837.

The common theme in these federal cases is that identifying characteristics unique to the plaintiffs were used in a context in which they were the only information as to the identity of the individual. The commercial advertisements in each case showed attributes of the plaintiff's identities which made it appear that the plaintiff was the person identified in the commercial. No effort was made to dispel the impression that the plaintiffs were the source of the personal attributes at issue. The commercials affirmatively represented that the plaintiffs were involved. See, e.g., Midler at 462 ("The [Motschenbacher] ad suggested that it was he.... In the same way the defendants here used an imitation to convey the impression that Midler was singing for them."). The proper interpretation of Motschenbacher, Midler, and Carson is that where identifying characteristics unique to a plaintiff are the only information as to the identity of the person appearing in an ad, a triable issue of fact has been raised as to whether his or her identity as been appropriated.

The case before this court is distinguishable from the factual showing made in Motschenbacher, Midler, and Carson. It is patently clear to anyone viewing the commercial advertisement that Vanna White was not being depicted. No reasonable juror could confuse a metal robot with Vanna White.

The majority contends that "the individual aspects of the advertisement ... [v]iewed together leave little doubt about the celebrity the ad is meant to depict." Majority Opinion at p. 1399. It derives this conclusion from the fact that Vanna White is "the only one" who "dresses like this, turns letters, and does this on the Wheel of Fortune game show." Id. In reaching this conclusion, the majority confuses Vanna White, the person, with the role she has assumed as the current hostess on the "Wheel of Fortune" television game show. A recognition of the distinction between a performer and the part he or she plays is essential for a proper analysis of the facts of this case. As is discussed below, those things which Vanna White claims identify her are not unique to her. They are, instead, attributes of the role she plays. The representation of those attributes, therefore, does not constitute a representation of Vanna White. See Nurmi v. Peterson, 10 U.S.P.Q.2d 1775 (C.D.Cal.1989) (distinguishing between performer and role).

Vanna White is a one-role celebrity. She is famous solely for appearing as the hostess on the "Wheel of Fortune" television show. There is nothing unique about Vanna White or the attributes which she claims identify her. Although she appears to be an attractive woman, her face and figure are no more distinctive than that of other equally comely women. She performs her role as hostess on "Wheel of Fortune" in a simple and straight-forward manner. Her work does not require her to display whatever artistic talent she may possess.

The majority appears to argue that because Samsung created a robot with the physical proportions of an attractive woman, posed it gracefully, dressed it in a blond wig, an evening gown, and jewelry, and placed it on a set that resembles the Wheel of Fortune layout, it thereby appropriated Vanna White's identity. But an attractive appearance, a graceful pose, blond hair, an evening gown, and jewelry are attributes shared by many women, especially in Southern California. These common attributes are particularly evident among game-show hostesses, models, actresses, singers, and other women in the entertainment field. They are not unique attributes of Vanna White's identity. Accordingly, I cannot join in the majority's conclusion that, even if viewed together, these attributes identify Vanna White and, therefore, raise a triable issue as to the appropriation of her identity.

The only characteristic in the commercial advertisement that is not common to many female performers or celebrities is the imitation of the "Wheel of Fortune" set. This set is the only thing which might possibly lead a viewer to think of Vanna White. The Wheel of Fortune set, however, is not an attribute of Vanna White's identity. It is an identifying characteristic of a television game show, a prop with which Vanna White interacts in her role as the current hostess. To say that Vanna White may bring an action when another blond female performer or robot appears on such a set as a hostess will, I am sure, be a surprise to the owners of the show. Cf. Baltimore Orioles, Inc. v. Major League Baseball Players Ass'n, 805 F.2d 663 (7th Cir.1986) (right to publicity in videotaped performances preempted by copyright of owner of telecast).

The record shows that Samsung recognized the market value of Vanna White's identity. No doubt the advertisement would have been more effective if Vanna White had appeared in it. But the fact that Samsung recognized Vanna White's value as a celebrity does not necessarily mean that it appropriated her identity. The record shows that Samsung dressed a robot in a costume usually worn by television game-show hostesses, including Vanna White. A blond wig, and glamorous clothing are not characteristics unique to the current hostess of Wheel of Fortune. This evidence does not support the majority's determination that the advertisement was meant to depict Vanna White. The advertisement was intended to depict a robot, playing the role Vanna White currently plays on the Wheel of Fortune. I quite agree that anyone seeing the commercial advertisement would be reminded of Vanna White. Any performance by another female celebrity as a game-show hostess, however, will also remind the viewer of Vanna White because Vanna White's celebrity is so closely associated with the role. But the fact that an actor or actress became famous for playing a particular role has, until now, never been sufficient to give the performer a proprietary interest in it. I cannot agree with the majority that the California courts, which have consistently taken a narrow view of the right to publicity, would extend law to these unique facts. . . .

The protection of intellectual property presents the courts with the necessity of balancing competing interests. On the one hand, we wish to protect and reward the work and investment of those who create intellectual property. In so doing, however, we must prevent the creation of a monopoly that would inhibit the creative expressions of others. We have traditionally balanced those interests by allowing the copying of an idea, but protecting a unique expression of it. Samsung clearly used the idea of a glamorous female game show hostess. Just as clearly, it avoided appropriating Vanna White's expression of that role. Samsung did not use a likeness of her. The performer depicted in the commercial advertisement is unmistakably a lifeless robot. Vanna White has presented no evidence that any consumer confused the robot with her identity. Indeed, no reasonable consumer could confuse the robot with Vanna White or believe that, because the robot appeared in the advertisement, Vanna White endorsed Samsung's product.

I would affirm the district court's judgment in all respects.

[Ed. Note: The preceding case was decided by a three-judge panel of the United States Court of Appeals for the 9th Circuit. Following the decision, the defendant petitioned for a rehearing of the case before all of the judges of the 9th Circuit as it may do under federal law. That petition was denied. However, a strong dissent was filed to that denial taking off where the dissent in the preceding case ended.]

WHITE v. SAMSUNG ELECTRONICS AMERICA, INC.

United States Court of Appeals for the Ninth Circuit (1993).
989 F.2d 1512.

KOZINSKI CIRCUIT JUDGE, with whom CIRCUIT JUDGES O'SCANNLAIN and KLEINFELD join, dissenting from the order rejecting the suggestion for rehearing en banc.

Saddam Hussein wants to keep advertisers from using his picture in unflattering contexts. Clint Eastwood doesn't want tabloids to write about him. Rudolf Valentino's heirs want to control his film biography. The Girl Scouts don't want their image soiled by association with certain activities. George Lucas wants to keep Strategic Defense Initiative fans from calling it "Star Wars." Pepsico doesn't want singers to use the word "Pepsi" in their songs. Guy Lombardo wants an exclusive property right to ads that show big bands playing on New Year's Eve. Uri Geller thinks he should be paid for ads showing psychics bending metal through telekinesis. Paul Prudhomme, that household name, thinks the same about ads featuring corpulent bearded chefs. And scads of copyright holders see purple when their creations are made fun of.

Something very dangerous is going on here. Private property, including intellectual property, is essential to our way of life. It provides an incentive for investment and innovation; it stimulates the flourishing of our culture; it protects the moral entitlements of people to the fruits of their labors. But reducing too much to private property can be bad medicine. Private land, for instance, is far more useful if separated from other private land by public streets, roads and highways. Public parks, utility rights-of-way and sewers reduce the amount of land in private hands, but vastly enhance the value of the property that remains.

So too it is with intellectual property. Overprotecting intellectual property is as harmful as underprotecting it. Creativity is impossible without a rich public domain. Nothing today, likely nothing since we tamed fire, is genuinely new: Culture, like science and technology, grows by accretion, each new creator building on the works of those who came before. Overprotection stifles the very creative forces it's supposed to nurture.

The panel's opinion is a classic case of overprotection. Concerned about what it sees as a wrong done to Vanna White, the panel majority erects a property right of remarkable and dangerous breadth: Under the majority's opinion, it's now a tort for advertisers to remind the public of a celebrity. Not to use a celebrity's name, voice, signature or likeness; not to imply the celebrity endorses a product; but simply to evoke the celebrity's image in the public's mind. This Orwellian notion withdraws far more from the public domain than prudence and common sense allow. It conflicts with the Copyright Act and the Copyright Clause. It raises serious First Amendment problems. It's bad law, and it deserves a long, hard second look.

Samsung ran an ad campaign promoting its consumer electronics. Each ad depicted a Samsung product and a humorous prediction: One showed a raw steak with the caption "Revealed to be health food. 2010 A.D." Another showed Morton Downey, Jr. in front of an American flag with the caption "Presidential candidate. 2008 A.D." The ads were meant to convey—humorously—that Samsung products would still be in use twenty years from now.

The ad that spawned this litigation starred a robot dressed in a wig, gown and jewelry reminiscent of Vanna White's hair and dress; the robot was posed next to a Wheel-of-Fortune-like game board. See Appendix. The caption read "Longest-running game show. 2012 A.D." The gag here, I take it, was that Samsung would still be around when White had been replaced by a robot.

Perhaps failing to see the humor, White sued, alleging Samsung infringed her right of publicity by "appropriating" her "identity." Under California law, White has the exclusive right to use her name, likeness, signature and voice for commercial purposes. Cal.Civ.Code § 3344(a); Eastwood v. Superior Court, 149 Cal.App.3d 409, 417, 198 Cal.Rptr. 342, 347 (1983). But Samsung didn't use her name, voice or signature, and it certainly didn't use her likeness. The ad just wouldn't have been funny had it depicted White or someone who resembled her—the whole joke was that the game show host(ess) was a robot, not a real person. No one seeing the ad could have thought this was supposed to be White in 2012.

The district judge quite reasonably held that, because Samsung didn't use White's name, likeness, voice or signature, it didn't violate her right of publicity. 971 F.2d at 1396–97. Not so, says the panel majority: The California right of publicity can't possibly be limited to name and likeness. If it were, the majority reasons, a "clever advertising strategist" could avoid using White's name or likeness but nevertheless remind people of her with impunity, "effectively eviscerat[ing]" her rights. To prevent this "evisceration," the panel majority holds that the right of publicity must extend beyond name and likeness, to any "appropriation" of White's "identity"—anything that "evoke[s]" her personality. Id. at 1398–99.

But what does "evisceration" mean in intellectual property law? Intellectual property rights aren't like some constitutional rights, absolute guarantees protected against all kinds of interference, subtle as well as blatant. They cast no penumbras, emit no emanations: The very point of intellectual property laws is that they protect only against certain specific kinds of appropriation. I can't publish unauthorized copies of, say, Presumed Innocent; I can't make a movie out of it. But I'm perfectly free to write a book about an idealistic young prosecutor on trial for a crime he didn't commit. So what if I got the idea from Presumed Innocent? So what if it reminds readers of the original? Have I "eviscerated" Scott Turow's intellectual property rights? Certainly not. All creators draw in part on the work of those who came before, referring to it, building on it, poking fun at it; we call this creativity, not piracy.

The majority isn't, in fact, preventing the "evisceration" of Vanna White's existing rights; it's creating a new and much broader property right, a right unknown in California law. It's replacing the existing balance between the interests of the celebrity and those of the public by a different balance, one substantially more favorable to the celebrity. Instead of having an exclusive right in her name, likeness, signature or voice, every famous person now has an exclusive right to anything that reminds the viewer of her. After all, that's all Samsung did: It used an inanimate object to remind people of White, to "evoke [her identity]." 971 F.2d at 1399.

Consider how sweeping this new right is. What is it about the ad that makes people think of White? It's not the robot's wig, clothes or jewelry; there must be ten million blond women (many of them quasi-famous) who wear dresses and jewelry like White's. It's that the robot is posed near the "Wheel of Fortune" game board. Remove the game board from the ad, and no one would think of Vanna White. . . . But once you include the game board, anybody standing beside it—a brunette woman, a man wearing women's clothes, a monkey in a wig and gown—would evoke White's image, precisely the way the robot did. It's the "Wheel of Fortune" set, not the robot's face or dress or jewelry that evokes White's image. The panel is giving White an exclusive right not in what she looks like or who she is, but in what she does for a living.

This is entirely the wrong place to strike the balance. Intellectual property rights aren't free: They're imposed at the expense of future creators and of the public at large. Where would we be if Charles Lindbergh had an exclusive right in the concept of a heroic solo aviator? If Arthur Conan Doyle had gotten a copyright in the idea of the detective story, or Albert Einstein had patented the theory of relativity? If every author and celebrity had been given the right to keep people from mocking them or their work? Surely this would have made the world poorer, not richer, culturally as well as economically.

This is why intellectual property law is full of careful balances between what's set aside for the owner and what's left in the public domain for the rest of us: The relatively short life of patents; the longer, but finite, life of copyrights; copyright's idea-expression dichotomy; the fair use doctrine; the prohibition on copyrighting facts; the compulsory license of television broadcasts and musical compositions; federal preemption of overbroad state intellectual property laws; the nominative use doctrine in trademark law; the right to make soundalike recordings. All of these diminish an intellectual property owner's rights. All let the public use something created by someone else. But all are necessary to maintain a free environment in which creative genius can flourish.

The intellectual property right created by the panel here has none of these essential limitations: No fair use exception; no right to parody; no idea-expression dichotomy. It impoverishes the public domain, to the detriment of future creators and the public at large. Instead of well-defined, limited characteristics such as name, likeness or voice, advertisers will now have to cope with vague claims of "appropriation of identity," claims often made by people with a wholly exaggerated sense of their own fame and significance. See pp. 1512–13 & notes 1–10 supra. Future Vanna Whites might not get the chance to create their personae, because their employers may fear some celebrity will claim the persona is too similar to her own. The public will be robbed of parodies of celebrities, and our culture will be deprived of the valuable safety valve that parody and mockery create.

Moreover, consider the moral dimension, about which the panel majority seems to have gotten so exercised. Saying Samsung "appropriated" something of White's begs the question: Should White have the exclusive right to something as broad and amorphous as her "identity"? Samsung's ad didn't simply copy White's schtick—like all parody, it created something new. True, Samsung did it to make money, but White does whatever she does to make money, too; the majority talks of "the difference between fun and profit," 971 F.2d at 1401, but in the entertainment industry fun is profit. Why is Vanna White's right to exclusive for-profit use of her persona—a persona that might not even be her own creation, but that of a writer, director or producer—superior to Samsung's right to profit by creating its own inventions? Why should she have such absolute rights to control the conduct of others, unlimited by the idea-expression dichotomy or by the fair use doctrine?

To paraphrase only slightly Feist Publications, Inc. v. Rural Telephone Service Co., 499 U.S. 340, 347–49, 111 S.Ct. 1282, 1289–90, 113 L.Ed.2d 358 (1991), it may seem unfair that much of the fruit of a creator's labor may be used by others without compensation. But this is not some unforeseen byproduct of our intellectual property system; it is the system's very essence. Intellectual property law assures authors the right to their original expression, but encourages others to build freely on the ideas that underlie it. This result is neither unfair nor unfortunate: It is the means by which intellectual property law advances the progress of science and art. We give authors certain exclusive rights, but in exchange we get a richer public domain. The majority ignores this wise teaching, and all of us are the poorer for it. . . . far. It is ironic that it is we who plant this kudzu in the fertile soil of our federal system. . . .

For better or worse, we are the Court of Appeals for the Hollywood Circuit. Millions of people toil in the shadow of the law we make, and much of their livelihood is made possible by the existence of intellectual property rights. But much of their livelihood—and much of the vibrancy of our culture—also depends on the existence of other intangible rights: The right to draw ideas from a rich and varied public domain, and the right to mock, for profit as well as fun, the cultural icons of our time.

In the name of avoiding the "evisceration" of a celebrity's rights in her image, the majority diminishes the rights of copyright holders and the public at large. In the name of fostering creativity, the majority suppresses it. Vanna White and those like her have been given something they never had before, and they've been given it at our expense. I cannot agree.

Vanna White

Ms. C3PO?

NOTES AND QUESTIONS

1. The *White* case is an extreme example of the lengths that courts have gone to protect the exploitation of famous personalities. Protection of persona is a relatively recent phenomena dating back perhaps no more than 100 years.

Only two decades ago a celebrity had no cause of action against an advertiser who imitated her voice. Until the 1970's any commercial value associated with celebrity was personal to the star and entered the public domain at death. As recently as the early 1950's celebrities could not assign the right to use their name and likeness. At the beginning of this century the law denied relief even to the living person whose name or likeness was the object of illicit appropriation. Clearly the law affords more protection to the commercial value of celebrity status now than at any previous time. Celebrity persona has become a heritable, alienable 'thing' from which the owner may arbitrarily exclude others. In other words, it has become property.

George M. Armstrong, Jr., The Reification of Celebrity: Persons as Property, 51 La. L. Rev. 443 (1991).

2.   While the *White* case relies heavily on state law, the two dissents suggest federal copyright or trademark laws may be implicated by the decision. Article I § 8 of the United States Constitution states that Congress has the power "to Promote the Progress of Science and Useful Arts, by securing for limited Times to Authors and Inventors the exclusive Right to their respective Writings and Discoveries." Pursuant to this constitutional authority, Congress has enacted copyright and patent laws to provide protection against the unauthorized use of so-called "intellectual property." Generally, copyrights apply to all forms of literary and artistic expression and the expressive elements of computer software. While ideas cannot be copyrighted, the way the idea is expressed can be. Patents apply to inventions which include, among other things, machines and processes. To obtain a patent, the inventor must demonstrate that the subject matter of the patent is novel, non-obvious, and useful. Trademarks are also a form of protected intellectual property; they protect symbols and words that are used to identify the source and nature of services or goods. With the development of computer software, the Internet, and biomedical engineering, interest in these laws has grown exponentially over the last several years. See generally R. Merges, P. Menell, M. Lemley, & T. Jorde, Intellectual Property in the New Technological Age (1997).

The length of protections varies considerably under the three laws. Under the current federal copyright laws, generally the holder of a copyright is protected for the life of the author plus seventy years; under federal patent law, the patent holder's exclusive property rights are limited in most cases to twenty years from the date of the filing of the patent application; under federal trademark law, rights in logos, names, or other indications of origin can last indefinitely. The nature of the protection afforded the holders of these interests is essentially to grant them a monopoly on the use of their work during the "protected period." Why does society grant copyright, patent and trademark protection? See also Richard Posner, Economic Analysis of the Law 48–59 (8th ed. 2010).

3.   The right protected in *White* is similar to the right protected in International News Service v. Associated Press, 248 U.S. 215 (1918). In INS, the Supreme Court held that AP had a "quasi property" right in the news that it gathered which could be protected from misappropriation by INS. AP complained that INS copied news published by AP from bulletin boards and from early editions of the newspaper on the East Coast and sold it to INS's customers on the West Coast. Thus, INS was able to distribute news to its customers at lower costs than AP could provide news to its customers. The

Court did not address whether there was a common law property right or a copyright in news, preferring to provide redress to AP on grounds that INS had engaged in a species of unfair competition called "misappropriation." In economic terms, INS was a "free rider."

A "free rider" is a person who takes advantage of a good or service without paying for it. Free riding, which is the cause of many market failures (see the preceding note on fugitive minerals), is fairly widespread in society. For example, the "discount" store that sells a complex consumer product, such as personal computers, often engages in free riding. When you are ready to purchase a personal computer, you go to a "full service" computer store where all the machines are displayed so that you can try them out. You take an hour of a trained salesperson's time determining the precise computer package that will fill your needs. Then you tell the salesperson that you will go home and "think about it." You immediately drive across town to a discount computer outlet, where all the computers are still in their factory cartons, and the sales staff knows absolutely nothing except the prices. The prices are much cheaper because the discount store has relied on the full service store to provide all the expensive point-of-sale information that was necessary to your decision.

INS was an even more outrageous free rider than the discount computer store in the above illustration. By copying AP's stories on the East Coast and wiring them to West Coast customers, INS was able to sell the same "product" as AP without doing any of the work.

Free riding can be a major economic problem. If it is too widespread in a particular market, the market may cease to perform efficiently. For example, the full service computer store will eventually be able to compete with the discount computer store only by cutting its own point-of-sale services. When that happens, customers will receive less information about computers, and they will likely respond by buying fewer of them. Likewise, if copying and wiring AP's news stories becomes too widespread, AP will not be able to compete with the free riders. As AP begins to lose customers, its costs per customer will go up and it will have to charge higher prices. (It costs the same amount to write a news story that will be sent to 100 newspapers as one that will be sent to 10 newspapers.) At the extreme, widespread free riding could drive AP out of business.

Both "private" and "public" solutions exist to the problem of free riding. For example, the computer manufacturer may solve the free riding problem by selling its product only through its own, company-owned stores. These stores can be closely monitored, and will have little incentive to engage in free riding. However, such a solution was probably not available to AP. Help with its free-rider problem had to come, if at all, from the government—either the legislature or the courts.

4. Hugo Zacchini, an entertainer known as the "human cannonball," brought an action against Scripps–Howard Broadcasting Company for damages resulting from the defendant's televising of the plaintiff's entire fifteen-second act. Zacchini alleged that he was " 'engaged in the entertainment business,' that the act he performs is one 'invented by his father and . . . performed only by his family for the last fifty years,' that respondent 'showed

and commercialized the film of his act without his consent,' and that such conduct was an 'unlawful appropriation of plaintiff's property'." In upholding Zacchini's claim and rejecting the defendant's claim that its conduct was protected under the U.S. Constitution, the Court stated:

> The broadcast of a film of petitioner's entire act poses a substantial threat to the economic value of that performance.... [T]his act is the product of petitioner's own talents and energy, the end result of much time, effort, and expense. Much of its economic value lies in the "right of exclusive control over the publicity given to his performance"; if the public can see the act free on television, it will be less willing to pay to see it at the fair. The effect of a public broadcast of the performance is similar to preventing petitioner from charging an admission fee.... [T]he broadcast of petitioner's entire performance ... goes to the heart of petitioner's ability to earn a living as an entertainer. Zacchini v. Scripps–Howard Broadcasting Co., 433 U.S. 562, 575–76 (1977).

5. Suppose a local newspaper publishes a report of a local news event that the local radio station later reads verbatim over the airwaves. Could the newspaper enjoin the radio station's activities? See Veatch v. Wagner, 14 Alaska 470, 116 F.Supp. 904 (D.Alaska 1953); Pottstown Daily News Pub. Co. v. Pottstown Broadcasting Co., 411 Pa. 383, 192 A.2d 657 (1963).

6. If your picture is used without your permission in a political advertisement, can you sue the candidate who used the picture? See Cox v. Hatch, 761 P.2d 556 (Utah 1988).

DAVIS v. DAVIS

Supreme Court of Tennessee (1992).
842 S.W.2d 588, cert. denied 507 U.S. 911 (1993).

DAUGHTREY, JUSTICE.

This appeal presents a question of first impression, involving the disposition of the cryogenically-preserved product of *in vitro* fertilization (IVF), commonly referred to in the popular press and the legal journals as "frozen embryos." The case began as a divorce action, filed by the appellee, Junior Lewis Davis, against his then wife, appellant Mary Sue Davis. The parties were able to agree upon all terms of dissolution, except one: who was to have "custody" of the seven "frozen embryos" stored in a Knoxville fertility clinic that had attempted to assist the Davises in achieving a much-wanted pregnancy during a happier period in their relationship.

I. Introduction

Mary Sue Davis originally asked for control of the "frozen embryos" with the intent to have them transferred to her own uterus, in a post-divorce effort to become pregnant. Junior Davis objected, saying that he preferred to leave the embryos in their frozen state until he decided whether or not he wanted to become a parent outside the bounds of marriage.

Based on its determination that the embryos were "human beings" from the moment of fertilization, the trial court awarded "custody" to Mary Sue Davis and directed that she "be permitted the opportunity to bring these children to term through implantation." The Court of Appeals reversed, finding that Junior Davis has a "constitutionally protected right not to beget a child where no pregnancy has taken place" and holding that "there is no compelling state interest to justify [ ] ordering implantation against the will of either party." The Court of Appeals further held that "the parties share an interest in the seven fertilized ova" and remanded the case to the trial court for entry of an order vesting them with "joint control . . . and equal voice over their disposition."

Mary Sue Davis then sought review in this Court, contesting the validity of the constitutional basis for the Court of Appeals decision. We granted review, not because we disagree with the basic legal analysis utilized by the intermediate court, but because of the obvious importance of the case in terms of the development of law regarding the new reproductive technologies, and because the decision of the Court of Appeals does not give adequate guidance to the trial court in the event the parties cannot agree.

We note, in this latter regard, that their positions have already shifted: both have remarried and Mary Sue Davis (now Mary Sue Stowe) has moved out of state. She no longer wishes to utilize the "frozen embryos" herself, but wants authority to donate them to a childless couple. Junior Davis is adamantly opposed to such donation and would prefer to see the "frozen embryos" discarded . . .

At the outset, it is important to note the absence of two critical factors that might otherwise influence or control the result of this litigation: When the Davises signed up for the IVF program at the Knoxville clinic, they did not execute a written agreement specifying what disposition should be made of any unused embryos that might result from the cryopreservation process. Moreover, there was at that time no Tennessee statute governing such disposition, nor has one been enacted in the meantime.

In addition, because of the uniqueness of the question before us, we have no case law to guide us to a decision in this case. Despite the fact that over 5,000 IVF babies have been born in this country and the fact that some 20,000 or more "frozen embryos" remain in storage, there are apparently very few other litigated cases involving the disputed disposition of untransferred "frozen embryos," and none is on point with the facts in this case.

But, if we have no statutory authority or common law precedents to guide us, we do have the benefit of extensive comment and analysis in the legal journals. In those articles, medical-legal scholars and ethicists have proposed various models for the disposition of "frozen embryos" when unanticipated contingencies arise, such as divorce, death of one or both of the parties, financial reversals, or simple disenchantment with the IVF process. Those models range from a rule requiring, at one extreme, that all embryos be used by the gamete-providers or donated for uterine transfer, and, at the other extreme, that any unused embryos be automatically discarded. Other formulations would vest control in the female gamete-provider—in every case, because of her greater physical and emotional contribution to the IVF process, or perhaps only in the event that she wishes to use them herself. There are also two "implied contract" models: one would infer from enrollment in an IVF program that the IVF clinic has authority to decide in the event of an impasse whether to donate, discard, or use the "frozen embryos" for research; the other would infer from the parties' participation in the creation of the embryos that they had made an irrevocable commitment to reproduction and would require transfer either to the female provider or to a donee. There are also the so-called "equity models": one would avoid the conflict altogether by dividing the "frozen embryos" equally between the parties, to do with as they wish;[2] the other would award veto power to the party wishing to avoid parenthood, whether it be the female or the male progenitor.

Each of these possible models has the virtue of ease of application. Adoption of any of them would establish a bright-line test that would dispose of disputes like the one we have before us in a clear and predictable manner. As appealing as that possibility might seem, we conclude that given the relevant principles of constitutional law, the existing public policy of Tennessee with regard to unborn life, the current state of scientific knowledge giving rise to the emerging reproductive technologies, and the ethical considerations that have developed in response to that scientific knowledge, there can be no easy answer to the question we now face. We conclude, instead, that we must weigh the interests of each party to the dispute, in terms of the facts and analysis set out below, in order to resolve that dispute in a fair and responsible manner.

II. The Facts

Mary Sue Davis and Junior Lewis Davis met while they were both in the Army and stationed in Germany in the spring of 1979. After a period of courtship, they came home to the United States and were married on April 26, 1980. When their leave was up, they then returned to their posts in Germany as a married couple.

Within six months of returning to Germany, Mary Sue became pregnant but unfortunately suffered an extremely painful tubal pregnancy, as a result of which she had surgery to remove her right fallopian tube. This tubal pregnancy was followed by four others during the course of the marriage. After her fifth tubal pregnancy, Mary Sue chose to have her left fallopian tube ligated, thus leaving her without functional fallopian tubes

---

2. Assuming that the parties do not change their current positions, in this case the result would be "the worst of both worlds": some of the frozen embryos would likely be destroyed, contrary to Mary Sue Davis's devout wish that they be implanted and given the opportunity to come to term; at the same time, the others would likely be implanted and might come to term, thus forcing Junior Davis into unwanted parenthood.

by which to conceive naturally. The Davises attempted to adopt a child but, at the last minute, the child's birth-mother changed her mind about putting the child up for adoption. Other paths to adoption turned out to be prohibitively expensive. *In vitro* fertilization became essentially the only option for the Davises to pursue in their attempt to become parents.

As explained at trial, IVF involves the aspiration of ova from the follicles of a woman's ovaries, fertilization of these ova in a petri dish using the sperm provided by a man, and the transfer of the product of this procedure into the uterus of the woman from whom the ova were taken. Implantation may then occur, resulting in a pregnancy and, it is hoped, the birth of a child.

Beginning in 1985, the Davises went through six attempts at IVF, at a total cost of $35,000, but the hoped-for pregnancy never occurred. Despite her fear of needles, at each IVF attempt Mary Sue underwent the month of subcutaneous injections necessary to shut down her pituitary gland and the eight days of intermuscular injections necessary to stimulate her ovaries to produce ova. She was anesthetized five times for the aspiration procedure to be performed. Forty-eight to 72 hours after each aspiration, she returned for transfer back to her uterus, only to receive a negative pregnancy test result each time.

The Davises then opted to postpone another round of IVF until after the clinic with which they were working was prepared to offer them cryogenic preservation, scheduled for November 1988. Using this process, if more ova are aspirated and fertilized than needed, the conceptive product may be cryogenically preserved (frozen in nitrogen and stored at sub-zero temperatures) for later transfer if the transfer performed immediately does not result in a pregnancy. The unavailability of this procedure had not been a hinderance to previous IVF attempts by the Davises because Mary Sue had produced at most only three or four ova, despite hormonal stimulation. However, on their last attempt, on December 8, 1988, the gynecologist who performed the procedure was able to retrieve nine ova for fertilization. The resulting one-celled entities, referred to before division as zygotes, were then allowed to develop in petri dishes in the laboratory until they reached the four-to eight-cell stage . . .

After fertilization was completed, a transfer was performed as usual on December 10, 1988; the rest of the four-to eight-cell entities were cryogenically preserved. Unfortunately, a pregnancy did not result from the December 1988 transfer, and before another transfer could be attempted, Junior Davis filed for divorce—in February 1989. He testified that he had known that their marriage "was not very stable" for a year or more, but had hoped that the birth of a child would improve their relationship. Mary Sue Davis testified that she had no idea that there was a problem with their marriage. As noted earlier, the divorce proceedings were complicated only by the issue of the disposition of the "frozen embryos."

III.   The Scientific Testimony

In the record, and especially in the trial court's opinion, there is a great deal of discussion about the proper descriptive terminology to be used in this case. Although this discussion appears at first glance to be a matter simply of semantics, semantical distinctions are significant in this context, because language defines legal status and can limit legal rights. Obviously, an "adult" has a different legal status than does a "child." Likewise, "child" means something other than "fetus." A "fetus" differs from an "embryo." There was much dispute at trial about whether the four-to eight-cell entities in this case should properly be referred to as "embryos" or as "preembryos," with resulting differences in legal analysis.

One expert, a French geneticist named Dr. Jerome Lejeune, insisted that there was no recognized scientific distinction between the two terms. He referred to the four-to eight-cell entities at issue here as "early human beings," as "tiny persons," and as his "kin." Although he is an internationally recognized geneticist, Dr. Lejeune's background fails to reflect any degree of expertise in obstetrics or gynecology (specifically in the field of infertility) or in medical ethics. His testimony revealed a profound confusion between science and religion. For example, he was deeply moved that "Madame [Mary Sue], the mother, wants to rescue babies from this concentration can," and he concluded that Junior Davis has a moral duty to try to bring these "tiny human beings" to term.

Dr. LeJeune's opinion was disputed by Dr. Irving Ray King, the gynecologist who performed the IVF procedures in this case. Dr. King is a medical doctor who had practiced as a sub-speciality in the areas of infertility and reproductive endocrinology for 12 years. He established the Fertility Center of East Tennessee in Knoxville in 1984 and had worked extensively with IVF and cryopreservation. He testified that the currently accepted term for the zygote immediately after division is "preembryo" and that this term applies up until 14 days after fertilization. He testified that this 14–day period defines the accepted period for preembryo research. At about 14 days, he testified, the group of cells begins to differentiate in a process that permits the eventual development of the different body parts which will become an individual.

Dr. King's testimony was corroborated by the other experts who testified at trial, with the exception of Dr. Lejeune. It is further supported by the American Fertility Society, an organization of 10,000 physicians and scientists who specialize in problems of human infertility . . .

Admittedly, this distinction is not dispositive in the case before us. It deserves emphasis only because inaccuracy can lead to misanalysis such as occurred at the trial level in this case. The trial court reasoned that if there is no distinction between embryos and preembryos, as Dr. Lejeune theorized, then Dr. Lejeune must also have been correct when he asserted that "human life begins at the moment of conception." From this proposition, the trial judge concluded that the eight-cell entities at issue were not preembryos but were "children in vitro." He then invoked the doctrine of *parens patriae* and held that it was "in the best interest of the children" to be born rather than destroyed. Finding that Mary Sue Davis was willing to provide such an opportunity, but that Junior Davis was not, the trial judge awarded her "custody" of the "children in vitro."

The Court of Appeals explicitly rejected the trial judge's reasoning, as well as the result. Indeed, the argument that "human life begins at the moment of conception" and that these four-to eight-cell entities therefore have a legal right to be born has apparently been abandoned by the appellant, despite her success with it in the trial court. We have neverthe-less been asked by the American Fertility Society, joined by 19 other national organizations allied in this case as amici curiae, to respond to this issue because of its far-reaching implications in other cases of this kind. We find the request meritorious.

IV. The "Person" vs. "Property" Dichotomy

One of the fundamental issues the inquiry poses is whether the preembryos in this case should be considered "persons" or "property" in the contemplation of the law. The Court of Appeals held, correctly, that they cannot be considered "persons" under Tennessee law . . .

Left undisturbed, the trial court's ruling would have afforded preembryos the legal status of "persons" and vested them with legally cognizable interests separate from those of their progenitors. Such a decision would doubtless have had the effect of outlawing IVF programs in the state of Tennessee. But in setting aside the trial court's judgment, the Court of Appeals, at least by implication, may have swung too far in the opposite direction . . .

The intermediate court's reliance on *York v. Jones,* is even more troublesome. That case involved a dispute between a married couple undergoing IVF procedures at the Jones Institute for Reproductive Medi-cine in Virginia. When the Yorks decided to move to California, they asked the Institute to transfer the one remaining "frozen embryo" that they had produced to a fertility clinic in San Diego for later implantation. The Institute refused and the Yorks sued. The federal district court assumed without deciding that the subject matter of the dispute was "property." The *York* court held that the "cryopreservation agreement" between the Yorks and the Institute created a bailment relationship, obligating the Institute to return the subject of the bailment to the Yorks once the purpose of the bailment had terminated. 717 F.Supp. at 424–425.

In this case, by citing to *York v. Jones* but failing to define precisely the "interest" that Mary Sue Davis and Junior Davis have in the preembryos, the Court of Appeals has left the implication that it is in the nature of a property interest. For purposes of clarity in future cases, we conclude that this point must be further addressed.

To our way of thinking, the most helpful discussion on this point is found not in the minuscule number of legal opinions that have involved "frozen embryos," but in the ethical standards set by The American Fertility Society, as follows:

> Three major ethical positions have been articulated in the debate over preembryo status. At one extreme is the view of the preembryo as a human subject after fertilization, which requires that it be accorded the rights of a person. This position entails an obligation to provide an opportunity for implantation to occur and tends to ban any action before transfer that might harm the preembryo or that is not immediately therapeutic, such as freezing and some preembryo research.
>
> At the opposite extreme is the view that the preembryo has a status no different from any other human tissue. With the consent of those who have decision-making authority over the preembryo, no limits should be imposed on actions taken with preembryos.
>
> A third view—one that is most widely held—takes an intermediate position between the other two. It holds that the preembryo deserves respect greater than that accorded to human tissue but not the respect accorded to actual persons. The preembryo is due greater respect than other human tissue because of its potential to become a person and because of its symbolic meaning for many people. Yet, it should not be treated as a person, because it has not yet developed the features of personhood, is not yet established as developmentally individual, and may never realize its biologic potential.

Report of the Ethics Committee of The American Fertility Society, *supra*, at 34S–35S.

Although the report alludes to the role of "special respect" in the context of research on preembryos not intended for transfer, it is clear that the Ethics Committee's principal concern was with the treatment accorded the transferred embryo. Thus, the Ethics Committee concludes that "special respect is necessary to protect the welfare of potential offspring ... [and] creates obligations not to hurt or injure the offspring who might be born after transfer [by research or intervention with a preembryo]." *Id.* at 35S ...

V.   *The Enforceability of Contract*

Establishing the locus of the decision-making authority in this context is crucial to deciding whether the parties could have made a valid contingency agreement prior to undergoing the IVF procedures and whether such an agreement would now be enforceable on the question of disposition. Under the trial court's analysis, obviously, an agreement of this kind would be unenforceable in the event of a later disagreement, because the trial court would have to make an ad hoc "best interest of the child" determination in every case. In its opinion, the Court of Appeals did not address the question of the enforceability of prior agreements, undoubtedly because that issue was not directly raised on appeal. Despite our reluctance to treat a question not strictly necessary to the result in the case, we conclude that discussion is warranted in order to provide the necessary guidance to all those involved with IVF procedures in Tennessee in the future—the health care professionals who administer IVF programs and the scientists who engage in infertility research, as well as prospective parents seeking to achieve pregnancy by means of IVF, their physicians, and their counselors.

We believe, as a starting point, that an agreement regarding disposition of any untransferred preembryos in the event of contingencies (such as the death of one or more of the parties, divorce, financial reversals, or abandonment of the program) should be presumed valid and should be enforced as between the progenitors. This conclusion is in keeping with the proposition that the progenitors, having provided the gametic material giving rise to the preembryos, retain decision-making authority as to their disposition.[3]

At the same time, we recognize that life is not static, and that human emotions run particularly high when a married couple is attempting to overcome infertility problems. It follows that the parties' initial "informed consent" to IVF procedures will often not be truly informed because of the near impossibility of anticipating, emotionally and psychologically, all the turns that events may take as the IVF process unfolds. Providing that the initial agreements may later be modified *by agreement* will, we think, protect the parties against some of the risks they face in this regard. But, in the absence of such agreed modification, we conclude that their prior agreements should be considered binding . . .

We are therefore left with this situation: there was initially no agreement between the parties concerning disposition of the preembryos under the circumstances of this case; there has been no agreement since; and there is no formula in the Court of Appeals opinion for determining the outcome if the parties cannot reach an agreement in the future.

In granting joint custody to the parties, the Court of Appeals must have anticipated that, in the absence of agreement, the preembryos would continue to be stored, as they now are, in the Knoxville fertility clinic. One problem with maintaining the status quo is that the viability of the preembryos cannot be guaranteed indefinitely. Experts in cryopreservation who testified in this case estimated the maximum length of preembryonic viability at two years.[4] Thus, the true effect of the intermediate court's opinion is to confer on Junior Davis the inherent power to veto any transfer of the preembryos in this case and thus to insure their eventual discard or self-destruction.

---

3. This situation is thus distinguishable from that in which a couple makes an agreement concerning abortion in the event of a future pregnancy. Such agreements are unenforceable because of the woman's right to privacy and autonomy. *See Planned Parenthood v. Danforth,* 428 U.S. 52, 96 S.Ct. 2831, 49 L.Ed.2d 788 (1976) (invalidating written consent of spouse as a prerequisite to abortion).

4. This two-year limit is apparently an estimate based on technological feasibility as of the time of trial. Our survey of law journal articles indicates other estimates of viability ranging from two to ten years.

As noted in Section I of this opinion, the recognition of such a veto power, as long as it applies equally to both parties, is theoretically one of the routes available to resolution of the dispute in this case. Moreover, because of the current state of law regarding the right of procreation, such a rule would probably be upheld as constitutional. Nevertheless, for the reasons set out in Section VI of this opinion, we conclude that it is not the best route to take, under all the circumstances.

VI. *The Right of Procreational Autonomy*

Although an understanding of the legal status of preembryos is necessary in order to determine the enforceability of agreements about their disposition, asking whether or not they constitute "property" is not an altogether helpful question. As the appellee points out in his brief, "[as] two or eight cell tiny lumps of complex protein, the embryos have no [intrinsic] value to either party." Their value lies in the "potential to become, after implantation, growth and birth, *children.*" Thus, the essential dispute here is not where or how or how long to store the preembryos, but whether the parties will become parents. The Court of Appeals held in effect that they will become parents if they both agree to become parents. The Court did not say what will happen if they fail to agree. We conclude that the answer to this dilemma turns on the parties' exercise of their constitutional right to privacy . . .

[Ed. Note: In this section the court engages in an extended discussion of the constitutional right of privacy under both the federal and Tennessee constitutions].

For the purposes of this litigation it is sufficient to note that, whatever its ultimate constitutional boundaries, the right of procreational autonomy is composed of two rights of equal significance—the right to procreate and the right to avoid procreation. Undoubtedly, both are subject to protections and limitations . . .

The equivalence of and inherent tension between these two interests are nowhere more evident than in the context of *in vitro* fertilization. None of the concerns about a woman's bodily integrity that have previously precluded men from controlling abortion decisions is applicable here. We are not unmindful of the fact that the trauma (including both emotional stress and physical discomfort) to which women are subjected in the IVF process is more severe than is the impact of the procedure on men. In this sense, it is fair to say that women contribute more to the IVF process than men. Their experience, however, must be viewed in light of the joys of parenthood that is desired or the relative anguish of a lifetime of unwanted parenthood. As they stand on the brink of potential parenthood, Mary Sue Davis and Junior Lewis Davis must be seen as entirely equivalent gamete-providers.

It is further evident that, however far the protection of procreational autonomy extends, the existence of the right itself dictates that decisional authority rests in the gamete-providers alone, at least to the extent that their decisions have an impact upon their individual reproductive status. As discussed in Section V above, no other person or entity has an interest sufficient to permit interference with the gamete-providers' decision to continue or terminate the IVF process, because no one else bears the consequences of these decisions in the way that the gamete-providers do . . .

The unique nature of this case requires us to note that the interests of these parties in parenthood are different in scope than the parental interest considered in other cases. Previously, courts have dealt with the child-bearing and child-rearing aspects of parenthood. Abortion cases have dealt with gestational parenthood. In this case, the Court must deal with the question of genetic parenthood. We conclude, moreover, that an interest in avoiding genetic parenthood can be significant enough to trigger the protections afforded to all other aspects of parenthood. The technological fact that someone unknown to these parties could gestate these preembryos does not alter the fact that these parties, the gamete-providers, would become parents in that event, at least in the genetic sense. The profound impact this would have on them supports their right to sole decisional authority as to whether the process of attempting to gestate these preembryos should continue. This brings us directly to the question of how to resolve the dispute that arises when one party wishes to continue the IVF process and the other does not.

VII. *Balancing the Parties' Interests*

Resolving disputes over conflicting interests of constitutional import is a task familiar to the courts. One way of resolving these disputes is to consider the positions of the parties, the significance of their interests, and the relative burdens that will be imposed by differing resolutions. In this case, the issue centers on the two aspects of procreational autonomy—the right to procreate and the right to avoid procreation. We start by considering the burdens imposed on the parties by solutions that would have the effect of disallowing the exercise of individual procreational autonomy with respect to these particular preembryos.

Beginning with the burden imposed on Junior Davis, we note that the consequences are obvious. Any disposition which results in the gestation of the preembryos would impose unwanted parenthood on him, with all of its possible financial and psychological consequences. The impact that this unwanted parenthood would have on Junior Davis can only be understood by considering his particular circumstances, as revealed in the record.

Junior Davis testified that he was the fifth youngest of six children. When he was five years old, his parents divorced, his mother had a nervous break-down, and he and three of his brothers went to live at a home for boys run by the Lutheran Church. Another brother was taken in by an aunt, and his sister stayed with their mother. From that day forward, he had monthly visits with his mother but saw his father only three more times before he died in 1976. Junior Davis testified that, as a boy, he had severe problems caused by separation from his parents. He said that it was especially hard to leave his mother after each monthly visit.

He clearly feels that he has suffered because of his lack of opportunity to establish a relationship with his parents and particularly because of the absence of his father.

In light of his boyhood experiences, Junior Davis is vehemently opposed to fathering a child that would not live with both parents. Regardless of whether he or Mary Sue had custody, he feels that the child's bond with the non-custodial parent would not be satisfactory. He testified very clearly that his concern was for the psychological obstacles a child in such a situation would face, as well as the burdens it would impose on him. Likewise, he is opposed to donation because the recipient couple might divorce, leaving the child (which he definitely would consider his own) in a single-parent setting.

Balanced against Junior Davis's interest in avoiding parenthood is Mary Sue Davis's interest in donating the preembryos to another couple for implantation. Refusal to permit donation of the preembryos would impose on her the burden of knowing that the lengthy IVF procedures she underwent were futile, and that the preembryos to which she contributed genetic material would never become children. While this is not an insubstantial emotional burden, we can only conclude that Mary Sue Davis's interest in donation is not as significant as the interest Junior Davis has in avoiding parenthood. If she were allowed to donate these preembryos, he would face a lifetime of either wondering about his parental status or knowing about his parental status but having no control over it. He testified quite clearly that if these preembryos were brought to term he would fight for custody of his child or children. Donation, if a child came of it, would rob him twice—his procreational autonomy would be defeated and his relationship with his offspring would be prohibited.

The case would be closer if Mary Sue Davis were seeking to use the preembryos herself, but only if she could not achieve parenthood by any other reasonable means. We recognize the trauma that Mary Sue has already experienced and the additional discomfort to which she would be subjected if she opts to attempt IVF again. Still, she would have a reasonable opportunity, through IVF, to try once again to achieve parenthood in all its aspects—genetic, gestational, bearing, and rearing.

Further, we note that if Mary Sue Davis were unable to undergo another round of IVF, or opted not to try, she could still achieve the child-rearing aspects of parenthood through adoption. The fact that she and Junior Davis pursued adoption indicates that, at least at one time, she was willing to forego genetic parenthood and would have been satisfied by the child-rearing aspects of parenthood alone.

VIII. Conclusion

In summary, we hold that disputes involving the disposition of preembryos produced by *in vitro* fertilization should be resolved, first, by looking to the preferences of the progenitors. If their wishes cannot be ascertained, or if there is dispute, then their prior agreement concerning disposition should be carried out. If no prior agreement exists, then the relative interests of the parties in using or not using the preembryos must be weighed. Ordinarily, the party wishing to avoid procreation should prevail, assuming that the other party has a reasonable possibility of achieving parenthood by means other than use of the preembryos in question. If no other reasonable alternatives exist, then the argument in favor of using the preembryos to achieve pregnancy should be considered. However, if the party seeking control of the preembryos intends merely to donate them to another couple, the objecting party obviously has the greater interest and should prevail.

But the rule does not contemplate the creation of an automatic veto, and in affirming the judgment of the Court of Appeals, we would not wish to be interpreted as so holding.

For the reasons set out above, the judgment of the Court of Appeals is affirmed, in the appellee's favor. This ruling means that the Knoxville Fertility Clinic is free to follow its normal procedure in dealing with unused preembryos, as long as that procedure is not in conflict with this opinion. Costs on appeal will be taxed to the appellant.

NOTES AND QUESTIONS

1. "Cryogenic preservation has caused controversy abroad as well. The Supreme Court of Israel initially rejected a divorced woman's decision to implant frozen pre-zygotes over the objections of her former husband. See Nachmani v. Nachmani, (Mar. 30, 1995, C.A. 5587/93). However, upon further review and reconsideration by the entire court (see, Gordon, Court Upholds Legitimacy of Second Hearings, Jerusalem Post, Mar. 3, 1996, at 12), a 7-to-4 majority awarded possession of the pre-zygotes to Mrs. Nachmani, finding that once fertilization had occurred through IVF, "the positive right" to be a parent overcame "the negative right not to be [one]" (Friedman, A Victory for Life, Westchester Jewish Week, Sept. 20, 1996, at 1, 39). Unfortunately attempts to obtain an English translation of the decision have been unsuccessful.

A significant case arose in Australia when the American "parents" of three frozen pre-zygotes perished in a plane crash without providing for the disposition of the pre-zygotes. A great debate raged, and the Australian state of Victoria ordered a study by the Waller Committee to consider the "social, ethical and legal issues arising from in vitro fertilization" (Davidoff, Frozen Embryos: A Need for Thawing in the Legislative Process, 47 SMU L.Rev. 131, 156 [1993] [hereinafter Davidoff, Frozen Embryos]). The Waller Committee recommended that IVF participants be required to execute written consent forms which, inter alia, provide for the disposition of the pre-zygotes (see, Davidoff, Frozen Embryos, supra, at 156–157). The Victoria Parliament passed the Infertility Medical Procedures Act in 1984 to govern such future controversies (see, Davidoff, Frozen Embryos, *supra*). Simultaneous therewith, the Warnock Commission released its report to the British government, setting forth 63 separate recommendations governing IVF procedures and facilities (see, Davidoff, Frozen Embryos, supra, at 157–158). Resulting legislation in Great Britain once again caused controversy and a debate raged over the fate of unclaimed frozen pre-zygotes due to be discarded as of August 1, 1996 (see, Ibrahim, Ethical Furor Erupts in Britain: Should Unclaimed Embryos Die?, N.Y. Times, Aug. 1, 1996, at A1, col. 1). Some other nations have adopted varying approaches to cope with the difficult issues posed by such cutting-edge reproductive technology (see, Lemonick, Sorry, Your Time Is Up, Time, Aug. 12, 1996, at 41)." Kass v. Kass, 235 A.D.2d 150, 172–73, 663 N.Y.S.2d 581, 596–97 (2d Dept.1997) (Dissenting Opinion).

2. The *Davis* court suggested that if the parties had signed an agreement providing for the disposition of the embryos that agreement would have controlled. However, in A.Z. v. B.Z., 431 Mass. 150, 725 N.E.2d 1051 (2000), the Massachusetts Supreme Judicial Court refused to enforce a signed agreement providing that if the husband and wife separated the embryos should be given to the wife for implantation. The court found the agreement ambiguous because it did not state that the parties intended to be bound by it in the face of a future disagreement. The court also stated that even if the agreement were clear, it would not be enforceable on "public policy" grounds against the parent seeking to prevent implantation. Do you agree? In J.B. v. M.B., 170 N.J. 9, 783 A.2d 707, 719 (2001), the court held that agreements regarding the disposition of embryos was enforceable "subject to the right of either party to change his or her mind about disposition up to the point of use or destruction of any stored preembryos." See also In re Marriage of Witten, 672 N.W.2d 768 (Iowa 2003) (holding that the disposition of the embryos depends upon the parties' contemporaneous mutual agreement and, in the absence of such agreement, the status quo is preserved, effectively meaning the embryos remain with the clinic); Roman v. Roman, 193 S.W.3d 40 (Tex. App. 2006) (enforcing the terms of the original agreement to discard unused embryos when the terms were clear and unambiguous).

Some IVF clinics require the parties to sign an agreement providing that if the parties divorce any unused embryos become the clinic's property. If you were the lawyer for a fertility clinic, would you recommend such a clause for its standard form contract?

3. Suppose that Mrs. Davis had prevailed. Would or should Mr. Davis be liable to support any biological children born as a result of the implantation of the embryos in Mrs. Davis? Section 706(a) of the Uniform Parentage Act (2002) provides that: "if a marriage is dissolved before placement of eggs, sperm, or embryos, the former spouse is not a parent of the resulting child unless the former spouse consented ... [in writing] that if assisted reproduction were to occur after a divorce, the former spouse would be a parent of the child." Subsection (b) further provides that consent once given can be revoked "at any time before placement of the eggs, sperm, or embryos [and] [a]n individual who withdraws consent ... is not a parent of the resulting child."

Similarly if consent to the placement of eggs, sperm, or embryos following a divorce is not given by the former spouse, or consent is revoked prior to such placement, a parent-child relationship does not exist between any resulting child and the former spouse. As a result the child cannot inherit from the former spouse and is not a child of the former spouse for class gift purposes. See Unif. Prob. Code § 2–120(j).

4.   Today a number of unused embryos are offered up by fertility clinics for "adoption." Embryos are often available for adoption because the biological parent(s) have had a child through IVF using some of the embryos but not all of them. If the embryos are not offered to other couples for "adoption" they are either destroyed, used for research, or stored indefinitely. "Embryo adoption," unlike the adoption of a living child, takes place without court approval. Little law exists to settle the rights of the biological parents and the "adopting parents."

5.   Suppose the Davises had not divorced but instead had moved to California and requested the IVF clinic to transfer the embryos to an IVF clinic in California. If the clinic refused, could they sue the clinic for conversion? See York v. Jones, 717 F.Supp. 421 (E.D.Va.1989) (holding sperm and egg donor could maintain an action for conversion).

6.   Suppose a married couple leaves seven embryos on deposit with a fertility clinic. As a result of the negligence of a clinic employee, the embryos are thawed and destroyed. Could the couple successfully sue the clinic for wrongful death? For conversion? For breach of a bailment contract? See, Jeter v. Mayo Clinic Arizona, 211 Ariz. 386, 121 P.3d 1256 (2005).

7.   The *Davis* trial court held that life began at conception and that the embryos were human beings. This holding earned immediate national attention and no doubt explained the enormous number of amici briefs filed in the appeals of *Davis*. Even admitting that embryos are life, does it necessarily follow they are "human beings?" In considering that question, is it sufficient to conclude the embryos are human merely because they come from the union of human sperm and ova or is there more that enters into the determination of when life is "human life?" The noted bioethicist, Professor Fletcher observes that:

> Synthetic concepts such as *human* and *man* and *person* require operational terms spelling out the which and what and when. Only in that way can we get down to cases—to normative decisions. There are always some people who prefer to be visceral and affective in their moral choices, with no desire to have any rationale for what they do. But *ethics* is precisely the business of rational, critical reflection (encephalic and not merely visceral) about the problems of moral agent—in biology and medicine as much as in law, government, education or anything else.

Fletcher, Indicators of Humanhood: A Tentative Profile of Man, 2 Hastings Cent. Rep. No. 5, 1 (1972). Professor Fletcher then catalogs characteristics of humanness. These are: (1) minimal intelligence (I.Q. 40 or over), (2) self-awareness, (3) self-control, (4) a sense of time, (5) a sense of futurity, (6) a sense of the past, (7) the capability to relate to others, (8) concern for others, (9) communication, (10) control of existence, (11) curiosity, (12) change and changeability, (13) balance of rationality and feeling, (14) idiosyncrasy, and (15) neo-cortical function. How would Professor Fletcher likely characterize the nature of embryos?

8. Those appellate courts that to date have considered the matter have refused to characterize embryos as either persons or property. Reflecting this view is the statement in *Davis* that "preembryos are not, strictly speaking, either 'persons' or 'property,' but occupy an interim category that entitles them to special respect because of their potential for human life." Davis v. Davis, 842 S.W.2d 588, 596 (1992).

Is "special respect" also accorded sperm and eggs because of their potentiality for human life or are they mere property? At some level, this issue arose in Hecht v. Superior Court, 16 Cal.App.4th 836, 20 Cal.Rptr.2d 275 (1993). Decedent, William Kane, bequeathed 15 vials of his sperm to Deborah Hecht, his girlfriend, for the purpose of her using them to become pregnant. His surviving children challenged the bequest on the grounds that the sperm were not property and, thus, could not be disposed of by his will. The court held that the sperm were property and, thus, could be the subject of a devise.[5] Subsequently, the children challenged the validity of the entire will but that suit was settled by an agreement between the children and Hecht. The agreement included provisions for the disposition of all of decedent's property. Under the agreement Hecht was to receive twenty percent of decedent's property, which would include three of the fifteen vials of sperm. Hecht subsequently attempted to use this sperm to become pregnant but the first two attempts failed. Before proceeding to use the third vial, her gynecologist asked whether she might be able to obtain possession of the other twelve vials and thus avoid his having to use a riskier medical procedure. Hecht then sued to obtain the remaining twelve vials but the trial court denied her request on the grounds that the property settlement agreement with Kane's children was determinative of her rights in the sperm. Hecht appealed this ruling. On appeal, the court held that Kane's sperm was a unique form of property and to subject it to division between Hecht and Kane's children would be inconsistent with the decedent's intent that it be used by Hecht for the purpose of becoming pregnant. Thus, Hecht's agreement to give up her rights to twelve vials was invalid. Hecht v. Superior Court, 59 Cal.Rptr.2d 222 (App. 1996) (depublished). The court expressly left open the question whether any child born to Hecht with Kane' sperm would be a child of Kane's for purpose of inheritance. Should any such child be Kane's child for this purpose? If Hecht gives birth to Kane's child, subsequent to his death, should the child be able to qualify for dependents' benefits under federal Social Security laws?

In Kievernagel v. Kievernagel, 166 Cal.App.4th 1024, 83 Cal. Rptr.3d 311 (2008), the court refused to allow a widow to compel a fertility clinic to distribute her deceased husband's sperm to her after he died, even though she wanted to use the sperm to conceive a child that would be biologically related to him. Prior to his death, the deceased husband had signed a form with the fertility clinic stating that if he should die his sperm should be discarded. The court found this a sufficient expression of his intent not to father a child after his death.

---

5. Sperm can also be the subject of a lifetime gift. *See,* Hall v. Fertility Institute of New Orleans, 647 So.2d 1348 (La.App. 1994).

9. Does a person have a property right in her body? For example, suppose a surgeon removes a spleen from her patient and uses that spleen to develop a cell line that is very effective in the treatment of certain cancers. The surgeon expects to earn $3 billion as a result of her discovery. To what extent does the patient have a claim to all or any portion of the $3 billion dollars? Would your answer depend on whether the surgeon had advised the patient of her expected use of the patient's spleen prior to the operation? See Moore v. Regents of the University of California, 51 Cal.3d 120, 271 Cal.Rptr. 146, 793 P.2d 479 (1990) (recovery permitted for failure to obtain patient's consent for use of the spleen but not on conversion theory). Suppose you conclude, as the California Supreme Court believed in *Moore,* that O has no property in her spleen, how would you decide the following cases:

> (a) Child had her tooth removed by the dentist. That evening Child placed tooth under her pillow in hopes of an exchange for money with the tooth fairy. During the night, the tooth is stolen by a thief. Does Child have a cause of action for conversion?
>
> (b) A has her hair cut at a local beauty shop. The hair stylist sells A's hair for $50 to a wig maker. Can A recover the $50? Suppose that before A left the beauty shop she asked to have her hair put in a bag so that she could take it with her, but the stylist refused? Can A recover her hair?
>
> (c) A seeks to recover her pap smear slides from a local hospital which, she alleges, the hospital has refused to give her. Hospital claims the slides are the property of the hospital relying on cases holding that X rays are the property of the radiologist who took them. A argues that tissue slides differ from X rays because they "contain human substances drawn from . . . [her] body which are incapable of being duplicated or reproduced." Is A entitled to the slides? See Cornelio v. Stamford Hospital, 1997 WL 430619 (Conn.Super. 1997).

If a removed organ is not the property of the person from whom it was removed, can it be the property of the person who removed the organ? For example, suppose Doctor Able removes a spleen from Patient John and stores the removed spleen in a freezer. Later, Thief takes the spleen. Can Able sue Thief for conversion? If you conclude Able can sue Thief for conversion, you must also be concluding that Able's property was stolen. Can the spleen be Able's property but not Patient's property as Moore suggests? Is an organ is not property, can it be the subject of an anatomical gift. See § 1.6, *infra.*

NOTE ON SURROGACY CONTRACTS

Couples for whom IVF is not a viable alternative may have to resort to a "surrogacy" arrangement. A surrogate is a woman who carries a fetus to term pursuant to the provisions of a contract with the "intended parents" to surrender custody of the child, when born, to the intended parents and to consent to the child's adoption by one or both of the intended parents. In the earliest years of surrogacy, a woman (the surrogate) was artificially insemi- nated with the sperm of a man. He and his wife would then have a contract with the surrogate under which the surrogate would agree to permit the wife to adopt the child. Because the husband was the child's biological father, it was not necessary for him to adopt the child. This type of surrogacy contract was held invalid as a matter of public policy in In the Matter of Baby M, 109 N.J. 396, 537 A.2d 1227 (1988). Today it is more common when using a surrogate to use either donor eggs or an adopted embryo. In such case, the surrogate has no genetic link to the resulting child. In Surrogate Parenting Associates, Inc. v. Commonwealth ex. rel. Armstrong, 704 S.W.2d 209 (Ky. 1986) the Kentucky Supreme Court upheld a surrogacy contract against a claim that it was an invalid agreement for the sale of a baby. Subsequently the Kentucky legislature abrogated that decision by enacting a statute invalidating surrogacy contracts where the surrogate was compensated. Ky. Rev. Stat. Ann. § 199.590(4). It now appears that such contracts are invalid in Arizona, District of Columbia, Indiana, Michigan, New York, North Dakota and Utah. Some allow them so long as the surrogate is not compensated. See, Kentucky, Louisiana, Nebraska, and Washington. Some exempt the arrangements from the crime of baby selling. See, Alabama, Iowa, and West Virginia. And, some allow them. Florida, Nevada, New Hampshire, and Virginia under certain circumstances.

The propriety of surrogacy contracts is sufficiently contentious that the Commissioners on Uniform State Laws, in adopting the Uniform Status of Children of Assisted Conception Act, included two alternative and inconsistent provisions in the proposed Uniform Act, one barring surrogacy contracts and the other permitting them under limited circumstances. States are free to adopt whichever alternative they choose. To date, North Dakota has adopted the alternative barring surrogacy, while Virginia has adopted the alternative permitting it. The Uniform Act followed on the heels of another proposal validating surrogacy contracts. See Model Human Reproductive Technologies and Surrogacy Act, 72 Iowa L. Rev. 943 (1987). See also Uniform Parentage Act §§ 801–809.

In Johnson v. Calvert, 5 Cal.4th 84, 19 Cal.Rptr.2d 494, 851 P.2d 776 (1993), the proposed surrogate had no biological relationship to the child. Rather an embryo resulting from the in vitro fertilization of the husband's sperm and the wife's egg were implanted in the surrogate. When the child was born, the surrogate sought to renege on the contract and keep the child. At the core of the court's decision was the notion that blood was thicker than water, that nature trumps nurture.

In *Johnson*, the surrogate argued that the contract should be voided as a matter of public policy because such contracts exploit poor women. The California Supreme Court rejected that argument stating that: "although common sense suggests that women of lesser means serve as surrogate mothers more than do wealthy women, there has been no proof that surrogacy contracts exploit poor women to any greater degree than economic necessity in general exploits them by inducing them to accept lower-paid or otherwise undesirable employment ... The argument that a woman cannot knowingly and intelligently agree to gestate and deliver a baby for intending parents carries overtones of the reasoning that for centuries prevented women from attaining equal economic rights and professional status under the law. To resurrect this view is both to foreclose a personal and economic choice on the part of the surrogate mother, and to deny intending parents what may be their only means of procreating a child of their own genes." Id.

at 97, 19 Cal.Rptr.2d at 503, 851 P.2d at 785. What do you think of this argument?

It is also possible for a child born to a surrogate to not be biologically related to any of the surrogate, the intended father, and the intended mother. While sperm banks have flourished for many years, recently egg banks have also been created with female donors often being paid tens of thousands of dollars for egg donations. Thus, it is possible for anonymously donated sperm and egg to be joined by in vitro fertilization with the resulting embryo implanted in the womb of a surrogate and the resulting child to be adopted by others, as the intended parents. Suppose the surrogate and a couple had a contract under which the surrogate agreed to surrender the child to the couple, but the surrogate reneges when the child is born. Should the surrogate be compelled to surrender the child to the intended parents where the intended parents are not the genetic parents?

§ 1.6 ACQUISITION OF PROPERTY RIGHTS BY GIFT

An owner of property enjoys a great number of rights with respect to it. The owner may have the right to possess the property and the right to pledge the property as security for a loan. The owner may have the right to exclude others from the property. Two important rights a property owner may have are the right to alienate the property during her life and the right to dispose of the property by her will. The right to alienate includes, among other things, both the right to sell and the right to give. Both sales and gifts represent transfers; the sale is premised on the receipt of consideration, and the gift is founded upon the intent to make a gratuitous transfer.

GRUEN v. GRUEN

Court of Appeals of New York (1986).
68 N.Y.2d 48, 505 N.Y.S.2d 849, 496 N.E.2d 869.

SIMONS, JUDGE.

Plaintiff commenced this action seeking a declaration that he is the rightful owner of a painting which he alleges his father, now deceased, gave to him. He concedes that he has never had possession of the painting but asserts that his father made a valid gift of the title in 1963 reserving a life estate for himself. His father retained possession of the painting until he died in 1980. Defendant, plaintiff's stepmother, has the painting now and has refused plaintiff's requests that she turn it over to him. She contends that the purported gift was testamentary in nature and invalid insofar as the formalities of a will were not met or, alternatively, that a donor may not make a valid inter vivos gift of a chattel and retain a life estate with a complete right of possession. Following a seven-day nonjury trial, Special Term found that plaintiff had failed to establish any of the elements of an inter vivos gift and that in any event an attempt by a donor to retain a present possessory life estate in a chattel invalidated a purported gift of it. The Appellate Division held that a valid gift may be made reserving a life estate and, finding the elements of a gift established in this case, it reversed and remitted the matter for a determination of value. That determination has now been made and defendant appeals directly to this court . . . from the subsequent final judgment . . . awarding plaintiff $2,500,000 in damages representing the value of the painting, plus interest. We now affirm.

The subject of the dispute is a work entitled "Schloss Kammer am Attersee II" painted by a noted Austrian modernist, Gustav Klimt. It was purchased by plaintiff's father, Victor Gruen, in 1959 for $8,000. On April 1, 1963 the elder Gruen, a successful architect with offices and residences in both New York City and Los Angeles during most of the time involved in this action, wrote a letter to plaintiff, then an undergraduate student at Harvard, stating that he was giving him the Klimt painting for his birthday but that he wished to retain the possession of it for his lifetime. This letter is not in evidence, apparently because plaintiff destroyed it on instructions from his father. Two other letters were received, however, one dated May 22, 1963 and the other April 1, 1963. Both had been dictated by Victor Gruen and sent together to plaintiff on or about May 22, 1963. The letter dated May 22, 1963 reads as follows:

Dear Michael:

I wrote you at the time of your birthday about the gift of the painting by Klimt.

Now my lawyer tells me that because of the existing tax laws, it was wrong to mention in that letter that I want to use the painting as long as I live. Though I still want to use it, this should not appear in the letter. I am enclosing, therefore, a new letter and I ask you to send the old one back to me so that it can be destroyed.

I know this is all very silly, but the lawyer and our accountant insist that they must have in their possession copies of a letter which will serve the purpose of making it possible for you, once I die, to get this picture without having to pay inheritance taxes on it.

Love,

s/Victor.

Enclosed with this letter was a substitute gift letter, dated April 1, 1963, which stated:

Dear Michael:

The 21st birthday, being an important event in life, should be celebrated accordingly. I therefore wish to give you as a present the oil painting by Gustav Klimt of Schloss Kammer which now hangs in the New York living room. You know that Lazette and I bought it some 5 or 6 years ago, and you always told us how much you liked it.

Happy birthday again.

Love,

    s/Victor.

Plaintiff never took possession of the painting nor did he seek to do so. Except for a brief period between 1964 and 1965 when it was on loan to art exhibits and when restoration work was performed on it, the painting remained in his father's possession, moving with him from New York City to Beverly Hills and finally to Vienna, Austria, where Victor Gruen died on February 14, 1980. Following Victor's death plaintiff requested possession of the Klimt painting and when defendant refused, he commenced this action.

The issues framed for appeal are whether a valid inter vivos gift of a chattel may be made where the donor has reserved a life estate in the chattel and the donee never has had physical possession of it before the donor's death and, if it may, which factual findings on the elements of a valid inter vivos gift more nearly comport with the weight of the evidence in this case, those of Special Term or those of the Appellate Division. The latter issue requires application of two general rules. First, to make a valid inter vivos gift there must exist the intent on the part of the donor to make a present transfer; delivery of the gift, either actual or constructive to the donee; and acceptance by the donee. . . . Second, the proponent of a gift has the burden of proving each of these elements by clear and convincing evidence. . . .

Donative Intent

There is an important distinction between the intent with which an inter vivos gift is made and the intent to make a gift by will. An inter vivos gift requires that the donor intend to make an irrevocable present transfer of ownership; if the intention is to make a testamentary disposition effective only after death, the gift is invalid unless made by will . . .

Defendant contends that the trial court was correct in finding that Victor did not intend to transfer any present interest in the painting to plaintiff in 1963 but only expressed an intention that plaintiff was to get the painting upon his death. The evidence is all but conclusive, however, that Victor intended to transfer ownership of the painting to plaintiff in 1963 but to retain a life estate in it and that he did, therefore, effectively transfer a remainder interest in the painting to plaintiff at that time. Although the original letter was not in evidence, testimony of its contents was received along with the substitute gift letter and its covering letter dated May 22, 1963. The three letters should be considered together as a single instrument . . . and when they are they unambiguously establish that Victor Gruen intended to make a present gift of title to the painting at that time. But there was other evidence for after 1963 Victor made several statements orally and in writing indicating that he had previously given plaintiff the painting and that plaintiff owned it. Victor Gruen retained possession of the property, insured it, allowed others to exhibit it and made necessary repairs to it but those acts are not inconsistent with his retention of a life estate. . . .

Defendant contends that even if a present gift was intended, Victor's reservation of a lifetime interest in the painting defeated it. She relies on a statement from Young v. Young, 80 N.Y. 422 that " '[a]ny gift of chattels which expressly reserves the use of the property to the donor for a certain period, or * * * as long as the donor shall live, is ineffectual' " (id., at p. 436, quoting 2 Schouler, Personal Property, at 118). The statement was dictum, however, and the holding of the court was limited to a determination that an attempted gift of bonds in which the donor reserved the interest for life failed because there had been no delivery of the gift, either actual or constructive (see, id., at p. 434; see also Speelman v. Pascal, 10 N.Y.2d 313, 319–320, 222 N.Y.S.2d 324, 178 N.E.2d 723). The court expressly left undecided the question "whether a remainder in a chattel may be created and given by a donor by carving out a life estate for himself and transferring the remainder" (Young v. Young, supra, at p. 440). We answered part of that question in Matter of Brandreth, 169 N.Y. 437, 441–442, 62 N.E. 563, supra when we held that "[in] this state a life estate and remainder can be created in a chattel or a fund the same as in real property". The case did not require us to decide whether there could be a valid gift of the remainder.

Defendant recognizes that a valid inter vivos gift of a remainder interest can be made not only of real property but also of such intangibles as stocks and bonds. Indeed, several of the cases she cites so hold. That being so, it is difficult to perceive any legal basis for the distinction she urges which would permit gifts of remainder interests in those properties but not of remainder interests in chattels such as the Klimt painting here. The only reason suggested is that the gift of a chattel must include a present right to possession. The application of Brandreth to permit a gift of the remainder in this case, however, is consistent with the distinction, well recognized in the law of gifts as well as in real property law, between ownership and possession or enjoyment . . . Insofar as some of our cases purport to require that the donor intend to transfer both title and possession immediately to have a valid inter vivos gift . . . they state the rule too broadly and confuse the effectiveness of a gift with the transfer of the possession of the subject of that gift. The correct test is " 'whether the maker intended the [gift] to have no effect until after the maker's death, or whether he intended it to transfer some present interest. . . .' " As long as the evidence establishes an intent to make a present and irrevocable transfer of title or the right of ownership, there is a present transfer of some interest and the gift is effective immediately. . . .

Defendant suggests that allowing a donor to make a present gift of a remainder with the reservation of a life estate will lead courts to effectuate otherwise invalid testamentary dispositions of property. The two have entirely different characteristics, however, which make them distinguishable. Once the gift is made it is irrevocable and the donor is limited to the rights of a life tenant not an owner. Moreover, with the gift of a remainder title vests immediately in the donee and any possession is postponed until the donor's death whereas under a will neither title nor possession vests immediately. Finally, the postponement of enjoyment of the gift is produced by the express terms of the gift not by the nature of the instrument as it is with a will. . . .

Delivery

In order to have a valid inter vivos gift, there must be a delivery of the gift, either by a physical delivery of the subject of the gift or a constructive or symbolic delivery such as by an instrument of gift, sufficient to divest the donor of dominion and control over the property. . . . As the statement of the rule suggests, the requirement of delivery is not rigid or inflexible, but is to be applied in light of its purpose to avoid mistakes by donors and fraudulent claims by donees. . . . Accordingly, what is sufficient to constitute delivery "must be tailored to suit the circumstances of the case. . . ." The rule requires that " '[t]he delivery necessary to consummate a gift must be as perfect as the nature of the property and the circumstances and surroundings of the parties will reasonably permit' " (citation omitted).

Defendant contends that when a tangible piece of personal property such as a painting is the subject of a gift, physical delivery of the painting itself is the best form of delivery and should be required. Here, of course, we have only delivery of Victor Gruen's letters which serve as instruments of gift. Defendant's statement of the rule as applied may be generally true, but it ignores the fact that what Victor Gruen gave plaintiff was not all rights to the Klimt painting, but only title to it with no right of possession until his death. Under these circumstances, it would be illogical for the law to require the donor to part with possession of the painting when that is exactly what he intends to retain.

Nor is there any reason to require a donor making a gift of a remainder interest in a chattel to physically deliver the chattel into the donee's hands only to have the donee redeliver it to the donor. As the facts of this case demonstrate, such a requirement could impose practical burdens on the parties to the gift while serving the delivery requirement poorly. Thus, in order to accomplish this type of delivery the parties would have been required to travel to New York for the symbolic transfer and redelivery of the Klimt painting which was hanging on the wall of Victor Gruen's Manhattan apartment. Defendant suggests that such a requirement would be stronger evidence of a completed gift, but in the absence of witnesses to the event or any written confirmation of the gift it would provide less protection against fraudulent claims than have the written instruments of gift delivered in this case.

Acceptance

Acceptance by the donee is essential to the validity of an inter vivos gift, but when a gift is of value to the donee, as it is here, the law will presume an acceptance on his part.... Plaintiff did not rely on this presumption alone but also presented clear and convincing proof of his acceptance of a remainder interest in the Klimt painting by evidence that he had made several contemporaneous statements acknowledging the gift to his friends and associates, even showing some of them his father's gift letter, and that he had retained both letters for over 17 years to verify the gift after his father died. Defendant relied exclusively on affidavits filed by plaintiff in a matrimonial action with his former wife, in which plaintiff failed to list his interest in the painting as an asset. These affidavits were made over 10 years after acceptance was complete and they do not even approach the evidence in Matter of Kelly (285 N.Y. 139, 148–149, 33 N.E.2d 62 [dissenting in part opn.], supra) where the donee, immediately upon delivery of a diamond ring, rejected it as "too flashy". We agree with the Appellate Division that interpretation of the affidavit was too speculative to support a finding of rejection and overcome the substantial showing of acceptance by plaintiff.

Accordingly, the judgment appealed from and the order of the Appellate Division brought up for review should be affirmed, with costs.

Notes and Questions

1. Gustav Klimt was a renowned Austrian painter. A number of his works were confiscated by the Nazis. Five, in particular, including the oil and gold-encrusted portrait "Adele Block–Bauer I" (1907) were seized from Ferdinand Bloch–Bauer who fled Austria in 1938. Following that seizure, the paintings were turned over by the Nazis to the Austrian government and publicly displayed in the Belvedere castle in Vienna for decades. Following a 7–year legal battle ending in 2006, the paintings, estimated at the time to be worth about $150,000,000, were awarded to Maria Altmann, a niece of the Bloch–Bauer family. The paintings were returned to Ms. Altmann and were most recently displayed in the Los Angeles County Museum of Art.

The estimate of value was clearly understated as shown by subsequent events. In June of 2006, Ronald S. Lauder, heir to the Estee–Lauder fortune, purchased the "Adele Bloch–Bauer I" for $135,000,000, the highest sum then ever paid for any painting. In November of 2006, "Adele–Bauer II" sold for $88,000,000, and the remaining paintings sold for just under $193,000,000.

The legal battle between Maria Altmann and Austria was partly played out in the United States Supreme Court. See Republic of Austria v. Altmann, 541 U.S. 677 (2004).

2. It is generally stated that in order to make a valid gift there must be intent, delivery, and acceptance.

As discussed in the principal case, the intent must be an intent to give an interest in property to the donee at the present time. A promise to make a gift in the future is unenforceable absent consideration. On the other hand, it is not necessary that the gifted interest be a presently possessory interest; it may become possessory in the future.[1] For example, suppose O gives D a note that states:

> I hereby give you all of my interest in ABC stock, the certificates to be delivered to you at the time of my death by X to whom I have given the stock with instructions to deliver to you at the time of my death.

This letter is capable of at least two interpretations. One, O intends to give D an interest in the stock now but also intends to withhold the possession and enjoyment of the stock from D until O dies. Presumably, O has reserved, at least by implication, the right to enjoy the dividends paid on the stock until she dies. Alternatively, the letter could be construed to give D no interest in the stock until O dies. As so construed the gift is ineffectual. It fails as a gift because O does not intend to give D any interest in the stock at the present time. It fails as a testamentary disposition because the writing is not executed with the formalities required by law. See chap. 4, *infra*. If O is dead at the time the court is asked to determine whether there was a gift, what factors should the court consider to determine O's intent? Compare Innes v. Potter, 130 Minn. 320, 153 N.W. 604 (1915), with Tygard v. McComb, 54 Mo.App. 85 (1893).

3.   Re-read Victor's letters to his son. Who do you think wrote them?

4.   Property transferred during a donor's life as a gift is subject to the federal estate tax (death tax) if the donor retained the right to the possession of the gifted property for her life. Int. Rev. Code § 2036(a). This provision causes such gifted property to be taxed in the same way as if the donor retained the property until death and bequeathed the property to the donee in her will.

Although Victor clearly intended to retain possession of the painting for his life (and in fact did), his lawyer recommended that he "doctor up" the transaction in order to avoid a paper trail that would result in an adverse tax consequence. In your judgment, is this ethical? Is it effective to accomplish the intended purpose?

If, as appears to be the case, the donor, acting under advice of counsel, executed instruments of gift which failed to reflect the actual fact that the donor retained possession of the painting for life, should that effect the validity of the gift for state law purposes?

5.   Most of the cases in which the validity of a gift is at issue are disputes concerning the effectiveness of the delivery.

In his classic law review article, The Requirement of Delivery in Gifts of Chattels and of Choses in Action Evidenced by Commercial Instruments, 21 Ill. L. Rev. 341, 348–349 (1926), Professor Mechem stated there were three reasons why delivery was required to affect a valid gift. First, "delivery makes vivid and concrete to the donor the significance of the act he is doing...." Second, "the act ... is as unequivocal to actual witnesses of the transaction

---

1. One of the geniuses of the common law property system was the recognition that interests in property could be created both *concurrently* and *successively*. When interests in property are created successively, one person has a present interest; another a future interest. A future interest can be quite valuable. The futurity of the interest in property merely refers to the fact that the right to the possession of the property is postponed to the future, typically when the present interest terminates. See chapter 4, *infra*.

as to the donor himself. . . ." Lastly, "the fact of delivery gives the donee . . . at least prima facie evidence . . . of the alleged gift." Which of these do you find most convincing?

To what extent, if any, is the delivery requirement distinct from the intent requirement? See Scherer v. Hyland, 75 N.J. 127, 380 A.2d 698 (1977) ("[T]he major purpose of the delivery requirement is evidentiary.").

The easiest delivery cases are those in which the subject matter of the gift is physically delivered by the donor to the donee in a ceremony in which witnesses can overhear the donor express to the donee the intent to make a gift. One suspects that these rarely occur, and clearly the litigated cases are never that unambiguous. Suppose, for example, that the subject matter of the gift is not physically delivered to the donee at the time the intent to make a gift is expressed, or, as in *Gruen*, the subject matter of the gift (a future interest in a painting) is incapable of a physical delivery. Suppose further that something else is delivered to the "donee." In the principal case, for example, the "something else" was a letter describing the subject matter of the gift. In other cases the something else might be some other physical object, such as a set of keys, which give the donee access to the subject matter of the gift.

Where the subject matter of the gift is incapable of a physical delivery, the delivery requirement may be satisfied by either a "constructive" or "symbolic" delivery.

A constructive delivery occurs when the donor delivers to the donee an object that permits the donee to gain possession of the subject matter of the gift. A symbolic delivery occurs when the donor delivers to the donee some object intended to represent the subject matter of the gift. See generally R. Brown, The Law of Personal Property (W. Raushenbush ed., 3d ed. 1975). Which of these substitute forms of delivery occurred in the principal case?

The courts are divided with respect to when either a constructive or a symbolic delivery will be an acceptable substitute for an actual delivery of the subject matter of the gift. For example, will the former be permitted only when it would be unreasonable to physically deliver the subject matter of the gift or will it be permitted if an actual delivery is merely inconvenient? How a court responds to that question can depend on whether the court conceives of delivery as a distinct requirement to effectuate a gift or merely as evidence of an intent to make a gift.

6. O gives A the keys to his safe deposit box in which there are three stock certificates and a life insurance policy. When O hands A the keys O says to A: "Here is the key to my safe deposit box, the contents are yours." Has O made an effective gift to A of the contents of the safe deposit box? Suppose O had a duplicate key to the safe deposit box or the bank required O's signature to gain entrance to the box. Same result? Bauernschmidt v. Bauernschmidt, 97 Md. 35, 54 A. 637 (1903); Harrison v. Foley, 206 F. 57 (8th Cir. 1913).

Suppose the stock certificates and life insurance policy were in a locked box in O's bedroom and O makes the foregoing statement to A as he hands A the keys to that box while A is visiting O in his bedroom. Same result? Cf. Newman v. Bost, 122 N.C. 524, 29 S.E. 848 (1898).

7. M tells her daughter that "I am giving you $500 which I have buried underneath the tree. To get to the tree go out the front door, turn left, walk 400 paces, turn right, walk 45 paces and turn right and continue walking until you come to a small bush. Turn 13 degrees west and dig down three feet to find the metal case the cash is in." If the daughter, following these directions, retrieves the cash, is there a completed gift? Is the gift complete if the daughter does not immediately retrieve the cash but does so only after M has died? See generally Waite v. Grubbe, 43 Or. 406, 73 P. 206 (1903).

8. How can a husband make a gift to his wife of the grand piano in their living room?

9. Father gave Daughter a check in the amount of $20,000 as a gift. Daughter forwarded the check to her bank with directions to purchase a certificate of deposit. Before her bank was able to process the check for payment Father died. When, after his death, the check was presented at the Father's bank for payment, that bank refused to honor the check on the grounds that the gift was revoked by the Father's death. Is the bank correct? See In re Estate of Bolton, 444 N.W.2d 482 (Iowa 1989).

10. In a number of cases the courts have had to consider the effectiveness of a gift where the subject matter of the gift (or something else intended to be a "stand in" for the subject matter of the gift) is delivered to a third person rather than the donee. The third person may be either an agent of the donor or a trustee for the donee. The characterization of this third party's role can affect the validity of the gift in light of the delivery requirement. If the third party to whom the subject matter of the gift is delivered is characterized as an agent of the donor, the gift is incomplete; if the third party is characterized as trustee for the donee, the gift is complete. What facts might be relevant in characterizing whether the third party is an agent of the donor or trustee of the donee?

ALBINGER v. HARRIS

Supreme Court of Montana (2002).
310 Mont. 27, 48 P.3d 711.

JUSTICE JAMES C. NELSON delivered the Opinion of the Court

Harris and Albinger met in June 1995, and began a troubled relationship that endured for the next three years, spiked by alcohol abuse, emotional turmoil and violence. Albinger presented Harris with a diamond ring and diamond earrings on December 14, 1995. The ring was purchased for $29,000. Days after accepting the ring, Harris returned it to Albinger and traveled to Kentucky for the holidays. Albinger immediately sent the ring back to Harris by mail. The couple set a tentative wedding date of June 27, 1997, but plans to marry were put on hold as Harris and Albinger separated and reconciled several times. The ring was returned to or reclaimed by Albinger upon each separation, and was re-presented to Harris after each reconciliation.

Albinger and Harris lived together in Albinger's home from August 1995 until April 1998. During this time, Albinger conferred upon Harris a new Ford Mustang convertible, a horse and a dog, in addition to the earrings and ring. Harris gave Albinger a Winchester hunting rifle, a necklace and a number of other small gifts. Albinger received a substantial jury award for injuries sustained in a 1991 railroad accident. He paid all household expenses and neither party was gainfully employed during their cohabitation.

On the night of February 23, 1997, during one of the couple's many separations, Albinger broke into the house where Harris was staying. He stood over Harris' bed, threatened her with a knife and shouted, "I'm going to chop your finger off, you better get that ring off." After severely beating Harris with a railroad lantern, Albinger forcibly removed the ring and departed. Harris sued for personal injuries and the county attorney charged Albinger by information with aggravated burglary, felony assault, and partner and family member assault. The next month, after another reconciliation, Harris requested the county attorney drop all criminal charges in exchange for Albinger's promise to seek anger management counseling and to pay restitution in the form of Harris' medical expenses and repair costs for damage to her friend's back door. Harris also directed her attorney to request the court dismiss the civil complaint without prejudice.

The parties separated again in late April 1998. Albinger told Harris to "take the car, the horse, the dog, and the ring and get the hell out ..." Harris moved from Great Falls, Montana to Kentucky, where she now resides. The parties dispute who was responsible for the end of the relationship. No reconciliation followed, marriage plans evaporated and Harris refused to return the ring.

Albinger filed a complaint on August 31, 1998, seeking recovery of the ring ...

At the conclusion of the trial, both parties submitted briefs discussing how the statute barring actions for breach of promise to marry, § 27–1–602, MCA, impacts an action to recover an engagement ring. The District Court found the ring to be a gift in contemplation of marriage, and reasoned that § 27–1–602, MCA, did not bar the action because the case could be decided on common-law principles, as opposed to contract theories. The court implied the existence of a condition attached to the gift of the engagement ring. Disregarding allegations of fault for "breaking" the engagement, the court concluded that the giver is entitled to the return of the ring upon failure of the condition of marriage.

On September 2, 1999, the District Court awarded the engagement ring or its reasonable value ... to Albinger ..., From this judgment, Harris appeals the disposition of the ring ...

In the instant case, the parties agree that the ring was a gift. The crux of the dispute today is whether a condition of marriage attached to the gift as a matter of law at the time Albinger presented the ring to Harris.

Harris contends the ring lost any association with a promise to marry after the first incidence of domestic violence. The couple canceled their June 1997 nuptials and never revived explicit wedding plans. In response to a question about the ring's symbolic relationship to a promise to marry after the couple's numerous break-ups, reconciliations, and incidents of domestic violence, Harris testified, "[A]fter a while you don't think about that stuff. You just resume life." Albinger argues that the ring was presented as a gift only upon the unspoken condition that the wedding take place.

The District Court found the ring at issue in this action to be an engagement ring given in contemplation of marriage, and not a gift in commemoration of another occasion or as consideration for any other anticipated acts on the part of Harris. The court noted Albinger proposed marriage to Harris on December 14, 1995, and presented her with the ring at that time. Harris accepted both the marriage proposal and the ring. Although the ring was reclaimed by or returned to Albinger numerous times during the ensuing years, both Albinger and Harris referred to the ring as an "engagement ring" with some consistency. We conclude that the court's characterization of the disputed gift as an engagement ring is supported by substantial evidence and is not clearly erroneous.

Legal ownership of the gift of an engagement ring when marriage plans are called off is an issue of first impression in Montana. In 1963, the Legislature barred access to the courts for actions arising from breach of the promise to marry. Sec. 2, Chap. 200, L.1963. The District Court determined that this action brought to recover an antenuptial gift is maintainable, notwithstanding § 27–1–602, MCA, which states:

> All causes of action for breach of contract to marry are hereby abolished. However, where a plaintiff has suffered actual damage due to fraud or deceit or a defendant has been unjustly enriched, the plaintiff may maintain an action for fraud or deceit or unjust enrichment and recover therein only the actual damage proved or for the benefit wrongfully obtained or restitution of property wrongfully withheld where such action otherwise is maintainable under existing law.

According to the District Court's analysis, the statute goes no further than to bar actions for general damages sustained by the loss of marriage such as humiliation, lost opportunities, emotional suffering and other non-specific consequences of the breach. We agree with the court's conclusion that the rights and duties of the parties regarding property exchanged "in contemplation of marriage" are still determined by existing law and common-law principles.

The District Court presents a cogent summary of common-law principles applied to antenuptial gift disputes in the wake of the abolition of breach of promise actions. Section 27–1–602, MCA, specifically preserves actions based upon fraud, deceit or unjust enrichment. Albinger levels no accusations of fraud or deceit, but nevertheless claims Harris is unjustly enriched by the value of the engagement ring.

The doctrine of unjust enrichment is an equitable means of preventing one party from benefitting by his or her wrongful acts, and, as such requires a showing of misconduct or fault to recover ... Albinger argues that the engagement ring was a conditional gift that he could revoke when the implied condition of marriage failed. Hence, Harris' refusal to return the ring upon demand constituted unjust enrichment. Harris contends she deserves the ring because Albinger repeatedly beat her, forcibly took the ring back, and was the one who finally ended the engagement by ordering Harris to move out of the residence where they had been living together.

The District Court declined to undertake a determination of which party was at fault in terminating the engagement. The court cited the following three reasons: 1) judicial holdings that fault is an inappropriate concern in matters of family relations; 2) pragmatic difficulties in discerning fault when the conduct of both parties likely contributes to the failure of a relationship; and, 3) aversion to concepts of legal "rightness" and "wrongness" regarding the choice of a marriage partner. We agree, and affirm that judicial fault-finding is irrelevant and immaterial in the adjudication of matters of antenuptial gifting under existing law, absent fraud or deceit.

The District Court employed the "conditional gift" theory advanced by Albinger to determine present ownership of the disputed engagement ring. The theory holds that an implied condition of marriage attaches to the gift of a ring upon initial delivery due to the ring's symbolic association with the promise to marry and, when the condition of marriage fails, the incomplete gift may be revoked by the giver. Albinger urges this Court to affirm the District Court's conclusion that the ownership of an engagement ring remains with the one who gave the ring when plans to marry are called off.

Only in engagement ring cases does precedent from other jurisdictions weigh heavily for conditional gift theory in the absence of an expressed condition ... Considering it "unduly harsh and unnecessary" to require a hopeful suitor to express any condition upon which a ring might be premised, many courts stepped in to impute the condition of marriage. *Fierro v. Hoel* (Iowa 1990), 465 N.W.2d 669, 671. In practice, courts presume the existence of the implied condition of marriage attaching to an engagement ring in the absence of an expressed intent to the contrary. *Fanning v. Iversen* (S.D.1995), 535 N.W.2d 770; *Brown v. Thomas* (1985), 127 Wis.2d 318, 379 N.W.2d 868; *Lyle v. Durham* (1984), 16 Ohio App.3d 1, 473 N.E.2d 1216. A party meets the burden of establishing the conditional nature of the gift by proving by a preponderance of the evidence that the ring was given in contemplation of marriage. *Fierro,* 465 N.W.2d at 671. "Not only does this rule of law establish a 'bright line' for situations where the parties involved are unlikely to have considered the necessity of making an 'agreement to the contrary,' but the rule also eliminates the need for a trial court to attempt the often impossible task of determining which, if either, party is at fault." *McIntire v. Raukhorst* (1989), 65 Ohio App.3d 728, 585 N.E.2d 456, 458.

Since the issue of ring ownership when the engagement ends without marriage is a matter of first impression, we will briefly review early breach of promise jurisprudence, look to some American customs associated with engagement rings, analyze the judicial imputation of a condition in the context of Montana gift law, and examine conditional gift theory in light of the constitutional prohibition against gender bias.

Abolition of Breach of Promise Actions

Historic breach of promise jurisprudence tended to view an engagement ring as either a pledge of personal property given to secure a marital promise or as consideration for the contract of marriage. See 44 A.L.R. 5th 1, §§ 8 and 9. When a contract to marry was abrogated, the jilted lover could seek redress in a breach of promise action that sounded in contract law, but availed the plaintiff of tort damages. "The law allows punitive or vindictive damages to be assessed by the jury; and all the circumstances attending the breach before, at the time, and after may be given in evidence in aggravation of damages." *Dupont v. McAdow* (1886), 6 Mont. 226, 232, 9 P. 925, 928. The plaintiffs were almost invariably women seeking economic relief for themselves, compensation for pregnancy and material support for children of the relationship. Whatever "heart balm" was awarded to assuage lost love, ruined reputation or foreclosed opportunities to marry well "rest[ed] in the sound discretion of the jury." Section 8685, RCM (1935).

By the mid–1930's, several state legislatures questioned the efficacy of court "interference with domestic relations" and passed statutes barring actions for breach of promise to marry, alienation of affections, criminal conversation and other inappropriate conduct of the "private realm." See Rebecca Rushnet, *Rules of Engagement* (1998), 107 Yale Law Review 2583, 2586–91. Commentators noted all of these actions "afforded a fertile field for blackmail and extortion by means of manufactured suits in which the threat of publicity is used to force a settlement." W. Page Keeton et al., *Prosser and Keeton on the Law of Torts* (5th ed.1984) § 124 at 929. "There is good reason to believe that even genuine actions of this type are brought more frequently than not with purely mercenary or vindictive motives [and] that it is impossible to compensate for such damage with what has derisively been called 'heart balm.' " *Prosser and Keeton,* § 124 at 929.

In the wake of "anti-heart balm" statutes that barred breach of contract to marry actions, courts heard a plethora of legal theories designed to involve them in settling antenuptial property disputes while avoiding the language of contract law. The results were mixed. Some courts allowed actions in replevin. See *Vann v. Vehrs* (2d Dist.1994), 260 Ill.App.3d 648, 198 Ill.Dec. 640, 633 N.E.2d 102 (to reclaim property which the other party allegedly no longer has a right to possess). Others entertained claims for restitution and unjust enrichment. See *Wilson v. Dabo* (1983), 10 Ohio App.3d 169, 461 N.E.2d 8 (to reclaim property transferred in reliance upon the promise to marry when the donor was the "non-breaching party"). Out of this legal morass, conditional gift analysis emerged as a popular way to resolve acrimonious engagement ring disputes. While some states pursue a fault-based determination for awarding the ring in equity, the modern wave aligns ring disposition with no-fault divorce property disposition and follows a bright-line rule of ring return.

Engagement Ring Symbology

The custom of giving expensive engagement rings is largely a mid-to late 20th Century phenomenon. Margaret F. Brinig, *Rings and Promises* (1990), 6 J.L. Econ. & Org. 203, 209. Nineteenth Century etiquette books struggled to identify proper gifts between men and women. Viviana A. Ziegler, *The Social Meaning of Money* (1994). Expensive or excessively intimate gifts, such as jewelry or wearing apparel, were fit for a kept woman, or perhaps a man's wife, but not as tokens of respectable courtship. *Ziegler,* at 99. Upper class men and women occasionally exchanged diamond rings as gifts during the 19th Century. *Ziegler,* at 99. The six-prong gold or platinum setting holding a raised, brilliant-cut diamond, which has become the classic engagement ring style, was created by Tiffany's in the 1870s. Anne Ward et al., *Rings Through the Ages* (1981), at 198. DeBeers' launched its national advertising campaign in 1939 that promised: "A diamond is forever." *Brinig,* at 206. To cultivate a no-return custom in America, the cartel threatened to cut off supply to dealers who bought diamonds back from purchasers. *Brinig,* at 209. An interesting correlation exists between the mid–20th Century increase in demand for costly diamond engagement rings and the statutory changes by state legislatures to abolish the breach of promise action. *Brinig,* at 206. After the Second World War, expensive rings became not just symbols of love, but tangible economic commitments in themselves, and appear to have gained significance as other economic incidents of marriage were in flux. See Reva B. Siegel, *Modernization of Marital Status Law: Adjudicating Wives Rights to Earnings, 1860–1930* (1994), 82 Geo. L.J. 2127, 2201–03. As courts closed to women seeking damages for breach of the promise to marry, the cost and the practice of giving engagement rings rose dramatically. *Brinig,* at 209. By the time Montana barred the breach of promise action, diamonds constituted over 80% of engagement ring sales. *Brinig,* at 205. Through the late 20th Century, rings remained personal tokens of affection; many couples who spurned the conventions of marriage still wore rings to bear witness to their union. *Ward,* at 146. Since 1980, however, engagement rings never exceeded 20% of diamond jewelry sales. *Brinig,* at 212.

This Court acknowledges the customary practice of presenting an engagement ring in conjunction with a promise to marry and we next examine the legal significance of that symbolic association in the context of Montana gift law.

Conditional Gift Theory

According to Montana law, "a gift is a transfer of personal property made voluntarily and without consideration." Section 70–3–101, MCA. The essential elements of an *inter vivos* gift are donative intent, voluntary delivery and acceptance by the recipient. *Marans v. Newland* (1962), 141 Mont. 32, 39, 374 P.2d 721, 724 (*citing O'Neil v. First Nat. Bank of Billings* (1911), 43 Mont. 505, 511, 117 P. 889, 890). Delivery, which manifests the intent of the giver, must turn over dominion and control of the property to the recipient. *In re Brown's Estate* (1949), 122 Mont. 451, 459, 206 P.2d 816, 821. Such a gift, made without condition, becomes irrevocable upon acceptance. *Marans,* 141 Mont. at 36, 374 P.2d at 723; *Fender v. Foust* (1928), 82 Mont. 73, 78, 265 P. 15, 16; *O'Neil v. First Nat. Bank of Billings* (1911), 43 Mont. 505, 511, 117 P. 889, 890. When clear and convincing evidence demonstrates the presence of the essential elements of donative intent, voluntary delivery and acceptance, the gift is complete and this Court will not void the transfer when the giver experiences a change of heart. See *Gross v. Gross* (1989), 239 Mont. 480, 781 P.2d 284 (father barred from revoking a gift of real property transferred to his son).

Another essential element of a gift is that it is given without consideration. Section 70–3–101, MCA. A purported "gift" that is part of the inducement for "an agreement to do or not to do a certain thing," becomes the consideration essential to contract formation. Sections 28–2–101 and 28–2–102, MCA. An exchange of promises creates a contract to marry, albeit an unenforceable one. Section 27–1–412(2), MCA. When an engagement ring is given as consideration for the promise to marry, a contract is formed and legal action to recover the ring is barred by the abolition of the breach of promise actions. Section 27–1–602, MCA.

The only revocable gift recognized by Montana law is a gift in view of death. *See* §§ 70–3–201, et seq., MCA. Also known as a gift *causa mortis,* such a gift is subject to the following conditions: 1) it must be made in contemplation, fear or peril of death; 2) the giver must die of the illness or peril that he or she fears or contemplates; and 3) the delivery must be made with the intent that the gift will only take effect if the giver actually dies. Section 70–3–201, MCA; *Nelson v. Wilson* (1928), 81 Mont. 560, 570, 264 P. 679, 682; *O'Neil,* 43 Mont. at 511, 117 P. at 890. Statutory law provides that a gift in view of death may be revoked by the giver at any time and is revoked by the giver's recovery from the illness or escape from the peril under which the gift was made. Section 70–3–203, MCA.

Albinger maintains he held a reversionary interest in the gift of the engagement ring grounded in an implied condition subsequent. Montana law recognizes the transfer of personal property subject to an express or implied condition which must be satisfied before title vests, as either a contract, § 28–1–405, MCA, or as a gift in view of death, §§ 70–3–201, et. seq., MCA. Since actions stemming from breach of the contract to marry are barred by our "anti-heart balm" statute, Albinger urges the Court to adopt a conditional gift theory patterned on the law relevant to a gift in view of death. Under Montana law, no gift is revocable after acceptance except a gift in view of death. While some may find marriage to be the end of life as one knows it, we are reluctant to analogize gifts in contemplation of marriage with a gift in contemplation of death. This Court declines the invitation to create a new category of gifting by judicial fiat.

Gender Bias

Article II, Section 4 of the Montana Constitution recognizes and guarantees the individual dignity of each human being without regard to gender. This Court and the Montana State Bar have recognized the harm caused by gender bias and sexual stereotyping in the jurisprudence and courtroom of this state. *In the Matter of the State Bar of Montana's Gender Fairness Steering Committee,* No. 90–231 (1990) (Petition and Order); *In re Marriage of Davies* (1994), 266 Mont. 466, 480–82, 880 P.2d 1368, 1378 (Nelson, J., concurring). In its Petition to the Supreme Court, the State Bar of Montana's Gender Fairness Steering Committee listed four forms of gender bias: a) denying rights or burdening people with responsibilities solely on the basis of gender; b) subjecting people to stereotypes about the proper behavior of men and women which ignore their individual situations; c) treating people differently on the basis of gender in situations in which gender should be irrelevant; and d) subjecting men or women as a group to a legal rule, policy, or practice which produces worse results for one group than the other.

The Montana Legislature made the social policy decision to relieve courts of the duty of regulating engagements by barring actions for breach of promise. While not explicitly denying access to the courts on the basis of gender, the "anti-heart balm" statutes closed courtrooms across the nation to female plaintiffs seeking damages for antenuptial pregnancy, ruined reputation, lost love and economic insecurity. During the mid–20th Century, some courts continued to entertain suits in equity for antenuptial property transfers. The jurisprudence that rose upon the implied conditional gift theory, based upon an engagement ring's symbolic associations with marriage, preserved a right of action narrowly tailored for ring givers seeking ring return. The bright-line rule of ring return on a no-fault basis, which Albinger urges this Court to adopt, sets forth as a matter of law "proper" post-engagement behavior in regard to this single gifted item. The proposed no-fault adjudication of a disputed engagement ring also ignores the particular circumstances of a couple's decision not to marry.

Conditional gift theory applied exclusively to engagement ring cases, carves an exception in the state's gift law for the benefit of predominately male plaintiffs. Montana's "anti-heart balm" statute bars all actions sounding in contract law that arise from mutual promise to marry, absent fraud or deceit, and bars all plaintiffs from recovering any share of expenses incurred in planning a canceled wedding. While antenuptial traditions vary by class, ethnicity, age and inclination, women often still assume the bulk of pre-wedding costs, such as non-returnable wedding gowns, moving costs, or non-refundable deposits for caterers, entertainment or reception halls. Consequently, the statutory "anti-heart balm" bar continues to have a disparate impact on women. If this Court were to fashion a special exception for engagement ring actions under gift law theories, we would perpetuate the gender bias attendant upon the Legislature's decision to remove from our courts all actions for breach of antenuptial promises.

Engagement Ring Disposition

To preserve the integrity of our gift law and to avoid additional gender bias, we decline to adopt the theory that an engagement ring is a gift subject to an implied condition of marriage. Judicial imputation of conditional gifting would stake new legal territory in Montana. "It is not the province of this court or any other court to assume to legislate by judicial interpretation, and to create in favor of any individual or any class of people an exception to the limitation set by the legislature." *Taylor v. Rann* (1938), 106 Mont. 588, 594, 80 P.2d 376, 379; see also Section 1–2–101, MCA.

The District Court found the engagement ring was voluntarily offered by Albinger on December 14, 1995, without consideration and with the present intent to voluntarily transfer dominion and control to Harris. Harris accepted the ring. Although the court implied a condition of marriage attaching to the gift as a matter of law, we do not. In our judgment, the gift was complete upon delivery, and a completed gift is not revocable. The fact that possession of the ring passed back and forth between Albinger and Harris during the course of their relationship bears no relevance to the issue of ring ownership. All of the elements of gifting must be present to transfer ownership, and the facts do not indicate re-gifting occurred. In fact, Albinger acknowledged Harris' ownership himself when he told Harris "to take the car, the horse, the dog and the ring" when she left the relationship. We hold that the engagement ring was an unconditional, completed gift upon acceptance and remains in Harris' ownership and control . . .

We reverse the District Court's conclusion of law and hold the engagement ring to be a gift given without implied or express condition. Montana gift law makes no provision for conditional gifting, except in the context of a gift in contemplation of death. We refrain from adopting permutations in the legal theory of gifting that have no legislated authority and serve to exacerbate gender bias . . .

JUSTICE TERRY N. TRIEWEILER concurring and dissenting.

Gender discrimination is a bad thing. I am glad the majority is against it. However, I regret that the majority has taken this opportunity to declare their good intentions because gender equity has about as much to do with this case as banking law. Furthermore, the parties in the District Court will be as surprised to hear about the basis on which this appeal has been resolved as I was when I read the proposed opinion. Principles of gender equity were never argued or even raised by the parties at any stage in the proceeding and the District Court had no opportunity to consider the relevance (or irrelevance) of Constitutional theory to any of the simple issues which were presented in the District Court ...

The simple fact is that if women are more likely to be the subject of an action to recover a conditional gift given in anticipation of a marriage which does not occur, it is because they are more frequently the recipient of the gift. Should we just prohibit gifts in anticipation of marriage altogether because men are more likely to have to pay for them? The possible implications of the majority's decision are just beyond my comprehension.

Before today, no court anywhere in the world has ever held that a conditional gift given in anticipation of marriage cannot be recovered if the condition on which it was given, the marriage, does not occur because to require its return would violate notions of gender fairness. Nowhere at any time. It is no wonder the parties did not think of it. Before embarking on this radical, unprecedented departure from traditional notions of contract and gift law, shouldn't we have at least asked the parties for their views? Shouldn't we at least have some record for the unfounded assumption that one gender is more likely to be affected than the other?

This is a simple case involving the law of conditional gifts, decided by the District Court based on findings which are fully supported by the evidence and law as it has been applied throughout the country. The District Court opinion is well reasoned and fair. It should be affirmed. Therefore, I dissent ...

The District Court ... found that the ring at issue ... was referred to throughout the couple's relationship as an "engagement ring." It found ... that the ring was presented to Michelle in contemplation of her marriage to Michael. The District Court found ... that each time, except for the last time, the couple broke up (and they broke up frequently), the ring was either returned by Michelle or taken back by Michael. These findings were fully supported by the evidence. For example, Michael testified as follows:

Q. Now, when you gave her the engagement ring, were you contemplating that you were going to get married?

A. That was the whole idea.

Q. Was there any way in your mind that the engagement ring was just a ring and she could keep it whether you were married or not?

A. No.

Q. Is it correct that it was always in contemplation of marriage?

A. Yes.

Q. Now, she testified that the engagement was on and off a couple of times at least; is that correct?

A. Yes.

Q. Okay. At any of those times when the engagement was off and the ring or excuse me, at any of those times that the engagement was off, was the ring delivered back to you?

A. Yes.

Q. Every time?

A. Yes.

Q. I guess with the exception of the time she got on the airplane?

A. Right. That would be, that would be the only time that I can recall . . .

Based on the District Court's findings, certain legal conclusions necessarily followed. First, the District Court concluded that courts in other jurisdictions have analyzed similar cases based on the theory of "conditional gift;" that the occurrence of the anticipated marriage was a condition on which the gift was given; and that because the condition was not fulfilled, plaintiff was entitled to recovery of the gift. The District Court was correct . . .

Elaine Marie Tomko, Annotation, *Rights in Respect of Engagement and Courtship Presents When Marriage Does Not Ensue*, 44 A.L.R. 5th 1, 18 (1996) . . .

However, the majority is not content to review the issues presented based on the facts which were proven and the legal authorities which have been submitted. The majority instead, without any factual basis in the record, explores what it finds are "some American customs associated with engagement rings" and turns this simple property dispute based on traditional rules of gift law into a battle of the sexes with constitutional implications. Considering the significance we have now attached to this case, does it strike anyone else as odd that we haven't asked the parties for any input on these critical issues?

The practical problems arising from the majority's impulsiveness become quickly apparent. For example, a predicate to its gender inequity approach is its conclusion that "anti-heart balm" statutes have "closed courtrooms across the nation to female plaintiffs seeking damages." What is the factual basis for assuming that women are more likely to seek damages for breach of a promise to marry than men? Tomko's annotation would suggest that gender is not a factor. She states that the purpose of heart balm statutes was originally "to avert perpetration of fraud by adventurers or adventuresses. . . ." 44 A.L.R. 5th at 27. There is no authority provided for the quantum leap taken by the majority. It must be so simply because the majority says so.

The next step in the majority's shaky syllogism is its unsupported conclusion that "[c]onditional gift theory applied exclusively to engagement ring cases carves an exception in the state's gift law for the benefit of predominantly male plaintiffs." Furthermore, the majority states that while "Montana's 'anti-heart balm' statute ... bars all plaintiffs from recovering any share of non-refundable expenses incurred in planning a cancelled wedding," it assumes that women usually incur these expenses. The majority's conclusion from these unsupported assumptions is that, therefore, we cannot, in fairness, enforce conditional gift law when it pertains to engagement rings.

First of all, either gender can given an engagement ring. For example, in *Vigil v. Haber* (1994), 119 N.M. 9, 888 P.2d 455, the parties exchanged engagement rings. However, their relationship deteriorated, the couple separated, and following their separation a hearing examiner determined that the parties should return the rings they had given each other. The plaintiff immediately returned the ring he had along with other of the defendant's possessions. However, the defendant objected to returning the engagement ring that had been given to her. The New Mexico Supreme Court held that the ring was a conditional gift dependant on the parties' marriage and should be returned. *Vigil,* 888 P.2d at 458. What if the roles had been reversed and the woman had returned the engagement ring given to her but the man had refused to do so? According to this Court, she would not be allowed to recover the engagement ring that she had given to her fiance, no matter how substantial the value and unfair the result because requiring the return of engagement rings is unfair to women.

The second problem with the majority's assumptions is the assumption that conditional gift law as it relates to gifts exchanged in anticipation of marriage only applies to wedding rings. It does not. For example, in *Pavlicic,* a case which disproves the theory that jurisprudence cannot be written in readable prose, the plaintiff was a 75–year–old man when the 26–year–old defendant asked for his hand in marriage. While he first protested on the basis of his age, she assured him that she was no longer interested in "young fellows" and prevailed upon him to make the commitment. Over the course of the next four years, she then prevailed upon him to pay the mortgage on her home, buy her two new cars, an engagement ring, a diamond for her mother's ring, remodel her house, and advance her $5000 to purchase a saloon which they could jointly operate. The problem was that after she received the money for the saloon, she disappeared. She was next seen in another town operating Ruby's bar and married to a man two years her junior. As noted by the Pennsylvania Supreme Court:

> When George emerged from the mists and fogs of his disappointment and disillusionment he brought an action in equity praying that the satisfaction of the mortgage on Sara Jane's property be stricken from the record, that she be ordered to return the gifts which had not been consumed, and pay back the moneys [sic] which she had gotten from him under a false promise to marry.

Pavlicic, 136 A.2d at 129.

The Pennsylvania Supreme Court held that George's action was not barred by the state's "Heart Balm Act" and that all gifts, not just the wedding ring, were conditional gifts in anticipation of marriage which must be returned or repaid. The Pennsylvania Supreme Court cited *Stanger v. Epler* (1955), 382 Pa. 411, 115 A.2d 197, 199, stating:

> A gift to a person to whom the donor is engaged to be married, made in contemplation of marriage, although absolute in form, is conditional; and upon breach of the marriage engagement by the donee the property may be recovered by the donor. See also 38 C.J.S. Gifts § 61.

Pavlicic, 136 A.2d at 131.

The point is that there is no reason to limit the law of "conditional gifts" in anticipation of marriage to engagement rings. There is precedent for applying it to all gifts in anticipation of marriage and had either of the parties had any forewarning that this Court would have launched into the gender equity issue on which it bases its opinion, they could have pointed that out.

Also predicate to the majority's decision is its conclusion that the District Court implied that marriage was a condition to the gift. However, as previously noted, the Court implied no such thing. The Court made a finding that the gift was given in anticipation of marriage based on the testimony that was presented. The majority has simply chosen, as a matter of law, to ignore those facts in favor of the social theory it has chosen to impose on the parties and the people of this state without the benefit of input from anyone else.

I dissent from the majority's conclusion that Montana, unlike any other jurisdiction which has considered this issue, should not apply traditional "conditional gift" or contract law to the resolution of the dispute between the parties. I dissent from the majority's interesting but inapplicable and factually unsupported social commentary and its interjection and ultimate reliance on constitutional theory which was never raised by any party, never considered by the District Court, and on which neither party had an opportunity to comment. The Opinion is based on sexual stereotypes, false assumptions unsupported by the record, constitutional theory never raised or considered by the parties or the District Court, and social theory that has nothing to do with the case as it was considered by the District Court or developed by the parties. In short, it breaks just about every rule of appellate decision-making.

I dissent from the majority's transformation of a simple case involving gift law to a soap box on which to analyze social customs and significant constitutional rights which have now been trivialized by their interjection in this case.

NOTES AND QUESTIONS

1. In a state adopting the conditional gift theory, should it make any difference which party, the donor or the donee, broke the engagement? Compare Wion v. Henderson, 24 Ohio App.3d 207, 494 N.E.2d 133 (1985) (no need to return the ring if the engagement is broken by the donor) with Lyle v. Durham, 16 Ohio App.3d 1, 473 N.E.2d 1216 (1984) (must return ring regardless of who breaks the engagement). See also Lindh v. Surman, 560 Pa. 1, 742 A.2d 643 (1999). Should the reason the engagement was broken be relevant? See Curtis v. Anderson, 106 S.W.3d 251 (Tex. App. 2003).

2. Does the majority assume that a gift to the man would not have to be returned if the marriage does not occur? If they don't assume that, where is the gender bias?

3. M and W publicly announce their engagement. Three months later, W's friends hold a wedding shower at which they give W fabulous gifts. One month after the wedding shower, M and W call off the engagement. Must the gifts be returned? If they don't have to be returned, how should they be divided between M and W?

4. H and W tell W's parents that W is pregnant. W's parents immediately throw a baby shower and H and W receive fabulous baby gifts. Unfortunately, two months later W miscarries. Must the baby shower gifts be returned? Suppose W aborts the baby. Same result?

5. Did Albinger make a tactical error in agreeing "that the ring was a gift?" How else might the presentation of the ring from him to her have been characterized and might that have made a difference to the outcome of the case?

6. In Syragakis v. Hopkins, 2001 WL 195012 (Conn.Super. 2001), the court held that a man who sued a defendant to recover an alleged engagement ring had the burden to prove that the ring was given as an engagement ring and not as an outright gift. The court found that burden was not met when the defendant claimed that when the man gave her the ring she told him she would not marry him. She testified that "she believed the purpose of [giving her a ring] was to keep other men away from her."

TENNESSEE DIVISION OF THE UNITED DAUGHTERS OF THE CONFEDERACY v. VANDERBILT UNIVERSITY

Court of Appeals of Tennessee (2005).
174 S.W.3d 98.

WILLIAM C. KOCH, JR., P.J. M.S.

This appeal involves a dispute stemming from . . . [Vanderbilt University's] decision to change the name of one of its dormitories. An organization that donated part of the funds used to construct the dormitory filed suit . . . asserting that the university's decision to rename the dormitory breached its seventy-year-old agreement with the university and requesting declaratory and injunctive relief and damages. Both the university and the donor organization filed motions for summary judgment. The trial court, granting the university's motion, determined that the university should be permitted to modify the parties' agreement regarding the dormitory's name because it would be "impractical and unduly burdensome" to require the university to continue to honor the agreement. The donor organization appealed. We have determined that the summary judgment must be reversed because the university has failed to demonstrate that it is entitled to a judgment as a matter of law. Furthermore, based on the essentially undisputed facts, we have determined that the donor organization is entitled to a partial summary judgment because the university has breached the conditions placed on the donor's gift and, therefore, that the university should be required to return the present value of the gift to the donor if it insists on renaming the dormitory.

Since 1902, the ... [Tennessee Division of the United Daughters of the Confederacy ("Tennessee U.D.C.)]." had been discussing the idea of raising funds for the construction of a women's dormitory for the use of descendants of Confederate soldiers at a college or university in Tennessee. Accordingly, [it] ... began discussions with Peabody College regarding underwriting the construction of a dormitory on the new campus.

On January 21, 1913, the Tennessee U.D.C. entered into a contract with the Peabody College trustees to raise $50,000 for the construction of a women's dormitory on the new campus. In return for this gift, the trustees agreed to allow women descendants of Confederate soldiers nominated by the Tennessee U.D.C. to live in the dormitory rent-free and to pay other dormitory expenses on an estimated cost basis. The contract reserved to the college the right to reject anyone nominated by the Tennessee U.D.C. and stipulated that the college would select the design and plan for the dormitory, would hold title to the building, and would control and manage it ...

[This contract was amended by a second contract which] ... stated that both parties desired that a "Confederate Memorial Hall" building be constructed on Peabody College's campus. The Tennessee U.D.C. agreed to pay over to the college treasurer the $17,421.47 it had already raised and to turn over further sums when they were collected. In return, the college agreed that when the funds reached a sufficient amount, it would construct a building on its property conforming to plans and specifications to be agreed upon by the parties, and that the building would be used for the purposes contemplated by the parties. In addition, the college agreed to invest the sums deposited by the Tennessee U.D.C., to pay the interest earned on these sums into the building fund annually, and to return the sums deposited, with interest, if the Tennessee U.D.C. decided to recall them.

In spite of the Great Depression, during the next six years the Tennessee U.D.C. managed to raise enough money to meet its original $50,000 goal. By that time, the Tennessee U.D.C. and Peabody College had decided that although a small women's dormitory could be constructed for

$50,000, they would both prefer to use the $50,000 as partial funding for the construction of a larger women's dormitory to be located on the campus quadrangle. Peabody College estimated that the larger dormitory would cost approximately $150,000 and had already applied to the National Recovery Administration for the extra funding.

Sometime in September of 1933, the Tennessee U.D.C. and Peabody College entered into a third written contract to reflect their new plans. The third contract expressly ratified and affirmed the 1913 and 1927 contracts. The Tennessee U.D.C. agreed to allow the college to use the original $50,000 and any additional sums raised by the Tennessee U.D.C. for the construction of a larger building, the plans and specifications of which had been examined, approved, and signed by representatives of the Tennessee U.D.C. The Tennessee U.D.C. agreed to this modification on the condition that the college allow the first two floors of the larger dormitory to be used for the purposes specified in the 1913 and 1927 contracts, and on the further condition that the college place on the building an inscription naming it "Confederate Memorial." . . .

From 1935 until the late 1970's, women descendants of Confederate soldiers nominated by the Tennessee U.D.C. and accepted by Peabody College lived in Confederate Memorial Hall rent-free. However, by the late 1970's, Peabody College found itself in increasingly dire financial straits . . . and it soon became evident that the college would either have to merge with another institution or face bankruptcy. . . . On April 28, 1979, the trustees of Vanderbilt and Peabody College entered into an agreement effectuating the merger. Under the terms of the merger agreement, Vanderbilt succeeded to all of Peabody College's legal obligations.

By the time of the merger, only four students nominated by the Tennessee U.D.C. were still living in Confederate Memorial Hall. Vanderbilt allowed these four students to continue living there at a reduced rental rate, but after they graduated, no other students nominated by the Tennessee U.D.C. were allowed to live in Confederate Memorial Hall rent-free or at a reduced rate.[1]

In 1987 and 1988, Vanderbilt spent approximately $2.5 million to renovate and upgrade Confederate Memorial Hall. During the following academic year, there was much discussion on the Vanderbilt campus regarding the propriety of retaining the name "Confederate Memorial Hall." A well publicized forum to discuss the issue was attended by Vanderbilt faculty, students, and staff, as well as representatives of the Tennessee U.D.C. and concerned citizens. Vanderbilt Chancellor Joe B. Wyatt later issued a statement announcing that he was not inclined to recommend renaming Confederate Memorial Hall based on the historical information currently available and because of "the absence of any indication that the naming of Confederate Memorial Hall by George Peabody College for Teachers was in any sense intended to support either slavery or any other form of prejudice toward Blacks."

---

1. Vanderbilt has continued to use the building as a dormitory to the present day.

Within a few months, the Vanderbilt Student Government Association passed a resolution recommending that Vanderbilt install a plaque on Confederate Memorial Hall explaining why it was named "Confederate." Vanderbilt officials, in consultation with representatives of student groups and the Tennessee U.D.C., agreed to place a plaque by the entrance to Confederate Memorial Hall explaining the contributions of the Tennessee U.D.C. and the resulting name of the building. The plaque was installed in 1989.[2]

Controversy over the name of Confederate Memorial Hall arose again in the spring of 2000 when the Vanderbilt Student Government Association passed a resolution calling on the administration to change the name of the building. The resolution stated that students, faculty, staff, and members of the administration had expressed great discontent with the name, that the name did not honor the heritage of all Vanderbilt students, faculty, and administrators, and that regardless of the original intent of the Tennessee U.D.C. in 1935, individuals at Vanderbilt felt offended by the name. The resolution noted that the demographic population of Vanderbilt had changed significantly since 1935[3] and that Vanderbilt respected all individuals regardless of their racial identity

E. Gordon Gee became the new chancellor of Vanderbilt in July 2000. In conversations with Vanderbilt students, faculty, and alumni over the next two years, the name of Confederate Memorial Hall was repeatedly identified as a major impediment to the progress of the university. In June 2002, Chancellor Gee discussed the matter with the executive committee of the Vanderbilt board of trust, and the executive committee decided that Chancellor Gee would handle the issue as an administrative matter. Chancellor Gee, without consulting the Tennessee U.D.C., then decided to change the name of "Confederate Memorial Hall" to "Memorial Hall," and his decision was made public in the fall of 2002.

Chancellor Gee's decision to rename Confederate Memorial Hall generated substantial public discussion. In September 2002, after the decision to rename the building was made public, Vanderbilt's vice chancellor for public affairs wrote to the Tennessee U.D.C. to explain Chancellor Gee's decision. The letter expressed gratitude to the Tennessee U.D.C. for its assistance to Peabody College in educating young teachers during a

---

2. The record on appeal does not contain a photograph of the plaque or a description of its wording as installed. However, the record contains a draft version of the plaque reflecting the following inscription:

CONFEDERATE MEMORIAL HALL CONSTRUCTED IN 1935 BY GEORGE PEABODY COLLEGE FOR TEACHERS, IN PART, WITH FUNDS RAISED AT PERSONAL SACRIFICE DURING THE GREAT DEPRESSION, BY TENNESSEE WOMEN OF THE UNITED DAUGHTERS OF THE CONFEDERACY, IN MEMORY OF THEIR FATHERS AND BROTHERS WHO FOUGHT IN THE WAR BETWEEN NORTH AND SOUTH, 1861–65. DEDICATED TO THE EDUCATION OF TEACHERS FOR A REGION SORELY IN NEED OF THEM. RENOVATED BY VANDERBILT UNIVERSITY IN 1988, FOR CONTINUED SERVICE TO ALL ITS STUDENTS. 1989

3. Vanderbilt did not admit African–American students to its graduate programs until 1953, and the first African–American undergraduates were not enrolled until 1964, the same year that Peabody admitted its first African–American undergraduate students. By the 2002–03 academic year, there were 371 African–American students in the Vanderbilt undergraduate student body.

difficult time in the nation's history and stated that the decision to rename the building had been made only after careful deliberation by the Vanderbilt administration, students, and faculty. In addition, the letter promised that the historic marker indicating the origins and historical significance of the building and the contributions of the Tennessee U.D.C. would remain in its current location. On October 3, 2002, Chancellor Gee met personally with representatives of the Tennessee U.D.C. and confirmed Vanderbilt's intention to rename Confederate Memorial Hall. Chancellor Gee also confirmed that the plaque by the entrance explaining the history of the building would remain in place.

On October 9, 2002, the Vanderbilt Student Government Association passed a resolution endorsing Chancellor Gee's decision to rename Confederate Memorial Hall. The resolution stated that the name of Confederate Memorial Hall had been under debate for fourteen years because of its negative association with slavery, that members of the Vanderbilt community had resolved not to live in Confederate Memorial Hall because of its name, and that Vanderbilt should strive to be a place where all students are challenged but not excluded from feeling a part of their campus and their dormitories. The resolution noted that names on buildings are usually a sign of pride and thankfulness for the contributions made to construct them, but that Vanderbilt was not proud of the legacy of slavery attached to the name of Confederate Memorial Hall or some of the actions of the United Daughters of the Confederacy.

On October 10, 2002, Chancellor Gee drafted a memorandum to the full Vanderbilt board of trust explaining his decision to rename the building. Chancellor Gee stated that former, current, and prospective students, faculty, and staff had identified the presence on the Vanderbilt campus of a building named "Confederate Memorial Hall" as a barrier to achieving an inclusive and welcoming environment that is essential for a world-class university. He also noted that some individuals had refused to live or attend events in the building, that the building was originally named "Confederate Memorial Hall" to commemorate values that do not reflect those of a university dedicated to educating all and meeting the aspirations of the broader society, and that assigning students to live in a dormitory so named implied an endorsement, if not a celebration, of a system that many people find offensive. Finally, Chancellor Gee observed that having a building on the campus named "Confederate Memorial Hall" strongly reinforced the worst stereotypes held by many people that Vanderbilt is an institution trapped in a long-distant past.

The Vanderbilt board of trust supported Chancellor Gee's decision to rename Confederate Memorial Hall. Since then, Vanderbilt has changed its maps, website, and correspondence to reflect the building's new name of "Memorial Hall." Vanderbilt has not yet removed the name "Confederate Memorial Hall" from the pediment on the front of the building but has indicated its unequivocal intention to do so. The 1989 plaque describing the history of the building and the contributions of the Tennessee U.D.C. remains in place by the entrance of the building.

On October 17, 2002, the Tennessee U.D.C. filed suit against Vanderbilt for breach of contract ... [alleging] that it had fully performed its obligations under the 1913, 1927, and 1933 contracts and that Vanderbilt's renaming of Confederate Memorial Hall constituted a breach of those contracts. The Tennessee U.D.C. sought an injunction to prevent Vanderbilt from removing the inscription on the pediment on the front of the building, a declaratory judgment specifying Vanderbilt's rights and obligations to the Tennessee U.D.C., and compensatory damages ...

Vanderbilt answered and on August 1, 2003 filed a motion for summary judgment. Vanderbilt framed the primary issue before the trial court as "whether Vanderbilt should be required to maintain a name on one of its campus buildings in spite of the fact that that name evokes racial animosity from a significant, though unfortunate, period of American history." Vanderbilt then turned its attention to its legal defenses. It advanced essentially five justifications for modifying its agreement with the Tennessee U.D.C. First, Vanderbilt claimed that none of the three contracts at issue specified precisely how the name "Confederate Memorial Hall" would be placed on the building and argued that the plaque installed by the entrance in 1989 constituted substantial compliance with any naming requirement in the three contracts.... Third, Vanderbilt argued that the Tennessee U.D.C. had received full consideration for its $50,000 donation because of the many women who had been allowed to live in the dormitory rent-free over the years and because the name "Confederate Memorial Hall" had remained on the building for almost seventy years. Fourth, Vanderbilt argued that principles of academic freedom prevented the court from requiring the maintenance of the name "Confederate" on the building.

The Tennessee U.D.C. opposed Vanderbilt's motion for summary judgment arguing (1) that the 1989 plaque did not constitute substantial compliance with Vanderbilt's contractual naming obligations ... (3) that "full consideration" for their contribution of more than $50,000 would require Vanderbilt to honor all of its contractual obligations for the full life of the building, and (4) that principles of academic freedom would not prevent the trial court from forcing Vanderbilt to comply with the terms of a contract that its predecessor-in-interest, Peabody College, had entered into freely. The Tennessee U.D.C. further argued that Chancellor Gee did not have the authority to change the name of Confederate Memorial Hall and that Vanderbilt's unilateral determination that the term "Confederate" had become offensive did not constitute a legally recognized basis for allowing Vanderbilt to breach its contractual obligations. Finally, the Tennessee U.D.C. sought a partial summary judgment holding that the 1913 contract, as amended by the 1927 and 1933 agreements, constituted a valid and binding contract between the Tennessee U.D.C. and Vanderbilt and that Vanderbilt had breached its contractual obligations by unilaterally deciding to rename Confederate Memorial Hall.

The trial court ... concluded that it would be "impractical and unduly burdensome for Vanderbilt to continue to perform that part of the contract pertaining to the maintenance of the name 'Confederate' on the building, and at the same time pursue its academic purpose of obtaining a racially diverse faculty and student body." The court found that Vanderbilt had "carried its burden of proof for modification of the contracts," declared that Vanderbilt sufficiently complied with its obligations under the 1913 and 1927 contracts by installation and maintenance of the plaque by the entrance to Confederate Memorial Hall, and held that, aside from the plaque, Vanderbilt could remove the name "Confederate" from the building without any further obligation to the Tennessee U.D.C. The Tennessee U.D.C. appealed . . .

In order to determine whether it is Vanderbilt or the Tennessee U.D.C. that is entitled to a judgment as a matter of law, we must first determine the precise nature of the legal relationship formed between the Tennessee U.D.C. and Peabody College by the 1913, 1927, and 1933 agreements. Although all three agreements use the word "contract," they do not purport to establish a typical commercial arrangement in which one party provides certain goods or services in return for a sum to be paid by the other party. Instead, the agreements indicate that the $50,000 to be raised by the Tennessee U.D.C. was to be transferred to Peabody College as a gift. Peabody College's status as a non-profit charitable organization dedicated to the advancement of education suggests the possibility of a donative intent on the part of the Tennessee U.D.C., and this possibility is confirmed by the plain language of the three agreements. The 1913 agreement repeatedly describes the $50,000 to be raised and turned over to Peabody College as a "gift" from the Tennessee U.D.C., and the 1927 and 1933 agreements do not in any way modify or retract this description.

The 1913, 1927, and 1933 contracts do not, however, describe the proposed transfer to Peabody College as a gift with no strings attached. The three contracts attach specific conditions to the gift, and the 1927 contract expressly reserves to the Tennessee U.D.C. the right to recall the gift if Peabody College fails or ceases to comply with these conditions. Where a party makes a donation to a charitable organization accompanied by conditions and a right to reclaim the donation if the conditions are not met, the law treats the arrangement between the parties as either a revocable charitable trust or a charitable gift subject to conditions. . . . [Here is it clear the donor intended to create a charitable gift subject to conditions].

Donors often seek to impose conditions on gifts to charitable organizations. . . . In the case of *inter vivos* transfers, the conditions are generally embodied in a gift agreement or a deed of conveyance. . . .

A conditional gift is enforceable according to the terms of the document or documents that created the gift. . . . If the recipient fails or ceases to comply with the conditions, the donor's remedy is limited to recovery of the gift. . . . Because noncompliance results in a forfeiture of the gift, the conditions must be created by express terms or by clear implication and are construed strictly. . . .

Taking all three contracts together, the gift from the Tennessee U.D.C. to Peabody College was subject to three specific conditions. First, Peabody College was required to use the gift to construct a dormitory on its campus conforming to plans and specifications approved by the Tennessee U.D.C. Second, Peabody College was required to allow women descendants of Confederate soldiers nominated by the Tennessee U.D.C. and accepted by Peabody College to live on the first and second floors of the dormitory without paying rent and paying all other dormitory expenses on an estimated cost basis. Third, Peabody College was required to place on the dormitory an inscription naming it "Confederate Memorial." The contracts do not specify the duration of these conditions. In such circumstances, the court must determine whether a duration can be inferred from the nature and circumstances . . . of the transaction. Given the nature of the project and the content of the conditions, we conclude that these conditions were not meant to bind Peabody College forever but instead were to be limited to the life of the building itself. Thus, as long as the building stands, these three conditions apply to the gift.

In its complaint, the Tennessee U.D.C. claimed that Vanderbilt had already violated the condition requiring an inscription on the building naming it "Confederate Memorial" by publicly and privately announcing its intention to rename the building "Memorial Hall" and that Vanderbilt planned to violate the condition further by removing or altering the inscription on the pediment. In its answer, Vanderbilt admitted its plans to rename the building "Memorial Hall" and to remove the word "Confederate" from the inscription on the pediment but denied that these actions would violate the conditions of the gift as reflected in the agreements between the parties. In its summary judgment papers and its brief on appeal, Vanderbilt argues that the Tennessee U.D.C. cannot succeed on its claim against Vanderbilt as a matter of law because the undisputed evidence in the record shows that Vanderbilt and Peabody College substantially performed their obligations under the contracts, that the Tennessee U.D.C. has already received full consideration for its original contribution, and that principles of academic freedom require that Vanderbilt be allowed to change the name of Confederate Memorial Hall without any further obligation to the Tennessee U.D.C. We find no merit in these arguments.

Vanderbilt's claim that the placement of a plaque by the entrance to the building describing the contributions of the Tennessee U.D.C. to the original construction constitutes substantial performance with the inscription condition cannot be taken seriously. The determination of whether a party has substantially performed depends on what it was the parties bargained for in their agreement. . . . Here, the 1933 contract expressly and unambiguously required Peabody College to place an inscription on the building naming it "Confederate Memorial," and we have already concluded that the parties intended the inscription to remain until the building was torn down. Peabody College complied with the condition by placing a large inscription in stone on the pediment of the building reading "Confederate Memorial Hall." Peabody College did so in conformity with Peabody College's own 1934 construction drawings which show these words in large incised lettering on the pediment of the building.

Vanderbilt continued to comply fully with this condition from its 1979 merger with Peabody College until 2002 when it announced its plans to remove the word "Confederate" from the building's pediment. It is doubtful that a party such as Vanderbilt that has willfully changed course after over twenty years of compliance with the literal terms of an agreement could ever rely on the doctrine of substantial performance.... Even if it could, no reasonable fact-finder could conclude that replacing a name written in stone in large letters on the pediment of a building with a plaque by the entrance constitutes substantial performance of a requirement to do the former.

Vanderbilt's argument that it should be excused from complying with the inscription condition contained in the 1933 contract because the Tennessee U.D.C. has already received enough value for its original contribution to the construction of the building is likewise without merit. The courts must interpret contracts as they are written, ... and will not make a new contract for parties who have spoken for themselves.... The courts do not concern themselves with the wisdom or folly of a contract, ... and are not at liberty to relieve parties from contractual obligations simply because these obligations later prove to be burdensome or unwise....

The same is true of conditions contained in a gift agreement. By entering into the 1913, 1927, and 1933 contracts, Peabody College necessarily agreed that the value of the gift it was receiving was worth the value of full performance of the conditions of the gift.... In short, Vanderbilt's unilateral assessment that Peabody College gave away too much in the 1913, 1927, and 1933 agreements does not constitute a legal defense that would excuse Vanderbilt from complying with the conditions of the original gift.

Vanderbilt's assertion that principles of academic freedom allow it to keep the gift from the Tennessee U.D.C. while ignoring the conditions attached to that gift is equally unavailing. As Vanderbilt correctly notes in its brief on appeal, the United States Supreme Court has long been solicitous of the independence of private colleges from government control.... However, the source of the obligation at issue in this case is not the government but Vanderbilt itself. The original obligation to place the inscription on Confederate Memorial Hall is contained in a private gift agreement voluntarily entered into between Peabody College and the Tennessee U.D.C. Vanderbilt's legal obligation to comply with the conditions of that gift agreement arises not from any action on the part of the government but from Vanderbilt's own decision to enter into a merger agreement with Peabody College in 1979 in which it agreed to succeed to Peabody College's legal obligations.

Moreover, we fail to see how the adoption of a rule allowing universities to avoid their contractual and other voluntarily assumed legal obligations whenever, in the university's opinion, those obligations have begun to impede their academic mission would advance principles of academic freedom. To the contrary, allowing Vanderbilt and other academic institutions to jettison their contractual and other legal obligations so casually would seriously impair their ability to raise money in the future by entering into gift agreements such as the ones at issue here ...

As noted above, where a donee fails or ceases to comply with the conditions of a gift, the donor's remedy is limited to recovery of the gift. However, it would be inequitable to allow Vanderbilt to "return" the gift at issue here simply by paying the Tennessee U.D.C. the same sum of money the Tennessee U.D.C. donated in 1933 because the value of a dollar today is very different from the value of a dollar in 1933. To reflect the change in the buying power of the dollar, the amount Vanderbilt must pay to the Tennessee U.D.C. in order to return the gift should be based on the consumer price index published by the Bureau of Labor Statistics of the United States Department of Labor. As attested by numerous Tennessee statutes, reference to the consumer price index is the most common way to calculate a change in the value of money over time under Tennessee law.... In addition, the Tennessee Supreme Court has endorsed the consumer price index as an accurate measure of the change in the purchasing power of a dollar.... Thus, on remand, if Vanderbilt continues to elect not to comply with the terms of the gift, it must pay the Tennessee U.D.C. in today's dollars the value of the original gift in 1933....

This court is well aware of the strong passions this case has generated on both sides. The depth of feeling is understandable given that the case touches on issues of heritage, identity, and racial justice. According to Vanderbilt, the maintenance of the inscription on the pediment of Confederate Memorial Hall forces Vanderbilt to send a message of racial hatred and exclusion that it no longer wishes to send. According to the Tennessee U.D.C., the inscription is not a symbol of racial intolerance and oppression, and Vanderbilt's decision to remove it is nothing less than an attempt to rewrite history in a manner that demeans its members' ancestors. It is not within the purview of this court to resolve the larger cultural and social conflicts regarding whether and how those who fought for the Confederacy should be honored or remembered. What this court has done is to resolve the existing legal dispute between the parties according to neutral principles of law. Our decision should not be viewed as an endorsement of either Vanderbilt's decision to change the name or the Tennessee U.D.C.'s desire to perpetuate it.

In summary, we have determined that the undisputed facts establish that the Tennessee U.D.C. gave a monetary gift to Vanderbilt's predecessor-in-interest subject to conditions and that Vanderbilt's predecessor-in-interest accepted the gift as well as the conditions that accompanied it. It is further undisputed that Vanderbilt now declines to abide by the conditions attached to the gift. Thus, because Vanderbilt has presented no legal basis for permitting it to keep the gift while refusing to honor the conditions attached to it, Vanderbilt must now either return the present value of the gift to the Tennessee U.D.C. or reverse its present course and agree to abide by the conditions originally placed on the gift.

Accordingly, we reverse the summary judgment entered in favor of Vanderbilt not because the record reveals disputed issues of material fact but rather because Vanderbilt has failed to demonstrate that it is entitled to a judgment as a matter of law. We have also determined that if Vanderbilt insists on changing the name of Confederate Memorial Hall, the Tennessee U.D.C. has demonstrated that it is entitled to a judgment as a matter of law on its motion for partial summary judgment. We remand the case with directions to calculate the present value of the Tennessee U.D.C.'s gift to Peabody College, to enter a judgment in favor of the Tennessee U.D.C. in that amount, and to make whatever further orders may be required. The costs of this appeal are taxed to Vanderbilt University for which execution, if necessary, may issue.

WILLIAM B. CAIN, J., concurring.

I concur in the exhaustive and expositive opinion prepared by Judge Koch. I write separately to emphasize two points.

First, the intent of the parties is not established alone by the provisions contained in their written contracts of 1913, 1927 and 1933. The Chancellor held: "However, the course of dealing between the parties persuades the court to conclude that it was the intention of the parties that *the building would be named 'Confederate Memorial Hall.'"

At the very least, from the time when the architect prepared the architectural drawings of the dormitory for George Peabody College for Teachers (July 12, 1934), there could be no doubt as to what the parties intended. For 68 years, until June of 2002 when Chancellor Gee determined to change the name, both parties honored the agreement....

Between the contracts of the parties and the conduct of the parties for nearly three-quarters of a century, the intent that the dormitory be named "Confederate Memorial Hall" is undisputed and, indeed, indisputable.

Second, the position of Vanderbilt is based on the misperception that somehow the dormitory is a memorial to the institution of slavery or, indeed, to the Confederate government. This assertion is in direct contradiction of the statement of former Vanderbilt Chancellor Joe B. Wyatt that historical information currently available reflected, "the absence of any indication that the naming of Confederate Memorial Hall by George Peabody College for Teachers was in any sense intended to support either slavery or any other form of prejudice toward blacks." The history of the dormitory has not changed since this 1989 statement of Chancellor Wyatt. Nothing in the record is so complete a repudiation of this assertion as the plaque prepared by Vanderbilt in 1989 to be placed on the dormitory. The inscription thereon reads: "Constructed in 1935 by George Peabody College for Teachers, in part, with funds raised at personal sacrifice during the Great Depression, by Tennessee women of the United Daughters of the Confederacy, in memory of their fathers and brothers who fought in the war between North and South, 1861–65."

While in the longer aftermath of history few will doubt that the outcome of the great war was a blessing to North and South alike, the word "confederate" has many meanings to many people. To those diminished few who would gladly fight the war again, it has an almost mystic significance. To the descendants of slaves whose "250 years of unrequited toil"[4] built a cotton empire and nourished it with blood, toil, tears and sweat until the Thirteenth Amendment to the United States Constitution swept the institution of slavery into the annals of history, it is a demeaning reminder of indignities and persecution. To others, it represents a remote chapter in history of little relevance to the global issues facing the world today. To the parties to this bilateral contract, its meaning under the record in this case cannot be clouded by any reasonable doubt. The plaque installed by Vanderbilt in 1989 said it all.

The institution of slavery was indefensible by any standards, and to the extent that the war was fought by the South in defense of slavery, no excuse can be made. There is another dimension to the struggle. A great majority of those who fought in the Confederate armies owned no slaves. Their homeland was invaded, and they rose up in defense of their homes and their farms. They fought the unequal struggle until nearly half their enlisted strength was crippled or beneath the sod. The dormitory is a memorial to them, and their place in history . . .

It is to the memory of these men that Confederate Memorial Hall was built and, to that end and at great personal sacrifice in the midst of the Great Depression that the United Daughters of the Confederacy raised and contributed to Peabody College more than one-third of the total cost of the construction of the dormitory.

I reluctantly concur in the remedy fashioned by Judge Koch, as I can think of no alternative other than the compulsion of a mandatory injunction, which, justified or not, leaves at least a perceived impediment to the primary mission of a renowned university.

NOTES AND QUESTIONS

1. The principal case involved an outright gift to a charitable organization that was subject to a condition the organization no longer wished to respect. The facts are a variation of a common problem arising from gifts to a charity, outright or in trust, where the terms have become impossible, illegal or impractical to carryout. In these circumstances, judicial proceedings can be brought to reform the terms of the gift to most closely approximate the intent of the donor while still avoiding a term of the gift which is impossible, illegal,

---

4. From Abraham Lincoln's 2nd inaugural address on March 4, 1865.

or impractical to carry out. This is known as "cy pres," meaning to reform to carry out the donor's intent as nearly as possible.

2. Section 6 of the Uniform Prudent Management of Institutional Funds Act provides that:

(a) If the donor consents in a record, an institution may release or modify, in whole or in part, a restriction contained in a gift instrument on the management, investment, or purpose of an institutional fund. A release or modification may not allow a fund to be used for a purpose other than a charitable purpose of the institution.

(b) The court, upon application of an institution, may modify a restriction contained in a gift instrument regarding the management or investment of an institutional fund if the restriction has become impracticable or wasteful, if it impairs the management or investment of the fund, or if, because of circumstances not anticipated by the donor, a modification of a restriction will further the purposes of the fund. The institution shall notify the [Attorney General] of the application, and the [Attorney General] must be given an opportunity to be heard. To the extent practicable, any modification must be made in accordance with the donor's probable intention.

(c) If a particular charitable purpose or a restriction contained in a gift instrument on the use of an institutional fund becomes unlawful, impracticable, impossible to achieve, or wasteful, the court, upon application of an institution, may modify the purpose of the fund or the restriction on the use of the fund in a manner consistent with the charitable purposes expressed in the gift instrument. The institution shall notify the [Attorney General] of the application, and the [Attorney General] must be given an opportunity to be heard.

(d) If an institution determines that a restriction contained in a gift instrument on the management, investment, or purpose of an institutional fund is unlawful, impracticable, impossible to achieve, or wasteful, the institution, [60 days] after notification to the [Attorney General], may release or modify the restriction, in whole or part, if:

(1) the institutional fund subject to the restriction has a total value of less than [$25,000];

(2) more than [20] years have elapsed since the fund was established; and

(3) the institution uses the property in a manner consistent with the charitable purposes expressed in the gift instrument.

If this act had been in effect in Tennessee at the time of the dispute involving Vanderbilt University, how might it have affected the outcome of the case?

3. A beloved professor of State University died in 1970. Anticipating, incorrectly, that other alums and other friends of the university would contribute substantial sums to honor the professor's memory, a rich alumnus of the university contributed $5,000 to State University to create scholarships in the professor's name for students attending the university from the

professor's rural hometown. Other gifts increased the fund to $7,500. There have been no additional contributions to the fund since 1974 although as a result of market forces the value of the fund is now $20,000.

As a result of dramatic demographic shifts, the high school in the professor's home town has closed and for the last 9 nears no one from that town has attended the university and no moneys have been distributed from the fund. The university president would like to use the fund to help finance construction of a new university building and name a room in the building for the deceased professor. Advise the president if she can.

FOSTER v. REISS

Supreme Court of New Jersey (1955).
18 N.J. 41, 112 A.2d 553.

VANDERBILT, C.J.

On April 30, 1951 the decedent, Ethel Reiss, entered a hospital in New Brunswick where she was to undergo major surgery. Just prior to going to the operating room on May 4, 1951, she wrote the following note in her native Hungarian language to her husband, the defendant herein:

"My Dearest Papa:

"In the kitchen, in the bottom of the cabinet, where the blue frying pan is, under the wine bottle, there is one hundred dollars. Along side the bed in my bedroom, in the rear drawer of the small table in the corner of the drawer, where my stockings are, you will find about seventy-five dollars. In my purse there is six dollars, where the coats are. Where the coats are, in a round tin box, on the floor, where the shoes are, there is two hundred dollars. This is Dianna's. Please put it in the bank for her. This is for her schooling.

"The Building Loan book is yours, and the Bank book, and also the money that is here. In the red book is my son's and sister's and my brother's address. In the letter box is also my bank book.

"Give Margaret my sewing machine and anything else she may want; she deserves it as she was good to me.

"God be with you. God shall watch your steps. Please look out for yourself that you do not go on a bad road. I cannot stay with you. My will is in the office of the former Lawyer Anekstein, and his successor has it. There you will find out everything.

"Your Kissing, loving wife,

"Ethel Reiss 1951–5–4."

She placed the note in the drawer of a table beside her bed, at the same time asking Mrs. Agnes Tekowitz, an old friend who was also confined in the hospital, to tell her husband or daughter about it—"In case my daughter come in or my husband come in, tell them they got a note over there and take the note." That afternoon, while the wife was in the operating room unconscious under the effects of ether, the defendant came to the hospital and was told about the note by the friend. He took the note from the drawer, went home, found the cash, the savings account passbook, and the building and loan book mentioned in the note, and has retained possession of them since that time.

The wife was admittedly in a coma for three days after the operation and the testimony is in dispute as to whether or not she recovered consciousness at all before her death on the ninth day. Her daughter, her son-in-law, Mrs. Waldner, an old friend and one of her executrices who visited her every day, and Mrs. Tekowitz, who was in the ward with her, said that they could not understand her and she could not understand them. The defendant, on the other hand, testified that while she was "awful poor from ether" after the operation, "the fourth, fifth and sixth days I thought she was going to get healthy again and come home. She talked just as good as I with you." The trial judge who saw the witnesses and heard the testimony found that

> "After the operation and until the date of her death on May 13, 1951 she was in a coma most of the time; was unable to recognize members of her family; and unable to carry on intelligent conversation * * * Mrs. Reiss was never able to talk or converse after coming out of the operation until her death."

The decedent's will gave $1 to the defendant and the residue of her estate to her children and grandchildren. The decedent's personal representatives and her trustees under a separation agreement with the defendant, brought this action to recover the cash, the passbook, and the building and loan book from the defendant, who in turn claimed ownership of them based on an alleged gift *causa mortis* from his wife. The trial court granted judgment for the plaintiffs, concluding that there had been no such gift. The Appellate Division of the Superior Court reversed, 31 N.J.Super. 496, 107 A.2d 24, and we granted the plaintiff's petition for certification to the Appellate Division, 16 N.J. 221, 108 A.2d 211.

The doctrine of *donatio causa mortis* was borrowed by the Roman law from the Greeks, 2 Bl.Com. 514, and ultimately became a part of English and then American common law, ... Blackstone has said that there is a gift *causa mortis* "when a person in his last sickness, apprehending his dissolution near, delivers or causes to be delivered to another the possession of any personal goods, to keep in case of his decease." 2 Bl.Com. 514. . . .

The modern description is similar:

> "A *donatio causa mortis* is a gift of personal property made by a party in expectation of death, then imminent, and upon the essential condition that the property shall belong fully to the donee in case the donor dies as anticipated, leaving the donee surviving him, and the gift is not in the meantime revoked, but not otherwise. . . . To constitute a valid gift *causa mortis,* it must be made in view of the donor's impending death; the donor must die of the disorder or peril; and there must be a delivery of the thing given. The donor must be

competent to make the gift; there must be an intent upon his part to do so; and an acceptance by the donee.... The delivery must be such as is actual, unequivocal and complete during the lifetime of the donor, wholly divesting him of the possession, dominion, and control thereof." Weiss v. Fenwick, 111 N.J.Eq. 385, 387–388, 162 A. 609, 610 (E. & A. 1932).

There is some doubt in the New Jersey cases as to whether as a result of a gift *causa mortis* the property remains in the donor until his death, ... or whether the transfer is considered absolute even though it is defeasible, ... In any event, a gift *causa mortis* is essentially of a testamentary nature and as a practical matter the doctrine, though well established, is an invasion into the province of the statute of wills:

> "Some quasi-testamentary acts,—such as gifts *causa mortis,* where delivery takes the place of the execution of a will,—may even enable essentially testamentary dispositions to be effected without compliance with the statutes governing wills. To be sure the delivery, actual or symbolic as the case may be, marks a gift *causa mortis* off from a strict testamentary disposition, but the revocable nature of the gift makes that distinction very slight, and in those jurisdictions where the title to the thing delivered as a gift *causa mortis* does not pass until the donor dies, the distinction becomes microscopic. Nevertheless the distinction is well established." Costigan, Constructive Trusts, 28 Harv.L.Rev. 237, at 240–241 (1915).

... Gifts *causa mortis* are not favored in the law. As stated in Buecker v. Carr, 60 N.J.Eq. 300, 305, 47 A. 34, 35 (Ch.1900), "gifts *mortis causa* are not favored in the law, for the reason that this mode of disposition permits property without limit of value to be transferred by mere delivery, and the proof thereof to be made when death has closed the lips of the claimed donor...."

The first question confronting us is whether there has been "actual, unequivocal, and complete delivery during the lifetime of the donor, wholly divesting him [her] of the possession, dominion, and control" of the property, Weiss v. Fenwick, supra, 111 N.J.Eq. 385, 388, 162 A. 609; ... In Keepers v. Fidelity Title and Deposit Co., supra, 56 N.J.L. 302, 28 A. 585, 586, 23 L.R.A. 184, the question was whether the delivery of the key to a box containing valuable papers was sufficient delivery to constitute a valid gift *causa mortis* of the papers therein, when the box, which was not in the presence or immediate control of the donor, did not pass into the actual possession of the donee during the lifetime of the donor. Justice Dixon in his opinion for the court reviewed the English and American authorities, and then concluded that there had not been that delivery required under New Jersey law:

> "The leading case on the subject of donations *mortis causa* is Ward v. Turner, 2 Ves.Sr. 431 (A.D.1752), where Lord Chancellor Hardwicke laid down the rule, with reference to delivery, which has ever since formed the basis whereon such gifts are supported. After showing that

the recognition of donations *mortis causa* by the common law was derived from the civil law, he declared that the civil law had been 'received in England, in respect of such donations, only so far as attended with delivery, or what the civil law calls "tradition;" that 'tradition or delivery is necessary to make a good donation *mortis causa.*' He further said: 'It is argued that, though some delivery is necessary, yet delivery of the thing is not necessary, but delivery of anything by way of a symbol is sufficient. But I cannot agree to that; nor do I find any authority for that in the civil law, which required delivery in some gifts, or in the law of England, which required delivery throughout. Where the civil law requires it, it requires actual tradition,—delivery over of the thing. So, in all the cases in this court, delivery of the thing given is relied on, and not in the name of the thing. . . . Yet, "he added, 'notwithstanding, delivery of the key of bulky goods, where wines, etc., are, has been allowed as delivery of the possession, because it is the way of coming at the possession, or to make use of the thing.' "

"On this footing, it has, in some instances, been adjudged that delivery of the key was sufficient delivery for a valid donation *mortis causa* of money or documents locked in a trunk or other receptacle, not within the presence or immediate control of the donor, and not otherwise transferred to the possession of the donee. . . .

We are not willing to approve the extreme views which have been adopted in the cases cited." (56 N.J.L. at pages 305–306, 307, 28 A. at page 586.)

In Cook v. Lum, supra, 55 N.J.L. 373, 26 A. 803, 804, our former Supreme Court stated that where choses in action were concerned delivery of the "donor's voucher of right or title" would be sufficient:

"The general legal principle regulating the subject of gifts of choses in action has long been established. It is to the effect that with respect to things both tangible and intangible mere words of donation will not suffice. With regard to the former class,—that is things corporeal,— there must be, in addition to the expression of a donative purpose, an actual tradition of the *corpus* of the gift whenever, considering the nature of the property and the circumstances of the actors, such a formality is reasonably practicable. In some instances, when the situation is incompatible with the performance of such ceremony, resort may be had to what has been called a 'symbolical delivery' of the subject. Touching things in action, as there can be no actual delivery of them, the legal requirement is that the donor's voucher of right or title must be surrendered to the donee. Such surrender is deemed equivalent to an actual handing over of things corporeal. To this extent the law of the subject is neither doubtful nor obscure. The difficulty supervenes as soon as the attempt is made to apply these rules to the ever variant conditions of the cases that are being presented for judicial examination. Even when the thing given has been a personal chattel, whether certain acts show a purpose to give consummated by a delivery of it has often been, and doubtless will be, a vexed question. The uncertainty in construing the circumstances is even greater when we have rights of action to deal with. There are a multitude of decisions which demonstrate the embarrassment inherent in this class of cases, but as these decisions, while all acknowledging the rules just indicated, are in truth nothing more than interpretations respectively of the facts of the particular case, and as such facts are unlike the juncture now present, it would serve no useful purpose to review or quote them in detail. There is no observed precedent, so far as circumstances are concerned, for the matter now before us. Many of these decisions may be found in the Encyclopedia of English and American Law, tit. 'Gift,' and any person who will examine this long train of cases will at once perceive that the principal difficulty has been to decide whether the evidence in hand in the given case showed a delivery of the subject of the gift in a legal point of view. But this was a maze not without its clue, for the cardinal principle as to what constituted a delivery that would legalize a gift was on all sides admitted, and was generally applied. The test was this: that the transfer was such that, in conjunction with the donative intention, it completely stripped the donor of his dominion of the thing given, whether that thing was a tangible chattel or a chose in action." (55 N.J.L. at pages 374–376, 26 A. at page 804).

Thus, under New Jersey law actual delivery of the property is still required except where "there can be no actual delivery" or where "the situation is incompatible with the performance of such ceremony." In the case of a savings account, where obviously there can be no actual delivery, delivery of the passbook or other indicia of title is required....

Here there was no delivery of any kind whatsoever. We have already noted the requirement so amply established in our cases, supra, 162 A. 609, of "actual, unequivocal and complete delivery during the lifetime of the donor, wholly divesting her of the possession, dominion, and control" of the property. This requirement is satisfied only by delivery by the *donor,* which calls for an affirmative act on her part, not by the mere taking of possession of the property by the donee.

Delivery itself, which we have been considering, is to be distinguished from donative intent, another element in gifts *causa mortis.* As stated in Madison Trust Co. v. Allen, supra, 105 N.J.Eq. 230, 235, 147 A. 546, 548, "the burden of proof is upon the alleged donee to clearly prove *both delivery and donative intent*" (emphasis supplied). This was clearly brought out by the court in Parker v. Copland, 70 N.J.Eq. 685, 64 A. 129, 130 (E. & A.1906):

"It necessarily follows from this that when a donor participates or concurs in a transaction, part of which is the retention by him, after the expression of his donative purpose, of every existing indicium of dominion over that to which such donative purpose referred, an enforceable gift has not been legally established; and this is true without regard to the clearness or cogency with which the donative purpose may have been indicated, for, in the above citation, it will be noted that the crucial test is not the strenuousness of the language in which the gift is couched, but in 'the transfer,' which is something that is both different from the donative intention and yet capable of acting in conjunction with it, so that both are necessary to the creation of an enforceable gift. The absence of either is as fatal to the gift as if both were lacking, just as a legacy may fail either because it is not found in the will or because the will itself is not legally executed. Indeed, an impressive illustration of this distinction would be the existence of a holographic will containing the most copious expressions of a donative intention, which, even though signed by the testator, would not in the least effectuate the purpose so expressed. This illustration, which for obvious reasons must not be pushed too far, serves to emphasize the point that, when two steps are required by law to complete a transaction, the excess of one cannot supply the lack of the other, a distinction not at all times regarded in the argument of the present appeal." (70 N.J.Eq. at pages 688–689, 64 A. at page 130).

Thus, an informal writing such as we have here does not satisfy the separate and distinct requirement of delivery, but rather there must be such delivery of the property that the donor stands absolutely deprived of his control over it. . . .

We must not forget that since a gift *causa mortis* is made in contemplation of death and is subject to revocation by the donor up to the time of his death it differs from a legacy only in the requirement of delivery. Delivery is in effect the only safeguard imposed by law upon a transaction which would ordinarily fall within the statute of wills. To eliminate delivery from the requirements for a gift *causa mortis* would be to permit any writing to effectuate a testamentary transfer, even though it does not comply with the requirements of the statute of wills.

Here we are concerned with three separate items of property—cash, a savings account represented by a bank passbook, and shares in a building and loan association represented by a book. There was no actual delivery of the cash and no delivery of the indicia of title to the savings account or the building and loan association shares. Rather, the donor set forth in an informal writing her desire to give these items to the defendant. Although the writing establishes her donative intent at the time it was written, it does not fulfill the requirement of delivery of the property, which is a separate and distinct requirement for a gift *causa mortis*. The cash, passbook, and stock book remained at the decedent's home and she made no effort to obtain them so as to effectuate a delivery to the defendant.

We disagree with the conclusion of the Appellate Division that the donee already had possession of the property, and therefore delivery was unnecessary. Assuming, but not deciding, the validity of this doctrine, we note that the house was the property of the deceased and, although defendant resided there with her, he had no knowledge of the presence of this property in the house, let alone its precise location therein; therefore it cannot be said that he had possession of the property.

Unlike some other jurisdictions New Jersey has resisted efforts to extend the doctrine of gifts *causa mortis,* recognizing it as a dangerous encroachment upon the policy embodied in the statute of wills. The words of Justice Dixon in his opinion for the court in Keepers v. Fidelity Title and Deposit Co., supra, 56 N.J.L. 302, 308, 28 A. 585, are equally applicable here.

> "We agree with the sentiment expressed in Ridden v. Thrall, 125 N.Y. 572, 26 N.E. 627 [11 L.R.A. 684], that 'public policy requires that the laws regulating gifts *causa mortis* should not be extended, and that the range of such gifts should not be enlarged.' When it is remembered that these gifts come into question only after death has closed the lips of the donor; that there is no legal limit to the amount which may be disposed of by means of them; that millions of dollars' worth of property is locked up in vaults, the keys of which are carried in the owners' pockets; and that, under the rule applied in those cases, such wealth may be transferred from the dying owner to his attendant, provided the latter will take the key, and swear that it was delivered to him by the deceased for the purpose of giving him the contents of the vault,—the dangerous character of the rule becomes conspicuous. Around every other disposition of the property of the dead, the legislative power has thrown safeguards against fraud and perjury; around this mode the requirement of actual delivery is the only substantial protection, and the courts should not weaken it by permitting the substitution of convenient and easily-proven devices." (56 N.J.L. at page 308, 28 A. at page 587).

Nor have our courts been alone in resisting further extension of the doctrine of gifts *causa mortis.* In the 1951 revision of Title 3 of the Revised Statutes of 1937 our Legislature abolished nuncupative wills as well as oral wills of soldiers and sailors, L.1951, c. 345, N.J.S. 3 A:1–1 et seq., N.J.S.A. It would certainly be a contradiction of legislative policy if, in the face of the legislative abolishment of nuncupative wills, our courts were to extend the doctrine of gifts *causa mortis,* "which are essentially of the same character and equally liable to objection." Schouler, On Wills, Executors and Administrators (1915 ed.) at 336.

But it is argued that the decedent's note to her husband in the circumstances of the case was an authorization to him to take possession of the chattels mentioned therein which when coupled with his taking of possession thereof during her lifetime was in law the equivalent of the delivery required in the Roman and common law alike and by all the decisions in this State for a valid gift *causa mortis.* Without accepting this contention, it is to be noted that it has no application to the present case, because here at the time the defendant obtained her note the decedent was in the operating room under ether and, according to the finding of the trial court, supra.

> "after the operation and until the date of her death on May 13, 1951 she was in a coma most of the time; was unable to recognize members of her family; and unable to carry on intelligent conversation ... Mrs. Reiss was never able to talk or converse after coming out of the operation until her death."

In these circumstances the note clearly failed as an authorization to the defendant to take possession of the chattels mentioned therein, since at the time he took the note from the drawer the decedent was under ether and according to the findings of the trial court unable to transact business until the time of her death. See section 122 of the Restatement of the Law of Agency:

> "The authority of the agent to make the principal a party to a transaction is terminated or suspended upon the happening of an event which deprives the principal of capacity to become a party to the transaction or deprives the agent of capacity to make the principal a party to it."

and comment (b) thereunder:

> "The power of the agent terminates although he has no notice of the principal's loss of capacity or of the event causing it. It also terminates although the contingency has been provided for and it has been agreed that the authority would not thereupon terminate."

* * *

The judgment of the Appellate Division of the Superior Court is reversed and the judgment of the Chancery Division of the Superior Court will be reinstated.

* * *

JACOBS, J. (with whom WACHENFELD and WILLIAM J. BRENNAN, JR., JJ., agree, dissenting.)

The decedent Ethel Reiss was fully competent when she freely wrote the longhand note which was intended to make a gift *causa mortis* to her husband Adam Reiss. On the day the note was written her husband duly received it, located the money and books in accordance with its directions, and took personal possession of them. Nine days later Mrs. Reiss died; in the meantime her husband retained his possession and there was never any suggestion of revocation of the gift. Although the honesty of the husband's claim is conceded and justice fairly cries out for the fulfillment of his wife's wishes, the majority opinion (while acknowledging that gifts *causa mortis* are valid in our State as elsewhere) holds that the absence of direct physical delivery of the donated articles requires that the gift be stricken down. I find neither reason nor persuasive authority anywhere which compels this untoward result. See Gulliver and Tilson, Classification of Gratuitous Transfers, 51 Yale L.J. 1, 2 (1941):

One fundamental proposition is that, under a legal system recognizing the individualistic institution of private property and granting to the owner the power to determine his successors in ownership, the general philosophy of the courts should favor giving effect to an intentional exercise of that power. This is commonplace enough but it needs constant emphasis, for it may be obscured or neglected in inordinate preoccupation with detail or dialectic. A court absorbed in purely doctrinal arguments may lose sight of the important and desirable objective of sanctioning what the transferror wanted to do, even though it is convinced that he wanted to do it.

Harlan F. Stone in his discussion of Delivery in Gifts of Personal Property, 20 Col.L.Rev. 196 (1920), points out that the rule requiring delivery is traceable to early notions of seisin as an element in the ownership of chattels as well as land; and he expresses the view that as the technical significance of seisin fades into the background, courts should evidence a tendency to accept other evidence in lieu of delivery as corroborative of the donative intent. See Philip Mechem, The Requirement of Delivery in Gifts of Chattels, 21 Ill.L.Rev. 341, 345 (1926). Nevertheless, the artificial requirement of delivery is still widely entrenched and is defended for modern times by Mechem (supra, at 348) as a protective device to insure deliberate and unequivocal conduct by the donor and the elimination of questionable or fraudulent claims against him. But even that defense has no applicability where, as here, the donor's wishes were freely and clearly expressed in a written instrument and the donee's ensuing possession was admittedly bona fide; under these particular circumstances every consideration of public policy would seem to point towards upholding the gift.

The delivery requirement has, for the most part, been applied in like fashion to gifts *causa mortis* and gifts *inter vivos*. See Brown, Personal Property (1936), 76, 137; Atkinson, Wills, (1937), 157. Cf. 4 Page, Wills (1941), 757. And although some courts have suggested that stricter attitude is called for in gifts *causa mortis* than in gifts *inter vivos,* other courts have adopted the opposite point of view. See e.g., In re Wasserberg (1915) 1 Ch. 195; Begovich v. Kruljac, 38 Wyo. 365, 267 P. 426, 60 A.L.R. 1046 (Sup.Ct.1928); Devol v. Dye, 123 Ind. 321, 24 N.E. 246, 7 L.R.A. 439 (Sup.Ct.1890). In the Begovich case, supra [38 Wyo. 365, 267 P. 429], the court said:

> ... gifts *causa mortis* are ordinarily resorted to by intending donors because the facilities for executing the more formal testamentary disposition are not available, or the death of the donor is so imminent in point of time as to preclude preparation of the formal documents. They are in their very nature emergency measures. Hence, though delivery cannot be dispensed with, since words may be easily misrepresented ... still we should naturally expect the courts to hold the requirements as to such delivery to be less strict than in connection

with gifts *inter vivos,* and that, in fact, is the holding of at least many of the courts.

* * *

And in the Devol case, supra, the Indiana Supreme Court, through Chief Justice Mitchell, said [123 Ind. 321, 24 N.E. 246]:

> Expressions are sometimes found in the books to the effect that gifts *causa mortis* are not favored in law because of the opportunity which they afford for the perpetration of frauds upon the estates of deceased persons by means of perjury and false swearing; but gifts of the character of those in question are not to be held contrary to public policy, nor do they rest under the disfavor of the law, when the facts are clearly and satisfactorily shown which make it appear that they were freely and intelligently made. Ellis v. Secor, 31 Mich. 185. While every case must be brought within the general rule upon the points essential to such a gift, yet, as the circumstances under which donations *mortis causa* are made must of necessity be infinite in variety, each case must be determined upon its own peculiar facts and circumstances. Dickeschied v. [Exchange] Bank, 28 W.Va. [340], 341; Kiff v. Weaver, 94 N.C. 274. The rule requiring delivery, either actual or symbolical, must be maintained, but its application is to be militated and applied according to the relative importance of the subject of the gift and the condition of the donor. The intention of a donor in peril of death, when clearly ascertained and fairly consummated within the meaning of well-established rules, is not to be thwarted by a narrow and illiberal construction of what may have been intended for and deemed by him a sufficient delivery. The rule which requires delivery of the subject of the gift is not to be enforced arbitrarily.

No helpful purpose would be served by further discussion of the history or wisdom of the delivery rule or its sympathetic or hostile application to gifts *causa mortis;* it would seem that under any reasoned point of view the particular facts in the instant matter should be deemed to constitute the required delivery. It must be remembered that the gift to Adam Reiss did not rest upon delivery of the note alone: it rested on the acknowledged fact that in accordance with the terms of the note the donee took physical possession of the donated articles and retained them until after the death of the donor. In his article on Gifts of Chattels without Delivery, 6 L.Quar.Rev. 446 (1890), Sir Frederick Pollock said:

> On principle it would seem that where A by word of mouth purports to give B a certain chattel, this will have the effect of a license to B to take that chattel peaceably wherever he may find it.

> For it would not be reasonable for A to treat B as a trespasser for acting upon A's expressed intention. The license is no doubt revocable until executed, and may be revoked either by the communication to B, by word or act, of A's will to that effect, or by A's death (which was the case of Irons v. Smallpiece) or perhaps by A's becoming insane. If

without any revocation the license is executed by B taking possession of the chattel, then, it is submitted, the property is irrevocably transferred to B. There would be great and obvious inconvenience in holding otherwise.

Similarly, Stone, supra, at 198, noted that "If the donor make oral gift of a chattel in the donor's possession to the donee, and the donee avails himself of the donor's license to possess himself of the chattel, the gift then becomes complete" without further delivery. Page in his treatise on Wills, supra, at 759, states flatly that "If the donor authorizes the donee to take physical possession of the property in question and the donee takes such possession before the donor dies, the donee's act in taking possession is sufficient delivery." Commonsensible decisions in England and in this country have applied these views to sustain gifts *causa mortis* where, as in the instant matter, the donee properly acquired possession before the donor's death.

* * *

The Davis case related to a *causa mortis* gift of a team of horses from a father to a son who lived with him; the court sustained a charge that where the donee and donor lived together, as in the case of husband and wife or parent and child, it was not necessary that the donated article be removed from the common residence and it was " 'sufficient if it appear that the donor has relinquished and the donee acquired a control of the property.' " See 101 N.W., at page 166. In the Champney case the court, in sustaining a gift *causa mortis,* held that where the donee already had possession no further formal delivery was necessary. See 39 N.Y., at page 116:

> Delivery of the subject-matter is, no doubt, essential to a gift, either *inter vivos* or *mortis causa*; but the object of delivery is to give possession, and, in this case, possession was already complete in the donee. No further delivery was necessary, nor was it possible, without first returning the property to the donor, that it might be redelivered to the donee, an idle and unmeaning ceremony.

To the same effect was the upholding of the gift *causa mortis* in the Cain case, where Justice Wills remarked (2 Q.B., at 289):

> Suppose a man lent a book to a friend, who expressed himself pleased with the book, whereupon the lender, finding that he had a second copy, told his friend that he need not return the copy he had lent him; it would be very strange if in such a case there were no complete gift, the book being in the possession of the intended donee.

When Ethel Reiss signed the note and arranged to have her husband receive it, she did everything that could reasonably have been expected of her to effectuate the gift *causa mortis*; and while her husband might conceivably have attempted to return the donated articles to her at the hospital for immediate redelivery to him, it would have been unnatural for him to do so. It is difficult to believe that our law would require such wholly ritualistic ceremony and I find nothing in our decisions to suggest it. The majority opinion advances the suggestion that the husband's authority to take possession of the donated articles was terminated by the wife's incapacity in the operating room and thereafter. The very reason she wrote the longhand note when she did was because she knew she would be incapacitated and wished her husband to take immediate possession, as he did. Men who enter hospitals for major surgery often execute powers of attorney to enable others to continue their business affairs during their incapacity. Any judicial doctrine which would legally terminate such power as of the inception of the incapacity would be startling indeed—it would disrupt commercial affairs and entirely without reason or purpose.

The New Jersey decisions dealing with gifts *causa mortis,* including the leading cases of Cook v. Lum, 55 N.J.L. 373, 26 A. 803 (Sup.Ct.1893), and Keepers v. Fidelity Title & Deposit Co., 56 N.J.L. 302, 28 A. 585, 23 L.R.A. 184 (E. & A.1893), relied upon by the majority, do not bear on the actual issue presented in the instant matter. In the Cook case the court held that delivery of a slip of paper referring to a sum of money which the donor had on deposit did not constitute delivery of the deposit (see Brown, supra, at 183); the donee there did not take possession of the deposit before the donor's death. In the Keepers case the court held that delivery of the key to a box did not constitute delivery of its contents (see Brown, supra, at 95); the donee there likewise did not take possession of the contents before the donor's death.

In the Cook case [55 N.J.L. 373, 26 A. 803] Chief Justice Beasley set forth the supposedly controlling principles which have been followed in our later cases and which do not in anywise impair the validity of the gift in the instant matter. Thus he noted that "there must be, in addition to the expression of a donative purpose, an actual tradition of the *corpus* of the gift whenever, considering the nature of the property and the circumstances of the actors, such a formality is reasonably practicable"; and further in his opinion he stated that "the test was this: that the transfer was such that, in conjunction with the donative intention, it completely stripped the donor of his dominion of the thing given." When the husband took possession of the donated articles in accordance with his wife's wishes and the decent dictates of the circumstances, he acquired complete dominion to the exclusion of the donor; in all justice this should satisfy the delivery requirement even in the eyes of those who adhere most technically to its ancient terms and tenor.

I would affirm the judgment of the Appellate Division.

NOTES AND QUESTIONS

1. The *Foster* court seems very concerned that validating gifts causa mortis undercuts the policies underlying statutes requiring certain formalities in the execution of testamentary dispositions. Generally, these requirements minimally include a writing that is signed by a testator and witnessed by two

witnesses. See generally chapter 4, *infra.* Are the court's concerns justified only in those cases where the donor intends that the donee take possession of the subject matter of the gift after the donor dies, or are they justified even if the donor intends the donee to take immediate possession of the gift?

2.   Suppose that Mrs. Reiss had handed the note to her husband rather than a third person to be delivered to her husband at a later time. Same result? Is the court imposing a stricter standard of delivery for gifts causa mortis?

3.   A gift causa mortis is a gift made in the apprehension of death. "The authorities all agree that this means something more than a realization of the general mortality of man and a desire to dispose of property before the final passing away of the donor. . . . The peril of death must be a reasonably present one."[2]

Suppose D, who is about to enter the hospital for a heart transplant, gives H a ring and says "I want you to have this, I might not make it." The operation is successful, but D dies three months later in the hospital from pneumonia. What arguments might the executor of D's estate raise to challenge the validity of the gift? Compare Ridden v. Thrall, 125 N.Y. 572, 26 N.E. 627 (1891) with Brind v. International Trust Co., 66 Colo. 60, 179 P. 148 (1919).

Is a gift causa mortis valid if the apprehension is death from suicide? Compare Pikeville Nat. Bank & Trust Co. v. Shirley, 281 Ky. 150, 135 S.W.2d 426 (1939) with In re Estate of Stockham, 193 Iowa 823, 186 N.W. 650 (1922). See also Scherer v. Hyland, 75 N.J. 127, 380 A.2d 698 (1977) ("[T]he major purpose of the delivery requirement is evidentiary.").

4.   A gift causa mortis is revocable by the donor at any time prior to her death and, according to the prevailing view, is revoked automatically if the donor does not die of the anticipated peril. Suppose the donor makes a gift causa mortis. The donor, however, recovers from the apprehended peril and does not ask the donee to return the subject matter of the gift. Two years later the donor dies unexpectedly of a heart attack, and the executor of the donor's estate demands that the donee return the gift to the executor to be disposed of as part of the donor's estate. What argument can you make in favor of the donee? Cf. Newell v. National Bank of Norwich, 214 A.D. 331, 212 N.Y.S. 158 (3d Dept. 1925).

5.   When Justice Sherman Minton resigned from the United States Supreme Court in 1956, President Eisenhower moved to fill the vacancy quickly. He sought to appoint Chief Justice Vanderbilt of the New Jersey Supreme Court, but Vanderbilt, not being in good health, recommended his younger colleague William J. Brennan for the position. Vanderbilt, it has been reported, described the future Supreme Court Justice as "possessed [of] the finest judicial mind that he had known."[3] Eisenhower accepted the Vanderbilt recommendation but later came to regret the appointment because of Brennan's liberal views. Once Eisenhower was asked if he made any mistakes as

2.   R. Brown, The Law of Personal Property 137 (W. Raushenbush ed., 3d ed. 1975) (citations omitted).

3.   Dwight D. Eisenhower, The White House Years: Mandate for Change, 1953–1956 (1963).

President. "Yes [he replied], two, and they are both sitting on the Supreme Court."[4]

ALCOR LIFE EXTENSION FOUNDATION
v. RICHARDSON

Court of Appeals, State of Iowa (2010).
785 N.W.2d 717.

MANSFIELD, J.

This dispute over a decedent's remains raises significant issues under the Revised Uniform Anatomical Gift Act, the Final Disposition Act, and Iowa law pertaining to disinterments.... In 2004 Orville Richardson made arrangements with Alcor Life Extension Foundation to take possession of his remains and cryopreserve his head after he passed away. When Orville died in 2009, however, Orville's relatives did not notify Alcor and instead had him buried. Alcor now appeals the district court's denial of its request for an order compelling the relatives to sign an approval for the disinterment of Orville's body at Alcor's expense. For the reasons set forth herein, we reverse and remand ...

Orville Richardson, born 1927, had a long career as a pharmacist in Burlington. Orville was married, but had no children, and his wife predeceased him. David Richardson and Darlene Broeker are Orville's brother and sister.

On June 1, 2004, Orville submitted a membership application to Alcor Life Extension Foundation. Alcor is a California nonprofit corporation registered as a tax exempt 501(c)(3) scientific organization engaged in the study and practice of cryonic suspension. Alcor defines cryonic suspension as "[t]he procedure of placing the bodies/brains of people who have been declared legally dead into storage at temperatures of $-100°C$ or lower, with the hope that future medical development will allow the restoration of life and health." In the membership application, Orville chose a method of suspension called "neurosuspension," wherein the member's brain or entire head is removed and cryopreserved.[5]

On December 15, 2004, Orville executed a series of documents authorizing Alcor to take possession of his remains upon his death so that his head and brain could undergo cryonic suspension. Among the documents was a "Last Will and Testament for Human Remains and Authorization of Anatomical Donation" made for "the purpose of furthering cryobiological and cryonic research." This document was signed in conjunction with ... [other documents having] the goal of cryonic suspension ... [with] "the hope of possible restoration to life and health at some time in the future."

---

4. Quoted by Elmo Richardson, The Presidency of Dwight D. Eisenhower at 108 (1978). The other Justice that Eisenhower referred to was Chief Justice Earl Warren.

5. According to the documentation, Orville's other remains would be cremated. Alcor would "retain or dispose of the cremated portion of the Member's remains ... consistent with legal requirements...."

At the time he signed these documents, Orville paid Alcor a lump sum lifetime membership fee of $53,500.

Orville's 2004 "Last Will and Testament for Human Remains and Authorization of Anatomical Donation" specifically stated:

[I]n accordance with the laws governing anatomical donations, I hereby:

a) donate my human remains to the Alcor Life Extension Foundation, Inc. ("Alcor"), a California non-profit corporation, . . . such donation to take place immediately after my legal death, and

b) direct that upon my legal death my human remains be delivered to Alcor or its agents or representatives, at such place as they may direct.

In the fall of 2007, Orville was no longer capable of living independently due to the onset of dementia. Accordingly, in April 2008, David and Darlene filed a petition with the district court seeking appointment as Orville's co-conservators. Darlene also filed a separate petition requesting she be appointed as Orville's guardian. These petitions were granted by separate orders on May 5, 2008.

On May 27, 2008, David and Darlene wrote to Alcor informing it of their recent appointment as co-conservators of Orville, and requesting that Alcor reissue an uncashed check discovered in Orville's files. As a result of the request, Alcor issued a replacement check to David and Darlene, the amount of which covered both that check and another uncashed check. The letter to David and Darlene enclosing the replacement check was written on Alcor letterhead, disclosing Alcor's full name, mission, address, website, officers, directors, and medical and scientific advisory boards.

Although it is unclear as to when, David and Darlene admitted that during Orville's lifetime, Orville discussed the subject of donating his brain or entire head for cryoic suspension, in their answer, David and Darlene state that they "tried to talk [Orville] out of such a plan and they emphatically told him they would have nothing to do with his plan." According to David and Darlene, Orville responded that he understood their position and the subject was never discussed thereafter. David and Darlene further assert in their answer that they never saw any contracts or agreements between Orville and Alcor, and that Orville never told them he had entered into such agreements.

Orville died intestate on February 19, 2009. The following day, David and Darlene were named co-administrators of Orville's estate. David and Darlene had Orville embalmed and then buried in Burlington on February 21, 2009.

On April 21, 2009, two months after Orville's burial, David wrote to Alcor requesting a refund of Orville's lifetime membership payment. The letter stated,

"Orville was my brother, and I'm aware he contracted with you several years back in the amount of approximately $50,000 to provide a potential service following his death.

Orville obviously did not utilize this service, and accordingly we request a refund of all funds to the Estate of Orville Martin Richardson."

A week later Alcor responded, questioning why it was not notified of Orville's death so that it could follow Orville's wishes.

Alcor soon demanded Orville's remains. When David and Darlene refused, Alcor filed a motion in the probate court for an expedited hearing. Alcor argued that Orville had made an anatomical donation to Alcor and that David and Darlene had no right to revoke it. Specifically, Alcor maintained that the Revised Uniform Anatomical Gift Act applied to Orville's transaction with Alcor, that section 142C.3(5) of that Act prohibits revocation of such a gift by anyone other than the donor, and that section 142C.8(8) makes the rights of a procurement organization superior to the rights of all other persons. As a remedy, Alcor asked the district court to order David and Darlene to obtain a permit for the disinterment of Orville's body. Alcor offered to pay all expenses associated with the disinterment. Alcor conceded that Iowa Code section 144.34 did not authorize the court to directly order disinterment, but argued the court could order Orville's brother and sister to execute an application for a disinterment permit with the Iowa Department of Public Health.

In their resistance, David and Darlene responded that they had no knowledge of the arrangement between Orville and Alcor and that Alcor had failed to contact them during Orville's lifetime despite its knowledge of their appointment as his co-conservators. They argued the transaction with Alcor was not covered by the Revised Uniform Anatomical Gift Act. In any event, they maintained that under the Final Disposition Act, Iowa Code § 144C (1)(f), they had the ultimate authority to dispose of Orville's remains.[6] David and Darlene further claimed that disinterment would be improper since it would not be for the purpose of autopsy or reburial.

The district court held a hearing on June 8, 2009. Arguments were presented, but no testimony was taken. In a June 15, 2009 ruling, the district court denied Alcor's requests for relief. The district court found the Final Disposition Act under Iowa Code chapter 144C to be controlling, and that Alcor could not qualify as a designee under the Act because Orville's declaration to Alcor was executed prior to the Act's effective date. Thus, the district court concluded that "David and Darlene were vested with the absolute right to control final disposition of Orville's remains

---

6. Iowa Code section 144C.5(1) confers the "right to control final disposition of a decedent's remains" upon a list of persons in order. The person with the first priority is a "designee ... acting pursuant to the decedent's designation." *Id.* § 144C.5(1)(a). Thereafter, the rights pass to the decedent's next of kin. *Id.* § 144C.5(1)(b)–(h). However, the "designation" provision applies only where the declaration was executed on or after July 1, 2008. *See* 2008 Iowa Acts ch. 1051, § 22. Accordingly, David and Darlene argued that they had the right to control final disposition of the body as Orville's next of kin.

after his death." The district court also agreed with David and Darlene that the disinterment statute did not apply in any event because Alcor was not seeking autopsy or reburial. Additionally, the district court found that it did not have authority to order David and Darlene to execute an application for a disinterment permit. Alcor appeals . . .

Four issues are raised on appeal: (1) whether Orville's arrangement with Alcor concerning the delivery of his body for cryonic suspension of his brain falls within Iowa's Revised Uniform Anatomical Gift Act; (2) whether Alcor, on the one hand, or David and Darlene, on the other, had the right to control the final disposition of Orville's remains; (3) whether a court has the authority to order David and Darlene to execute a consent to disinterment, assuming that Alcor prevailed on the first two issues; and (4) if so, whether the district court should have exercised that authority under the facts and circumstances of this case . . .

Our primary goal in interpreting a statute is to ascertain and give effect to the legislature's intent . . . In determining intent, we consider not only the words used by the legislature, but also the statute's subject matter, the object sought to be accomplished, the purpose to be served, underlying policies, and the consequences of various interpretations . . . We assess a statute in its entirety, and look for a reasonable interpretation that best achieves the statute's purpose and avoids absurd results . . .

Absent a statutory definition or an established meaning in the law, we give words their ordinary and common meaning by considering the context within which they are used. . . . Where the legislature has not defined words of the statute, we may refer to prior decisions of this court and others, similar statutes, dictionary definitions, and common usage . . . In the absence of instructive Iowa legislative history, we also look to the comments and statements of purpose contained in Uniform Acts to guide our interpretation of a comparable provision in an Iowa Act.

Statutes relating to the same subject matter are to be considered in light of their common purposes and should be harmonized. . . . "[W]hen two pertinent statutes cannot be harmonized, the court will apply the statute that deals with the subject 'in a more definite and minute way,' as opposed to a statute that 'deals with [the] subject in a general and comprehensive manner.' " . . .

The original Uniform Anatomical Gift Act was approved by the National Conference of Commissioners on Uniform State Laws (NCCUSL) in 1968. The 1968 Act was intended to "encourage the making of anatomical gifts" by eliminating uncertainty as to the legal liability of those authorizing and receiving anatomical gifts, while respecting dignified disposition of human remains. Prefatory Note to Unif. Anatomical Gift Act of 1968.

The most significant contribution of the 1968 Act was to create a right to donate organs, eyes, and tissue. This right was not clearly recognized at common law. By creating this right, individuals became empowered to donate their parts or their loved one's parts to save or improve the lives of others . . .

By 1987, the introduction of new immunosuppressive drugs and improvements in surgical techniques for transplanting organs and tissues enhanced the capacity to perform transplants, thereby increasing the demand for organs . . . Accordingly, it had become "apparent that the public policy instituted in 1969 (by promulgation of the Uniform Anatomical Gift Act in 1968) [was] not producing a sufficient supply of organs to meet the current or projected demand for them." . . . In addition, it was noted that although many Americans supported organ donation, very few actually participated in organ donation programs. . . . Therefore, NCCUSL decided to revise the 1968 Act. The proposed amendments were meant to "simplify the manner of making an anatomical gift and require that the intentions of a donor be followed."

The 1987 revisions were adopted in only twenty-six states . . . As a result, the non-uniformity actually became a hindrance to the policy of encouraging donations . . . Therefore, in 2006, NCCUSL again revised the Act. One of the major changes in the 2006 revision was the strengthening of the respect due to a donor's decision to make an anatomical gift . . . While the 1987 revision provided that a donor's anatomical gift was "irrevocable," it was common practice for procurement organizations to seek affirmation from the donor's family. . . . The 2006 revision ended this practice. Specifically, the 2006 revision "intentionally disempower[ed] families from making or revoking anatomical gifts in contravention of a donor's wishes. Thus, under the strengthened language of this [act], if a donor had made an anatomical gift, there is no reason to seek consent from the donor's family as they have no right to give it legally". *Id.*

The drafters noted the "possible tension between a donor's autonomous decision to be a donor with the interest of surviving family members," but decided it was necessary to "favor[ ] the decision of the donor over the desires of the family." Revised Unif. Anatomical Gift Act of 2006 § 8 cmt. The drafters went on to specifically note:

> This section does not affect property rights families might otherwise have in a decedent's body under other law, such as the right to dispose of a decedent's body after the part that was the subject of the anatomical gift has been recovered. In fact, language in Section 11(h) confirms the family's right to dispose of the donor's body after the donor's parts have been recovered for transplantation, therapy, research, or education. *Id.* . . .

According to the RUAGA, "an anatomical gift of a donor's body or part may be made during the life of the donor for the purposes of transplantation, therapy, research, or education." Iowa Code § 142C.3(1). The donor may make an anatomical gift by will, *id.* § 142C.3(2)(a)(2), and the will "takes effect upon the donor's death whether or not the will is probated." *Id.* § 142C.3(2)(d). Once an anatomical gift is made by a donor, it is given preclusive effect. *Id.* § 142C.3(5). Accordingly, when a donor makes an anatomical gift or amendment and no contrary indication by the donor is shown, "a person other than the donor is prohibited from making, amending, or revoking an anatomical gift of a donor's body or part." *Id.* § 142C.3(5)(a).

Anatomical gifts may be made to and received by several different persons, including "appropriate person[s] for research and education." *Id.* § 142C.5(1). If the anatomical gift appropriately passes to a person entitled to receive an anatomical gift, "the rights of a person to whom the part passes ... are superior to the rights of all other persons with respect to the part." *Id.* § 142C.8(8).

The RUAGA did not become effective in Iowa until July 1, 2007, three years after Orville had entered into his arrangements with Alcor. Nonetheless, both parties appear to concede that the 2006 Revised Act is the relevant law for us to consider. *See* Iowa Code § 142C.13 (indicating that chapter 142C is intended to be retroactive and stating, "This chapter applies to an anatomical gift, or amendment to, revocation of, or refusal to make an anatomical gift, whenever made.").

The parties initially focus on whether Alcor is an "appropriate person for research" such as to be able to receive anatomical gifts. *See* Iowa Code § 142C.5(1)(a) (stating that an anatomical gift may be made to a "hospital, accredited medical or osteopathic medical school, dental school, college, or university, organ procurement organization, or other appropriate person for research or education"). In *Alcor Life Extension Found., Inc. v. Mitchell*, 7 Cal.App.4th 1287, 1292, 9 Cal.Rptr.2d 572 (1992), the California Court of Appeal held that Alcor could receive bodies under the Uniform Anatomical Gift Act as it then existed. This is the only reported decision of which we are aware involving Alcor or cryonic suspension. There, Alcor did not have a license from California to function as a "procurement organization," the donee category into which Alcor sought classification. The California Uniform Anatomical Gift Act at that time required any recipient that was a "procurement organization" to be "licensed, accredited, or approved" under state law. However, the court affirmed the trial court's injunction in favor of Alcor and against the State of California based on the particular facts of that case. California had previously allowed post-mortem transfers of bodies to Alcor, but then made a "sudden and unexplained about-face with respect to Alcor's status," and failed to establish procedures for Alcor to become such a "procurement organization," thus placing Alcor in an untenable "catch–22." *Id.*

In the present case, though, Alcor does not argue that it qualifies as an "organ procurement organization," we presume because this now requires a designation by the *federal* government, which we assume Alcor does not have ... Instead, as noted, Alcor maintains that it is an "other appropriate person for research." *Id.* § 142C.5(1)(a).

From the record before us, which includes the Internal Revenue Service's determination that Alcor qualifies for tax-exempt status ..., as well as documents indicating Alcor's bona fides as an organization engaged in research in cryopreservation, we believe that Alcor meets the definition of an "appropriate person for research." *See* Revised Unif. Anatomical Gift Act of 2006 § 11 cmt. ("[A]n anatomical gift of a body for research or education can be made to a named organization. These gifts typically occur as the result of a whole body donation to a particular institution in the donor's will or as the result of a prior arrangement between a donor and a particular research or educational institution.").

However, as we see it, another key inquiry presented by this case is whether a transaction whereby an individual *pays* an organization for the future cryonic suspension of his body or body part constitutes an "anatomical gift" so as to implicate the RUAGA. This particular question was not raised by the parties or addressed by the district court. Therefore, we question whether it was preserved for our review. Nonetheless, because it is subsumed within the larger issue of whether RUAGA applies, we will address it.

In the classic situation covered by the RUAGA, of course, the organ donor is engaged in pure altruism. He or she receives no satisfaction other than the knowledge that he or she is providing either the "gift of life" to an unknown third party or a specimen for medical research. Here, the transaction involved a payment from Orville and services to be rendered in return by Alcor. To the outside observer, it looks like a bargained-for contract.

An "anatomical gift" is defined as "a donation of all or part of the human body effective after the donor's death, for the purposes of transplantation, therapy, research, or education." Iowa Code § 142C.2(3). As the plain language states, a person must be making a donation or gift. Normally, to meet the requirements of a gift in Iowa, there must be (1) donative intent, (2) delivery, and (3) acceptance. . . . The intent of the grantor is the controlling element. *Id.* Section 142C.6 of the RUAGA supersedes the common law principle that a gift requires delivery to be effective. *See* Iowa Code § 142C.6 ("A document of gift does not require delivery during the donor's lifetime to be effective."). However, the RUAGA does not by its terms displace the common law principles regarding donative intent. *See* Restatement (Third) of Prop.: Wills & Other Donative Transfers § 6.1 cmt.b. (2003) (discussing donative intent and noting that "[t]he relevant criterion is intent to transfer an ownership interest gratuitously, as opposed to engaging in an exchange transaction or making an involuntary transfer"); . . .

Orville's intent is reflected in the documents he executed with Alcor. Based upon these documents, one might argue that Orville lacked the necessary donative intent to make a gift. The documents are referred to collectively as an "Agreement" and there are obligations on both sides. The documents reveal that Orville's motivation was the possibility of being restored in the future to life and health. Alcor agreed to undertake certain tasks toward that end. Alcor was paid to undertake those tasks.

We note also that the 2006 version of the Uniform Act was proposed so that individuals would be "empowered to donate their parts or their loved one's parts *to save or improve the lives of others.*" Prefatory Note to Unif. Anatomical Gift Act of 2006 (emphasis added).

Thus, we have some concerns whether the transaction between Orville and Alcor falls within the statutory definition of an "anatomical gift." However, we conclude here that a transaction where the putative donor compensates a qualified donee for preserving all or part of the donated body does not take the transaction outside the scope of the RUAGA, even if in a strict common-law sense it may not qualify as a "gift." We reach this conclusion for several reasons. First, we note that the documents executed by Orville characterize the arrangement as an "anatomical donation" and state that he has "made this donation for the purpose of furthering cryobiological and cryonic research." These statements are entitled to some deference.... Second, we note that section 142C.10 of the RUAGA, which generally prohibits the sale or purchase of body parts, allows "reasonable payment" for the "preservation" or "disposal" of a part. While this language is not directly on point, it suggests that paying for preservation of part or all of a body is not enough to place a transaction outside the RUAGA that otherwise would fall within its terms. Third, whenever an exchange transaction is not regarded as a gift, it is almost invariably because the putative donor received compensation in return, not because the donor provided the donee with something in addition to the gift.... Nonetheless, for the future, we agree with certain commentators that legislative clarification would be beneficial in this area. *See generally* Adam A. Perlin, *"To Die in Order to Live": The Need for Legislation Governing Post–Mortem Cryonic Suspension,* 36 Sw. U. L. Rev. 33, 52 (2007) (noting uncertainty surrounding the status of cryonic suspension under the 1968 and 1987 versions of the Uniform Anatomical Gift Act: "Although by its terms the UAGA ... seems to plausibly encompass cryonics institutes, it is highly debatable whether this interpretation is the one that will prevail.").

In addition to the RUAGA, Iowa also recently adopted the Final Disposition Act. *See* 2008 Iowa Acts ch. 1051. This Act responds to a perceived need for clarity as to who will determine the disposition of a decedent's remains. ... Iowa's Act establishes a series of priorities. A designee acting pursuant to the "decedent's declaration" has the highest priority. Iowa Code § 144C.5(1)(a). However, if there is no designee, the decision falls to the decedent's next of kin. *Id.* § 144C.5(1)(b)–(h).

David and Darlene argue, and the district court found, that Orville did not execute a declaration covered by the Final Disposition Act, because a valid declaration must be executed on or after the law's effective date of July 1, 2008. *See* 2008 Iowa Acts ch. 1051, § 22. Therefore, they contend that, as his next of kin, they had the right to dispose of his remains as they saw fit. However, this argument only goes so far, because it does not address whether the RUAGA or the Final Disposition Act prevails in the event of a conflict between the two. We agree with Alcor that the legislature resolved such conflicts in favor of the RUAGA. First, the RUAGA expressly provides that "the rights of a person to whom a part passes under section 142C.5 are superior to the rights of all other persons with respect to the part." *Id.* § 142C.8(8). Furthermore, the Final Disposition Act directly gives precedence to the RUAGA. Iowa Code section 144C.10(4) states, "The rights of a donee created by an anatomical gift pursuant to section 142C.11[7] are superior to the authority of a designee under a declaration executed pursuant to this chapter." Since a valid designee would have the highest priority conferred by the Final Disposition Act, this provision effectively reinforces that rights under the RUAGA take precedence over rights under the Final Disposition Act. Thus, we conclude that the rights of Alcor as a donee of an anatomical gift under the RUAGA are superior to David and Darlene's dispositional rights conferred by the Final Disposition Act.

[Ed. Note: The court, having concluded that Alcor's rights were superior to Orville's family' rights to control his burial, then addressed the question of whether a mandatory injunction was an appropriate remedy to compel Orville's family to sign a disinterment order that that Orville's body could be exhumed to allow Alcor to retrieve Orville's head. The court concluded that it was appropriate to compel them to sign a disinterment order for the reasons stated in the following sections of the opinion.]

First and foremost, Orville clearly wanted to undergo cryonic suspension, and our state historically has ranked the decedent's preferences highly. . . .

Second, Alcor has no adequate remedy at law. There is no substitute for Orville's remains. David and Darlene argue that Alcor's "remedy" may be to keep the approximately $50,000 it received (although they previously asked Alcor to return those funds). Alternatively, David and Darlene argue that transfer of Orville's remains to Alcor at this point would be a "meaningless act," given the amount of time they have already been in the ground, and the unlikelihood that cryonic preservation could ever be successful. However, the problem with both arguments is that our legal tradition considers human remains very special and unique, regardless of their worldly value. As the supreme court said many years ago:

> It is true that it was the pride of Diogenes and his disciples of the ancient school of Cynics to regard burial with contempt, and to hold it utterly unimportant whether their bodies should be burned by fire, or devoured by beasts, birds, or worms, and some of the French philoso-

---

7. Iowa Code section 142C.11 is the right chapter but the wrong section. The rights of an anatomical gift donee are established by Iowa Code sections 142C.3 and 142C.5, not 142C.11 which concerns immunity. However, we have the power to judicially construe legislative enactments to correct inadvertent clerical errors that frustrate obvious legislative intent. *State v. Dann*, 591 N.W.2d 635, 639 (Iowa 1999) (also citing cases). We exercise that authority here. We note also that the legislature rectified the error this past session, and section 144C.10(4) now states, "The rights of a donee created by an anatomical gift pursuant to chapter 142C are superior to the authority of a designee under a declaration executed pursuant to this chapter." *See* Iowa Legis. Serv. S.F. 2138 (West 2010). [Ed. Note: The Iowa legislature following this case corrected the cross reference.]

phers of modern days have, in a kindred spirit, descanted upon the "glorious nothingness" of the grave, and that "nameless thing," a dead body, but the public sentiment and secular jurisprudence of civilized nations hold the grave and the dead body in higher and better regard.

King v. Frame, 204 Iowa 1074, 1078, 216 N.W. 630, 632 (1927). We quote this passage not to suggest that David and Darlene attach less importance to the remains of their sibling than Alcor does. Rather, our point is simply that if the equities strongly favor one side in a dispute over human remains, as we believe they do, it is not a sufficient response to argue that an adequate remedy at law exists.

Third, the record indicates David and Darlene knew of Orville's decision to entrust his remains to Alcor at the time they arranged for burial, notwithstanding their assertion that they had not seen a contract between Alcor and Orville. David and Darlene admit in their unverified answer that "during his lifetime" they were "advised by Orville he wanted his head severed and frozen." It is further undisputed that during the conservatorship, David and Darlene corresponded with Alcor and received a substantial replacement check from it. The check was accompanied by a letter that would have put David and Darlene on notice as to the nature of this entity, i.e., that Alcor had entered into a financial arrangement with Orville. Given the size of the check (nearly $5000), we find it implausible that David and Darlene would have paid no attention to the identity of the party that issued it and its reasons for doing so. It would have been part of their job as co-conservators to inform themselves as to Orville's affairs. . . .

Also, by April 21, 2009, two months after Orville's burial, David and Darlene indisputably knew of the entire arrangement between Orville and Alcor, since they wrote seeking a refund of the "approximately $50,000" Orville had paid for a "potential service." David and Darlene are noticeably silent as to when and how they acquired this information.

In short, from the record before us, we conclude that David and Darlene decided to bury Orville despite knowledge he had made different arrangements for his remains. This in our view tips the equities further in Alcor's favor. Had David and Darlene notified Alcor at the time of Orville's death, and allowed this dispute to be resolved at that time, the practical difficulties in this case would not exist. Alcor would not be seeking a mandatory injunction forcing David and Darlene "to sign an Application they find abhorrent"; indeed, disinterment would be unnecessary. It seems unfair and inequitable, in our view, for David and Darlene to rely on obstacles to injunctive relief that exist only because of their own efforts to create a fait accompli.

David and Darlene implicitly concede that "who knew what and when?" is relevant, because they fault Alcor for not advising them of Orville's instructions for his remains. The implication is that if they had known of those arrangements, this might be a different case. We agree that "who knew what and when?" is relevant, but draw a different conclusion from this record. Alcor had no way of knowing that Orville had died or that his relatives were having him buried. By contrast, on this record, we find that David and Darlene were aware of Orville's having made a plan for disposition of his remains with Alcor. . . .

Based on the foregoing considerations, and the specific facts of this case, we conclude that Alcor was entitled to its requested mandatory injunction directing David and Darlene to execute the application for a disinterment permit, with Alcor bearing all the burden and expense of disinterment. Despite the novelty of cryogenics, and the statutory complexity involved in this case, we believe this outcome is largely dictated by two longstanding and relatively straightforward traditions: first, our historic deference to the testator's wishes regarding the method and location of burial; and, second, the ability of courts of equity to fashion a suitable remedy when one party has violated another's rights. . . .

We reverse and remand for entry of an order directing David Richardson and Darlene Broeker to execute an approval of the application for disinterment, and for further proceedings consistent with this opinion.

NOTES AND QUESTIONS

1. The Uniform Anatomical Gift Act (2006) makes it possible for individuals to donate organs, tissue, or eyes for transplantation or research purposes. A donor may make an anatomical gift effective upon the donor's death by signing a donor card, a driver's license, or inserting an appropriate symbol electronically on an electronic donor registry. Under both the 1987 and 2006 versions of the Act, if a donor makes an anatomical gift, the donor's family cannot alter the gift after the donor dies. If an individual does not make an anatomical gift during life, then the individual's family can make an anatomical gift on the individual's behalf at the time of the individual's death unless the individual, during life, signed a refusal that barred family members from making an anatomical gift. Poll data suggests that where families know of the deceased's desire to be an organ donor, they would make a gift on his or her behalf. See S. Kurtz and M. Saks, The Transplant Paradox: Overwhelming Public Support for Organ Donation vs. Under–Supply of Organs, The Iowa Organ Procurement Study, 21 J. Corp. L. 767 (1996).

2. Typically, when a prospective donor of an organ is near death the hospital where the prospective donor is a patient will contact an appropriate "organ procurement organization." This organization will determine whether the prospective donor has signed up to be an organ donor and, if not, will contact the prospective donor's family to seek a gift from them on the prospective donor's behalf. The organ procurement organization will also conduct minimal tests and review appropriate medical records to determine if the prospective donor is a suitable donor. Prospective donors may be suitable for any or all of organ, tissue, or eye donation.

3. There is a critical shortage of organs available for transplantation in the United States. In 2011 over 112,000 individuals were on the waiting list

for life-saving or life-enhancing organs. At the same time there about 8,000 cadaveric organ donors. While the number of persons on the waiting list tends to increase each year, the number of cadaveric donors tends to remain constant. To a limited extent, the growing gap between supply and demand is satisfied by gifts from living donors. Nonetheless, the gap is enormous.

A number of suggestions have been made to increase the supply of organs for transplantation. These include: (1) presumed consent laws under which potential donors would be presumed to want to be organ donors unless they, or their family members, opted out; (2) conscription laws under which useable organs would be removed as a matter of course from cadavers; and (3) mandated choice laws under which persons would be required as a condition to obtaining a driver's license or social security card to express a preference to be, or not to be, an organ donor. A recent study of 834 Iowans suggested that a slight majority favored the third proposal—mandated choice—but only a minority favored presumed consent. See S. Kurtz and M. Saks, The Transplant Paradox: Overwhelming Public Support for Organ Donation vs. Under–Supply of Organs, The Iowa Organ Procurement Study, 21 J. Corp. L. 767 (1996). Currently both federal and state laws bar the sale of organs for transplantation. See National Organ Transplant Act of 1984. The interviewees in the Iowa Organ Procurement Study also rejected the use of financial incentives to entice organ donations but strongly supported the proposition that a member of a donor's family could receive a preference for an organ if a family member later needed an organ. See also Hansmann, The Economics and Ethics of Markets for Human Organs, Organ Transplantation Policy Issues 58 (James F. Blumstein & Frank A. Sloan eds., 1989), Caplan, Beg, Borrow, or Steal: The Ethics of Solid Organ Procurement, Organ Substitution Technology 59 (Deborah Mathieu ed. 1988).

4. In *Alcor*, the gift was for research as distinguished from transplantation. Given that Mr. Richardson had been embalmed, why would Alcor have gone to the lengths that it did to secure Mr. Richardson's head?

5. Can you construct an argument that, *even accepting* that Alcor is a research organization, it cannot be the donee of an anatomical gift?

6. On his death bed a man signed a "donation form" specifying that he wanted to donate his "kidneys" to his friend Paul who was in need of a kidney transplant. When the man died his kidney was flown to another location where Paul was in the medical intensive care unit. Paul's transplant surgeon refused to transplant the kidney into Paul because there was an aneurysm in the kidney. In the meantime the man's other kidney was transplanted into a third person. When Paul discovered that the man's other kidney had been transplanted into a third person, he sued for conversion or, in the alternative, damages. Assuming the other kidney could have successfully been transplanted into Paul, can Paul successfully sue for conversion to recover the kidney? Can he successfully sue for damages? Cf. Colavito v. New York Organ Donor Network, Inc., 8 N.Y.3d 43, 827 N.Y.S.2d 96, 860 N.E.2d 713 (2006) (denying donee of directed donation of a kidney remedy of conversion or damages when the donated kidneys were not a match for the donee and thus could not be successfully transplanted into the donee).

7.   The 1987 Version of the Uniform Anatomical Gift Act authorized a coroner under limited circumstances to donate the eyes of decedents under the coroner's jurisdiction. In some states, this authority was broadened to include solid organs as well. Generally, the coroner was empowered to make an anatomical gift if no family members could be located within a reasonable period of time to make the gift. In a series of cases, the federal courts held that, if coroners failed to comply with procedures to discover the whereabouts of families before making anatomical gifts of their loved ones parts, the families could sue for deprivation of property without due process of law. See, e.g., Brotherton v. Cleveland, 923 F.2d 477 (6th Cir. 1991). The Uniform Anatomical Gift Act (2006) deletes the authority of the coroner to make an anatomical gift from the body of a decedent under the coroner's jurisdiction unless there are no other persons having a priority to make a gift available for that purpose. See generally Unif. Anatomical Gift Act (2006), § 9.

CHAPTER 2

SOME POWERS AND OBLIGATIONS OF POSSESSORS

■ ■ ■

§ 2.1 POWERS

PORTER v. WERTZ

Supreme Court, Appellate Division, First Department (1979).
68 A.D.2d 141, 416 N.Y.S.2d 254, aff'd, 53 N.Y.2d 696,
421 N.E.2d 500, 439 N.Y.S.2d 105 (1981).

BIRNS, JUSTICE:

Plaintiffs-appellants, Samuel Porter and Express Packaging, Inc. (Porter's corporation), owners of a Maurice Utrillo painting entitled "Chateau de Lion–sur–Mer", seek in this action to recover possession of the painting or the value thereof from defendants, participants in a series of transactions which resulted in the shipment of the painting out of the country. The painting is now in Venezuela.

Defendants-respondents Richard Feigen Gallery, Inc., Richard L. Feigen & Co., Inc. and Richard L. Feigen, hereinafter collectively referred to as Feigen, were in the business of buying and selling paintings, drawings and sculpture.

The amended answer to the complaint asserted, *inter alia,* affirmative defenses of statutory estoppel (UCC, § 2–403) and equitable estoppel.[1] The trial court, after a bench trial, found statutory estoppel inapplicable but sustained the defense of equitable estoppel and dismissed the complaint.

On this appeal, we will consider whether those defenses, or either of them, bar recovery against Feigen. We hold neither prevents recovery.

---

1. We note that the appeal is from the trial court's determination that equitable estoppel constitutes a bar to the action. However, because the enactment of statutory estoppel (UCC, § 2–403) was intended to embrace prior uniform statutory provisions and case law thereunder (so as "to continue unimpaired all rights acquired under the law of agency or of apparent agency or ownership or other estoppel"), and to state a unified and simplified policy on good faith purchase of goods (see Practice Commentary, Alfred A. Berger and William J. O'Connor, Jr., McKinney's Cons.Laws of N.Y., Book 62½, p. 395), we find it necessary to enter into some discussion of section 2–403 of the Uniform Commercial Code.

Porter, the owner of a collection of art works, bought the Utrillo in 1969. During 1972 and 1973 he had a number of art transactions with one Harold Von Maker who used, among other names, that of Peter Wertz.[2] One of the transactions was the sale by Porter to Von Maker in the spring of 1973 of a painting by Childe Hassam for $150,000, financed with a $50,000 deposit and 10 notes for $10,000 each.... [Ed. note: A later dispute arose between Porter and Von Maker regarding these notes. The dispute resulted in their signing an agreement in which, among other things,] Von Maker acknowledged that he had received the Utrillo from Porter together with a certain book[3] on Utrillo, that both "belong to (Porter)", that the painting was on consignment with a client of Von Maker's, that within 90 days Von Maker would either return the painting and book or pay $30,000 therefor, and that other than the option to purchase within said 90–day period, Von Maker had "no claim whatsoever to the Utrillo painting or Book." ...

At the very time that Von Maker was deceitfully assuring Porter he would return the Utrillo and book or pay $30,000, Von Maker had already disposed of this painting by using the real Peter Wertz to effect its sale for $20,000 to Feigen. Von Maker ... had made the availability of the Utrillo known to Feigen. When Wertz, at Von Maker's direction, appeared at the Feigen gallery with the Utrillo, he was met by Feigen's employee, Mrs. Drew–Bear. She found a buyer for the Utrillo in defendant Brenner. In effecting its transfer to him, Feigen made a commission. Through a sale by Brenner the painting is now in Venezuela, S.A.

We agree with the conclusion of the trial court that statutory estoppel does not bar recovery.

The provisions of statutory estoppel are found in section 2–403 of the Uniform Commercial Code. Subsection 2 thereof provides that "any entrusting of possession of goods to a merchant who deals in goods of that kind gives him power to transfer all rights of the entruster to a buyer in the ordinary course of business." Uniform Commercial Code, section 1–201, subdivision 9, defines a "buyer in [the] ordinary course of business" as "a person who in good faith and without knowledge that the sale to him is in violation of the ownership rights or security interest of a third party in the goods buys in ordinary course from a person in the business of selling goods of that kind...."

In order to determine whether the defense of statutory estoppel is available to Feigen, we must begin by ascertaining whether Feigen fits the definition of "[a] buyer in [the] ordinary course of business." (UCC, § 1–201[9].) Feigen does not fit that definition, for two reasons. First, Wertz, from whom Feigen bought the Utrillo, was not an art dealer—he was not

2. As will be seen, Peter Wertz was a real person, at least an acquaintance of Von Maker, who permitted Von Maker to use his name. Von Maker's true name was Harold Maker, presumably he was born in New Jersey. Apparently Maker added the prefix "Von" to his name to indicate nobility of birth.

3. The book, entitled "Petrides on Utrillo", was purchased by Porter in 1971 in Paris for the sum of $200.00.

"a person in the business of selling goods of that kind." (UCC, § 1–201[9].) If anything, he was a delicatessen employee.[4] Wertz never held himself out as a dealer. Although Feigen testified at trial that before he (Feigen) purchased the Utrillo from Wertz, Sloan, who introduced Wertz to Feigen told him (Feigen) that Wertz was an art dealer, this testimony was questionable. It conflicted with Feigen's testimony at his examination before trial where he stated he did not recall whether Sloan said that to him.[5] Second, Feigen was not "a person . . . in good faith" (UCC, § 1–201[9]) in the transaction with Wertz. Uniform Commercial Code, section 2–103, subdivision (1)(b), defines "good faith" in the case of a merchant as "honesty in fact and the observance of reasonable commercial standards of fair dealing in the trade." Although this definition by its terms embraces the "reasonable commercial standards of fair dealing in the trade", it should not—and cannot—be interpreted to permit, countenance or condone commercial standards of sharp trade practice or indifference as to the "provenance", *i.e.*, history of ownership or the right to possess or sell an object d'art, such as is present in the case before us.

We note that neither Ms. Drew–Bear nor her employer Feigen made any investigation to determine the status of Wertz, *i.e.*, whether he was an art merchant, "a person in the business of selling goods of that kind." (UCC, § 1–201[9].) Had Ms. Drew–Bear done so much as call either of the telephone numbers Wertz had left, she would have learned that Wertz was employed by a delicatessen and was not an art dealer. Nor did Ms. Drew–Bear or Feigen make any effort to verify whether Wertz was the owner or authorized by the owner to sell the painting he was offering. Ms. Drew–Bear had available to her the Petrides volume on Utrillo which included "Chateau de Lion–sur–Mer" in its catalogue of the master's work.[6] Although this knowledge alone might not have been enough to put Feigen on notice that Wertz was not the true owner at the time of the transaction, it could have raised a doubt as to Wertz's right of possession, calling for further verification before the purchase by Feigen was consummated. Thus, it appears that statutory estoppel provided by Uniform Commercial Code, section 2–403(2), was not, as Trial Term correctly concluded, available as a defense to Feigen.

---

4. Wertz is described as a seller of caviar and other luxury food items (because of his association with a Madison Avenue gourmet grocery) and over whom the Trial Term observed, Von Maker "cast his hypnotic spell . . . and usurped his name, his signature and his sacred honor."

5. Feigen's explanation for his changed version was that after his examination before trial and before the trial, his memory was "jogged" by Lipinsky, who had introduced Sloan to Feigen.

In connection with Feigen's claim that Wertz was a dealer, it is observed that on a previous appeal, Porter v. Wertz, et al., defendants, and Richard Feigen Gallery, Inc., et al., appellants, 56 A.D.2d 570, 392 N.Y.S.2d 10, this court unanimously affirmed an order of Special Term denying appellants' motion for summary judgment in that there was an issue of fact as to whether Wertz was a dealer or a collector. If a dealer, appellants claimed, as they do now, the applicability of UCC, § 2–403(2).

6. Page 32 of that book clearly contained a reference to the fact that that painting, at least at the time of publication of the book in 1969, was in the collection of Mrs. Donald D. King of New York, supposedly the party from whom Porter obtained it.

We disagree with the conclusion of the trial court that the defense of equitable estoppel (see *Zendman v. Harry Winston, Inc.*, 305 N.Y. 180, 111 N.E.2d 871) raised by Feigen bars recovery.

We pause to observe that although one may not be a buyer in the ordinary course of business as defined in the Uniform Commercial Code, he may be a good-faith purchaser for value and enjoy the protection of pre-Code estoppel.... We now reach the question whether the defense of equitable estoppel has been established here.

In general terms:

Equitable estoppel or estoppel in pais is the principle by which a party is absolutely precluded, both at law and in equity, from denying, or asserting the contrary of, any material fact which, by his words or conduct, affirmative or negative, intentionally or through culpable negligence, he has induced another, who was excusably ignorant of the true facts and who had a right to rely upon such words or conduct, to believe and act upon them thereby, as a consequence reasonably to be anticipated, changing his position in such a way that he would suffer injury if such denial or contrary assertion were allowed. An estoppel in pais can arise only when a person, either by his declarations or conduct, has induced another person to act in a particular manner. The doctrine prohibits a person, upon principles of honesty and fair and open dealing, from asserting rights the enforcement of which would, through his omissions or commissions, work fraud and injustice.

(21 N.Y. Jur., Estoppel, § 15 [citing cases].)

As the Court of Appeals reiterated in *Zendman v. Harry Winston, Inc.*, supra, an " 'owner may be estopped from setting up his own title and the lack of title in the vendor as against a *bona fide* purchaser for value where the owner has clothed the vendor with possession and other indicia of title (46 Am.Jur., Sales, § 463).' " Indeed, "[t]he rightful owner may be estopped by his own acts from asserting his title. If he has invested another with the usual evidence of title, or an apparent authority to dispose of it, he will not be allowed to make claim against an innocent purchaser dealing on the faith of such apparent ownership (*Smith v. Clews*, 114 N.Y. 190, 194, 21 N.E. 160, 161)."

In *Zendman v. Harry Winston, Inc.*, supra, a diamond merchant in New York City sent a ring to Brand, Inc., a corporation which conducted auctions on the boardwalk in Atlantic City, New Jersey, with a memorandum reciting that the ring was for examination only and that title was not to pass until the auctioneer had made his selection, and had notified the sender of his agreement to pay the indicated price and the sender had indicated acceptance thereof by issuing a bill of sale. The ring was placed in a public show window at the auctioneer's place of business, remaining there for more than a month, before being sold to the plaintiff at a public auction. Under circumstances where it was demonstrated that the defendant had permitted other pieces of jewelry it owned to be exhibited and sold by the auctioneer, it was held that the defendant by his conduct was estopped from recovering the ring from the plaintiff.

In the case at bar, Porter's conduct was not blameworthy. When the first promissory note was dishonored, he retained Bishop's investigative service and informed the FBI of the financial transactions concerning the series of notes. His attorney obtained a comprehensive agreement covering several paintings, within which was the assurance (now proven false) by Von Maker that he still controlled the Utrillo. Although Porter had permitted Von Maker to possess the painting, he conferred upon Von Maker no other indicia of ownership. Possession without more is insufficient to create an estoppel (Zendman v. Harry Winston, Inc., supra, 305 N.Y. at 186–187, 111 N.E.2d at 874–875).

We find that the prior art transactions between Porter and Von Maker justified the conclusion of the trial court that Porter knew that Von Maker was a dealer in art. Nevertheless, the testimony remains uncontradicted, that the Utrillo was not consigned to Von Maker for business purposes, but rather for display only in Von Maker's home (compare Zendman v. Harry Winston, Inc., supra). In these circumstances, it cannot be said that Porter's conduct in any way contributed to the deception practiced on Feigen by Von Maker and Wertz.

Finally, we must examine again the position of Feigen to determine whether Feigen was a purchaser in good faith.

In purchasing the Utrillo, Feigen did not rely on any indicia of ownership in Von Maker. Feigen dealt with Wertz, who did not have the legal right to possession of the painting. Even were we to consider Wertz as the agent of Von Maker or merge the identities of Von Maker and Wertz insofar as Feigen was concerned, Feigen was not a purchaser in good faith. As we have commented, neither Ms. Drew–Bear nor Feigen made, or attempted to make, the inquiry which the circumstances demanded.

The Feigen claim that the failure to look into Wertz's authority to sell the painting was consistent with the practice of the trade does not excuse such conduct. This claim merely confirms the observation of the trial court that "in an industry whose transactions cry out for verification of ... title ... it is deemed poor practice to probe.... " Indeed, commercial indifference to ownership or the right to sell facilitates traffic in stolen works of art. Commercial indifference diminishes the integrity and increases the culpability of the apathetic merchant. In such posture, Feigen cannot be heard to complain.

In the circumstances outlined, the complaint should not have been dismissed. Moreover, we find ... that plaintiffs-appellants are the true owners of the Utrillo painting and are entitled to possession thereof, that defendants-respondents wrongfully detained that painting and are obligated to return it or pay for its value at the time of trial....

* * *

Accordingly, the judgment of the Supreme Court, New York County, ... should be reversed and vacated, on the law and the facts, the complaint reinstated, judgment entered in favor of plaintiffs-appellants on liability, and the matter remanded for an assessment of damages....

All concur.

NOTES AND QUESTIONS

1. Maurice Utrillo (1883–1955) was born Maurice Valadon in Montmarte, France, the illegitimate son of Marie–Clemente Valadon. He was given the name Utrillo by a family friend when he was eight years old. He began drinking at the age of sixteen and was in and out of sanitariums throughout his life in his combat with alcoholism. His artistic talents nonetheless flourished. By the age of fourteen he was already a world famous painter, able to capture vivid texture and color in his street scenes and architectural structures. In 1928, France awarded him the Legion of Honor for his painting achievements. He is considered one of the most popular artists of the modern French period. Throughout his life, he continued to sign all his paintings "Maurice Utrillo, V." to signify that he was born a Valadon.

2. As a general proposition, a person cannot convey a better title to property than he has. Following the logic of this principle, if T steals a painting from O, T cannot convey a good title to that painting to B who purchases the property from T even if B was a bona fide purchaser. See generally Autocephalous Greek–Orthodox Church of Cyprus v. Goldberg & Feldman Fine Arts, Inc., 717 F. Supp. 1374 (S.D. Ind.1989). Since both O and B are innocent parties, a holding that O prevails against B effectively shifts the risk of loss resulting from T's failure of title to B.

A tension exists, however, between the general principle protecting the interest of the true owner from theft and the interests of society to foster commerce. The tension is magnified if the title to the articles in commerce is best evidenced only by the fact that the seller has possession of the goods. Thus, courts developed a number of important exceptions to the application of the general rule. Two such exceptions arose where: (1) the seller had a voidable title rather than a void title; and (2) the owner had entrusted the goods to a merchant dealing in those types of goods. Both of these exceptions are codified in Section 2–403 of the Uniform Commercial Code which provides:

> (1) A purchaser of goods acquires all title which his transferor had or had power to transfer except that a purchaser of a limited interest acquires rights only to the extent of the interest purchased. A person with voidable title has power to transfer a good title to a good faith purchaser for value. When goods have been delivered under a transaction of purchase the purchaser has such power even though
>
> > (a) the transferor was deceived as to the identity of the purchaser, or
> >
> > (b) the delivery was in exchange for a check which is later dishonored, or
> >
> > (c) it was agreed that the transaction was to be a "cash sale", or

(d) the delivery was procured through fraud punishable as larcenous under the criminal law.

(2) Any entrusting of possession of goods to a merchant who deals in goods of that kind gives him power to transfer all rights of the entruster to a buyer in ordinary course of business.

(3) "Entrusting" includes any delivery and any acquiescence in retention of possession regardless of any condition expressed between the parties to the delivery or acquiescence and regardless of whether the procurement of the entrusting or the possessor's disposition of the goods have been such as to be larcenous under the criminal law.

Section 1–201(b)(9) defines the "buyer in ordinary course of business" as follows:

"Buyer in ordinary course of business" means a person that buys goods in good faith, without knowledge that the sale violates the rights of another person in the goods, and in the ordinary course from a person, other than a pawnbroker, in the business of selling goods of that kind. A person buys goods in the ordinary course if the sale to the person comports with the usual or customary practices in the kind of business in which the seller is engaged or with the seller's own usual or customary practices.

3. The following comparison of the conveyancing rule in the first sentence of section 2–403 and the good faith purchaser rule is helpful in understanding the rationale underlying Section 2–403. It appears in Dolan, The U.C.C. Framework: Conveyancing Principles and Property Interests, 59 B.U. L. Rev. 811, 812–815 (1979):

The [Uniform Commercial] Code's conveyancing rules ... begin with the shelter, or umbrella, principle: the taker receives everything the transferor had to convey. . . .

The security of property principle manifested in [this rule] ... applies to all conveyances unless contrary, identifiable policies dictate limitations on it. Good faith purchase, the second of the first three basic conveyancing principles, is the first such limitation.

In direct opposition to the security of property postulate that one cannot give what one does not have, the good faith purchase rule permits the taker to receive interests greater than those his transferor possessed. Courts have rationalized this departure from the logic of the shelter principle in two ways. Some assert that it is a question of the fault or negligence of the true owner or his creditor. These cases emphasize the culpability of a property owner who does not take care to protect his interest in the property when introducing it into the channels of commerce. He thereby misleads an innocent purchaser who relies on the appearance that the owner's negligence has created. Other courts view the issue as essentially an economic one. These cases opt for the good faith purchase principle as commercially convenient and regard indiscriminate use of the security of property approach as wasteful.

Both doctrines evolved in response to perceived needs. The propertied classes reacted against the primitive rule that strength determined ownership. Staunch notions that a man should never be stripped of property without his consent flowed naturally from the prairie frontier and from high seas traversed by privateers, and demanded the development of rules upholding security of property in the face of a lawless taking. The good faith purchase doctrine responded to a different set of needs. It is no accident that [judges] ... and others familiar with mercantile practices readily accepted the argument that strict adherence to the security of property dogma would strangle commercial intercourse, whose advancement demanded freeing the buyer from the duty of costly title inquiry.

It is fair to say, then, that property owners preferred security of property while the merchant class preferred security of purchase. Much of the history of commercial law has been a dispute between these competing interests. The Code properly accepts the validity of both doctrines and uses first one and then the other pursuant to a well-defined pattern. Specifically, in the process of balancing the elements of fairness to the parties, culpability for ownership misunderstandings, and commercial celebrity, the Code employs the good faith purchase principle to facilitate and protect transactions that are regular.

Judge Posner has also provided keen economic insights supporting the protection of bona fide purchasers who deal with entrusters and not thieves. He writes:

A entrusts his overcoat to B with directions to pawn it, and B, misunderstanding, sells it to C. Provided C does not know or have reason to know that B was not authorized to sell the overcoat to him, C will acquire a good title to it. This is a simple case of A's being the lower-cost avoider of the mistake than C. But now suppose that B was not A's agent, but stole the overcoat from A and sold it to C without giving C any reason to suspect he was buying stolen merchandise. C will not acquire a good title; a thief cannot pass good title to his purchaser. Although A could prevent the erroneous transfer at lower cost than C by taking greater precautions against theft, allowing C to obtain a good title would encourage theft. Thieves would get higher prices from their "fences," because the fences could (provided they took steps to throw the buyer off the scent) get higher prices in the resale market; people will pay more for an assured than a clouded title. We do not want an efficient market in stolen goods.

Posner, Economic Analysis of Law 80 (7th ed. 2007).

4. The decision in the principal case was affirmed by the New York Court of Appeals. See Porter v. Wertz, 53 N.Y.2d 696, 439 N.Y.S.2d 105, 421 N.E.2d 500 (1981). It found that section 2–403 was inapplicable because (1) even accepting that Wertz was an art merchant, he was not the merchant to whom Porter entrusted the Utrillo painting, (2) Wertz was not an art merchant, and (3) the sale was not in the ordinary course of Wertz's business because Wertz did not deal in goods of that kind. The court stated that "[t]he 'entruster provision' of the Uniform Commercial Code is designed to enhance the reliability of commercial sales by merchants (who deal with the kind of goods sold on a regular basis) while shifting the risk of loss through fraudulent transfer to the owner of the goods, who can select the merchant to whom he entrusts his property. It protects only those who purchase from the

merchant to whom the property was entrusted in the ordinary course of the merchant's business." Id. at 698, 439 N.Y.S.2d at 105–106, 421 N.E.2d at 500–01. Is this view consistent with the Dolan analysis in the preceding note?

The Court of Appeals also rejected the estoppel argument. In so doing it stated:

> An estoppel might arise if Porter had clothed Peter Wertz with ownership of or authority to sell the Utrillo painting and the Feigen Gallery had relied upon Wertz' apparent ownership or right to transfer it. But Porter never even delivered the painting to Peter Wertz, much less create apparent ownership in him; he delivered the painting to Von Maker for his own personal use. It is true ... that Von Maker used the name Peter Wertz in his dealings with Porter, but the Appellate Division found that the Feigen Gallery purchased from the actual Peter Wertz and that there was insufficient evidence to establish the claim that Peter Wertz had been described as an art dealer by Henry Sloan. Nothing Porter did influenced the Feigen Gallery's decision to purchase from Peter Wertz a delicatessen employee.

Id. at 700, 439 N.Y.S.2d at 106–07, 421 N.E.2d at 501–502.

5. O owns a watch that O entrusts to B for repairs. B sells the watch to P, who believes that B is authorized to sell him the watch. After O determines that B sold the watch to P, O sues P to recover the watch. What result? Zendman v. Harry Winston, Inc., 305 N.Y. 180, 111 N.E.2d 871 (1953).

Suppose O had delivered the watch to B only after B personally appeared in O's shop and fraudulently represented to O that he was a jewelry salesman and that he wanted to show the watch to a prospective purchaser. B then sells the watch to P. O sues P to recover the value of the watch. What result? Would your answer differ if B delivered the watch to P to discharge a prior debt that B owed to P? See Baehr v. Clark, 83 Iowa 313, 49 N.W. 840 (1891). See also U.C.C. § 1–201(44) (providing that "a person gives 'value' for rights if he acquires them ... as security for or in total or partial satisfaction of a pre-existing claim").

Suppose B had not personally appeared in O's shop but had written O a letter requesting that O send B the watch to show a prospective purchaser. O did so mistakenly thinking that B was in fact B–1, a person to whom O had previously sold watches. B sells the watch to P. If O sues P to recover the value of the watch, what result? See generally Brown, The Law of Personal Property § 9.7 at 202–205 (W. Raushenbush ed., 3d ed. 1975).

6. Owner left a bag of clothing with the local Goodwill store. Goodwill is a national organization that trains disabled persons in the sale and merchandising of used goods, including clothing and silver. Mistakenly, $3,500 of silver flatware also was included in this bag. Ms. Lucky purchased the silver from Goodwill. Thereafter, Owner sued to recover the silver from Ms. Lucky. What arguments might each of the parties raise in support of their claim to own the silver, and if you were the judge in this case, how would you rule? See Kahr v. Markland, 187 Ill. App. 3d 603, 135 Ill. Dec. 196, 543 N.E.2d 579 (1989).

7. SuperStore is a local truck dealer that both services and sells trucks. O brings his truck to the service department for repairs. When the repairs are

completed, the service manager takes the truck to that area of the store where used trucks are sold and places a sign on the windshield reading $12,000. B purchases the truck from SuperStore. When O sues to recover the truck, B defends by relying on the entrusting provisions of the Uniform Commercial Code. O responds by arguing that the service and sales departments are separate merchants and that B did not entrust the truck to the sales department. Is O's argument persuasive? See In re Fred Madore Chevrolet–Pontiac–Oldsmobile, 219 B.R. 938 (D.N.H.1998). See also Sutton v. Snider, 33 P.3d 309 (Okla. Civ. App. 2001).

8. In Graffman v. Espel, 1998 WL 55371 (S.D.N.Y.1998), the owner of a Picasso painting sued to recover the painting from a buyer. The buyer bought the painting from an art dealer to whom it had been entrusted by the owner. The owner, relying on *Porter*, claimed that the buyer failed to act in "good faith" because he had not checked on the provenance of the painting before buying it. The court rejected that argument and distinguished *Porter* on the grounds that in *Porter* the buyer was an art dealer, whereas the buyer in *Graffman* was not. Therefore, the buyer was under no obligation to adhere to commercial standards applicable to art dealers. Do you agree?

§ 2.2 OBLIGATIONS

LAPLACE v. BRIERE

Superior Court of New Jersey, Appellate Division (2009).
404 N.J. Super. 585, 962 A.2d 1139.

CHAMBERS, J.

The unusual facts of this case require us to visit the common law principles governing bailment and conversion, not often encountered today.

Plaintiff Michael R. LaPlace brought this suit to recover for the loss of his horse which died while boarding at a stable owned by defendants Pierre Briere, trading as Pierre Briere Quarter Horses, and Pierre Briere Quarter Horses, LLC ("Briere stable") and while being exercised by defendant Charlene Bridgwood. The trial court granted summary judgment for the defendants and denied plaintiff's motion for partial summary judgment on the issue of liability. Plaintiff now appeals. . . .

The [question] . . . presented by this appeal is whether . . . the stable where the horse was boarded and where the death occurred may be liable under the law of bailment under these circumstances. We answer [this question] in the negative, and we affirm the granting of summary judgment to defendants and the denial of partial summary judgment to plaintiff. . . .

We now turn to whether Briere stable may be held liable to plaintiff under bailment law. We will first address whether a bailment relationship existed between plaintiff and Briere stable at the time of the horse's death. If it did, then we will consider whether Briere stable is liable under bailment law for the loss of the horse.

A bailment may be created by contract, either express or implied, or by operation of law or statute.... A bailment arises when a person leaves his chattel on the premises of another "if the latter is given primary control of the chattel for the time being." *Moore's Trucking Co. v. Gulf Tire & Supply Co.,* 18 *N.J.Super.* 467, 469–70, 87 *A.*2d 441 (App.Div.) (listing as examples of bailments: "jewelry checked with a swimming pool attendant; diamonds delivered to a retail jeweler 'on memorandum' for sale; automobile placed in shop to be washed; airplane stored in a hangar," (citations omitted)), *certif. denied,* 10 *N.J.* 22, 89 *A.*2d 306 (1952); *see also State v. Goodmann,* 390 *N.J.Super.* 259, 266–67, 915 *A.*2d 79 (App.Div.2007) (holding that film left with a store for developing gave rise to a bailment); *Jasphy v. Osinsky,* 364 *N.J.Super.* 13, 15, 18, 834 *A.*2d 426 (App.Div.2003) (noting that a bailment arose when plaintiff left her three fur coats with defendant for storage and cleaning). A bailment has been explained in the following way:

> A bailment is created by the delivery of personal property by one person to another in trust for a specific purpose, pursuant to an express or implied contract to fulfill that trust. Inherent in the bailment relationship is the requirement that the property be returned to the bailor, or duly accounted for by the bailee, when the purpose of the bailment is accomplished, or that it be kept until it is reclaimed by the bailor.

[8A *Am.Jur.2d Bailments* § 1 (1997).]

Notably, for a bailment to arise, the bailor must have "possession and primary control" over the chattel. *City of Jersey City v. Liggett & Myers Tobacco Co.,* 14 *N.J.* 112, 115, 101 *A.*2d 555 (1953). During the bailment arrangement, the bailee has sole custody and control and exclusive possession of the chattel.... Nonetheless, the bailee still "must deal with the property during the term of the bailment according to the bailor's instructions." [citation omitted]

Briere stable denies that a bailment relationship existed because it contends that it did not have complete and exclusive control over the horse. It argues that plaintiff and his family had complete access and control over the horse in that they would ride the horse and transport it to shows at their discretion at any time. It maintains that at most there was joint control of the horse between Briere stable and plaintiff, and hence no bailment arose.

In making this argument, Briere stable relies on *Della Cerra v. Burns,* 69 *N.J.Super.* 110, 173 *A.*2d 564 (App.Div.1961). In that case, the owner of a car had left his vehicle with a garage for repair work.... In accordance with past practices between the parties, the car was left on the street, unlocked, with the key under the mat, so that the owner could pick it up after hours.... The car was then taken by an unknown person and became involved in an automobile accident.... The court determined that under the circumstances, the garage did not have primary control over the car.... Rather, the garage and owner had joint control over the car at the time of the theft, and hence, there was no bailment.... By analogy, Briere stable attempts to argue that it and plaintiff had joint control over the horse and hence no bailment existed. *Della Cerra* would be analogous here if, with plaintiff's consent, the horse had been left tied to a post on the side of road outside Briere's property waiting for plaintiff to pick it up. That of course did not happen here. At the time this horse died, it was residing at Briere stable solely under the care of Briere stable. Briere stable provided it with shelter, food, water, training, grooming, and on occasion arranged for its medical care and shoeing. Plaintiff was not present at the time to exercise any control over the horse. Accordingly, we conclude that when plaintiff delivered his horse to Briere stable and left it in Briere stable's care for safekeeping, a bailment arrangement arose.

Certainly, at the times when plaintiff had removed the horse from the stable, Briere stable no longer had physical possession and control of the animal, and the bailment relationship was suspended or temporarily terminated. However, once plaintiff returned the horse to the stable and he and his family left, his actual possessory control over the horse reverted to Briere stable which once again assumed its exclusive actual possession and primary control over the animal, and the bailment resumed.

Since a bailment relationship existed at the time the horse died, we must now consider whether, under the facts presented, Briere stable is liable for the loss. A bailee is not an insurer of the goods.... However, where goods subject to a bailment are not returned or are damaged or lost, the bailor may be able to recover under theories of either conversion or negligence. *Lembaga Enters., Inc. v. Cace Trucking & Warehouse, Inc.,* 320 *N.J.Super.* 501, 507, 727 A.2d 1026 (App.Div.), *certif. denied,* 161 *N.J.* 334, 736 A.2d 527 (1999).

We will first address whether Briere stable can be held liable under a conversion theory applicable to bailees. A bailee commits the tort of common law conversion when it commits "an unauthorized act of dominion over the bailor's property inconsistent with its rights in that property." *Ibid.* A bailee's intentional or negligent conduct can give rise to a claim of conversion, even though it acted in good faith. *Ibid.* For example, a bailee will be liable for conversion due to its negligent conduct if the bailee "mistakenly destroys or disposes of the goods ... although there is no intent to steal or destroy the goods." *Ibid.*

The bailor's "proof of delivery, demand and failure to return the goods" gives rise to "a prima facie case of conversion." *Charles Bloom & Co. v. Echo Jewelers,* 279 *N.J.Super.* 372, 381, 652 A.2d 1238 (App.Div. 1995). Once a prima facie case is established, the bailee then has the burden of producing evidence to show what happened to the goods.... Without this rule, the bailor, who was not in possession of the goods, would be in a difficult position to show what occurred.... As one court has explained:

A bailee who accepts responsibility for goods should have the burden of producing evidence as to the fate of those goods. To hold otherwise would place an impossible burden on a plaintiff. How is a plaintiff to present sufficient evidence of conversion when knowledge of the fate of the goods is available only to defendant?

[*Joseph H. Reinfeld, Inc. v. Griswold & Bateman Warehouse Co.,* 189 *N.J.Super.* 141, 143–44, 458 *A.*2d 1341 (Law Div.1983) (involving forty cases of whiskey missing from defendant's warehouse).] However, the burden of proof remains with the bailor. *Id.* at 144–45, 458 *A.*2d 1341. Once the bailee has produced evidence explaining what happened to the chattel, the bailor then must prove its claim of conversion. *Ibid.*

Here plaintiff has made out a prima facie case of conversion in that he delivered the horse and it has not been returned. Briere stable, however, has come forward with proofs establishing the circumstances under which the horse died, namely that it was being exercised by Bridgwood when it reared up, fell, began bleeding profusely from the nose, and died. Plaintiff has come forward with no further proofs to show that Briere stable converted the horse. Further, as noted, Bridgwood's conduct did not constitute conversion, so Briere stable cannot be liable for conversion due to her conduct. The sole fact that Briere stable was unable to return the horse due to its death does not mean it is liable for the loss. *See Gouled v. Holwitz,* 95 *N.J.L.* 277, 113 *A.* 323 (Sup.Ct.1921) (holding that the bailee was not liable for the death of a horse despite the provision in the bailment agreement requiring that the horse be returned in "good condition" where, during the bailment, the horse came down with spinal meningitis and was thereafter shot by an agent from the Society for the Prevention of Cruelty to Animals over the bailee's protest, since an implied condition in the bailment was that the horse would continue to live). Based on this state of the evidence, plaintiff cannot sustain his ultimate burden of proving that Briere stable is liable under a theory of conversion.

We now turn to whether Briere stable may be held liable under a theory of negligence. In a bailment for mutual benefit, a bailee has a duty to exercise reasonable care for the safekeeping of the subject of the bailment and will be liable for any loss caused by its failure to do so. *Charles Bloom & Co. v. Echo Jewelers, supra,* 279 *N.J.Super.* at 380, 652 *A.*2d 1238. When proofs are presented showing that goods were damaged while in the care of a bailee, a presumption of negligence arises and in those circumstances, a prima facie case is established against the bailee. *McGlynn v. Parking Auth. of Newark,* 86 *N.J.* 551, 556, 432 *A.*2d 99 (1981) (citing *Bachman Chocolate Mfg. Co. v. Lehigh Warehouse & Transp. Co.,* 1 *N.J.* 239, 242, 62 *A.*2d 806 (1949) (proof that cocoa beans were damaged when stored in the bailee's warehouse established a prima facie case of negligence against the bailee)). The presumption of negligence, however, may be rebutted by the bailee "with evidence showing that the loss was not caused by his negligence or that he exercised due care." *Ibid.; Jasphy v. Osinsky, supra,* 364 *N.J.Super.* at 19, 834 *A.*2d 426. The burden of proof always remains with the plaintiff. *Bachman Chocolate Mfg. Co. v. Lehigh Warehouse & Transp. Co., supra,* 1 *N.J.* at 242, 62 A.2d 806.

As with the conversion claim, here plaintiff made out a prima facie case of negligence by showing that his horse died in Briere stable's care during the bailment. Briere stable then came forward with evidence showing that the horse was undergoing ordinary exercises by a person experienced in handling and exercising horses, when it died. These proofs presented by Briere stable are devoid of any evidence of negligence causing the death of the horse, and thus rebut the presumption of negligence. Plaintiff has failed to come forward with any additional proofs to establish that the horse was negligently exercised or that the exercise was a proximate cause of its death.

Furthermore, even if we were to presume that Briere stable negligently allowed Bridgwood to exercise the horse or that she negligently did so or that a material issue of fact is presented on the question of negligence, there still is no showing that Bridgwood's conduct was a proximate cause of the horse's death. Nor can we presume that proximate cause is present here. The rebuttable presumptions in favor of a bailor against a bailee for negligence or conversion are in place because the chattel is in the exclusive control of the bailee who is in a unique position to explain what happened to the chattel. *See Joseph H. Reinfeld, Inc. v. Griswold & Bateman Warehouse Co., supra,* 189 *N.J.Super.* at 143–44, 458 A.2d 1341. Operation of that presumption on the issue of proximate cause in this case makes no sense since determining the cause of death was uniquely within the control of plaintiff. Since plaintiff owned the animal, his consent was required for further examination and a necropsy. Plaintiff still bears the ultimate burden of proof, and under a negligent cause of action, he must show both negligence and that the negligence was a proximate cause of the harm. This he cannot do.

As a result, since no rational factfinder could determine, based on these proofs, that Briere stable was negligent or converted the horse, Briere stable cannot be held liable for the death of the horse under bailment law. Summary judgment in favor of Briere stable was properly granted.

We affirm the grant of summary judgment in favor of defendants and the denial of plaintiff's motion for partial summary judgment.

NOTES AND QUESTIONS

1. Bailment arrangements are a common feature of everyday life. For example, a bailment arises when a person borrows her neighbor's snowblower while her snowblower is in the repair shop. Likewise, bailments arise when a person takes her clothes to a dry cleaner to be cleaned, when a family entrusts its possessions to a moving company to move from their present home to another, or when a friend requests that you take care of her car while she is on vacation. In each of these illustrations, consider whether the benefits of

the bailment are primarily for the benefit of the bailor or the bailee or whether there are mutual benefits for each party.

As discussed in *LaPlace*, where the bailment is for the mutual benefit of the parties, the bailee has a duty to exercise "reasonable care" over the property. Thus, under the common law, the bailee would be liable only for his ordinary negligence. On the other hand, under the common law, if a bailment was primarily for the benefit of the bailor (say your neighbor asks you to take care of her cat over the weekend), the bailee was only responsible to exercise slight care over the goods and was thus liable only for gross negligence. But, if the bailment was primarily for the benefit of the bailee (say your neighbor borrows your lawnmower to cut his lawn), then the bailee was responsible to take great care with respect to the goods and was liable for slight negligence. Does this tripartite distinction make sense? Or, should the characterization of bailments be collapsed into one category to the effect that the bailee's obligation over the bailed goods is measured by "the amount and kind of care that would be exercised by an ordinarily prudent person in the same or similar circumstances." See Peet v. Roth Hotel Company, 191 Minn. 151, 253 N.W. 546, 547 (1934). Or, is that just saying the same thing?

2. At the heart of the bailment contract is the bailee's promise that it will return the bailed goods to the bailor. If the bailee fails to return the goods because they have been lost, stolen or destroyed, or if the goods are returned to the bailor in damaged condition, the bailee is liable to the bailor if the bailee was negligent. On the other hand, if the bailee fails to return the goods to the bailor because the bailee actually delivered them to the wrong person (someone other than the bailor or a designee of the bailor)—a so-called "misdelivery"—the bailee is absolutely liable to the bailor. See, e.g., Fireman's Fund Ins. Co. v. Wagner Fur, Inc., 760 F. Supp. 1101 (S.D.N.Y.1991); Rensch v. Riddle's Diamonds of Rapid City, Inc., 393 N.W.2d 269 (S.D.1986). The absence of negligence or presence of good faith is no defense. Misdelivery is equivalent to the bailee's conversion of the bailor's goods.

O loses her watch. F finds the watch. T tells F that he owns the watch and accurately describes both the watch and the place where F found the watch. F gives the watch to T. Subsequently O sues F to recover the value of the watch, claiming that F is absolutely liable to O because F was a bailee and delivered the watch to the wrong person. What result? Cf. Cowen v. Pressprich, 202 A.D. 796, 194 N.Y.S. 926 (1st Dept.1922) (reversing lower court judgment holding that the defendant stockbroker with whom bonds were inadvertently deposited was liable for delivering the bonds to the wrong person).

BROWN, THE LAW OF PERSONAL PROPERTY § 11.8 AT 289–293 (W.D. RAUSHENBUSH ED., 3D ED. 1975)

Burdens of Proof and Presumptions

In the ordinary trial of an action at law, the plaintiff who asserts a cause of action has the burden or obligation in the first instance of furnishing evidence to show the existence of that cause. If he fails to do so, his action must fail and be dismissed. When, however, the plaintiff has assumed this initial burden and has put in evidence those facts, which the substantive law regards as sufficient to authorize a recovery by the plaintiff, then, unless the defendant proceeds further, not only will the case not be dismissed but, if the plaintiff's evidence is credible, it will be the duty of the court to have judgment entered for the plaintiff. Thus the burden of proceeding with the evidence has now shifted to the defendant who must either put in evidence controverting that of the plaintiff or of some new affirmative defense, for example that a debt sued upon has been paid. Suppose now that the defendant has thus proceeded and put in evidence which, if credible, is a good defense to the plaintiff's action. In such an event, the burden of proceeding has again shifted to the plaintiff who must in order to avoid a judgment in favor of the defendant, introduce evidence to controvert that of the defendant.

Distinct from this burden of going ahead with the evidence is the burden of persuading the jury or other trier of the facts, as to the existence of those facts in the case, upon the finding of which depends the judgment, either for the plaintiff or for the defendant. The testimony is, of course, often conflicting and contradictory, so that it cannot be said with certainty what the true fact situation is. In such a situation, the jury must be instructed which of the two parties has the burden of persuading the jury by a preponderance of evidence concerning the truth of the disputed facts in issue. The determination of this question is often decisive of the case. Suppose, for example, that the plaintiff has deposited valuables with the defendant for safe-keeping and that the same have been destroyed by fire of an unknown origin. If the bailor has the burden of proving that the bailee was negligent the bailor cannot recover; for, not knowing the cause of the fire, he cannot show that the bailee failed in his duty of due care. If, on the other hand, the bailee must convince the jury that he was careful he will likely be defeated, for he also cannot show that the fire may not have been due to some carelessness on his part. The difference between the burden of going forward with the evidence and the burden of persuading the jury by a preponderance of the evidence seems clear. Unfortunately, the term "burden of proof" has been used to describe both of these two burdens and in reading the cases it is frequently difficult to decide in which sense the court employed the phrase.

Affecting vitally the problem of the burden of proof in both of the above mentioned senses is the doctrine of presumptions. A presumption occurs in legal terminology when the trier of fact, whether court or jury, is required from the proof of one fact to assume some other fact not directly testified to. A well-known example is the presumption that a person is dead, when he has been shown to have been absent for seven years without being heard from. Presumptions may be purely logical inferences. From the usual course of events, it may ordinarily follow that when fact A exists, fact B is also present. Presumptions may also be permitted to aid a party in his proof, when it appears that the only evidence of the ultimate fact to be established is in the possession of his adversary. Presumptions may also be raised for reasons of general social policy. The courts may in some instances believe that certain activities are so fraught with possibilities of injury to third persons, that the parties engaging in them should be required to prove that injuries resulting therefrom were not due to the fault of the actor, instead of requiring the injured party to prove, as in the normal case, that the injury was due to the fault of the actor.

There has been much controversy over the question whether the effect of a presumption is merely to shift the burden of going ahead with the evidence to the party against whom the presumption applies, or whether, although such party has put in evidence to controvert the effect of the presumption, it still has weight with the jury as affecting the burden of persuasion. The traditional view undoubtedly is that a presumption, when once rebutted by evidence, is dead and of no effect, and is to be ignored by the jury in determining the truth or falsity of the ultimate fact, which it was said to infer. However, some courts and legal writers take the position that a presumption based on logical inferences, with no countervailing social policy to prevent, still has weight with the jury in determining the burden of presumption.

* * *

NOTES AND QUESTIONS

1. Ordinarily the bailor establishes a prima facie case that he is entitled to recover from the bailee if the bailor establishes that (1) he had prior possession of the bailed goods, (2) he delivered the goods to the bailee under a contract of bailment, and (3) the bailee failed to redeliver the goods to the bailor. Once the bailor has established a prima facie case, if the bailee introduces no evidence to rebut it, the bailor is entitled to recovery. In other words, the bailor's *prima facie* case requires no showing relating to why the goods were not returned to the bailor.

If there is a good reason the bailee failed to return the goods to the bailor, the burden of coming forward with that evidence rests on the bailee. For example, the bailee might claim the goods were destroyed by fire. Ordinarily if such a defense is raised the bailee will prevail unless the bailor also can establish by a preponderance of the evidence that, but for the bailee's negligence, the fire would not have occurred, i.e., the bailee was negligent and that negligence resulted in the loss of the goods. Thus, while presenting a prima facie case creates on the defendant a burden to come forward with a reason (evidence) to excuse a return of the goods, the ultimate burden of proof on the issue of negligence remains with the plaintiff-bailor.

Placing the burden of proof on the issue of negligence on the bailor can be particularly onerous when the goods have been in exclusive possession of the bailee, and the bailor may not have sufficient knowledge of, or access to, the facts that would establish whether the bailee was negligent. In recognition of this difficulty, some courts shift the burden of proof on the issue of negligence to the bailee to prove that it was *not* negligent. See, e.g., Peet v. Roth Hotel

Company, 191 Minn. 151, 253 N.W. 546 (1934). Which is the better approach? Which approach is adopted in *LaPlace*?

2. As noted above, proof of prima facie cases requires that the delivery be under a contract of bailment. The existence of bailment contract was partially at issue in *Peet* where the hotel claimed there was no contract because of a mistake relating to the value of the allegedly bailed goods. The court, however, held that such a mistake did not result in there being no bailment contract. Effectively, in *Peet,* the bailee was held to bear the risk of its mistaken belief as to the value of the ring. Alternatively, the court could have held that the bailor was under an obligation to disclose the value of the ring to the bailee and that for her failure to do so, the bailee could either limit its liability to whatever amount it reasonably believed the ring was worth or claim there was no bailment contract. What argument might be made to support this alternate rule? Which of these two approaches represents the better view? Suppose the value of the ring was not based upon the qualities of its material and workmanship but rather upon the fact that it had been given by Napoleon to Josephine. Should the bailee in this case have been held liable for the entire value of the ring?

3. In many cases a bailor will have a personal property insurance policy on the bailed goods that should compensate the bailor for the value of any bailed goods that the bailor cannot recover from the bailee. If the bailor's insurance company pays the bailor the value of the lost or damaged goods and thereafter the bailor sues the bailee, can the bailee offset his liability by the amount the bailor's insurer paid to the bailor? When the insurer has paid the bailor, in all likelihood the insurer will be subrogated to the rights of the bailor against the bailee. If the insurer recovers more from the bailee than it paid to the bailor, must it remit the excess to the bailor? Can the bailee limit the insurer's recovery to that amount the insurer paid to the bailor?

ELLISH v. AIRPORT PARKING COMPANY OF AMERICA, INC.

Supreme Court, Appellate Division, Second Department (1973).
42 A.D.2d 174, 345 N.Y.S.2d 650, aff'd 33 N.Y.2d
764, 350 N.Y.S.2d 411, 305 N.E.2d 490.

HOPKINS, ACTING PRESIDING JUSTICE.

About to leave on a flight from John F. Kennedy International Airport on September 1, 1966, the plaintiff parked her automobile in a lot operated by the defendant under an agreement with the Port of New York Authority. When she returned on September 5, 1966, her automobile had disappeared. Claiming that the defendant was responsible for the loss, she brought this suit. The Civil Court granted judgment in her favor, finding that the transaction was a bailment (Ellish v. Airport Parking Co. of Amer., 66 Misc.2d 470, 321 N.Y.S.2d 635). The Appellate Term reversed and dismissed the complaint, finding that no bailment had been created (Ellish v. Airport Parking Co. of Amer., 69 Misc.2d 837, 331 N.Y.S.2d 283). By permission of the Appellate Term the plaintiff appeals.

We affirm the order of Appellate Term. Under the circumstances of this case we do not find the defendant liable for the plaintiff's loss.

The case was submitted to the Civil Court under an agreed statement of facts.... Briefly stated, the parties stipulated that the plaintiff drove into the parking lot at the airport, receiving from an automatic vending machine a ticket stamped with the date and time of entry. On one side the ticket was labelled "License to Park" and stated that the lot provided self-service parking; it warned the holder that the lot was not attended and that the car should be locked. On the other side the ticket contained the words in smaller print: "This contract licenses the holder to park one automobile in this area at holder's risk." Further, it provided that the defendant was not responsible for the theft of the automobile.

Upon the plaintiff's receipt of the ticket, a gate opened, permitting the entry of the automobile into the lot. The plaintiff drove the automobile into a parking space, locked it and took the keys with her. Under the practice of the defendant, on leaving the lot, the holder of the ticket would drive to the point of exit, present the ticket to a cashier and pay the amount due based on the time elapsed. If the driver did not have a ticket, the cashier would demand proof of ownership of the automobile. The defendant employed personnel to maintain the lot and to check automobiles left overnight in order to make certain that the cashiers collected proper fees. The lot was patrolled by Port of New York Authority police, in the same manner as the airport.

Since the parties stipulated that neither had any knowledge concerning the disappearance of the automobile from the parking lot, the plaintiff could succeed in the action only by the existence of a duty on the part of the defendant to account for the loss of the automobile while standing in the lot. At common law when a chattel was placed by the owner in the possession of another under an agreement by the latter to deliver it on demand, a convenient short hand expression of a duty cast on the bailee was found by establishing a presumption of negligence if the bailee did not come forward with a satisfactory explanation to rebut the presumption ..., though the burden of proof on the whole case remained on the owner ... The rule thus reflected the judgment that the party last in possession of the chattel was better able to account for its loss.

A bailment is, of course, merely a special kind of contract; it describes a result which in many instances does not flow from the conscious promises of the parties made in a bargaining process but from what the law regards as a fair approximation of their expectations.... Hence, in formulating a rule to determine the extent of the liability of the defendant, we must concern ourselves with the realities of the transaction in which the parties engaged. The nature of the circumstances themselves leads to the determination whether the transaction should be considered a bailment, in which event the defendant is liable to the plaintiff, or whether the transaction should be considered a license to occupy space, in which event the defendant is not liable to the plaintiff.

Parking lots generally accommodate the free use of automobiles in urban areas. Automobiles are so much a part of urban life that it is necessary for both municipalities and private operators to make space available for parking. The parking lots scarcely resemble the traditional warehouses of the professional bailee with their stress on security and safekeeping. Rather, they are designed to meet the need of providing temporary space in crowded urban centers for a highly mobile means of transportation. In the case before us, the parking lot at the airport was designed to facilitate the passage of patrons of airlines by private automobiles to the point of their departure and arrival. As the use of air transportation is a major interest in our social and economic life, it is important that a fair rule, easy to apply, should govern the relationship of the parties to the transaction.

Against this general background we think these considerations are paramount:

1.   The service provided by the defendant to the plaintiff was clearly a space for her automobile to stand while she was away on her trip. That space was located in a lot where many other automobiles were similarly standing and to which the operators of the automobiles and others were given access. The plaintiff was not treated differently from the other automobile operators; nor was she led to believe that the lot would not be open to others.

2.   The service provided by the defendant was impersonal. The plaintiff was aware that the defendant had no employees either to deliver the ticket for the automobile or to park the automobile. She accepted the ticket from an automatic dispensing device and she parked the car herself, choosing her own space, not at the direction of the defendant.

3.   The plaintiff retained as much control as possible over the automobile. She locked the car and kept the keys. She did not expect or desire the defendant to move the automobile in her absence.

4.   The plaintiff followed the directions contained in the ticket she received. In her favor, we think that the plaintiff should not be closely bound by the terms of the ticket, for plainly it was a contract of adhesion. The plaintiff was hardly in a position to bargain over the conditions of the ticket and, indeed, the condition of nonliability for theft sought to be imposed by the defendant is unenforceable under the public policy of our statute (General Obligations Law, § 5–325). Nevertheless, it is still the fact that the plaintiff heeded the warning of the ticket to lock her automobile.

5.   We can draw the reasonable inference from the agreed statement of facts ... that, since the plaintiff followed the directions in the ticket, she read the other warnings which it contained to the effect that the lot was not attended and that the parking of her car was at her own risk. Thus, any expectation that the defendant would take special precautions to protect her car while she was away could not reasonably have been in her mind.

6. The actual operation of an airport parking lot must have been apparent to her. Thousands of automobiles were constantly entering and leaving the airport, many of which were using the parking lot that her car occupied. The plaintiff, seeing the confusion and bustle, should have realized the gigantic task which an individual check-out of each automobile would require—a task which she was aware the defendant did not undertake, since the ticket which she received did not identify her automobile.

In the absence of any proof of neglect by the defendant, then, we do not think that the defendant should be held responsible for the loss of the automobile. Other courts considering parking lots at airports have concluded as we do....

We do not find Dunham v. City of New York, 264 App.Div. 732, 34 N.Y.S.2d 289, in which we allowed recovery for the loss of an automobile parked in a lot at the World's Fair held in 1939, a precedent requiring us to hold for the plaintiff here. In Dunham, though the motorist locked his car after parking it and retained the keys, an attendant gave a ticket to the motorist before parking and directed him to the space to be occupied, thereby giving the appearance of the acceptance of custody for the car. Here, instead, the defendant by its procedures of impersonal parking disclaimed any appearance of custody.

We are of the opinion that liability should not be determined by ancient labels and characteristics not connected with present-day practices. It is one thing for the owner of a livery stable to have to explain the disappearance of a horse from its stall to the owner, but it is not at all the same for the operator of a parking lot at a busy airport to have to explain the disappearance from the lot of one of the thousands of cars parked there daily. Unless proof of negligence is present on the part of the operator of the lot, the risk of loss must be assumed by the owner of the automobile.

We therefore should affirm the order of the Appellate Term, without costs.

SHAPIRO, JUSTICE (dissenting).

My learned brother, Mr. Justice Hopkins, has aptly stated the question here to be determined when he says: "The nature of the circumstances themselves leads to the determination whether the transaction should be considered a bailment, in which event the defendant is liable to the plaintiff, or whether the transaction should be considered a license to occupy space, in which event the defendant is not liable to the plaintiff." He concludes that "the realities of the transaction in which the parties engaged" establish that when the plaintiff placed her automobile in the defendant's enclosed parking lot (from which she was not free to remove it without paying the accrued parking charges) she merely obtained "a license to occupy space". I cannot subscribe to that view.

We start with the undisputed fact that the plaintiff was a captive customer of the defendant. There was no public street on which she could park her car; nor did she have a choice of parking facilities. If she was to come to the airport by automobile—which she had a right to do and the doing of which was encouraged by the defendant's operation of a commercial parking lot there—she had no choice of accommodations. She could not pick out a parking lot in which the operator would take her keys and park her car. It was the defendant's lot or none at all. Under such circumstances and considering the fact that the plaintiff was not free to leave with her automobile until she had first paid the charges due thereon, it seems to me that "the realities of the transaction in which the parties engaged" clearly show a sufficient retention of control by the defendant over the plaintiff's car to make the defendant liable for the loss in the absence of the defendant's giving any explanation for the loss.

Although the majority recognizes that "the condition of nonliability for theft sought to be imposed by the defendant (by virtue of the terms of the ticket-receipt which the plaintiff received from the automatic machine) is unenforceable under the public policy of our statute (General Obligations Law, § 5–325)," it nevertheless draws the inferences, improperly I believe, "that the plaintiff heeded the warning of the ticket to lock her automobile" and that, since the plaintiff followed that direction on the ticket, she must have "read the other warnings which it contained to the effect that the lot was not attended and that the parking of her car was at her own risk" and that therefore "any expectation that the defendant would take special precautions to protect her car while she was away could not reasonably have been in her mind." But those successive assumptions, heaped upon one another, proceed on the theory that the plaintiff, and others like her, approached this parking lot with *tabula rasa*—that she knew what to do only from reading the instructions on the ticket. That assumption, in my opinion, lacks validity. Every driver these days is familiar with parking lot procedures and does not have to examine a ticket (with printing usually too small to be readily readable) to know what to do when he enters a self-service parking lot. Every driver knows that airport parking lots are fenced in and attended at all times because he knows that he must pay the full parking fee due when he comes to retrieve his car. The lot operator's retention of the right to payment when the car owner comes for his car, it seems to me, carries with it a concomitant representation that the car will be there at that time, since, at least to that extent, the parking lot operator has retained control over the car. Such awareness by a patron of his obligation to pay when he returns for his car is inconsistent with any implication of acceptance by him of the risk of an unexplained disappearance of the car from the lot.

Neither do we believe that the plaintiff's observations of the confusion and bustle which unfortunately characterize the operations of our huge airports at heavy-use periods should have led her to realize that the parking lot operator owed her no duty of seeking to ascertain that the check she had received when entering the parking lot with her car was the same check presented by the person leaving the lot with her car. Would not the patron have reason to believe, from the fact that the lot was fenced in and its exit gate manned throughout the day and night, that his car was safer there than on the streets or in an unmanned, unpatrolled and unfenced lot and that the lot operator was accepting supervision and control, though limited in degree, of his car?

To buttress its conclusion that the defendant should not "be held responsible for the loss of the automobile," the majority says that other courts considering parking lots at airports have concluded as the majority does (Wall v. Airport Parking Co. of Chicago, 41 Ill.2d 506, 244 N.E.2d 190; St. Paul Fire & Marine Ins. Co. v. Zurich Ins. Co., 250 So.2d 451 (La.App.); Equity Mut. Ins. Co. v. Affiliated Parking, 448 S.W.2d 909 (Mo.App.)). However, these three cases are not at all persuasive. All three use as their keystone the outworn limitation of the law of bailment. Wall v. Airport Parking Co. of Chicago (supra) follows the reasoning of Greene Steel & Wire Co. v. Meyers Bros. Operations, 44 Misc.2d 646, 254 N.Y.S.2d 299 (App.Term, 1st Dept.) although the Greene case did not deal with the loss of an automobile, but with damage to it.[1] In the St. Paul case the court based its decision on the ground that in Louisiana the self-service long-term airport parking lot from which the car was stolen was an exception to the general rule that parking lots are treated as compensated depositories against which negligence need not be proved in cases of vehicle loss or theft, because its operation was so "restricted and structured so as to make it *clear* that the patron-motorist merely leases parking space rather than making a deposit of his car" (250 So.2d p. 453). In the Equity Mutual case the rejection of the plaintiff's claim was based on the erroneous premise that it could recover only if there was "such delivery to the bailee as would entitle him to exclude the possession of anyone else, even the owner, for the period of the bailment" (448 S.W.2d p. 914).

Parking lots where the operators retained dominion over any cars parked in the lots until the cars were returned to their owners have traditionally been held to be liable for loss or damage unless the owners rebutted the presumption of negligence by showing reasonable care. Modern technology has allowed parking lot operators at airports to dispense with attendants at the entrances of the lots who insured that the

---

1. There are a number of appellate decisions dealing with the problem of the liability of parking lot operators for loss of cars left with them (Galowitz v. Magner, 208 App.Div. 6, 203 N.Y.S. 421; Chamberlain v. Station Parking Serv., 251 App.Div. 825, 297 N.Y.S. 694; Dunham v. City of New York, 264 App.Div. 732, 34 N.Y.S.2d 289; Greene Steel & Wire Co. v. Meyers Bros. Operations, 44 Misc.2d 646, 254 N.Y.S.2d 299 (App.Term, 1st Dept.)). The only one which is directly in point is our decision in Dunham, which the majority attempts to distinguish on the factual ground that in Dunham, though the motorist locked his car after parking it and retained the keys, his ticket-receipt was given to him on entrance by an attendant instead of by a machine and the attendant directed the motorist to the space to be occupied. But this difference in no way lessens the essential impersonal nature of the procedure used by the parking lot operator in allocating space for the car; nor does it do away with the fact that the motorist, by locking the car and keeping the keys, retains exactly the same form of partial control of his car as if he himself chose the vacant spot in which to leave his car and received his ticket-receipt from a ticket-dispensing machine. Thus, if anything, Dunham, which is the only appellate case dealing with the theft of an automobile from an airport parking lot, squarely supports the appellant's position.

license numbers and makes of the cars were recorded on the receipts so as to help insure that the holders of the receipts were in fact the owners of the cars when they were taken out of the lots. This cutting of costs of operation, while retaining sufficient dominion of the cars parked in their lots by means of fencing and manned exit gates to insure payment of the fees due as a condition of releasing parked cars to their owners, has caused the operators to seek to avoid liability for loss or damage by claiming that their more automatic method of operation eliminates the presumption of negligence in case of loss they formerly had to rebut. In our view, the shift to lessened personal contact between the lot operator's employees and his patrons in no way changes the basic nature of the relationship between the lot operator and his patrons so long as he retains dominion over the cars parked in his lot and can withhold their return until he is paid the full fee due for the parking. It would be ironic if the operator's use of additional cost-saving devices were read as lessening his responsibility to use due care in protecting cars parked with him from damage or theft. If he fences in the lot, mans its exits at all hours so that his employees control every removal of cars from the lot, and patrols the lot nightly to record all cars left overnight, he is clearly responsible to exercise a reasonable effort to use his facilities to prevent or at least minimize theft of cars from the lot. And if a theft does occur he must rebut the presumption of negligence that arises therefrom by showing that he used reasonable care to avoid thefts.

Airport long-term parking lots are not public streets or open parking areas. Patrons who must use such lots are made aware of this by the fact that the lots are fenced in and their exits are guarded at all times. Such patrons expect the use of due care by the operator to prevent removal of their cars without the receipts given them by the lot operator (by a machine), the more so because they have no choice but to use the lot and pay the fee imposed. If they find their cars gone when they return, they should be able to recover for the loss unless the operator can show that the loss occurred despite his exercise of due care. Such a result is in accord with both public policy and with the public interest in facilitating air travel.

For the foregoing reasons the order of the Appellate Term should be reversed and the judgment of the Civil Court in favor of the plaintiff should be reinstated.

NOTES AND QUESTIONS

1. Precisely what benefit would inure to plaintiff if the transaction had been characterized as a bailment rather than a license? Should the liability of the defendant depend upon the characterization of the relationship between the defendant and the plaintiff?

2. In Samples v. Geary, 292 S.W. 1066 (Mo. Ct. App.1927), the bailor had deposited a coat in the bailee's checkroom. The bailor's fur piece was concealed in the coat. When the coat was returned, the fur piece was missing.

The court held that the bailee was not liable for the missing fur piece. See also Ziva Jewelry, Inc. v. Car Wash Headquarters, Inc., 897 So.2d 1011 (Ala. 2004) (car wash to whom car bailed not liable for over $800,000 of jewelry in trunk of car lost when bailed car was stolen by a thief). By contrast, in Insurance Co. of North America v. Solari Parking, Inc., 370 So.2d 503 (La.1979) plaintiff parked his car in a parking garage located in a tourist area of New Orleans. The back seat and the trunk were packed with plaintiff's clothing. The court held that the bailee-parking lot was liable not only for the stolen car, but also the contents in both the back seat and the trunk. To what extent are these two cases reconcilable?

3. In Peet v. Roth Hotel Co., 191 Minn. 151, 253 N.W. 546 (1934), a woman brought a valuable diamond ring to the hotel for delivery to one of the hotel guests. The hotel's clerk took the ring from the woman and placed it in an envelope marked with the name of the guest. Shortly thereafter, the envelope with the ring was stolen. In the woman's action to recover the value of the ring, the hotel defended by claiming no bailment contract was formed because the woman failed to disclose the high value of the ring to the hotel clerk. The court rejected that argument, placing the risk of mistake of value on the bailee. Do you agree? How might a bailee protect herself in these circumstances?

4. A, an electrician, brought his car to B's garage to have B test the car to determine whether it complied with the state's motor vehicle inspection laws. While the car was at B's garage, it was stolen. A's insurance carrier reimbursed A for the value of the car. However, it did not reimburse A for the value of his tools which were in the trunk of the car because the insurance policy did not purport to insure contents. Therefore, A sued B to recover the value of the tools. What result? Compare Gilchrist v. Winmar J. Ford, Inc., 77 Misc. 2d 847, 355 N.Y.S.2d 261 (Dist. Ct.1974) with Swarth v. Barney's Clothes, Inc., 40 Misc. 2d 423, 242 N.Y.S.2d 922 (App. Term 1963). Should the reason A brought his car to B affect whether B should be liable for items concealed in the car?

5. Suppose A bails his car in a hotel parking lot. He takes his suitcase into the hotel for the night. However, A leaves his daughter's fully packed suitcase in the trunk of the car. A is taking that suitcase to his daughter who lives in a dormitory at State U. During the night, A's car is stolen. A sues the hotel to recover the value of the car, the suitcase, and its contents. You represent the hotel. What defenses might you raise and how successful do you think you will be? See Traylor v. Hyatt Corporation, 122 Ga. App. 633, 178 S.E.2d 289 (1970).

6. Negligent bailees have attempted to limit their liability to bailors in one of two ways. First, bailees have attempted to include within the contract of bailment a provision that bailors waive all rights to sue bailees for their negligence. In other words, bailees disclaim any liability for their own negligence. Second, bailees have attempted to limit the amount of their liability to a specific dollar amount. There are a number of variations on this second alternative, including, for example, limiting liability to a specific dollar amount unless the bailor declares the goods to have a higher value and possibly charging a higher rate if a higher value is declared. Attempts to limit

or eliminate liability may be done by the posting of signs (not always conspicuously) or the inclusion of a limitation of liability on some claim check or other written evidence of the bailment contract.

The predominant American view is that a provision that attempts to waive or limit the bailee's liability is void if the bailor is unaware of the provision. Nonetheless, many courts have held that even though the bailor is aware of the bailee's attempt to limit its liability in negligence, such a provision is void on public policy grounds. The provision is void because of the view that it is inappropriate for a person to exempt himself from liability for his own negligence. On the other hand, some courts uphold clauses that merely limit liability to a specific sum but do not disclaim all liability. Is there a point where a limitation of liability to a specific amount is the same as a disclaimer of liability?

The Restatement (Second) of Contracts § 195 (1979) would support the notion that a bailee could limit its liability to a specific dollar amount or could disclaim its liability unless the harm was caused "intentionally or recklessly."

Suppose the bailor and bailee enter into an agreement that if the goods are lost or damaged, the bailee will be liable to the bailor even if the bailee was not negligent. Would such a provision be valid? Assuming the provision is valid, why would a bailee agree to be liable for lost or damaged goods where neither the loss nor damage results from the bailee's negligence?

7. A bailee's liability may also be limited by statute or treaty. For example, under the terms of the Warsaw Convention, an airline's liability for loss of baggage on an international flight is limited to $640.

8. In Allen v. Hyatt Regency–Nashville Hotel, 668 S.W.2d 286 (Tenn. 1984), the court found a bailment under the following facts:

Appellant is the owner and operator of a modern high-rise hotel in Nashville fronting on the south side of Union Street. Immediately to the rear, or south, of the main hotel building there is a multi-story parking garage with a single entrance and a single exit to the west, on Seventh Avenue, North. As one enters the parking garage at the street level, there is a large sign reading "Welcome to Hyatt Regency–Nashville." There is another Hyatt Regency sign inside the garage at street level, together with a sign marked "Parking." The garage is available for parking by members of the general public as well as guests of the hotel, and the public are invited to utilize it.

On the morning of February 12, 1981, appellee's husband, Edwin Allen, accompanied by two passengers, drove appellee's new 1981 automobile into the parking garage. Neither Mr. Allen nor his passengers intended to register at the hotel as a guest. Mr. Allen had parked in this particular garage on several occasions, however, testifying that he felt that the vehicle would be safer in an attended garage than in an unattended outside lot on the street. The single entrance was controlled by a ticket machine. The single exit was controlled by an attendant in a booth just opposite to the entrance and in full view thereof. Appellee's husband entered the garage at the street level and took a ticket which was automatically dispensed by the machine. The machine activated a barrier gate which rose and permitted Mr. Allen to enter the garage. He drove to the fourth floor level, parked the vehicle, locked it, retained the ignition key, descended by elevator to the street level and left the garage. When he returned several hours later, the car was gone, and it has never been recovered. Mr. Allen reported the theft to the attendant at the exit booth, who stated, "Well, it didn't come out here." The attendant did not testify at the trial.

Mr. Allen then reported the theft to security personnel employed by appellant, and subsequently reported the loss to the police. Appellant regularly employed a number of security guards, who were dressed in a distinctive uniform, two of whom were on duty most of the time. These guards patrolled the hotel grounds and building as well as the garage and were instructed to make rounds through the garage, although not necessarily at specified intervals.

Id. at 287.

Do you agree that a bailment was created? Would the *Ellish* court agree?

9. O parked her automobile on B's property without B's permission. B called the local police to have O's car towed off of B's property, which the police did in conformity with a local ordinance. The car was taken by the towing company to its enclosed lot where it was vandalized in the middle of the night. O seeks damages from the towing company, claiming it was a bailee who acted negligently. Do you agree the towing company was a bailee? If it was a bailee, are there sufficient facts to conclude it acted negligently? See Hadfield v. Gilchrist, 343 S.C. 88, 538 S.E.2d 268 (Ct. App. 2000).

CHAPTER 3

POSSESSION LEADING TO TITLE: ADVERSE POSSESSION

■ ■ ■

§ 3.1 RIGHTS OF POSSESSOR OF LAND

Suppose A enters into possession of O's land without having title to that land. To what extent does A's possession give A rights in the land against persons other than O?

TAPSCOTT v. COBBS

Court of Appeals of Virginia (1854).
52 Va. (11 Grat.) 172.

[Action brought on behalf of Mrs. Cobbs against Tapscott to recover the possession of certain lands originally owned by Thomas Anderson who died in 1800. Under the terms of Anderson's will his executors were authorized to sell the land.

Sometime between 1820 and 1825, the executors of Anderson's estate agreed to sell the land to Sarah Lewis. She entered upon the land, improved it, and remained in possession until her death in 1835.

It also appeared that the executors of Anderson's estate sold the land to Robert Rives. Apparently neither Rives nor Lewis paid for the land, although under the terms of a separate purchase agreement between them relating to other lands, Rives agreed to pay the purchase price for Lewis.

Mrs. Cobbs was the heir of Mrs. Lewis. No evidence was submitted to show that Mrs. Cobbs or anyone claiming under her took possession of the land after Mrs. Lewis' death.

Tapscott entered into possession of the land in 1842 without any claim or color of title.]

DANIEL, J. It is no doubt true, as a general rule, that the right of a plaintiff in ejectment to recover, rests on the strength of his own title, and is not established by the exhibition of defects in the title of the defendant, and that the defendant may maintain his defense by simply showing that the title is not in the plaintiff, but in some one else. And the rule is

196

usually thus broadly stated by the authorities, without qualification. There are, however, exceptions to the rule as thus announced, as well established as the rule itself. As when the defendant has entered under the title of the plaintiff he cannot set up a title in a third person in contradiction to that under which he entered. Other instances might be cited in which it is equally as well settled that the defendant would be estopped from showing defects in the title of the plaintiff. In such cases, the plaintiff may, and often does recover, not by the exhibition of a title good in itself, but by showing that the relations between himself and the defendant are such that the latter cannot question it. The relation between the parties stands in the place of title; and though the title of the plaintiff is tainted with vices or defects that would prove fatal to his recovery in a controversy with any other defendant in peaceable possession, it is yet all sufficient in a litigation with one who entered into the possession under it, or otherwise stands so related to it that the law will not allow him to plead its defects in his defense.

Whether the case of an intrusion by a stranger without title, on a peaceable possession, is not one to meet the exigencies of which the courts will recognize a still further qualification or explanation of the rule requiring the plaintiff to recover only on the strength of his own title, is a question which, I believe, has not as yet been decided by this court. And it is somewhat remarkable that there are but few cases to be found in the English reporters in which the precise question has been decided or considered by the courts.

The cases of Read & Morpeth v. Erington, Croke Eliz. 321; Bateman v. Allen, Ibid. 437; and Allen v. Rivington, 2 Saund. R. 111, were each decided on special verdicts, in which the facts with respect to the title were stated. In each case it was shown that the plaintiff was in possession, and that the defendant entered without title or authority; and the court held that it was not necessary to decide upon the title of the plaintiff, and gave judgment for him. In the report of Bateman v. Allen it is said that Williams Sergeant moved, "that for as much as in all the verdict it is not found that the defendant had the *primer* possession, nor that he entered in the right or by the command of any who had title, but that he entered on the possession of the plaintiff without title, his entry is not lawful;" and so the court held.

And in Read & Morpeth v. Erington, it was insisted that for a portion of the premises the judgment ought to be for the defendant, in as much as it appeared from the verdict that the title to such portion was outstanding in a third party; but the court said it did not matter, as it was shown that the plaintiff had entered, and the defendant had entered on him.

I have seen no case overruling these decisions. It is true that in Haldane v. Harvey, 4 Burr. R. 2484, the general doctrine is announced that the plaintiff must recover on the strength of his own title; and that the "possession gives the defendant a right against every man who cannot show a good title." But in that case the circumstances under which the defendant entered, and the nature of the claim by which he held, do not appear; and the case, therefore, cannot properly be regarded as declaring more than the general rule.

* * *

... In this country the cases are numerous, and to some extent conflicting.... I have found no case in which the question seems to have been more fully examined or maturely considered than in Sowder, & c. v. McMillan's heirs, 4 Dana's R. 456. The views of the learned judge (Marshall) who delivered the opinion in which the whole court concurred, are rested on the authority of several cases in Kentucky, previously decided, on a series of decisions made by the Supreme court of New York, and on the three British cases of Bateman v. Allen, Allen v. Rivington, and Read & Morpeth v. Erington, before mentioned. "These three cases (he says) establish unquestionably the right of the plaintiff to recover when it appears that he was in possession, and that the defendant entered upon and ousted his possession, without title or authority to enter; and prove that when the possession of the plaintiff and an entry upon it by the defendant are shown, the right of recovery cannot be resisted by showing that there is or may be an outstanding title in another; but only by showing that the defendant himself either has title or authority to enter under the title."

"It is a natural principle of justice, that he who is in possession has the right to maintain it, and if wrongfully expelled, to regain it by entry on the wrongdoer. When titles are acknowledged as separate and distinct from the possession, this right of maintaining and regaining the possession is, of course, subject to the exception that it cannot be exercised against the real owner, in competition with whose title it wholly fails. But surely it is not accordance with the principles of justice, that he who ousts a previous possession, should be permitted to defend his wrongful possession against the claim of restitution merely by showing that a stranger, and not the previous possessor whom he has ousted, was entitled to the possession. The law protects a peaceable possession against all except him who has the actual right to the possession, and no other can rightfully disturb or intrude upon it. While the peaceable possession continues, it is protected against a claimant in the action of ejectment, by permitting the defendant to show that a third person and not the claimant has the right. But if the claimant, instead of resorting to his action, attempt to gain the possession by entering upon and ousting the existing peaceable possession, he does not thereby acquire a rightful or a peaceable possession. The law does not protect him against the prior possessor. Neither does it indulge any presumption in his favor, nor permit him to gain any advantage by his own wrongful act."

* * *

To the same effect are the decisions in New Jersey, Connecticut, Vermont and Ohio....

In Delaware, North Carolina, South Carolina, Indiana, and perhaps in other states of the Union, the opposite doctrine has been held.

In this state of the law, untrammeled as we are by any decisions of our own courts, I feel free to adopt that rule which seems to me best calculated to attain the ends of justice. The explanation of the law (as usually announced) given by Judge Marshall in the portions of his opinion which I have cited, seems to me to be founded on just and correct reasoning; and I am disposed to follow those decisions which uphold a peaceable possession for the protection as well of a plaintiff as of a defendant in ejectment, rather than those which invite disorderly scrambles for the possession, and clothe a mere trespasser with the means of maintaining his wrong, by showing defects, however slight, in the title of him on whose peaceable possession he has intruded without shadow of authority or title.

The authorities in support of the maintenance of ejectment upon the force of a mere prior possession, however, hold it essential that the prior possession must have been removed by the entry or intrusion of the defendant; and that the entry under which the defendant holds the possession must have been a trespass upon the prior possession. Sowder v. McMillan's heirs, 4 Dana's R. 456. And it is also said that constructive possession is not sufficient to maintain trespass to real property; that actual possession is required, and hence that where the injury is done to an heir or devisee by an abator, before he has entered, he cannot maintain trespass until his re-entry. 2 Tucker's Comm. 191. An apparent difficulty, therefore, in the way of a recovery by the plaintiffs, arises from the absence of *positive* proof of their possession at the time of the defendant's entry. It is to be observed, however, that there is no proof to the contrary. Mrs. Lewis died in possession of the premises, and there is no proof that they were vacant at the time of the defendant's entry. And in Gilbert's Tenures 37, (in note,) it is stated, as the law, that as the heir has the right to the hereditaments descending, the law presumes that he has the possession also. The presumption may indeed, like all other presumptions, be rebutted: but if the possession be not shown to be in another, the law concludes it to be in the heir.

The presumption is but a fair and reasonable one; and does, I think, arise here; and as the only evidence tending to show that the defendant sets up any pretense of right to the land, is the certificate of the surveyor of Buckingham, of an entry by the defendant, for the same, in his office, in December 1844; and his possession of the land must, according to the evidence, have commenced at least as early as some time in the year 1842; it seems to me that he must be regarded as standing in the attitude of a mere intruder on the possession of the plaintiffs.

Whether we might not in this case presume the whole of the purchase money to be paid, and regard the plaintiffs as having a perfect equitable title to the premises, and in that view as entitled to recover by force of such title; or whether we might not resort to the still further presumption in their favor, of a conveyance of the legal title, are questions which I have not thought it necessary to consider; the view, which I have already taken of the case, being sufficient, in my opinion, to justify us in affirming the judgment.

Judgment affirmed.

NOTES AND QUESTIONS

1. The *Tapscott* court applies the principle that a prior peaceful possessor prevails over a subsequent possessor. (Have you seen this principle applied in other contexts?) In reading the facts, it appears, however, that the plaintiff offered no "positive proof" of her prior peaceful possession at the time of the defendant's entry. Nonetheless, the court presumes she was in prior peaceful possession. Why does the court engage in that presumption? Is the court trying to accomplish more than merely applying the principle that a prior peaceful possessor prevails over a subsequent possessor? In considering these questions, might the fact that Mrs. Lewis died be important?

2. Suppose O owns Blackacre, and A forcibly evicts O from the property. B, who has no connection with O, subsequently sues A for possession of Blackacre. Does B prevail because A did not enter Blackacre peaceably?

3. To what extent is the rule of Tapscott v. Cobbs consistent with the previously considered rule that a defendant cannot defeat an action for possession by a prior possessor by showing a better title in a third person?

4. The *Tapscott* court states that "[i]t is no doubt true, as a general rule, that the right of a plaintiff to recover, rests on the strength of his own title, and is not established by the exhibition of defects in the title of the defendant, and the defendant may maintain his defense by simply showing that the title is not in the plaintiff but in some one else." Is the holding of the case consistent with this view, or does the court create an exception to it?

5. A person who enters land under "color of title" enters under apparent authority evidenced by a document that, for one reason or another, is defective. Should the rule of Tapscott v. Cobbs apply where the *subsequent* possessor enters in good faith and under color of title? See Vick v. Georgia Power Co., 178 Ga. 869, 174 S.E. 713 (1934).

6. Ordinarily for a plaintiff to establish a good paper title to real property, the plaintiff must show an unbroken chain of title to the so-called "root of title." To illustrate, suppose the root of title with respect to certain lands called "Blackacre" began with a United States grant of Blackacre to A in consideration for A's services to his country during the War of 1812. Subsequently, A deeded all of his rights in Blackacre to B, who in turn deeded all his rights to C, who in turn deeded all his right to D, and so forth. Ultimately, Z deeds Blackacre to plaintiff. If the parties to the prior deeds were dead, or for any other reason were unavailable to testify in court to the fact that they deeded their interest in Blackacre, plaintiff might establish his title against someone claiming a superior title by introducing the prior deeds into evidence. The ability to introduce the prior deeds into evidence, however, might depend upon whether they had been properly recorded. See generally

chapter 16, infra. If the deeds were not properly recorded and other evidence of ownership is unavailable, plaintiff might have a difficult time in proving title. How does the rule of Tapscott v. Cobbs aid a true owner in establishing a right to ejectment against a wrongful possessor?

7.   In Bradshaw v. Ashley, 180 U.S. 59 (1901), plaintiff, a prior possessor, sued to recover the possession of real property located in Washington, D.C. from a subsequent possessor who without claim or color of title had ousted plaintiff from possession. Plaintiff was unable to establish good paper title. In upholding plaintiff's claim, the Court stated:

> Generally speaking, the presumption is that the person in possession is the owner in fee. If there be no evidence to the contrary, proof of possession, at least under a color of right, is sufficient proof of title. Therefore, when in an action of ejectment the plaintiff proves that on the day named he was in the actual, undisturbed and quiet possession of the premises, and the defendant thereupon entered and ousted him, the plaintiff has proved a *prima facie* case, the presumption of title arises from the possession, and unless the defendant prove a better title, he must himself be ousted. Although he proves that some third person, with whom he in no manner connects himself, has title, this does him no good, because the prior possession of the plaintiff was sufficient to authorize him to maintain it as against a trespasser, and the defendant being himself without title, and not connecting himself with any title cannot justify an ouster of the plaintiff. This is only an explanation of the principle that the plaintiff recovers upon the strength of his own title. His title by possession is sufficient, and it is a title, so far as regards a defendant who only got into possession by a pure tort, a simple act of intrusion or trespass, with no color or pretense of title.

Id. at 63–64.

The court also observed that if defendant entered when the land was vacant and the plaintiff relies only on a constructive possession as evidence of a prior peaceful possession, plaintiff must also show that plaintiff had not abandoned the property. *[handwritten margin note: "# 8 f there was proof"]*

8.   In considering whether a prior possessor who is not the true owner can recover damages from a defendant for the wrongful taking of personal property, one concern has been the possibility that the defendant might have to pay double damages. Is that concern present in Tapscott v. Cobbs? Suppose that the plaintiff had brought an action for damages rather than for possession. Should the rule of Tapscott v. Cobbs apply?

In Winchester v. Stevens Point, 58 Wis. 350, 17 N.W. 3 (1883), the plaintiff brought an action against the defendant municipality for damages for permanent injury to the premises caused by flooding resulting from a dam built by the defendant. The plaintiff alleged that she was the owner of the property, but at trial, she could not prove a paper title because the rules of evidence would not permit her to introduce into the record certain deeds in her chain of title that had been improperly recorded in the local land records office. The court denied the plaintiff any recovery because she had alleged a good paper title but failed to prove it at the trial. (Plaintiff in Bradshaw v. Ashley, supra, apparently also attempted to prove a good paper title but failed). The court's opinion further suggests that even if plaintiff had relied merely on her prior possession, she would still have lost. The court likened the action to a condemnation proceeding in which "it is understood the plaintiff must show title, and that title will not be presumed from evidence of possession under claim of title." See chapter 10 (condemnation).

Is the *Winchester* court simply rejecting the application of the rule of Tapscott v. Cobbs in a suit for damages, or does likening the plaintiff's action to a condemnation proceeding suggest that something else may have motivated the court to reach the conclusion that it did given that the defendant was a governmental body?

9. O owned Blackacre. O died in 1994. Under the terms of O's will, O devised Blackacre to A for life, remainder to B. Under this devise, A is entitled to the possession of Blackacre for life. At A's death, B is entitled to the possession of Blackacre. Even though B's right to the possession of Blackacre is postponed until A's death, during A's life, B has a legally recognized property interest in Blackacre that can be judicially protected in an appropriate proceeding. For example, B might have the right to enjoin A from damaging Blackacre in any way that would destroy the future value of Blackacre to B. See generally chapter 4.

In 1998, T enters Blackacre and cuts timber. Assuming A's rights to the timber were worth $5 and B's rights were worth $10, if A sues T for the act of cutting timber, what amount, if any, can A recover from T? Compare Zimmerman v. Shreeve, 59 Md. 357 (1883) with Rogers v. Atlantic, Gulf & Pacific Co., 213 N.Y. 246, 107 N.E. 661 (1915). See also Restatement of Property § 118 (1936), providing that the life tenant can recover "the difference between the value of the estate for life before and its value after" the injury and cannot recover "damages . . . to the interests subsequent to such estate for life."

§ 3.2   INTRODUCTION TO THE LAW OF ADVERSE POSSESSION

All states have statutes limiting the time that a civil action can be brought by a plaintiff who seeks a judicial remedy to a perceived wrong. In most cases, the time period begins to run from the date the wrong occurs. In some cases, however, the time period may begin to run from the time the person entitled to bring the action discovers, or should have discovered, that she has been wronged.

A true owner of real property (ordinarily the person whose ownership is reflected by the public land records) may bring an action to recover its possession from any person who enters or takes possession of the property without the true owner's permission. The state where the real property is located will have a statute of limitations limiting the time period in which the true owner may sue to recover the possession of the real property. No uniform time period exists throughout the states. A number of eastern states provide for a twenty year period while the southern and midwestern states tend to have periods ranging between ten and fifteen years. In

California, the period is five years. Some states also shorten the period of time if the possessor entered under color of title or paid taxes on the property. Additionally, there are substantial differences in the complexity of the various statutes of limitations. For example, Ariz. Rev. Stat. Ann. § 12–526 (1982) provides that: "[a] person who has a cause of action for recovery of any lands . . . from a person having peaceable and adverse possession thereof . . . shall commence an action therefor within ten years after the cause of action accrues, and not afterward." By contrast, Mich. Comp. Laws Ann. § 600.5801 (West 1998) provides that:

> No person may bring . . . any action for the recovery or possession of . . . or make any entry upon any lands unless, after the claim or right to make the entry first accrued to himself or to someone through whom he claims, he commences the action or makes the entry within the periods of time prescribed by this section.
>
> (1) When the defendant claims title to the land in question by or through some deed made upon the sale of the premises by an executor, administrator, guardian or testamentary trustee; or by a sheriff or other proper ministerial officer under the order, judgment, process, or decree of a court or legal tribunal . . . within this state, or by a sheriff upon a mortgage foreclosure sale the period of limitation is 5 years.
>
> (2) When the defendant claims title under some deed made by an officer of this state or of the United States who is authorized to make deeds upon the sale of lands for taxes assessed and levied within this state the period of limitation is 10 years.
>
> (3) When the defendant claims title through a devise in any will, the period of limitation is 15 years after the probate of the will in this state.
>
> (4) In all other cases under this section, the period of limitation is 15 years.

The running of a statute of limitations on a cause of action to recover the possession of real property has a twofold effect. First, it extinguishes the true owner's cause of action.

Second, it effectively results in the possessor acquiring a better title to the property than anyone in the whole world. This occurs because the true owner can no longer sue to recover the possession of the property from the so-called adverse possessor. Alternatively, the adverse possessor can sue to recover the possession of the real property from anyone because, as against others in the world, the adverse possessor has the prior possession and, therefore, the best title. This effect of the running of the statute of limitations has prompted one commentator to observe:

> Title by adverse possession sounds, at first blush, like title by theft or robbery, a primitive method of acquiring land without paying for it. When the novice is told that by the weight of authority not even good faith is a requisite, the doctrine [of adverse possession] apparently

affords an anomalous instance of maturing a wrong into a right contrary to one of the most fundamental axioms of the law. Ballantine, Title By Adverse Possession, 32 Harv. L. Rev. 135 (1918).

Because of the extreme consequences to the true owner resulting from the running of the statute of limitations on an action to recover the possession of real property, the courts have developed five criteria which must be met in order for the possessor to successfully claim a title by adverse possession. Of course, questions as to whether the five criteria have been satisfied arise only if the true owner sues for possession after the period set forth in the statute of limitations runs from the date of the possessor's entry. If the true owner sues to recover possession before the statutory period has run, no question arises with respect to whether the possessor satisfied the criteria. Thus, the imposition of the criteria gives courts leeway to avoid the effects of the running of the statute of limitations in an appropriate case. The five criteria are that the possession must be (1) actual, (2) open and notorious, (3) exclusive, (4) continuous, and (5) hostile and under claim of right. Additional criteria may also be imposed in certain states. Can you find support for the five criteria in the statutes quoted above, or are they crafted wholly out of judicial cloth?

Two conflicting policies frequently are cited as justifying the doctrine of adverse possession. One policy seeks to punish the true owner for sitting on his rights too long. The other seeks to reward the possessor for using the land in a socially beneficial way. In addition to these views, which focus on the relative merits and demerits of the true owner and the possessor, there may be a greater societal interest favoring the doctrine of adverse possession as a method to quiet title to land where there are deficiencies or irregularities in the paper title as well as a policy interest in assuring that real property remains in the stream of commerce. An appreciation of these policies may help to explain facially irreconcilable decisions in this area. Do these policies suggest reasons why the courts have crafted the five criteria necessary to acquire a title by adverse possession?

Must it follow that upon a running of the statute of limitations and complete satisfaction of the five elements necessary to acquire a title by adverse possession, the adverse possessor acquires a good title even as against the true owner? For example, might a better rule be that the adverse possessor acquires merely a right to purchase the property from the true owner at its then fair market value? See, Merrill, Property Rules, Liability Rules, and Adverse Possession, 79 Nw. U. L. Rev. 1122 (1984).

§ 3.3   THE ACTUAL, OPEN, CONTINUOUS AND EXCLUSIVE REQUIREMENTS

JARVIS v. GILLESPIE

Supreme Court of Vermont (1991).
155 Vt. 633, 587 A.2d 981.

CHIEF JUSTICE ALLEN:

Defendant, grantee of a quitclaim deed from the Town of Waterville for a 1.2–acre parcel of land, contests the trial court's ruling that title to the parcel had previously passed from the Town of Waterville to plaintiff by way of adverse possession. We affirm.

The Town of Waterville acquired title to the parcel in 1935 from the administrator of the estate of the then owner. In 1932, the owner had mortgaged the parcel to the Town in order to receive public assistance. The Town provided support for the owner until his death, after which the administrator of the owner's estate deeded the parcel over to the Town.

In 1947, plaintiff purchased over 200 acres of land which surround the disputed parcel on three sides. The fourth side of the parcel is bounded by a road.

On May 7, 1986, the Town of Waterville, by quitclaim deed, conveyed the disputed parcel to defendant. Shortly thereafter, defendant went to the property and removed "No Trespassing" signs which plaintiff had posted on the property. Plaintiff replaced the signs and built a wooden fence on the property.

On February 24, 1988, plaintiff filed a declaratory judgment action to establish his ownership of the disputed parcel by way of adverse possession. . . . Defendant contested the action by denying plaintiff's claims and by asserting as an affirmative defense that plaintiff could not gain title . . . because lands given to a public use are exempted from adverse possession claims by 12 V.S.A. § 462.

The trial court found that at various times between the years 1947 and 1986 plaintiff had used the land for a variety of purposes, such as grazing cattle and horses, parking vehicles, as a staging area for a logging operation on surrounding property, and to store slab wood from a sawmill which was located on adjacent property. The court also found that during that period plaintiff, at various times, maintained a fence on the roadside boundary of the parcel, tapped maple trees on the parcel, planted trees on the parcel, cut Christmas trees and firewood from the parcel, posted "No Trespassing" signs on the parcel, and built a loading ramp on the parcel for the logging operation which remained in use to load and unload his tractor after the logging operation ceased. The court found that these uses were clearly visible from the road which abutted the parcel. Further, the court found that plaintiff was the only person to make use of the property for any reason during the period and that neither the Town of Waterville nor the public made any use of the parcel during that time.[1]

From these facts, the court concluded that plaintiff had established title to the property by adverse possession. The court further concluded that the exemption provided in 12 V.S.A. § 462 did not apply in this instance because the property was not given to a public use. Defendant then brought this appeal. . . .

Defendant . . . contends that the trial court erred in finding that plaintiff had established all the elements necessary to gain title to the parcel by adverse possession. One acquires title by adverse possession through " 'open, notorious, hostile and continuous' possession of another's property for a period of fifteen years." Moran v. Byrne, 149 Vt. 353, 355, 543 A.2d 262, 263 (1988) (quoting Laird Properties New England Land Syndicate v. Mad River Corp., 131 Vt. 268, 277, 305 A.2d 562, 567 (1973)). The claimant has the burden of establishing all of these elements. Laird, 131 Vt. at 279, 305 A.2d at 569.

Defendant argues that except for the logging operation in 1971 and 1972 and storing the slab wood in 1983 and 1984, none of plaintiff's uses of the parcel constituted sufficient possession to establish adverse possession. Defendant relies on case law asserting that certain acts, such as tapping trees or cutting timber, by themselves are insufficient to establish possession. See Caskey v. Lewis, 54 Ky. (15 B. Mon.) 27, 32 (1854) (occasional use for sugaring and cutting timber and firewood did not constitute possession); Adams v. Robinson, 6 Pa. 271, 272 (1847) (annual use of land as a sugar camp constituted a succession of trespasses rather than occupancy). Such a general proposition, however, is not conclusive of the particular controversy before us. "The ultimate fact to be proved in an adverse possession case is that the claimant has acted toward the land in question as would an average owner, taking properly into account the geophysical nature of the land." 7 R. Powell, The Law of Real Property ¶ 1013[2][h], at 91–62 (1990); see Laird, 131 Vt. at 280, 305 A. 2d at 569 (acts needed to give rise to constructive possession must be consistent with the nature of the property). Thus, although certain of the acts of possession taken by a claimant may not be sufficient to establish posses-

---

1. The pertinent findings read: 17. Between the years 1951 and 1961, Plaintiff tapped several maple trees on the disputed parcel in connection with his sugaring operation. The tapping of the maple trees was visible to the public in the early spring of each of those years. 19. In the late 1940s, Plaintiff planted twenty-five to thirty trees on the disputed parcel. 20. From the mid 1950s until 1972, Plaintiff used the disputed parcel to cut Christmas trees and firewood, to load logs, to drive his tractor on and off, and to park his vehicles. He also constructed a loading ramp on the parcel. 21. Plaintiff utilized the premises each and every year from the mid 1950s to 1972 for one of the uses noted above. [T]he Plaintiff's use of the parcel was visible to the public. 22. In 1972 and 1973, the disputed parcel was used as a staging area for a logging operation. This logging operation was not conducted personally by Plaintiff but was undertaken by a person hired by Plaintiff. 23. From 1974 through 1982, Plaintiff cut firewood from the logs left on the land by the men conducting the logging operation, parked his vehicles on the disputed parcel, used the loading ramp for loading and unloading his tractor while working in the woods and continued to act and consider the disputed parcel to be his own. 30. At all times during the period from 1947 to 1986, Plaintiff was the exclusive person to utilize the disputed parcel. Plaintiff used the disputed parcel consistent with a rural and agricultural purpose, which was seasonal in nature. [This note appeared in a portion of the opinion omitted from these materials].

sion in all circumstances, each case must be examined individually, viewing the claimant's acts in light of the nature of the land.

In this case, the land is a 1.2–acre parcel surrounded on three sides by 280 acres of plaintiff's land and bounded on the fourth side by a road. The area in which it is located is rural and agricultural in nature. In 1947 there were no buildings on the property and there had not been any for many years. Grazing cattle and horses, cutting hay, planting and tapping trees, and cutting firewood and Christmas trees are the types of acts which are consistent with the nature of the parcel.

Defendant contends, however, that these acts are not the uses an average owner would have made of the parcel. He argues that because at one point before 1947 there had been a house on the parcel, because the parcel is flat, open, dry and well drained, because more trees could have been planted on it, and because defendant plans to build a house upon it, plaintiff did not use the parcel as an average owner might. We do not agree. Simply because a parcel may be susceptible to uses other than those to which the claimant chose to put it does not necessarily lead to the conclusion that the claimant failed to act toward the parcel as an average owner would have. " 'The possession is gauged by the actual state of the land, and not with reference to its capability of being changed into another state which would reasonably admit of a different character of possession.' " Bergen v. Dixon, 527 So.2d 1274, 1278 (Ala.1988) (quoting Goodson v. Brothers, 111 Ala. 589, 595, 20 So. 443, 445 (1896)). Plaintiff used the parcel for purposes which were consistent with its condition as he found it. He was not required to change nor necessarily improve the land, but was merely required to perform acts of possession which were consistent with the parcel's nature. Plaintiff's acts, while not necessarily sufficient to constitute possession of every piece of land, were sufficient to establish his possession of this parcel of rural, agricultural land. . . .

Another basis for the argument raised by defendant is that the acts of possession were merely fragmentary and occasional. "To constitute continuous possession of lands, the law does not require the occupant to be present on the site at all times. The kind and frequency of the acts of occupancy, necessary to constitute continuing possession, are dependent on the nature and condition of the premises as well as the uses to which it is adapted." There may be lapses of time between acts of possession. Montgomery v. Branon, 129 Vt. 379, 386, 278 A.2d 744, 748 (1971) (quoting Amey v. Hall, 123 Vt. 62, 67, 181 A.2d 69, 73 (1962)).

The uses made of the parcel from 1965 until 1986 consisted of cutting firewood and Christmas trees, parking vehicles, staging the logging operation, building the loading ramp, loading and unloading a tractor using the ramp, storing slab wood, cutting brush, and posting "No Trespassing" signs. Further, plaintiff testified that although there were times when he had not been on the parcel for as long as a month, he was never absent for as long as a year.

This Court has held that using property only at certain times of the year for certain activities and not using it for the rest of the year can constitute sufficiently continuous use for adverse possession. Thibault v. Vartuli, 143 Vt. 178, 181, 465 A.2d 248, 250 (1983) (using island only in summer for recreational activities); Montgomery, 129 Vt. at 386, 278 A.2d at 748 (using hunting camp only during season); Amey, 123 Vt. at 67–68, 181 A.2d at 73 (using logging camp only during cutting times). Although plaintiff did not use the parcel constantly, he used it each year during certain seasons in ways which were both consistent with the season and with the nature of the parcel. The uses, therefore, were more than fragmentary and occasional, and were sufficiently continuous. Thus, plaintiff established a continuous period of use from 1965 until 1986, which is more than sufficient to satisfy the statutory requirement of fifteen years.

Defendant also contends that plaintiff's acts were not open and notorious. Acts of possession are deemed sufficiently open and notorious if they are conducted in a manner which would put a person of ordinary prudence on notice of the claim. Waterman v. Moody, 92 Vt. 218, 238–39, 103 A. 325, 334 (1918). As the parcel bordered on the road, anyone passing would have been able to see plaintiff's activities. Further, there was testimony from a former town lister and from the town clerk, who had worked in the town clerk's office since 1939, that they both knew that plaintiff claimed to own the parcel. There was no error in finding plaintiff's possession to be open and notorious.

Lastly, defendant argues that the plaintiff's acts were not hostile because they "were beneficial to the Town." Hostility, when used in the context of adverse possession, does not require the presence of ill will toward the actual owner nor destructiveness toward the land. Grubb v. State, 433 N.W.2d 915, 918 (Minn.Ct.App.1988); Sinicropi v. Town of Indian Lake, 148 A.D.2d 799, 800, 538 N.Y.S.2d 380, 381 (1989); 7 R. Powell, The Law of Real Property ¶ 1013[2][c], at 91–23 to 91–26 (1990). Rather, what is required is that the adverse possessor intends to claim the land and treat it as his own. Lathrop v. Levarn, 83 Vt. 1, 4, 74 A. 331, 331–32 (1909). The trial court properly found that plaintiff's claim was hostile.

Defendant argues that while the parcel was owned by the Town of Waterville it was exempt from adverse possession claims by 12 V.S.A. § 462. The statute reads: "Nothing contained in this chapter [relating to the limitations of actions] shall extend to lands given, granted, sequestered or appropriated to a public, pious or charitable use, or to lands belonging to the state." 12 V.S.A. § 462. While we have applied the statute in the past, we have yet to face the issue presented by this case, namely, how to determine whether property owned by a municipality is "given, granted, sequestered or appropriated to a public . . . use."

Defendant urges that the proper focus of such an inquiry is whether the Town was acting in its "governmental capacity" or its "proprietary capacity" when it acquired the property. The significance of this distinction, defendant contends, is that land which is acquired or held by a municipality in its governmental capacity is within the meaning of the statutory phrase "given ... to a public ... use." We do not find this argument persuasive.

Other jurisdictions which have faced the question are split. New Hampshire, for example, in applying N.H. Rev. Stat. Ann. § 477:34 (1983), which reads "[n]o person shall acquire by prescription a right to ... any public ground by ... occupying it adversely for any length of time," has held that " 'mere retention of title, without more,' " is a public use for lands owned by a municipality. Kellison v. McIsaac, 131 N.H. 675, 681, 559 A.2d 834, 837 (1989) (quoting McInnis v. Town of Hampton, 112 N.H. 57, 60, 288 A.2d 691, 694 (1972).) This, in essence, exempts all municipal lands from adverse possession claims. This standard, however, is in conflict with our statute which only exempts lands given to a "public, pious, or charitable use." Our statute does not provide a blanket exemption for municipally owned lands, which it easily could have, as evidenced by the provision exempting state-owned land. Therefore, we decline to follow New Hampshire's example.

We find the approach of the Supreme Court of Connecticut to be more in accord with our statute. In American Trading Real Estate Properties, Inc. v. Town of Trumbull, 215 Conn. 68, 574 A.2d 796 (1990), the court held that land which is owned by a municipality is presumed to be given to a public use. Id. at 80, 574 A.2d at 802. However, this presumption can be rebutted by demonstrating that the town has abandoned any plans for the land. Id. Evidence to be considered in determining this issue may include the reason the property was acquired by the town, uses the town has made of the property since acquisition, and whether the town has manifested an intention to use the property in the future.

This standard is a simple, balanced approach for determining which municipal lands are given to a public use and thereby exempt from claims of adverse possession. It allows a municipality to be protected from adverse possession claims on property which it is not using at present but may have future plans for or on property which it has set aside as open space or to be left in its natural state for the benefit of the community and the environment. It does not, however, clash with 12 V.S.A. § 462 by giving a town a blanket exemption to adverse possession claims. It provides only for a presumption that the property is given to a public use which can be rebutted by evidence to the contrary.

In *American Trading,* the court reviewed an older Connecticut case which found that a piece of property could be adversely possessed although it was owned by a municipality because it was not given to a public use. Id. at 81, 574 A.2d at 802 (examining Goldman v. Quadrato, 142 Conn. 398, 114 A.2d 687 (1955)). Goldman involved a claim of adverse possession against a piece of property which a city had acquired by tax foreclosure. Goldman, 142 Conn. at 400, 114 A.2d at 689. The city then did nothing with the property for twenty-four years until it conveyed it to a private individual. Id. The American Trading court found that Goldman was in accord with the rebuttable-presumption standard because the city acquired the property only to protect its fisc from a delinquent taxpayer, because the city never used the property for any reason, and because the city, by selling the property to a private individual, manifested "no intention to develop the property, then or later, for any public purpose whatsoever." American Trading, 215 Conn. at 81, 574 A.2d at 802.

The facts of the case at hand are very similar to those of Goldman. The Town of Waterville acquired the parcel in 1935 as settlement for the support it had provided for the owner. The Town then did nothing with the parcel for fifty-one years. Finally, in 1986, the Town conveyed the property to defendant by quitclaim deed.

Based on these facts, we find that plaintiff has carried his burden of rebutting the presumption that the parcel, while owned by the Town of Waterville, was given to a public use. The Town acquired the parcel as settlement of a debt, the parcel was not used by the public while the Town had title, and by conveying the parcel to defendant, a private individual, the Town manifested that it had no intention of ever using the parcel for a public use. Therefore, the trial court properly concluded that the parcel was not given to a public use and that it was not exempt from claims of adverse possession by 12 V.S.A. § 462.

Affirmed.

NOTES AND QUESTIONS

1. "The common law doctrine and application of adverse possession has a long history. As early as 2250 B.C. the Code of Hammurabi discussed adverse possession and the misuse of land, including provisions that punished land waste, rewarded long-term development, and allowed one who worked the land of another for three years to take and keep the land. . . . In England, the history of adverse possession can be traced back to the Norman Conquest in 1066. See Gardiner at 125. The common law doctrine of adverse possession was applied to resolve land disputes between colonists in Virginia as early as 1646, where it was used 'in an effort to help resolve the proverbial conflicts between speculators and squatters.' Critique at 823 n. 29. The first statutory recognition of adverse possession in the New World appeared in a 1715 statute of limitations in North Carolina. . . .

"With the western migration of pioneers, the federal government initially prohibited settlement of the western lands unless purchased from the government, but that requirement was gradually relaxed; anti-squatting prohibitions were abandoned, recognition of preemptive purchase rights were extended, and land was distributed to military veterans. . . . Eventually, with the 1852 passage of the Homestead Act, land was freely available to such settlers. Id. At the same time, whereas the courts had originally followed the English example of requiring that the adverse possessor engage in activities giving notice to an inspecting owner such as residence, cultivation, fencing, and other improvements, American courts began to focus upon acts by the adverse possessor in keeping with the nature and character of the land involved. *Id.* at 538–39. The policy behind favoring adverse possession was the same as that of land distribution: favoring the productive use of the land. *Id.* at 534–40; *see also* Netter at 219 (adverse possession rewards the use of land and punishes those who sit on their rights)."

Fraley v. Minger, 829 N.E.2d 476 (Ind. 2005).

2. In order to acquire a title by adverse possession, the possessor must take actual possession of the real property. The actuality requirement has given rise to much spirited litigation in those cases where the possessor has neither enclosed nor substantially improved the real property. The lack of such activity, however, does not foreclose the possessor from acquiring a title by adverse possession assuming the other requirements have been satisfied. The critical test to determine whether possession has been actual seems to be whether the possessor's activities are consistent with how a reasonable owner of the land in question might have used the land. In answering this question, the peculiarities of the land may be particularly important. An early exposition of this test was laid down in Ewing's Lessee v. Burnet, 36 U.S. (11 Pet.) 41 (1837), involving the adverse possession of a gravel pit. The Court stated:

> It is well settled, that to constitute an adverse possession, there need not be a fence, building or other improvement made …; it suffices for this purpose, that visible and notorious acts of ownership are exercised over the premises in controversy, for … [the statutory period], after an entry under claim … of title. So much depends on the nature and situation of the property, the uses to which it can be applied, or to which the owner or claimant may choose to apply it, that it is difficult to lay down any precise rule, adapted to all cases…. Neither actual occupation, cultivation nor residence, are necessary to constitute actual possession … when the property is so situated as not to admit of any permanent useful improvement, and the continued claim of the [adverse possessor] … has been evidenced by public acts of ownership, such as he would exercise over property which he claimed in his own right, and would not exercise over property which he did not claim.

Id. at 52–53.

State statutes may require certain kinds of activities in order for the possessor to acquire title by adverse possession even though such activities are not judicially required in the absence of a statute. For example, some states require the possessor to pay the taxes on the property. Cal. Civ. Proc. Code § 325 (West 1982). See also Comment, Payment of Taxes As A Condition of Title By Adverse Possession: A Nineteenth Century Anachronism, 9 Santa Clara Lawyer 244 (1969).

The actual requirement tends to reward the exploitation of land. This phenomenon underlies the concerns of John Sprankling who wrote:

> Adverse possession evolved in England as a method to protect the true owner of land by barring ancient (and presumably frivolous) claims, much like a modern statute of limitations. In a heavily populated, agricultural country lacking an effective title recording system, long-term possession was optimum evidence of ownership. Under these circumstances, it was

reasonable to expect that the true owner of property would either reside there or, at least, inspect it frequently enough to detect trespassers and bring a timely suit in ejectment. On the other hand, lengthy possession uninterrupted by litigation could be construed as community acknowledgement that the occupant was the true owner. Under this approach, the key elements of adverse possession—actual possession, hostility, exclusivity, continuity, openness and notoriety—afforded constructive notice to the world of the occupant's title claim.

The courts of the new United States initially followed the English model of adverse possession by requiring evidence that the adverse claimant had engaged in activities likely to afford notice to an inspecting owner: residence, cultivation, fencing or other improvement.

Nineteenth-century American courts, however, transformed the doctrine in order to promote the development of wilderness land. They slowly abandoned the requirement of residence, cultivation, or improvement in cases involving such lands; in stead, they adopted a new yardstick, which measured the acts required for adverse possession by the nature and character of the land involved. The paradigm adverse possession suit of the era was a contest between E, an absentee owner holding title, and F, a settler or other adverse claimant who had put the land to productive use. By lowering the legal threshold for adverse possession of wilderness land, courts tended to transfer title from idle owner E to proven user F, whose development track record predicted future exploitation.

The new "wild lands" standard had no logical link with constructive notice. Under this calculus, adverse possession of wilderness land could be premised on infrequent, inconspicuous actions that were unlikely to afford notice to anyone. Thus, for example, berry picking and occasional timber cutting, seasonal sheep grazing, and the sporadic use of forest as wood lot all sufficed to vest title in nineteenth-century claimants. Accordingly, it became much easier to adversely possess wilderness than developed land. As a twentieth-century jurist later explained, adverse possession law evolved "when much of the continental United States was unsurveyed wilderness" such that "the courts adopted a public policy that as much land should be put to use as possible."

* * *

Just as in the nineteenth century, it is easier to adversely possess wilderness land than nonwilderness land. Almost all jurisdictions still use a reduced adverse-possession threshold for wilderness. This standard is based not on what reasonable notice requires, but rather on what economic use the existing condition of the land allows. As a result, adverse possession of wilderness may be founded on occasional activities that leave behind no visible traces. Applying this standard, twentieth-century courts have transferred title to adverse possessors based on such limited activities as harvesting natural hay, seasonal stock grazing, and cutting small amounts of timber. In a modern New York case, for example, the owner of 260 acres of wild forest land lost title to an adverse claimant whose only activities were tree cutting, occasional hunting, and paying taxes on the land.

Modern adverse possession law threatens environmental damage. It encourages the adverse claimant to place wilderness land in at least minimal economic use—such as grazing or logging—in order to acquire title. It also encourages the true owner to do the same—so as to negate the exclusive possession element of adverse possession, and thus retain title— by undertaking similar exploitative activities suited to the primitive condition of the property. Such timber cutting or grazing may in turn cause soil erosion, sediment pollution in streams, and injury to undergrowth, ultimately degrading wilderness quality.

More importantly, adverse possession tends to transfer wilderness land from the preservationist owner to the exploitative claimant. Once vested with title, the successful adverse claimant is free to clear the property, thereby destroying its wilderness value.

John G. Sprankling, The Antiwilderness Bias in American Property Law, 63 U. Chi. L. Rev. 519, 538–539, 573 (1996). See also John G. Sprankling, An Environmental Critique of Adverse Possession, 79 Cornell L. Rev. 816 (1994).

3. In most cases, a possession that is actual will also be open and notorious. What function does the "open and notorious" requirement serve? If the possession of the adverse possessor is open and notorious, will the statute of limitations run if the true owner was not actually aware that someone was in possession of her land?

Suppose a possessor was unable to establish acts of possession that are sufficiently open and notorious to meet the standards of adverse possession. Could the possessor nonetheless acquire a title by adverse possession if the true owner was actually aware that the possessor was present on the land? See Houston v. United States Gypsum Co., 652 F.2d 467 (5th Cir. 1981) (holding that while acts of possession might not be sufficient to satisfy the open and notorious requirement, adverse possessor prevailed where true owner had actual notice of adverse claim because its attorney had received a map from the possessor with marks showing portions of land claimed adversely).

4. O and A are adjoining landowners. A discovers the entrance to an underground cave on his property. After unsealing the cave and making all appropriate improvements, A exploits the cave for commercial purposes by charging the public an admission price to view the cave. In fact, most of the cave runs under the land of O although neither O nor A was aware of that fact until after the statute of limitations had run when O caused a survey to be made of the cave. O sues A to recover the possession of the cave running under his land. What result? Marengo Cave Co. v. Ross, 212 Ind. 624, 10 N.E.2d 917 (1937).

Suppose immediately after A discovered the entrance to the cave but before the statute had run, A conveyed all right, title, and interest to the cave to X, reserving to himself all rights to the surface land but giving the right of ingress and egress over the land to X for the use of X and his invitees. X improves the cave and opens it to the public. Twenty years later (the statutory period), O, under whose land most of the cave runs, sues X to recover possession of the cave. Same result?

5. In order to acquire a title by adverse possession, the possessor must be in possession throughout the entire statutory period. This is not to say that the possessor may not take a vacation. Rather, there must not be any substantial interruption of the possession. Assume the statutory period to acquire a title by adverse possession is ten years. In 1994, A–1, the adjoining neighbor of O, goes into possession of the easterly 20′ strip of O's land. Except during the months of February and March of 1997, A–1 stores lumber on this 20′ strip. In February and March of 1997, A–1's lumber stock had been completely sold, and during those two months, cement contractors employed by O to work on his property stored supplies and equipment on the 20′ strip. In 2005, O brings an action to recover the strip from A–1. What result? See Mendonca v. Cities Service Oil Co., 354 Mass. 323, 237 N.E.2d 16 (1968). Suppose O's employees had used the strip for only one day. Same result?

6. Assume the statutory period to acquire a title by adverse possession is ten years. In 1990, A–2 goes into possession of O's land and adversely possesses the same for five years. In 1995, A–2 transfers all of his rights to the land to A–3, who immediately goes into possession and remains in possession until 2004 when O sues A–3 for possession. What result? If, prior to 1995, O had sued A–2 for possession, O would clearly prevail because A–2 would not have been in possession for ten years. Further, if A–3 can prevail against O only on the basis of *her* time in possession, O would win as against A–3 because A–3 has not been in possession for ten years. Therefore, A–3 can acquire title by adverse possession as against O *only if the periods of possession of A–2 (five years) and A–3 (more than five years) can be aggregated together so that more than ten years have run on O's cause of action.* In those cases where the possession of one possessor can be aggregated to the possession of another to satisfy the time period under the applicable statute of limitations, it is said that the periods of possession of the two possessors are "tacked" together.

Tacking is permitted when the two possessors are found to be in "privity" with each other. Privity exists when the subsequent possessor[2] enters with the permission of the prior possessor. Permission may be evidenced by a written instrument or by less formal means. It can also occur where the subsequent possessor claims as heir or devisee of the prior possessor. For tacking to occur it is essential that "the predecessor passes ... [the property] to the successor by mutual consent, as distinguished from the case where a possessor abandons possession generally, and another, finding the premises unoccupied, enters without contact or relation with the former...." Illinois Steel Co. v. Paczocha, 139 Wis. 23, 28–29, 119 N.W. 550, 552 (1909).

Tacking may occur not only for the purpose of aggregating times of possession but also true owners' causes of action. For example, suppose A enters O's land in 2000. O dies in 2008 and H, who is O's sole heir, inherits the title to the land possessed by A. If H fails to bring an action to recover

---

2. A possessor is something more than a squatter. The term "squatter" is difficult to define, but it, like its more pejorative cousin, "mere squatter", is clearly intended to describe, clearly in a derogatory manner, a possessor whose acts of possession are deemed insufficient (often for reasons the court never makes clear) to give rise to an adverse possession claim. The failure often relates to the continuous and actual requirements. In some sense, therefore, the "squatter" stands somewhere between a trespasser and an adverse possessor.

possession of the land from A by 2010, in a state with a ten year statute of limitations, A will acquire title to the land by adverse possession. Which policy, if any, underlying the law of adverse possession explains why tacking is permitted?

In each of the following cases, assume, unless otherwise stated, a ten year statute of limitations and that A enters O's land—Blackacre—in 2000 and at all times A, or an individual in privity with A, is in actual, open, exclusive, continuous and hostile possession of Blackacre. When, if at all, will O lose O's title by adverse possession and to whom?

(a) In 2009, B forcefully removes A from Blackacre, and O sues B to recover possession of Blackacre in 2014. *Tacking*

(b) A dies in 2008, and A's heir, H, goes into possession of Blackacre immediately upon A's death. O sues H in 2014. *Tacking*

(c) A dies in 2008 leaving a will under which A devises Blackacre to C for life and directs that, upon C's death, Blackacre should pass to D. C immediately takes possession of Blackacre and dies in 2015. In 2016, O sues D to recover the possession of Blackacre. See 3 Amer. L. Prop. §§ 15.4, 15.10 (A.J. Casner ed. 1952). *Tacking*

(d) O dies in 2005 leaving a will under which O devises Blackacre to H for life and, upon H's death, directs that Blackacre should pass to M. H dies in 2010. M sues A in 2015 to recover possession of Blackacre. See 3 Amer. L. Prop. supra, § 15.8. *Tacking*

(e) Suppose in 1998, two years prior to A's entry on Blackacre, O had *No tacking* died devising Blackacre to X for life and, upon X's death, directed that Blackacre should pass to Z. A enters in 2000. X dies in 2011, and in 2015, Z *Tacking* sues A for possession. What result? See 3 Amer. L. Prop. supra, § 15.8.

7. O owns a five acre tract of land known as Blackacre located in a state with a ten year statute of limitations. In 1990, A–1 goes into possession of all of Blackacre. In 2005, A–1 conveys by written instrument all of his rights in Blackacre to A–2. However, the deed from A–1 to A–2 only describes the easterly three acres of Blackacre. A–2 goes into possession of all five acres of Blackacre. If O sued A–2 in 2014, can O recover any portion of Blackacre from A–2? See Brand v. Prince, 43 A.D.2d 638, 349 N.Y.S.2d 222 (3d Dept. 1973), *aff'd*, 35 N.Y.2d 634, 364 N.Y.S.2d 826, 324 N.E.2d 314 (1974).

8. O is the record owner of Blackacre located in a state with a ten year statute of limitations. A–1 enters in 2000 and remains in possession for a sufficient period that as against O, A–1 acquires a title by adverse possession. In 2015, A–1 orally conveys Blackacre to A–2. This conveyance, because it is oral, is invalid under the Statute of Frauds. In 2017, O sues A–2 for possession. O claims that when A–1 acquired a title to Blackacre by adverse possession, A–1 could only transfer that title by a valid conveyance or by will. Furthermore, O argues that A–2 only has been in possession for two years and that A–2 cannot tack her possession to A–1's possession. What result? See Evans v. Hogue, 296 Or. 745, 681 P.2d 1133 (1984).

9. Where the nature of the land is such that seasonal possession would be consistent with the possessory acts of a true owner, a tension exists between the policy of rewarding the possessor because of his actual occupation

of the land and the policy of penalizing the true owner who sits on his rights too long. For example, suppose O owns land in the mountains ideally suited only for a summer retreat and that A possesses the land only during the summer months for each of ten seasons. If local law requires that an action be brought within ten years after the cause of action accrues and O sues in the eleventh year, can O prevail on the theory that either A's possession was not continuous or that it was not actual, open, and notorious throughout each year? See Madson v. Cohn, 122 Cal. App. 704, 10 P.2d 531 (1932) (acts insufficient to establish title by adverse possession), Monroe v. Rawlings, 331 Mich. 49, 49 N.W.2d 55 (1951) (seasonal use sufficient to establish title by adverse possession); Winchester v. Porretto, 432 S.W.2d 170 (Tex. Civ. App. 1968) (adverse possession not established).

10. All states provide that under certain circumstances, the running of a statute of limitations is tolled if the person entitled to bring the cause of action *at the time the cause of action* accrues has a disability. The most frequently covered disabilities are minority, insanity, or imprisonment. The precise effect of disabilities on the running of a statute of limitations varies from state to state. In some states, an additional period of time to bring the action after the disability terminates is allowed even though the ordinary statute of limitations has run. See, e.g., Ohio Rev. Code Ann. § 2305.04 (West 2004) (person with a disability has ten years after disability terminates to bring action even though twenty-one year statute has run). In others, the ordinary statute of limitations does not begin to run until the disability terminates. See, e.g., Ariz. Rev. Stat. Ann. § 12–528 (2003). See also Fla. Stat. Ann. § 95.051 (West 2002). See generally 3 Amer. L. Prop. supra, § 15.12. In addition, under certain circumstances, the statute is tolled for members of the military. See Serviceman Civil Relief Act, 50 App. USCA § 526(a), providing that "the period of a servicemember's military service may not be included in computing any period limited by law, regulation, or order for the bringing of any action or proceeding in a court, or in any board, bureau, commission, department, or other agency of a State (or political subdivision of a State) or the United States by or against the servicemember or the servicemember's heirs, executors, administrators, or assigns."

Why would states provide for a tolling of the statute of limitations during a period of disability? Are tolling statutes consistent with the policies underlying the adverse possession doctrine? As Professor Epstein observes, ordinarily the status of either the plaintiff or defendant does not affect the entitlements that the parties would otherwise have. Nonetheless, the law is otherwise with respect to adverse possession. See Epstein, Past and Future: The Temporal Dimension in the Law of Property, 64 Wash. U. Law. Q. 667 (1986).

Ohio Rev. Code § 2305.04 (West 2004) provides as follows:

An action to recover the title to or possession of real property shall be brought within twenty-one years after the cause of action accrued, but if a person entitled to bring the action is, at the time the cause of action accrues, within the age of minority or of unsound mind, the person, after the expiration of twenty-one years from the time the cause of action accrues, may bring the action within ten years after the disability is removed.

The State of Bliss has enacted a statute of limitations identical to that provided by Ohio law. Under the laws of Bliss, a person attains majority at the age of eighteen. O owns real property in Bliss known as Blackacre. A enters Blackacre on September 1, 2000. In each of the following cases, in what year, if any, will A acquire title to Blackacre by adverse possession?

(a) O was under no disability in 2000. O is alive and well today.

(b) O was under no disability in 2000. In 2007, however, O was declared to be mentally incompetent. O is alive and mentally incompetent today.

(c) O was under no disability in 2000. O died in 2009 survived by H, his only heir. H was age 2 in 2009. H is still a minor today.

Suppose H was age 23 when O died but mentally incompetent. Same result?

(d) O was age 2 in 2000. O will be 18 in 2016.

Suppose O had been age 15 in 2000. Same result?

(e) O was age 13 in 2000. In 2005, O was declared mentally incompetent, and O is mentally incompetent today.

(f) O was both age 13 and mentally incompetent in 2000. O is mentally incompetent today. Suppose O dies tomorrow. What result?

(g) The whereabouts of O in 2000 and today are unknown.

11. Another requirement to acquire a title by adverse possession is that the possession must have been exclusive. Possession can be exclusive even though others used the property during the possessor's time of possession if the use by others can be characterized as permissive. See, e.g., Peters v. Juneau–Douglas Girl Scout Council, 519 P.2d 826 (Alaska 1974). Ordinarily, the exclusivity requirement is not met if the true owner was concurrently in possession of the property with the adverse possessor. But see Nevells v. Carter, 122 Me. 81, 119 A. 62 (1922) (where parent-true owner lived on farm concurrently with son who took possession with parent's permission following parent's request that son care for parent and property. The court concluded that parent's possession was subordinate to son's possession).

12. If A enters O's land with O's permission, the entry is not wrongful, and A cannot claim adversely to O. For example, if O leases property to A for ten years and A enters the land, A cannot claim adversely to O. However, suppose at the end of the ten year period A remains in possession. In this case, it may be unclear whether A is claiming adversely to O or whether some form of a new tenancy arises by operation of law between A and O. Generally, if a tenant holds over beyond the term of a lease, the landlord may elect to treat the tenant as a tenant for a certain period of time or as a trespasser. How such election is manifested is considered in Chapter 7. Thus, if A intends to have her possession characterized as adverse to O, it would be necessary that A communicate to O by word or act a repudiation of any rightful possession of the property. In the absence of a repudiation, A's wrongful possession would not commence until the landlord elected to treat the tenant as a trespasser. See generally 3 Amer. L. Prop. § 15.6 (A.J. Casner ed. 1952).

13. If two or more persons own real property concurrently, each has the right to take sole possession of the property. See generally chapter 5 for the

rights of concurrent owners. Thus, if A and B own real property concurrently and A goes into sole possession of the property, A's possession, without more, is not adverse to B, the other owner of the property. B would have no cause of action to eject A. However, under certain circumstances, A may claim adversely to B. Thus, as the court stated in Johnson v. James, 237 Ark. 900, 903, 377 S.W.2d 44, 46 (1964):

> It is well settled that possession by a tenant in common [a kind of concurrent owner] is presumed to be possession by all cotenants and where a family relationship exists, then stronger and more cogent evidence of adverse possession or hostile acts of ownership are required than where no such relationship exists.... We have also held that knowledge of adverse possession must be made known to other cotenants directly or by notorious acts of such an unequivocal character that notice may be presumed and, further, that acts of possession, payment of taxes, enjoyment of rents and profits, and the making of improvements are consistent with a cotenancy and do not necessarily amount to disseizin.... However, we have held that when the acts of ownership of a cotenant are of such a notorious nature as to amount to a declaration of hostility to other cotenants for more than ... [the statutory period], that title by adverse possession is vested in the occupant....

See also Zaslow v. Kroenert, 29 Cal.2d 541, 176 P.2d 1 (1946) (ouster[3] occurs when cotenant in possession refuses other cotenant the right to enter into possession); Whittington v. Cameron, 385 Ill. 99, 52 N.E.2d 134 (1943) (ouster occurs if cotenant in possession with knowledge of cotenant not in possession purports to convey all interests to third person and grantee enters into possession). The heightened notice requirement follows from the fact that cotenants are fiduciaries to each other and thus are not expected to act wrongfully towards each other. Thus, a court in a Hawaii case observed:

> [B]ecause of the general fiduciary relationship between cotenants, a tenant in common claiming by adverse possession must prove that he [or she] acted in *good faith* towards the cotenants during the statutory period. In most circumstances, this requirement of good faith will in turn mandate that the tenant claiming adversely must *actually notify* his [or her] cotenants that he [or she] is claiming against them. In the following exceptional circumstances, however, good faith is satisfied by less than actual notice: where the tenant in possession has *no reason to suspect* that a cotenancy exists; or where the tenant in possession makes a *good faith, reasonable effort to notify* the cotenants but is unable to locate them; or where the tenants out of possession already have actual knowledge that the tenant in possession is claiming adversely to their interests. In these limited circumstances, the notice requirement will be satisfied by constructive notice and "open and notorious possession."

Petran v. Allencastre, 91 Hawai'i 545, 985 P.2d 1112, 1121–22 (Haw. Ct. App. 1999).

---

3. Ouster does not require a physical eviction of one person by another. Ouster is a physical occupation that excludes others with a right to be in possession. See generally Parker v. Shecut, 349 S.C. 226, 562 S.E.2d 620 (2002).

14. O owns Blackacre located in a state with a ten-year statute of limitations. O dies on June 1, 1995, survived by two children, A and B, who would be O's heirs in the absence of a will. O left a will under the terms of which Blackacre is bequeathed to A. However, although A and B know of the terms of the will, it is not offered for probate in the local state court having jurisdiction of O's estate. Under state law if a will is not probated within five years of a testator's death, it cannot be probated, and in such a case, title to the decedent's property passes to the decedent's heir or, if more than one, to the heirs as tenants in common. If the will is probated within the five-year period, the title of the devisees under the "relation back" doctrine is deemed to begin on the date of the decedent's death, not the date the will is probated.

A goes into possession of Blackacre immediately upon O's death and remains in exclusive possession of Blackacre until August 1, 2005, on which date B commences a suit claiming that A has improperly excluded B from any enjoyment of the property. A claims title by adverse possession.

Assuming that during the ten-year period A has satisfied all of the general requirements of adverse possession, can A satisfy the further requirement that knowledge of the adverse possession be communicated to the other cotenant? See Johnson v. James, 237 Ark. 900, 377 S.W.2d 44 (1964); Ruick v. Twarkins, 171 Conn. 149, 367 A.2d 1380 (1976) (exclusive possession which was open, visible, and notorious under a claim of title, and without license or consent from cotenants for the statutory period, fulfilled the requirement of communication). But see Westheimer v. Neustadt, 362 P.2d 110, 111–12 (Okla. 1961) (cotenant's possession of property, collecting rents, paying taxes, and representing to lessee that he owned the property was held insufficient notice to cotenants that he was denying their rights). See also 3 Amer. L. Prop. supra, § 15.7; Note, Real Property–Adverse Possession Between Cotenants, 56 Mich. L. Rev. 1360 (1958).

Assuming that A did communicate his intent to exclude B, would B's cause of action commence in 1995 when O died or on June 1, 2000 when the time period expired for the probating of O's will?

How rigorously must A satisfy the general requirements of adverse possession? For example, could A's adverse possession claim be defeated if (i) B visited A on Blackacre from time to time during the statutory period, (ii) B paid the taxes on Blackacre because the tax authorities never sent the bill to A, and B never asked A for any reimbursement, (iii) A rented the property to C and periodically sent B a check for one half of the rents, or (iv) B periodically rendered advice to A on how Blackacre should be maintained?

15. Landlord leases property to Tenant for a period of eight years. In the sixth year of the lease, Landlord dies. Tenant continues to occupy the premises for the balance of the term and continues in possession for another thirteen years. At the end of that time, Landlord's heir sues Tenant to recover possession of the property. Tenant claims title by adverse possession. What result? See Estate of Wells v. Estate of Smith, 576 A.2d 707, 711–12 (D.C. 1990) wherein the court stated:

> Possession that is initially permissive can be changed to hostile possession only by the most unequivocal conduct on the part of the adverse claimant since it is presumed that permission continues and possession is

not hostile.... Thus, some jurisdictions require a tenant to surrender possession of the property to the landlord, followed by a reentry into possession by the tenant to show sufficient repudiation of a tenancy.... Evidence of the occupant's recognition of a superior title can be fatal....

On the other hand, when the claim of right is in some way asserted so that the owner knows of the claim, possession can become adverse....

In the absence of actual notice to the owner, the tenant's acts of ownership must be of such an open, notorious, and hostile character that the owner can be deemed to have known of it. For example, in Adams v. Johnson, the Supreme Court of Minnesota held that a cotenant who occupied land undisturbed for fifty years as a sole owner, paid all taxes and insurance, and retained all of the profits from farming operations as well as made substantial improvements to the farm, overcame the presumption that one cotenant holds land with the implicit permission of others. 271 Minn. 439, 136 N.W.2d 78 (1965). Similarly, in Johnson v. James, the Supreme Court of Arkansas held that where one cotenant has lived on and had sole and exclusive possession of the property in question for thirty-six years, exercising such acts of ownership as payment of taxes, enjoyment of rents, payment of insurance made payable to him, together with possession of an unprobated will giving him the property, about which the non-claiming cotenant was aware, and where the non-claiming cotenant never asserted any claim to the property until it was acquired by eminent domain proceedings, the claimant successfully asserted a claim of adverse possession. 237 Ark. 900, 377 S.W.2d 44, 47 (1964). See also Holtzman v. Douglas, 168 U.S. 278, 283, 18 S.Ct. 65, 67, 42 L.Ed. 466 (1897) (requiring that adverse possession be brought home to true owner); Root v. Woolworth, 150 U.S. 401, 415, 14 S.Ct. 136, 140, 37 L.Ed. 1123 (1893) (same); Zeller's Lessee v. Eckert, 45 U.S. 289, 296, 11 L.Ed. 979 (1846) (same). There is, however, no general rule as to the nature of the tenant's disclaimer of the owner's title and adverse holding and acts of ownership such as the payment of taxes when performed in a slightly different context, while tending to support a claim of possession, do not in themselves work a divestiture of title.

16. O dies and under the terms of O's will, O devises Blackacre to A for life. O's will further provides that upon A's death Blackacre should pass to B. A enters into possession of Blackacre and remains in exclusive possession of Blackacre for over ten years, the statutory period. Ordinarily possession by a life tenant is not hostile toward the remainderman. (Do you see why?) Suppose, however, that A erroneously believes he owns the real property and B (the remainderman) has no interest in it. Has A acquired title to Blackacre by adverse possession as against all the world, including B? See Piel v. Dewitt, 170 Ind. App. 63, 351 N.E.2d 48 (1976) (statute of limitations did not run against remaindermen who had insufficient notice of adverse possession). Cf. Armstrong v. Cities Service Gas Co., 210 Kan. 298, 502 P.2d 672 (1972) (statute of limitations ran against remainderman who had knowledge of adverse possession). But see Wallace v. Magie, 214 Kan. 481, 522 P.2d 989 (1974) (remainderman barred by statute even if he did not know of adverse possession).

Suppose during A's life B goes into exclusive possession of Blackacre and remains in possession for over ten years. Would B acquire title to Blackacre by adverse possession? See Lucas v. Brown, 396 So.2d 63 (Ala. 1981) (since a remainderman has no right to possession during the life of the life tenant, possession by the remainderman would be adverse to the possession of the life tenant).

17.   As a general matter, one cannot acquire title to state or federally owned land by adverse possession. This rule is reflected in both case law and, in some states, by statute or constitutional provisions. The rule is rationalized on the ground that state or federally owned lands are held in trust for the people and such lands should not therefore be lost because of the failure of governmental officials to properly discharge the duties of their office. See generally State v. Barkdoll, 99 Wis. 2d 163, 298 N.W.2d 539 (1980). Some states, on the other hand, have enacted statutes that would permit a possessor to acquire a title by adverse possession against the state in certain cases. See, e.g., N.Y. Real Prop. Acts. Law § 501 (McKinney 1979); N.Y. C.P.L.R. § 211(c) (McKinney 1972) (extending, however, the time period in which the state may bring the action); Mass. Ann. Laws ch. 260 § 31 (Michie/Law. Co-op. 1980) (land of Commonwealth and its political subdivisions may be adversely possessed after running of a twenty years period.) However, in these states, the courts have tended to interpret the statutes narrowly or to go to extraordinary measures to find that the possessor failed in some respect to satisfy the five requisites for acquiring a title by adverse possession. As evident from the *Jarvis* case, while adverse possession against the state may be statutorily proscribed, adverse possession against a municipality of the state may be possible depending upon the language of the state statute. Does the *Jarvis* court's analysis apply as well to state-owned lands?

It is extremely rare for one state to claim adverse possession against another state, but the States of New York and New Jersey came pretty close to that in the dispute culminating in New Jersey v. New York, 523 U.S. 767 (1998).

In 1834, New Jersey and New York entered into a compact (agreement) setting the boundary line between the two states at the middle of the Hudson River. New York was granted sovereignty over Ellis Island despite its location on the New Jersey side of the river. However, under the agreement, New Jersey retained sovereignty over the submerged lands surrounding the island.

In 1890, the United States government began to use Ellis Island as the point of entry for the millions of immigrants coming to this country, and over the next forty two years, it added some 24.5 acres of landfill to the submerged lands surrounding the original three-acre island. In 1954, immigration to the United States through Ellis Island ceased, and since then, the island was developed as a national historic site.

New York and New Jersey each claim the acreages attributable to the federal government's landfill. Rather than argue adverse possession, New York argued a closely analogous claim based on prescription. New York argued that its prescriptive acts from 1890 through 1954 were evidenced by the following facts: (1) it recorded vital statistics (five birth certificates, five death certificates, and four marriage certificates) for residents of the island,

(2) New York statutes included the island in state voting districts and also included island residents on state voter lists, (3) the belief of the islanders that they lived in New York, and (4) the federal government believed that the filled portions belonged to New York. In rejecting these claims, the Court noted that none of these facts were sufficient to put New Jersey on notice of New York's adverse claims. The Court also rejected the argument that New Jersey had acquiesced to New York's claims.

Can a state claim adverse possession against an individual? Should it depend on whether the state requires that an adverse possessor have paid property taxes? See State v. Serowiecki, 892 N.E.2d 194 (Ind. Ct. App. 2008).

18. If O fails to sue the adverse possessor on time and loses title to the adverse possessor, has O made a gift to the adverse possessor for federal gift tax purposes? While O's failure to timely sue is not a gift for property law purposes (because it lacks donative intent), the test for a taxable gift under federal law does not require intent. Rather, a taxable gift under federal gift tax law arises whenever a property owner transfers the property to another for less than adequate and full consideration in money or money's worth. Clearly, that is what happens when O fails to timely enforce an ejectment action. If O has made a gift under these circumstances, would that mean that any person who allows the statute of limitations to run on a lawsuit makes a taxable gift to the person who could have been sued, or is adverse possession unique?

§ 3.4 STATE OF MIND

Hostility

One of the most frequently litigated issues in the law of adverse possession is whether the possessor had the requisite "state of mind" to satisfy the hostile and under claim of right requirement. As noted in the *Jarvis* case, supra, "hostility ... does not require the presence of ill will toward the actual owner nor destructiveness toward the land.... Rather, what is required is that the adverse possessor intends to claim the land and treat it as his own." A similar approach was adopted by the court in Peters v. Juneau–Douglas Girl Scout Council, 519 P.2d 826 (Alaska 1974). In *Peters*, the court, commenting upon the hostility requirement and its purposes, stated:

> The trial court based its finding that Peters failed to satisfy the hostility requirement on its belief that Peters' possession was permissive and therefore subservient to the true owner's legal title. In so concluding, the trial court erred. We find that Peters satisfied the hostility requirement.
>
> > The great majority of the cases establish convincingly that the alleged requirements of claim of title and of hostility of possession mean only that the possessor must use and enjoy the property continuously for the required period as the average owner would use it, without the consent of the true owner and therefore in

actual hostility to him irrespective of the possessor's actual state of mind or intent.

The test for determining the existence of the requisite degree of hostility is a fairly objective one. The question is whether or not the claimant acted toward the land as if he owned it. His beliefs as to the true legal ownership of the land, his good faith or bad faith in entering into possession (*i.e.*, whether he claimed a legal right to enter, or avowed himself a wrongdoer), all are irrelevant. An early Minnesota case, Carpenter v. Coles, 75 Minn. 9, 77 N.W. 424 (1898), put it quite succinctly when it said:

> The misapprehension on the subject arises from the somewhat misleading, if not inaccurate, terms frequently used in the books to express this adverse intent, such as "claim of right," "claim of title," and "claim of ownership." These terms, when used in this connection, mean nothing more than the intention of the disseisor to appropriate and use the land as his own to the exclusion of all others. To make a disseisin it is not necessary that the disseisor should enter under color of title, or should either believe or assert that he had a right to enter. It is only necessary that he enter and take possession of the lands as if they were his own, and with the intention of holding for himself to the exclusion of all others.

From the standpoint of the true owner, the purpose of the various requirements of adverse possession—that the nonpermissive use be actual, open, notorious, continuous, exclusive and hostile—is to put him on notice of the hostile nature of the possession so that he, the owner, may take steps to vindicate his rights by legal action. Where the user has acted, without permission of the true owner, in a manner inconsistent with the true owner's rights, the acts alone (without any explicit claim of right or intent to dispossess) may be sufficient to put the true owner on notice of the nonpermissive use. Ottavia v. Savarese, 338 Mass. 330, 155 N.E.2d 432, 435 (1959). See Amer. L. Prop. § 15.4, at 771–785; Restatement of Property § 458 cmt. a, d. "[T]he physical facts of entry and continued possession may themselves evidence an intent to occupy and to hold as of right sufficient in law to support the acquisition of rights by prescription." Ottavia v. Savarese, supra, at 435, citing Holmes v. Johnson, 324 Mass. 450, 86 N.E.2d 924 (1949).

"The intent with which the occupant holds possession is normally determined by what he does upon the land. [Citation omitted.] Where the land is used in the manner that an owner would use it there is a presumption that the possession is adverse. [Citation omitted.]" Springer v. Durette, 217 Or. 196, 342 P.2d 132, 135 (1959).

519 P.2d at 831–32.

NOTES AND QUESTIONS

1. Notwithstanding the relatively objective and easily satisfied tests relating to the actual, open, continuous, and exclusive requirements, many courts read much more into the hostility requirement. Many courts require the possessor to have an intent to claim what the possessor knows is not his; others require that the possessor have a good faith claim to the property.

The notion that a claim of adverse possession can be defeated merely because the possessor lacks a certain state of mind is inconsistent with the idea that a cause of action for possession is running against the true owner from the date of the possessor's wrongful entry. For example, suppose A enters O's land in 1990 and remains in open, actual, continuous, and exclusive possession for over ten years. If a court concludes that A does not acquire a title by adverse possession because A lacked hostility, then, even though A has been in possession for more than ten years, the court must necessarily conclude that the statute has not run against O. But logic suggests that if the statute has not run against O, it must have been because O had no cause of action for possession against A commencing in 1990 at the time of A's physical entry. This is a preposterous idea since at any time between 1990 and 2000 (assuming a ten year statute), O, the true owner, could have sued A for possession and won. Given this absurdity, why might a court want to have a requirement of hostility?

Professor Helmholz has suggested that the reason the courts have not addressed this logical quagmire is because they consistently ask the wrong question in adverse possession cases. He says:

> The recent cases on adverse possession seldom approach the subject by asking when a cause of action accrued against the possessor. If this is the "basic question," as the American Law of Property insists it is, then it is a question the courts are practically unanimous in disregarding. Instead, they focus on whether or not the trespasser has fulfilled the five positive requirements of adverse possession: that is, hostility under claim of right, actual possession, openness and notoriety, exclusivity, and continuity. In other words, the judges routinely ask the question: Has the trespasser met a series of affirmative tests? They regularly refrain from asking: When could the record owner have brought suit to oust the trespasser?

Helmholz, Adverse Possession and Subjective Intent, 61 Wash. U. L.Q. 331, 334 (1983).

For a response, see Cunningham, Adverse Possession and Subjective Intent: A Reply to Professor Helmholz, 64 Wash. U. L.Q. 1 (1986); Merrill, Property Rules, Liability Rules, and Adverse Possession, 79 Nw. U. L. Rev. 1122 (1985). But see Helmholz, More on Subjective Intent: A Response to Professor Cunningham, 64 Wash. U. L.Q. 65 (1986).

Professor Helmholz also observed something quite startling and dichotomous between the observations of academic commentators and observable empirical evidence. He found that although academic commentators almost uniformly reject the notion that a subjective state of mind is relevant, "where courts allow adverse possession to ripen into title, bad faith on the part of the possessor seldom exists. Where the possessor knows that he is trespassing, valid title does not accrue to him simply by the passage of years." Helmholz, Adverse Possession and Subjective Intent, 61 Wash. U. L.Q. 331, 347 (1983).

2. Suppose A enters O's land knowing he did not own it and intending to leave it if and when the true owner appeared to claim the land. Would this intent defeat A's claim to title by adverse possession if A remains in possession beyond the statutory period? In Patterson v. Reigle, 4 Pa. 201, 204–205, 45 Am. Dec. 684, 685–686 (1846), the court stated:

> It has been determined that one already in possession estops himself by declarations of submission addressed to the owner; and it would seem he might do so by a general declaration explanatory of the nature of his entry. But there is a presumption which lasts till it is rebutted, that an intruder enters to hold for himself; and it is not to be doubted that a trespasser entering to gain a title, though conscious that he is a wrong-doer, will accomplish his object, if the owner ... [does] not enter or prosecute his claim within the prescribed period. But to do so, it is necessary that his possession be adverse from the first; and to infer that he intended it to be otherwise, would impute to him an inconsistency of purpose. Was there evidence to rebut the presumption that the entry and possession of ... [the possessors] were adverse to the title? No declaration by them was inconsistent with an intention to hold the land as long as they could, or ... evincive [sic] of a design to give it up before they should be compelled to do so by the appearance of a claimant whom they could not resist. They were conscious they had no title themselves, and they said so; they were conscious they could not resist him who had it, and they said so; but they did not say that they meant not to acquire a title to it for themselves. Whatever they did say, was predicated on the expected appearance of the owner while he continued to be so; for they certainly did not mean to purchase the land from any one else. [One of the possessors] ... testified that he and ... [the other possessor] settled on the land "to hold it till a better owner came for it;" but the holder of the title would lose it, and cease to be the better owner at the end of one-and-twenty years [the statutory period]. They intended to hold adversely to all the world till the title should be produced to them, and consequently as adversely to the owner before he disclosed himself as to anyone else. The sum of the evidence is that ... [the possessors] entered to hold the land as long as they could; and they consequently gained the title to it by the statute of limitations.

But see Smeberg v. Cunningham, 96 Mich. 378, 56 N.W. 73 (1893).

3. Suppose O orally gifts Blackacre to B who immediately enters into possession of Blackacre. The state's statute of frauds requires all transfers of real property to be in writing; thus, this gift is invalid under state law. Fifteen years later, O dies and the executor of O's estate sells Blackacre to C, who then sues B in ejectment. B claims title by adverse possession. Assuming a ten year statute of limitations and that B's possession was otherwise open, notorious, continuous, exclusive, and actual, who wins? See Vezey v. Green, 35 P.3d 14 (Alaska 2001).

Claim Clubs, Disputes of Titles,
and the Priority Principle

The vastness of this continent and the continuous movement of peoples westward presented unique problems for the settlement of disputes regarding the ownership of land. This was particularly true when settlers took possession of land in areas where no formal local government existed, no judiciary existed for the settlement of "title disputes," and paper titles derived from grants from the federal government, which acquired the land by purchase or conquest and perhaps conveyed its title to persons who never took possession of the land. Many of the early settlers were "squatters" knowingly having no legal title to the land.[1] In order to protect their interests, settlers organized "claim clubs" where disputes could be quickly settled so that economic investments in the land could be secured against intrusions. These clubs, acting as de facto government land registry offices, clothed themselves with judicial authority to punish crimes against property.

The priority principle largely governed the resolution of disputes regarding "titles." The principle applied whether the possessor who was first in time was a cultivator or a speculator. Absentee owners were much disfavored in the adjudications of the claim clubs with their lands either confiscated or financially and disproportionately burdened by taxes to finance local improvements. The priority principle "also meant the superiority of the rules of the community which existed before the formal government.... [It] made men hurry on. It made them insist that early arrival was no mere fact of history or biography, but a virtue for which riches were not too great a reward."[2]

The first in time principle is reflected in the nickname of the Oklahoma football team, the "Sooners." The Sooners were some 100,000 settlers who in 1889 were lined up on the border of the Oklahoma District "waiting for the starting guns to be fired by army officers." Under the rules, someone who reached a parcel "sooner" than anyone else and asserted a claim, acquired title. "Within a few hours the 1,920,000 acres ... [of the District] had been taken."[3]

The hostility requirement has proved most difficult in the so-called "mistaken boundary" line cases. In these cases, a dispute concerning the ownership of land arises between two neighbors, generally involving slight encroachments by one upon the land of the other. In connection with such disputes, consider the following case.

---

1. Daniel Boorstin reports that "[i]n Illinois, for example, before the end of 1828, about two-thirds of the population were 'squatters'—settlers on land that still technically belonged to the United States government." Boorstin, The Americans: The National Experience 74 (1965).

2. Id. at 78.

3. Id. at 81.

MANNILLO v. GORSKI

Supreme Court of New Jersey (1969).
54 N.J. 378, 255 A.2d 258.

HANEMAN, J.

Plaintiffs filed a complaint in the Chancery Division seeking a mandatory and prohibitory injunction against an alleged trespass upon their lands. Defendant counterclaimed for a declaratory judgment which would adjudicate that she had gained title to the disputed premises by adverse possession under N.J.S. 2A:14–6, N.J.S.A., which provides:

> Every person having any right or title of entry into real estate shall make such entry within 20 years next after the accrual of such right or title of entry, or be barred therefrom thereafter.

After plenary trial, judgment was entered for plaintiffs. Mannillo v. Gorski, 100 N.J.Super. 140, 241 A.2d 276 (Ch.Div.1968). Defendant appealed to the Appellate Division. Before argument there, this Court granted defendant's motion for certification. . . .

The facts are as follows: In 1946, defendant and her husband entered into possession of premises in Keansburg known as Lot No. 1007 in Block 42, under an agreement to purchase. Upon compliance with the terms of said agreement, the seller conveyed said lands to them on April 16, 1952. Defendant's husband thereafter died. The property consisted of a rectangular lot with a frontage of 25 feet and a depth of 100 feet. Plaintiffs are the owners of the adjacent Lot 1008 in Block 42 of like dimensions, to which they acquired title in 1953.

In the summer of 1946 Chester Gorski, one of the defendant's sons, made certain additions and changes to the defendant's house. He extended two rooms at the rear of the structure, enclosed a screened porch on the front, and put a concrete platform with steps on the west side thereof for use in connection with a side door. These steps were built to replace existing wooden steps. In addition, a concrete walk was installed from the steps to the end of the house. In 1953, defendant raised the house. In order to compensate for the resulting added height from the ground, she modified the design of the steps by extending them toward both the front and the rear of the property. She did not change their width.

Defendant admits that the steps and concrete walk encroach upon plaintiffs' lands to the extent of 15 inches. She contends, however, that she has title to said land by adverse possession. N.J.S.A. 2A:14–6, quoted above. Plaintiffs assert contrawise that defendant did not obtain title by adverse possession as her possession was not of the requisite hostile nature. They argue that to establish title by adverse possession, the entry into and continuance of possession must be accompanied by an intention to invade the rights of another in the lands, *i.e.*, a knowing wrongful taking. They assert that . . . defendant's encroachment was not accompanied by an intention to invade plaintiffs' rights in the land, but rather by the mistaken belief that she owned the land, and that therefore an essential requisite to establish title by adverse possession, i.e., an intentional tortious taking, is lacking.

The trial court concluded that defendant had clearly and convincingly proved that her possession of the 15–inch encroachment had existed for more than 20 years before the institution of this suit and that such possession was "exclusive, continuous, uninterrupted, visible, notorious and against the right and interest of the true owner." There is ample evidence to sustain this finding except as to its visible and notorious nature, of which more hereafter. However, the judge felt impelled by existing New Jersey case law, holding as argued by plaintiffs above, to deny defendant's claim and entered judgment for plaintiffs. 100 N.J.Super., at 150, 241 A.2d 276. The first issue before this Court is, therefore, whether an entry and continuance of possession under the mistaken belief that the possessor has title to the lands involved, exhibits the requisite hostile possession to sustain the obtaining of title by adverse possession.

The first detailed statement and acceptance by our then highest court, of the principle that possession as an element of title by adverse possession cannot be bottomed on mistake, is found in Folkman v. Myers, 93 N.J.Eq. 208, 115 A. 615 (E. & A.1921), which embraced and followed that thesis as expressed in Myers v. Polkman, 89 N.J.L. 390, 99 A. 97 (Sup.Ct.1916). It is not at all clear that this was the common law of this State prior to the latter case. An earlier opinion, Davock v. Nealon, 58 N.J.L. 21, 32 A. 675 (Sup.Ct.1895), held for an adverse possessor who had entered under the mistaken belief that he had title without any discussion of his hostile intent. However, the court in Myers v. Folkman, *supra*, at p. 393, 99 A. at p. 98, distinguished Davock from the case then under consideration by referring to the fact that "Charles R. Myers *disclaims* any intent to claim what did not belong to him, and apparently never asserted a right to land outside the bounds of his title...." (Emphasis supplied) The factual distinction between the two cases, according to *Myers,* is that in the later case there was not only an entry by mistake but also an articulated disclaimer of an intent by the entrant to claim title to lands beyond his actual boundary. *Folkman,* although apparently relying on *Myers,* eliminated the requirement of that decision that there be expressed an affirmative disclaimer, and expanded the doctrine to exclude from the category of hostile possessors those whose entry and continued possession was under a mistaken belief that the lands taken were embraced within the description of the possessor's deed. In so doing, the former Court of Errors and Appeals aligned this State with that branch of a dichotomy which traces its genesis to Preble v. Maine Cent. R. Co., 85 Me. 260, 27 A. 149, 21 L.R.A. 829 (Sup.Jud.Ct.Me.1893) and has become known as the Maine doctrine. In *Preble,* the court said at 27 A. at p. 150:

> There is every presumption that the occupancy is in subordination to the true title, and, if the possession is claimed to be adverse, the act of the wrongdoer must be strictly construed, and the character of the possession clearly shown. Roberts v. Richards, 84 Me. 1, 24 Atl.Rep. 425, and authorities cited. 'The intention of the possessor to claim adversely,' says Mellen, C.J., in Ross v. Gould, supra [5 Me. 204], 'is an essential ingredient in disseisin.' And in Worcester v. Lord, supra

[56 Me. 266] the court says: 'To make a disseisin in fact, there must be an intention on the part of the party assuming possession to assert title in himself.' Indeed, the authorities all agree that this intention of the occupant to claim the ownership of land not embraced in his title is a necessary element of adverse possession; and in case of occupancy by mistake beyond a line capable of being ascertained this intention to claim title to the extent of the occupancy must appear to be absolute, and not conditional; otherwise the possession will not be deemed adverse to the true owner. It must be an intention to claim title to all land within a certain boundary on the face of the earth, whether it shall eventually be found to be the correct one or not. If, for instance, one in ignorance of his actual boundaries takes and holds possession by mistake up to a certain fence beyond his limits, upon the claim and in the belief that it is the true line, with the intention to claim title, and thus, if necessary, to acquire 'title by possession' up to that fence, such possession, having the requisite duration and continuity, will ripen into title. Hitchings v. Morrison, 72 Me. 331, is a pertinent illustration of this principle. See, also, Abbott v. Abbott, 51 Me. 575; Ricker v. Hibbard, 73 Me. 105.

If, on the other hand, a party through ignorance, inadvertence, or mistake occupies up to a given fence beyond his actual boundary, because he believes it to be the true line, but has no intention to claim title to that extent if it should be ascertained that the fence was on his neighbor's land, an indispensable element of adverse possession is wanting. In such a case the intent to claim title exists only upon the condition that the fence is on the true line. The intention is not absolute, but provisional, and the possession is not adverse.

This thesis, it is evident, rewards the possessor who entered with a premeditated and predesigned "hostility"—the intentional wrongdoer and disfavors an honest, mistaken entrant. 3 American Law of Property (Casner ed. 1952), § 104, at 773, 785; Bordwell, "Disseisin and Adverse Possession," 33 Yale L.J. 1, 154 (1923); Darling, "Adverse Possession in Boundary Cases," 19 Ore.L.Rev. 117 (1940); Sternberg, "The Element of Hostility in Adverse Possession," 6 Temp.L.Q. 206 (1932); Annotation, "Adverse possession involving ignorance or mistake as to boundaries— modern views," 80 A.L.R.2d 1171 (1961).

The other branch of the dichotomy relies upon French v. Pearce, 8 Conn. 439 (Sup.Ct.Conn.1831). The court said in *Pearce* on the question of the subjective hostility of a possessor, at pp. 442, 445–446:

Into the recesses of his [the adverse claimant's] mind, his motives or purposes, his guilt or innocence, no enquiry is made....

... The very nature of the act [entry and possession] is an assertion of his own title, and the denial of the title of all others. It matters not that the possessor was mistaken, and had he been better informed, would not have entered on the land.

8 Conn. at 442, 445–446.

The Maine doctrine has been the subject of much criticism in requiring a knowing wrongful taking. The criticism of the Maine and the justification of the Connecticut branch of the dichotomy is well stated in 6 Powell, Real Property (1969) ¶ 1015, pp. 725–28:

Do the facts of his possession and of his conduct as if he were the owner, make immaterial his mistake, or does such a mistake prevent the existence of the prerequisite claim of right. The leading case holding the mistake to be of no importance was French v. Pearce, decided in Connecticut in 1831.... This viewpoint has gained increasingly widespread acceptance. The more subjectively oriented view regards the 'mistake' as necessarily preventing the existence of the required claim of right. The leading case on this position is Preble v. Maine Central R.R., decided in 1893. This position is still followed in a few states. It has been strongly criticized as unsound historically, inexpedient practically, and as resulting in better treatment for a ruthless wrongdoer than for the honest landowner.... On the whole the law is simplified, in the direction of real justice, by a following of the Connecticut leadership on this point.

Again, 4 Tiffany, Real Property (3d ed. 1939), § 1159, pp. 474–475, criticizes the employment of mistake as negating hostility as follows:

... Adopting this view, it is only in so far as the courts, which assert the possible materiality of the mistake, recognize a contrary presumption, of an intention on the part of the wrongful possessor not to claim title if he is mistaken as to the boundary, that the assertion of the materiality of mistake as to boundary becomes of substantial importance. That the presumption is properly in favor of the adverse or hostile character of the possession rather than against it has been previously argued, but whatever presumption in this regard may be recognized, the introduction of the element of mistake in the discussion of the question of adverse possession is, it is submitted, unnecessary and undesirable. In no case except in that of a mistake as to boundary has the element of mistake been regarded as having any significance, and there is no reason for attributing greater weight thereto when the mistake is as to the proper location of a boundary than when it is a mistake as to the title to all the land wrongfully possessed. And to introduce the element of mistake, and then limit its significance by an inquiry as to the intention which the possessor may have as to his course of action in case there should be a mistake, an intention which has ordinarily no existence whatsoever, is calculated only to cause confusion without, it is conceived, any compensating advantage.

Our Appellate Division in Predham v. Holfester, 32 N.J.Super. 419, 108 A.2d 458 (App.Div.1954) although acknowledging that the Maine doctrine had been severely criticized felt obliged because of *stare decisis* to adhere thereto. See also Rullis v. Jacobi, 79 N.J.Super. 525, 528, 192 A.2d 186 (Ch.Div.1963).

We are in accord with the criticism of the Maine doctrine and favor the Connecticut doctrine for the above quoted reasons. As far as can be seen, overruling the former rule will not result in undermining any of the values which *stare decisis* is intended to foster. The theory of reliance, a cornerstone of *stare decisis,* is not here apt, as the problem is which of two mistaken parties is entitled to land. Realistically, the true owner does not rely upon entry of the possessor by mistake as a reason for not seeking to recover possession. Whether or not the entry is caused by mistake or intent, the same result eventuates—the true owner is ousted from possession. In either event his neglect to seek recovery of possession, within the requisite time, is in all probability the result of a lack of knowledge that he is being deprived of possession of lands to which he has title.

Accordingly, we discard the requirement that the entry and continued possession must be accompanied by a knowing intentional hostility and hold that any entry and possession for the required time which is exclusive, continuous, uninterrupted, visible and notorious, even though under mistaken claim of title, is sufficient to support a claim of title by adverse possession.

However, this conclusion is not dispositive of the matter *sub judice.* Of equal importance under the present factual complex, is the question of whether defendant's acts meet the necessary standard of "open and notorious" possession. It must not be forgotten that the foundation of so-called "title by adverse possession" is the failure of the true owner to commence an action for the recovery of the land involved, within the period designated by the statute of limitations. The justifications for the doctrine are aptly stated in 4 Tiffany, Real Property (3d ed. 1939) § 1134, p. 406 as follows:

> The desirability of fixing, by law, a definite period within which claims to land must be asserted has been generally recognized, among the practical considerations in favor of such a policy being the prevention of the making of illegal claims after the evidence necessary to defeat them has been lost, and the interest which the community as a whole has in the security, of title. The moral justification of the policy lies in the consideration that one who has reason to know that land belonging to him is in the possession of another, and neglects, for a considerable period of time, to assert his right thereto, may properly be penalized by his preclusion from thereafter asserting such right. It is, apparently, by reason of the demerit of the true owner, rather than any supposed merit in the person who has acquired wrongful possession of the land, that this possession, if continued for the statutory period, operates to debar the former owner of all right to recover the land.

See also 5 Thompson, Real Property (1957 Replacement), 497.

In order to afford the true owner the opportunity to learn of the adverse claim and to protect his rights by legal action within the time specified by the statute, the adverse possession must be visible and notorious. In 4 Tiffany, *supra* (Supp.1969, at 291), the character of possession for that purpose, is stated to be as follows:

> ... [I]t must be public and based on physical facts, including known and visible lines and boundaries. Acts of dominion over the land must be so open and notorious as to put an ordinarily prudent person on notice that the land is in actual possession of another. Hence, title may never be acquired by mere possession, however long continued, which is surreptitious or secret or which is not such as will give unmistakable notice of the nature of the occupant's claim.

See also 5 Thompson, *supra*, § 2546; 6 Powell, Real Property, ¶ 1013 (1969).

Generally, where possession of the land is clear and unequivocal and to such an extent as to be immediately visible, the owner may be presumed to have knowledge of the adverse occupancy. In Foulke v. Bond, 41 N.J.L. 527, 545 (E. & A.1879), the court said:

> Notoriety of the adverse claim under which possession is held, is a necessary constituent of title by adverse possession, and therefore the occupation or possession must be of that nature that the real owner is *presumed to have known* that there was a possession adverse to his title, under which it was intended to make title against him. (Emphasis supplied)

However, when the encroachment of an adjoining owner is of a small area and the fact of an intrusion is not clearly and self-evidently apparent to the naked eye but requires an on-site survey for certain disclosure as in urban sections where the division line is only infrequently delineated by any monuments, natural or artificial, such a presumption is fallacious and unjustified. See concurring opinion of Judge (now Justice) Francis in Predham v. Holfester, 32 N.J.Super. 419, 428–429, 108 A.2d 458 (App.Div. 1954). The precise location of the dividing line is then ordinarily unknown to either adjacent owner and there is nothing on the land itself to show by visual observation that a hedge, fence, wall or other structure encroaches on the neighboring land to a minor extent. Therefore, to permit a presumption of notice to arise in the case of minor border encroachments not exceeding several feet would fly in the face of reality and require the true owner to be on constant alert for possible small encroachments. The only method of certain determination would be by obtaining a survey each time the adjacent owner undertook any improvement at or near the boundary, and this would place an undue and inequitable burden upon the true owner. Accordingly we hereby hold that no presumption of knowledge arises from a minor encroachment along a common boundary. In such a case, only where the true owner has actual knowledge thereof may it be said that the possession is open and notorious.

It is conceivable that the application of the foregoing rule may in some cases result in undue hardship to the adverse possessor who under an innocent and mistaken belief of title has undertaken an extensive improvement which to some extent encroaches on an adjoining property.

In that event the situation falls within the category of those cases of which Riggle v. Skill, 9 N.J.Super. 372, 74 A.2d 424 (Ch.Div.1950), affirmed 7 N.J. 268, 81 A.2d 364 (1951) is typical and equity may furnish relief. Then, if the innocent trespasser of a small portion of land adjoining a boundary line cannot without great expense remove or eliminate the encroachment, or such removal or elimination is impractical or could be accomplished only with great hardship, the true owner may be forced to convey the land so occupied upon payment of the fair value thereof without regard to whether the true owner had notice of the encroachment at its inception. Of course, such a result should eventuate only under appropriate circumstances and where no serious damage would be done to the remaining land as, for instance, by rendering the balance of the parcel unusable or no longer capable of being built upon by reason of zoning or other restrictions.

We remand the case for trial of the issues (1) whether the true owner had actual knowledge of the encroachment, (2) if not, whether plaintiffs should be obliged to convey the disputed tract to defendant, and (3) if the answer to the latter question is in the affirmative, what consideration should be paid for the conveyance. The remand, of course, contemplates further discovery and a new pretrial.

Remanded for trial in accordance with the foregoing.

NOTES AND QUESTIONS

1. Does the Maine doctrine encourage perjury? If so, is that a good reason to abandon that rule?

2. The court in the principal case, in overruling its prior adherence to the Maine doctrine, adopts the so-called Connecticut rule that possession is hostile even though the possessor did not subjectively intend to claim title to what he did not own. Adoption of this view, however, is not a "vindication of the view that simple possession is all that matters, because the cases show that it is the very absence of a desire to trespass upon another's land that makes the Connecticut rule preferable." Helmholz, Adverse Possession and Subjective Intent, 61 Wash. U. L.Q. 331, 339–40 (1983).

3. The decision in the principal case to overturn its prior adherence to the Maine rule did not necessarily result in the possessor prevailing in her adverse possession claim. Why? Does the rule adopted by the court adequately take into account the competing policies underlying the doctrine of adverse possession?

4. A doctrine related to adverse possession is the doctrine of "prescription," or "adverse use," commonly applied to easements. The doctrine is developed further in chapter 8.

5. Two other doctrines may be invoked to adjust the competing claims of adjoining landowners where encroachments arise by mistake. These are "acquiescence" and "estoppel." See chapter 15.

CARPENTER v. RUPERTO

Supreme Court of Iowa (1982).
315 N.W.2d 782.

McCormick, Justice.

Plaintiff Virginia Carpenter appeals from an adverse decree in her action to quiet title to land adjacent to her residential premises based on a theory of adverse possession. . . . We affirm on the merits of the appeal and dismiss the cross-appeal for want of jurisdiction. . . .

Plaintiff and her husband moved in 1951 to a home which they purchased in southeast Des Moines. Plaintiff's husband subsequently died, but plaintiff has lived on the premises continuously. Her lot has a frontage of 40 feet and is 125 feet long. . . .

A larger undeveloped lot bounded plaintiff's property to the north. . . .

Defendants and their predecessors have held record title to this lot at all material times.

The property which plaintiff claims to have acquired by adverse possession is the south 60 feet of defendants' lot. Thus, the property in dispute is a 60 by 125 foot parcel adjacent to the north boundary of plaintiff's lot.

When plaintiff and her husband moved into their home in July 1951, the lot north of their property was a cornfield. Although plaintiff was not certain of the location of the northern boundary of her lot, she knew her lot's dimensions, and she knew it did not include the cornfield. In 1952 the corn was not planted as far south on the adjacent lot. Concerned about rats and the threat of fire, and desiring additional yard for their children, plaintiff and her husband cleared several feet of the property to the north, graded it, and planted grass seed on it. Since that time plaintiff has used the land as an extension of her yard. She planted peony bushes on it during the 1950's, installed a propane tank on it approximately 30 feet north of her lot in 1964, constructed a dirt bank on the city right of way to divert water from that parcel in 1965, and put in a driveway infringing five feet onto the land in 1975.

The remainder of defendants' lot was planted in corn until approximately 1957. The lot was owned by Abraham and Beverly Rosenfeld from July 1960 until February 1978. During that period the only use Rosenfelds made of the property was to store junk and debris on it. Except for the strip used by plaintiff, the lot was overgrown with brush and weeds. The Rosenfelds paid all taxes and special assessments on the property. Plaintiff and her husband at one time obtained the Rosenfelds' permission to keep a horse on the lot. On one occasion in the 1960's plaintiff examined the plat of defendants' lot in the courthouse to see if it ran all the way to a street to the north. When defendant McCormick purchased his interest in the lot in 1978, he was aware of the possibility of a boundary dispute because of the location of plaintiff's propane tank and driveway. He and the other defendants were unsuccessful in their efforts to settle the dispute with plaintiff, who subsequently brought this action.

In seeking to establish her ownership of the disputed parcel, plaintiff alleged she had "for more than thirty (30) years last past been in open, exclusive, hostile, adverse and actual possession under claim of right." The trial court held in part that she did not establish her possession was under a claim of right. The court reasoned that a claim of right must be made in good faith and that plaintiff was not in good faith because she knew someone else had title to the land. Although the court found plaintiff had not proved her claim of adverse possession, it ordered defendants to "do equity" by deeding to her the strip of land her driveway was on and to pay the costs of moving the propane tank to her lot. The appeal and cross-appeal followed.

. . . The doctrine of adverse possession is based on the ten-year statute of limitations for recovery of real property in section 614.1(5), The Code. One claiming title by adverse possession must establish hostile, actual, open, exclusive and continuous possession, under a claim of right or color of title, for at least ten years, by clear and positive proof. Because the law presumes possession under regular title, the doctrine is strictly construed. . . .

As permitted, plaintiff relied on claim of right rather than color of title. In contending the trial court erred in finding she failed in her proof of this element, she attacks the viability of the principal case relied on by the trial court, *Goulding v. Shonquist,* 159 Iowa 647, 141 N.W. 24 (1913). Its facts are analogous to those here.

In *Goulding* the individual also cleared land adjacent to his house. The land was overrun with brush and willows and was frequented by hunters. After clearing it, the individual used the land as a pasture and garden. In finding he did not establish good faith claim of right, the court said:

> When he moved into his present property, the lands in question were objectionable because they were frequented by hunters, and for that reason he and his wife thought they ought to clear them up. He says he supposed they were part of the old river bed or waste land upon which anyone could enter. No other facts are offered by defendant as a reason for entering into the possession of the land at that time. Whether the title to the land was in the state or some other person, the defendant knew that he had no title and that he had no claim of title, and no right whatever to enter into the possession, and his possession was not in good faith for that reason.

Id. at 651, 141 N.W. at 25. The court quoted a statement from *Litchfield v. Sewell,* 97 Iowa 247, 251, 66 N.W. 104, 106 (1896), that "that there can be no such thing as adverse possession where the party knows he has no title, and that, under the law, he can acquire none by his occupation."

Plaintiff argues that it is inconsistent to say ownership can be acquired by claim of right as an alternative to color of title and at the same time say ownership cannot be acquired by a person who knows he does not have title. She also argues that the good faith requirement was eliminated by the court's decision in *I–80 Associates, Inc.* Although we agree it is an overstatement to say ownership cannot be acquired by a person who knows he does not have title, plaintiff is incorrect in her argument that good faith is not an essential component of claim of right. Moreover, we agree with the trial court that plaintiff did not prove this element of her adverse possession claim.

The overbreadth of the statement that title cannot be obtained through adverse possession by one who knows he has no title is demonstrated in *Litchfield, Goulding* and subsequent decisions. In *Litchfield* the court rejected the adverse possession claim of a person in possession of land under a quitclaim deed from a squatter. In finding an absence of good faith, the court noted the adverse possession doctrine "has no application to one who actually knows that he has no claim, or title, or right to a title." 97 Iowa at 250, 66 N.W. at 106. Under this holding a mere squatter or one who claims under a squatter cannot have a good faith claim of right to the property, but mere knowledge by the person that he has no title is not preclusive. A claim of right by a squatter is a false claim. To permit a squatter to assert a claim of right would put a premium on dishonesty. See 4 H. Tiffany, *Real Property* § 1147 at 792 (3d ed. 1975). One of the main purposes of the claim of right requirement is "to bar mere squatters from the benefits of adverse possession." 7 R. Powell, *Real Property* ¶ 1015 (Rohan ed. 1981). As in *Litchfield*, the possessor in Goulding not only knew that he had no title but that he had no claim of title or any right to enter into possession of the property. He was a mere squatter.

Policy

Knowledge of a defect in title is not alone sufficient to preclude proof of good faith:

> One is not deprived of the benefit of the statute of limitations merely because his claim of right is unenforceable or his title is known to be defective. The doctrine of adverse possession presupposes a defective title. It is not based on, but is hostile to, the true title. If the statute were to run only in favor of a valid title, it would serve no purpose. The holder of such a title has no need to invoke the statute. Where bad faith is held to negative an alleged claim of right, it is only another way of saying that such claim has been disproved.

Creel v. Hammans, 234 Iowa 532, 535, 13 N.W.2d 305, 307 (1944).

Nevertheless, when knowledge of lack of title is accompanied by knowledge of no basis for claiming an interest in the property, a good faith claim of right cannot be established. For example, a mere exchange of quitclaim deeds by persons who know legal title is in another will not support a claim of right:

> It is evident the claim and possession of George C. Abel could not have been in good faith. There was no reason why he and his brother

should believe they had any right to divide and apportion between themselves the real estate of their father while he was an insane patient in the state hospital. They must be held to have known the quitclaim deeds they exchanged gave them no title. At best, they proceeded upon what proved to be an unfounded assumption that their father would never be discharged from the adjudication of insanity. No claim of ownership by adverse possession will be sustained upon such a foundation. Plaintiff's position at this point does not appeal to a court of equity.

Abel v. Abel, 245 Iowa 907, 920, 65 N.W.2d 68, 75 (1954).

... The requirement of good faith was implicitly reaffirmed in a subsequent case, *Pearson v. City of Guttenberg*, 245 N.W.2d 519, 532 (Iowa 1976). We now confirm that good faith, as explained in this case, is essential to adverse possession under a claim of right.

We believe plaintiff failed to prove a good faith claim of right in the present case. She knew her lot did not include the cornfield north of it. She knew someone else had title to it and she had no interest in it or claim to it. This is not a case of confusion or mistake. At the time she entered possession of the disputed land, plaintiff knew she had no legal right to do so. To say that one can acquire a claim of right by merely entering possession would recognize squatter's rights. Possession for the statutory period cannot be bootstrapped into a basis for claiming a right to possession.

We hold that the trial court was right in rejecting plaintiff's claim....

Affirmed on the appeal; dismissed on the cross-appeal.

NOTES AND QUESTIONS

1. Under what circumstances could a possessor in a mistaken boundary line case establish a "good faith" claim?

2. Does the holding in *Carpenter* place Iowa in the Maine or the Connecticut camp?

3. Does the holding of *Carpenter* apply as well to non-mistaken boundary line cases? If so, how could the possessor in such case establish "good faith"?

4. In Jasperson v. Scharnikow, 150 F. 571, 572 (9th Cir. 1907), the court stated that: "This idea of acquiring title by larceny does not go in this country. A man must have a bona fide claim, or believe in his own mind that he has got a right as owner, when he goes upon land that does not belong to him, in order to acquire title by occupation and possession."

5. Restatement of Property § 458 cmt. d (1944) provides that "it is not necessary in order that a use be adverse that it be made either in the belief or under a claim that it is legally justified. The essential quality is that it be not made in subordination to those against whom it is claimed to be adverse. Yet he who claims a right in himself is impliedly asserting an absence of any right

in another inconsistent with the right claimed. Hence one who uses under a claim of right in himself is denying a use by the permission of another."

6.   Most courts require the possessor to establish her claim by clear and convincing evidence.

> The bottom line is that the function of the legal process is to minimize the risk of erroneous decisions.... The law should not allow the land of one to be taken by another, without a conveyance or consideration, merely upon slight presumption or probabilities. The relevant evidence in an adverse action must necessarily expand over a ten year period. A preponderance standard, in our judgment, would create the risk of increasing the number of cases whereby land is erroneously taken from the title owner under spurious adverse possession claims. This heightened standard of clear and convincing is one way to impress the factfinder with the importance of the decision, and thereby reduce the chances that spurious claims of adverse possession will be successful. Having concluded that the preponderance standard falls short of meeting the demands of fairness and accuracy in the factfinding process in the adjudication of adverse possession claims, we hold that the burden is upon the party who claims title by adverse possession to prove by clear and convincing evidence all elements essential to such title. To the extent that a different standard is intimated in our previous decisions, we herein expressly reject such intimations.

Brown v. Gobble, 196 W.Va. 559, 564–565, 474 S.E.2d 489, 494–495 (1996).

7.   In her provocative article, Efficient Trespass, The Case for Bad Faith Adverse Possession, 100 Nw. U. L. Rev. 1037, 1037–38 (2006), Professor Lee Anne Fennell notes that "the 'bad faith' adverse possession claimant—the trespasser who knows that the land she occupies is not her own—is an anomalous figure in the law. While not disqualified from gaining title to land in many jurisdictions, the bad faith claimant tends to fare poorly in court and suffers regular drubbings in law review articles. Meanwhile, judicial and scholarly approval is lavished on her 'good faith' counterpart, the encroacher who labors under the misimpression that he occupies his own land. In this Article, I challenge this consensus view. Instead of triggering moral condemnation and legal disadvantage, a claimant's knowledge of the encroachment should be a prerequisite for obtaining title under a properly formulated doctrine of adverse possession. Many courts and commentators have supported an objective standard under which both knowing and inadvertent encroachers can fulfill the 'hostility' requirement in adverse possession law. But I go further to argue that only the claimant who knew that she was encroaching—and who documented that awareness—should be able to take title to land through adverse possession."

She continues: "This surprising position follows logically from a wide-lensed look at the appropriate place of adverse possession in the overall framework of modern property law. When considered as part of a system that contains other, superior mechanisms for addressing problems such as innocent improvements and old title defects, adverse possession can best be understood as a doctrine of efficient trespass. It should work in concert with legal remedies that apply before the statute of limitations runs to test the relative·valuations of record owners and encroachers and to winnow out those situations in which consensual market transactions cannot accomplish transfers of land to much higher-valuing users." Id. at 1038–39.

The Innocent Improver Doctrine

Suppose A and B are adjoining landowners. A mistakenly extends his garage six feet upon B's land. Prior to the running of the statute of limitations, B sues A to remove the garage from his land. A claims that B should be required to convey to her the strip on which the garage encroaches. What result? At common law, the landowner was entitled to have the encroacher remove the encroaching structure. Should that be the result when the cost of the encroachment to build or remove is substantial compared to the negligible harm to the landowner? Should that be the result when the encroachment enhances the value of the landowner's property? In either of these cases, the courts traditionally held that the landowner could compel the removal of the structure. More modern courts may look at the relative hardship to the parties and, at least where the encroacher acted by mistake, deny the landowner the remedy of compulsory removal and require the encroacher to pay for the land. See, e.g,. Williams v. South & South Rentals, Inc., 82 N.C. App. 378, 346 S.E.2d 665, 669 (1986):

> Where the encroachment is minimal and the cost of removing the encroachment is most likely substantial, two competing factors must be considered in fashioning a remedy. On the one hand, without court intervention, a defendant may well be forced to buy plaintiff's land at a price many times its worth rather than destroy the building that encroaches. On the other hand, without the threat of a mandatory injunction, builders may view the legal remedy as a license to engage in private eminent domain. The process of balancing the hardships and the equities is designed to eliminate either extreme. Factors to be considered are whether the owner acted in good faith or intentionally built on the adjacent land and whether the hardship incurred in removing the structure is disproportionate to the harm caused by the encroachment. Mere inconvenience and expense are not sufficient to withhold injunctive relief. The relative hardship must be disproportionate.

In Somerville v. Jacobs, 153 W.Va. 613, 170 S.E.2d 805 (1969), the possessor mistakenly built a warehouse on a lot owned by another. When the landowner claimed to own the building, the possessor sued for equitable relief. The court stated:

> The controlling question for decision is whether a court of equity can award compensation to an improver for improvements which he has placed upon land not owned by him, which, because of mistake, he had reason to believe he owned, which improvements were not known to the owner until after their completion and were not induced or permitted by such owner, who is not guilty of any fraud or inequitable

conduct, and require the owner to pay the fair value of such improvements or, in the alternative, to convey the land so improved to the improver upon his payment to the owner of the fair value of the land less the value of the improvements....

... [T]hough the cases are conflicting the decisions in some jurisdictions, upon particular facts, recognize and sustain the jurisdiction of a court of equity to award compensation to the improver to prevent unjust enrichment to the owner and in the alternative to require the owner to convey the land to the improver upon his payment to the owner of the fair value of the land less the improvements....

To prevent such unjust enrichment of the defendants, and to do equity between the parties, this Court holds that an improver of land owned by another, who through a reasonable mistake of fact and in good faith erects a building entirely upon the land of the owner, with reasonable belief that such land was owned by the improver, is entitled to recover the value of the improvements from the landowner and to a lien upon such property which may be sold to enforce the payment of such lien, or, in the alternative, to purchase the land so improved upon payment to the landowner of the value of the land less the improvements and such landowner, even though free from any inequitable conduct in connection with the construction of the building upon his land, who, however, retains but refuses to pay for the improvements must, within a reasonable time, either pay the improver the amount by which the value of his land has been improved or convey such land to the improver upon the payment by the improver to the landowner of the value of the land without the improvements.

153 W.Va. at 616–17, 629, 170 S.E.2d at 807, 813.

JUDGE CAPLAN filed a strong dissent stating:

What of the property owner's right? The solution offered by the majority is designed to favor the plaintiff, the only party who had a duty to determine which lot was the proper one and who made a mistake. The defendants in this case, the owners of the property, had no duty to perform and were not parties to the mistake. Does equity protect only the errant and ignore the faultless? Certainly not.

In my opinion for the court to permit the plaintiff to force the defendants to sell their property contrary to their wishes is unthinkable and unpardonable. This is nothing less than condemnation of private property by private parties for private use. Condemnation of property (eminent domain) is reserved for government or such entities as may be designated by the legislature. Under no theory of law or equity should an individual be permitted to acquire property by condemnation. The majority would allow just that.

153 W.Va. at 635, 170 S.E.2d at 816–17.

What effect will the rule of the case have on other landowners contemplating additions to their property with respect to the care they will take to make sure the improvement does not encroach on a neighbor's land? What effect will the judgment have on other landowners trying to negotiate the sale of a strip of land where one of the parties has built an encroaching structure? What could the defendant have done to protect himself at some earlier point in time? Should the rule be limited to encroachments resulting from mistake and made in good faith? Is this consistent with the court's approach in the *Mannillo* case?

To what extent, if any, should the doctrines of acquiescence or estoppel apply in the case of possession of a large tract of land as against an absentee owner?

In some states, statutes govern the right of possessors to compensation from landowners with respect to improvements to the land. For example, Iowa Code ch. 560 (West Supp. 1984–85), entitled "Occupying Claimants," provides that where a possessor has "color of title" as peculiarly defined by the statute and "has in good faith made valuable improvements" upon the land of another, no judgment for possession shall be issued unless the provisions of the chapter have been satisfied. The chapter then provides that the owner shall compensate the improver for the value of the improvement. Failing that, the improver may purchase the land from the owner and, failing that, the parties shall hold the land and improvements as tenants in common. "Color of title" for the purpose of this statute means, among other things, that the possessor, or his predecessors, occupied the land for at least five continuous years. To what extent does this Iowa law differ from the rights of the possessor and owner recognized in the principal case or in *Somerville?*

Color of Title and Constructive Adverse Possession

Claim of right or hostility should not be confused with the concept of an entry under color of title. Entry under color of title refers to the situation where the possessor claims he has entered the land under the terms of a written instrument that purports to convey a title to the possessor but which instrument for one reason or another is defective or invalid. For example, A might enter O's land under a deed from B, believing that B had owned the property. Similarly, A may have purchased the land at a tax or other judicial sale and entered under a sheriff's deed that was improperly executed or properly executed following a sale that did not comply with the statutory procedures for affecting the tax sale. As a final example, A may have entered under the authority of a will that was not probated. While most states do not require entry under color of title to establish a title by adverse possession, a few states do impose this requirement. See 3 Amer. L. Prop. § 15.1 (A.J. Casner ed. 1952). Nonetheless, if the possessor enters under color of title, that fact may be helpful to establish the requisite hostility.

Two other benefits may flow from an entry under color of title. First, in some jurisdictions, if the possessor enters under color of title, the statutory period for acquiring a title by adverse possession may be shortened from the period required where there is an entry without color of title. See generally 7 R. Powell, Real Property 1014 (P. Rohan ed. 1984).

Second, if the possessor entered under an instrument that described a larger tract of land than the possessor actually possesses, actual possession of only a part of the tract may be constructive adverse possession of the whole. Under certain circumstances, therefore, if the possessor actually occupies only a portion of the tract for the entire statutory period, the possessor will acquire a title by adverse possession to the whole tract described in the instrument. Should the size of the tract described in the written instrument affect whether actual possession of only a part of the described tract is constructive possession of the unoccupied portion of the tract? See 3 Amer. L. Prop. § 15.11 (A.J. Casner ed. 1952).

Finally, in jurisdictions requiring the payment of taxes in order to acquire a title by adverse possession, the statute seldom runs unless the occupant has color of title. Do you see why?

NOTES AND QUESTIONS

1. In 1995, A receives an invalid deed describing a tract of four acres known as Blackacre. A enters the easterly two acres of Blackacre and remains in actual possession of this portion of Blackacre for longer than the prescribed period. However, during the entire period of A's occupation, O, the true owner of Blackacre, has been in actual occupation of the westerly two acres of Blackacre. In 2006, A sues O in ejectment claiming that he has acquired a title by adverse possession to all of Blackacre. What result? See Elliott v. Hensley, 188 Ky. 444, 222 S.W. 507 (1920); Patrick v. Goolsby, 158 Tenn. 162, 11 S.W.2d 677 (1928); 3 Amer. L. Prop. § 15.11 (A.J. Casner ed. 1952).

Suppose A–1, rather than O, had been in possession of the westerly two acres of Blackacre and that A–1 had entered in 1994 and had remained in actual possession until 2006 when A sued A–1 for possession. What result? See Bradley v. West, 60 Mo. 33 (1875); 3 Amer. L. Prop. § 15.11 (A.J. Casner ed. 1952).

2. Lots 1–4 are four contiguous lots owned by O. A enters Lot 1 under an invalid deed from X describing both Lot 1 and Lot 3. If A remains in actual, open, exclusive, and continuous possession of Lot 1 under claim of right for more than the statutory period, will A acquire a title by adverse possession to both Lots 1 and 3 if they are contiguous? If they are not contiguous? See Southern Coal and Iron Co. v. Schwoon, 145 Tenn. 191, 239 S.W. 398 (1921); 3 Amer. L. Prop. § 15.11 (A.J. Casner ed. 1952).

Suppose Lots 1 and 3 are contiguous, but Lot 1, the lot A actually entered, is owned by O and Lot 3, which is also described in the deed, is owned by O–1. Will A acquire title by adverse possession to Lot 3 if A is in actual possession only of Lot 1 during the entire statutory period?

3. If A acquires a title by adverse possession against O, is the nature of that title the same as O's title prior to the running of the statute? From what date is A's title deemed to have commenced? This issue is important if coincidentally with the time period during which O had a cause of action for

possession, O had other causes of actions against A. Additionally, questions can arise as to the effect of A's title on others having an interest in the property derived from O, such as O's mortgagees and judgment creditors.

Generally, title by adverse possession relates back to the date of the possessor's entry but is subject to any interest outstanding against the property against which no cause of action ran during the period that the possessor was in adverse possession. Thus, easements, covenants, and liens against the property in existence at the time of entry generally continue to be valid as against the adverse possessor after the statute of limitations has run on the true owner's cause of action for possession. This rule generally does not apply, however, if the adverse possessor interfered with such an interest at the same time he possessed the land. In that case the statute of limitations would also run against the owner of such interest. Similarly, the adverse possessor's title is subject to the dower claim of the prior owner's spouse to the extent it is still inchoate.

Ordinarily, the possessor can acquire no better title than the owner of the cause of action had. Thus, if the owner who had a cause of action was merely a life tenant, the possessor will only acquire an estate measured by the life tenant's life and will not acquire a good title as against the holder of the remainder interest. Is this consistent with the policies underlying the concept of adverse possession?

Lastly, because of the relation back rule, the true owner's other causes of action against the possessor will expire simultaneously with the running of the statute of limitations on the action for possession. For example, ordinarily, if A enters O's land and O sues A prior to the running of the statute of limitations, O can recover not only possession but also damages equal to the fair rental value of the property during the period of the unauthorized possession. O's right to receive damages from A is a separate cause of action from O's cause of action against A for possession. Once A acquires a title to the property by adverse possession, however, any outstanding cause of action O may have to recover the fair rental value of the property from A also expires even though the statute of limitations on O's action for damages has not expired. Likewise, any cause of action O might have against A for damages resulting from waste expires once A acquires title by adverse possession. Why should O's other causes of action against A expire?

NOTE: EFFICIENCY, COMPENSATION, AND ADVERSE POSSESSION

A legal rule is efficient if it maximizes social wealth. The unregulated market is the greatest maximizer of social wealth, for it uses the price system to assign things to those who place the highest value on them. A market transaction will not occur unless each party to the transaction thinks it makes him better off; if both parties are "richer" as a result of the transaction, and no one else is adversely affected, then society as a whole is richer.

Can the law of adverse possession be defended as economically efficient? What is the economic justification for a rule that lets one person "steal" another's land simply by occupying it for a specified length of time? There are several explanations for adverse possession, many of them "economic"—i.e., they purport to explain how society has more wealth as a result of adverse possession. One of these is that the law of adverse possession aids in "quieting," or clearing, ambiguous titles to real estate. If the written record is unclear, the law effectively creates some presumptions in favor of the current possessor, assuming she has been there long enough. The effect is to make the market for real property operate much more smoothly. More will be said of this rationale for adverse possession later in this note, and it is discussed at length in chapter 16.

A second, frequently given explanation for adverse possession law is that it tends to assign land to active claimants at the expense of inactive ones. Assuming the former are more valuable to society, adverse possession efficiently places the land where it will make the greatest contribution.

This second rationale does not withstand close analysis, however. First, the notion that non-development of property is inefficient is untrue. A reasonable person who holds land for the future rather than developing it today has calculated that the value of future development is greater than the value of present development. Keeping land undeveloped for a time is frequently efficient—for precisely the same reason that harvesting corn in September and selling it in February can be efficient. If the record title owner has been merely holding land while the occupier has been developing it, there may be a difference of opinion about which strategy is more profitable—but it does not follow automatically that the development is more efficient. If the land really does have a higher value in the hands of the developer than the record owner, we would expect the developer to purchase it.

As a result, we cannot be certain that it is socially preferable in any particular case to award the land to the possessor rather than the record title holder. It has been suggested that one way to ensure that the land is given to the person who values it more (and whose use is thus presumed to be more valuable to society) is to force the occupier to compensate the record owner for his losses. The possessor will do this only if he places a greater value on the land than the record owner does. Suppose an investor buys a farm, which he values at $500 per acre. Unknown to him, someone else occupies an acre of the farm for the statutory period and all other requirements for adverse possession have been met. However, suppose that the court awards the acre to the occupier *only* if the latter agrees to pay the record owner $500. If the occupier values the possessed land at $500 or more, he will be willing to pay; if he values it at less than $500, he will not. In short, a rule requiring compensation will assign the land to the person who places the greater value on it, which is precisely the way the free market would assign the land. See Comment, Compensation for the Involuntary Transfer of Property Between Private Parties: Application of a Liability Rule to the Law of Adverse Possession, 79 Nw. U. L. Rev. 758 (1984).

The principal problem with this argument is that the compensation award is unnecessary to make adverse possession efficient. Even without the award, the possessed land should be given to the person who places the highest value on it. In the above example, suppose that the possessor in fact values the acre of land at only $100. The court gives a traditional award of adverse possession, without awarding compensation. In this case the *record owner* of the land will probably pay the possessor for the right to retain the land. They will complete this transaction at some price between $100 and $500. For example, if the record owner pays the possessor $300, both parties will be $200 better off. In short, whether or not compensation is ordered, we would expect the land to go to the person who places the greater value on it.

Although an award of compensation will not determine whether adverse possession is efficient, it has a great deal to do with the resulting distribution of wealth between the parties. The compensation requirement makes the possessor relatively poorer and the record owner relatively richer, regardless of which person ends up owning the land. As a result one might argue that although a compensation requirement is not necessary to create efficient outcomes in the law of adverse possession, it results in fairer treatment of record owners.

The case against compensation is strong, however. First, *the compensation requirement is the status quo when the requirements of adverse possession are not met.* That is, the market for real property tends to assign *all* land to its most efficient user, whether or not that land is being adversely possessed. In the above example, if the possessor, who valued the land at only $100 per acre, were really the record owner, his neighbor, who values the land at $500 per acre, would buy it from him at some price between $100 and $500. We use the law of adverse possession to *depart* from the general free market rule that requires payment when one person takes another's property in a commercial transaction.[4]

Second, a compensation requirement would substantially undermine the use of adverse possession as a title clearing device. One of the most common uses of adverse possession is to clear land titles in favor of a known current occupant when the record claimant is unknown, long deceased, or the record title appears to be in many persons scattered over a wide area. To say that the current occupant obtains title by adverse possession only upon payment of compensation to the record owners is to require exactly what the title lawyer is hoping to avoid—the duty of having to locate and identify the claims of many people who might be difficult or impossible to find.

§ 3.5 ADVERSE POSSESSION OF CHATTELS

SOLOMON R. GUGGENHEIM FOUNDATION v. LUBELL

Court of Appeals of New York (1991).
77 N.Y.2d 311, 567 N.Y.S.2d 623, 569 N.E.2d 426.

WACHTLER, JUDGE

The backdrop for this replevin action (*see*, CPLR art. 71) is the New York City art market, where masterpieces command extraordinary prices at auction and illicit dealing in stolen merchandise is an industry all its own. The Solomon R. Guggenheim Foundation, which operates the Gug-

---

4. Actually, the situation is a little more complicated. The market permits the landowner to refuse to sell his land at any price. A rule of adverse possession plus compensation would give the record owner the fair market value, but it would force him to make the transaction. See Merrill, Property Rules, Liability Rules, and Adverse Possession, 79 Nw. U. L. Rev. 1122 (1984).

genheim Museum in New York City, is seeking to recover a Chagall gouache worth an estimated $200,000. The Guggenheim believes that the gouache was stolen from its premises by a mailroom employee sometime in the late 1960s. The appellant Rachel Lubell and her husband, now deceased, bought the painting from a well-known Madison Avenue gallery in 1967 and have displayed it in their home for more than 20 years. Mrs. Lubell claims that before the Guggenheim's demand for its return in 1986, she had no reason to believe that the painting had been stolen.

On this appeal, we must decide if the museum's failure to take certain steps to locate the gouache is relevant to the appellant's statute of limitations defense. In effect, the appellant argues that the museum had a duty to use reasonable diligence to recover the gouache, that it did not do so, and that its cause of action in replevin is consequently barred by the statute of limitations. The Appellate Division rejected the appellant's argument. We agree with the Appellate Division that the timing of the museum's demand for the gouache and the appellant's refusal to return it are the only relevant factors in assessing the merits of the statute of limitations defense. We see no justification for undermining the clarity and predictability of this rule by carving out an exception where the chattel to be returned is a valuable piece of art. Appellant's affirmative defense of laches remains viable, however, and her claims that the museum did not undertake a reasonably diligent search for the missing painting will enter into the trial court's evaluation of the merits of that defense. Accordingly, the order of the Appellate Division should be affirmed. The gouache, known alternately as "Menageries" or "Le Marchand de Bestiaux" ("The Cattle Dealer"), was painted by Marc Chagall in 1912, in preparation for an oil painting also entitled "Le Marchand de Bestiaux." It was donated to the museum in 1937 by Solomon R. Guggenheim.

The museum keeps track of its collection through the use of "accession cards," which indicate when individual pieces leave the museum on loan, when they are returned and when they are transferred between the museum and storage. The museum lent the painting to a number of other art museums over the years. The last such loan occurred in 1961–62. The accession card for the painting indicates that it was seen in the museum on April 2, 1965. The next notation on the accession card is undated and indicates that the painting could not be located.

Precisely when the museum first learned that the gouache had been stolen is a matter of some dispute. The museum acknowledges that it discovered that the painting was not where it should be sometime in the late 1960s, but claims that it did not know that the painting had in fact been stolen until it undertook a complete inventory of the museum collection beginning in 1969 and ending in 1970. According to the museum, such an inventory was typically taken about once every ten years. The appellant, on the other hand, argues that the museum knew as early as 1965 that the painting had been stolen. It is undisputed, however, that the Guggenheim did not inform other museums, galleries or artistic organizations of the theft, and additionally, did not notify the New York City Police, the FBI, Interpol or any other law enforcement authorities. The museum asserts that this was a tactical decision based upon its belief that to publicize the theft would succeed only in driving the gouache further underground and greatly diminishing the possibility that it would ever be recovered. In 1974, having concluded that all efforts to recover the gouache had been exhausted, the museum's Board of Trustees voted to "deaccession" the gouache, thereby removing it from the museum's records.

Mr. and Mrs. Lubell had purchased the painting from the Robert Elkon Gallery for $17,000 in May of 1967. The invoice and receipt indicated that the gouache had been in the collection of a named individual, who later turned out to be the museum mailroom employee suspected of the theft. They exhibited the painting twice, in 1967 and in 1981, both times at the Elkon Gallery. In 1985, a private art dealer brought a transparency of the painting to Sotheby's for an auction estimate. The person to whom the dealer showed the transparency had previously worked at the Guggenheim and recognized the gouache as a piece that was missing from the museum. She notified the museum, which traced the painting back to the defendant. On January 9, 1986, Thomas Messer, the museum's director, wrote a letter to the defendant demanding the return of the gouache. Mrs. Lubell refused to return the painting and the instant action for recovery of the painting, or, in the alternative, $200,000, was commenced on September 28, 1987. In her answer, the appellant raised as affirmative defenses the statute of limitations, her status as a good faith purchaser for value, adverse possession, laches, and the museum's culpable conduct. The museum moved to compel discovery and inspection of the gouache and the defendant cross-moved for summary judgment. In her summary judgment papers, the appellant argued that the replevin action to compel the return of the painting was barred by the three year statute of limitations because the museum had done nothing to locate its property in the twenty year interval between the theft and the museum's fortuitous discovery that the painting was in Mrs. Lubell's possession. The trial court granted the appellant's cross motion for summary judgment, relying on DeWeerth v. Baldinger (836 F.2d 103), an opinion from the United States Court of Appeals for the Second Circuit. The trial court cited New York cases holding that a cause of action in replevin accrues when demand is made upon the possessor and the possessor refuses to return the chattel. The court reasoned, however, that in order to avoid prejudice to a good faith purchaser, demand cannot be unreasonably delayed and that a property owner has an obligation to use reasonable efforts to locate its missing property to ensure that demand is not so delayed. Because the museum in this case had done nothing for twenty years but search its own premises, the court found that its conduct was unreasonable as a matter of law. Consequently, the court granted Mrs. Lubell's cross motion for summary judgment on the grounds that the museum's cause of action was time-barred. . . .

In DeWeerth v. Baldinger [836 F.2d 103 (1987)] which the trial court in this case relied upon in granting Mrs. Lubell's summary judgment motion, the Second Circuit took note of the fact that New York case law treats thieves and good faith purchasers differently and looked to that difference as a basis for imposing a reasonable diligence requirement on the owners of stolen art. Although the court acknowledged that the question posed by the case was an open one, it declined to certify it to this Court (*see*, 22 NYCRR § 500.17), stating that it did not think that it "[would] recur with sufficient frequency to warrant use of the certification procedure" (836 F.2d at 108). Actually, the issue has recurred several times in the three years since DeWeerth was decided (*see*, e.g., The Republic of Turkey v. The Metropolitan Museum of Art, No. 87 Civ. 3750[VLB], slip op. [S.D.N.Y. July 16, 1990]), including the case now before us. We have reexamined the relevant New York case law and we conclude that the Second Circuit should not have imposed a duty of reasonable diligence on the owners of stolen art work for purposes of the statute of limitations.

While the demand and refusal rule is not the only possible method of measuring the accrual of replevin claims, it does appear to be the rule that affords the most protection to the true owners of stolen property. Less protective measures would include running the three year statutory period from the time of the theft even where a good faith purchaser is in possession of the stolen chattel, or, alternatively, calculating the statutory period from the time that the good faith purchaser obtains possession of the chattel (*see generally*, Weil, Repose, 8 IFAR reports, at 6–7 [August–September 1987]). Other states that have considered this issue have applied a discovery rule to these cases, with the statute of limitations running from the time that the owner discovered or reasonably should have discovered the whereabouts of the work of art that had been stolen (*see*, e.g., O'Keeffe v. Snyder, 83 N.J. 478, 416 A.2d 862; Cal.Civ.Proc.Code § 338[c]).

New York has already considered—and rejected—adoption of a discovery rule. In 1986, both houses of the New York State Legislature passed Assembly Bill 11462–A (Senate Bill 3274–B), which would have modified the demand and refusal rule and instituted a discovery rule in actions for recovery of art objects brought against certain not-for-profit institutions. This bill provided that the three year statute of limitations would run from the time these institutions gave notice, in a manner specified by the statute, that they were in possession of a particular object. Governor Cuomo vetoed the measure, however, on advice of the United States Department of State, the United States Department of Justice and the United States Information Agency (*see*, 3 U.S. Agencies Urge Veto of Art–Claim Bill, N.Y. Times, July 23, 1986, C15, col. 1). In his veto message, the Governor expressed his concern that the statute "[did] not provide a reasonable opportunity for individuals or foreign governments to receive notice of a museum's acquisition and take action to recover it before their rights are extinguished." The Governor also stated that he had been advised by the State Department that the bill, if it went into effect, would have caused New York to become "a haven for cultural property stolen abroad since such objects [would] be immune from recovery under the limited time periods established by the bill."

The history of this bill and the concerns expressed by the Governor in vetoing it, when considered together with the abundant case law spelling out the demand and refusal rule, convince us that rule remains the law in New York and that there is no reason to obscure its straightforward protection of true owners by creating a duty of reasonable diligence. Our case law already recognizes that the true owner, having discovered the location of its lost property, cannot unreasonably delay making demand upon the person in possession of that property. . . . Here, however, where the demand and refusal is a substantive and not a procedural element of the cause of action (*see*, Solomon R. Guggenheim Foundation v. Lubell, 153 A.D.2d, at 147; Menzel v. List, 22 A.D.2d 647; compare, CPLR § 206 [where a demand is necessary to entitle a person to commence an action, the time to commence that action is measured from when the right to make demand is complete]), it would not be prudent to extend that case law and impose the additional duty of diligence before the true owner has reason to know where its missing chattel is to be found.

Further, the facts of this case reveal how difficult it would be to specify the type of conduct that would be required for a showing of reasonable diligence. Here, the parties hotly contest whether publicizing the theft would have turned up the gouache. According to the museum, some members of the art community believe that publicizing a theft exposes gaps in security and can lead to more thefts; the museum also argues that publicity often pushes a missing painting further under-ground. In light of the fact that members of the art community have apparently not reached a consensus on the best way to retrieve stolen art (*see*, B. Burnham, Art Theft: Its Scope, Its Impact and Its Control), it would be particularly inappropriate for this Court to spell out arbitrary rules of conduct that all true owners of stolen art work would have to follow to the letter if they wanted to preserve their right to pursue a cause of action in replevin. All owners of stolen property should not be expected to behave in the same way and should not be held to a common standard. The value of the property stolen, the manner in which it was stolen, and the type of institution from which it was stolen will all necessarily affect the manner in which a true owner will search for missing property. We conclude that it would be difficult, if not impossible, to craft a reasonable diligence requirement that could take into account all of these variables and that would not unduly burden the true owner.

Further, our decision today is in part influenced by our recognition that New York enjoys a worldwide reputation as a preeminent cultural center. To place the burden of locating stolen artwork on the true owner and to foreclose the rights of that owner to recover its property if the burden is not met would, we believe, encourage illicit trafficking in stolen art. Three years after the theft, any purchaser, good faith or not, would be able to hold onto stolen art work unless the true owner was able to establish that it had undertaken a reasonable search for the missing art. This shifting of the burden onto the wronged owner is inappropriate. In our opinion, the better rule gives the owner relatively greater protection and places the burden of investigating the provenance of a work of art on the potential purchaser.

Despite our conclusion that the imposition of a reasonable diligence requirement on the museum would be inappropriate for purposes of the statute of limitations, our holding today should not be seen as either sanctioning the museum's conduct or suggesting that the museum's conduct is no longer an issue in this case. We agree with the Appellate Division that the arguments raised in the appellant's summary judgment papers are directed at the conscience of the court and its ability to bring equitable considerations to bear in the ultimate disposition of the painting. As noted above, although appellant's statute of limitations argument fails, her contention that the museum did not exercise reasonable diligence in locating the painting will be considered by the trial judge in the context of her laches defense. The conduct of both the appellant and the museum will be relevant to any consideration of this defense at the trial level, and as the Appellate Division noted, prejudice will also need to be shown (153 A.D.2d at 149). On the limited record before us there is no indication that the equities favor either party. Mr. & Mrs. Lubell investigated the provenance of the gouache before the purchase by contacting the artist and his son-in-law directly. The Lubells displayed the painting in their home for more than 20 years with no reason to suspect that it was not legally theirs. These facts will doubtless have some impact on the final decision regarding appellant's laches defense. Because it is impossible to conclude from the facts of this case that the museum's conduct was unreasonable as a matter of law, however, Mrs. Lubell's cross motion for summary judgment was properly denied.

We agree with the Appellate Division, for the reasons stated by that court, that the burden of proving that the painting was not stolen properly rests with the appellant Mrs. Lubell. We have considered her remaining arguments, and we find them to be without merit. Accordingly, the order of the Appellate Division should be affirmed, with costs, and the certified question answered in the affirmative.

NOTES AND QUESTIONS

1. Analyzed from the perspective of the requirements of adverse possession, would the display of the painting on the walls in the home of the Lubells be sufficiently open? See DeWeerth v. Baldinger, 658 F. Supp. 688 (S.D.N.Y. 1987), rev'd 836 F.2d 103 (2d Cir. 1987).

2. In O'Keeffe v. Snyder, 83 N.J. 478, 416 A.2d 862 (1980), a suit was brought to recover possession of an allegedly stolen painting many years after the date of the alleged theft. The trial court held that the cause of action accrued on the date of the alleged theft even though plaintiff was unaware of

the actual location of the painting. The Supreme Court rejected this rule in favor of a discovery rule. It stated:

> The discovery rule provides that, in an appropriate case, a cause of action will not accrue until the injured party discovers, or by exercise of reasonable diligence and intelligence should have discovered, facts which form the basis of a cause of action.... The rule is essentially a principle of equity, the purpose of which is to mitigate unjust results that otherwise might flow from strict adherence to a rule of law....
>
> ... [T]he discovery rule applies to an action for replevin of a painting under N.J.S.A. 2A:14. O'Keeffe's cause of action accrued when she first knew, or reasonably should have known through the exercise of due diligence, of the cause of action, including the identity of the possessor of the paintings. See N. Ward, Adverse Possession of Loaned or Stolen Objects Is Possession Still 9/10ths of the Law?, published in Legal Problems of Museum Administration (ALI–ABA 1980) at 89–90....
>
> In determining whether O'Keeffe is entitled to the benefit of the discovery rule, the trial court should consider, among others, the following issues: (1) whether O'Keeffe used due diligence to recover the paintings at the time of the alleged theft and thereafter; (2) whether at the time of the alleged theft there was an effective method, other than talking to her colleagues, for O'Keeffe to alert the art world; and (3) whether registering paintings with the Art Dealers Association of America, Inc. or any other organization would put a reasonably prudent purchaser of art on constructive notice that someone other than the possessor was the true owner.

83 N.J. at 491, 493–94, 416 A.2d at 869–70.

Two judges filed strong dissents. Judge Handler wrote:

> The Court today rules that if a work of art has been stolen from an artist, the artist's right to recover his or her work from a subsequent possessor would be barred by the statute of limitations if the action were not brought within six years after the original theft. This can happen even though the artist may have been totally innocent and wholly ignorant of the identity of the thief or of any intervening receivers or possessors of the stolen art. The Court would grudgingly grant some measure of relief from this horrendous result and allow the artist to bring suit provided he or she can sustain the burden of proving "due diligence" in earlier attempting to retrieve the stolen artwork. No similar duty of diligence or vigilance, however, is placed upon the subsequent receiver or possessor, who, innocently or not, has actually trafficked in the stolen art. Despite ritualistic disavowals, the Court's holding does little to discourage art thievery. Rather, by making it relatively more easy for the receiver or possessor of an artwork with a "checkered background" to gain security and title than for the artist or true owner to reacquire it, it seems as though the Court surely will stimulate and legitimatize art thievery.
>
> I believe that there is a much sounder approach in this sort of case than one that requires the parties to become enmeshed in duplicate or cumulative hearings that focus on the essentially collateral issues of the statute

of limitations and its possible tolling by an extended application of the discovery doctrine. The better approach ... is one that enables the parties to get to the merits of the controversy. It would recognize an artist's or owner's right to assert a claim against a newly-revealed receiver or possessor of stolen art as well as the correlative right of such a possessor to assert all equitable and legal defenses.... By dealing with the merits of the claims instead of the right to sue, such an approach would be more conducive to reconciling the demands for individual justice with societal needs to discourage art thievery.

83 N.J. at 507–08, 416 A.2d at 878.

3. At common law, the statute of limitations on an action to recover the possession of personal property began to run not when the owner discovered the location of the personalty, but rather when the possession became hostile to the rights of the owner. See, e.g., Isham v. Cudlip, 33 Ill. App. 2d 254, 179 N.E.2d 25 (1962). In those cases where the owner delivered possession of the personal property to the possessor, the statute began to run when she demanded a return of the goods and the demand was refused. Further, in adverse possession of chattels cases, the courts, while recognizing the open and notorious requirement, have had to grapple with the problem of concealment and the potential status of the defendant as a bona fide purchaser.

4. The time periods under the statute of limitations for the recovery of chattels tend to be shorter than the period provided for the recovery of the possession of real property. Two to six-year statutes are common. What policies, if any, justify the shorter period of time?

5. Over the last few years, there has been increasing public interest over the settlement of claims arising from art stolen by Nazis during the Second World War. Much of this art was stolen from Jewish families who ultimately perished in the Holocaust. Later, some of the art was found in the vaults of museums, such as the Hermitage in St. Petersburg where art confiscated by the Soviets following their invasion of Nazi Germany was stored; others found their way into private collections as a result of purchase by persons ignorant or indifferent to the provenance of the artwork. The competing claims of buyers and heirs of Nazi victims are being pursued both in Europe and the United States. To some extent the ability of the heirs to successfully reclaim the art depends on how disputes over the proper function of a statute of limitations are resolved. Compare the following:

Ashton Hawkins, Richard Rothman, & David Goldstein, A Tale of Two Innocents: Creating An Equitable Balance Between the Rights of Former Owners and Good Faith Purchasers of Stolen Art, 64 Fordham L. Rev. 49, 49–54 (1995):

> Art theft has probably been with us for almost as long as there has been art, which is to say, virtually forever. As the value of art transactions has expanded, now totalling billions of dollars annually, the theft of art and the trade in stolen art has kept pace. Stolen art frequently returns to the stream of commerce, where it is often obtained by an innocent good faith purchaser for value who is unaware of the theft many years ago. When the former owner finally locates the art in the possession of this good faith purchaser and commences an action against this innocent purchaser

for conversion or replevin, the courts are faced with the unpleasant dilemma of allocating rights and burdens between these two innocent victims of the thief, who is typically either unknown or judgment-proof.

At the heart of the stolen art problem—virtually dispositive in many cases—is the question of the appropriate statute of limitations, i.e., how long after the theft can the former owner sue the current holder of the art? This problem arises from a fundamental principle of law, combined with the unique attributes of art. Anglo–American law is well-settled that neither a thief nor a good faith purchaser from the thief, nor even subsequent good faith purchasers, can pass good title. Indeed, the tort of conversion is unique in that it permits a plaintiff to recover property or money damages from a defendant who is by definition innocent of any wrongdoing or of inflicting harm on the plaintiff, regardless of the defendant's ability to recover against the actual wrongdoer. Despite this unusual situation, courts have, for statute of limitations purposes, treated innocent purchasers no less harshly—and often more harshly—than "guilty" tortfeasors.

The statute of limitations problem is heightened with respect to valuable works of art because, unlike most forms of personal property, art is frequently nonperishable (often lasting for centuries); easily transportable (the art trade, legitimate and otherwise, is notable for its internationalism) and hence, easily concealed; readily identified; nonfungible; and often of dramatically increasing value. Thus, it is not uncommon for claims to recover stolen art to be made decades after the theft, often against innocent purchasers....

The 1991 decision of the New York Court of Appeals—the highest court in the art market capital of the world—in Solomon R. Guggenheim Foundation v. Lubell exemplifies this judicial failure to balance the rights of the two innocents. In Guggenheim—an action to recover a stolen painting from a good faith purchaser—the court held that the statute of limitations does not begin to run until the former owner locates, demands, and is refused the return of its property, regardless of the former owner's failure to exercise diligence in locating the stolen work. As a result of this decision, New York effectively has no statute of limitations for the recovery of stolen property, and innocent purchasers are perpetually at risk of a claim of theft by a former owner.

Although the court in Guggenheim expressed a fear that a less "owner-friendly" rule would turn New York into a haven for stolen art, its decision instead threatens to turn New York into a haven for questionable litigation of ancient claims, and thereby may have a chilling effect on legitimate art transactions and art exhibitions in the state. Moreover, rather than helping to solve or to ameliorate the widespread and serious problems involving art theft, Guggenheim's view of the law has exacerbated them, permitting former owners to avoid taking the steps that might lead to the recovery of stolen art, and thus preventing innocent purchasers of stolen art from becoming new victims of the thief.

The fundamental flaw in Guggenheim ... is its failure to consider that it had two "innocents" before it—the innocent theft victim and the innocent purchaser. Instead, the court absolved the former owner, as a matter of law, of any duty of diligence under the applicable statute of limitations to attempt to locate its missing art. The court harshly treated the innocent purchaser as worse than the thief, holding that the innocent purchaser could challenge the owner's delay only through the equitable defense of laches. Under a laches defense, the burden falls on the purchaser to show that the former owner unreasonably delayed in bringing suit and that the purchaser was unduly prejudiced by the unreasonable delay. This fact-intensive inquiry can rarely be resolved without protracted litigation. Guggenheim simply failed to give proper weight to the value of repose both to settled commercial relations and to the proper functioning of the legal system.

Under Guggenheim's inflexible application of New York's unique demand and refusal rule, former owners will be able to prevail over innocent purchasers even after decades of inaction in attempting to locate the missing work. . . .

As a direct result of Guggenheim, there is a growing concern on the part of art dealers, collectors, and museums regarding art transactions and exhibitions of artworks in New York. Guggenheim confirms that the courts are institutionally ill-equipped to achieve a proper balance of the competing interests at stake. Unless a proper balance is restored between the rights and duties of innocent former owners and purchasers, New York's "worldwide reputation as a preeminent cultural center," including both the commerce and display of art, with its many museums, galleries, private collectors, auction houses, and resident artists, will be jeopardized.

The appropriate balancing of rights and duties among former owners, sellers, and purchasers would appear to require a legislative, rather than a judicial, solution. . . .

More specifically, this article proposes that the accrual of the statute of limitations for an art theft victim's claim for conversion or replevin would depend on whether the former owner or subsequent purchaser avails themself of the special procedures set forth in the proposed statute. Under these procedures, a former owner who "registered" expeditiously the stolen work with a confidential, user-financed international computerized stolen art registry would be protected against a limitations claim by subsequent purchasers. Correspondingly, a purchaser who consulted the registry at the time of purchase would be protected by a three-year limitations period from the date of purchase.

Thus, a registered owner's time to commence suit would be tolled indefinitely against a subsequent purchaser, so long as the owner exercised reasonable diligence in searching for the art, while the three-year statute would begin to run in favor of the purchaser at the time he checked the registry and found that the work in question had not been registered. The registry would notify the registered owner that an inquiry had been made by a prospective purchaser and confidential records would be kept of such inquiries. If neither party availed itself of the registry, the proposed statute would apply a discovery rule. Issues of retroactivity and lack of knowledge of the registries are also addressed.

Steven Bibas, The Case Against the Statutes of Limitations for Stolen Art: 103 Yale L.J. 2437, 2437–39 (1994):

In the mid–1960's, a mailroom clerk at the Guggenheim Museum in New York City stole a Marc Chagall watercolor entitled The Cattle Dealer. Museum officials did not notify the police, the FBI, Interpol, or other museums or galleries of the theft. In 1967, Jules and Rachel Lubell bought The Cattle Dealer from a reputable New York gallery and displayed it in their home for over two decades. After learning of the painting's location in 1985, museum officials demanded its return. When Mrs. Lubell refused, the museum began a lawsuit that dragged on for years. Mrs. Lubell claimed ownership as an adverse possessor and under the statute of limitations. In 1991, the New York Court of Appeals sent the case back to the trial court for a determination of the relative blameworthiness of the parties, further prolonging the litigation.

The balancing-test approach adopted by the New York Court of Appeals in Guggenheim exemplifies one of several tangled threads in the law of stolen chattels. Many of the commentators who have written about statutes of limitations for personal property advocate adverse possession, a doctrine borrowed from land law. Other authors endorse a multi-factor balancing of the equities called the discovery rule, an approach similar to the one adopted in Guggenheim. Related doctrines, such as the due diligence and laches rules, also balance the relative equities of the parties.

All of these approaches are flawed. Adverse possession, a doctrine that works well for real estate, is not suited to the very different realm of movable, concealable personal property. Because it ignores an owner's diligence, adverse possession doctrine hurts diligent owners who have reported thefts but are unable to find their property. Since multi-factor balancing tests do not automatically award title to theft victims, they do not adequately deter trafficking in stolen goods. Adverse possession law and balancing tests do not automatically reward theft reporting, nor does either doctrine routinely penalize the purchase of stolen property. Thus, neither approach creates adequate incentives to report thefts and deter the buying of stolen art. Judges and academics have been too preoccupied with ex post dispute resolution to see the ex ante impact of their rules upon future behavior. Therefore, current approaches fuel the market for stolen goods and encourage more thefts.

This Note's thesis is simple: victims of art thefts who promptly report the thefts to the police and to a computerized theft database should never be legally barred from recovering their property. In other words, statutes of limitations should not apply to actions brought by owners who have promptly taken two simple steps to protect their legal titles. Often, a so-called bona fide purchaser (BFP) is negligent when investigating title to an artwork. Now that an international computerized art-theft registry is available, buyers should be encouraged to check the registry and should be held liable if they fail to do so.

Posner, Economic Analysis of Law 91 (5th ed. 1998):

It can be argued, however, that there should be an exception [from the rule protecting bona fide purchasers, see ch. 2] for durable goods, in particular, works of art. Many works of art were stolen during World War II . . . so if the original owner has done nothing to try to recover the work in all that time, shouldn't he be barred? Isn't there a danger that if an owner of a work of art can never be certain that a previous owner won't jump out of the woodwork and take the work back people will be reluctant to exhibit their art for fear of alerting a previous owner? But the other side of this coin is that original owners will take additional precautions to prevent the theft of their art—and these precautions may include not exhibiting it widely—if they know that they will not be able to get the art back if it is stolen and sold to a bona fide purchaser. The cost of the additional precautions to the owner, if he can't recover the art stolen from him, has to be balanced against the cost of additional efforts by the purchaser to prevent the discovery of the art and additional search costs by original owners to discover their stolen art, if the original owner can get it back. If the purchaser-concealment and owner-search costs under the original-owner-wins system do not greatly exceed the owner-precaution costs under the bona-fide-purchaser-wins system, then the undesirability of making stolen goods more readily marketable should tip the balance against allowing the bona fide purchaser from a thief to acquire title.

Other barriers might also be raised to bar claimants' recovery of Nazi art. For example, if the art is in the possession of a foreign country, there might be a claim of sovereign immunity. In 2004 the United States Supreme Court held in a case of admittedly limited application that the Foreign Sovereign Immunities Act did not apply to conduct that occurred prior to its enactment. See Republic of Austria v. Altmann, 541 U.S. 677 (2004). The facts of the case tell an interesting story about the provenance of so-called Nazi art.

In 1998 an Austrian journalist, granted access to the Austrian Gallery's archives, discovered evidence that certain valuable works in the Gallery's collection had not been donated by their rightful owners but had been seized by the Nazis or expropriated by the Austrian Republic after World War II. The journalist provided some of that evidence to respondent, who in turn filed this action to recover possession of six Gustav Klimt paintings. Prior to the Nazi invasion of Austria, the paintings had hung in the palatial Vienna home of respondent's uncle, Ferdinand Bloch–Bauer, a Czechoslovakian Jew and patron of the arts. Respondent claims ownership of the paintings under a will executed by her uncle after he fled Austria in 1938. She alleges that the Gallery obtained possession of the paintings through wrongful conduct in the years during and after World War II. . . .

Born in Austria in 1916, respondent Maria V. Altmann escaped the country after it was annexed by Nazi Germany in 1938. She settled in California in 1942 and became an American citizen in 1945. She is a niece, and the sole surviving named heir, of Ferdinand Bloch–Bauer, who died in Zurich, Switzerland, on November 13, 1945.

Prior to 1938 Ferdinand, then a wealthy sugar magnate, maintained his principal residence in Vienna, Austria, where the six Klimt paintings and other valuable works of art were housed. His wife, Adele, was the subject of two of the paintings. She died in 1925, leaving a will in which she "ask[ed]" her husband "after his death" to bequeath the paintings to the Gallery. App. 187a,[1] The attorney for her estate advised the Gallery that Ferdinand intended to comply with his wife's request, but that he was not legally obligated to do so because he, not Adele, owned the paintings. Ferdinand never executed any document transferring ownership of any of the paintings at issue to the Gallery. He remained their sole legitimate owner until his death. His will bequeathed his entire estate to respondent, another niece, and a nephew.

On March 12, 1938, in what became known as the "Anschluss," the Nazis invaded and claimed to annex Austria. Ferdinand, who was Jewish and had supported efforts to resist annexation, fled the country ahead of the Nazis, ultimately settling in Zurich. In his absence, according to the complaint, the Nazis "Aryanized" the sugar company he had directed, took over his Vienna home, and divided up his artworks, which included the Klimts at issue here, many other valuable paintings, and a 400–piece porcelain collection. A Nazi lawyer, Dr. Erich Führer, took possession of the six Klimts. He sold two to the Gallery in 1941 and a third in 1943, kept one for himself, and sold another to the Museum of the City of Vienna. The immediate fate of the sixth is not known. 142 F.Supp.2d, at 1193.

In 1946 Austria enacted a law declaring all transactions motivated by Nazi ideology null and void. This did not result in the immediate return of looted artwork to exiled Austrians, however, because a different provision of Austrian law proscribed export of "artworks ... deemed to be important to [the country's] cultural heritage" and required anyone wishing to export art to obtain the permission of the Austrian Federal Monument Agency. Seeking to profit from this requirement, the Gallery and the Federal Monument Agency allegedly adopted a practice of "forc[ing] Jews to donate or trade valuable artworks to the [Gallery] in exchange for export permits for other works."

The next year Robert Bentley, respondent's brother and fellow heir, retained a Viennese lawyer, Dr. Gustav Rinesch, to locate and recover property stolen from Ferdinand during the war. In January 1948 Dr. Rinesch wrote to the Gallery requesting return of the three Klimts purchased from Dr. Führer. A Gallery representative responded, asserting-falsely, according to the complaint-that Adele had bequeathed the paintings to the Gallery, and the Gallery had merely permitted Ferdinand to retain them during his lifetime.

Later the same year Dr. Rinesch enlisted the support of Gallery officials to obtain export permits for many of Ferdinand's remaining works of art.

---

1. Adele's will mentions six Klimt paintings, Adele Bloch–Bauer I, Adele Bloch–Bauer II, Apple Tree I, Beechwood, Houses in Unterach am Attersee, and Schloss Kammer am Attersee III. The last of these, Schloss Kammer am Attersee III, is not at issue in this case because Ferdinand donated it to the Gallery in 1936. The sixth painting in this case, Amalie Zuckerkandl, is not mentioned in Adele's will. For further details, see 142 F.Supp.2d 1187, 1192–1193 (C.D.Cal.2001).

In exchange, Dr. Rinesch, purporting to represent respondent and her fellow heirs, signed a document "acknowledg[ing] and accept[ing] Ferdinand's declaration that in the event of his death he wished to follow the wishes of his deceased wife to donate" the Klimt paintings to the Gallery. *Id.*, at 177a, ¶ 56. In addition, Dr. Rinesch assisted the Gallery in obtaining both the painting Dr. Führer had kept for himself and the one he had sold to the Museum of the City of Vienna. At no time during these transactions, however, did Dr. Rinesch have respondent's permission either "to negotiate on her behalf or to allow the [Gallery] to obtain the Klimt paintings." *Id.*, at 178a, ¶ 61.

In 1998 a journalist examining the Gallery's files discovered documents revealing that at all relevant times Gallery officials knew that neither Adele nor Ferdinand had, in fact, donated the six Klimts to the Gallery. The journalist published a series of articles reporting his findings, and specifically noting that Klimt's first portrait of Adele, "which all the [Gallery] publications represented as having been donated to the museum in 1936," had actually been received in 1941, accompanied by a letter from Dr. Führer signed " 'Heil Hitler.' " *Id.*, at 181a, ¶ 67.

In response to these revelations, Austria enacted a new restitution law under which individuals who had been coerced into donating artworks to state museums in exchange for export permits could reclaim their property. Respondent—who had believed, prior to the journalist's investigation, that Adele and Ferdinand had "freely donated" the Klimt paintings to the Gallery before the war—immediately sought recovery of the paintings and other artworks under the new law. A committee of Austrian Government officials and art historians agreed to return certain Klimt drawings and porcelain settings that the family had donated in 1948. After what the complaint terms a "sham" proceeding, however, the committee declined to return the six paintings, concluding, based on an allegedly purposeful misreading of Adele's will, that her precatory request had created a binding legal obligation that required her husband to donate the paintings to the Gallery on his death. *Id.*, at 185a.

Respondent then announced that she would file a lawsuit in Austria to recover the paintings. Because Austrian court costs are proportional to the value of the recovery sought (and in this case would total several million dollars, an amount far beyond respondent's means), she requested a waiver. The court granted this request in part but still would have required respondent to pay approximately $350,000 to proceed. When the Austrian Government appealed even this partial waiver, respondent voluntarily dismissed her suit and filed this action in the United States District Court for the Central District of California.

Id. at 680–85.

It has been reported that the Adele Bloch–Bauer I painting had been sold for about $135,000,000 and is currently in the collection of Ronald Lauder and the Adele Bloch–Bauer II has been sold for over $88,000,000 and the remaining four paintings have been sold for over $192,000,000.

CHAPTER 4

ESTATES IN LAND AND FUTURE INTERESTS

■ ■ ■

§ 4.1 INTRODUCTION

In this chapter we study an area of property law that has perplexed law students, lawyers and judges since the 12th century. The American law relating to estates in land has its antecedents in the land law of England, and an understanding of the English law is essential to put the American law in its proper perspective. Generally, the states have adopted the so-called common law scheme of estates as it existed in England, with such variations as are warranted in light of American political institutions, traditions and economics. In England, land ownership was primarily a source of wealth, status and power. While land has these attributes in the United States as well, from earliest times land in this country has also been viewed as an article of commerce. During the 19th century, for example, when much of American land law was formulated, land was often used for investment speculation in the same ways that stocks and bonds are today.

Although American land law has changed dramatically over time, in many cases effective representation of a client requires an understanding of outmoded rules that can affect the outcome of the client's case. Perhaps more importantly, statutes and cases that purport to repeal or overturn prior rules can only be understood if the rule that is rejected, and the policies underlying that rule are understood. In this context, therefore, Holmes' statement that "[u]pon this point a page of history is worth a volume of logic"[1] was never more true.

While the rules embodied under the heading of the common law scheme of estates may not be entirely logical (particularly viewed from the vantage point of 21st century America), a definite elegance attaches to them, and, but for some minor exceptions, they give great intellectual satisfaction to one who sees how the pieces of the puzzle nicely fit together. In traveling this road, however, students should expect to be frustrated and confused. Such is the nature of an endeavor where complete understanding is lacking until all pieces of the puzzle are known. We

---

1. New York Trust Co. v. Eisner, 256 U.S. 345, 349 (1921).

259

begin with a giant step back in time to lay the foundations for your understanding of this fascinating area of the law of property.

BAKER, INTRODUCTION TO ENGLISH LEGAL HISTORY, 3RD ED. 1990 AT 255–294

The most fundamental distinction in the English law of property was between real property (realty) and personal property (personalty). Land is a place to live for man and beast, a source of food and of all other commodities, including—if one has enough to let—money. It outlives its inhabitants, is immune from destruction by man, and therefore provides a suitably firm base for institutions of government and wealth. Control of land could not, indeed, be readily divorced from power and jurisdiction, from "lordship". Land for this reason became the subject of feudal tenure, which will be explained presently. Schemes of provision for the interests of successive members of landed families led in due course to an elaborate system of rules governing inheritance and estates, which will be considered in a later chapter. Personalty, on the other hand, was not subject to tenure, inheritance or future estates.... In Roman law, and to some extent in the later common law, another fundamental distinction is that between ownership (a legal right) and possession (a fact). But the word "owner" does not seem to have been much used by medieval lawyers: ownership is not an immutable legal idea, any more than the French equivalent "property". The Latin word for ownership, dominium, is particularly confusing, since in medieval times it is also the word for lordship. Certainly the starting point of our story is not ownership or property; it is tenure.

Tenure

Tenure is the name given to the relationship whereby a tenant "holds" land of a lord. Holding, as opposed to owning, must be explained in terms of the "feudal system" which was the economic basis of society at the time of the Norman conquest. Unfortunately, like many other short-hand expressions, the term "feudal system" is an anachronism, a useful modern label for certain common features of medieval life which had no contemporary name given to them ... [T]enure was not in origin a legal concept at all, but a social fact, or a set of common assumptions: a state of affairs beyond precise legal definition.

We know that feudal institutions of a kind existed in Anglo–Saxon England, and elsewhere in contemporary Europe, in the sense that the occupation of land was commonly associated with vassalage, with bonds between lords and their men. Land given to reward a vassal was his "fee"....

It is no accident, however, that feudalism suddenly comes into clear focus under William I. The conquest of England in 1066, and its ensuing occupation and settlement by a French elite, necessarily led to a renegotiation of landholding arrangements. The Normans displaced the English nobility who, having fought against the conqueror, were deemed traitors. In reallocating what had been forfeited, the important assumption was made that all land is held ultimately of the king.... The reallocation began in the 1070s, when the tenancies in chief—those held directly of the Crown—were concentrated in the hands of a few Norman families. In return for their holdings the tenants in chief owed the king loyalty and military service. The chief lords parcelled out their dominions in like manner, keeping some for themselves and distributing the rest in return for the loyalty and service of their own tenants. The transaction whereby a grantee of land was admitted to hold it as tenant of the grantor, in return for services, is now called "subinfeudation": contemporaries called it an "entry in the fee" of the grantor. The process of subinfeudation created a chain of tenures from the king down to the men who actually occupied the land....

The relationship between Norman lord and tenant may be seen as contractual.... It was the conquest which brought this contractual aspect to the fore, since the reallocation of the 1070s and 1080s was in fact a series of bargains, however unequal, whereby the duties owed by vassals became express terms. Every man's holding, except at the lowest level (where no bargaining occurred), had its fixed quota of services. The tenant bound himself to perform what had been settled as the consideration for his holding, and he forfeited his interest if he committed a fundamental breach of his contract by failing in the service, by committing an unpardonable crime, or by being unfaithful. The lord in return protected the tenant as his man, guaranteed his security of tenure, and held court for him and for all his other tenants. But tenure was much more than a commercial bargain. It was a life-long bond, comparable in some respects with marriage, which also began by contract.... The special relationship was sealed by the ceremony of homage, when the tenant knelt and placed his hands between those of his lord and swore to become his man in life and limb and earthly honour against all men except the king.

A typical Norman baron would have held numerous parcels of land from the king or from other barons. Some of these would have been retained for his own use: his "demesne land". Most would have been subinfeudated to tenants, in consideration of services defined to meet his needs.... The same held true of lesser landowners, except for the very poorest who had only enough land to work by themselves; these last were always tenants, never lords, the men at the end of the feudal chain....

The Variety of Services

The nature of a lord's moral obligations to his sworn men was universal; the bond of homage and the receipt of service tied him, according to the common understanding of society, to warrant (guarantee) his men's tenancies against adverse claims and to do them justice. But the tenant's obligations were almost infinitely variable. At the upper end of the feudal order, as organised by the Normans, there were three main kinds of tenure: military, civil and spiritual. The principal military tenure was *knight-service*, whereby the tenant was obliged in time of war to provide one mounted soldier in combat order for every knight's fee which he held ... Civilian services were similarly provided for by feudal grants. Tenants in chief who were bound to perform personal services for the king were said to hold by *grand serjeanty*; and of this there were as many forms as there were services to be done, from looking after the king's wine to holding his head when he felt seasick. Other tenants might be required to provide things, such as horses, arrows or armour for military uses, wine or food for the king's palace, sheep-skins or wax for his bureaucracy. Such services, when due from tenants in chief, were called *petty serjeanty*. Spiritual tenure arose when grants were made to ecclesiastical bodies to hold by the regular celebration of *divine service*, or the general duty of saying prayers for the soul of the donor without any service being expressed (*frankalmoin*, free alms).

At the lower level the services were not always defined. The duties of the peasant were chiefly agricultural....

Under a hypothetically perfect and complete feudal economy, the type of tenure would have denoted not merely the services due from a tenant but also his status and way of life. The king at the top had the greatest bargaining power, the peasant at the bottom none. Everyone had his place in the hierarchy: tenure, rank and economic position were interdependent. Knight-service and serjeanty denoted high rank; villeinage was the servile state of the peasant. Life was not, however, as neat as this in reality: or, if it once was, it did not long remain so. A man might hold different lands for different kinds of service, or the same land for a mixture of services. It was quite possible for a tenant to hold part of his lands by knight-service and another part by socage. Moreover, tenure by knight-service did not make the tenant a knight, any more than tenure in villeinage made him a villein. When legal theory formed, there was no objection to a knight holding land in villeinage, or a villein by knight-service.

In any case, the feudal economy was not one in which land was the only medium of payment; even if it had been, the kind of bargaining which occurred under William I could not recur with every passing generation. Within two centuries of the Norman conquest, at most, the concept of buying services with land was dead. The main reason was that inheritance and alienability, both engrafted onto the system at an early stage, worked against the contractual nature of the feudal relationship. The military system may have been the first to founder. Armies were only intermittently needed, and only by the king. Service was normally limited to forty days in the year, with no provision for training. It is unlikely whether any army after Norman times was raised solely by the feudal levy, and the last serious levy of any kind was in 1327. Inheritance created additional problems. When knight's fees descended or were alienated to women, children, old men, or monasteries, personal service became impossible. The division of estates upon inheritance by coheirs or upon partial subinfeudation created fractions of knight's fees, and no tenant could be expected to find a fraction of a knight. Then again, the services fixed by an ancestor might not meet the requirements of the next generation; methods of warfare changed, and cavalry lost some of its importance to artillery. The only answer to such problems was to collect money from the tenants and use it to pay mercenaries. This was effected with respect to most knight's fees within the century after 1066. Actual knight-service was replaced by *scutage*, a payment based on the number of knights to be provided. When the king went to war, the rate of scutage was proclaimed and levied proportionately on the tenants of knight's fees. Probably these payments did not exempt tenants in chief from personal service, but if they were not inclined to the sword they could buy licenses to stay at home. By the fourteenth century scutage itself had become largely obsolete, and money for wars was raised by other forms of taxation.

Similar commutations were made of other kinds of service.... By the middle of the thirteenth century hardly any personal services were being paid for with land, except at the lowest level. Knight-service and serjeanty were no longer exacted, while most others had been commuted into monetary quit-rents which were losing value through inflation to the point where many were hardly worth collecting. Feudal services, the original raison d'être of the feudal system, had therefore lost much of their economic significance two centuries before Littleton. Yet, as we shall see, the legal importance of tenure continued unabated.

Feudalism and Land Ownership

If the question were posed, whether under the early feudal system the land was owned by the lord or the tenant, one could not give a direct answer without [being] misleading. Feudal tenure was the antithesis of ownership as we know it. Before the advent of the common law, the tenant enjoyed few of the privileges which we now attribute to an owner. He could not do what he liked with the land. He could not sell it without the lord's consent. He could not pass it on to others by will, and there was no legally enforceable right of succession in his family after his death. His only protection against dispossession by the lord was the lord's moral or social obligation to protect his own men. The tenant's interest therefore stopped short at possession, which is a fact and not a legal right. The fact of being in possession as a feudal tenant was called "seisin", which originally was associated with the act of homage which clinched the lord's acceptance of his man....

In this feudal world, then, we should think in terms of seisin rather than ownership. The tenant was seised of the land, and the lord was seised of the tenant's services, but neither of them "owned" the land in any absolute sense. Even if the land came back to the lord, he was then seised of it as tenant of someone else. Only the king was not a tenant; but no king after William I had the kind of control exercised in the 1070s, and no one thought of the lord king as being in any meaningful sense *owner* of all the land in England....

[B]y the early 1200s the Norman system of feudal economy, of buying services with land, was virtually dead; existing services, if demanded at all, were mostly turned into rent and were losing value through inflation; military service had become little more than abstract theory; and yet tenure was if anything growing in legal importance. The reason is that services were not the only right which the common law gave to the lord. The casual side-effects of tenure were becoming at least as valuable as the services, and in many cases more so. . . .

[Ed. Note: There were a number of feudal incidents. These included:]

1. Aids

The omnipotent lord might exact financial contributions ("aids") from his tenants to assist him in meeting any financial difficulties. Since a power of random confiscation was inconsistent with the status of free men, it was curtailed by law. By Magna Carta, aids were limited to three cases: where the lord needed money to ransom himself from captivity, or to knight his eldest son, or to provide a dowry for his eldest daughter. . . .

2. Fines on alienation

Because tenure was a personal relationship, alienation of the land by substitution—that is, by replacing one tenant with another—required the consent of the lord. And if real consent was required, it could be charged for: the fine for licence to alienate. The fine was not generally payable on subinfeudation, which did not disturb the relationship between the vendor and his lord. Fines for alienation were abolished when alienation by subinfeudation was ended in 1290. . . .

3. Relief and primer seisin

On the death of a tenant, the land went back ("reverted") to the lord. If the tenant's interest had been merely for life, the lord was then free to choose a new tenant. But if the tenant's interest had been inheritable, the lord was bound to admit the tenant's heir in his place. Before inheritance was defined and protected by the common law, lords might seize the land and take the profits for themselves until the heir bought back the land by paying "relief"; unscrupulous lords might even frustrate inheritance by demanding excessive relief. When the law began to protect inheritance, the lord might still claim to take the deceased tenant's land into his hands until the new tenant did homage; this "primer seisin" entitled the lord to the profits during the feudal limbo, and was also a security to ensure that the tenant paid relief. The common law necessarily regulated such claims, which if abused would obstruct the heir's emergent legal rights. As early as the 1160s, the relief for a knight's fee was fixed at five pounds and other reliefs had to be reasonable; the reasonable relief for socage land was held to be one year's profits. Primer seisin was abolished in 1267, except for the king's rights over his tenants in chief, in the latter case it remained a valuable royal prerogative until the seventeenth century.

4. Escheat

If a tenant in fee died without leaving an heir, the land necessarily fell to the lord by way of escheat. Likewise, if the tenant was convicted of felony, his land fell to the lord. This latter kind of escheat was later called "forfeiture". Forfeiture in its original sense occurred when a tenant committed treason: in that case his land went to the Crown, and the rights of mesne lords were extinguished. . . .

6. Wardship and marriage

If a deceased tenant's heir was under age, and so unable to perform his feudal obligations, he was subject to wardship. The land came back to the lord during the infancy, so that he might be compensated out of the income for the loss of services, and the lord in return was supposed to raise the ward, seeing if need be to his military training. The common law did not suppress wardship; but some regulation was necessary. The very least requirement was that the heir should inherit all the capital that his ancestor left, and so Magna Carta forbade guardians to commit waste in their wards' lands. In respect of the income, however, a difference arose between military tenure and socage. The guardian in socage, usually a near relative of the infant heir, was effectively turned into a trustee who (after 1267) could be compelled to render an account to the heir when he came of age at 14. In the case of military tenure, by contrast, the guardian was the feudal lord and there was no accountability: even when actual military service was no longer exacted, guardians unashamedly helped themselves to the profits of the land until the ward was 21.

Guardians received into ward not only the heir's land but also the heir's body. Perhaps this originated as a form of protection for the ward—apologists argued that grasping relatives could not be trusted with the heir's life—but again it was exploited for profit. The guardian was entitled to select a suitable marriage for the ward, and because arranging marriages for young heirs and heiresses involved substantial transfers of wealth, this right could be highly valuable. No marriage could be forced on unwilling children, because consent was a requisite of true matrimony; but if a ward declined a suitable marriage when it was offered, he or she had to compensate the lord to the value of the marriage. And if a ward married without the lord's consent, he or she incurred the penalty (after 1236) of remaining in ward until the lord had received double the value of the marriage. The only legal concession made to the infant was that a guardian should not disparage his ward by offering a marriage with someone who was either legally unsuitable (such as a widow, a bastard, or a villein) or physically unsuitable (such as a leper, a deformed or blind person, or a woman beyond the age of child-bearing).

The Value of Incidents

Those incidents which were fixed in monetary terms suffered the same economic fate as the services. But those which were tied to the value of the land, or gave a right to take the profits of the land, were inflation-proof. The most profitable for lords, and the most onerous to tenants, were therefore those incidents which attached on a descent to an heir, especially if the heir held by knight-service and (as often happened) was under age. Being casual windfalls, these death duties did not provide a regular source of income except for great lords who had many tenants. But until means were found of avoiding descents, the incidents fell due whenever a tenant in fee died, and that was an event he could not avoid. The greatest profits of all came to the Crown, which was ultimate lord of all land in the realm and also had special prerogative rights which other lords did not possess. On the death of a tenant in chief, the king's escheator seized all his lands until an inquisition post mortem had ascertained the king's rights. In addition to the rights of a common lord, the king had primer seisin (a year's profits) and priority as to wardship before all other lords of whom lands had been held. . . .

Quia Emptores Terrarum 1290

Once the system of paying for services with land became obsolete, the principal feudal aspect of conveyancing was that the method chosen might affect the value of the lord's incidents. If property was sold to raise money, the vendor could either put the purchaser in his place as tenant (substitution) or make the purchaser his own tenant (subinfeudation). The latter was preferable for the vendor, because it did not require the lord's approval, and because the vendor retained a seignory which might yield occasional profits, perhaps even an escheat. The purchaser, on the other hand, lost nothing by subinfeudation that he would have gained by substitution. The only loser was the vendor's lord. When his tenant died possessed of the land in demesne, leaving an infant heir, the lord had wardship of the land and could take the full profits during the minority. But if the tenant had in his lifetime subinfeudated for a worthless service, taking payment in ready money, the lord had wardship only of the seignory (that is, the worthless service). The true value of the land, instead of being reflected in rent-service which would benefit the lord, had been converted into cash which went into the vendor's pocket. Furthermore, the likelihood of an escheat was reduced as more tenants were inserted in the chain. Alienation by substitution could harm the lord in a different way: for instance, if an old tenant substituted a young man with a long life-expectancy. The greater evil, however, was seen as subinfeudation.

The statute *Quia emptores terrarum* was passed to solve this problem and affords clear proof that the incidents were by 1290 more important than the services. In order to protect the incidents, the statute enacted that alienation was thenceforward to be by substitution, which was to be allowed without fine. As a consequence, no mesne tenures in fee simple have been created since 1290, and as mesne tenures have lapsed over the years most of the land in England has come to be held in chief of the Crown. . . .

Evasion and Preservation of Incidents

An equally important legal consequence of the incidents of tenure followed from the constant attempts of lawyers to arrange their clients' property interests in such a way that they attracted the least burdens. The incidents which most needed avoidance were relief, wardship and primer seisin, all of which arose when a tenant died and the fee descended to his heir. Now, these were not simply death duties, but inheritance duties; and, if death could not be avoided, inheritance could. The essence of most feudal tax-dodges was therefore to ensure that land did not descend to an heir. Provision against descent had to be made during the tenant's lifetime, because at common law land could not be disposed of by will. We have already noticed an early device for achieving the object by grants in mortmain; but that way had been stopped in 1215. Another method, which generally had no legal success, was to create a succession of life interests so that the tenant and his heir and his heir's heir, and so on *ad infinitum*, each had separate life estates under the original grant and took nothing by descent. Another was for a father to convey the land during his lifetime to the heir apparent, or to the heir apparent jointly with himself so that the heir would take by survivorship and not by inheritance. Few fathers thought such a course wise. A fourth device was a collusive grant to friends on condition that they would convey the land back to the heir when he attained his majority. Each form of evasion was countered at an early date by legislation or by judicial decision. But all were superseded by the institution of the "use", which enabled the real owner of land to hide behind a legal facade. . . .

The distinction between the legal and beneficial ownership of property has become the foundation of the modern system of estates in land. But the technical distinction between legal and equitable estates could hardly have been invented, and indeed we must seek its origin not in legal thought but in a miscellany of factual situations requiring recognition in conscience if not in law. The situations arose whenever a feudal tenant was personally obliged, either by contract or by the requirements of good faith, to allow another person to have the beneficial enjoyment of land vested in himself. Such an arrangement did not in the beginning have a technical name. The nominal owner was obliged in conscience to observe the trust reposed in him, and in Latin he was said to hold the property *ad commodum* or *ad opus* (to the benefit) of the beneficiary.

. . . The holding *ad opus* therefore of necessity involved a separation of the title as recognised by law from the true ownership as acknowledged in fact. . . .

The most fruitful of the devices discovered in the fourteenth century was that which enabled a landowner to avoid the rule prohibiting wills of land. A dying tenant could grant the land to a group of friends and neighbours on trust to regrant it after his death to such beneficiary as he should name. This enabled the land in effect to be devised, and since title did not pass by descent the feudal incidents were avoided as well. But here again there was an advantage in making the arrangement permanent: The power to devise did not need to await the deathbed. It made sense for any landowner to vest his land in feoffees to perform his will: that is to carry out any immediate instructions during his life, and his last will after his death. The machinery was informal. If the feoffor made it a formal condition of the feoffment that the feoffees should perform their trust, the condition was enforced by the law with unbending exactitude; if it was unperformed, the land automatically returned to the feoffor or his heirs. Only the heir, however, could enter for breach after the feoffor's death; therefore if the condition was to convey the land after his death to someone other than the heir, this means of enforcement was useless. Moreover, if the condition was to allow someone else the full rights of beneficial ownership, it was arguably repugnant and void. The solution was not to impose a condition at all, but to make the feoffment merely on trust that the feoffees would perform the will. The feoffees then held the title solely to the use of the feoffor. Whatever he directed, they were expected to obey. This was very convenient to the feoffor. He remained the absolute owner in effect, because he continued to possess the land for his own benefit and take the profits, and he could sell the fee whenever he wished by directing the feoffees to convey to his purchaser. Yet he could in addition, if he so wished, defer selection of his successors to the point of his own death. Thus the landowner achieved the power of disposing of the land by last will or by *inter vivos* conveyance, as he pleased. It was this attribute of the holding *ad opus*, the permanent arrangement giving the beneficial owner the power to devise without impairing his other powers, which principally assured its establishment as a common institution. It also ensured that the device had to be a mere trust, because the effect of a will was necessarily to disinherit the only person capable of enforcing a condition. . . .

Each of the arrangements just described began as a temporary expedient which was found to have advantageous effects if extended into a permanent state of affairs. The permanent institution which resulted was called a "use", the law French word for *opus*; and the beneficiary, when not the feoffor himself, was called *cestui que use*. The trusting of feoffees with lands in use was a fact of life long before it had any legal consequences. The common law took no notice of a mere trusting, without a condition. As far as the common law was concerned, the cestui que use had "no more to do with the land than the greatest stranger in the world", and if he remained in possession he was technically only a tenant at sufferance of the feoffees. It was said in 1464 that the feoffees could sue the cestui que use for trespass if he felled timber, and the proposition was often approved in later cases as a statement of abstract theory. Yet the feoffees, being charged with a fiduciary duty, were not supposed to obstruct the wishes of the cestui que use or derive any benefit from the land for themselves. By choosing a substantial group of feoffees, usually lawyers, the feoffor ensured against individual unscrupulousness. But difficulties were bound to arise as such feoffments became more common, and those difficulties required a legal solution.

The first recourse may have been to the ecclesiastical courts, especially when wills were involved. We know, for instance, that in 1375 a group of feoffees were excommunicated for conveying land (allegedly under duress) contrary to the feoffor's will. But the Chancery was also an obvious resort, since the feoffees were clearly bound by ties of conscience which were not recognised in the courts of common law. The origins of the Chancery jurisdiction over uses are elusive, but it was well established by the 1420s, and in the course of the fifteenth century uses accounted for much of the chancellor's business.

The principles established by the courts in the fifteenth century turned the interest of the beneficiary into a new kind of ownership, analogous to what was later called the "equitable estate". If the feoffees died, the trust passed to the heir of the last survivor; if the feoffees alienated the land, the trust passed to the purchaser, unless he bought for value without notice of the trust, in which case alone his conscience was clear. A use could also be raised by implication. If the legal owner of land bargained and sold it to another, then before the conveyance an implied use was raised in favour of the purchaser, which the chancellor would protect by specific performance. And if the legal owner enfeoffed another without any consideration being given, or any express use declared, the feoffee held the land to the use of the feoffor and his heirs. The recognition of this "resulting" use, perhaps as early as 1465, confirms how usual it had become for feoffments to be made on secret or undisclosed trusts, or to perform the feoffor's will generally. By 1500 it could be asserted that the greater part of the land in England was held in use. . . .

The main reason why so much land had come to be vested in feoffees to uses during the fifteenth century, at any rate by major landowners, was that it provided an escape from the automatic certainty of the legal rules of succession; by last will the landowner could provide for younger sons, daughters, bastards, remote relations, or charities, could vary the provision given by law to his widow, and could charge the payment of his debts and legacies on real property. These objects could be achieved either by directing the feoffees to convey property directly to the devisees, or by directing them to sell or let the property and apply the proceeds as instructed. Whichever course was taken, it was the use and not the legal title which passed on the testator's death.

The flexibility made possible by uses was accompanied by two problems. The first was that conveyancing was rendered less certain. The use could be transferred informally, without "livery of seisin", and could even pass by word of mouth. Purchasers of land might therefore find themselves adversely affected by a hidden use. This problem was eased by the statute of 1484, but other uncertainties continued to be a source of complaint well into the sixteenth century.

Second, and this was the cause of all the trouble which came in Tudor times, the employment of uses deprived lords, and most of all the Crown, of valuable feudal revenues. It is unlikely that this was the prime motive behind uses, but it was their inevitable result and doubled their attraction. The machinery displaced inheritance and, therefore, the incidents which attached on inheritance; even if the beneficiary died intestate, there was no descent of the land to which incidents could attach. Of course, incidents would attach if a sole feoffee died; but a plurality of feoffees, besides providing safety in numbers, also ensured that there would never be a descent. The feoffees were joint tenants, and so if one feoffee died the others absorbed his share by the *jus accrescendi*; so long as numbers were kept up, if necessary by reconveyance, there was an "unassailable mortmain". It was unassailable because the lord had living tenants to whom the feudal rules applied; and that being so, if the lord suffered loss, it was *damnum absque injuria*. Once this became common knowledge, it was foolish for anyone to leave land vested in his own name. By vesting it in others he paradoxically became a more absolute owner than the common law allowed: he was released from the most burdensome incidents of feudalism, and from the inflexible rules of inheritance, and the estate was also freed from claims by the widow to dower. As a result of the use, feudal revenue from reliefs and wardships in chivalry was by 1500 becoming virtually obsolete. Littleton's account of feudal law might well have seemed like an obituary.

Tudor Legislation and Fiscal Feudalism

In the century between 1391 and 1490 little was done to preserve the financial profits of feudalism against the encroachments of uses. Weak efforts were made in the fifteenth century by royal advisers to amplify the scope of existing legislation, and to control feoffments to uses by tenants in chief; but no king before Henry VII set about plugging the loopholes which uses had made in the earlier law. The inertia has been attributed to the turmoil of the wars of the roses, in which kings lacked the political strength to stem tax avoidance by their own supporters; but more recently it has been suggested that the problem was only of limited extent before the development of the common recovery in the 1470s. When a tenant in tail suffered a recovery to uses, no fine for alienation was due to the Crown and therefore control by that means was impossible. But Henry VII and Henry VIII determined to revive at least some of the feudal revenues which had belonged to their predecessors, and which they needed to defray the expense of government and of supporting themselves in royal state. Ad hoc parliamentary taxation did not have as much to commend it as a regular feudal revenue which could be collected simply by enforcing the old law of the land.

Henry VII did not tackle the main problem, the will of land, but by statutes of 1490 and 1504 the heir of an intestate cestui que use was subjected to the same incidents as if his ancestor had died seised. Just as the 1484 statute had treated the beneficiary as having the powers of the legal tenant for conveyancing purposes, so the statutes of Henry VII showed how beneficiaries could be treated as having the liabilities of the legal tenant for tax purposes. They ended a glaring anomaly, and were seen chiefly as closing a gap in the Statute of Marlborough, but they were not designed to and in fact did not greatly enrich the Crown. They only applied on intestacy, and perhaps served largely as a reminder to make wills. It was Henry VIII who, for revenue purposes, raised feudalism from the grave. Historians have given to this artificial revival the name "fiscal feudalism". . . .

The king's counsel were able to take advantage of two lines of thought on uses. The Common Pleas judges, in applying the statute of 1484, were coming to the view that uses were governed by the common law. If that were taken to its logical conclusion, wills of uses would be void, because wills of land were void. The other line of thought was that separating the legal and beneficial ownership was innately deceitful, and that chancellors in enforcing uses had been naively countenancing large-scale fraud and undermining the common law. On this argument, uses might not be binding in conscience after all. The author of a "replication" to *Doctor and Student* proclaimed uses to be an "untrue and crafty invention" to deprive the king and his subjects of their feudal incidents. "What a falseness," he wrote, "to speak and do one thing, and think another clean contrary to the same." Thomas Audley, as reader of the Inner Temple in 1526, and doubtless keen to propagate the new government policy, complained of landowners who had pursued uses "for the evil purpose of destroying the good laws of the realm, which now by reason of these trusts and confidences is turned into a law called conscience, which is always uncertain and depends for the greater part on the whim of the judge in conscience. . . ." Seven years later Audley himself became that judge in conscience, placed by the king in a position to put his preaching into practice; as indeed he did. With the assistance of the king's secretary Thomas Cromwell, appointed to sit beside him as master of the rolls in 1534, he assembled the judges to discuss a test case adjourned from the common-law side of the Chancery. The question was whether a will made by a tenant in chief, Lord Dacre, which would have deprived the king of his wardship and primer seisin, was valid. The judges, having been coerced or coaxed by Henry VIII into apparent unanimity, declared that it was against the nature of land to be devisable by will, and that a will of the use of land was just as invalid as a will of the land itself. The decision flew in the face of previous learning, and is perhaps the only case in English legal history in which the Crown, unable to push a bill through parliament, managed to change the common law instead. The decision accomplished more than what parliament had rejected, since there was no longer any concession as to two thirds; and within a few months the Commons were persuaded to assent to a new measure concerning uses. The reason why the Commons gave way in 1536 was not merely that their theoretical position had been undermined. If all wills were invalid in 1535, regardless of any fraud, merely because it was against the nature of land to pass by will, it followed that wills had always been invalid, and that any title dependent on a devise by will was invalid. The decision must have thrown into doubt many titles throughout the country. A significant clause in the 1536 bill provided that wills of persons dying before 1536 should be accounted as valid and effectual as they had been until recent decisions had brought their validity into doubt. The effect was to reverse *Lord Dacre's Case* as to the past. Almost certainly this was the inducement which persuaded the Commons to accept without demur the sweeping legislative change which was to govern thenceforth.

The Statute of Uses 1536 carried the royal policies to the extreme of abolishing the power to devise for the future. This it achieved, without actually mentioning wills, by the neat statutory fiction called "executing the use". Wills had only been valid where the legal title was vested in feoffees to uses, and therefore if uses were extirpated there could be no wills. The simple abolition of uses would nevertheless have been absurd, because its effect would have been that most of the land in England would have become beneficially vested in the lawyers who happened to be acting as feoffees. The legal title had instead to be taken from those feoffees and given to the beneficiaries. The statute accordingly provided that where A was seised of property to the "use, trust or confidence" of B, then B was thereafter to be deemed to be seised of the property "to all intents, purposes and constructions in the law, of and in such like estates as [he] had or shall have in use". In other words, whenever A was seised of property to the use of B, the statute effected a notional or fictional livery of seisin from A to B. B, the cestui que use, was to be statutory owner of the legal estate, and the feoffee (A) merely a channel through which the seisin passed in an instant of time to B. A similar fictional livery of seisin occurred if A covenanted to stand seised to the use of B, or bargained and sold the land to B in which case there was an (implied use). The purpose and effect of executing the use was that the beneficial owner of land would always die seised, so that his last will was ineffective at common law and the feudal incidents attached on the descent to his heir. The common-law position was so completely restored that the Crown regained its prerogative rights in addition to wardship and relief.

Financially, the statute was a tremendous success. And as a piece of legal draftsmanship it was greatly admired by later generations: Francis Bacon called it the "most perfectly and exactly conceived and penned of any law in the book". Yet at the time of its passing it aroused much popular opposition. It not only restored feudal incidents, but it imposed compulsory primogeniture on a society which had accustomed itself to wills; moreover it did so for socage tenants, who were of little interest for revenue purposes, as well as for tenants by knight-service. The Duke of Norfolk soon pronounced it the worst act ever made, and it was one of the statutes attacked by the Pilgrimage of Grace in 1536. A lawyer prominent in that protest urged that landowners be allowed to leave part of their lands by will, so that they could pay their debts and provide for their children's marriages, or else lawyers would seek out loopholes in the legislation. The king loftily told the protesters that the statute did not concern them, as "base commons"; and yet within four years the government in effect accepted the demand, and retreated to the one-third compromise proposed in 1529. The Statute of Wills 1540 conferred for the first time the legal power to dispose of freeholds by will, save that tenants by knight-service had to leave at least one third to descend. The preamble to the statute referred to the king's "grace, goodness and liberality" towards his loving subjects; but it was a major political retreat. The retreat had little to do with the pilgrims of 1536, whose other demands had been ignored, save that their intellectual threat clearly struck home. The lawyer's pen was mightier than mere wails of protest . . .

NOTES AND QUESTIONS

1. "The basic idea of feudal land 'ownership,' . . . was that it was *tenurial* in character—more a *holding* of land on good behavior than ownership as we think of it today." T. Bergin & P. Haskell, Preface to Estates In Land and Future Interests 4 (2d ed. 1984). Except in a few states, the concept of tenure did not gain any foothold in the United States. See generally 1 Amer. Law Prop. § 1.41 (A.J. Casner ed. 1952). On the other hand, as will be seen, the classification of estates as developed under English common law evidences lasting staying power.

2. A number of texts have been written on the common-law scheme of estates. Three texts students will find particularly helpful are T. Bergin & P. Haskell, Preface to Estates in Land and Future Interests (2d ed. 1984), S. Kurtz, Moynihan's Introduction to the Law of Real Property (5th ed. 2011), and H. Hovenkamp & S. Kurtz, The Law of Property, An Introductory Survey (5th ed. 2001). For a more complete treatment of the history of estates in land, students can refer to A. Simpson, An Introduction to the History of the Land Law (2d ed. 1986) and W. Holdsworth, An Historical Introduction to the Land Law (1927). See also L. Simes & A. Smith, The Law of Future Interests (2d ed. 1956).

The Classification of Common Law Estates in Land

The common law scheme of estates differentiates between possessory estates and future interests. A possessory (present) estate is an interest in property that includes, as at least one of its privileges, the right to the current possession of the property. A future estate (or interest) is an interest in property where the right to possession of the property is postponed into the future.[1] The fact that possession is postponed, however, should neither suggest that the future interest is valueless or even less valuable than a present possessory estate, nor that the holder of the future interest has no other present rights in the property.

---

1. Restatement (Third) of Property § 25.1 adopts the same concept by providing that "a future interest is an ownership interest in property that does not currently entitle the owner to possession or enjoyment of the property. The owner's right to possession or enjoyment is postponed until some time in the future and may be contingent or vested."

For example, if O conveys property to A for life and upon A's death to B, A is presently entitled to the possession of the property; B has a future interest, and his possession of the property (or the possession of whoever succeeds to B's interest should B die before A) is postponed until A dies. Nonetheless, B's interest may actually be more valuable than A's interest. For instance, this would be true if A were quite old and B very young. Furthermore, during A's lifetime, B's interest may be sold, mortgaged, and gifted to another, and if B were to predecease A, B's interest could be disposed of by B's will. Thus, even though B has a future interest, that interest is alienable, devisable, and descendible. On the other hand, A's interest albeit possessory is neither descendible nor devisable, although it is alienable. Thus, classification of an interest as present or future tells you nothing more about that interest other than whether it is possessory.

The common law distinguished between so-called "freehold" estates and "non-freehold" estates. Roughly speaking a freehold estate was a possessory estate of which the holder was "seized." The concept of seisin referred to the fact that the holder was entitled to possession of the property subject to the obligations of feudal incidences of tenure discussed in the Baker excerpt. Conversely, the holder of a non-freehold estate was entitled to mere occupancy. Thus, the holder of a non-freehold estate was not burdened by the incidents of tenure. Historically, as well as today, non-freehold estates were associated with the landlord-tenant relationship. As might be expected, holders of freehold estates generally were entitled to greater protection as well as respect within the feudal system. In this chapter the focus is on freehold estates; in chapter 7 the focus turns toward the landlord-tenant relationship.

Types of Estates

There are five types of possessory freehold estates. These are:

(a) The "fee simple absolute,"

(b) The "fee simple determinable,"

(c) The "fee simple on condition subsequent,"

(d) The "fee tail" (which was the successor to the "fee simple conditional"), and

(e) The "life estate."

There are three types of possessory non-freehold estates. These are:

(a) The "term for years,"

(b) The "tenancy at will," and

(c) The "periodic tenancy."

In some instances these estates might be followed by a future interest in another person or class.

If someone has a future interest in the same property in which someone else has a present interest (whether that present interest is a freehold or non-freehold estate), the future interest is classified as either a "reversionary interest," a "remainder," or an "executory interest."

A reversionary interest is an interest retained by the grantor. There are three types of reversionary interests:

(a) The "possibility of reverter,"

(b) The "right of entry for condition broken" (also known as a "power of termination"), and

(c) The "reversion."

Remainders and executory interests are future interests that are transferred by a grantor to a third party. There are four types of remainders and two types of executory interests. The four types of remainders are:

(a) The "indefeasibly vested remainder,"

(b) The "contingent remainder,"

(c) The "vested remainder subject to open (or partial divestment)," and

(d) The "vested remainder subject to complete divestment."

The two types of executory interests are:

(a) The "shifting executory interest," and

(b) The "springing executory interest."

Executory interests were not recognized as valid common-law estates until after the enactment of the Statute of Uses, 27 Hen. 8, c. 10 (1535) (effective in 1536). They were recognized earlier as valid estates in the courts of equity. Thus, after the Statute of Uses it was possible to create the entire range of future interests as legal, as well as equitable estates.

It is ironic that the states adhere to the classification of estates as developed at common law because England, the birthplace of our land law, did away with the classification system in 1925. In England today, only the fee simple absolute and the term for years are recognized as legal estates while the other estates are valid only if held as equitable estates in trust. See Law of Property Act of 1925, 15 & 16 Geo. V, c. 20.

The following chart highlights these present and future estates:

ESTATES IN LAND

Present Interest	Words to Create at Common Law	Future Interest In Grantor	In Third Person
FREEHOLD ESTATES			
Fee simple absolute	"and his heirs"	None	None
Fee simple determinable	"so long as," "while" "during"	Possibility of Reverter	Executory Interests
Fee simple on (or subject to a) condition subsequent	"provided that," "on condition" "but if"	Right of entry for condition broken or power of termination	Executory Interests [2]
Fee tail [3]	"and the heirs of (his or her) body"	Reversion	Remainders
Life estate	"for life"	Reversion	Remainders Executory Interests
NON–FREEHOLD ESTATES			
Term for years	"for ___ years"	Reversion	Remainders Executory Interests
Tenancy at will	"at will"	Reversion	Remainders Executory Interests
Periodic tenancy	e.g., month to month	Reversion	Remainders Executory Interests

The Third Restatement of Property recommends a reclassification of the estates system, particularly for the fee simple estates, other than the fee simple absolute, and for all future interests. References to the recommendations are made throughout this chapter.

---

2. Entries expressed in the plural indicate that more than one type of the named interest may be created.

3. Prior to 1285 words that created a fee tail created a "fee simple conditional." The grantor's estate was called a possibility of reverter.

§ 4.2   THE FEE SIMPLE ABSOLUTE

WHITE v. BROWN
Supreme Court of Tennessee (1977).
559 S.W.2d 938.

BROCK, JUSTICE.

This is a suit for the construction of a will. The Chancellor held that the will passed a life estate, but not the remainder, in certain realty, leaving the remainder to pass by inheritance to the testatrix's heirs at law. The Court of Appeals affirmed.

Mrs. Jessie Lide died on February 15, 1973, leaving a holographic will which, in its entirety, reads as follows:

"April 19, 1972

"I, Jessie Lide, being in sound mind declare this to be my last will and testament. I appoint my niece Sandra White Perry to be the executrix of my estate. I wish Evelyn White to have my home to live in and *not* to be *sold*.

"I also leave my personal property to Sandra White Perry. My house is not to be sold.

Jessie Lide"

(Underscoring by testatrix).

Mrs. Lide was a widow and had no children. Although she had nine brothers and sisters, only two sisters residing in Ohio survived her. These two sisters quitclaimed any interest they might have in the residence to Mrs. White. The nieces and nephews of the testatrix, her heirs at law, are defendants in this action.

Mrs. White, her husband, who was the testatrix's brother, and her daughter, Sandra White Perry, lived with Mrs. Lide as a family for some twenty-five years. After Sandra married in 1969 and Mrs. White's husband died in 1971, Evelyn White continued to live with Mrs. Lide until Mrs. Lide's death in 1973 at age 88.

Mrs. White, joined by her daughter as executrix, filed this action to obtain construction of the will, alleging that she is vested with a fee simple title to the home. The defendants contend that the will conveyed only a life estate to Mrs. White, leaving the remainder to go to them under our laws of intestate succession. The Chancellor held that the will unambiguously conveyed only a life interest in the home to Mrs. White and refused to consider extrinsic evidence concerning Mrs. Lide's relationship with her surviving relatives. Due to the debilitated condition of the property and in accordance with the desire of all parties, the Chancellor ordered the property sold with the proceeds distributed in designated shares among the beneficiaries.

I.

Our cases have repeatedly acknowledged that the intention of the testator is to be ascertained from the language of the entire instrument when read in the light of surrounding circumstances.... But, the practical difficulty in this case, as in so many other cases involving wills drafted by lay persons, is that the words chosen by the testatrix are not specific enough to clearly state her intent. Thus, in our opinion, it is not clear whether Mrs. Lide intended to convey a life estate in the home to Mrs. White, leaving the remainder interest to descend by operation of law, or a fee interest with a restraint on alienation. Moreover, the will might even be read as conveying a fee interest subject to a condition subsequent (Mrs. White's failure to live in the home).

In such ambiguous cases it is obvious that rules of construction, always yielding to the cardinal rule of the testator's intent, must be employed as auxiliary aids in the courts' endeavor to ascertain the testator's intent.

In 1851 our General Assembly enacted two such statutes of construction, thereby creating a statutory presumption against partial intestacy.

Chapter 33 of the Public Acts of 1851 (now codified as T.C.A. §§ 64–101 and 64–501) reversed the common law presumption[1] that a life estate was intended unless the intent to pass a fee simple was clearly expressed in the instrument. T.C.A. § 64–501 provides:

> "Every grant or devise of real estate, or any interest therein, shall pass all the estate or interest of the grantor or devisor, unless the intent to pass a less estate or interest shall appear by express terms, or be necessarily implied in the terms of the instrument."

Chapter 180, Section 2 of the Public Acts of 1851 (now codified as T.C.A. § 32–301) was specifically directed to the operation of a devise. In relevant part, T.C.A. § 32–301 provides:

> "A will ... shall convey all the real estate belonging to [the testator] or in which he had any interest at his decease, unless a contrary intention appear by its words and context."

Thus, under our law, unless the "words and context" of Mrs. Lide's will clearly evidence her intention to convey only a life estate to Mrs. White, the will should be construed as passing the home to Mrs. White in fee. "'If the expression in the will is doubtful, the doubt is resolved against the limitation and in favor of the absolute estate.'" ...

Several of our cases demonstrate the effect of these statutory presumptions against intestacy by construing language which might seem to convey an estate for life, without provision for a gift over after the termination of such life estate, as passing a fee simple instead. In *Green v. Young*, 163 Tenn. 16, 40 S.W.2d 793 (1931), the testatrix's disposition of all of her property to her husband "to be used by him for his support and comfort during his life" was held to pass a fee estate. Similarly, in

---

1. Because the feudal lord granted land solely as compensation for personal services, the grant was for no longer than the life of the grantee. Later the grant was extended to the sons and other issue of the grantee under the designation of "heirs." Heirs were thus entitled to stand in the place of their ancestor after his death if mentioned in the grant—but only if specifically mentioned. Thereafter, the word "heirs," when used in a conveyance to a man "and his heirs," came to include collateral as well as lineal heirs, ultimately indicating that such grantee took an estate which would pass to his heirs or the heirs of anyone to whom he alienated it. That is, "heirs" ceased to be a word of purchase and became a word of limitation. 1 Tiffany, Real Property § 28 (3d ed. 1939).

Williams v. Williams, 167 Tenn. 26, 65 S.W.2d 561 (1933), the testator's devise of real property to his children "for and during their natural lives" without provision for a gift over was held to convey a fee. And, in *Webb v. Webb*, 53 Tenn.App. 609, 385 S.W.2d 295 (1964), a devise of personal property to the testator's wife "for her maintenance, support and comfort, for the full period of her natural life" with complete powers of alienation but without provision for the remainder passed absolute title to the widow.

II.

Thus, if the sole question for our determination were whether the will's conveyance of the home to Mrs. White "to live in" gave her a life interest or a fee in the home, a conclusion favoring the absolute estate would be clearly required. The question, however, is complicated somewhat by the caveat contained in the will that the home is "not to be sold"—a restriction conflicting with the free alienation of property, one of the most significant incidents of fee ownership. We must determine, therefore, whether Mrs. Lide's will, when taken as a whole, clearly evidences her intent to convey only a life estate in her home to Mrs. White.

Under ordinary circumstances a person makes a will to dispose of his or her entire estate. If, therefore, a will is susceptible of two constructions, by one of which the testator disposes of the whole of his estate and by the other of which he disposes of only a part of his estate, dying intestate as to the remainder, this Court has always preferred that construction which disposes of the whole of the testator's estate if that construction is reasonable and consistent with the general scope and provisions of the will.... A construction which results in partial intestacy will not be adopted unless such intention clearly appears....

It has been said that the courts will prefer any reasonable construction or any construction which does not do violence to a testator's language, to a construction which results in partial intestacy....

The intent to create a fee simple or other absolute interest and, at the same time to impose a restraint upon its alienation can be clearly expressed. If the testator specifically declares that he devises land to A "in fee simple" or to A "and his heirs" but that A shall not have the power to alienate the land, there is but one tenable construction, viz., the testator's intent is to impose a restraint upon a fee simple. To construe such language to create a life estate would conflict with the express specification of a fee simple as well as with the presumption of intent to make a complete testamentary disposition of all of a testator's property. By extension, as noted by Professor Casner in his treatise on the law of real property:

> "Since it is now generally presumed that a conveyor intends to transfer his whole interest in the property, it may be reasonable to adopt the same construction, [conveyance of a fee simple] even in the

absence of words of inheritance, if there is no language that can be construed to create a remainder." 6 *American Law of Property* § 26.58 (A.J. Casner ed. 1952).

In our opinion, testatrix's apparent testamentary restraint on the alienation of the home devised to Mrs. White does not evidence such a clear intent to pass only a life estate as is sufficient to overcome the law's strong presumption that a fee simple interest was conveyed.

Accordingly, we conclude that Mrs. Lide's will passed a fee simple absolute in the home to Mrs. White. Her attempted restraint on alienation must be declared void as inconsistent with the incidents and nature of the estate devised and contrary to public policy. *Nashville C & S.L. Ry. v. Bell*, 162 Tenn. 661, 39 S.W.2d 1026 (1931).

The decrees of the Court of Appeals and the trial court are reversed and the cause is remanded to the chancery court for such further proceedings as may be necessary, consistent with this opinion. Costs are taxed against appellees.

HARBISON, JUSTICE, dissenting.

With deference to the views of the majority, and recognizing the principles of law contained in the majority opinion, I am unable to agree that the language of the will of Mrs. Lide did or was intended to convey a fee simple interest in her residence to her sister-in-law, Mrs. Evelyn White.

The testatrix expressed the wish that Mrs. White was "to have my home to live in and *not* to be *sold*". The emphasis is that of the testatrix, and her desire that Mrs. White was not to have an unlimited estate in the property was reiterated in the last sentence of the will, to wit: "My house is not to be sold."

The testatrix appointed her niece, Mrs. Perry, executrix and made an outright bequest to her of all personal property.

The will does not seem to me to be particularly ambiguous, and like the Chancellor and the Court of Appeals, I am of the opinion that the testatrix gave Mrs. White a life estate only, and that upon the death of Mrs. White the remainder will pass to the heirs at law of the testatrix.

The cases cited by petitioners in support of their contention that a fee simple was conveyed are not persuasive, in my opinion. Possibly the strongest case cited by the appellants is *Green v. Young*, 163 Tenn. 16, 40 S.W.2d 793 (1931), in which the testatrix bequeathed all of her real and personal property to her husband "to be used by him for his support and comfort during his life." The will expressly stated that it included all of the property, real and personal, which the testatrix owned at the time of her death. There was no limitation whatever upon the power of the husband to use, consume, or dispose of the property, and the Court concluded that a fee simple was intended.

In the case of *Williams v. Williams*, 167 Tenn. 26, 65 S.W.2d 561 (1933), a father devised property to his children "for and during their natural lives" but the will contained other provisions not mentioned in the majority opinion which seem to me to distinguish the case. Unlike the provisions of the present will, other clauses in the *Williams* will contained provisions that these same children were to have "all the residue of my estate personal or mixed of which I shall die possessed or seized, or to which I shall be entitled at the time of my decease, to have and to hold the same to them and their executors and administrators and assigns forever."

Further, following some specific gifts to grandchildren, there was another bequest of the remainder of the testator's money to these same three children. The language used by the testator in that case was held to convey the fee simple interest in real estate to the children, but its provisions hardly seem analogous to the language employed by the testatrix in the instant case.

In the case of *Webb v. Webb*, 53 Tenn.App. 609, 385 S.W.2d 295 (1964), the testator gave his wife all the residue of his property with a clear, unqualified and unrestricted power of use, sale or disposition. Thereafter he attempted to limit her interest to a life estate, with a gift over to his heirs of any unconsumed property. Again, under settled rules of construction and interpretation, the wife was found to have a fee simple estate, but, unlike the present case, there was no limitation whatever upon the power of use or disposition of the property by the beneficiary.

On the other hand, in the case of *Magevney v. Karsch*, 167 Tenn. 32, 65 S.W.2d 562 (1933), a gift of the residue of the large estate of the testator to his daughter, with power "at her demise [to] dispose of it as she pleases...." was held to create only a life estate with a power of appointment, and not an absolute gift of the residue. In other portions of the will the testator had given another beneficiary a power to use and dispose of property, and the Court concluded that he appreciated the distinction between a life estate and an absolute estate, recognizing that a life tenant could not dispose of property and use the proceeds as she pleased. 167 Tenn. at 57, 65 S.W.2d at 569.

In the present case the testatrix knew how to make an outright gift, if desired. She left all of her personal property to her niece without restraint or limitation. As to her sister-in-law, however, she merely wished the latter have her house "to live in", and expressly withheld from her any power of sale.

The majority opinion holds that the testatrix violated a rule of law by attempting to restrict the power of the donee to dispose of the real estate. Only by thus striking a portion of the will, and holding it inoperative, is the conclusion reached that an unlimited estate resulted.

In my opinion, this interpretation conflicts more greatly with the apparent intention of the testatrix than did the conclusion of the courts below, limiting the gift to Mrs. White to a life estate. I have serious doubt that the testatrix intended to create any illegal restraint on alienation or to violate any other rules of law. It seems to me that she rather emphatically intended to provide that her sister-in-law was not to be able to sell the house during the lifetime of the latter—a result which is both legal and consistent with the creation of a life estate.

In my opinion the judgment of the courts below was correct and I would affirm.

NOTES AND QUESTIONS

1. "The estate in 'fee simple' absolute is the present interest in land that is unlimited in duration. 'Absolute ownership' is the present interest in personal property that is unlimited in duration." Restatement (Third) of Property, § 24.2 (2012).

2. At common law the magic words necessary to create a fee simple absolute were "and (his or her) heirs." Thus, if O conveys Blackacre to "A and her heirs," the state of the title would be fee simple absolute in A. If, by contrast, O conveys Blackacre to "A in fee simple absolute," omitting the phrase "and his heirs," A took a mere life estate.[2] As noted in the *White* case, Tennessee abolished by statute the requirement that the phrase "and his heirs" be included in a disposition to create a fee simple absolute. Rather, Tennessee law now presumes that a conveyance or devise conveys or devises the entire estate of the grantor or testator. See also N.Y. Real Prop. Law § 245 (McKinney 1968); Ohio Rev. Code Ann. § 5301.02 (Page 1981); Cal.Civ. Code § 1072 (West 1982); 2 R. Powell, Real Property ¶ 184–185 (P. Rohan ed. 1990). Thus, if O who owns a fee simple absolute conveys Blackacre to A without any other language denoting the nature of A's estate, A has a fee simple absolute.

In some states the common-law formalistic rule has been overturned by the courts. While approximately three-fourths of the states have abolished the common-law formalistic requirements, the statutes of each state must be carefully studied for local nuances. In a few states, e.g., South Carolina and Maine, some vestiges of the common-law rules remain.

In a jurisdiction that has abolished the common-law requirement in favor of a rule similar to that of Tennessee, suppose O conveys Blackacre to A. How can we determine what estate O conveys to A? Suppose O conveyed Blackacre to A prior to the enactment of a statute eliminating the necessity of including the phrase "and his heirs" in a deed to convey a fee simple absolute. Could the statute be applied retroactively to O's conveyance to A and, therefore, ripen A's estate into a fee simple absolute? See U.S. Const. amend. XIV (no state can deprive a person of property without due process of law). But see Texaco, Inc. v. Short, 454 U.S. 516 (1982), reprinted in chapter 17. Cf. Faucheaux v. Alton Ochsner Med. Foundation Hosp. & Clinic, 470 So.2d 878 (La. 1985)(statute granting immunity to a hospital for its torts committed

---

2. This rule did not apply to devises, nor did it apply to a conveyance to a corporation. However, the words "and its successors" were required to convey a fee simple absolute to a corporation.

prior to enactment of the statute cannot be applied to an existing cause of action which was the equivalent of a vested property right).

Suppose a state does not enact a statute similar to the Tennessee statute. After O's conveyance to A, however, A seeks a declaratory judgment in state court that A owns the property in fee simple absolute. (If A only had a life estate then upon A's death the property would revert back to O). If the state court determines in this case of first impression that the common-law rule was not a part of the state's received common law and that A has a fee simple absolute, would that determination be unconstitutional? Cf. *Dennen v. Searle*, 149 Conn. 126, 176 A.2d 561 (1961). Suppose after the state court determines that A has a fee simple absolute, O sues the attorney who prepared the deed for damages. O argues that because he only intended to convey a life estate to A and the attorney fully understood O's intent, the attorney was negligent in failing to expressly limit A's interest to a life estate. What result?

In *White*, the statute provided that a devise passes the testator's entire interest in the property "unless the intent to pass a less estate or interest shall appear by express terms, or be necessarily implied in the terms of the instrument." Furthermore, the court notes that in construing wills doubts about the meaning of language that might create a limitation should be resolved in favor of finding an absolute estate. How is the statutory language and the preceding principle of will construction implicated in *White*?

3. At common law, if O conveys Blackacre to A and his heirs, what, if anything, do A's heirs take? The answer is nothing. The reason lies in the distinction between so-called "words of purchase" and "words of limitation." Words of purchase are those words that describe the person or persons who take the property by conveyance or devise. In that sense the word "purchase" is a misnomer since the person who takes may be a purchaser but alternatively could be a donee of a gift or a beneficiary under a will. Words of limitation, on the other hand, are the words that define the quantitative estate (in terms of time) that the "purchaser" takes. In the conveyance to "A and his heirs," the word "A" is the word of purchase, and the phrase "and his heirs" are words of limitation.

NOTE ON THE MATHEMATICS OF ESTATES

Underlying the common law classification of present and future estates is a unique concept of "quantity" that gives the law of estates its own arithmetic. The nature of a fee simple absolute—the so-called highest and best estate known to the common law—is that the holder of a fee simple absolute has an estate of possibly infinite duration. Since the holder cannot live to infinity, the estate passes to the holder's successors, who may be his transferees, heirs or devisees. Thus, properly speaking, in terms of the concept of estates in land, even if O conveys his fee simple absolute in Blackacre to A, O's estate in Blackacre has not come to an end; rather it has merely been transferred to A.

The reason an estate in fee simple absolute is an estate of infinite duration is that no event can occur that will terminate the duration of the estate *because of any limitation or condition set forth in the instrument of conveyance*. Other events, of course, such as condemnation, may terminate the estate of the holder of a fee simple absolute, but this terminating event is external to the terms of the conveyance itself. And, even in this case, it can be said the estate has simply been conveyed to the condemning authority pursuant to a "forced sale."

The instrument of conveyance may attach words of limitation or words of condition to the estate that will result in its termination prior to infinity. In all such cases, some other estate or estates in the same land must be simultaneously created in the governing instrument or must arise by operation of law at the time of the conveyance. The value of the quantities of all such estates in the same land always aggregate to infinity. Thus, classifying estates is simply a matter of arithmetic. To put it somewhat differently, the sum of the quantities of all estates existing in the same land simultaneously must equal a fee simple absolute—that is, they must sum to infinity. To illustrate, if O conveys Blackacre to A for life, some other estate must also exist in Blackacre such that the sum of the quantity interest of that estate when added to an estate measured by A's life will equal infinity. That estate is O's reversion, which at A's death will become possessory as a fee simple absolute.

Under the law of merger, discussed later in this chapter, the "reassembly" of all estates by transfer to the same person once again causes them to collapse into a fee simple absolute.

4. In the *White* case, the court is construing the terms of a decedent's last will. Prior to the enactment of the Statute of Wills in 1540, 32 Hen. 8, c. 1, the owner of an estate could not devise (transfer by will) an estate in land that would be recognized in the common law courts. Rather, the holder's estate would pass to his heirs.[3] Under the prevailing but not the exclusive English inheritance system, property descended according to rules of primogeniture. Under this system, property passed to the intestate's eldest son or the representative of that son. Only in the absence of male heirs would the property pass equally to the intestate's female descendants.

The right to devise property by will was recognized in the Statute of Wills, supra, provided the testator complied with numerous statutory formalities designed to assure that the document truly reflected the "will" of the testator. While all states have enacted some version of the Statute of Wills, the states vary significantly with respect to the formal requirements demanded for a will to be validly executed. The provisions of Section 2–502 of the Uniform Probate Code are strikingly liberal in reducing the formalities to a minimum. Section 2–502(a) provides:

(a) Except as provided in subsection (b) [relating to holographic wills] . . . a will must be:

(1) in writing;

(2) signed by the testator or in the testator's name by some other individual in the testator's conscious presence and by the testator's direction; and

---

3. Heirs are those persons who inherit the estate of an intestate, a person who dies without a valid will. To be an heir, the person must survive the intestate. Thus, persons now living who would be the heirs of a living person at such person's death are merely heirs apparent. Heirs apparent have no interest in a living person's property.

(3) either:

(A) signed by at least two individuals, each of whom signed within a reasonable time after the individual witnessed either the signing of the will as described in paragraph (2) or the testator's acknowledgement of that signature or acknowledgment of the will; or

(B) acknowledged by the testator before a notary public or other individual authorized by law to take acknowledgements.

The Uniform Probate Code further provides that if a document was not executed with even the minimum formalities required by Section 2–502 it can be "treated as if it had been executed in compliance with that section if the proponent of the document or writing establishes by clear and convincing evidence that the decedent intended the document or writing to" be his will. Unif. Prob. Code § 2–503. This "dispensing power" is a major change from the common law's strict compliance doctrine which voided documents intended to be wills for any deviation from the formalities required by the wills statute. See generally Langbein, Substantial Compliance With the Wills Act, 88 Harv. L. Rev. 489 (1975). Similarly, Restatement (Third) of Property (Wills and Other Donative Transfers) § 3.3 provides that: "A harmless error in executing a will may be excused if the proponent establishes by clear and convincing evidence that the decedent adopted the document as his or her will." At least one state has judicially adopted this approach. In re Ranney, 124 N.J. 1, 589 A.2d 1339 (1991).

5.   A decedent who dies without a will is said to have died "intestate," and the decedent is called an "intestate." Unlike the English common law, however, in the United States and as a general matter if property passes by intestacy to decedent's children (because they alone are his heirs), it passes to them without regard to their gender. In other words, no state follows the English rule of primogeniture. Male and female children take equally. In this country, if an intestate dies without any descendants, the intestate's heirs are either ancestors or collateral relatives as determined by the applicable state statute.

6.   It was generally assumed there is no constitutional right to inherit property. Consider the following statement by the Iowa Supreme Court:

The right to take property by devise or descent is a statutory privilege, and not a natural right. Such matters are strictly within legislative control. . . . Neither our state nor our Federal Constitution secures the right to anyone to control or dispose of his property after his death, nor the right to anyone, whether of kin or not, to take it by inheritance. . . . The legislature may restrict the succession of estates or decedents in any manner, and, if it pleased, could absolutely repeal the statute of wills and of descent and distribution. It could, in the exercise of its sovereignty, take any or all property, upon the death of the owner, for the payment of decedent's debts, and apply the residue to public uses. In re Estate of Emerson, 191 Iowa 900, 905, 183 N.W. 327, 329 (1921).

Compare the preceding view with that of the United States Supreme Court in Hodel v. Irving, 481 U.S. 704 (1987), challenging the validity of Section 207 of the Indian Land Consolidation Act. This statute provided that:

"No undivided fractional interest in any tract of trust or restricted land within a tribe's reservation or otherwise subjected to a tribe's jurisdiction shall descend by intestacy or devise but shall escheat to that tribe if such interest represents 2 per centum or less of the total acreage in such tract and has earned to its owner less than $100 in the preceding year before it is due to escheat." In holding the statute unconstitutional, the Court stated:

> But the character of the Government regulation here is extraordinary.... [T]he regulation here amounts to virtually the abrogation of the right to pass on a certain type of property—the small undivided interest—to one's heirs. In one form or another, the right to pass on property—to one's family in particular—has been part of the Anglo–American legal system since feudal times.... Even the United States concedes that total abrogation of the right to pass property is unprecedented and likely unconstitutional.... Moreover, this statute effectively abolishes both descent and devise of these property interests even when the passing of the property to the heir might result in consolidation of property—as for instance when the heir already owns another undivided interest in the property.... Since the escheatable interests are not, as the United States argues, necessarily de minimis, nor, as it also argues, does the availability of inter vivos transfer obviate the need for descent and devise, a total abrogation of these rights cannot be upheld.

> In holding that complete abolition of both the descent and devise of a particular class of property may be a taking, we reaffirm the continuing vitality of the long line of cases recognizing the States', and where appropriate, the United States', broad authority to adjust the rules governing the descent and devise of property without implicating the guarantees of the Just Compensation Clause.... The difference in this case is the fact that both descent and devise are completely abolished; indeed they are abolished even in circumstances when the governmental purpose sought to be advanced, consolidation of ownership of Indian lands, does not conflict with the further descent of the property. Id. at 716–18.

7. At common law, and generally under the laws of each state, the intestate's surviving spouse was not an heir of the intestate. At common law the surviving spouse was entitled to an estate of either dower, if a female, or curtesy, if a male. Most states have abolished the estates of dower and curtesy and have substituted a statutory share for the surviving spouse. See chapter 6.

The typical Statute of Wills contemplates that at least two witnesses attest to the execution of the testator's will although in a few states three witnesses are required. Some states also permit so-called holographic wills to be admitted to probate. See Unif. Prob. Code § 2–502(b). Generally, a holographic will is an unwitnessed will entirely in the testator's handwriting. Holographic wills generally are prepared by testators without the aid of a lawyer. Assuming that Miss Lide prepared her will without the assistance of counsel, what effect, if any, would that assumed fact have on the inclination of the court to construe the will the way that it did?

The defendants in the *White* case are the decedent's nieces and nephews, the descendants of her predeceased brothers and sisters, whom the court describes as heirs at law. After reviewing the decedent's will, how is it that they might have an interest in the decedent's home?

8.   The nomenclature of inheritance includes not only the word "heirs" but also the words "issue," "ancestors," "collaterals," and "escheat." Issue is synonymous with "descendants" and includes the named ancestor's entire line of lineal descendants. Thus, it includes not only children (who are issue of the first generation) but also grandchildren, great-grandchildren and so forth. Ancestors include parents, grandparents, great-grandparents and so forth. Collaterals are blood relatives who are neither issue nor ancestors and who are related to each other through a common ancestor. Collaterals would include siblings, nieces and nephews, cousins, uncles and aunts and the like. Lastly, escheat refers to the phenomenon that occurs if it is determined that a person has died without any known living heirs. In this case, the intestate's property passes to the state. In many cases a determination that a person dies without heirs is only shorthand for the conclusion that after a reasonable search, no heirs of the intestate could be found.

9.   An estate in fee simple absolute is alienable, devisable, and descendible. Since the estate is alienable, the holder of the estate can transfer it to another by gift or by sale. Likewise, the holder can mortgage the interest or create other liens thereon. Since the estate is devisable, the holder of the estate can transfer it to another by will and, since the estate is descendible, if the holder of the estate dies leaving no valid will and without having alienated the estate during his life, the estate will pass to the holder's heirs. The fact that under limited circumstances the estate in fee simple absolute may pass to the holder's heirs tends to create the confusion that the heirs are purchasers under the terms of the conveyance to the holder of the fee simple absolute. As discussed above, however, the heirs take nothing under the conveyance, and if in fact they take the estate upon the holder's death, they take from the holder by operation of state inheritance laws and not from the holder's grantor. In that sense the heirs of the holder of the estate are "purchasers" from the holder of the estate.

10.   There are both forfeiture and disabling restraints against the alienation of property. A forfeiture restraint attempts to prohibit the ability of the owner to convey the property by providing that an attempted conveyance will result in the forfeiture of the owner's interest. See Restatement (Second) of Property, § 3.1. A disabling restraint attempts to prohibit the ability of the owner of property to convey the property by providing that any transfer is void. However, the interest of the owner who purported to make the transfer is unaffected. Restatement (Second) of Property § 3.1. According to the Restatement, both disabling and forfeiture restraints on a fee simple are void. Restatement (Second) of Property §§ 4.1, 4.2.

In the *White* case the court holds, in common with the Restatement of Property, that the attempted restraint on alienation was void as "inconsistent with the incidents and nature of the estate devised and contrary to public policy." Why is a restraint on alienation of a fee simple contrary to public policy? If the court had held that the devisee took a legal life estate, would the restraint have been valid?

A legal life estate is a life estate of which the holder at common law was seized. On the other hand, if the life estate exists in a trust (a legal device that separates the administrative and management burdens associated with the ownership of property from the benefits of ownership, and that is the present day equivalent of the historic common law "use"), the holder of the life estate has an *equitable* life estate. She is not seized of the land; rather seisin is in the trustee (the manager) who has legal title and the power to alienate the property held in the trust. Generally, a restraint on the alienation of an *equitable* life estate is valid. Thus, if O conveys property to T in trust to pay the income from the property to A for life, O can validly restrain the alienation of A's equitable life estate. Why isn't a restraint on the alienation of an equitable life estate invalid?

11. It is interesting that both the majority and dissent rely in part on Williams v. Williams, 167 Tenn. 26, 65 S.W.2d 561 (1933), to rationalize their conclusions. The majority cites *Williams* for the proposition that a devise for life can be construed to transfer a fee simple absolute; the dissent (which accurately details the other provisions of the will being construed in *Williams*) states that the *Williams* case is distinguishable. Which opinion, in your judgment, properly uses *Williams* as authority?

12. To what extent, if any, was the result in the *White* case dictated by the relationship between the decedent and Mrs. White or the relationship of the decedent to her relatives who claimed a share of the property as heirs of the decedent?

§ 4.3 FEE SIMPLE DETERMINABLE AND FEE SIMPLE ON CONDITION SUBSEQUENT ("FEE SIMPLE DEFEASIBLES")

If O transfers Blackacre "to A (and his heirs) so long as the premises are not used as a tavern," A has a fee simple determinable, and O retains a possibility of reverter. In that conveyance, what are the words of purchase and the words of limitation? The nature of O's interest is that upon the use of the premises as a tavern by A (or A's successors), A's estate automatically ends, and the possession of the property reverts to O, whose possibility of reverter ripens into a fee simple absolute.

By contrast, if O conveys Blackacre "to A (and his heirs) provided that if the premises are used as a tavern, O may re-enter and claim the premises," A has a fee simple on condition subsequent, and O has a right of entry for condition broken or a power of termination. (In this conveyance, are the words "provided that if the premises are used as a tavern" words of limitation, words of purchase or something else?) If the premises are used as a tavern, A's estate does *not automatically* end. Rather, O must exercise the retained right of re-entry. If O sues A for possession without first notifying A that he elects to re-enter, has O properly terminated the fee simple on condition subsequent? See Dunham, Possibil-

Rev = FSA(D)
Term = FSA(CS)

ity of Reverter and Powers of Termination—Fraternal or Identical Twins?, 20 U.Chi.L.Rev. 215 (1953).

Where the terms of an instrument are ambiguous as to whether the grantee has a fee simple determinable or a fee simple on condition subsequent subject to a right of re-entry, the courts tend to presume that the latter estate was created. Why do the courts prefer the latter? See 2 R. Powell, Real Property ¶ 188 (P. Rohan ed. 1990).

The characterization of a conveyance as either creating a fee simple determinable with a resulting possibility of reverter in the grantor or, alternatively, a fee simple on condition subsequent with a resulting power of termination in the grantor can ultimately affect the ownership of property. To illustrate, suppose:

1. In 1949, Mr. and Mrs. Hutton, who owned Blackacre in fee simple absolute, conveyed it to the Y School "for school purposes only, otherwise to revert to the grantors."

2. In 1951, Mr. Hutton died intestate. His future interest (possibility of reverter or power of termination, depending on whether Y School had a fee simple determinable or fee simple on condition subsequent) passed by intestacy to his heir. Depending upon the underlying state law, this would have been either Mrs. Hutton or his son, Harry. While in many states today, Mrs. Hutton would be the sole heir, in 1951 it would more likely have been Harry and Mrs. Hutton in some percentile share.

3. In 1969, Mrs. Hutton died intestate, and her interest(s) passed to her son and heir, Harry.

4. In 1973, Y School began to use the premises for storage purposes.

5. In May, 1977, Harry conveys to P.

A statute in the jurisdiction, contrary to the law of most jurisdictions, provides that possibilities of reverters and powers of termination are neither alienable nor devisable, but they are descendible. Under what circumstances would P have a fee simple absolute? Under what circumstances would P have nothing? See Mahrenholz v. County Board of School Trustees of Lawrence County, 93 Ill.App.3d 366, 48 Ill.Dec. 736, 417 N.E.2d 138 (1981).

ALBY v. BANC ONE FINANCIAL

Supreme Court of Washington (2006).
156 Wash.2d 367, 128 P.3d 81.

JOHNSON, J.

The issue in this case is whether a restriction in a deed, which provides that the deeded property automatically reverts to the grantor if the property is mortgaged or encumbered during the life of the grantor, is a valid restraint on alienation. We find the clause to be reasonable and justified by the interests of the parties and, therefore, valid. We affirm the Court of Appeals. . . .

In 1992, Eugene and Susan Alby sold part of their family farm to their niece, Lorri Brashler, and her husband, Larry Brashler. Although the property's market value was $100,000, the parties agreed to a purchase price of $15,000. The contract and the deed contained nearly identical clauses providing for automatic reverter to the Albys if the property were subdivided, mortgaged, or otherwise encumbered during either of the Albys' lifetimes. The restriction at issue provided:

> RESERVATION in favor of the Grantors, their heirs and assigns, an automatic reverter, should the property conveyed herein ever be mortgaged or encumbered within the life time of either Grantor. . . .

The parties included these restrictions as a means of ensuring that the land remained within the family during the Albys' lifetimes. . . .[2] The parties recorded the real estate contract on April 28, 1992. After the Brashlers satisfied their obligations under the contract, the warranty deed was recorded on September 27, 1996.

Notwithstanding the restrictions, the Brashlers obtained a loan for $92,000 from First Union Mortgage Corporation by executing a deed of trust for the property on February 26, 1999. This loan was recorded on March 3, 1999. The Brashlers executed a second deed of trust to obtain a second loan for $17,250 from CIT Group on March 31, 1999. This loan was recorded on April 2, 1999. CIT Group assigned the loan to petitioner, Banc One Financial (Banc One). The Brashlers defaulted on their payments on their first loan and the lender held a trustee's sale on October 27, 2000. Banc One purchased the property at the sale for $100,822.16 and recorded the trustee's deed on November 2, 2000.[3]

---

2. Susan Alby's uncontested affidavit states:

Because this piece of property had been in the ALBY family for several generations, GENE and I wanted to make sure that the property always stayed in the family. After several discussions with LORRI about what she and her husband, LARRY R. BRASHLER, could afford to pay for the home, my husband GENE and I decided that $15,000.00 was what LORRI and her husband could afford, even though we believed the property and home was of considerably greater valued [sic]. Since we were so concerned about the property staying in the family, we consulted with an attorney . . . to make a contract with the proper and appropriate language so that LORRI and her husband could not do three things:

1. Sell the property to someone who was not a member of the family;

2. Divide the property in any way; and

3. Encumber the property with a mortgage or deed of trust.

We even told LORRI that we would buy the property back from her and her husband should they ever decide that they did not want it.

My husband GENE ALBY, now deceased, received this property from his mother. His father had received part of this property from his father who immigrated to the United States from Norway. This property has been in the ALBY family for all these generations and *for this reason,* my husband and I had the [attorney] place the necessary language in the real estate contract and deed that should LORRI and her husband attempt to do any of the above mentioned acts, the property would automatically revert back to us.

CP at 39–40 (emphasis added) (Although neither the contract nor the deed contains restrictions on selling the property to someone who is not a member of the family, the Albys reserved a right of first refusal in the contract).

3. Because the deed containing the restrictions had been recorded, Banc One had actual or constructive notice of the reversion that was created when the Brashlers mortgaged the property.

On April 18, 2002, Susan Alby filed a quiet title action in Stevens County Superior Court against Banc One, arguing the title to the property automatically reverted to her when the Brashlers encumbered the property. On competing motions for summary judgment, the trial court quieted title in Banc One and declared the clause void against public policy as an unreasonable restraint on alienation. The Court of Appeals reversed, concluding that the clause is valid because it is not a restraint on alienation and even if it were, the restraint is reasonable. *Alby v. Banc One Fin.*, 119 Wash.App. 513, 82 P.3d 675 (2003). We granted review to determine whether the clause is a restraint on alienation, and if so, whether it is reasonable. . . .

The first step in resolving the dispute in this case is to identify the type of interest conveyed. Banc One and Susan Alby agree that the interest conveyed to the Brashlers is a fee simple determinable. A "fee simple determinable" is an estate that will automatically end and revert to the grantor if some specified event occurs. BLACK'S LAW DICTIONARY 649 (8th ed.2004). We agree that the Albys conveyed a fee simple determinable interest to the Brashlers because the estate would revert to the Albys if the property were mortgaged or encumbered during their lifetimes.

Though we conclude the transferred estate is a fee simple determinable estate, that conclusion does not end the analysis. Fee simple determinable estates are subject to the rule against restraints on alienation, which prohibits undue or unreasonable restraints on alienation. *Black's Law Dictionary* defines a "restraint on alienation" as:

> [a] restriction, usu[ally] in a deed of conveyance, on a grantee's ability to sell or transfer real property; a provision that conveys an interest and that, even after the interest has become vested, prevents or discourages the owner from disposing of it at all or from disposing of it in particular ways or to particular persons.

Black's, *Supra,* at 1340.

Here we have a restraint on alienation because the clause prevented the Brashlers from disposing of the property in a particular way: they could not mortgage or encumber the property without the property automatically reverting to the Albys. Additionally, though the clause did not directly prevent the Brashlers from selling the property, it limited the property's marketability because it prevented potential buyers from financing the purchase of the property.

Because we find the prohibition on mortgaging or encumbering to be a restraint on alienation, we must next determine the validity of the restraint. Washington follows the reasonableness approach to restraints on alienation. "Unreasonable restraints on alienation of real property are . . . invalid; reasonable restraints on alienation . . . are valid if justified by the *legitimate interests of the parties*." *McCausland v. Bankers Life Ins.*

[Ed. Note: See chapter 16 with respecting to recording statutes and the notice they provide to buyers and mortgagees].

Co., 110 Wash.2d 716, 722, 757 P.2d 941 (1988) (emphasis added). In determining whether a restraint is reasonable, we balance the utility of the purpose served by the restraint against the injurious consequences that are likely to flow from its enforcement.[4] *See* Restatement (Third) of Property § 3.4, at 440 (2000). Whether a restraint is limited in scope or time is often highly significant. 17 William B. Stoebuck & John W. Weaver, Washington Practice: Real Estate: Property Law § 1.26, at 50 (2d ed.2004). In addition to the scope and duration of the restraint, we look at the purpose of the restraint and whether the restraint is supported by consideration.

The balance in this case is between the operation of a free market in land and the right to maintain property in family ownership for a limited time period. Family ownership is not always subordinated to immediate and free alienability. The fact that restraints may negatively affect marketability does not necessarily render them unreasonable. The Albys conveyed a restrained interest in long-held family property to their niece and her husband for a substantially reduced price with the purpose of maintaining family ownership of the property through the Albys' lifetimes. This restraint prevents the property from being mortgaged or encumbered but does not restrict the right to sell or transfer the property. The restraint has a limited scope of preventing only mortgaging or encumbering, a limited duration of the Albys' lifetimes, and a legitimate purpose of keeping the property in the family. The restraint is also supported by the consideration apparent in the significantly reduced purchase price. The recorded deed provides notice to potentially affected parties. Balancing the relevant factors, we conclude that the potentially injurious consequences of not mortgaging or encumbering the property and reducing its marketability are outweighed by the utility of enforcing the limited restraint to keep the property in the family for the Albys' lifetimes.

We next consider the legitimate interests of the parties. The Albys have a legitimate interest in keeping the property in the family and in preventing the property from being lost through foreclosure. The Brashlers have a legitimate interest in realizing the right to freely dispose of their property. However, the Brashlers' interest in free alienation is limited by the fact that they agreed to the restraint in consideration for the substantially reduced price. Enforcement of the restraint still provides the Brashlers with a legitimate interest in owning the property with every aspect of absolute ownership except the right to mortgage or encumber the property. Both parties also have legitimate interests in enforcing the terms of their contract.

---

4. Restraints on alienation of land are used for a variety of legitimate purposes: retaining land in families; preserving affordable housing; furthering conservation, preservation, and charitable purposes to which land is devoted; and facilitating land investment and creating investment opportunities. Potentially harmful consequences that may flow from restraints on alienation include impediments to the operation of a free market in land, limits on the prospects for improvement, development, and redevelopment of land, and limits on the mobility of landowners and would-be purchasers. Restatement (Third) of Property § 3.4 cmt. c at 442 (2000).

When evaluating the reasonableness of any agreement placing a restraint on alienation, courts should be reluctant to invoke common law principles disfavoring restraints to invalidate a bargained for contract freely agreed to by the parties. The parties here contracted to transfer property with the purpose of keeping the family farm in the family during the lifetimes of the grantors. We find nothing unreasonable about this purpose. We conclude that the restraint, which prevents the Brashlers from mortgaging or encumbering the property, is reasonable and justified by the legitimate interests of the parties. Accordingly, we affirm the Court of Appeals and remand to superior court with directions to enter summary judgment in favor of and quieting title in Susan Alby.

OWENS, SANDERS, FAIRHURST, and J.M. JOHNSON, JJ., concur.

ALEXANDER, C.J. (dissenting).

I disagree with the majority's determination that Susan Alby placed a valid restraint on alienation of her niece's property and that the Court of Appeals should be affirmed. While I agree that a reasonableness test applies to restraints on alienation, I would hold that the restraint in this case was not reasonable because the cherished value that our state places on free alienability outweighs the value to the Alby family of maintaining the property in family ownership.

We determine whether a restraint on alienation is reasonable or unreasonable based on "factual determinations and consideration of the equities," *Morris v. Woodside,* 101 Wash.2d 812, 818, 682 P.2d 905 (1984), and on an assessment of the "legitimate interests of the parties." *Erickson v. Bank of Cal.,* 97 Wash.2d 246, 249, 643 P.2d 670 (1982). Determining reasonableness also requires "weighing the utility of the restraint against the injurious consequences of enforcing the restraint." Restatement (Third) of Property § 3.4, at 440 (2000).

Thus, we first consider the "legitimate interests of the parties ..." Eugene and Susan Albys' interest was keeping the property in the Alby family. Lorri and Larry Brashlers' interest, on the other hand, was that of realizing the right of a property owner to freely dispose of his or her property interest, which, as this court has recognized, is among the " 'fundamental attribute[s] of property ownership.' " *Manufactured Hous. Cmtys. v. State,* 142 Wash.2d 347, 364, 13 P.3d 183 (2000) (quoting *Guimont v. Clarke,* 121 Wash.2d 586, 595, 854 P.2d 1 (1993)). As has been observed in the *Restatement (Second) of Property,*

> [i]f the full benefits which flow from the freedom to alienate an interest in property ... are to be obtained, the owner of such interest must be able to take advantage of any of the existing methods of transferring property. Any restraint which interferes with the power to alienate in some manner, though it leave the owner of the estate free to alienate in other ways, may substantially hinder him in disposing of the property.

Restatement (Second) of Property § 4.2 cmt. n at 183 (1983).

According to Susan Alby, the parties here "freely contracted for the exchange," Answer to Pet. for Review at 11, with full knowledge and after an opportunity to freely negotiate the terms of their bargain. She argues that, although the Brashlers' right to exercise one of the incidents of property ownership was limited by the terms of the deed, this limitation was reflected in the selling price of the property as they paid significantly below market price.

However, nothing in the record supports the claim that the Albys and the Brashlers bargained for a reduction in price in exchange for an estate that did not include the full right of alienation or that the reduction in price was consideration for conveyance of a reduced estate. The real estate contract that the parties signed indicated that the Albys considered the sale of the property to Lorri Brashler to be "in essence a gift to her." Clerk's Papers (CP) at 7. Indeed, Susan Alby's own affidavit reflects that the property was sold to the Brashlers at a reduced price, not in exchange for agreeing to a lesser estate, but as a favor to Lorri Brashler. She stated that

> [a]fter several discussions with LORRI about what she and her husband, LARRY R. BRASHLER, could afford to pay for the home, my husband GENE, and I decided that $15,000.00 was what LORRI and her husband could afford, even though we believed the property and home was of considerably greater valued [sic].

CP at 40. Susan Alby's affidavit also suggests that the Albys placed the restraint on alienation into the contract and deed *after* having agreed with the Brashlers on a selling price. For the foregoing reasons, I believe that the sale of the property at a reduced price was not a bargained-for exchange in consideration for the conveyance of a reduced estate.

Susan Alby notes that the restraint imposed on the alienability of the property in this case was limited both in scope and duration because it was a restriction on mortgaging or encumbering only and expired upon the death of both of the grantors. However, this limitation effectively rendered the property unalienable during the life of the grantors. The duration of the restriction is unknown; it could be a significant period of time, depending on Susan Alby's longevity.[5] During this period, the Brashlers would effectively be relegated to the status of leaseholders of the property, with the right of possession only. Furthermore, the restriction "runs with the land" and therefore limits the rights of not only the Brashlers, the immediate purchasers of the property, but all subsequent purchasers, for the lifetime of the grantor.

The utility of maintaining property in family ownership has been viewed in the law as subordinate to the value of free alienability of property. 3 John A. Borron, Jr., Simes & Smith: The Law of Future Interests § 1117 (3d ed.2004). The doctrine of restraint on alienation and

---

5. Over 14 years have elapsed since the relevant language was placed in the real estate contract and deed. Because Susan Alby is now only 66 years of age, the restriction, if not void, could be in effect for many more years.

other common law doctrines such as the rule against perpetuities arose, in large part, to ensure that the desire of individuals to retain ownership of property within their family did not harm the economic interests of the nation by destroying the free market for property. *Id.* Despite the long history of this principle, the majority asserts that "[f]amily ownership is not always subordinated to immediate and free alienability." Majority at 84. It cites no authority for this assertion, which dismisses the doctrine recognized in *Simes & Smith* that society has a stronger interest in the free alienability of property than in fostering family dynasties.

Maintaining the property within the Alby family no doubt has certain value, to Susan Alby individually and to her family. Continued ownership of the property would allow them to maintain possession over land to which they no doubt have an emotional attachment. However, allowing Susan Alby to limit the alienability of the property for the sole purpose of maintaining it in the Alby family has injurious consequences both to the Brashlers and to the general public. The Brashlers are deprived of their right to freely dispose of their property, a right recognized as being one of the " 'fundamental attribute[s] of property ownership.' " *Manufactured Hous. Cmtys.*, 142 Wash.2d at 364, 13 P.3d 183 (quoting *Guimont,* 121 Wash.2d at 595, 854 P.2d 1). Further, the property is effectively removed from the marketplace, causing economic consequences affecting society as a whole.

For the foregoing reasons, I would hold that the clause in the Alby/Brashler deed providing for automatic reversion of the property if it is mortgaged or encumbered during the life of either grantor is unreasonable and, therefore, void. Accordingly, I would reverse the Court of Appeals and remand to the superior court for reinstatement of the summary judgment in favor of Banc One.

MADSEN and BRIDGE, JJ., concur.

CHAMBERS, J. (dissent).

I respectfully dissent. But first, I agree with my colleagues that Eugene and Susan Alby conveyed a fee simple determinable estate with the possibility of reverter. Majority at 83; *see also* Roger A. Cunningham, et al., The Law of Property § 2.3, at 35 (2d ed.1993). The appropriate next question, as the majority properly notes, is whether the reservation was an unreasonable restraint on alienation. Majority at 83. We also agree that the Court of Appeals was in error when it concluded that the encumbrance clauses in the fulfillment deed did not operated as a restraint on alienation. *Black's Law Dictionary* defines a "restraint on alienation" as:

> [a] restriction, usu[ally] in a deed of conveyance, on a grantee's ability to sell or transfer real property; a provision that conveys an interest and that, even after the interest has become vested, prevents or discourages the owner from disposing of it at all or from disposing of it in particular ways or to particular persons. Restraints on alienation are generally unenforceable as against public policy favoring the free alienability of land.

Black's Law Dictionary 1340 (8th ed.2004). The clause clearly qualifies.

I part company with my colleagues because the encumbrance clause at issue in this case was, in my view, an unreasonable restraint on alienation because it prevented Lorri and Larry Brashler, or their successors, from transferring their interest in the property in a particular and very common way: by way of mortgage or encumbrance. The encumbrance clause also had the effect of seriously discouraging disposition of the property by limiting the ability of a potential buyer to finance the purchase primarily through a mortgage.

It is, however, primarily the majority and Chief Justice Alexander's discussion of reasonableness with which I take issue. Given the nature of the estate and the restraint, I would hold that the restraint was per se unreasonable. It was only after the real estate contract was satisfied and the warranty deed vesting title to the property in the Brashlers had been recorded, that the Brashlers attempted to obtain a loan by executing a deed of trust for the property. After the Brashlers had paid the $15,000 purchase price and recorded the warranty deed, the automatic reverter restraint was, in my view, per se unreasonable and so holding would clarify the law.[6]

Restraints on alienation fall into two categories: direct and indirect. 3 John A. Borron, Jr., Simes & Smith: The Law of Future Interests § 1112, at 3 (3d ed. 2004) (Simes & Smith). Direct restraints are those provisions in an instrument which, by their terms or implications, "purport[ ] to prohibit or penalize the exercise of the power of alienation" of property. 3 Simes & Smith, *supra,* § 1112, at 3.

Direct restraints take one of three forms: promissory, disabling, or forfeiture. 3 Simes & Smith, *supra,* § 1131, at 14. A promissory restraint is an agreement by the holder of an interest not to alienate, with contractual liability, if the agreement is breached. A disabling restraint is a provision in the document creating the interest that renders void any attempt to alienate the interest. Black's Law Dictionary 494 (8th ed.2004) (a disabling restraint places "[l]imits on the alienation of property"); *cf.* 17 William B. Stoebuck & John W. Weaver, Washington Practice: Real Estate: Property Law § 1.26, at 50 (2d ed.2004) ("restraint [that] is stated in the form of a prohibition; the transferor in some way forbids the transferee from alienating."). A forfeiture restraint is a condition that terminates the fee upon an attempt to alienate. 3 Simes & Smith, *supra,* § 1131, at 14. Such a restraint exists when "an instrument of conveyance provides that if the grantee attempts to alienate, the land shall go to the grantor by way of possibility of reverter or right of entry or to a third person by way of executory interest." 17 Stoebuck & Weaver, *supra,*

---

6. Assuming that the goal of the Albys was to convey an estate which would keep the whole parcel of land in the family for their life times, there are better ways they could have accomplished this. For example, they could have given the Albys fee simple and retained for themselves a life estate.

§ 1.26, at 50; *see also* Restatement (Second) of Property § 3.2, at 147 (1983).

The automatic reverter clause here is a direct forfeiture restraint. Although there are no Washington decisions on point, the general rule is that even limited forfeiture restraints that interfere with the alienability of property if unreasonable, are void. 17 Stoebuck & Weaver, *supra*, § 1.26, at 51; 3 Simes & Smith, *supra*, § 1131, at 14.

It is desirable that the law be clear, understandable, and predictable. The reasonableness test embraced by the majority and dissent does not promote predictability. To send every contested restraint to a court hearing to balance the interests sought to be protected by the restraint against the benefits of alienability serves neither clarity nor predictability. I would hold that where, as here, the condition of payment has been satisfied and a warranty deed is transferred and recorded, a direct and automatic reverter upon the attempt to alienate is unreasonable as a matter of law. I therefore respectfully dissent.

NOTES AND QUESTIONS

1. The parties agreed that the deed created a fee simple determinable. Do you agree?

2. To what extent, if any, does the law of Washington state differ from the common law rule relating to restraints on alienation. To what extent, if at all, is the dissent of Justice Chambers consistent with or different from the common law rule?

3. In 2000, O transferred Blackacre "to the X Church to be used by the church solely for the purpose of maintaining a church school." What kind of interest is created in the X Church and O, if any, by this grant?

In 2006, the X Church ceases to use the property as a church school although it remains in possession of Blackacre. Assuming the jurisdiction has a statute providing that actions to recover the possession of real property must be brought within ten years after the cause of action accrues, when will O's cause of action, if any, expire? Does it make any difference whether the conveyance is construed to create a fee simple determinable or a fee simple on condition subsequent subject to a power of termination? If it does, how would the estate passing to the X Church likely be classified and why? See Dunham, Possibility of Reverter and Powers of Termination—Fraternal or Identical Twins?, 20 U.Chi.L.Rev. 215 (1953).

4. In 1900, O conveyed Blackacre "to Y County provided the land be used as a storage area for county vehicles." O reserved the power to re-enter the land if it was not so used. From 1900 until 1935, Y County used the area for the storage of county vehicles. Since 1935, however, the land has been used as a public park. In 1983, the county brought an action against O's heir to quiet its title to the land. What arguments can you make in support of the county's position and the heirs' position? See Metropolitan Park District of Tacoma v. Unknown Heirs of John L. Rigney, 65 Wash.2d 788, 399 P.2d 516 (1965).

5.   In 1980, O conveyed Blackacre, a 180 acre tract of land, "to Z so long as no liquor is sold on the premises." Z died in 1985. Under the applicable state inheritance law, one-third of Blackacre was set aside for Z's surviving spouse, and the remainder was set aside for Z's children. See generally chapter 6, infra (discussion of marital property rights). Thereafter the spouse and children brought a partition action to sever their tenancy in common, and the court approved a partition under which 60 distinct acres were set off to the spouse and 120 distinct acres were set off to the children. In 2000, the children sold liquor on the 120 acres set aside to them in the partition action. What are O's rights, if any, in the 60 acres of Blackacre set aside to the spouse in the decree of partition? See generally Restatement of Property § 54, Appendix 5–11 (1936); Amer.L.Prop. § 5.29 (A.J. Casner ed. 1952).

Suppose O conveys his 100 acre farm "to A and his heirs so long as liquor is not consumed on the land." Five years later A subdivides the land into 400 residential lots and sells all of them. Five years later one purchaser drinks liquor in his home. O now claims that all 400 homeowners have lost the title to their land. Do you agree? See Storke v. Penn Mutual Life Ins. Co., 390 Ill. 619, 61 N.E.2d 552 (1945).

6.   Should a retained possibility of reverter or power of termination be void as a "restraint on alienation" either because it restricts the use of property or deflates the value of the property from what it would have been if the holder of the present estate had a fee simple absolute? See Prieskorn v. Maloof, 128 N.M. 226, 991 P.2d 511 (1999).

7.   A number of jurisdictions have enacted statutes designed to terminate possibilities of reverter and rights of re-entry for condition broken where the holders of these future interests fail to file periodically in the local land records office a statement that they intend to enforce their future interests in the event the limitation or condition attached to the present fee simple estate occurs. See, e.g., Iowa Code § 614.24 (2011). Other states have statutes that bar the enforcement of these future interests unless an action to enforce them is brought within a fixed period *after the limitation or condition has occurred.* See, e.g., 735 Ill. Comp. Stat. Ann. 5/13–102 (West 2011). In some states, actions to enforce such future interests are barred unless brought within a fixed period after the fee simple determinable or fee simple on condition subsequent is created. Absent such statutes, at common law these future interests lasted in perpetuity. But see City of Casper v. J.M. Carey & Brothers, 601 P.2d 1010 (Wyo.1979) (enforcing the restriction only if the duration is "reasonable"). Are statutes that have the effect of extinguishing possibilities of reverters and rights of re-entry for condition broken constitutional or are they unconstitutional because they are either ex post facto laws, statutes impairing contract rights or statutes that deprive persons of property without due process of law? Compare Trustees of Schools of Township No. 1 v. Batdorf, 6 Ill.2d 486, 130 N.E.2d 111 (1955) (upholding validity of Illinois statute) and Presbytery of Southeast Iowa v. Harris, 226 N.W.2d 232 (Iowa 1975) (upholding validity of Iowa statute) with Board of Education v. Miles, 15 N.Y.2d 364, 259 N.Y.S.2d 129, 207 N.E.2d 181 (1965) (holding invalid the New York statute). For a more thorough discussion of these statutes, see chapter 16, infra.

8. In some cases the grantor of a fee simple determinable or a fee simple on condition subsequent may not retain a future interest in the property. Rather the grantor, with the creation of the fee simple estate, simultaneously conveys a future interest to a transferee. For example, O deeds Blackacre to the X Church so long as the premises are used for church purposes over the next 10 years and, if not so used, then to C and his heirs. Or, O might convey to the X Church, but if the property ceases to be used for church purposes over the next 10 years, then to C and his heirs.

In both cases, C has a future interest rather than O. C's interest is called a "shifting executory interest." In the first case the church has a fee simple determinable; in the second the church has a fee simple subject to an executory interest. Interestingly, in each case, C's interest automatically becomes possessory if the X Church fails to use the premises for church purposes within the ten-year period. C need not exercise any "right of entry." See generally Gutierrez v. Rodriguez, 30 S.W.3d 558 (Tex.Ct.App.2000).

9. The Third Restatement of Property abandons the distinction between the fee simple determinable and the fee simple on condition subsequent, preferring to classify each of these as "fee simple defeasibles." It provides: "The estate in fee simple defeasible is a present interest that terminates upon the happening of a stated event that might or might not occur. The subcategories historically known as the fee simple determinable, the fee simple subject to a condition subsequent, and the fee simple subject to an executory limitation are no longer recognized but are absorbed under the term fee simple defeasible." Restatement (Third) of Property, § 24.3 (2012).

§ 4.4 FEE TAIL AND FEE SIMPLE CONDITIONAL

Once the early common law courts held that the words "and his heirs" were only words of limitation and created no interest in the heirs of the named grantee, the grantor's intent to create an estate in the grantee that was not alienable became frustrated. Thus, the practice developed whereby the grantor would convey to "A and the heirs of his body." The apparent intent of this conveyance was to limit A's interest to a life estate with successive life estates in A's heirs (typically A's eldest son) until A's descendants became extinct. If A's descendants became extinct, the property would revert back to O or O's heirs. The purpose of the conveyance was to preserve the estate for the benefit of A and A's descendants. Courts, however, viewed such conveyances as inconsistent with societal goals of furthering the alienability of land and held that as soon as a child was born alive to A, A could convey a fee simple absolute in the land to another. This conveyance would extinguish the interest of A's descendants and the grantor's possibility of reverter. As so construed, the interest of A was called a fee simple conditional. If neither A nor a later descendant conveyed the land to another in fee simple absolute and A's line of lineal descendants became extinct, the property would revert to the grantor. Under this construction of the disposition to "A and the heirs of his body," the grantor's intent could be easily subverted. For example, upon birth of his issue, A could convey a fee simple absolute to a third party who could then reconvey the property to A. By this "strawman" conveyance, A could effectively convert the fee simple conditional into a fee simple absolute.

In 1285, the Statute de Donis Conditionalibus, 13 Edw. I, c 1 (1285), was enacted for the purpose of restoring the original purpose of the conveyance to create successive life estates in A and A's descendants. Thereafter, A's estate was known as a fee tail, and the grantor's estate was classified as a reversion. A was frequently called the tenant-in-tail.

If A's entire line of lineal descendants (issue) became extinct (an event that could happen many years after A died), the property would revert to the grantor. An estate in Blackacre that terminates when the line of descendants becomes extinct assures that, so long as a family has descendants, Blackacre remains in the family, perhaps for many generations.[1] Furthermore, if the current generation of descendants is effectively limited to a life estate, then the property for all intents and purposes is inalienable.

A practice developed among holders of fee tails to engage in what was known as a common recovery. The effect of the common recovery (a collusive lawsuit) was to substitute an uncollectible money judgment for the future estate that the descendants of the tenant-in-tail had in the entailed land and to vest a fee simple absolute in that land in the tenant-in-tail. By 1472, the courts readily acquiesced in the use of the common recovery as a way to convert the fee tail into a fee simple absolute. Later attempts by conveyancers to restrict grantees from entering into a common recovery proved to no avail. This ultimately led to the preference for the creation of life estates followed by the now familiar remainders and executory interests.

Once the fee tail was recognized, four kinds of fee tails could be created. The fee tail general (O to "A and the heirs of his body"); the fee tail male (O to "A and the male heirs of his body"); the fee tail female (O to "A and the female heirs of his body"); and the fee tail special (O to "A and the heirs of his body by B"). The fee tail general could pass to any male heir, or absent a male descendant and if primogeniture applied, to the female heirs of A's body, whereas the fee tail male and the fee tail female limited the entailment to either the male or female descendants. The fee tail special was often used by A's father-in-law to assure that the estate would descend only to issue born to A and the father-in-law's daughter, B. If B died before issue was born, A's estate was classified as a fee tail special with possibility of issue extinct.

---

1. For example, suppose O conveyed to A and the heirs of A's body. A dies in 1750 survived by child B who dies in 1795 survived by grandchild C who dies in 1845 survived by great-grandchild D who dies in 1906 without descendants. Under these facts A's line of lineal descendants becomes extinct in 1906, and A's fee tail estate would end *even though A died in 1750.*

The fee tail estate received a rather cool reception in the United States. In most states, words that at common law would have created a fee tail create a fee simple absolute in the grantee. A few states have simply abolished the fee tail but make no provision for what kind of estate is created by the words "and the heirs of his body." In others, the grantee receives a life estate and the grantee's descendants a remainder. See, e.g., Mo. Stat. § 442.470; see generally H. Hovenkamp & S. Kurtz, The Law of Property, An Introductory Survey at 103 (5th ed. 2001).

Although for all practical purposes the fee tail has been abolished in the United States, on occasion the law relating to fee tails rears its ugly head. In Robins Island Preservation Fund, Inc. v. Southold Development Corporation, 959 F.2d 409 (2d Cir. 1992), yes 1992, the resolution of a modern day dispute involving whether a seller had marketable title depended upon whether the State of New York had properly attained the interest of a descendant of a fee tail male. Here's what happened:

1. In 1715, Joseph Wickham, Sr. purchased Robins Island.

2. In 1734, Joseph Wickham, Sr. devised the island to his son Joseph Wickham, Jr. "and to the male heirs of his body lawfully begotten or to be begotten forever." This conveyance created a fee tail male in Joseph.

3. In 1749, Joseph, the tenant-in-tail, died and Robins Island passed to his son, Parker Wickham in fee tail male.

4. In 1779 the New York State Legislature passed the Act of Attainder declaring British loyalists as *ipso facto* convicted of "adherence" to the British. As punishment, all property owned by the "attained" individuals was declared to be immediately forfeited to the State of New York. Parker Wickham, the then owner of the fee tail male, was a loyalist and as a result of the 1779 statute his interest as tenant-in-tail of Robins Island was forfeited to the State of New York under the statute.

5. In 1782, the New York Legislature abolished the estate tail, converting lands that once were fee tails into fee simples.

6. In 1783, after the Provisional Treaty of Peace was signed between the United States and Great Britain, New York began to physically seize the land declared confiscated by the 1779 Act of Attainder. Parker Wickham fled to Connecticut where he remained until his death in 1785. At the same time, his eldest son, Joseph Parker Wickham, his heir apparent, left the United States for Great Britain.

7. In 1784, the New York State Legislature passed an act for the sale of estates confiscated pursuant to the 1779 Act of Attainder. Under that Act, Robins Island was sold to Benjamin Tallmedge and Caleb Brewster in fee simple. SDC, the appellee in the case, claims title to Robins Island as the successor-in-interest to these two individuals.

The court held that when New York "attained" the interest of Parker Wickham, the loyalist, it also attained the interest of those with an interest in the tail, i.e., Joseph and the more remote descendants of his father, Parker. That gave the estate to the State in New York, which estate, by the act of 1792, was elevated into a fee simple estate.

NOTES AND QUESTIONS

1. Suppose in the year 1500 O made both of the following conveyances: (1) O conveys Blackacre to A and the heirs of her body and then to B and his heirs. (2) O conveys Greenacre to A and her heirs but if A dies without issue then to B and his heirs. At common law, what estate does A take in Blackacre and Greenacre? What does the phrase "die without issue" mean? See, H. Hovenkamp & S. Kurtz, The Law of Property, An Introductory Survey at 147 (5th ed. 2001). With respect to the conveyance of Greenacre, suppose A died in 1520 survived by a son, S, age 21, who died in 1568 survived by a child, GC, (a grandchild of A) who died in 1635 without any descendants. When, if at all, can it be determined whether A died with or without issue?

2. Suppose each conveyance in note 1 was made by O in 1980 and in a jurisdiction that has abolished the fee tail estate by a statute that provides that any conveyance that conveys to A a fee tail shall be construed to give A a fee simple absolute. Should this statute affect the meaning of the phrase "die without issue" and the classification of B's future interest?

3. The Third Restatement of Property states that the "fee tail is not recognized in American law." Restatement (Third) of Property, § 24.4 (2012).

§ 4.5 LIFE ESTATES AND REVERSIONS

Of all of the possible estates in land, the life estate is the easiest to understand. If O conveys an estate "to A for life," A's estate terminates at A's death and, upon A's death, the property reverts to O. Since A's estate comes to its natural end at A's death, A's estate is neither devisable nor descendible. On the other hand, A's estate is alienable, although any transferee from A can acquire no greater estate than A has. If O conveys Blackacre to A for life, O has a reversion. A reversion is "the interest remaining in the grantor, or in the successor in interest of a testator, who transfers a vested estate of a lesser quantum than that of the vested estate which he has."[1] These interests arise by operation of law and are always vested.

It is also possible for O to convey Blackacre "to A for the life of B." In this case A has an estate *per autre vie,* an estate measured by the life of another.

NOTES AND QUESTIONS

1. The Restatement (Third) of Property defines a life estate as "a present interest that terminates on the death of an individual whose life serves as the governing life. A life estate can be qualified by language specifying one or more events that can terminate the estate before or extend

---

1. Amer.Law Prop. § 4.16 (A.J. Casner ed. 1952).

the estate beyond the death of the individual whose life serves as the governing life." Restatement (Third) of Property, § 24.5 (2012).

2.   O conveys Blackacre "to A for life." A conveys the life estate "to B." If B dies during A's lifetime, state the title. If A dies during B's lifetime, state the title. Suppose A conveys the life estate "to B for life." State the title. If B dies during A's lifetime, state the title. If A dies during B's lifetime, state the title.

3.   If O conveys Blackacre "to A for life," is it clear whose life measures the duration of A's estate? If not, what are the possibilities? In resolving this question, should it make any difference what estate O had? See generally Restatement of Property § 108 comment a (1936). If you believe the conveyance is ambiguous, how would you have drafted the conveyance to avoid the ambiguity?

4.   Suppose O conveys Blackacre "to A for the life of O." State the title.

5.   H dies in 1992. Under his will he devises Blackacre "to his wife, W, so long as she remains unmarried." H devises the remainder of his estate to C. Subsequently W dies bequeathing her entire estate to Z. W never remarried. At W's death, who owns Blackacre, C or Z? If it depends, upon what does it depend? Compare Dickson v. Alexandria Hospital, 177 F.2d 876 (4th Cir. 1949) with Mouser v. Srygler, 295 Ky. 490, 174 S.W.2d 756 (1943).

6.   Suppose O conveys Blackacre "to A for life, then to B for life." Given that B could predecease A, would you conclude that during A's life B has no interest in Blackacre? If you conclude B has an interest in Blackacre, is it a valuable interest?

7.   O conveys Blackacre "to A for life." O dies during A's lifetime survived by H, who would be O's sole heir if O died intestate. In fact O died leaving a will under which O bequeathed "my entire estate to X." At A's death, who owns Blackacre? Suppose prior to A's death O had conveyed the reversion to Y. If H, X, and Y survive A, who owns Blackacre?

Suppose prior to A's death O had conveyed the reversion to A. At the time of this conveyance, what is the state of the title?

8.   The law of waste was developed to protect the holders of future interests from acts of a present possessor that would unreasonably result in the devaluation of the future interest. Waste may be either "voluntary" or "permissive." Voluntary waste occurs when the holder of the present interest undertakes some affirmative act that unreasonably devalues the future interest. For example, under English common law a life tenant commits an act of voluntary waste if he demolishes a building on the premises even though that act increases the value of the real estate. This view, however, was rejected in Melms v. Pabst Brewing Co., 104 Wis. 7, 79 N.W. 738 (1899) where the court held that the destruction of a building that enhanced the value of the property was not actionable as waste. In *Melms* the property became more valuable without a personal residence on it because the neighborhood had changed from residential to commercial. But see Brokaw v. Fairchild, 135 Misc. 70, 237 N.Y.S. 6 (N.Y.Sup.Ct. 1929), aff'd, 231 A.D. 704, 245 N.Y.S. 402 (1930), aff'd, 256 N.Y. 670, 177 N.E. 186 (N.Y. 1931) (refusing to allow the destruction of testator's personal residence in order to build an apartment house notwith-

standing a substantial change of neighborhood, where to do so would violate the testator's intent and do substantial damage to the remainder interest). A life tenant can be immunized from actions for waste by the creator of the life estate. See, e.g., Marshall v. Marshall, 268 Ga. 687, 492 S.E.2d 188 (1997).

Permissive waste occurs when the holder of the present interest fails to undertake some act that the present interest holder is legally under a duty to perform to protect the future interest. For example, permissive waste occurs when the life tenant fails to maintain a building upon the premises. Underlying the notion of permissive waste is the idea that the possessor has failed to perform some legal duty. The difficulty with relying on the doctrine of permissive waste to protect the holder of a future interest is that the law may not be clear whether a duty is imposed upon the possessor that the possessor has failed to perform. Whether a duty is imposed on the possessor may depend on the duration of the possessory interest, the reasonableness of the conduct and the condition of the premises at the time the possessory interest commenced. See generally W. Stoebuck & D. Whitman, The Law of Property § 4.3 (2000).

Holders of a future interest may recover damages from the possessor for either voluntary or permissive waste. In certain states, they may recover treble damages or cause the possessor's estate to be forfeited. Generally, these remedies are available only if the holder of the future interest has an estate that in all events will become possessory or if the holder joins in the action all possible takers of all future interests in the property. In addition, courts may enjoin the possessor from committing future waste. While historically a plaintiff might be denied equitable relief if damages at law were sufficient, courts today are less likely to adhere to that position, and in fact, in actions seeking an injunction, the courts may also grant the plaintiff an accounting from the possessor to recompense the holder of the future interests for prior acts of waste. An injunction may also issue in favor of a plaintiff whose future interest may not become possessory. The probability, however, that the interest will become possessory may influence the likelihood that the court will grant an injunction. See Brokaw v. Fairchild, 135 Misc. 70, 237 N.Y.S. 6 (1929). This necessarily places a premium on joining all holders of future interests in the property in the lawsuit seeking an injunction.

Suppose O transfers Blackacre "to A for life, remainder to such of B's children who survive A." During his life, A undertakes to remove timber from Blackacre and B's only then living child sues for damages and to enjoin A from removing any further timber from the property. Why would a court be more reluctant to award damages to B's child than an injunction? Could some relief be fashioned that would ameliorate judicial concerns about awarding the child damages? Suppose the value of the timber to A is $100. Is that also the value of the timber to B?

9. "Problems of waste can arise whenever interests in property are divided among different persons having present and future interests, e.g., life tenants and remaindermen or reversioners; landlord and tenants. Each interest holder will desire to have the property used, or not used, in such manner as will maximize his own economic self interest. Tensions between these

interests arise when the maximizing use for one interest holder does not maximize the interest of the other.

More than one person may have a property right in the same thing.... Property rights in real estate may be divided between a life tenant and a remainderman.... A life tenant will have an incentive to maximize not the value of the property, that is, the present value of the entire stream of future earnings obtainable from it, but only the present value of the earnings stream obtainable during his expected lifetime. He will therefore want [for example] to cut timber before it has attained its mature growth—even though the present value of the timber would be greater if the cutting of some or all of it were postponed—if the added value will enure to the remainderman. The law of waste forbade this. There might seem to be no need for a law of waste, because the life tenant and the remainderman would negotiate an optimal plan for exploiting the property. But since the tenant and remainderman have only each other to contract with, the situation is ... one of bilateral monopoly, and transaction costs may be high. Also, the remaindermen may be children who do not have the legal capacity to make binding contracts; they may even be unborn children."

R. Posner, Economic Analysis of Law 73–74 (7th ed. 2006).

A bilateral monopoly exists when a monopoly buyer is forced to negotiate with a monopoly seller. The result is a situation where there is no established market price, and the participants may negotiate at length before they come to an agreement.

Posner then observes that the "law of waste has largely been supplanted by a more efficient method of administering property ... the trust. By placing property in trust, the grantor can split the beneficial interest as many ways as he pleases without worrying about divided ownership. The trustee will manage the property as a unit, maximizing its value and allocating that value among the trust's beneficiaries in the proportions desired by the grantor." Id. at 74.

A trust is a recognized legal entity that separates the administrative and management burdens associated with the ownership of property from the economic benefits associated with the ownership of property. Beneficial interests in trust ("equitable interests") can be divided among successive interest holders in much the same way as legal interests in land can be divided. Thus, if O owns Blackacre and desires to give A an interest in Blackacre so long as A lives, with a remainder in A's children, O could convey Blackacre "to A for life, remainder to A's children." Alternatively, O could convey Blackacre "to T to hold in trust to pay the income to A for life (the trust law analog to a present possessory legal life estate) and upon A's death, to distribute the principal of the trust (consisting of Blackacre) to A's children."

If O transfers property to T in trust, T holds the legal title to the property and has the power to sell, lease, mortgage, etc. In other words, T has the fee simple absolute in the property. However, T cannot administer the property in any way that is inconsistent with the interests of the trust beneficiaries. This obligation is imposed upon T by the law of trusts. Thus, T cannot give away the property. The income beneficiaries of the trust will enjoy the income earned on the property, and the remaindermen will benefit from any increase in the value of the property held in the trust. None of the beneficiaries are burdened by the management and administrative responsibilities associated with property ownership. In the basic property course, the treatment of present and future estates centers around the creation of legal estates for the most part; in more advanced courses on wealth transfers, the focus tends to be on trusts and, truthfully, that is the more relevant way to consider present and future interests in that most of them created today are created by way of a trust. Generally, however, the estate rules applicable to legal interests apply to equitable interests as well, with some important exceptions.

10. Suppose you represent a client who wishes to leave Blackacre to her husband for his life and upon his death to their children. In considering whether to advise the client to convey a legal life estate to the husband or, alternatively, to transfer Blackacre to a trust, consider the following questions:

(a) If during the husband's life it became advisable to lease the property, could the husband convey a leasehold interest that would extend beyond the term of his life? Could a trustee? Would it be desirable to have the flexibility to lease the property for a term that might extend beyond the husband's lifetime?

(b) If during the husband's life it became advisable to either sell Blackacre or give a lien thereon to secure the repayment of monies borrowed to improve the property, could the husband convey a good title or grant a mortgage? Could the trustee? If you conclude the husband can sell the property, does that mean he can also exhaust the sales proceeds?

(c) If during the husband's life, $50,000 was needed to repair Blackacre, would the husband have the responsibility to make that repair? If Blackacre were devised in trust, who would have the obligation to make the repair?

§ 4.6 THE CLASSIFICATION OF FUTURE INTERESTS IN TRANSFEREES

The arithmetic of estates is such that the sum of all interests in property must equal a fee simple absolute. In other words, the durational attributes of all estates in the same property must aggregate to infinity. Thus if O, who owns a fee simple absolute, conveys only a life estate to A, the sum total of A's life estate and O's reversion equals a fee simple absolute. If O, in addition to creating the life estate in A, also transfers a future interest to another, the total of the interests transferred and any interest retained must also equal a fee simple absolute.

The preceding materials have considered three types of future interests: the possibility of reverter, the right of entry for condition broken and the reversion. These are the three types of future interests that can be retained by a grantor. There are also a number of future interests that may be created in transferees. The future interests that may be created in transferees are: the indefeasibly vested remainder, the vested remainder subject to complete divestment, the vested remainder subject to open (or partial divestment), the contingent remainder, the shifting executory interest, and the springing executory interest. Some of these future interests are subject to certain rules that may affect their validity or whether they will ever become possessory. These rules are: The Rule of Destructibility, The Rule in Shelley's Case, The Doctrine of Worthier Title and the Rule Against Perpetuities. Before considering these rules, however, it is necessary to classify an interest created by a conveyance or devise to determine whether it might be subject to one or more of them.

A. Remainders

A remainder is any "future interest limited in favor of a transferee in such a manner that it can become a present interest upon the expiration of all prior interests simultaneously created, and cannot divest any interest except an interest left in the transferor."[1] For example, if O conveys Blackacre to "A for life, and then to B," B has a type of remainder.

As used in the definition of a remainder, a present interest refers to an interest of which the holder was *seized* at common law. Therefore, the present interest cannot be a term for years, a periodic tenancy or a tenancy at will.

Given the requirement that a remainder interest cannot divest the present interest of any other transferee, generally only a life estate or fee tail can be the present possessory estate on whose heels the remainder interest follows. Both of these present possessory estates terminate upon the happening of a limitation whereas the other present possessory estates terminate upon the happening of a condition.[2] A limitation was perceived by the common law as inherent in the estate created. For example, a life estate inherently terminates at the death of someone. On the other hand, a condition was perceived as being *attached* to an estate. For example, a fee simple on condition subsequent is an estate of potentially infinite duration, which nevertheless could be terminated "prematurely" upon the happening of a stated condition.

In order for an interest to be classified as a remainder it is sufficient that it is an interest that is *capable* of becoming possessory upon the termination of the preceding estate. It is not necessary for a future interest to be classified as a remainder that it *must* become possessory upon the termination of the preceding estate. On the other hand, if the future interest is limited in such a manner that it is incapable of becoming possessory upon the termination of the preceding estate, the interest cannot be a remainder.

There are four kinds of remainders that could ripen into a fee simple (or fee tail) if they ever became possessory. They are: (1) the vested

---

1. Restatement of Property § 156(1) (1936).

2. An exception to this rule is that the future interest following a fee simple determinable is an executory interest and not a remainder even though if a fee simple determinable terminates, it does so upon the happening of a limitation and not a condition. The unsatisfactory historical rationale for this exception was that a fee could not be limited on another fee. See also Restatement of Property § 156(2) (1936).

remainder (sometimes called the indefeasibly vested remainder), (2) the contingent remainder, (3) the vested remainder subject to open and (4) the vested remainder subject to complete divestment.

A vested remainder is a remainder limited in favor of a born or ascertained person(s) where the person(s) (or their transferees, heirs or devisees) are "certain to acquire a present interest at some time in the future, and [are] also certain to be entitled to retain permanently thereafter the present interest so acquired."[3] The vested remainder is alienable, devisable and descendible.[4] The classification of a remainder as indefensibly vested means only that in all events the interest will become possessory, albeit at some time in the future. It does not mean that it will necessarily become possessory in the designated remaindermen. It may become possessory in the designated remainderman or in her transferees, heirs, or devisees as substituted remaindermen.

Unlike the vested remainder, the contingent remainder is an interest that may or may not become possessory. A contingent remainder is a remainder limited in favor of (1) an unborn person, (2) an unascertained person or (3) a person who is either born or ascertained but whose interest is subject to the occurrence or nonoccurrence of a *condition precedent*. Generally, contingent remainders are alienable, and they are devisable and descendible unless conditioned (expressly or impliedly) upon survivorship.

A vested remainder subject to open (also known as the vested remainder subject to partial divestment) is a remainder limited in favor of a class. A class is a group of persons collectively described, (such as children, brothers and sisters, heirs, descendants, nieces and nephews, etc.). The class gift is vested if (1) there is at least one living member of the class and (2) there are no unmet conditions precedent attached to the gift. It is subject to open if new persons can join the class. A class is closed if no additional persons may join the class.[5] If a class is closed and requirements (1) and (2) are satisfied, the remainder is an indefeasibly vested remainder in a class of persons. The interest of a member of such a class is alienable, devisable, and descendible.

For example, suppose O conveys Blackacre "to A for life, and upon A's death to B's children." At the time of the conveyance B has two children, C and D. B is still alive. Because there is a child of B living and there are no conditions attached to the gift, it is vested. Because B is alive, however, the class gift is open because B could produce or adopt more children. If B

---

3. Restatement of Property § 157(a) comment f (1936).

4. Under the Unif. Prob. Code § 2–707, a remainder *in a trust* is impliedly conditioned on survivorship. Thus, if the remainderman does not survive to the time of distribution (typically the death of the life income beneficiary of the trust), the remainder interest fails. The UPC extends this rule to other future interests in trust as well. The rule does not apply to legal remainders; thus the rules for legal and equitable estates differ.

5. The class closing rules are discussed, infra. The Restatement (Third) of Property defines a class gift as "a disposition to beneficiaries who take as members of a group. Taking as members of a group means that the identities and shares of the beneficiaries are subject to fluctuation." Restatement (Third) of Property, § 13.1 (2012).

were to die during A's lifetime, how would that affect the interest of C and D?

Last, a vested remainder subject to complete divestment is a remainder limited in favor of a born or ascertained person or in a class that is vested subject to open, but is subject to the occurrence or nonoccurrence of a *condition subsequent* such that the remainder may not become possessory or, if it becomes possessory, may not remain possessory in infinity. For example, if O conveys Blackacre "to A for life and upon A's death to B and his heirs but if C marries D, then to D and her heirs," B has a vested remainder subject to complete divestment.

Generally, a vested remainder subject to complete divestment is alienable and it is devisable and descendible unless the interest is subject to an express or implied condition of survivorship.

B. Executory Interests

There are two kinds of executory interests: the shifting executory interest and the springing executory interest. A shifting executory interest is a future interest created in a transferee that in order to become possessory must, upon the occurrence or non-occurrence of an event, divest a present interest of another transferee or a vested interest of another transferee.[6] Since the preceding estate must be an estate that is divested, such estate must terminate upon the happening of a condition rather than a limitation.[7] The interest that is divested is an interest of a transferee and not an interest that has been retained by the transferor. For example, if O conveys Blackacre "to A for life and upon A's death to B and his heirs but if C marries D, then to D and her heirs," D has a shifting executory interest. D's interest divests B's vested remainder subject to complete divestment.

A springing executory interest is a future interest limited in favor of a transferee that in order to become possessory must divest the transferor of a retained interest after some period of time during which there is no transferee entitled to a present interest. For example, if O conveys Blackacre "to A upon her marriage," she has a springing executory interest which, if it ever becomes possessory, will divest O of his interest in Blackacre.

For purpose of the definition of a springing executory interest, the present interest refers to an interest of which the holder would, at common law, be seized. In other words, if there is a *transferee* entitled to possession, the future interest following that present interest can only be a springing executory interest if the present interest is a term for years, a periodic tenancy or a tenancy at will. If the present estate immediately preceding the future interest is a life estate, the future interest cannot be

---

6. Restatement of Property §§ 25(1), 158 (1936).

7. Two exceptions to this rule are that the future interest following the fee simple determinable and the fee simple conditional (both of which, if they terminate, terminate upon the happening of a limitation) is an executory interest and not a remainder. Restatement of Property § 25(2) (1936).

a springing executory interest. On the other hand, if there is a "gap" between a life estate and the future interest, the future interest is a springing executory interest. Thus, if O conveys Blackacre "to A for life and one day after A dies, to B," B has a springing executory interest.

Generally both shifting and springing executory interests are alienable, devisable and descendible.[8]

At common law, executory interests were not recognized as valid legal estates although they were recognized as valid in the courts of equity. In order to create an executory interest that could be recognized in the courts of equity, it was necessary for the grantor to transfer seisin in the property to a trustee to hold for the use of another. This so-called "use" was the forerunner of the modern day trust. The use was utilized not only to create executory interests but also to create equitable remainders that could avoid the Rule of Destructibility, the Rule in Shelley's case and important feudal incidents, such as the feudal inheritance taxes known as reliefs. By 1536, uses had become so prevalent that a coalition of the king who was concerned with the loss of revenues and the legal conveyancing bar which was concerned with the loss of business was able to persuade Parliament to enact the Statute of Uses.[9] This statute provided that if any person (T) was seized of property for the use of another person (B), the person for whose benefit the use was created (B) had a legal estate of the same character as the equitable estate. Thus, executory interests were executed into valid common law estates.

Interests in property may be classified at any time from the moment of their creation and thereafter. Of course, changes in the facts and circumstances after the time the interest is created may result in a change in the classification of interests. In other words, interests may change their colors. For example, if O conveys Blackacre to A for life, remainder to B, B has a vested remainder at the time of the conveyance. Why? But, the state of the title will change at A's death, at which time B will have a fee simple absolute. Why?

NOTES AND QUESTIONS

1. O owns Blackacre in fee simple absolute. In each of O's following conveyances, state the title at the time of the conveyance and at such other time as may be indicated.

(a) To A for life and upon A's death to B and his heirs.

(b) To A for life and upon A's death to B and his heirs if B attains the age of 21.

(c) To A for life and, if B survives A, then to B and her heirs. Suppose three years later, A dies. State the title. Suppose A and B die under such circumstances that from all outward appearances it cannot be determined who survived whom. State the title.

---

8. But see note 4, supra.

9. 27 Hen. VIII, c. 10 (effective May 1, 1536).

(d) To A for life and upon A's death to B's heirs. B dies during A's life survived by X as his sole heir. At B's death, state the title. If X survives A, state the title. If X survives B but dies before A, state the title.

(e) To A for life and upon A's death and, if B marries A's widow, then to B and his heirs. State the title.

2.　When future interests are created in two or more persons or classes of persons, generally the interests are classified in the order in which they are set forth in the governing instrument. Therefore, in each of the two following conveyances, B's interest must be classified before C's interest can be classified. Before attempting to state the titles in each of these two conveyances, first consider in each conveyance what are the (1) words of purchase, (2) the words of limitation, and (3) the words of condition. Next, review the definitions of contingent remainders, vested remainders subject to divestment and shifting executory interests and make sure you know which future interests, if any, are subject to a condition precedent or a condition subsequent.

(a) To A for life and upon A's death if B survives A then to B and his heirs but if B does not survive A then to C and his heirs.

(b) To A for life and upon A's death to B and his heirs but if B dies before A then to C and his heirs.

Although the common law and both the First and Second Restatements of Property classify the interests of B and C in the two preceding examples differently, the Third Restatement of Property classifies the interests of B and C in both examples as contingent. Section 25.3 of the Restatement (Third) of Property provides that: "a future interest is either contingent or vested. A future interest is contingent if it might not take effect in possession or enjoyment. A future interest is vested if it is certain to take effect in possession or enjoyment. A contingent or vested future interest may additionally be classified according to the present interest into which the future interest will ripen once and if it takes effect in possession or enjoyment—as a fee simple absolute (or absolute ownership), a fee simple defeasible, a life estate, or a term of years." Under the Third Restatement, how would the interests of B and C in the preceding two examples be classified?

(c) To A for life and one day after A dies to B and his heirs.

(d) To B and his heirs 21 years from now.

(e) To A for life and upon A's death to B and his heirs but, if B dies without issue, then to C and his heirs. In thinking about this problem, consider again how the phrase "die without issue" might be construed.

(f) To A for life and upon A's death to A's children and their heirs. At the time of the conveyance A has no children. One year later A has one child. State the title. The next year A has another child. State the title. The next year A has a third child. State the title. The next year A dies. State the title. Suppose, in the year A's first child is born, A desires to rent Blackacre to B for ten years. You represent B. What advice would you give B?

Suppose that at the time of the conveyance A has a child C–1 living. Thereafter child C–2 is born. C–1 dies during A's lifetime leaving her spouse S as the sole devisee under her will. A dies survived by S and by C–2. State the title.

(g) To A for life, and upon A's death to A's children and their heirs but if none of A's children survive A, then to B and his heirs. At the time of conveyance, A, B and A's two children, C and D, are living. State the title. Three years later C and D die. State the title.

3. The right of an adopted child to be treated like a biological child for purposes of inheritance and claiming rights as a beneficiary under a will has evolved dramatically over time. At one time, the law excluded the adopted child from claiming as an heir or beneficiary absent an expressly stated intent to the contrary. This exclusion was consistent with common law notions relating to the importance of "blood lines." Over time, however, and no doubt attributable to the increasing number of adoptions, both the courts and the legislatures began to look more favorably upon adopted children. Today, statutes like Sections 2–118, 2–119, and 2–705 of the Uniform Probate Code equate adopted children and biological children for purposes of intestate succession and the inclusion of adopted children as members of a class in a gift to a class under either a deed or a will.

The Uniform Probate Code also treats children born-out-of-wedlock as the children of their genetic parents (absent adoption). See Unif. Prob. Code § 2–117. Recent amendments to that Code also address the parent-child relationship resulting from assisted reproductive technologies and surrogacy. See Unif. Prob. Code §§ 2–120; 2–121.

4. Suppose O conveys Blackacre to A for life, then to A's children. A dies survived by seven children, namely,

(a) Baker, A's biological child born to A in wedlock,

(b) Carrie, A's biological child born to A out-of-wedlock,

(c) Darla, an adopted child of A,

(d) Edna, a step-child of A,

(e) Freda, a biological child of A who had been adopted by Hanna (no relation of A),

(f) George, a gestational child of A but a biological child of Nick and Martha who A carried to term under the provisions of a surrogacy contract between A, Nick, and Martha,

(g) Harry, a biological child of A's husband and Rita who Rita carried to term under the provisions of a surrogacy contract between A, her husband, and Rita.

Upon A's death, who owns Blackacre?

NOTE ON THE VALUATION OF LIFE ESTATES AND FUTURE INTERESTS

Before proceeding to a fuller consideration of the various future interests, it is appropriate to dispel any lingering notion that the holder of a future interest has a valueless interest. In fact, the holder of a future interest may actually have an interest that is more valuable than the present interest that precedes it. For example, suppose O conveys Blackacre, having a fair market value of $100,000, to A for life and upon A's death to B. Under the terms of this conveyance B's interest will become possessory in all events when A dies. A's death, of course, is an event that is sure to occur in the future. While during her life A is entitled to the possession of Blackacre, when A dies, B (or B's successor in interest) will acquire the estate in fee simple absolute, an estate of conceptually infinite duration. Whose interest is more valuable, A's interest or B's interest?

In order to answer that question, we must first consider what it means when we say Blackacre has a fair market value (i.e., present value) of $100,000. To an economist, the *present value* of property represents the free market's assessment of the property's future income stream in perpetuity.[10] A and B have present and future estates in this income stream that can be separately valued, but necessarily the aggregate value of the respective interests of A and B will equal the property's present fair market value. Remember the whole is equal to the sum of its parts. A's interest in that present value is limited by A's life expectancy; B's interest represents the remaining value in the property (i.e., the present value of the income stream in perpetuity less the present value of the income stream for A's life).

How should A's life estate be valued? The value of A's interest is a function of two distinct variables. The first variable was the interest rate assumed to measure present value. The higher the assumed interest rate, the greater the value A's interest would be in relationship to the value of B's interest. The second variable was A's life expectancy. For example, suppose Blackacre had a fair market value of $100,000 and for purposes of calculating present value we use a 6% rate of return. If $100,000 produced income of $6,000 a year, the value of A's income interest would be the *present value* of the right to receive an annuity of $6,000 for A's life. A's life expectancy would then have to be determined from standard mortality tables. Are there any determinants of value that the common law overlooked?

What is meant by the present value of money to be received in the future? The present value of money is that amount of money one would pay currently that if invested at an agreed upon rate of return would yield a given amount of money in the future. To illustrate, how much would A pay B today in exchange for B's promise to give A $1 one year from now? If the assumed interest rate were 7%, A would pay that amount (X) which invested at the rate of 7% would equal $1 in a year.[11] The present value of A's right to receive $7,000 annually for his life equals the sum of the

---

10. The concept of an income stream might be viewed in at least two ways. Under one viewpoint, an income stream represents the present value of the income from property held in perpetuity. Under the other, the concept of an income stream contemplates that the property will be held for a period short of infinity. In this case, the income stream is the present value of the income and profits realized when the property is disposed of at the end of the holding period. These concepts, in fact, express the same idea since the profits realized on a disposition are the immediate realization of the present value of the future income that would have been earned if the property had been held in perpetuity.

11. $X + .07X = \$1$. Therefore, $X = .93$.

present value of the right to receive $7,000 one year from now, plus the present value of the right to receive $7,000 two years from now, etc.

Fortunately, in many cases, published tables have simplified the calculation. For example, if the value of A's life estate is important for federal estate tax purposes, published tables include the appropriate factor taking account of both A's life expectancy and an assumed rate of interest. Under one such table, if A is age 27, the appropriate factor to value A's life estate is .93554. If the fair market value of Blackacre is $100,000, A's life interest is valued at $93,554. What is the value of B's interest? If A is age 89 the values of A's and B's interest change dramatically. Using those same tables, A's interest is valued at $25,062 and B's interest is valued at $74,938.

With respect to the valuation of possibilities of reverter, contingent remainders and other interests that are not certain to become possessory, see the note on "Just Compensation" and future interests in chapter 9.

NOTE ON CLASS GIFT CLOSING RULES

If a gift is limited in favor of a class of persons, new persons may join the class until such time as it is determined that the class is "closed." Thus, once a class gift is closed, *no new members may join the class.* A class gift may close in one of two ways: physiologically or under the "rule of convenience."

A class gift can close in one of two ways—physiologically or under the "rule of convenience." A class closes physiologically whenever that person who is capable of giving birth to or adopting class members dies. For example, if O conveys Blackacre to A for life and then to B's children, the class gift to B's children closes physiologically when B dies. For this purpose, however, if B, a male, dies survived by a wife who is pregnant and the fetus is later born alive, the resulting child is included in the class.

Under the "rule of convenience," which is a rule of judicial construction that can give way to a contrary intent, a class closes whenever any member of the class is entitled to demand possession of his or her share. A remainderman is entitled to demand possession of his share when the preceding possessory estate has terminated and there is no conditions precedent outstanding with respect to the person who can make the demand. For example, in the preceding example, if both B and X, a child of B, survive A, the class closes at A's death under the rule of convenience because X can demand possession of his or her share at that time. Because the rule of convenience is a rule of construction, a governing instrument can direct that a class gift close physiologically only even though it might have closed earlier under the rule of convenience. For example, in In re Estate of Earle, 369 Pa. 52, 85 A.2d 90 (1951), decedent died bequeathing property to every male child of his sons who "shall bear the name of Earle." At decedent's death there were already a number of living grandchildren to whom, under the rule of convenience, the property could have passed. Nonetheless, the court held that the class remained open until the death of the last survivor of the children of the decedent who survived the decedent.

Once a class closes no new members can join the class. Thus, in the conveyance A for life and then to B's children, suppose B and X (a child of B) survive A. One year later B has another child, Y. Y cannot join the class because Y was conceived and born after the class closed. See generally Restatement (Second) of Property § 26.2. See also, Restatement (Third) of Property, § 15.1 (2012) "Unless the language or circumstances establish that the transferor had a different intention, a class gift that has not yet closed physiologically closes to future entrants on the distribution date if a beneficiary of the class gift is then entitled to distribution." In amplification of this rule the comments state: the term "distribution date" with respect to a class gift refers to the time when an immediate or a postponed class gift is to take effect in possession or enjoyment. The distribution date for an immediate class gift taking effect on the death of the testator is the time of death of the testator, not the beginning or end of the calendar day of the testator's death and not when the testator's estate is actually distributed. The distribution date for a postponed class gift taking effect in possession or enjoyment on the death of the income beneficiary is the time of death of the income beneficiary, not the beginning or end of the calendar day of the income beneficiary's death and not when the principal of the trust is actually distributed. *Id.* cmt. b.

The fact that a class closes doesn't mean that those persons in the class at the time of closing cannot "fall out of" the class. Members of a class can fall out of the class if they later fail to satisfy some condition attached to the gift. For example, suppose O deeds property to A for life, then to B's children who attain age 21. A dies survived by B and by B's two children, C, age 22, and D, age 18. Because C can demand possession of his share (do you see why?) the class closes at A's death even though B is still living. At that time both C and D are members of the class. However, if D fails to attain age 21, D will fall out of the class. If that occurs, then only C will take Blackacre in fee simple. If D reaches age 21, then C and D will share the ownership of Blackacre.

In each of the following testamentary bequests from T, when will the class close?

(a) To B's children who survive me. B and three children of B survive T.

(b) To A for life and upon A's death to such of A's children as survive A.

(c) To A for life and upon A's death to such of B's children who attain age 21. B and one child of B, age 14, survive A. One year after A dies, B has another child. Eight years after A dies B has another child. Will this child join the class and, if it depends, upon what does it depend?

Suppose B had died in A's lifetime survived by two children, X and Y. When will the class close and who are the members of the class?

NOTE ON THE IMPORTANCE OF CLASSIFICATION

Professor Powell has suggested at least nine situations in which the classification of an interest may be important, although some of these situations are only of historical but of no practical interest today.[14] The principal areas in which the classification of a future interest can make a difference are:

---

14. R. Powell, Future Interests 13–14 (1961). See also Dukeminier, Contingent Remainders and Executory Interests: A Requiem for the Distinction, 43 Minn.L.Rev. 13 (1958).

1. *Alienability.* At common law, vested remainders were alienable *inter vivos* while contingent remainders were for the most part inalienable. Most American jurisdictions, however, hold that both vested and contingent remainders are alienable. In jurisdictions where contingent remainders are inalienable, however, creditors of the holder of the contingent interest may not be able to reach that interest in satisfaction of their claims. The Third Restatement of Property provides that: "all future interests are alienable and are also devisable and inheritable if the owner's death does not terminate the interest, unless the transferor has imposed a valid restraint on alienation." Restatement (Third) of Property § 25.2 cmt. f (2012).

2. *Inheritability.* At common law, both vested and contingent remainders were inheritable unless, in the case of a contingent remainder, the nature of the contingency was such that the interest terminated at the death of the contingent remainderman. Thus, if O conveyed Blackacre to A for life and upon A's death to B and his heirs if B survived A, B's remainder interest was not inheritable if B predeceased A since B's death terminated that interest. Most American jurisdictions follow this rule, although at least two jurisdictions[15] hold that a contingent remainder expressly conditioned upon an event other than survivorship is impliedly conditioned on the remainderman being alive when that event occurs. In these jurisdictions, therefore, contingent remainders are not inheritable.

3. *Acceleration.* The possession of a vested remainder accelerates if the preceding life estate prematurely terminates, whereas a contingent remainder will ordinarily not accelerate upon the premature termination of the preceding estate. Thus, if O conveys Blackacre to A for life and upon A's death to B and his heirs, and prior to her death A renounces the life estate, B's vested remainder interest will accelerate and become possessory. On the other hand, if B's interest was expressly conditioned upon B surviving A, B's contingent remainder would not accelerate. However, the rule that contingent remainders do not accelerate is often avoided by first construing an instrument to determine whether any purpose would be served in light of the grantor's intent to deny acceleration or whether anyone would be harmed by permitting acceleration. If B's interest does not accelerate, who is entitled to the possession of Blackacre until A dies?

Section 2–1106(b)(4) of the Uniform Probate Code (rejecting the common-law distinction) provides that: "upon the disclaimer of a preceding interest, a future interest held by a person other than the disclaimant takes effect as if the disclaimant had died or ceased to exist immediately before the time of distribution, but a future interest held by the disclaimant is not accelerated in possession or enjoyment."

4. *Destructibility.* At common law, contingent remainders were destructible.[16] Neither vested remainders nor executory interests were destructible.

5. *Rule Against Perpetuities.* The most important difference lies in the application of the Rule Against Perpetuities to the future interest. Indefeasibly vested remainders and vested remainders in an individual or in a class

---

15. Arkansas and North Carolina.

16. See § 4.7, infra.

which are closed from the moment of creation or which are subject to complete divestment are not subject to the Rule. On the other hand, vested remainders subject to open, contingent remainders, and executory interests are subject to the Rule.

Classification aside, some of the more perplexing issues raised by the creation of future interests relate to the circumstances under which conditions of survivorship are to be implied in the governing instrument. In other words, in the absence of an express condition that someone must survive to take, when will the courts imply a condition of survivorship? This issue is raised in the following case.

IN RE ESTATE OF HOUSTON

Supreme Court of Pennsylvania (1964).
414 Pa. 579, 201 A.2d 592.

BELL, CHIEF JUSTICE.

This appeal involves the important questions—was testator's gift of principal contingent or vested, and if vested, when vested and who took thereunder?

Henry H. Houston died a resident of Philadelphia County on June 21, 1895. His will was executed on February 2, 1892. At that time he had a wife, Sallie S. Houston; a married son, Samuel F. Houston; a married daughter, Sallie Houston Henry; and an unmarried daughter, Gertrude Houston, who married and became Gertrude Houston Woodward on October 9, 1894. All of these children survived the testator.[17] At the time of testator's death he had six living grandchildren; six other grandchildren were born after his death.

Testator executed a lengthy will, including a lengthy trust. The will contains 64 items and covers 25 printed pages. Testator provided in "Item Fifty-ninth: All the rest residue and remainder of my estate real and personal wheresoever the same may be I give devise and bequeath to the Executors hereinafter named in trust to pay over the *net income*[18] arising therefrom in the manner following." There then follow five separate gifts of a specified amount to be paid annually to five of testator's cousins "*during her [or his] life.*" These are followed by 11 directions to pay out of the said income the sum of specified dollar amounts annually to named individuals *during their respective lives, and at the death of each,* he provided: "I direct to be paid out of the principal of the residuary estate the sum of [specified] Dollars in equal shares *to each of his children who may be living at the time of his decease;* the children of any deceased child taking however their deceased parents share." There then followed three additional gifts to a Church, and an annual gift to a sister-in-law during her life upon certain conditions.

---

17. Mr. Houston had had three other children, who predeceased him, unmarried and without issue. . . .

18. Italics throughout, ours.

We come then to Paragraph *Twenty-second* of Item Fifty-ninth which, relevantly, is the most important part of the will, and reads:

"Twenty-second: All the rest, residue, and remainder of the *net income* of my estate including herein such income as may fall into and become a part of the residue by reason of the death of any of the beneficiaries hereinbefore mentioned, I direct shall be paid and distributed one fourth thereof to my beloved wife Sallie S. Houston *during her life*. One fourth thereof to my daughter Sallie H. Henry *during her life,* one fourth thereof to my son Samuel F. Houston *during his life* and one fourth thereof to my daughter Gertrude Houston *during her life*. On the death of my said wife I direct that the one fourth of the income payable to her shall thereafter be payable to my said children in equal shares *during their lives* (sic). and should any of my said children be dead *leaving children* at the time of the death of their mother I direct that the said income be *paid to the children* of such deceased child until the death of my last surviving child. On the death of any one of my said children *without leaving lawful issue him or her surviving* I direct that the income heretofore payable to such deceased child shall be paid to my wife and *surviving children* in equal shares and if either of the said children shall *then be dead leaving issue,* such issue shall take the deceased parents share. On the death of any one of my said *children* leaving *lawful issue him or her surviving,* I direct that the *income* to which such deceased child would have been entitled if living, shall be paid in equal shares to and among his or her children and the issue of deceased children, *if any there be,* such issue taking their deceased parents share, until the death of my last surviving child. *On the death of my last surviving child* I direct that *the whole of the principal* of the trust estate shall be distributed *in equal portions to and among my grand-children,* the children of any deceased grandchild taking their deceased parents share."

Both appellants and appellees also point out, although each draw a different conclusion therefrom, that testator specifically provided for the spouse of each of his then married children. For example, in the Fifth Item of his will testator gave his son-in-law $100,000, and in the Sixth Item, his daughter-in-law $100,000, in the 6% bonds of the International Navigation Company. He also made many bequests to his relatives, in-laws, and friends, some without any gift over, most of them, however, with a gift over upon or in the event of the death of the first legatee or life tenant.

Sallie S. Houston, testator's widow, died intestate on November 13, 1913; his daughter, Sallie Houston Henry, died on July 6, 1938; his son, Samuel F. Houston, died May 2, 1952; and testator's *last surviving child,* his daughter, Gertrude Houston Woodward, died on October 2, 1961.

(1) Samuel F. Houston (testator's son) had four children, three of whom still survive. The fourth, Henry H. Houston II, born April 5, 1895,

was killed in action in World War I, on October 18, 1918. His father, Samuel F. Houston, was his sole heir.

(2) Sallie Houston Henry (testator's daughter) had two children (daughters) who survived testator's last living child. She also had a son, T. Charlton Henry, who predeceased his mother, leaving a wife and two daughters who are still living. Charlton willed his entire estate to his wife.

(3) Gertrude Houston Woodward (testator's daughter) had three children who survived her and two who predeceased her. Her son, H.H. Houston Woodward, was born February 27, 1896, and was killed in action in World War I on April 1, 1918. Another child of Mrs. Woodward, Gertrude Houston Woodward, Jr., who was born April 21, 1909, died March 6, 1934. Each of these children died intestate and unmarried. The sole heirs of each of these deceased children were their parents, Gertrude H. Woodward and Dr. George Woodward.

If the remainders for testator's *grandchildren* were vested at testator's death, or became vested on birth after testator's death, subject in both cases to being *divested in favor of their children* if any such grandchild predeceased testator's last surviving child, the principal of the residuary trust (which is carried at over $25,000,000, but is allegedly worth approximately $145,000,000) will be divided into *12 equal parts*— eight of such parts being for testator's eight living grandchildren; three of such parts for the heirs (or personal representatives) of testator's three grandchildren who died after testator's death but before the death of testator's last surviving child (Mrs. Woodward), intestate and unmarried; and one such part for the two (living) daughters of testator's deceased grandson, T. Charlton Henry.

If, however, the remainders were contingent upon testator's grandchildren or their children living at the death of testator's last surviving child (Mrs. Woodward), testator's remainder estate would be divided into and distributed in nine *equal* parts—eight such parts to testator's eight living grandchildren, and the ninth part to the two living daughters per stirpes of testator's deceased grandchild, T. Charlton Henry.

The Orphans' Court unanimously held (in scholarly opinions) that testator gave a vested interest in the principal of his residuary trust estate in equal portions to his grandchildren who (a) survived him, or (b) were born after his death, the children of any deceased grandchild taking their deceased parent's share—and consequently divided (and awarded) the principal into 12 equal parts.

We first place ourselves in the armchair of the testator and remember that the intention of the testator is the polestar in the construction of every will.

Pertinent Principles of Law

In Lewis' Estate, 407 Pa. 518, 180 A.2d 919, the Court, (quoting from Burleigh's Estate, 405 Pa. 373, 376, 175 A.2d 838) recently said (page 520 of 407 Pa., page 920 of 180 A.2d):

" 'It is now hornbook law (1) that the testator's intent is the polestar and must prevail; and (2) that his intent must be gathered from a consideration of (a) all the language contained in the four corners of his will and (b) his scheme of distribution and (c) the circumstances surrounding him at the time he made his will and (d) the existing facts; and (3) that technical rules or canons of construction should be resorted to only if the language of the will is ambiguous or conflicting or the testator's intent is for any reason uncertain. . . .' "

This law is stated and reiterated in a myriad cases before and several after Lewis' Estate. In Walton's Estate, 409 Pa. 225, page 231, 186 A.2d 32, page 35, the Court once again pertinently said:

'No rule regarding wills is more settled than the great General Rule that the testator's intent, if it is not unlawful, must prevail': Collins Estate, 393 Pa. 519, 522, 143 A.2d 45, 47. We reiterate what by now is hornbook law: 'The testator's intention is the polestar in the construction of every will and that intention must be ascertained from the language and scheme of his [entire] will [together with the surrounding facts and circumstances]; *it is not what the Court thinks he might or would or should have said in the existing circumstances,* or even what the Court thinks he meant to say, but *what is the meaning of his words.*" . . .

Appellants' Contentions

Appellants vigorously contend—and this is their principal contention—that the testator intended to give the remainder (principal) of his trust estate to, and *only to living* persons, and that he demonstrated this intent *impliedly* in his gift of this remainder (principal) and very many times *expressly* throughout his entire will, and particularly in other gifts in this *Twenty-second* paragraph. Numerous times throughout the prior provisions of this will, testator made absolute gifts to then living persons *or to those surviving* a life beneficiary, *or to the living* members of a class, after the death of a named life beneficiary. Moreover, in this very *Twenty-second* paragraph of Item Fifty-ninth, as well as in other paragraphs of Item Fifty-ninth of his will, testator gave the income from a particular trust *only to living persons.* From a consideration of his *entire* will, and particularly from his gift of *income* only to *living* persons in this Twenty-second paragraph, appellants argue that testator must have meant and intended to give the *principal* of this large trust estate to his *then living* descendants, namely, to such of his grandchildren and the children per stirpes of his deceased grandchildren as were living at the death of his (testator's) last surviving child. Appellants further contend (1) that this construction is fortified by testator's evident intent to keep this residuary trust estate in his family blood line, since (a) he made no provision therein for a spouse of a deceased grandchild, nor (b) did he give a deceased grandchild a power of appointment, and (2) that this construction would obviously have the desirable result of a colossal tax saving for his descendants. This reasoning is plausible and appealing but unfortunately has three serious weaknesses.

First and most important, appellants' interpretation glosses over or ignores the clear language of testator's gift of the principal *in equal portions to his grandchildren per capita,* which at first blush certainly creates in the grandchildren a *vested* interest. Moreover, this language—at least prima facie—shows a different intent from testator's *gift of income to his grandchildren per stirpes.* Secondly, in 11 paragraphs in his very *Fifty-ninth Item* of his will, as well as in many prior items in his will, testator made gifts conditional upon survivorship, *thus clearly demonstrating that he knew how to make a contingent gift, i.e., conditional upon survivorship when that was his intention.* The third weakness of appellants' contentions is the oft repeated statement that testator demonstrated in the language of his entire will that he wished to leave his property *only to living* persons. This is substantially but not entirely correct.[19]

Appellees' Contentions

Appellees' basic contentions are twofold: (1) Testator gave the *principal* of his trust estate *clearly* and *unquestionably* to his *grandchildren per capita,* and this is in striking contrast with his gift of *income* to his grandchildren *per stirpes;* and (2) All the canons of construction require that the gift of principal be construed to be *vested* in testator's grandchildren, subject to subsequent divesting upon the happening of one particular event.

Analysis of Testator's Language

When we read and reread and very carefully analyze all of testator's will from its four corners, and of course particularly the language of the *Twenty-second* paragraph of the Fifty-ninth item—we believe that he gave and intended to give the whole of the principal of his residuary trust estate (after the death of his last surviving child) to his *grandchildren per capita,* or if any grandchild was at that time dead and had left children, such children should take their deceased parent's share. In order to adopt appellants' interpretation and that of the dissenting opinion, we would

---

19. While this statement was not challenged by any of the attorneys, a careful analysis of the testator's gifts of income will show that in possible although remote contingencies a *living party* is not provided for or apparently required in the gifts of income in the following instances: For example, in the provision for the wife's one-fourth of the income, there is no provision covering the contingency which would occur if one of the children of testator's deceased children should die before the death of testator's last surviving child. Next, with respect to the gift of income on the death of any of testator's children *without leaving issue,* a similar hiatus or unprovided for contingency occurs, viz., if any one of the issue of testator's other surviving children dies before the death of testator's last surviving child. The third unprovided for, although likewise remote, contingency is that in the gift of income, upon the death of testator's wife, to the children and issue of one of testator's deceased children, there is no provision for the contingency that would arise in the event that one of the living issue who were receiving income should die before the death of testator's last surviving child.

All of this indicates, sometimes clearly and at other times very remotely, that the testator did not in every instance make his gifts conditional upon survivorship or living, and therefore it cannot be accurately said that testator demonstrated in the income provisions of this *Twenty-second paragraph* that he always wished to leave his income *only* to living persons.

have to change and rewrite the testator's gift of principal by *interpolating* the words "then living," so that the testator's gift of principal *as changed* would read: "On the death of my last surviving child, I direct that the whole of the principal of the trust estate shall be distributed in equal portions to and among my '*then living*' grandchildren, the '*then living*' children of any deceased grandchild taking their deceased parent's share."

Expressing the same thought in more technical language, we believe testator gave and intended to give a *vested* interest in this *principal per capita* (a) to those of his grandchildren who were living at the time of his death and (b) those subsequently born—such gifts to *vest in possession* at the death of testator's last surviving child, *subject to being divested* in one instance *only*, viz., *if any such grandchild was deceased leaving children.* In that particular event, the children of any such deceased grandchild were given their parent's interest (or share) per stirpes.

We are impressed by the fact that in this meticulously drawn will—in spite of the fact that throughout his entire will and throughout this very *Twenty-second* paragraph, testator had repeatedly demonstrated that he knew how to make a gift, contingent upon survival—testator was careful not to say that he gave this principal in equal shares to his grandchildren *who were living at the death* of testator's last surviving child, with a substitutionary gift to the *then living children* of any deceased grandchild per stirpes. The gift of principal to his *grandchildren per capita* was express and absolute; no prior condition or limitation or contingency of survivorship was attached thereto. This clearly expressed gift of principal to his grandchildren per capita was subject only to one condition, a condition subsequent, viz., that if a grandchild was deceased at the death of testator's last surviving child leaving children, such deceased grandchild's children should take their deceased parent's share. Testator's grandchildren were his designated legatees, and if any grandchild was deceased at the termination of the last life estate, leaving children, the deceased grandchild was the source and fountainhead of the interest of his children.

This gift of principal to testator's grandchildren *per capita*, we repeat once more, is in striking contrast to his gift of *income* to his grandchildren *per stirpes*. While a contingent interest can be created either expressly or by implication, the thought keeps recurring: If testator in this skillfully drawn will intended to give the principal of his remainder estate *to and only to* his grandchildren who *survived* his last living child, and to the children of his deceased grandchildren who were *then living,* why didn't he say so, when he had so often and so clearly created contingent interests in this very residuary trust as well as in other items throughout his will? It is both clear and certain that there was no express contingent gift of principal; moreover, considering the will in this particular paragraph and as a whole, we believe there was no contingent gift of principal by implication.

Part II

Our interpretation of testator's intention as expressed in and by his will, is further *supported* by the canons of construction respecting vested and contingent interests.

Vested or Contingent Interests

Whether a gift is contingent, or vested, or vested subject to ... [being] divested, has perplexed or vexed the Courts for centuries. Where a testator's language is ambiguous, or for any reason his intent is uncertain, Courts are aided in their discovery of his intent, by a consideration of whether the gift is vested or contingent. The rules as to vesting are (with but a few minor exceptions) well settled, although (as we shall see) they are at times difficult of application and the cases are not always consistent or harmonious in their application of the rules or indeed in the language setting forth the rules.

In Gray, The Rule Against Perpetuities, 4th Ed., the law is well stated:

" '101. Vested and Contingent Remainders. Since contingent remainders have been recognized, the line between them and vested remainders is drawn as follows: A remainder is vested in A., when throughout its continuance, A., ... [has] the right to the immediate possession, whenever and however the preceding freehold estates may determine. A remainder is contingent if, in order for it to come into possession, the fulfilment of some condition precedent other than the determination of the preceding freehold estates is necessary.

" '102. A remainder is none the less vested because it may terminate before the remainder-man comes into possession; thus if land be given to A. for life, remainder to B. for life, B. may die before A., yet the remainder is vested, for during its continuance, namely the life of B., it is ready to come into possession whenever and however A.'s estate determines. This result is not affected by the fact that the termination of the remainder is contingent; that is, that it is subject to a condition subsequent. *For instance, if land is devised to A. for life, remainder to B. and his heirs, but if B. dies unmarried then to C. and his heirs, B.'s remainder is vested, although it is possible that he may die unmarried in A.'s lifetime.*

* * *

" '108. Common Law Rule.... Whether a remainder is vested or contingent depends upon the language employed. If the conditional element is incorporated into the description of, or into the gift to, the remainderman, then the remainder is contingent; *but if, after words giving a vested interest, a clause is added divesting it, the remainder is vested.* Thus on a devise to A. for life, remainder to his children, but if any child dies in the lifetime of A. his share to go to those who survive, *the share of each child is vested,* subject to be divested by its death. But on a devise to A. for life, remainder to such of his children as survive him, the remainder is contingent.' "

* * *

This was and long prior to 1892 had been the well recognized law of Pennsylvania, as it was gradually expounded over the years.

In Newlin's Estate, 367 Pa. 527, pages 532, 533, 534, 80 A.2d 819, pages 823–824, the Court stated at length the pertinent principles which previously had been severally iterated:

"If a bequest is to a class who take at the death of a life tenant, the fact that the members of the class are unknown or even not in being at the death of the testator, or that their interest is subject to be increased or decreased or divested by subsequent events, will not render the gift contingent or violate the rule against perpetuities. In re Edwards' Estate, 255 Pa. 358, 99 A. 1010; Id., 360 Pa. 504, 62 A.2d 763; . . . .

" 'Where an estate is given to a life tenant, with remainder to the children of the life tenant, the estate vests at once upon the birth of each child, subject to open and let in after-born children, . . . without regard to the question of whether or not a child survives the life tenant'. In re Edwards' Estate, 255 Pa. 358, 361, 99 A. 1010, 1011; In re Edwards' Estate, 360 Pa. 504, 508, 62 A.2d 763. . . . "

" 'Where a bequest is to a class, the vesting is not postponed because of uncertainty as to who, if any, may be the constituents of the class at the time fixed for the enjoyment of it. If there is a present right to a future possession, though that right may be defeated by some future event, contingent or certain, there is nevertheless a vested estate'. In re McCauley's Estate, 257 Pa. 377, 382, 101 A. 827, 829; In re Reed's Estate, 307 Pa. 482, 484, 161 A. 729."

. . .

The law leans to vested rather than to contingent estates, and the presumption is that a legacy is vested. [In re] Carstensen's Estate, 196 Pa. 325, 46 A. 495; [In re] Tatham's Estate, 250 Pa. 269, 95 A. 520; [In re] Neel's Estate, 252 Pa. 394, 97 A. 502; [In re] Rau's Estate [254 Pa. 464, 98 A. 1068], supra and 'the presumption that a legacy was intended to be vested applies with far greater force where a testator is making provision for a child or a grandchild, than where the gift is to a stranger or to a collateral relative.' Wengerd's Estate, 143 Pa. 615, 22 Atl. 869, 13 L.R.A. 360.

The intention of a testator or settlor to create a contingent interest must appear clearly and plainly[20] otherwise the interest will be construed to be vested, or vested subject to be divested.

---

20. Several cases state that an interest will not be construed to be contingent unless it is *impossible* to construe it as vested. The word "impossible" is an unfortunate expression, as many

A myriad cases state, we repeat, that a Court is to place itself in the armchair of a testator and determine his intent from his language and the circumstances surrounding him at the time he made his will.

However, where a testator uses words which have a legal or technical meaning, " 'they are to be so interpreted according to the law in effect at the testator's death unless the will contains a clearly expressed intention to the contrary' ": Farmers Trust Co., [Executor] v. Wilson [et ux.,] 361 Pa. 43, 46, 63 A.2d 14, 17, and cases therein cited:. . . .

There can be no doubt that when Mr. Houston's will was written and at the time of his death, and for a century prior thereto, his gifts of the principal or remainder of his trust estate created a vested interest in his grandchildren,[21] and since the will itself evidences the hand of an expert will-draftsman[22] it is persuasive that testator intended this gift to be vested rather than contingent.

To summarize: We conclude that the language and scheme of testator's will, particularly the *Twenty-second* paragraph of Item Fifty-ninth, disclose an intention to make a vested gift of principal to his grandchildren, with no provision or condition, or any necessity for their surviving testator's last surviving child, but with one divesting condition, viz., if any grandchild of testator was deceased at the death of testator's last surviving child, such deceased grandchild's portion or share was to be distributed to his children.

We reach this construction of the will with regret because (a) it gives a share of the principal to descendants long dead, and (b) it would permit strangers to testator's blood (a deceased grandchild's spouse, or his legatees, or his heirs under the intestate laws) to receive a substantial portion of his estate without any express gift and (c) it greatly depletes, by colossal unforeseeable taxation, the property which the testator desired and intended to go to his descendants. However, such sentiments or results are not legally sufficient to allow us to ignore or distort testator's language, or rewrite his will. It is not what the Court thinks testator might or should or would have said if he could have foreseen the existing circumstances and conditions, but what he actually did say.

We agree with the lower Court that the family agreements upon which appellants rely, have no relevancy or bearing upon the issues herein

---

people believe that nothing is impossible. Several other cases use the expression "clear, plain and manifest" while others use "clear, plain and indisputably" or "indisputable." However, we believe that it is fair and correct to say that an analysis of these authorities discloses an intention in each of the prior cases to express the same meaning, albeit in different language. The variety of language used to express this test has caused such confusion that we deem it wise to herein use and apply the test hereinabove set forth in this opinion, since it appears to be the fairest and most correct test.

21. Unless other provisions of the will contain a clearly expressed intention to the contrary. Section 14 of the Wills Act. . . .

22. Item Sixty-third provides, "In all matters requiring legal services or advice" the executors and trustees should consult "my attorney William W. Porter"; Porter was also a subscribing witness.

presented, viz., the testamentary intention of the testator, and therefore deem discussion of them unnecessary.

Notwithstanding the very able argument of counsel for the appellants, the Decree must be affirmed.

Decree affirmed, all costs to be paid out of the principal of the residuary trust estate.

JONES, J., concurs in the result.

ROBERTS, J., files a dissenting Opinion in which MUSMANNO, J., joins.

ROBERTS, JUSTICE (dissenting).

My reading and study of decedent's will and our past decisions[23] preclude me from joining the majority. In my view, the majority have incorrectly construed testator's gift of residuary principal.

Although almost three-quarters of a century span the years between decedent's will and its present construction, his intention, as expressed in his will and reflected by the circumstances surrounding his armchair, must prevail.

All must agree that the best evidence of decedent's intention is his language.

"And, while the words employed in a will necessarily constitute the gauge of the testator's intent (Ludwick's Estate, 269 Pa. 365, 371, 112 A. 543), a construction that would lead to a highly improbable result is to be avoided, if at all possible; and a meaning conformable to the testator's plausible intent should be ascribed to his words if agreeable to reason: Riegel v. Oliver, 352 Pa. 244, 247, 42 A.2d 602, 161 A.L.R. 177." Fahey's Estate, 360 Pa. 497, 500, 61 A.2d 880, 881 (1948).

In seeking to ascertain the intention and meaning of decedent's language, this Court has said:

"The proper course of procedure for the interpreter of a testamentary writing is not to apply rules of construction until all reasonable effort to deduce a meaning from the writing itself has been exhausted with no understandable and sensible result." Buzby's Estate, 386 Pa. 1, 8, 123 A.2d 723, 726 (1956).

In reality, this controversy is governed by that portion of decedent's will which provides:

"On the death of my last surviving child I direct that the whole of the principal of the trust estate shall be distributed in equal portions to and among my grand-children, the children of any deceased grand-child taking deceased parents share."

This language, testator's meaning and his intention are clear. I agree with the majority that canons of construction should be resorted to only if

---

23. Keeping in mind, of course, that no will or testamentary trust has an exact twin or even a reasonably identical relative. This is due in part to the special and individual circumstances surrounding a testator.

the language of the will is ambiguous or testator's intent is uncertain. Lewis' Estate, 407 Pa. 518, 180 A.2d 919 (1962). Yet the majority's conclusion appears to be based upon (rather than supported by) rules of construction despite the clarity of testator's words and intention.

Furthermore, proper construction of this gift does not require the application of the presumption that an interest is vested rather than contingent. Basically, this presumption, even though a very ancient one, is itself merely a rule of construction. To counterbalance the absoluteness of the presumption of vesting the "pay and divide rule" was developed over many years. With the proper abolition of the "pay and divide rule" by Mr. Justice, now Chief Justice Bell, speaking for a unanimous Court, in Dickson's Estate, 396 Pa. 371, 152 A.2d 680 (1959), this counter-balancing effect was destroyed. Thus, we must now avoid routine use of the presumption of vesting as an absolute rule but must apply it as it was originally intended, as a helpful rule of construction. Application of the presumption here requires the reopening of estates long closed with all the attending legal and practical difficulties. I fear this presumption may have unduly influenced the majority in its determination, thereby achieving the "highly improbable result" to be avoided under Fahey's Estate, supra.

As the testator in his armchair contemplated the future and reflected upon the objects of his bounty, particularly the members of his immediate family, he was keenly aware from tragic personal experience that children may and unfortunately do predecease their parents. In his lifetime, he and his wife endured three such unfortunate losses.[24] While he undoubtedly, hoped and prayed that his children, as parents, would be spared such tragedies, he could not and did not ignore the teachings of his own experience.

In view of testator's personal experiences, it is difficult and almost impossible to conclude that his gift to "my grandchildren, the children of any deceased grandchild taking deceased parents share" is an expression of intention that his estate eventually pass to deceased grandchildren. I can find no indication anywhere in his will or in the relevant attending circumstances to suggest that this alert, well-informed and well-advised testator, who created trusts for many years in the future for many persons, and whose obvious and primary purpose was to benefit his descendants, intended to or did direct that the ultimate distribution of trust principal devolve through short-term, intermittent estates of deceased grandchildren. This is precisely what testator sought to avoid. His constant reference throughout his will to living persons announced and repeated that he was thinking, writing and providing for living persons only.

If, as the majority concludes, testator's gift was to grandchildren without reference to survival at the time of distribution and irrespective of whether deceased grandchildren were survived by children, he could have

---

24. Daughters Cornelia Bonnell Houston and Eleanor Anne Houston died in 1857 and 1875, respectively. Henry H. Houston, Jr., died in 1879.

achieved that gift by ending with the phrase "in equal portions to and among my grandchildren." However, by adding "the children of any deceased grand-child taking deceased parents share," he sought to, and did, make clear that his gifts were to living persons and not to deceased grandchildren who left no children. In the case of a deceased grandchild who left children, he specifically provided a gift for such children. However, as to other deceased grandchildren—those leaving no children—the will is entirely silent. If, as the majority holds, testator intended them as beneficiaries also, is it likely that he would have said nothing about them? It is more likely that deceased grandchildren dying without children are not mentioned because testator did not intend them to benefit if they predeceased his last surviving child. Similarly, testator would not have awarded to such deceased grandchildren the same freedom to pass (by will or intestacy) the trust property as he granted to living grandchildren, a privilege not granted to deceased grandchildren leaving issue.

It seems clear to me that testator intended and his will provided that at the death of his last child, the principal should be distributed equally to his then living grandchildren, and if there were deceased grandchildren who left children, they (great-grandchildren) would take the share their parents would have taken.

In providing only for living grandchildren and the living children of deceased grandchildren, testator was carrying out his considered scheme of distribution and avoiding the incidents and consequences of almost immediate successive devolutions through estates of deceased persons. "The exclusion of estates of deceased persons is the ordinary intention of a testator."

The majority reaches its conclusion with three expressed regrets:

" . . . (a) it gives a share of the principal to descendants long dead, and (b) it would permit strangers to testator's blood (a deceased grand-child's spouse, or his legatees, or his heirs under the intestate laws) to receive a substantial portion of his estate without any express gift, and (c) it greatly depletes, by colossal unforeseeable taxation, the property which the testator desired and intended to go to his descendants."

In my view, the first two majority regrets (a and b) are more than expressions of regret. I deem each to be a very persuasive factor in revealing testator's intention. Together they very strongly support the conclusion that testator created contingent and not vested gifts for his grandchildren. Each justifies and certainly both require a result contrary to that reached by the majority.

I regard the majority's tax regret as simply a regret, since it deals with tax circumstances and consequences unknown to this nineteenth century testator. However, in lieu of the majority's tax regret, it is suggested that the pyramiding of estate administration costs and expenses and the resulting diminution of assets occasioned by early and almost immediate successive administrations constitute a proper indication of testator's intention. These circumstances lend added support to the conclusion that testator's gifts of principal were to living grandchildren.

I dissent and would direct that the trust corpus be divided into nine equal shares.

NOTES AND QUESTIONS

1. The following Houston family tree should assist you in your understanding of the case:

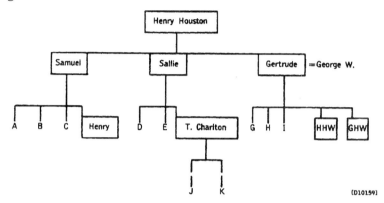

At Gertrude's death, A, B, C, D, E, J, K, G, H, and I survived. All of Henry's other descendants predeceased Gertrude.

2. The value of the Houston trust that was the subject of the litigation was approximately $145,000,000, and the dispute involved whether the pie should have been divided into ⅑ or ¹⁄₁₂ shares. After reading the case, however, you should have a sense that some other concerns may have been even more paramount to the litigants. What might these concerns have been?

3. The court makes reference to a "per stirpes" distribution. For further discussion of this see note 2 in Section 4.9, infra.

4. The court states that the will was meticulously drawn. If that characterization implies that the decedent had employed very able and sophisticated counsel, would you agree?

5. The court discusses the common law preference for the early vesting of estates. Why might the common law have preferred an early vesting of estates? Should that preference prevail today?

6. As the court notes in construing ambiguous instruments, courts attempt to find and then apply the testator's intent. In attempting to ascertain that intent some courts willingly look to evidence extrinsic to the document; others refuse to do so. To what extent do the majority and the dissent look to extrinsic evidence? Assuming courts are willing to look to extrinsic evidence to construe ambiguous instruments, what kind of evidence would be probative? What should courts do in construing ambiguous instruments where no evidence of intent is available? To what extent are prior cases appropriate precedents to aid in the construction of an ambiguous instru-

ment? To what extent are courts engaging in a vain and useless act when they seek to find intent?

7.   If you had been the testator's counsel, what would you have done to avoid the possibility of future litigation to construe the meaning of the will?

8.   Suppose the testator's will provided only that "on the death of the last surviving child I direct that the whole of the principal of the trust estate shall be distributed in equal portions to and among my grandchildren." Would the case have been decided in the same way?

9.   One of the arguments in favor of implying a condition of survivorship was that if no such condition was implied, the interest of a grandchild who predeceased the surviving life tenant leaving no issue who survived the life tenant could pass to "strangers of blood." Is this a persuasive argument? Does it prove too much?

10.   Section 2–707(b)(1) of the Uniform Probate Code provides that "a future interest . . . [in a trust] is contingent on the beneficiary's surviving the distribution date." The distribution date is that date on which the future interest is to become possessory. If this statute had applied to the Houston trust, would the result of the case have changed?

11.   Suppose T devises Blackacre to A for life, and upon A's death to "my children, C and D, or their heirs." C predeceases A survived by Child X who would have been C's only heir. C's will devised all of C's property to Y. D also predeceased A survived by Y who would have been D's heir. However, prior to D's death D had conveyed all of D's rights in Blackacre to Z. To whom should Blackacre be distributed upon A's death? See Rowett v. McFarland, 394 N.W.2d 298 (S.D. 1986).

12.   Could the creation of an alternative gift in the issue of a deceased child evidence an intent that in no event would the testator have wanted the share of a deceased class member to pass through that decedent's estate? This was the conclusion reached in Martino v. Martino, 35 S.W.3d 252, 254 (Tex.Ct.App. 2000) ("This substitution [children for deceased parent] indicates that [the decedent] did not wish that the devise should pass through the deceased class member's estate.")

§ 4.7   DESTRUCTIBILITY OF CONTINGENT REMAINDERS

Suppose O conveyed Blackacre to A for life and upon A's death to A's eldest child if he shall attain the age of 21. At common law, A, during his life, would be seized of Blackacre and would be responsible for the performance of all feudal duties associated with a freehold estate. If A's eldest child survived A and was then 21, such child would then be seized of Blackacre and would succeed to the responsibilities associated with the ownership of a freehold estate. But suppose when A died his eldest child had not then attained the age of 21. Since the vesting of such child's estate was conditioned upon his reaching age 21, such child's interest would not vest at A's death, and if one had to await such child attaining age 21 then seisin would be in abeyance until it was known whether or not that condition would occur. During this suspended period (or gap), no transferee of O would have been responsible for the performance of the feudal obligations. From a feudal perspective, this was a sufficiently intolerable situation that the rule developed that *if a contingent remainder did not vest before, or at the time of, the termination of the preceding freehold estate, it was destroyed, and the property reverted to the grantor.* Interestingly, when the rule was applied the remainder interest was forever destroyed. It was not brought back to life if the condition later occurred. Thus in the preceding example, if A died survived by his eldest child who was under the age of 21, the child's contingent remainder was destroyed and O's reversion ripened into a fee simple absolute. If A's child later reached 21, O retained the fee simple absolute. This rule is called the Rule of Destructibility of Contingent Remainders.

The application of the Rule of Destructibility was limited to legal, not equitable, contingent remainders; it did not apply to executory interests; it did not apply to interests in personal property. Thus, after the enactment of the Statute of Uses executing equitable future interests into legal future interests, attempts to save executed contingent remainders from destructibility were made by seeking to have such interests re-classified as executory interests. These attempts, however, were squelched when the court in Purefoy v. Rogers, 2 Wms. Saunders 380, 85 Eng.Rep. 1181 (K.B.1671), held that if a future interest could have been classified as a contingent remainder before the enactment of the Statute of Uses, it must be similarly classified after the enactment of the Statute of Uses.

Your client wishes to avoid the Rule of Destructibility but create both a life estate in A and a future interest in B if B reaches age 21. What do you advise your client to do?

At common law, if a life estate and the next vested estate came into the same hands, they merged to give the life tenant a fee simple. For example, if O deeds property to A for life, then to B and his heirs and B sells the remainder to A, A would have both the life estate and the remainder. The estates would merge to give A a fee simple absolute.

When both the doctrine of merger and the Rule of Destructibility applied, if a life estate and the next *vested* estate came into the same hand, the two estates merged and destroyed any outstanding contingent remainder. For example, if O conveyed Blackacre to A for life and upon A's death to such of A's children who survived A, the children of A had a contingent remainder. If O later died intestate leaving A as his sole heir, O's reversion would pass to A. In such case, A would have the life estate and the next vested estate (O's reversion), and they would merge to destroy the contingent remainder in A's children. Cf. Abo Petroleum Corp. v. Amstutz, 93 N.M. 332, 600 P.2d 278 (1979) (holding that Rule of Destructibility was not part of New Mexico law but noting that if it were, the contingent remainder in the preceding example would have been destroyed).

An exception to the destructibility by merger rule was that if the life estate and the next vested estate were created *simultaneously* in the same person with the creation of a contingent remainder in another person, the life estate and the next vested estate did not merge to destroy the contingent remainder. Suppose O conveys Blackacre to A for life, and upon A's death to A's first-born daughter and the heirs of her body and, if A has no daughter, then to A and his heirs. Assuming that at the time of the conveyance A has no daughter, the state of the title is a life estate in A, a contingent remainder in tail in A's first born daughter, and a vested remainder in A. Do you see why? While A has both the life estate and the next vested estate, they do not merge to destroy the contingent remainder in tail in A's first born daughter. If A sought to destroy that contingent remainder in tail, what could A do? Since this exception applied only where a fee tail or a remainder in tail was created, its importance is primarily historical.

Suppose T died and devised Blackacre in her will to her daughter, D, for life and upon D's death to such of D's children who survive D. T devised the residue of her estate to her daughter D. At T's death, state the title. Suppose further that one year after T died D conveyed "all of my right, title and interest in Blackacre" to B. At this point, state the title. Suppose you represent A, a prospective purchaser of Blackacre, who shortly after T died consults you to determine if there is any way she might acquire a fee simple absolute in Blackacre. How would you advise A?

The Rule of Destructibility did not apply to equitable contingent remainders. Why?

Suppose O conveys Blackacre to A for life and upon A's death to such of A's children as survive A and attain the age of 21. A dies survived by two children, ages 22 and 14. Is the interest of the 14 year old child of A destroyed? Simonds v. Simonds, 199 Mass. 552, 85 N.E. 860 (1908); L. Simes & A. Smith, The Law of Future Interests § 205 (2d ed. 1956).

Suppose O conveys Blackacre to A for life and upon A's death to A's children who attain the age of 21. A dies survived by two children, ages 19 and 15. If the Rule of Destructibility does not apply, at A's death what is the state of the title? Suppose A dies survived by a child age 22 and a child age 18. What is the state of the title?

The Rule of Destructibility was abolished in England in 1877 and in at least three-fourths of the states by statute or judicial decision. The rule still appears to survive in Florida. See Blocker v. Blocker, 103 Fla. 285, 137 So. 249 (1931); In re Rentz' Estate, 152 So.2d 480 (Fla.App. 3 Dist.1963). There is scholarly disagreement whether it exists in Arkansas, North Carolina, South Carolina, Tennessee, Oregon, and Pennsylvania. See generally 2A R. Powell, Real Property ¶ 314 (P. Rohan ed. 1990). See also Dukeminier, Contingent Remainders and Executory Interests: A Requiem for the Distinction, 43 Minn.L.Rev. 13 (1958); Fetters, Destructibility of Contingent Remainders, 21 Ark.L.Rev. 145 (1967); Jones & Heck,

Destructibility of Contingent Remainders in Tennessee, 42 Tenn.L.Rev. 761 (1975).

The Third Restatement of Property takes the view that the rule of destructibility is "not recognized as part of American law." Restatement (Third) of Property § 25.5 (2012).

§ 4.8 THE RULE IN SHELLEY'S CASE

Under the Rule in Shelley's Case, if a grantor conveys a life estate to A *and* by the same instrument purports to create a remainder in A's heirs *and* if both estates are legal estates or both estates are equitable, the remainder is a fee simple in A. A similar rule applied if the remainder were limited in favor of the heirs of A's body, although in that case the remainder would be a fee tail in A. Thus, if O conveys Blackacre to A for life and upon A's death to A's heirs, A has a life estate and A also has a remainder. *The Rule in Shelley's Case does nothing more.* On its face the Rule did not apply to executory interests.

In the preceding example, A has the life estate and the next vested estate (by operation of the Rule in Shelley's Case), then under the separate doctrine of merger, both estates merge, and A has a fee simple absolute. In some cases, however, A will not have the next vested estate and therefore A's future interest will not merge with A's life estate. For example, suppose O conveys Blackacre to A for life and upon A's death to B and the heirs of his body, remainder to A's heirs. Under the Rule in Shelley's Case, the remainder following B's vested remainder in tail is in A. Does A's remainder merge with A's life estate to give A the fee simple absolute?

Suppose O conveys Blackacre to A for life and upon A's death if A's daughter Jane survives A then to such daughter and the heirs of her body, remainder to A's heirs. State the title.

The Rule in Shelley's Case was designed to make property more marketable by eliminating the purported contingent remainder in A's heirs. It also increased feudal death taxes by assuring that if A died intestate the property passed to A's heirs from A (a taxable event) rather than from the grantor by purchase (a nontaxable event).

The Rule in Shelley's Case is a rule of law and not a rule of construction. See Society National Bank v. Jacobson, 54 Ohio St.3d 15, 560 N.E.2d 217 (1990). What does this mean and what difference does it make? Notwithstanding that the Rule in Shelley's Case is the law in some states, the Third Restatement states "the Rule in Shelley's Case is not recognized as part of American Law. A remainder interest in favor of the life tenant's heirs (or the heirs of the body of the life tenant) passes to the life tenant's heirs (or the heirs of the body of the life tenant), not to the life tenant." Restatement (Third) of Property, § 16.2 (2012). This position is consistent with the Second Restatement but not the First Restatement of Property.

1. Assuming the Rule in Shelley's Case applies, in each of the following conveyances, state the title:

(a) O conveys Blackacre to A for life and upon A's death to B for life and upon B's death to B's heirs.

(b) O conveys Blackacre to A for life and if A returns from Iowa to A's heirs.

(c) O conveys Blackacre to A for life and upon A's death to B for life and upon the death of the survivor of A and B to A's heirs.

(d) O conveys Blackacre to A for life and one day after A dies to A's heirs.

2. The Rule in Shelley's Case was abolished in England in 1925 and has been abolished in almost all states. See 2A Richard R. Powell, The Law of Real Property, ¶ 380 (Rev. ed. 1996). Often statutes or decisions overturning the Rule apply prospectively only. Thus, the Rule may continue to haunt us for many years.

3. What policy, if any, continues to justify the Rule in Shelley's Case?

§ 4.9 THE DOCTRINE OF WORTHIER TITLE

The Doctrine of Worthier Title at common law had two branches: the inter vivos branch and the testamentary branch. Under the inter vivos branch, a conveyance of a remainder or executory interest to the heirs of the grantor was void, and the grantor retained the reversion. Thus, if O conveyed Blackacre to A for life and upon A's death to O's heirs, A had a life estate, O had a reversion, and O's heirs had nothing. If O later dies testate leaving her entire estate to B, who would not have been O's heir, then B succeeds to O's reversion, and O's heir takes nothing. Then, when A dies B, the devisee under O's will, takes a fee simple absolute.

In common with the Rule in Shelley's Case, this branch of the doctrine aided the marketability of property and caused it to pass by descent rather than purchase, thereby subjecting the property to feudal inheritance taxes.

Under the testamentary branch, a devise to the heir of the testator was void if it purported to give to the devisee an interest of the same quality and quantity that the devisee would have taken if the testator had died intestate. Thus if T died and bequeathed his entire estate to his son, who would have been T's sole heir if T had died intestate, the devise would be void, and the son would take T's entire estate by descent rather that devise. The testamentary branch also was designed to cause property to pass to the heir of the decedent by descent rather than devise, thereby subjecting the property to feudal inheritance taxes. The testamentary branch appears to have been applied in a recent adverse possession case. Apparently, in South Carolina one adverse possessor's time in possession cannot be tacked on to the time of another adverse possessor except when the second possessor succeeds to the right of possession from the first possessor by operation of law. Under this rule, the time of possession of an intestate and an heir (but not a testator and devisee) can be tacked to each other. Suppose, however, a testator who is adversely possessing Blackacre bequeaths his entire estate, including whatever interest he has in Blackacre, to the only person who would be his heir. Can the testator's time of possession and the time of possession of the devisee named in the will be tacked together for purposes of determining whether the statute of limitations had run? Yes, if the testamentary branch of the doctrine of worthier title applies because the devise would be void and the named legatee would take as heir. See Catawba Indian Tribe of South Carolina v. State of South Carolina, 978 F.2d 1334, 1345–47 (4th Cir.1992).

At common law the Doctrine of Worthier Title was a rule of law. Like the Rule in Shelley's Case, it would not give way to a contrary intent. Since Doctor v. Hughes, 225 N.Y. 305, 122 N.E. 221 (1919), however, the doctrine of worthier title in this country has operated more as a rule of construction rather than a rule of law. Therefore, the doctrine could give way to a contrary intent. As a rule of construction, it has engendered much litigation respecting whether the grantor intended to retain a reversion or convey a contingent remainder to his or her heirs. In Doctor v. Hughes, Justice Benjamin Cardozo not only advanced the notion that the doctrine was only a rule of construction; he extended the operation of the doctrine to dispositions of personal property as well as real property.

NOTES AND QUESTIONS

1. The staying power of the inter vivos branch of the Doctrine of Worthier Title has been much greater than the Rule in Shelley's Case. The inter vivos branch has been legislatively abolished in eleven states. In many states, however, the doctrine survives but only as a rule of construction. At least one state has abolished the testamentary branch by statute and it now appears that this branch is not recognized in any state. Only recently Iowa, one of the last states to appear to recognize the testamentary branch, abolished the doctrine. See In re Estate of Kern, 274 N.W.2d 325 (Iowa 1979). Most recently, the Third Restatement of Property decreed: "The doctrine of worthier title is not recognized as part of American law, neither as a rule of law nor as a rule of construction. An inter vivos transfer purporting to create a future interest in the transferor's heirs or next of kin creates a future interest in the transferor's heirs or next of kin, not a reversionary interest in the transferor." Restatement (Third) of Property, § 16.3 (2011).

2. When a remainder becomes distributable among the grantor's heirs, the question arises whether the property should be distributed among them per capita or per stirpes. When property is distributed per capita among a group of persons, each person takes an equal share. When property is distributed per stirpes, living descendants of a closer degree of relationship to the named ancestor take to the exclusion of their own descendants and the ultimate takers of the property may not necessarily take equal shares. To illustrate, consider the following family tree:

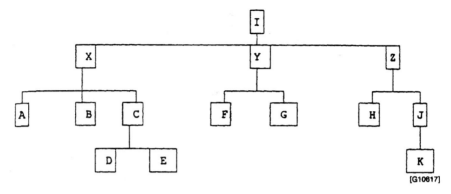

[G10617]

If I dies survived by all of I's thirteen descendants, namely, X, Y, Z, A, B, C, D, E, F, G, H, J, and K, each of them takes an equal $\frac{1}{13}$ share if I's descendants take per capita. If I's descendants take per stirpes, then X, Y, and Z take equal $\frac{1}{3}$ shares and their descendants A, B, C, D, and E (in the case of X), F and G (in the case of Y), and H, J, and K (in the case of Z) take nothing.

Suppose I is survived by no children but by A, B, C, D, E, F, G, H, J, and K. Again, under a per capita distribution, each of them takes $\frac{1}{10}$. Under a per stirpes distribution, D and E take nothing because their immediate ancestor C is alive to take, and K takes nothing because K's immediate ancestor J is alive to take. While only A, B, C, F, G, H, and J take under a per stirpes approach, the size of their shares depends upon whether the initial division of shares is made at the first generation where there is at least one living member (grandchildren of I in this case) or at the first generation period regardless of whether any members of that generation are living. Under the former, each of I's descendants take an equal $\frac{1}{7}$ share. Under the latter, A, B, and C divide X's $\frac{1}{3}$ share among themselves with each taking a $\frac{1}{9}$ share; F and G divide Y's $\frac{1}{3}$ share between themselves as H and J divide Z's $\frac{1}{3}$ share between themselves. Thus, F, G, H, and J each take $\frac{1}{6}$.

§ 4.10   THE RULE AGAINST PERPETUITIES

The Rule Against Perpetuities is one of the most confounding rules encountered by students of the law. This Rule is studied primarily in upperclass courses in Wills, Trusts and Estate Planning. Thus, the following materials are intended only as a brief introduction. See also, S. Kurtz, Moynihan's Introduction to the Law of Real Property, 5th (2011) at 259–266.

As crystalized by Professor Gray, the common-law Rule Against Perpetuities states that "no interest is good unless it must vest, if at all, not later than twenty-one years after some life in being at the creation of the interest." J. Gray, Rule Against Perpetuities § 201 (4th ed. 1942). As so stated, the Rule is concerned with the remoteness of vesting and therefore applies only to interests that for purposes of the Rule are nonvested from the moment of their creation. These interests are contingent remainders, vested remainders limited in favor of a class, and executory interests. The Rule does not apply to interests retained by a grantor because these interests are vested. See, e.g., Collins v. Church of God of Prophecy, 304 Ark. 37, 800 S.W.2d 418 (1990) (possibility of reverter not subject to the Rule).

A simple illustration of the operation of the common-law Rule may prove helpful. Suppose O conveys Blackacre to A for life and upon A's death to such of A's children as attain age twenty-five. Under the common-law Rule, the remainder in favor of A's children is void because A might die survived by a child under the age of four who could not reach the age of twenty-five within twenty-one years of A's death (or be assured of not reaching age 25 within 21 years of A's death). The gift was void even though when A died all of his surviving children were over the age of four and, thus, would either reach or fail to reach age 25 within 21 years of A's death. In other words, the validity of the remainder interest was determined on the basis of events that *might-have-been*, given the facts and circumstances in existence at the time of the creation of the non-vested interest, and not upon subsequent events that actually happen.

There are at least three justifications for the Rule. First, "the rule against perpetuities provides an adjustment or balance between the desire of the current owner of property to prolong indefinitely into the future his control over the devolution and use thereof and the desire of the person who will in the future become the owner of the affected land or other thing, to be free of the dead hand."[1] Second, "the rule against perpetuities contributes to the probable utilization of wealth of society."[2] Third, the "rule against perpetuities aids in the keeping of property responsive to the meeting of the exigencies of its current owners."[3] As you study the following materials consider whether all or any of these rationales are persuasive.

CONNECTICUT BANK AND TRUST COMPANY v. BRODY

Supreme Court of Connecticut (1978).
174 Conn. 616, 392 A.2d 445.

HOUSE, CHIEF JUSTICE.

This action was brought in the Superior Court in Hartford County by the plaintiff, successor trustee of a trust created by the will of William C. Skinner, seeking a decree advising the trustee as to its rights, powers and authority in connection with the administration of that trust. The appearing and nondefaulted parties, ... joined in a stipulation of facts and a request that the Superior Court reserve the action for the advice of this court. The court granted the request and reserved the case for the advice of this court with respect to eleven specific questions.

---

1. Restatement (Second) of Property at 9–13 (Tent. Draft No. 2 (1979)).
2. Id.
3. Id.

The parties properly stipulated to all the relevant facts, but it is unnecessary for the purposes of this opinion to recite them in full detail. A summary will suffice: William C. Skinner, to whom we will refer as the testator, was a resident of Hartford. He executed a will on August 6, 1920, and died, a widower, on March 8, 1922, leaving a large estate. His will was duly presented for probate to the Probate Court for the district of Hartford and, on March 18, 1922, the will was proved and approved by that court. On September 26, 1927, a final administration account on the estate was filed and accepted, and the then Phoenix State Bank and Trust Company qualified as trustee of a testamentary trust created by article fourteenth of the will. The plaintiff trust company is successor trustee of that trust, and the principal of the trust consists entirely of personalty which is located within the state.

Article fourteenth of the will, in its entirety, provided: "Fourteenth: All the rest and residue of my property of every kind and nature, and wheresoever situated, I divide into three equal parts, and one of said parts I do hereby give, devise and bequeath to the Phoenix National Bank of Hartford, Connecticut, in trust, to hold the same for the use and benefit of my children, my grandchildren and my great grandchildren; and I hereby direct said Bank as Trustee to pay the income from said one-third of my residuary estate equally to my three children, share and share alike, during their lives and the life of each of them. Upon the decease of my last surviving child, it is my will that said Bank as Trustee should pay the entire income of said trust fund to my grand-children, share and share alike, during the term of the lives of my several grand-children. If either of my children should die leaving issue him or her surviving, it is my will that the issue of such deceased child should take that portion of the income which would have gone to the parent if living, until my last surviving child shall have deceased, and upon the happening of that event, it is my will that the entire income of said trust estate shall be divided equally between my grand-children, share and share alike. Upon the death of my last surviving grandchild, it is my will that said trust should terminate, and said trust fund then remaining should be divided equally per capita among my great grand-children. The remaining two-thirds of said residuum I do hereby give, devise and bequeath to my children, to be divided between them, share and share alike, to them and their heirs and assigns forever."

It will be noted that the trust res consists of one-third of the residue of the testator's estate. During the life of his three children, the income was to be paid equally to them, share and share alike, the issue of any child dying taking per stirpes the share that the parent would have taken if living, until the last surviving child of the testator died. Upon the death of the testator's last surviving child, the entire income of the trust was to be paid, share and share alike, to the testator's grandchildren for the term of the lives of the grandchildren and upon the death of the last surviving grandchild the trust should terminate and the trust fund then remaining should be divided equally per capita among the testator's great-grandchildren.

On the death of the testator in 1922, he was survived by his three children: Roberts K. Skinner, born in 1880; Marjorie R. S. Trumbull, born in 1881; and William C. Skinner, Jr. born in 1888. All three of them have since died.

The testator was also survived by five grandchildren, four of whom are still living. One grandchild, Roberts K. Skinner, Jr., hereinafter referred to as Roberts, Jr., died in 1973 and is survived by three children.

Subsequent to the death of the testator, twelve great-grandchildren were born, including the three children of his now deceased grandson, Roberts, Jr. At the present time, all of these grandchildren and great-grandchildren are living, with the exception of the grandson, Roberts, Jr. Upon his death on November 6, 1973, questions arose as to the proper disposition of the one-fifth of the trust income which, until his death, was being paid to him under the provisions of the trust as a member of the class of grandchildren. The trust contains no express provision as to the disposition of the income of the trust payable to a member of the class of grandchildren in the event of the death of a member prior to the time fixed for the termination of the trust. The trust only provides that upon the death of the last surviving grandchild, that is, after the expiration of the second set of life estates in favor of the grandchildren, the great-grandchildren are to receive the trust fund then remaining equally, per capita. It is the questionable validity of the gift of the remainder interest to the testator's great grandchildren and the gift of the trust income to his grandchildren as a class during their lives with no express provision as to the disposition of that income in the event of the death of a grandchild prior to the time fixed for the termination of the trust on the death of the last grandchild which have given rise to the present proceedings and the necessity for a resolution of the following ... issues which have been briefed and argued by all the parties with commendable thoroughness: (1) Whether any provisions of the trust created by article fourteenth of the will of William C. Skinner violate the rule against perpetuities and are, therefore, invalid. (2) If any provision of the trust violates the rule against perpetuities, should the trust be terminated immediately or be allowed to continue until expiration of the second set of life estates, that is, until the death of the testator's last surviving grandchild? ...

The rule against perpetuities is deeply rooted in our common law and much has been written about its history and development. See 61 Am. Jur.2d, Perpetuities and Restraints on Alienation, § 6; Restatement, 4 Property, pt. 1; 6 American Law of Property, pt. 24; 2 Scott, op. cit. § 124.1; Leach, "Perpetuities in a Nutshell," 51 Harv.L.Rev. 638. "The rule against perpetuities, generally stated, is that 'no interest is good unless it must vest, if at all, not later than twenty-one years after some life in being at the creation of the interest' or (as the case may be) twenty-one years and the period of gestation. Gray, [The Rule Against] Perpetuities (3d Ed.) § 201;.... Its usual application and effect is to prohibit or invalidate attempts to create by limitation, whether executory or by way of remainder, future interests or estates the vesting of which is postponed beyond the prescribed period." *Wilbur v. Portland Trust Co.*, 121 Conn. 535, 537, 186 A. 499, 500.

The rule against perpetuities was early recognized as a principle of our common law....

The underlying and fundamental purpose of the rule is founded on the public policy in favor of free alienability of property and against restricting its marketability over long periods of time by restraints on its alienation. The rule "is not a rule of construction but a positive mandate of law to be obeyed irrespective of the question of intention, and is to be applied even if the accomplishment of the expressed intent of the testator is made impossible.... The proper procedure is to determine the true construction of the will or deed involved, just as if there was no such thing in existence as the rule against perpetuities, and then to apply the rule rigorously, in complete disregard of the wishes and intentions of the testator or grantor." 61 Am.Jur.2d, op. cit. § 9.

Under the will of the testator in the present case, the testamentary scheme was for title in the residuary share to vest ultimately in his great-grandchildren after life estates in his children as a class and then in his grandchildren as a class.

With respect to the first estate—to the testator's own children—there is, of course, no problem as they were lives in being at the time of the testator's death and the creation of these life estates involves no problem with the rule against perpetuities.

The provisions for life estates to the testator's grandchildren with remainder over to great-grandchildren, however, very much involve the application of the rule and we conclude that the gift to the great-grandchildren does violate the rule against perpetuities and is invalid. See, generally, annot., "Validity, under rule against perpetuities, of gift in remainder to creator's great-grandchildren, following successive life estates to children and grandchildren," 18 A.L.R.2d 671. As that annotation notes, the determination of the validity of the gift of remainder to great-grandchildren, following successive life estates to children and grandchildren depends upon the particular facts of each case, but the "determining factor ... is the character of the secondary life estate to grandchildren." Id., p. 673. The crucial question is whether the grandchildren can be regarded as "lives in being" as of the testator's death. If so, then they can be considered measuring lives for the purpose of applying the rule that an interest must vest, if at all, not later than *twenty-one years after some life in being at the creation of the interest.*

As will have been noted, the testator provided that upon the death of his last surviving child the trustee was to "pay the entire income of ... [the] trust fund to my grand-children, share and share alike, during the term of the lives of my several grand-children" and that "[u]pon the death of my last surviving grandchild, it is my will that said trust should terminate, and said trust fund then remaining should be divided equally per capita among my great grand-children." In the case of each generation, the gift was to a class "grand-children" and "great grand-children" and in the case of the grandchildren, unlike the testator's provision for survivorship among his own children, he made no express provision for any alternative distribution in the event of the death of a grandchild "during the term of the lives of my several grand-children." The conclusion is inescapable that the gifts were in each instance class gifts and the testator intended to designate as his beneficiaries in each instance a group capable of future change in number rather than specific individuals. See Restatement, 4 Property § 279. Unlike the circumstances in *Beers v. Narramore*, 61 Conn. 13, 22 A. 1061, and *Willis v. Hendry*, 127 Conn. 653, 20 A.2d 375, it cannot be found that the testator was referring to particular persons rather than classes of persons.

As the parties stipulated at the time of his death the testator was survived by three children and five grandchildren. Until the death of all of his children, there remained the possibility that another grandchild would be born. The law recognizes such an event as among the possibilities. " 'For the purpose of applying the rule against perpetuities, both men and women are considered capable of having issue so long as they live.' *Jee v. Audley*, 1 Cox Ch. 324; *In re Sayer's Trusts*, L.R. 6 Eq. 318, 319; 71 Law Times, 186; Gray on Perpetuities, § 215, 376. The law looks forward from the time the limitation is made to see what may be, not backward to see what has been. It regards the possible, not the actual. *Rand v. Butler*, 48 Conn. 293; *Tingier v. Chamberlin*, 71 Conn. 466, 42 A. 718; *Thomas v. Gregg*, 76 Md. 169, 24 A. 418." *White v. Allen*, 76 Conn. 185, 189, 56 A. 519, 521. In Connecticut, the rule as stated in the *White* case has long been observed. "The presumption that the possibility of issue is never extinct so long as a person lives is settled law in this country as it pertains to the validity of titles and the distribution of property. [Citations omitted.]" *Willimantic Investors, Inc. v. Covell*, 147 Conn. 34, 39, 156 A.2d 473, 475; Restatement, 4 Property § 377.

Applying these principles to the present case, it is apparent that the gift to the grandchildren was a gift to a class which at the time of the testator's death was subject to being opened to let in members born after the death of the testator. "Gifts to a group designated as children, grandchildren and the like have been so uniformly construed by us as made to a class which opens to let in after-born members that the words have acquired a definite significance." *Westport Paper–Board Co. v. Staples*, 127 Conn. 115, 124, 15 A.2d 1, 5; *Hill v. Birmingham*, 131 Conn. 174, 177–78, 38 A.2d 604. It follows that since it was possible that another grandchild of the testator might be born at some undetermined time after his death and thus become a member of the grandchildren class of beneficiaries, then the grandchildren cannot be regarded as "lives in being" for the purpose of applying the rule. It was the *children* of the testator who were the measuring lives and since a great-grandchild could have been born more than twenty-one years after the death of the children, the provision for the great-grandchildren violated the rule against perpetuities. . . .

We have not overlooked the existence in some jurisdictions of the so-called "wait and see" . . . doctrine pursuant to which a gift, which would be void under the certainty-of-vesting requirement of the common-law rule against perpetuities, may be validated by the occurrence of events which happen within the prescribed period. See annot., "Perpetuities—Rule Against," 20 A.L.R.3d 1094; 61 Am.Jur.2d, Perpetuities and Restraints on Alienation, § 26. Discussion in Tentative Draft No. 1, "Restatement of the Law Second, Property," Division I, pt. 1 and appendix (March 15, 1978). This is not the common-law rule in Connecticut. . . .

Having concluded that the remainder interest in the great-grandchildren is void under the rule, we must determine whether the life estate in the grandchildren is so inextricably intertwined with the void remainder that it too must fail. Such a determination can only be made by looking to the intent of the testator to ascertain the function of the life estate in the general testamentary scheme. See Restatement, 4 Property § 402; annots., 28 A.L.R. 375; 75 A.L.R. 124; 168 A.L.R. 321, "Prior estate as affected by remainder void for remoteness."

Although, in general, an effort will be made to preserve a life estate even when it is followed by a void remainder; annot., 28 A.L.R. 375, 400; this can be accomplished only when the testator's primary intention "is not frustrated by cutting out the bad part." *Russell v. Hartley*, 83 Conn. 654, 659, 78 A. 320, 322. "If the leading and primary object was to accumulate a fund for illegal distribution; or if the trusts were strictly subservient or auxiliary to such a distribution so as to be themselves tainted with the illegality; or if they are so connected therewith that they cannot be separated and carried into effect without involving consequences substantially and materially different from what the testator intended, then they, too, must fall with the illegal distribution." *Andrews v. Rice*, 53 Conn. 566, 571, 5 A. 823, 825; *Leake v. Watson*, 60 Conn. 498, 515–16, 21 A. 1075.

In the case before us, the provision for the benefit of the grandchildren appears to serve no function other than to preserve a portion of the testator's estate intact for ultimate distribution to his great-grandchildren. There is no indication that a primary purpose of the life estate in the grandchildren was to see that they were comfortably provided for during their lifetimes, as might be inferred were there a provision for invasion of the corpus of the trust. See *Russell v. Hartley*, supra; *Leake v. Watson*, supra. Nor is there evidence that an underlying purpose was to preclude the possibility that the spouse of a grandchild might gain control of a portion of the testator's estate. See *Andrews v. Rice*, supra. Thus, the only apparent purpose of the life estates to the grandchildren was to postpone the distribution to the great-grandchildren. Because we have found that the provision for postponed distribution to the great-grandchildren violates the rule against perpetuities, the provision for the grandchildren, which is clearly subservient or auxiliary to the disposition of the remainder, must fail as well.

It is also significant to note that the will of the testator does not indicate any intention that each of his grandchildren should have a separate life estate in a separate share and that each such separate share should vest separately at the death of such grandchild in the issue of that grandchild. Rather the entire corpus of the trust was to be held first for the benefit of all the testator's children for their lives, and on the death of the last survivor of them the same corpus was to be held for the benefit of his grandchildren as a class until the last of them should die at which time the same undivided corpus should, as a remainder, vest in his great-grandchildren per capita. We conclude, as did the court in *North Carolina National Bank v. Norris*, 21 N.C.App. 178, 203 S.E.2d 657, in similar circumstances, that the doctrine of separability is not applicable.

Before answering the specific questions reserved by the Superior Court, it is pertinent to note the existence of one more well-settled legal principle. Since the testator's attempted gifts to his grandchildren and great-grandchildren must fail and these gifts were from a portion of the residue of his estate and the will made no other provision for distribution, the subject property must pass as intestate property of the testator. . . .

* * *

In this opinion the other judges concurred.

NOTES AND QUESTIONS

1. The devise in the *Brody* case can be restated as follows: T devises property "to my children for their lives, then to my grandchildren for their lives and upon the death of the survivor of my children and grandchildren equally to my great-grandchildren."

2. The court refers to the testator's children as lives in being. Under the common law rule, a nonvested interest is good under the Rule only if there is some life (or lives) in being at the creation of the interest[4] within whose life or within twenty-one years of whose death there is absolute certainty the nonvested interest will vest or fail to vest. While the testator's children are lives in being, they are not lives in being within twenty-one years of whose death there is *absolute certainty* the remainder gift to the great-grandchildren will vest or fail. In other words, they are not lives that validate the future interest in the great-grandchildren. Can you construct a scenario that would demonstrate how the remainder in the great-grandchildren might vest too remotely?

It is not essential that the validating measuring lives be mentioned in the governing instrument. For example, if T devises Blackacre "to such of my grandchildren as attain the age of twenty-one" the gift is valid under the Rule

---

4. Interests created by deed are deemed created at the time of delivery; interests created by will are deemed created at the time of the testator's death.

even though more grandchildren of T may be born after T dies. Do you see why? If you are having difficulty, ask yourself whether there is any life or lives in being at T's death within twenty-one years of whose death there is *absolute certainty* the gift to the grandchildren who reach twenty-one will vest or fail.

Suppose O deeded Blackacre "to such of my grandchildren as attain the age of twenty-one" and at the time of the conveyance O has no grandchildren. Is the gift to the grandchild valid under the common law Rule?

3.   The *Brody* case is unusual in applying what is known as the doctrine of "infectious invalidity." In other words, the court voids the grandchildren's interest even though that interest does not violate the Rule. Not to do so, the court concluded, would result in a disposition of the testator's property inconsistent with the testator's overall estate plan. Do you agree with the court?

4.   A nonvested interest is valid under the Rule if it must timely vest. For this purpose, a vested remainder subject to open vests when the class closes; a contingent remainder in a class vests when the class closes *and* all conditions precedent for each and every member of the class occur; a springing executory interest vests when the interest becomes possessory, and a shifting executory interest vests when it either becomes possessory or becomes a vested remainder. See generally Kurtz, The Iowa Rule Against Perpetuities: A State of Little or No Law, 65 Iowa L.Rev. 177 (1979).

In each of the following dispositions, what interests are not vested from the moment of their creation and do they, if they are not vested, violate the common-law Rule?

(a) T devises property to A for life and upon A's death to such of A's grandchildren as attain the age of twenty-one.

(b) T devises property to A's grandchildren who reach the age of twenty-one. At T's death A and three grandchildren of A survive T. The oldest grandchild is age 15. If A's oldest grandchild at T's death was age 23 rather than age 15, how would that change the analysis?

(c) O conveys Blackacre to his son for life and upon his son's death to his son's widow for her life and upon the death of the survivor of his son and his son's widow to such of their issue as shall then be living. At the time of the conveyance the son and his wife, Alice, are then living.

(d) T devises Blackacre to such of his grandchildren who are living at the time T's will is admitted to probate. T dies survived by three children and two grandchildren. Would the results change if all of T's children predeceased T?

5.   The court in the *Brody* case notes that under the terms of the testator's will the testator did not bequeath each grandchild a separate life estate in a separate share that would terminate at his or her death in favor of his or her children. If the will had done so, however, the gift to the children of each grandchild who survived the testator would have been valid under the subclass exception. This exception can be illustrated as follows: Suppose T devises property to X in trust to pay the income to A for life and upon A's death to pay the income to each of A's surviving children for life and, as each

child of A who survives A dies, to distribute the share of corpus proportionate to the number of children that survived A to such child's issue. If A and three children of A, namely, B, C and D, survived T, the effect of this disposition is that three separate trusts are created: a trust for A for life, then for B for life, remainder to B's issue; a trust for A for life, then for C for life, remainder to C's issue; and a trust for A for life, then for D for life, remainder to D's issue. If A dies survived by a child E, born after T died, the remainder in favor of the issue of E is void. Do you see why?

6. The court in the *Brody* case specifically rejects the application of the wait-and-see analytical approach. Under the wait-and-see approach a nonvested interest is good if it *actually vests* or fails to vest within the lives in being plus twenty-one year period. Wait-and-see was first judicially adopted in New Hampshire. See, Merchants National Bank v. Curtis, 98 N.H. 225, 97 A.2d 207 (1953). Other jurisdictions have followed the New Hampshire lead by statute or case law.

To illustrate wait-and-see, suppose O deeds property to A for life, then to A's children who attain age 25. Under the common-law Rule, the contingent remainder in A's children who attain age 25 is void because of the possibility that A might die survived by one or more children under age four who could not, of course, be guaranteed to reach (or fail to reach) age 25 within 21 years of A's death. But suppose that A's youngest child living at A's death was over age 4. Under wait-and-see the contingent remainder is good because it will vest or fail no later than 21 years after A dies.

Let's try another example. Suppose T dies and under T's will, T bequeaths her entire estate to A "when A's will is probated." A's interest is classified as a springing executory interest. Do you see why? Because A's interest is a springing executory interest, for purposes of the Rule, it vests when A's interest becomes possessory. Because we do not know when T's will might be probated, it is possible (albeit unlikely) that A's interest will become possessory more than 21 years after A's death and the death of any other individual alive at T's death. But, because A's interest in not subject to a survivorship contingency, if A is deceased when T's will is probated, A's interest would become possessory (i.e, vest) in A's estate. Since it is possible for A's interest to vest more than 21 years after A's death and the death of any other individual alive at T's death, it is void under the Rule. Alternatively, under wait-and-see, A's interest is good so long as T's will is actually probated within A's lifetime or within 21 years of A's death.

The *Brody* court specifically refuses to validate the gift to the great-grandchildren under the wait-and-see analytical approach. What facts, if they turn out to be true, would establish that the great-grandchildren's interest timely vests or fails under the wait-and-see rule?

Jurisdictions that follow wait-and-see must also resolve whose lives may be taken into account to determine the validity of a nonvested interest. Two distinct statutory approaches are reflected in the various state statutes. Under Ky.Rev.Stat.Ann. § 381.216 (Baldwin 1985) any life can be a measuring life if such life is *causally related* to the vesting or failing of the interest. A life is causally related if such life has some effect on the vesting or failing of the nonvested interest. Under Iowa Code § 558.68 (1985) a list of statutory measuring lives is compiled. This list might include lives not causally related to the vesting or failing of a nonvested interest. The Iowa statute is modeled after the Restatement (Second) of Property § 1.3 (Tent.Draft No. 2 1979). See Kurtz, The Iowa Rule Against Perpetuities—Reform At Last, Restatement Style: Wait–and–See and Cy Pres, 69 Iowa L.Rev. 705 (1984).

The Commissioners on Uniform State Laws have adopted the Uniform Statutory Rule Against Perpetuities which also appears as sections 2–901–906 of the Uniform Probate Code. This rule has been adopted in Alaska, Arizona, California, Colorado, Connecticut, District of Columbia, Georgia, Hawaii, Indiana, Kansas, Massachusetts, Michigan, Minnesota, Montana, Nebraska, Nevada, New Jersey, New Mexico, North Carolina, North Dakota, Oregon, South Carolina, South Dakota, Tennessee, Utah, Virginia, Washington and West Virginia. It validates a nonvested interest that is certain to vest within the common law perpetuity period and an interest that might not vest, but actually vests or terminates, within 90 years after the interest is created. This 90 year period, therefore, is akin to the wait-and-see reform. Nonvested interests that cannot vest within the 90 year period can be reformed "in a manner that most closely approximates the transferor's manifested plan of distribution" to avoid invalidity. Unif. Prob. Code § 2–903. See generally Waggoner, The Uniform Statutory Rule Against Perpetuities, 21 Real Prop. Prob. & Tr. J. 569 (1986). For criticism of the Uniform Act, see Bloom, Perpetuities Refinement: There is an Alternative, 62 Wash. L. Rev. 23 (1987); Dukeminier, The Uniform Statutory Rule Against Perpetuities: Ninety Years in Limbo, 34 UCLA L. Rev. 1023 (1987).

7. In addition to the wait-and-see reforms, many jurisdictions have adopted the cy pres reform. See, e.g., Fla.Stat. § 689.22(2) (1983); Iowa Code § 558.68 (1985); Ohio Rev.Code Ann. § 2131.08 (Baldwin 1978). Under cy pres a court can reform a nonvested interest to assure that it will timely vest or fail to vest. For example, if O conveys property to A for life and upon A's death to such of A's children that attain age 25, the remainder is void under the common law Rule. If the remainder had been limited to A's children who attain age twenty-one, the remainder would be good. Thus, a court, in exercise of its cy pres power, might reduce the age contingency from twenty-five to twenty-one if necessary to assure that the remainder will timely vest or fail under the Rule.

8. In recent years a number of states and the District of Columbia have either abolished the rule or expanded significantly upon the concept of a 90–year term. States that have abolished the rule include: Arizona, Colorado, Delaware (for trusts of personalty), Idaho, Illinois, Maine, Maryland, Missouri, Nebraska, New Hampshire, New Jersey, Ohio, Rhode Island, South Dakota, Virginia, and Wisconsin. Alaska allows a trust for 1,000 years, Delaware (110 years for trusts of realty), Florida for 360 years, Nevada for 365 years, Utah for 1,000 years, Washington for 150 years and Wyoming for 1,000 years. Why don't these latter states simply abolish the rule?

9. Violations of the Rule Against Perpetuities have proved to be a fertile source for litigation to adjudicate the validity of property interests and to establish attorney malpractice. In the infamous case of Lucas v. Hamm, 56 Cal.2d 583, 15 Cal.Rptr. 821, 364 P.2d 685 (1961), cert. denied 368 U.S. 987

(1962), the California Supreme Court held that as a matter of law an attorney could not be liable in malpractice for drafting a will that violated the Rule.[5] In Wright v. Williams, 47 Cal.App.3d 802, 809 n. 2, 121 Cal.Rptr. 194, 199 n. 2 (1975), however, a lower California court stated that "[T]here is reason to doubt that the ultimate conclusion of Lucas v. Hamm is valid in today's state of the art. Draftsmanship to avoid the rule against perpetuities seems no longer esoteric."

Subsequently, the Iowa Supreme Court addressed the issue of when the statute of limitations on an action for malpractice would run against an attorney who prepared a will that violated the Rule. The attorney argued that the cause of action commenced on the date of the testator's death on the theory that everyone knows the law; therefore the beneficiaries of the void interest should have known as of the testator's death that their interest was void. The beneficiaries argued that the statute of limitations ran from the date they first actually learned the will violated the Rule. The court held the statute ran from the date of the testator's death. Millwright v. Romer, 322 N.W.2d 30 (Iowa 1982). In a sharp dissent, Justice Harris stated: "In all respects, the basis for the majority holding escapes me. Question: How do we bar a claim that a lawyer was negligent for misunderstanding the rule against perpetuities? Answer: By pretending lay persons understand it." Id. at 34.

10. In a complete departure from the law of any state, statutory or judicial, the Third Restatement (calling into question the proper role of a restatement) adopts a novel approach to the Rule. In lieu of tying the Rule to the timely vesting of an interest, it focuses exclusively on timely termination. It provides in Section 27.1:

(a) A trust or other donative transfer is subject to judicial modification under § 27.2 to the extent that the trust or other disposition does not terminate on or before the expiration of the perpetuity period, except that if, upon the expiration of the perpetuity period, the share of a beneficiary is distributable upon reaching a specified age and the beneficiary is then younger than the earlier of the specified age or the age of 30, the beneficiary's share may, without judicial modification, be retained in trust until the beneficiary reaches or dies before reaching the earlier of the specified age or the age of 30.

(b) The perpetuity period expires at the death of the last living measuring life. The measuring lives are as follows:

(1) Except as otherwise provided in paragraph (2), the measuring lives constitute a group composed of the following individuals: the transferor, the beneficiaries of the disposition who are related to the transferor and no more than two generations younger than the transferor, and the beneficiaries of the disposition who are unrelated to the transferor and no more than the equivalent of two generations younger than the transferor.

(2) In the case of a trust or other property arrangement for the sole current benefit of a named individual who is more than two generations

---

5. In reflecting on this case an English commentator has stated: "[I]t is to be hoped that on the standard of professional competence ... [Lucas v. Hamm] will prove to be a slur on the profession which, like the mule, will display neither pride of ancestry nor hope of posterity." Megarry, Comment, 81 L.Q.Rev. 478, 481 (1965).

younger than the transferor or more than the equivalent of two generations younger than the transferor, the measuring life is the named individual.

How would this apply in the context of a gift or bequest of a legal estate in Blackacre? For example, suppose O conveys Blackacre to B and his heir thirty years from now? At common law, B's interest was void because there was no "guaranty" it would vest within the lifetime of B or any other person living when B's springing executory interest is created. But, if it is to be valid under the Third Restatement, it is not because it timely terminates, but rather because it becomes a fee simple absolute in a timely manner, i.e., the time period specified in subsection (b)(1).

For the Third Restatement to become law anywhere, states would have to abandon the Statutory Rule Against Perpetuities, as well as doctrines relating to wait-and-see and cy pres—a tall order.

HANSEN v. STROECKER

Supreme Court of Alaska (1985).
699 P.2d 871.

MATTHEWS, JUSTICE.

On December 31, 1971, James B. Hansen and W.G. Stroecker signed an agreement entitled "Option to Purchase."[6] Under the terms of the agreement, Stroecker paid $1,500.00 to Hansen in exchange for an option to purchase some seven parcels....

The agreement does not state when the option was to be exercised. Further, it does not state who was to have the property surveyed so that the parcels' price per square foot could be calculated....

Hansen died on June 20, 1976. Stroecker had the property surveyed in July of 1980 and on August 25, 1980, he sent a check for the balance of

---

6. The agreement provides in relevant part:

James B. Hansen, the undersigned, for and in consideration of the sum of $1,500.00 in hand paid by W.G. Stroecker, the receipt of which is hereby acknowledged, does by these presents grant to said W.G. Stroecker an option to purchase the following described tract of land situated in Section 5, Township 9 South Range 10 East Fairbanks Meredian [sic] in the Fairbanks Recording District, Fourth Judicial District, State of Alaska.

The total purchase price to be determined after the calculation of engineering data determining the total area in square feet. The total purchase price to be calculated on the following basis:

$500.00 for each of two 150′ X 100′ foot lots fronting 100′ directly on the slough, surplusage if any in frontage on the river to be calculated and added to purchase price at the rate of $.0333 per square foot. The tier of lots next adjoining the river frontage lots also measuring 150′ X 100′ their price to be $250.00 for each lot. Any additional land lying westerly of these four lots and bounded by the East boundary of the Old Richardson Highway to be purchased at the rate of $0.1667 per square foot.

It is to be understood, however, that any land lying southerly of the south boundary line of the lots hereinabove specified, (said South boundary lines running parallel with the E–W quarter section line) and being bounded to the southwest by the Old Richardson Highway and on easterly side bounded by the first course of the tract of land herein optioned, the same being triangular in shape is to be conveyed to the optionee without payment of a purchase price, and is a gift.

A rough sketch map is attached hereto to aid in clarrification [sic] of the intent of the parties.

Terms of the purchaser [sic]: cash upon delivery of a warranty deed containing an acceptable legal description; the $1,500.00 delivered herewith to be applied on the purchase price.

This option shall be binding upon the heirs devisees and assigns of the parties herein.

the purchase price, $1,028.00, to the attorney for Mrs. Hansen. Mrs. Hansen refused to deliver to Stroecker a deed to the property. Stroecker brought this action for specific performance of the agreement.

Stroecker moved for summary judgment. Mrs. Hansen opposed on the grounds that the agreement was void because it violated the rule against perpetuities and that the agreement could not be enforced because Stroecker had unreasonably delayed his exercise of the option. The superior court granted Stroecker's motion and ordered Mrs. Hansen to deliver to Stroecker a deed for the property. Stroecker moved, as the prevailing party, for an award of attorney's fees. The court, without explanation, denied this motion. Both parties appealed. Hansen seeks to have this court reverse the decision on the merits, while Stroecker urges a remand on the issue of attorney's fees.

The trial court concluded that the agreement was not an option but a real estate contract which conveyed a vested interest to Stroecker when the contract was signed. The court therefore found there to be no violation of the rule against perpetuities. In our view, the court's conclusion that the contract was a real estate contract rather than an option depends upon the resolution of conflicting extrinsic evidence which can be accomplished only at trial. However, it is unnecessary to remand for a trial because, assuming that the contract is an option, it does not violate the variant of the rule against perpetuities which we conclude was effective in this case.

The rule against perpetuities, in its general common law form, is this: "No interest is good unless it must vest, if at all, not later than twenty-one years after some life in being at the creation of the interest." Gray, Rule Against Perpetuities § 201 (4th Ed.1942). The interest in question must be examined as of the time of its creation; it must be certain to vest within the period of perpetuities. Leach, Perpetuities in a Nutshell, 51 Harv.L.Rev. 638, 642 (1938). Thus, if anything might happen, no matter how unlikely, which would cause the interest to vest later than twenty-one years after the death of all lives in being at the creation of the interest, the interest is void. Id. at 643.

Under this traditional approach, it is clear that options "in gross"[7] to purchase real estate violate the rule against perpetuities when the time for their exercise is not limited to the period of perpetuities. See Restatement of Property § 393 (1944); 5 Powell on Real Property ¶ 771[2], at 73 (1980); Annot., 66 A.L.R.3d 1294, 1296 (1975). In this case the agreement, viewed most favorably to Mrs. Hansen, creates an option in gross which was not by its terms required to be exercised within the period of

---

7. An option "in gross" is one which is not connected with a present interest in the questioned property. 5 Powell on Real Property ¶ 771[2] (1980). Options in gross should be distinguished from other types of options which are connected to an estate in land. An example would be an option to purchase real property at the end of a leasehold estate. Such options are generally held not to violate the rule against perpetuities. See Restatement of Property § 395 (1944).

perpetuities. It therefore would be void under the traditional conception of the rule against perpetuities.

Stroecker urges us, however, to apply AS 34.27.010. This provision, enacted in 1983, provides: In determining if an interest would violate the rule against perpetuities, the period of perpetuities shall be measured by actual rather than possible events. However, the period of perpetuities may not be measured by a life whose continuance does not have a causal relationship to the vesting or failure of the interest. An interest that would violate the rule against perpetuities as modified by this section shall be reformed, within the limits of that rule, to approximate most closely the intention of the creator of the interest. The first two sentences of this statute adopt an approach to the rule commonly referred to as "wait-and-see." The last sentence gives the court the power to reform interests, which is known as "cy pres." The wait-and-see approach requires the court to judge an interest's validity by what actually happens, rather than what might happen. Thus, if AS 34.27.010 applies to this case, the option will not violate the rule, since it was actually exercised in 1980, well within the period of perpetuities.

However, AS 34.27.010 does not apply here because of AS 01.10.090,[8] which prohibits retrospective application of a statute unless clearly provided for by the statute. . . .

Even though the statutory wait-and-see approach does not apply to this case, this does not mean that the general common law approach must. We have never had occasion to adopt the general rule against perpetuities and are not precluded from adopting the wait-and-see approach.

Several courts from other states have adopted or used wait-and-see in at least a limited sense. Merchants Nat. Bank v. Curtis, 98 N.H. 225, 97 A.2d 207, 212 (1953); Warner v. Whitman, 353 Mass. 468, 233 N.E.2d 14, 16–17 (1968); Phelps v. Shropshire, 254 Miss. 777, 183 So.2d 158, 161–62 (1966); Grynberg v. Amerada Hess Corp., 342 F.Supp. 1314, 1321–22 (D.Colo.1972) (applying Mississippi law); Story v. First National Bank & Trust Co., 115 Fla. 436, 156 So. 101, 104–06 (1934). Other courts have adopted a cy pres approach, exhibiting willingness to reform instruments to comply with the rule. See In re Estate of Chun Quan Yee Hop, 52 Hawaii 40, 469 P.2d 183 (1970) (adoption of cy pres); In re Foster's Estate, 190 Kan. 498, 376 P.2d 784 (1962) (excision of part of will which would invalidate gift); Carter v. Berry, 243 Miss. 321, 140 So.2d 843 (Miss.1962) (limited cy pres—reduction of the age contingency).

In Curtis, the New Hampshire Supreme Court could see no harm in the wait-and-see approach: There is no logical justification for deciding the problem as of the date of the death of the testator on facts that might have happened rather than facts which actually happened. It is difficult to see how the public welfare is threatened by a vesting that might have been postponed beyond the period of perpetuities but actually was not. 97 A.2d at 212. The Massachusetts Supreme Court in Warner, a case similar to

---

8. AS 01.10.090 states: "No statute is retrospective unless expressly declared therein."

this one, applied Massachusetts's limited wait-and-see statute[9] retroactively, even though the statute applied prospectively only. The court explained:

> Although the statute operates prospectively, the Legislature has clearly expressed the policy of the Commonwealth and we feel that this court is justified in applying that policy to the provisions under consideration.

> The policy behind the rule against perpetuities is not violated if the trust instrument is given the construction we have placed on it. Property was not in fact tied up beyond the period of the rule. 233 N.E.2d at 17.

The authors of the Restatement (Second) of Property endorse the wait-and-see approach even though they acknowledge that it is "the present minority view." Restatement (Second) of Property § 1.4 (1981). The primary reason they favor wait-and-see is that the traditional approach voids reasonable limitations that would, in fact, vest within the period of perpetuities. See id. at Reporter's Note. Further, bad limitations easily can be made "good" by a skilled draftsman who includes a savings clause providing that all limitations in the instrument must vest within twenty-one years after the death of the lives in being at the creation of the instrument. Thus, all the general rule does is to put a premium on skilled draftsmanship, while unfairly trapping and punishing the uninitiated.

> The adoption of the wait-and-see approach in this Restatement is largely motivated by the equality of treatment that is produced by placing the validity of all non-vested interests on the same plane, whether the interest is created by a skilled draftsman or one not so skilled.

Id., introductory note at 13.

We are persuaded by these authorities that the wait-and-see approach should be adopted as the common law rule against perpetuities in Alaska. Therefore, the agreement in this case is not void, because Stroecker exercised his option well within the period of perpetuities. The superior court's conclusion that the agreement was not void is therefore sustained.

NOTES AND QUESTIONS

1. In United Virginia Bank/Citizens & Marine v. Union Oil Co., 214 Va. 48, 197 S.E.2d 174 (1973), a suit was brought to determine the validity of an option to purchase certain real estate for 120 days to begin "at the time the City of Newport News, Virginia acquires the right of way of Boxley Boulevard Extension and new U.S. 60." Id. at 49, 197 S.E.2d at 175. In holding the option void under the common-law Rule the court stated:

---

9. Mass.Gen.Laws Ann. ch. 184A, § 1 (West 1977) provides: In applying the rule against perpetuities to an interest in real or personal property limited to take effect at or after the termination of one or more life estates in, or lives of, persons in being when the period of said rule commences to run, the validity of the interest shall be determined on the basis of facts existing at the termination of such one or more life estates or lives.

Sanford argues, however, that it was "the dominant intent" of the parties to the option agreement that the city would acquire the rights-of-way in question, if at all, within a reasonable time and that such time "under the circumstances of this case is less than 21 years." This being true, Sanford asserts, we should exercise the *cy pres* power of the judiciary and imply into the terms of the option agreement a provision that the contingency of the city's acquisition of the rights-of-way would occur within a reasonable time not more than 21 years from the date of the agreement. This, Sanford concludes, would effectuate the intention of the parties and avoid a construction of the agreement which would violate the rule against perpetuities.

The answer to his argument is three-fold. In the first place, "the dominant intent" Sanford refers to does not appear from the option agreement itself or from any other source. Secondly, the asserted intent related to acts which parties other than those privy to the agreement must perform to bring about occurrence of the agreed contingency. So whatever may have been the intent of the contracting parties, it is of little moment. Lastly, assuming, without deciding, that the power of *cy pres* is otherwise available in a case such as this, it may not be employed in Virginia as a vehicle to alter an agreement so as to evade the rule against perpetuities. 214 Va. at 52, 197 S.E.2d at 177.

2. Some courts take the view that the common-law Rule Against Perpetuities does not apply to a right of first refusal. For example, in Old Port Cove Holdings, Inc. v. Old Port Cove Condominium Ass'n One, Inc., 986 So.2d 1279 (Fla. 2008) the court upheld a first refusal right against the claim it was void under the Rule Against Perpetuities on the grounds that such a right creates neither a legal or equitable interest in property but is merely a "contractual right." The court reasoned that the Rule is a rule of property law not contract law. Would you agree with this reasoning?

3. Section 2–904 of the Uniform Probate Code expressly provides that the Statutory Rule Against Perpetuities is inapplicable to nonvested interests arising out of a nondonative transfer. While there are limited exceptions to this exclusion, Section 2–904 would encompass arms' length negotiated options for consideration. A similar approach is taken by Restatement (Third) of Property, § 27.3 (2011).

CHAPTER 5

CONCURRENT ESTATES

■ ■ ■

§ 5.1 INTRODUCTION

In Chapter 4 we considered, among other things, some consequences flowing from the fact that two or more persons had *successive* interests in the same property. This chapter focuses on problems arising because two or more persons have *concurrent* interests in the same property. A "concurrent interest" exists "whenever two or more persons have a concurrent and equal right to the possession and use of the same parcel of land."[1] At common law there were five types of concurrent estates. For all practical purposes, only three of these survive in the United States, namely, the tenancy in common, the joint tenancy with right of survivorship ("joint tenants"), and the tenancy by the entirety.[2]

Where two or more persons hold title as tenants in common, each tenant is equally entitled to the right to possess all of the property subject to the tenancy. In other words, each co-tenant has an undivided interest in the whole. Each co-tenant has an interest that is alienable during his life, devisable by his will, and descendible to his heirs should he die intestate owning such interest. Persons can be tenants in common without regard to whether they acquired their interest at the same time and under the same instrument. Furthermore, tenants in common need not necessarily have an equal interest in the property.

Conversely, at common law, joint tenants with right of survivorship were persons having a concurrent interest in property whose interest also satisfied the so-called four unities test. The four unities were:

---

1. W. Stoebuck & D. Whitman, The Law of Property, 3rd ed. § 5.1 at 176 (2000).

2. The other common law concurrent estates were the tenancy in coparcenary (where two or more persons inherited by intestate succession interests in land) and tenancy in partnership.

The former estate was similar to a tenancy in common in that each tenant had an interest that passed to his heirs at his death. At common law, coparceners were daughters. If the intestate died survived by a son (or a representative of the son) the son would take the entire estate under the laws of primogeniture.

The latter estate, the tenancy in partnership, was necessitated by the common law prohibition against partnerships holding title to real estate. The need for this tenancy has been eliminated by the Uniform Partnership Act and similar statutes.

Another form of concurrent ownership is community property. See Chapter 6.

Unity:	Meaning:
Time	Joint tenants acquired their concurrent interests at the same time.
Title	Joint tenants acquired their concurrent interests under the same instrument.
Interest	Each joint tenant had an identical percentage share of the concurrent estate.
Possession	Each joint tenant had an identical share respecting duration, quality and right to possession.

In some states, statutes have either abolished or modified the four unities test relating to the joint tenancy. See, e.g., Wis. Stat. § 700.19(5) (abolishing the common-law requirements of unity of title and time). In others the test has been judicially abolished in favor of an "intent test," meaning that if the parties intended to create a joint tenancy, it is not necessary that the four unities test be met. See In re Estate of Bates, 492 N.W.2d 704 (Iowa App. 1992).

The critical difference between a tenancy in common and a joint tenancy with right of survivorship is the "right of survivorship." Unlike tenants in common who each have an interest that is alienable, devisable, and descendible, joint tenants have an interest that is alienable but is *not* devisable or descendible. Thus, if two persons own real property as joint tenants with a right of survivorship and one joint tenant dies, the survivor owns the entire property in fee simple, assuming that the joint tenancy was never severed as a result of a lifetime alienation. The survivor owns the entire interest in fee simple not because he or she inherited the interests of the deceased joint tenant but because as each joint tenant dies, his interest in the property is extinguished. This survivorship feature of the joint tenancy with right of survivorship continues to make this form of concurrent ownership very popular. This is particularly so for married persons where the surviving spouse becomes sole owner of the joint tenancy property when the first spouse dies without the need to probate the deceased spouse's will or commence an administration of the first spouse's estate. Unfortunately, there are certain adverse death and income tax consequences associated with joint tenancies. See, Int. Rev.Code. §§ 1014; 2040.

During the existence of a joint tenancy with right of survivorship, each joint tenant has an alienable interest. If the right to alienate is exercised the alienation severs the joint tenancy and converts it into a tenancy in common between the transferee and the other co-tenant(s). Therefore, the effect of a severance is to terminate the right of survivorship with respect to that part that is severed. Where there are three or more joint tenants, alienation by one severs that joint tenant's undivided interest from the joint tenancy but the remaining joint tenants continue to hold their remaining interest, as among themselves, as joint tenants with right of survivorship.

If a grantor or testator conveyed or devised property to two or more persons who were not married to each other, at common law it was presumed that a joint tenancy with right of survivorship was intended.[3] This presumption does not prevail in the majority of states today.[4] Rather, a majority of states by statute presume that, unless the conveyance or will otherwise provides, a conveyance to two or more persons creates a tenancy in common. Likewise, when property passes by intestacy to two or more heirs, the property passes to the heirs as tenants in common. While the evidence is scanty why the common law preference for joint tenancy was abandoned, it has been suggested that the change reflected the probable intent of the grantor.[5]

The most effective method to create a joint tenancy with right of survivorship is by a conveyance or devise to "A and B as joint tenants with right of survivorship and not as tenants in common." Other formulae may give rise to a dispute whether a joint tenancy or tenancy in common was intended.

A tenancy by the entirety is a form of joint tenancy that, in addition to the four unities mentioned above, requires the unity of marriage as well. Thus, this tenancy can only be created in persons married to each other. Because this tenancy cannot be unilaterally severed, the right of survivorship is effectively indestructible.[6] The tenancy by the entirety exists in about half of the states[7] in its pristine or some modified form. In other states it has been abolished. Where these tenancies have been abolished a conveyance of a concurrent estate to a husband and wife creates either a tenancy in common or a joint tenancy with right of survivorship.[8]

NOTES AND QUESTIONS

1. O conveys Blackacre "to A and B, jointly." State the title. See *Montgomery v. Clarkson*, 585 S.W.2d 483 (Mo.1979).

2. In 2010, A and B own Blackacre as joint tenants with right of survivorship. In 2011, A conveys all of his right, title and interest in Blackacre to C. After this conveyance, what is the state of the title? Michigan recognizes two types of joint tenancies: the ordinary joint tenancy and the joint tenancy with "full rights of survivorship." In the latter joint tenancy, the tenants have concurrent life estates and each of them has a contingent remainder that ripens into a fee simple in whichever of them survives. The survivorship

---

3. 2 Amer.L.Prop. § 6.1, n.16 (A.J. Casner ed. 1952). A joint tenancy, however, did not arise by inheritance. The concurrent estate that arose at common law by inheritance was the tenancy in coparcenary.

4. Id. at § 5.3.

5. 1 Am.Jurist & L.Mag. 77 (1829).

6. The tenancy by the entirety can be severed if *both* spouses convey the property to a third party.

7. States recognizing the tenancy by the entirety include: Alaska, Arkansas, Delaware, District of Columbia, Florida, Hawaii, Illinois, Indiana, Kentucky, Maryland, Massachusetts, Michigan, Mississippi, Missouri, New Jersey, New York, North Carolina, Oklahoma, Oregon, Pennsylvania, Rhode Island, Tennessee, Vermont, Virginia, and Wyoming.

8. See Chapter 6, infra.

feature of this joint tenancy is not extinguished if either joint tenant conveys his interest to a third person who takes subject to the contingent remainder. See, Albro v. Allen, 434 Mich. 271, 454 N.W.2d 85 (1990). See also Sanderson v. Saxon, 834 S.W.2d 676 (Ky.1992) (joint tenant cannot defeat survivor's interest by lifetime conveyance of her interest).

3. In 2008, O conveys Blackacre to A, B and C, as joint tenants with right of survivorship and not as tenants in common. In 2010, A conveys all of his rights in Blackacre to D. B dies in 2012 survived by X who would be B's sole heir if B died intestate. In fact B died testate leaving his entire estate to Y. D, X, Y and C all survive B. State the title. Cf. Giles v. Sheridan, 179 Neb. 257, 137 N.W.2d 828 (1965).

4. In 2008, O conveys Blackacre to A, B and C, as joint tenants with right of survivorship. In 2010, A conveys all of her rights in Blackacre to B. What is the state of the title? See Rendle v. Wiemeyer, 374 Mich. 30, 131 N.W.2d 45 (1964), rehearing denied 374 Mich. 30, 132 N.W.2d 606 (1965); Jackson v. O'Connell, 23 Ill.2d 52, 177 N.E.2d 194 (1961).

5. In 2008, O conveys Blackacre to A, B and C, as joint tenants with right of survivorship. In 2012, A and B exchange deeds in which A conveys all of her rights in Blackacre to B and B conveys all of his rights in Blackacre to A. What is the state of the title?

6. In 2008, O conveys Blackacre to A and B, as joint tenants with right of survivorship. In 2011, A conveys to A and C. What are the respective interests of A, B and C in Blackacre? See, Johnson v. MacIntyre, 356 Md. 471, 740 A.2d 599 (1999).

7. O owned Blackacre in fee simple absolute in 2011. In that year, O conveyed Blackacre to O and A as joint tenants with right of survivorship. Is this conveyance effective to create a joint tenancy between O and A? See, W. Stoebuck, & D. Whitman, The Law of Property, 3rd ed. § 5.3 at 187 (2000). See also Mass. Gen. Laws Ann. ch. 184, § 8 (West 1977); Strout v. Burgess, 144 Me. 263, 68 A.2d 241 (1949).

8. Tenants in common, unlike joint tenants, do not *necessarily* have the same percentage interest in the property, although ordinarily they will. For example, if O dies intestate survived by two children, A and B, each of them has a fifty percent interest in any property they inherit as tenants in common. On the other hand, if A and B purchase Blackacre as tenants in common and A contributes sixty percent of the purchase price and B forty percent of the purchase price, they have 60–40 shares in Blackacre unless they otherwise agree to a different division. The fact that tenants in common have different percentage interests in the estate does not affect their individual rights to the possession of the whole although it may affect other sticks in their bundle of ownership rights. As noted in Garcia v. Andrus, 692 F.2d 89, 92 (9th Cir.1982):

> [T]he percentage of ownership has nothing to do with the right of possession. That is, a one-third owner has the right to possess the entire parcel, just as the two-thirds owner does.

> However, numerous other elements of control do follow the percentage of ownership. For example, if a co-tenant obtains a loan and mortgages the

property, he is able to mortgage only his percentage ownership interest. If one co-tenant rents the whole property to a third party, he must share the proceeds with his co-tenants in accordance with their respective percentages of ownership.... Thus, sharing of benefits that flow from the land, other than the right of possession of each co-tenant, generally follows the percentage of ownership in the land.

§ 5.2   RIGHTS OF CO–TENANTS AS BETWEEN THEMSELVES

CUMMINGS v. ANDERSON

Supreme Court of Washington, En Banc (1980).
94 Wash.2d 135, 614 P.2d 1283.

ROSELLINI, JUSTICE.

In September 1973, the petitioner and the respondent, contemplating marriage, bought the purchaser's interest in a contract for the sale of a single-family residence in Enumclaw and assumed the obligations of the underlying contract. They paid $2,500 for the assignment of the purchaser's interest. The contract called for monthly payments of $150, including interest, and the payment of the balance in full on or before August 1, 1975. It provided for forfeiture upon default.

The assignment was made to the petitioner and the respondent as tenants in common, and, according to the testimony of the attorney who advised them in this transaction, they intended to acquire the property as equal owners.

The evidence showed that both parties contributed to the down payment, neither of them having assets sufficient to pay for the interest which they bought from the purchaser. They used their separate funds for a part of it and obtained a loan for the balance. From the circumstances, it is evident that they planned to pay the balance owed on the real estate contract, as well as the balance of the loan, with community funds which would belong to both of them. From these facts, it can be inferred that they intended to contribute equally in the purchase of the property.

The respondent in her answer to the petition tacitly acknowledges that the obligations of the parties were equal.

In February 1974, the parties were married. They lived in the residence, with the petitioner's two teenaged children and the respondent's four younger children, until August 1974, when the respondent left the home, taking her children and substantially all of the community personalty, including the cash in the joint bank account. She was granted a default dissolution in March 1975, the decree making no disposition of the property of the parties.

At the time of the respondent's departure from the residence, the parties had paid $2,828.92 toward the purchase of the property and $16,350.16 remained to be paid. They had no discussion regarding their rights in the property or their future obligations. The respondent did not communicate with the petitioner and made no offer to participate in making the payments necessary for acquisition of the property, nor did she assert a right to occupy the property or to receive rent for the petitioner's occupancy of it. He remained in possession and continued to make the payments under the contract, paying also the taxes and insurance premiums. At the time this action was brought, he had reduced the unpaid balance to $8,763.85. He had arranged with the sellers to assume their mortgage obligations instead of paying the full balance of the purchase price in August 1975.

Shortly before the final payment became due under the original contract, the respondent, who had remarried after the dissolution, offered to purchase the petitioner's interest in the contract for the sum of $1,000. This offer was rejected. She then brought this suit for partition, claiming a one-half interest in the purchaser's equity, and demanding one-half of the rental value of the premises during the period that the residence had been occupied by the petitioner alone.

At the trial, the respondent testified she had left the premises to protect her children from involvement in and observation of the sexual activities of the petitioner's son, then in his early teens. She said that she had told the petitioner that one of them would have to leave, and he had said it would have to be her. His testimony was that she had left the home without notice and without explanation. She did not contend that her departure had been occasioned by any conduct or omission of the petitioner.

The trial court found that the respondent had not been ousted by the petitioner. Because the evidence was uncertain with respect to the contributions made by the parties prior to the respondent's departure, the court found that their contributions had been equal. It further found that the respondent had made her own division of the property when she took with her the bulk of the community personalty, which the court found to have a value in excess of $1,400, and that she had abandoned her interest in the real property, as well as her obligations under the contract of purchase. Its judgment quieted title to the purchasers' interest in the petitioner, and ordered that he obtain a release of the respondent from any liability under the real estate contract.

The Court of Appeals, Division One, affirmed the lower court's finding that there had been no ouster of the respondent, as well as its conclusion that the petitioner was not obliged to pay rent for his exclusive occupancy of the premises. It held, however, that the interests of the parties in the property were fixed as of the date of their purchase of the vendee's interest and their assumption of the contract obligations. Accordingly, it awarded the respondent a one-half interest in the purchasers' equity, allowing the petitioner a lien on that interest for one-half of the amount which he had paid out in maintaining the contract, one-half of the value of improvements which he had made, and one-half of the value of the community personal property taken by the respondent.

It is agreed that the parties' interest in this property was held as tenants in common. The petitioner urges that the court was in error in holding that the respondent had acquired a one-half interest in the purchasers' equity, which was not affected by her subsequent abandonment of her obligations under the contract. He argues that, because the survival of the purchasers' interest depended upon the fulfillment of the obligations under the contract, the respondent's abandonment of those obligations manifested an intent to also abandon any interest which she had acquired as of that date. Alternatively he argues that, even if it cannot be said that she abandoned her existing interest as of that date, that interest was proportionate to her investment in the property, and she acquired no further interest thereafter.

The respondent, on the other hand, maintains that because the status of the property was established as of the date of acquisition, the respective interests of the parties were fixed as of that date. The evidence was undisputed, and the trial court found that the parties intended to acquire the property as equal owners. It is the theory of the respondent that nothing which happened thereafter could alter her interest.

Where, as here, the character of ownership is that of cotenancy, and the instrument by which the property was acquired is silent as to the respective interests of the co-owners, it is presumed that they share equally. However, when in rebuttal it is shown that they contributed unequally to the purchase price, a presumption arises that they intended to share the property proportionately to the purchase price. *Iredell v. Iredell*, 49 Wash.2d 627, 305 P.2d 805 (1957). Annot., *Presumption and proof as to shares of respective grantees or transferees in conveyance or transfer to two or more persons as tenants in common, silent in that regard.* 156 A.L.R. 515 (1945). The Illinois Supreme Court in *People v. Varel*, 351 Ill. 96, 100, 184 N.E. 209, 211 (1932), said:

> Where title to property is taken in the name of two persons as co-tenants and their contributions to the purchase price of the property are unequal and their relationship is not such that a gift from one to the other is presumed to be intended, they will in equity be held to own the property in the proportions of their contributions to the purchase price.

The presumption that co-tenants intend their interests to be proportionate to their contributions to the purchase price was applied in *Iredell*, even though the relationship of the parties was that of husband and wife.

In *West v. Knowles*, 50 Wash.2d 311, 311 P.2d 689 (1957), we said that where property is held by the parties as tenants in common, the courts will presume that they intended to share the property in proportion to the amount contributed, where it can be traced, otherwise they share it equally. . . .

* * *

The equitable principle involved in these cases is in harmony with the rule that while a co-tenant cannot at his own suit recover for improvements placed upon the common estate without the request or consent of his co-tenant, yet a court of equity, in a partition suit, will give the co-tenant the fruits of his industry and expenditures, by allotting to him the parcel so enhanced in value or so much thereof as represents his share of the whole tract. That rule is stated and followed in *Bishop v. Lynch*, 8 Wash.2d 278, 111 P.2d 996 (1941), citing A. Freeman, *Cotenancy and Partition* § 509 (2d ed. 1886).

* * *

A partition proceeding is an equitable one, in which the court has great flexibility in fashioning relief for the parties. *Leinweber v. Leinweber*, 63 Wash.2d 54, 385 P.2d 556 (1963). Here, the trial court correctly held that the respondent, having abandoned her obligations under the contract, could no longer be heard to say that her interest was equal to that of the petitioner, who alone made the payments necessary to preserve the equity existing at that time and avoid forfeiture. There appears no reason why the petitioner should have intended to donate to the respondent the benefit of one-half of the payments which he made after their relationship terminated, nor is it contended that he had any legal or equitable duty to do so.

We are mindful that tenants in common have certain fiduciary duties toward each other. See 4A R. Powell, *The Law of Real Property* ¶ 605 (P. Rohan ed. 1979).[1] There is no showing that such a duty was breached here.

The intent of the parties at the inception of this undertaking cannot be permitted to govern their rights at this juncture, since their original purpose has been frustrated by the change in their relationship to each other and to the property, a change for which the petitioner was not responsible. When that change occurred, the respondent found it no longer practical or expedient to further pursue the acquisition of the property. Her actions manifested to the petitioner that she was abandoning her obligations, and warranted the conclusion that any further payments made by him would inure to his sole benefit, except to the extent that they preserved the respondent's existing equity in the property.

However, we cannot agree with the trial court's conclusion that the respondent, by abandoning her obligations, lost the interest which she had already acquired in the property. As the cases which we have cited indicate, a very strong showing of intentional abandonment is necessary before a co-tenant will be held to have lost such an interest. Here, it is true that the respondent took most of the community personal property

---

1. "Two situations give rise to most of the problems involving the existence and extent of fiduciary relations between tenants in common. These are (1) the effort by one co-tenant to buy in and later to assert a superior title to the detriment of his co-tenants; and (2) the making of an agreement with the other co-tenants, in which some advantage is gained by 'overreaching' the others." R. Powell, *supra* at 619.

when she left the home of the parties, but that property did not represent one-half of the value of the property of the parties. Her interest in the real estate contract at that time was approximately 7.38 percent of the purchase price. Adding the value of the personal property, $1,400, to the amount of the purchase price which had been paid, which was $2,828.92, and taking no account of the probable increase in value of the investment due to inflation, the property of the parties was worth $4,228.92. The share of each would have been $2,114.46. When it is also considered that the personal property taken by the respondent was due to depreciate in value, while the real property was destined to increase in value, the inequity of denying her the benefit of her investment in that property is apparent.

We conclude that the respondent has an equity in the real property which bears the same ratio to the total equity as the ratio of her investment to the total investment of the parties. The petitioner is entitled to have offset against that interest a corresponding portion of the taxes and insurance premiums which he has paid. While he did some remodeling in the interior of the house, he did not prove that these changes resulted in an increase in its market value. The rule is that improvements placed upon the property by one co-tenant cannot be charged against the other co-tenant unless they were either necessary or actually enhanced the value of the property. *In re Estate of Foster*, 139 Wash. 224, 246 P. 290 (1926). Accordingly, the petitioner is not entitled to an offset for these improvements.

The respondent urges reversal of the Court of Appeals upon the question of her entitlement to rent. She relies upon the conduct of the petitioner's son as constituting ouster, but cites no authority which supports that contention.

It is the rule in Washington that, in the absence of an agreement to pay rent, or limiting or assigning rights of occupancy, a co-tenant in possession who has not ousted or actively excluded the co-tenant is not liable for rent based upon his occupancy of the premises. *Fulton v. Fulton*, 57 Wash.2d 331, 357 P.2d 169 (1960). In order for ouster to exist, there must be an assertion of a right to exclusive possession....

An appealing argument is made that, in a situation such as this, where the property is not adaptable to double occupancy, the mere occupation of the property by one co-tenant may operate to exclude the other....

Had the respondent not abandoned her obligations under the contract of purchase at a time when over four-fifths of the purchase price remained to be paid, we would be much inclined to agree that she is entitled to receive rent. Under the circumstances as they exist, she has not demonstrated a sufficient equitable interest to warrant this extension of the rule.

Upon payment to the respondent of an amount sufficient to compensate her for her interest, less the offsets we have approved, the petitioner may have title to the purchasers' interest quieted in him.

The decision of the Court of Appeals, Division One, is reversed (*Cummings v. Anderson*, 22 Wash.App. 634, 590 P.2d 1297 (1979)), except as affirmed or modified herein, and the cause is remanded to the Superior Court for King County with directions to proceed accordingly.

NOTES AND QUESTIONS

1. In *Robinson v. Delfino*, 710 A.2d 154, 156–57 n. 8 (R.I.1998), the court said: "[i]t has been facetiously noted that there are two ways to start a civil action in this state. The first is [by initiating an appropriate action under the Rhode Island statute], and the second is by opening a joint bank account with right of survivorship." The following notes suggest there is a great deal of truth to this wisdom.

2. Disputes concerning the rights of co-tenants among themselves generally are unaffected by the fact that the co-tenants are tenants in common or joint tenants with right of survivorship. Broadly speaking, litigation among co-tenants falls into one of three categories—contribution, accounting, and partition. See generally H. Hovenkamp & S. Kurtz, The Law of Property, An Introductory Survey § 6.5 (5th ed. 2001).

3. (a) A and B are co-tenants of Blackacre. Each owns an undivided one-half interest in Blackacre. A goes into possession of Blackacre but A does not exclude B. Is A liable to B for one half of the fair rental value of the premises? See, e.g., Martin v. Martin, 878 S.W.2d 30 (Ky.Ct.App.1994). Suppose A wrongfully excludes B from Blackacre. Is A liable to B for one-half of the property's fair rental value? See, Cox v. Cox, 138 Idaho 881, 71 P.3d 1028 (2003).

(b) If A leases the property to X, is A accountable to B for one-half of the rents? Under the English Statute of 4 Anne, c 16, § 27 (1704), a co-tenant was liable to account to her co-tenant for rents and profits she received in excess of her proportionate share in the real property. This statute was construed to apply only to rents received by a co-tenant from a lessee. It did not compel the co-tenant in possession to pay the co-tenant out of possession her share of the property's fair rental value. See generally 2 Amer.L.Prop. § 6.14 (A.J. Casner ed. 1952). The Statute of Anne has either been legislatively adopted or construed to be part of the received common law in most of the United States.

> In most of these jurisdictions, the duty to account has been limited almost as narrowly as in England, but the co-tenant who derives income from a non-tortious use of the land that permanently reduces its value has generally been required to account to the other co-tenants. In a minority of American jurisdictions, the duty to account applies more broadly whenever one co-tenant derives any income from the sole possession of the property in the form of rents or otherwise. And in a few states, a co-tenant in sole possession must account for the reasonable rental value of the land even if he derives no actual income from it. But there is no duty to account for income produced by improvements on the land made by the occupying co-tenant alone.[2]

2. W. Stoebuck & D. Whitman, The Law of Property, 3rd ed. § 5.8 at 205–206 (2000) (footnotes omitted).

Which of the various views makes most sense economically? Can the distinction drawn by the Statute of Anne be justified on non-economic grounds?

The foregoing rules apply absent an ouster by the co-tenant in possession of the co-tenant out of possession. If an ouster has occurred, the co-tenant out of possession is entitled to his share of the fair rental value of the premises from the co-tenant in possession. How can one determine whether an ouster has occurred?

> The practical borderline between privileged occupancy of the whole by a single co-tenant and unprivileged greedy grabbing which subjects the greedy one to liability to his co-tenants is not crystal clear. Occupation of the whole by one co-tenant only is never presumed to be adverse to the other co-tenants. Special facts, however, can make it clear that the occupying co-tenant has ousted his co-tenants and has claimed as an individual more than his due as a co-tenant. In this situation, the wrongfully acting co-tenant must compensate his co-tenants unless his wrongful claim has ripened into an adverse ownership.[3]

Even though a co-tenant in possession may not be liable for rent to the co-tenant out of possession, should imputed rent be taken into account if the property is sold and the proceeds of sale become distributable between the co-tenants? For example, suppose A and B are co-tenants of Blackacre. A takes possession; B does not. The fair rental value of Blackacre is $12,000 annually. Over five years A incurs $10,000 of expenses. A and B then sell Blackacre for $100,000. As will be seen, A may be entitled to receive $5,000 from B as B's share of the expenses. Is B entitled to receive half of Blackacre's fair rental value over the five year period from A? See generally Esteves v. Esteves, 341 N.J.Super. 197, 775 A.2d 163 (App.Div.2001).

(c) While A is in exclusive possession of Blackacre he commits an act which, if committed by a tenant of a landlord, would be considered to be waste. Is A liable to B for the act of waste? Compare Clark v. Whitfield, 218 Ala. 593, 119 So. 631 (1929) with McCord v. Oakland Quicksilver Mining Co., 64 Cal. 134, 27 P. 863 (1883).

(d) During the period A is in possession of Blackacre, A spends $5,000 for necessary repairs. Can A recoup one-half of each expense from B as the payments are made? See 2 Amer.L.Prop. § 6.18 (A.J. Casner ed. 1952). If A did not recoup any share of the costs of the repairs as they were paid, can A seek contribution from B in either an accounting or partition? To what extent, if at all, can B question the propriety of a repair expense with respect to its amount, character and necessity? Id. Why might it be reasonable to conclude that A can recoup the costs of repairs only upon an accounting or partition and not as they are expended?

(e) Suppose A makes a permanent improvement to Blackacre costing A $75,000. If B knew that A intended to make this improvement but did not object, can A receive contribution from B prior to a final accounting or partition? See, Shelangowski v. Schrack, 162 Iowa 176, 143 N.W. 1081 (1913).

---

3. 4A R. Powell, Real Property ¶ 603 (P. Rohan ed. 1982).

(f) In 2010, A pays the local county treasurer $1,500 for the property taxes on Blackacre. Can A seek immediate reimbursement from B if B, although not ousted from Blackacre, is not in possession of any part of Blackacre, or must A await an accounting or partition proceeding? May B offset any tax contribution to A by the reasonable rental value of A's exclusive, nonadverse possession? See, Ward v. Pipkin, 181 Ark. 736, 27 S.W.2d 523 (1930) (no contribution if rental value of co-tenant's use exceeds amount of taxes). But see, Baird v. Moore, 50 N.J.Super. 156, 141 A.2d 324 (App.Div.1958) (co-tenant not in possession may not offset rental value if possession of the co-tenant is not adverse). See also 2 Amer.L.Prop. § 6.17 (A.J. Casner ed. 1952).

(g) How would your answers to the foregoing be affected if A had excluded B from the possession of Blackacre?

4. It is often said that co-tenants stand in a fiduciary capacity to each other. As fiduciaries, co-tenants cannot deal with the property in their own self-interest if the effect of such self-dealing would be to affect adversely the other co-tenant's title. Suppose A and B own Blackacre as co-tenants. They inherited Blackacre from O. At O's death Blackacre was subject to a $10,000 mortgage which the mortgagee forecloses because neither A nor B paid off the mortgage. If A purchases Blackacre at the foreclosure sale, to what extent, if at all, will A continue to hold Blackacre for the benefit of A and B? Compare Carpenter v. Carpenter, 131 N.Y. 101, 29 N.E. 1013 (1892) with Jackson v. Baird, 148 N.C. 29, 61 S.E. 632 (1908). See also Massey v. Prothero, 664 P.2d 1176 (Utah 1983).

5. Tenancies in common and joint tenancies may be terminated by either a voluntary or an involuntary partition. A voluntary partition occurs when the co-tenants exchange deeds setting off to each co-tenant from the parcel they owned as co-tenants separate parcels in which only one of them has any interest. For example suppose A and B own Blackacre as tenants in common.

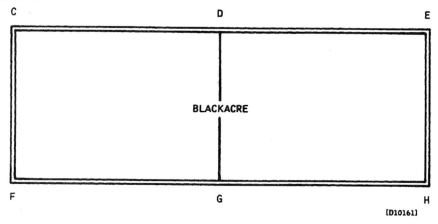

They could affect a partition by A conveying to B all of her rights in portion CDGF and B conveying to A all of her rights in portion DEHG. After this exchange of deeds, A owns DEHG in fee simple absolute and B owns CDGF in fee simple absolute.

If the co-tenants who seek partition cannot voluntarily determine an appropriate division, any co-tenant can seek an involuntary partition by filing an action for partition with the court.[4] A partition will be accompanied by an accounting in which one or more of the co-tenants may be charged for rents and profits, waste, allocable costs of repairs and improvements, taxes, etc. If one co-tenant has made an improvement, then to the extent practicable, the court will direct a partition that will allocate the improved portion to the improver. Furthermore, if the court determines that a physical partition is impracticable, it may order that the real property be sold and the proceeds allocated among the co-tenants as their shares are determined by the accounting. Under what circumstances would a court be justified in directing a sale of the property and division of the sales proceeds rather than a partition of the property?

6. O conveys Blackacre to A and B as joint tenants with right of survivorship and not as tenants in common. In consideration for that transfer A pays O the entire purchase price of $75,000. Six years later, B brings an action to force the sale of Blackacre and for an equal division of the proceeds of sale between A and B. A, however, argues that A should first be reimbursed the $75,000. Is A right? See, Cunningham v. Hastings, 556 N.E.2d 12 (Ind.Ct.App.1990). Would it make any difference if O had conveyed to A and B as tenants in common?

7. O allegedly gave a rocking chair to his child, A, as a gift causa mortis. O later died and under the terms of his will O bequeathed all of his tangible personal property "in equal shares to my son, A, and my daughter, B." In upholding B's claim that the gift causa mortis was invalid for want of delivery and the rocking chair passed to A and B under the foregoing provisions of the will, the court stated that:

> In view of the nature of the claim herein, [the court directs the executor] not to attempt to sell the chair to a third party and, since the property cannot reasonably be divided and/or sold that the use of the rocking chair be shared equally. Although it may sound strange, substantial justice would prevail if the respondent, Arthur C. McDowell, were to have the use of the chair up to and including July 1, 1973, on which date he is then directed to make the rocking chair available to the executrix, who will take possession of it until the end of December 1973. The executrix is then directed to return the chair to her brother for a six month period. This arrangement to continue unless terminated voluntarily between parties or until one or the other is deceased. Since the chair has only nominal and/or sentimental value, it again would appear that substantial justice would prevail if on the death of either the brother or sister the chair becomes the sole property of the survivor thereof and such direction shall accordingly be contained in the order embracing this decision. In re Estate of McDowell, 74 Misc.2d 663, 664–65, 345 N.Y.S.2d 828, 830 (Sur.1973).

What kind of co-tenancy did the siblings have in the rocking chair?

---

4. Actions for partition are not available for tenants by the entirety.

8. Suppose O conveys Blackacre to A for life and upon A's death to B and C. During A's life can B and C compel a partition of Blackacre? Suppose the remainder had been limited to "such of B and C who survive A." Same result? See generally 2A R. Powell, Real Property ¶ 290 (P. Rohan ed. 1990).

9. Suppose A and B, co-tenants of Blackacre, enter into an agreement that neither of them shall ever seek to partition the property. Is the agreement valid? See, Raisch v. Schuster, 47 Ohio App.2d 98, 352 N.E.2d 657 (1975). Would the agreement be valid if they agreed not to seek partition for the next five years? See, e.g., Ex parte Watts, 130 N.C. 237, 41 S.E. 289 (1902).

10. Mom owns Blackacre in fee simple absolute. She recently attended a seminar in which she heard that probate costs lots of money and that use of a joint tenancy with right of survivorship can avoid probate and, thus, save money. She then conveys Blackacre to herself and her son as joint tenants with right of survivorship in a state that does not strictly adhere to the four unities test. Subsequently, the son incurs $40,000 of valid gambling debts. His creditors seek to enforce their judgment against the son against Blackacre. Can they?

11. A and B are good friends but are not romantically attached to each other. They have both recently been accepted to the same medical school. In lieu of renting an apartment to live in they decide to buy Blackacre as co-tenants. One year after purchasing Blackacre, B asks A if it would be alright if B's boyfriend moves in with them, sleeping, of course, in B's room. A says no. Can A prevent B's boyfriend from moving in?

§ 5.3 SEVERANCE OF CONCURRENT ESTATES

TENHET v. BOSWELL

Supreme Court of California (1976).
18 Cal.3d 150, 133 Cal.Rptr. 10, 554 P.2d 330.

MOSK, JUSTICE.

A joint tenant leases his interest in the joint tenancy property to a third person for a term of years, and dies during that term. We conclude that the lease does not sever the joint tenancy, but expires upon the death of the lessor joint tenant.

Raymond Johnson and plaintiff Hazel Tenhet owned a parcel of property as joint tenants. Assertedly without plaintiff's knowledge or consent, Johnson leased the property to defendant Boswell for a period of 10 years at a rental of $150 per year with a provision granting the lessee an "option to purchase." Johnson died some three months after execution of the lease, and plaintiff sought to establish her sole right to possession of the property as the surviving joint tenant. After an unsuccessful demand upon defendant to vacate the premises, plaintiff brought this action to have the lease declared invalid. The trial court sustained demurrers to the complaint, and plaintiff appealed from the ensuing judgment of dismissal.

* * *

An understanding of the nature of a joint interest in this state is fundamental to a determination of the question whether the present lease severed the joint tenancy. Civil Code section 683 provides in part: "A joint interest is one owned by two or more persons in equal shares, by a title created by a single will or transfer, when expressly declared in the will or transfer to be a joint tenancy...." This statute, requiring an express declaration for the creation of joint interests, does not abrogate the common law rule that four unities are essential to an estate in joint tenancy: unity of interest, unity of time, unity of title, and unity of possession....

The requirement of four unities reflects the basic concept that there is but one estate which is taken jointly; if an essential unity is destroyed the joint tenancy is severed and a tenancy in common results. (*Swartzbaugh v. Sampson* (1936) 11 Cal.App.2d 451, 454, 54 P.2d 73; 2 Am.Law of Prop. (1952) § 6.2, p. 9.) Accordingly, one of two joint tenants may unilaterally terminate the joint tenancy by conveying his interest to a third person.... Severance of the joint tenancy, of course, extinguishes the principal feature of that estate—the *jus accrescendi* or right of survivorship. Thus, a joint tenant's right of survivorship is an expectancy that is not irrevocably fixed upon the creation of the estate ... it arises only upon success in the ultimate gamble—survival—and then only if the unity of the estate has not theretofore been destroyed by voluntary conveyance ... by partition proceedings ... by involuntary alienation under an execution ... or by any other action which operates to sever the joint tenancy.

Our initial inquiry is whether the partial alienation of Johnson's interest in the property effected a severance of the joint tenancy under these principles. It could be argued that a lease destroys the unities of interest and possession because the leasing joint tenant transfers to the lessee his present possessory interest and retains a mere reversion.... Moreover, the possibility that the term of the lease may continue beyond the lifetime of the lessor is inconsistent with a complete right of survivorship.

On the other hand, if the lease entered into here by Johnson and defendant is valid only during Johnson's life, then the conveyance is more a variety of life estate *pur autre vie* than a term of years. Such a result is inconsistent with Johnson's freedom to alienate his interest during his lifetime.

We are mindful that the issue here presented is "an ancient controversy, going back to Coke and Littleton." (2 Am.Law of Prop. (1952) § 6.2, p. 10.) Yet the problem is like a comet in our law: though its existence in theory has been frequently recognized, its observed passages are few. Some authorities support the view that a lease by a joint tenant to a third person effects a complete and final severance of the joint tenancy.... Such a view is generally based upon what is thought to be the English common law rule....

Others adopt a position that there is a temporary severance during the term of the lease. If the lessor dies while the lease is in force, under this view the existence of the lease at the moment when the right of survivorship would otherwise take effect operates as a severance, extinguishing the joint tenancy. If, however, the term of the lease expires before the lessor, it is reasoned that the joint tenancy is undisturbed because the joint tenants resume their original relation.... The single conclusion that can be drawn from centuries of academic speculation on the question is that its resolution is unclear.

As we shall explain, it is our opinion that a lease is not so inherently inconsistent with joint tenancy as to create a severance, either temporary or permanent.... Under Civil Code sections 683 and 686 a joint tenancy must be expressly declared in the creating instrument, or a tenancy in common results. This is a statutory departure from the common law preference in favor of joint tenancy.... Inasmuch as the estate arises only upon express intent, and in many cases such intent will be the intent of the joint tenants themselves, we decline to find a severance in circumstances which do not clearly and unambiguously establish that either of the joint tenants desired to terminate the estate....

If plaintiff and Johnson did not choose to continue the joint tenancy, they might have converted it into a tenancy in common by written mutual agreement.... They might also have jointly conveyed the property to a third person and divided the proceeds. Even if they could not agree to act in concert, either plaintiff or Johnson might have severed the joint tenancy, with or without the consent of the other, by an act which was clearly indicative of an intent to terminate, such as a conveyance of her or his entire interest. Either might also have brought an action to partition the property, which, upon judgment, would have effected a severance. Because a joint tenancy may be created only by express intent, and because there are alternative and unambiguous means of altering the nature of that estate, we hold that the lease here in issue did not operate to sever the joint tenancy.

III

Having concluded that the joint tenancy was not severed by the lease and that sole ownership of the property therefore vested in plaintiff upon her joint tenant's death by operation of her right of survivorship, we turn next to the issue whether she takes the property unencumbered by the lease.

In arguing that plaintiff takes subject to the lease, defendant relies on *Swartzbaugh v. Sampson* (1936) ... 11 Cal.App.2d 451, 54 P.2d 73. In that case, one of two joint tenants entered into lease agreements over the objection of his joint tenant wife, who sought to cancel the leases. The court held in favor of the lessor joint tenant, concluding that the leases were valid.

But the suit to cancel the lease in *Swartzbaugh* was brought during the lifetime of both joint tenants, not as in the present case after the death of the lessor. Significantly, the court concluded that "a lease to all of the joint property by one joint tenant is not a nullity but is a valid and supportable contract *in so far as the interest of the lessor in the joint property is concerned.*" (Italics added; *id.* at p. 458, 54 P.2d at p. 77.) During the lifetime of the lessor joint tenant, as the *Swartzbaugh* court perceived, her interest in the joint property was an undivided interest in fee simple that encompassed the right to lease the property.

By the very nature of joint tenancy, however, the interest of the nonsurviving joint tenant extinguishes upon his death. And as the lease is valid only "in so far as the interest of the lessor in the joint property is concerned," it follows that the lease of the joint tenancy property also expires when the lessor dies.

This conclusion is borne out by decisions in this state involving liens on and mortgages of joint tenancy property. In *Zeigler v. Bonnell* (1942) ... 52 Cal.App.2d 217, 126 P.2d 118, the Court of Appeal ruled that a surviving joint tenant takes an estate free from a judgment lien on the interest of a deceased co-tenant judgment debtor. The court reasoned that "The right of survivorship is the chief characteristic that distinguishes a joint tenancy from other interests in property.... The judgment lien of [the creditor] could attach only to the interest of his debtor.... That interest terminated upon [the debtor's] death." (*Id.* at pp. 219–220, 126 P.2d at p. 119.) After his death "the deceased joint tenant had no interest in the property, and his judgment creditor has no greater rights." (*Id.* at p. 220, 126 P.2d at p. 120.)

A similar analysis was followed in *People v. Nogarr* (1958) 164 Cal.App.2d 591, 330 P.2d 858, which held that upon the death of a joint tenant who had executed a mortgage on the tenancy property, the surviving joint tenant took the property free of the mortgage. The court reasoned (at p. 594, 330 P.2d at p. 861) that "as the mortgage lien attached only to such interest as [the deceased joint tenant] had in the real property[,] when his interest ceased to exist the lien of the mortgage expired with it." (Accord, *Hamel v. Gootkin* (1962) 202 Cal.App.2d 27, 20 Cal.Rptr. 372 (applying the *Nogarr* holding to a trust deed).)

As these decisions demonstrate, a joint tenant may, during his lifetime, grant certain rights in the joint property without severing the tenancy. But when such a joint tenant dies his interest dies with him, and any encumbrances placed by him on the property become unenforceable against the surviving joint tenant. For the reasons stated a lease falls within this rule.

Any other result would defeat the justifiable expectations of the surviving joint tenant. Thus if A agrees to create a joint tenancy with B, A can reasonably anticipate that when B dies A will take an unencumbered interest in fee simple. During his lifetime, of course, B may sever the tenancy or lease his interest to a third party. But to allow B to lease for a term continuing after his death would indirectly defeat the very purposes of the joint tenancy. For example, for personal reasons B might execute a 99–year lease on valuable property for a consideration of one dollar a year. A would then take a fee simple on B's death, but would find his right to use the property—and its market value—substantially impaired. This circumstance would effectively nullify the benefits of the right of survivorship, the basic attribute of the joint tenancy.

On the other hand, we are not insensitive to the potential injury that may be sustained by a person in good faith who leases from one joint tenant. In some circumstances a lessee might be unaware that his lessor is not a fee simple owner but merely a joint tenant, and could find himself unexpectedly evicted when the lessor dies prior to expiration of the lease. This result would be avoided by a prudent lessee who conducts a title search prior to leasing, but we appreciate that such a course would often be economically burdensome to the lessee of a residential dwelling or a modest parcel of property. Nevertheless, it must also be recognized that every lessee may one day face the unhappy revelation that his lessor's estate in the leased property is less than a fee simple. For example, a lessee who innocently rents from the holder of a life estate is subject to risks comparable to those imposed upon a lessee of joint tenancy property.

More significantly, we cannot allow extraneous factors to erode the functioning of joint tenancy. The estate of joint tenancy is firmly embedded in centuries of real property law and in the California statute books. Its crucial element is the right of survivorship, a right that would be more illusory than real if a joint tenant were permitted to lease for a term continuing after his death. Accordingly, we hold that under the facts alleged in the complaint the lease herein is no longer valid.

It is ordered that the judgment dated June 18, 1973, be and it is hereby amended to read as follows:

> "It is ordered, adjudged and decreed that Defendant, W.W. Boswell, Jr., have judgment against Plaintiff of dismissal of said First, Second and Third Causes of Action of said Third Amended Complaint and the Plaintiff, with respect to said defendant, take nothing by said First, Second and Third Causes of Action of said Third Amended Complaint."

As amended, the judgment is reversed.

NOTES AND QUESTIONS

1. Whether the leasing of a joint tenant's interest severs the joint tenancy has been the subject of much dispute. This dispute is reflected by three different views courts have taken on the question. Tenhet discusses two of them—namely, the lease severs the joint tenancy or does not. The third view is that the lease severs the joint tenancy only if the leasing joint tenant dies during the term of the lease.

2. For a case reaching the opposite result from the principal case, see, Alexander v. Boyer, 253 Md. 511, 253 A.2d 359 (1969). Recently, the Pennsyl-

vania Supreme Court held that a joint tenancy with right of survivorship was not severed when one of the joint tenants executed an oil and gas lease. In re Estate of Quick, 588 Pa. 485, 905 A.2d 471 (2006) (the court noted that if all the joint tenants signed the lease that would not sever the joint tenancy).

3.　A and B own Blackacre as tenants in common. Without B's consent, A leases Blackacre to C for five years. Can B successfully sue C prior to the termination of the lease term to void the lease? See, Morgan v. Maddox, 216 Ga. 816, 120 S.E.2d 183 (1961) (tenants in common); Swartzbaugh v. Sampson, 11 Cal.App.2d 451, 54 P.2d 73 (1936) (joint tenants with right of survivorship). Suppose B had not consented to the lease. However, after A executed the lease, B collected one-half of the rents from A. Same result? See Land Clearance for Redevelopment Authority of Kansas City v. Dunn, 416 S.W.2d 948 (Mo.1967).

4.　Suppose A and B are joint tenants of Blackacre. A goes into exclusive possession of Blackacre. In order to borrow funds to make improvements to Blackacre, A borrows $100,000 from a local bank and executes a mortgage on Blackacre to secure repayment of the loan. Does the execution of the mortgage sever the joint tenancy?

Whether the execution of a mortgage severs the joint tenancy may depend on the particular state's view of the effect of a mortgage. Some states consider the execution of a mortgage to have the same effect as a conveyance. (See the note on mortgages in Chapter 17.) In these so-called "title theory" states, the execution of the mortgage severs the joint tenancy. The joint tenancy is severed even if the mortgage is discharged before either co-tenant dies. See, e.g., Eder v. Rothamel, 202 Md. 189, 95 A.2d 860 (1953). In other jurisdictions the execution of a mortgage merely creates a lien on the real property. In so-called "lien theory" states, generally the execution of the mortgage does not result in a severance of the joint tenancy. See, e.g., American National Bank & Trust Co. of Shawnee v. McGinnis, 571 P.2d 1198 (Okl.1977); Harms v. Sprague, 105 Ill.2d 215, 85 Ill.Dec. 331, 473 N.E.2d 930 (1984). But see, General Credit Company v. Cleck, 415 Pa.Super. 338, 609 A.2d 553 (1992) (mortgage by one joint tenant severs joint tenancy in a lien theory state). See generally W. Stoebuck & D. Whitman, The Law of Property, 3rd ed. at 191 (2000). Which view is implicit in the *Tenhet* decision?

5.　H and W own Blackacre as joint tenants with right of survivorship. H executes a contract to sell his interest in Blackacre to A for $100,000. The contract dated January 1, 2011, provides that A shall pay H the purchase price on May 5, 2012, on which date H shall deliver a deed to Blackacre to A. On March 3, 2012, H dies. Under the terms of H's will he leaves his entire estate to X. Is X entitled to any share of the proceeds or does W own Blackacre in fee simple absolute as the surviving joint tenant? See, Naiburg v. Hendriksen, 370 Ill. 502, 19 N.E.2d 348 (1939). Suppose the contract of sale had been executed by H and W and the contract had provided that on May 5, 2012, they would convey Blackacre to A. Same result? Compare In re Estate of Baker, 247 Iowa 1380, 78 N.W.2d 863 (1956) with Watson v. Watson, 5 Ill.2d 526, 126 N.E.2d 220 (1955).

6. In those jurisdictions where tenancies by the entirety are still recognized the right of either tenant to sever the estate is curtailed. See generally H. Hovenkamp & S. Kurtz, The Law of Property, 5th ed. 163 (2001).

LAKATOS v. ESTATE OF BILLOTTI

Supreme Court of Appeals of West Virginia (1998).
203 W.Va. 553, 509 S.E.2d 594.

MAYNARD, J.

The appellants, Andrew and Virginia Lakatos, parents of Carolyn Sue Billotti, deceased, appeal the December 1, 1997 order of the Circuit Court of Monongalia County, West Virginia. The circuit court held that Carolyn Billotti's estate is not entitled to any interest in the property Carolyn Billotti owned in joint tenancy with her husband, Frank J. Billotti. We disagree.

Frank J. Billotti and Carolyn Sue Billotti owned three parcels of real estate. One parcel was owned as tenants in common without the right of survivorship and two parcels were owned as joint tenants with the right of survivorship. On October 9, 1982, Frank Billotti murdered his wife and two daughters. Carolyn Billotti died intestate; her only heirs at law were her husband, Frank Billotti, and her parents, Andrew and Virginia Lakatos, the appellants in this case. Frank Billotti was convicted of the murders and was sentenced to life in prison without the possibility of parole. Billotti died in prison on November 28, 1996.

On November 15, 1982, shortly after he committed the murders, Frank Billotti conveyed without consideration the two properties he held in joint tenancy with his wife to his mother, Rose Ann Billotti, the appellee in this case. On January 11, 1990, Rose Ann Billotti conveyed the two properties to a straw party, Ellen F. Harner. Contemporaneously, Ellen F. Harner conveyed the property to Frank J. Billotti and Rose Ann Billotti by deed of even date therewith.

The appellants filed a complaint in circuit court, seeking partition of the three parcels of real estate which were owned by Carolyn Billotti and Frank Billotti. The court granted the request in part and denied the request in part. The request for partition of the property held as tenants in common was granted and the court ordered the property be sold at public auction. . . . [T]he court denied the request for partition of the two parcels held in joint tenancy. The appellants appeal the circuit court's order as it relates to the denial of partition of the properties held in joint tenancy.

On appeal, the appellants contend the circuit court erred in denying their request for partition of the two properties which were held in joint tenancy with survivorship. They argue they are entitled to partition of the properties because West Virginia law prohibits Frank Billotti from profiting from the murder of his wife . . .

We begin by reviewing this Court's previous opinions regarding the public policy considerations of this important issue in West Virginia. This Court has on prior occasions plainly and unequivocally stated its aversion to permitting a murderer to profit from his or her wrongful act. In *Johnston v. Metropolitan Life Ins. Co.,* 85 W.Va. 70, 100 S.E. 865 (1919), the wife who was named as the beneficiary under a life insurance policy was denied the right to recover the proceeds of the policy upon the death of her husband whom she had murdered. The *Johnston* Court stated:

> It would be monstrous for the courts to lend their aid to anyone for the purpose of enriching himself by the commission of murder, and to entertain suit on behalf of the beneficiary to recover upon this policy of insurance would be doing that very thing. It is against the policy of our law to reward one for the commission of crime, and whenever the effect of the enforcement of a right which one would otherwise have would be to give him an advantage by reason of his felonious act, the courts will decline to entertain it.

Id. at 71–72, 100 S.E. at 866. . . .

West Virginia's "slayer statute," W.Va.Code § 42–4–2, was enacted after the *Johnston* decision . . . , was a codification of the policy espoused in *Johnston* and was enacted to arrange for the disposition of property withheld from the killer because *Johnston* left the proceeds of the policy with the insurance company. W.Va.Code § 42–4–2 (1931) reads as follows:

> No person who has been convicted of feloniously killing another, or of conspiracy in the killing of another, shall take or acquire any money or property, real or personal, or interest therein, from the one killed or conspired against, either by descent and distribution, or by will, or by any policy or certificate of insurance, *or otherwise;* but the money or the property to which the person so convicted would otherwise have been entitled shall go to the person or persons who would have taken the same if the person so convicted had been dead at the date of the death of the one killed or conspired against, unless by some rule of law or equity the money or the property would pass to some other person or persons. (ed. note: emphasis added).

We now must determine if this code section applies to property held in joint tenancy with the right of survivorship. W.Va.Code § 42–4–2 was discussed in *State ex rel. Miller v. Sencindiver,* 166 W.Va. 355, 275 S.E.2d 10 (1980). In *Miller,* Dorothy and George Taylor owned property as joint tenants with survivorship. Dorothy killed George, was indicted for murder, but pleaded guilty to involuntary manslaughter. Their son sued to divest Dorothy's title to the property. After listing the states which had adopted legislation to sever jointly held estates when a cotenant intentionally kills the co-owner, the *Miller* Court determined, "We have no such statute, unless the 'or otherwise' in Code, 42–4–2 has that effect. And we believe it does not." *Miller* at 358, 275 S.E.2d at 12. The Court reasoned that "[t]he Taylors' rights were established by their deed and did not involve descent or inheritance." *Id.* at 359, 275 S.E.2d at 13 (citations omitted). In other words, W.Va.Code § 42–4–2, which is included in the chapter titled "Descent and Distribution," did not apply to a survivorship created in a deed pursuant to W.Va.Code § 36–1–20, which is included in the chapter titled "Estates and Property."

The *Miller* Court acknowledged that many courts have analyzed this problem from the perspective that equity prevents one from profiting from his wrong and went on to discuss the four methods courts have used to deal with the property issue:

> Some find that title held in joint tenancy with survivorship is vested by the original conveyance and subsequent acts, even if equitably wrong, cannot divest a tenant of rights to acquire a survivorship estate. Others limit the wrongdoer's estate, creating a constructive trust by which the property is held for those who would have acquired it were it not for the killing. Some sever the estate into a tenancy in common[.] Three courts have deprived the killer of all portions of the tenancy. (Citations omitted)....

This Court finally "decline[d] to decide that a joint tenancy with survivorship created by prior conveyance is vested property that may be divested by the killing of one's cotenant." *Miller* at 361, 275 S.E.2d at 14 (footnote omitted). The ultimate result was that Dorothy was entitled to sole ownership of the property in spite of the fact she shot and killed her husband.

We no longer believe this decision accurately reflects the clear and actual intent of the Legislature. When our slayer statute, W.Va.Code § 42–4–2, was adopted, the phrase "or otherwise" was included in the statute, and the phrase is found following a list of methods by which one may take property. The list includes descent and distribution, will, or by any policy or certificate of insurance. The words "or otherwise" contained in W.Va.Code § 42–4–2 (1931) mean, in addition to descent and distribution, will, and policy or certificate of insurance, any and every other way one could take property, including joint tenancy with the right of survivorship. To the extent that *State ex rel. Miller v. Sencindiver, supra,* is inconsistent with this holding, it is overruled.

The Supreme Court of Montana's reasoning in *In re Cox' Estate,* 141 Mont. 583, 380 P.2d 584 (1963), is persuasive. In that case, a husband and wife, Jess and Bess Cox, held jointly owned property. Jess murdered his wife, then committed suicide. Jess's heirs thereupon sought to inherit the entire property. The Montana court found that Jess became an "involuntary trustee" of Bess's share for the benefit of her heirs. The court said:

> "If we accept the petitioner's view, then we must believe that the Legislature contemplated a situation where a joint owner would feloniously kill the other joint owner, thereby taking all, and approved such a result. We cannot believe that such an abhorrent result was contemplated by the Legislature."

* * *

We, too, find it unthinkable that our Legislature contemplated giving the fruits of his crime to one who commits a homicide, and find inherent in the statute dealing with joint property the reservation that the felonious killer shall not benefit by his wrong.

Id. at 589–90, 380 P.2d at 587–88.

Likewise, the West Virginia Legislature did not contemplate giving the fruits of his or her crime to one who commits a homicide. When one joint tenant murders his or her cotenant, W.Va.Code § 42–4–2 (1931) controls who acquires or takes the property. W.Va.Code § 42–4–2 specifically states, in part, that "the money or the property to which the person so convicted would otherwise have been entitled shall go to the person or persons who would have taken the same if the person so convicted had been dead at the date of the death of the one killed . . ., unless by some rule of law or equity the money or the property would pass to some other person or persons." This plain statutory language clearly provides that upon the death of the victim, the total estate held in a joint tenancy passes in its entirety to the person or persons who would have taken the same if the slayer had predeceased the victim. If Frank Billotti had died before his wife, Carolyn would have taken the entire property which would have passed to her heirs at the time of her death. We reach that same result today. The entire property at issue here passes to Carolyn's heirs.

Even in the complex and sophisticated world of modern law, we still treasure and revere our ancient equitable maxims. These principles of law became equitable maxims because the simple, immutable truths which they contain are so basically and universally fair that they are without dispute obvious to all. Aside from our slayer statute, the old equitable maxim *nemo ex suo delicto meliorem suam conditionem facere potest,* which we commonly state as no man should profit from his own wrong, but which literally means no one can make his condition better by his own misdeed, supports the conclusion we reach today.

Having concluded that W.Va.Code § 42–4–2 (1931) applies to this case, we find the statute controls who takes the property. As Carolyn Billotti's heirs, Andrew and Virginia Lakatos own the entire property. Rose Billotti takes nothing.

The decision of the Circuit Court of Monongalia County is reversed.

Reversed.

NOTES AND QUESTIONS

1. Do you agree with the result in *Lakatos*? Was it compelled by the applicable statute? If not, should the court have deferred to the legislature to change the statute?

2. Many courts hold that where the slayer and victim owned property as joint tenants with rights of survivorship, the slayer and the victim's estate become tenants in common upon the victim's death. See, e.g, Duncan v.

Vassaur, 550 P.2d 929 (Ok. 1976). In Preston v. Chabot, 138 Vt. 170, 412 A.2d 930 (1980) the court held that the slayer was entitled to the entire tenancy by the entirety as the survivor but held one half of the property in a constructive trust for the benefit of the victim's estate. The effect of the holding is that one-half of the property belongs to the slayer; one-half to the victim's estate. Why not simply hold that the slayer and the victim's estate hold as tenants in common? Compare, In re Estate of Thomann, 649 N.W.2d 1 (Iowa 2002) (refusing to impose a constructive trust on B's share where the state's slayer statute did not provide such a remedy because "unlike an inheritance in which the prospective beneficiary/murderer has no ownership interest prior to the victim's death, the murderer owns his proportional interest in joint tenancy property from the moment the joint tenancy is established").

PORTER v. PORTER

Supreme Court of Alabama (1985).
472 So.2d 630.

ALMON, JUSTICE.

This is an appeal by Mary Jane Porter from a partial summary judgment rendered in favor of Martha Porter. The issue is whether a divorce decree destroyed a joint tenancy with right of survivorship in real estate.

The appellant, Mary Jane Porter, and the late Denis M. Porter were married in 1948. In 1963 they purchased a house and lot in Jefferson County [as joint tenants with right of survivorship] ...

The appellant and Denis Porter were divorced in 1976. The final judgment of divorce contained the following references to the real property in question:

> [Fifth] (b) Defendant/Cross–Plaintiff [Mary Jane Porter] shall have the right to exclusive occupancy to the former residence of the parties, property now jointly owned by them until a change in circumstances warrants a modification of this Decree in this respect ...

Sometime after his divorce from appellant, Denis Porter married Martha Porter, appellee, and remained married to her until his death in 1983. There was no modification of the final judgment of divorce in regard to the real property, and neither Denis Porter nor appellant attempted to convey his or her interest in the real property prior to the death of Denis Porter.

Appellee, as executrix of the estate of Denis Porter (later substituted as Martha Porter, individually) filed a complaint for the sale of the property for division. She alleged that Denis Porter's estate was a tenant in common in the property with appellant, claiming that the final judgment of divorce terminated the survivorship provisions of the 1963 deed and made the parties joint owners of the property subject to a sale for division upon petition of either party. Appellant denied any termination of the joint tenancy and moved for summary judgment upon the pleadings and uncontradicted facts presented. Appellee answered by also moving for summary judgment.

The trial court entered a decree of partial summary judgment, finding that "Plaintiff [appellee] and Defendant [appellant] are co-tenants in the property ... and each owns a one-half (1/2) undivided interest therein." . . .

At common law a joint tenancy could be severed by destruction of one of the four unities, i.e., time, title, interest, and possession. Shrout v. Seale, 287 Ala. 215, 250 So.2d 592 (1971); II W. Blackstone, Commentaries on the Laws of England, 180–82.

The issue [in this case] is whether the divorce decree destroyed the unity of possession and converted the joint tenancy with right of survivorship into a tenancy in common by granting exclusive occupancy of the house to appellant. The major distinction between a tenancy in common and a joint tenancy is that the interest held by tenants in common is devisable and descendible, whereas the interest held by joint tenants passes automatically to the last survivor. Thus, if the granting of exclusive possession to appellant destroyed the joint tenancy and converted it into a tenancy in common, appellee would own a half interest in the property through Mr. Porter's will. If the joint tenancy was not destroyed, appellant would own the entire interest by virtue of being the survivor.

Unity of possession requires that the property be held by one and the same undivided possession. 4 G. Thompson, Commentaries on the Modern Law of Real Property, § 1776 (1979). Unity of possession means that all joint tenants have a common right to possess and enjoy the property. II American Law of Property, § 6.1 (1952). Possession by one cotenant is presumed to be possession by all. 4A R. Powell, The Law of Real Property, ¶ 603 (Rohan ed. 1982).

Appellee argues that since the divorce decree gave appellant "exclusive occupancy" that means she was given exclusive "possession." This argument concludes that the unity of possession is destroyed, the joint tenancy is destroyed, and a tenancy in common results.

When one or all of the unities of time, title, and interest are destroyed the joint tenancy is severed and a tenancy in common results. II Tiffany, Real Property, § 425 (3rd ed.). This result follows from the rule of law that a tenancy in common requires only one unity, that of possession. Van Meter v. Grice, 380 So.2d 274 (Ala.1980). II W. Blackstone, supra, at 191.

Thus, if we assume that by granting exclusive occupancy to the appellant the unity of possession was destroyed, then the joint tenancy was severed. No other recognized common law joint estate arose and we are left with the conclusion that the divorce court either granted absolute ownership to one of the parties or partitioned the property or some variation of the above. This result is contrary to the divorce decree. The granting of exclusive possession of the house to appellant did not destroy the unity of possession. The divorce decree provides that appellant shall have exclusive occupancy of the house "until a change in the circumstances warrants a modification of this decree in this respect." This retention of jurisdiction, with respect to the jointly owned property, indicates that the court left itself an option to later modify the occupancy or terminate the joint tenancy. This retention of jurisdiction to later modify the decree also indicates that the exclusive occupancy given to the appellant was temporary as opposed to permanent. . . . The mere temporary division of property held by joint tenants, without an intention to partition, will not destroy the unity of possession and amount to a severance of the joint tenancy. . . .

Appellee argues that the divorce decree, when read in its entirety, severs the joint tenancy. No portion of the divorce decree, other than that quoted at the beginning of this opinion, sheds any light on the present controversy. Thus, we must discern from the previously quoted portion of the divorce decree if the joint tenancy was severed.

The decree refers to the property as "jointly owned" and the parties as "joint owners." These are the only attempts by the court to characterize the cotenancy in common law terms. The term "jointly" is consistent with either a joint tenancy or a tenancy in common. . . .

The lower court relied on Watford v. Hale . . . and Mann v. Bradley . . . in holding that the divorce decree severed the joint tenancy. Suffice it to say that each of these cases involved a property settlement agreement which expressed the intent of the parties to sell the jointly owned property and divide the proceeds equally. We do not deem these cases controlling under the facts in this case.

A divorce does not necessarily sever a joint tenancy. Although divorcing parties are usually desirous of settling all their property rights, there is no requirement that the divorce modify the previous ownership . . . A divorce decree which is silent with respect to property held jointly with a right of survivorship does not automatically destroy the existing survivorship provisions . . . The divorce decree is effectively silent as to the status of the property. To hold that the divorce decree severed the joint tenancy in this case would be to convey the property by implication. Real property cannot be conveyed by implication. . . .

The divorce decree did not destroy the joint tenancy with right of survivorship. Consequently, the property vested in the appellant upon the death of her joint tenant, Mr. Porter. The judgment is therefore reversed and the cause remanded.

Reversed and remanded.

NOTES AND QUESTIONS

1. Because joint tenancy property is a commonly owned asset for married couples and the divorce rate is quite high, the effect of a divorce on the title to joint tenancy property is a recurring problem. Divorcing couples should negotiate how the divorce will affect their respective interests in the

joint tenancy property and the judicial degree affecting the couples' property rights should be clear with respect to its effect on that title. In the absence of any agreement or decree, divorce does not ordinarily terminate the joint tenancy. However, if the couple owned property as tenants by the entirety (a form of joint tenancy to which the unity of marriage is added), divorce terminates the tenancy by the entirety because the divorce severs the unity of marriage. If a couple holding title as tenants by entirety divorce, is their title converted to a joint tenancy or a tenancy in common? Steltz v. Shreck, 128 N.Y. 263, 28 N.E. 510, 40 N.Y.St.Rep. 267 (1891).

2. Husband and Wife owned property as joint tenants with right of survivorship. The couple later divorced and in the decree the court directed that certain property shall remain "in joint tenancy." Subsequent Husband conveyed his undivided one-half interest in the property to a revocable trust. One month later, he died. Wife claims the entire property as the surviving joint tenant; the trustee claims one-half the property as tenant in common with the Wife. Is Wife or trustee correct? See, Smolen v. Smolen, 114 Nev. 342, 956 P.2d 128 (1998).

3. Husband and Wife own Blackacre as joint tenants with right of survivorship. Husband later conveys his undivided half interest to himself as tenant in common. At Husband's death a dispute arises between Wife, claiming to own all of Blackacre as the survivor and the Husband's heirs who claim to own half of Blackacre through Husband's estate. Who owns Blackacre? See, In re Estate of Carpenter, 140 Cal.App.3d 709, 189 Cal.Rptr. 651 (1983).

§ 5.4   BANK ACCOUNTS

IN THE MATTER OF THE ESTATE OF INGRAM

Supreme Court of Oklahoma (1994).
874 P.2d 1282.

SUMMERS, JUSTICE:

The first question is whether a will severs a valid joint tenancy so that jointly held property passes through the estate rather than to the surviving joint tenant. We hold that it does not. The second question is whether bank accounts described as "joint", but lacking, as far as we can find, any language of "survivorship", create a valid joint tenancy. We find that under the facts of this case they do not.

Lola Jane Ingram established a savings account and a checking account, and on each of these accounts named as a co-signor Shirley Gazalski, one of her daughters. Ingram later created three certificates of deposit, each of which named Gazalski as a co-tenant in a joint tenancy relationship. The CD's specifically established joint tenancy with the right of survivorship.

Four days prior to her death, at the request of her other children, Ingram, the mother, wrote a holographic will which stated that she wanted her entire estate "including bank account and CD" divided equally among her four children: Doyle Ingram, Shirley Gazalski, Zeda Jenkins and Norma Goss. The will appointed Gazalski as the personal representative of Ingram's estate. After the mother's death, Gazalski kept the money from the checking and savings accounts as well as the three certificates of deposit. She sold mother's house and car and distributed the proceeds equally among the four children.

The other three children objected to the final accounting presented by Gazalski, arguing that their mother's intent was to include the bank accounts and the certificates of deposit in the estate. At the hearing before the trial court, Gazalski, who had cared for her mother on a day to day basis, testified that her mother intended for the bank accounts and the certificates of deposit to be hers. She stated that her mother told her that the proceeds from the sale of the house and car were to be divided, but that the bank accounts and certificates of deposit were in a joint tenancy so that Gazalski would receive them.

On cross examination Gazalski agreed that she did not receive the interest from the certificates of deposit, and that the interest had been claimed, for income tax purposes, by her mother. She also testified that she contributed none of the money held in the accounts or the CD's. Gazalski testified that she never used any of the funds in the bank accounts for her personal benefit, although her mother told her that she use could the money if she so chose.

Norma Goss testified that her mother told her that Gazalski's name was on the accounts so that someone would be able to pay her bills. Goss also stated that Ingram never talked to her about the certificates of deposit or the bank accounts, but did state that she wanted "everything" divided among her four children. Goss did not know what Ingram intended to be included in "everything."

The trial court held that the bank accounts and the certificates of deposit were to be included in the estate, and were not the property of Gazalski as a joint tenant. The Court of Appeals, Division III, affirmed, stating that (1) there was no express language of joint tenancy in the documentation of the bank accounts and (2) that there was sufficient evidence to support the trial court's ruling with regard to the certificates of deposit. We reverse and remand in part, directing that certificates of deposit not be included as property of the estate. As to the bank accounts, we affirm.

The Certificates of Deposit

The three certificates of deposit established by Ingram totalled $63,000.00 at the time of her death. The language on the face of the certificates specifically stated that the certificates were payable to "said depositor(s), or if more than one depositor as joint tenants with the right of survivorship." Both Ingram's and Gazalski's names appeared on the face of all three certificates.

A joint tenancy can be created in two ways: (1) By express language in the instrument ... and (2) by actions of the party creating the joint tenancy which show an intention to create the essential elements of joint ownership and survivorship. *Raney v. Diehl,* 482 P.2d 585, 590 (Okla. 1971); *Dyer v. Vann,* 359 P.2d 1061 (Okla.1961). When the owner of property transfers funds or property to herself and another by a written agreement which meets the requirements of a joint tenancy, a joint tenancy is created with the right of survivorship. *Raney,* 482 P.2d at 590; *Barton v. Hooker,* 283 P.2d 514 (Okla.1955).

The distinguishing characteristic of joint tenancy is the right of survivorship. *Clovis v. Clovis,* 460 P.2d 878, 881 (Okla.1969). *Mercer v. Mercer,* 365 P.2d 554 (Okla.1961); See also *Shackelton v. Sherrard,* 385 P.2d 898, 901 (Okla.1963). "A joint tenancy simply creates a present estate which, absent severance of the tenancy during the life of both tenants, assures the surviving joint tenant absolute ownership of the whole subject matter of the joint tenancy." *Clovis,* 460 P.2d at 882.

In *Alexander v. Alexander,* 538 P.2d 200 (Okla.1975), we analyzed certificates of deposit appearing to be in joint tenancy. The deceased had established certificates of deposit in his name and the name of his niece and nephew. The certificates specifically stated on the face of the documents that they were held "as joint tenants and not as tenants in common with right of survivorship." *Id.* at 201. The wife of the deceased urged that the certificates were merely incomplete gifts to the niece and nephew, or in the alternative, that the certificates were only a constructive trust. We disagreed, stating that there was no doubt that the certificate's language created a joint tenancy in accordance with the statute. The Court further stated that there was no indication that the deceased intended a constructive trust. Rather, the express language on the face of the documents showed his intent to be the creation of a joint tenancy. *Id.* at 203.

In the present case, the language on the face of the certificates established a joint tenancy. Both parties were listed as joint tenants, and the certificate provided that the parties had the right of survivorship. Children urge that even if there was a joint tenancy, it was severed by Ingram's subsequently executed will. In the alternative, they urge by implication that the joint tenancy was created only for convenience, and was more in the nature of a constructive trust, with the intended beneficiaries being all four children.

As for their first argument, we do not agree that the joint tenancy was severed by the will. A joint tenancy can be severed, but only during the lifetime of the tenant who would sever. *Littlefield v. Roberts,* 448 P.2d 851, 855 (Okla.1969); *Shackelton,* 385 P.2d at 901. The reason the argument fails is that at the death of one tenant, the title to the property passes by operation of law to the surviving tenant. *Littlefield,* 448 P.2d at 855.

In *Littlefield,* property was placed in joint tenancy by a deed conveying to a mother and one of her daughters. The mother's will, executed after the joint tenancy deed, stated that the property subject to the deed was to be split among her children. The will even stated that the deed was one of convenience; however, no such language appeared in the deed itself. While we agreed that the will may show that the mother's intent changed after the execution of the deed, the will did not operate as a severance, because it had no effect until her death. A joint tenancy cannot be severed after the death of the party who would sever. Thus, the daughter, as the surviving joint tenant, was the owner of the property.

In *Shackelton*, 385 P.2d at 901, we held that the acts of one of the joint tenants operated to sever the joint tenancy. There, land was placed in a joint tenancy between a husband and wife. Later, the husband deeded his part of the land to his son. We held that the second deed of the husband was inconsistent with a joint tenancy, and destroyed the required unity of interest. Since the inconsistent act occurred during the lifetime of the husband, a severance of the joint tenancy resulted.

Likewise, in *Clovis v. Clovis*, 460 P.2d at 882, the mother executed a joint tenancy deed, naming herself and her son as joint tenants. The deed was executed under fraudulent circumstances, and the mother then attempted to cancel the joint tenancy. The court held that the joint tenancy was severed because a joint tenancy can be severed during the lifetime of the tenant. *Id.*

Our case is controlled by *Alexander* and *Littlefield*. Unlike *Shackelton* and *Clovis*, here the mother's act claimed as one of severance was the execution of a will which did not take effect until her death. Thus no severance was accomplished during her lifetime. While the will may be evidence of a changed intent, no act occurred prior to her death which terminated the joint tenancies as established by the certificates of deposit. The Children presented no evidence other than the will to support their argument for severance. When Ingram died, the surviving joint tenant Gazalski became the sole owner of the certificates of deposit. *See Peyton v. McCaslin*, 417 P.2d 316, 320 (Okla.1966) (property in a joint tenancy becomes the sole and separate property of the surviving tenant at the death of the designating owner and tenant).

As for the Children's other argument that the certificates of deposit were held in a constructive trust, we find that they failed to meet their heavy burden of proving such a trust. Equity can be invoked when the circumstances surrounding a joint tenancy show that the surviving joint tenant was only to hold legal title while the beneficial title was intended to inure to another. *Peyton*, 417 P.2d at 320.

> If one obtains the legal title to property by fraud or by violation of confidence or fiduciary relationship, or in any other unconscientious manner so that he cannot equitably retain the property which really belongs to an other, equity carries out its theory of a double ownership, equitable and legal, by imposing a constructive trust upon the property in favor of the one who is in good conscience entitled to it, and who is considered in equity as the beneficial owner.

Id. at 321, citing as authority *Powell v. Chastain,* 318 P.2d 859 (Okla. 1957); *McCaleb v. McKinley,* 80 Okla. 38, 194 P. 105 (1920).

A constructive trust is an involuntary or implied trust which arises by operation of law. *Cacy,* 619 P.2d at 202 (Okla.1980). It is imposed against an individual when the individual obtains legal right to property through fraudulent, abusive means, or by means "against equity and good conscience." *Id.* The primary reason for imposing a constructive trust is to avoid unjust enrichment. *Easterling,* 651 P.2d at 680. However, "unfairness" is not reason enough to impose a trust:

> [A]n element of unfairness in allowing the legal title holder to retain the property is not sufficient to justify the imposition of a constructive trust. There must also be some active wrongdoing on the part of the person against whom recovery is sought. . . .

Robison v. Graham, 799 P.2d 610, 616 (Okla.1990) quoting, *Easterling,* 651 P.2d at 680–81.

The burden of proving a constructive trust is on the person or persons asserting it. *Peyton,* 417 P.2d at 321. Before a court will recognize and enforce a constructive trust, the evidence must be "clear, unequivocal, and decisive." *Id.* A mere preponderance of the evidence is insufficient to prove a constructive trust, the evidence must lead to but one conclusion and leave no reasonable doubt as to the existence of the trust. *Easterling v. Ferris,* 651 P.2d 677, 681 (Okla.1982); *Cacy v. Cacy,* 619 P.2d 200, 202 (Okla.1980); *Perdue v. Hartman,* 408 P.2d 293 (Okla.1965). This heavy burden is necessary to protect the security of titles. *Regal v. Riegel,* 463 P.2d 680 (Okla.1969).

The Children assert that the will, combined with Goss' testimony, is sufficient evidence to support the constructive trust. They do not allege fraud or duress by Gazalski. In fact, they do not allege any wrongdoing by Gazalski. Gazalski testified that she cared daily for her mother, and that the mother herself arranged the joint tenancy. We do not find the evidence presented by the children to be so "clear, unequivocal, and decisive" as is required to impose a constructive trust. *Peyton,* 417 P.2d at 321.

The certificates of deposit, formerly being in joint tenancy, are now owned by Gazalski as the surviving tenant. The joint tenancy was not severed by the will, and there is insufficient evidence to show a constructive trust. The trial court erred in including the certificates in the estate.

The Bank Accounts

Unlike the certificates of deposit, the bank accounts do not expressly state that they include the right of survivorship. The photocopy of the front side of the signature cards provided that both the savings account and the checking account were "joint." The cards also state that the account is governed by the rules and regulations on the back of the cards. However, a photocopy of the back of the cards is not in the record before this Court. Thus, the only express language indicating the possibility of a joint tenancy is use of the word "joint" in connection with the checking and savings accounts.

The usual and safe way to create a joint tenancy is for the grantor to use the words "as joint tenants with right of survivorship", or similar language, in the grant of the property. *See Alexander,* 538 P.2d at 201. This language helps to show the intent of the grantor and to overcome statutory or common law presumptions of tenancies in common. Powell, *The Law of Property* § 616[1] (1993). Some states have enacted statutes to require such language. *See Ephran v. Frazier,* 840 S.W.2d 81 (Tex.Ct.App. 1992).

Here, we do not find a joint tenancy created by express language. The signature cards make no mention of "tenancy" or "survivorship", nor is there any other language to suggest it. In *Guilinger v. Guilinger,* 433 P.2d 946, 947 (Okla.1967), we found that the bank account in question was not a joint tenancy, even though the signature card, as here, provided that the account was "joint." We held that this alone was not sufficient to create a joint tenancy by express language.[1] We then looked at the circumstances surrounding the account, and found no intent to create a joint tenancy.

As stated above, there are two ways in which a joint tenancy can be created. Clearly, the record on appeal does not contain the usual express language creating joint tenancy bank accounts, because such words as "with right of survivorship", or "or survivor", or even the initials "JTWRS" do not appear. However, a joint tenancy may be found to exist if the intentions of the grantor may be shown to clearly so indicate.

From review of our decisions it appears we recognize two categories of joint tenancies with right of survivorship. First those falling within the statute, supra, created by written instrument expressly declaring the relationship. *Second, those not created with words of joint tenancy or survivorship, but which are determined to exist because the party initiating the relationship' * * * intentionally and intelligently created essential elements of joint ownership and survivorship.'*

Raney v. Diehl, 482 P.2d at 590, quoting *Dyer v. Vann,* 359 P.2d 1061 (Okla.1961). (Emphasis added, citations omitted). When considering the evidence as to whether a joint tenancy is created in the second way mentioned, it is not critical that specific words like "survivorship" or "joint ownership" are omitted. *Dyer v. Vann,* 359 P.2d at 1063.

Raney set out five factors to consider when faced with the question of whether a joint tenancy was created in the absence of the usual language: (1) the owner's unqualified expression of intent to create the relationship of joint tenant at that time; (2) whether the establishment of the account was in the form advised by a bank officer upon the owner's inquiry as to the means of accomplishing a joint tenancy; (3) whether accessibility to the account was given to both parties after the creation of the account; (4)

---

1. On the reverse side of the card in *Guilinger* was a printed form setting up a joint account with right of survivorship, and a place for signatures if survivorship was desired. Neither party signed on the reverse of the card.

whether both tenants have consented to discretional use of the account; and (5) whether there was an exercise of possessory rights by any of the joint tenants. *Id.* at 591. *See also Hendricks v. Grant County Bank,* 379 P.2d 693 (Okla.1963); *Dyer v. Vann,* 359 P.2d at 1063. These factors must be considered as a whole; one is not determinative of the issue.

In the present case, we have no evidence which shows that it was the unqualified intention of the owner to create a joint tenancy with right of survivorship. Nor do we have any evidence that inquiry was made to a bank official or any other person about the ramifications of a joint tenancy account. Both parties did have access to the accounts, but the record indicates that possessory rights were exercised only by Ingram. Since Gazalski had access to the accounts, she could have used the money in the accounts. However, she testified that she did not use any of the money in the account prior to Ingram's death.

There is insufficient evidence to show that the bank accounts were intended to be in joint tenancy. The record before us does not include evidence of the other side of the signature cards, which were said to have contained the rules and regulations governing the accounts. The evidence presented as to the intent of the deceased is not such that we are persuaded that a joint tenancy with right of survivorship was intended.

Conclusion

The Order of the District Court finding no joint tenancy ownership with respect to the bank checking account and savings account is affirmed. Those accounts are properly part of the estate. That part of the Order placing the certificates of deposit in the estate is reversed. The CD's are the property of surviving joint tenant, Gazalski. The opinion of the Court of Appeals is vacated, and the case is remanded for conclusion in a manner consistent with this opinion.

NOTES AND QUESTIONS

1. Many cases involving joint bank accounts involve the question of whether the survivor is entitled to the balance in the account as of the death of the first joint tenant. In most of these cases, in common with the principal case, the first joint tenant to die was also the sole depositor of funds into the account. However, disputes can arise during the lives of both owners of the account particularly when one of them has withdrawn funds from the account and especially when one has withdrawn more than half of the funds on deposit. If this occurs at least two resolutions are possible. First, whoever withdraws funds from the account might be entitled to all of the withdrawn funds. Second, if one of the co-owners withdraws more than one-half of the account, he might be accountable to the other co-owner for the excess on the theory that the withdrawal severs the joint tenancy and creates a tenancy in common in the withdrawn funds. See, e.g., In re Carson's Estate, 431 Pa. 311, 245 A.2d 859 (1968).

Withdrawals may also affect the right of survivorship that might otherwise exist. For example, suppose H and W are joint owners of a bank account which, if there were no withdrawals, would belong solely to W upon H's death. However, two days before H dies, W withdraws all of the funds from the account. Under the terms of H's will, he leaves his entire estate to X. Can the executor of H's estate compel W to turn over one-half of the withdrawn funds to the estate for distribution to X? See, In re Estate of Kohn, 43 Wis.2d 520, 168 N.W.2d 812 (1969). See also note 6 infra.

In Estate of Propst, 50 Cal.3d 448, 268 Cal.Rptr. 114, 788 P.2d 628 (1990), the California Supreme Court held that a joint bank account co-tenant could unilaterally sever the joint tenancy by withdrawing the funds and depositing them in a new account in his name alone. The court indicated that some duty to account would arise if the joint tenants had agreed not to unilaterally sever. It refused to imply that duty, however. While the court appeared to liken its rule to that involving real property, it also observed that a unilateral severance of a joint tenancy in real property leaves the co-tenants as tenants in common and does not result in the non-severing co-tenant being deprived of all interest in the property.

On the other hand, in Dent v. Wright, 322 Ark. 256, 909 S.W.2d 302 (1995) the court reiterated its stand that if a joint tenant withdraws all of the funds in a joint tenancy bank account, she is liable to the other for the amount withdrawn that exceeds her share in the account. Statutes that protect banks for paying the funds to one joint tenant to the exclusion of the other are not intended to shield one joint tenant from the claims of the other for making an excessive withdrawal.

2. Two theories that courts use to sustain the validity of the survivorship feature of joint bank accounts are the contract theory and the gift theory. Under the contract theory the survivor is entitled to the balance in the account at the death of the other co-owner by virtue of the contract between the depositor and the bank. Because the survivor is entitled to the balance in the account as a third party beneficiary of that contract, it is generally irrelevant that the deceased co-owner retained the passbook or other evidences of the account until death and that the survivorship right was not effectuated by a will. See, e.g., Perry v. Leveroni, 252 Mass. 390, 147 N.E. 826 (1925); Rhorbacker v. Citizens Bldg. Ass'n Co., 138 Ohio St. 273, 34 N.E.2d 751 (1941); Wisner v. Wisner, 82 W.Va. 9, 95 S.E. 802 (1918).

Under the gift theory, the validity of the survivorship feature of joint bank accounts depends upon ordinary principles of gift law. Thus, the survivor is entitled to the entire balance in the account if there has been an intent to make a gift coupled with delivery and acceptance. See, Kepner, The Joint and Survivorship Account—A Concept Without a Name, 41 Calif.L.Rev. 596, 598 (1953). A difficulty in sustaining such accounts under the gift theory arises if the depositor retains the tangible indicia of the account, such as the passbook or checkbook. This fact, however, has generally not deterred the courts from upholding the validity of such accounts under the gift theory. Thus, in Burns v. Nolette, 83 N.H. 489, 492–93, 144 A. 848, 850 (1929) the court stated:

> If the donor intended to pass to the defendant a present right to draw upon the account, retaining a like right to herself during life, was there a present completed gift? The test of a valid gift is said to be whether his

dominion and power to revoke are gone ... [A] delivery of the subject matter to the donee or to some person for him, so as to divest the title and possession of the donor, must be shown. ... The question is whether, admitting another to an equal control, but without retaining a right in the donor to the funds withdrawn by the donee, is such a divesting of the donor's control as satisfies the test before stated. It seems to us that it is. The donee's present right is complete. He can draw from the account so long as funds remain. That right is what was given to him. It might subsequently prove valueless, if the donor withdrew the whole deposit. But for what it was worth it was a completed gift. No further act of the donor was required. No act of hers could defeat the right, although she might render it of no value. On the other hand, he could destroy her reserved right by a like proceeding.

3. A depositor's motive in opening a joint account may be to allow the other joint tenant to withdraw funds from the account merely as a convenience to the depositor. This arrangement, for example, is attractive to older persons who are house bound and desire to give their children access to their bank accounts. Would evidence of this motive be sufficient to overcome the survivorship feature in jurisdictions that have adopted the gift theory? See, In re Estate of Michaels, 26 Wis.2d 382, 132 N.W.2d 557 (1965). The contract theory? See generally R. Brown, The Law of Personal Property 183–85 (W. Raushenbush 3d ed. 1975). If a parent opens a joint account with one child, should that child bear the burden to prove the account was not opened for the parent's convenience but was intended as a gift? See, In re Estate of Penna, 322 N.J.Super. 417, 731 A.2d 95 (1999) (daughter, in order to claim entitlement to the account, must show that the creation of the joint account was free of undue influence and intended as an *inter vivos* gift).

If a depositor wants a child to be able to write checks on the account but does not want to create a co-tenancy in the account, what options are available to the depositor?

4. P deposits $5,000 into a joint bank account in the name of herself and D, as joint tenants with right of survivorship. P's will purports to revoke the joint tenancy by a direction that "all funds jointly on deposit in my name and the name of D, I give to X." How should the account be distributed between D and X? Cf. In re Estate of Boldt, 342 N.W.2d 463 (Iowa 1983).

The provisions of the Uniform Probate Code have markedly altered the law relating to so-called "multiple party accounts." While a joint bank account is customarily created by express words evidencing the "right of survivorship," Section 6–204(b) provides that "a contract of deposit that does not contain provisions in substantially the form provided in subsection (a) [setting forth a statutory form to create a multiple party account] is governed by the provisions of this part applicable to the type of account that most nearly conforms to the depositor's intent." Under Sections 6–212 and 6–213(a), all multiple party accounts are payable to the surviving party unless a contrary intent is evidenced by a writing given to the financial institution where the account is located. Multiple party accounts cannot be revoked by will. Unif. Prob. Code § 6–213(b). Furthermore, "during the lifetime of all parties, an account belongs to the parties in proportion to the net contribution of each to the sums on deposit, unless there is clear and convincing evidence to the contrary." Unif. Prob. Code § 6–211(b).

Suppose O deposits $100,000 into a joint bank account in the name of O and B. B's creditors seek to attach $50,000 from this account to satisfy a claim against B. Under the Uniform Probate Code, can B's creditor attach the account? Suppose three days before O dies, O withdraws the entire $100,000 and deposits that amount in a new account in O's name alone. At O's death, does the new account, or any portion thereof, pass to B or does the entire account pass to the successors of O's estate?

5. There are some important differences between a joint tenancy in land and joint tenancy bank accounts. First, co-owners of real estate generally have an undivided interest in the whole; neither can exclude the other from the use and enjoyment of the property. However, in many jurisdictions the "donee-nondepositor" cannot compel the donor-depositor to share the funds with her. In that sense the donee-nondepositor's rights to the funds attach only if she survives the donor-depositor. Likewise, in many jurisdictions the donee-nondepositor can be required to reimburse the donor-depositor for withdrawals if the withdrawals were contrary to the intent of the donor-depositor. Lastly, the creditors of the donee-nondepositor generally cannot reach the entirety of the funds to satisfy their claims against the donee-nondepositor. On the other hand, the donor-depositor's creditors can reach all funds she has contributed to the account in satisfaction of their claims. See generally Hines, Personal Property Joint Tenancies: More Law, Fact and Fancy, 54 Minn. L.Rev. 509 (1970).

6. Joint tenancy bank accounts are often called the "poor man's will." Another form of bank deposits that competes for that accolade is the so-called "Totten Trust" or "Tentative Trust Account." These accounts are evidenced by a deposit in a bank in the name of A, the depositor, "in trust for B." Unlike the joint bank account, during A's life only A has the right to make withdrawals from this account. B's rights are limited to taking the balance of the account, if any, at A's death. The validity of this device was upheld in Matter of Totten, 179 N.Y. 112, 125–26, 71 N.E. 748, 752 (1904) where the court stated:

> A deposit by one person of his own money in his own name as trustee for another, standing alone, does not establish an irrevocable trust during the lifetime of the depositor. It is a tentative trust merely, revocable at will, until the depositor dies or completes the gift in his lifetime by some unequivocal act or declaration, such as delivery of the pass book or notice to the beneficiary. In case the depositor dies before the beneficiary without revocation, or some decisive act or declaration of disaffirmance, the presumption arises that an absolute trust was created as to the balance on hand at the death of the depositor.

In many jurisdictions Totten trusts are validated by statute. See, e.g., Unif.Prob.Code § 6–111 which has been adopted in many states.

During the depositor's lifetime, the depositor's creditors can reach the trust assets to satisfy their claims against the depositor. At the depositor's death his creditors can reach the trust assets only after the assets of the depositor's probate estate have been exhausted. Thus, the beneficiary of the

Totten Trust is preferred to the heirs or devisees of the depositor's estate with respect to claims filed against the estate not exceeding the value of the probate estate. See, Unif.Prob.Code § 6–107.

Analogous to the Totten Trust is the so-called POD ("pay-on-death") accounts. E.g., "A POD B". Where POD accounts are valid, B is entitled to the balance of the account, if any, remaining at A's death. Some states hold them to be invalid on the theory that they are at cross purposes with the policies underlying the Statute of Wills. See generally Note, Disposition of Bank Accounts: The Poor Man's Will, 53 Colum.L.Rev. 103, 113 (1953). Many state statutes permit POD accounts even though they are commonly used as will substitutes. See, e.g., Unif.Prob.Code § 6–212(b). See also Unif. Prob. Code § 6–201 et seq.

CHAPTER 6

PROPERTY AND COHABITANTS

■ ■ ■

§ 6.1 INTRODUCTION

It goes without saying that when persons marry, many things change. In today's American society, it can also be said that when persons "cohabit" many things change as well. Cohabitants, as used in the title to this chapter, are persons who are either married to each other or who see their relationship as similar to a traditional marriage, even though the outside world and the law may view them differently.

Marriage and cohabitation raise a number of legal issues, including the division of property at the death of one of the parties and the division of property acquired by them during the marriage or period of cohabitation when the relationship goes sour. These and other related issues are explored in the following materials.

§ 6.2 DOWER AND CURTESY: THE OUTMODED COMMON LAW

At common law, a surviving spouse was not entitled to a share of the deceased spouse's estate as an heir. The surviving spouse, however, was entitled to some protection from total disinheritance through the estate of dower (in the case of a widow) or the estate of curtesy (in the case of a widower).

Generally, a widow was entitled to receive a life estate in one-third of all lands of which her deceased husband had been seized of a beneficial legal but not an equitable estate at any time during the marriage in which he had an estate capable of inheritance by issue of their marriage. This so-called "dower" interest could not be defeated by the husband's lifetime transfer of real estate unless the wife had released her dower interest with respect to the transferred land. Likewise, dower could not be defeated by the claims of the husband's creditors or by the husband's testamentary transfers. Dower was said to be "inchoate" during the marriage; it became "consummate" if the wife survived her husband. Since the widow's dower was carved out of the deceased husband's estate, the duration of the dower

390

estate could not exceed the duration of the deceased husband's estate. For example, if the husband had an estate in Blackacre for "so long as Blackacre was used for residential purposes," the widow's dower estate was subject to the same limitation. Thus the widow had an estate that would terminate at her death or, if earlier, when the property no longer was used for residential purposes.

At common law, a husband had a greater interest in his wife's property than she had in his property. Upon marriage, the husband acquired a life estate in all real estate owned by the wife and capable of inheritance by issue of the marriage. This estate terminated upon the death of the first of the husband and wife to die. This estate was known as the tenancy "by marital right." Upon birth of a first child, however, the husband's estate ripened into a life estate measured solely by the husband's life. The live birth of a child was so important to the husband's entitlement to the life estate that it was common for male witnesses to stand outside of the "birthing room" who could later testify that the child was "heard to cry within the four walls." In this case the husband's life estate became possessory even though the child died soon after birth. The husband's estate was called curtesy initiate during the wife's life; if the husband survived the wife the estate was called curtesy consummate.

§ 6.3 THE PROPERTY RIGHTS OF A SURVIVING SPOUSE: MODERN APPROACHES

The common law estates of dower and curtesy have been supplanted by more general statutes of inheritance that guarantee the surviving spouse a fixed percentage of the deceased spouse's real and personal property if the deceased spouse dies intestate. The intestate share of the spouse can be as little as one-third and as great as 100% depending on the applicable state laws. See, e.g., Unif. Prob. Code § 2–102. Even in those states where the surviving spouse's percentage share is not 100%, the spouse may be entitled to a minimum share that assures that in smaller estates the spouse receives everything. For example, under the Uniform Probate Code, if the intestate is survived by a spouse and children, the spouse is entitled to the first $150,000 if all the children also are the spouse's children.

If the deceased spouse dies testate, most states provide a so-called "elective" share for the surviving spouse which the spouse may elect to claim in lieu of the share, if any, provided for the spouse under the deceased spouse's will. In many cases the elective share will be a smaller share of the estate than the surviving spouse would receive if the deceased spouse had died intestate. In addition, some states by statute or case law permit the surviving spouse to claim an elective share of property transferred during the decedent's life where decedent retained certain economic benefits in such property.[1]

In order to claim an elective share, typically the surviving spouse must file a notice of election with the personal representative of the deceased spouse's estate within some time period fixed by state law, for example, six months. If the spouse does not make a timely election, the spouse is deemed to have waived the right to claim an elective share.

Under some elective share statutes, the surviving spouse is entitled to a fixed share of the deceased spouse's estate. Therefore, a surviving spouse who had been married to the decedent for 20 years would be treated identically with a surviving spouse who had been married to the decedent for two years. Under Section 2–201 of the Uniform Probate Code, however, the size of the elective share is determined in part by the duration of the marriage between the decedent and the surviving spouse. If they were married 15 or more years to each other, the elective share equals 50% of the augmented estate. If they were married only two years, the elective share is 6% of the augmented estate. If they were married less than one year, the elective share cannot exceed $50,000.

The abolition of dower and curtesy in favor of spousal elective shares largely is explained by the fact that much wealth today is in the form of personal rather that real property.[2] However, even today it probably is true that for people with smaller estates real property, in the form of the family home, continues to be the principal asset. Significant wealth evidenced in the form of personal property is limited to persons with sizable portfolios of stocks, bonds, certificate of deposits and other forms of intangible personal property.

The abolition of dower and curtesy may also be explained by the widespread use of joint tenancies between spouses with respect to both personal and real property and tenancies by the entirety between spouses with respect to the family home. Use of the marital joint tenancy obviates the need for the estates of dower and curtesy to provide financial security for the surviving spouse.

NOTES AND QUESTIONS

1. W's father, O, conveys Blackacre to H and the heirs of his body with W. They are childless. W dies and thereafter H remarries W–2. They have two children. H later dies survived by W–2 and the two children. Can W–2 claim common law dower in Blackacre?

2. Suppose O conveys Blackacre to A and B as joint tenants with right of survivorship. A dies survived by his wife, W, and by B. Can W claim common law dower in Blackacre?

3. O is the sole owner of all of the common stock of Beaumont Acres, Inc., a corporation which owns vast acres of real estate in Bloomington Valley.

---

1. See, e.g., Newman v. Dore, 275 N.Y. 371, 9 N.E.2d 966 (1937). See also, Unif.Prob.Code § 2–202 et seq. (augmented estate).

2. 2 R. Powell, The Law of Real Property ¶ 209 (P. Rohan ed. 1985).

Shares of stock are personal property. At O's death, can her husband claim curtesy in the real estate owned by the corporation? If not, how effective are the common law estates of dower and curtesy in providing a surviving spouse with financial security?

4. Suppose O died owning Blackacre in fee simple absolute. O was survived by his wife, W, and his son, S, who is O's sole heir. Under the common law, how should Blackacre be distributed between W and S? Three years after O dies S dies survived by his wife, Y, and his son, J. S is also survived by his mother, W. State the title to Blackacre?

5. Only a surviving spouse is entitled to the statutory intestate or forced share set aside under state law for surviving spouses. If two persons married and later divorced, the survivor of them would not be entitled to an intestate or forced share because the survivor would not be a "surviving spouse." On the other hand, if the married couple separated but were not divorced, or if they were in the process of divorcing when one of them died but the divorce was not yet final, the survivor would be entitled to an intestate or forced share. Recently there has been litigation whether a post-operative male-to female transsexual was entitled to claim a marital share of the estate of "her" deceased husband. If the marriage was valid, the answer is yes; if the marriage was invalid, the answer was no. Compare M.T. v. J.T., 140 N.J.Super. 77, 355 A.2d 204, cert. denied, 71 N.J. 345, 364 A.2d 1076 (1976) (marriage valid) with In re Estate of Gardiner, 273 Kan. 191, 42 P.3d 120 (2002) (marriage invalid).

§ 6.4 TENANTS BY THE ENTIRETY

UNITED STATES v. CRAFT

Supreme Court of the United States (2002).
535 U.S. 274.

JUSTICE O'CONNOR delivered the opinion of the Court.

This case raises the question whether a tenant by the entirety possesses "property" or "rights to property" to which a federal tax lien may attach. ... Relying on the state law fiction that a tenant by the entirety has no separate interest in entireties property, the United States Court of Appeals for the Sixth Circuit held that such property is exempt from the tax lien. We conclude that, despite the fiction, each tenant possesses individual rights in the estate sufficient to constitute "property" or "rights to property" for the purposes of the lien, and reverse the judgment of the Court of Appeals.

I

In 1988, the Internal Revenue Service (IRS) assessed $482,446 in unpaid income tax liabilities against Don Craft, the husband of respondent Sandra L. Craft, for failure to file federal income tax returns for the years 1979 through 1986. ... When he failed to pay, a federal tax lien attached to "all property and rights to property, whether real or personal, belonging to" him. ...

394 PROPERTY & COHABITANTS CH. 6

At the time the lien attached, respondent and her husband owned a piece of real property in Grand Rapids, Michigan, as tenants by the entirety. . . . After notice of the lien was filed, they jointly executed a quitclaim deed purporting to transfer the husband's interest in the property to respondent for one dollar. . . .When respondent attempted to sell the property a few years later, a title search revealed the lien. The IRS agreed to release the lien and allow the sale with the stipulation that half of the net proceeds be held in escrow pending determination of the Government's interest in the property. . . .

Respondent brought this action to quiet title to the escrowed proceeds. The Government claimed that its lien had attached to the husband's interest in the tenancy by the entirety. . . . The District Court granted the Government's motion for summary judgment, holding that the federal tax lien attached at the moment of the transfer to respondent, which terminated the tenancy by the entirety and entitled the Government to one-half of the value of the property. . . .

Both parties appealed. The Sixth Circuit held that the tax lien did not attach to the property because under Michigan state law, the husband had no separate interest in property held as a tenant by the entirety. 140 F.3d 638, 643 (C.A.6 1998). It remanded to the District Court to consider the Government's alternative claim that the conveyance should be set aside as fraudulent. . . .

On remand, the District Court concluded that where, as here, state law makes property exempt from the claims of creditors, no fraudulent conveyance can occur. 65 F.Supp.2d 651, 657–658 (W.D.Mich.1999) . . .

[On appeal, the government claims] . . . that its lien attached to the husband's interest in the entireties property. . . .

We granted certiorari to consider the Government's claim that respondent's husband had a separate interest in the entireties property to which the federal tax lien attached. . . .

II

Whether the interests of respondent's husband in the property he held as a tenant by the entirety constitutes "property and rights to property" for the purposes of the federal tax lien statute, 26 U.S.C. § 6321, is ultimately a question of federal law. The answer to this federal question, however, largely depends upon state law. The federal tax lien statute itself "creates no property rights but merely attaches consequences, federally defined, to rights created under state law." . . . Accordingly, "[w]e look initially to state law to determine what rights the taxpayer has in the property the Government seeks to reach, then to federal law to determine whether the taxpayer's state-delineated rights qualify as 'property' or 'rights to property' within the compass of the federal tax lien legislation." Drye v. United States, 528 U.S. 49, 58, 120 S.Ct. 474, 145 L.Ed.2d 466 (1999).

A common idiom describes property as a "bundle of sticks"—a collection of individual rights which, in certain combinations, constitute property. See B. Cardozo, Paradoxes of Legal Science 129 (1928) (reprint 2000); see also Dickman v. Commissioner, 465 U.S. 330, 336, 104 S.Ct. 1086, 79 L.Ed.2d 343 (1984). State law determines only which sticks are in a person's bundle. Whether those sticks qualify as "property" for purposes of the federal tax lien statute is a question of federal law.

In looking to state law, we must be careful to consider the substance of the rights state law provides, not merely the labels the State gives these rights or the conclusions it draws from them. Such state law labels are irrelevant to the federal question of which bundles of rights constitute property that may be attached by a federal tax lien. In Drye v. United States, supra, we considered a situation where state law allowed an heir subject to a federal tax lien to disclaim his interest in the estate. The state law also provided that such a disclaimer would "creat[e] the legal fiction" that the heir had predeceased the decedent and would correspondingly be deemed to have had no property interest in the estate. Id., at 53, 120 S.Ct. 474. We unanimously held that this state law fiction did not control the federal question and looked instead to the realities of the heir's interest. We concluded that, despite the State's characterization, the heir possessed a "right to property" in the estate—the right to accept the inheritance or pass it along to another—to which the federal lien could attach. Id., at 59–61, 120 S.Ct. 474.

III

We turn first to the question of what rights respondent's husband had in the entireties property by virtue of state law. In order to understand these rights, the tenancy by the entirety must first be placed in some context.

English common law provided three legal structures for the concurrent ownership of property that have survived into modern times: tenancy in common, joint tenancy, and tenancy by the entirety. 1 G. Thompson, Real Property § 4.06(g) (D. Thomas ed. 1994) (hereinafter Thompson) ... The common law characterized tenants in common as each owning a separate fractional share in undivided property. [7 R. Powell & P. Rohan, Real Property § 51.01[3] (M. Wolf ed. 2001) (hereinafter Powell)] ... § 50.01[1]. Tenants in common may each unilaterally alienate their shares through sale or gift or place encumbrances upon these shares. They also have the power to pass these shares to their heirs upon death. Tenants in common have many other rights in the property, including the right to use the property, to exclude third parties from it, and to receive a portion of any income produced from it. Id., §§ 50.03–50.06.

Joint tenancies were the predominant form of concurrent ownership at common law, and still persist in some States today. 4 Thompson § 31.05. The common law characterized each joint tenant as possessing the entire estate, rather than a fractional share: "[J]oint-tenants have one and the same interest ... held by one and the same undivided possession." 2 W. Blackstone, Commentaries on the Laws of England 180 (1766). Joint tenants possess many of the rights enjoyed by tenants in common: the right to use, to exclude, and to enjoy a share of the property's income. The main difference between a joint tenancy and a tenancy in common is that a joint tenant also has a right of automatic inheritance known as "survivorship." Upon the death of one joint tenant, that tenant's share in the property does not pass through will or the rules of intestate succession; rather, the remaining tenant or tenants automatically inherit it. Id., at 183; 7 Powell § 51.01[3]. Joint tenants' right to alienate their individual shares is also somewhat different. In order for one tenant to alienate his or her individual interest in the tenancy, the estate must first be severed—that is, converted to a tenancy in common with each tenant possessing an equal fractional share. Id., § 51.04[1]. Most States allowing joint tenancies facilitate alienation, however, by allowing severance to automatically accompany a conveyance of that interest or any other overt act indicating an intent to sever. Ibid.

A tenancy by the entirety is a unique sort of concurrent ownership that can only exist between married persons. 4 Thompson § 33.02. Because of the common-law fiction that the husband and wife were one person at law (that person, practically speaking, was the husband, see J. Cribbet et al., Cases and Materials on Property 329 (6th ed. 1990)), Blackstone did not characterize the tenancy by the entirety as a form of concurrent ownership at all. Instead, he thought that entireties property was a form of single ownership by the marital unity. Orth, Tenancy by the Entirety: The Strange Career of the Common–Law Marital Estate, 1997 B.Y.U.L. Rev. 35, 38–39. Neither spouse was considered to own any individual interest in the estate; rather, it belonged to the couple.

Like joint tenants, tenants by the entirety enjoy the right of survivorship. Also like a joint tenancy, unilateral alienation of a spouse's interest in entireties property is typically not possible without severance. Unlike joint tenancies, however, tenancies by the entirety cannot easily be severed unilaterally. 4 Thompson § 33.08(b). Typically, severance requires the consent of both spouses, id., § 33.08(a), or the ending of the marriage in divorce, id., § 33.08(d). At common law, all of the other rights associated with the entireties property belonged to the husband: as the head of the household, he could control the use of the property and the exclusion of others from it and enjoy all of the income produced from it. Id., § 33.05. The husband's control of the property was so extensive that, despite the rules on alienation, the common law eventually provided that he could unilaterally alienate entireties property without severance subject only to the wife's survivorship interest. Orth, supra, at 40–41.

With the passage of the Married Women's Property Acts in the late 19th century granting women distinct rights with respect to marital property, most States either abolished the tenancy by the entirety or altered it significantly. 7 Powell § 52.01[2]. Michigan's version of the estate is typical of the modern tenancy by the entirety. Following Blackstone, Michigan characterizes its tenancy by the entirety as creating no individual rights whatsoever: "It is well settled under the law of this state that one tenant by the entirety has no interest separable from that of the other.... Each is vested with an entire title." Long v. Earle, 277 Mich. 505, 517, 269 N.W. 577, 581 (1936). And yet, in Michigan, each tenant by the entirety possesses the right of survivorship. Mich. Comp. Laws Ann. § 554.872(g) (West Supp. 1997), recodified at § 700.2901(2)(g) (West Supp. Pamphlet 2001). Each spouse—the wife as well as the husband—may also use the property, exclude third parties from it, and receive an equal share of the income produced by it. See § 557.71 (West 1988). Neither spouse may unilaterally alienate or encumber the property, Long v. Earle, supra, at 517, 269 N.W., at 581; Rogers v. Rogers, 136 Mich.App. 125, 134, 356 N.W.2d 288, 292 (1984), although this may be accomplished with mutual consent, Eadus v. Hunter, 249 Mich. 190, 228 N.W. 782 (1930). Divorce ends the tenancy by the entirety, generally giving each spouse an equal interest in the property as a tenant in common, unless the divorce decree specifies otherwise. Mich. Comp. Laws Ann. § 552.102 (West 1988).

In determining whether respondent's husband possessed "property" or "rights to property" within the meaning of 26 U.S.C. § 6321, we look to the individual rights created by these state law rules. According to Michigan law, respondent's husband had, among other rights, the following rights with respect to the entireties property: the right to use the property, the right to exclude third parties from it, the right to a share of income produced from it, the right of survivorship, the right to become a tenant in common with equal shares upon divorce, the right to sell the property with the respondent's consent and to receive half the proceeds from such a sale, the right to place an encumbrance on the property with the respondent's consent, and the right to block respondent from selling or encumbering the property unilaterally.

IV

We turn now to the federal question of whether the rights Michigan law granted to respondent's husband as a tenant by the entirety qualify as "property" or "rights to property" under § 6321. The statutory language authorizing the tax lien "is broad and reveals on its face that Congress meant to reach every interest in property that a taxpayer might have." United States v. National Bank of Commerce, 472 U.S., at 719–720, 105 S.Ct. 2919. "Stronger language could hardly have been selected to reveal a purpose to assure the collection of taxes." Glass City Bank v. United States, 326 U.S. 265, 267, 66 S.Ct. 108, 90 L.Ed. 56 (1945). We conclude that the husband's rights in the entireties property fall within this broad statutory language.

Michigan law grants a tenant by the entirety some of the most essential property rights: the right to use the property, to receive income produced by it, and to exclude others from it. See Dolan v. City of Tigard, 512 U.S. 374, 384, 114 S.Ct. 2309, 129 L.Ed.2d 304 (1994) ("[T]he right to exclude others" is " 'one of the most essential sticks in the bundle of rights that are commonly characterized as property'") (quoting Kaiser Aetna v. United States, 444 U.S. 164, 176, 100 S.Ct. 383, 62 L.Ed.2d 332 (1979)); Loretto v. Teleprompter Manhattan CATV Corp., 458 U.S. 419, 435, 102 S.Ct. 3164, 73 L.Ed.2d 868 (1982) (including "use" as one of the "[p]roperty rights in a physical thing"). These rights alone may be sufficient to subject the husband's interest in the entireties property to the federal tax lien. They gave him a substantial degree of control over the entireties property, and, as we noted in Drye, "in determining whether a federal taxpayer's state-law rights constitute 'property' or 'rights to property,' [t]he important consideration is the breadth of the control the [taxpayer] could exercise over the property." 528 U.S., at 61, 120 S.Ct. 474 (internal quotation marks omitted).

The husband's rights in the estate, however, went beyond use, exclusion, and income. He also possessed the right to alienate (or otherwise encumber) the property with the consent of respondent, his wife. Loretto, supra, at 435, 102 S.Ct. 3164 (the right to "dispose" of an item is a property right). It is true, as respondent notes, that he lacked the right to unilaterally alienate the property, a right that is often in the bundle of property rights. See also post, at 1429–1430. There is no reason to believe, however, that this one stick—the right of unilateral alienation—is essential to the category of "property."

This Court has already stated that federal tax liens may attach to property that cannot be unilaterally alienated. In United States v. Rodgers, 461 U.S. 677, 103 S.Ct. 2132, 76 L.Ed.2d 236 (1983), we considered the Federal Government's power to foreclose homestead property attached by a federal tax lien. Texas law provided that " 'the owner or claimant of the property claimed as homestead [may not], if married, sell or abandon the homestead without the consent of the other spouse.' " Id., at 684–685, 103 S.Ct. 2132 (quoting Tex. Const., Art. 16, § 50). We nonetheless stated that "[i]n the homestead context ..., there is no doubt ... that not only do both spouses (rather than neither) have an independent interest in the homestead property, but that a federal tax lien can at least attach to each of those interests." 461 U.S., at 703, n. 31, 103 S.Ct. 2132; cf. Drye, supra, at 60, n. 7, 120 S.Ct. 474 (noting that "an interest in a spendthrift trust has been held to constitute 'property for purposes of § 6321' even though the beneficiary may not transfer that interest to third parties").

Excluding property from a federal tax lien simply because the taxpayer does not have the power to unilaterally alienate it would, moreover, exempt a rather large amount of what is commonly thought of as property. It would exempt not only the type of property discussed in Rodgers, but also some community property. Community property states often provide that real community property cannot be alienated without the consent of both spouses. See, e.g., Ariz. Rev. Stat. Ann. § 25–214(C) (2000); Cal. Fam. Code Ann. § 1102 (West 1994); Idaho Code § 32–912 (1996); La. Civ. Code Ann., Art. 2347 (West Supp. 2002); Nev. Rev. Stat. § 123.230(3) (1995); N. M. Stat. Ann. § 40–3–13 (1999); Wash. Rev. Code § 26.16.030(3) (1994). Accordingly, the fact that respondent's husband could not unilaterally alienate the property does not preclude him from possessing "property and rights to property" for the purposes of § 6321.

Respondent's husband also possessed the right of survivorship—the right to automatically inherit the whole of the estate should his wife predecease him. Respondent argues that this interest was merely an expectancy, which we suggested in Drye would not constitute "property" for the purposes of a federal tax lien. 528 U.S., at 60, n. 7, 120 S.Ct. 474 ("[We do not mean to suggest] that an expectancy that has pecuniary value ... would fall within § 6321 prior to the time it ripens into a present estate"). Drye did not decide this question, however, nor do we need to do so here. As we have discussed above, a number of the sticks in respondent's husband's bundle were presently existing. It is therefore not necessary to decide whether the right to survivorship alone would qualify as "property" or "rights to property" under § 6321.

That the rights of respondent's husband in the entireties property constitute "property" or "rights to property" "belonging to" him is further underscored by the fact that, if the conclusion were otherwise, the entireties property would belong to no one for the purposes of § 6321. Respondent had no more interest in the property than her husband; if neither of them had a property interest in the entireties property, who did? This result not only seems absurd, but would also allow spouses to shield their property from federal taxation by classifying it as entireties property, facilitating abuse of the federal tax system. Johnson, After Drye: The Likely Attachment of the Federal Tax Lien to Tenancy-by-the-Entireties Interests, 75 Ind. L. J. 1163, 1171 (2000) ...

Respondent argues that, whether or not we would conclude that respondent's husband had an interest in the entireties property, legislative history indicates that Congress did not intend that a federal tax lien should attach to such an interest. In 1954, the Senate rejected a proposed amendment to the tax lien statute that would have provided that the lien attach to "property or rights to property (including the interest of such person as tenant by the entirety)." S. Rep. No. 1622, 83d Cong., 2d Sess., p. 575 (1954). We have elsewhere held, however, that failed legislative proposals are "a particularly dangerous ground on which to rest an interpretation of a prior statute," Pension Benefit Guaranty Corporation v. LTV Corp., 496 U.S. 633, 650, 110 S.Ct. 2668, 110 L.Ed.2d 579 (1990), reasoning that " '[c]ongressional inaction lacks persuasive significance because several equally tenable inferences may be drawn from such inaction, including the inference that the existing legislation already incorporated the offered change' " Central Bank of Denver, N.A. v. First Interstate Bank of Denver, N.A., 511 U.S. 164, 187, 114 S.Ct. 1439, 128 L.Ed.2d 119 (1994). This case exemplifies the risk of relying on such legislative history. As we noted in United States v. Rodgers, 461 U.S., at 704, n. 31, 103 S.Ct. 2132, some legislative history surrounding the 1954 amendment indicates that the House intended the amendment to be nothing more than a "clarification" of existing law, and that the Senate rejected the amendment only because it found it "superfluous." See H. R.

Rep. No. 1337, 83d Cong., 2d Sess., A406 (1954) (noting that the amendment would "clarif[y] the term 'property and rights to property' by expressly including therein the interest of the delinquent taxpayer in an estate by the entirety"); S. Rep. No. 1622, 83d Cong., 2d Sess., 575 (1954) ("It is not clear what change in existing law would be made by the parenthetical phrase. The deletion of the phrase is intended to continue the existing law").

The same ambiguity that plagues the legislative history accompanies the common-law background of Congress' enactment of the tax lien statute. Respondent argues that Congress could not have intended the passage of the federal tax lien statute to alter the generally accepted rule that liens could not attach to entireties property. See Astoria Fed. Sav. & Loan Assn. v. Solimino, 501 U.S. 104, 108, 111 S.Ct. 2166, 115 L.Ed.2d 96 (1991) ("[W]here a common-law principle is well established ... the courts may take it as given that Congress has legislated with an expectation that the principle will apply except 'when a statutory purpose to the contrary is evident' "). The common-law rule was not so well established with respect to the application of a federal tax lien that we must assume that Congress considered the impact of its enactment on the question now before us. There was not much of a common-law background on the question of the application of federal tax liens, as the first court of appeals cases dealing with the application of such a lien did not arise until the 1950's. United States v. Hutcherson, 188 F.2d 326 (C.A.8 1951); Raffaele v. Granger, 196 F.2d 620 (C.A.3 1952). This background is not sufficient to overcome the broad statutory language Congress did enact, authorizing the lien to attach to "all property and rights to property" a taxpayer might have.

We therefore conclude that respondent's husband's interest in the entireties property constituted "property" or "rights to property" for the purposes of the federal tax lien statute. We recognize that Michigan makes a different choice with respect to state law creditors: "[L]and held by husband and wife as tenants by entirety is not subject to levy under execution on judgment rendered against either husband or wife alone." Sanford v. Bertrau, 204 Mich. 244, 247, 169 N.W. 880, 881 (1918). But that by no means dictates our choice. The interpretation of 26 U.S.C. § 6321 is a federal question, and in answering that question we are in no way bound by state courts' answers to similar questions involving state law. As we elsewhere have held, " 'exempt status under state law does not bind the federal collector.' " Drye v. United States, 528 U.S., at 51, 120 S.Ct. 474. See also Rodgers, supra, at 701, 103 S.Ct. 2132 (clarifying that the Supremacy Clause "provides the underpinning for the Federal Government's right to sweep aside state-created exemptions") ...

The judgment of the United States Court of Appeals for the Sixth Circuit is accordingly reversed, and the case is remanded for proceedings consistent with this opinion.

It is so ordered.

JUSTICE SCALIA, with whom JUSTICE THOMAS joins, dissenting.

. . .

I write separately to observe that the Court nullifies (insofar as federal taxes are concerned, at least) a form of property ownership that was of particular benefit to the stay-at-home spouse or mother. She is overwhelmingly likely to be the survivor that obtains title to the unencumbered property; and she (as opposed to her business-world husband) is overwhelmingly unlikely to be the source of the individual indebtedness against which a tenancy by the entirety protects. It is regrettable that the Court has eliminated a large part of this traditional protection retained by many States.

JUSTICE THOMAS, with whom JUSTICE STEVENS and JUSTICE SCALIA join, dissenting.

The Court today allows the Internal Revenue Service (IRS) to reach proceeds from the sale of real property that did not belong to the taxpayer, respondent's husband, Don Craft, because, in the Court's view, he "possesse[d] individual rights in the [tenancy by the entirety] estate sufficient to constitute 'property and rights to property' for the purposes of the lien" created by 26 U.S.C. § 6321 . . . The Court does not contest that the tax liability the IRS seeks to satisfy is Mr. Craft's alone, and does not claim that, under Michigan law, real property held as a tenancy by the entirety belongs to either spouse individually. Nor does the Court suggest that the federal tax lien attaches to particular "rights to property" held individually by Mr. Craft. Rather, borrowing the metaphor of "property as a 'bundle of sticks'—a collection of individual rights which, in certain combinations constitute property," . . . the Court proposes that so long as sufficient "sticks" in the bundle of "rights to property" "belong to" a delinquent taxpayer, the lien can attach as if the property itself belonged to the taxpayer . . .

This amorphous construct ignores the primacy of state law in defining property interests, eviscerates the statutory distinction between "property" and "rights to property" drawn by § 6321, and conflicts with an unbroken line of authority from this Court, the lower courts, and the IRS. Its application is all the more unsupportable in this case because, in my view, it is highly unlikely that the limited individual "rights to property" recognized in a tenancy by the entirety under Michigan law are themselves subject to lien. I would affirm the Court of Appeals and hold that Mr. Craft did not have "property" or "rights to property" to which the federal tax lien could attach.

I

Title 26 U.S.C. § 6321 provides that a federal tax lien attaches to "all property and rights to property, whether real or personal, belonging to" a delinquent taxpayer. It is uncontested that a federal tax lien itself "creates no property rights but merely attaches consequences, federally defined, to rights created under state law." United States v. Bess, 357 U.S.

51, 55, 78 S.Ct. 1054, 2 L.Ed.2d 1135 (1958) (construing the 1939 version of the federal tax lien statute). Consequently, the Government's lien under § 6321 "cannot extend beyond the property interests held by the delinquent taxpayer," United States v. Rodgers, 461 U.S. 677, 690–691, 103 S.Ct. 2132, 76 L.Ed.2d 236 (1983), under state law. Before today, no one disputed that the IRS, by operation of § 6321, "steps into the taxpayer's shoes," and has the same rights as the taxpayer in property or rights to property subject to the lien. B. Bittker & M. McMahon, Federal Income Taxation of Individuals ¶ 44.5[4][a] (2d ed. 1995 and 2000 Cum. Supp.) (hereinafter Bittker). I would not expand " 'the nature of the legal interest' " the taxpayer has in the property beyond those interests recognized under state law. Aquilino v. United States, 363 U.S. 509, 513, 80 S.Ct. 1277, 4 L.Ed.2d 1365 (1960) (citing Morgan v. Commissioner, 309 U.S. 78, 82, 60 S.Ct. 424, 84 L.Ed. 1035 (1940)).

A

If the Grand Rapids property "belong[ed] to" Mr. Craft under state law prior to the termination of the tenancy by the entirety, the federal tax lien would have attached to the Grand Rapids property. But that is not this case. As the Court recognizes, pursuant to Michigan law, as under English common law, property held as a tenancy by the entirety does not belong to either spouse, but to a single entity composed of the married persons. See ante, at 1422. Neither spouse has "any separate interest in such an estate." Sanford v. Bertrau, 204 Mich. 244, 249, 169 N.W. 880, 882 (1918); see also Long v. Earle, 277 Mich. 505, 517, 269 N.W. 577, 581 (1936) ("Each [spouse] is vested with an entire title and, as against the one who attempts alone to convey or incumber such real estate, the other has an absolute title"). An entireties estate constitutes an indivisible "sole tenancy." See Budwit v. Herr, 339 Mich. 265, 272, 63 N.W.2d 841, 844 (1954); see also Tyler v. United States, 281 U.S. 497, 501, 50 S.Ct. 356, 74 L.Ed. 991 (1930) ("[T]he tenants constitute a unit; neither can dispose of any part of the estate without the consent of the other; and the whole continues in the survivor"). Because Michigan does not recognize a separate spousal interest in the Grand Rapids property, it did not "belong" to either respondent or her husband individually when the IRS asserted its lien for Mr. Craft's individual tax liability. Thus, the property was not property to which the federal tax lien could attach for Mr. Craft's tax liability.

The Court does not dispute this characterization of Michigan's law with respect to the essential attributes of the tenancy by the entirety estate. However, relying on Drye v. United States, 528 U.S. 49, 59, 120 S.Ct. 474, 145 L.Ed.2d 466 (1999), which in turn relied upon United States v. Irvine, 511 U.S. 224, 114 S.Ct. 1473, 128 L.Ed.2d 168 (1994), and United States v. Mitchell, 403 U.S. 190, 91 S.Ct. 1763, 29 L.Ed.2d 406 (1971), the Court suggests that Michigan's definition of the tenancy by the entirety estate should be overlooked because federal tax law is not controlled by state legal fictions concerning property ownership. Ante, at 1420. But the Court misapprehends the application of Drye to this case.

Drye, like Irvine and Mitchell before it, was concerned not with whether state law recognized "property" as belonging to the taxpayer in the first place, but rather with whether state laws could disclaim or exempt such property from federal tax liability after the property interest was created. Drye held only that a state-law disclaimer could not retroactively undo a vested right in an estate that the taxpayer already held, and that a federal lien therefore attached to the taxpayer's interest in the estate. 528 U.S., at 61, 120 S.Ct. 474 (recognizing that a disclaimer does not restore the status quo ante because the heir "determines who will receive the property—himself if he does not disclaim, a known other if he does"). Similarly, in Irvine, the Court held that a state law allowing an individual to disclaim a gift could not force the Court to be "struck blind" to the fact that the transfer of "property" or "property rights" for which the gift tax was due had already occurred; "state property transfer rules do not transfer into federal taxation rules." 511 U.S., at 239–240, 114 S.Ct. 1473 (emphasis added). See also Mitchell, supra, at 204, 91 S.Ct. 1763 (holding that right to renounce a marital interest under state law does not indicate that the taxpayer had no right to property before the renunciation).

Extending this Court's "state law fiction" jurisprudence to determine whether property or rights to property exist under state law in the first place works a sea change in the role States have traditionally played in "creating and defining" property interests. By erasing the careful line between state laws that purport to disclaim or exempt property interests after the fact, which the federal tax lien does not respect, and state laws' definition of property and property rights, which the federal tax lien does respect, the Court does not follow Drye, but rather creates a new federal common law of property. This contravenes the previously settled rule that the definition and scope of property is left to the States. See Aquilino, supra, at 513, n. 3, 80 S.Ct. 1277 (recognizing unsoundness of leaving the definition of property interests to a nebulous body of federal law, "because it ignores the long-established role that the States have played in creating property interests and places upon the courts the task of attempting to ascertain a taxpayer's property rights under an undefined rule of federal law").

B

That the Grand Rapids property does not belong to Mr. Craft under Michigan law does not end the inquiry, however, since the federal tax lien attaches not only to "property" but also to any "rights to property" belonging to the taxpayer. While the Court concludes that a laundry list of "rights to property" belonged to Mr. Craft as a tenant by the entirety, it does not suggest that the tax lien attached to any of these particular rights. Instead, the Court gathers these rights together and opines that there were sufficient sticks to form a bundle, so that "respondent's husband's interest in the entireties property constituted 'property' or 'rights to property' for the purposes of the federal tax lien statute." ...

But the Court's "sticks in a bundle" metaphor collapses precisely because of the distinction expressly drawn by the statute, which distinguishes between "property" and "rights to property." The Court refrains from ever stating whether this case involves "property" or "rights to property" even though § 6321 specifically provides that the federal tax lien attaches to "property" and "rights to property" "belonging to" the delinquent taxpayer, and not to an imprecise construct of "individual rights in the estate sufficient to constitute 'property and rights to property' for the purposes of the lien." ...

Rather than adopt the majority's approach, I would ask specifically, as the statute does, whether Mr. Craft had any particular "rights to property" to which the federal tax lien could attach. He did not. Such "rights to property" that have been subject to the § 6321 lien are valuable and "pecuniary," i.e., they can be attached, and levied upon or sold by the Government. Drye, 528 U.S., at 58–60, and n. 7, 120 S.Ct. 474. With such rights subject to lien, the taxpayer's interest has "ripen[ed] into a present estate" of some form and is more than a mere expectancy, id., at 60, n. 7, 120 S.Ct. 474, and thus the taxpayer has an apparent right "to channel that value to [another]," id., at 61, 120 S.Ct. 474.

In contrast, a tenant in a tenancy by the entirety not only lacks a present divisible vested interest in the property and control with respect to the sale, encumbrance, and transfer of the property, but also does not possess the ability to devise any portion of the property because it is subject to the other's indestructible right of survivorship. Rogers v. Rogers, 136 Mich.App. 125, 135–137, 356 N.W.2d 288, 293–294 (1984). This latter fact makes the property significantly different from community property, where each spouse has a present one-half vested interest in the whole, which may be devised by will or otherwise to a person other than the spouse. See 4 G. Thompson, Real Property § 37.14(a) (D. Thomas ed. 1994) (noting that a married person's power to devise one-half of the community property is "consistent with the fundamental characteristic of community property": "community ownership means that each spouse owns 50% of each community asset"). See also Drye, 528 U.S., at 61, 120 S.Ct. 474 ("[I]n determining whether a federal taxpayer's state-law rights constitute 'property' or 'rights to property,' the important consideration is the breadth of the control the taxpayer could exercise over the property") (emphasis added, citation and brackets omitted).

It is clear that some of the individual rights of a tenant in entireties property are primarily personal, dependent upon the taxpayer's status as a spouse, and similarly not susceptible to a tax lien. For example, the right to use the property in conjunction with one's spouse and to exclude all others appears particularly ill suited to being transferred to another, see ibid., and to lack "exchangeable value," id., at 56, 120 S.Ct. 474.

Nor do other identified rights rise to the level of "rights to property" to which a § 6321 lien can attach, because they represent, at most, a contingent future interest, or an "expectancy" that has not "ripen[ed] into a present estate." Id., at 60, n. 7, 120 S.Ct. 474 ("Nor do we mean to suggest that an expectancy that has pecuniary value and is transferable under state law would fall within § 6321 prior to the time it ripens into a present estate"). Cf. Bess, 357 U.S., at 55–56, 78 S.Ct. 1054 (holding that no federal tax lien could attach to proceeds of the taxpayer's life insurance policy because "[i]t would be anomalous to view as 'property' subject to lien proceeds never within the insured's reach to enjoy"). By way of example, the survivorship right wholly depends upon one spouse outliving the other, at which time the survivor gains "substantial rights, in respect of the property, theretofore never enjoyed by [the] survivor." Tyler, 281 U.S., at 503, 50 S.Ct. 356. While the Court explains that it is "not necessary to decide whether the right to survivorship alone would qualify as 'property' or 'rights to property' " under § 6321, ante, at 1424, the facts of this case demonstrate that it would not. Even assuming both that the right of survivability continued after the demise of the tenancy estate and that the tax lien could attach to such a contingent future right, creating a lienable interest upon the death of the nonliable spouse, it would not help the IRS here; respondent's husband predeceased her in 1998, and there is no right of survivorship at issue in this case.

Similarly, while one spouse might escape the absolute limitations on individual action with respect to tenancy by the entirety property by obtaining the right to one-half of the property upon divorce, or by agreeing with the other spouse to sever the tenancy by the entirety, neither instance is an event of sufficient certainty to constitute a "right to property" for purposes of § 6321. Finally, while the federal tax lien could arguably have attached to a tenant's right to any "rents, products, income, or profits" of real property held as tenants by the entirety, Mich. Comp. Laws Ann. § 557.71 (West 1988), the Grand Rapids property created no rents, products, income, or profits for the tax lien to attach to . . .

Accordingly, I conclude that Mr. Craft had neither "property" nor "rights to property" to which the federal tax lien could attach.

II

That the federal tax lien did not attach to the Grand Rapids property is further supported by the consensus among the lower courts. For more than 50 years, every federal court reviewing tenancies by the entirety in States with a similar understanding of tenancy by the entirety as Michigan has concluded that a federal tax lien cannot attach to such property to satisfy an individual spouse's tax liability. This consensus is supported by the IRS' consistent recognition, arguably against its own interest, that a federal tax lien against one spouse cannot attach to property or rights to property held as a tenancy by the entirety.

That the Court fails to so much as mention this consensus, let alone address it or give any reason for overruling it, is puzzling. While the positions of the lower courts and the IRS do not bind this Court, one would be hard pressed to explain why the combined weight of these judicial and administrative sources—including the IRS' instructions to its own employees—do not constitute relevant authority . . .

NOTES AND QUESTIONS

1. What happens to a tenancy by the entirety when the marriage ends in a divorce? As the New York Court of Appeals has stated:

> The common law soon recognized that in addition to death a legal dissolution of the unity of husband and wife would necessarily affect the continuing validity of a tenancy by the entirety. In holding that an absolute divorce terminates a tenancy by the entirety, Judge Peckham observed: "When the idea upon which the creation of an estate by the entirety depends is considered, it seems to me much the more logical as well as plausible view to say that as the estate is founded upon the unity of husband and wife, and it never would exist in the first place but for such unity; anything that terminates the legal fiction of the unity of two separate persons ought to have an effect upon the estate whose creation depended upon such unity." [citation omitted]

> Upon termination of a tenancy by the entirety through divorce, the parties become tenants in common. . . . Since an annulment also alters the legal relationship between husband and wife, it has also been held to result in conversion of a tenancy by the entirety into a tenancy in common. . . . Where, however, husband and wife separate without the aid of a judicial decree, they remain one legal person; and, therefore, they continue to own property acquired as tenants by the entirety just as they did prior to their separation. Kahn v. Kahn, 43 N.Y.2d 203, 207, 401 N.Y.S.2d 47, 49, 371 N.E.2d 809, 811 (1977).

In some jurisdictions, if tenants by the entirety are divorced, the court may allocate the entirety property to one spouse in order to provide for an "equitable division of property." See N.J.Stat.Ann. § 2A:34–23 (West Supp. 1986).

Unlike co-tenants, neither spouse is entitled to sever the tenancy by the entirety by a compulsory partition. Severance of the tenancy can result only from the voluntary acts of the parties. See Branstetter v. Branstetter, 36 N.C.App. 532, 245 S.E.2d 87 (1978).

2. States that recognize the tenancy by the entirety differ regarding the right of one spouse to alienate his or her interest and the power of one spouse's creditor to reach the property. Most states that recognize such tenancy take the view that neither spouse can unilaterally transfer his or her interest and also bar each spouse's creditors from attaching the property. A small number of such states are to the contrary. See generally S. Kurtz, Moynihan's Introduction to the Law of Real Property, 4th ed., 3rd ed. at 286–288 (2005).

3. Suppose O transfers Blackacre to H and W, who are married to each other, and to Y. What is the state of the title? In jurisdictions recognizing the tenancy by the entirety, H and W can hold their one-half share as tenants by the entirety and in common with Y who owns an undivided one-half interest in Blackacre. See, e.g., West Chicago Park Commissioners v. Coleman, 108 Ill. 591 (1884).

4. Suppose O conveys property to H and W, as tenants by the entirety. H and W, however, are not legally married. What is the state of the title? Compare Bove v. Bove, 394 Pa. 627, 149 A.2d 67 (1959) (joint tenants) with Wright v. Kayner, 150 Mich. 7, 113 N.W. 779 (1907).

5. H and W–1 own Blackacre as tenants by the entirety. H murders W–1. After his subsequent release from prison, he marries W–2, and through a straw device conveys Blackacre to himself and W–2 as tenants by the entirety. H dies in 1985 and under the terms of this will leaves all of his property to W–2. H is survived by W–2 and by A and B, his two children from his marriage to W–1. A and B claim to own an undivided one-half interest in Blackacre. W–2 claims to own all of Blackacre. What theories would support these competing contentions? See Preston v. Chabot, 138 Vt. 170, 412 A.2d 930 (1980).

6. At common law, a woman's husband controlled the disposition of her real property and was entitled to the rents and profits from that property. Additionally, his creditors could reach her property in satisfaction of his debts. In part to assure that married women were entitled to the same rights over their property as unmarried women as well as to protect married women from impoverishment because of their spendthrift husbands, the states in the mid–1830s began enacting so-called Married Women's Property Acts. "The first statutes appeared in Arkansas and Florida territories in the mid–1830s, but the first major state act was that of Mississippi, which came hard on the heels of the devastating Panic of 1837. The New York State act, passed in 1848 . . . emerged as the national model. . . . The first wave of married women's property acts freed wives' estates from the debts of their husbands, leaving the traditional marital estate and coverture rules intact. Subsequent legislation extended the sweep of these laws by taking into account the changing workplace where women entered in small but growing numbers in the late nineteenth century."[1]

States are divided on whether married women's property acts are inconsistent with the creation of a tenancy by the entirety. Compare, Morrill v. Morrill, 138 Mich. 112, 101 N.W. 209 (1904) (acts have no effect on validity of tenancy by the entirety) with Fay v. Smiley, 201 Iowa 1290, 207 N.W. 369 (1926) (tenancy not valid in Iowa). In 1918, the Tennessee Supreme Court held that by enacting the Married Women's Property Act, the tenancy by the entirety was abolished. Gill v. McKinney, 140 Tenn. 549, 205 S.W. 416 (1918). A couple of years later the Tennessee legislature responded by enacting a statute restoring such tenancy to the types of tenancies that could be created. A recent case, Roberts v. Bailey, 338 S.W.3d 540 (2010), involved a conveyance made to a married couple purporting to create a tenancy by the entirety

---

1. K. Hall, W. Wiecek, & P. Winkelman, American Legal History, Cases and Materials 267–268 (1991). Coverture was the name that described the rights a husband had to control his wife's property.

during the period between the time Gill was decided and the subsequent legislative response. The court held that no tenancy by the entirety was created.

7. Where property is held by spouses as tenants by the entirety, the government's right to a forfeiture of the property because one of the spouses uses the property for illegal purposes is limited. See, United States v. Parcel Known As 1500 Lincoln Avenue, 949 F.2d 73 (3d Cir.1991) (government's right to forfeit husband's interest in property used for illegal purposes limited to a lien against the property; wife's right to possession during spouses' lifetimes, her right to avoid unilateral conveyances, and her right of survivorship not affected by the government lien). However, where the spouses owned an automobile as joint tenants with right of survivorship and the car was used in a crime, the Supreme Court held that the property could forfeit to the State of Michigan as a nuisance. The Court reasoned that the spouse who did not engage in the illegal activity (prostitution) was subject to having her interest forfeited because she, as an owner, had entrusted the property to her husband who was involved in the illegal activity. Bennis v. Michigan, 516 U.S. 442 (1996).

§ 6.5 COMMUNITY PROPERTY INTERESTS

YOUNGER, COMMUNITY PROPERTY, WOMEN AND THE LAW SCHOOL CURRICULUM, 48 N.Y.U.L.REV. 211, 214–223 (1974)

The notion of marital community is much older than common law principles. Its sources are the Code of Hammurabi, the Twelve Tables of Gortyn and the Fuero Juzgo, or Visigothic Code. Stemming from a way of life said to be classless and democratic and spread, incidentally, by people said to be barbaric, the community property system would seem to have been well-suited to the American frontier. Had it survived in England until the first landings at Jamestown and Plymouth the predominant American pattern might have been different. However, the English rejected the marital community in the thirteenth century; it arrived in the New World, therefore, as part of the civil law systems of the Spanish and the French. At one time it enjoyed fairly wide recognition in America, existing "in every one of the southern tier of states" as well as a number of those northern ones which formed part of the Northwest Territory. In lasting impact, however, the civil law community was no match for the English common law. In some jurisdictions it was viewed as a transplanted but rootless "exotic" and was soon displaced. In others—Louisiana, Texas and California—it was retained despite the omnipresence of the rival system in other areas of law. In still other states—Nevada, New Mexico, Arizona, Washington and Idaho—it was adopted anew after a test of married life under common law property rules. In Louisiana the civil law governed not only marital property but everything else as well; in Texas it applied to marital property, land and civil procedure; and in California, Nevada, New

Mexico, Arizona, Washington, and Idaho, it governed marital property only. The common law was the source of all other rules.

It is not always clear why the states rejected, retained or adopted the marital community. Of the retaining states, Louisiana was the first to take a firm stand by prohibiting acceptance of the common law as a unit in the Constitution of 1812. Texas formally retained the marital community in 1840 and California followed suit in 1850; together the two influenced its adoption in the other five community states. Only in California, however, does the record show that the relative merits of common law and community systems were actually discussed. The occasion was the California Constitutional Convention of 1849; the focal point was the proposed inclusion in the state constitution of a provision defining the wife's separate estate. One delegate made his personal preferences crystal clear: he saw the constitutional definition and the community system as a way to attract wives. Calling on all fellow bachelors at the Convention to vote accordingly, he anticipated the migration of rich, marriageable women to California. Another delegate lent his support for a less selfish reason: the common law "annihilated" married women. While he himself could "stand" the system, he entreated the Convention not to impose its "despotic provisions" on wives. The advocates of the common law rallied to its defense. To this group there was nothing more natural than the notion of woman's inferior place. Delegate Lippit, citing the sad example of France, described its capital as a "spectacle of domestic disunion" where, he assured the Convention, two-thirds of the married couples were living apart. Civil law principles caused such disorder by "setting the wife up as an equal, in everything whatever, to the husband" and "raising her from the condition of head clerk to partner." Delegate Botts was even more emphatic. In his eyes, common law marital rules were "beautiful," "admirable" and "beneficial"; husbands were better protectors of wives than the law; the opposition's plan "to make the wife independent of the husband" was contrary to "nature" and "wisdom"; and the "doctrine of woman's rights" was the doctrine of "those mental hermaphrodites, Abby Folsom, Fanny Wright, and the rest of that tribe."

Both factions were overreacting, for the community system, as it ultimately developed in this country, offered nothing for married women to celebrate or married men to fear. Basically, it created a community. The members, of course, were husband and wife. Community property, or "common" property as it was called in early American statutes, included everything acquired by either spouse after marriage, except for gifts and inheritances. Common property was said to belong to both spouses as partners in marriage. In theory, it followed, the wife's interest in the common property was that of a full "partner"—a startling contrast to the common law in which all was vested in the husband. In practice, however, the two systems had like effect. The wife was a decidedly inferior partner; in fact, her partnership interest began at the partnership's end. While the marriage and the community lasted, the husband was vested with the sole management and control of its assets, generally enjoying the same power of disposition over them as he had over his separate estate. Until dissolution of the marriage and the community, the wife's interest seemed suspended. As the Louisiana Code frankly provided, she had "no sort of right" in community assets "until her husband be dead." She was then entitled to sue his heirs if she could prove he had fraudulently sold community assets in order to injure her. The exact nature of the wife's interest gave rise to much discussion, since courts then, as now, felt the need to match theory and practice so as to justify the law's preference for husbands. Some were forthright: the husband, they said, was made manager of the community because the community property was really his. According to others, the husband was given control of the community not because he was its exclusive owner, but because someone must manage it and the law chose him. Of course, both spouses might have been designated joint managers of community assets, or management responsibilities might have been apportioned between them. Neither of these schemes, however, was part of early American law.

The other aspect of the community system which differed theoretically from the common law was its clear recognition of wife's separate estate. . . . If the wife seemed thus endowed with a separate estate, she was not to be permitted to use it. Its management, like that of her interest in the community, was vested by law in the husband. Written consent of both spouses, however, was required for its sale. Louisiana alone stood true to the Spanish heritage, allowing the wife to administer her own paraphernal property. But there, too, the husband's authorization or, if he failed to give it, that of the court was required for sale. In California the restriction on the wife's power to sell her separate property was soon attacked. How could the husband's consent be required in view of the state constitution? The California Supreme Court considered the question and upheld the restriction. Conceding that the framers, by defining the wife's separate estate, "swept out of existence many of the disabilities of the wife and some of the most important rights of the husband," the court unaccountably found the state legislators free to restore them.

In justification of American lawmakers, it might be said that in making the husband manager of the community, they were merely following Spanish law, expressing legitimate concern for the rights of creditors or giving effect to the reality of most marriages in which the husband was the sole wage-earner and provider. In making him manager of the wife's separate estate as well, they ignored the Spanish law and had no other excuses with which to justify their action. In fact, they were influenced by the common law and its insistence on the husband's superior place. Thus they acted purely on the basis of sex.

Judicial motive is harder to assess in cases dealing with another significant question that arose early in the American community property states. In two cases, one in California and the other in Texas, creditors of the husband tried to reach dividends of stock purchased with the wife's separate funds and cotton grown on her separate land by slaves who were her separate property. The question before each court was the nature of these "fruits" of the wife's separate estate: were they to be treated as her separate property or as part of the community fund? The Texas Supreme Court characterized the cotton as community property, which could therefore be reached by the husband's creditors. The California Supreme Court held that the dividends were part of the wife's separate estate and thus were immune from suits by creditors of the husband. In reaching opposite conclusions both courts said they were acting in the best interests of the wife. Neither statement can be summarily dismissed. The California ruling, followed in all community property states except Texas, Louisiana and Idaho, increased the wife's separate property and kept it safe from the husband's debts. If the husband had separate property and the wife had none, the California rule, applied reciprocally to the husband, increased his separate estate instead of the community in which wife had a share. It thus worked to the disadvantage of the wife who stayed home as the husband's dependent, with no source of capital except the community. The Texas ruling, on the other hand, worked to her advantage by adding the increment of the husband's separate property to the community rather than to his separate estate. The effect upon a propertied or earning married woman was mixed: she was protected against her husband's misuse of his control over her separate property to increase his own separate estate; but she was exposed to the extent that the increment of her separate property, when added to the community, became subject to his debts. In making a final evaluation of the companion rulings, one must discount any advantage to the propertied wife from the California rule and to the dependent wife from the Texas rule. Whether labeled "separate" or "community" property, the increment of the wife's separate estate remained in the husband's control. Since wives, in the eyes of the law, were supposed to stay at home and be supported by husbands—and a century ago most of them did—the Texas view (increasing community assets and, theoretically at least, the wife's compensation for services) was probably the fairer of the two.

Thus, by the turn of the century, the stage was set for forty-two common law and eight community property states; and so it remained except for short-lived conversions to community property by the then territory of Hawaii and the states of Michigan, Nebraska, Oklahoma, Oregon and Pennsylvania. These departures were motivated by the hope of securing tax advantages for married residents, not by legislative concern for women's rights. Static in terms of the number of jurisdictions embracing it, the community system has nevertheless undergone significant substantive change since its American reception. The first modification, now completely effective, has been the freeing of wives via Married Women's Property Acts to manage, control and otherwise deal with their separate estates. The second, not yet effected in all eight states but equally important in terms of women's rights, has been a discernible trend toward revesting wives with their full "partnership" interests in community assets, including the right during marriage to manage and control them.

The philosophy underlying the community property system is that the husband and wife are essentially equal partners in property acquired as a result of their work effort by either one of them during the marriage. Thus, each spouse's earnings and all property bought with those earnings belong to the community. Property acquired by either spouse but not as a result of work effort remains the separate property of each spouse. Therefore, property acquired by either spouse during the marriage as a result of a gift, bequest or inheritance is the separate property of each spouse. Likewise property acquired by either spouse prior to the marriage is the separate property of such spouse. In all community property states[1] there is a presumption that property acquired during the marriage is community property.

While each spouse in a community property state has the power to sell, mortgage, lease or otherwise dispose of his or her interest in separate property, generally the spouses share the management power over the community property. However, the community property states have idiosyncratic nuances with respect to the rights of the spouses to manage community property. In all community property states, however, each spouse has the unrestricted right to dispose by will of his or her one-half of the community property and, of course, all of his or her separate property. See, e.g., Ariz.Rev.Stat. § 14–3101(A) (Supp.1991); Tex.Rev.Civ. Stat.Prob. Code § 58 (Vernon 1992). If a spouse dies intestate, community property state laws differ respecting the disposition of the deceased spouse's share of the community and of his or her separate property. For example, in California, Idaho, Nevada, New Mexico and Washington, the intestate spouse's share of the community passes to the surviving spouse; in Arizona and Texas the surviving spouse may have to share the deceased spouse's community property interest with children. See Ariz.Rev.Stat. § 14–2102 (1985); Tex.Rev.Civ.Stat.Ann.Prob. Code § 45 (Vernon 1980).

Community property state laws also vary respecting the rights of a spouse's creditors to reach the community property to satisfy the spouse's separate obligations. The extent to which creditors of one spouse can reach community property depends upon whether their claims arose in contract or tort, whether the claim accrued prior to or after the marriage and on the nature of the particular community asset. Creditors of community obligations, on the other hand, can reach the community assets in satisfaction of their claims. They can also reach the separate assets of the debtor spouse although in some community property states they can only do so after the community property has been exhausted.

The community is dissolved by death, divorce, dissolution or annulment. When the community is dissolved by divorce, dissolution, or annulment the property settlement can be affected by the characterization of property as either separate or community. In some states each spouse must receive his or her separate property; in others separate property is in the "pot" for purposes of making an "equitable distribution." In some

---

1. Arizona, California, Idaho, Louisiana, Nevada, New Mexico, Texas, and Washington.

states all community property is divided equally between the spouses; in others it is in the "pot" for purposes of making an equitable distribution.

For a detailed analysis of community property laws, see, W. McClanahan, Community Property Law in the United States (1982); W. de Funiak & M. Vaughn, Principles of Community Property (2d ed. 1971); W. Reppy & C. Samuel, Community Property in the United States (2d ed. 1982).

UNIFORM MARITAL PROPERTY
ACT PREFATORY NOTE

9A U.L.A. 21–26 (Supp.1976).

"The institution of property is the embodiment of accidents, events, and the wisdom of the past. It is before us as clay into which we can introduce the coloration and configuration representing our wisdom. How great, how useful this new ingredient may be will largely determine the future happiness, and perhaps the continued existence of our society." Powell, The Law of Real Property (Rohan 4th ed. 1977).

Marriages have beginnings and endings. For their participants, the period between these points is the marriage. This Act is a property law. It functions to recognize the respective contributions made by men and women during a marriage. It discharges that function by raising those contributions to the level of defined, shared and enforceable property rights at the time the contributions are made.

The challenge to create such a framework is not new. Basic differences in approaches to marital economics go back for many centuries.

* * *

In modern times the challenge was well articulated twenty years ago by the Report of the Committee on Civil and Political Rights to the President's Commission on the Status of Women. In 1963 that Report said:

Marriage is a partnership to which each spouse makes a different but equally important contribution. This fact has become increasingly recognized in the realities of American family living. While the laws of other countries have reflected this trend, family laws in the United States have lagged behind. Accordingly, the Committee concludes that during marriage each spouse should have a legally defined and substantial right in the earnings of the other spouse and in the real and personal property acquired as a result of such earnings, as well as in the management of such earnings and property. Such right should survive the marriage and be legally recognized in the event of its termination by annulment, divorce, or death. This policy should be appropriately implemented by legislation which would safeguard either spouse against improper alienation of property by the other.

In the twenty years after those words much has changed regarding the institution of marriage, even though the challenge has not been fully met.

* * *

Statistics are not the only evidence of dramatic change. State houses have reflected it. Beginning with California at the end of the 60's and promulgation of the Uniform Marriage and Divorce Act in the early 70's, no-fault divorce has swept the statute books. In 1983 Illinois and South Dakota stand alone in adhering to fault-based divorce, and efforts to change to no-fault continue in Illinois. "Equitable distribution" of property became the handmaiden of no-fault divorce in the Uniform Marriage and Divorce Act and in most other reforms. Forty-one traditional common law jurisdictions now use some form of property division as a principal means of resolving economic dilemmas on dissolution. Adding the eight community property jurisdictions in which such a division is an inherent aspect of spousal property rights yields a total of 49. . . .

The ferment of change has not been limited to dissolution. The Uniform Probate Code was promulgated in 1969. . . . Article II of the Code contains the concept of an augmented estate. It borrows heavily from New York's 1966 version of the idea. It is an advance on traditional forced-share procedures, operating by the creation of a larger universe of property against which a spousal right of election is exercisable. It accomplishes this by penetrating the veil of title and other techniques which have developed to insulate assets from the reach of forced-share statutes. In the official comment to the Code the augmented estate provisions are described as preventing arrangements by the owner of wealth which would transmit property to others than a surviving spouse by means other than probate for the deliberate purpose of defeating the rights of a surviving spouse.

It is worth noting that the Code's provisions, as well as conventional forced-share provisions in common law states, leave a gap. They transform assets into a sharing mode in a meaningful way only when the "have-not" spouse survives. If the sequence of death is the opposite, the have-not spouse has no power to dispose of assets over which he or she has no title in any common law jurisdiction.

* * *

Obviously the "everything to each other" mode is confined to dispositions at death. An imposing body of case law testifies to a paradigm shift in this view when the question of "Who should get what and when?" is asked at a dissolution! And it is the equitable distribution court's demanding role in the judicial process to monitor and referee the ensuing contests in the divorce courts. Burgeoning advance sheets clearly indicate just how difficult the referee's job is when it must be done well over a million times a year!

In 1981 yet another shift was added to the catalog of change. After years of debate, tax-free interspousal transfers entered the stage under the auspices of the Economic Recovery Tax Act of 1981. Wall Street Journal columnist Vermont Royster furnished a characteristically succinct summary of it all:

> "The marriage ceremony may say you two are now one and even include that phrase about with all my worldly goods I thee endow. The Internal Revenue Service has always taken a different view. It's wanted its share.
>
> . . . wait until January 1, 1982, and . . . after that magic date you can share with your spouse an much as you please of those worldly goods . . . without so much as a by-your-leave from the federal tax man. In 1982 no more gift and estate taxes between spouses." Wall St. J., Sept. 2, 1981.

Heavy economic responsibilities of married couples and methods of coping with them point to yet another trend line of the last few decades. It is that of the two-worker households in which sharing the burden of producing family income is becoming routine. In more than half of American marriages with two spouses present there is a working wife and the number is growing. When there are children, the ratio is even higher. In more than two-thirds of current upper income marriages ($24,000 or more) there are two wage earners. Sharing of responsibility for wages from outside the home is altering traditional spousal roles and particularly economic roles, rights, and responsibilities.

Thus the stage is set by substantial social and legislative change in the duration of marriages and in the economics of the termination of marriages by dissolution and death.

The Uniform Marital Property Act makes its appearance on that stage to offer a means of establishing present shared property rights of spouses during the marriage. This approach is bottomed on two propositions. The first is creation of an immediate sharing mode of ownership. The second proposition is that the sharing mode during marriage is an ownership right already in existence at the end of a marriage. . . .

* * *

What are the root concepts?

FIRST: Property acquired during marriage by the effort of spouses is shared and is something the couple can truly style as "ours." Rather than an evanescent hope, the idea of sharing implicit in viewing property as "ours" becomes reality as a result of a present, vested ownership right which each spouse has in all property acquired by the personal efforts of either during the marriage. That property is "marital property." . . .

Except for its income, property brought into the marriage or acquired afterward by gift or devise is not marital but "individual property." Its appreciation remains individual property. However, the income of that property becomes marital property, so that all income of a couple is marital property. . . .

Property already owned when the Act becomes effective or owned by couples moving into an adopting state will take on the characteristics of marital property only at death or marital dissolution and then only if it would have been marital property under the Act had the Act been in effect when and where the property was acquired. Prior to death or dissolution the Act ordains no change in the classification of property of a couple acquired at a time when the Act did not apply.

* * *

SECOND: The system which the Act creates to manage and control marital property accords a considerable measure of individual option. "Management and control" is a phrase of art in the Act. Basically management and control rights flow from the form in which title to property is held. If only one spouse holds property there is no requirement for the other spouse to participate in management and control functions. If both spouses hold property they must both participate in management and control unless the holding is in an alternative ("A or B") form. Couples can select their own options as they deem appropriate. . . . Management and control is different from ownership. Ownership rights are not lost by relinquishing or even neglecting management and control rights. In essence, the Act's management and control system is substantially similar to the existing procedures of title based management in common law states. . . .

To guard against possible abuses by a spouse with sole title, a court can implement the addition of the name of the other spouse to marital property so that it is held, managed and controlled by both spouses.

* * *

The rule on gifts of marital property to third parties provides a safe harbor for smaller gifts. Unless aggregate gifts of marital property by one spouse to a third party in a calendar year are less than a specified dollar amount or are reasonable in amount with respect to the economic position of the spouses when made, both spouses must join in making the gift. A failure to procure that joinder renders the gift voidable at the option of the non-participating spouse. . . .

THIRD: The varying patterns of today's marriages are accommodated by an opportunity to create custom systems by "marital property agreements." Full freedom to contract with respect to virtually all property matters is possible under the Act. By a marital property agreement a couple could opt out of the provisions of the Act in whole or in part. Conversely, they could opt in by agreeing that the Act's provisions will apply to all or a part of the property they own before they became subject to its terms.

As a protection and to ease matters of proof, the Act requires that marital property agreements be made in writing and signed by both spouses.... Marital property agreements are enforceable without consideration.

FOURTH: On dissolution the structure of the Act as a property statute comes into full play. The Act takes the parties "to the door of the divorce court" only. It leaves to existing dissolution procedures in the several states the selection of the appropriate procedures for dividing property. On the other hand the Act has the function of confirming the ownership of property as the couple enters the process. Thus reallocation of property derived from the effort of both spouses during the marriage starts from a basis of the equal undivided ownership that the spouses share in their marital property. A given state's equitable distribution or other property division procedures could mean that the ownership will end that way, or that it could be substantially altered, but that will depend on other applicable state law and judicial determinations. An analogous situation obtains at death, with the Act operating primarily as a property statute rather than a probate statute.

At divorce and death special provisions will apply to property of a couple acquired before the Act applied to that couple. If any of that property would have been marital property under the Act, had the Act been in effect when and where it was acquired, then such property will be treated as if it were marital property at divorce. Property of the deceased spouse having that characteristic will be treated in that manner at death. This represents a deferred approach to reclassification of the property of spouses which does not otherwise have the characteristics of marital property due to the time or place of its acquisition. The deferral is to the time of marital termination at divorce or death. Those are events at which states have long altered the classification of their citizens' property by equitable distribution provisions or by forced share and augmented estate provisions. The Act builds on those established patterns already followed by the states by creating the deferred classification with respect to property owned by couples before the Act applied to them....

* * *

FIFTH: Creditors may have claims that arise before marriage and after marriage. The premarital creditor is denied a bonanza by a marriage. (Section 8(b)(iii)). That creditor can only reach what would have been reached had there been no marriage. Postmarital obligations may subject both marital and individual property to claims. Obligations incurred by a spouse during marriage are presumed to be incurred in the interest of the marriage and the family and those obligations may be satisfied from all marital property and the other property of the incurring spouse....

SIXTH: Bona fide purchasers of property for value are protected in their transactions with spouses by reliance on the manner in which property is held. They are under no duty to look "underneath" the manner of holding and are fully protected for not doing so. . . .

* * *

IN RE MARRIAGE OF BROWN

Supreme Court of California (1976).
15 Cal.3d 838, 126 Cal.Rptr. 633, 544 P.2d 561.

TOBRINER, JUSTICE.

Since French v. French (1941) 17 Cal.2d 775, 778, 112 P.2d 235, California courts have held that nonvested pension rights are not property, but a mere expectancy, and thus not a community asset subject to division upon dissolution of a marriage. . . . Properly raised in the present case by appellant Gloria Brown, the issue of division of nonvested pension rights upon dissolution of a marriage again confronts this court.

Upon reconsideration of this issue, we have concluded that French v. French should be overruled and that the subsequent decisions which rely on that precedent should be disapproved. As we shall explain, the French rule cannot stand because nonvested pension rights are not an expectancy but a contingent interest in property; furthermore, the French rule compels an inequitable division of rights acquired through community effort. Pension rights, whether or not vested, represent a property interest; to the extent that such rights derive from employment during coverture, they comprise a community asset subject to division in a dissolution proceeding.

Before we turn to the facts of this appeal we must devote a few words to terminology. Some decisions that discuss pension rights, but do not involve division of marital property, describe a pension right as "vested" if the employer cannot unilaterally repudiate that right without terminating the employment relationship. . . . As we explain later, we believe that these decisions correctly define the point at which a pension right becomes a property interest. In divorce and dissolution cases following French v. French, however, the term "vested" has acquired a special meaning; it refers to a pension right which is not subject to a condition of forfeiture if the employment relationship terminates before retirement. We shall use the term "vested" in this latter sense as defining a pension right which survives the discharge or voluntary termination of the employee.

As so defined, a vested pension right must be distinguished from a "matured" or unconditional right to immediate payment. Depending upon the provisions of the retirement program, an employee's right may vest after a term of service even though it does not mature until he reaches retirement age and elects to retire. Such vested but immature rights are frequently subject to the condition, among others, that the employee survive until retirement.

The issue in the present case concerns the nonvested pension rights of respondent Robert Brown. General Telephone Company, Robert's employer, maintains a noncontributory pension plan in which the rights of the employees depend upon their accumulation of "points," based upon a combination of the years of service and the age of the employee. Under this plan, an employee who is discharged before he accumulates 78 points forfeits his rights; an employee with 78 points can opt for early retirement at a lower pension, or continue to work until age 63 and retire at an increased pension.

Gloria and Robert Brown married on July 29, 1950. When they separated in November of 1973, Robert had accumulated 72 points under the pension plan, a substantial portion of which is attributable to his work during the period when the parties were married and living together.[2] If he continues to work for General Telephone, Robert will accumulate 78 points on November 30, 1976. If he retires then, he will receive a monthly pension of $310.94; if he continues his employment until normal retirement age his pension will be $485 a month.

Relying on the French rule, the trial court held that since Robert had not yet acquired a "vested" right to the retirement pension, the value of his pension rights did not become community property subject to division by the court. It divided the remaining property, awarding Gloria the larger share but directing her to pay $1,742 to Robert to equalize the value received by each spouse. The court also awarded Gloria alimony of $75 per month. Gloria appeals from the portion of the interlocutory judgment that declares that Robert's pension rights are not community property and thus not subject to division by the court.[3]

As we have stated, the fundamental theoretical error which led to the inequitable division of marital property in the present case stems from the seminal decision of French v. French, supra, 17 Cal.2d 775, 112 P.2d 235. Mrs. French claimed a community interest in the prospective retirement pay of her husband, an enlisted man in the Fleet Reserve. The court noted that "under the applicable statutes the [husband] will not be entitled to such pay until he completes a service of 14 years in the Fleet Reserve and complies with all the requirements of that service." (P. 778, 112 P.2d p. 236.) It concluded that "At the present time, his right to retirement pay is an expectancy which is not subject to division as community property." (Ibid.)

In 1962 the Court of Appeal in Williamson v. Williamson, 203 Cal. App.2d 8, 21 Cal.Rptr. 164, explained the French rule, asserting that "To the extent that payment is, at the time of the divorce, subject to conditions which may or may not occur, the pension is an expectancy, not subject to

---

2. Since it concluded that nonvested pension rights are not divisible as a community asset, the trial court did not determine what portion of Robert's pension rights is owned by the community.

3. Gloria appealed also from the trial court's ruling that the parties' interest in the stock benefit purchase plan of General Telephone Company and all present shares owned by the parties in General Telephone Company are the separate property of Robert. Her briefs on appeal, however, do not discuss the stock benefit purchase plan or the ownership of the shares. At oral argument counsel informed us that these assets are connected to the pension program and governed by the same legal principles.

division as community property." (203 Cal.App.2d at p. 11, 21 Cal.Rptr. at p. 167.)

Subsequent cases, however, have limited the sweep of French, holding that a vested pension is community property even though it has not matured ... or is subject to conditions within the employee's control ... But although we have frequently reiterated the French rule in dictum ... we have not previously had occasion to reexamine the merits of that rule.

Throughout our decisions we have always recognized that the community owns all pension rights attributable to employment during the marriage.... The French rule, however, rests on the theory that nonvested pension rights may be community, but that they are not property; classified as mere expectancies, such rights are not assets subject to division on dissolution of the marriage.

We have concluded, however, that the French court's characterization of nonvested pension rights as expectancies errs. The term expectancy describes the interest of a person who merely foresees that he might receive a future beneficence, such as the interest of an heir apparent ... or of a beneficiary designated by a living insured who has a right to change the beneficiary ... As these examples demonstrate, the defining characteristic of an expectancy is that its holder has no enforceable right to his beneficence.

Although some jurisdictions classify retirement pensions as gratuities, it has long been settled that under California law such benefits "do not derive from the beneficence of the employer, but are properly part of the consideration earned by the employee." (In re Marriage of Fithian, supra, 10 Cal.3d 592, 596, 111 Cal.Rptr. 369, 371, 517 P.2d 449, 451.) Since pension benefits represent a form of deferred compensation for services rendered ... the employee's right to such benefits is a contractual right, derived from the terms of the employment contract. Since a contractual right is not an expectancy but a chose in action, a form of property ... an employee acquires a property right to pension benefits when he enters upon the performance of his employment contract.

* * *

Although, as we have pointed out, ... courts have previously refused to allocate this right in a nonvested pension between the spouses as community property on the ground that such pension is contingent upon continued employment, we reject this theory. In other situations when community funds or effort are expended to acquire a conditional right to future income, the courts do not hesitate to treat that right as a community asset. For example, in Waters v. Waters (1946) 75 Cal.App.2d 265, 170 P.2d 494, the attorney husband had a contingent interest in a suit pending on appeal at the time of the divorce; the court held that his fee, when and if collected, would be a community asset. Indeed in the several recent pension cases the courts have asserted that vested but immature pensions are community assets although such pensions are commonly subject to the condition that the employee survive until retirement. . . .

We conclude that French v. French, and subsequent cases erred in characterizing nonvested pension rights as expectancies and in denying the trial courts the authority to divide such rights as community property. This mischaracterization of pension rights has, and unless overturned, will continue to result in inequitable division of community assets. Over the past decades, pension benefits have become an increasingly significant part of the consideration earned by the employee for his services. As the date of vesting and retirement approaches, the value of the pension right grows until it often represents the most important asset of the marital community. . . . A division of community property, which awards one spouse the entire value of this asset, without any offsetting award to the other spouse, does not represent that equal division of community property contemplated by Civil Code section 4800.

The present case illustrates the point. Robert's pension rights, a valuable asset built up by 24 years of community effort, under the French rule would escape division by the court as a community asset solely because dissolution occurred two years before the vesting date. If, as is entirely likely, Robert continues to work for General Telephone Company for the additional two years needed to acquire a vested right, he will then enjoy as his separate property an annuity created predominantly through community effort. This "potentially whimsical result," . . . cannot be reconciled with the fundamental principle that property attributable to community earnings must be divided equally when the community is dissolved.

Respondent does not deny that if nonvested pension rights are property, the French rule results in an inequitable division of that property. He maintains, however, that any inequity can be redressed by an award of alimony to the nonemployee spouse. Alimony, however, lies within the discretion of the trial court; the spouse "should not be dependent on the discretion of the court . . . to provide her with the equivalent of what should be hers as a matter of absolute right." (In re Marriage of Peterson, . . . 41 Cal.App.3d 642, 651, 115 Cal.Rptr. 184, 191.)

Respondent and amicus further suggest that a decision repudiating the French rule would both impose severe practical burdens upon the courts and restrict the employee's freedom to change his place or terms of employment. We shall examine these contentions and point out why they do not justify a continued refusal by the courts to divide nonvested pension rights as a community asset.

In dividing nonvested pension rights as community property the court must take account of the possibility that death or termination of employment may destroy those rights before they mature. In some cases the trial court may be able to evaluate this risk in determining the present value of those rights. . . . But if the court concludes that because of uncertainties affecting the vesting or maturation of the pension that it should not attempt to divide the present value of pension rights, it can instead award each spouse an appropriate portion of each pension payment as it is paid. This method of dividing the community interest in the pension renders it unnecessary for the court to compute the present value of the pension rights, and divides equally the risk that the pension will fail to vest. . . .

As respondent points out, an award of future pension payments as they fall due will require the court to continue jurisdiction to supervise the payments of pension benefits. Yet this obligation arises whenever the court cannot equitably award all pension rights to one spouse, whether or not such rights are vested; the claim of mere administrative burden surely cannot serve as support for an inequitable substantive rule which distinguishes between vested and nonvested rights. Despite the administrative burden such an award imposes, courts in the past have successfully divided vested pension rights by awarding each spouse a share in future payments. . . . Courts can divide nonvested pension rights in like fashion.

Moreover, the practical consequence of the French rule has been historically that the court must often award alimony to the spouse who, deprived of any share in the nonvested pension rights, lacks resources to purchase the necessities of life. . . . Judicial supervision of alimony awards, undertaken in the past, entails far more onerous a burden than supervision of future pension payment.

As to the claim that our present holding will infringe upon the employee's freedom of contract, we note that judicial recognition of the nonemployee spouse's interest in vested pension rights has not limited the employee's freedom to change or terminate his employment, to agree to a modification of the terms of his employment (including retirement benefits), or to elect between alternative retirement programs. We do not conceive that judicial recognition of spousal rights in nonvested pensions will change the law in this respect. The employee retains the right to decide, and by his decision define, the nature of the retirement benefits owned by the community.

* * *

We conclude that our decision today should not apply retroactively to permit a nonemployee spouse to assert an interest in nonvested pension rights when the property rights of the marriage have already been adjudicated by a decree of dissolution or separation which has become final as to such adjudication, unless the decree expressly reserved jurisdiction to divide such pension rights at a later date (see Civ.Code, § 4800). Our decision will apply retroactively, however, to any case in which the property rights arising from the marriage have not yet been adjudicated, to such rights if such adjudication is still subject to appellate review, or if in such adjudication the trial court has expressly reserved jurisdiction to divide pension rights.

For the foregoing reasons we conclude that the holding of French v. French, supra, 17 Cal.2d 775, 112 P.2d 235 that nonvested pension rights cannot constitute community property subject to division upon dissolution of the marriage must be overruled.

In sum, we submit that whatever abstract terminology we impose, the joint effort that composes the community and the respective contributions of the spouses that make up its assets, are the meaningful criteria. The wife's contribution to the community is not one whit less if we declare the husband's pension rights not a contingent asset but a mere "expectancy." Fortunately we can appropriately reflect the realistic situation by recognizing that the husband's pension rights, a contingent interest, whether vested or not vested, comprise a property interest of the community and that the wife may properly share in it.

The judgment of the superior court is reversed and the cause remanded for further proceedings consistent with the views expressed herein.

Notes and Questions

1. If the husband's pension rights can terminate by death or employment termination, the valuation of those rights becomes highly conjectural. The valuation of pension rights is complicated by the fact that in so-called "contributory pension plans" both the employee and the employer contribute to the pension plan. Employer contributions toward a pension plan are a form of deferred compensation. Employer contributions prior to the divorce arguably should enter into the calculation of an equitable division of property in the same way they would have if the employer had paid its cash contributions currently to the employee who had then saved the cash. If the employee continues to work after the divorce and the employer contributes to the pension plan, it is questionable whether the former spouse should reap any advantage from that contribution if he or she could not have reached any of the employed spouse's income earned after the divorce.

Ordinarily the courts have wide discretion in making an equitable division of property taking into account pension rights. As the court stated in Bloomer v. Bloomer, 84 Wis.2d 124, 135–36, 267 N.W.2d 235, 240–41 (1978):

> There are at least three ways in which the value [of pension rights] can be determined.... First, the ... court could consider the amount of the ... [employed spouse's] contributions to the fund, plus interest, and award [the non-employed spouse] an appropriate share.... Second, the ... court could attempt to calculate the present value of ... [the employed spouse's] retirement benefits when they vest under the plan.... Under this approach, the benefits payable in the future would have to be discounted for interest in the future, for mortality (the probability that ... [the employed spouse] will die before qualifying for the benefits), and for vesting (since ... [the employed spouse] will have to continue to work at least until age fifty-five before qualifying for fully vested pension rights).... The benefits would then have to be calculated with respect to ... [the employed spouse's] life expectancy as a retiree. This calculation involves considerable uncertainty, and the amount yielded changes as different assumptions are used with respect to mortality, job turn-over, etc.... The third method, which has been used widely in

other states ... is to determine a fixed percentage for ... [the unemployed spouse] of any future payments ... [the employed spouse] receives under the plan, payable to her as, if, and when paid to ... [the employed spouse].... Under this approach, of course, it is unnecessary to determine the value of the pension fund at all. The court need do no more than determine the appropriate percentage to which the non-employee spouse is entitled.

2. The Brown court indicates that its decision will not limit "the employee's freedom to change or terminate his employment, to agree to a modification of the terms of his employment (including retirement benefits), or to elect between alternative retirement programs." Does this mean that the former spouse could not enjoin the employed former spouse from changing jobs if the change was motivated by a desire to infringe upon the amounts that would otherwise be payable to the former spouse? If the employed spouse is free to terminate his employment and possibly extinguish the opportunity of the former spouse to share in the pension, what does that suggest about the efficacy of the third way pension benefits may be equitably divided?

3. The law of the domicile of the spouses at the time property is acquired determines whether the acquired property is community property or common-law property. The status of the property as community or common-law does not change if the spouses later change their domicile unless they agree to the contrary. Understanding these rules is essential to the proper planning of the estates of married couples moving between common-law states and community property states. See, generally, Johanson, The Migrating Client: Estate Planning for the Couple from a Community Property State, 9 U of Miami Inst. Est. Plan. ¶ 800 (1975).

§ 6.6   IS EDUCATION A MARITAL ASSET?

O'BRIEN v. O'BRIEN

Court of Appeals of New York (1985).
66 N.Y.2d 576, 498 N.Y.S.2d 743, 489 N.E.2d 712.

SIMONS, JUDGE.

In this divorce action, the parties' only asset of any consequence is the husband's newly acquired license to practice medicine. The principal issue presented is whether that license, acquired during their marriage, is marital property subject to equitable distribution under Domestic Relations Law § 236(B)(5). Supreme Court held that it was and accordingly made a distributive award in defendant's favor. On appeal to the Appellate Division, a majority of that court held that plaintiff's medical license is not marital property.... It modified the judgment and remitted the case to Supreme Court for further proceedings, specifically for a determination of maintenance and a rehabilitative award (106 A.D.2d 223, 485 N.Y.S.2d 548). The matter is before us by leave of the Appellate Division.

We now hold that plaintiff's medical license constitutes "marital property" within the meaning of Domestic Relations Law § 236(B)(1)(c) and that it is therefore subject to equitable distribution pursuant to subdivision 5 of that part. . . .

I

Plaintiff and defendant married on April 3, 1971. At the time both were employed as teachers at the same private school. Defendant had a bachelor's degree and a temporary teaching certificate but required 18 months of postgraduate classes at an approximate cost of $3,000, excluding living expenses, to obtain permanent certification in New York. She claimed, and the trial court found, that she had relinquished the opportunity to obtain permanent certification while plaintiff pursued his education. At the time of the marriage, plaintiff had completed only three and one-half years of college but shortly afterward he returned to school at night to earn his bachelor's degree and to complete sufficient premedical courses to enter medical school. In September 1973 the parties moved to Guadalajara, Mexico, where plaintiff became a full-time medical student. While he pursued his studies defendant held several teaching and tutorial positions and contributed her earnings to their joint expenses. The parties returned to New York in December 1976 so that plaintiff could complete the last two semesters of medical school and internship training here. After they returned, defendant resumed her former teaching position and she remained in it at the time this action was commenced. Plaintiff was licensed to practice medicine in October 1980. He commenced this action for divorce two months later. At the time of trial, he was a resident in general surgery.

During the marriage both parties contributed to paying the living and educational expenses and they received additional help from both of their families. They disagreed on the amounts of their respective contributions but it is undisputed that in addition to performing household work and managing the family finances defendant was gainfully employed throughout the marriage, that she contributed all of her earnings to their living and educational expenses and that her financial contributions exceeded those of plaintiff. The trial court found that she had contributed 76% of the parties' income exclusive of a $10,000 student loan obtained by defendant. Finding that plaintiff's medical degree and license are marital property, the court received evidence of its value and ordered a distributive award to defendant.

Defendant presented expert testimony that the present value of plaintiff's medical license was $472,000. Her expert testified that he arrived at this figure by comparing the average income of a college graduate and that of a general surgeon between 1985, when plaintiff's residency would end, and 2012, when he would reach age 65. After considering Federal income taxes, an inflation rate of 10% and a real interest rate of 3% he capitalized the difference in average earnings and reduced the amount to present value. He also gave his opinion that the present value of defendant's contribution to plaintiff's medical education was $103,390. Plaintiff offered no expert testimony on the subject.

The court, after considering the life-style that plaintiff would enjoy from the enhanced earning potential his medical license would bring and defendant's contributions and efforts toward attainment of it, made a distributive award to her of $188,800, representing 40% of the value of the license, and ordered it paid in 11 annual installments of various amounts beginning November 1, 1982 and ending November 1, 1992. The court also directed plaintiff to maintain a life insurance policy on his life for defendant's benefit for the unpaid balance of the award and it ordered plaintiff to pay defendant's counsel fees of $7,000 and her expert witness fee of $1,000. It did not award defendant maintenance.

A divided Appellate Division, relying on its prior decision in Conner v. Conner, 97 A.D.2d 88, 468 N.Y.S.2d 482 and the decision of the Fourth Department in Lesman v. Lesman, 88 A.D.2d 153, 452 N.Y.S.2d 935, appeal dismissed 57 N.Y.2d 956, concluded that a professional license acquired during marriage is not marital property subject to distribution. It therefore modified the judgment by striking the trial court's determination that it is ... and remitted the case for further proceedings.

On these cross appeals, defendant seeks reinstatement of the judgment of the trial court. Plaintiff contends that the Appellate Division correctly held that a professional license is not marital property....

II

The Equitable Distribution Law contemplates only two classes of property: marital property and separate property (Domestic Relations Law § 236[B][1][c], [d]). The former, which is subject to equitable distribution, is defined broadly as "all property acquired by either or both spouses during the marriage and before the execution of a separation agreement or the commencement of a matrimonial action, regardless of the form in which title is held" (Domestic Relations Law § 236[B][1][c] [emphasis added]; see § 236[B][5][b], [c]). Plaintiff does not contend that his license is excluded from distribution because it is separate property; rather, he claims that it is not property at all but represents a personal attainment in acquiring knowledge. He rests his argument on decisions in similar cases from other jurisdictions and on his view that a license does not satisfy common-law concepts of property. Neither contention is controlling because decisions in other States rely principally on their own statutes, and the legislative history underlying them, and because the New York Legislature deliberately went beyond traditional property concepts when it formulated the Equitable Distribution Law.... Instead, our statute recognizes that spouses have an equitable claim to things of value arising out of the marital relationship and classifies them as subject to distribution by focusing on the marital status of the parties at the time of acquisition. Those things acquired during marriage and subject to distribution have been classified as "marital property" although, as one commentator has observed, they hardly fall within the traditional property concepts because there is no common-law property interest remotely resembling marital property. "It is a statutory creature, is of no meaning whatsoever during the normal course of a marriage and arises full-grown, like Athena, upon the signing of a separation agreement or the commencement of a matrimonial action. [Thus] [i]t is hardly surprising, and not at all relevant, that traditional common law property concepts do not fit in parsing the meaning of 'marital property' " (Florescue, "Market Value", Professional Licenses and Marital Property: A Dilemma in Search of a Horn, 1982 N.Y.St.Bar Assn.Fam.L.Rev. 13 [Dec.]). Having classified the "property" subject to distribution, the Legislature did not attempt to go further and define it but left it to the courts to determine what interests come within the terms of section 236(B)(1)(c).

We made such a determination in Majauskas v. Majauskas, 61 N.Y.2d 481, 474 N.Y.S.2d 699, 463 N.E.2d 15, holding there that vested but unmatured pension rights are marital property subject to equitable distribution. Because pension benefits are not specifically identified as marital property in the statute, we looked to the express reference to pension rights contained in section 236(B)(5)(d)(4), which deals with equitable distribution of marital property, to other provisions of the equitable distribution statute and to the legislative intent behind its enactment to determine whether pension rights are marital property or separate property. A similar analysis is appropriate here and leads to the conclusion that marital property encompasses a license to practice medicine to the extent that the license is acquired during marriage.

Section 236 provides that in making an equitable distribution of marital property, "the court shall consider: . . . (6) any equitable claim to, interest in, or direct or indirect contribution made to the acquisition of such marital property by the party not having title, including joint efforts or expenditures and contributions and services as a spouse, parent, wage earner and homemaker, and to the career or career potential of the other party [and] . . . (9) the impossibility or difficulty of evaluating any component asset or any interest in a business, corporation or profession" (Domestic Relations Law § 236[B][5][d][6], [9] [emphasis added]). Where equitable distribution of marital property is appropriate but "the distribution of an interest in a business, corporation or profession would be contrary to law" the court shall make a distributive award in lieu of an actual distribution of the property (Domestic Relations Law § 236[B][5][e] [emphasis added]). The words mean exactly what they say: that an interest in a profession or professional career potential is marital property which may be represented by direct or indirect contributions of the non-title-holding spouse, including financial contributions and nonfinancial contributions made by caring for the home and family.

The history which preceded enactment of the statute confirms this interpretation. Reform of section 236 was advocated because experience had proven that application of the traditional common-law title theory of property had caused inequities upon dissolution of a marriage. The Legislature replaced the existing system with equitable distribution of marital property, an entirely new theory which considered all the circumstances of the case and of the respective parties to the marriage (Assembly Memorandum, 1980 N.Y.Legis.Ann., at 129–130). Equitable distribution was based on the premise that a marriage is, among other things, an economic partnership to which both parties contribute as spouse, parent, wage earner or homemaker (id., at 130; see, Governor's Memorandum of Approval, 1980 McKinney's Session Laws of N.Y., at 1863). Consistent with this purpose, and implicit in the statutory scheme as a whole, is the view that upon dissolution of the marriage there should be a winding up of the parties' economic affairs and a severance of their economic ties by an equitable distribution of the marital assets. Thus, the concept of alimony, which often served as a means of lifetime support and dependence for one spouse upon the other long after the marriage was over, was replaced with the concept of maintenance which seeks to allow "the recipient spouse an opportunity to achieve [economic] independence" (Assembly Memorandum, 1980 N.Y.Legis.Ann., at 130).

The determination that a professional license is marital property is also consistent with the conceptual base upon which the statute rests. As this case demonstrates, few undertakings during a marriage better qualify as the type of joint effort that the statute's economic partnership theory is intended to address than contributions toward one spouse's acquisition of a professional license. Working spouses are often required to contribute substantial income as wage earners, sacrifice their own educational or career goals and opportunities for child rearing, perform the bulk of household duties and responsibilities and forego the acquisition of marital assets that could have been accumulated if the professional spouse had been employed rather than occupied with the study and training necessary to acquire a professional license. In this case, nearly all of the parties' nine-year marriage was devoted to the acquisition of plaintiff's medical license and defendant played a major role in that project. She worked continuously during the marriage and contributed all of her earnings to their joint effort, she sacrificed her own educational and career opportunities, and she traveled with plaintiff to Mexico for three and one-half years while he attended medical school there. The Legislature has decided, by its explicit reference in the statute to the contributions of one spouse to the other's profession or career (see, Domestic Relations Law § 236[B][5][d][6], [9]; [e]), that these contributions represent investments in the economic partnership of the marriage and that the product of the parties' joint efforts, the professional license, should be considered marital property. . . .

Plaintiff's principal argument, adopted by the majority below, is that a professional license is not marital property because it does not fit within the traditional view of property as something which has an exchange value on the open market and is capable of sale, assignment or transfer. The position does not withstand analysis for at least two reasons. First, as we have observed, it ignores the fact that whether a professional license constitutes marital property is to be judged by the language of the statute which created this new species of property previously unknown at common law or under prior statutes. Thus, whether the license fits within traditional property concepts is of no consequence. Second, it is an overstatement to assert that a professional license could not be considered property even outside the context of section 236(B). A professional license is a valuable property right, reflected in the money, effort and lost opportunity for employment expended in its acquisition, and also in the enhanced earning capacity it affords its holder, which may not be revoked without due process of law (see, Matter of Bender v. Board of Regents, 262 App.Div. 627, 631, 30 N.Y.S.2d 779; People ex rel. Greenberg v. Reid, 151 App.Div. 324, 326, 136 N.Y.S. 428). That a professional license has no market value is irrelevant. Obviously, a license may not be alienated as may other property and for that reason the working spouse's interest in it is limited. The Legislature has recognized that limitation, however, and has provided for an award in lieu of its actual distribution (see, Domestic Relations Law § 236[B][5][e]).

Plaintiff also contends that alternative remedies should be employed, such as an award of rehabilitative maintenance or reimbursement for direct financial contributions. . . .

The statute does not expressly authorize retrospective maintenance or rehabilitative awards and we have no occasion to decide in this case whether the authority to do so may ever be implied from its provisions. . . . It is sufficient to observe that normally a working spouse should not be restricted to that relief because to do so frustrates the purposes underlying the Equitable Distribution Law. Limiting a working spouse to a maintenance award, either general or rehabilitative, not only is contrary to the economic partnership concept underlying the statute but also retains the uncertain and inequitable economic ties of dependence that the Legislature sought to extinguish by equitable distribution. Maintenance is subject to termination upon the recipient's remarriage and a working spouse may never receive adequate consideration for his or her contribution and may even be penalized for the decision to remarry if that is the only method of compensating the contribution. As one court said so well, "[t]he function of equitable distribution is to recognize that when a marriage ends, each of the spouses, based on the totality of the contributions made to it, has a stake in and right to a share of the marital assets accumulated while it endured, not because that share is needed, but because those assets represent the capital product of what was essentially a partnership entity" (Wood v. Wood, 119 Misc.2d 1076, 1079, 465 N.Y.S.2d 475). The Legislature stated its intention to eliminate such inequities by providing that a supporting spouse's "direct or indirect contribution" be recognized, considered and rewarded (Domestic Relations Law § 236[B][5][d][6]).

Turning to the question of valuation, it has been suggested that even if a professional license is considered marital property, the working spouse is entitled only to reimbursement of his or her direct financial contributions (see, Note, Equitable Distribution of Degrees and Licenses: Two Theories Toward Compensating Spousal Contributions, 49 Brooklyn L.Rev. 301, 317–322). By parity of reasoning, a spouse's down payment on real estate or contribution to the purchase of securities would be limited to the money contributed, without any remuneration for any incremental value in the asset because of price appreciation. Such a result is completely at odds with the statute's requirement that the court give full consideration to both direct and indirect contributions "made to the acquisition of such marital property by the party not having title, including joint efforts or expenditures and contributions and services as a spouse, parent, wage earner and homemaker" (Domestic Relations Law 236[B][5][d][6] [emphasis added]). If the license is marital property, then the working spouse is entitled to an equitable portion of it, not a return of funds advanced. Its value is the enhanced earning capacity it affords the holder and although fixing the present value of that enhanced earning capacity may present problems, the problems are not insurmountable. Certainly they are no more difficult than computing tort damages for wrongful death or diminished earning capacity resulting from injury and they differ only in degree from the problems presented when valuing a professional practice for purposes of a distributive award, something the courts have not hesitated to do.... The trial court retains the flexibility and discretion to structure the distributive award equitably, taking into consideration factors such as the working spouse's need for immediate payment, the licensed spouse's current ability to pay and the income tax consequences of prolonging the period of payment.

* * *

[A]nd, once it has received evidence of the present value of the license and the working spouse's contributions toward its acquisition and considered the remaining factors mandated by the statute (see, Domestic Relations Law § 236[B][5][d][1]–[10]), it may then make an appropriate distribution of the marital property including a distributive award for the professional license if such an award is warranted. When other marital assets are of sufficient value to provide for the supporting spouse's equitable portion of the marital property, including his or her contributions to the acquisition of the professional license, however, the court retains the discretion to distribute these other marital assets or to make a distributive award in lieu of an actual distribution of the value of the professional spouse's license (see, Majauskas v. Majauskas, 61 N.Y.2d 481, 493, 474 N.Y.S.2d 699, 463 N.E.2d 15, supra).

Accordingly, in view of our holding that plaintiff's license to practice medicine is marital property, the order of the Appellate Division should be modified, with costs to defendant, by reinstating the judgment and the case remitted to the Appellate Division for determination of the facts, including the exercise of that court's discretion (CPLR 5613), and, as so modified, affirmed. Question certified answered in the negative.

MEYER, JUDGE (concurring).

I concur in Judge Simons' opinion but write separately to point up for consideration by the Legislature the potential for unfairness involved in distributive awards based upon a license of a professional still in training.

An equity court normally has power to " 'change its decrees where there has been a change of circumstances' " (People v. Scanlon, 11 N.Y.2d 459, 462, 230 N.Y.S.2d 708, 184 N.E.2d 302, on second appeal 13 N.Y.2d 982, 244 N.Y.S.2d 781, 194 N.E.2d 689). The implication of Domestic Relations Law § 236(B)(9)(b), which deals with modification of an order or decree as to maintenance or child support, is, however, that a distributive award pursuant to section 236(B)(5)(e), once made, is not subject to change. Yet a professional in training who is not finally committed to a career choice when the distributive award is made may be locked into a particular kind of practice simply because the monetary obligations imposed by the distributive award made on the basis of the trial judge's conclusion (prophecy may be a better word) as to what the career choice will be leaves him or her no alternative.

The present case points up the problem. A medical license is but a step toward the practice ultimately engaged in by its holder, which follows after internship, residency and, for particular specialties, board certification. Here it is undisputed that plaintiff was in a residency for general surgery at the time of the trial, but had the previous year done a residency in internal medicine. Defendant's expert based his opinion on the difference between the average income of a general surgeon and that of a college graduate of plaintiff's age and life expectancy, which the trial judge utilized, impliedly finding that plaintiff would engage in a surgical practice despite plaintiff's testimony that he was dissatisfied with the general surgery program he was in and was attempting to return to the internal medicine training he had been in the previous year. The trial judge had the right, of course, to discredit that testimony, but the point is that equitable distribution was not intended to permit a judge to make a career decision for a licensed spouse still in training. Yet the degree of speculation involved in the award made is emphasized by the testimony of the expert on which it was based. Asked whether his assumptions and calculations were in any way speculative, he replied: "Yes. They're speculative to the extent of, will Dr. O'Brien practice medicine? Will Dr. O'Brien earn more or less than the average surgeon earns? Will Dr. O'Brien live to age sixty-five? Will Dr. O'Brien have a heart attack or will he be injured in an automobile accident? Will he be disabled? I mean, there is a degree of speculation. That speculative aspect is no more to be taken into account, cannot be taken into account, and it's a question, again, Mr. Emanuelli, not for the expert but for the courts to decide. It's not my function nor could it be."

The equitable distribution provisions of the Domestic Relations Law were intended to provide flexibility so that equity could be done. But if the assumption as to career choice on which a distributive award payable over a number of years is based turns out not to be the fact (as, for example, should a general surgery trainee accidentally lose the use of his hand), it should be possible for the court to revise the distributive award to conform to the fact. And there will be no unfairness in so doing if either spouse can seek reconsideration, for the licensed spouse is more likely to seek reconsideration based on real, rather than imagined, cause if he or she knows that the nonlicensed spouse can seek not only reinstatement of the original award, but counsel fees in addition, should the purported circumstance on which a change is made turn out to have been feigned or to be illusory.

IN RE MARRIAGE OF FRANCIS

Supreme Court of Iowa (1989).
442 N.W.2d 59.

NEUMAN, JUSTICE.

This appeal involves the thorny economic issues surrounding what has come to be called the "advanced degree/divorce decree"[1] dissolution of marriage action.

On the day he was admitted to medical school, appellant Thomas Francis proposed marriage to appellee Diana Mora Francis. Like countless couples before them, they pledged to one another their support and commitment to a shared future. Six years and two children later, however, their marriage is at an end. And while Tom stands at the threshold of his career as a physician specializing in family practice, Diana ponders her future from the vantage point of one who has helped support the family through medical school and two years of residency on the modest income generated by her in-home day care business.

The fighting issue, as framed by the trial court and reiterated by the parties on appeal, is this: What compensation, if any, should Diana receive for her contribution to Thomas' increased earning capacity due to his education received during the marriage? For over a decade this court has recognized that a spouse's contribution to that increased earning potential is a factor properly considered in the award of alimony and an equitable division of the parties' assets. See In re Marriage of Horstmann, 263 N.W.2d 885, 891 (Iowa 1978). Yet precisely because each dissolution action must be decided on its unique facts and circumstances, no predictable method of valuing that contribution or distributing the fruits of that increased potential has been settled upon.

Here the trial court awarded Diana a $100,000 lump sum property award payable with interest in ten annual installments, along with a three-year rehabilitative alimony award totaling $54,000. On appeal from these judgments, Thomas concedes that Diana is entitled to something but challenges the size and nature of the awards on three principal grounds: first, that the court based its $100,000 on the erroneous legal conclusion that a medical education constitutes an asset for the purpose of equitable distribution; second, that the trial court based its award on calculations that were speculative, incomplete, and misleading; and, third, that the record does not support Diana's need for rehabilitative alimony. Addition-

1. An apt, but somewhat cynical, label derived from one coined by the Wisconsin Supreme Court in Haugan v. Haugan, 117 Wis.2d 200, 206, 343 N.W.2d 796, 799–800 (1984).

ally, Thomas challenges his obligation to pay $1000 towards Diana's attorney fees and resists the payment of similar fees on appeal. . . .

We are persuaded that the trial court neither misapplied legal doctrine nor erroneously misconstrued the evidence so as to compensate Diana far beyond her contribution to the marriage, as Thomas suggests. We conclude, however, that for marriages of short duration which are devoted almost entirely to the educational advancement of one spouse and yield the accumulation of few tangible assets, alimony—rehabilitative, reimbursement, or a combination of the two—rather than an award of property, furnishes a fairer and more logical means of achieving the equity sought under Horstmann and its progeny. Accordingly, with some modification, we affirm the trial court.

I. Several well settled rules guide our decision. Principal among them is the rule that an advanced degree or professional license in and of itself is not an asset for property division purposes. . . .

Nevertheless, the future earning capacity flowing from an advanced degree or professional license is a factor to be considered in the division of property and the award of alimony. . . . Insofar as the advanced professional degree creates an expectancy of higher future earnings, the degree may and should be taken into account in calculating that future earning capacity. . . .

Prior Iowa cases have interchangeably used property awards and alimony as means of compensating a nonprofessional spouse for the contribution made to the other spouse's advanced degree or professional license. Janssen, 348 N.W.2d [251] at 254 (substantial periodic alimony rather than lump sum property award equitably adjusts parties' finances); Horstmann, 263 N.W.2d at 891 (husband's potential for increased earning capacity made possible "with the aid of his wife's efforts" pertinent to both equitable distribution of assets and whether alimony should be awarded); Stewart, 356 N.W.2d [611] at 612–13 (enhanced earning capacity factored in issue of alimony but properly rejected when supporting spouse made comparable career advancement during marriage); Estlund, 344 N.W.2d [276] at 280 (wife's contributions, as homemaker and breadwinner, to husband's law degree properly considered upon issue of equitable division of property). These decisions are in harmony with statutes that direct the trial courts to consider such contributions in the awarding of property and spousal support. . . .

It must be remembered, however, that the purposes of property division and alimony are not the same. Property division is based on each partner's right to "a just and equitable share of the property accumulated as the result of their joint efforts." In re Marriage of Hitchcock, 309 N.W.2d 432, 437 (Iowa 1981). Alimony, on the other hand, is a stipend to a spouse in lieu of the other spouse's legal obligation for support. In re Marriage of Wegner, 434 N.W.2d 397, 398 (Iowa 1988).

Recently, such court-ordered stipends have taken on new forms to accommodate the broad range of functions that alimony may serve. See H.

Clark, The Law of Domestic Relations in the United States 641–44 (2d ed. 1988). The Utah Court of Appeals nicely summarized the need for such flexibility this way:

> In [long-term marriages], life patterns have largely been set, the earning potential of both parties can be predicted with some reliability, and the contributions and sacrifices of the one spouse in enabling the other to attain a degree have been compensated by many years of the comfortable lifestyle which the degree permitted. Traditional alimony analysis works nicely to assure equity in such cases. In another kind of recurring case, . . . where divorce occurs shortly after the degree is obtained, traditional alimony analysis would often work hardship because, while both spouses have modest incomes at the time of divorce, the one is on the threshold of a significant increase in earnings. Moreover, the spouse who sacrificed so the other could attain a degree is precluded from enjoying the anticipated dividends the degree will ordinarily provide. Nonetheless, such a spouse is typically not remote in time from his or her previous education and is otherwise better able to adjust and to acquire comparable skills, given the opportunity and the funding. In such cases, alimony analysis must become more creative to achieve fairness, and an award of "rehabilitative" or "reimbursement" alimony, not terminable upon remarriage, may be appropriate. . . .

With these principles in mind, we consider the contentions of the parties.

Thomas begins by asserting that the trial court erroneously characterized his medical education and license as marital assets properly subject to equitable division. We find no merit in the contention. The trial court specifically found that the "degree . . . obtained by Thomas [is] not property." It then went on to correctly cite Horstmann, Janssen, and Estlund for the proposition that it is the potential for increased future earning capacity made possible by Thomas' degree, with Diana's assistance, "that constitutes the asset for distribution by the Court."[2]

We are persuaded, however, by Thomas' assertion that alimony, not a property award, is the proper vehicle by which to achieve equity upon the dissolution of this marriage.

As previously stated in this opinion, alimony has traditionally taken the place of support that would have been provided had the marriage continued. A calculation of future earning capacity, in a case like the present one, essentially represents a value placed on the income to be derived from the advanced degree achieved during the marriage. The amount that would have been the student spouse's contribution to the future support of the parties is logically tied, if not wholly determined by,

---

2. In light of the precedent earlier cited in this opinion, we differ with the court of appeals' recent suggestion in In re Marriage of Wagner, 435 N.W.2d 372, 374–76 (Iowa App.1988) that "potential increase in earning capacity is not, [as distinguished from the degree] in and of itself, the asset to which a value is fixed and then divided." (Emphasis added.) We find such a view in direct conflict with Horstmann, 263 N.W.2d at 891.

future earning capacity. Thus the court's duty to look at the future earning capacity of the spouses tracks more closely with a concern for loss of anticipated support, reimbursable through alimony, than through division of as-yet-unrealized tangible assets.

The alimony of which we speak is designed to give the "supporting" spouse a stake in the "student" spouse's future earning capacity, in exchange for recognizable contributions to the source of that income—the student's advanced education. As such, it is to be clearly distinguished from "rehabilitative" or "permanent" alimony.

Rehabilitative alimony was conceived as a way of supporting an economically dependent spouse through a limited period of re-education or retraining following divorce, thereby creating incentive and opportunity for that spouse to become self-supporting. See Krauskopf, Rehabilitative Alimony: Uses and Abuses of Limited Duration Alimony, 21 Fam.L.Q. 573, 581 (1988) (hereinafter Krauskopf); Sackett & Munyon, Alimony: A Retreat from Traditional Concepts of Spousal Support, 35 Drake L.Rev. 297, 314 (1985–86) (hereinafter Sackett); see also In re Marriage of Bevers, 326 N.W.2d 896, 900 (Iowa 1982).

Because self-sufficiency is the goal of rehabilitative alimony, the duration of such an award may be limited or extended depending on the realistic needs of the economically dependent spouse, tempered by the goal of facilitating the economic independence of the ex-spouses. See Krauskopf, 21 Fam.L.Q. at 582. As in the case of "traditional" alimony, payable for life or so long as a spouse is incapable of self-support, a change in status (e.g., remarriage) may alter the support picture and warrant a modification. See In re Marriage of Shima, 360 N.W.2d 827, 828 (Iowa 1985) (remarriage shifts the burden on recipient to prove extraordinary circumstances requiring continuation of alimony).

"Reimbursement" alimony, on the other hand, which is predicated upon economic sacrifices made by one spouse during the marriage that directly enhance the future earning capacity of the other, should not be subject to modification or termination until full compensation is achieved. Similar to a property award, but based on future earning capacity rather than a division of tangible assets, it should be fixed at the time of the decree. In recognition of the personal nature of the award and the current tax laws, however, a spouse's obligation to pay reimbursement alimony must terminate upon the recipient's death. See I.R.C. § 71(b)(1)(D) (Tax Reform Act of 1986); cf. Green v. Commissioner, 855 F.2d 289, 294 (6th Cir.1988).

We think the case before us exemplifies the situation calling for an award of reimbursement alimony rather than a property settlement. Not only does such an award bear a closer resemblance to support than a division of assets, alimony carries tax benefits to the payor and assurance to the payee that the award will not be discharged in bankruptcy. See I.R.C. § 215; 11 U.S.C. § 523(a)(5). The trial court's decree must be modified accordingly.

Whether classified as a property division or alimony, Thomas objects to the court's award of $100,000 as a "windfall to Diana far in excess of any equitable return on the contributions she made during the marriage." We thus turn to the record to evaluate the size of the award in light of the facts presented.

The parties were legally married in May 1982, but had lived together since the birth of their son, Michael, in November 1980. At the time of their marriage, neither party was employed and neither had significant assets of any kind. Thomas had completed his bachelor's degree and one year of graduate study. Diana had completed all but her thesis and oral examination required for a master's degree in early childhood development. She received that degree in June 1983. The parties' second child, Melissa, was born in March 1984.

From the outset of their marriage, Thomas and Diana agreed that Diana would care for their children and earn income for the family by caring for other people's children in their home. This arrangement continued throughout the marriage except for a brief period shortly after Melissa was born.

Meanwhile, Thomas entered medical school at Southern Illinois University in the fall of 1982. After one year he transferred to the University of Illinois at Springfield where he obtained his medical degree in 1986, graduating in the top twenty-five percent of his class. The family then moved to Iowa City so that Thomas could enroll in the University's three-year residency program for physicians specializing in family practice.

By November 1986, the parties were experiencing marital difficulties. In June 1987, Thomas petitioned for dissolution of marriage. Trial was held in June 1988.

From the date of their marriage through the date of trial, the parties supported themselves on income from a variety of sources. During the summer before medical school began, Thomas worked as a gardener and earned approximately $1200. Diana earned roughly $5000 per year from her in-home day care business. Thomas' parents contributed $11,500 and Diana's mother gave them $12,000. Student loans accounted for $45,500 over the six-year period.

Once Thomas obtained his medical degree, his earnings went up substantially. In 1986 he earned $8700, while his salary for 1987 was $29,337. At the time of trial, he was earning approximately $3000 per month from a combination of resident's salary and "moonlighting" as an emergency room physician.

The parties strenuously dispute their relative contributions to child rearing and housekeeping tasks throughout the marriage. Thomas claims that he contributed thirty to fifty percent of those services and that Diana should not be credited for child care or homemaking during those hours in which she was caring for other children as well as her own. Diana argues that Thomas' devotion to his medical studies, as demonstrated by his class rank and a successful residency, greatly limited his available time at home.

The district court specifically found Thomas' testimony lacking in credibility with regard to his alleged substantial contribution to the maintenance of the household. It did conclude, however, that Thomas' educational loans, combined with the income he has earned since the parties' separation, has furnished the bulk of the family's financial support. From our review of the record, we discover no reason to differ with these findings.

The parties' principal argument is over the testimony of Dr. Richard Stevenson, professor of finance and acting treasurer of the University of Iowa. He was engaged by Diana, in his words, "to value the capital that was contributed by Mrs. Francis to the medical education received during the marriage of Dr. Francis." Thomas' counsel objected to the introduction of this testimony on the ground that the expert's analysis placed a value on the degree itself, contrary to the dictates of Horstmann. Thomas renews that contention on appeal. We are convinced, however, that Dr. Stevenson's calculations, and the district court's ultimate award, were based on Diana's contribution to Thomas' future earning capacity, not the value of Thomas' medical license.

As background for his economic analysis, Dr. Stevenson took into account the facts previously related concerning the age, education, work experience and financial contributions of the parties. To those figures he added the sum of $64,095 for the estimated present value of Diana's homemaker services (at $6.70 per hour) over the six-year period. Adding this sum to her day care earnings, Diana's capital investment in obtaining Thomas' medical education equalled approximately fifty percent of the total capital committed.

Based upon 1987 figures reported in a journal of medical economics that surveys physicians' earnings by speciality and other classifications (such as geography, type of practice, age, experience, etc.), Dr. Stevenson calculated the after-tax present value of Thomas' future income as a family practice physician to be $1,615,735. He then subtracted the sum of $807,206, a figure representing the estimated future income of a male in the 30–34 age bracket with a five-year undergraduate degree. The difference ($808,529) represents the additional income accruing as a result of the medical degree.

Applying a 30/70 capital to labor ratio, Dr. Stevenson then determined that thirty percent of the present value of Thomas' future earnings, or $242,559, is attributable to capital contributed to acquiring the education. He then reduced that figure by one-half to reflect Diana's contribution to "the capital needed to obtain the medical education and to support the family until the divorce was filed." Thus his estimation of Diana's contribution to Thomas' future earning capacity equals $121,279.

The district court recognized that Dr. Stevenson's final figure was based on many assumptions and that his prediction of Thomas' future earnings could not be exact. Moreover, the court noted that the professor did not consider the benefit gained by Diana in her achievement of a master's degree during the marriage. Consequently, "to compensate Diana for her contribution to Thomas' increased future earning capacity," the court ordered Thomas to pay Diana the sum of $100,000, payable in annual installments of $10,000 each commencing July 1, 1989.

Thomas attacks the trial court's award by challenging virtually every aspect of Dr. Stevenson's calculations. But for his own opinions, however, Thomas offered no evidence to controvert the assumptions upon which the calculations were based. He certainly did not challenge the estimated annual income projections, reduced to present value. He merely begrudges Diana her contribution to the accumulation of that income.

In Horstmann, we approved an award that represented the cost of the education towards an advanced degree. See Horstmann, 263 N.W.2d at 891. We noted, however, that other methods could have been used to measure future earning capacity. Id. Similar cases have authorized awards representing the value of services, as a percentage of future earning capacity, contributed to the attainment of the degree. See Wagner, 435 N.W.2d at 374–76; Berger, 431 N.W.2d at 388–90.

We note that other states, while recognizing the need for something akin to the "reimbursement alimony" outlined in division II of this opinion, limit the supporting spouse's compensation to the financial contributions made towards tuition, living expenses and other costs of the education.... Other jurisdictions speak of compensating the supporting spouse through an award of alimony, but not based on the student's future earning capacity.... In keeping with the standard established in Horstmann, however, courts in Iowa are not confined to reimbursing supporting spouses solely for the expense of the advanced degree itself.

We find no error in the formula used here to measure Thomas' future earning capacity and Diana's contribution to its attainment. Thomas concedes a willingness to pay Diana $60,000 for her contribution. The trial court's figure of $100,000 finds ample support in the record and we are not persuaded to reduce or overturn it.

Just prior to trial, Diana learned of a program in St. Louis that would train her in Montessori pre-school theory and thereby enhance her re-entry into the early childhood education field. The program included seven weeks of training at a cost of $1200 followed by a one-year internship and guaranteed placement as a teacher in a Montessori school. The district court found that Diana was in need of support during this training period and that she was entitled to rehabilitative alimony in the sum of $500 per month during the internship and $1000 per month for four years thereafter to become established in her field.

Thomas strongly opposes this additional award, claiming that with her master's degree and her in-home day care experience, Diana is fully able to support herself without further education or training. In fact, Thomas claims, such a generous alimony award would allow Diana "to attain a standard of living greater than that which she experienced during the marriage."

Diana responds by contending that Thomas' attitude toward rehabilitative alimony would "freeze the inequities of the present moment into perpetuity." We find considerable merit in her retort. Diana may have a master's degree, but she has devoted the last six years of her life to raising her own children and caring for three others at the rate of $230 per week. It is not fair to expect that she support herself this way indefinitely, nor is it realistic to assume that she will become immediately marketable in some more lucrative endeavor.

Like the district court, we view the St. Louis Montessori program as a reasonable way of facilitating Diana's re-entry into the work force. In view of the guaranteed placement feature of the program, however, we think one-year's rehabilitative alimony is sufficient and the decree must be modified accordingly . . . .

Summary. In lieu of the $100,000 judgment entered by the trial court in Diana's favor, we direct that the trial court order Thomas to pay Diana reimbursement alimony of $10,000 per year for a period of ten years commencing July 1, 1989. Interest at the rate of ten percent per annum shall accrue on any payment not made within thirty days of its due date. This alimony judgment shall not be subject to modification but shall terminate in the event of Diana's death.

The district court's order for rehabilitative alimony commencing August 1, 1988, is affirmed as modified by the reduction to one year and increase in amount to $1000 per month. The trial court's judgment for attorney fees is affirmed. Diana's request for attorney fees on appeal is denied. Costs for this action are assessed against the appellant.

NOTES AND QUESTIONS

1. There is a growing awareness that judicial awards of either alimony or an equitable distribution of property likely are biased in favor of the husband. These findings from the Executive Summary of the Report of the Florida Supreme Court Gender Bias Study Commission 4–7 (1990) illustrate the point:

> Men customarily retain more than half of the assets of the marriage and leave with an enhanced earning capacity. The remaining family members are left with less than half of the marital assets and a severely diminished earning capacity.

> A homemaker's contributions of time and energy, as well as the opportunities she has foregone, often are minimized by Florida courts. Many judges are especially reluctant to acknowledge that these contributions are a genuine resource of the marriage.

> Post-divorce families headed by women are the fastest growing segment of those living in poverty.

Older women whose marriages end in divorce are most likely either to have abandoned their own aspirations or to have devoted their lives to furthering their husbands' careers. They are not adequately compensated by application of the present system of alimony and equitable division of marital assets.

In many areas of the state, the courts have virtually abandoned permanent alimony or substituted in its place unrealistic rehabilitative alimony awards.

Many judges fail to award permanent alimony, preferring instead to use the vehicle of equitable distribution. Yet, because men usually have a greater earning potential, women are disadvantaged by "equitable" distribution when marital assets are too slight to provide sufficient income.

In equitable distribution, men generally receive sixty-five to seventy-five percent of the marital assets compared to twenty-five to thirty-five percent for women.

The major asset of most marriages is the earning capacities of the partners.

The Commission recommends that Florida adopt a community property system as a way of rectifying this discriminatory treatment. It further recommends that presumptively property should be divided evenly upon divorce; that spousal awards for marriages of long duration should be designed to equalize the standards of living of post-divorce households at the time of dissolution rather than merely maintaining the standard of living established during the marriage. The Commission also recommends that periodic alimony for equitable distribution purposes should not end upon remarriage or death.

Much spirited litigation in dissolution cases concerns whether the working spouse who supported the other spouse who was in school is entitled only to recoup "out-of-pocket" expenses, has a property interest in the professional degree, or, alternatively, whether the amounts expended by the working spouse were an investment in the schooled spouse's future earning potential to be taken into account in an equitable division of property. How do the two principal cases resolve this issue? What economic and non-economic factors affect the approach a court should take? This issue becomes critically important where for one reason or another alimony is unavailable as is the modern trend.[3] See generally Erickson, Spousal Support Toward the Realization of Educational Goals: How the Law Can Ensure Reciprocity, 1978 Wis.L.Rev. 947; Ellman, The Theory of Alimony, 77 Calif. L. Rev. 1 (1989) (discussing the redefinition of alimony as "compensable marital investment").

2. Should the working spouse have the option either to recoup the expenses incurred on behalf of the schooled spouse or have the schooled spouse's future earning capacity enter into the calculation of an equitable division of property? If the working spouse should have such an option, under what circumstances would the working spouse prefer one option over the other?

---

3. When alimony is available and the court retains jurisdiction to modify an alimony award, it may take account of later changes in circumstances and modify the amount of alimony.

3.　Did the *O'Brien* court take into account all of the husband's contributions toward the value of the education? Can you think of any contributions he might have made that the court did not allude to? If the working-spouse has contributed toward the education of the schooled-spouse and has deferred his own education, shouldn't the schooled-spouse be required to make a comparable contribution towards the education of the working-spouse?

Suppose H and W marry immediately after H receives his medical degree. Thereafter, H supports W while she earns her law degree. Two years after W earns her law degree and five years after H earned his medical degree they divorce. Should either of them be able to take into account the future earnings of the other in determining an equitable division of property?

4.　Suppose an adult child supports a parent who has quit a job and returned to school. If thereafter the parent disinherits the child, should the child have a claim for reimbursement against the parent's estate?

5.　Both *O'Brien* and *Francis* raise the question of whether a degree is property or is otherwise to be taken into account in a divorce settlement. But what about other achievements of the marital partner? For example, in Elkus v. Elkus, 169 A.D.2d 134, 140, 572 N.Y.S.2d 901, 904 (1st Dept.1991), the issue was whether the value of a career as a performing artist and its accompanying celebrity status is marital property subject to equitable division. In holding that it is, the court stated:

> While it is true that the plaintiff was born with talent, and, while she had already been hired by the Metropolitan Opera at the time of her marriage to the defendant, her career, at this time, was only in the initial stages of development. During the course of the marriage, the defendant's active involvement in the plaintiff's career, in teaching, coaching, and critiquing her, as well as in caring for their children, clearly contributed to the increase in its value. Accordingly, to the extent the appreciation in the plaintiff's career was due to the defendant's efforts and contributions, this appreciation constitutes marital property.

6.　The two principal cases reflect differing judicial attitudes regarding the appropriateness of treating the university degree as property. While most courts are willing to take enhanced earning capacity into account in structuring a settlement for the divorcing couple, few have gone as far as New York in treating the degree itself as property. The failure to treat the degree as property has been criticized.

> The question of human capital and whether it is property within the context of marriage and divorce has been one of the "hot" topics in legal scholarship since the early seventies. The issue centers around whether enhancements to human capital or earning capacity which occurred during marriage should be considered marital property at the time of divorce. The factual scenario giving rise to the issue is fairly simple, "so common as to be a cliche." The wife and husband decide that the wife will forego her career opportunities and invest her time and energy in furthering the husband's career.
>
> She agrees to make this sacrifice with the expectation of receiving a benefit in the future: a return on her investment, through the husband's

enhanced earning power. This phenomenon has been given a variety of names: the diploma dilemma, putting-hubby-through, the "enhanced-spouse/other spouse" conundrum.

The problem arises when, after getting his degree, or finally reaching the point where the couple can expect a significant return on their joint investment, the husband decides to get a divorce. Not only does the wife lose her investment in his capital growth, but her own human capital has significantly depreciated because she delayed her own career opportunities. In addition, she has endured a lower standard of living during the marriage thus far. Resources which were expended on enhancing the husband's human capital, were unavailable for day-to-day living expenses, vacations, and accumulation of more traditional property, such as stocks, bonds, and real-estate. And because the husband was not working, she relinquished the benefits of the money he would have earned.

At this time, only New York clearly and consistently treats human capital as marital property. Michigan's policy is unsettled, with some panels of the court treating it as property; others not. Some states have dealt with the issue statutorily; other courts, while refusing to acknowledge human capital as property, have used a variety of other theories to provide some form of compensation to the wife. These theories include reimbursement, equitable restitution, quasi-contract, reimbursement support, equitable reimbursement, reimbursement alimony, classic maintenance, maintenance recognizing future earning capacity, lump-sum alimony, alimony-in-gross rehabilitative alimony, or whatever the court deems equitable.

Academicians are not in agreement that enhanced capacity should be considered property. Some think it a bad idea, with the potential for adverse consequences as likely as positive ones. Others think recognizing human capital as property is simply unnecessary and would continue to use alternative legal theories. Still others are equally convinced that justice requires that enhanced earning capacity be considered property in order to adequately compensate the wife. Commentators do appear to agree that the economic situation of divorced women and their children continues to deteriorate, while divorced men, in general, continue to fare fairly well. Numerous proposals are being put forth to alleviate some of this disparity.

The primary arguments underlying the reluctance to define enhanced earning capacity as property are: it doesn't fit within the traditional legal conceptions of property; valuation of future earning capacity is too difficult; and considering enhanced earning capacity as property would probably require long-term financial entanglement between the parties, thus thwarting the goal of a clean break. In other words, it's not property because it's not property; it's not property because if it were, it would be too difficult to assess its value; it's not property because if it were, requiring the husband to pay over a long period of time would keep the parties financially entangled and prohibit their establishing a new life.

Davis, Enhanced Earning Capacity/Human Capital: The Reluctance to Call it Property, 17 Women's Rts. L. Rep. 109–113 (1996).

Connecticut also refuses to treat the advanced degree as property. In Simmons v. Simmons, 244 Conn. 158, 708 A.2d 949, 956–57 (1998) the court stated:

> We agree that an advanced degree has no inherent value extrinsic to the recipient. Its only value rests in the possibility of the enhanced earning capacity that it might afford sometime in the future. The possibility of future earnings, however, represents a mere expectancy, not a present right. We previously have concluded that "[t]he terms 'estate' and 'property,' as used in the statute . . . connote presently existing interests. 'Property' entails 'interests that a person has already acquired in specific benefits.' " . . .

> In this regard, we find the rationale of the Supreme Court of Pennsylvania persuasive. In Hodge v. Hodge, 513 Pa. 264, 520 A.2d 15 (1986), the court denied a professional degree the status of property, concluding that "[i]n instances such as the one now before the Court, the real value being sought is not the diploma but the future earned income of the former spouse which will be attained as a result of the advanced degree. The property being sought is actually acquired subsequent to the parties' separation. Thus, the future income sought cannot be 'marital property' because it has not been earned. If it has not been earned, it has not been acquired during the marriage." (Emphasis in original.) Id., at 269, 520 A.2d 15.

> The court in Hodge went on to note that "the contribution made by one spouse to another spouse's advanced degree plays only a small part in the overall achievement." Id. In the same vein, the Supreme Court of Appeals of West Virginia, concluded that "[o]n the whole, a degree of any kind results primarily from the efforts of the student who earns it. Financial and emotional support are important, as are homemaker services, but they bear no logical relation to the value of the resulting degree." Hoak v. Hoak, 179 W.Va. 509, 513, 370 S.E.2d 473 (1988). The defendant maintains in her reply brief that this assertion "reflects a paleolithic view of marriage" that is inconsistent with the partnership theory of marriage embraced in Connecticut. We disagree.

> The defendant reminds us that "the primary aim of property distribution is to recognize that marriage is, among other things, 'a shared enterprise or joint undertaking in the nature of a partnership to which both spouses contribute—directly and indirectly, financially and nonfinancially—the fruits of which are distributable at divorce.' " (Emphasis added.) Krafick v. Krafick, supra, 234 Conn. at 795, 663 A.2d 365. She argues that the only way to effectuate this purpose in these circumstances is to conclude that the plaintiff's medical degree is marital property. We disagree.

> There are other ways to compensate the defendant for her contribution to the plaintiff's degree without subjecting it to classification as property subject to equitable distribution. See B. Herring, supra, 19 J. Marshall L.Rev. 1 (analyzing variety of solutions adopted by courts). Furthermore, while we have acknowledged that the marital union is akin to a partnership, we have never held that it is an actual economic partnership. The parties to a marriage do not enter into the relationship with a set of

ledgers and make yearly adjustments to their capital accounts. "Marriage is not a business arrangement, and this Court would be loathe to promote any more tallying of respective debits and credits than already occurs in the average household." ... Reducing the relationship, even when it has broken down, to such base terms serves only to degrade and undermine that relationship and the parties.

Where the couple divorces after the professional practice has been fully established, the nonprofessional spouse may be entitled to share in the practice's future income stream even though the court does not treat the professional degree itself as marital property. This is because the professional practice may be treated as a marital asset subject to equitable distribution. See, Mace v. Mace, 818 So.2d 1130 (Miss.2002).

7.   Suppose H, a high school graduate, fully supports W and their child while W obtains her college degree. Shortly after earning that degree, H and W divorce. H agrees to pay W $350 a month in child support, calculated by reference to H's salary at the time of the divorce. Two years later, H quits his job in order to enroll in college so that he can obtain both a college and then a medical degree. As a college student, H's income is drastically reduced. Can H successfully seek a reduction in the amount of his child support payments? See, Harvey v. Robinson, 665 A.2d 215 (Me.1995).

8.   In addition to disagreeing about whether a degree is subject to division upon divorce, divorcing couples often fight over whether the noncustodial parent of a minor child has an obligation to provide for the child's college education. Since parents (even noncustodial parents) are obligated to support their minor children, this issue arises because most children now attend college after they have obtained their age of majority. There is a division of authority regarding whether the noncustodial parent is obligated to provide for the college education of the adult child. Compare Milne v. Milne, 383 Pa.Super. 177, 556 A.2d 854 (1989) (holding noncustodial parent obligated to provide child with college education) with Dowling v. Dowling, 679 P.2d 480 (Alaska 1984) (parent not obligated). The Florida courts have also rejected the obligation of parents generally to provide adult children with a college education, finding such obligation at best moral. See Grapin v. Grapin, 450 So.2d 853 (Fla.1984). However, other courts have voiced strong sentiments in requiring parents to provide their children with a college education. In Pass v. Pass, 238 Miss. 449, 118 So.2d 769, 773 (1960) the court said:

> [W]e are living today in an age of keen competition, and if the children of today who are to be the citizens of tomorrow are to take their rightful place in a complex order of society and government, and discharge the duties of citizenship as well as meet with success the responsibilities devolving upon them in their relations with their fellow man, the church, the state and nation, it must be recognized that their parents owe them the duty to the extent of their financial capacity to provide for them the training and education which will be of such benefit to them in the discharge of the responsibilities of citizenship. It is a duty which the parent not only owes to his child, but to the state as well, since the stability of our government must depend upon a well-equipped, a well-

trained, and well-educated citizenship. We can see no good reason why this duty should not extend to a college education. Our statutes do not prohibit it, but they are rather susceptible of an interpretation to allow it. The fact is that the importance of a college education is being more and more recognized in matters of commerce, society, government, and all human relations, and the college graduate is being more and more preferred over those who are not so fortunate. No parent should subject his worthy child to this disadvantage if he has the financial capacity to avoid it.

9.   Almost all of the cases in this area involve divorces sought shortly after one of the spouses completed his or her professional education. In Root v. Root, 65 P.3d 41 (Wyo. 2003), a husband in a long-term marriage sought a greater share of assets than were awarded to him by the trial court based upon his support of his wife while she obtained a medical degree. Said the appellate court:

> The husband contends he facilitated the wife's efforts to obtain her medical degree by supporting her while she went to medical school, at the expense of his own career, which allowed her to ultimately earn substantially more money than he was earning. He described accepting lateral transfers instead of promotions in order to remain close to the wife and support her and their family during her schooling. He claimed he was the primary financial support and caretaker for the family during this time and he gave up attending law school because the parties could not marry and pursue both careers at the same time. The husband claims his deference to the wife's career resulted in her earning approximately $143,500 annually while he was earning approximately $57,450 annually from his federal employment ($44,450) and his part-time employment with the pathology business ($13,000). On this basis, he argues the trial court abused its discretion by refusing to consider awarding him more than half of the marital assets to offset the sacrifices he made and the corresponding detrimental impact to his earning capacity.

> [As provided by Wyoming statutory law, the] court shall make such disposition of the property of the parties as appears just and equitable, having regard for the respective merits of the parties and the condition in which they will be left by the divorce, the party through whom the property was acquired and the burdens imposed upon the property for the benefit of either party and children.

> The decision letter dispels the husband's accusation the [trial] court arbitrarily refused to consider his argument and instead reflects the court carefully considered his position and sets out the explicit reasons why the court concluded the facts did not support an increase in the proportion of the property awarded to the husband:

> [The husband] is not entitled to any reimbursement for career changes and adjustments. These are the compromises which are made by virtually every party to a marriage. [The wife] could just as well claim that she would have entered a more lucrative specialty if she had been single. [The husband] does not cite any law which allows a party to

receive compensation for what he or she might have been able to earn as a single person.

[The husband] is not entitled to reimbursement for [the wife] having obtained a medical degree during the marriage. This is not a case where [the wife] filed for divorce shortly after graduation and left [the husband] without significant income or assets. Both parties had college degrees at marriage. [The husband] has a good job. Both benefitted from [the wife's] medical degree. [The husband] received compensation as an employee of the pathology business. They have accumulated a substantial amount of property . . .

The trial court was not persuaded that the husband's support for the wife's education made a significant difference in the equities . . .

§ 6.7 PROPERTY RIGHTS OF UNMARRIED COHABITANTS

POSIK v. LAYTON

District Court of Appeal of Florida, 5th Dist. (1997).
695 So.2d 759.

HARRIS, JUDGE.

Emma Posik and Nancy L.R. Layton were close friends and more. They entered into a support agreement much like a prenuptial agreement. The trial court found that the agreement was unenforceable because of waiver. We reverse.

Nancy Layton was a doctor practicing at the Halifax Hospital in Volusia County and Emma Posik was a nurse working at the same facility when Dr. Layton decided to remove her practice to Brevard County. In order to induce Ms. Posik to give up her job and sell her home in Volusia County, to accompany her to Brevard County, and to reside with her "for the remainder of Emma Posik's life to maintain and care for the home," Dr. Layton agreed that she would provide essentially all of the support for the two, would make a will leaving her entire estate to Ms. Posik, and would "maintain bank accounts and other investments which constitute non-probatable assets in Emma Posik's name to the extent of 100% of her entire non-probatable assets." Also, as part of the agreement, Ms. Posik agreed to loan Dr. Layton $20,000 which was evidenced by a note. The agreement provided that Ms. Posik could cease residing with Dr. Layton if Layton failed to provide adequate support, if she requested in writing that Ms. Posik leave for any reason, if she brought a third person into the home for a period greater than four weeks without Ms. Posik's consent, or if her abuse, harassment or abnormal behavior made Ms. Posik's continued residence intolerable. In any such event, Dr. Layton agreed to pay as liquidated damages the sum of $2,500 per month for the remainder of Ms. Posik's life.

It is apparent that Ms. Posik required this agreement as a condition of accompanying Dr. Layton to Brevard. The agreement was drawn by a lawyer and properly witnessed. Ms. Posik, fifty-five years old at the time of the agreement, testified that she required the agreement because she feared that Dr. Layton might become interested in a younger companion. Her fears were well founded. Some four years after the parties moved to Brevard County and without Ms. Posik's consent, Dr. Layton announced that she wished to move another woman into the house. When Ms. Posik expressed strong displeasure with this idea, Dr. Layton moved out and took up residence with the other woman.

Dr. Layton served a three-day eviction notice on Ms. Posik. Ms. Posik later moved from the home and sued to enforce the terms of the agreement and to collect on the note evidencing the loan made in conjunction with the agreement. Dr. Layton defended on the basis that Ms. Posik first breached the agreement. Dr. Layton counterclaimed for a declaratory judgment as to whether the liquidated damages portion of the agreement was enforceable.

The trial judge found that because Ms. Posik's economic losses were reasonably ascertainable as to her employment and relocation costs, the $2,500 a month payment upon breach amounted to a penalty and was therefore unenforceable. The court further found that although Dr. Layton had materially breached the contract within a year or so of its creation, Ms. Posik waived the breach by acquiescence. Finally, the court found that Ms. Posik breached the agreement by refusing to continue to perform the house work, yard work and cooking for the parties and by her hostile attitude which required Dr. Layton to move from the house. Although the trial court determined that Ms. Posik was entitled to quantum meruit, it also determined that those damages were off-set by the benefits Ms. Posik received by being permitted to live with Dr. Layton. The court did award Ms. Posik a judgment on the note executed by Dr. Layton.

Although neither party urged that this agreement was void as against public policy, Dr. Layton's counsel on more than one occasion reminded us that the parties had a sexual relationship. Certainly, even though the agreement was couched in terms of a personal services contract, it was intended to be much more. It was a nuptial agreement entered into by two parties that the state prohibits from marrying. But even though the state has prohibited same-sex marriages and same-sex adoptions, it has not prohibited this type of agreement. By prohibiting same-sex marriages, the state has merely denied homosexuals the rights granted to married partners that flow naturally from the marital relationship. In short, "the law of Florida creates no legal rights or duties between live-ins." Lowry v. Lowry, 512 So.2d 1142 (Fla. 5th DCA 1987). (Sharp, J., concurring specially). This lack of recognition of the rights which flow naturally from the break-up of a marital relationship applies to unmarried heterosexuals as well as homosexuals. But the State has not denied these individuals their right to either will their property as they see fit nor to privately commit by contract to spend their money as they choose. The State is not thusly condoning the lifestyles of homosexuals or unmarried live-ins; it is merely recognizing their constitutional private property and contract rights.

Even though no legal rights or obligations flow as a matter of law from a non-marital relationship, we see no impediment to the parties to such a relationship agreeing between themselves to provide certain rights and obligations. Other states have approved such individual agreements. In Marvin v. Marvin, 18 Cal.3d 660, 134 Cal.Rptr. 815, 557 P.2d 106 (1976), the California Supreme Court held:

> [W]e base our opinion on the principle that adults who voluntarily live together and engage in sexual relations are nonetheless as competent as any other persons to contract respecting their earnings and property rights. . . . So long as the agreement does not rest upon illicit meretricious consideration, the parties may order their economic affairs as they choose. . . .

In Whorton v. Dillingham, 202 Cal.App.3d 447, 248 Cal.Rptr. 405 (1988), the California Fourth District Court of Appeal extended this principle to same-sex partners. We also see no reason for a distinction.

The Ohio Court of Appeal also seemed to recognize this principle in Seward v. Mentrup, 87 Ohio App.3d 601, 622 N.E.2d 756, 757 (1993):

> Appellant contends that she is entitled to a legal or equitable division of the property accumulated by the parties' joint efforts during the time they lived together. It is appellant's belief that her relationship with appellee was "more like a marriage," and that consequently, she is entitled to reimbursement for money she contributed toward capital improvements to appellee's residence. . . .

The evidentiary materials clearly indicate that there were no written contracts or agreements governing the parties' [lesbian] relationship . . .

Based upon Lauper [v. Harold, 23 Ohio App.3d 168, 492 N.E.2d 472, 474 (1985)], a property division, per se, applies only to marriages. We see no reason to deviate from this position. Accordingly, the trial court had no authority to divide property absent a marriage contract or similar agreement, and the court correctly granted summary judgment to appellee on appellant's breach of contract claim. (Emphasis added).

In a case involving unmarried heterosexuals, a Florida appellate court has passed on the legality of a non-marital support agreement. In Crossen v. Feldman, 673 So.2d 903 (Fla. 2d DCA 1996), the court held:

> Without attempting to define what may or may not be "palimony," this case simply involves whether these parties entered into a contract for support, which is something that they are legally capable of doing.

Addressing the invited issue, we find that an agreement for support between unmarried adults is valid unless the agreement is inseparably based upon illicit consideration of sexual services. Certainly prostitution, heterosexual or homosexual, cannot be condoned merely because it is performed within the confines of a written agreement. The parties, represented by counsel, were well aware of this prohibition and took pains to assure that sexual services were not even mentioned in the agreement. That factor would not be decisive, however, if it could be determined from the contract or from the conduct of the parties that the primary reason for the agreement was to deliver and be paid for sexual services. See Bergen v. Wood, 14 Cal.App.4th 854, 18 Cal.Rptr.2d 75 (1993). This contract and the parties' testimony show that such was not the case here. Because of the potential abuse in marital-type relationships, we find that such agreements must be in writing. The Statute of Frauds (section 725.01, Florida Statutes) requires that contracts made upon consideration of marriage must be in writing. This same requirement should apply to non-marital, nuptial-like agreements. In this case, there is (and can be) no dispute that the agreement exists.

The obligations imposed on Ms. Posik by the agreement include the obligation "to immediately commence residing with Nancy L.R. Layton at her said residence for the remainder of Emma Posik's life...." This is very similar to a "until death do us part" commitment. And although the parties undoubtedly expected a sexual relationship, this record shows that they contemplated much more. They contracted for a permanent sharing of, and participating in, one another's lives. We find the contract enforceable.

We disagree with the trial court that waiver was proved in this case. Ms. Posik consistently urged Dr. Layton to make the will as required by the agreement and her failure to do so was sufficient grounds to declare default. And even more important to Ms. Posik was the implied agreement that her lifetime commitment would be reciprocated by a lifetime commitment by Dr. Layton—and that this mutual commitment would be monogamous. When Dr. Layton introduced a third person into the relationship, although it was not an express breach of the written agreement, it explains why Ms. Posik took that opportunity to hold Dr. Layton to her express obligations and to consider the agreement in default.

We also disagree with the trial court that Ms. Posik breached the agreement by refusing to perform housework, yard work, provisioning the house, and cooking for the parties. This conduct did not occur until after Dr. Layton had first breached the agreement. One need not continue to perform a contract when the other party has first breached. City of Miami Beach v. Carner, 579 So.2d 248 (Fla. 3d DCA 1991). Therefore, this conduct did not authorize Dr. Layton to send the three-day notice of eviction which constituted a separate default under the agreement.

We also disagree that the commitment to pay $2,500 per month upon termination of the agreement is unenforceable as a penalty. We agree with Ms. Posik that her damages, which would include more than mere lost wages and moving expenses, were not readily ascertainable at the time the contract was created. Further, the agreed sum is reasonable under the circumstances of this case. It is less than Ms. Posik was earning some four years earlier when she entered into this arrangement. It is also less than

Ms. Posik would have received had the long-term provisions of the contract been performed. She is now in her sixties and her working opportunities are greatly reduced.

We recognize that this contract, insisted on by Ms. Posik before she would relocate with Dr. Layton, is extremely favorable to her. But there is no allegation of fraud or overreaching on Ms. Posik's part. This court faced an extremely generous agreement in Carnell v. Carnell, 398 So.2d 503 (Fla. 5th DCA 1981). In Carnell, a lawyer, in order to induce a woman to become his wife, agreed that upon divorce the wife would receive his home owned by him prior to marriage, one-half of his disposable income and one-half of his retirement as alimony until she remarried. Two years after the marriage, she tested his commitment. We held:

> The husband also contends that the agreement is so unfair and unreasonable that it must be set aside ... "The freedom to contract includes the right to make a bad bargain." (Citation omitted). The controlling question here is whether there was overreaching and not whether the bargain was good or bad. 398 So.2d at 506.

Contracts can be dangerous to one's well-being. That is why they are kept away from children. Perhaps warning labels should be attached. In any event, contracts should be taken seriously. Dr. Layton's comment that she considered the agreement a sham and never intended to be bound by it shows that she did not take it seriously. That is regrettable.

We affirm that portion of the judgment below which addresses the promissory note and attorney's fees and costs associated therewith. We reverse that portion of the judgment that fails to enforce the parties' agreement.

AFFIRMED in part; REVERSED in part and REMANDED for further action consistent with this opinion. . . .

PETERSON, CHIEF JUDGE, concurring specially.

Partially quoting from Crossen v. Feldman, 673 So.2d 903 (Fla. 2d DCA 1996), "this case simply involves whether [Emma Posik and Nancy L. R. Layton] ... entered into a contract for support, which is something that they are legally capable of doing."

In the instant case, two persons entered into a lifetime personal services contract—Posik managed a household exclusively for Layton, who was engaged in a demanding medical practice, and Layton was to provide monetary support and living quarters for Posik, who sacrificed her own professional career as a nurse to manage a household. Posik's reward, if she outlived Layton, and if Layton fared well in her professional endeavors, was a golden parachute—Layton's assets upon Layton's death. Each and every term of this agreement could have been included in one between a single invalid or an elderly married couple who seek the companionship and household services of a housekeeper, cook or a practical or professional nurse, in which no sexual relationship was involved.

The result reached by us in this case should not be interpreted as anything more than a recognition that legally competent individuals may exercise their constitutional private property and contract rights. Much has been included in the opinion about the lifestyles of the litigants in this case because of arguments presented at trial and on appeal. But as Judge Harris accurately points out, neither this contract, nor the parties' testimony, reflects that the reason for this agreement was the delivery and payment for a sexual relationship or a same sex marriage, both of which are not recognized by the laws of Florida.

NOTES AND QUESTIONS

1. The rights arising by law that are enjoyed by married persons and of which unmarried lesbian and gay people now are universally deprived, in whole or in part, are numerous. Some of these are:

a. The right of inheritance (particularly in the case of intestacy);

b. The right to claim an elective share;

c. The right to serve as a fiduciary of each other's estates;

d. The right to file joint tax returns;

e. The right to claim dependency deductions and status;

f. The right to claim estate and gift tax benefits;

g. The right to sue for infliction of emotional distress by injury to the partner, for loss of consortium, wrongful death and other personal injuries;

h. The right to claim marital communication privilege;

i. The right to participate in end-of-life care decisions or other health care decisions for a partner;

j. The right to share in property if the relationship ends during the partners' lives,

k. The right to adopt a partner's biological child;

l. The right to visit the partner in jail, hospitals, mental institutions, and other places restricted to family members;

m. The right to purchase health insurance on each other's lives, and

n. The right to bereavement leaves and family medical leaves.

See, Dunlap, The Lesbian and Gay Marriage Debate: A Microcosm of Our Hopes and Troubles in the Nineties, 1 Law and Sexuality 63 (1991).

Because some of these can be created by contract, a written agreement to govern the rights of partners in a same-sex relationship is of paramount importance. For example, same-sex couples can enter into agreements governing the distribution of property in the event of separation or death. They can also sign appropriate documents to assure each has a role in making health care decisions for each other. Additionally, in some states one of the partners can sign a consent for the other to adopt the signor's biological child without the signor having to surrender the signor's parental rights.

2. In the celebrated decision of Marvin v. Marvin, 18 Cal.3d 660, 670–671, 134 Cal.Rptr. 815, 822, 557 P.2d 106, 113 (1976) involving the actor Lee Marvin the court stated:

> Although the past decisions hover over the issue in the somewhat wispy form of the figures of a Chagall painting, we can abstract from those decisions a clear and simple rule. The fact that a man and woman live together without marriage, and engage in a sexual relationship, does not in itself invalidate agreements between them relating to their earnings, property, or expenses. Neither is such an agreement invalid merely because the parties may have contemplated the creation or continuation of a nonmarital relationship when they entered into it. Agreements between non-marital partners fail only to the extent that they rest upon a consideration of meretricious sexual services.

An agreement that failed was found to exist in Jones v. Daly, 122 Cal.App.3d 500, 508, 176 Cal.Rptr. 130 (1981). In Jones the partner's services were limited to "lover, companion, homemaker, traveling companion, house-keeper and cook...." In finding the agreement to divide property and provide support unenforceable, the court stated:

> "According to the allegations of the complaint, the agreement provided that the parties would share equally the earnings and property accumu-lated as a result of their efforts while they lived together and that Daly would support plaintiff for the rest of his life. Neither the property sharing nor the support provision of the agreement rests upon plaintiff's acting as Daly's traveling companion, housekeeper or cook as distin-guished from acting as his lover. The latter service forms an inseparable part of the consideration for the agreement and renders it unenforceable in its entirety." Jones v. Daly, 122 Cal.App.3d at 509, 176 Cal.Rptr. at 130

Contracts to share earnings and assets upheld in Marvin are rejected in Illinois as a disguised attempt to revive common-law marriage. See, Hewitt v. Hewitt, 77 Ill.2d 49, 31 Ill.Dec. 827, 394 N.E.2d 1204 (1979). In New York, express agreements between cohabitants to share earnings and assets will be upheld but will not be implied merely from the fact of cohabitation. See Morone v. Morone, 50 N.Y.2d 481, 413 N.E.2d 1154, 429 N.Y.S.2d 592 (1980). On the other hand, in Washington a presumption of joint ownership of assets can arise where a marriage-like arrangement of long duration existed, at least for heterosexual couples. See, Connell v. Francisco, 127 Wash.2d 339, 898 P.2d 831 (1995).

3. What kind of protection is afforded to the cohabitants in the absence of a finding of a contract or agreement to pool their income and resources? If a contract or agreement is a necessary requirement, to what extent will courts infer such an agreement merely from such acts of the parties as opening a bank account in the names of both parties jointly or naming each other the beneficiary of a life insurance policy on the life of the other? See, Morone v. Morone, 50 N.Y.2d 481, 413 N.E.2d 1154, 429 N.Y.S.2d 592 (1980). If a contract is required, to what extent must it comply with the Statute of Frauds? Cf. Botis v. Estate of Kudrick, 421 N.J.Super. 107, 22 A.3d 975 (2011)

(reciting New Jersey statute expressly extending the requirements of the statute of frauds to a palimony contract).

4. Cohabitants may have difficulties establishing property entitlements not only upon separation but also upon the death of one of the cohabitants. To date, no state extends the protection of dower, curtesy or statutory shares in lieu thereof to cohabitants. However, Professor Lawrence Waggoner, Reporter for the Uniform Probate Code, has proposed a statute that would create an intestate share for a "committed partner" which is roughly equivalent to what many states now provide for a surviving spouse. To be a "committed partner," the survivor and the decedent must "have been sharing a common household ... in a marriage-like relationship." The concepts of common household and marriage-like relationship are defined as follows:

> (c) [Common Household.] For purposes of subsections (b) and (e), "sharing a common household" or "shared a common household" means that the decedent and the individual shared the same place to live, whether or not one or both had other places to live and whether or not one or both were physically residing somewhere else at the decedent's death. The right to occupy the common household need not have been in both of their names.

> (d) [Marriage-like Relationship; Factors.] For purposes of subsection (b), a "marriage-like relationship" is a relationship that corresponds to the relationship between marital partners, in which two individuals have chosen to share one another's lives in a long-term, intimate and committed relationship of mutual caring. Although no single factor or set of factors determines whether a relationship qualifies as marriage-like, the following factors are among those to be considered:

> (1) the purpose, duration, constancy and degree of exclusivity of the relationship;

> (2) the degree to which the parties intermingled their finances, such as by maintaining joint checking, credit card, or other types of accounts, sharing loan obligations, sharing a mortgage or lease on the household in which they lived or on other property, or titling the household in which they lived or other property in joint tenancy;

> (3) the degree to which the parties formalized legal obligations, intentions and responsibilities to one another, such as by one or both naming the other as primary beneficiary of life insurance or employee benefit plans or as agent to make health care decisions;

> (4) whether the couple shared in co-parenting a child and the degree of joint care and support given the child;

> (5) whether the couple joined in a marriage or a commitment ceremony, even if the ceremony was not of a type giving rise to a presumption under subsection (e)(3); and

> (6) the degree to which the couple held themselves out to others as married or the degree to which the couple held themselves out to others as emotionally and financially committed to one another on a permanent basis.

(e) [Presumption.] An individual's relationship with the decedent is presumed to have been marriage-like if:

(1) during the [six] year period next preceding the decedent's death, the decedent and the individual shared a common household for periods totaling at least [five] years;

(2) the decedent or the individual registered or designated the other as his [or her] domestic partner with and under procedures established by an organization and neither partner executed a document terminating or purporting to terminate the registration or designation;

(3) the decedent and the individual joined in a marriage or a commitment ceremony conducted and contemporaneously certified in writing by an organization; or

(4) the individual is the parent of a child of the decedent, or is or was a party to a written co-parenting agreement with the decedent regarding a child, and if, in either case, the child lived before the age of 18 in the common household of the decedent and the individual.

(f) [Force of the Presumption]. If a presumption arises under subsection (e) because only one of the listed factors is established, the presumption is rebuttable by a preponderance of the evidence. If more than one of the listed factors is established, the presumption can only be rebutted by clear and convincing evidence.

5.   Over the last fifteen years, there has been an ongoing debate whether gay and lesbian couples should be permitted to marry. In Europe, Belgium, Iceland, the Netherlands, Norway, Portugal, and Spain permit such marriages. So does Argentina, Canada, South Africa and Sweden. In 2003, Massachusetts became the first state in this country to permit gay marriages. Subsequently, Connecticut, District of Columbia, Iowa, New Hampshire, New York, Vermont and Washington, have validated same-sex marriages by legislation or judicial decision. California, New Jersey, Maryland, and Rhode Island to some extent recognize same-sex marriages that were performed in other states.

6.   Under the Full Faith and Credit Clause of the United States Constitution, each state is obliged to give full faith and credit to the public acts, records and judicial proceedings of the other states. If any state were to validate same-sex marriages, it is not clear whether this clause would require the other states to recognize those marriages even though not permitted by the laws of the other states. The answer to that question would depend on how the Full Faith and Credit Clause was interpreted. However, in 1996 Congress adopted the Defense of Marriage Act, 28 U.S.C. § 1738C & 1 U.S.C. § 7. (Known as "DOMA")

(DOMA) provides that no state would be required to give full faith and credit to a same-sex marriage valid in another state. It also provides that for purposes of federal laws and entitlements, such as social security, welfare, and the tax laws, the word "spouse" means only a person of the opposite sex who is a husband or wife and the word "marriage" means only a marriage between a man and a woman. This Act could arguably violate the U.S. Constitution on the grounds that Congress is not the interpreter of the full faith and credit clause nor the "equal protection" clause. The constitutionality of DOMA is slowly working its way through the courts.

Twenty-nine states have state constitutional amendments that bar same-sex marriages. Most states have statutes which limit marriage to two persons of the opposite-sex.

7.   A number of state and federal laws create default property rights for married persons that do not apply to cohabitants. For example, state intestacy laws create marital property rights for a surviving spouse. These laws apply when the first spouse dies without a will. State laws also provide default rules that apply to the division of property and support upon divorce in the absence of the couples' agreement to the contrary. Because of the exponential growth in the number of couples that cohabit but do not marry, there is a growing need to address what the appropriate default property rules should be for such couples when the relationship ends by death or otherwise. The need for such laws is evident from the following demographic analysis:

> There is widespread recognition that U.S. households have changed dramatically in the latter half of the twentieth century. The changes include an increased number of blended families, single-parent households, and unmarried same-sex and opposite-sex committed couples, including some with children. The transformation taking place in U.S. households implicates property law and vice versa. In recognition of the changing U.S. household and the symbiotic relationship between wealth transmission and family, we undertook an empirical study designed to assess public attitudes about the inclusion of surviving committed partners as heirs. This Article reports our findings.

> In 1994, approximately 7% of the nation's couples were in unmarried committed relationships. Data from surveys of "unmarried partner households" indicate about 30%, or approximately 1.7 million, of unmarried households are likely to be headed by same-sex couples. The number of opposite-sex committed relationships is growing at a more rapid pace than the number of same-sex relationships. Opposite-sex households increased at a 28% rate between 1990 and 1994 as compared to just 4% for same-sex households. A significant minority of same-sex couples (between 8 and 9%) and an even greater percentage of opposite-sex couples (35%) have children under the age of fifteen living with them.

Fellows, Johnson, Chiericozzi, Hale, Lee, Preble, Varan, Committed Partners and Inheritance: An Empirical Study, 16 Law & Inequality: A Journal of Theory and Practice1–3 (1998).

CHAPTER 7

LEASEHOLD ESTATES

. . .

§ 7.1 INTRODUCTION

Over the last few decades, the law of landlord and tenant has undergone a remarkable transformation. For centuries the tenant's view of the slant of the law was encapsulated in the idea that the tenant had one "right"—the right to pay rent. Although that view was somewhat exaggerated, it is true that for many centuries the focus of the law of landlord and tenant concentrated on the landlord's rights and remedies rather than on the tenant's rights and remedies. In part this focus was dictated by the conceptualization of the lease as a type of conveyance of real estate with the effect that, during the term of the lease when the tenant was entitled to the exclusive possession of the property, the tenant was more akin to a purchaser. In part this focus also was dictated by the fact that, because early leases related to land and not improvements, there was little need to consider whether any ongoing obligations should be inherent in the landlord-tenant relationship. Fundamental changes in the nature of leased property and the sociological transformation of America from an agricultural to an urban society presaged a transformation of landlord-tenant law as well. This story is developed as this chapter unfolds.

While the historical roots are somewhat obscure, leasehold estates appear to have begun as a device to avoid ecclesiastical prohibitions on the charging of interest.[1] The origin of leases coupled with the fact that the tenant was not obligated to perform the incidences of feudal tenure led to their characterization as nonfreehold estates and, correspondingly, their relatively low place on the feudal ladder.

§ 7.2 CLASSIFICATION OF TENANCIES

As the law of landlord and tenant developed, four kinds of tenancies or leasehold interests were recognized: the tenancy for a term for years,

---

1. See, Hicks, The Contractual Nature of Real Property Leases, 24 Baylor L.Rev. 443, 448 (1972). Professor Hicks illustrates this as follows: "A, in consideration of a lump sum amount of money, would grant a term of years to B of sufficient duration to allow B to recoup both his consideration and a profit." Id.

the periodic tenancy, the tenancy at will, and the tenancy at sufferance. The principal distinction among these four types of tenancies relates to whether notice is required to terminate the tenancy by either the landlord or the tenant, and the time in which any required notice must be given. What function is served by a requirement of notice to terminate?

A. Term for Years

A lease for a term for years is a lease "for any fixed or computable period of time."[1] In other words, it is a tenancy with a fixed beginning date and a fixed ending date. The length of the term is irrelevant to the classification of the tenancy as a term for years. Thus, a tenancy to commence on January 1, 1993, and to end on January 31, 1993, is a term for years even though the length of the term is only one month. Courts have also upheld the validity of leases for an extended term for years. See, e.g., Monbar, Inc. v. Monaghan, 18 Del.Ch. 395, 162 A. 50 (1932) (2000 years); Ralston Steel Car Co. v. Ralston, 112 Ohio St. 306, 147 N.E. 513 (1925) (99–year lease perpetually renewable). Some states, however, have imposed restrictions on the duration of tenancies for a term for years in order to prevent the creation of extremely long tenancies. See, e.g., Cal. Civ. Code § 718 (West 1982) (restricting leases of municipal property to 55 years, leases of land within a city to 99 years); S.D. Codified Laws Ann. § 43–32–2 (1983) (restricting leases of agricultural lands to 20 years). If a lease provides for a term in excess of the length permitted by law, the effect of the restriction on the tenancy varies. For example, in Waldo v. Jacobs, 152 Mich. 425, 116 N.W. 371 (1908), the court treated the lease as completely void. However, in Robertson v. Hays, 83 Ala. 290, 3 So. 674 (1888), the court held that only the term in excess of the term permitted by law was void. As a general matter, leases for an extended period of time are the exclusive province of the commercial rental market. Residential leases, if a term for years, tend to run from one to three years. Why does the duration of tenancies in commercial and residential leases vary?

No notice is required to terminate a tenancy for a term for years, other than the notice provided by the lease. The lease may provide that the term for years will terminate prior to the date fixed in the agreement because of the happening of some condition or limitation. For example, a lease agreement will commonly provide that, if the tenant fails to pay rent on the due date or within any grace period, the landlord may elect to terminate the tenancy and proceed to evict the tenant.

Unless the terms of the lease otherwise provide, a tenancy for a term for years is alienable, devisable, and descendible.

---

1. Restatement (Second) of Property § 1.4 (1977). But the Third Restatement states that "The term of years is a present interest that terminates on the expiration of a term that is measured in one or more years, in units of a year, or in multiples or divisions thereof. A term of years can be qualified by language that specifies one or more events that can terminate the estate before or extend the estate beyond the expiration of the term." Restatement (Third) of Property, § 24.6 (2012).

Customarily the tenancy for a term for years is created by a written instrument executed by both the landlord and the tenant. In fact, most states' Statutes of Frauds provide that an oral lease for a term of more than one year is void, although these statutes often provide that if the tenant enters under an oral lease of more than one year and pays rent, a periodic tenancy arises that is not subject to the statute.[2]

B. Periodic Tenancy

According to the Restatement (Second) of Property, a periodic tenancy is a tenancy that will "endure until one of the parties has given the required notice to terminate the tenancy at the end of a period."[3] Periodic tenancies have definite durations, such as one week, one month, or one year, but at the end of the term the lease is automatically renewed for a like period unless either the landlord or the tenant gives *proper* notice of intent to terminate the tenancy to the other. Because of the automatic renewal feature, these tenancies have been characterized as leaseholds having indefinite durations that require minimum advance notice of intent to terminate.[4]

At common law a year-to-year periodic tenancy required six months notice to terminate. Leases of shorter durations required a notice to terminate that equaled the period of the lease, provided the notice did not exceed six months. Thus, a month's notice was necessary to terminate a month-to-month tenancy; a week's notice was necessary to terminate a week-to-week tenancy and so on. The notice to terminate must have been received by the party to whom it was delivered no later than the last day of the period. If the notice was not received by that date the termination was ineffective as to that period. However, the notice was sufficient to terminate the tenancy at the end of the subsequent period. For example, if a month-to-month tenant, whose tenancy began on the 20th of each month and ended on the 19th of each succeeding month, sent her landlord a notice of termination on October 21 stating that she was terminating the tenancy on November 19, the notice of termination would be ineffective to terminate the tenancy on November 19 because the landlord would not have received one month's notice. The notice would be effective, however, to terminate the tenancy as of December 19.

State laws in many jurisdictions have shortened the length of notice required to terminate a periodic tenancy. See, e.g., N.C.Gen.Stat. § 42–14 (1997) (year to year periodic tenancy terminable by notice of one month or more before the end of the tenancy; month-to-month tenancy terminable by seven days notice; week to week tenancy terminable by two days notice). Other states have permitted a month-to-month tenancy to be terminated at any time during the period provided sufficient notice is

---

2. See generally, 1 Amer.L.Prop. §§ 3.18–3.21 (A.J. Casner ed. 1952); 2 R. Powell, The Law of Real Property ¶ 222 (P. Rohan ed. 1985).

3. Restatement (Second) of Property § 1.5 (1977).

4. H. Hovenkamp & S. Kurtz, The Law of Property at 89 (5th ed. 2001).

given in advance of the termination date. See, e.g., Cal.Civ.Code § 1946 (West 1985).

C. Tenancy at Will

A tenancy at will is a tenancy of potentially infinite duration which at common law could be terminated at any time by either party without prior notice to the other.[5] According to the Restatement (Second) of Property, the death of either landlord or tenant terminates a tenancy at will.[6] Many states, concerned by the disadvantages to both landlords and tenants if tenancies are terminable without notice, have modified the no notice requirement by requiring some notice to terminate the tenancy at will. See, e.g., Ala.Code § 35–9–3 (1995) (10 days notice required to terminate an express tenancy at will). Even at common law there were limits on the no prior notice rule. For example, under the doctrine of "emblements" an agricultural tenant with planted but unharvested annual crops at the time a notice of termination was given had the right to tend the crops to maturity and harvest them. See 2 W. Blackstone, Commentaries on the Laws of England 144–45 (1761).

A lease that can be terminated at the will of only the landlord or only the tenant, but not both, is not a tenancy at will. At best it is a determinable term for years. According to the Restatement (Second) of Property "[a] tenancy terminable at the will of one of the parties only may under all the circumstances present an unconscionable arrangement and, if so, the tenancy will be terminable at the will of either party...."[7]

D. Tenancy at Sufferance

A tenancy at sufferance is not a tenancy at all. This tenancy arises when a tenant (typically a tenant of a term for years) enters the landlord's property rightfully but remains in possession of the property after the termination of the tenancy. This tenant, known to the law as a "holdover," is not really a tenant within the proper meaning of that word. At the moment of holding over, this tenant is a mere trespasser in possession of the property without the consent of the landlord. Because this tenant was once in rightful possession of the property, however, his initial entry did not amount to a trespass. The landlord may elect to treat the holdover as either a trespasser and initiate an action to evict the tenant or, alternatively, as a periodic tenant. If such an election is made, the period begins to run from the date the tenant first became a holdover tenant, i.e., at the termination of the preceding lease. The holdover tenancy doctrine will be explored later in greater detail.

Notes and Questions

1. L and T enter into a lease dated January 1, 2006. The lease agreement provides that the term of the lease will commence on January 1, 2006,

---

5. Cf., Restatement (Second) of Property § 1.6 (1977).

6. Restatement (Second) of Property, § 1.6 comment e (1977).

7. Id. at comment g.

but the agreement provides no date of termination. The lease also provides that "T shall pay L rent of $6000 annually, said rent to be paid in equal monthly installments of $500." What kind of tenancy has been created and what notice, if any, is required to terminate this tenancy?

2. L and T enter into a month-to-month tenancy of an apartment commencing on March 1, 2012. On April 15, 2012, T dies. L knows T died. On May 1, 2012, T's spouse vacates the apartment. On June 1, 2012, L sues T's estate for May rent claiming that the tenancy had not been terminated. Is L correct? Suppose L later sues T's estate for June rent. Can L prevail? See Restatement (Second) of Property § 1.5 comment f (1977).

3. L leases an apartment to T for a term to commence on February 1, 2009, and to terminate on January 31, 2011. At 5:00 P.M. on January 31, 2011, three painters employed by L to repaint the apartment for the new tenant arrive and request T to permit them to enter and paint the premises. Can T refuse them the right to enter the apartment? See Fox v. Nathans, 32 Conn. 348 (1865); Buchanan v. Whitman, 151 N.Y. 253, 45 N.E. 556 (1896). See also Restatement (Second) of Property § 1.4 comment d (1977).

4. Ace Development Corporation has constructed a new shopping center and leases space in the building to Florence's Flower Shop. The lease provides:

the term of this lease shall commence on July 1, 2010 and shall continue through June 30, 2011 and for successive annual periods thereafter. Rent under this agreement is payable in monthly installments of $1000.

Governing state law provides that "a lease of real property for a term not specified by the parties or for a term automatically renewable at the end of the term is deemed renewed at the end of the term implied by law or stated in the lease agreement unless one party provides written notice to the other of his or her intention to terminate the same, at least as long before the expiration thereof as the term of the leasing itself, not exceeding sixty days...."

On May 15, 2012, Florence consults you concerning how she can terminate the lease. She advises you that on April 29, 2012, she sent a letter to her landlord stating that the flower shop would move to a different location and would vacate the leased premises on June 30, 2012. Unfortunately, a delay occurred in the mail and the landlord did not receive her letter until May 3, 2007. The landlord claims the lease has been automatically renewed for another year. She wants to know if her notice to terminate complied with the statute. Cf. UCC § 1–201(26). Assuming the notice was defective, when does the leasehold terminate?

5. Robert signed a printed form lease providing that Lou was granted a term to commence on May 1 and to end when Lou terminates the lease. Three years later Robert notifies Lou to vacate the premises within thirty days. Lou claims he has a determinable life estate. Robert claims the lease created a tenancy at will. Who is correct? See Garner v. Gerrish, 63 N.Y.2d 575, 483 N.Y.S.2d 973, 473 N.E.2d 223 (1984).

§ 7.3 THE LEASE

One of the first legal documents a law student is likely to encounter is the lease, and it can be a truly imposing document. Typically the lease includes words and phrases foreign to common vocabulary often hidden within text readable only with a magnifying glass. All too often the residential tenant believes the lease is presented to him on a take it or leave it basis and that the housing market is sufficiently constricted so that the tenant has little or no other housing alternatives. How valid these beliefs are, however, is open to question as some of the following readings will demonstrate. Before considering the extent to which tenants have any bargaining power in the negotiation of leases, the student should read the following "plain English" lease form devised as a response to Section 5–702 of the New York General Obligations Law requiring leases, among other legal documents, to be in "plain language."

By this agreement, made on _____(1)_____, 19_(2)_____, between _____ (3)_____, hereinafter called lessor, and _____(4)_____, hereinafter called lessee, lessor grants, demises, and lets to lessee, and lessee hires and takes as tenant of lessor, Apartment No. _____(5)_____ of the building situated at _____(6)_____ [*street address*], in the City of _____(7)_____, County of _____(8)_____, State of New York, to be used and occupied by lessee as a residence and for no other use or purpose whatsoever, for a term of _____(9)_____ years beginning _____(10)_____, 19_(11)_____, and ending _____(12)_____, 19_ (13)_____, at a rental of _____ (14)_____ Dollars ($_____), payable monthly, in advance, during the entire term of this contract at the office of lessor, at _____(15)_____, in the City of _____(16)_____, County of _____(17)_____, State of New York, or to any other person or agent and at any other time that lessor may designate.

It is further mutually agreed between the parties as follows:

1. Lessee shall not assign this lease or sublet the premises, or any part thereof; or use or permit the use of the premises, or any part thereof, for any purpose other than as above stipulated; or make any alterations therein, or additions thereto, without the written consent of lessor. Lessor expressly covenants that such consent shall not be unreasonably or arbitrarily refused. All additions, fixtures, or improvements made by lessee, except movable household furniture, to become the property of lessor and remain on the premises as a part thereof, and be surrendered with the leased premises at the termination of this lease.

2. All personal property placed in the leased premises, or in the basement, storage rooms, or any other part of the building, shall be at the risk of lessee or the owner of such personal property. Lessor shall not be liable for any loss or damage to such personal property or for any injury to lessee arising from the accidental bursting or leaking of water or steam

pipes, or from any act of negligence of any cotenant, occupant of the building, or any person other than lessor, his agents, servants, and employees.

3. Without charge to lessee, during the proper seasons and during reasonable hours, lessor will furnish _____ (18)_____ [steam *or other type*] for heating the premises, and, also during reasonable hours, hot and cold water. Reasonable hours shall be determined by lessor. In the event the heating apparatus shall need repair, or if from some other causes beyond the control of lessor, including federal, state, or municipal control, or shortage or inferior quality of fuel, it should be necessary, in the determination of lessor, to cut off, reduce, or stop the production of heat, lessor shall not be liable for any damage arising out of the failure to furnish such heating or water service. Should any of the electrical equipment belonging to the leased premises, or the building, become unserviceable, lessor shall have a reasonable time, after notification, to determine the responsibility, and have the same repaired, without any liability to lessee for damage or inconvenience.

4. In the event the leased premises are destroyed or rendered untenantable by fire, storm, earthquake, or other casualty not caused by the negligence of lessee, this lease shall be at an end from such time except for the purpose of enforcing rights that may have then accrued hereunder. The rental shall then be accounted for between lessor and lessee up to the time of such injury or destruction of said premises, lessee paying up to said date and lessor refunding the rents collected beyond such date. Should a part only of the leased premises thereby be rendered untenantable, the rental shall abate in the proportion which the injured part bears to the whole leased premises, and such part so injured shall be restored by lessor as speedily as practicable, after which the full rent shall recommence and the lease continue according to its terms.

5. In the event possession cannot be delivered to lessee on commencement of the lease term, through no fault of lessor or its agents, there shall be no liability on lessor or its agents, but the rental herein provided shall abate until possession is given. Lessor or its agents shall have _____(19)_____ days in which to give possession, and if possession is tendered within such time, lessee agrees to accept the leased premises and pay the rental herein provided from that date. In the event possession cannot be delivered within such time, through no fault of lessor or its agents, then this lease and all rights hereunder shall be at an end.

6. The prompt payment of the rent, monthly, in advance, as specified; the performance of all other covenants contained herein; and the faithful observance of the rules and regulations printed on this lease and hereby made a part of this covenant, and of such other and further rules or regulations as may be hereafter made by lessor, are conditions on which the lease is made and accepted. Any failure on the part of lessee to comply with the provisions of the lease or of any present rules and regulations or any that may be hereafter prescribed by lessor, shall at lessor's option

work a forfeiture of this contract and all of lessee's rights hereunder, and thereupon lessor, his agents or attorneys, shall have the right to re-enter the leased premises and remove all persons therefrom and lessee hereby expressly waives any and all notice required by law to terminate tenancy, and also waives any and all legal proceedings to recover possession of the leased premises. Lessee expressly agrees that on violation of any of the covenants of this lease, or of present or future rules and regulations, lessor, his agents or his attorneys, may immediately re-enter the leased premises and dispossess lessee without legal notice or the institution of any legal proceedings whatsoever.

Should it become necessary for lessor to employ an attorney to enforce any of the conditions or covenants hereof, including the collection of rentals or gaining possession of the premises, lessee agrees to pay all expenses so incurred, including reasonable attorney's fees.

7. Lessor, or his agents, shall have the right to enter the leased premises during all reasonable hours to inspect the same or to make repairs, additions, or alterations as may be deemed necessary for the safety and comfort of tenants, or for the preservation of the leased premises or the building, or to exhibit the leased premises, and to put and keep upon the doors or windows thereof a notice indicating that said premises are for rent, at any time within _____ (20)_____ days before the expiration day of this lease. The right of entry shall likewise exist for the purpose of removing placards, signs, fixtures, alterations, or additions, which do not conform to this agreement or to the rules and regulations of the building.

8. Lessee agrees to maintain the leased premises in the same condition, order and repair as they are at the commencement of the lease term, excepting only reasonable wear and tear arising from the use thereof under this agreement, and to make good to lessor, immediately on demand, any damage to the heating or water apparatus or electric lights or wires, or any fixtures, appliances or appurtenances of the leased premises, or of the building, caused by act or neglect of lessee or any person or persons in the employ or under the control of lessee.

9. If lessee abandons or vacates the leased premises or is dispossessed for cause by lessor before the termination of this lease, or any renewal thereof, lessor may, on giving _____ (21)_____ days' written notice to lessee, declare this lease forfeited and shall, in such event, make reasonable efforts to relet the premises. Lessee shall be liable to lessor for all damages suffered by lessor by reason of such forfeiture. Damages shall include, but shall not be limited to, the following: (1) all actual damages suffered by lessor, until the property is relet, including reasonable expenses incurred in reletting or in attempting to relet; (2) the difference between the rent received when the property is relet and the rent reserved under this lease.

Until the premises have been relet, lessee agrees to pay to lessor, on the same days as rental payments are due under this lease, the actual damages suffered by lessor since the last payment, either of rent or damages, was made.

After the premises have been relet, lessee agrees to pay to lessor, on the last day of each rental period, the difference between the rent received for the period from reletting and the rent reserved under this lease for that period.

10.   Lessor's failure to take advantage of any default on the part of lessee shall not be construed as a waiver thereof, nor shall any custom or practice that may grow up between the parties in the course of administering this instrument be construed to waive or to lessen the right of lessor to insist on the performance of the provisions hereof.

In witness whereof, the parties hereto have duly executed this lease the day and year first above written.

[Signatures]

[Acknowledgments]

Rules and Regulations of Apartments (Applicable to
the premises rented by the foregoing lease)

1.   The sidewalks, courts, entry passages, halls, and stairways shall not be obstructed by lessees, or used by them for any purpose other than that of ingress and egress.

2.   The front porches are not common property for all lessees and each lessee's use of the porches must be limited to that portion directly in front of his apartment.

3.   Where an apartment has a rear entrance, service must be made through the rear only.

4.   When practical, lessees will be required to have their household goods brought into and taken out of the building through the rear entrance.

5.   Employees of lessees, except nurses accompanying lessees' children, will be permitted to have ingress and egress only by entrances appropriately indicated or marked by lessor.

6.   Lessees and their employees shall maintain order in the building and shall not make or permit any improper noises in the building or interfere in any way with other tenants or those having business with them.

7.   The use of all pianos, radios, television sets, phonographs, and other musical devices must discontinue at _____ (22)_____ o'clock p.m. No musical instruments shall be played for practice at any time and the giving of music lessons, vocal or instrumental, in the building is prohibited.

8.   The lessor acknowledges the lessee's right to have parties, or a large number of guests, provided that good order prevails and boisterous

conduct is avoided. Continued violations of this regulation will, at the option of the lessor, void this lease.

9. No play wagons, bicycles, motorcycles, motorbikes, or other vehicles shall be allowed in the corridors, halls, elevators, or elsewhere in the building and the lessor reserves the right to remove any and all objectionable items and nuisances, and the failure to remove them promptly does not constitute a waiver in this regard.

10. Dogs, cats, and other pet animals or birds are strictly prohibited in this building.

11. The floors, skylights, and windows that reflect or admit light into any place in the building shall not be covered or obstructed by lessee. The bathroom facilities and other water apparatus shall not be used for any other purposes than those for which they were constructed, and no sweepings, rubbish, rags, ashes, or other substances shall be thrown therein. Any damage resulting to them, to the heating apparatus, or to any other equipment from misuse shall be paid for by the lessee who caused it.

12. Nothing shall be thrown by lessee or his servants out of the windows or doors, or down the passage of skylights of the building.

13. All lessees and occupants must observe strict care not to leave their windows open when it rains or snows, and for any default shall make good any injury sustained by other tenants, or by the lessor, through damage to paint, plastering, or other parts of the building.

14. No lessee shall do, or permit anything to be done, in said premises, or bring or keep anything therein, that shall in any way increase the rate of fire insurance on the leased premises, or bring or keep anything therein that will interfere with the rights of other tenants, or in any way injure or annoy them, or conflict with the laws relating to fires, or with the regulations of the Fire Department, or with any insurance policy on the building or any part thereof, or conflict with any of the rules and ordinances of the Board of Health.

15. All nonemergency reports of repairs needed and of irregularities to which lessor's attention should be directed must be made in writing to lessor's office.

16. No painting or wall papering shall be done, or alterations made to any part of the building by putting up or changing any partition, door, or window, and no nailing, boring, or screwing into the woodwork or plastering shall be done, without the consent of the lessor.

17. All glass, locks, and trimmings in or on the doors and windows, belonging to the building, shall be kept whole, and whenever any part thereof shall be broken, the same immediately shall be replaced or repaired and put in order under the direction, and to the satisfaction, of the lessor, and shall be left whole and in good repair, in the same number and kind, and with the same kind of keys as received by the lessee on entering into possession of any part of the building or during his tenancy.

18. If the lessee desires awnings outside or shades inside the windows, other than those provided by the lessor, they must be of such shape, color, material, and make as may be prescribed by the lessor, and must be constructed or attached at lessee's expense.

19. Any lessee installing or causing to be installed an additional lock in the entrance door of his apartment shall, within _____ (23)_____ days after such installation, deliver a duplicate key to such lock to the lessor at his office, and all locks so installed are to remain after the termination of the lessee's tenancy for the benefit of the lessor.

20. Lessee, at the termination of his lease, must return all keys to doors, closets, and storerooms.

21. As many keys for outside doors or mailboxes will be furnished as lessee desires. A deposit of _____ (24)_____ [amount] per key is required, but the deposit will be refunded when the keys are returned to the lessor.

22. All garbage must be placed in a sanitary can at the rear hall door, between the hours of _____ (25)_____ and _____ (26)_____ o'clock a.m. daily; cans will be provided by the lessor and garbage so deposited will be removed by the janitor.

23. No janitor service other than for the removal of garbage is to be provided under this lease.

24. Special stipulations: _____ (27)_____

NOTES AND QUESTIONS

1. Section 5–702 of the New York General Obligations Law also provides that:

> Any . . . lessor who fails to comply with . . . [the statute] shall be liable to a consumer who is a party to a written agreement governed by . . . [the statute] in an amount equal to any actual damages sustained plus a penalty of fifty dollars. . . . No action . . . may be brought after both parties to the agreement have fully performed their obligation under such agreement, nor shall any . . . lessor who attempts in good faith to comply with . . . [the statute] be liable for such penalties.
>
> b. A violation of . . . [the statute] shall not render any such agreement void or voidable nor shall it constitute:
>
> > 1. A defense to any action or proceeding to enforce such agreement; or
> >
> > 2. A defense to any action or proceeding for breach of such agreement.

What facts could a lessor establish to demonstrate good faith compliance?

The penalty provisions under the act are decidedly mild. What legislative purpose is served by limiting liability in this manner? Is this statute as clear as it requires leases to be? For example, what does it mean that a lease should be written in a "clear" manner? How are the "common and every day meanings" of words to be determined? Lastly, what does it mean to be "plain?" Consider the following comments in Ross, On Legalities and Linguistics: Plain Language Legislation, 30 Buffalo L.Rev. 317, 329–30 (1981):

"Plain" can have three distinguishable meanings when applied to a written document. Every document is, first, a physical object that the reader must perceive, thus "plain" can refer to *legibility,* or the ease with which a document's printed language can be read. Second, every document arranges language in a certain order or sequence, thus "plain" can refer to *coherence,* or the manner in which a document's parts relate to one another. Third, a document contains words and sentences that vary in their degree of intelligibility, thus "plain" can refer to the *semantic clarity,* or the degree to which readers can comprehend the language. Of course, these meanings of "plain" are mutually dependent. It is difficult to understand either an illegible document or a document containing nonsensical words or sentences, even if printed in boldface type and carefully numbered in sequence. These distinctions are crucial, however, if valid judgments about language are to [be] made, for the more emphasis a statute places on legibility and the less on semantic clarity, the easier that statute is to comply with but the less effective it will be in protecting consumers from obscure terms unfavorable to their interests. In other words, the more quantifiable the criteria used to define plain language, the less effective a statute may prove in reforming, in any meaningful way, obscure standardized contracts.

2. "The basic principle underlying ... [the New York statute] is the common law doctrine that a party cannot be held bound by contract provisions not likely to have been comprehended (and thus agreed to) by the party."[8] Is this principle consistent with the statutory dictate that the violation of the statute is not a defense to an action to enforce the agreement?

3. At least two important doctrines, one ancient, the other modern, of landlord tenant law are not reflected in the terms of this lease. These are the implied covenant of quiet enjoyment and the implied warranty of habitability. These doctrines result in certain promises being implied by law in the terms of a lease. After you have come to understand these doctrines, consider whether the parties to the lease might not prefer, if they can, to incorporate and, if possible, perhaps limit the application of these doctrines by express provisions in the lease.

Are Residential Leases Coercive Contracts?

It is often assumed that tenants sign leases on a take it or leave it basis and make no attempt to negotiate the terms of their leases. The reason for these assumptions appears to be the belief that the residential landlord and residential tenant have unequal bargaining power. See, e.g., Note, The Form 50 Lease: Judicial Treatment of an Adhesion Contract, 111 U.Pa.L.Rev. 1197 (1963); Berger, Hard Leases Make Bad Law, 74 Colum.L.Rev. 791 (1974). A study of tenants living in Ann Arbor, Michi-

---

8. Givens, Practice Commentary, N.Y.Gen.Oblig.Law § 5–702 (McKinney's Supp.1986).

gan, casts a great deal of suspicion on these assumptions as well as others relating to the landlord tenant relationship. Of six hypotheses tested, five were:

(1) that few tenants do more than check the rent and occupancy dates before signing a lease; (2) that tenants would be unable to identify fine-print terms contained within their leases; (3) that tenants do not understand fine-print terms; (4) that tenants would view fine-print terms as inequitable; (5) that the standard-form lease is neither negotiated nor negotiable. . . .

We surmised that few tenants do more than check the rent provision and occupancy dates of their leases before signing them; particularly, it seemed doubtful that tenants would take care to scrutinize the fine-print terms following these initial items of immediate economic concern. It was, therefore, somewhat surprising to find . . . that about half of the tenants involved in the study declared that they had read carefully all paragraphs of any leases they signed. Related to the assumption about the intensiveness with which tenants peruse their leases before signing them was the further assumption that tenants would not be able to identify many of the "fine-print" terms in their lease. The results of the study suggest a great degree of variance in this "recognition" factor, ranging from minimal awareness of protection afforded the lessor who is unable to give occupancy on the agreed date to widespread realization of the presence in one's lease of a tenant's repair obligation or a requirement of lessor's consent to subletting.

Particular conviction lay behind our supposition that tenants have a very inadequate understanding of the terms of their leases; accordingly, it was somewhat perplexing to find tenants blithely professing that many selected fine-print terms were readily comprehensible. However, the accuracy of these expressions of self-assurance was brought into question by the somewhat poor comprehension of typical lease terms demonstrated by our sample tenants when they were asked to apply such terms to hypothetical fact situations. In short, tenants, despite their declarations to the contrary, do not always appreciate the latent ambiguity of legal language.

. . . A remarkably high percentage of the tenants in the sample . . . found certain conventional terms to be "reasonably fair," but at the same time almost unanimously stigmatized, as either somewhat or grossly unfair, a standard personal-injury exemption clause.

A primary working hypothesis of the study was that the standard-form lease is neither a negotiated nor a negotiable document. The former of these twin aspects proved to be largely true; few persons tried to bargain about fine-print terms. The latter assumption, on the other hand, was shown to be questionable; tenants who requested alteration in lease terms achieved a limited measure of success. It is dangerous, however, to make broad generalizations from our data

§ 7.3 THE LEASE **469**

about the negotiability of leases. While there is some measure of negotiation on matters of immediate impact such as the amount of rent and the length of the lease, there proved to be little negotiation about more typical fine-print terms, especially when such terms dealt with remote, though serious, contingencies rather than problems of frequent occurrence. . . .

The preconceived notion that at first blush seems to be most in conflict with the empirical data is the belief that tenants will be unable to secure alterations in fine-print terms even if they attempt to negotiate. But when the data, which does reveal some bargaining success, is subject to close scrutiny, it is evident that the small number of tenants who secured alteration in these terms had only a limited degree of success and are generally persons whose occupational skills make them better equipped than the average person for the bargaining process.[9]

This view should be contrasted with the view of Professor Berger of Columbia University who writes, after surveying most of the landlord tenant cases decided in the New York courts between 1970 and 1972:

> Most tenants will barely glance at the . . . [lease] they sign. The few who read it through carefully will find much they do not understand or do not like, and much whose potential for mischief they do not grasp. A lawyer beside them would help little, since there are few terms that a landlord will negotiate in or out. If the tenant does not want to sign, he can go down the street. But, of course, the landlord down the street with equally uninviting space uses an equally uninviting and unnegotiable form.[10]

Can the differences in these views be explained by the differences in the New York City and Ann Arbor rental markets?

Both Mueller and Berger comment on the extensive use of so-called "form leases," which are concerned primarily with the landlord's rights and remedies. Could the extensive use of "form leases" be explained only by the presence of unequal bargaining power between landlords and tenants? Could the use of "form leases" result in cost savings that ultimately benefit the tenants through lower rents? Consider the following:

> Many contracts . . . are offered on a take-it-or-leave-it basis. The seller hands the purchaser a standard printed contract that sets forth sometimes in numbing detail, the respective obligations of the parties. The purchaser can sign it or not as he pleases but there is no negotiation over terms. It is an easy step from the observation that there is no negotiation to the conclusion that the purchaser lacked a free choice and therefore should not be bound by onerous terms. But there is an innocent explanation: The seller is just trying to avoid the

---

9. Mueller, Residential Tenants and Their Leases: An Empirical Study, 69 Mich.L.Rev. 247, 250, 274–75 (1970).

10. Berger, Hard Leases Make Bad Law, 74 Colum.L.Rev. 791 (1974).

costs of negotiating and drafting a separate agreement with each purchaser. These costs ... are likely to be very high for a large company that has many contracts. Consistent with the innocent explanation, large and sophisticated buyers, as well as individual consumers, often make purchases pursuant to printed form contracts.

The sinister explanation is that the seller refuses to dicker separately with each purchaser because the buyer has no choice but to accept his terms. This assumes an absence of competition. If one seller offers unattractive terms, a competing seller, wanting sales for himself, will offer more attractive terms. The process will continue until the terms are optimal. All the firms in the industry may find it economical to use standard contracts and refuse to negotiate with purchasers. But what is important is not whether there is haggling in every transaction; it is whether competition forces sellers to incorporate in their standard contracts terms that protect the purchasers.

Under monopoly, by definition, the buyer has no good alternatives to dealing with the seller, who is therefore in a position, within limits, to compel the buyer to agree to terms that in a competitive market would be bettered by another seller. It does not follow, however, that the buyer will be indifferent to the terms of the contract offered by the seller. On the contrary, since a monopolized product will be priced higher than it would be under competition, prospective buyers will invest more, rather than less, in search; and one form of consumer search is careful reading of the terms of a contract.[11]

Are there reasons for thinking that the market for rental properties is not very competitive? See the Note on the economics of rent control at the end of this chapter.

§ 7.4 FORMAL REQUIREMENTS OF A LEASE

At the heart of the landlord-tenant relationship is an agreement between the parties respecting the tenant's rightful possession of real property owned by the landlord. The essential terms of this agreement must include an identification of the landlord and the tenant, an adequate description of the premises that are the subject of the lease, the amount of the rent (and the times when rent is payable), and the term of the lease. See McCarter v. Uban, 166 N.W.2d 910 (Iowa 1969); Cook v. Hargis, 164 Colo. 368, 435 P.2d 385 (1967).

In certain cases the lease must also be in writing. For example, Section 1624 of the California Civil Code provides that:

The following contracts are invalid, unless they, or some note or memorandum thereof, are in writing and subscribed by the party to be charged or by the party's agent....

(c) An agreement for the leasing for a longer period than one year....

---

11. Posner, Economic Analysis of Law 127–28 (5th ed. 1998).

The California statute requires a writing only for leases of more than one year. Leases of shorter duration need not be in writing. In common with most oral agreements, however, evidentiary problems often will exist should a party seek to enforce its terms.

NOTES AND QUESTIONS

1. L and T enter into an oral lease of Blackacre for a term of five years. T goes into actual possession of Blackacre and remains in possession for two years at which time L seeks to evict T on the grounds that the lease is invalid. What result? Compare Guardian Equipment Corp. v. Whiteside, 18 B.R. 864 (S.D.Fla.1982) (possession coupled with significant improvements takes lease out from under the statute) with Grundstein v. Suburban Motor Freight, 92 Ohio App. 181, 107 N.E.2d 366 (1951) (term for years invalid; periodic tenancy created). See also W. Stoebuck & D. Whitman, The Law of Property, § 6.15 at 261–63 (3rd ed. 2000).

2. If L and T enter into an oral lease for more than one year, is the entire lease void or is the lease void only for the term in excess of one year? Mahon v. Sahration, 310 Mich. 563, 17 N.W.2d 753 (1945).

3. Section 1.402 of the Uniform Residential Landlord and Tenant Act (hereafter referred to as URLTA),[1] applicable only to leases of residential real estate, provides that:

(a) If the landlord does not sign and deliver a written rental agreement signed and delivered to him by the tenant, acceptance of rent without reservation by the landlord gives the rental agreement the same effect as if it had been signed and delivered by the landlord.

(b) If the tenant does not sign and deliver a written rental agreement signed and delivered to him by the landlord, acceptance of possession and payment of rent without reservation gives the rental agreement the same effect as if it had been signed and delivered by the tenant.

(c) If a rental agreement given effect by the operation of this section provides for a term longer than one year, it is effective for only one year.

Does section 1.402 apply to entry under an oral lease for a term of more than one year?

In New Jersey landlords are prohibited from removing tenants except for good cause. The applicable statutes list thirteen grounds upon which a landlord would have good cause to remove a tenant. Among these are: (1) nonpayment of rent; (2) wilful or grossly negligent injury to the leased premises; (3) tenant's violations of rules and regulations; (4) landlord's determination to remove premises from the residential rental market; and (5) tenant's failure to agree to reasonable changes in the provisions of the lease which the landlord seeks to make at the termination of the existing term and which the tenant is notified of prior to the end of the term.

---

1. URLTA has been enacted in Alabama, Alaska, Arizona, Connecticut, Florida, Hawaii, Iowa, Kansas, Kentucky, Michigan, Mississippi, Montana, Nebraska, New Mexico, Oklahoma, Oregon, Rhode Island, South Carolina, Tennessee, Virginia, and Washington.

4. L and T enter into a written agreement dated January 1, 2006, providing that on September 1, 2006, T will be entitled to take possession of Blackacre for a term of five years ending on August 31, 2011. On July 1, 2006, T advises L that T has found other premises to rent and T wishes to terminate the agreement. In such case L's rights against T may depend upon whether the agreement of January 1, 2006, is characterized as a "lease to commence in the future" or a contract to make a lease.

> A good many decisions deal with whether an agreement is a lease to commence *in futuro* or only a contract to make a lease. The major consequence of this distinction is the measure of damages to the landowner if the alleged tenant defaults. If the agreement is a lease, damages are the unpaid rent, whereas damages are only the difference between the agreed rent and fair rental value if the agreement is a contract.... Ultimately it is a question of fact whether the parties intended a contract or a lease. Factors may be whether they use the word "lease" or an equivalent, whether they intend to draw up a later agreement, and whether a document contains legally required elements for a lease. The fact that the tenant is not to have possession immediately is of little consequence, for leases to commence *in futuro* are unexceptional, as we have seen. Even if the transaction is found to be a purported contract to lease, it may still be abortive for indefiniteness, on the contract law principle that a contract ... must contain the essential elements of the final agreement sufficiently for a court to enforce it. Thus, we still face questions similar to those faced with a lease itself, whether parties, premises, term, and so forth are spelled out with adequate specificity.[2]

L and T enter into an agreement under which T agrees to lease Blackacre from L for $50 a month for a period during which at all times the fair rental value of Blackacre is $40 a month. What is the amount of damages or rents L can recover from T if T breaches the agreement and if (a) the agreement is merely a contract to make a lease or (b) the agreement is a lease to commence *in futuro*? Economically, how are L and T affected by the characterization of the agreement?

§ 7.5   THE NECESSITY OF DELIVERING POSSESSION

HANNAN v. DUSCH

Supreme Court of Appeals of Virginia (1930).
154 Va. 356, 153 S.E. 824.

PRENTIS, C.J.

The declaration filed by the plaintiff, Hannan, against the defendant, Dusch, alleges that Dusch had on August 31, 1927, leased to the plaintiff certain real estate in the city of Norfolk, Va., therein described, for fifteen years, the term to begin January 1, 1928, at a specified rental; that it thereupon became and was the duty of the defendant to see to it that the

---

2. W. Stoebuck & D. Whitman, The Law of Property § 6.13, at 260 (3rd ed. 2000).

premises leased by the defendant to the plaintiff should be open for entry by him on January 1, 1928, the beginning of the term, and to put said petitioner in possession of the premises on that date; that the petitioner was willing and ready to enter upon and take possession of the leased property, and so informed the defendant; yet the defendant failed and refused to put the plaintiff in possession or to keep the property open for him at that time or on any subsequent date; and that the defendant suffered to remain on said property a certain tenant or tenants who occupied a portion or portions thereof, and refused to take legal or other action to oust said tenant or tenants or to compel their removal from the property so occupied. Plaintiff alleged damages which he had suffered by reason of this alleged breach of the contract and deed, and sought to recover such damages in the action. There is no express covenant as to the delivery of the premises nor for the quiet possession of the premises by the lessee.

The defendant demurred to the declaration on several grounds, one of which was "that under the lease set out in said declaration the right of possession was vested in said plaintiff and there was no duty as upon the defendant, as alleged in said declaration, to see that the premises were open for entry by said plaintiff."

The single question of law therefore presented in this case is whether a landlord, who without any express covenant as to delivery or possession leases property to a tenant, is required under the law to oust trespassers and wrongdoers so as to have it open for entry by the tenant at the beginning of the term; that is, whether without an express covenant there is nevertheless an implied covenant to deliver possession.

For an intelligent apprehension of the precise question it may be well to observe that some questions somewhat similar are not involved.

It seems to be perfectly well settled that there is an implied covenant in such cases on the part of the landlord to assure to the tenant the legal right of possession; that is, that at the beginning of the term there shall be no legal obstacle to the tenant's right of possession. This is not the question presented. Nor need we discuss in this case the rights of the parties in case a tenant rightfully in possession under the title of his landlord is thereafter disturbed by some wrongdoer. In such case the tenant must protect himself from trespassers, and there is no obligation on the landlord to assure his quiet enjoyment of his term as against wrongdoers or intruders.

Of course, the landlord assures to the tenant quiet possession as against all who rightfully claim through or under the landlord.

The discussion then is limited to the precise legal duty of the landlord in the absence of an express covenant, in case a former tenant, who wrongfully holds over, illegally refuses to surrender possession to the new tenant. This is a question about which there is a hopeless conflict of the authorities. It is generally claimed that the weight of the authority favors the particular view contended for. There are, however, no scales upon which we can weigh the authorities. In numbers and respectability they may be quite equally balanced.

It is then a question about which no one should be dogmatic, but all should seek for that rule which is supported by the better reason.

* * *

It is conceded by all that the two rules, one called the English rule, which implies a covenant requiring the lessor to put the lessee in possession, and that called the American rule, which recognizes the lessee's legal right to possession, but implies no such duty upon the lessor as against wrongdoers, are irreconcilable.

The English rule is that, in the absence of stipulations to the contrary, there is in every lease an implied covenant on the part of the landlord that the premises shall be open to entry by the tenant at the time fixed by the lease for the beginning of his term. . . .

* * *

It must be borne in mind, however, that the courts which hold that there is such an implied covenant do not extend the period beyond the day when the lessee's term begins. If after that day a stranger trespasses upon the property and wrongfully obtains or withholds possession of it from the lessee, his remedy is against the stranger and not against the lessor.

It is not necessary for either party to involve himself in uncertainty, for by appropriate covenants each may protect himself against any doubt either as against a tenant then in possession who may wrongfully hold over by refusing to deliver the possession at the expiration of his own term, or against any other trespasser.

* * *

King v. Reynolds, 67 Ala. 229, 42 Am.Rep. 107, has been said to be the leading case in this country affirming the English rule. . . .

* * *

Another case which supports the English rule is Herpolsheimer v. Christopher, 76 Neb. 352, 107 N.W. 382, 111 N.W. 359, 360. . . . In that case the court gave these as its reasons for following the English rule: "We deem it unnecessary to enter into an extended discussion, since the reasons pro and con are fully given in the opinions of the several courts cited. We think, however, that the English rule is most in consonance with good conscience, sound principle, and fair dealing. Can it be supposed that the plaintiff in this case would have entered into the lease if he had known at the time that he could not obtain possession on the 1st of March, but that he would be compelled to begin a lawsuit, await the law's delays, and follow the case through its devious turnings to an end before he could hope to obtain possession of the land he had leased? Most assuredly not. It is unreasonable to suppose that a man would knowingly contract for a lawsuit, or take the chance of one. Whether or not a tenant in possession intends to hold over or assert a right to a future term may nearly always be known to the landlord, and is certainly much more apt to be within his knowledge than within that of the prospective tenant. Moreover, since in an action to recover possession against a tenant holding over the lessee would be compelled largely to rely upon the lessor's testimony in regard to the facts of the claim to hold over by the wrongdoer, it is more reasonable and proper to place the burden upon the person within whose knowledge the facts are most apt to lie. We are convinced, therefore, that the better reason lies with the courts following the English doctrine, and we therefore adopt it, and hold that ordinarily the lessor impliedly covenants with the lessee that the premises leased shall be open to entry by him at the time fixed in the lease as the beginning of the term."

In commenting on this line of cases, Mr. Freeman says this: "The above rule practically prohibits the landlord from leasing the premises while in the possession of a tenant whose term is about to expire, because notwithstanding the assurance on the part of the tenant that he will vacate on the expiration of his term, he may change his mind and wrongfully hold over. It is true that the landlord may provide for such a contingency by suitable provisions in the lease to the prospective tenant, but it is equally true that the prospective tenant has the privilege of insisting that his prospective landlord expressly agree to put him in possession of the premises if he imagines there may be a chance for a lawsuit by the tenant in possession holding over. It seems to us that to raise by implication a covenant on the part of the landlord to put the tenant into possession is to make a contract for the parties in regard to a matter which is equally within the knowledge of both the landlord and tenant."

So let us not lose sight of the fact that under the English rule a covenant which might have been, but was not, made is nevertheless implied by the court, though it is manifest that each of the parties might have provided for that and for every other possible contingency relating to possession by having express covenants which would unquestionably have protected both.

Referring then to the American rule: Under that rule, in such cases, "the landlord is not bound to put the tenant into actual possession, but is bound only to put him into legal possession, so that no obstacle in the form of a superior right of possession will be interposed to prevent the tenant from obtaining actual possession of the demised premises. If the landlord gives the tenant a right of possession he has done all that he is required to do by the terms of an ordinary lease, and the tenant assumes the burden of enforcing such right of possession as against all persons wrongfully in possession, whether they be trespassers or former tenants wrongfully holding over." This quoted language is Mr. Freeman's, and he cites these cases in support thereof:....

So that, under the American rule, where the new tenant fails to obtain possession of the premises only because a former tenant wrongfully holds over, his remedy is against such wrongdoer and not against the landlord—this because the landlord has not covenanted against the wrongful acts of another and should not be held responsible for such a tort, unless he has expressly so contracted. This accords with the general rule as to other wrongdoers, whereas the English rule appears to create a specific exception against lessors. It does not occur to us now that there is any other instance in which one clearly without fault is held responsible for the independent tort of another in which he has neither participated nor concurred, and whose misdoings he cannot control.

* * *

Mr. Freeman supports the American rule with the calm cogency which should be convincing. He summarizes this conclusion thus: "The gist of the reason advanced in favor of the English rule is that under the American rule, in case the demised premises are in the possession of a person wrongfully holding over or of some trespasser at the beginning of the tenant's term, and the tenant is forced to resort to litigation to oust the one in such possession, all he obtains by his lease is a chance for a lawsuit. It is conceded that under the English rule it becomes the duty of the tenant to maintain his possession at his own expense after once being placed in possession. It is also conceded that if the premises are withheld by the landlord or someone holding a paramount title, that the tenant has a right of recovery against the landlord for a breach of his covenant of quiet possession. It must be conceded also that if the premises are withheld from the possession of the tenant by reason of the wrongful act of a trespasser or of some former tenant who wrongfully holds over, the tenant has a right to recover his damages from such person. In other words, the tenant is protected, no matter in what manner the possession is withheld from him. It is, of course, true that the tenant will suffer delay in obtaining possession if he is forced to sue for it, but so would the landlord under the same circumstances. It is not, we believe, customary for a person who contracts in respect to any subject to insure the other party against lawsuits. Indeed, both the landlord and tenant have a right to presume that a former tenant will vacate at the end of his term, and that no one will unlawfully prevent the new tenant from going into possession. To sue or be sued is a privilege or misfortune which may occur to anyone. We believe that the American, or New York rule as it is sometimes called, under which it is held that there is no implied covenant that the premises shall be open to entry by the tenant at the time fixed for the beginning of the term, but merely that the tenant shall have a right to the possession at that time is more in accord with substantial justice to both the landlord and tenant, and in accordance with the general course of business dealings in respect to insurance against the chances of a lawsuit in a court of justice."

There are some underlying fundamental considerations. Any written lease, for a specific term, signed by the lessor, and delivered, is like a deed signed, sealed, and delivered by the grantor. This lease for fifteen years is and is required to be by deed. It is a conveyance. During the term the tenant is substantially the owner of the property, having the right of possession, dominion, and control over it. Certainly, as a general rule, the lessee must protect himself against trespassers or other wrongdoers who disturb his possession. It is conceded by those who favor the English rule that, should the possession of the tenant be wrongfully disturbed the second day of the term, or after he has once taken possession, then there is no implied covenant on the part of his landlord to protect him from the torts of others. The English rule seems to have been applied only where the possession is disturbed on the first day, or, perhaps more fairly expressed, where the tenant is prevented from taking possession on the first day of his term; but what is the substantial difference between invading the lessee's right of possession on the first or a later day? To apply the English rule you must imply a covenant on the part of the landlord to protect the tenant from the tort of another, though he has entered into no such covenant. This seems to be a unique exception, an exception which stands alone in implying a contract of insurance on the part of the lessor to save his tenant from all the consequences of the flagrant wrong of another person. Such an obligation is so unusual and the prevention of such a tort so impossible as to make it certain, we think, that it should always rest upon an express contract.

For the reasons which have been so well stated by those who have enforced the American rule, our judgment is that there is no error in the judgment complained of.

We are strengthened in this view by the only expression which we know of in this jurisdiction.

In McGhee v. Cox, 116 Va. 718, 723, 82 S.E. 701, 702, Ann.Cas.1916E, 843, this is said: "The general rule is that a lease becomes complete and takes effect upon its execution, unless otherwise specifically provided, and entry by the lessee is not necessary to give it effect. The plaintiffs were not bound to put the defendants into actual possession of the leased premises. They were only bound to put them into legal or constructive possession; that is, to have the premises open to entry without any obstacle in the form of a superior right to prevent the defendants from obtaining actual possession. 24 Cyc. 1049, 1050; Taylor on Landlord & Tenant, §§ 86 and 15; Gardner v. Keteltas, 3 Hill (N.Y.) 330, 38 Am.Dec. 637, 638."

While doubtless this precise question was not directly in issue in that case, the language is nevertheless clear and pertinent. It is the restrained expression of a learned and careful judge (Buchanan), who was not given to thoughtless words or to the common judicial vice of writing over-much....

We are confirmed in our view by the Virginia statute, providing a summary remedy for unlawful entry or detainer, Code, § 5445 et seq. The adequate, simple, and summary remedy for the correction of such a wrong provided by that statute was clearly available to this plaintiff. It specifically provides that it shall lie for one entitled to possession in any case in which a "tenant shall detain the possession of land after his right has expired, without the consent of him who is entitled to the possession." Section 5445.

Certainly there should be co-operation between the lessor and lessee to impose the resulting loss upon such a trespasser, but whatever other equities may have arisen, when the plaintiff found that the premises which he had leased were occupied by a wrongdoer who unlawfully refused to surrender possession, it is manifest that he (the lessee, Hannan) had the right to oust the wrongdoer under this statute. His failure to pursue that remedy is not explained. . . .

* * *

The plaintiff alleges in his declaration as one of the grounds for his action that the defendant suffered the wrongdoer to remain in possession, but the allegations show that he it was who declined to assert his remedy against the wrongdoer, and so he it was who permitted the wrongdoer to retain the possession. Just why he valued his legal right to the possession so lightly as not to assert it in the effective way open to him does not appear. Whatever ethical duty in good conscience may possibly have rested upon the defendant, the duty to oust the wrongdoer by the summary remedy provided by the unlawful detainer statute clearly rested upon the plaintiff. The law helps those who help themselves, generally aids the vigilant, but rarely the sleeping, and never the acquiescent.

Affirmed.

Notes and Questions

1. In your judgment, and after reviewing the court's discussion of the reasons underlying the English and American rules, did the court adopt the correct view? See, Weissenberger, The Landlord's Duty to Deliver Possession: The Overlooked Reform, 46 U.Cin.L.Rev. 937 (1978). For additional citations to the division of authority in this country, see, Special Project, Developments in Contemporary Landlord–Tenant Law: An Annotated Bibliography, 26 Vand.L.Rev. 689, 719–20 (1973).

2. The *Hannan* court states that landlords and tenants can specifically negotiate a covenant that the landlord will deliver actual possession of the leased premises to the tenant. Is this a viable option?

Suppose a state has adopted the English rule. Can L and T agree in the lease agreement that if there is a holdover tenant, L will not be liable to T for any of T's resulting damages? See Duane Reade, Inc. v. Reade Broadway Associates, 274 A.D.2d 301, 710 N.Y.S.2d 566 (1st Dept.2000).

3. The effect of the English rule is to impose upon a landlord a duty to remove a prior tenant ("PT") who wrongfully holds over beyond the term of the lease. If the new tenant desires to obtain possession of premises wrongfully occupied by PT rather than damages, does it make any difference whether

the *duty* to evict PT resides with the landlord so long as there is a *right* in the new tenant to remove PT if the landlord fails to perform its duty?

4. Generally for breach of the implied covenant to deliver possession of the leased premises the tenant may terminate the lease and recover damages. The measure of damages for the landlord's breach of the covenant to deliver possession of the leased premises (the "English" rule) is the difference between the fair rental value of the leased premises and the promised rent. Additionally, special damages, if proved, can be awarded to the tenant. See generally Annot., 88 A.L.R.2d 1024, 1032 (1963). See also Restatement (Second) of Property § 10.2 (1977). Lost profits would be compensable as special damages but in many cases the tenant is unable to collect these because the tenant is unable to prove the amount of lost profits.

5. In *Hannan*, the court states that the tenant could avail himself of Virginia's unlawful entry and detainer statute. Unlawful entry and detainer statutes (also known as "summary proceedings statutes") generally provide an expeditious procedure by which landlords can remove tenants who fail to pay rent or hold over beyond the term of the lease. These statutes obviate the need for the landlord to pursue more traditional civil proceedings that could result in long delays before the matter is heard by the court and judgment rendered. Summary eviction statutes severely restrict the kinds of cases in which landlords may expedite proceedings to obtain possession (e.g., tenants failure to pay rent; tenant remaining in possession after the expiration of the lease term). See § 7.11, infra. Would the *Hannan* court have decided the case differently if the Virginia unlawful entry and detainer statute had not been available for the tenant's use?

6. L leases an apartment to T–1 for a term of three years ending on May 31, 2007. On March 1, 2007, L leases the same apartment to T–2 for a term to commence on June 1, 2007. T–1 remains in possession on June 1, 2007. Assuming the jurisdiction follows the American rule can T–2 sue T–1 for possession? Generally, if a tenant holds over beyond the term specified in the lease, the landlord may elect to treat the tenant as a periodic tenant at the same rent provided in the lease or as a trespasser and elect to evict the tenant. Would T–2 succeed to these rights? See United Merchants' Realty & Improvement Co. v. Roth, 193 N.Y. 570, 86 N.E. 544 (1908).

If L sues T–1 on June 1, 2007, to recover the possession of the premises, can T–1 defend on the basis that as of that date T–2 and not L is entitled to the possession of the property? See Eells v. Morse, 208 N.Y. 103, 101 N.E. 803 (1913). How would T–2's remedies be affected if L had advised T–2 that in all likelihood T–1 would hold over beyond the original term?

7. URLTA § 2.103 adopts the English view. It provides:

> At the commencement of the term a landlord shall deliver possession of the premises to the tenant in compliance with the rental agreement and Section 2.104. The landlord may bring an action for possession against any person wrongfully in possession and may recover the damages provided in Section 4.301(c).

This covenant is not waivable. See URLTA § 1.403. If the landlord fails to deliver possession section 4.102 provides:

(a) If the landlord fails to deliver possession of the dwelling unit to the tenant as provided in Section 2.103, rent abates until possession is delivered and the tenant may

(1) terminate the rental agreement upon at least [5] day's written notice to the landlord and upon termination the landlord shall return all prepaid rent and security; or

(2) demand performance of the rental agreement by the landlord and, if the tenant elects, maintain an action for possession of the dwelling unit against the landlord or any person wrongfully in possession and recover the actual damages sustained by him.

(b) If a person's failure to deliver possession is willful and not in good faith, an aggrieved person may recover from that person an amount not more than [3] months' periodic rent or [threefold] the actual damages sustained, whichever is greater, and reasonable attorney's fees.

The provisions of URLTA § 2.103 should be compared with Restatement (Second) of Property § 6.2 (1977), which also adopts the English view but permits the parties to expressly waive that rule. For breach of the landlord's obligation to deliver possession of the leased premises tenant may terminate the lease and recover damages.

8. L leases Blackacre for a term beginning on January 1, 2007, and ending on December 31, 2007. T takes possession of Blackacre on January 1, 2007. On March 10, 2007, T learns that L had previously leased Blackacre to T–1 for a like term. On April 1, 2007, T fails to pay the rent due that month and sues L to recover the rents paid for January through March of 2007, and to terminate the lease. What result? See Campbell v. Hensley, 450 S.W.2d 501 (Ky.1970).

9. L leases Blackacre to T for a term of five years commencing on January 1, 2007. On that date Blackacre was unoccupied. Blackacre is located in California and T was moving to California from New York. T was delayed in moving and did not arrive in California until January 10, 2007. On that date X, a trespasser, was in possession of Blackacre. Can T terminate the lease? See King v. Reynolds, 67 Ala. 229 (1880); Sloan v. Hart, 150 N.C. 269, 63 S.E. 1037 (1909). Suppose X was in possession of Blackacre on January 1, 1998, but L was unaware of this fact. Can T terminate the lease? See Restatement (Second) of Property § 6.2 comment c (if third person improperly in possession on date tenant entitled to possession, tenant can terminate the lease) & comment d (1977) (landlord after reasonable notice must act promptly to remove trespassers).

10. Does a tenant have a correlative duty to take possession of leased premises at the commencement of the tenancy? The general rule is no. See Stevens v. Mobil Oil Corp., 412 F.Supp. 809 (E.D. Mich. 1976), aff'd 577 F.2d 743 (6th Cir. 1978).

Suppose, however, the landlord's interest would be adversely affected if the tenant failed to take possession on the commencement date. For example, suppose the leased premises are a nonconforming use under the zoning laws (see chapter 10), such that once a present use grandfathered in under the present zoning laws ceases, the premises become subject to the zoning laws and can no longer be used as they currently are by the landlord. L leases these premises to T so long as the premises are used in the same manner they have previously been used by L. T fails to commence his tenancy immediately upon the commencement date of the lease and the premises become subject to a different use restriction. Can L sue T for damages? Compare Childs v. Goode, 261 Ark. 382, 548 S.W.2d 827 (1977) with Powell v. Socony Mobil Oil Co., 113 Ohio App. 507, 179 N.E.2d 82 (1960). Would your answer depend on whether T knew the premises were a nonconforming use? On whether the lease expressly required tenant to take possession?

Similarly, suppose L leased T space in a shopping center under a so-called percentage lease entitling L to a percentage of T's gross sales receipts as part of the rent. If T fails to take possession on the commencement date, can L sue T for lost rents? See, Evans v. Grand Union Co., 759 F.Supp. 818, 822 (M.D.Ga. 1990) (It appears to be the law in Georgia that if the parties to a lease contemplate that the amount of rent to be generated by the percentage payment clause will be substantially greater than the minimum monthly rent, it is possible to infer a covenant of continuous use and operation).

§ 7.6 PROBLEMS REGARDING USE OF LEASED PREMISES

§ 7.6.1 USE RESTRICTIONS IMPOSED UPON THE TENANT BY THE LANDLORD

Many leases restrict the kinds of activities the tenant may conduct on the leased premises or require that the tenant adhere to certain behavioral standards. The following clauses are illustrative of the kinds of restrictions the landlord may impose upon the tenant:

Occupancy: The Apartment may be occupied only by Tenant and the Tenant's immediate family and used by them for living purposes only.

Restrictions on Use: Tenant agrees not to install any dishwashing, clothes washing or drying machines, electric stoves or garbage disposal units or heating, ventilating, air conditioning equipment in the Apartment, nor place in the Apartment any water-filled furniture without the Landlord's prior written approval.

No aerial or antenna may be erected on the roof or exterior walls of the building in which the Apartment is located without the Landlord's prior written approval.

No dogs, cats or other animals shall be kept in the Apartment, or brought into the building, by the Tenant, unless it is expressly permitted in writing by the Landlord. Landlord's consent, if given, shall be revocable by Landlord at any time for good cause. In no event shall any dog be permitted on any passenger elevator or in any public portion of the building unless carried or on a leash, nor on any grass or garden plot under any condition. The strict adherence to this clause is a material requirement of the Lease Agreement. Any failure by Tenant, or Tenant's immediate family, to conform to this provision is a serious violation of an important obligation hereunder and the Landlord, in the case of such violation, may elect to terminate this lease.

Use restrictions of the foregoing kind are commonly found in modern day leases. Your lease probably has similar clauses. Are all of these clauses enforceable? If they are, should they be? For example, the foregoing lease restrictions forbid the keeping of pets in the apartment without the written consent of the landlord. While this restriction is perfectly under-standable from the landlord's perspective, should it be enforced against a tenant who goes blind and needs a "seeing eye" dog? Compare Fla.Stat. Ann. § 413.08(4)(a)–(c) (West 1997) with Cal.Civ.Code § 54.1 (West Supp. 1997). Is the restriction enforceable against a tenant living in a high-crime area where safety is best maintained by multiple door locks and dober-mans? What if the tenant in the high-crime area keeps a dachshund rather than a doberman in the apartment? See East River Hous. Corp. v. Matonis, 62 Misc.2d 588, 309 N.Y.S.2d 240 (1970), order reversed, 34 A.D.2d 937, 312 N.Y.S.2d 461 (1970). Cf., Triangle Mgmt. Corp. v. Inniss, 62 Misc.2d 1095, 312 N.Y.S.2d 745 (Civ.Ct.1970).

> Suppose the lease signed by the tenant contains the following clause:

> Tenant agrees to be bound by such rules and regulations regarding the Tenant's occupancy as the landlord shall establish from time to time. Landlord shall furnish copies of such rules and regulations to Tenant.

Since the tenant has not specifically had an opportunity to bargain with the landlord over the specifics of future rules and regulations, is the preceding clause unconscionable? If the clause is not unconscionable, suppose that six months after the lease term begins the landlord amends the rules to prohibit dogs on the premises. Would this new rule be binding upon the tenant? Would your judgment be affected by the fact that at the time the lease was signed the tenant had a dog? By whether the landlord knew the tenant had a dog when the lease was executed? In this connec-tion consider the following provisions of Section 3.102 of URLTA:

> (a) A landlord, from time to time, may adopt a rule or regulation, however described, concerning the tenant's use and occupancy of the premises. It is enforceable against the tenant only if

> (1) its purpose is to promote the convenience, safety, or welfare of the tenants in the premises, preserve the landlord's property from abu-sive use, or make a fair distribution of services and facilities held out for the tenants generally;

> (2) it is reasonably related to the purpose of which it is adopted;

> (3) it applies to all tenants in the premises in a fair manner;

> (4) it is sufficiently explicit in its prohibition, direction, or limitation of the tenant's conduct to fairly inform him of what he must or must not do to comply;

(5) it is not for the purpose of evading the obligations of the landlord; and

(6) the tenant has notice of it at the time he enters into the rental agreement, or when it is adopted.

(b) If a rule or regulation is adopted after the tenant enters into the rental agreement that works a substantial modification of his bargain it is not valid unless the tenant consents to it in writing.

Commercial leases frequently restrict the kinds of commercial activities that can be conducted on the leased premises. For instance, a lease for space in a shopping mall may require that the premises be used solely for retail sales of merchandise or services and perhaps limit the kinds of merchandise or service that can be sold on the leased premises. Thus, with such a restriction the tenant could not convert the use of the premises from a shoe store to a travel agency. Why might a landlord want to restrict the use of the premises in this way? Suppose the landlord leases a service station to the tenant, and under the terms of the lease the tenant is limited to selling petroleum products and providing automobile repair services. Can the tenant convert one of the service station bays into an automatic car wash? See Boyd v. Shell Oil Co., 454 Pa. 374, 311 A.2d 616 (1973). Can the tenant close one of the bays and convert it into a convenience food store in order to compete with a convenience food store located next to the service station that is also selling gasoline? Cf. Grossenbacher v. Daly, 287 S.W. 781 (Mo.App.1926) (permitting a restrictive use to be expanded by a business custom).

How should ambiguous lease provisions be construed? For example, suppose the lease prohibits the tenant from having "pets" on the premises. If the tenant keeps goldfish on the premises has she violated the terms of the lease? Generally the policy of the law is to construe lease use restrictions against the party drafting the lease and to construe ambiguities in a way that least restricts the use of the land.

What remedies should be available if the tenant actually breaches a use covenant? Damages and injunctive relief are clearly available. Eviction is also a possibility. The tenant's defenses are few. Unconscionability and waiver are two possibilities.

For many years it was common for leases to contain restrictions on who could live in an apartment. Typical restrictions might require that couples be married to each other or that only members of the tenant's immediate family reside in the premises. Often restrictions were couched in terms of race, gender, religion, sex, or national origin. Early civil rights laws sought to prohibit restrictions based on race, but over the years these laws have been broadened. Today, for example, The Civil Rights Act of 1968, Title VIII ("The Fair Housing Act" or FHA), 42 U.S.C.A. § 3604, makes it illegal, with respect to covered dwellings, to refuse to rent a dwelling to "any person because of race, color, religion, sex, familial status, or national origin." See generally chapter 12, infra.

§ 7.6.2 SUPERCEDING ILLEGALITY AND COMMERCIAL FRUSTRATION

Governments may prohibit the making of a lease for a particular purpose or the making of a lease if the premises are in a certain condition. For example, a law might provide that neither the landlord nor the tenant shall rent any apartment in which housing code violations exist.[1] This law makes illegal the very act of leasing certain buildings. Alternatively, the law may make certain activities illegal without making the leasing of the premises for such purposes also illegal. For example, municipal zoning ordinances may make a particular use of land illegal without also making illegal the act of leasing the premises in a residential area for that otherwise illegal purpose.

If both landlord and tenant intend that the leased premises will be used only for an illegal purpose neither party may enforce the terms of the lease. Thus, if both the landlord and the tenant intend that the premises be used only for the operation of a gambling casino, the lease is unenforceable, assuming state law prohibits gambling casinos. While the lease may be unenforceable, the landlord is entitled to bring an action to recover possession of the property. Lozano v. Brant, 172 Cal.App.2d 650, 343 P.2d 177 (1959). Suppose the tenant knows the premises are to be used for an illegal purpose, but the landlord only suspects that they may be so used. Is this sufficient to demonstrate that the landlord also intended that the premises be used for an illegal purpose? Should a higher standard be imposed on the landlord such as actual knowledge of, or acquiescence in, the illegal use or a showing of actual intent or active participation in the illegal use? Generally courts are satisfied by a showing of knowledge and acquiescence, although a few courts require actual intent or active participation. See generally Musco v. Torello, 102 Conn. 346, 128 A. 645 (1925) (lease void if landlord knows tenant will use premises for illegal purpose); Hoefeld v. Ozello, 290 Ill. 147, 125 N.E. 5 (1919) (lease void only if landlord participates in the illegal activity).

If the tenant's use of the premises is illegal under some circumstances but legal under others, the lease is unenforceable if both parties intended that the premises be used only for the illegal purpose. If the landlord did not intend that the premises be used for illegal purposes, the lease is enforceable by the landlord.

> Violations of zoning ordinances present a special situation. In some cases in which the lease is for a purpose that violates zoning [laws], the courts have held the leasing valid or invalid on the principles [discussed above].... Other courts, however, refuse to apply the illegality invalidity doctrine, at least where, as is usually the case, zoning ordinances allow for nonconforming uses, variances, special permits, and the like. These courts reason that the parties may have

---

1. See Brown v. Southall Realty Co., 237 A.2d 834 (D.C.App.1968), infra.

written their lease intending that zoning relief would be obtained, though it would seem to be a question of fact whether they did so. Some courts may simply feel zoning restrictions are different from, say, an ordinance or statute prohibiting prostitution. In any event, a tenant who is concerned about zoning should always expressly reserve a power to terminate if the intended use cannot be made.[2]

The Restatement (Second) of Property § 9.2 (1977) provides that:

Except to the extent the parties to a lease validly agree otherwise, if the use of the leased premises intended by the parties becomes illegal after the lease is made and without the fault of the tenant, the tenant may:

(1) terminate the lease ... at the time the use becomes illegal if no other use is permitted; and

(2) terminate the lease ... even though some other use is permitted under the terms of the lease, if it would be unreasonable to place on the tenant the burdens of the lease after converting to the other use.

Why should the risk of subsequent illegality be borne by the landlord with respect to the tenant's obligation to pay rent?

The Restatement (Second) of Property § 9.3 (1977) provides:

Except to the extent the parties to a lease validly agree otherwise, if the use of the leased property intended by the parties is frustrated by governmental action, other than action that makes the use illegal or that involves a taking by eminent domain, and if the governmental action was not reasonably foreseeable by the tenant at the time the lease was made, the tenant may terminate the lease....

This section of the Restatement (Second) of Property, addresses the issue of so-called "commercial frustration." Commercial frustration occurs when the performance of the lease is possible but "the expected value of performance to the party seeking to be excused has been destroyed by a fortuitous event, which supervenes to cause an actual but not literal failure of consideration." Further, "[t]he question in cases involving frustration is whether the equities of the case, considered in the light of sound public policy, require placing the risk of a disruption or complete destruction of the contract equilibrium on ... [the tenant] or ... [the landlord] under the circumstances of a given case...." Lloyd v. Murphy, 25 Cal.2d 48, 53–54, 153 P.2d 47, 50 (1944). The doctrine is analogous to the more general contractual doctrine known as "impossibility," although there are some differences. Impossibility occurs when the performance of either party to the contract becomes illegal, difficult or expensive, dangerous, or literally impossible. Frustration involves the situation where the purposes the parties intended are frustrated but performance is still possible. See generally 6 A. Corbin on Contracts § 1322 (1962); Restatement (Second) of Contracts § 285 comment a (1977).

---

2. W. Stoebuck & D. Whitman, The Law of Property § 6.27 at 278–279 (3rd ed.2000).

A number of requirements must be met for a tenant to be relieved from performance under a lease because of commercial frustration. These are: (1) the landlord must have known of the tenant's intended use; (2) there must have been either total or near total frustration; and (3) the cause of the frustration must not have been reasonably foreseeable at the time the lease was executed. See generally Restatement (Second) of Property § 9.3 Reporter's Note No. 3 (1977).

NOTES AND QUESTIONS

1. Suppose L leases Blackacre to T who operates a college bar on the premises. The lease provides that "Tenant agrees to use the premises for the sale of alcoholic beverages only." Last year the state legislature enacted a law increasing the drinking age in the state from 18 to 21. Because over 90% of the undergraduates in the community are under the age of 21, business at T's bar decreases by 80%. T consults you to determine whether she can terminate the lease. What advice would you give T? See, e.g., Mid–Continent Petroleum Corp. v. Barrett, 297 Ky. 709, 181 S.W.2d 60 (1944) (service station lease terminated when government rationed gasoline, prohibited the sale of tires and restricted the sale of new automobiles). But see, Lloyd v. Murphy, 25 Cal.2d 48, 153 P.2d 47 (1944) (although sole purpose of lease was to permit tenant to sell new cars, government war-time restrictions on sale of new cars resulting in loss of profits is not sufficient to relieve tenant of lease obligations).

Suppose the lease had provided that "Tenant agrees to lease premises for use as a tavern. Lessor agrees that in the course of using the premises as a tavern, the tenant shall be permitted to employ musicians to provide live entertainment and to permit dancing." Same result? See The Stratford, Inc. v. Seattle Brewing & Malting Co., 94 Wash. 125, 162 P. 31 (1916). Cf. Deibler v. Bernard Bros., Inc., 385 Ill. 610, 53 N.E.2d 450 (1944).

2. Suppose L and T enter into a five year lease for space in a shopping mall. T intends to use the space for a "small, intimate bar." T assumed there would be no problem obtaining a liquor license and therefore failed to make the lease contingent on his obtaining a liquor license. T applied for the license but it was denied because only a limited number of licenses could be issued for the area of the community in which the mall was located and all of them had been issued. Can T terminate the lease? Cf., Maryland Trust Co. v. Tulip Realty Co. of Maryland, 220 Md. 399, 153 A.2d 275 (1959).

§ 7.6.3 WARRANTY OF FITNESS FOR A PARTICULAR PURPOSE

At common law a landlord did not warrant that the premises were fit for a particular purpose. Absent an express provision in the lease to the contrary, the tenant bore the risk that the premises could not be used for the tenant's intended activities. In other words, the bromide "*caveat emptor*" applied in the lease as well as the sales context. The courts justified this conclusion upon the grounds that the tenant could have secured an express warranty that the premises were fit for a particular purpose or could have inspected the premises prior to executing the lease to determine whether they were suitable for the tenant's needs. See, e.g., Anderson Drive–in Theatre, Inc. v. Kirkpatrick, 123 Ind.App. 388, 110 N.E.2d 506 (1953). Does the absence of an implied warranty that the premises are fit for a particular purpose make sense today? Did it make sense 100 years ago? See generally 1 Amer.L.Prop. § 3.45 (A.J. Casner ed. 1952).

One early exception to the "no warranty-take it 'as is' " rule related to a short-term lease of a furnished home. In Ingalls v. Hobbs, 156 Mass. 348, 350, 31 N.E. 286 (1892) the court held that for such a lease there was a warranty that the premises were habitable. Stated the court:

> [T]here are good reasons why a different rule should apply to one who hires a furnished room, or a furnished house, for a few days, or a few weeks or months. Its fitness for immediate use of a particular kind, as indicated by its appointments, is a far more important element entering into the contract than when there is a mere lease of real estate. One who lets for a short term a house provided with all furnishings and appointments for immediate residence may be supposed to contract in reference to a well-understood purpose of the hirer to use it as a habitation. An important part of what the hirer pays for is the opportunity to enjoy it without delay, and without the expense of preparing it for use. It is very difficult, and often impossible, for one to determine on inspection whether the house and its appointments are fit for the use for which they are immediately wanted, and the doctrine caveat emptor, which is ordinarily applicable to a lessee of real estate, would often work injustice if applied to cases of this kind. It would be unreasonable to hold, under such circumstances, that the landlord does not impliedly agree that what he is letting is a house suitable for occupation in its condition at the time.

As will be seen, the courts have moved away from the common-law "no warranty" rule at least with respect to the issue of whether there is an implied warranty that structures leased for residential purposes are habitable. To some extent this movement builds upon one of two early exceptions to the common-law "no warranty" rule. The first exception was that if the tenant's use of the premises was restricted to a particular purpose, the landlord warrants that the premises are fit for that purpose. See, Woolford v. Electric Appliances, 24 Cal.App.2d 385, 75 P.2d 112 (1938). The second exception is reflected in the *Ingalls* case.

A tenant may have a right to terminate the lease or seek damages or a defense in a suit for nonpayment of rent if the tenant was fraudulently induced to enter the lease. The utility of this alternative fraud theory of recovery is in most cases highly conjectural if any one or more of the following apply: (1) the doctrine of *caveat emptor,* (2) the prospective tenant fails to ask specific questions about the premises or has not reduced to writing the landlord's responses to specific questions, (3) issues of latent defects are not involved, or (4) the tenant has not relied upon the statements made by the landlord. Is silence golden in this area? In other words, under what circumstances will the landlord have an obligation to disclose more than latent defects?

Although at common law the landlord did not warrant that the premises were fit for a particular purpose, the landlord was bound to disclose to a tenant the presence of any "latent" defects in the premises of which the landlord either had knowledge or could have discovered after the exercise of reasonable care, and of which the tenant either did not know or could not reasonably have discovered. If the landlord failed to disclose such defects and the tenant or members of the tenant's family were injured because of such defects, the landlord could be held liable in tort. See, e.g., Marsh v. Bliss Realty, Inc., 97 R.I. 27, 195 A.2d 331 (1963); Anderson v. Hamilton Gardens, Inc., 4 Conn.Cir. 255, 229 A.2d 705 (1966). See also Perkins v. Marsh, 179 Wash. 362, 37 P.2d 689 (1934) (failure to disclose latent defect is fraud and tenant allowed to rescind lease or defend action for rent).

§ 7.7 INTERFERENCE WITH THE TENANT'S USE AND ENJOYMENT OF THE PREMISES

At common law, with one important exception, lease covenants were independent unless the lease otherwise provided. Therefore, the failure of one party to perform a covenant in the lease did not excuse the other party from performing her covenant under the lease. For example, suppose L and T entered into a lease under which the landlord was obligated to make certain repairs. L failed to make the repairs, but L's failure to make repairs did not excuse T from the obligation to pay rent. T, on the other hand, would have a cause of action for damages against L for L's breach of the covenant to make repairs. Similarly, if the tenant failed to pay rent, the landlord could not sue for possession unless the landlord expressly reserved that remedy.

The one exception to the "independent covenant" rule was the implied covenant of quiet enjoyment. Under this covenant, the landlord promises that during the term of the tenancy neither the landlord, anyone claiming through the landlord or a third person having a superior title to the leased premises would disturb the tenant in the tenant's use and enjoyment of the premises. If the landlord breached this implied covenant the tenant could terminate the lease and sue for damages.

The landlord's implied covenant of quiet enjoyment is not breached if the tenant's possession is disturbed by a mere wrongdoer. Rather the disturbance must be by a party having a superior or paramount title. For example, suppose O conveys Blackacre to A for 15 years, then to B. Thereafter, A leases the property to T for 20 years. At the end of A's term B successfully sues T for possession. T has a cause of action against A for breach of the implied covenant of quiet enjoyment because B, who has a paramount title to Blackacre, dispossessed T. Could T assert a breach of the covenant of quiet enjoyment if T knew of B's interest? See Restatement (Second) of Property § 4.3 comment f (1977).

The implied covenant of quiet enjoyment is not breached merely because someone has a title paramount to the landlord's title. Rather, breach occurs only when the holder of the paramount title interferes with the tenant's possession. See Restatement (Second) of Property, § 4.3 (1977).

The implied covenant of quiet enjoyment is also breached if the landlord wrongfully interferes with T's use, enjoyment or possession of the premises. Wrongful actual evictions typify a landlord's breach of this covenant. Generally, if the landlord wrongfully evicts the tenant, the tenant can sue for damages or possession. Furthermore, the tenant can cease paying rent or terminate the lease. See Restatement (Second) of Property §§ 6.1, 10.1, 10.2 (1977). These remedies are also available if the tenant is wrongfully evicted by the landlord from only a portion of the premises on the theory that the landlord cannot apportion its wrong. See Fifth Ave. Bldg. Co. v. Kernochan, 221 N.Y. 370, 117 N.E. 579 (1917).

NOTES AND QUESTIONS

1. L leases an apartment to T. Without any notice to T, L enters T's apartment by using his master key. Assuming the lease is silent on landlord's right to enter T's apartment, does L's entry entitle T to terminate the lease? Would your answer to this question depend on the reason L entered the premises? For example, suppose water was leaking from T's toilet into a downstairs apartment, and L needed to enter T's apartment to fix the toilet. What result? Alternatively, suppose L was suspicious that T was not taking very good care of the apartment and entered to learn whether there was any damage in the premises and whether T was keeping it clean. What result?

2. L leases an apartment to T. The lease includes a provision authorizing T to park her car in the rear of the apartment building in a parking lot which is accessible from the street by means of a driveway adjoining the building. The landlord blocks off T's use of the driveway thereby depriving T the use of the parking lot. Can T terminate the lease? See Briargrove Shopping Center Joint Venture v. Vilar, Inc., 647 S.W.2d 329 (Tex.App.1982).

§ 7.7.1 CONSTRUCTIVE EVICTION

Over time the courts also adopted the doctrine of constructive eviction as an appropriate extension of the law relating to the right of a tenant to terminate a lease because of a wrongful actual eviction. A constructive eviction occurs when the landlord wrongfully performs, or fails to perform, some duty that the landlord is obligated to undertake resulting in the tenant's substantial loss of the use and enjoyment of the leased premises. The basic elements of a common-law constructive eviction are:

1.   The landlord must wrongfully perform or fail to perform some obligation that the landlord is under some expressed or implied duty to perform;

2.   As a result of the landlord's commission or omission there must be a substantial interference with the tenant's use and enjoyment of the premises;

3.   The tenant must give the landlord notice of the interference and a reasonable opportunity to remedy the interference; and

4.   If after such notice the landlord fails to remedy the interference, the tenant must vacate the premises within a reasonable time.

Once the tenant has vacated the premises after a proper constructive eviction, tenant's obligation to pay further rents terminates. Tenant may terminate the lease and sue the landlord for damages.

The current Restatement (Second) of Property (Landlord and Tenant) § 6.1 would liberalize the common law in several significant ways. It provides that the landlord breaches his obligation to the tenant if "the landlord, or someone whose conduct is attributable to him, interferes with a permissible use of the leased premises by the tenant." For purposes of this rule, the Restatement takes the position that the interference must be more than insignificant. This appears to be a more liberal standard than the common law "substantial" standard. It also rejects the common-law requirement that the tenant vacate the premises because "it makes the law completely unavailable to tenants who for one reason or another cannot move." Reporter's Note 6. It also, under certain circumstances, makes the landlord responsible for the acts of third persons, including other tenants in the building, that interfere with the tenant's use and enjoyment if the third-person's conduct could be legally controlled by the landlord.

The following case illustrates what could happen when a tenant complains about the actions of another tenant that allegedly interfere with the complaining tenant's use and enjoyment of the premises. As you review this case, consider whether the complaining tenant—Levins, in the case—could have vacated the premises and, if sued for rent, successfully asserted a constructive eviction defense.

LOUISIANA LEASING COMPANY v. SOKOLOW

Civil Court of the City of New York, Queens Co. (1966).
48 Misc.2d 1014, 266 N.Y.S.2d 447.

DANIEL E. FITZPATRICK, JUSTICE.

This is a proceeding to remove the respondents from the premises of the petitioner upon the ground that they are objectionable tenants. The applicable clauses in the lease between the parties contain the following: "15. No Tenant shall make or permit any disturbing noises in the building by himself, his family, servants, employees, agents, visitors and licensees, nor do or permit anything by such persons that will interfere with the rights, comforts or convenience of other tenants." Paragraph 9 of said lease states in part as follows: "9. Tenant and Tenant's family, servants, employees, agents, visitors, and licensees shall observe faithfully and comply strictly with the Rules and Regulations set forth on the back of this lease, * * *. Tenant agrees that any violation of any of said Rules and Regulations by Tenant or by a member of Tenant's family, or by servants, or employees, or agents, or visitors, or licensees, shall be deemed a substantial violation by Tenant of this lease and of the Tenancy."

The landlord alleges that the noise from respondents' apartment is destroying the peace and quiet of the new tenants immediately underneath them. The claim is and the proof attempted to establish that the noise is of such a character as to constitute a violation of the provisions of the lease set out above. The respondents have been in possession over two and one-half years and their lease runs until December 31, 1966. It is significant that the respondents over that period gave no evidence of being objectionable until the new tenants, the Levins, moved in last October. From the court's opportunity to observe them, both the respondents and the tenants below seem to be people who under other circumstances would be congenial and happy neighbors. It is unfortunate that they have had to come to court to face each other in an eye-ball to eye-ball confrontation.

The respondents are a young couple with two small children, ages 4 and 2. It was admitted by them that the children do run and play in their apartment, but they say that they keep shoes off their feet when at home. The father says that he does walk back and forth at various times when at home, particularly to the refrigerator during the TV commercials and, also, to other areas of the apartment as necessity requires, but denies that he does this excessively or in a loud or heavy manner. They maintain that whatever noises emanate from their apartment are the normal noises of everyday living.

The tenants below, the Levins, are a middle-aged couple who go to business each day. They are like many others of our fellow citizens, who daily go forth to brave the vicissitudes of the mainstream of city life. At the end of the toilsome day, like tired fish, they are only too happy to seek out these quiet backwaters of the metropolis to recuperate for the next day's bout with the task of earning a living. They have raised their own child and are past the time when the patter of little feet overhead is a welcome sound. They say they love their new apartment and that it is just what they have been looking for and would hate to have to give it up because of the noise from above. Mrs. Levin is associated with the publisher of a teen-age magazine and realizes that she is in a bind between her desire for present comfort and the possible loss of two future subscribers. She consequently hastens to add that she loves children and has no objection to the Sokolows because of them—that it is solely the noise of which she complains. So we have the issue.

The landlord's brief states that in its 'view, the conduct that is even more objectionable than the noise, is the uncooperative attitude of the Tenants'. This observation is probably prompted by testimony to the effect that Mr. Sokolow, one of the upstairs tenants, is reported to have said "This is my home, and no one can tell me what to do in my own home". This is a prevalent notion that stems from the ancient axiom that a man's home is his castle.

The difficulty of the situation here is that Mr. Sokolow's castle is directly above the castle of Mr. Levin. That a man's home is his castle is an old Anglo-legal maxim hoary with time and the sanction of frequent repetition. It expressed an age when castles were remote, separated by broad moors, and when an intruder had to force moat and wall to make his presence felt within. The tranquility of the King's Peace, the seclusion of a clandestine romance and the opportunity, like Hamlet, to deliver a soliloquy from the ramparts without fear of neighborly repercussions were real. Times however change, and all change is not necessarily progress as some sage has perceptively reminded us. For in an era of modernity and concentrated urban living, when high-rise apartment houses have piled castle upon castle for some twenty or more stories in the air, it is extremely difficult to equate these modern counterparts with their draw-bridged and turreted ancestors. The builders of today's cubicular confusion have tried to compensate for the functional construction by providing lobbies in Brooklyn Renaissance that rival in decor the throne room at Knossos. They have also provided built-in air-conditioning, closed circuit television, playrooms and laundromats. There are tropical balconies to cool the fevered brow in the short, hot northern summer; which the other nine months serve as convenient places to store the floor mop and scrub pail. On the debit side they also contain miles of utility and sanitary piping which convey sound throughout the building with all the gusto of the mammoth organ in the Mormon Tabernacle at Salt Lake City. Also, the prefabricated or frugally plastered walls have their molecules so critically near the separation level that they oppose almost no barrier at all to alien sounds from neighboring apartments. This often forces on into an embarrassingly auditory intimacy with the surrounding tenants. Such are the hazards of modern apartment house living. One of my brother justices, the Honorable Harold J. Crawford, has opined that in this day in our large cities it is fruitless to expect the solitude of the sylvan glen.... In this we concur. Particularly so, when we consider that all of us are daily assaulted by the "roaring traffic's boom", the early-morning carillon of the garbage cans and the determined whine of homing super-sonic jets. Further, children and noise have been inseparable from a time whence the mind of man runneth not to the contrary. This Court, therefore, is not disposed to attempt anything so schizophrenic at this late date.

Weighing the equities in this difficult controversy, the court finds that the Sokolows were there first, with a record as good tenants. The Levins underneath seem to be good tenants also. This was attested to by the superintendent who was called upon to testify. He made the understatement of the year when he said, "I kept out of the middle of this fight. It's near Christmas and this is no time for me to fight with tenants"—a piece of homely pragmatism which would have gladdened the heart of William James.

In his own crude way the superintendent may have suggested the solution to this proceeding. This is a time for peace on earth to men of good will. As the court noted above, they are all nice people and a little mutual forbearance and understanding of each other's problems should resolve the issues to everyone's satisfaction.

The evidence on the main question shows that in October the respondents Sokolow were already in a fixed relationship to the landlord. The Levins, on the other hand, were not—their position was a mobile one. They had the opportunity to ascertain what was above them in the event they decided to move in below. They elected to move in and afterwards attempted to correct the condition complained of. Since upon the evidence the overhead noise has been shown to be neither excessive nor deliberate, the court is not constrained to flex its muscles and evict the respondents. Upon the entire case the respondents are entitled to a final order dismissing the petition.

NOTES AND QUESTIONS

1. Why was Louisiana Leasing concerned that the noise in the Sokolow's apartment would disturb other tenants? In considering this question, review the quoted clauses in the Sokolow's lease.

2. Suppose you were counsel to the Levins. Would you advise them to vacate the premises and then, if sued for rent, rely on the constructive eviction defense?

Can a tenant abandon the premises and later defend claiming a constructive eviction because other tenants in the building were noisy and disturbed the tenant's peace? See, Gottdiener v. Mailhot, 179 N.J.Super. 286, 431 A.2d 851 (1981); Eskanos & Supperstein v. Irwin, 637 P.2d 403 (Colo.Ct.App.1981).

There is a split of authority whether a tenant can claim constructive eviction as a result of the landlord's failure to control the behavior of others. In general, before the landlord can be found to have breached his obligation because of the behavior of third persons, more than the mere landlord-tenant relationship between the landlord and the third person must be shown. Permission or authorization, express or implied, from the landlord is necessary in order to attribute a third-party's behavior to the landlord.

3. In light of the court's decision, could a landlord, now concerned that future tenants might be discouraged from renting in a building where there was noisy children, discriminate against couples with children? See generally, chapter 12, infra.

4. Typically, a constructive eviction case involves allegations that the landlord breached a duty to (1) provide heat or other utilities, (2) make repairs the landlord covenanted to make, (3) remedy unsafe, unhealthy, or

unsanitary conditions on the premises, such as rodents or insect infestation, or (4) remove nuisances on the premises, such as a house of prostitution. Historically, however, the courts were reluctant to imply a duty upon the landlord the breach of which could give rise to a constructive eviction defense.[1] Therefore, unless the duty was expressed in the lease, the tenant who moved when the premises became untenantable would not likely prevail with a constructive eviction defense. Illustrative of this conservative approach was the historic treatment of the obligation to repair.

At common law, and absent a contrary provision in the lease, the landlord was not obligated to repair the leased premises. Rather, the obligation to repair was imposed upon the tenant. Precisely what the scope of the tenant's duty to repair was, however, unclear, particularly because the obligation to repair did not include the obligation to make improvements. Distinguishing between a repair and an improvement took all of Solomon's talents. The tenant's duty was often expressed in the concept that the tenant was obligated to make all "ordinary and necessary" or "minor" repairs. On the other hand, the tenant was not obligated to restore or repair premises destroyed by "acts of god" or other casualties not resulting from the tenant's negligence. Interestingly, at common law, if the premises were totally destroyed by fire or similar calamity, the tenant was not excused from the obligation to pay rent. This result appears to flow from the independent nature of the lease covenant and the conceptualization of the lease as primarily a conveyance rather than a contract imposing continuing rights, duties and obligations.[2]

> The rule that the tenant must make repairs was probably fair when applied in an agrarian economy where the materials for repairs were simple and at hand, and the tenant capable of making them himself. At least as concerns the actual making of repairs, the rule seems archaic and completely out of harmony with the facts when applied in a complicated society to urban dwellings occupied by persons on salary or weekly wage. Common experience indicates that the tenant in such cases seldom makes or is expected to make repairs even of the minor type covered by the common law duty ... It would seem that the lessor is in the better position, from the viewpoint of economic situation and interest, to make repairs, and that the tenant ought to have no duty in the absence of a specific covenant.[3]

URLTA § 2.104(2) & (4) provides that the landlord shall "make all repairs and do whatever is necessary to put and keep the premises in a fit and habitable condition" and shall "maintain in good and safe working order and condition all electrical, plumbing, sanitary, heating, ventilating, air-conditioning, and other facilities and appliances...." These provisions apply to leases of apartments and single family residences. See also Restatement (Second) of Property § 5.5 (1977). With respect to a single family residence, the landlord and the tenant may agree to shift the obligation to repair or make specific

---

1. This discussion is tempered by recent developments in which the courts have implied a warranty of habitability in residential leases.

2. Numerous courts and legislatures have overturned this common law rule.

3. 1 Amer.L.Prop. § 3.78 at 347–48 (A.J. Casner ed. 1952).

maintenance tasks to the tenant. URLTA § 4.106 authorizes the tenant to terminate the lease of premises wholly destroyed by fire.

Suppose L leases T a single family residence. The lease does not purport to shift any of L's repair and maintenance obligations to T. If L refuses to change the furnace filters, is L in violation of the statute? Suppose L had expressly obligated himself to make repairs. If L breaches this covenant what are T's remedies?

5.   In recent years, concern over physical safety resulting from crime has led some tenants to claim constructive eviction on the grounds that the landlord failed to keep the premises (typically common hallways) free of criminal activity. While courts generally have been sympathetic to the tenant's concerns, as evidenced by the following passage, they have not held that landlords have anything but a duty to act reasonably.

> While the landlord has some duty to provide secure common areas in an apartment complex, he is not an insurer of the premises against criminal activity. Unfortunately, criminal activity pervades virtually every community. The risk that criminal activity will interfere with a tenant's possession and enjoyment of property must be allotted between the parties. Generally, as in the case before us, where the lease does not place the burden of providing security from criminal activity, the tenant may expect only that reasonable precautions will be taken by the landlord. Nothing more than reasonable security arises from the covenant of quiet enjoyment. This holding is in accord with cases in other jurisdictions.

Sciascia v. Riverpark Apartments, 3 Ohio App.3d 164, 444 N.E.2d 40 (1981).

6.   Suppose L covenants to provide T with electrical service and air conditioning twenty-four hours a day in T's four-room office suite. Due to L's negligence, service is chronically discontinued in two of the four rooms. Although T can use the remaining two rooms, T is unable to use the two rooms which are frequently subject to a cessation of services. May T remain in possession of the two rooms which have electrical service but suspend the payment of all rent on a theory of "partial constructive eviction." Compare Barash v. Pennsylvania Terminal Real Estate Corp., 26 N.Y.2d 77, 308 N.Y.S.2d 649, 256 N.E.2d 707 (1970) with East Haven Associates Inc. v. Gurian, 64 Misc.2d 276, 313 N.Y.S.2d 927 (Civ.Ct.1970). See also Note, Partial Constructive Eviction: The Common Law Answer in the Tenant's Struggle for Habitability, 21 Hastings L. J. 417 (1970).

7.   Under the traditional common-law rule, in order for a tenant to successfully claim constructive eviction the tenant had to vacate the premises within a reasonable time. Compare K & S Enterprises v. Kennedy Office Supply Co., 135 N.C.App. 260, 520 S.E.2d 122 (1999) (where tenant vacated three years and one month after leaks began, tenant did not vacate within a reasonable time) with Zurel USA, Inc. v. Magnum Realty Corp., 279 A.D.2d 520, 719 N.Y.S.2d 276 (2001) (delay of four months not unreasonable for a commercial tenant to remove in an "orderly manner"). This "vacation requirement" often put the tenant between a rock and a hard place. In Charles E. Burt, Inc. v. Seven Grand Corp., 340 Mass. 124, 163 N.E.2d 4 (1959) the court permitted a tenant to bring a declaratory judgment action seeking an order that if the tenant were to remove from the premises and was later sued

for rent, the tenant could claim a constructive eviction. How effective would this alternative be for residential tenants?

8. Traditionally, the constructive eviction doctrine provided certain advantages for a tenant. With the advent of the implied warranty of habitability, however, the usefulness of the doctrine for residential tenants has diminished. The implied warranty of habitability has some significant advantages over the constructive eviction doctrine. The primary advantage is that the tenant can avail himself of the implied warranty without having to vacate the premises. Nonetheless, in jurisdictions where the implied warranty has not yet been accepted, for interferences that the implied warranty does not reach and for commercial leases, the constructive eviction doctrine remains the most viable way for the tenant to extricate himself from an intolerable situation.

9. Over time, courts expanded the constructive eviction defense to include cases where a landlord was found to have breached an implied, rather than an express, duty. L leases an apartment to T for five years. After notice to the landlord and a reasonable opportunity to correct the situation, T vacates the apartment and defends L's action for rent on the ground that a house of prostitution was maintained in the neighboring apartment. If you conclude T can maintain a constructive eviction defense, what duty did the landlord breach? Compare Phyfe v. Dale, 72 Misc. 383, 130 N.Y.S. 231 (1911) with Dyett v. Pendleton, 8 Cow. 727 (N.Y.1826). Cf., Blackett v. Olanoff, 371 Mass. 714, 358 N.E.2d 817 (1977) (constructive eviction defense upheld where tenant abandoned premises as a result of noise emanating from a nearby bar owned by the landlord, although operated by a third party).

10. A tenant who has been constructively evicted is no longer liable for future rents and may recover damages from the landlord. As a general rule the amount of damages is the difference between the fair rental value of the premises for the balance of the term and the promised rent. See 1 Amer. L.Prop. § 3.52 (A.J. Casner ed. 1952). Can the tenant also recover special damages such as lost profits?

11. One of the requirements for a constructive eviction is that there be a *substantial* interference with the tenant's use and enjoyment of the premises. Does this mean that the interference must be continuous or is it sufficient if the interference is only intermittent? See Reste Realty Corp. v. Cooper, 53 N.J. 444, 251 A.2d 268 (1969).

12. The requirements of the constructive eviction doctrine create a number of barriers to its effective use by the tenant and a number of risks to tenants who vacate the premises and then assert constructive eviction as a defense. If the tenant must vacate the premises, what must the tenant do if alternative housing or commercial space is not readily available? If the tenant remains on the premises until alternative space becomes available, can the landlord avoid the constructive eviction defense on the ground that the tenant failed to move from the premises within a reasonable time? If the tenant vacates the premises in a timely manner, the tenant may still be held liable for unpaid future rents if it is later determined that the landlord did not fail to perform a duty or that the landlord's action or inaction did not substantially interfere with the tenant's use and enjoyment of the premises. Is there anything the tenant can do to avoid these risks?

§ 7.7.2   ILLEGALITY BECAUSE OF LACK OF HABITABILITY

In response to a growing crisis in urban slums, a number of legal scholars in the 1960s began to write of the shortcomings of the constructive eviction doctrine and to advocate for the development of an implied warranty of habitability analogous to the warranty of merchantability widely recognized in other forms of commercial arrangements. The ideas advanced by these scholars soon caught the attention of a few courts in the United States which began to lay the judicial groundwork for the full-blown doctrine that has been widely accepted today. One potential intellectual barrier to the adoption of the implied warranty of habitability was the rule treating lease covenants as independent. While the doctrine of constructive eviction was an early example of treating lease covenants as dependent, it was never articulated as an exception to the independent covenant rule. But at least as early as 1961, one court was willing to treat the promise to pay rent and the warranty of fitness (a variant of the warranty of habitability) as mutually dependent. See Pines v. Perssion, 14 Wis.2d 590, 111 N.W.2d 409 (1961). Like most common-law doctrines, the implied warranty of habitability developed in stages on the two critical issues of duration and scope. An early important case on both scope and duration was Lemle v. Breeden, 51 Haw. 426, 51 Haw. 478, 462 P.2d 470 (1969).

Lemle was a case marked by unusual facts in that it did not involve the paradigm urban ghetto apartment, but rather a palatial single family home in the Diamond Head area of Honolulu that was rat infested as the tenants discovered on their first night of occupancy.

In *Lemle,* the court held there was an implied warranty that the premises were habitable and fit for the use intended. The opinion is vague whether this warranty applies only as of the commencement of the lease or continues throughout the lease. It appears to lean towards the former. Of course, limiting the warranty only to conditions existing at the time the lease commenced provides little protection for tenants living in dwellings that become untenantable after the lease began through no fault of their own. The *Lemle* court further held that the remedies of "damages, reformation and rescission" were available for breach of the warranty of habitability.

Rescission is the contract analog to constructive eviction. If the tenant elects to rescind the lease, can the tenant remain in possession of the premises? Can the landlord evict the tenant? If the tenant elects to rescind the lease, does the rescission take effect on the date the lease commenced or the date the tenant notified the landlord of his intent to rescind? If the former, is the tenant liable to the landlord for rent between the date the lease commenced and the date the tenant vacated the premises?

As for damages, the *Lemle* court was non-specific regarding how they were to be calculated. The court was also vague regarding whether a tenant who does not vacate can reduce the amount of rents owed by the amount of the damages attributable to a breach of the warranty. Lastly, the court did not explain what kind of reformation would be appropriate.

In Brown v. Southall Realty Co., 237 A.2d 834 (DC Ct. App. 1968) a landlord owned an apartment in the District of Columbia. The landlord knew conditions existed in the apartment which rendered it uninhabitable under the provisions of the DC Housing Code. The landlord also knew (as everyone in DC should know) that a local ordinance provided that: "no persons shall rent or offer to rent any habitation, or the furnishings thereof, unless such habitation and its furnishings are in a clean, safe and sanitary condition, in repair, and free from rodents or vermin."

Notwithstanding the landlord's knowledge of the uninhabitable nature of the apartment and the DC housing code ban on its rental, the landlord leased the apartment to a tenant. Subsequently the tenant stopped paying rent. The landlord then sued for possession for nonpayment of rent. The tenant defended on the grounds that the landlord knew the premises were uninhabitable at the commencement of the lease and that that it was illegal to lease the apartment in its uninhabitable condition. Because the lease was illegal, defendant argued, no rent was due. The court agreed and denied landlord's petition for possession.

Although the holding of Brown v. Southall Realty Co. is quite narrow, historically the decision is important in the progression from a world in which there were no warranties to a world in which, at least for residential tenants, there is an implied warranty of habitability. *Brown* gave birth to the so-called "illegality defense." Suppose the local housing code did not make it expressly illegal to lease premises that were in an unsafe or unsanitary condition. Would the illegality defense be available? Cf., Warshawsky v. American Automotive Products Co., 12 Ill.App.2d 178, 138 N.E.2d 816 (1956) (noting that courts distinguish between cases where the act of leasing is illegal and where only the use is illegal). See also Posnanski v. Hood, 46 Wis.2d 172, 174 N.W.2d 528 (1970) (Housing Code contemplates only administrative remedies).

A number of issues are raised by the illegality defense. For example, if it is the existence of Housing Code violations that demonstrate the unsafe or unsanitary conditions of the leased premises, how serious must, or trivial can, they be? Suppose the landlord did not know that the premises were unsafe or unsanitary and no Housing Code violations had been filed against the landlord. Is the illegality defense available? See Diamond Housing Corp. v. Robinson, 257 A.2d 492 (D.C.App.1969).

If the tenant had entered under an illegal lease and paid three-months rent to the landlord before it was determined that the lease was illegal, could the tenant sue to recover the three-months rent? In this connection should it matter whether the tenant also knew that the premises were unsafe or unsanitary at the time the leasehold commenced? Should it matter that the tenant also knew or should have known that entering into a lease of premises deemed uninhabitable under the housing code was illegal?

If a tenant successfully defends an action for possession or rent on the illegality theory, can the tenant remain in possession of the premises wholly rent free? See William J. Davis, Inc. v. Slade, 271 A.2d 412 (D.C.App.1970) (landlord entitled to reasonable rental value of the premises during period the tenant was in possession of premises under an illegal lease).

What are the relative advantages and disadvantages of the illegality defense when compared to the constructive eviction defense? Does *Brown* apply if the premises were safe and sanitary at the commencement of the lease but became unsafe or unsanitary only after the term commenced?

§ 7.7.3 THE IMPLIED WARRANTY OF HABITABILITY

WADE v. JOBE

Supreme Court of Utah (1991).
818 P.2d 1006.

DURHAM JUSTICE:

In June 1988, defendant Lynda Jobe (the tenant) rented a house in Ogden, Utah, from plaintiff Clyde Wade (the landlord). Jobe had three young children. Shortly after she took occupancy, the tenant discovered numerous defects in the dwelling, and within a few days, she had no hot water. Investigation revealed that the flame of the water heater had been extinguished by accumulated sewage and water in the basement which also produced a foul odor throughout the house. The tenant notified the landlord, who came to the premises a number of times, each time pumping the sewage and water from the basement onto the sidewalk and relighting the water heater. These and other problems persisted from July through October 1988.

In November 1988, the tenant notified the landlord that she would withhold rent until the sewage problem was solved permanently. The situation did not improve, and an inspection by the Ogden City Inspection Division (the division) in December 1988 revealed that the premises were unsafe for human occupancy due to the lack of a sewer connection and other problems. Within a few weeks, the division made another inspection, finding numerous code violations which were a substantial hazard to the health and safety of the occupants. The division issued a notice that the property would be condemned if the violations were not remedied.

After the tenant moved out of the house, the landlord brought suit in the second circuit court to recover the unpaid rent. The tenant filed a counterclaim, seeking an offset against rent owed because of the uninhabitable condition of the premises and seeking damages ... [and other relief]

. . .

At trial, the landlord was awarded judgment of unpaid rent of $770, the full rent due under the parties' original agreement.... [On appeal, the court was asked to consider the following:] ... may a tenant recover at common law for breach of a warranty of habitability? ...

I. WARRANTY OF HABITABILITY

At common law, the leasing of real property was viewed primarily as a conveyance of land for a term, and the law of property was applied to landlord/tenant transactions. At a time when the typical lease was for agricultural purposes, it was assumed that the land, rather than any improvements, was the most important part of the leasehold. *See generally* 2 R. Powell, *The Law of Real Property* ¶ 221[1], at 16–7 to–9, ¶ 233, at 16B–39 to–40 (1991); *Javins v. First Nat'l Realty Corp.,* 428 F.2d 1071, 1077 (D.C.Cir.), *cert. denied,* 400 U.S. 925, 91 S.Ct. 186, 27 L.Ed.2d 185 (1970). Under the rule of caveat emptor, a tenant had a duty to inspect the premises to determine their safety and suitability for the purposes for which they were leased before entering a lease. Moreover, absent deceit or fraud on the part of the landlord or an express warranty to the contrary, the landlord had no duty to make repairs during the course of the tenancy. *See Jespersen v. Deseret News Publishing Co.,* 119 Utah 235, 225 P.2d 1050, 1053 (1951). Under the law of waste, it was the tenant's implied duty to make most repairs. *See Cluff v. Culmer,* 556 P.2d 498, 499 (Utah 1976).

Unlike tenants in feudal England, most modern tenants bargain for the use of structures on the land rather than the land itself ... Modern tenants generally lack the necessary skills or means to inspect the property effectively or to make repairs.... Moreover, the rule of caveat emptor assumes an equal bargaining position between landlord and tenant. Modern tenants, like consumers of goods, however, frequently have no choice but to rely on the landlord to provide a habitable dwelling.... Where they exist, housing shortages, standardized leases, and racial and class discrimination place today's tenants, as consumers of housing, in a poor position to bargain effectively for express warranties and covenants requiring landlords to lease and maintain safe and sanitary housing. *Javins,* 428 F.2d at 1079; *Green v. Superior Court,* 10 Cal.3d 616, 111 Cal.Rptr. 704, 709, 517 P.2d 1168, 1173 (1974).

In consumer law, implied warranties are designed to protect ordinary consumers who do not have the knowledge, capacity, or opportunity to ensure that goods which they are buying are in safe condition. *See Henningsen v. Bloomfield Motors, Inc.,* 32 N.J. 358, 161 A.2d 69, 78 (1960); Utah Code Ann. §§ 70A–2–314 to –316 (implied warranties contained in Uniform Commercial Code). The implied warranty of habitability has been adopted in other jurisdictions to protect the tenant as the party in the less advantageous bargaining position.

The concept of a warranty of habitability is in harmony with the widespread enactment of housing and building codes which reflect a legislative desire to ensure decent housing. *See Hall v. Warren,* 632 P.2d

848, 850 (Utah 1981). It is based on the theory that the residential landlord warrants that the leased premises are habitable at the outset of the lease term and will remain so during the course of the tenancy. *See Javins,* 428 F.2d at 1081. The warranty applies to written and oral leases, *see Javins,* 428 F.2d at 1077 n. 29, and to single-family as well as to multiple-unit dwellings. The warranty of habitability has been adopted, either legislatively or judicially, in over forty states and the District of Columbia. *See* 2 R. Powell, *The Law of Real Property* ¶ 233[2], at 16B–50 to –51 n. 42 (cases), ¶ 233[3], at 16B–64 (statutes) (1991).

In recent years, this court has conformed the common law in this state to contemporary conditions by rejecting the strict application of traditional property law to residential leases, recognizing that it is often more appropriate to apply contract law. *See Reid v. Mutual of Omaha Ins. Co.,* 776 P.2d 896, 902 n. 3 (Utah 1989); *Williams v. Melby,* 699 P.2d at 726–27; *Hall v. Warren,* 632 P.2d at 850. Similarly, we have expanded landlord liability in tort. *See Williams; Hall; Stephenson v. Warner,* 581 P.2d 567 (Utah 1978) (landlord must use ordinary care to ensure leased premises are reasonably safe). Consistent with prevailing trends in consumer law, products liability law, and the law of torts, we reject the rule of caveat emptor and recognize the common law implied warranty of habitability in residential[1] leases.

The determination of whether a dwelling is habitable depends on the individual facts of each case. To guide the trial court in determining whether there is a breach of the warranty of habitability, we describe some general standards that the landlord is required to satisfy. We note initially that the warranty of habitability does not require the landlord to maintain the premises in perfect condition at all times, nor does it preclude minor housing code violations or other defects. Moreover, the landlord will not be liable for defects caused by the tenant. *See Javins,* 428 F.2d at 1082 n. 62; *Hinson v. Delis,* 26 Cal.App.3d 62, 102 Cal.Rptr. 661 (1972); *Marini v. Ireland,* 56 N.J. 130, 265 A.2d 526 (1970). Further, the landlord must have a reasonable time to repair material defects before a breach can be established.

As a general rule, the warranty of habitability requires that the landlord maintain "bare living requirements," *see Academy Spires, Inc. v. Brown,* 111 N.J.Super. 477, 268 A.2d 556, 559 (1970), and that the premises are fit for human occupation. *See Mease v. Fox,* 200 N.W.2d 791 (Iowa 1972); *Hilder v. St. Peter,* 144 Vt. 150, 478 A.2d 202, 208 (1984). Failure to supply heat or hot water, for example, breaches the warranty. A breach is not shown, however, by evidence of minor deficiencies such as the malfunction of venetian blinds, minor water leaks or wall cracks, or a need for paint. *See Academy Spires, Inc. v. Brown,* 268 A.2d at 559.

Substantial compliance with building and housing code standards will generally serve as evidence of the fulfillment of a landlord's duty to provide habitable premises. Evidence of violations involving health or

---

1. We do not decide whether the warranty is implied in commercial leases.

safety, by contrast, will often sustain a tenant's claim for relief. *See Green v. Superior Court,* 517 P.2d at 1182–83. At the same time, just because the housing code provides a basis for implication of the warranty, a code violation is not necessary to establish a breach so long as the claimed defect has an impact on the health or safety of the tenant. *Hilder v. St. Peter,* 478 A.2d at 209.

In the instant case, in support of her claim that the premises were not in habitable condition, the tenant presented two city housing inspection reports detailing numerous code violations which were, in the words of the trial judge, "a substantial hazard to the health and safety of the occupants." Those violations included the presence of raw sewage on the sidewalks and stagnant water in the basement, creating a foul odor. At trial, the tenant testified that she had repeatedly informed the landlord of the problem with the sewer connection and the resulting lack of hot water, but the landlord never did any more than temporarily alleviate the problem. The landlord did not controvert the evidence of substantial problems. At trial, the court granted judgment for the landlord, concluding that Utah law did not recognize an implied warranty of habitability for residential rental premises. As discussed above, we have now recognized the warranty. We therefore remand this case to the trial court to determine whether the landlord has breached the implied warranty of habitability as defined in this opinion. If the trial court finds a breach of the warranty of habitability, it must then determine damages.

A. Remedies

Under traditional property law, a lessee's covenant to pay rent was viewed as independent of any covenants on the part of the landlord ... Even when a lessor expressly covenanted to make repairs, the lessor's breach did not justify the lessee's withholding rent. Under the prevailing contemporary view of the residential lease as a contractual transaction, however, ... the tenant's obligation to pay rent is conditioned upon the landlord's fulfilling his part of the bargain. The payment of rent by the tenant and the landlord's duty to provide habitable premises are, as a result, dependent covenants.

Once the landlord has breached his duty to provide habitable conditions, there are at least two ways the tenant can treat the duty to pay rent. The tenant may continue to pay rent to the landlord or withhold the rent.[2] If the tenant continues to pay full rent to the landlord during the period of uninhabitability, the tenant can bring an affirmative action to establish the breach and receive a reimbursement for excess rents paid. Rent withholding, on the other hand, deprives the landlord of the rent due

---

2. In addition, some jurisdictions recognize rent application, also known as "repair and deduct," allowing the tenant to use the rent money to repair the premises. Because this remedy has not been relied on or sought in the instant case, we do not at this time make a ruling on its availability in Utah.

during the default, thereby motivating the landlord to repair the premises. *See* 2 R. Powell, *The Law of Real Property* ¶ 228[6][d], at 16A–51 (1990).[3]

Some jurisdictions have taken the position that the tenant is entitled to an abatement only against the withheld rent in a rent collection case, holding that damages for the uninhabitable conditions existing prior to the tenant's withholding must be recovered in a separate action. *See C.F. Seabrook Co. v. Beck,* 174 N.J.Super. 577, 417 A.2d 89 (1980). We reject this reasoning; it is more in keeping with the policy behind our adoption of the warranty of habitability to provide for retroactive abatement of the rent during the period of the landlord's default whether or not the tenant withholds rent.[4]

B. Damages

In general, courts have applied contract remedies when a breach of the warranty of habitability has been shown ... One available remedy, therefore, is damages. Special damages may be recovered when, as a foreseeable result of the landlord's breach, the tenant suffers personal injury, property damage, relocation expenses, or other similar injuries.... General damages recoverable in the form of rent abatement or reimbursement to the tenant are more difficult to calculate.

Several different measures for determining the amount of rent abatement to which a tenant is entitled have been used by the courts. The first of these is the fair rental value of the premises as warranted less their fair rental value in the unrepaired condition.... Under this approach, the contract rent may be considered as evidence of the value of the premises as warranted.... Another measure is the contract rent less the fair rental value of the premises in the unrepaired condition.... Methodological difficulties inherent in both of these measures ... combined with the practical difficulties of producing evidence on fair market value,[5] however, limit the efficacy of those measures for dealing with residential leases. For this reason, a number of courts have adopted what is called the "percentage diminution" (or percentage reduction in use) approach which places more discretion with the trier of fact.[6]

---

3. The majority of jurisdictions that permit rent withholding allow the tenant to retain the funds subject to the discretionary power of the court to order the deposit of the rent into escrow. *See* 2 R. Powell, *The Law of Real Property* ¶ 228[6][d], at 16A–54 (1990). Like the court in *Javins,* we think this type of escrow account would provide a useful protective procedure in the right circumstances.

4. Before the tenant may receive a rent abatement, she must put the landlord in breach by giving her actual or constructive notice of the defects and a reasonable time in which to make repairs....

5. Under either approach, at least one market value is almost certain to require expert testimony. The production of such testimony will increase the cost, in time and money, of the typical case.

6. ... A fourth, hybrid measure, adopted by the Restatement (Second) of Property, uses the ratio of the fair rental value of the unrepaired premises to the fair rental value of the habitable unit as the percentage applied to the agreed rent. Restatement (Second) of Property, Landlord & Tenant § 11.1 (1976). The Restatement approach has been rejected by at least one court as "mind boggling." *See Cazares v. Ortiz,* 168 Cal.Rptr. at 112.

Under the percentage diminution approach, the tenant's recovery reflects the percentage by which the tenant's use and enjoyment of the premises has been reduced by the uninhabitable conditions... In applying this approach, the trial court must carefully review the materiality of the particular defects and the length of time such defects have existed.[7] ... It is true that the percentage diminution approach requires the trier of fact to exercise broad discretion and some subjective judgment to determine the degree to which the defective conditions have diminished the habitability of the premises. It should be noted, however, that despite their theoretical appeal, the other approaches are not objectively precise either.... Furthermore, they involve the use of an expert witness's subjective opinion of the "worth" of habitable and uninhabitable premises.

As the foregoing discussion demonstrates, the determination of appropriate damages in cases of a breach of the warranty of habitability will often be a difficult task. None of the approaches described above is inherently illegitimate, but we think that the percentage diminution approach has a practical advantage in that it will generally obviate the need for expert testimony and reduce the cost and complexity of enforcing the warranty of habitability. We acknowledge the limitation of the method but conclude that it is as sound in its result as any other and more workable in practice. We will have to depend on development of the rule in specific cases to determine whether it will be universally applicable....

... We remand this case to the trial court to determine whether the landlord breached the implied warranty of habitability as defined in this opinion. If the trial court determines that he was not in breach, the landlord will be entitled to payment for all the past due rent. If the trial court determines that his breach of the warranty of habitability totally excused the tenant's rent obligation (i.e., rendered the premises virtually uninhabitable), the landlord's action to recover rent due will fail. If the trial court determines that the landlord's breach partially excused the tenant's rent obligation, the tenant will be entitled to percentage rent abatement for the period during which the house was uninhabitable.

NOTES AND QUESTIONS

1. Should the adoption of the implied warranty of habitability and the rejection of the centuries old caveat emptor rule have been left to the legislature? See Pugh v. Holmes, 486 Pa. 272, 405 A.2d 897 (1979). In *Pugh* the argument was made, but rejected, that the court should refrain from implying a warranty of habitability, because the Pennsylvania legislature had partially acted by providing tenants with a remedial judicial procedure to address claims that the premises were uninhabitable. This argument is part of a larger argument, generally unsuccessful, that courts should not find any implied warranty in contravention of such an established legal principle as "let the buyer beware," and that changes in the law are more appropriately

---

7. These are presumably the same factors considered by an expert in determining fair market values under the other two approaches.

made by the legislature. This view was most recently expressed in P.H. Inv. v. Oliver, 778 P.2d 11 (Utah App.1989), where the court refused to imply the warranty as an inappropriate exercise of judicial power. The court reasoned that the legislature was the more appropriate branch to "weigh the conflicting interests of lessors and tenants." Id. at 13. Do you agree? The Oliver case was reversed following the Wade decision. See P.H. Inv. v. Oliver, 818 P.2d 1018 (Utah 1991).

2. What societal goal are courts and legislatures that adopt the implied warranty of habitability attempting to promote?

3. Courts regularly wrestle with the question of the property scope of the warranty. In Pugh v. Holmes, 253 Pa.Super. 76, 87, 384 A.2d 1234, 1240 (1978) the court stated:

> In order to constitute a breach of the implied warranty of habitability ... the defect must be of a nature and kind which will render the premises unsafe, or unsanitary and thus unfit for living therein.... Materiality is a question of fact to be decided by the trier of fact on a case-by-case basis. Among those factors to be considered in determining whether a breach is material are 1) whether the condition violates a housing law, regulation or ordinance; 2) the nature and seriousness of the defect; 3) the effect of the defect on safety and sanitation; 4) the length of time for which the condition has persisted; and 5) the age of the structure. This proposed list of factors is not designed to be exclusive; the lower court, in its discretion may consider any other factors it deems appropriate.

How does this standard compare with the standard set forth in the principal case?

Recently a New York Civil Court was presented with a novel claim relating to the implied warranty of habitability. In Poyck v. Byrant, 13 Misc.3d 699, 820 N.Y.S.2d 774 (Civ. Ct. 2006), tenants claimed a breach of the implied warranty of habitability and constructive eviction because of second-hand smoke in the common hallways of the building complex. They claimed that, notwithstanding their repeated complaints, the landlord failed to solve the problem caused by other tenants in the building. Stated the court:

> While there appears to be no reported cases dealing with secondhand smoke in the context of implied warranty of habitability, secondhand smoke is just as insidious and invasive as the more common conditions such as noxious odors, smoke odors, chemical fumes, excessive noise, and water leaks and extreme dust penetration. Indeed, the U.S. Surgeon General, the New York State Legislature and the City of New York City Counsel declared that there is a substantial body of scientific research that breathing secondhand smoke poses a significant health hazard. U.S. Surgeon General's report on *The Health Consequences of Involuntary Smoking* (December, 1986); New York Public Health Law § 1399–n(1) ... Therefore, this Court holds as a matter of law that secondhand smoke qualifies as a condition that invokes the protections of [the statute] under the proper circumstances ...

Id. at 776–77.

4. Section 2–104 of the Uniform Residential Landlord and Tenant Act incorporates a form of the implied warranty and did so in 1972 long before the concept had been recognized in many states. That section provides that:

(a) A landlord shall

(1) comply with the requirements of applicable building and housing codes materially affecting health and safety;

(2) make all repairs and do whatever is necessary to put and keep the premises in a fit and habitable condition;

(3) keep all common areas of the premises in a clean and safe condition;

(4) maintain in good and safe working order and condition all electrical, plumbing, sanitary, heating, ventilating, air-conditioning, and other facilities and appliances, including elevators, supplied or required to be supplied by him;

(5) provide and maintain appropriate receptacles and conveniences for the removal of ashes, garbage, rubbish, and other waste incidental to the occupancy of the dwelling unit and arrange for their removal; and

(6) supply running water and reasonable amounts of hot water at all times and reasonable heat [between [October 1] and [May 1]] except where the building that includes the dwelling unit is not required by law to be equipped for that purpose, or the dwelling unit is so constructed that heat or hot water is generated by an installation within the exclusive control of the tenant and supplied by a direct public utility connection ...

(c) The landlord and tenant of a single family residence may agree in writing that the tenant perform the landlord's duties specified in paragraphs (5) and (6) of subsection (a) and also specified repairs, maintenance tasks, alterations, and remodeling, but only if the transaction is entered into in good faith.

(d) The landlord and tenant of any dwelling unit other than a single family residence may agree that the tenant is to perform specified repairs, maintenance tasks, alterations, or remodeling only if

(1) the agreement of the parties is entered into in good faith and is set forth in a separate writing signed by the parties and supported by adequate consideration;

(2) the work is not necessary to cure noncompliance with subsection (a)(1) of this section; and

(3) the agreement does not diminish or affect the obligation of the landlord to other tenants in the premises.

As a counterpoint, however, Section 3.101 provides that:

A tenant shall

(1) comply with all obligations primarily imposed upon tenants by applicable provisions of building and housing codes materially affecting health and safety;

(2) keep that part of the premises that he occupies and uses as clean and safe as the condition of the premises permit;

(3) dispose from his dwelling unit all ashes, garbage, rubbish, and other waste in a clean and safe manner;

(4) keep all plumbing fixtures in the dwelling unit or used by the tenant as clear as their condition permits;

(5) use in a reasonable manner all electrical, plumbing, sanitary, heating, ventilating, air-conditioning, and other facilities and appliances including elevators in the premises;

(6) not deliberately or negligently destroy, deface, damage, impair, or remove any part of the premises or knowingly permit any person to do so; and

(7) conduct himself and require other persons on the premises with his consent to conduct themselves in a manner that will not disturb his neighbors' peaceful enjoyment of the premises.

5. Must the landlord have notice of the uninhabitable conditions in order for the tenant to press any claim based upon the implied warranty of habitability? According to the *Wade* court, the answer is yes. While most courts have not specifically required that the landlord have notice in fact, in most cases the landlord had knowledge of the uninhabitable conditions. See also Restatement (Second) of Property § 10.1 (1977).

The *Wade* court required the tenant to give the landlord notice of the condition of the premises and a reasonable opportunity to make necessary repairs. Not all courts have imposed this requirement. See Knight v. Hallsthammar, 29 Cal.3d 46, 171 Cal.Rptr. 707, 623 P.2d 268 (1981).

6. The courts that have embraced the implied warranty of habitability have based their holdings on a contract theory and have adopted remedies for breach of the implied warranty typically available for breach of contract. In other words, damages, rescission, and reformation. Rescission of the contract, i.e., termination of the lease, has been accepted by some courts. See, e.g., Lemle v. Breeden, 51 Haw. 426, 51 Haw. 478, 462 P.2d 470 (1969); Mease v. Fox, 200 N.W.2d 791 (Iowa 1972). However, rescission is not necessarily a viable remedy for tenants who cannot afford to move or rent alternative housing or for tenants located in areas of severe housing shortages.

Additionally, some courts have suggested in dicta that the tenant, under certain circumstances, may demand specific performance. See, e.g., Pugh v. Holmes, 486 Pa. 272, 405 A.2d 897 (1979). No reported appellate case has yet held that this remedy is available. Where does *Wade* come out on this question? See, e.g., Javins v. First National Realty Corp., 428 F.2d 1071 (D.C.Cir.1970), cert. denied, 400 U.S. 925 (1970). Interestingly, this may in fact turn out to be the most potent weapon in the tenant's arsenal. Why?

Damages also are available to a tenant for the landlord's breach of the implied warranty, but again it is quite rare for a tenant to initiate a suit to recover damages. Damages are available to a tenant who remains in possession or who removes from the premises, terminates the lease, and sues for damages.

As a practical matter, the force of the implied warranty comes from the tenant's use of the doctrine as a defense to the landlord's action to recover rents or possession. In almost all the cases the courts have agreed that if the tenant has wrongfully withheld rent because there has been no breach of the implied warranty of habitability, the landlord can recover possession. Conversely, if the tenant's obligation to pay rent is wholly suspended because of the landlord's breach of the warranty, the landlord may not recover possession of the premises. See Javins v. First Nat'l. Realty Corp., 428 F.2d 1071 (D.C.Cir.1970), cert. denied 400 U.S. 925 (1970) (if the obligation to pay rent is wholly suspended and the landlord makes the necessary repairs, the obligation to pay rents resumes). More difficult problems arise where some, but not all, of the rent obligation is appropriately suspended because there has been less than a complete breach of the implied warranty. There are at lease five approaches to determine how much rent should abate in this case. These are:

(a) The percentage diminution approach: Damages (or the amount of rent reduction) equals the promised rent multiplied by the percentage of the use of the premises lost as a result of the breach. This is the method adopted in the *Wade* case. See also Academy Spires, Inc. v. Brown, 111 N.J.Super. 477, 487–88, 268 A.2d 556, 562 (Dist.Ct.1970). Thus, if the tenant loses one-fourth of the use of premises, damages or rent reduction equal one-fourth of the promised rent. How is this percentage to be determined?

(b) The Restatement approach: According to the Restatement (Second) of Property § 11.1 (1977):

> If the tenant is entitled to an abatement of the rent, the rent is abated to the amount of that proportion of the rent which the fair rental value after the event giving the right to abate bears to the fair rental value before the event. Abatement is allowed until the default is eliminated or the lease terminates, whichever first occurs.

Is this the correct way proportionately to reduce rent? Consider the following:

> If the fair rental value of the premises in "suitable" condition (that is, in substantial compliance with the housing code) would be $100 a month, and if at the beginning of the tenancy the fair rental value of the premises in their existing, dilapidated condition is $20 a month, and if the contract rent is $30 a month, is the tenant entitled to reduce his rent by the amount of $24 a month to the sum of $6 a month? *Answer:* yes.[7]

(c) The fair rental value approach #1: Damages (or the amount of rent reduction) equal the difference between the promised rent and the fair rental value of the premises during the period in which the warranty was breached. See Kline v. Burns, 111 N.H. 87, 276 A.2d 248 (1971); Lane v. Kelley, 57 Or.App. 197, 643 P.2d 1375 (1982), review denied 293 Or. 394, 650 P.2d 927 (1982). For example, if T agreed to rent premises for $75 a month but because the premises were in an unsafe or unsanitary condition the premises were only worth $50 a month, T's damages would equal $25 a month.

---

7. Meyers, The Covenant of Habitability and the American Law Institute, 27 Stan.L.Rev. 879, 883 (1975).

(d) The fair rental value approach #2: Damages equal the difference between the fair rental value of the premises if the premises had been in their warranted condition and the fair rental value of the premises in their "as is" condition. See, e.g., Green v. Superior Court, 10 Cal.3d 616, 638, 111 Cal.Rptr. 704, 719, 517 P.2d 1168, 1183 (1974); Teller v. McCoy, 162 W.Va. 367, 253 S.E.2d 114 (1978) (if the fair rental value of the premises in their warranted condition is the same as the promised rent, then the damages under this approach equal the damages under approach #1). For example, if T leased premises having a fair market value as warranted of $90 for only $75 a month but in fact the premises because of their unsafe or unsanitary condition only had a fair rental value of $50, T's damages would equal $40. Conceptually, what is the measure of damages compensating T for?

In Mease v. Fox, 200 N.W.2d 791, 797 (Iowa 1972), the Iowa Supreme Court held that this measure of damages was appropriate only if the tenant remained in possession of the premises and paid rent. If the tenant removed from the premises the appropriate measure of damages was the difference, if any, between the fair rental value of the premises as warranted and the promised rent (i.e., $15 in the preceding case). Do you agree?

Why does *Wade* reject the fair rental value approach? Do these reasons have merit? Are the difficulties of that approach any greater than the difficulties associated with the other approaches?

(e) The tort approach: Under this approach the tenant could recover for emotional distress and discomfort and punitive damages in addition to any loss of rental value as measured by one of the foregoing methods. See Moskovitz, The Implied Warranty of Habitability: A New Doctrine Raising New Issues, 62 Calif.L.Rev. 1444 (1974); Sax & Hiestand, Slumlordism as a Tort, 65 Mich.L.Rev. 869 (1967). See also Fair v. Negley, 257 Pa.Super. 50, 390 A.2d 240 (1978).

7.   The implied warranty of habitability has been widely adopted judicially throughout the United States. A large number of states have adopted the warranty by statute although these statutes vary as to specificity in detailing the standard of habitability required. Compare Mich.Comp.Laws Ann. § 554.139 (West Supp.1986) (requiring keeping premises "fit for the use intended by the parties") with URLTA § 2.104(a) (adopted in thirteen states and elaborating on warranty components with regard to plumbing, heating, electrical systems, etc.). The statutes also vary in applicability. Compare Nev.Rev.Stat. § 118A.180 (Michie 1986) (act applies only where landlord owns at least seven units) with Iowa Code Ann. § 562A.5 (West Supp.1986) (implying coverage of nearly all residential rental living arrangements). Some of the states that have adopted the implied warranty by judicial decision have also enacted statutes codifying the warranty.

If a state has codified the warranty following a judicial decision adopting the warranty, does that mean the judicial warranty is no longer effective? See Foisy v. Wyman, 83 Wash.2d 22, 515 P.2d 160 (1973) (judicial warranty applies to rental of house on a farm, a category excepted from the URLTA based statute).

8.   To what kinds of property should the implied warranty of habitability extend? Can the reasoning underlying the warranty be applied to commercial

leases, leases of single family residences or farms? See generally McArdle v. Courson, 82 Ill.App.3d 123, 37 Ill.Dec. 402, 402 N.E.2d 292 (1980); Greenfield & Margolis, An Implied Warranty of Fitness in NonResidential Leases, 45 Albany L.Rev. 855 (1981). But see Reste Realty Corp. v. Cooper, 53 N.J. 444, 251 A.2d 268 (1969).

Should the implied warranty apply to dwelling units in public housing projects? See Alexander v. United States Department of Housing and Urban Development, 555 F.2d 166 (7th Cir.1977), aff'd 441 U.S. 39 (1979). But see Casenote, Implied Warranty of Habitability in Federal Housing Projects: Alexander v. United States Department of Housing and Urban Development, 19 B.C.L.Rev. 343 (1978).

To what other kinds of dwelling units should the implied warranty apply? Only units covered by a local housing code? See Winchester Management Corp. v. Staten, 361 A.2d 187 (D.C.App.1976) (Yes). Only urban residential property? See Steele v. Latimer, 214 Kan. 329, 521 P.2d 304 (1974) (suggesting such a distinction). Does the size of the building matter? See Jack Spring, Inc. v. Little, 50 Ill.2d 351, 280 N.E.2d 208 (1972) (only multiple unit buildings); Nev.Rev.Stat.Ann. §§ 118A.180, 118A.290 (1977) (buildings with five or more dwelling units). But see Lensey Corp. v. Wong, 83 Ill.App.3d 207, 38 Ill.Dec. 612, 403 N.E.2d 1066 (1980) (applying implied warranty to single family residences).

9. On what source did the *Wade* court rely to find the implied warranty—the housing code, evolving common law principles, or both? Judicial decisions are often unclear on the source of the implied warranty. What consequences might flow from a determination that the warranty is based upon the housing code or common law?

10. By what standards should breaches of the implied warranty be measured? Just how egregious must the breach be? The case law appears to fall into five categories. In the first group the standard used to measure the implied warranty is the local housing code. Although the implication is that a single breach of any provision of the housing code would be sufficient to result in a breach of the implied warranty, no court has taken that strict a position. Rather, the decisions finding a breach of the implied warranty based upon housing code violations have factually involved multiple violations of the housing code. Thus, the issue of the impact of only one violation has been left to the academics. See Steele v. Latimer, 214 Kan. 329, 521 P.2d 304 (1974) (concurring opinion argues that only defects rendering the premises unsafe, unsanitary or uninhabitable result in breach); Glyco v. Schultz, 35 Ohio Misc. 25, 289 N.E.2d 919 (Mun.1972).

In several other jurisdictions the measure of the implied warranty has been substantial compliance with the housing code. This is the approach taken in Javins v. First Nat'l Realty Corp., 428 F.2d 1071 (D.C.Cir.1970), cert. denied 400 U.S. 925 (1970). In essence, it requires proof of conditions affecting habitability before finding a breach because substantial compliance with the housing code would mean, assuming the housing code has any force, the dwelling is habitable. This measure avoids de minimis violation problems and strikes a balance between the nuisance and hassle of mandating repair of small violations with the tenant's need for an effective warranty.

A third approach finds a breach of the implied warranty of habitability if the defect is substantial. In Mease v. Fox, 200 N.W.2d 791, 796 (Iowa 1972), for example, the court held that latent defects must be "in facilities and utilities vital to the use of the premises for residential purposes," and patent defects must be violations of the housing code sufficient to render the premises "unsafe, or unsanitary and unfit for living therein." The nature of the defect, its effect on safety and sanitation and its duration were among the factors the court considered.

A fourth approach uses the housing code as a relevant standard by which to judge whether the implied warranty has been breached. The housing code, however, is not the only standard. Rather, the standard is whether the defect would "render the premises uninhabitable in the eyes of a reasonable person," Berzito v. Gambino, 63 N.J. 460, 469, 308 A.2d 17, 22 (1973), or whether the dwelling is fit for human occupation, Boston Housing Authority v. Hemingway, 363 Mass. 184, 293 N.E.2d 831 (1973). This test is flexible enough to allow the fact finder to conclude that a breach exists where conditions render a dwelling uninhabitable though no housing code provision is violated. See, e.g., Park Hill Terrace Associates v. Glennon, 146 N.J.Super. 271, 369 A.2d 938 (1977) (air conditioning failure a breach of the implied warranty).

Lastly, the standard of the warranty is measured without reference to a housing code but in favor of a general test of "habitability." Thus, the question is merely whether the premises are habitable. This is a common statutory test. See, e.g., Alaska Stat. § 34.03.100 (1985); Or.Rev.Stat. § 91.770 (1984). See also Restatement (Second) of Property § 5.1 (1977) (premises not suitable for residential purposes).

Which approach is adopted by the *Wade* court?

It is clear that the implied warranty applies to latent defects. However, there has been judicial language that questions the applicability of the warranty to patent defects existing when the parties entered into the lease. Compare Marini v. Ireland, 56 N.J. 130, 265 A.2d 526 (1970) with Boston Housing Authority v. Hemingway, 363 Mass. 184, 293 N.E.2d 831 (1973). If, as most courts agree, the warranty is a continuing promise on the landlord's part that from the inception of the lease and throughout its duration the premises will be habitable, is it relevant whether the defect is latent or patent at the commencement of the lease?

11. The issue of the application of the implied warranty to patent defects and the tenant's acceptance of the premises with these defects is closely related to the issue whether the implied warranty is waivable. As a matter of public policy, should the implied warranty be waivable? Courts are divided on this issue. Compare Javins v. First National Realty Corp., 428 F.2d 1071 (D.C.Cir.1970), cert. denied, 400 U.S. 925 (1970) with Mease v. Fox, 200 N.W.2d 791 (Iowa 1972). URLTA § 2.104 incorporates the implied warranty of habitability and makes that warranty an obligation of the landlord. URLTA § 1.403 makes a waiver of that warranty unenforceable. On the other hand, Restatement (Second) of Property § 5.6 (1977), appears to allow landlord and tenant to alter the landlord's obligations "with respect to the condition of the leased property . . . unless . . . [their agreement is] unenforceable in whole or

in part because ... [it is] unconscionable or significantly against public policy." Comment e to this section of the Restatement states that "[a]n agreement or provision may be against public policy if it will materially and unreasonably obstruct achievement of a well defined statutory, regulatory, or common law policy."

Is the "non-waivable" rule consistent with how damages for the breach of the implied warranty are measured? In a jurisdiction in which the warranty is waivable, what other doctrines are available to bar a landlord's claim that a tenant waived the warranty?

12. Is the implied warranty waivable by a tenant's agreement to pay rent equal to the property's fair market value computed by reference to the property's uninhabitable condition? In Miller v. C.W. Myers Trading Post, Inc., 85 N.C.App. 362, 370, 355 S.E.2d 189, 194 (1987), the court stated:

> The rental or lease of residential premises for a price that is "fair" or below fair rental value does not absolve the landlord of his statutory obligation to provide fit premises and is not a defense to plaintiffs' claims. The implied warranty of habitability entitles a tenant in possession of leased premises to the value of the premises as warranted, which may be greater than the rent agreed upon or paid.

See also Foisy v. Wyman, 83 Wash.2d 22, 515 P.2d 160 (1973) (tenant can assert breach of the implied warranty as a defense to action for possession for nonpayment of rent even though the tenant knew of a substantial number of defects when he rented premises and rent was reduced to take account of these defects).

13. Can the implied warranty be used to defend an action for possession or rent if the tenant caused the premises to become uninhabitable? To what extent can the actions of other tenants in the building that cause the premises to become uninhabitable be cited by the landlord to defeat the assertion of the implied warranty as a defense?

14. The *Wade* court also upheld the tenant's right to repair the premises and deduct the cost of the repair from future rents. See also Marini v. Ireland, 56 N.J. 130, 265 A.2d 526 (1970). The repair and deduct remedy is also adopted in the Restatement (Second) of Property § 11.2 (1977), providing that "[i]f the tenant is entitled to apply his rent to eliminate the landlord's default, the tenant, after proper notice to the landlord, may deduct from his rent reasonable costs incurred in eliminating the default." How viable is the repair and deduct remedy if the cost of the repair is substantial? Why might a landlord object to this remedy if the tenant is merely discharging what would otherwise be the landlord's legal obligation to repair? Is the tenant limited to making repairs in the leased premises or may the tenant make repairs to items in the common areas of the buildings? Can the tenant waive the right to utilize the repair and deduct remedy? See Restatement (Second) of Property § 11.2 comment a (1977). URLTA § 4.103 provides that:

> (a) If the landlord fails to comply with the rental agreement or Section 2.104 [relating to the landlord's obligation to maintain the premises], and the reasonable cost of compliance is less than [$100], or an amount equal to [one-half] the periodic rent, whichever amount is greater, the tenant

may recover damages for the breach under Section 4.101(b) or may notify the landlord of his intention to correct the condition at the landlord's expense. If the landlord fails to comply within [14] days after being notified by the tenant in writing or as promptly as conditions require in case of emergency, the tenant may cause the work to be done in a workmanlike manner and, after submitting to the landlord an itemized statement, deduct from his rent the actual and reasonable cost or the fair and reasonable value of the work, not exceeding the amount specified in this subsection.

(b) A tenant may not repair at the landlord's expense if the condition was caused by the deliberate or negligent act or omission of the tenant, a member of his family, or other person on the premises with his consent.

15. Another remedy available to tenants in some jurisdictions is "rent withholding." Under this remedy a tenant may be permitted to deposit rents with the court until the defects are cured and during such time the tenant may not be evicted by the landlord. In some jurisdictions the courts are further authorized to appoint an administrator of the rent deposits who is permitted to apply the deposited rents towards the making of repairs. How effective is rent withholding to assure that the necessary repairs are made to make the premises habitable?

The rent withholding statutes vary significantly among the states. See, e.g., Mo.Rev.Stat. §§ 441.500–441.640 (Supp.1985); N.J.Stat.Ann. §§ 2A:42–85 to 2A:42–96 (West Supp.1985); N.Y. Real Prop.Acts.Law §§ 769–782 (McKinney 1979); Pa.Stat.Ann. tit. 35, § 1700–1 (Purdon's Cum.Supp.1986). See also Restatement (Second) of Property § 11.3 (1977). In Javins v. First National Realty Corp., 428 F.2d 1071 (D.C.Cir.1970), cert. denied, 400 U.S. 925 (1970), the court approved of rent withholding and deposit with the court even in the absence of enabling legislation as an "excellent protective procedure." Id. at 1083, n.67. See generally Rosen, Receivership: A Useful Tool for Helping to Meet the Needs of Low Income People, 3 Harv.C.R.–C.L.L.Rev. 311 (1968).

16. Has the implied warranty of habitability improved the housing stock of America? Two empirical studies of the effects of the implied warranty in two California rental markets were unable to draw any definitive conclusions on this question. The studies were designed in part to measure the impact of Green v. Superior Court, 10 Cal.3d 616, 111 Cal.Rptr. 704, 517 P.2d 1168 (1974) in which the California Supreme Court adopted the implied warranty of habitability. See Note, The Great *Green* Hope: The Implied Warranty of Habitability in Practice, 28 Stanford L.Rev. 729 (1976); Heskin, The Warranty of Habitability Debate: A California Case Study, 66 Calif.L.Rev. 37 (1978). The first study concluded that, although the implied warranty was "not being extensively used … few low income tenants receive the legal advice necessary to make use of this innovation in landlord-tenant law." Note, The Great *Green* Hope, supra at 776. However, the study found that "if the implied warranty of habitability is intended to shift some bargaining power from landlords to tenants in litigation, the rule has had some success. Thus, as of the time of this study, the primary effect of *Green* probably has not been to

improve housing quality, but rather to give tenants more favorable results in landlord-tenant litigation." Id. at 776.

The Heskin study further found that the impact of the implied warranty has not been found in the court records but in the offices of legal service attorneys who use the warranty to effect out-of-court settlements. This study indicates, however, that the "horribles" that were predicted to accompany the importation of the implied warranty into California law have not materialized on either side of the issue.

> The opponents of *Green* point to eastern slums with deteriorated tenements, fleeing investors and massive abandonment, arguing that anything, including the warranty, that places additional pressures on the landlords can only drive California toward the eastern situation. Proponents argue instead that *Green* will slow that decline. The proponents argue that the nature of the housing market in low-income areas necessitates legal intervention, and that there is money which can be diverted to repair of the property. All parties seem to assume that *Green* addresses a pervasive problem of California's low-income housing stock. . . .

> [S]ix factors [limit] the enforcement of the warranty. The first among these was the perceived hostility of the local branch of the municipal court. Second, the lawyers responded to their perception of the court's attitude with a conservative interpretation and application of the law. Third, the lawyers were overworked and not fully prepared to exploit the [Green] case's potential. Fourth, the language of the *Green* decision is ambiguous, making it difficult for lawyers to explain the law to their clients and to enforce it according to their clients' desires. Fifth, the clients had a variety of problems that limited their ability to engage in and sustain litigation. Last, the tenant unions, which the proponents expected to expand the use of *Green,* did not materialize.

Heskin, The Warranty of Habitability Debate: A California Case Study, supra at 43, 59.

17.   At common law the landlord was not liable to the tenant for injuries sustained by the tenant resulting from defects on the leasehold premises. Is this rule consistent with the common law's characterization of a lease? Is it consistent with the characterization of a leasehold today? The common-law rule was subject to a number of important exceptions. For example, the landlord was liable for injuries resulting from defects in the common areas. See also Restatement (Second) of Property, § 17.3 (1977). Likewise, if the landlord undertook to make repairs and did so in a negligent way and the tenant was injured because of the negligent manner in which the repairs were made, the landlord could be liable to the tenant. See, e.g., Jordan v. Savage, 88 Ill.App.2d 251, 232 N.E.2d 580 (1967).

Restatement (Second) Property § 17.1 (1977) rejects the common law no liability rule. It provides that the landlord is liable for harms caused to the tenant as a result of conditions involving an unreasonable risk of physical harm existing when the tenant took possession if (1) the tenant did not know or have reason to know of the condition or the risk involved and (2) the landlord knew or had reason to know of the condition, realizes or should have realized the risk and had reason to expect that the tenant would not have discovered the condition or realized the risk. Would the landlord be liable to the tenant under this section if the tenant was injured subsequent to the landlord's transfer of its reversion to a third person? See Restatement (Second) of Property, § 17.1 comment 1 (1977).

Suppose a landlord and a tenant enter into a lease providing that the landlord is not liable for injuries the tenant incurs upon the leased premises. Is this "exculpatory clause" valid? Compare Walston v. Birdnest Apartments, Inc., 395 So.2d 45 (Ala.1981) (exculpatory clause in residential lease valid with respect to "passive" negligence) with Cappaert v. Junker, 413 So.2d 378 (Miss.1982) (exculpatory clause in residential lease invalid). Should the validity of an exculpatory clause depend upon whether it is in a commercial or a residential lease?

In Cardona v. Eden Realty Co., 118 N.J.Super. 381, 383, 288 A.2d 34, 35 (1972), an exculpatory clause was held invalid notwithstanding that "the landlord recited that it had no public liability insurance and if the tenant desired to eliminate the exculpatory clause, written notice thereof should be given the landlord, in which event the rent would be increased by $2 a month."

18. Can the imposition of tort liability for "slumlordism" more effectively improve the quality of housing in the United States than the implied warranty of habitability can? See Sax & Hiestand, Slumlordism as a Tort, 65 Mich.L.Rev. 869 (1967); Blum & Dunham, Slumlordism as a Tort—A Dissenting View, 66 Mich.L.Rev. 451 (1968); Sax, Slumlordism as a Tort—A Brief Response, 66 Mich.L.Rev. 465 (1968).

19. Many leases contain a "no pets" clause barring tenants from having pets in the apartment. Suppose Landlord leases an apartment to Tenant who in violation of the "no pets" clause has a small dog in her apartment. One day the dog runs out of the apartment and bites the up-stairs tenant's 4–year old son, causing substantial injuries. Does the child have a cause of action against the landlord for damages resulting from his injuries? See, Amyotte v. Rolette County Housing Authority, 658 N.W.2d 324 (N.D. 2003).

20. On July 11, 1987, the New York Times reported that a Los Angeles Municipal Court found a Beverly Hills neurosurgeon guilty of repeatedly violating health and fire-safety codes in the neglected, vermin-infested apartment buildings he owned in the Los Angeles area. The doctor was sentenced to 30 days in jail and to an additional 30 days house arrest in a one-room apartment in one of his buildings. Additionally, the court directed that he would be allowed to supply his own security guard, reading material and a television, and would be allowed to leave the room only to use a bathroom shared by other building residents. The prosecuting attorney, commenting on the court's decision, indicated that if slumlords had to face the possibility of actually having to live under the same conditions as their tenants, they might think twice about letting the condition of their buildings deteriorate so badly.

AN ECONOMIC NOTE ON WARRANTIES IN LEASES

A warranty is nothing more than a mechanism for assigning the risk that a particular unpleasant thing will happen. If a landlord "warrants" that she has title to the property or that the property is free from structural defects, then the landlord has assumed the risk of liability should someone else be found to have title, or the property be found to be defective.

As a general rule, the most efficient way to assign risks is to give them to the party who can either avoid them or bear them at the lowest cost. To illustrate, suppose that a certain event, X, might occur that would damage either L or T, who are the parties to a lease, by $3,000. The likelihood that X will occur is 50% if no preventative measures are taken. In that case the "expected cost" of X (that is, the cost of X, discounted by the probability that it will occur) is $1,500. Suppose, however, that L can prevent the event from occurring at a cost of $100, while T can prevent the event from occurring at a cost of $1,000.

In this situation it makes sense to assign the risk, or liability in case the event should occur, to L. L will spend $100 to prevent the event from occurring, and the "social cost" (the cost to society as a whole) of preventing the event will be $100. On the other hand, if the risk of X's occurrence should be assigned to T, the social cost of preventing X will be $1,000. By assigning the cost to T rather than L social costs increase by $900 (this and the following analysis, of course, avoids the wealth transfer implications that flow from assigning the risk to L who will be out $100 at a savings of $1,000 to T and thus $900 to society as a whole. In other words, assigning the cost to L depletes her wealth by $100 so others may benefit).

Consider this example. Suppose that a title search through the land records, which will establish that L has good title to the leased property, costs $1,000. A title search needs to be done very rarely if the property is not sold— i.e., once L has done a title search she can be reasonably confident throughout the entire period she owns the property that she has a good title. L might own this property for ten years, and have ten different tenants, each of whom stays one year. Under these circumstances the social cost of assigning the risk of a title failure to L is lower than if the risk were assigned to each of the ten tenants. L can do a title search that will give L substantial confidence in the quality of her title for the entire ten year period that L owns the property and rents it to others. However, if each successive tenant had to bear the risk of L's failure of title, each of them will have to search the title himself to make sure that L has good title. This may mean ten title searches instead of one. T–2 will not be able to accept T–1's title search because during the interval L may have done something to the property that adversely affects the title. Only the landlord is in a position to have knowledge about such things without doing a title search. It is much cheaper overall to assign the risk of title failure to the landlord. Thus, the covenant of quiet enjoyment effectively warrants to the tenant that the landlord has good title, and the landlord will be liable to the tenant in the event of a title failure.

While this argument is pretty good, as far as it goes, it does not explain one important thing. Why should the law *imply* a covenant of good title on the part of the landlord? That is, what justifies the legal rule that the landlord warrants good title even though the parties have not explicitly bargained that the landlord would include such a warranty in the lease? As a general rule, when two parties bargain with respect to a particular unwanted occurrence, they will agree to assign the risk to the person who can bear it at the lowest cost. For example, the landlord owning the property for ten years can do a title search at an amortized cost of $100 a year. The tenant, who is only renting the property for one year, will pay $1,000 for title protection for that year. When the parties sit down to bargain over their lease, they should reach a bargain that maximizes their joint wealth. If the tenant agrees to do the title search, that will reduce by $1,000 the maximum rent he is willing to pay to the landlord. The landlord would be much better off collecting that $1,000 from the tenant as rents and doing the title search herself, for only $100 of the costs of the title search will be attributed to the first year's tenancy. The landlord will then be $900 better off, and the tenant will be no worse off. Knowing this, the tenant may bargain to pay only $500 more in rents, rather than $1,000 more; so the parties will end up sharing the savings that accrue when the landlord rather than the tenant does the title search. However, the parties will *not* agree that the tenant should do the title search.

The best explanation of why the covenant of quiet enjoyment is *implied* in leases is that the above description of the bargaining process describes what transpires in a perfectly functioning market. However, markets, like people, are not perfect, and some are less perfect than others. The market for real property is particularly imperfect because each parcel, and therefore each transaction, is quite unique. If it can be shown that it is virtually *always* more efficient for the landlord to bear the risk of loss of title, but that forcing the parties to bargain with respect to this issue will make the bargaining process too complex and costly, then it might make sense to *imply* the covenant of quiet enjoyment. By implying this covenant the parties effectively can forget about it in their contracting process. This might permit the parties to concentrate on the things that are worth bargaining about because the outcomes vary from one lease to another—such as the duration of the lease and the amount of rent to be paid.

With only a little imagination, the preceding arguments can be extended to warranties of habitability in residential leases. As a basic premise it may almost always be more efficient for the landlord to ensure habitability than it is for the tenant. For example, if the landlord fixes the roof, the expense can be amortized over several years and perhaps over a large number of tenants; on the other hand, if the tenant fixes the roof he loses the benefit of the repair as soon as the lease terminates. In the case of warranties of habitability in residential leases there is some reason to believe that imperfections in the market frequently prevent the parties from arriving at efficient solutions. One important problem is that the parties, particularly prospective tenants, are untrained in the bargaining process and may not know what makes an apartment habitable and how to bargain for it. They could hire attorneys to represent them, but in that case the cost of bargaining could rise substantially. There is also a problem of lopsided availability of information. The landlord presumably has better information concerning a building's defects than a tenant does. To be sure, the tenant could hire an engineer to examine the building, but once again, the costs of bargaining would rise. If the meaning of the term "habitable housing" is more or less the same for all tenants—that is, if all of them would seek the same thing when they bargained for their own individual standards of habitability anyway—then it might be far more efficient for the state simply to create such a standard of habitability and imply it in residential leases.

For a number of reasons, however, the same argument does not apply to warranties of tenantability in commercial leases. Principally, the variations among commercial lessees are much greater than they are among residential lessees. For example, it might be easy to conclude that minimum standards of habitability for a residence in the Midwest include a working furnace or heater. However, commercial leases include not only law offices (which presumably need heaters) but also airplane hangars, storage sheds, and warehouses, where heat may not be necessary. It is relatively easy to produce a generalized list of things that constitute "habitability" in a residence; it is virtually impossible to compile a list of factors constituting "tenantability" for commercial leases.

Another problem of commercial leases is that they are often of very long duration and commercial tenants often need buildings modified to suit their own peculiar needs. As a result, it is not at all uncommon for tenants under long-term leases to agree to make their own modifications.

In short, two important elements—uniformity from one tenant to the next and an almost unexceptionable rule that the landlord can comply more cheaply than the tenant—suggest that warranties of habitability should be implied in residential leases. These elements are not necessarily present in commercial leases, where the warranty is best negotiated on an individual basis.

§ 7.7.4 THE IMPLIED WARRANTY OF SUITABILITY

DAVIDOW v. INWOOD NORTH PROFESSIONAL GROUP–PHASE I

Supreme Court of Texas (1988).
747 S.W.2d 373.

SPEARS, JUSTICE.

This case presents the question of whether there is an implied warranty by a commercial landlord that the leased premises are suitable for their intended commercial purpose. Respondent Inwood North Professional Group—Phase I sued petitioner Dr. Joseph Davidow for unpaid rent on medical office space leased by Dr. Davidow. The jury found that Inwood materially breached the lease agreement and that the defects rendered the office space unsuitable for use as a medical office. The trial court rendered judgment that Inwood take nothing and that Dr. Davidow recover damages for lost time and relocation expenses. The court of appeals reversed the trial court judgment and rendered judgment that Inwood recover unpaid rents for the remainder of the lease period and that Dr. Davidow take nothing. . . . We affirm in part and reverse . . . in part.

Dr. Davidow entered into a five-year lease agreement with Inwood for medical office space. The lease required Dr. Davidow to pay Inwood

$793.26 per month as rent. The lease also required Inwood to provide air conditioning, electricity, hot water, janitor and maintenance services, light fixtures, and security services. Shortly after moving into the office space, Dr. Davidow began experiencing problems with the building. The air conditioning did not work properly, often causing temperatures inside the office to rise above eighty-five degrees. The roof leaked whenever it rained, resulting in stained tiles and rotting, mildewed carpet. Patients were directed away from certain areas during rain so that they would not be dripped upon in the waiting room. Pests and rodents often infested the office. The hallways remained dark because hallway lights were unreplaced for months. Cleaning and maintenance were not provided. The parking lot was constantly filled with trash. Hot water was not provided, and on one occasion Dr. Davidow went without electricity for several days because Inwood failed to pay the electric bill. Several burglaries and various acts of vandalism occurred. Dr. Davidow finally moved out of the premises and discontinued rent payments approximately fourteen months before the lease expired.

Inwood sued Dr. Davidow for the unpaid rent and costs of restoration. Dr. Davidow answered by general denial and the affirmative defenses of material breach of the lease agreement, a void lease, and breach of an implied warranty that the premises were suitable for use as a medical office. The jury found that Inwood materially breached the lease, that Inwood warranted to Dr. Davidow that the lease space was suitable for a medical office, and that the lease space was not suitable for a medical office. . . .

With one justice dissenting, the court of appeals reversed the trial court judgment and rendered judgment in favor of Inwood for unpaid rent. The court of appeals held that because Inwood's covenant to maintain and repair the premises was independent of Dr. Davidow's covenant to pay rent, Inwood's breach of its covenant did not justify Dr. Davidow's refusal to pay rent. The court of appeals also held that the implied warranty of habitability does not extend to commercial leaseholds and that Dr. Davidow's pleadings did not support an award of affirmative relief.

Inwood contends that the defense of material breach of the covenant to repair is insufficient as a matter of law to defeat a landlord's claim for unpaid rent. In Texas, the courts have held that the landlord's covenant to repair the premises and the tenant's covenant to pay rent are independent covenants. . . . Thus, a tenant is still under a duty to pay rent even though his landlord has breached his covenant to make repairs. . . .

This theory of independent covenants in leases was established in early property law prior to the development of the concept of mutually dependent covenants in contract law. At common law, the lease was traditionally regarded as a conveyance of an interest in land, subject to the doctrine of caveat emptor. The landlord was required only to deliver the right of possession to the tenant; the tenant, in return, was required to pay rent to the landlord. Once the landlord delivered the right of possession, his part of the agreement was completed. The tenant's duty to pay rent continued as long as he retained possession, even if the buildings on the leasehold were destroyed or became uninhabitable. The landlord's breach of a lease covenant did not relieve the tenant of his duty to pay rent for the remainder of the term because the tenant still retained everything he was entitled to under the lease—the right of possession. All lease covenants were therefore considered independent....

In the past, this court has attempted to provide a more equitable and contemporary solution to landlord-tenant problems by easing the burden placed on tenants as a result of the independence of lease covenants and the doctrine of caveat emptor. See, e.g., Kamarath v. Bennett, 568 S.W.2d 658 (Tex.1978); Humber v. Morton, 426 S.W.2d 554 (Tex.1968). In Kamarath v. Bennett, we reexamined the realities of the landlord-tenant relationship in a modern context and concluded that the agrarian common-law concept is no longer indicative of the contemporary relationship between the tenant and landlord. The land is of minimal importance to the modern tenant; rather, the primary subject of most leases is the structure located on the land and the services which are to be provided to the tenant. The modern residential tenant seeks to lease a dwelling suitable for living purposes. The landlord usually has knowledge of any defects in the premises that may render it uninhabitable. In addition, the landlord, as permanent owner of the premises, should rightfully bear the cost of any necessary repairs. In most instances the landlord is in a much better bargaining position than the tenant. Accordingly, we held in Kamarath that the landlord impliedly warrants that the premises are habitable and fit for living. We further implicitly recognized that the residential tenant's obligation to pay rent is dependent upon the landlord's performance under his warranty of habitability. Kamarath, 568 S.W.2d at 660–61.

When a commercial tenant such as Dr. Davidow leases office space, many of the same considerations are involved. A significant number of commentators have recognized the similarities between residential and commercial tenants and concluded that residential warranties should be expanded to cover commercial property. See, e.g., Chused, Contemporary Dilemmas of the Javins Defense: A Note on the Need for Procedural Reform in Landlord–Tenant Law, 67 Geo.L.J. 1385, 1389 (1979); Greenfield & Margolies, An Implied Warranty of Fitness in Nonresidential Leases, 45 Albany L.Rev. 855 (1981); Levinson & Silver, Do Commercial Property Tenants Possess Warranties of Habitability?, 14 Real Estate L.J. 59 (1985); Note, Landlord–Tenant—Should a Warranty of Fitness be Implied in Commercial Leases?, 13 Rutgers L.J. 91 (1981); see also Restatement (Second) of Property s 5.1 reporter's note at 176 (1977).

It cannot be assumed that a commercial tenant is more knowledgeable about the quality of the structure than a residential tenant. A businessman cannot be expected to possess the expertise necessary to adequately inspect and repair the premises, and many commercial tenants lack the financial resources to hire inspectors and repairmen to assure the suitability of the premises. Note, supra, at 111. Additionally, because commercial tenants often enter into short-term leases, the tenants have limited economic incentive to make any extensive repairs to their premises. Levinson & Silver, supra, at 68. Consequently, commercial tenants generally rely on their landlords' greater abilities to inspect and repair the premises. Id.

In light of the many similarities between residential and commercial tenants and the modern trend towards increased consumer protection, a number of courts have indicated a willingness to apply residential property warranties to commercial tenancy situations.... [citations omitted]

There is no valid reason to imply a warranty of habitability in residential leases and not in commercial leases. Although minor distinctions can be drawn between residential and commercial tenants, those differences do not justify limiting the warranty to residential leaseholds. Therefore, we hold there is an implied warranty of suitability by the landlord in a commercial lease that the premises are suitable for their intended commercial purpose. This warranty means that at the inception of the lease there are no latent defects in the facilities that are vital to the use of the premises for their intended commercial purpose and that these essential facilities will remain in a suitable condition. If, however, the parties to a lease expressly agree that the tenant will repair certain defects, then the provisions of the lease will control.

We recognized in Kamarath that the primary objective underlying a residential leasing arrangement is "to furnish [the tenant] with quarters suitable for living purposes." Kamarath, 568 S.W.2d at 661. The same objective is present in a commercial setting. A commercial tenant desires to lease premises suitable for their intended commercial use. A commercial landlord impliedly represents that the premises are in fact suitable for that use and will remain in a suitable condition. The tenant's obligation to pay rent and the landlord's implied warranty of suitability are therefore mutually dependent.

The existence of a breach of the implied warranty of suitability in commercial leases is usually a fact question to be determined from the particular circumstances of each case. Among the factors to be considered when determining whether there has been a breach of this warranty are: the nature of the defect; its effect on the tenant's use of the premises; the length of time the defect persisted; the age of the structure; the amount of the rent; the area in which the premises are located; whether the tenant waived the defects; and whether the defect resulted from any unusual or abnormal use by the tenant. Kamarath, 568 S.W.2d at 661.

The jury found that Inwood leased the space to Dr. Davidow for use as a medical office and that Inwood knew of the intended use. The evidence and jury findings further indicate that Dr. Davidow was unable to use the space for the intended purpose because acts and omissions by Inwood rendered the space unsuitable for use as a medical office. The jury findings establish that Inwood breached the implied warranty of suitability. Dr.

Davidow was therefore justified in abandoning the premises and discontinuing his rent payments. . . .

NOTES AND QUESTIONS

1. In light of the court's definition of the warranty of suitability, how important is it for a tenant to communicate its intended use to the landlord? How is the warranty affected if the tenant subsequently changes the use of the premises?

2. Assuming it is important to communicate the tenant's intended use to the landlord, how specific must that communication be? For example, Dr. Davidow's needs would vary considerably depending upon whether he was a general practitioner or a radiologist.

3. Do you agree there is little difference between the commercial tenant and the residential tenant, as the court suggests? If not, why not?

4. To what extent is the warranty waivable?

5. L owns an apartment building with commercial space on the first floor. L leases space on the first floor to a store that sells greeting cards and space immediately above on the second floor to a family of four. How do the warranties L owes these tenants differ? How are they the same?

§ 7.8 RETALIATORY EVICTION

ROBINSON v. DIAMOND HOUSING CORPORATION

United States Court of Appeals for the District of Columbia (1972).
463 F.2d 853.

J. SKELLY WRIGHT, CIRCUIT JUDGE:

In Edwards v. Habib, . . . 397 F.2d 687 (1968), cert. denied, 393 U.S. 1016, . . . (1969), this court held that a tenant may assert the retaliatory motivation of his landlord as a defense to an otherwise proper eviction. In Brown v. Southall Realty Co., D.C.App., 237 A.2d 834 (1968), the District of Columbia Court of Appeals held that a lease purporting to convey property burdened with substantial housing code violations was illegal and void and that hence the landlord was not entitled to gain possession for rent due under the invalid lease. . . . The case before us involves the intersection of these two principles. Specifically, it raises the question whether a landlord who has been frustrated in his effort to evict a tenant for nonpayment of rent by successful assertion of a *Southall Realty* defense may automatically accomplish the same goal by serving a 30–day notice to quit.

Appellant argues that she should be permitted to show that her landlord, Diamond Housing, was motivated by a retaliatory intent when it served the notice to quit. Diamond Housing contends that a retaliatory eviction defense has no place in a situation where, as here, the landlord is unable or unwilling to make the repairs on the premises that would entitle it to rent under *Southall Realty* and alleges an intent to take the property off the housing market. When the District of Columbia Court of General Sessions granted summary judgment to appellee, appellant renewed her arguments in the District of Columbia Court of Appeals. That court affirmed, holding:

> "... [T]he retaliatory defense of Edwards v. Habib ... is not available to a tenant in a case such as this where she was successful in a prior Landlord and Tenant action and is being evicted after the expiration of a thirty-day notice because the landlord wishes to withdraw the property from the rental market. The *Edwards* case involved a situation where the landlord attempted to evict the tenant because of her complaints to the housing authorities and it should be, we think, limited to its facts."

Robinson v. Diamond Housing Corp., D.C.App., 267 A.2d 833, 835 (1970).

We can find nothing about the *Edwards* principle which necessitates such a drastic limitation on its applicability. Indeed the prohibition against retaliatory evictions generally, without limitation to the facts of *Edwards,* and in terms applicable to *Southall Realty* rights, has become part of the housing code of the District of Columbia. We see no reason why the rights protected in *Southall Realty* and *Javins* should be rendered nugatory by a restrictive reading of *Edwards* or by a judicial failure to respect the legislative will. We are therefore of the view that appellant should have been given the opportunity to prove the facts necessary to make out an *Edwards* defense and that the trial judge erred in aborting this opportunity by prematurely granting summary judgment. It follows that the decision of the District of Columbia Court of Appeals must be reversed....

The saga begins on May 2, 1968, when Mrs. Robinson and her four children moved into a row house owned by Diamond Housing in Northwest Washington. Mrs. Robinson signed a lease making her a month-to-month tenant with the apparent understanding that the landlord would repair the deteriorating condition of the premises. *See* Diamond Housing Corp. v. Robinson, L & T No. 62391–68, opinion and order of Judge Belson, October 16, 1968, Transcript of Record in DCCA No. 4864 at 6–7. When the landlord failed to keep this promise, Mrs. Robinson began withholding rent, and Diamond Housing sued for possession. Mrs. Robinson defended on the ground that substantial housing violations existed at the time the lease was signed and that the lease was therefore unenforceable under the principles announced in Brown v. Southall Realty Co., *supra.* Specifically, Mrs. Robinson introduced evidence showing that large pieces of plaster were missing throughout the house, that there was no step from the front walk to the front porch, that the front porch was shaky and unsafe, that there was a wall in the back bedroom which was not attached to the ceiling and which moved back and forth when pressed, that nails protruded along the side of the stairway, that there was a pane of glass missing from the living room window, and that the window frame in the kitchen was so far out of position that one could see into the back yard through the space between it and the wall. See Transcript of Record in DCCA No. 4864 at 7–8. At the completion of the trial, the jury returned a special verdict finding that housing code violations existed at the inception of the lease rendering the premises unsafe and unsanitary. Id. at 10–11. The trial court then granted judgment to Mrs. Robinson, as required by *Southall Realty. Id.* at 17.

Unwilling to admit defeat, Diamond Housing instituted a second suit for possession on the theory that, since the lease was void, Mrs. Robinson was a trespasser and hence no longer entitled to possession. When the trial court granted Mrs. Robinson's motion to dismiss, Diamond Housing appealed to the District of Columbia Court of Appeals. That court affirmed, holding that "an agreement entered into in violation of the law creates no rights upon the wrongdoer. The defense of illegality does not rescind the illegal agreement, but merely prevents a party from using the courts to enforce such an agreement." Diamond Housing Corp. v. Robinson, D.C.App., 257 A.2d 492, 495 (1969). (Footnote omitted.) It followed that Mrs. Robinson, "having entered possession under a void and unenforceable lease, was not a trespasser but became a tenant at sufferance." Ibid. The court added, however, that Mrs. Robinson's tenancy, "like any other tenancy at sufferance, may be terminated on thirty days' notice. The Housing Regulations do not compel an owner of housing property to rent his property. Where, as here, it has been determined that the property when rented was not habitable, that is, not safe and sanitary, and should not have been rented, and if the landlord is unwilling or unable to put the property in a habitable condition, he may and should promptly terminate the tenancy and withdraw the property from the rental market, because the Regulations forbid both the rental and the occupancy of such premises." Ibid. (Footnote omitted.)

Seizing upon this dicta, Diamond Housing instituted a third action for possession, this time on the basis of a 30–day notice. In support of its action, Diamond filed an affidavit stating that it was unwilling to make the repairs necessary to put the housing in compliance with the housing code and that it presently intended to take the unit off the rental market. In defense, Mrs. Robinson asserted that she was being evicted in retaliation for successfully asserting her *Southall Realty* rights in the previous actions, and that the eviction was therefore illegal under the principles announced in Edwards v. Habib, *supra*. Mrs. Robinson also argued that the eviction was barred under general equitable principles since Diamond Housing, having allowed its housing to fall into disrepair, lacked the requisite "clean hands."

On this record, Diamond Housing moved for summary judgment. In an oral opinion, Judge Hyde recognized that "there wouldn't be but one way this issue [Diamond's retaliatory motive] could be decided by the jury, because as a matter of fact, I should think that if the landlord is honest at all, he would admit that he's upset, angry, wanted the tenant out of there. . . ."[1] Nonetheless, the court found that "[i]t would seem to be the height of absurdity to permit retaliation, at this juncture, even to be entertained," . . . and granted Diamond's motion.

A panel of this court recently had occasion to observe that there is an "apparently rising incidence of possessory actions based on notices to quit following closely on the heels of possessory actions based on nonpayment of rent." Cooks v. Fowler, 141 U.S.App.D.C. 236, 240, 437 F.2d 669, 673 (1970). This trend is disturbing because, if judicially encouraged, it would vitiate tenants' rights recognized in *Southall Realty* and *Javins* and now protected by statute in the District of Columbia. *See* Regulations §§ 2902.1, 2902.2. . . .

The *Javins* and *Southall Realty* decisions—as well as the District of Columbia regulations patterned after them—were based on the express premise that private remedies for housing code violations would increase the stock of livable low-cost housing in the District. If exercise of those remedies leads instead to eviction of tenants and abandonment of what little low-cost housing remains in the District, the great goal of "a decent home and a suitable living environment for every American family," Section 1 of the Housing Act of 1937, 50 Stat. 888, as amended by the Housing Act of 1949, 63 Stat. 413, will be frustrated. Cf. 84 Harv.L.Rev. 729, 733–734 (1971).

Of course, if the housing market is structured in such a way that it is impossible for landlords to absorb the cost of bringing their units into compliance with the housing code, there may be nothing a court can do to prevent vigorous code enforcement from driving low-cost housing off the market. But the most recent scholarship on the subject indicates this danger is largely imagined. In fact, it appears that vigorous code enforcement plays little or no role in the decrease in low-cost housing stock. When code enforcement is seriously pursued, market forces generally prevent landlords from passing on their increased costs through rent increases. See generally Ackerman, Regulating Slum Housing Markets On Behalf of the Poor: Of Housing Codes, Housing Subsidies and Income Redistribution Policy, 80 Yale L.J. 1093 (1971). The danger stems not from the possibility that landlords might take low-cost units off the market altogether, but rather from the possibility that they will do so selectively in order to "make an example" of a troublesome tenant who has the temerity to assert his legal rights in court. We can be fairly confident that most landlords will find ownership of property sufficiently profitable—even with vigorous code enforcement—to remain in business. But it is undoubtedly true that the same landlords would be able to make a greater profit if the housing code were enforced laxly or not at all. There is thus a real danger that landlords may find it in their interest to

---

1. Even counsel for Diamond seems to have conceded that a jury would find the landlord to have been motivated by retaliatory purposes. At one point in oral argument he stated, "Any jury is going to have to practically say that there is retaliation. Certainly, it's understandable—only human nature, that a person who can't collect the rent is going to try and get them out. That's going to be the basic reason." Transcript of Record in DCCA No. 5194 at 39.

sacrifice the profits derived from operation of a few units in order to intimidate the rest of their tenants.

Fortunately, this is a danger with which the law is better equipped to deal. While the judiciary may be powerless to control landlords who no longer wish to remain landlords, it can prevent landlords from conducting their business in a way that chills the legally protected rights of tenants.... Indeed, this court's decision in Edwards v. Habib, supra, was premised on the belief that retaliatory evictions had a "chilling effect" on assertion of rights protected by the housing code, and that the courts could and should eliminate this inhibition. The *Edwards* court expressly recognized the vital role which private tenants play in the District's system of housing code enforcement, and held that it would violate congressional intent to permit eviction of tenants for the purpose of preventing exercise of private remedies.

It would thus appear, at first blush at least, that the *Edwards* principle should control disposition of this case. Applying this principle Diamond Housing would prevail if it were able to prove to the satisfaction of a jury that it evicted Mrs. Robinson because it could not afford to repair the premises, or for some other valid reason, or for no reason at all. But questions of motivation are particularly inappropriate for resolution on a motion for summary judgment.

* * *

There is also the possibility—indeed, the trial judge viewed it as a near certainty—that the jury would find Mrs. Robinson's eviction to be based on an illicit motive. Given the legal sufficiency of the *Edwards* defense, Mrs. Robinson should have been permitted to make her case if she could, and the factual issue should have been left in the hands of a jury.

This argument assumes, however, that an *Edwards* defense is in fact legally sufficient in this situation. Although the broad principles which underlie *Edwards* would seem squarely applicable, it is possible that something special about this fact pattern would make it unwise or impermissible to utilize *Edwards* here. Diamond Housing takes the position that this case is, in fact, special and that the special circumstances surrounding it make an application of *Edwards* unjust. Diamond's argument begins with the premise—apparently shared by the District of Columbia Court of Appeals—that *Edwards* should be narrowly "limited to its facts." Since *Edwards* involved reporting of code violations to city officials while this case involves setting up those violations as a defense to an action for eviction, it is contended that *Edwards* does not compel reversal here. Moreover, Diamond argues that, even if *Edwards* is more broadly read, it still should not be applied to a case such as this where the landlord is prevented from collecting rent by *Southall Realty,* refuses to repair the premises, and wishes to take the housing off the market altogether. Closely allied to this contention is the further argument that Mrs. Robinson is precluded from remaining in possession by Section 2301 of the Housing Regulations which makes it illegal to occupy premises which are in violation of the Regulations. Finally, Diamond argues that in any event this case is now moot since Mrs. Robinson has voluntarily surrendered possession and Diamond has chosen to forego any claim it might have to back rent.

We have carefully examined each of these arguments and have concluded that none of them sufficiently distinguishes this case from *Edwards* or precludes application of the District of Columbia law against retaliatory evictions. If we resolve all reasonable doubts in favor of appellant—as we must when reviewing a summary judgment, ... it becomes plain that a jury might find Diamond Housing to be using the eviction machinery to punish Mrs. Robinson for exercising her legal rights. *Edwards* squarely holds that the state's judicial processes may not be so used, and nothing which has transpired since *Edwards* was decided has caused us to change our view. Indeed, if anything, the creation by the District of Columbia City Council of new private remedies for code violations since *Edwards* reinforces our belief in the necessity for a broad retaliatory eviction defense. If the housing code were effectuated solely by a system of comprehensive public enforcement, the situation might perhaps be different. But by legislating a system of private remedies conforming to the *Javins* and *Southall Realty* decisions, the City Council has made plain that the code is to be enforced in large part through the actions of private tenants. Having put at least some of its eggs in the private enforcement basket, the legislature should not at the same time be taken as having authorized use of legal processes by those who seek to frustrate private enforcement. The right to a decent home is far too vital for us to assume that government has taken away with one hand what it purports to grant with the other.

* * *

It must nonetheless be conceded that implementing the legislative will in this fact situation leads to some difficulties and ambiguities. For example, Diamond Housing argues that permitting a retaliatory eviction defense here may mean that it will never be able to recover possession of its property. Nonreceipt of rent is a continuing injury, Diamond argues, and it will always want to remove the tenant so as to remove the source of injury. Yet ironically, so long as it is motivated by this goal, the *Edwards* defense will prevent achievement of it. Thus Diamond fears that its shotgun marriage to Mrs. Robinson may last till death do them part.

Moreover, Diamond points out, it is not trying to evict Mrs. Robinson so that it may rent the premises to someone else. It does not want a quickie divorce in order to permit a hasty remarriage. Rather, if freed from Mrs. Robinson, Diamond promises to beat a strategic retreat to a monastery where it will go and sin no more. Thus Diamond says that it intends to take the unit off the market altogether when Mrs. Robinson leaves—the very thing which this court has suggested a landlord do when he is unwilling or unable to repair the premises. See Whetzel v. Jess

Fisher Management Co., 108 U.S.App.D.C. 385, 392, 282 F.2d 943, 950 (1960). There is nothing in the Housing Regulations which prevents it from going out of business, Diamond argues. Whatever limitations the law imposes on how it chooses its tenants, Diamond claims an absolute right to choose not to have any tenants.

In order to clarify these and other ambiguities inherent in the *Edwards* defense, attorneys for Mrs. Robinson have suggested that we formulate comprehensive guidelines for the circumstances under which a landlord may evict his tenants when the premises contain unremedied housing code violations. Cf. American Bar Foundation, Model Residential Landlord–Tenant Code § 2–407 (tent. draft 1969). We respectfully decline this invitation. We do so primarily because we think the *Edwards* rule, as supplemented by District law, is largely self-explanatory and its ramifications are best elucidated on a case-by-case basis. We are also motivated, however, by the fear, generated in part by this case, that any such guidelines would become the basis for mechanical legal decisions by judges, whereas we believe the matter is best left to the sound discretion of juries under proper instructions. Whether the landlord's action is retaliatory is, after all, a question of fact, see Edwards v. Habib, supra, 130 U.S.App.D.C. at 141, 397 F.2d at 702, and we would not be justified in taking it away from the jury merely because it is "hard." Cf. United States v. Leazer, 148 U.S.App.D.C. 356, 361, 460 F.2d 864, 869 (1972) (Chief Judge Bazelon, concurring). As the Supreme Court has made plain, "Trial by affidavit is no substitute for trial by jury which so long has been the hallmark of 'even handed justice.' " Poller v. Columbia Broadcasting System, Inc., supra, 368 U.S. at 473, 82 S.Ct. at 491. This is especially true where, as here, the matter for decision involves a complex of moral and empirical judgments best left in the hands of representatives of the community as a whole. Cf. United States v. Bennett, 148 U.S.App.D.C. 364, 368, 460 F.2d 872, 876 (1972).

But while we are unwilling to write comprehensive guidelines for application of the *Edwards* defense, we do feel it may be useful to clarify some of the confusion which has evidently surrounded it. These clarifications should, in turn, be incorporated into appropriate instructions which the trial judge should give to the jury when it considers the underlying factual question. First, then, it should be noted that the *Edwards* defense deals with the landlord's subjective state of mind—that is, with his motive. If the landlord's actions are motivated by a desire to punish the tenant for exercising his rights or to chill the exercise of similar rights by other tenants, then they are impermissible.

It is commonplace, however, that a jury can judge a landlord's state of mind only by examining its objective manifestations.... Thus when the landlord's conduct is "inherently destructive" of tenants' rights, or unavoidably chills their exercise, the jury may, under well recognized principles, presume that the landlord intended this result.... An unexplained eviction following successful assertion of a *Javins* or *Southall Realty* defense falls within this inherently destructive category and hence gives rise to the presumption. Once the presumption is established, it is then up to the landlord to rebut it by demonstrating that he is motivated by some legitimate business purpose rather than by the illicit motive which would otherwise be presumed.... We wish to emphasize, however, that the landlord's desire to remove a tenant who is not paying rent is not such a legitimate purpose. *Southall Realty* and the housing code guarantee the right of a tenant to remain in possession without paying rent when the premises are burdened with substantial housing code violations making them unsafe and unsanitary. The landlord of such premises who evicts his tenant because he will not pay rent is in effect evicting him for asserting his legal right to refuse to pay rent. This, of course, is the very sort of reason which, according to *Edwards* and the housing code, will not support an eviction.

Thus Diamond Housing is correct when it asserts it will never be able to evict Mrs. Robinson so long as it is motivated by a desire to rid itself of a tenant who is not paying rent. But it does not follow that Diamond will be burdened by its unwanted tenant forever. If Diamond comes forward with a legitimate business justification—other than the mere desire to get rid of a tenant exercising *Southall Realty* rights—it may be able to convince a jury that it is motivated by this proper concern. For example, if Diamond brought the premises up to housing code standards so that rent was again due and then evicted the tenant for some unrelated, lawful reason, the eviction would be permissible. Similarly, if Diamond were to make a convincing showing that it was for some reason impossible or unfeasible to make repairs, it would have a legitimate reason for evicting the tenant and taking the unit off the market.[2]

It does not follow, however, that mere desire to take the unit off the market is by itself a legitimate business reason which will justify an eviction. Expression of such a desire begs the further question of why the landlord wishes to remove the unit. If he wishes to remove the unit for some sound business reason, then of course he is free to do so. But such a removal, following a tenant's *Southall Realty* defense, is as inherently destructive of tenants' rights as an ordinary eviction. Therefore, a landlord who fails to come forward with a substantial business reason for removing a unit from the market—such as, for example, his financial inability to make the necessary repairs[3] may be presumed to have done so for an illicit reason.[4]

* * *

---

2. We do not mean to suggest, however, that it would be permissible for Diamond to make a showing that it is unable to repair the premises and then evict Mrs. Robinson in order to rent to another tenant. Such a course of action is perhaps the most destructive of tenants' rights of all, since it can be explained only in terms of a desire to punish the complaining tenant. It would be permissible, however, for Diamond to force Mrs. Robinson to vacate on a temporary basis if it could show that repair of the premises was not feasible while she remained in possession.

3. We do not mean to suggest that this is the only legitimate business reason for taking a unit off the market. The legitimacy of other reasons can be decided as they are asserted on a case-by-case basis.

4. The same principles, of course, apply to retaliatory sale of the premises if the sale is intended to lead to ultimate eviction of the tenant.

It should be plain from the above discussion that the landlord's assertion that he wishes to remove the property from the market, even when coupled with the assertion that he is unwilling to remedy housing code violations, is legally insufficient to justify summary judgment over a *Southall Realty* defense. Indeed, the offer to take the unit off the market is totally irrelevant to the issue of motive unless it is accompanied by the further declaration that the landlord is unable to correct housing code violations which preclude his receipt of rent. But while inability to repair *is* a legitimate business reason which would justify removing the unit from the market, even this allegation is not sufficient to justify summary judgment. . . .

Thus the landlord's mere allegation that he is removing the unit from the market because he cannot afford to make repairs does not mean that the jury will find that he is *in fact* unable to make the necessary repairs. Moreover, even if the jury makes such a finding, it still does not follow that judgment for the landlord is compelled. We must remember that we are dealing with a question of subjective motive, and that objective factors are relevant only as indicia of motive. Thus the mere existence of a legitimate reason for the landlord's actions will not help him if the jury finds that he was in fact motivated by some illegitimate reason. . . . In cases of mixed motives, the jury will have the difficult task of weighing one against the other and determining which was the causative factor. . . . None of this is to say that the landlord may not go out of business entirely if he wishes to do so or that the jury is authorized to inspect his motives if he chooses to commit economic harakiri. There would be severe constitutional problems with a rule of law which required an entrepreneur to remain in business against his will. . . .

* * *

We do not pretend that allowing Mrs. Robinson to assert an *Edwards* defense will solve the housing crisis in the District of Columbia. That crisis is the product of a constellation of social and economic forces over which no court—and indeed perhaps no legislature—can exercise full control. But while the judicial process is not a *deus ex machina* which can magically solve problems where the legislature and the executive have failed, neither is it a mere game of wits to be played without regard for the well-being of the helpless spectators. We cannot expect judges to solve the housing dilemma, but at least they should avoid affirmative action which makes it worse. The District's legislative body has formulated a comprehensive plan, including criminal sanctions, public inspections, subsidies and rent withholding, to tackle our housing difficulties. In the end, that plan may not work. But if it fails, at least the failure should be caused by inherent weaknesses rather than by judicial subversion.

Thus all we hold today is that when the legislature creates a broad based scheme for dealing with a problem in the public interest, courts should not permit private, selfishly motivated litigants to undermine it. This result is required by the clear wording of the applicable statute, by the dictates of legislatively declared social policy, and, in the final analysis, by respect for the separation of powers and the rule of law.

Reversed and remanded with instructions.

ROBB, CIRCUIT JUDGE (dissenting):

* * *

The majority suggests that its decision will promote the development of more and better low-cost housing. This reasoning passes my understanding. In my judgment the majority's Draconian treatment of landlords will inevitably discourage investment in housing for rental purposes.

I dissent. I would affirm the judgment of the District of Columbia Court of Appeals.

NOTES AND QUESTIONS

1. Traditionally landlords have been free to refuse to renew a lease at the end of the fixed term or to terminate a periodic tenancy for any reason. The law as it developed was loath to interfere with the landlord's right to control who would be the landlord's tenant. The retaliatory eviction doctrine represents a significant curtailment of the landlord's right. What policies support the doctrine?

2. To whom should the retaliatory eviction defense be available? Should it be available only to residential tenants? See William C. Cornitius, Inc. v. Wheeler, 276 Or. 747, 556 P.2d 666 (1976); Rossow Oil Co. v. Heiman, 72 Wis.2d 696, 242 N.W.2d 176 (1976). Is the defense available to a tenant residing in a luxury high rise along Chicago's North Michigan Avenue? May a commercial tenant claim retaliatory eviction? Ontell v. Capitol Hill E.W. Ltd., 527 A.2d 1292 (D.C..1987).

3. Should a tenant who has vacated property following a landlord's retaliatory act be able to sue the landlord for damages? In Murphy v. Smallridge, 196 W.Va. 35, 468 S.E.2d 167 (1996), the court held that tenants could sue their landlord for damages resulting from his retaliation against them for their complaints about his garbage dumping even though the tenants had vacated the premises. In holding that retaliatory eviction can be an affirmative cause of action as well as a defense to an action for possession, the court, consistent with its prior law, required that the retaliation be for an act of the tenant that was an incident of the tenancy. How should damages be calculated?

4. Suppose T, a month-to-month tenant in a mobile home park, encourages other residents of the park to organize a "union" to bargain with L for changes in the rules and regulations governing the tenants in the park. L serves a thirty-day notice of termination on T because of these activities. Can T treat the notice as invalid because of L's retaliatory motive? If L sues to evict T, can T defend on the basis of her First Amendment free speech guarantees under the Federal Constitution? See Seidelman v. Kouvavus, 57 Ill.App.3d 350, 14 Ill.Dec. 922, 373 N.E.2d 53 (1978).

5.   Typical of the statutes incorporating the retaliatory eviction defense in Section 5.101 of URLTA. It provides:

(a) Except as provided in this section, a landlord may not retaliate by increasing rent or decreasing services or by bringing or threatening to bring an action for possession after:

(1) the tenant has complained to a governmental agency charged with responsibility for enforcement of a building or housing code of a violation applicable to the premises materially affecting health and safety; or

(2) the tenant has complained to the landlord of a violation under Section 2.104 [relating the landlord's obligation to maintain the premises]; or,

(3) the tenant has organized or become a member of a tenant's union or similar organization.

* * *

(c) Notwithstanding ... [the foregoing], a landlord may bring an action for possession if:

(1) the violation of the applicable building or housing code was caused primarily by lack of reasonable care by the tenant, a member of his family, or other person on the premises with his consent; or

(2) the tenant is in default in rent; or

(3) compliance with the applicable building or housing code requires alteration, remodeling, or demolition which would effectively deprive the tenant of use of the dwelling unit.

Section 5.101(a) begins by proscribing certain landlord conduct: the landlord is forbidden to increase rent, reduce services or evict or threaten to evict a tenant for engaging in certain conduct. One key feature common to some statutes is a provision forbidding the landlord from refusing to renew a lease. This provision is important to tenants with terms of years whose terms would likely be renewed but for the landlord's retaliatory motive. In some state statutes the language is not as specific as URLTA's language. Rather, the statute includes a catchall phrase that bans a landlord's attempt to alter the terms of the lease or increase the tenant's obligations. See Mass.Gen.Laws Ann. ch. 186 § 18 (Michie 1981).

In Helfrich v. Valdez Motel Corp., 207 P.3d 552 (Alaska 2009), tenant claimed that landlord's eviction of tenant was in retaliation for the tenant bringing a tort action against landlord when tenant slipped and fell on the landlord's premises. Because a tort action for a slip and fall is not an action seeking to vindicate rights under the state residential landlord tenant act, the act's anti-retaliation provision is inapplicable.

6.   URLTA protects the tenant's right to make complaints to governmental authorities responsible for housing code enforcement relating to health and safety violations as well as complaints to the landlord for the landlord's failure to perform its maintenance obligations under the statute. This scheme is fairly typical of most state statutes. But see R.I. Gen.Laws § 34–20–10

(1984) (broadening the protection afforded to tenants). Because of the basic theory used by most courts to rationalize the adoption of the implied warranty of habitability (i.e., the public policy of encouraging habitable housing), most states that have only a judicially created retaliatory eviction defense limit it to activities concerned with improving the habitability of rented dwellings. See, e.g., Dickhut v. Norton, 45 Wis.2d 389, 173 N.W.2d 297 (1970). Some states have been more liberal in determining what tenant activities are protected. See, e.g., S.P. Growers Ass'n v. Rodriguez, 17 Cal.3d 719, 131 Cal.Rptr. 761, 552 P.2d 721 (1976).

Suppose the tenant complains to the police that the landlord is using a portion of the premises for illegal purposes. If following that complaint the landlord terminates the tenant's periodic tenancy, can the tenant raise the defense of retaliation? See Barela v. Superior Court, 30 Cal.3d 244, 178 Cal.Rptr. 618, 636 P.2d 582 (1981).

7. Two of the perplexing problems facing courts that have adopted the defense of retaliatory eviction are (1) establishing standards indicating that a retaliatory motive has dissipated and (2) determining who bears the burden of proof on this question. URLTA § 5.101(b) attempts to resolve these issues by providing that

[i]n an action by or against the tenant, evidence of a complaint within [1] year before the alleged act of retaliation creates a presumption that the landlord's conduct was in retaliation. The presumption does not arise if the tenant made the complaint after notice of a proposed rent increase or diminution of services. "Presumption" means that the trier of fact must find the existence of the fact presumed unless and until evidence is introduced which would support a finding of its nonexistence.

See also Wash.Rev.Code Ann. § 59.18.250 (Supp.1985) (incorporating 90 day period); Ariz.Rev.Stat.Ann. § 33–1381(B) (1974) (six months period).

Should the tenant be protected from a retaliatory eviction only for "good faith" complaints to the housing authorities? If not, how can the landlord be protected against the tenant who reports minor Housing Code infractions to the housing authorities knowing the authorities will "harass" the landlord? Should the landlord be protected against the tenant who reports housing code violations to the authorities immediately before the end of the term or immediately after the tenant hears rumors the landlord intends to increase rents or not renew a lease?

8. In many cases the landlord's reasons for seeking to evict the tenant or terminate a periodic tenancy may be varied and only one of them may be the desire to retaliate. What weight should be given to the fact that a retaliatory motive is only one of the reasons the landlord desires to evict the tenant? The courts that have judicially recognized the retaliatory eviction defense have developed three distinct tests. See Comment, California's Common Law Defense Against Landlord's Retaliatory Conduct, 22 U.C.L.A. L.Rev. 1161 (1975). The first of these, and the most restrictive, is the test adopted in Wisconsin where the court held that in order for the eviction to be retaliatory and thus improper, it must be shown that the landlord's retaliatory motive was his *sole* motive for evicting the tenant. See Dickhut v. Norton, 45 Wis.2d 389, 173 N.W.2d 297 (1970). Other jurisdictions, such as the District of

Columbia, have taken a more liberal approach. For example, in the principal case retaliation need only be a causative factor. See also Windward Partners v. Delos Santos, 59 Haw. 104, 577 P.2d 326 (1978) (retaliation must be a primary motive). An even more liberal approach is the independent motivation test which establishes an improper retaliatory eviction when the tenant is evicted at least partly in retaliation, even if the primary purpose of the eviction was the tenant's failure to pay rent or some other legitimate reason. See Parkin v. Fitzgerald, 307 Minn. 423, 240 N.W.2d 828 (1976). URLTA takes what might be called a middle approach. See URLTA § 5.101(b). What are the relevant advantages and disadvantages of each approach?

9.   L owns two apartment buildings. Building A is a high rise luxury apartment house that has been profitable for L. The other is an uninhabitable building known as Building B. The tenants in Building B stopped paying rent after successfully asserting a *Brown* illegality defense in L's prior action to evict them for non-payment of rent. Nine months have passed since L sought to evict them. L now seeks to terminate their periodic tenancies, but their attorney claims that L's retaliatory motive has not been dissipated as evidenced by the fact that L has not repaired Building B even though by taking account of the profits from Building A, L can financially afford to make the repairs. How do you respond to this argument? Suppose Building A was owned by the Building A Corporation and Building B by the Building B Corporation, and L was the sole shareholder and President of each corporation. Same result?

10.   In *Robinson,* Judge Wright assumes that the cost of bringing the premises up to Code will be borne by the landlord who would be unable to pass these costs along to the tenants as increased rents. Since he does not question the propriety of that assumption, we can only assume he believes that is an appropriate social policy. Do you?

11.   What economic assumptions underlie the decision in *Robinson*? The court relies on the economic analysis reflected in Ackerman, Regulating Slum Housing Markets On Behalf of the Poor: Of Housing Codes, Housing Subsidies and Income Redistribution Policy, 80 Yale L.J. 1093 (1971). Among other things, Professor Ackerman argued (1) that landlords charge excessive rents and (2) as a result of that they could easily afford to bear the cost of bringing rental housing up to Code. The following excerpts, one responding to Professor Ackerman's study and the other written much earlier, call Professor Ackerman's conclusions into question.

CUNNINGHAM, THE NEW IMPLIED AND STATUTORY WARRANTIES OF HABITABILITY IN RESIDENTIAL LEASES: FROM CONTRACT TO STATUS

16 Urban L.Ann. 3, 138–153 (1979).

VI.   Conclusion: The Consequences of Recognizing the Residential Tenant's Right to a Habitable Dwelling

A.   Theories as to the Economic Consequences

It is obvious that effective enforcement of the new right of the residential tenant to a habitable dwelling (through exercise of the new tenant remedies) will subject landlords to increased costs for maintenance and operation, taxes, insurance, and litigation. Depending on supply and demand conditions in the rental housing market, landlords may either absorb the increased costs and operate at a lower profit, pass on the increased costs (or part of them) in the form of higher rents, or abandon their rental properties. Legislators and courts generally have failed to consider the possibility that landlords may adopt one or both of the latter options, in response to enforcement of the new tenant's right to a habitable dwelling, thus harming the very class of persons primarily sought to be protected by legislatures and courts—low-income tenants. One of the few cases in which this possibility is mentioned is Robinson v. Diamond Housing Corp., where Judge Skelly Wright said:

> [I]f the housing market is structured in such a way that it is impossible for landlords to absorb the cost of bringing their units into compliance with the [housing] code, there may be nothing a court can do to prevent vigorous housing code enforcement from driving low cost housing off the market. But the most recent scholarship on the subject indicates this danger is largely imagined. In fact, it appears that vigorous code enforcement plays little or no role in the decrease in low cost housing stock. When code enforcement is seriously pursued, market forces generally prevent landlords from passing on their increased costs through rent increases.

Unfortunately, the article cited by Judge Wright was entirely theoretical, lacking any empirical basis. Although the article did not explicitly consider the economic impact of widespread assertion of the new tenant's right to a habitable dwelling, Professor Ackerman's theoretical analysis of the economic consequences of effective housing code enforcement is clearly relevant to the issue here under consideration. For present purposes, Professor Ackerman's principal conclusions with respect to the economic effects of housing code enforcement can be summarized as follows:[5]

---

5. This summary is adapted from Komesar, *Return to Slumville: A Critique of the Ackerman Analysis of Housing Code Enforcement and the Poor*, 82 Yale L.J. 1175, 1177 (1973)[hereinafter cited as Komesar]. Professor Ackerman's article at 80 Yale L.J. 1093 (1971) deals, of course, with a great many other issues in addition to the impact of strict housing code enforcement on the cost and supply of low-income housing. Ackerman is primarily concerned with the relationship between housing codes, housing subsidies, and income redistribution policy. Professor Ackerman does, however, offer the following comment on private tenant remedies near the end of his article:

> [L]ocalized rent-withholding actions cannot be expected to be terribly successful in vindicating the "decent home" interest if they simply induce the isolated target landlord to improve his building. For in the medium run—if not the short run—the landlord will succeed in increasing his rent substantially as the residents of the surrounding slum find the improved apartments more desirable. Consequently, whatever virtue rent strikes may have in giving the poor a sense of self-respect, they will frequently be rather ineffective income redistribution devices. The same may be said for even more drastic remedies, like receiverships and the suggestion that slum-lordism be made a tort. If, however, rent withholding and similar actions are more than sporadic and isolated affairs, their value as a redistributive device holds greater promise.... [I]f tenant organizations can achieve broad effectiveness throughout a particular Slumville, a properly drawn rent withholding statute may provide a mechanism by which tenant organizations may themselves take on the task of enforcing the code on a wide ranging basis. And, as we have shown, comprehensive code enforcement permits a significant possibility of substantial income redistribution in a wide range of situations.

Id. at 1095–96.

* If the supply of slum housing units is fixed and unresponsive to increased costs of production, and the demand is responsive to changes in rent, the increased costs imposed on landlords by effective code enforcement will not be passed on to tenants in the form of increased rent;

* The additional costs imposed on landlords by effective code enforcement will have little effect on investment in either low-income housing or housing in general, and therefore no substantial decrease in the supply of low-income rental housing will occur; and

* Improved housing will not cause any substantial immigration of tenants into an area, and hence it is unlikely that rents will increase because of increased demand for improved housing.

Professor Ackerman's conclusions have been severely criticized by Professors Komesar,[6] Posner,[7] Hirsch et al.,[8] and Abbott.[9] Professor Komesar attacks Ackerman's seemingly unrealistic assumptions that the supply of low-income housing is fixed and unresponsive to increased costs of production and that the demand is responsive to changes in rent. Professor Posner concludes that effective housing code enforcement would in fact result in higher rents and a decrease in the housing supply for low-income tenants, and that assertion of the new tenant remedies for breach of a statutory or implied warranty would tend to produce these results.[10] As Posner points out, in the absence of government subsidies all costs that result from housing code enforcement must come either out of "the rentals paid by tenants or the rent of the land obtained by the landlords."[11] Posner further concludes, without citing any empirical evidence, that "tenants forced to pay higher rentals to cover the cost of compliance ... will be made worse off."[12]

6. Komesar, id.

7. R. Posner, Economic Analysis of Law 259–63 (1972) [hereinafter cited as R. Posner; Posner offers an updated discussion at pp. 504–507 (7th ed. 2007)—eds.].

8. Hirsch, Hirsch & Margolis, *Regression Analysis of the Effects of Habitability Laws Upon Rent: An Empirical Observation on the Ackerman–Komesar Debate,* 63 Calif.L.Rev. 1098 (1975) [hereinafter cited as *Regression Analysis*].

9. Abbott, *Housing Policy, Housing Codes and Tenant Remedies: An Integration,* 56 B.U.L.Rev. 1, 108–11 (1976).

10. R. Posner, supra.

11. Id. at 260.

Economic rent is an especially unpromising source of the funds necessary to comply with the housing code, because the use of land for slum housing generally does not generate substantial rent. In New York and Chicago, where the abandonment of slum dwellings by their owners has become a common phenomenon, the value of much land in slum areas, and hence its rent, must be at or near zero. Even if the land itself has some value, the rent from using it for slum housing may be zero, depending on the other uses to which the land might be put.... In any case, the result of housing code enforcement is quite likely to be a reduction in the stock of housing available to the poor, albeit the housing that is available will be of higher quality than before.

Id.

12. Id. at 260. However, Posner subsequently says more cautiously:

There is no assurance that the poor will be on balance better off. Furthermore, the renters in this case who bear a part of the cost of compliance are likely to include a number of almost-poor people for whom ownership of slum property represents a first step in the escape from poverty.

Id. at 260–61.

Hirsch et al. assert that Ackerman's conclusions can be questioned on the ground that his abstract model may depart too far from reality, and that while his assumption of a perfectly inelastic supply of housing may be appropriate in the very short-run, it is contradicted both by empirical evidence and by theories as to the supply of low-income housing advanced by other economists. They further conclude, on the basis of an application of supply and demand concepts to the analysis of the effect of habitability laws, that except under the most unlikely circumstances, housing costs must increase if a law is enforced so as to impose additional costs on landlords; if tenants feel that they derive no benefit from the law, price increases will be less than the additional costs imposed on landlords, and if tenants place some positive value on the law, price increases will be larger—perhaps large enough to offset completely the additional costs associated with provision of the new, higher quality of housing. Hirsch et al. also recognize that even though tenants are forced to pay higher rents because of habitability laws this fact does not necessarily mean that tenants are worse off since the benefits received by tenants by virtue of such laws may exceed the rent increases. The authors suggest, however, that "habitability laws are unlikely to effect a redistribution of wealth in favor of indigent tenants."

Professor Abbott is critical of Ackerman's analysis because he doubts that the conditions postulated for income redistribution from the landlord class to the generally poorer tenant class by means of effective housing code enforcement are likely to occur in any real-world housing market. Abbott's analysis of the probable effect of strict code enforcement distinguishes between several different types of residential neighborhoods: (1) sound neighborhoods with stable or rising property values; (2) deteriorated neighborhoods with rising property values; (3) sound neighborhoods with declining property values; and (4) deteriorated neighborhoods with stable or declining property values. He also deals with the problem on the alternative assumptions that the low-income housing market structure is competitive and monopolistic. His ultimate conclusion is that, "whatever it achieves, housing code enforcement is costly to the low income housing consumer who is most likely to occupy units generating substantial code compliance costs" because "[h]e is forced either to pay increased rents or to consume less housing, resulting in overcrowding"; and further, that "[e]ven when part or all of the cost is absorbed by the owner, the result may be withdrawal of units from the market, causing dislocation costs, increased crowding and higher prices for those consumers who remain."

NOTES AND QUESTIONS

1. Professor Meyers [The Covenant of Habitability and the American Law Institute, 27 Stan.L.Rev. 879 (1975)] has addressed the problem of the economic impact of the implied warranty of habitability on the welfare of low-income tenants. His conclusions are generally similar to those of Professor

Abbott. Meyers distinguishes four categories of housing (rather than neighborhood types) that may be affected by the implied warranty: (1) dwellings which substantially comply with the housing code and hence will be relatively unaffected by the implied warranty; (2) dwellings which do not comply with the housing code and are considered unsuitable for residential use but which can be brought up to code standards by additional investment that can be recovered through higher rents; (3) dwellings which do not comply with the housing code and are considered unsuitable for residential use but which can be brought up to code standards by an expenditure that will reduce the landlord's rate of return (because rents cannot be raised enough to cover repair costs) but will not eliminate a positive return on "sunk capital"; and (4) dwellings which do not comply with the housing code and are considered unsuitable for residential use, for which the costs of repair to meet code standards (together with other expenses) will result in a negative return on "sunk capital." Professor Meyers' conclusions, briefly stated, are as follows: Housing in category-two will be brought into compliance with the implied warranty, with the result that tenants will either have to pay higher rents or move elsewhere. Low-income tenants in category-three housing will be benefited by the implied warranty in the short-run, for as long as the landlord recovers from rents all his out-of-pocket costs (including the cost of repairs plus interest on his investment in repairs) he is likely to make the repairs, at least while he has some equity in the property. But in the long-run the quantity of category-three housing will decrease because the operating costs associated with increased building age will take their toll faster than normal and the housing will be forced into a deficit position and removed from the market prematurely; and no new category-three property will be built since, while present owners need only cover their operating costs, potential owners must be able to cover their initial capital costs. Category-four housing will be withdrawn from the rental market, and low-income tenants as a class will be injured.[13]

2. Judges Posner and Easterbrook (formerly Professors Posner and Easterbrook) strongly argue that legislation designed to facially strengthen the rights of tenants against landlords ultimately will result in increased rents and better housing for the middle class. In Chicago Board of Realtors, Inc. v. City of Chicago, 819 F.2d 732 (7th Cir. 1987), they voted to uphold a Chicago Residential Landlord and Tenant Ordinance even though seriously questioning its economic wisdom.

> The new ordinance rewrites present and future leases of apartments in Chicago to give tenants more legal rights than they would have without the ordinance. It requires the payment of interest on security deposits; requires that those deposits be held in Illinois banks; allows (with some limitations) a tenant to withhold rent in an amount reflecting the cost to him of the landlord's violating a term in the lease; allows a tenant to

---

13. Since no one knows how the nation's substandard housing stock is divided among categories two, three and four, one can summarize even more concisely as follows: some proportion of the substandard rental housing stock would be upgraded and rents would be raised to cover the added costs; some proportion would be upgraded even though rents could not be raised, since landlords could still upgrade it without incurring a deficit; and some portion would be abandoned as soon as the owner determines that income will not cover the expenses of required repairs and concludes that this deficit is likely to persist. Id. at 893.

make minor repairs and subtract the reasonable cost of the repair from his rent; forbids a landlord to charge a tenant more than $10 a month for late payment of rent (regardless of how much is owing); and creates a presumption (albeit rebuttable) that a landlord who seeks to evict a tenant after the tenant has exercised rights conferred by the ordinance is retaliating against the tenant for the exercise of those rights.

The stated purpose of the ordinance is to promote public health, safety, and welfare and the quality of housing in Chicago. It is unlikely that this is the real purpose, and it is not the likely effect. Forbidding landlords to charge interest at market rates on late payment of rent could hardly be thought calculated to improve the health, safety, and welfare of Chicagoans or to improve the quality of the housing stock. But it may have the opposite effect. The initial consequence of the rule will be to reduce the resources that landlords devote to improving the quality of housing, by making the provision of rental housing more costly. Landlords will try to offset the higher cost (in time value of money, less predictable cash flow, and, probably, higher rate of default) by raising rents. To the extent they succeed, tenants will be worse off, or at least no better off. Landlords will also screen applicants more carefully, because the cost of renting to a deadbeat will now be higher; so marginal tenants will find it harder to persuade landlords to rent to them. Those who do find apartments but then are slow to pay will be subsidized by responsible tenants (some of them marginal too), who will be paying higher rents, assuming the landlord cannot determine in advance who is likely to pay rent on time. Insofar as these efforts to offset the ordinance fail, the cost of rental housing will be higher to landlords and therefore less will be supplied—more of the existing stock than would otherwise be the case will be converted to condominia and cooperatives and less rental housing will be built.

The provisions of the ordinance requiring that interest on security deposits be paid and that those deposits be kept in Illinois banks are as remote as the provision on late payment from any concern with the health or safety of Chicagoans, the quality of housing in Chicago, or the welfare of Chicago as a whole. Their only apparent rationale is to transfer wealth from landlords and out-of-state banks to tenants and local banks—making this an unedifying example of class legislation and economic protectionism rolled into one. However, to the extent the ordinance seeks to transfer wealth from landlords to tenants it could readily be undone by a rent increase; the ordinance puts no cap on rents. Cf. Coase, The Problem of Social Cost, 3 J. Law & Econ. 1 (1960).

The provisions that authorize rent withholding, whether directly or by subtracting repair costs, may seem more closely related to the stated objectives of the ordinance; but the relation is tenuous. The right to withhold rent is not limited to cases of hazardous or unhealthy conditions. And any benefits in safer or healthier housing from exercise of the right are likely to be offset by the higher costs to landlords, resulting in higher rents and less rental housing.

The ordinance is not in the interest of poor people. As is frequently the case with legislation ostensibly designed to promote the welfare of the poor, the principal beneficiaries will be middle-class people. They will be people who buy rather than rent housing (the conversion of rental to owner housing will reduce the price of the latter by increasing its supply); people willing to pay a higher rental for better-quality housing; and (a largely overlapping group) more affluent tenants, who will become more attractive to landlords because such tenants are less likely to be late with the rent or to abuse the right of withholding rent—a right that is more attractive, the poorer the tenant. The losers from the ordinance will be some landlords, some out-of-state banks, the poorest class of tenants, and future tenants. . . .

A growing body of empirical literature deals with the effects of governmental regulation of the market for rental housing. The regulations that have been studied, such as rent control in New York City and Los Angeles, are not identical to the new Chicago ordinance, though some—regulations which require that rental housing be "habitable"—are close. The significance of this literature is not in proving that the Chicago ordinance is unsound, but in showing that the market for rental housing behaves as economic theory predicts: if price is artificially depressed, or the costs of landlords artificially increased, supply falls and many tenants, usually the poorer and the newer tenants, are hurt. See, e.g., Olsen, An Econometric Analysis of Rent Control, 80 J.Pol.Econ. 1081 (1972); Rydell et al., The Impact of Rent Control on the Los Angeles Housing Market, ch. 6 (Rand Corp. N–1747–LA, Aug. 1981); Hirsch, Habitability Laws and the Welfare of Indigent Tenants, 61 Rev.Econ. & Stat. 263 (1981). The single proposition in economics from which there is the least dissent among American economists is that "a ceiling on rents reduces the quantity and quality of housing available." Frey et al., Consensus and Dissension Among Economists: An Empirical Inquiry, 74 Am.Econ.Rev. 986, 991 (1984) (tab. 2).

Id. at 741–42.

§ 7.9 TRANSFERS OF A LEASEHOLD INTEREST

JABER v. MILLER

Supreme Court of Arkansas (1951).
219 Ark. 59, 239 S.W.2d 760.

GEORGE ROSE SMITH, JUSTICE.

This is a suit brought by Miller to obtain cancellation of fourteen promissory notes, each in the sum of $175, held by the appellant, Jaber. The plaintiff's theory is that these notes represent monthly rent upon a certain business building in Fort Smith for the period beginning January 1, 1950, and ending March 1, 1951. The building was destroyed by fire on December 3, 1949, and the plaintiff contends that his obligation to pay rent then terminated. The defendant contends that the notes were given not for rent but as deferred payments for the assignment of a lease formerly held by Jaber. The chancellor, in an opinion reflecting a careful study of the matter, concluded that the notes were intended to be rental payments and therefore should be canceled.

In 1945 Jaber rented the building from its owner for a five-year term beginning March 1, 1946, and ending March 1, 1951. The lease reserved a monthly rent of $200 and provided that the lease would terminate if the premises were destroyed by fire. Jaber ... transferred the lease to Norber & Son. Whether this instrument of transfer is an assignment or a sublease is the pivotal issue in this case.

In form the document is an assignment rather than a sublease. It is entitled "Contract and Assignment." After reciting the existence of the five-year lease the instrument provides that Jaber "hereby transfers and assigns" to Norber & Son "the aforesaid lease contract ... for the remainder of the term of said lease." It also provides that "in consideration of the sale and assignment of said lease contract" Norber & Son have paid Jaber $700 in cash and have executed five promissory notes for $700 each, due serially at specified four-month intervals. Norber & Son agree to pay to the owner of the property the stipulated rental of $200 a month, and Jaber reserves the right to retake possession if Norber & Son fail to pay the rent or the notes. The instrument contains no provision governing the rights of the parties in case the building is destroyed by fire.

Later on the plaintiff, Miller, obtained a transfer of the lease from Norber & Son. Miller, being unable to pay the $700 notes as they came due, arranged with Jaber to divide the payments into monthly installments of $175 each. He and the Norbers accordingly executed the notes now in controversy, which Jaber accepted in substitution for those of the original notes that were still unpaid. When the premises burned Miller contended that Jaber's transfer to Norber & Son had been a sublease rather than an assignment and that the notes therefore represented rent. Miller now argues that, under the rule that a sublease terminates when the primary lease terminates, his sublease ended when the fire had the effect of terminating the original lease.

In most jurisdictions the question of whether an instrument is an assignment or a sublease is determined by principles applicable to feudal tenures. In a line of cases beginning in the year 1371 the English courts worked out the rules for distinguishing between an assignment and a sublease. See Ferrier, "Can There be a Sublease for the Entire Term?", 18 Calif.L.Rev. 1. The doctrine established in England is quite simple: If the instrument purports to transfer the lessee's estate for the entire remainder of the term it is an assignment, regardless of its form or of the parties' intention. Conversely, if the instrument purports to transfer the lessee's estate for less than the entire term—even for a day less—it is a sublease, regardless of its form or of the parties' intention.

The arbitrary distinction drawn at common law is manifestly at variance with the usual conception of assignments and subleases. We think of an assignment as the outright transfer of all or part of an existing lease, the assignee stepping into the shoes of the assignor. A sublease, on the other hand, involves the creation of a new tenancy between the sublessor and the sublessee, so that the sublessor is both a tenant and a landlord. The common law distinction is logical only in the light of feudal property law.

In feudal times every one except the king held land by tenure from some one higher in the hierarchy of feudal ownership. "The king himself holds land which is in every sense his own; no one else has any proprietary right in it; but if we leave out of account this royal demesne, then every acre of land is 'held of' the king. The person whom we may call its owner, the person who has the right to use and abuse the land, to cultivate it or leave it uncultivated, to keep all others off it, holds the land of the king either immediately or mediately. In the simplest case he holds it immediately of the king; only the king and he have rights in it. But it well may happen that between him and the king there stand other persons; Z holds immediately of Y, who holds of X, who holds of V, who holds . . . of A, who holds of the king." Pollock and Maitland, History of English Law (2d Ed.), vol. I, p. 232. In feudal law each person owed duties, such as that of military service or the payment of rent, to his overlord. To enforce these duties the overlord had the remedy of distress, being the seizure of chattels found on the land.

It is evident that in feudal theory a person must himself have an estate in the land in order to maintain his place in the structure of ownership. Hence if a tenant transferred his entire term he parted with his interest in the property. The English courts therefore held that the transferee of the entire term held of the original lessor, that such a transferee was bound by the covenants in the original lease, and that he was entitled to enforce whatever duties that lease imposed upon the landlord. The intention of the parties had nothing to do with the matter; the sole question was whether the first lessee retained a reversion that enabled him to hold his place in the chain of ownership.

The injustice of these inflexible rules has often been pointed out. Suppose that A makes a lease to B for a certain rental. B then executes to C what both parties intend to be a sublease as that term is generally understood, but the sublease is for the entire term. If C in good faith pays his rent to B, as the contract requires, he does so at his peril. For the courts say that the contract is really an assignment, and therefore C's primary obligation is to A if the latter elects to accept C as his tenant. Consequently A can collect the rent from the subtenant even though the sublessor has already been paid. For a fuller discussion of this possibility of double liability on the part of the subtenant see Darling. "Is a Sublease for the Residue of a Lessee's Term in Effect an Assignment?", 16 Amer. L.Rev. 16, 21.

Not only may the common law rule operate with injustice to the subtenant; it can be equally harsh upon the sublessor. Again suppose that

A makes a lease to *B* for a certain rental. *B* then makes to *C* what *B* considers a profitable sublease for twice the original rent. But *B* makes the mistake of attempting to sublet for the entire term instead of retaining a reversion of a day. The instrument is therefore an assignment, and if the original landlord acquires the subtenant's rights there is a merger which prevents *B* from being able to collect the increased rent. That was the situation in Webb v. Russell, 3 T.R. 393, 100 Eng.Reprint 639. The court felt compelled to recognize the merger, but in doing so Lord Kenyon said: "It seems to me, with all the inclination which we have to support the action (and we have hitherto delayed giving judgment in the hopes of being able to find some ground on which the plaintiff's demand might be sustained), that it cannot be supported. The defence which is made is made of a most unrighteous and unconscious nature; but unfortunately for the plaintiff the mode which she has taken to enforce her demand cannot be supported." Kent, in his Commentaries (14th Ed.), p. 105, refers to this case as reaching an "inequitable result"; Williams and Eastwood, in their work on Real Property, p. 206, call it an "unpleasant result." Yet when the identical question arose in California the court felt bound to hold that the same distasteful merger had taken place. Smiley v. Van Winkle, 6 Cal. 605.

A decided majority of the American courts have adopted the English doctrine in its entirety. Tiffany, Landlord & Tenant, § 151. A minority of our courts have made timid but praiseworthy attempts to soften the harshness of the common law rule. In several jurisdictions the courts follow the intention of the parties in controversies between the sublessor and the sublessee, thus preserving the inequities of feudal times only when the original landlord is concerned. . . .

In other jurisdictions the courts have gone as far as possible to find something that might be said to constitute a reversion in what the parties intended to be a sublease. In some States, notably Massachusetts, it has been held that if the sublessor reserves a right of re-entry for nonpayment of rent this is a sufficient reversionary estate to make the instrument a sublease. . . . But even these decisions have been criticized on the ground that at common law a right of re-entry was a mere chose in action instead of a reversionary estate. See, for example, Tiffany, supra, § 151.

The appellee urges us to follow the Massachusetts rule and to hold that since Jaber reserved rights of re-entry his transfer to Norber & Son was a sublease. We are not in sympathy with this view . . .

In Arkansas the distinction between a sublease and an assignment has been considered in only one case, and then in such circumstances that the litigants were in agreement as to the law. In Pennsylvania Min. Co. v. Bailey, 110 Ark. 287, 161 S.W. 200, the transcript in this court at first contained an instrument purporting to transfer possession for only ten years out of a term of about eighteen years. The appellant accordingly argued that the instrument was a sublease under the orthodox common law rule. The appellee then had the transcript amended to show that the original lessee had later executed an instrument purporting to transfer the entire remaining term. In view of this amendment to the transcript the appellee merely adopted the appellant's argument as to the distinction between an assignment and a sublease. It was therefore to be expected that the court would announce the traditional view, since both parties were urging that position. In one other case, Crump v. Tolbert, 210 Ark. 920, 198 S.W.2d 518, we adverted by dictum to the customary distinction between the two instruments.

In this state of the law we do not feel compelled to adhere to an unjust rule which was logical only in the days of feudalism. The execution of leases is a very practical matter that occurs a hundred times a day without legal assistance. The layman appreciates the common sense distinction between a sublease and an assignment, but he would not even suspect the existence of the common law distinction. As Darling, supra, puts it: "Every one knows that a tenant may in turn let to others, and the latter thereby assumes no obligations to the owner of the property; but who would guess that this could only be done for a time falling short by something—a day or an hour is sufficient—of the whole term? And who, not familiar with the subject of feudal tenures, could give a reason why it is held to be so?" It was of such a situation that Holmes was thinking when he said: "It is revolting to have no better reason for a rule than that so it was laid down in the time of Henry IV. It is still more revolting if the grounds upon which it was laid down have vanished long since, and the rule simply persists from blind imitation of the past." The Path of the Law, 10 Harv.L.Rev. 457, 469. The rule now in question was laid down some years before the reign of Henry IV.

The English distinction between an assignment and a sublease is not a rule of property in the sense that titles or property rights depend upon its continued existence. A lawyer trained in common law technicalities can prepare either instrument without fear that it will be construed to be the other. But for the less skilled lawyer or for the layman the common law rule is simply a trap that leads to hardship and injustice by refusing to permit the parties to accomplish the result they seek.

For these reasons we adopt as the rule in this State the principle that the intention of the parties is to govern in determining whether an instrument is an assignment or a sublease. If, for example, a tenant has leased an apartment for a year and is compelled to move to another city, we know of no reason why he should not be able to sublease it for a higher rent without needlessly retaining a reversion for the last day of the term. The duration of the primary term, as compared to the length of the sublease, may in some instances be a factor in arriving at the parties' intention, but we do not think it should be the sole consideration. The Bailey case, to the extent that it is contrary to this opinion is overruled.

In the case at bar it cannot be doubted that the parties intended an assignment and not a sublease. The document is so entitled. All its language is that of an assignment rather than that of a sublease. The consideration is stated to be in payment for the lease and not in satisfaction of a tenant's debt to his landlord. The deferred payments are evidenced by promissory notes, which are not ordinarily given by one making a lease. From the appellee's point of view it is unfortunate that the assignment makes no provision for the contingency of a fire, but the appellant's position is certainly not without equity. Jaber sold his merchandise at public auction, and doubtless at reduced prices, in order to vacate the premises for his assignees. Whether he would have taken the same course had the contract provided for a cancellation of the deferred payments in case of a fire we have no way of knowing. A decision either way works a hardship on the losing party. In this situation we do not feel called upon to supply a provision in the assignment which might have been, but was not, demanded by the assignees.

Reversed.

NOTES AND QUESTIONS

1. Most of the litigation surrounding assignment and sublet concerns commercial leases, probably because most residential leases are either month-to-month or for a term of year of 1–2 years.

2. As noted in the *Jaber* case, there are two distinct approaches to resolving the issue of whether a transfer of a leasehold interest is an assignment or a sublease. The common law's formalistic rule treated any transfer of a leasehold interest as a sublease if the transferor (called the "sublessor" under the sublease and "lessee" under the main lease) retained a reversionary interest that would become possessory in the future, even if the duration of the reversionary interest was only one day. See Walgreen Arizona Drug Co. v. Plaza Center Corp., 132 Ariz. 512, 647 P.2d 643 (App.1982). By contrast, if the transferor (called the "assignor") transferred the entire balance of the term to the transferee (called the "assignee"), the transfer was characterized as an assignment.

The alternative to the formalistic approach is best exemplified in the *Jaber* case. This alternative prefers to characterize the transfer as an assignment or sublease in accordance with the intentions of the parties. Does the *Jaber* approach mean that the transferor's intent controls the characterization of the transfer as an assignment or sublease?

3. How does the transferor's retention of a right of entry affect the characterization of a transfer of a leasehold as either an assignment or sublet? Is a retained right of entry the equivalent of a reversion such that the transferor is deemed to have made a sublet or is the retention of such right merely evidence of the intent of the parties? The courts are split on these questions. Compare Spears v. Canon de Carnue Land Grant, 80 N.M. 766, 461 P.2d 415 (1969) with Danaj v. Anest, 77 Ill.App.3d 533, 33 Ill.Dec. 19, 396 N.E.2d 95 (1979).

Restatement (Second) of Property § 15.1 comment i (1977) provides that:

> [t]he tenant may transfer his entire interest under the lease, usually referred to as an assignment of his lease ... If the tenant makes a

transfer of the leased property for less than the balance of the term, he has made a sublease of the leased property. The tenant has made a sublease, even though the transfer is initially for the balance of the term, if the right to possession of the leased property may return to him upon the occurrence of some event.

Does the Restatement follow the common law formalistic test or the intent test?

4. A lease prohibition against assignment or sublet is a restraint on alienation. Unlike restraints on the alienation of a fee simple, however, they are upheld. Why? Although valid, restraints on the alienation of leaseholds are strictly construed. Thus, if the lease only prohibits an assignment the tenant is free to sublet the premises; if the lease only prohibits a sublet the tenant is free to assign the premises. How can the landlord easily overcome these rules?

5. Can a prohibition against an assignment or sublet of a leasehold be implied? See Restatement (Second) of Property § 15.1 comment c (1977).

6. The characterization of a transfer of a leasehold interest as an assignment or sublet can affect the enforceability of lease covenants among the lessor, the transferor, and the transferee of the leasehold interests. Lease covenants are either real covenants or personal covenants, a distinction which is considered in greater detail in chapter eight. A real covenant is enforceable against the lessee as well as subsequent transferees with whom the lessor is in privity of estate. On the other hand, personal covenants can be enforced only against the original parties to the contract and subsequent persons who promise to be bound by the terms of the contract. These persons are said to be in privity of contract. Two important real covenants are the tenant's covenant to pay rent and the landlord's or tenant's covenant to make repairs on the leased premises.

7. At the creation of the leasehold estate between landlord and tenant, the parties are in both privity of contract and privity of estate. Privity of contract arises by virtue of the lease agreement, which is a form of contract. The parties also are in privity of estate because they both have an estate in the same land and the landlord's right to possession succeeds immediately to the tenant's possession. If the tenant assigns the leasehold interest to T–2, privity of estate now exists between the landlord and T–2 because at the termination of T–2's estate the possession of the property will revert to the landlord. Privity of estate no longer exists between the landlord and the original tenant. Because the assignment of the leasehold interest does not in and of itself effect a termination of the lease agreement, the landlord and the original tenant continue to be in privity of contract. Consider the following:

(a) Suppose L leases Blackacre to T who assigns her leasehold to T–2. If T–2 fails to pay L rent, can L sue T–2 and, if so, on what theory? See Bloor v. Chase Manhattan Mortgage & Realty Trust, 511 F.Supp. 17 (S.D.N.Y.1981). Can L sue T and, if so, on what theory? See, Price v. S.S. Fuller, Inc., 639 P.2d 1003 (Alaska 1982). What might T do in order to avoid being liable to L in the event T–2 defaults in the payment of rent? If L sues T and wins, can T recover from T–2 the rents T paid L? See Prospect Realty, Inc. v. Bishop, 33 Conn.Supp. 622, 365 A.2d 638 (1976); Crowley v. Gormley, 59 A.D. 256, 69 N.Y.S. 576 (2d Dept.1901).

(b) Suppose T–2 assigns the lease to T–3 who then fails to pay rent. Can L sue T–3 for the unpaid rents? Can L sue T–2? See Bloor v. Chase Manhattan Mortgage & Realty Trust, 511 F.Supp. 17 (S.D.N.Y.1981). But see Stark v. American National Bank, 100 S.W.2d 208 (Tex.Civ.App. 1936). Can L sue and collect rents for the same rental period from both T–2 and T–3?

(c) If L breached its duty to make repairs, can either T–2 or T–3 sue L for specific performance or damages? Can T sue?

(d) If T promises to repair the leased property and thereafter assigns the lease to T–1, does T–2 assume the obligation to repair merely by reason of the assignment?

8. An assignee may establish privity of contract between herself and the landlord by expressly assuming the terms of the lease. Hollywood Shopping Plaza, Inc. v. Schuyler, 179 So.2d 573 (Fla.Dist.Ct.App.1965). What are the implications to the assignee if she assumes the lease terms and thereafter assigns the premises to another assignee who later defaults in the payment of rent? See Stevenson v. Allen, 94 Ga.App. 123, 93 S.E.2d 794 (1956).

9. When does privity of estate begin? There are two possible times. It can arise when the right to possession begins or when the tenant takes actual possession. Compare Williams v. Safe Deposit & Trust Co., 167 Md. 499, 175 A. 331 (1934) with Gillette Brothers v. Aristocrat Restaurant, 239 N.Y. 87, 145 N.E. 748 (1924). Does it make a difference?

10. If L leases property to T who thereafter sublets his interest to S, a landlord tenant relationship arises between T and S. Since at the termination of S's interest possession of the property will revert to T, S and T are in privity of estate. See Reed v. South Shore Foods, Inc., 229 Cal.App.2d 705, 40 Cal.Rptr. 575 (1964). They are also in privity of contract. Furthermore, since the sublet does not terminate the lease agreement between L and T and when T's interest terminates possession of the property will revert to L, both L and T remain in privity of estate and privity of contract notwithstanding the sublet. Many courts continue to follow the common-law rule that no privity of estate or contract exists between L and S. See Mac Enterprises, Inc. v. Del E. Webb Dev. Co., 132 Ariz. 331, 645 P.2d 1245 (App.1982).

(a) L leases Blackacre to T who sublets Blackacre to S. S fails to pay rent to either L or T. Can L sue T for the unpaid rents and, if so, under what theory? Can L sue S for the unpaid rents and, if so, under what theory? See Rittenberg v. Donohoe Construction Co., 426 A.2d 338 (D.C.1981). But see Ky.Rev.Stat. § 383.180(2) (1972). Suppose S had promised T to pay the rents to L. If S fails to pay L rent, can T sue S? Can L sue S? See Manges v. Willoughby, 505 S.W.2d 379 (Tex.Civ.App.1974).

(b) L leases Blackacre to T for $400 a month. T subleases Blackacre to S for $500 a month. Is L or T entitled to the additional rent of $100 a month? Suppose S pays T the promised rent but T fails to pay L. Can L sue S for possession? See International Industries, Inc. v. United Mortgage Co., 96 Nev. 150, 606 P.2d 163 (1980). What rights does S have against T? See, e.g., USA Petroleum Corp. v. Jopat Building Corp., 343 So.2d 501 (Ala.1977).

11. L leases Blackacre to T for a term of five years. At the time the leasehold interest commences Blackacre is habitable. Two years later T assigns the lease to T–1 for the balance of the term. At that time the premises are uninhabitable because of damage to Blackacre caused by T. If L sues T–1 for possession for T–1's failure to pay rent, can T–1 defend on the basis of the implied warranty of habitability? Suppose the premises become uninhabitable after the assignment and through no cause of T. Same result? Would the results change if T sublet Blackacre to T–1? Suppose the lease prohibited T from assigning or subletting Blackacre without L's consent and L consented to the assignment or sublet, as the case may be. What result?

12. Upon the creation of a leasehold estate the tenant acquires a non-freehold estate and the landlord retains a reversion. Reversions are alienable, devisable, and descendible. If the landlord transfers its reversion to another, the transferee of the reversion comes into privity of estate with the tenant and privity of estate between the transferor and the tenant ceases. On the other hand, privity of contract continues to exist between the transferor and the tenant and between the transferee of the reversion and the tenant, provided that the transferee agrees to be bound by the terms of the lease.

KENDALL v. ERNEST PESTANA, INC.

Supreme Court of California (1985).
40 Cal.3d 488, 220 Cal.Rptr. 818, 709 P.2d 837.

BROUSSARD, JUSTICE.

This case concerns the effect of a provision in a commercial lease[1] that the lessee may not assign the lease or sublet the premises without the lessor's prior written consent. The question we address is whether, in the absence of a provision that such consent will not be unreasonably withheld, a lessor may unreasonably and arbitrarily withhold his or her consent to an assignment.[2] This is a question of first impression in this court.

I.

... The lease at issue is for 14,400 square feet of hangar space at the San Jose Municipal Airport. The City of San Jose, as owner of the property, leased it to Irving and Janice Perlitch, who in turn assigned their interest to respondent Ernest Pestana, Inc. . . . Prior to assigning their interest to respondent, the Perlitches entered into a 25–year sublease with one Robert Bixler commencing on January 1, 1970. The sublease covered an original five-year term plus four 5–year options to renew. The rental rate was to be increased every 10 years in the same

---

1. We are presented only with a commercial lease and therefore do not address the question whether residential leases are controlled by the principles articulated in this opinion.

2. Since the present case involves an assignment rather than a sublease, we will speak primarily in terms of assignments. However, our holding applies equally to subleases. The difference between an assignment and a sublease is that an assignment transfers the lessee's entire interest in the property whereas a sublease transfers only a portion of that interest, with the original lessee retaining a right of reentry at some point during the unexpired term of the lease. . . .

proportion as rents increased on the master lease from the City of San Jose. The premises were to be used by Bixler for the purpose of conducting an airplane maintenance business.

Bixler conducted such a business under the name "Flight Services" until, in 1981, he agreed to sell the business to appellants Jack Kendall, Grady O'Hara and Vicki O'Hara. The proposed sale included the business and the equipment, inventory and improvements on the property, together with the existing lease. The proposed assignees had a stronger financial statement and greater net worth than the current lessee, Bixler, and they were willing to be bound by the terms of the lease.

The lease provided that written consent of the lessor was required before the lessee could assign his interest, and that failure to obtain such consent rendered the lease voidable at the option of the lessor.[3] Accordingly, Bixler requested consent from the Perlitches' successor-in-interest, respondent Ernest Pestana, Inc. Respondent refused to consent to the assignment and maintained that it had an absolute right arbitrarily to refuse any such request. The complaint recites that respondent demanded "increased rent and other more onerous terms" as a condition of consenting to Bixler's transfer of interest. . . .

II.

The law generally favors free alienability of property, and California follows the common law rule that a leasehold interest is freely alienable. . . . Contractual restrictions on the alienability of leasehold interests are, however, permitted. . . . "Such restrictions are justified as reasonable protection of the interests of the lessor as to who shall possess and manage property in which he has a reversionary interest and from which he is deriving income." (Schoshinski, American Law of Landlord and Tenant (1980) § 8:15, at pp. 578–579. See also 2 Powell on Real Property, ¶ 246[1], at p. 372.97.)

The common law's hostility toward restraints on alienation has caused such restraints on leasehold interests to be strictly construed against the lessor. (See Schoshinski, supra, § 8.16, at pp. 583–588; 2 Powell, supra, ¶ 246[1], at pp. 372.97, 372.100). . . .

Nevertheless, a majority of jurisdictions have long adhered to the rule that where a lease contains an approval clause (a clause stating that the lease cannot be assigned without the prior consent of the lessor), the lessor may arbitrarily refuse to approve a proposed assignee no matter

---

3. Paragraph 13 of the sublease between the Perlitches and Bixler provides: "Lessee shall not assign this lease, or any interest therein, and shall not sublet the said premises or any part thereof, or any right or privilege appurtenant thereto, or suffer any other person (the agents and servants of Lessee excepted) to occupy or use said premises, or any portion thereof, without written consent of Lessor first had and obtained, and a consent to one assignment, subletting, occupation or use by any other person, shall not be deemed to be a consent to any subsequent assignment, subletting, occupation or use by another person. Any such assignment or subletting without this consent shall be void, and shall, at the option of Lessor, terminate this lease. This lease shall not, nor shall any interest therein, be assignable, as to the interest of lessee, by operation of a law [sic], without the written consent of Lessor."

how suitable the assignee appears to be and no matter how unreasonable the lessor's objection.... The harsh consequences of this rule have often been avoided through application of the doctrines of waiver and estoppel, under which the lessor may be found to have waived (or be estopped from asserting) the right to refuse consent to assignment....

The traditional majority rule has come under steady attack in recent years. A growing minority of jurisdictions now hold that where a lease provides for assignment only with the prior consent of the lessor, such consent may be withheld only where the lessor has a commercially reasonable objection to the assignment, even in the absence of a provision in the lease stating that consent to assignment will not be unreasonably withheld....[4]

For the reasons discussed below, we conclude that the minority rule is the preferable position....

The impetus for change in the majority rule has come from two directions, reflecting the dual nature of a lease as a conveyance of a leasehold interest and a contract.... The policy against restraints on alienation pertains to leases in their nature as conveyances. Numerous courts and commentators have recognized that "[i]n recent times the necessity of permitting reasonable alienation of commercial space has become paramount in our increasingly urban society." (Schweiso v. Williams, supra, 150 Cal.App.3d at p. 887, 198 Cal.Rptr. 238....)

Civil Code section 711 provides: "Conditions restraining alienation, when repugnant to the interest created, are void." It is well settled that this rule is not absolute in its application, but forbids only unreasonable restraints on alienation.... Reasonableness is determined by comparing the justification for a particular restraint on alienation with the quantum of restraint actually imposed by it....

One commentator explains as follows: "The common-law hostility to restraints on alienation had a large exception with respect to estates for years. A lessor could prohibit the lessee from transferring the estate for years to whatever extent he might desire. It was believed that the objectives served by allowing such restraints outweighed the social evils implicit in the restraints, in that they gave to the lessor a needed control over the person entrusted with the lessor's property and to whom he must look for the performance of the covenants contained in the lease. Whether this reasoning retains full validity can well be doubted. Relationships between lessor and lessee have tended to become more and more imper-

---

4. The minority rule has also been espoused in jurisdictions where there appears to be conflicting or uncertain authority. North Carolina: See Sanders v. Tropicana (1976) 31 N.C.App. 276, 229 S.E.2d 304 [minority rule]; L & H Inv., Ltd. v. Belvey Corp. (W.D.N.C.1978) 444 F.Supp. 1321, 1325 [minority rule, applying North Carolina law]; but see Isbey v. Crews (1981) 55 N.C.App. 47, 284 S.E.2d 534 [majority rule]. Louisiana: Gamble v. New Orleans Housing Mart, Inc. (La.App.1963) 154 So.2d 625 [minority rule]; Associates Comm. Corp. v. Bayou Management Inc. (La.App.1982) 426 So.2d 672 [minority rule]; but see Illinois Central Gulf R. Co. v. Int'l Harvester Co. (La.1979) 368 So.2d 1009, 1014–1015 [majority rule]. Massachusetts: Granite Trust Bldg. Corp. v. Great A. & P. Tea Co. (D.Mass.1940) 36 F.Supp. 77 [minority rule, applying Massachusetts law; dicta].

sonal. Courts have considerably lessened the effectiveness of restraint clauses by strict construction and liberal applications of the doctrine of waiver. With the shortage of housing and, in many places, of commercial space as well, the allowance of lease clauses forbidding assignments and subleases is beginning to be curtailed by statutes." (2 Powell, supra, ¶ 246[1], at pp. 372.97–372.98, fns. omitted.)[5]

The Restatement Second of Property adopts the minority rule on the validity of approval clauses in leases: "A restraint on alienation without the consent of the landlord of a tenant's interest in leased property is valid, but the landlord's consent to an alienation by the tenant cannot be withheld unreasonably, unless a freely negotiated provision in the lease gives the landlord an absolute right to withhold consent." (Rest.2d Property, § 15.2(2) (1977), ...)[6] A comment to the section explains: "The landlord may have an understandable concern about certain personal qualities of a tenant, particularly his reputation for meeting his financial obligations. The preservation of the values that go into the personal selection of the tenant justifies upholding a provision in the lease that curtails the right of the tenant to put anyone else in his place by transferring his interest, but this justification does not go to the point of allowing the landlord arbitrarily and without reason to refuse to allow the tenant to transfer an interest in leased property." (Id., com. a.) Under the Restatement rule, the lessor's interest in the character of his or her tenant is protected by the lessor's right to object to a proposed assignee on reasonable commercial grounds. (See id., reporter's note 7 at pp. 112–113.) The lessor's interests are also protected by the fact that the original lessee remains liable to the lessor as a surety even if the lessor consents to the assignment and the assignee expressly assumes the obligations of the lease. . . .

The second impetus for change in the majority rule comes from the nature of a lease as a contract. As the Court of Appeal observed in Cohen v. Ratinoff, supra, "[s]ince Richard v. Degan & Brody, Inc. [espousing the majority rule] was decided, . . . there has been an increased recognition of and emphasis on the duty of good faith and fair dealing inherent in every contract." (Id., 147 Cal.App.3d at p. 329, 195 Cal.Rptr. 84.) Thus, "[i]n every contract there is an implied covenant that neither party shall do anything which will have the effect of destroying or injuring the right of the other party to receive the fruits of the contract. . . ." (Universal Sales Corp. v. Cal. etc. Mfg. Co. (1942) 20 Cal.2d 751, 771, 128 P.2d 665. See also Bleecher v. Conte (1981) 29 Cal.3d 345, 350, 173 Cal.Rptr. 278, 626

---

5. Statutes have been enacted in at least four states prohibiting lessors from arbitrarily refusing consent to the assignment of leases. Alaska Stat., § 34.03.060 (1975) [residential leases only]; Del.Code Ann., tit. 25, § 5512, subd. (b) (1974) [residential, commercial and farm leases]; Hawaii Rev.Stat., § 516–63 [residential leases only]; N.Y.Real Prop.Law § 226–b (McKinney 1982) [residential leases only].

This rule has also been adopted by a number of jurisdictions as a matter of common law. (See ante, pp. 822–823 of 220 Cal.Rptr., pp. 842–843 of 709 P.2d.)

6. This case does not present the question of the validity of a clause absolutely prohibiting assignment, or granting absolute discretion over assignment to the lessor. We note that under the Restatement rule such a provision would be valid if freely negotiated.

P.2d 1051.) "[W]here a contract confers on one party a discretionary power affecting the rights of the other, a duty is imposed to exercise that discretion in good faith and in accordance with fair dealing." (Cal. Lettuce Growers v. Union Sugar Co. (1955) 45 Cal.2d 474, 484, 289 P.2d 785. See also Larwin–Southern California, Inc. v. J.G.B. Inv. Co. (1979) 101 Cal. App.3d 626, 640, 162 Cal.Rptr. 52.) Here the lessor retains the discretionary power to approve or disapprove an assignee proposed by the other party to the contract; this discretionary power should therefore be exercised in accordance with commercially reasonable standards. "Where a lessee is entitled to sublet under common law, but has agreed to limit that right by first acquiring the consent of the landlord, we believe the lessee has a right to expect that consent will not be unreasonably withheld." (Fernandez v. Vazquez, supra, 397 So.2d at p. 1174; accord, Boss Barbara, Inc. v. Newbill, supra, 638 P.2d at p. 1086.)[7]

Under the minority rule, the determination whether a lessor's refusal to consent was reasonable is a question of fact. Some of the factors that the trier of fact may properly consider in applying the standards of good faith and commercial reasonableness are: financial responsibility of the proposed assignee; suitability of the use for the particular property; legality of the proposed use; need for alteration of the premises; and nature of the occupancy, i.e., office, factory, clinic, etc. . . .

Denying consent solely on the basis of personal taste, convenience or sensibility is not commercially reasonable. . . . Nor is it reasonable to deny consent "in order that the landlord may charge a higher rent than originally contracted for." (Schweiso v. Williams, supra, 150 Cal.App.3d at p. 886, 198 Cal.Rptr. 238. . . .) This is because the lessor's desire for a better bargain than contracted for has nothing to do with the permissible purposes of the restraint on alienation—to protect the lessor's interest in the preservation of the property and the performance of the lease covenants. " '[T]he clause is for the protection of the landlord in its ownership and operation of the particular property—not for its general economic protection.' " (Ringwood Associates v. Jack's of Route 23, Inc., . . . [153 N.J. Super. 294, 379 A.2d 508 (1977)] quoting Krieger v. Helmsley–Spear, Inc. (1973) 62 N.J. 423, 302 A.2d 129, ...)

In contrast to the policy reasons advanced in favor of the minority rule, the majority rule has traditionally been justified on three grounds. Respondent raises a fourth argument in its favor as well. None of these do we find compelling.

First, it is said that a lease is a conveyance of an interest in real property, and that the lessor, having exercised a personal choice in the selection of a tenant and provided that no substitute shall be acceptable

---

7. Some commentators have drawn an analogy between this situation and the duties of good faith and reasonableness implied in all transactions under the Uniform Commercial Code. (U.Com.Code §§ 1–203, 2–103(b); see also U.Com.Code § 1–102, com. 1 [permitting application of the U.Com.Code to matters not expressly within its scope]. See Comment, The Approval Clause in a Lease: Toward a Standard of Reasonableness, supra, 17 U.S.F.L.Rev. 681, 695; see also Levin, Withholding Consent to Assignment: The Changing Rights of the Commercial Landlord (1980) 30 De Paul L.Rev. 109, 136.)

without prior consent, is under no obligation to look to anyone but the lessee for the rent. (Gruman v. Investors Diversified Services, ... 247 Minn. 502, 78 N.W.2d 377, 380; see also Funk v. Funk, ... 102 Idaho 521, 633 P.2d 586, 591 (Bakes, C.J., dis.).) This argument is based on traditional rules of conveyancing and on concepts of freedom of ownership and control over one's property....

A lessor's freedom at common law to look to no one but the lessee for the rent has, however, been undermined by the adoption in California of a rule that lessors—like all other contracting parties—have a duty to mitigate damages upon the lessee's abandonment of the property by seeking a substitute lessee. (See Civ.Code, § 1951.2.) Furthermore, the values that go into the personal selection of a lessee are preserved under the minority rule in the lessor's right to refuse consent to assignment on any commercially reasonable grounds. Such grounds include not only the obvious objections to an assignee's financial stability or proposed use of the premises, but a variety of other commercially reasonable objections as well. (See, e.g., Arrington v. Walter E. Heller Int'l Corp. (1975) 30 Ill.App.3d 631, 333 N.E.2d 50 [desire to have only one "lead tenant" in order to preserve "image of the building" as tenant's international headquarters]; Warmack v. Merchants Nat'l Bank of Fort Smith (Ark.1981) 612 S.W.2d 733 [desire for good "tenant mix" in shopping center]; List v. Dahnke (Colo.App.1981) 638 P.2d 824 [lessor's refusal to consent to assignment of lease by one restaurateur to another was reasonable where lessor believed proposed specialty restaurant would not succeed at that location].) The lessor's interests are further protected by the fact that the original lessee remains a guarantor of the performance of the assignee. (See ante, p. 825 of 220 Cal.Rptr., p. 844 of 709 P.2d.)

The second justification advanced in support of the majority rule is that an approval clause is an unambiguous reservation of absolute discretion in the lessor over assignments of the lease. The lessee could have bargained for the addition of a reasonableness clause to the lease (i.e., "consent to assignment will not be unreasonably withheld"). The lessee having failed to do so, the law should not rewrite the parties' contract for them. (See Gruman v. Investors Diversified Services, supra, 78 N.W.2d at pp. 381–382; Funk v. Funk, supra, 633 P.2d at pp. 590, 592 (Bakes, C.J., dis.))....

The third justification advanced in support of the majority rule is essentially based on the doctrine of stare decisis. It is argued that the courts should not depart from the common law majority rule because "many leases now in effect covering a substantial amount of real property and creating valuable property rights were carefully prepared by competent counsel in reliance upon the majority viewpoint." (Gruman v. Investors Diversified Services, ... 78 N.W.2d at p. 381.... As pointed out above, however, the majority viewpoint has been far from universally held and has never been adopted by this court. Moreover, the trend in favor of the minority rule should come as no surprise to observers of the changing state of real property law in the 20th century. The minority rule is part of an increasing recognition of the contractual nature of leases and the implications in terms of contractual duties that flow therefrom. (See Green v. Superior Court (1974) 10 Cal.3d 616, 624, 111 Cal.Rptr. 704, 517 P.2d 1168.) We would be remiss in our duty if we declined to question a view held by the majority of jurisdictions simply because it is held by a majority. As we stated in Rodriguez v. Bethlehem Steel Corp. (1974) 12 Cal.3d 382, 115 Cal.Rptr. 765, 525 P.2d 669, the "vitality [of the common law] can flourish only so long as the courts remain alert to their obligation and opportunity to change the common law when reason and equity demand it." (Id., at p. 394, 115 Cal.Rptr. 765, 525 P.2d 669.))

A final argument in favor of the majority rule is advanced by respondent and stated as follows: "Both tradition and sound public policy dictate that the lessor has a right, under circumstances such as these, to realize the increased value of his property." Respondent essentially argues that any increase in the market value of real property during the term of a lease properly belongs to the lessor, not the lessee. We reject this assertion. One California commentator has written: "[W]hen the lessee executed the lease he acquired the contractual right for the exclusive use of the premises, and all of the benefits and detriment attendant to possession, for the term of the contract. He took the downside risk that he would be paying too much rent if there should be a depression in the rental market.... Why should he be deprived of the contractual benefits of the lease because of the fortuitous inflation in the marketplace[?] By reaping the benefits he does not deprive the landlord of anything to which the landlord was otherwise entitled. The landlord agreed to dispose of possession for the limited term and he could not reasonably anticipate any more than what was given to him by the terms of the lease. His reversionary estate will benefit from the increased value from the inflation in any event, at least upon the expiration of the lease." (Miller & Starr, Current Law of Cal. Real Estate (1977) 1984 Supp., § 27:92 at p. 321.)

Respondent here is trying to get more than it bargained for in the lease. A lessor is free to build periodic rent increases into a lease, as the lessor did here. (See ante, p. 821 of 220 Cal.Rptr., p. 840 of 709 P.2d.) Any increased value of the property beyond this "belongs" to the lessor only in the sense, as explained above, that the lessor's reversionary estate will benefit from it upon the expiration of the lease. We must therefore reject respondent's argument in this regard....[8]

IV.

In conclusion, both the policy against restraints on alienation and the implied contractual duty of good faith and fair dealing militate in favor of adoption of the rule that where a commercial lease provides for assignment only with the prior consent of the lessor, such consent may be

---

8. Amicus Pillsbury, Madison & Sutro request that we make clear that, "whatever principle governs in the absence of express lease provisions, nothing bars the parties to commercial lease transactions from making their own arrangements respecting the allocation of appreciated rentals if there is a transfer of the leasehold." This principle we affirm; we merely hold that the clause in the instant lease established no such arrangement.

withheld only where the lessor has a commercially reasonable objection to the assignee or the proposed use. Under this rule, appellants have stated a cause of action against respondent Ernest Pestana, Inc.

The order sustaining the demurrer to the complaint, which we have deemed to incorporate a judgment of dismissal, . . . is reversed.

NOTES AND QUESTIONS

1. Under the traditional common law and in the absence of a contrary provision in the lease, if the lease prohibited an assignment or sublet without the landlord's consent, the landlord could unreasonably withhold consent. The Restatement (Second) of Property § 15.2(2) (1977) rejects this rule by providing that if the lease prohibits an assignment or sublet without the consent of the landlord the "landlord's consent . . . cannot be withheld unreasonably, unless a freely negotiated provision in the lease gives the landlord an absolute right to withhold consent." "A reason for refusing consent, in order for it to be reasonable, must be objectively sensible and of some significance and not be based on mere caprice or whim or personal prejudice."[9] The landlord's refusal is reasonable if it is based upon one of the following grounds: (1) lack of financial responsibility, (2) the identity, business character, or reputation of the proposed transferee, (3) the legality of the proposed use, or (4) the nature of the occupancy, e.g., office, residential, factory, etc. See American Book Co. v. Yeshiva University Development Foundation, Inc., 59 Misc.2d 31, 297 N.Y.S.2d 156 (1969). Accord, Van Sloun v. Agans Bros., Inc., 778 N.W.2d 174 (IA 2010).

Who bears the burden of proof that the landlord's consent has been unreasonably withheld? See Broad & Branford Place Corp. v. J.J. Hockenjos Co., 132 N.J.L. 229, 39 A.2d 80 (1944).

Suppose L and T enter into a lease that provides that T may not assign the lease without L's prior written consent, which consent shall not be unreasonably withheld. T desires to assign to T–1, but L is concerned about T–1's financial responsibility. T, therefore, undertakes to guarantee the rent obligation in the event of T–1's default in the payment of rent. If L continues to withhold its consent, has L acted unreasonably? See Riggs v. Murdock, 10 Ariz.App. 248, 458 P.2d 115 (1969). If it is determined that L withheld its consent unreasonably, can T recover damages from L? Cf., Rock County Savings & Trust Co. v. Yost's, Inc., 36 Wis.2d 360, 153 N.W.2d 594 (1967). Can T or T–1 sue L for specific performance?

2. L and T enter into a five-year lease. The lease prohibits T's assignment or sublet of the leasehold without L's prior written consent. T proposed to assign the premises to T–2, and L consented to the assignment. T–2 now desires to assign the leasehold to T–3. Is L's consent required? Under the ancient Rule in Dumpor's Case, 4 Coke 119, 76 Eng.Rep. 1110 (1603), once the landlord has consented to the first assignment, his consent is not necessary to any other assignment. The Rule has been followed in America. See generally Schoshinski, American Law of Landlord and Tenant § 8:17

---

9. Restatement (Second) of Property, § 15.2 comment g (1977).

(1980). Most courts have refused to extend the rule of that case to sublets. Id. Does that make sense? In light of the fact that the landlord can avoid the application of the Rule by conditioning his consent to the first assignment by a reservation of the right to consent to all further assignments, does the Rule in Dumpor's Case make sense? A number of courts refuse to apply the Rule at all; others apply the Rule to both assignments and sublets. See generally 1 Amer.L.Prop. § 3.58 (A.J. Casner ed. 1952).

3.   L and T Corporation entered into a ten-year lease of Blackacre. The lease prohibited assignments and sublets without L's written consent. Four years later, T Corporation dissolved and its assets were distributed to T, as the sole shareholder of T Corporation. T entered into possession of Blackacre. L sues to evict T on the grounds that T is an assignee but that L did not consent to the assignment. Is L correct? See Shakey's Inc. v. Caple, 855 F.Supp. 1035 (E.D.Ark.1994).

§ 7.10   TERMINATION OF LEASEHOLD ESTATES AND REVERSION OF THE PREMISES

Suppose a tenant who is dissatisfied with the terms of the lease or the conditions of the premises simply moves out of (i.e., abandons) the premises. Can the landlord treat the lease as rescinded? Can the landlord lease the premises to another tenant even though the original term has not expired? Must the landlord seek a new tenant? If the landlord leases the premises to the new tenant what are the consequences if the terms of the new lease and the old lease differ, particularly as to rent?

Before exploring the consequences of the tenant's abandonment of the premises the term "abandonment" should be defined. Generally an "abandonment of the leased property by the tenant occurs when he vacates the leased property without justification and without any present intention of returning and he defaults in the payment of the rent."[1]

Suppose a tenant abandons the leased premises. Can the landlord agree to consider the lease terminated? What facts might give rise to a finding of either an express or implied agreement to terminate the lease? Obviously, the landlord and the tenant are free to agree to a termination of the lease and the tenant's obligation to pay rents due in the future. The process is formally known as "acceptance of the surrender." It generally takes two forms. An express acceptance of the surrender must be for consideration and satisfy any relevant provisions of the Statute of Frauds because, among other things, it is a conveyance of real property. An acceptance of the surrender may also occur by operation of law. This occurs "when the parties to a lease do some act so inconsistent with the subsisting relation of landlord and tenant as to imply they have both agreed to consider the surrender as effectual.... Thus, a surrender cannot be effected by the actions of only one party.... To constitute a

---

1.   Restatement (Second) of Property, § 12.1 comment i.

surrender by operation of law, there must be some decisive, unequivocal act by the landlord which manifests the lessor's acceptance of the surrender."[2]

Intent is crucial in determining whether the actions of the parties constitute a surrender by operation of law. Generally the intent of the tenant to abandon is readily determined from the fact that the tenant is no longer in possession of the leased property. On the other hand, the landlord's response can be decidedly ambiguous and subject to various interpretations respecting the landlord's intent. Would the following actions by the landlord constitute an acceptance of the surrender: (1) acceptance of the keys to the leased premises, (2) reletting the premises to another tenant for the balance of the original term, (3) reletting the premises to another tenant for a term extending beyond the original term?

SOMMER v. KRIDEL

Supreme Court of New Jersey (1977).
74 N.J. 446, 378 A.2d 767.

PASHMAN, J.

We granted certification in these cases to consider whether a landlord seeking damages from a defaulting tenant is under a duty to mitigate damages by making reasonable efforts to re-let an apartment wrongfully vacated by the tenant. Separate parts of the Appellate Division held that, in accordance with their respective leases, the landlords in both cases could recover rents due under the leases regardless of whether they had attempted to re-let the vacated apartments. Although they were of different minds as to the fairness of this result, both parts agreed that it was dictated by *Joyce v. Bauman*, 113 N.J.L. 438, 174 A. 693 (E. & A. 1934), a decision by the former Court of Errors and Appeals. We now reverse and hold that a landlord does have an obligation to make a reasonable effort to mitigate damages in such a situation. We therefore overrule *Joyce v. Bauman* to the extent that it is inconsistent with our decision today.

I

A.

Sommer v. Kridel

This case was tried on stipulated facts. On March 10, 1972 the defendant, James Kridel, entered into a lease with the plaintiff, Abraham Sommer, owner of the "Pierre Apartments" in Hackensack, to rent apartment 6–L in that building.[3] The term of the lease was from May 1,

---

2. Grueninger Travel Service v. Lake County Trust Co., 413 N.E.2d 1034, 1038–39 (Ind.App. 1980).

3. Among other provisions, the lease prohibited the tenant from assigning or transferring the lease without the consent of the landlord. If the tenant defaulted, the lease gave the landlord the option of re-entering or re-letting, but stipulated that failure to re-let or to recover the full rental would not discharge the tenant's liability for rent.

1972 until April 30, 1974, with a rent concession for the first six weeks, so that the first month's rent was not due until June 15, 1972.

One week after signing the agreement, Kridel paid Sommer $690. Half of that sum was used to satisfy the first month's rent. The remainder was paid under the lease provision requiring a security deposit of $345. Although defendant had expected to begin occupancy around May 1, his plans were changed. He wrote to Sommer on May 19, 1972, explaining

> I was to be married on June 3, 1972. Unhappily the engagement was broken and the wedding plans cancelled. Both parents were to assume responsibility for the rent after our marriage. I was discharged from the U.S. Army in October 1971 and am now a student. I have no funds of my own, and am supported by my stepfather.

> In view of the above, I cannot take possession of the apartment and am surrendering all rights to it. Never having received a key, I cannot return same to you.

> I beg your understanding and compassion in releasing me from the lease, and will of course, in consideration thereof, forfeit the 2 month's rent already paid.

> Please notify me at your earliest convenience.

Plaintiff did not answer the letter.

Subsequently, a third party went to the apartment house and inquired about renting apartment 6–L. Although the parties agreed that she was ready, willing and able to rent the apartment, the person in charge told her that the apartment was not being shown since it was already rented to Kridel. In fact, the landlord did not re-enter the apartment or exhibit it to anyone until August 1, 1973. At that time it was rented to a new tenant for a term beginning on September 1, 1973. The new rental was for $345 per month with a six week concession similar to that granted Kridel.

Prior to re-letting the new premises, plaintiff sued Kridel in August 1972, demanding $7,590, the total amount due for the full two-year term of the lease. Following a mistrial, plaintiff filed an amended complaint asking for $5,865, the amount due between May 1, 1972 and September 1, 1973. The amended complaint included no reduction in the claim to reflect the six week concession provided for in the lease or the $690 payment made to plaintiff after signing the agreement. Defendant filed an amended answer to the complaint, alleging that plaintiff breached the contract, failed to mitigate damages and accepted defendant's surrender of the premises. He also counterclaimed to demand repayment of the $345 paid as a security deposit.

The trial judge ruled in favor of defendant. Despite his conclusion that the lease had been drawn to reflect "the 'settled law' of this state," he found that "justice and fair dealing" imposed upon the landlord the duty to attempt to re-let the premises and thereby mitigate damages. He also held that plaintiff's failure to make any response to defendant's unequivocal offer of surrender was tantamount to an acceptance, thereby terminating the tenancy and any obligation to pay rent. As a result, he dismissed both the complaint and the counterclaim. The Appellate Division reversed in a per curiam opinion, 153 N.J.Super. 1 (1975), and we granted certification. 69 N.J. 395, 354 A.2d 323 (1976).

B.

Riverview Realty Co. v. Perosio

This controversy arose in a similar manner. On December 27, 1972, Carlos Perosio entered into a written lease with plaintiff Riverview Realty Co. The agreement covered the rental of apartment 5–G in a building owned by the realty company at 2175 Hudson Terrace in Fort Lee. As in the companion case, the lease prohibited the tenant from subletting or assigning the apartment without the consent of the landlord. It was to run for a two-year term, from February 1, 1973 until January 31, 1975, and provided for a monthly rental of $450. The defendant took possession of the apartment and occupied it until February 1974. At that time he vacated the premises, after having paid the rent through January 31, 1974.

The landlord filed a complaint on October 31, 1974, demanding $4,500 in payment for the monthly rental from February 1, 1974 through October 31, 1974. Defendant answered the complaint by alleging that there had been a valid surrender of the premises and that plaintiff failed to mitigate damages. The trial court granted the landlord's motion for summary judgment against the defendant, fixing the damages at $4,050 plus $182.25 interest.[4]

The Appellate Division affirmed the trial court, holding that it was bound by prior precedents, including *Joyce v. Bauman, supra.* 138 N.J.Super. 270, 350 A.2d 517 (App.Div.1976). Nevertheless, it freely criticized the rule which it found itself obliged to follow:

> There appears to be no reason in equity or justice to perpetuate such an unrealistic and uneconomic rule of law which encourages an owner to let valuable rented space lie fallow because he is assured of full recovery from a defaulting tenant. Since courts in New Jersey and elsewhere have abandoned ancient real property concepts and applied ordinary contract principles in other conflicts between landlord and tenant there is no sound reason for a continuation of a special real property rule to the issue of mitigation. . . . [138 N.J.Super. at 273–74, 350 A.2d at 519; citations omitted]

We granted certification. 70 *N.J.* 145, 358 *A.*2d 191 (1976).

---

4. The trial court noted that damages had been erroneously calculated in the complaint to reflect ten months rent. As to the interest awarded to plaintiff, the parties have not raised this issue before this Court. Since we hold that the landlord had a duty to attempt to mitigate damages, we need not reach this question.

II

As the lower courts in both appeals found, the weight of authority in this State supports the rule that a landlord is under no duty to mitigate damages caused by a defaulting tenant.... This rule has been followed in a majority of states, Annot. 21 *A.L.R.*3d 534, § 2[a] at 541 (1968), and has been tentatively adopted in the American Law Institute's Restatement of Property. *Restatement (Second) of Property,* § 11.1(3) (Tent. Draft No. 3, 1975).

Nevertheless, while there is still a split of authority over this question, the trend among recent cases appears to be in favor of a mitigation requirement....

The majority rule is based on principles of property law which equate a lease with a transfer of a property interest in the owner's estate. Under this rationale the lease conveys to a tenant an interest in the property which forecloses any control by the landlord; thus, it would be anomalous to require the landlord to concern himself with the tenant's abandonment of his own property....

For instance, in *Muller v. Beck*, [110 A. 831 (Sup.Ct.1920)] where essentially the same issue was posed, the court clearly treated the lease as governed by property, as opposed to contract, precepts.[5] The court there observed that the "tenant had an estate for years, but it was an estate qualified by this right of the landlord to prevent its transfer," 94 N.J.L. at 313, 110 A. at 832, and that "the tenant has an estate with which the landlord may not interfere." Id. at 314, 110 A. at 832. Similarly, in *Heckel v. Griese, supra*, the court noted the absolute nature of the tenant's interest in the property while the lease was in effect, stating that "when the tenant vacated, ... no one, in the circumstances, had any right to interfere with the defendant's possession of the premises." ...

Other cases simply cite the rule announced in Muller v. Beck, supra, without discussing the underlying rationale....

Yet the distinction between a lease for ordinary residential purposes and an ordinary contract can no longer be considered viable. As Professor Powell observed, evolving "social factors have exerted increasing influence on the law of estates for years." 2 *Powell on Real Property* (1977 ed.), § 221[1] at 180–81. The result has been that

> [t]he complexities of city life, and the proliferated problems of modern society in general, have created new problems for lessors and lessees and these have been commonly handled by specific clauses in leases. This growth in the number and detail of specific lease covenants has reintroduced into the law of estates for years a predominantly contractual ingredient. [Id. at 181]

Thus in 6 Williston on Contracts (3 ed. 1962), § 890A at 592, it is stated:

---

5. It is well settled that a party claiming damages for a breach of contract has a duty to mitigate his loss.

> There is a clearly discernible tendency on the part of courts to cast aside technicalities in the interpretation of leases and to concentrate their attention, as in the case of other contracts, on the intention of the parties, ...

See also Javins v. First National Realty Corp., 138 U.S.App.D.C. 369, 373, 428 F.2d 1071, 1075 (D.C.Cir.1970), cert. den. 400 U.S. 925, 91 S.Ct. 186, 27 L.Ed.2d 185 (1970) ("the trend toward treating leases as contracts is wise and well considered"); . . . .

This Court has taken the lead in requiring that landlords provide housing services to tenants in accordance with implied duties which are hardly consistent with the property notions expressed in *Muller v. Beck, supra*, ... See *Braitman v. Overlook Terrace Corp.*, 68 N.J. 368, 346 A.2d 76 (1975) (liability for failure to repair defective apartment door lock); *Berzito v. Gambino*, 63 N.J. 460, 308 A.2d 17 (1973) (construing implied warranty of habitability and covenant to pay rent as mutually dependent); *Marini v. Ireland*, 56 N.J. 130, 265 A.2d 526 (1970) (implied covenant to repair); *Reste Realty Corp. v. Cooper*, 53 N.J. 444, 251 A.2d 268 (1969) (implied warranty of fitness of premises for leased purpose). In fact, in *Reste Realty Corp. v. Cooper, supra*, we specifically noted that the rule which we announced there did not comport with the historical notion of a lease as an estate for years. 53 N.J. at 451–52, 251 A.2d 268. And in *Marini v. Ireland, supra*, we found that the "guidelines employed to construe contracts have been modernly applied to the construction of leases." 56 N.J. at 141, 265 A.2d at 532.

Application of the contract rule requiring mitigation of damages to a residential lease may be justified as a matter of basic fairness.[6] Professor McCormick first commented upon the inequity under the majority rule when he predicted in 1925 that eventually

> the logic, inescapable according to the standards of a "jurisprudence of conceptions" which permits the landlord to stand idly by the vacant, abandoned premises and treat them as the property of the tenant and recover full rent, . . . [will] yield to the more realistic notions of social advantage which in other fields of the law have forbidden a recovery for damages which the plaintiff by reasonable efforts could have avoided. [McCormick, "The Rights of the Landlord Upon Abandonment of the Premises by the Tenant," 23 Mich.L.Rev. 211, 221–22 (1925)]

Various courts have adopted this position. See Annot., supra, § 7(a) at 565, and ante at 770–771.

The pre-existing rule cannot be predicated upon the possibility that a landlord may lose the opportunity to rent another empty apartment because he must first rent the apartment vacated by the defaulting tenant. Even where the breach occurs in a multi-dwelling building, each

---

6. We see no distinction between the leases involved in the instant appeals and those which might arise in other types of residential housing. However, we reserve for another day the question of whether a landlord must mitigate damages in a commercial setting. . . .

apartment may have unique qualities which make it attractive to certain individuals. Significantly, in *Sommer v. Kridel*, there was a specific request to rent the apartment vacated by the defendant; there is no reason to believe that absent this vacancy the landlord could have succeeded in renting a different apartment to this individual.

We therefore hold that antiquated real property concepts which served as the basis for the pre-existing rule, shall no longer be controlling where there is a claim for damages under a residential lease. Such claims must be governed by more modern notions of fairness and equity. A landlord has a duty to mitigate damages where he seeks to recover rents due from a defaulting tenant.

If the landlord has other vacant apartments besides the one which the tenant has abandoned, the landlord's duty to mitigate consists of making reasonable efforts to re-let the apartment. In such cases he must treat the apartment in question as if it was one of his vacant stock.

As part of his cause of action, the landlord shall be required to carry the burden of proving that he used reasonable diligence in attempting to re-let the premises. We note that there has been a divergence of opinion concerning the allocation of the burden of proof on this issue. See Annot., *supra*, § 12 at 577. While generally in contract actions the breaching party has the burden of proving that damages are capable of mitigation, ... here the landlord will be in a better position to demonstrate whether he exercised reasonable diligence in attempting to re-let the premises....

III

The *Sommer v. Kridel* case presents a classic example of the unfairness which occurs when a landlord has no responsibility to minimize damages. Sommer waited 15 months and allowed $4658.50 in damages to accrue before attempting to re-let the apartment. Despite the availability of a tenant who was ready, willing and able to rent the apartment, the landlord needlessly increased the damages by turning her away. While a tenant will not necessarily be excused from his obligations under a lease simply by finding another person who is willing to rent the vacated premises, *see, e.g., Reget v. Dempsey–Tegler & Co.*, 70 Ill.App.2d 32, 216 N.E.2d 500 (Ill.App.1966) (new tenant insisted on leasing the premises under different terms); *Edmands v. Rust & Richardson Drug Co.*, 191 Mass. 123, 77 N.E. 713 (1906) (landlord need not accept insolvent tenant), here there has been no showing that the new tenant would not have been suitable. We therefore find that plaintiff could have avoided the damages which eventually accrued, and that the defendant was relieved of his duty to continue paying rent. Ordinarily we would require the tenant to bear the cost of any reasonable expenses incurred by a landlord in attempting to re-let the premises, *see Ross v. Smigelski, supra*, 166 N.W.2d at 248–49; 22 Am.Jur.2d, Damages, § 169 at 238, but no such expenses were incurred in this case.[7]

---

7. As to defendant's counterclaim for $345, representing the amount deposited with the landlord as a security deposit, we note that this issue has not been briefed or argued before this

In *Riverview Realty Co. v. Perosio*, no factual determination was made regarding the landlord's efforts to mitigate damages, and defendant contends that plaintiff never answered his interrogatories. Consequently, the judgment is reversed and the case remanded for a new trial. Upon remand and after discovery has been completed, R. 4:17 et seq., the trial court shall determine whether plaintiff attempted to mitigate damages with reasonable diligence, see Wilson v. Ruhl, supra, 356 A.2d at 546, and if so, the extent of damages remaining and assessable to the tenant. As we have held above, the burden of proving that reasonable diligence was used to re-let the premises shall be upon the plaintiff. See Annot., *supra*, § 11 at 575.

In assessing whether the landlord has satisfactorily carried his burden, the trial court shall consider, among other factors, whether the landlord, either personally or through an agency, offered or showed the apartment to any prospective tenants, or advertised it in local newspapers. Additionally, the tenant may attempt to rebut such evidence by showing that he proffered suitable tenants who were rejected. However, there is no standard formula for measuring whether the landlord has utilized satisfactory efforts in attempting to mitigate damages, and each case must be judged upon its own facts. *Compare Hershorin v. La Vista, Inc.*, 110 Ga.App. 435, 138 S.E.2d 703 (App.1964) ("reasonable effort" of landlord by showing the apartment to all prospective tenants); *Carpenter v. Wisniewski*, 139 Ind.App. 325, 215 N.E.2d 882 (App.1966) (duty satisfied where landlord advertised the premises through a newspaper, placed a sign in the window, and employed a realtor); *Re Garment Center Capitol, Inc.*, 93 F.2d 667, 115 A.L.R. 202 (2 Cir.1938) (landlord's duty not breached where higher rental was asked since it was known that this was merely a basis for negotiations); *Foggia v. Dix*, 265 Or. 315, 509 P.2d 412, 414 (1973) (in mitigating damages, landlord need not accept less than fair market value or "substantially alter his obligations as established in the pre-existing lease"); with *Anderson v. Andy Darling Pontiac, Inc.*, 257 Wis. 371, 43 N.W.2d 362 (1950) (reasonable diligence not established where newspaper advertisement placed in one issue of local paper by a broker); *Scheinfeld v. Muntz T.V., Inc.*, 67 Ill.App.2d 8, 214 N.E.2d 506 (Ill.App.1966) (duty breached where landlord refused to accept suitable subtenant); *Consolidated Sun Ray, Inc. v. Oppenstein*, 335 F.2d 801, 811 (8th Cir.1964) (dictum) (demand for rent which is "far greater than the provisions of the lease called for" negates landlord's assertion that he acted in good faith in seeking a new tenant).

IV

The judgment in *Sommer v. Kridel* is reversed. In *Riverview Realty Co. v. Perosio*, the judgment is reversed and the case is remanded to the trial court for proceedings in accordance with this opinion.

Court, and apparently has been abandoned. Because we hold that plaintiff breached his duty to attempt to mitigate damages, we do not address defendant's argument that the landlord accepted a surrender of the premises.

Notes and Questions

1. A substantial number of states, if not the majority, refuse to impose a duty to mitigate on the landlord. States applying the no-mitigation rule justify that rule on a number of grounds. For example, in Stonehedge Square Limited Partnership v. Movie Merchants, Inc., 552 Pa. 412, 416, 715 A.2d 1082, 1084 (1998), the court stated:

> The established [no mitigation] rule has the virtue of simplicity. If the landlord is required to relet the premises, there is unlimited potential for litigation initiated by the tenant concerning the landlord's due diligence, whether the landlord made necessary repairs which would be required to rent the premises, whether the landlord was required to borrow money to make repairs, whether the landlord hired the right agents or a sufficient number of agents to rent the premises, whether the tenants who were refused should have been accepted, and countless other questions in which the breaching tenant is permitted to mount an assault on whatever the landlord did to mitigate damages, alleging that it was somehow deficient. This potential for complexity, expense, and delay is unwelcome and would adversely affect the existing schema utilized to finance commercial development ...

> There is a fundamental unfairness in allowing the breaching tenant to require the nonbreaching landlord to mitigate the damages caused by the tenant. This unfairness takes the form of depriving the landlord of the benefit of his bargain, forcing the landlord to expend time, energy and money to respond to the tenant's breach, and putting the landlord at risk of further expense of lawsuits and counterclaims in a matter which he justifiably assumed was closed.

The court also noted that where the tenant was free under the lease to assign or sublet the premises, the tenant could easily mitigate by finding an appropriate transferee.

It has also been said that another reason to reject imposing a mitigation requirement on the landlord is that a duty to mitigate unfairly requires the lessor to seek new tenants continually. Wohl v. Yelen, 22 Ill.App.2d 455, 161 N.E.2d 339 (1959) (residential lease).

2. The *Sommer* case represents the modern view on the obligation of a landlord to mitigate damages resulting from the tenant's abandonment of the premises. See also Vawter v. McKissick, 159 N.W.2d 538 (Iowa 1968); Wright v. Baumann, 239 Or. 410, 398 P.2d 119 (1965), appeal after remand, 254 Or. 175, 458 P.2d 674 (1969); R. Schoshinski, American Law of Landlord and Tenant § 10:12 (1980 & Supp.1992). The duty to mitigate is also reflected in URLTA § 4.203(c) and the Model Residential Landlord and Tenant Code § 2–308(4) (Tent. Draft 1969). In jurisdictions in which the duty to mitigate is not the law, the landlord and the tenant are, of course, free to impose a mitigation requirement on the landlord by contract. Whitehorn v. Dickerson, 419 S.W.2d 713, 718 (Mo.Ct.App.1967). There are a number of significant reasons to require mitigation, including: (1) avoiding economic waste, (2) encouraging the productive use of a scarce resource (real estate), and (3) discouraging

victims from "passively suffering economic loss which could be averted by reasonable efforts." See generally, Davis, Better Late Than Never: Texas Landlords Owe a Duty to Mitigate Damages When a Tenant Abandons Leased Property: Austin Hill Country Realty, Inc. v Palisades Plaza, Inc., 28 Tex. Tech. L. Rev. 1281 (1997).

Suppose the landlord either fails to mitigate entirely or mitigates unreasonably. Does this release the tenant from any further liability? See URLTA § 4.203(c) ("If the landlord fails to use reasonable efforts to rent the dwelling unit at a fair rental ... the rental agreement is deemed to be terminated by the landlord as of the date the landlord has notice of the abandonment.")

The majority of courts imposing the mitigation requirement have concluded that the landlord is entitled to damages even though it has not attempted to mitigate, but that the amount of damages are to be reduced by the fair rental value of the premises. What rationales support these differing approaches? See, e.g., Isbey v. Crews, 55 N.C.App. 47, 284 S.E.2d 534 (1981).

In contrast to the URLTA mitigation rule, the Restatement (Second) of Property § 12.1(3) (1977) rejects mitigation. In justification of its surprising position the Reporter states: "Abandonment of property is an invitation to vandalism, and the law should not encourage such conduct by putting a duty of mitigation of damages on the landlord."[8]

3.   Does the duty to mitigate apply to commercial leases? In Ringwood Associates, Ltd. v. Jack's of Route 23, Inc., 153 N.J.Super. 294, 379 A.2d 508 (Law Div.1977), aff'd 166 N.J.Super. 36, 398 A.2d 1315 (App.Div.1979), the court held there was such a duty. See also Frenchtown Square Partnership v. Lemstone, Inc., 99 Ohio St.3d 254, 791 N.E.2d 417 (2003). Would imposing a duty to mitigate on residential but not commercial leases make sense?

4.   Can the duty to mitigate be waived? In considering this question, review the *Sommer* case and see if the parties purported to waive the duty to mitigate.

Suppose a lease contains a "liquidated damages" clause providing that if the tenant breaches the lease in any material respect the landlord, in lieu of all other remedies, can terminate the lease and recover $5,000 from the tenant. Is this clause valid in a jurisdiction requiring a landlord to mitigate?

5.   If the landlord is under a duty to mitigate damages what actions should the landlord take to meet this legal obligation? What standards does the *Sommer* court apply? Would merely listing the property for rent be sufficient? See Wilson v. Ruhl, 277 Md. 607, 356 A.2d 544 (1976). Is it reasonable to negotiate with only one prospective tenant at a time? Is it necessarily unreasonable only to agree to a relet at a higher rent than the rent provided for in the lease of the abandoning tenant? See Jefferson Development Co. v. Heritage Cleaners, 109 Mich.App. 606, 311 N.W.2d 426 (1981); MAR–SON, Inc. v. Terwaho Enterprises, Inc., 259 N.W.2d 289 (N.D. 1977). Is advertising the property once in a local newspaper sufficient? See Anderson v. Andy Darling Pontiac, Inc., 257 Wis. 371, 43 N.W.2d 362 (1950).

---

8.   Restatement (Second) of Property, § 12.1, comment i (1977).

Who should bear the burden of proof on the issue of whether the landlord has fulfilled the duty to mitigate? The case law is divided. Compare Stewart Title & Trust of Tucson v. Pribbeno, 129 Ariz. 15, 628 P.2d 52 (App.1981) (burden on tenant) with Williams v. Kaiser Aluminum & Chemical Sales, Inc., 396 F.Supp. 288 (N.D.Tex.1975) (burden on party who causes breach to show that losses could have been avoided).

6. The more traditional view of the landlord's rights upon a tenant's wrongful abandonment of the premises would be that:

> If a tenant wrongfully abandons leased premises before the expiration of the term, the landlord may, at his election, at once enter and terminate the contract and recover the rent due up to the time of abandonment, he may suffer the premises to remain vacant and sue on the contract for the entire rent, or he may give notice to the tenant of his refusal to accept a surrender when such notice can be given, and sublet the premises for the unexpired term for the benefit of the lessee to reduce his damages.[9]

What purpose is served by a rule that actually forces the landlord to keep rental property vacant?

While the phrase "acceptance of surrender" suggests that the landlord forgoes any other rights it has against the tenant, under certain circumstances the landlord may accept the surrender and also sue for damages. See Sagamore Corp. v. Willcutt, infra.

If you represented a landlord, what risks would you advise are posed by the traditional rule? Is the court suggesting there is, or should be, a difference in law between the landlord who takes actual possession of the abandoned premises and the landlord who "sublets" them for the benefit of the abandoning tenant? Are there any circumstances in which the landlord would be justified in taking actual possession of the abandoned premises?

How does one determine whether the landlord has relet for the abandoning tenant's benefit or the landlord's benefit? Is the act of reletting deemed to be for the tenant's benefit if the landlord notifies the tenant to that effect, see Hurwitz v. Kohm, 594 S.W.2d 643 (Mo.App.1980); Casper National Bank v. Curry, 51 Wyo. 284, 65 P.2d 1116 (1937), Restatement (Second) of Property § 12.1(3)(b) (1977), or must the tenant consent to the reletting? See Leo v. Santagada, 45 Misc.2d 309, 256 N.Y.S.2d 511 (City Ct.1964). How might a landlord protect itself at the time of the lease negotiations? Note how this matter is resolved by the "plain English" lease printed at the beginning of this chapter?

7. L owns a commercial building. L rents the left half to T–1 and the right half to T–2. T–1 wrongfully abandons the premises. Thereafter L rents the left half to T–2 for a term that ends when T–1's term would have ended. Has L accepted T–1's surrender of the premises? See McGrath v. Shalett, 114 Conn. 622, 159 A. 633 (1932) (no acceptance of surrender).

8. T–1 wrongfully abandons Blackacre and thereafter L relets to T–2. In order to induce T–2 to lease the premises L substantially alters and remodels Blackacre. Do L's actions amount to an acceptance of the surrender? Compare

9. Conner v. Warner, 52 Okl. 630, 152 P. 1116 (1915).

Airport Assoc. v. Hawaii Air Gunnery, Inc., 8 B.R. 979 (D.Haw.1981) with Guaranty Bank & Trust Co. v. Mid–State Ins. Agency, Inc., 383 Mass. 319, 418 N.E.2d 1249 (1981).

9. Suppose L and T–1 negotiate a lease providing that T–1 cannot assign the leasehold without L's consent "which consent cannot be unreasonably withheld." T–1 desires to terminate the lease and proposes that L rent the premises to T–2 for the balance of the term. Notwithstanding that in all respects T–2 is a desirable tenant, L refuses to consent to assignment. If L later sues T–1 for unpaid rents, can T–1 reasonably argue that the proposed assignment clause imposed a duty to mitigate on L and reduce his damages by the amount T–2 would have paid L in rents? See also Cal.Civ.Code § 1951.4 (West 1985).

10. L leases an apartment to T who has two small children for a term of two years. Three months later a registered sex offender moves into the adjacent apartment. Can T terminate the lease? See Knudsen v. Lax, 17 Misc.3d 350, 842 N.Y.S.2d 341 (Co.Ct. 2007). Suppose T's husband abuses both T and the children. Can T terminate the lease?

SAGAMORE CORP. v. WILLCUTT

Supreme Court of Connecticut (1935).
120 Conn. 315, 180 A. 464.

BANKS, JUDGE.

The complaint alleged that on October 1, 1934, the plaintiff leased to the defendant for the term of one year from that date certain premises for the annual rental of $480 payable at the rate of $40 a month on the first day of each month in advance, that the defendant occupied the premises until February 1, 1935, on which day he moved out and thereafter notified the plaintiff that he would no longer comply with the terms of the lease and would pay no further rent, and that as a result of the defendant's breach of the lease the plaintiff has suffered as damages the difference between the rental specified in the lease and the reasonable rental value of the premises for the remainder of the term. The defendant's demurrer to the complaint, stated in four paragraphs, makes a single claim; that the breach of a covenant to pay rent creates no debt until the time stipulated for payment arrives, that the defendant owes the plaintiff no duty except to pay the rent on the first of each month during the remainder of the term, and consequently the plaintiff is not entitled, in an action brought before the expiration of the term of the lease, to recover damages for the defendant's anticipatory breach of his covenant to pay rent.

The lessee has abandoned the leased premises and refused to pay any further rent. The lessor in such a situation has two courses of action open to him. He may accept the surrender of the premises, thereby terminating the lease and effecting a rescission of the contract, or he may refuse to accept the surrender. In the latter case he may let the property lie idle and collect the balance of the rent due under the lease, or he may take possession of the property and lease it to others, in which case he may recover from the original lessee the balance of the rent due under his lease less the rent received from the new lessee. Whether the taking possession of the premises constitutes a rescission of the contract depends upon his intent. . . . The action in that case is one to recover the rent which the lessee has covenanted to pay, and of course cannot be maintained until such rent becomes due and payable under the terms of the lease. By bringing this action for damages for breach of contract, the plaintiff has manifested its intention to accept the surrender of the premises, and has acquiesced in the termination of the lease and the rescission of the contract. Its action is one for damages for the breach by the defendant of his covenant to pay rent.

The arguments and briefs of counsel appear to have proceeded largely upon the assumption that the breach arose out of the repudiation by the defendant of his obligation to pay rent which would accrue in the future and therefore constituted an anticipatory breach, or, more accurately, a breach by anticipatory repudiation of his contract. A positive statement to the promisee that the promisor will not perform his contract constitutes an anticipatory repudiation which is a total breach of contract, except in cases of a contract originally unilateral and not conditional on some future performance by the promisee and of a contract originally bilateral that has become unilateral and similarly unconditional by full performance by one party. . . . Where the contract was originally unilateral or has become so by the performance of one party, no breach can arise before the time fixed in the contract for some performance. There must be some dependency of performance in order to make anticipatory breach possible. Restatement, op. cit., Comment e. A lease is primarily a conveyance of an interest in land and its execution by the lessor may be said to constitute performance on his part, making the instrument, when considered as a contract, a unilateral agreement with no dependency of performance which would make an anticipatory breach possible. This, we take it, is the basis of the distinction which the defendant claims to exist between a covenant to pay rent in a lease of real estate and an ordinary executory contract.

But the plaintiff is not obliged to rely solely upon the rules controlling a right to recover for an anticipatory breach arising out of the defendant's repudiation of his obligation to pay rent to accrue in the future. The complaint alleges that the rent was payable on the first day of each month in advance, that the defendant moved out on the first day of February, 1935, and thereafter notified the plaintiff that he would pay no further rent. This can only be construed as an allegation of a refusal to pay the rent which had fallen due on that date as well as that to accrue in the future. This constituted a present breach of his covenant to pay rent when due. Granting the defendant's contention that a covenant to pay rent creates no debt until the time stipulated for payment arrives, that time had arrived, so far as the rent due February 1st was concerned, and his failure to pay that rent constituted a breach of the covenants of his lease. The question remains whether this was a total or only a partial breach. If the former, the plaintiff would be entitled to maintain this action to recover the damages alleged in its complaint; if the latter, it would be limited to those resulting from the refusal to pay the rent due on February 1st. Considering a lease as a unilateral contract, or a bilateral contract that has been wholly performed by the lessor, the covenant to pay rent at certain fixed periods is a contract for the payment of money in installments, and the failure to pay any installment of rent as it falls due would constitute a partial breach of the lessee's contract.... But when such a partial breach is accompanied or followed by a repudiation of the entire contract, the promisee may treat it as a total breach.... Defendant's failure to pay the rent due on February 1st, considered alone, constituted a breach only of his agreement to pay that particular installment of rent. His subsequent statement to the plaintiff that he would no longer comply with the terms of the lease and would pay no further rent was a repudiation of his entire contract. The breach thereupon became a total one justifying an immediate action by the plaintiff to recover the damages which would naturally follow from such a breach.

* * *

There is no error.

In this opinion, the other Judges concurred.

NOTES AND QUESTIONS

1. How does the *Sagamore* court measure the amount of the landlord's damages? Does the court's measure of damages expressly or impliedly take into account the duty to mitigate?

If the promised rent equals the fair rental value of the premises, what, if anything, can the landlord recover from the tenant? If the measure of damages takes into account the reasonable rental value of the premises, how is such value to be proved? Under what circumstances would the promised rent not equal the reasonable rental value? How probative of reasonable rental value would the rents payable by a new tenant be if the landlord found the new tenant within thirty days of the tenant's abandonment? Within nine months? Should the court's measure of damages be applied if the landlord relet the premises within one month of the abandonment?

2. L leases Blackacre to T for a term of twelve months. T abandons the premises in the fourth month. At that time T is in default of rent for March and April. Can L sue T for the unpaid April rent and later sue T for the unpaid March rent? Lekse v. Municipal Court, 138 Cal.App.3d 188, 187 Cal.Rptr. 698 (1982) (landlord cannot split cause of action). Can L sue T for the remaining eight months rent? Will L's rights be affected if the lease provides that if T wrongfully abandons the premises all rents due in the future become immediately due and payable? How does the "plain language" lease handle this issue?

At common law, the landlord could sue an abandoning tenant for rents only as the rents came due or for past due rents. In other words, the landlord could only sue for rents accrued to the date the suit was filed. The landlord could not sue for rents payable in the future. The rationale for this rule was that the independent covenant to pay rent created no enforceable rights in the landlord until the rent payment was due and the promise to pay rent was breached. The rule posed risks for the landlord who was unwilling to await the termination of the lease before suing for all unpaid rents. The rule also imposed additional litigation costs on the landlord who sued periodically to recover rents currently due. The common-law rule continues to be applied in many jurisdictions. See, e.g., General Development Corp. v. Wilbur–Rogers Atlanta Corp., 28 Ohio App.2d 35, 273 N.E.2d 908 (1971).

In order to avoid the harshness of the common-law rule, landlords often include so-called "acceleration clauses" in leases. An acceleration clause provides that if the tenant wrongfully abandons the premises all rents due in the future become immediately due and payable.[10] Jurisdictions are divided on the validity of such acceleration clauses. Compare Ricker v. Rombough, 120 Cal.App.2d Supp. 912, 261 P.2d 328 (1953) (invalid) with Aurora Business Park Associates v. Michael Albert, Inc., 548 N.W.2d 153 (Iowa 1996) (valid). If the clause is upheld, can the landlord accelerate the unpaid rents and also relet the property to a new tenant? If the acceleration clause is valid can the landlord collect more than the present value of the rents payable in the future?

3. If the court permits the landlord to sue for rent due in the future, how much can the landlord collect from the tenant? For example, suppose the tenant abandons the premises at the end of the fifth year of a ten-year term. Under the terms of the lease, tenant was obligated to pay rent of $100 a month. Since there are sixty months left of the original term, can the landlord recover $6,000, more than $6,000, or less than $6,000? How is the amount of the recovery affected if the landlord has a duty to mitigate damages? Suppose the original term of the lease had been fifty years and tenant abandoned after five years. Does the fact that there are forty-five years remaining on the original term affect the calculation of damages? See Hawkinson v. Johnston, 122 F.2d 724 (8th Cir.1941), cert. denied, 314 U.S. 694 (1941).

Suppose that tenant had been in arrears for seven months at the time of the abandonment. Would awarding the landlord $700 damages for those seven months adequately compensate the landlord?

4. L and T enter into a 20 year lease under which T promises to pay L $1,000 a month rent plus 3% of T's monthly profits from the sale of widgets. During the first 15 years of the lease, T paid L an average of $2,000 a month rent. T, who recently reached age 65, desires to retire, to cease operations and to terminate the lease. T claims that it only owes L $1,000 for each remaining month of the lease. L claims T should pay L $2,000 rent for each remaining month of the lease. Is L correct? See College Block v. Atlantic Richfield Co., 206 Cal.App.3d, 1376, 254 Cal.Rptr. 179 (1988) (covenant of continue operations can be implied in percentage leases "in order for the lessor to receive that for which the lessor bargained," particularly, where the base guaranteed rent is insubstantial); Columbia East Associates v. Bi–Lo, Inc., 299 S.C. 515, 386 S.E.2d 259 (App.1989) (tenant, which was an anchor store at a mall, has

---

10. Landlords use acceleration clauses to accelerate rents due in the future for many other breaches by the tenant.

obligation of continued operations where landlord intended tenant to be a principal attraction for customers to come to the mall).

5. At common law, lease covenants were independent. Thus, breach of a covenant by the tenant did not necessarily entitle the landlord to terminate the lease and sue for possession. For example, if the tenant failed to pay rent the landlord was entitled to sue for rents but not recover possession. The lease could specifically provide, however, that if the tenant failed to pay rents the landlord could elect to terminate the lease and sue for possession.

Suppose the tenant breaches one or more terms of the lease but refuses to surrender possession of the premises to the landlord, even though such breach amounts to a termination of the lease. What options does the landlord have? Can the landlord forcibly remove the tenant from the premises? While the tenant is physically off the premises can the landlord change the locks so that the tenant can not reenter? The law has long frowned upon such self-help remedies, and often landlords will be liable for punitive type damages for exercising self-help eviction procedures. By contrast, statutes have been enacted providing the landlord with an expeditious judicial procedure for obtaining possession of the premises in cases where the tenant has breached the terms of the lease. These statutes are referred to as summary procedures or forceful (forcible) entry and detainer acts.

6. The tenant is obligated to return the premises to the landlord in substantially the same condition as the premises were in at the commencement of the lease, ordinary wear and tear excepted. Consistent with this obligation the tenant could not commit waste. Waste could occur if the tenant destroyed, altered, or even improved the premises. The rigidness with which the doctrine of waste might be applied varies with the courts; some courts hold the tenant liable for any action that technically is waste; others impose a substantiality requirement. Thus, one court has stated that waste is such "change as to effect a vital and substantial portion of the premises; as would change its characteristic appearance; the fundamental purpose of the erection, or the uses contemplated, or a change of such a nature as would affect the very realty itself extraordinary in scope and effect or unusual in expenditure." Pross v. Excelsior Cleaning & Dyeing Co., 110 Misc. 195, 201, 179 N.Y.S. 176, 179–80 (Mun.Ct.1919).

Additionally, at common law the tenant was obligated not to permit the premises to fall into a state of disrepair. The tenant was required to return the premises to the landlord in the same condition in which he found them at the commencement of the lease, ordinary wear and tear excepted. Thus, in the absence of a contrary provision in the lease, the tenant, not the landlord, had the duty to make repairs. What arguments might justify the common-law rule? Should the common-law rule apply in an urban environment? Should it continue to apply to rural leases? See generally 1 Amer.L.Prop. § 3.78 (A.J. Casner ed. 1952). While the tenant had a duty to repair, this duty did not extend to the replacement or restoration of a building that was destroyed by fire or other casualty or had fallen into such a state of disrepair that it had to be demolished. Id.

The landlord and the tenant could expressly covenant concerning the duty to repair. Suppose L and T covenant that T shall maintain the premises in good repair. Does that covenant enlarge T's common law duty? Suppose the covenant had been that T shall maintain the premises in good order and repair, ordinary wear and tear excepted? How does this differ from a general covenant to repair? Is the measure of the duty determined by the condition of the building at the commencement of the lease or at the termination of the lease?

Most courts hold that if the tenant grants the landlord a general covenant to repair, the tenant must rebuild the premises if they are destroyed by fire. Compare Willis v. Wrenn's Ex'x, 141 Va. 385, 127 S.E. 312 (1925) with Wattles v. South Omaha Ice & Coal Co., 50 Neb. 251, 69 N.W. 785 (1897). Does this rule seem inappropriately harsh? Is there any justification for the rule? This rule has been changed by statute in some jurisdictions. See, e.g., Mo.Rev.Stat. § 441.010 (1978).

Suppose L leases a building to T for 10 years. In the seventh year of the lease the building is destroyed by fire. If T has covenanted to rebuild the building, at what point of time after the destruction of the building can it be said that T is in breach of the covenant and L is entitled to damages?

Suppose T lives in a rent controlled apartment and L is unwilling or unable to make repairs and minor improvements to the premises. If T, for example, repairs the ceiling by replacing it with sheetrock, has an electrician install four additional electrical outlets in the apartment, and has a carpenter install a wooden closet in the apartment, has the tenant committed waste? Rumiche Corp. v. Eisenreich, 40 N.Y.2d 174, 386 N.Y.S.2d 208, 352 N.E.2d 125 (1976).

7.   L leases Blackacre to T for a term of ten years. During the term of the lease T installs wall-to-wall carpeting on the premises, lighting fixtures and window air conditioners. At the termination of the lease can T remove these items from the premises? Should the answer depend on whether T was a residential or commercial tenant? See generally R. Brown, The Law of Personal Property § 16.8 (W. Raushenbush ed., 3d ed. 1975).

8.   L leases an apartment to T for a period of three years. Two months prior to the termination date fixed in the lease T dies of a heart attack in the apartment. T's body, however, was not discovered for 7 days and as a result of decomposition the apartment had to be fumigated. This cost $6,000. Does T's death terminate the lease? Should L or T's estate be responsible for paying the $6,000? Kennedy v. Kidd, 557 P.2d 467 (Okl.App.1976). If you conclude L should bear this cost, would you change your mind if T had committed suicide in the apartment?

Suppose a tenant's spouse died in the apartment while the tenant was away on a business trip. When the tenant returned the tenant found the spouse had decomposed and the premises needed fumigation. Would tenant or landlord be liable for the cost of fumigation?

NOTE ON SUMMARY PROCEEDINGS

It has long been the policy of our law to discourage landlords from taking the law into their own hands, and our decisions and statutory law have looked with disfavor upon any use of self-help to dispossess a tenant in circumstances which are likely to result in breaches of the peace. We gave early recognition to this policy in Lobdell v. Keene, 85 Minn. 90, 101, 88 N.W. 426, 430 (1901), where we said:

> "The object and purpose of the legislature in the enactment of the forcible entry and unlawful detainer statute was to prevent those claiming a right of entry or possession of lands from redressing their own wrongs by entering into possession in a violent and forcible manner. All such acts tend to a breach of the peace, and encourage high-handed oppression. The law does not permit the owner of land, be his title ever so good, to be the judge of his own rights with respect to a possession adversely held, but puts him to his remedy under the statutes."[11]

Summary eviction statutes are intended as an alternative and discouragement to the use of self-help. While the statutes vary from state to state, generally they provide that if the landlord gives notice to the tenant (usually three days) of his intent to terminate the lease because of the tenant's breach, the landlord may file an eviction proceeding in the court to recover possession of the premises. The court will hear the proceeding usually within thirty days and determine whether the landlord is entitled to a judgment for possession. Under the summary eviction statutes as initially conceived, the tenant had few defenses, particularly if the landlord sued for possession because of nonpayment of rent. With the recognition of the implied warranty of habitability and the dependency of covenants rule, however, tenants can defend an action for nonpayment of rent on the grounds that the obligation to pay rent was suspended because of the landlord's breach of the implied warranty of habitability. Raising this defense and bringing evidence before the court to prove the defense necessarily diminishes the "summariness" of the eviction proceeding. Could a state constitutionally deny the right of the tenant to raise the implied warranty of habitability as a defense in a summary proceeding for possession based upon non-payment of rent? Lindsey v. Normet, 405 U.S. 56 (1972).

NOTE ON SECURITY DEPOSITS

Landlords generally require tenants to post so-called "security deposits" to protect the landlord against tenant's damage to the premises. American case law reflects a rich number of disputes between landlords and tenants relating to security deposits. See generally R. Schoshinski, Amer. Law of Landlord & Tenant §§ 6:27–6:44 (1980 & Supp.1992). This case law, however, has largely been replaced by statutory schemes covering security deposits. At least forty-one states have enacted statutes of one kind or another that address basic security deposit issues, including a ceiling on the amount of the deposit, the use of the deposit by landlord during the term of the lease, the landlord's obligation to return the deposit and the consequences of the landlord's failure to account for and return the deposit.

URLTA is fairly typical of the state statutes although it contains some features not common in other statutory schemes. Of course, since URLTA is limited to residential leases, its provisions are inapplicable to commercial

---

11. Berg v. Wiley, 264 N.W.2d 145, 149–50 (Minn.1978).

leases. URLTA § 2.101(a) limits the size of the security deposit to one month's rent. While this is fairly typical, some states have higher ceilings on the amount of the security deposit. See, e.g., Mich.Comp.Laws Ann. § 554.602 (West Supp.1986) (1½ months); Iowa Code Ann. § 562A.12(1) (West Supp. 1986) (2 months). Are there justifications in support of more than a one month ceiling on the security deposit?

URLTA § 2.101 applies to security deposits "however denominated. . . ." The purpose of this provision is to ensure that amounts denominated as prepaid rents, but which are in fact intended to be security deposits are also regulated. Not all state statutes are similarly worded. Some state statutes go beyond regulating money received, which is intended to be a security deposit, and cover any money received from the tenant in advance. See, e.g., Mass. Gen.Laws Ann. ch. 186 § 15B (West Supp.1986).

URLTA § 2.101(b) requires that the landlord return the deposit, less any amounts owed to the landlord for accrued rent or damages, within fourteen days after the termination of the tenancy, the delivery of possession, and the tenant's demand for the deposit. Contrasted with the thirty day return provisions of other state statutes, URLTA is fairly liberal in the tenant's favor. Nearly all statutes have a provision obliging the landlord to return the funds within a reasonable period of time following the termination of the tenancy. URLTA restricts the landlord to using the deposit to offset damages arising from the tenant's obligation not to commit waste and to occupy the premises in a manner consistent with health and safety. Michigan statutes additionally permit the landlord to deduct from the deposit an amount of the tenant's unpaid utility bills. Mich.Comp.Laws Ann. § 554.607(b) (West Supp. 1986). Additionally, URLTA and other state statutes require the landlord to itemize damages. While URLTA does not do so, some states place the burden of proof on the landlord to show the extent of its loss and that the tenant caused the alleged damages. See also Cal.Civ.Code § 1950.5(h) (West Supp. 1986) (landlord has burden to prove reasonableness of amounts claimed).

URLTA § 2.101(c) provides that if the landlord fails to comply with his obligations to timely return the deposit and to itemize any reductions the tenant can recover the amount due. Additionally, the tenant can recover damages equal to, depending upon local option, the amount due or twice the amount wrongfully withheld, as well as reasonable attorney fees incurred in collecting the money. Some state statutes deny the landlord rights to any of the deposit if it fails to comply with the statutes governing the duty to return the deposit at the termination of the tenancy. See, e.g., Ill.Ann.Stat. ch. 80 § 101 (Smith–Hurd Supp.1986); Colo.Rev.Stat. § 38–12–103(2) (1982).

One issue often regulated by state statute is ignored by URLTA, namely the landlord's use of the deposit during the term of the tenancy. According to the comments to URLTA § 2.101, the difficulties of administration and accounting for the deposit justify the absence of any regulation of the landlord's use of the deposit. Many states have departed from this position. For instance, in New York the landlord must place the deposit in trust. N.Y.Gen.Oblig.Law § 7–103 (McKinney 1978). Others require the funds to be placed in escrow. Del.Code Ann. tit. 25, § 5511(b) (1975). The general purpose of these statutes is to prevent commingling of the funds of the landlord and the tenant. Michigan law permits the landlord to use the deposit for its personal benefit provided the landlord posts a bond to secure the return of the money to the tenant.

Lastly, some states require the landlord to pay the tenant interest on the deposit or to pay the tenant any income actually earned on the deposit. See Mass.Gen.Law Ann. ch. 186 § 15B(3)(b) (West Supp.1986). The landlord is generally permitted to deduct from the interest earned some amount to compensate it for the administrative burdens imposed by requiring that interest be earned and paid to the tenant. N.J.Stat.Ann. § 46:8–19(b) (West Supp.1986) (landlord entitled to a 1% fee for administrative expenses).

§ 7.11   THE HOLDOVER TENANT

A holdover tenant is a tenant who, after the termination of the lease, fails to surrender possession of the premises to the landlord. Since by definition a tenant is a person in the rightful possession of the land of another, to call a tenant a "holdover" is somewhat of a misnomer since the holdover tenant is no longer in rightful possession of the premises. Neither is such tenant a mere trespasser since a trespasser is one who enters wrongfully.

What are the lessor's options when a tenant holds over beyond the termination of the tenancy? What are the tenant's options? To the extent either the landlord or the tenant has options, what factors affect which option they shall elect?

COMMONWEALTH BUILDING CORP. v. HIRSCHFIELD

Appellate Court of Illinois, 1st District, 1st Division (1940).
307 Ill.App. 533, 30 N.E.2d 790.

MATCHETT, JUSTICE.

In a suit for rent to the amount of $3,300, on trial by jury, there was a verdict for plaintiff in the sum of $1,100. There were motions by each of the parties for judgment non obstante veredicto, which were in each case denied, and a motion by defendant for a new trial, which was allowed on August 1, 1940. This appeal is by leave from that order.

The material (and as we think, uncontradicted) facts are that the defendant with his family was in possession of an apartment used for residence purposes, under a written lease with the plaintiff, which by its terms expired September 30, 1938. The lease contained a clause (paragraph 11 not abstracted) providing that if defendant held over he would become liable for double rent. Mr. Kishin was the bookkeeper for plaintiff. He was also an attorney employed by the firm of Pennish and Rashbaum, and Mr. Pennish was managing director of this building. It contained thirteen floors comprising twenty-four apartments, twelve of seven rooms each and twelve of nine rooms each. The apartment leased by defendant was known as 3–A. It contained nine rooms, and the rent paid by defendant under his lease was $275 per month. The business office of defendant was at 544 N. Wells street.

Mr. Fleury was engineer in charge of the building, and Mr. Danny was his assistant. Mr. Zeri was a janitor-helper. There was an elevator in the front of the building used exclusively by passengers and an elevator in the back of the building used exclusively for deliveries and general service. The passenger elevator was operated by an attendant. The freight elevators were operated without an attendant by the use of electricity applied by pushing buttons.

Defendant determined to move at the expiration of his lease, and about two months before the lease expired so notified plaintiff by registered mail. Defendant employed the Federal Storage and Moving Company to do the necessary work and transportation of goods to that end. Two packers delivered boxes and barrels and necessary material for the packing of breakables on September 27. The breakable goods were packed in boxes and barrels and September 29 part of the household goods (including large items of furniture) were moved out by way of the elevator in the rear. Six to ten van loads were moved out on September 29; forty to fifty barrels (including cases). The moving continued for three days, the 28th, 29th and 30th of September.

While this was going on Danny was washing the walls and removing trash and garbage. Most of the goods had been moved out by the 30th, the day on which the lease expired. The work was, however, not quite completed. There had been some delay in getting the use of the elevators. Defendant gave evidence tending to show that the servants of plaintiff were responsible for this, but the evidence is denied by them and they on the contrary say they gave assistance. This would seem to be true as Mrs. Hirschfield testified she tipped them as a reward for their help. At any rate, when the lease expired at 12 o'clock on the night of September 30, the family was not yet out and with the servants slept in the apartment. Carpets and the bedroom furniture had not been removed but were promptly taken out on the following day, October 1.

At about 10 o'clock on the morning of October 1, Mr. Pennish, for plaintiff, served upon defendant at his office in Wells street, a notice as follows: "In view of the fact that you did not vacate possession of your apartment within the time provided for in your lease, the undersigned has elected, and does hereby elect, to treat you as a hold-over tenant for another year, and you are accordingly requested to pay October rent immediately."

While the law is otherwise in England (16 R.C.L., § 684, p. 1163) it was decided in New York in the early case of Conway v. Starkweather, 1 Denio 113, 114, that a tenant who holds over after the expiration of his term may, at the election of the landlord, be held to be either a trespasser or tenant for another similar term. Later New York decisions adhere to that rule . . ., although the later case of Herter v. Mullen, 159 N.Y. 28, 53

N.E. 700, 44 L.R.A. 703, 70 Am.St.Rep. p. 517, seems to decide that the holding must be voluntary on the part of the tenant.

The New York rule was adopted by the Illinois Supreme Court in the case of Clinton Wire Cloth Co. v. Gardner et al., 99 Ill. 151, and has been followed in subsequent cases based upon the theory, however, that the rule is to be applied only where the holding is voluntary. . . .

The argument for strict adherence to the New York rule is based upon the necessity for certainty as between landlords and tenants with regard to their respective rights. In a note to Herter v. Mullen, supra, in the American State Reports, it is said: "It is a universal rule that if premises are let for a year or from year to year, and the tenant holds over, the landlord may elect to treat him as a tenant from year to year, or when the renting is for a shorter period and the tenant holds over, he may be deemed to hold upon the terms upon which he entered, and the landlord may recover rent of him according to the terms of the original contract or lease. . . . or the landlord may at his election treat the tenant holding over as a trespasser and may bring ejectment against him without any previous notice, unless the holding over has been such that it may be presumed that the landlord has assented thereto. . . ."

* * *

An examination of the cases discloses that usually they proceed upon one of two theories. First, that the voluntary action of the tenant is such as to disclose the right of the landlord to assume an intention on the tenant's part to create a second tenancy, or, secondly, that the action of the tenant is such that the court will as a matter of law hold the tenant liable for a second lease upon the principal of quasi contract that justice may prevail. Williston on Contracts, Vol. 6, § 1836.

On the undisputed facts of this case we think plaintiff is not entitled to recover upon either theory. The uncontradicted evidence recited above shows no grounds on which a voluntary agreement for a new tenancy could be inferred. Defendant was vacating the premises with reasonable speed and in good faith. The representatives of the landlord were present, knew and assisted them in getting their goods out of the apartment and were given extra pay for doing so. There is not a scintilla of evidence from which the jury could reasonably find there was any intention on the part of defendant to continue the lease. Unfortunately, notwithstanding good faith, the removal of the last piece of furniture was delayed for a few hours. The tenant and his family did not arise at midnight and move out. They waited until the rising of the sun. Shortly thereafter the landlord availed himself of this supposed ancient rule of law and served notice of his intention to collect from defendant $3,300 for his delict. There is nothing either in word or deed of the tenant that indicates an intention on his part to renew. Every action indicated the contrary intention. Defendant, therefore, cannot be held on the theory of a voluntary contract. Nor in our opinion can defendant be held on the theory of quasi contract that justice required an absolute presumption of a contract for another tenancy. The lease provided for precisely such a contingency. The provision was in substance (paragraph 11 not abstracted) that if the tenant failed to move at the expiration of the lease, he should pay double the usual rent for the actual time of his occupancy. This is the agreement of the parties and is reasonable. The claim of plaintiff is highly penal in its nature. It has been held in New York that the rule is not applicable in such a case. Pickett v. Bartlett, 107 N.Y. 277, 14 N.E. 301. In Green v. Kroeger, 67 Mo.App. 621, under similar circumstances the court said: "In this case the lease by express terms provides for the rights of the parties in the contingency of a holding over after its expiration. By the clause to that effect it is distinctly provided that the continued occupancy of the premises after the end of the term shall entitle the lessor to recover double rent from the occupiers 'for all such time.' This clause did not deprive the lessor of his option to retake the premises at the expiration of the lease, but in case of his failure so to do or to make a new agreement with the lessees, it deprived him of the power to do more than recover double rent for the time he should permit the lessees to hold over after the expiration of the lease."

There are no Illinois decisions so far as we are informed to the contrary. We hold the motion of defendant for judgment in his favor notwithstanding the verdict should have been allowed. . . .

Reversed, with judgment here for the defendant.

McSURELY, J., concurs.

O'CONNOR, PRESIDING JUSTICE (specially concurring).

I agree with what is said in the foregoing opinion and the result reached but I think it ought to be said that the claim made by plaintiff for $3,300 shocks the conscience of the court. It is wholly without merit and ought not to be entertained by any court of justice. As stated in the opinion, defendant had the right to remain in the premises all day of the 30th of September and it is common knowledge in Chicago, of which we take judicial notice, that some leases of apartments expire on the 30th of April and others on the 30th of September, and that a lease to a succeeding tenant begins the first of May and others on the first of October. And everyone knows that tenants who are vacating on the 30th of April or on the 30th of September, as the case might be, have not completed their moving on the last day covered by their respective leases, there being a great many persons moving at those times so that it is physically impossible to do so. But in such cases the "rule of reason" must constantly be kept in mind. . . .

Under this rule which is in every case whether we realize it or not, it is not every dereliction however slight which will give rise to a cause of action.

NOTES AND QUESTIONS

1. As the principal case suggests, if a tenant wrongfully holds over beyond the termination of the tenancy, the landlord, at common law, has the option to treat the tenant as a holdover tenant for another term or to treat the tenant as a trespasser and sue for possession. Thus, potential for hardship to the tenant is great. What policy justified allowing the landlord the election to treat the tenant as a holdover or as a trespasser? Does the rule benefit only landlords as a class or do tenants as a group also benefit from the rules? See generally R. Schoshinski, American Law of Landlord & Tenant, § 2:23 (1980 & Supp.1986). Is the *Hirschfield* case merely a rejection of the harshness of the common-law rule?

2. At common law how much time should the landlord be permitted before it must make a decision which option it will select? As might be expected, the case law suggests the landlord must make its election within a reasonable time. Is that a helpful standard? What constitutes a reasonable time? If the landlord elects to evict the tenant two months after the expiration of the term of the lease, has the landlord acted within a reasonable time? Should the law simply have required the landlord to make the election within one month?

3. Can the landlord change an election once it has been made? For example, suppose L elects to treat T as a holdover for another year and one month later sues to evict T. Can L recover? See, e.g., Crechale & Polles, Inc. v. Smith, 295 So.2d 275 (Miss.1974). Suppose L does nothing within a reasonable time after the termination of the lease. What is the tenant's status? Is the tenant a periodic tenant or a trespasser? Compare W.H. Hobbs & Son v. Grand Trunk Ry. Co., 93 Vt. 392, 108 A. 199 (1919) with Beach Realty Co. v. Wildwood, 105 N.J.L. 317, 144 A. 720 (Err. & App.1929).

4. If the landlord elects to treat the tenant as a holdover for a new term is a periodic tenancy or a tenancy for a term for years created? Compare Brach v. Amoco Oil Co., 677 F.2d 1213 (7th Cir.1982) with Grisham v. Lowery, 621 S.W.2d 745 (Tenn.App.1981). Although there is a split of authority, most states hold that a periodic tenancy results. Among the states holding that a periodic tenancy is created, there is a split as to the nature of the period. Compare Vernon v. Kennedy, 50 N.C.App. 302, 273 S.E.2d 31 (1981) and Makin v. Mack, 336 A.2d 230 (Del.Ch.1975) (year-to-year) with Madison Bldg. Ass'n v. Eckert, 49 Ohio App. 210, 196 N.E. 789 (1934) (month-to-month).

Restatement (Second) of Property § 14.4 (1977), takes the position that a periodic tenancy results from landlord's election and the term equals the length of the period for which rent is computed. Thus, if rent is computed on a monthly basis, the holdover tenancy is a month-to-month tenancy. In no event, however, can the holdover be for a period more than a year-to-year.

URLTA § 4.301 provides that if the tenant remains in possession of the premises beyond the term of the lease the landlord may (1) sue for possession and, under certain circumstances, recover up to three months rent or damages, whichever is greater, or (2) treat the tenant as a month-to-month tenant.

5. The *Hirschfield* case is somewhat unusual in that it involves an express election by the landlord to treat the holdover as a tenant for year-to-year. Most cases involve only an implied election one way or the other. Suppose the landlord leases the premises to another. Is that an implied election? Brown v. Music, Inc., 359 P.2d 295 (Alaska 1961). Suppose the landlord accepts rent checks from the tenant. Is that an implied election? Grisham v. Lowery, 621 S.W.2d 745 (Tenn.App.1981). Suppose landlord accepts a rent check while the parties are negotiating the terms of a new lease. Is that an implied election? Rottman v. Bluebird Bakery, Inc., 3 Wis.2d 309, 88 N.W.2d 374 (1958).

6. In Herter v. Mullen, 159 N.Y. 28, 53 N.E. 700 (1899), cited in the *Hirschfield* case, the tenant held over because the tenant's mother was too ill to move at the time the lease terminated. The tenant remained in possession of one room of the leased apartment for fifteen days. The court held that the tenant was liable for the amount of damages landlord actually suffered, including lost profits, but refused to hold the tenant liable as a periodic tenant for year-to-year. The court found that one could be held for another period only if the holding over had been voluntary and not the result of an accident or act of God. Is this the reasoning of the principal case? How far can one stretch this reasoning? Suppose the tenant wants to leave at the end of the term but is unable to do so because of a severe housing shortage in the locale. Can the landlord elect to treat the tenant as a holdover or can the tenant plead the *Herter* defense? See Shull v. Hatfield, 240 Mo.App. 275, 202 S.W.2d 916 (1947). Suppose the tenant has leased new premises but is unable to vacate the old premises when its lease terminates because the new premises are unavailable due to a construction workers' strike. Same result? Suppose the landlord and the tenant are negotiating a new lease and, believing an agreement is within reach, the tenant holds over beyond the end of the term. Subsequently the negotiations collapse and the landlord seeks to hold tenant liable for a new term. What result? See Lawson v. West Virginia Newspaper Publishing Co., 126 W.Va. 470, 29 S.E.2d 3 (1944).

7. L and T enter into a lease requiring T to surrender the premises in the same condition as they were at the beginning of the term. For the two-month period following the end of the term, T had workmen on the premises to make repairs necessary to comply with T's obligations under the lease. L claims that because the repairs were made by T following the end of the term, T is a holdover tenant. Do you agree? Suppose T timely vacates the premises at the end of the term but retains the keys. Can L treat T as a holdover? See Consumers Distributing Co. Ltd. v. Hermann, 107 Nev. 387, 812 P.2d 1274 (1991).

8. Suppose the landlord sends notice to the tenant that the rent will be increased at the end of the lease term from $240 a month to $325 a month, and that if the tenant wishes to remain in possession she will be required to pay the increased rents. The tenant fails to respond to this written notice and holds over beyond the end of the term. Can the landlord hold the tenant liable for the increased rents? See generally Garrity v. United States, 107 Ct.Cl. 92,

67 F.Supp. 821 (1946); Heckman v. Walker, 167 Neb. 216, 92 N.W.2d 548 (1958). But see Iorio v. Donnelly, 343 Mass. 772, 178 N.E.2d 28 (1961). What if the tenant sends landlord a written notice that the tenant refuses to pay the increased rent and then holds over? Compare Sheriff v. Kromer, 232 Ill.App. 589 (1924) with Palagonia v. Pappas, 79 Misc.2d 830, 361 N.Y.S.2d 236 (Dist.Ct.1974).

Suppose the tenant sends a notice to the landlord that it will continue the tenancy beyond the end of the lease terms but only on covenants different from those contained in the lease. The landlord fails to respond to this notice and state law provides that if landlord fails to respond to tenant's notice of an intent to hold over, a new periodic tenancy is created. Is such a tenancy also created upon the terms stated by the tenant in the notice? Routman v. Bohm, 194 Pa.Super. 413, 168 A.2d 612 (1961).

§ 7.12 RENT CONTROL

Rent control is government regulation of the maximum rents that landlords may charge their tenants. Most rent control involves residential tenants, although a few ordinances apply to commercial tenants as well.

Rent control legislation is usually local, not state. While the local ordinances vary greatly, most have a few points in common. When first passed, they identify some "base" rent for each rental unit in the controlled area—usually the rent that was being charged on some specified date before the passage of the ordinance. Typically, new rental units that come on the market after the ordinance becomes effective may have the initial rent established by agreement between the landlord and the first tenant. This becomes the base rent for that unit. Some ordinances provide that housing built after the ordinance takes effect are not subject to rent control.

Under many rent control ordinances landlords are permitted a uniform maximum periodic rent increase—for example, a five percent increase once a year. A rent stabilization board created by the ordinance meets periodically (generally once a year) to compute the allowable increase. The board may consider such factors as the inflation rate or the cost of living index, any unusual changes in property taxes or utility bills that affected the entire community, and perhaps some factors on the demand side of the market, such as the unemployment rate. It will then produce a maximum allowable rent increase for that year. Landlords generally may exact less than the maximum, but not more. Most statutes additionally provide a process by which landlords (and often tenants) may request a separate hearing for consideration of an unusual situation justifying a larger (or smaller) increase than the statute permits.

PENNELL v. CITY OF SAN JOSE

Supreme Court of the United States (1988).
485 U.S. 1.

CHIEF JUSTICE REHNQUIST delivered the opinion of the Court.

This case involves a challenge to a rent control ordinance enacted by the City of San Jose, California, that allows a hearing officer to consider, among other factors, the "hardship to a tenant" when determining whether to approve a rent increase proposed by a landlord. Appellants Richard Pennell and the Tri–County Apartment House Owners Association sued in the Superior Court of Santa Clara County seeking a declaration that the ordinance, in particular the "tenant hardship" provisions, are "facially unconstitutional and therefore ... illegal and void." * * *

At the heart of the Ordinance is a mechanism for determining the amount by which landlords subject to its provisions may increase the annual rent which they charge their tenants. A landlord is automatically entitled to raise the rent of a tenant in possession by as much as eight percent; if a tenant objects to an increase greater than eight percent, a hearing is required before a "Mediation Hearing Officer" to determine whether the landlord's proposed increase is "reasonable under the circumstances." The Ordinance sets forth a number of factors to be considered by the hearing officer in making this determination, including "the hardship to a tenant." Because appellants concentrate their attack on the consideration of this factor, we set forth the relevant provision of the Ordinance in full:

> "§ 5703.29 Hardship to Tenants. In the case of a rent increase or any portion thereof which exceeds the standard set in Section 5703.28(a) or (b), then with respect to such excess and whether or not to allow same to be part of the increase allowed under this Chapter, the Hearing Officer shall consider the economic and financial hardship imposed on the present tenant or tenants of the unit or units to which such increases apply. If, on balance, the Hearing Officer determines that the proposed increase constitutes an unreasonably severe financial or economic hardship on a particular tenant, he may order that the excess of the increase which is subject to consideration under subparagraph (c) of Section 5703.28, or any portion thereof, be disallowed. Any tenant whose household income and monthly housing expense meets [certain income requirements] shall be deemed to be suffering under financial and economic hardship which must be weighed in the Hearing Officer's determination. The burden of proof in establishing any other economic hardship shall be on the tenant."

If either a tenant or a landlord is dissatisfied with the decision of the hearing officer, the Ordinance provides for binding arbitration. A landlord who attempts to charge or who receives rent in excess of the maximum rent established as provided in the Ordinance is subject to criminal and civil penalties. * * *

[W]e first address appellants' contention that application of the Ordinance's tenant hardship provisions violates the Fifth and Fourteenth Amendments' prohibition against taking of private property for public use without just compensation. In essence, appellants' claim is as follows: § 5703.28 of the Ordinance establishes the seven factors that a Hearing Officer is to take into account in determining the reasonable rent increase. The first six of these factors are all objective, and are related either to the landlord's costs of providing an adequate rental unit, or to the condition of the rental market.[1] Application of these six standards results in a rent that is "reasonable" by reference to what appellants' contend is the only legitimate purpose of rent control: the elimination of "excessive" rents caused by San Jose's housing shortage. When the Hearing Officer then takes into account "hardship to a tenant" pursuant to § 5703.28(c)(7) and reduces the rent below the objectively "reasonable" amount established by the first six factors, this additional reduction in the rent increase constitutes a "taking." This taking is impermissible because it does not serve the purpose of eliminating excessive rents—that objective has already been accomplished by considering the first six factors—instead, it serves only the purpose of providing assistance to "hardship tenants." In short, appellants contend, the additional reduction of rent on grounds of hardship accomplishes a transfer of the landlord's property to individual hardship tenants; the Ordinance forces private individuals to shoulder the "public" burden of subsidizing their poor tenants' housing. * * *

We think it would be premature to consider this contention on the present record. As things stand, there simply is no evidence that the "tenant hardship clause" has in fact ever been relied upon by a Hearing Officer to reduce a rent below the figure it would have been set at on the basis of the other factors set forth in the Ordinance. In addition, there is nothing in the Ordinance requiring that a Hearing Officer in fact reduce a proposed rent increase on grounds of tenant hardship. Section 5703.29 does make it mandatory that hardship be considered—it states that "the Hearing Officer shall consider the economic hardship imposed on the present tenant"—but it then goes on to state that if "the proposed increase constitutes an unreasonably severe financial or economic hardship * * * he may order that the excess of the increase" be disallowed. § 5703.29. Given the "essentially ad hoc, factual inquir[y]" involved in the takings analysis, Kaiser Aetna v. United States, 444 U.S. 164, 175, 100 S.Ct. 383, 390, 62 L.Ed.2d 332 (1979), we have found it particularly important in takings cases to adhere to our admonition that "the constitutionality of statutes ought not be decided except in an actual factual setting that makes such a decision necessary." * * * [T]he mere fact that a Hearing Officer is enjoined to consider hardship to the tenant in fixing a landlord's rent, without any showing in a particular case as to the

1. [The other six factors that the ordinance required the hearing officer to take into account were: (1) the cost of servicing the landlord's debt (mortgage); (2) the rental history of the unit; (3) the physical condition of the unit; (4) changes in the amount of services the landlord provided; (5) any additional financial information supplied by the landlord; and (6) the market value for similar units. San Jose Municipal Ordinance 19696, § 5703.28(c) (1979)—ed.]

consequences of that injunction in the ultimate determination of the rent, does not present a sufficiently concrete factual setting for the adjudication of the takings claim appellants raise here. * * *

Appellants also urge that the mere provision in the Ordinance that a Hearing Officer may consider the hardship of the tenant in finally fixing a reasonable rent renders the Ordinance "facially invalid" under the Due Process and Equal Protection Clauses, even though no landlord ever had its rent diminished by as much as one dollar because of the application of this provision. The standard for determining whether a state price-control regulation is constitutional under the Due Process Clause is well established: "Price control is 'unconstitutional . . . if arbitrary, discriminatory, or demonstrably irrelevant to the policy the legislature is free to adopt. . . .' " Permian Basin Area Rate Cases, 390 U.S. 747, 769–770, 88 S.Ct. 1344, 1361 (1968) (quoting Nebbia v. New York, 291 U.S. 502, 539, 54 S.Ct. 505, 517, 78 L.Ed. 940 (1934)). In other contexts we have recognized that the Government may intervene in the marketplace to regulate rates or prices that are artificially inflated as a result of the existence of a monopoly or near monopoly. . . . Accordingly, appellants do not dispute that the Ordinance's asserted purpose of "prevent[ing] excessive and unreasonable rent increases" caused by the "growing shortage of and increasing demand for housing in the City of San Jose. . . ." They do argue, however, that it is "arbitrary, discriminatory, or demonstrably irrelevant" for appellees to attempt to accomplish the additional goal of reducing the burden of housing costs on low-income tenants by requiring that "hardship to a tenant" be considered in determining the amount of excess rent increase that is "reasonable under the circumstances" pursuant to § 5703.28. As appellants put it, "The objective of alleviating individual tenant hardship is . . . not a 'policy the legislature is free to adopt' in a rent control ordinance."

We reject this contention, however, because we have long recognized that a legitimate and rational goal of price or rate regulation is the protection of consumer welfare. * * * Here, the Ordinance establishes a scheme in which a Hearing Officer considers a number of factors in determining the reasonableness of a proposed rent increase which exceeds eight percent and which exceeds the amount deemed reasonable under either §§ 5703.28(a) or 5703.28(b). The first six factors of § 5703.28(c) focus on the individual landlord—the Hearing Officer examines the history of the premises, the landlord's costs, and the market for comparable housing. Section 5703.28(c)(5) also allows the landlord to bring forth any other financial evidence—including presumably evidence regarding his own financial status—to be taken into account by the Hearing Officer. It is in only this context that the Ordinance allows tenant hardship to be considered and, under § 5703.29, "balance[d]" with the other factors set out in § 5703.28(c). Within this scheme, § 5703.28(c) represents a rational attempt to accommodate the conflicting interests of protecting tenants from burdensome rent increases while at the same time ensuring that landlords are guaranteed a fair return on their investment. We accordingly find that the Ordinance, which so carefully considers both the individual circumstances of the landlord and the tenant before determining whether to allow an additional increase in rent over and above certain amounts that are deemed reasonable, does not on its face violate the Fourteenth Amendment's Due Process Clause.

We also find that the Ordinance does not violate the Amendment's Equal Protection Clause. Here again, the standard is deferential; appellees need only show that the classification scheme embodied in the Ordinance is "rationally related to a legitimate state interest." As we stated in Vance v. Bradley, 440 U.S. 93, 99 S.Ct. 939, 59 L.Ed.2d 171 (1979), "we will not overturn [a statute that does not burden a suspect class or a fundamental interest] unless the varying treatment of different groups or persons is so unrelated to the achievement of any combination of legitimate purposes that we can only conclude that the legislature's actions were irrational." In light of our conclusion above that the Ordinance's tenant hardship provisions are designed to serve the legitimate purpose of protecting tenants, we can hardly conclude that it is irrational for the Ordinance to treat certain landlords differently on the basis of whether or not they have hardship tenants. The Ordinance distinguishes between landlords because doing so furthers the purpose of ensuring that individual tenants do not suffer "unreasonable" hardship; it would be inconsistent to state that hardship is a legitimate factor to be considered but then hold that appellees could not tailor the Ordinance so that only legitimate hardship cases are redressed.

For the foregoing reasons, we hold that it is premature to consider appellants' claim under the Takings Clause and we reject their facial challenge to the Ordinance under the Due Process and Equal Protection Clauses of the 14th Amendment. The judgment of the Supreme Court of California is accordingly

Affirmed.

JUSTICE SCALIA, with whom JUSTICE O'CONNOR joins, concurring in part and dissenting in part.

Appellants * * * contend that any application of the tenant hardship provision of the San Jose Ordinance would effect an uncompensated taking of private property because that provision does not substantially advance legitimate state interests and because it improperly imposes a public burden on individual landlords. I can understand how such a claim—that a law applicable to the plaintiffs is, root and branch, invalid—can be readily rejected on the merits, by merely noting that at least some of its applications may be lawful. But I do not understand how such a claim can possibly be avoided by considering it "premature." Suppose, for example, that the feature of the rental ordinance under attack was a provision allowing a Hearing Officer to consider the race of the apartment owner in deciding whether to allow a rent increase. It is inconceivable that we would say judicial challenge must await demonstration that this provision has actually been applied to the detriment of one of the plaintiffs. There is no difference, it seems to me, when the facial, root-and-branch challenge rests upon the Takings Clause rather than the Equal Protection Clause. * * *

* * * Appellants contend that providing financial assistance to impecunious renters is not a state interest that can legitimately be furthered by regulating the use of property. Knowing the nature and character of the particular property in question, or the degree of its economic impairment, will in no way assist this inquiry. * * *

Today's holding has no more basis in equity than it does in precedent. Since the San Jose Ordinance does not require any specification of how much reduction in rent is attributable to each of the various factors that the Hearing Officer is allowed to take into account, it is quite possible that none of the many landlords affected by the ordinance will ever be able to meet the Court's requirement of a "showing in a particular case as to the consequences of [the hardship factor] in the ultimate determination of the rent[.]" There is no reason thus to shield alleged constitutional injustice from judicial scrutiny. I would therefore consider appellants' takings claim on the merits. * * *

Traditional land-use regulation (short of that which totally destroys the economic value of property) does not violate [the Takings clause] because there is a cause-and-effect relationship between the property use restricted by the regulation and the social evil that the regulation seeks to remedy. Since the owner's use of the property is (or, but for the regulation, would be) the source of the social problem, it cannot be said that he has been singled out unfairly. Thus, the common zoning regulations requiring subdividers to observe lot-size and set-back restrictions, and to dedicate certain areas to public streets, are in accord with our constitutional traditions because the proposed property use would otherwise be the cause of excessive congestion. The same cause-and-effect relationship is popularly thought to justify emergency price regulation: When commodities have been priced at a level that produces exorbitant returns, the owners of those commodities can be viewed as responsible for the economic hardship that occurs. Whether or not that is an accurate perception of the way a free-market economy operates, it is at least true that the owners reap unique benefits from the situation that produces the economic hardship, and in that respect singling them out to relieve it may not be regarded as "unfair." That justification might apply to the rent regulation in the present case, apart from the single feature under attack here. Appellants do not contest the validity of rent regulation in general. They acknowledge that the City may constitutionally set a "reasonable rent" according to the statutory minimum and the six other factors that must be considered by the Hearing Officer. * * * Appellants' only claim is that a reduction of a rent increase below what would otherwise be a "reasonable rent" under this scheme may not, consistently with the Constitution, be based on consideration of the seventh factor—the hardship to the tenant as defined in § 5703.29. I think they are right. * * *

The traditional manner in which American government has met the problem of those who cannot pay reasonable prices for privately sold necessities—a problem caused by the society at large—has been the distribution to such persons of funds raised from the public at large through taxes, either in cash (welfare payments) or in goods (public housing, publicly subsidized housing, and food stamps). Unless we are to abandon the guiding principle of the Takings Clause that "public burdens ... should be borne by the public as a whole," this is the only manner that our Constitution permits. The fact that government acts through the landlord-tenant relationship does not magically transform general public welfare, which must be supported by all the public, into mere "economic regulation," which can disproportionately burden particular individuals. Here the City is not "regulating" rents in the relevant sense of preventing rents that are excessive; rather, it is using the occasion of rent regulation (accomplished by the rest of the Ordinance) to establish a welfare program privately funded by those landlords who happen to have "hardship" tenants.

The politically attractive feature of regulation is not that it permits wealth transfers to be achieved that could not be achieved otherwise; but rather that it permits them to be achieved "off budget," with relative invisibility and thus relative immunity from normal democratic processes. * * *

I would hold that the seventh factor in § 5703.28(c) of the San Jose Ordinance effects a taking of property without just compensation.

BRASCHI v. STAHL ASSOCIATES COMPANY

Court of Appeals of New York (1989).
74 N.Y.2d 201, 544 N.Y.S.2d 784, 543 N.E.2d 49.

TITONE, JUDGE.

In this dispute over occupancy rights to a rent-controlled apartment, the central question to be resolved on this request for preliminary injunctive relief ... is whether appellant has demonstrated a likelihood of success on the merits ... by showing that, as a matter of law, he is entitled to seek protection from eviction under New York City Rent and Eviction Regulations 9 NYCRR 2204.6(d).... That regulation provides that upon the death of a rent-control tenant, the landlord may not dispossess "either the surviving spouse of the deceased tenant or some other member of the deceased tenant's family who has been living with the tenant...." Resolution of this question requires this court to determine the meaning of the term "family" as it is used in this context.

I.

Appellant, Miguel Braschi, was living with Leslie Blanchard in a rent-controlled apartment located at 405 East 54th Street from the summer of 1975 until Blanchard's death in September of 1986. In November of 1986, respondent, Stahl Associates Company, the owner of the apartment building, served a notice to cure on appellant contending that he was a mere licensee with no right to occupy the apartment since only Blanchard was the tenant of record. In December of 1986 respondent served appellant with a notice to terminate informing appellant that he had one month to vacate the apartment and that, if the apartment was not vacated, respondent would commence summary proceedings to evict him.

Appellant then initiated an action seeking a permanent injunction and a declaration of entitlement to occupy the apartment. By order to show cause appellant then moved for a preliminary injunction ... enjoining respondent from evicting him until a court could determine whether he was a member of Blanchard's family within the meaning of 9 NYCRR 2204.6(d). After examining the nature of the relationship between the two men, Supreme Court concluded that appellant was a "family member" within the meaning of the regulation and, accordingly, that a preliminary injunction should be issued. The court based this decision on its finding that the long-term interdependent nature of the 10–year relationship between appellant and Blanchard "fulfills any definitional criteria of the term 'family.'"

The Appellate Division reversed, concluding that section 2204.6(d) provides noneviction protection only to "family members within traditional, legally recognized familial relationships" (143 A.D.2d 44, 45, 531 N.Y.S.2d 562). Since appellant's and Blanchard's relationship was not one given formal recognition by the law, the court held that appellant could not seek the protection of the noneviction ordinance. After denying the motion for preliminary injunctive relief, the Appellate Division granted leave to appeal to this court, certifying the following question of law: "Was the order of this Court, which reversed the order of the Supreme Court, properly made?" We now reverse.

II.

* * *

It is fundamental that in construing the words of a statute "[t]he legislative intent is the great and controlling principle" ... [citations omitted] Indeed, "the general purpose is a more important aid to the meaning than any rule which grammar or formal logic may lay down" (United States v. Whitridge, 197 U.S. 135, 143, 25 S.Ct. 406, 408, 49 L.Ed. 696). Statutes are ordinarily interpreted so as to avoid objectionable consequences and to prevent hardship or injustice.... Hence, where doubt exists as to the meaning of a term, and a choice between two constructions is afforded, the consequences that may result from the different interpretations should be considered.... In addition, since rent-control laws are remedial in nature and designed to promote the public good, their provisions should be interpreted broadly to effectuate their purposes.... Finally, where a problem as to the meaning of a given term arises, a court's role is not to delve into the minds of legislators, but rather to effectuate the statute by carrying out the purpose of the statute as it is embodied in the words chosen by the Legislature....

The present dispute arises because the term "family" is not defined in the rent-control code and the legislative history is devoid of any specific reference to the noneviction provision. All that is known is the legislative purpose underlying the enactment of the rent-control laws as a whole. Rent control was enacted to address a "serious public emergency" created by "an acute shortage in dwellings," which resulted in "speculative, unwarranted and abnormal increases in rents" (L.1946 ch. 274, codified, as amended, at McKinney's Uncons. Laws of N.Y. § 8581 et seq.). These measures were designed to regulate and control the housing market so as to "prevent exactions of unjust, unreasonable and oppressive rents and rental agreements and to forestall profiteering, speculation and other disruptive practices tending to produce threats to the public health * * * [and] to prevent uncertainty, hardship and dislocation" (id.). Although initially designed as an emergency measure to alleviate the housing shortage attributable to the end of World War II, "a serious public emergency continues to exist in the housing of a considerable number of persons" (id.). Consequently, the Legislature has found it necessary to continually reenact the rent-control laws, thereby providing continued protection to tenants.

To accomplish its goals, the Legislature recognized that not only would rents have to be controlled, but that evictions would have to be regulated and controlled as well (id.). Hence, section 2204.6 of the New York City Rent and Eviction Regulations (9 NYCRR 2204.6), which authorizes the issuance of a certificate for the eviction of persons occupying a rent-controlled apartment after the death of the named tenant, provides, in subdivision (d), noneviction protection to those occupants who are either the "surviving spouse of the deceased tenant or some other member of the deceased tenant's family who has been living with the tenant [of record].... " The manifest intent of this section is to restrict the landowners' ability to evict a narrow class of occupants other than the tenant of record. The question presented here concerns the scope of the protections provided. Juxtaposed against this intent favoring the protection of tenants, is the over-all objective of a gradual "transition from regulation to a normal market of free bargaining between landlord and tenant" (see, e.g., Administrative Code of City of New York § 26–401). One way in which this goal is to be achieved is "vacancy decontrol," which automatically makes rent-control units subject to the less rigorous provisions of rent stabilization upon the termination of the rent-control tenancy....

Emphasizing the latter objective, respondent argues that the term "family member" as used in 9 NYCRR 2204.6(d) should be construed, consistent with this State's intestacy laws, to mean relationships of blood, consanguinity and adoption in order to effectuate the over-all goal of orderly succession to real property. Under this interpretation, only those entitled to inherit under the laws of intestacy would be afforded noneviction protection.... Further, as did the Appellate Division, respondent relies on our decision in Matter of Robert Paul P., 63 N.Y.2d 233, 481

N.Y.S.2d 652, 471 N.E.2d 424, arguing that since the relationship between appellant and Blanchard has not been accorded legal status by the Legislature, it is not entitled to the protections of section 2204.6(d), which, according to the Appellate Division, applies only to "family members within traditional, legally recognized familial relationships" (143 A.D.2d 44, 45, 531 N.Y.S.2d 562)....

Respondent's reliance on Matter of Robert Paul P. (supra) is also misplaced, since that case, which held that one adult cannot adopt another where none of the incidents of a filial relationship is evidenced or even remotely intended, was based solely on the purposes of the adoption laws ... and has no bearing on the proper interpretation of a provision in the rent control laws.

We also reject respondent's argument that the purpose of the noneviction provision of the rent-control laws is to control the orderly succession to real property in a manner similar to that which occurs under our State's intestacy laws.... The noneviction provision does not concern succession to real property but rather is a means of protecting a certain class of occupants from the sudden loss of their homes. The regulation does not create an alienable property right that could be sold, assigned or otherwise disposed of and, hence, need not be construed as coextensive with the intestacy laws. Moreover, such a construction would be inconsistent with the purposes of the rent-control system as a whole, since it would afford protection to distant blood relatives who actually had but a superficial relationship with the deceased tenant while denying that protection to unmarried lifetime partners. Finally, the dissent's reliance on Hudson View Props. v. Weiss, 59 N.Y.2d 733, 463 N.Y.S.2d 428, 450 N.E.2d 234 is misplaced. In that case we permitted the eviction of an unrelated occupant from a rent-controlled apartment under a lease explicitly restricting occupancy to "immediate family." However, the tenant in Hudson View conceded "that an individual not part of her immediate family" occupied the apartment (id., at 735, 463 N.Y.S.2d 428, 450 N.E.2d 234), and, thus, the sole question before us was whether enforcement of the lease provision was violative of the State or City Human Rights Law. Whether respondent tenant was, in fact, an "immediate family" member was neither specifically addressed nor implicitly answered....

Contrary to all of these arguments, we conclude that the term family, as used in 9 NYCRR 2204.6(d), should not be rigidly restricted to those people who have formalized their relationship by obtaining, for instance, a marriage certificate or an adoption order. The intended protection against sudden eviction should not rest on fictitious legal distinctions or genetic history, but instead should find its foundation in the reality of family life. In the context of eviction, a more realistic, and certainly equally valid, view of a family includes two adult lifetime partners whose relationship is long term and characterized by an emotional and financial commitment and interdependence. This view comports both with our society's traditional concept of "family" and with the expectations of individuals who live in such nuclear units.... [1] In fact, Webster's Dictionary defines "family" first as "a group of people united by certain convictions or common affiliation" (Webster's Ninth New Collegiate Dictionary 448 [1984]; see, Ballantine's Law Dictionary 456 [3d ed. 1969] ["family" defined as "[p]rimarily, the collective body of persons who live in one house and under one head or management"]; Black's Law Dictionary 543 [Special Deluxe 5th ed. 1979]). Hence, it is reasonable to conclude that, in using the term "family," the Legislature intended to extend protection to those who reside in households having all of the normal familial characteristics.[2] Appellant Braschi should therefore be afforded the opportunity to prove that he and Blanchard had such a household.

This definition of "family" is consistent with both of the competing purposes of the rent-control laws: the protection of individuals from sudden dislocation and the gradual transition to a free market system. Family members, whether or not related by blood, or law who have always treated the apartment as their family home will be protected against the hardship of eviction following the death of the named tenant, thereby furthering the Legislature's goals of preventing dislocation and preserving family units which might otherwise be broken apart upon eviction.[3] This approach will foster the transition from rent control to rent stabilization by drawing a distinction between those individuals who are, in fact, genuine family members, and those who are mere roommates ... or newly discovered relatives hoping to inherit the rent-controlled apartment after the existing tenant's death.[4]

The determination as to whether an individual is entitled to noneviction protection should be based upon an objective examination of the relationship of the parties. In making this assessment, the lower courts of this State have looked to a number of factors, including the exclusivity

---

1. Although the dissent suggests that our interpretation of "family" indefinitely expands the protections provided by section 2204.6(d) ... its own proposed standard—legally recognized relationships based on blood, marriage or adoption—may cast an even wider net, since the number of blood relations an individual has will usually exceed the number of people who would qualify by our standard.

2. We note that the concurrer apparently agrees with our view of the purposes of the noneviction ordinance (concurring opn., at p. 215, at p. 791 of 544 N.Y.S.2d, at p. 56 of 543 N.E.2d), and the impact this purpose should have on the way in which this and future cases should be decided.

3. We note, however, that the definition of family that we adopt here for purposes of the noneviction protection of the laws is completely unrelated to the concept of "functional family," as that term has developed under this court's decisions in the context of zoning ordinances ... [citations omitted] Those decisions focus on a locality's power to use its zoning powers in such a way as to impinge upon an individual's ability to live under the same roof with another individual. They have absolutely no bearing on the scope of noneviction protection provided by section 2204.6(d).

4. Also unpersuasive is the dissent's interpretation of the "roommate" law which was passed in response to our decision in Hudson View Props. v. Weiss, 59 N.Y.2d 733, 463 N.Y.S.2d 428, 450 N.E.2d 234. That statute allows roommates to live with the named tenant by making lease provisions to the contrary void as against public policy ... The law also provides that "occupant's" (roommates) do not automatically acquire "any right to continued occupancy in the event that the tenant vacates the premises." ... Occupant is defined as "a person, other than a tenant or a member of a tenant's immediate family." ... However, contrary to the dissent's assumption that this law contemplates a distinction between related and unrelated individuals, no such distinction is apparent from the Legislature's unexplained use of the term "immediate family."

and longevity of the relationship, the level of emotional and financial commitment, the manner in which the parties have conducted their everyday lives and held themselves out to society, and the reliance placed upon one another for daily family services.... These factors are most helpful, although it should be emphasized that the presence or absence of one or more of them is not dispositive since it is the totality of the relationship as evidenced by the dedication, caring and self-sacrifice of the parties which should, in the final analysis, control. Appellant's situation provides an example of how the rule should be applied.

Appellant and Blanchard lived together as permanent life partners for more than 10 years. They regarded one another, and were regarded by friends and family, as spouses. The two men's families were aware of the nature of the relationship, and they regularly visited each other's families and attended family functions together, as a couple. Even today, appellant continues to maintain a relationship with Blanchard's niece, who considers him an uncle. In addition to their interwoven social lives, appellant clearly considered the apartment his home. He lists the apartment as his address on his driver's license and passport, and receives all his mail at the apartment address. Moreover, appellant's tenancy was known to the building's superintendent and doormen, who viewed the two men as a couple. Financially, the two men shared all obligations including a household budget. The two were authorized signatories of three safe-deposit boxes, they maintained joint checking and savings accounts, and joint credit cards. In fact, rent was often paid with a check from their joint checking account. Additionally, Blanchard executed a power of attorney in appellant's favor so that appellant could make necessary decisions— financial, medical and personal—for him during his illness. Finally, appellant was the named beneficiary of Blanchard's life insurance policy, as well as the primary legatee and coexecutor of Blanchard's estate. Hence, a court examining these facts could reasonably conclude that these men were much more than mere roommates.

Inasmuch as this case is before us on a certified question, we conclude only that appellant has demonstrated a likelihood of success on the merits, in that he is not excluded, as a matter of law, from seeking noneviction protection. Since all remaining issues are beyond this court's scope of review, we remit this case to the Appellate Division so that it may exercise its discretionary powers in accordance with this decision. Accordingly, the order of the Appellate Division should be reversed and the case remitted to that court for a consideration of undetermined questions. The certified question should be answered in the negative.

BELLACOSA, JUDGE (concurring).

My vote to reverse and remit rests on a narrower view of what must be decided in this case than the plurality and dissenting opinions deem necessary. The issue is solely whether petitioner qualifies as a member of a "family", as that generic and broadly embracive word is used in the anti-eviction regulation of the rent-control apparatus. The particular anti-eviction public policy enactment is fulfilled by affording the remedial protection to this petitioner on the facts advanced on this record at this preliminary injunction stage. The competing public policy of eventually restoring rent-controlled apartments to decontrol, to stabilization and even to arm's length market relationships is eclipsed in this instance, in my view, by the more pertinently expressed and clearly applicable anti-eviction policy. Courts, in circumstances as are presented here where legislative intent is completely indecipherable (Division of Housing and Community Renewal, the agency charged with administering the policy, is equally silent in this case and on this issue), are not empowered or expected to expand or to constrict the meaning of the legislatively chosen word "family," which could have been and still can be qualified or defined by the duly constituted enacting body in satisfying its separate branch responsibility and prerogative. Construing a regulation does not allow substitution of judicial views or preferences for those of the enacting body when the latter either fails or is unable or deliberately refuses to specify criteria or definitional limits for its selected umbrella word, "family", especially where the societal, governmental, policy and fiscal implications are so sweeping. . . . For then, "the judicial function expands beyond the molecular movements, in Holmes' figure, into the molar". . . . [citation omitted] . . .

The application of the governing word and statute to reach a decision in this case can be accomplished on a narrow and legitimate jurisprudential track. The enacting body has selected an unqualified word for a socially remedial statute, intended as a protection against one of the harshest decrees known to the law—eviction from one's home. Traditionally, in such circumstances, generous construction is favored. Petitioner has made his shared home in the affected apartment for 10 years. The only other occupant of that rent-controlled apartment over that same extended period of time was the tenant-in-law who has now died, precipitating this battle for the apartment. The best guidance available to the regulatory agency for correctly applying the rule in such circumstances is that it would be irrational not to include this petitioner and it is a more reasonable reflection of the intention behind the regulation to protect a person such as petitioner as within the regulation's class of "family". In that respect, he qualifies as a tenant in fact for purposes of the interlocking provisions and policies of the law. Therefore, under CPLR 6301, there would unquestionably be irreparable harm by not upholding the preliminary relief Supreme Court has decreed; the likelihood of success seems quite good since four Judges of this court, albeit by different rationales, agree at least that petitioner fits under the beneficial umbrella of the regulation; and the balance of equities would appear to favor petitioner.

SIMONS, JUDGE (dissenting).

I would affirm. The plurality has adopted a definition of family which extends the language of the regulation well beyond the implication of the words used in it. In doing so, it has expanded the class indefinitely to include anyone who can satisfy an administrator that he or she had an emotional and financial "commitment" to the statutory tenant. Its interpretation is inconsistent with the legislative scheme underlying rent regulation, goes well beyond the intended purposes of 9 NYCRR 2204.6(d), and produces an unworkable test that is subject to abuse. The concurring opinion fails to address the problem. It merely decides, ipse dixit, that plaintiff should win. Preliminarily, it will be helpful to briefly look at the legislative scheme underlying rent regulation. . . .

Rent regulation in New York is implemented by rent control and rent stabilization. Rent control is the stricter of the two programs. In 1946 the first of many "temporary" measures was enacted to address a public emergency created by the shortage of residential accommodations after World War II. That statute, and the statutes and regulations which followed it, were designed to monitor the housing market to prevent unreasonable and oppressive rents. These laws regulate the terms and conditions of rent-controlled tenancies exclusively; owners can evict tenants or occupants only on limited specified grounds . . . and only with the permission of the administrative agency. . . .

Central to any interpretation of the regulatory language is a determination of its purpose. There can be little doubt that the purpose of section 2204.6(d) was to create succession rights to a possessory interest in real property where the tenant of record has died or vacated the apartment. . . . It creates a new tenancy for every surviving family member living with decedent at the time of death who then becomes a new statutory tenant until death or until he or she vacates the apartment. The State concerns underlying this provision include the orderly and just succession of property interests (which includes protecting a deceased's spouse and family from loss of their longtime home) and the professed State objective that there be a gradual transition from government regulation to a normal market of free bargaining between landlord and tenant. Those objectives require a weighing of the interests of certain individuals living with the tenant of record at his or her death and the interests of the landlord in regaining possession of its property and rerenting it under the less onerous rent-stabilization laws. The interests are properly balanced if the regulation's exception is applied by using objectively verifiable relationships based on blood, marriage and adoption, as the State has historically done in the estate succession laws, family court acts and similar legislation. . . . The distinction is warranted because members of families, so defined, assume certain legal obligations to each other and to third persons, such as creditors, which are not imposed on unrelated individuals and this legal interdependency is worthy of consideration in determining which individuals are entitled to succeed to the interest of the statutory tenant in rent-controlled premises. Moreover, such an interpretation promotes certainty and consistency in the law and obviates the need for drawn out hearings and litigation focusing on such intangibles as the strength and duration of the relationship and the extent of the emotional and financial interdependency. . . . So limited, the regulation may be viewed as a tempered response, balancing the rights of landlords with those of the tenant. To come within that protected class, individuals must comply with State laws relating to marriage or adoption. Plaintiff cannot avail himself of these institutions, of course, but that only points up the need for a legislative solution, not a judicial one. . . .

Aside from these general considerations, the language itself suggests the regulation should be construed along traditional lines. Significantly, although the problem of unrelated persons living with tenants in rent-controlled apartments has existed for as long as rent control, there has been no effort by the State Legislature, the New York City Council or the agency charged with enforcing the statutes to define the word "family" contained in 9 NYCRR 2204.6(d) and its predecessors and we have no direct evidence of the term's intended scope. The plurality's response to this problem is to turn to the dictionary and select one definition, from the several found there, which gives the regulation the desired expansive construction.[5] I would search for the intended meaning by looking at what the Legislature and the Division of Housing and Community Renewal (DHCR), the agency charged with implementing rent control, have done in related areas. These sources produce persuasive evidence that both bodies intend the word family to be interpreted in the traditional sense.

The legislative view may be found in the "roommate" law enacted in 1983 (Real Property Law § 235–f, L.1983, ch. 403). That statute granted rights to persons living with, but unrelated to, the tenant of record. The statute was a response to our unanimous decision in Hudson View Props. v. Weiss, 59 N.Y.2d 733, 463 N.Y.S.2d 428, 450 N.E.2d 234; see, legislative findings to ch. 403, set out as note after Real Property Law § 226–b, McKinney's Cons. Laws of N.Y., Book 49, at 130. In Hudson View the landlord, by a provision in the lease, limited occupancy to the tenant of record and the tenant's "immediate family". When the landlord tried to evict the unmarried heterosexual partner of the named tenant of record, she defended the proceeding by claiming that the restrictive covenant in the lease violated provisions of the State and City Human Rights Laws prohibiting discrimination on the basis of marital status. We held that the exclusion had nothing to do with the tenants' unmarried status but depended on the lease's restriction of occupancy to the tenant and the tenant's "immediate family". Implicitly, we decided that the term "immediate family" did not include individuals who were unrelated by blood, marriage or adoption, notwithstanding "the close and loving relationship" of the parties. The Legislature's response to Weiss was measured. It enacted Real Property Law § 235–f(3), (4) which provides that occupants

---

5. For example, the definitions found in Black's Law Dictionary 543 (Special Deluxe 5th ed.) are: "family. The meaning of word 'family' necessarily depends on field of law in which word is used, purpose intended to be accomplished by its use, and facts and circumstances of each case * * * Most commonly refers to group of persons consisting of parents and children; father, mother and their children; immediate kindred, constituting fundamental social unit in civilized society * * * A collective body of persons who live in one house and under one head or management. A group of blood-relatives; all the relations who descend from a common ancestor, or who spring from a common root. A group of kindred persons * * * Husband and wife and their children, wherever they may reside and whether they dwell together or not" (citations omitted). The term is similarly defined in the other dictionaries cited in the plurality opinion.

of rent-controlled accommodations, whether related to the tenant of record or not, can continue living in rent-controlled and rent-stabilized apartments as long as the tenant of record continues to reside there. Lease provisions to the contrary are rendered void as against public policy (subd. [2]). Significantly, the statute provides that no unrelated occupant "shall * * * acquire any right to continued occupancy in the event the tenant vacates the premises or acquire any other rights of tenancy" (subd. [6]). Read against this background, the statute is evidence the Legislature does not contemplate that individuals unrelated to the tenant of record by blood, marriage or adoption should enjoy a right to remain in rent-controlled apartments after the death of the tenant (see, Rice, The New Morality and Landlord–Tenant Law, 55 N.Y.S. Bar J. [No. 6] 33, 41[postscript]).

There is similar evidence of how DHCR intends the section to operate. Manifestly, rent stabilization and rent control are closely related in purpose. Both recognize that, because of the serious ongoing public emergency with respect to housing in the City of New York, restrictions must be placed on residential housing. The DHCR promulgates the regulations for both rent-regulation systems, and the eviction regulations in rent control and the exceptions to them share a common purpose with the renewal requirements contained in the Rent Stabilization Code (compare, 9 NYCRR 2204.6[d], with 9 NYCRR 2523.5[b]). In the Rent Stabilization Code, the Division of Housing and Community Renewal has made it unmistakably clear that the definition of family includes only persons related by blood, marriage or adoption. Since the two statutes and the two regulations share a common purpose, it is appropriate to conclude that the definition of family in the regulations should be of similar scope.

Specifically, the rent-stabilization regulations provide under similar circumstances that the landlord must offer a renewal lease to "any member of such tenant's family * * * who has resided in the housing accommodation as a primary resident from the inception of the tenancy or commencement of the relationship" (9 NYCRR 2523.5[b][1]; see also 2523.5[b][2]). family for purposes of these two provisions is defined in section 2520.6(o) as: "A husband, wife, son, daughter, stepson, stepdaughter, father, mother, stepfather, stepmother, brother, sister, nephew, niece, uncle, aunt, grandfather, grandmother, grandson, granddaughter, father-in-law, mother-in-law, son-in-law, or daughter-in-law of the tenant or permanent tenant". All the enumerated relationships are traditional, legally recognized relationships based on blood, marriage or adoption. That being so, it would be anomalous, to say the least, were we to hold that the agency, having intentionally limited succession rights in rent-stabilized accommodations to those related by blood, marriage or adoption, intended a different result for rent-controlled accommodations; especially so when it is recognized that rent control was intended to give way to rent stabilization and that the broader the definition of family adopted, the longer rent-controlled tenancies will be perpetuated by sequentially created family members entitled to new tenancies. These expressions by the

Legislature and the DHCR are far more probative of the regulation's intended meaning than the majority's selective use of a favored dictionary definition.

Finally, there are serious practical problems in adopting the plurality's interpretation of the statute. Any determination of rights under it would require first a determination of whether protection should be accorded the relationship (i.e., unmarrieds, nonadopted occupants, etc.) and then a subjective determination in each case of whether the relationship was genuine, and entitled to the protection of the law, or expedient, and an attempt to take advantage of the law. Plaintiff maintains that the machinery for such decisions is in place and that appropriate guidelines can be constructed. He refers particularly to a formulation outlined by the court in 2–4 Realty Assocs. v. Pittman, 137 Misc.2d 898, 902, 523 N.Y.S.2d 7, which sets forth six different factors to be weighed. The plurality has essentially adopted his formulation. The enumeration of such factors, and the determination that they are controlling, is a matter best left to Legislatures because it involves the type of policy making the courts should avoid (see, People v. Allen, 27 N.Y.2d 108, 112–113, 313 N.Y.S.2d 719, 261 N.E.2d 637, supra), but even if these considerations are appropriate and exclusive, the application of them cannot be made objectively and creates serious difficulties in determining who is entitled to the statutory benefit. Anyone is potentially eligible to succeed to the tenant's premises and thus, in each case, the agency will be required to make a determination of eligibility based solely on subjective factors such as the "level of emotional and financial commitment" and "the manner in which the parties have conducted their everyday lives and held themselves out to society" (plurality opn. . . .).

By way of contrast, a construction of the regulation limited to those related to the tenant by blood, marriage or adoption provides an objective basis for determining who is entitled to succeed to the premises. That definition is not, contrary to the claim of the plurality, "inconsistent with the purposes of the system" and it would not confer the benefit of the exception on "distant blood relatives" with only superficial relationships to the deceased (plurality opn.). Certainly it does not "cast an even wider net" than does the plurality's definition (plurality opn. . . .). To qualify, occupants must not only be related to the tenant but must also "[have] been living with the tenant" (see, 22 NYCRR 2204.6[d]). We applied the "living with" requirement in 829 Seventh Ave. Co. v. Reider, 67 N.Y.2d 930, 502 N.Y.S.2d 715, 493 N.E.2d 939, when construing the predecessor to section 2204.6(d), and refused to extend the exception to a woman who occupied an apartment for the five months before the death of her grandmother, the statutory tenant, because she was not "living with" her grandmother. We held that the granddaughter, to be entitled to the premises under the exception, was required to prove more than blood relationship and co-occupancy; she also had to prove an intention to make the premises her permanent home. Since she had failed to establish that intention, she was not entitled to succeed to her grandmother's tenancy.

That ruling precludes the danger the plurality foresees that distant relatives will be enabled to take advantage of the exception contained in section 2204.6(d) (cf., 9 NYCRR 2523.5[b][1], [2]).

Rent control generally and section 2204.6, in particular, are in substantial derogation of property owners' rights. The court should not reach out and devise an expansive definition in this policy-laden area based upon limited experience and knowledge of the problems. The evidence available suggests that such a definition was not intended and that the ordinary and popular meaning of family in the traditional sense should be applied. If that construction is not favored, the Legislature or the agency can alter it. . . .

Accordingly, I would affirm the order of the Appellate Division.

* * *

Notes and Questions

1. In Yee v. City of Escondido, 503 U.S. 519 (1992), the Supreme Court also brushed aside a takings clause challenge to a mobile home rent control ordinance. That decision is noted in chapter ten.

Courts have generally struck down city rent control ordinances under either federal or state law if the provisions failed to guarantee the property owner a "fair" rate of return. For example, in Birkenfeld v. Berkeley, 17 Cal.3d 129, 130 Cal.Rptr. 465, 550 P.2d 1001 (1976), the California Supreme Court struck down an ordinance that rolled back all rents in the city to 1971 levels and confined landlords to the base rent for an indefinite time until the adjustment board should permit an increase. The court found that the ordinance was confiscatory. However, Kavanau v. Santa Monica Rent Control Bd., 16 Cal.4th 761, 782–786, 66 Cal.Rptr.2d 672, 941 P.2d 851 (1997), then held that if a controlled rent was set so low as to be confiscatory, the municipality could avoid a penalty by permitting a future rent increase sufficiently large to offset the earlier rent found to be too low. See also Galland v. City of Clovis, 24 Cal.4th 1003, 16 P.3d 130, 103 Cal.Rptr.2d 711 (2001) (*Kavanau*-style offsetting rent increase precludes subsequent damage action by landlord).

In *City of Monterey v. Del Monte Dunes at Monterey, Ltd.,* 526 U.S. 687 (1999), the Supreme Court suggested that a legislative enactment can be an unconstitutional taking if it substantially impairs the value of property without substantially advancing a legitimate state interest. However, in Lingle v. Chevron, 544 U.S. 528 (2005), the Supreme Court made clear that the "advancing a legitimate state interest" formulation was not a part of federal takings jurisprudence (see Ch. 10). Since then several lower courts have backed away from holding that rent control ordinances were unconstitutional because they did not advance a legitimate state interest. For example, in *Cashman v. City of Cotati,* 374 F.3d 887 (9th Cir.2004), the owners of mobile home parks, challenged a "vacancy deconrol" provision in a mobile home rent control ordinance that "prevent[ed] mobile home park owners from charging a new base rent for a mobile home space when ownership of a mobile home coach is transferred and the coach remains in place." The court initially found a taking, seeing no legitimate state interest in a provision that permitted incumbent tenants rather than the land owner to capture the present value of increased value of the combination of land-plus-mobile-mobile home. However, the court later withdrew its opinion in light of *Lingle*, supra.

2. What do you think about Justice Scalia's observation in his *Pennell* dissent that the Court would ordinarily permit an immediate facial challenge to an ordinance that permitted consideration of a person's race. Why not do the same with respect to alleged takings? Does it matter that virtually all statutes that explicitly make race a qualification are unconstitutional, while price regulations are generally unconstitutional only when they deny the regulated person or firm a reasonable return?

3. Rent control ordinances differ in their treatment of new tenants. Under so-called "vacancy decontrol" ordinances, the landlord may establish a new rental rate with each *new* tenant at whatever price the market will bear. However, once the tenant moves in, future rent increases will be restricted to the amount authorized by the ordinance or the rent stabilization board. Other ordinances compute all permissible future rent increases on the original base, regardless of the number of tenant changes.

Under vacancy decontrol ordinances, prevailing rents tend to track the market rate. Although each individual tenant is protected from excessive rent increases for the duration of his tenancy, the average tenant may not stay in the same apartment for more than two or three years. When a vacancy occurs, the landlord will charge the next tenant the market rate. As a result, rents citywide can increase much faster than the rent control ordinance appears to permit. Such ordinances give no protection to the prospective tenant seeking an apartment. If anything, that tenant ends up paying more than he would pay in an uncontrolled community (see the discussion of the economics of rent control below).

One common problem in municipalities that have ordinances with vacancy decontrol is that landlords have an incentive to evict a tenant who has been in an apartment a long time and is currently paying a lower rent than the market will bear. Such ordinances prohibit evictions except in specified circumstances, typically: (1) the tenant's failure to pay rent or violation of another covenant in the lease; (2) the landlord's decision to take the property off the rental market; (3) the landlord's decision to live in the property herself, or to lease it to a member of her immediate family; or (4) substantial renovation of the property during which continued occupancy will be impossible.

Some ordinances recognize limitations even to these exceptions. For example, New York City's ordinance permits a landlord to evict a tenant for his own occupancy or that of his immediate family, unless the tenant is at least 62 years old, has been a tenant for 20 years or more, or has a medical disability. See Guerriera v. Joy, 64 N.Y.2d 747, 485 N.Y.S.2d 979, 475 N.E.2d 446 (1984).

4. In a vacancy decontrol jurisdiction the landlord can raise the rent only at the time of a vacancy. Suppose that A, a law student, enters into a lease with L. A short time later A asks the landlord if B and C can move in as

roommates. A few months after that A vacates, but B and C remain. Has a "vacancy" been created, entitling L to raise the rent to B and C? Is it relevant that L agreed to let B and C move in? See Sullivan v. Brevard Associates, 66 N.Y.2d 489, 498 N.Y.S.2d 96, 488 N.E.2d 1208 (1985).

5. Clearly, if a rent control ordinance is successful, a landlord will be earning less than she could earn in an unregulated market. Can a landlord "cheat" on the ordinance and earn the competitive return? Perhaps not by renting the property, but maybe by selling it to someone else. The suppressed rents will depress the sale price, however; property that cannot be rented for its full market value cannot be sold for its full market value either, *if* the new owner is going to rent it to someone as well. One alternative is for the owner to convert the multi-unit apartment building into condominiums, whose sale price is unregulated. Suppose, for example, that a ten-unit building would have a value in an unregulated market of $1,000,000. A fair market rate of return on this building might be gross rents of 10% of value, which is $10,000 per unit yearly, or about $835 monthly. As a result of rent control, however, the maximum rental is $650 per month, which gives the building a market value of $650 × 12 months × 10 units × 10, or $780,000.

Although the owner cannot charge more than $650 per month rental, she can divide the building into ten condominiums and sell each for the market price, about $100,000, and thus receive the full market value of the building. One result of rent control is that landlords have converted large numbers of apartment buildings into condominiums. Some cities have responded with ordinances that place strict limits on the number of such "condo conversions" that can take place annually. See Bronstein v. Prudential Ins. Co. of Am., 390 Mass. 701, 459 N.E.2d 772 (1984); City of West Hollywood v. Beverly Towers, Inc., 52 Cal.3d 1184, 278 Cal.Rptr. 375, 805 P.2d 329 (1991).

6. Other cities have responded to the problem addressed in the previous note with ordinances that simply forbid the landlord from going out of the residential rental business. Restrictions such as these would probably be an unconstitutional taking of property if they were applied to a landlord who could not receive a fair rate of return on the property in its present use. They may be constitutional, however, if they are applied only to landlords whose rate of return is reasonable. In Fresh Pond Shopping Center, Inc. v. Callahan, 464 U.S. 875 (1983) the Supreme Court had the opportunity to consider the validity of a Cambridge, Mass., antidemolition ordinance under both the takings clause and the due process clause of the United States Constitution. The Supreme Court dismissed the appeal for want of a substantial federal question, thus implicitly suggesting that the application of the ordinance did not violate any federal constitutional provisions. The U.S. Supreme Court's work load is such, however, that it sometimes dismisses appeals for want of a substantial federal question even when the federal question is probably substantial. As a result its action in *Fresh Pond* should be characterized as ambiguous. Nevertheless, in a dissent from the dismissal then Justice Rehnquist noted that the dismissal was tantamount to an affirmance on the merits. 464 U.S. at 875.

Relying heavily on *Fresh Pond,* the California Supreme Court upheld a similar ordinance in Nash v. Santa Monica, 37 Cal.3d 97, 207 Cal.Rptr. 285,

688 P.2d 894 (1984). The Santa Monica ordinance required a landlord who sought to demolish a residential rental building and did not intend to rebuild to obtain a demolition permit, to be granted only upon a finding that (1) the building was not inhabited by persons of low or moderate income; (2) could not be afforded by people of low or moderate income; (3) removal of the building would not adversely affect the local housing supply; *and* (4) the owner could not make a reasonable return on his investment. A landlord who was not earning a reasonable rate of return on his building could nevertheless not tear it down if the building were occupied by people of low or moderate income. In this case, however, Nash admitted that the building was earning a reasonable rate of return. He simply wanted to go out of the business of being a residential landlord. How would this ordinance fare under *Pennell, supra*?

In response to *Nash*, the California Legislature passed the Ellis Act, which effectively permits a residential landlord to go out of business. Calif. Gov't Code § 7060–7060.7. The statute's basic provision is: "No public entity . . . shall, by statute, ordinance, or regulation, or by administrative action implementing any statute, ordinance, or regulation, compel the owner of any residential real property to offer, or to continue to offer, accommodations in the property for rent or lease." Bullock v. San Francisco, 221 Cal.App.3d 1072, 271 Cal.Rptr. 44 (1990), held that the Act pre-empted San Francisco's attempts to restrain owners of residential hotels from turning them into tourist hotels.

7. See Frey, et al., Consensus and Dissension Among Economists: an Empirical Inquiry, 74 Amer. Econ. Rev. 986, 988–991 (1984), which notes that less than two percent of American economists randomly surveyed disagreed with the statement that a "ceiling on rents reduces the quantity and quality of housing available." See also Michael A. Goldberg, On Systemic Balance: Flexibility and Stability in Social, Economic, and Environmental Systems 18 (1989) (rent control is "the most efficient technique known to destroy a city— except for bombing").

8. A municipality may enact rent control legislation only if it has a legislative grant of this power from the state. Many municipalities rely on home rule provisions to give them this power. A home rule provision is a statute or state constitutional amendment that gives the municipality substantial regulatory power over activities occurring within its borders. Other municipalities may rely on a rent control enabling act, which is a special legislative grant that permits the municipality to regulate rents but nothing else. In the absence of such enabling legislation from the states, municipalities would not have the power to regulate rents. However, just to make sure, some states have passed statutes forbidding their municipalities from engaging in rent control. See, e.g., Wash.Rev.Code § 35.21.830 (Supp.1986) (stating that control of rents is a matter of "state-wide significance and is preempted by the state.") See also Colo.Rev.Stat. § 38–12–301 (1982); and Town of Telluride v. Lot Thirty–Four Venture, 3 P.3d 30 (Colo.2000, en banc), which applied this statute to strike down a municipal ordinance that attempted to limit the rents on new housing to a specified number of dollars per square foot of space.

RENT CONTROL AND THE ANTITRUST LAWS

In Fisher v. Berkeley, 475 U.S. 260 (1986), the Supreme Court upheld a municipal rent control ordinance against a charge that it was preempted by § 1 of the Sherman Act, one of the federal antitrust laws. The Court recognized that municipal regulation of rents constituted a kind of "price fixing." However, it held that section 1 of the Sherman Act requires not only price fixing but also an *agreement* between two or more persons to engage in price fixing. The Court was unwilling to characterize the relationship between the Rent Stabilization Board, which determined maximum prices, and the landlords complying with the Board's orders, as an "agreement."

NOTE: THE ECONOMICS OF RENT CONTROL

Rent control turns privately-owned rental housing into a price-regulated public utility. There may be some important similarities between the market for urban housing and the markets served by some utilities. For example, price regulation may be justified by "market failures" that prevent an unregulated market from operating efficiently. Defenders of rent control generally cite price "gouging"—that is, the landlords' charging of unfairly high, or monopoly, rents—as the chief rationale for rent control.

But the market for rental housing differs substantially from public utility markets. First of all, today most price regulated public utilities are monopolies; in fact they are "natural monopolies" (markets that can be served most cheaply by a single firm). By contrast, the market for urban housing is competitively structured. In most cities even a very large landlord has a small percentage of the market. A market containing many competing providers ordinarily does not require price controls. Competition would tend to drive prices to the competitive level, unless the landlords were fixing prices. However, it is difficult to imagine that tens of thousands of landlords in New York City or Chicago could be engaged in price-fixing? Is rent "gouging" plausible?

Two phenomena have been presented as justifications for rent control. One is the fact that the supply of rental housing has not been able to keep up with the demand, largely because of legal and physical restrictions on the building of new rental housing. The other is the problem of "economic rents."

The market for rental housing is structured "competitively" in the sense that the housing is provided by a large number of relatively small suppliers in the same market. However, if the supply of a product is restricted artificially, it will clear the market at a high price even if there are a large number of suppliers. Suppose, for example, that widgets cost $1.00 to produce and 100 people produce them. Demand for widgets in a competitive market would be 1000 widgets per year. In such a market widgets would be sold at the cost price of $1.00; economic "cost" includes a reasonable profit. Suppose, however, that each widget maker is permitted by law to produce only one widget per year. In that case the widgets must be rationed. In an unregulated market they will be rationed by price. Even though there are 100 widget sellers, each seller will know that he can obtain far more than the competitive price for his widget. The widgets will end up going to the customers who are willing to pay the most for them. If the market clearing price is $3.00 (i.e., if there are 100 buyers willing to pay $3.00 or more for a widget) the sellers will obtain high monopoly profits even though they are "competitors."

There is some reason to believe that the market for urban housing is analogous to the market described above. The amount of available space in cities is finite and much of that space has already been filled, particularly if the city has severe restrictions on housing density or on the amount of new construction. Although construction may sometimes be possible at the out-skirts of the city, the "market" for housing of a certain kind may be quite small. For example, many low income persons who cannot afford to pay much for housing are also without automobiles of their own; they must live fairly close to their place of employment. Quite simply, given a particular area of urban land, there may be more people willing to pay the competitive price for housing in that area than there are housing units available. In that case, the units will be rationed to those willing to pay the most, and they will end up bringing more than a competitive price. In the short run, rent control will tend to force rents back to the competitive "equilibrium" level—i.e., the level that would exist if there were no artificial restrictions on the supply.

The second phenomenon that might justify rent control is the problem of "economic rents." A "rent" is a high profit that a particular seller earns because she has been blessed with a lower cost source of supply than is available to her competitors. For example, suppose that one farmer has more fertile soil than his competitors, and can produce wheat for $1.00 a bushel while others have costs of $2.00 a bushel. In such a situation the market price for wheat, established by competition, will probably be $2.00 per bushel. The fact that one farmer has very low costs will have little effect on the market price, since he has much too small a share of the market. If he is already using his fertile soil to full capacity he cannot increase his market share at the same low costs. He will simply make a very high profit by selling wheat at the market price; that is, he earns monopoly returns even though the market is "competitive."

Economic rents are common in the market for housing because housing is durable, often lasting for a century or more. Further, the costs of land and housing construction have increased dramatically over the past several dec-ades. A city such as San Francisco has many fine Victorian houses that cost $3000 or $4000 to build at the turn of the century. They may have been purchased by their current owners forty years ago for $25,000, and may be worth more than $300,000 today. As a result residential property owners who have similar units to put on the market have widely different investments in those units. The "replacement cost" of a unit of housing might be $100,000. In such a market rents must be sufficient to give a fair rate of return to the $100,000 investment, or else no one will build new housing. At the same time, other landlords have similar but older units in which their investment is far lower.

Whether or not such differing cost structures justify price regulation, they nonetheless make such regulation very difficult. Public utilities frequent-ly experience the problem that some groups of customers cost much more to serve than others. For example, single-family homes may cost far more per home to connect to the telephone or electric system than do apartment buildings. However, the telephone company charges both classes of subscribers the same amount. Effectively, it makes more money from one set of customers than from another set. In this situation one set of customers may be seen as "subsidizing" another set. This kind of price discrimination is often considered desirable in public utility markets, because it makes the service more nearly universal: if every utility customer were charged the full cost of providing him with utilities, certain high cost customers would not be able to afford them.

Although different groups of consumers of rental housing impose different costs on their landlords, these costs cannot be shifted back and forth very easily, because there are a large number of landlords. For this reason, the rent control authority cannot create a single public utility price as the telephone or electric company may do.

The problem is illustrated in Figure One. The figure shows a declining demand curve D—that is, the more units of housing that are available on the market, the lower the "market clearing" price (the price at which all units will be rented). Likewise, because of the presence of economic rents, the supply curve S slopes up sharply. A rental unit built today would have to rent at price Pc in order to be a profitable investment. However, a landlord who purchased a unit ten years ago could profitably charge rental Pb, while one who owned his unit for thirty years could charge price Pa. If supply and demand are balanced in the market, rental rates will gravitate toward Pc, the current replacement rate. If rents were any lower than that, new housing would not be built. Incidentally, if either A or B *sold* his rental unit, it would bring a price of C on the current market; that is, anticipated rents would be capitalized into the purchase price and the new buyer would obtain only a competitive rate of return. This is because the value of the property to the new buyer is its expected income stream, and it can be rented for price Pc, just as a new unit. Of course, if older buildings are less attractive to tenants or have higher maintenance costs, these prices will have to be adjusted accordingly.

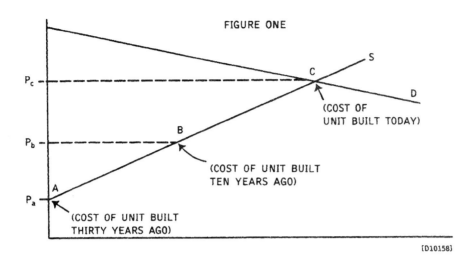

FIGURE ONE

[D10158]

If the rent control ordinance sets the rental rate at any price less than Pc, no new units will be built, although some owners of older housing may earn a good rate of return on their initial investment. Any *single* rental rate (for example, $300 per month for all one-bedroom apartments) would tend to give some landlords monopoly rents, while others would fail to earn a competitive rate of return. For this reason the rent control ordinance cannot establish a single price for all units. Rather, it tries to regulate C's rental rates at Pc (that is, builders of new units will obtain the unregulated competitive rate, sufficient to encourage their investment), B's rental rates at point Pb, and A's rental rates at point Pa. If the ordinance does this effectively, no monopoly returns will be earned by landlords, and there will be no disincentive to new construction of rental housing. Other municipalities may obtain the same result by regulating rents at a somewhat lower rate, but exempting all new construction from the rent control ordinance. By making the cost of the mortgage a factor in determining rents, the ordinance at issue in *Pennell*, *supra*, effectively permitted the rent control board to assess relatively higher rents to apartments that were new and for which their owners paid a relatively higher price, and relatively lower rents to older apartments where the historical investment was smaller.

People commonly view rent control ordinances as benefiting tenants and harming landlords. However, this oversimplifies the situation. Rent control almost always injures landlords. However, it benefits some tenants while it injures others. The benefited tenants are the stable tenants who have an apartment and live there a long time. The injured tenants are generally those entering the community or those who wish to move frequently. In the case of vacancy control ordinances, rent control can create severe shortages that make apartments very difficult to find. In the case of vacancy decontrol ordinances, rent control can actually force new tenants to pay *higher* rentals than would prevail in an unregulated market. This is so for two reasons. First, to the extent that any rent control ordinance depresses the supply of housing, unregulated units will be rationed by price and the price will be higher. Second, landlords in multi-unit buildings will often find it easy to "subsidize" the rents from their old, low rent tenants by charging higher rents to new tenants.

Finally, as noted above, several states are quite hostile toward rent control, and some actually forbid it by statute. One likely reason for this hostility is the adverse impact that rent control ordinances can have on adjacent communities. To the extent that city A's rent control ordinance creates housing shortages in A, unsuccessful hunters will be forced to find housing in adjoining cities B and C. The result will be an increase in demand for housing in B and C, new growth pressures, and—worst of all—higher rents. Eventually B and C may be forced to respond with their own rent control ordinances.

CHAPTER 8

"PRIVATE" CONTROLS OF LAND
USE: SERVITUDES

■ ■ ■

§ 8.1 THE LAW OF SERVITUDES:
AN INTRODUCTION

This chapter and the ones that follow deal with legal restrictions on the use of land. Other parts of the law also deal with such restrictions—for example, the law of defeasible fees discussed in chapter four. More precisely, these chapters deal with legal obligations that can be imposed on land owners or occupiers *regardless* of the estate they own.

The term "servitudes" refers to easements, real covenants, and equitable servitudes. We think of these as "private" legal mechanisms for controlling land use and access. The word "private" is placed in quotation marks because in law nothing is purely private. Even a contract between two persons may have to be enforced in a court, which is a very "public" institution. Private land use and access controls may be distinguished from those presented in the following chapters on "public" controls (such as zoning laws) in that they are created either by individual negotiation, or else by litigation under common law rules. By contrast, public controls are almost always statutory or constitutional, and their creation and enforcement are most often initiated by the government itself.

Servitudes are essentially *contractual* mechanisms for controlling land use or access. That is, the controls arise out of a bargaining process, generally between adjacent or nearby landowners, or between successive owners of the same land. The documents in which these agreements are contained are not always called "contracts." Often, particularly in the case of easements, they are "conveyances," or deeds. The distinction is often important, as discussed below. Nevertheless, both easements and covenants are contractual in the sense that they are the product of bargaining that takes place in the market for property rights. Knowing this will help you understand why certain interests are created, why the law protects the interests that it does, and perhaps where the law has gone wrong.

Many people find the law of servitudes particularly confusing. In fact, many are so confused that they leave the subject thinking they know less than they did when they began and wishing they had never heard of servitudes, or—in a few documented cases—they abandon the study of law altogether. Although it is important that we have a set of legal rules determining when a promise respecting the use of land can be enforced, why must the rules be so complicated, and why must courts follow them so erratically? Entering the study of servitudes is a little like diving into a swamp at night, swimming and floundering in terror, and emerging quite fortuitously on some unknown shore in the morning. When it is all over you're sorry that it happened, you don't understand anything you saw but you know that you didn't like it, and you are extremely grateful that you blundered out. Fortunately, falling into a swamp can, in most cases, be avoided. Unfortunately for a property lawyer, the study of servitudes cannot be.

In the case of servitudes, however, an ounce of history is worth several pounds of logic. We have a complicated tripartite system of servitudes (easements, covenants and equitable servitudes) because the law has developed along three quite different paths. *Easements* are very old, and had always been viewed by the courts as grants of property interests. They could not be created by mere contract. They are usually created by deed, and they can be created by "prescription," which is similar to adverse possession. Because easements were considered to be "interests in land," questions about whether the easement would "run with the land"—i.e., whether it would pass from owner to owner as the property was transferred—were relatively simple.

The real covenant, by contrast, is in form a *contract,* even though most real covenants are contained in conveyances of property interests, such as deeds or leases. Real covenants came to prominence in the United States late in the nineteenth century. As late as 1885, when Justice Holmes, then on the Supreme Judicial Court of Massachusetts, wrote Norcross v. James, 140 Mass. 188, 2 N.E. 946 (1885), it was widely believed that the only kinds of covenants conveyed by deeds were either easements or warranties of title.[1] Holmes' opinion in *Norcross* did nothing to dispel that belief.

Two phenomena explain the rise of the real covenant in the United States. First, industrialization required more sophisticated and flexible land use devices if property owners in relatively dense, highly developed areas, were to live together peacefully. In form, the contract seemed to permit an almost infinite variety of private arrangements. Secondly, during this period, American law developed extremely formalistic rules in which the contract became the most highly regarded social control device. This era, sometimes known as the age of "liberty of contract," gave privately negotiated contracts substantial protection from interference by state law makers. As a result, people came to believe that they could really

---

1. Deed warranties of title are discussed in chapter 16.

do what *they* wanted with their property, rather than what the state wanted, provided they expressed their wishes in a binding contract.[2]

The same legal formalism that permitted the rise of the real covenant, or "running" contract affecting land use, also explains its macabre complexities. The requirements of horizontal and vertical privity of estate, and an elaborate but ambiguous "touch and concern" requirement, are both the product of an age that was frequently more fascinated by the logic of legal rules than by the effect those rules had on people's lives and affairs.

Equitable servitudes differ from both easements and real covenants because they developed in a completely different court system—the British equity courts. However, equitable servitudes did not really mature in the United States as a private land use control device until the twentieth century. At the risk of some oversimplification, courts began to apply the concept of equitable servitudes in situations where the technical requirements of the law of easements or real covenants could not be met, but fairness seemed to dictate that a promise be enforced against someone who had acquired a land interest with notice of that particular obligation. As a result, promises that could not be enforced in law could be enforced in equity.

The Restatement (Third) of Property: Servitudes (2000) is the American Law Institute's attempt at simplifying the law of servitudes. The Restatement aspires to modernize the law of servitudes, in part, by reducing uncertainty and "unnecessary formalities." The American Law Institute describes the Restatement as "enabling toward private governance, so long as there is full disclosure to prospective and current participants and so long as decisions are made according to established and fair procedures." Real covenants, equitable servitudes, easements, profits, and irrevocable licenses are treated integrally as parts of one body of law under the Restatement rather than as separate and independent doctrines each governed by separate and independent rules. While not binding on courts, the Restatement can be persuasive authority and so, for this reason, this Chapter discusses the important distinctions between the Restatement and the common law.

This chapter should enable you to see the important legal differences in the three private land use control devices that collectively are called servitudes. But it will also force you to consider whether these three complex legal devices are really necessary.

---

2. For historical discussions of liberty of contract in American law, see H. Hovenkamp, Enterprise and American Law: 1836–1937 at 171–206 (1991); L. Friedman, A History of American Law 337–63 (2d ed. 1985); M. Horwitz, The Transformation of American Law, 1870–1960: The Crisis of Legal Orthodoxy 29–39 (1992).

§ 8.2   THE CREATION OF SERVITUDES

§ 8.2.1   EASEMENTS BY GRANT, RESERVATION, OR OTHER FORM OF AGREEMENT

WILLARD v. FIRST CHURCH OF CHRIST, SCIENTIST, PACIFICA

Supreme Court of California, In Bank (1972).
7 Cal.3d 473, 102 Cal.Rptr. 739, 498 P.2d 987.

PETERS, ASSOCIATE JUSTICE.

In this case we are called upon to decide whether a grantor may, in deeding real property to one person, effectively reserve an interest in the property to another. We hold that in this case such a reservation vests the interest in the third party.

Plaintiffs Donald E. and Jennie C. Willard filed an action to quiet title to a lot in Pacifica against the First Church of Christ, Scientist (the church). After a trial judgment was entered quieting the Willards' title. The church has appealed.

Genevieve McGuigan owned two abutting lots in Pacifica known as lots 19 and 20. There was a building on lot 19, and lot 20 was vacant. McGuigan was a member of the church, which was located across the street from her lots, and she permitted it to use lot 20 for parking during services. She sold lot 19 to one Petersen, who used the building as an office. He wanted to resell the lot, so he listed it with Willard, who is a realtor. Willard expressed an interest in purchasing both lots 19 and 20, and he and Petersen signed a deposit receipt for the sale of the two lots.

* * *

At the time he agreed to sell lot 20 to Willard, Petersen did not own it, so he approached McGuigan with an offer to purchase it. She was willing to sell the lot provided the church could continue to use it for parking. She therefore referred the matter to the church's attorney, who drew up a provision for the deed that stated the conveyance was "subject to an easement for automobile parking during church hours for the benefit of the church on the property at the southwest corner of the intersection of Hilton Way and Francisco Boulevard ... such easement to run with the land only so long as the property for whose benefit the easement is given is used for church purposes." Once this clause was inserted in the deed, McGuigan sold the property to Petersen, and he recorded the deed.

Willard paid the agreed purchase price and received Petersen's deed 10 days later. He then recorded this deed, which did not mention an easement for parking by the church. While Petersen did mention to Willard that the church would want to use lot 20 for parking, it does not appear that he told him of the easement clause contained in the deed he received from McGuigan.

Willard became aware of the easement clause several months after purchasing the property. He then commenced this action to quiet title against the church. At the trial, which was without a jury, McGuigan testified that she had bought lot 20 to provide parking for the church, and would not have sold it unless she was assured the church could thereafter continue to use it for parking. The court found that McGuigan and Petersen intended to convey an easement to the church, but that the clause they employed was ineffective for that purpose because it was invalidated by the common law rule that one cannot "reserve" an interest in property to a stranger to the title.

The rule derives from the common law notions of reservations from a grant and was based on feudal considerations. A reservation allows a grantor's whole interest in the property to pass to the grantee, but revests a newly created interest in the grantor.[1] While a reservation could theoretically vest an interest in a third party, the early common law courts vigorously rejected this possibility, apparently because they mistrusted and wished to limit conveyance by deed as a substitute for livery by seisin. * * * Insofar as this mistrust was the foundation of the rule, it is clearly an inapposite feudal shackle today. Consequently, several commentators have attacked the rule as groundless and have called for its abolition.

California early adhered to this common law rule. In considering our continued adherence to it, we must realize that our courts no longer feel constricted by feudal forms of conveyancing. Rather, our primary objective in construing a conveyance is to try to give effect to the intent of the grantor. In general, therefore, grants are to be interpreted in the same way as other contracts and not according to rigid feudal standards. The common law rule conflicts with the modern approach to construing deeds because it can frustrate the grantor's intent. Moreover, it produces an inequitable result because the original grantee has presumably paid a reduced price for title to the encumbered property. In this case, for example, McGuigan testified that she had discounted the price she charged Petersen by about one-third because of the easement.

* * *

The highest courts of two states have already eliminated the rule altogether, rather than repealing it piecemeal by evasion. In Townsend v. Cable (Ky.1964) 378 S.W.2d 806, the Court of Appeals of Kentucky abandoned the rule. It said: "We have no hesitancy in abandoning this archaic and technical rule. It is entirely inconsistent with the basic principle followed in the construction of deeds, which is to determine the intention of grantor as gathered from the four corners of the instrument."

* * *

Relying on *Townsend*, the Supreme Court of Oregon, in Garza v. Grayson (1970) 255 Or. 413, 467 P.2d 960, rejected the rule because it was

---

1. The effect of a reservation should be distinguished from an exception, which prevents some part of the grantor's interest from passing to the grantee. The exception cannot vest an interest in the third party, and the excepted interest remains in the grantor. (6 Powell, Real Property ¶ 892).

"derived from a narrow and highly technical interpretation of the meaning of the terms 'reservation' and 'exception' when employed in a deed", and did not sufficiently justify frustrating the grantor's intention. Since the rule may frustrate the grantor's intention in some cases even though it is riddled with exceptions, we follow the lead of Kentucky and Oregon and abandon it entirely.

Willard contends that the old rule should nevertheless be applied in this case to invalidate the church's easement because grantees and title insurers have relied upon it. He has not, however, presented any evidence to support this contention, and it is clear that the facts of this case do not demonstrate reliance on the old rule. There is no evidence that a policy of title insurance was issued, and therefore no showing of reliance by a title insurance company. Willard himself could not have relied upon the common law rule to assure him of an absolute fee because he did not even read the deed containing the reservation. This is not a case of an ancient deed where the reservation has not been asserted for many years. The church used lot 20 for parking throughout the period when Willard was purchasing the property and after he acquired title to it, and he may not claim that he was prejudiced by lack of use for an extended period of time.

The determination whether the old common law rule should be applied to grants made prior to our decision involves a balancing of equitable and policy considerations. We must balance the injustice which would result from refusing to give effect to the grantor's intent against the injustice, if any, which might result by failing to give effect to reliance on the old rule and the policy against disturbing settled titles. The record before us does not disclose any reliance upon the old common law rule, and there is no problem of an ancient title. Although in other cases the balancing of the competing interests may warrant application of the common law rule to presently existing deeds, in the instant case the balance falls in favor of the grantor's intent, and the old common law rule may not be applied to defeat her intent.

Willard also contends that the church has received no interest in this case because the clause stated only that the grant was "subject to" the church's easement, and not that the easement was either excepted or reserved. In construing this provision, however, we must look to the clause as a whole which states that the easement "is given." Even if we assume that there is some ambiguity or conflict in the clause, the trial court found on substantial evidence that the parties to the deed intended to convey the easement to the church.

The judgment is reversed.

NOTES AND QUESTIONS

1. The *Willard* court suggests that early common law courts forbad reservations vesting interests in third parties because they wanted to limit the use of deeds as a substitute for the ceremony of livery by seisin. The court is probably wrong. The holder of an easement, which is a nonpossessory interest, was never held to have seisin. As a result, easements had always been

transferred by grant rather than by feoffment with livery of seisin. Livery of seisin as a predecessor to the modern deed is discussed in chapter 15.

Most easements are created by deed, sometimes by a separate deed creating only the easement, sometimes by a deed which also grants a possessory interest in certain property. Both of these are called easements by grant. Sometimes someone sells the possessory interest in real property but retains a right to travel across that property or to use it for some other specified purpose. An easement created this way is called an easement by reservation, or an easement by exception.

Historically, the common law had great difficulty with easements created by reservation. It viewed the easement created by reservation as a *grant* of the possessory interest in Blackacre from O to A, and then a *regrant* from A to O of the easement in Blackacre for O's benefit. However, if the deed at issue was a "deed poll," commonly used in America, it bore the signature of only the grantor, O, of the underlying possessory interest. The deed did not bear A's signature as grantor of anything. The Statute of Frauds generally requires that grants of land bear the signature of the grantor. In England this problem was generally avoided by widespread use of "deeds of indenture," which bore the signatures of both grantor and grantee. American courts generally solved the problem by holding that the grantee's acceptance of a deed reserving an easement was an acceptance of all its terms, and implicitly a regrant of the reserved interest back from the grantee. However, a third party grantee of the easement did not likely "accept" anything, and perhaps did not even know about the creation of the interest. Hence the hostility toward easements reserved in favor of third parties. These legal gymnastics are recounted in 3 R. Powell, Powell on Real Property ¶ 407 (P. Rohan, ed. 2002).

An easement is said to be "appurtenant" if it benefits a particular piece of property. An appurtenant easement creates a "dominant" estate (the estate benefitted by the easement) and a "servient" estate (the estate against which the easement can be asserted). By contrast, an easement is "in gross" if a particular person is benefitted rather than a particular parcel of land. An easement in gross has a servient estate but no dominant estate. Which kind of easement is at issue in *Willard*? Suppose the Church of Christ, Scientist, moves to a bigger building down the street, selling the old building at the corner of Hilton Way and Francisco Boulevard to the First Baptist Church. The following Sunday both the Christian Scientists and the Baptists show up at the parking lot. Which congregation has the right to use it?

2. See the Restatement:

Restatement (First) of Property (1936): § 9. Estate

The word "estate," as it is used in this Restatement, means an interest in land which

      (a) is or may become possessory; and

      (b) is ownership measured in terms of duration.

Restatement (First) of Property (1944): § 450. Easement

An easement is an interest in land in the possession of another which

(a) entitles the owner of such interest to a limited use or enjoyment of the land in which the interest exists;

(b) entitles him to protection as against third persons from interference in such use or enjoyment;

(c) is not subject to the will of the possessor of the land;

(d) is not a normal incident of the possession of any land possessed by the owner of the interest, and

(e) is capable of creation by conveyance.

Is an easement an "estate"? The nearly unanimous answer is no. According to the Restatement, an "estate" must either be possessory or must be capable of becoming possessory. An easement is neither. Yet, easements appurtenant and most easements in gross can be alienated and devised. If an interest capable of being sold, given away or inherited is not an "estate," then what is it?

3. Compare with *Willard*, Estate of Thomson v. Wade, 69 N.Y.2d 570, 516 N.Y.S.2d 614, 615, 509 N.E.2d 309, 310 (1987), which expressly rejected the *Willard* rule that an easement may be created in favor of a third party. The court reasoned:

> Plaintiff invites us to abandon [the traditional] rule and adopt the minority view which would recognize an interest reserved or excepted in favor of a stranger to the deed, if such was the clearly discernible intent of the grantor. * * * Although application of the stranger-to-the-deed rule may, at times, frustrate a grantor's intent, any such frustration can readily be avoided by the direct conveyance of an easement of record from the grantor to the third party. The overriding considerations of the "public policy favoring certainty in title to real property, both to protect bona fide purchasers and to avoid conflicts of ownership, which may engender needless litigation" persuade us to decline to depart from our settled rule. We have previously noted that in this area of law, "where it can reasonably be assumed that settled rules are necessary and necessarily relied upon, stability and adherence to precedent are generally more important than a better or even a 'correct' rule of law."

By contrast, in Uhes v. Blake, 892 P.2d 439 (Colo.App.1995), a Colorado court followed *Willard* and recognized an easement granted to a third party.

4. One problem with grants of easements to third parties is that they complicate title searches by splitting the chain of title in a way that can be detected only by a careful reading of every deed in the chain of title. While title searchers have a duty to read every deed carefully, oversights are bound to occur. See chapter 16. Another difficulty with permitting grantors to reserve easements in third persons is that ambiguous language may result which makes the grantor's purpose unclear. In *Willard* the deed from McGuigan to Petersen stated that it was "subject to" an easement in the church for parking purposes. The most obvious meaning of "subject to" is that the church *already owned* an easement, and that the deed merely recognized the outstanding easement as an encumbrance on the land. But, what if the existence of such easements is uncertain? A grantor who conveys land "subject to road and street easements" may simply be attempting to protect

herself from a later lawsuit, just in case it turns out that such easements already exist. If so, the grantee will not have an action against the grantor for breach of warranty of title should such an easement later be found. See Camino Sin Pasada Neighborhood Assn. v. Rockstroh, 119 N.M. 212, 889 P.2d 247 (App.1994), which noted the ambiguity in "subject to" and concluded that a court should look at surrounding circumstances to determine whether the parties intent was to create an easement, or merely to recognize one that already existed.

5.   The Restatement (Third) of Property: Servitudes § 2.6 (2000) allows the reservation of an easement in favor of a third party. "The benefit of a servitude may be granted to a person who is not a party to the transaction that creates the servitude." Nevertheless, the majority of jurisdictions still likely follow the rule of no reservations or exceptions of easements in favor of third parties. Jurisdictions that continue to follow this view stress the importance of certainty of title and of protecting bona fide purchasers. See The Law of Easements & Licenses in Land § 3:9 (2011).

6.   What is the distinction between a reservation of an easement and an exception of an easement? The *Willard* court sites to Powell, Real Property in a footnote but the explanation may be confusing. Technically, the phrase "reserve an easement" implies that a new interest is created in the grantor. In contrast, the term "exception of an easement" implies that the easement that is being withheld from the grant is a preexisting interest in the grantor. As will become more clear when we discuss the concept of quasi-easements, the notion of the exception of an easement is conceptually troublesome because an individual cannot, at the same time, own the fee simple and an easement in the same land. If this were not confusing enough, the terms "reservation" and "exception" are often used interchangeably without an appreciation for their technical distinctions. Today, most courts disregard these technical distinctions and, instead, construe the language used so as to effectuate the intention of the parties. See The Law of Easements & Licenses in Land § 3:7 (2011).

7.   Suppose a client wants to sell the possessory interest in land to one party, but transfer an easement for parking purposes to another. How would you structure the transaction in a jurisdiction that does not follow *Willard*?

§ 8.2.2   THE IRREVOCABLE LICENSE

SHEARER v. HODNETTE

Civil Court of Appeals of Alabama (1995).
674 So.2d 548. Certiorari Denied, 1996.

L. CHARLES WRIGHT, J.

In 1957 six joint owners of a private drive leading to their respective river-front lots executed an instrument, giving the right to use the northernmost 900 feet of the drive to Retired Circuit Court Judge and Mrs. Robert E. Hodnette, Jr. The document was prepared by Judge Hodnette, who was then a practicing attorney. It provided that the Hodnettes would be granted the personal right to use the road "as a road for ingress and egress to and from said property owned by [the Hodnettes] and that portion on which they contemplate building a home." The Hodnettes gave one dollar in consideration for the use of the road. They also agreed to "contribute pro rata to the upkeep" of the road. Judge Hodnette wrote a letter to the landowners, describing the Hodnettes' intent in securing use of the private drive. That letter contained the following pertinent information: * * * "[W]e contemplate starting construction on our home in the very near future and if you are agreeable to granting us the right to use a portion of the road it will save us considerable expense in building a parallel road....

"I call your attention further to the fact that under this instrument we have expressly stated that the right of use is granted to my wife and me personally, and that there is an exclusion in the instrument stating that it shall not be considered as granting an easement to run with my land. The effect of these two provisions is to ensure that in the event we sold all of the property the right of use of the road would not follow the subsequent owners...."

The Hodnettes have used the road continuously for 37 years. Since 1957 their usage of the road has extended beyond the 900 feet referred to in the document....

Approximately six years ago, the Hodnettes granted the Mobile Water and Sewer Board an easement down the length of their property to provide water and sewerage service for all the homes served by the private road. In exchange for granting the easement, the Water and Sewer Board put a gravel drive on the Hodnettes' property, which parallels the private road. At the same time the Water and Sewer Board also widened and repaved the private road at issue.

* * * [The Hodnettes] concede that they can gain access to their home via the gravel drive on their property and do not absolutely need to use the private road. However, the private road is in better condition and is much more convenient for the Hodnettes, who are retired senior citizens, than the gravel drive.

In 1994 Lee Shearer, one of the landowners, dug a ditch across the entrance to the Hodnettes' home, making it impossible for the Hodnettes to gain access to their home from the private road. * * *

Thereafter, the Hodnettes filed an action in the Circuit Court of Mobile County, requesting a temporary restraining order and further, upon final hearing, a permanent injunction prohibiting Shearer from damaging the entrance and requiring her to repair the damage done to it. The trial court granted the temporary restraining order. Following a hearing on the Hodnettes' application for a permanent injunction, the trial court entered an order in favor of the Hodnettes. * * *

Initially, we must determine what right, if any, the Hodnettes possess in the private road. Shearer alleges that the 1957 document conveyed to the Hodnettes a license to use the private road. She concedes that oral permission extended the Hodnettes' original grant to include use of the private road beyond the original 900 feet granted. She contends that the Hodnettes no longer have a right to use the road because she has withdrawn her permission for them to do so. The Hodnettes, on the other hand, maintain that the 1957 document, and the oral extension of that document, created an enforceable easement which is not revocable during their lives.

Traditionally, easements could be created only by deed, by prescription, or by adverse use. Cleek v. Povia, 515 So.2d 1246 (Ala.1987). Several additional means of establishing easements were outlined in Helms v. Tullis, 398 So.2d 253 (Ala.1981): (1) by express conveyance, (2) by reservation or exception, (3) by implication, (4) by necessity, (5) by contract, and (6) by reference to boundaries and maps. * * *

The 1957 document provided: "It is further understood and agreed by and between the parties that the right to use said property as a road shall be considered a personal right and this instrument shall not be considered as granting an easement to run with the said described land. . . ." We find from the face of the document that the parties' intent was to convey a "license" to the Hodnettes for their personal use of the private road. The document is not ambiguous. It states this intent in plain and simple language.

At common law the term "license" denoted the doing of an act, i.e., the giving of one's consent. Camp v. Milam, 291 Ala. 12, 277 So.2d 95 (1973). Its revocability is grounded on this concept. "Since the granting of a license is the giving of one's permission to another to do a certain thing . . ., this license is revocable at the will of the licensor, simply by the withdrawing of his permission." A license does not pass any interest in the property to the licensee. It only makes an action lawful, which without a license would have been unlawful.

Not all licenses, however, are revocable at the will of the licensor. "A license coupled with an interest" or an "executed license" are exceptions to the general rule of revocability. Rhodes v. Otis, 33 Ala. 578 (1859). In *Camp*, the Supreme Court explained the exception in the following manner: "Thus, when expenditures contemplated by the licensor have been made by the licensee, the license, having been acted upon so as to greatly benefit the licensor, is said to have been executed. An executed license, for the reasons founded upon the equitable principle of estoppel, becomes irrevocable and confers upon the licensee a substantive equitable right in the property."

We find that the exception to the general rule applies to the facts of this case. The 1957 document and the oral extension gave the Hodnettes a license to use the private road for ingress and egress to and from their property. The Hodnettes expended money for the upkeep of the road. The easement across their property, which they granted to the Water and Sewer Board, also made it possible for the private road to be paved and widened at no expense to the landowners. We find that the Hodnettes' expenditures and their grant of an easement to the Water and Sewer Board conferred benefits upon the landowners, thus making the license to use the private road an executed, irrevocable license.

Although irrevocable, the license during the lifetime of the Hodnettes is by its nature personal. It is not an interest which runs with the land, nor can it be assigned, conveyed, or inherited. The use of the private road under this license may never ripen into an easement by prescription, however long continued. Although Shearer has no right to enjoin the Hodnettes from using the private road, the Hodnettes' use remains that use as contemplated by the parties in 1957.

NOTES AND QUESTIONS

1. A license, like an easement, is a right to enter or do something on the land of another. Unlike an easement, the license is revocable at the will of the licensor. A license is not an estate in nor even an "interest" in land. Licenses are frequently created orally.

As the *Shearer* court notes, however, under the law of many states a license can turn into an irrevocable license, sometimes called an "easement by estoppel" or a "license coupled with an interest," if the licensee spends resources in a way that was contemplated by the licensor when the license was given. The expenditure must be reasonable, given the license offer in question. The Alabama court adds the requirement that the expenditure must somehow have benefitted the licensor—i.e., that the expenditure was a form of consideration; however, neither the Restatement, infra, nor the majority case law imposes this requirement. See, e.g., McCoy v. Hoffman, 295 S.W.2d 560 (Ky.1956); Ricenbaw v. Kraus, 157 Neb. 723, 61 N.W.2d 350 (1953). Typically, the licensor gives the licensee permission to build a roadway, dig a ditch or lay an underground pipe across the licensor's property. The operative requirement to create an easement by estoppel is not that the licensor benefit from the expenditures made by the licensee, but that the licensor reasonably should have contemplated that such expenditures by the licensee would be necessary. Shrewsbury v. Humphrey, 183 W.Va. 291, 395 S.E.2d 535 (1990).

2. What is "reasonable" reliance on an offer of a license? Wouldn't a reasonable person know that a license is revocable at will and refuse to make any expenditure until she had a guarantee of something more permanent, such as a written grant of an easement? Not all states hold that a license plus reliance expenditures can turn into an easement by estoppel. For example, in Henry v. Dalton, 89 R.I. 150, 155–56, 151 A.2d 362, 366 (1959), the court held that no matter how reasonable and how great the reliance expenditures, the license was terminable at the will of the licensor. The Rhode Island court cited a public policy of preventing the "burdening of lands with restrictions founded upon oral agreements...." Doyle v. Peabody, 781 P.2d 957 (Alaska 1989), held that the license was revocable but the licensee may be able to recover some of his unrealized expenditures from the licensor. This may be a way of solving the problem of unrecorded interests in land without giving licensors too great an incentive to revoke at will.

3. Note how the Restatement (First) of Property (1944) deals with the problem of licenses:

§ 512. Definition of "License"

The term "license," as used in this Chapter, denotes an interest in land in the possession of another which

   (a) entitles the owner of the interest to a use of the land, and

   (b) arises from the consent of the one whose interest in the land used is affected thereby, and

   (c) is not incident to an estate in the land, and

   (d) is not an easement.

§ 513. License Coupled With An Interest

A license coupled with an interest is one which is incidental to the ownership of an interest in a chattel personal located on the land with respect to which the license exists.

§ 514. Licenses Analogous, As To Use, Easements

A privilege to use land in the possession of another is a license if, though the use privileged is of such a character that the privilege to make it could be created as an easement,

   (a) its creation lacks a formal requirement necessary to the creation of an easement, or

   (b) it is created to endure at the will of the possessor of the land subject to the privilege.

§ 519. Revocation

(1) Except as stated in Subsections (2), (3) and (4), a license is terminable at the will of the possessor of the land subject to it.

(2) In the termination of the license of one who has entered upon land under a license, the licensee must be given a reasonable opportunity to remove himself and his effects from the land.

(3) A license coupled with an interest can be terminated only to such an extent as not to prevent the license from being effective to protect the interest with which it is coupled.

(4) A licensee under such a license as is described in § 514 who has made expenditures of capital or labor in the exercise of his license in reasonable reliance upon representations by the licensor as to the duration of the license, is privileged to continue the use permitted by the license to the extent reasonably necessary to realize upon his expenditures.

The "license coupled with an interest" described in the Restatement generally refers to the situation in which one buys chattels located on the property of another. In the absence of an agreement concerning how the buyer will take possession of the chattels, she generally has an implied license to enter the property in order to pick up what she has purchased. Bohle v. Thompson, 78 Md.App. 614, 554 A.2d 818 (1989) (timber purchaser acquired irrevocable license to enter land to remove timber).

Some states flatly reject the Restatement. For example, in Kitchen v. Kitchen, 465 Mich. 654, 641 N.W.2d 245 (2002), the Michigan Supreme Court held that the Statute of Frauds required that all durable property interests be manifested in a suitable writing. As a result an oral license could be revoked notwithstanding the licensee's reasonable reliance. ". . . [I]n order to constitute a permanent interest, plaintiffs' alleged license would have to have been conveyed through a deed or conveyance in compliance with the statute of frauds."

4. A discount grocery store advertises very low prices and in the advertisement invites customers to "check and compare" its prices with those charged by others. The plaintiff drives "a substantial number of miles" to the grocery store and begins writing down prices in order to compare them against the prices of others. At that point the store's manager tells the plaintiff that it is against store policy to permit customers to write down prices and the plaintiff must either stop or else leave the store. Is the plaintiff a licensee? Can the license be revoked any time the store pleases, or has the customer acquired an irrevocable license? Compare Mosher v. Cook United, Inc., 62 Ohio St.2d 316, 405 N.E.2d 720 (1980) with Feldt v. Marriott Corp., 322 A.2d 913 (D.C.App.1974).

5. Distinguishing between an easement and a license can be difficult at times but it must be done. The intention of the parties is critical. Factors that indicate that an agreement is a license rather than an easement include: (1) the agreement is oral; (2) the holder is not entitled to be protected from interference from third parties; (3) the interest is not transferable (though some easements are nonassignable); and/or (4) the agreement contains an express reservation of a right of revocation. In contrast, agreements: (1) of a set duration; (2) that create an entitlement to use a particular part of the burdened estate or to make improvements; and (3) that involve substantial consideration, suggest an easement. The Law of Easements & Licenses in Land §§ 1:4, 1:5 (2011). See also, Gilman v. Blocks, 44 Kan.App.2d 163, 235 P.3d 503 (2010) (construing access agreement to pond); Barlow v. Spaziani, 63 A.D.3d 1225, 880 N.Y.S.2d 369 (2009) (prescriptive easement case stating that permission to use a driveway "can be implied from neighborly cooperation or a familial relationship"); Blackburn v. Lefebvre, 976 So.2d 482 (Ala. Civ. App. 2007) (finding a boat-slip agreement was a license even when the agreement referred to an easement and discussing factors to consider when determining the nature of the interest created); Benham v. Morton & Furbish Agency, 929 A.2d 471 (Maine 2007) (discussing factors pointing to a license in a lodging context); Section 514 of The Restatement (First) of Property, supra. The Restatement (Third) of Property: Servitudes § 1.2 comment g (2000) states that executed parol licenses are easements and that irrevocable licenses become easements by estoppels.

§ 8.2.3 EASEMENTS BY IMPLICATION AND NECESSITY

ROMANCHUK v. PLOTKIN

Supreme Court of Minnesota (1943).
215 Minn. 156, 9 N.W.2d 421.

PETERSON, JUSTICE.

In 1915 defendants acquired the real property at the northeast corner of Twelfth avenue north and Humboldt avenue north in Minneapolis, on which there was a duplex dwelling near the corner facing Twelfth avenue, known as 1312 Twelfth avenue north, and a small dwelling toward the rear facing Humboldt, known as 1206 Humboldt avenue north. Both houses were equipped with plumbing serviced by a common sewer drain which connected with the public sewer in Humboldt avenue.

On February 23, 1921, defendants acquired the real property now owned by plaintiffs, located immediately east of the duplex and known as 1310 Twelfth avenue north. At that time this property was without plumbing and sewer connection. There has not been, nor is there now, a public sewer in Twelfth avenue north. In 1922 defendants installed plumbing in the house at 1310 Twelfth avenue, which they connected with a sewer drain they laid below the basement floor and underground extending from the rear of the house across the properties of the parties into the basement of the duplex, where it was connected with the sewer drain from the duplex to the street. After this connection was made the one sewer drain connecting with the public sewer in Humboldt avenue serviced the three houses on defendants' property. * * *

On February 25, 1921, two days after defendants became the owners of 1310 Twelfth avenue north and about one year before they installed the plumbing and made the sewer connection there, they executed a mortgage of the property, with the appurtenances thereto belonging, to one Margaret Roggeman. The mortgage contained the usual covenants of a warranty deed. In July, 1936, Margaret Roggeman acquired title through foreclosure of the mortgage. She did not inspect the property either when she took the mortgage or when she foreclosed it. She dealt through an agent, who afterwards looked after the renting and who, out of rents collected, paid defendant Plotkin for cleaning and repairing the sewer.

On August 8, 1938, plaintiffs purchased the property from Roggeman. They dealt through Roggeman's agent. Plaintiff Nicholas Romanchuk testified that he observed the drainpipes in an unfinished and unused part of the basement. Over objection, he also testified that the agent told him that the sewer drain connected with the public sewer in the street.

Neither the mortgage to Roggeman nor the deed to plaintiffs mentions any easement in the sewer across defendants' land.

In 1941 the common drain connecting these properties with the city sewer became clogged, necessitating repairs. Plaintiffs' proportionate share of the repairs was $25, of which they paid five dollars prior to trial and the balance during the trial.

On October 22, 1941, defendant Samuel Plotkin notified plaintiffs that on November 5, 1941, the connection of the sewer drain serving their property with the drain to the sewer in the street would be severed. Plaintiffs then brought this action to enjoin defendants from disconnecting their sewer connection and to compel them to remove the fence.

The court below found that plaintiffs had an easement for the use and maintenance of the sewer drain across defendants' property connecting with the sewer in Humboldt avenue north, subject to the requirement that they pay their proportionate share of the cost of repairing and maintaining the same, and that the fence encroached one foot and five inches on plaintiffs' land. As conclusions it ordered judgment enjoining defendants to refrain from interfering with plaintiffs' use of the sewer drain and from severing the connection of their sewer drain with the sewer leading to the street. * * *

Here, defendants contend that the finding that plaintiffs are entitled to an easement for the use and maintenance of the sewer drain across defendants' land is without basis, because (a) the severance of ownership occurred when the Roggeman mortgage was given, which was prior to the installation of the sewer drain on plaintiffs' property and the connection thereof with the one across their other property; (b) the use of the sewer drain across defendants' property to Humboldt avenue was not apparent but, on the contrary, was concealed by the fact that the sewer pipes were underground; and (c) the use thereof was not necessary to the beneficial use of plaintiffs' property.

The doctrine of implied grant of easement is based upon the principle that where, during unity of title, the owner imposes an apparently permanent and obvious servitude on one tenement in favor of another, which at the time of severance of title, is in use and is reasonably necessary for the fair enjoyment of the tenement to which such use is beneficial, then, upon a severance of ownership, a grant of the dominant tenement includes by implication the right to continue such use. That right is an easement appurtenant to the estate granted to use the servient estate retained by the owner. Under the rule that a grant is to be construed most strongly against the grantor, all privileges and appurtenances that are obviously incident and necessary to the fair enjoyment of the property granted substantially in the condition in which it is enjoyed by the grantor are included in the grant.

* * *

Prior to the severance and while there is unity of title, the use is generally spoken of as a quasi-easement appurtenant to the dominant tenement.

* * *

It is commonly said that three things are essential to create an easement by implication upon severance of unity of ownership, viz.: (1) a separation of title; (2) the use which gives rise to the easement shall have been so long continued and apparent as to show that it was intended to be permanent; and (3) that the easement is necessary to the beneficial enjoyment of the land granted.

* * *

Defendants contend that the sewer was not an apparent quasi-easement at the time of severance of ownership, upon the theory that the severance took place when the mortgage was given, which was approximately one year before the sewer drain was installed on plaintiffs' property, citing Mt. Holyoke Realty Corp. v. Holyoke Realty Corp., 284 Mass. 100, 187 N.E. 227. In Massachusetts and some other states a mortgage of real property conveys the title subject to defeasance upon payment of the mortgage debt or upon fulfillment of the conditions of the mortgage. We do not follow that rule. Under Minn.St.1941, § 559.17 (Mason St.1927, § 9572), the rule that a mortgage of real estate conveyed the legal title was abrogated and the rule adopted that a mortgage creates a lien in favor of the mortgagee as security for his debt with right of ownership and possession in the mortgagor until foreclosure and expiration of the period of redemption. * * * Where a mortgage on real estate creates a lien, the execution of the mortgage does not effect a severance of title, but the foreclosure of the mortgage does.

* * *

Under the title theory, a use created after the giving of a mortgage does not give rise to an easement in favor of the mortgagee . . . but, under the lien theory, it does and passes to the purchaser at the foreclosure sale. In Cannon v. Boyd, 73 Pa. 179, the court held, without any particular discussion of the distinction in question, that an implied easement passed to the purchaser under mortgage foreclosure sale where the use on which it was based came into existence after the execution of the mortgage, but prior to the foreclosure sale.

It cannot be seriously contended that the sewer in question was not continuous and permanent. It is urged, however, that, since the sewer, both in plaintiffs' house and outside in plaintiffs' and defendants' yards, was underground, it was not apparent. "Apparent" does not necessarily mean "visible." The weight of authority sustains the rule that "apparent" means that indicia of the easement, a careful inspection of which by a person ordinarily conversant with the subject would have disclosed the use, must be plainly visible. An underground drainpipe, even though it is buried and invisible, connected with and forming the only means of draining waste from plumbing fixtures and appliances of a dwelling house, is apparent, because a plumber could see the fixtures and appliances and readily determine the location and course of the sewer drain.

* * *

In Larsen v. Peterson, 53 N.J.Eq. 88, 93, 94, 30 A. 1094, 1097, is an elaborate discussion of the principle as applied to underground water pipes leading from a well to a pump inside a house, where the pump was visible but the pipes were not. The court said:

> "In the case in hand the controlling fact is that the pump was there visible and in use, and by its connection with the invisible pipe leading to *some* fountain the house conveyed to complainant was supplied with water. . . .
>
> ". . . In short, in my opinion all that is meant by 'apparent,' in that connection, is that the parties should have either actual knowledge of the *quasi*-easement or knowledge of such facts as to put them upon inquiry."

In the instant case the plumbing fixtures and their connection with the sewer pipes were plainly visible. The pipes extended from the rear of plaintiffs' house toward defendants' duplex. A plumber easily could have ascertained that the pipes, although underground and invisible, extended under the duplex, where they connected with the drain leading from the duplex to the sewer in the street.

The authorities are in conflict as to what is meant by "necessary" in this connection. Some hold that "necessary" means substantially the same as indispensable. Others hold that it means reasonably necessary or convenient to the beneficial enjoyment of the property.

* * * The weight of authority supports the view that "necessary" does not mean indispensable, but reasonably necessary or convenient to the beneficial use of the property. * * * In 17 Am.Jur., Easements, p. 985, § 79, the text states:

> "As heretofore stated, the prevailing rule, to which, however, there is some dissent, is that the necessity requisite to the creation of an easement by implication is not an absolute necessity, but that a reasonable necessity suffices. Generally, in order to support an easement as to drainage or sewage by implied grant the easement must be reasonably necessary or convenient to the beneficial enjoyment of the property. Where it appears that property is sold fully equipped with visible plumbing and appliances to carry off waste and water, it has been held that there can be no serious dispute that the use of the drainpipe is reasonably necessary for the convenient and comfortable enjoyment of the property and passes upon conveyance of the property without specific mention."

* * *

As a word of caution, we do not hold that in all cases the existence of the three characteristics mentioned are necessary to create an easement by implication. Rules of construction are mere aids in ascertaining the meaning of writings, whether they are statutes, contracts, deeds, or mortgages. Being such, they are neither ironclad nor inflexible and yield to manifestation of contrary intention.

* * * [A]n implied easement to the use of the sewer across defendants' land passed under the mortgage and the foreclosure thereof and that plaintiffs became the owners of the easement as grantees of the purchaser at the mortgage foreclosure sale.

* * *

Affirmed.

NOTES AND QUESTIONS

1. Easements can be implied in favor of grantees (i.e., by implied grant) and grantors (i.e., by implied reservation). Most are implied in favor of grantees. In many states the legal standards are stricter when the grantor seeks implication. The reasons are clear. First, the grantor usually drafts the instrument making the grant and is responsible for its contents. Second, the grantor is in a much better position to know about the existence of the easement to be implied. This does not mean that the current grantor always has actual knowledge of the existence or need for an easement. He may be mistaken about the location of boundaries, or the easement may be hidden and left over from a previous owner (for example, an underground drain line or water pipe).

The Restatement (First) of Property §§ 474–476 (1944) speaks of easements such as the one in *Romanchuk* as arising "by implication from the circumstances under which the conveyance was made." The Restatement then suggests that implication requires an inference that the parties to the conveyance intended to create the easement. In determining whether there was such an intention, the Restatement looks to eight factors: whether the claimant is grantor or grantee; the terms of the conveyance; the consideration given; whether the claim is against a simultaneous grantee; the extent of the necessity to the claimant of the easement; whether there are reciprocal benefits to grantor and grantee; the manner in which the land was used before the conveyance; and the extent to which the prior use may have been known to the parties.

When the claimant is the grantor, courts sometimes say the necessity for the easement must be somewhat stronger than when the claimant is the grantee. See Otero v. Pacheco, 94 N.M. 524, 612 P.2d 1335 (App.1980); Van Sandt v. Royster, 148 Kan. 495, 83 P.2d 698 (1938). The distinction between "strict" and "reasonable" necessity is not crystal clear. The Restatement tries to distinguish the two, but is not particularly helpful. Restatement of Property § 476 comment g (1944) defines strict necessity as meaning that the property "cannot be effectively used" without the easement. Recent decisions appear not to take the necessity requirement very seriously. For example, see Granite Properties Limited Partnership v. Manns, 117 Ill.2d 425, 111 Ill.Dec. 593, 512 N.E.2d 1230 (1987) which found the necessity requirement to be met even though there was evidence that an alternative location for a driveway would have been suitable.

In Harrison v. Heald, 360 Mich. 203, 103 N.W.2d 348 (1960), the grantor initially owned a parcel containing one house in which she lived and another

house that she rented to tenants. She built a sidewalk between the two
houses, which serviced both of them. Later she sold the parcel containing the
rental house, thinking that she had kept the strip of land containing the
sidewalk on the retained land. However, the deed description actually included the strip of land containing the sidewalk. A controversy later arose when
subsequent grantees attempted to block the sidewalk. The Michigan Supreme
Court held that the easement could be implied in favor of the grantor under
these circumstances.

2. The courts have had some difficulty with the concept of "severance"
of title creating an easement by implication. As *Romanchuk* notes, under a
common law mortgage the mortgagee (typically, the lender) takes legal title to
the property. Under this "title theory" the properties were already severed
when the mortgage was created, prior to the construction of the sewerline.
But today nearly all states follow the "lien theory," under which the mortgage is treated as a security device only and title is considered for most
purposes as resting in the mortgagor (typically, the borrower).

What if the property is leased rather than sold? Has a qualifying severance occurred? See, Schmidt v. Eger, 94 Mich.App. 728, 736, 289 N.W.2d 851,
856 (1980), which concluded that the real issue was whether the claimant of
the easement acquired possession; thus the lease constituted a severance. Cf.
United States v. O'Connell, 496 F.2d 1329 (2d Cir.1974), which concluded that
when shareholders in one corporation sold the quasi-dominant estate to
another corporation which they also owned, no severance occurred. And see
Lake George Park v. Mathwig, 548 N.W.2d 312 (Minn.App.1996), concluding
that when the grantor conveyed an undivided one half interest to the grantee
by a contract for deed which had not yet become possessory, no severance
occurred.

NOTE: THE LOGIC AND ECONOMICS OF IMPLIED EASEMENTS

The logic of implied easements goes something like this: originally a
single owner owns a parcel that is subsequently divided into two parcels.
During the period of unified ownership the owner does something that makes
one part of the parcel dependent upon the other part. Common examples: the
property contains two buildings and the owner connects them with a sewer,
water or other kind of utility line; or she builds a sidewalk or driveway that
connects one part of the property to the other. During the period of common
ownership this structure is not an "easement," since there are not separate
dominant and servient estates. After severance, however, when the issue of
implication arises, courts commonly refer to such structures as they existed
during unity of title as "quasi-easements." See H. Hovenkamp & S. Kurtz,
The Law of Property 367–371 (5th ed. 2001).

An easement is efficient if the benefits it creates to the dominant estate
(or, in the case of easements in gross, the owner) are greater than the losses
imposed on the servient estate, and no other property interests are affected.
In a perfectly functioning market only efficient easements are likely to be
created. Do you see why? The legal rules that permit implied easements are
efficient if the implied easements are themselves efficient, as described above,

and would have been produced in a perfectly functioning market. If that is the case, however, why were the easements not expressly created by grant as they should have been? The answer in most cases involving implied easements is that some kind of "market failure" prevented an express easement from being created. A market failure is an imperfection in a market that keeps it from operating efficiently. One of the most common causes of market failures is lack of information by one or both of the participants in a market. Markets perform most efficiently when all participants have ready access to complete information, both about market conditions and about the product that is being bought and sold. The less complete the information held by the parties, the more likely that a failure will occur—i.e., that a buyer will pay more than a competitive price or fail to obtain the kind and quality of product that she wants, or that the seller will sell at too low a price or sell more than he intended to sell.

As a general matter, quasi-easements are efficient at the time they are created, even though the market for easements is highly imperfect (see the note on the market for easements, infra.) This is so because when an implied easement is originally constructed as a "quasi-easement" there is no market transaction at all; rather, one owner controls both the benefitted land that will become the dominant estate and the burdened land that will become the servient estate. If the quasi-easement were not efficient—that is, if the benefits created for the benefitted part of the owner's land were worth less than the costs imposed on the burdened part of the land—then the owner would not build the easement. For example, if access to the back of a farm along a certain driveway was worth $1000 a year to a farmer, but construction of the roadway necessitated the destruction of a field at the front of the farm that was worth $1500.00 per year, the farmer would not build the driveway. If he did, he would be poorer by $500.00 per year, not including the cost of building the driveway. The sewer line easement in the *Romanchuk* case was almost certainly efficient or else it would not have been built when the houses connected by the line had the same owner.

It seems that the law of implied easements is a pretty good idea. It preserves efficient easements that probably would have been preserved in a perfectly functioning market, but were inadvertently not preserved because the parties did not have good information about what they were buying and selling.

However, one rule of implied easements makes little sense when the easements are implied in favor of grantees: the requirement that at the time of severance the quasi-easement must have been "apparent." The *Romanchuk* court went to some lengths to show that an underground sewerline was "apparent" at the time the title was severed. Other courts have had similar problems with underground drains and sewerlines, but most have managed to conclude that the easements were apparent. See, e.g., Van Sandt v. Royster, 148 Kan. 495, 83 P.2d 698 (1938); Sievers v. Flynn, 305 Ky. 325, 204 S.W.2d 364 (1947). But in cases where the grantee is the person seeking implication, it makes far more sense to grant the easement if it were *concealed* at the time of severance.

Presumably, a prospective buyer of property who knew that the sewerline ran across adjoining property retained by the grantor would insist on an express easement for the sewerline. For example, a buyer who saw that the driveway for the property she was buying ran across property retained by the seller would certainly ask for such an easement. Failure to ask when the buyer has actual knowledge of the existence of the driveway suggests that the buyer did not want the driveway easement, perhaps because she intended to enter the property somewhere else. Easements should be *implied*—i.e., created in favor of someone who did not bargain for them in a transaction—only when lack of information explains the failure to bargain. This suggests that before an easement will be implied in favor of a grantee, the grantee should show that the quasi-easement relationship was *concealed* at the time of the transaction, and that this explains why the grantee did not bargain for it.

By contrast, when the grantor seeks implication of the easement, it is more sensible to require that the quasi-easement was apparent at the time of severance. The inference is strong that the seller intended to retain the use that was clearly visible on the surface but neglected to do so because he was mistaken about where the property line was. Likewise, if the quasi-easement is apparent we can infer that the buyer intended to take the property subject to the use imposed on it by the grantor.

The general rule is that only affirmative easements (rights to use the land of another) can be implied based upon prior use. Implied reciprocal negative easements as part of a common development scheme or plan are the exception to this rule.

> Upon dividing a large tract of land into residential building lots for sale, the grantor often will impose various covenants, conditions, and restrictions upon the use of those lots to ensure the uniform and orderly development of the entire subdivision by all of the original purchasers, as well as their successors in interest. The question of whether the grantor intended to create reciprocal negative easements on lots within the subdivision by establishment of a common scheme of development typically arises in situations where the restrictions imposed are not uniform, or have been omitted from some of the original or subsequent deeds to the lots. In an action to enjoin the defendant-owner of one of the lots from violating the restrictions, the court will need to determine, from the surrounding circumstances, whether a general plan of development exists, whether the defendant's lot is part of that general plan, and whether the defendant had actual or constructive notice of the restrictions.

62 Am. Jur. Proof of Facts 3d 1 (originally published in 2001). The Restatement only allows for affirmative easements to be implied from prior use. The Restatement (Third) of Property: Servitudes § 2.12 cmt. b (2000).

Negative Easements: The term "negative easement" refers to the duty of an owner of land not to use the land in certain ways. The four traditional categories of negative easements are easements for light, support, air flow and for the flow of artificial streams. Thus, a negative easement gives the holder of the easement the right to prevent the owner of the burdened estate from using the burdened estate in such a manner as to interfere with the free flow of light, air and artificial streams to the dominant estate and to require the owner not to use the burdened estate in a manner that would disturb the support of buildings on the dominant estate. Courts have been hesitant to expand the category of negative easements, with the exception of the conservation easement. The National Conference of Commissioners on Uniform State Laws promulgated the Uniform Conservation Easement Act which permits restrictions to attach to land for the benefit of natural resources and historic sites. See Carol Necole Brown, A Time to Preserve: A Call for Formal Private–Property Rights in Perpetual Conservation Easements, 40 Ga. L. Rev. 85 (2005). See also Michael A. Heller, The Boundaries of Private Property, 108 Yale L.J. 1163 (1999).

ROY v. EURO–HOLLAND VASTGOED, B.V.

District Court of Appeal of Florida (1981).
404 So.2d 410.

DOWNEY, JUDGE.

Appellants Maurice A. Roy and Lillian A. Roy seek reversal of a final judgment denying them a way of necessity over appellees' property so that appellants will have ingress and egress to their landlocked property.

* * *

The Roys own the north 200 feet of the south 500 feet of Tract 1, Block 33, St. Lucie Inlet Farms, according to the plat thereof recorded in Plat Book 1, page 98, public records of Martin County, Florida. The Appellee, Euro–Holland Vastgoed, B.V., is the owner of Tracts 2, 6, and 7 and a portion of Tracts 1 and 8, all in Block 33 of St. Lucie Inlet Farms subdivision.

* * *

In 1910 Henry H. Buckman was the owner of all of the above described land. The property was subdivided and in March, 1913, Buckman conveyed the north 200 feet of the south 500 feet of Tract 1 of Block 33 to Frank and John Coventry. At the time of said conveyance there was no access to the above described parcel except over the remainder of Buckman's property, which remainder abutted a public right of way. The parcel was conveyed five times thereafter, the fifth conveyance being to the Roys. Having no means of ingress and egress to their property, the Roys instituted this suit requesting the court to declare the existence of a right of way of necessity over appellee's property pursuant to the authority of § 704.01(1), Florida Statutes (1979).

After a non-jury trial the court entered final judgment in favor of the defendant-appellees. This judgment, which effectively denied the Roys' claim to a common law easement of necessity, was based on appellees' contention, and the trial court's conclusion, that the Roys had not proven the following necessary elements for relief: 1) unity of title in a common source, and 2) reasonable necessity for such an easement for the beneficial use and enjoyment of the Roys' property. We disagree with the trial court's conclusion and reverse.

By means of § 704.01(1), Florida Statutes, the Legislature codified the common law rule of an implied grant of a way of necessity and also provided for a statutory way of necessity for landlocked property that could not qualify under the common law rule. We are here dealing with the common law way of necessity, which § 704.01 described as follows:

> *IMPLIED GRANT OF WAY OF NECESSITY.*—The common law rule of an implied grant of a way of necessity is hereby recognized, specifically adopted, and clarified. Such an implied grant exists where a person has heretofore granted or hereafter grants lands to which there is no accessible right-of-way except over his land, or has heretofore retained or hereafter retains land which is inaccessible except over the land which he conveys. In such instances a right-of-way is presumed to have been granted or reserved. Such an implied grant or easement in lands or estates exists where there is no other reasonable and practicable way of egress, or ingress and same is reasonably necessary for the beneficial use or enjoyment of the part granted or reserved. An implied grant arises only where a unity of title exists from a common source other than the original grant from the state or United States; provided, however, that where there is a common source of title subsequent to the original grant from the state or United States, the right of the dominant tenement shall not be terminated if title of either the dominant or servient tenement has been or should be transferred for nonpayment of taxes either by foreclosure, reversion, or otherwise.

The general rule and the rule applicable in Florida with reference to easements for ways of necessity is found in 25 Am.Jur.2d, Easements and Licenses, § 34, pp. 447–448:

> A way of necessity is an easement founded on an implied grant or implied reservation. It arises where there is a conveyance of a part of a tract of land of such nature and extent that either the part conveyed or the part retained is shut off from access to a road to the outer world by the land from which it is severed or by this land and the land of strangers. In such a situation there is an implied grant of a way across the grantor's remaining land to the part conveyed, or conversely, an implied reservation of a way to the grantor's remaining land across the portion of the land conveyed. The order in which two parcels of land are conveyed makes no difference in determining whether there is a right of way by necessity appurtenant to either.

> A way of necessity results from the application of the presumption that whenever a party conveys property he conveys whatever is necessary for the beneficial use of that property and retains whatever is necessary for the beneficial use of land he still possesses. Such a way is of common-law origin, and is presumed to have been intended by the parties. A way of necessity is also said to be supported by the rule of public policy that lands should not be rendered unfit for occupancy or successful cultivation. (Footnotes omitted.)

Thus, in order for the owner of a dominant tenement to be entitled to a way of necessity over the servient tenement both properties must at one time have been owned by the same party (that is another way of saying that one seeking the grant of a way of necessity must show unity of ownership or common source of title).

* * *

In addition, the common source of title must have created the situation causing the dominant tenement to become landlocked. A further requirement is that at the time the common source of title created the problem the servient tenement must have had access to a public road. The rationale of the rule demonstrates the necessity of the foregoing requirements. The easement is founded upon an implied grant or implied reservation which arises from the supposed intention of the parties that the party conveying or reserving the landlocked parcel intends to convey or retain whatever is necessary for the beneficial use of property conveyed or reserved.

In the case at bar Buckman owned all of the above described property presently owned by both the Roys and Euro–Holland. Thus, Buckman is the common source of title. Buckman also created the situation landlocking the Roys' property and necessitating the easement for ingress and egress. Finally, at the time of the conveyance from Buckman to the Coventrys the remainder of Buckman's property had access to a public road. Accordingly, the law implies the grant of a way of necessity over Buckman's remaining property so that Buckman's grantees and their successors in title would have access to said road from the landlocked property. As this court noted in Reyes v. Perez, 284 So.2d 493 (Fla. 4th DCA 1973), such an easement is created at the time of the original conveyance.

As we mentioned earlier, appellees and the trial court seemed to be of the view that the common source of title could not be a remote grantor in the chain of title, but must be the immediate grantor of the present owners. This is not our understanding of the law, since we believe the relevant rules are the following:

> [I]f at one time there has been unity of title, the right to a way of necessity may lie dormant through several transfers of title and yet pass with each transfer as appurtenant to the dominant estate and be exercised at any time by the holder of title. 25 Am.Jur.2d, Easements and Licenses, § 35, p. 449 (footnote omitted).

* * *

A way of necessity over remaining lands of the grantor, created by implied grant upon the severance of land, being appurtenant to the granted land, passes by each conveyance to subsequent grantees thereof. Hence, a subsequent grantee of land which is not used by the common owner at the time of the severance of the larger tract may, when the use of such way becomes necessary to the enjoyment of the land, claim it under the remote deed of severance. Id., § 95, p. 501 (footnote omitted).

Many of the cases and the writers on this question talk in terms of "tracing back" in the chain of title to the common source. Thus, "tracing back" would seem to indicate going back beyond the immediate grantor. Therefore, we hold that the common source of title need not be the immediate grantor but is any common source in the chain of title to the two estates which meets the other criteria for creation of a way of necessity over the property of another.

Finally, appellees contend there was no adequate showing of necessity. Appellees seem to feel that proof was required to show a present use of the property which makes access immediately necessary where in the past there has been no pressing need therefor. If this is a correct characterization of appellees' position then they have misconceived the impact of the term "necessity" as it is used in this context.

An easement for a way of necessity is not implied or granted if there is other reasonable access to the property which will enable the owner to achieve the beneficial use and enjoyment of the property. As Thompson states in his work on real property:

> The doctrine of ways of necessity is applicable only when conditions existing at the time of division or severance call for its enforcement. The term "necessity" is to be understood as meaning that there exists no other reasonable mode of enjoying the dominant tenement without the easement. 2 Thompson on Real Property, § 364, p. 405, (footnotes omitted).

The claimant is not entitled to an option or an election as between several adequate means of access. The fact that one means of access may be more convenient than another does not suffice. Id. at p. 409.

Accordingly, we hold that an easement for a way of necessity was created in favor of the Roys' above described property. Therefore, we reverse the judgment appealed from and remand the cause for further proceedings wherein the trial court should declare, locate, and define the easement based upon evidence adduced by the parties for that purpose.

Notes and Questions

1. Why would anyone purchase landlocked property without making provisions for a way of entry and exit? Why should a court help someone who has neglected to do so? Should it matter if the property was acquired by devise or gift rather than by purchase?

2. The *Roy* court gives an "efficiency" explanation for the doctrine of easement by necessity: it prevents landlocked parcels from being underutilized. Is this true? Suppose that I own a landlocked parcel and it is worth $1000 to me to have a right of way to enter it. You own an adjoining parcel which will be injured by $800 if made subject to such an easement. We will

negotiate and I will acquire the easement at some price between $800 and $1000. By contrast, if the easement is worth $1000 to me, but it injures your property by $1500, then we will not complete the transaction. The social cost of the easement would be $500 greater than its social value. This could happen, for example, if I own a vacant lot and you own an apartment building that takes up your entire lot. The only way I can access my vacant and undeveloped property is to compel you to destroy part of your developed property. A properly functioning market will create the easement *only* if the easement is efficient—i.e., if the benefits that it produces are larger than the burdens. The doctrine of easement by necessity creates the easement whether or not it is efficient.

Some states have passed statutes that effectively require the claimant of an easement by necessity to compensate the owner of the servient estate for the acquired easement. For example, a Washington statute provides that:

> An owner, or one entitled to the beneficial use, of land which is so situated with respect to the land of another that it is necessary for its proper use and enjoyment to have and maintain a private way of necessity . . . may condemn and take lands of such other sufficient in area for the construction and maintenance of such private way of necessity. . . .

Wash.Rev.Code § 8.24.010 (2011).

Under this statute the easement would be taken only if its value to the claimant was greater than the loss imposed upon the servient estate. Otherwise the claimant would not be willing to pay the damages. See Shields v. Garrison, 91 Wash.App. 381, 957 P.2d 805 (1998), which held that when a landowner used the statute to claim a way of necessity over a neighbor's established road the measure of damages equalled the value of the road to the claimant, not merely nominal damages given that the roadway already existed and the plaintiff's use would cause no incremental harm. Further, the court concluded, the cost of building the roadway would be a fair measure of its value to the plaintiff.

Has the statute made Washington courts any more willing to find easements by necessity? The cases have held that the statute creates a private eminent domain power without a public use requirement (which may be prohibited by the federal constitution—see chapter ten), and have construed it strictly. See Brown v. McAnally, 97 Wash.2d 360, 644 P.2d 1153 (1982); Beeson v. Phillips, 41 Wash.App. 183, 702 P.2d 1244 (1985). The Alabama Supreme Court has held that such a statute must be very narrowly construed, and will permit such a private use of eminent domain power only where there are no reasonable alternatives to the claimed easement. Cater v. Nichols, 772 So.2d 1117 (Ala.2000) (necessity not shown where plaintiff could have built a bridge across a creek in order to obtain alternative access). But compare Bickel v. Hansen, 169 Ariz. 371, 819 P.2d 957 (Ariz. App.1991), which interpreted a similar provision (in dicta) to permit private condemnation where strict necessity could not be shown.

3. The common law rule and the statute applied in *Roy* permit assertion of an easement by necessity only against the owner of land whose severance caused the property to become landlocked. For example, if O, the owner of

Blackacre Ranch, carves out a parcel at the back end that is landlocked, the buyer might be able to assert an easement by necessity over that portion of Blackacre that O retained. But he would not be able to assert such an easement over adjoining Greenacre, even if that way would be shorter or more convenient. See Jordan v. Shea, 791 A.2d 116 (Me.2002), which applied this principle. Accord, Loomis v. Luraski, 306 Mont. 478, 36 P.3d 862 (2001). By the same token, property that has become landlocked merely by an act of nature, such as a river whose altered course obstructs a road, could not claim an easement by necessity at common law. The common law viewed the doctrine as a "transaction fixer" giving grantees access where it assumed the parties intended to do so but forgot. It did not create a general right of access just because the land owner needed it.

4. While the courts often say that the "necessity" required for an easement by necessity is absolute, they are still willing to make exceptions. See Berge v. State, 181 Vt. 1, 915 A.2d 189 (2006), which concluded that the landowner made out the requirements for an easement by necessity even though he was still able to reach his land by taking a boat across a pond:

> Without use of the road across State land, plaintiff would have no reasonably consistent, practical means of reaching his property; rather, he would be subject to the constant vicissitudes of motor boats, weather, and water conditions. In addition, he would have virtually no access for those periods of the year when the pond could not be safely traversed because of ice or snow.

Contrast Dee v. King, 73 Vt. 375, 50 A. 1109 (1901), concluding that the necessity requirement was not shown when the landowner still had access over a circuitous, winding road over a hill, forcing him to carry only very light loads. The court held that "extreme inconvenience" is not the same thing as necessity.

5. What if the necessity that initially gave rise to the easement subsequently ends? For example, suppose a neighbor graciously gives the landowner an easement over the neighbor's land, thereby providing adequate access. Once the necessity no longer exists, the easement by necessity terminates, automatically. If the landowner later becomes landlocked again, the prior easement by necessity *does not automatically revive*. The landlocked owner will have to establish the elements of an easement implied by necessity again.

§ 8.2.4 PRESCRIPTION

FISCHER v. GRINSBERGS
Supreme Court of Nebraska (1977).
198 Neb. 329, 252 N.W.2d 619.

BRODKEY, JUSTICE.

This is an appeal from a District Court judgment dismissing a petition which prayed for injunctive relief on the basis of an alleged acquisition of a prescriptive easement for the purpose of access to a garage, over a driveway located along and on both sides of the property line between two adjacent lots of land in Lincoln, Nebraska. We reverse and remand with directions to grant the injunctive relief requested.

On June 5, 1975, Viola M. Fischer, plaintiff and appellant herein, filed a petition in the District Court for Lancaster County, alleging that she had acquired a prescriptive easement over part of a driveway located on the property of the defendants and appellants, Valdemars and Parsala Grinsbergs. The petition alleged that plaintiff and defendants owned adjoining lots of land in Lincoln, Nebraska; that a driveway runs parallel to the boundary line between the two lots, and is situated on both sides of that boundary; that plaintiff has acquired a prescriptive easement over the driveway for the purpose of access to her garage by virtue of adverse possession; and that the defendants had interfered with plaintiff's use of the driveway. The petition prayed that defendants be enjoined from interfering with plaintiff's use of the driveway.

* * *

It appears from the record that prior to 1945 a cinder driveway ran along and on both sides of the property line between Lots 25 and 26. There is, however, no evidence as to how and under what circumstances this cinder driveway was originally constructed. The driveway ran from South 16th Street toward the back of the lots, and then branched in a "Y" shape toward garages located on each lot. In 1945, the driveway was made into a concrete driveway. The owners of the lots in 1945, Benjamin McConnel and Paul Baldwin, both worked on the new concrete driveway, and each paid one-half of the costs. Subsequent to 1945, until at least 1972, the owners and/or tenants of Lots 25 and 26 both used the driveway as a means of access to their respective garages without any controversy. It is undisputed that the owners or tenants of Lot 25 frequently and openly used the driveway, helped repair it, and helped scoop snow from it in winter months. It is also undisputed that, to the knowledge of the parties and witnesses, no written agreement in regard to the driveway ever existed between the current or prior owners of the lots.

In 1972 an attorney for the defendants wrote the plaintiff, stating that the plaintiff could no longer use the driveway. Apparently there had been a survey of the lots in 1972, which showed that 6 or 7 feet of the driveway were on the property of the defendants; and that 2 to 3 feet of it were on plaintiff's property. No action resulted from the letter written in 1972, and the plaintiff or her tenants continued to use the driveway as a means of access to her garage.

In 1975 the defendants tore up the part of the driveway on their property, and replaced it with new concrete. In so doing, a small portion of the old cement on plaintiff's property was destroyed, but most of it remained intact. The defendant then built a barrier or fence on the property line, effectively preventing plaintiff from using the driveway as a means of access to her garage. Photographs admitted into evidence indicate that plaintiff's house is located so near the property line that it is impossible for her to build a driveway which would lie entirely on her property and be wide enough to permit passage of an automobile to her garage. The evidence does not show the reason for the defendants' decision to prevent plaintiff from using the driveway.

With regard to the issue of whether the defendants or previous owners of Lot 26 had ever given owners of Lot 25 permission to use their part of the driveway, there was no evidence that express permission had ever been given. Leonard Corr, who had an interest in Lot 25 from 1949 to 1959, stated that he had no real knowledge of whether Paul Baldwin, who owned Lot 26 from 1945 to 1952 ever gave the owners of Lot 25 permission to use his part of the driveway. Corr had never discussed the matter with the defendants, who became owners of Lot 26 in 1954. Corr stated that he "assumed" that the owners of Lot 26 granted permission to use their part of the driveway, but had no knowledge of this fact.

Edwin V. Fischer, plaintiff's husband, stated that he "assumed," on the basis of defendants' "inaction" on the matter, that they had given permission to use the driveway; but he clarified this statement by stating unequivocally that to his knowledge the defendants had never given him or anyone else permission to use the driveway. The defendant, Mr. Grinsbergs, gave no testimony whatsoever on the issue of permission. He stated that no written agreement existed in regard to the driveway, and that he had received no explanation in regard to it when he acquired Lot 26 in 1954. He stated that Leonard Corr, previous owner of Lot 25, had told him that the driveway was on the Grinsbergs' property. Mr. Grinsbergs stated that he had never requested that plaintiff or her tenants not use the driveway.

Following the submission of briefs in the case, the trial court entered judgment in favor of the defendants on April 28, 1976, and made the following findings: (1) [t]hat the use of the driveway was a permissive use, (2) that there was not an agreement made between the parties or the prior owners of the real estate in question which would constitute an agreement sufficient to constitute an easement, and (3) the evidence was insufficient to establish a location for the easement claimed by the plaintiff. In accordance with these findings, the trial court dismissed plaintiff's petition. Plaintiff's motion for new trial was overruled, and she has now appealed to this court.

* * *

The general rules applicable to prescriptive easements are well settled in this state, and are set forth in Jurgensen v. Ainscow, 155 Neb. 701, 53 N.W.2d 196 (1952) as follows: "The use and enjoyment which will give title by prescription to an easement is substantially the same in quality and characteristics as the adverse possession which will give title to real estate. It must be adverse, under a claim of right, continuous and uninterrupted, open and notorious, exclusive, and with the knowledge and acquiescence of the owner of the servient tenement, for the full prescriptive period."

* * *

It is also established law that a permissive use is not adverse, and cannot ripen into an easement.

* * *

There is no question under the evidence in this case that plaintiff's use of the driveway was continuous, uninterrupted, and open and notorious for a period exceeding 10 years. The evidence was undisputed that plaintiff or her predecessors openly used the driveway without interruption from at least 1945 to 1975. Use of predecessors in title may be tacked on to plaintiff's use to meet the 10–year requirement. See 25 Am.Jur.2d, Easements and Licenses, § 58, p. 467. Plaintiff's use also was "exclusive" under the meaning of that word as applied in cases involving prescriptive easements.

* * *

Acquiescence and knowledge of the defendants were also established under the test set forth in Jurgensen v. Ainscow, supra, as acquiescence means "passive assent or submission, quiescence, consent by silence," and the owner is charged with the knowledge when the claimant's use has been open, notorious, visible, uninterrupted, and undisputed.

The primary question remaining, therefore, is whether plaintiff's use was adverse and under a claim of right, since the other requirements of establishing a prescriptive easement have been met. Nebraska law is clear and well established that where "the evidence establishes the open, visible, continuous, and unmolested use of the land for a period of time sufficient to acquire an easement by adverse user, the use will be presumed to be under a claim of right. In such a case the owners of the servient estate, in order to avoid the acquisition of an easement by prescription, have the burden of rebutting the prescriptive right by showing that the use was permissive." Smith v. Bixby, 196 Neb. 235, 242 N.W.2d 115 (1976). The presumption of adversity and claim of right which exists when there has been open, visible, continuous, and unmolested use for the prescriptive period of 10 years is well established in a long line of Nebraska cases.

* * *

As long ago as 1912, this court stated in Majerus v. Barton, 92 Neb. 685, 139 N.W. 208 (1912), that if a person proves uninterrupted and open use for the necessary period without evidence to explain how the use began, the presumption is raised that the use is adverse and under the claim of right, and the burden is on the owner of the land to show that the use was by license, agreement, or permission. The presumption of adverse use and claim of right, when applicable prevails unless it is overcome by a preponderance of the evidence.

* * *

Plaintiff relies on the above cases and contends in her brief that the presumption of adverse use and claim of right is applicable in this case, and that the defendants did not overcome this presumption by a preponderance of the evidence. The defendants contend that the presumption is not applicable in this case, and argue that the trial court was correct in finding that plaintiff's use of the driveway was permissive.

The defendants rely on three cases: Bone v. James, 82 Neb. 442, 118 N.W. 83 (1908); Stubblefield v. Osborn, 149 Neb. 566, 31 N.W.2d 547 (1948); and Scoville v. Fisher, 181 Neb. 496, 149 N.W.2d 339 (1967). In *Bone*, the claimant of the easement admitted that he used the land by permission of the owner, and the court appropriately found that no prescriptive easement was acquired when the use was permissive.

In *Stubblefield*, the plaintiff sought to establish an easement over the defendant's land for the purpose of hunting. The court said: "In the instant case the evidence by the plaintiffs shows the original entry and use to have been permissive. The plaintiffs did not inform Bolton that they claimed a right-of-way and perpetual easement across his land. They crossed the land on occasions to go hunting, as did others. There was no claim of right or exclusive use. The most that can be said as to their crossing the lands in question is that it was permissive only, a neighborly act on the part of the owners or tenants on the land."

In *Scoville*, the plaintiff sought to establish an easement over the town lot of the defendant. The lot was unenclosed and unimproved, and was used by the public generally for parking and other purposes. The evidence showed that the original use of the lot was permissive, and the court held that "when an owner permits his unenclosed and unimproved land to be used by the public, or by his neighbors generally, a user thereof by a neighboring landowner, and others, however frequent, will be presumed to be permissive and not adverse in the absence of any attendant circumstances indicative to the contrary." The court noted the general rule that a presumption of adversity arises when there has been open, visible, continuous, and unmolested use for the prescriptive period, but stated that this general rule must be interpreted in the light of the facts of each case. The court stated: "Here we have unenclosed land with no defined pathway across it and where, paraphrasing Stubblefield v. Osborn, supra, the most that can be said of the plaintiff, the public, and the many other various users of the whole area was that their use was permissive only, a neighborly act on the part of the owners or tenants on the land. Applicable here is what this court said in Burk v. Diers, 102 Neb. 721, 169 N.W. 263, as follows: 'Oftentimes farmers or owners of city lots, out of mere generosity and neighborly feeling, permit a way over their land to be used, when the entire community knows that the use is permissive only, without thought of dedication or adverse user. This use ought not to deprive the owner of his property, however long continued. Such rule would be a prohibition of all neighborhood accommodations in the way of travel.' "

A review of *Stubblefield* and *Scoville* indicates that those cases present different and distinguishable factual situations from the one presented in the present case. It would appear that the cases cited earlier in which the presumption of adversity and claim of right was applied, control in this case. The defendants' claim that the presumption does not apply in this case is not supported by the case law.

If we apply the presumption of adverse holding referred to, the evidence clearly does not sustain the trial court's finding that plaintiff's use of the driveway was a permissive use. Defendants, in their brief, do not contend that the presumption was rebutted, but argue that the presumption should not apply. There was no evidence whatsoever that the defendants, or their predecessors in title, gave permission to use the part of the driveway on their land. Defendant Grinsbergs, in his own testimony, said nothing at all about granting permission. Our conclusion is that the defendants failed to overcome the presumption referred to by a preponderance of the evidence.

A second issue raised by the parties is whether the mutual use of a driveway by adjoining landowners can ripen into a prescriptive easement. Defendants claim it cannot, relying on two Michigan cases, Wilkinson v. Hutzel, 142 Mich. 674, 106 N.W. 207 (1906); and Hopkins v. Parker, 296 Mich. 375, 296 N.W. 294 (1941). *Hopkins* is clearly distinguishable on the facts from the present case, and the court found that the use by the claimant was permissive at inception, and therefore not adverse.

Wilkinson, however, does generally support the defendants' position. In that case predecessors of the parties had established a private right-of-way between two adjoining lots of land for the mutual convenience of both landowners. Both owners used the way for more than 30 years, until one owner blocked the way. The court found that from the beginning there was an accommodation agreement between the parties for their mutual convenience, and that there was no hostile and adverse use by either owner as against the other. The court stated that the way was based on a license which was revocable at any time by either party.

The *Wilkinson* case, however, represents a minority position, and must be read in conjunction with a later Nebraska decision, Jensen v. Showalter, 79 Neb. 544, 113 N.W. 202 (1907). In *Jensen* neighboring landowners established an alley along the boundary between their properties, each contributing 6 feet of land. The alley was used continuously by both landowners until one blocked it with a fence built along the division line. There was no written agreement in regard to the alley, and no easement by deed was involved. The court first noted the following rule: "The defendant claims that the agreement between the parties was a mere license, one to the other, to use their respective share of the lots in question for an alley for their mutual convenience, and that such license is revokable [sic] by either one at their pleasure. The rule is well established that, where one enjoys a right of way under a claim of right, the owner of the land has the burden of proving that the use of the easement was under some license, indulgence, or special contract inconsistent with the right claimed by the other party." Reviewing numerous cases from other jurisdictions, the court concluded that an agreement of the kind involved in the case gave to the parties a prescriptive right in the alley. The court specifically found the *Wilkinson* case to be inapplicable. See 79 Neb. at p. 548, 113 N.W. 202, 203. Plaintiff relies on the *Jensen* case, pointing out that the evidence showed that the owners of Lots 25 and 26 agreed in 1945 to construct a driveway, and each paid for one-half of the cost.

The following statement in 28 C.J.S. Easements § 18j, p. 673, should also be noted: "As stated in Corpus Juris, which has been cited and quoted with approval, while there are some decisions to the contrary, the weight of authority is to the effect that, where adjoining proprietors lay out a way or alley between their lands, each devoting a part of his own land to that purpose, and the way or alley is used for the prescriptive period by the respective owners or their successors in title, neither can obstruct or close the part which is on his own land; and in these circumstances the mutual use of the whole of the way or alley will be considered adverse to a separate and exclusive use by either party. However, where the owners of land used an alleyway for their mutual convenience, the user being occasional, permissive, and for broken periods of time, no right of way in the alley was established by prescription."

* * * It appears that the overwhelming weight of authority favors the plaintiff's position that her use of the driveway was not permissive, and we conclude that the trial court erred in holding that her use of the driveway was permissive.

* * *

The final finding of the trial court was that the evidence was insufficient to establish a location for the easements by the plaintiff. We believe this finding to be erroneous. It is true that a claimed easement must not be such that the extent of the claim is too indefinite for a determinate description.

* * *

In the present case, however, deeds covering the lots in question were admitted into evidence, and the testimony was undisputed that the driveway extended approximately 6 feet on the defendants' land and 3 feet on plaintiff's land. Photographs showed the location of the driveway in relation to the houses and garages on the lots. We do not believe that a more precise description of the claimed easement is necessary to afford injunctive relief, especially since the driveway to the garages has existed for years. The extent of an easement is determined from the use actually made of the property during the running of the prescriptive period. Jurgensen v. Ainscow, supra; Hopkins v. Hill, supra. In this case it is clear the easement would be limited to the width of the driveway as is reasonably necessary for access to plaintiff's garage. See Smith v. Bixby, supra.

We conclude, therefore, that the presumption of adversity and claim of right applies in this case, and the defendants did not rebut that presumption, although it was their burden to do so. It is clear that plaintiff is entitled to a prescriptive easement under the facts of this case, and the evidence appears sufficient to establish a location for the easement claimed.

* * *

The judgment must be reversed and the cause remanded with directions to grant the injunctive relief requested by plaintiff.

NOTES AND QUESTIONS

1. Why don't adverse possession statutes apply to easements?

2. Can you think of another theory, previously developed in this chapter, under which Ms. Fischer might have won the right to keep her driveway?

3. The law of prescriptive easements has developed along two different, and fundamentally inconsistent, legal theories. The "lost grant" theory rests on the legal fiction that a long period of visible access to the property of another is best explained by a "grant" that had been made to the claimant's predecessor by the predecessor of the person against whom the claim is made. See Stoebuck, The Fiction of Presumed Grant, 15 Kan.L.Rev. 17 (1966), strongly urging that courts abandon this theory.

The "adverse possession" theory is similar to the general theory of adverse possession of possessory interests, except that in most states it is a product of the common law, not of statute (see generally chapter 3). The court generally adopts the period created by the adverse possession statute as the prescriptive period. The principal difference between this theory and the law of adverse possession is the *absence* of any requirement that the claimant's use be "exclusive" vis-a-vis the record owner. Many easements are shared by the owners of the dominant and servient estates. A second difference is that prescription requires adverse "use" for the prescriptive period, while adverse possession requires adverse "possession" for the statutory period. The difference lies in the intensity of the claimant's use. For example, one who merely entered property on one side and exited from the other side daily for twenty years, never making any improvements, would almost certainly not be able to show "possession," even if his use were exclusive. By contrast, this use might easily be sufficient to establish prescription.

The most unfortunate aspect of the two theories of prescription is that the theories are not only different, they are logically inconsistent, and the same facts that will establish prescription under one theory will tend to undermine it under the other theory. This is particularly problematic for a jurisdiction that has precedents approving both theories. The lost grant theory is built on a fictional *permissive* use. Evidence of acquiescence and approval by the owner against whom the easement is claimed tends to support the claimant's position. See, e.g., Dartnell v. Bidwell, 115 Me. 227, 230, 98 A. 743, 745 (1916) ("Proof of acquiescence by the owner is held essential by all authorities. It raises the presumption of a grant. . . . Where the adverse use has continued for 20 years without interruption or denial on the part of the owner, and with his knowledge, his acquiescence is conclusively presumed.").

In contrast, under the adverse possession theory relied upon increasingly by modern courts, permission tends to defeat the prescriptive claim. Lunt v. Kitchens, 123 Utah 488, 260 P.2d 535 (1953). The trend in the cases is to grant the prescriptive easement if the use has continued for the required period and there is not clear evidence that the owner of the servient interest expressly gave the claimant a revocable license. See, e.g., Dieck v. Landry, 796 So.2d 1004 (Miss.2001) (claimant simply used strip of land without asking, but clearly the landowner knew claimant was trespassing; easement created).

4. Subjective intent continues to play a role in easement by prescription, even though the trend is to the contrary. See Wilfon v. Cyril Hampel 1985 Trust, 105 Nev. 607, 781 P.2d 769 (1989), holding that no prescriptive easement could arise where the claimant thought he was using a roadway with the landowner's permission. Contrast Nelson v. Davis, 262 Va. 230, 546 S.E.2d 712 (2001) (easement by prescription created even though users mistakenly believed that there was a recorded easement by grant over the claimed strip of land). And see Cardenas v. Kurpjuweit, 116 Idaho 739, 742, 779 P.2d 414, 417 (1989), which rejected

> the curious doctrine that a claimant's subjective state of mind may determine whether he is entitled to a prescriptive easement. This state of mind doctrine is illogical. The "adversity" of a claimant's use lies in its derogation from the exclusive rights of the landowner; it does not lie in the claimant's state of mind. Regardless of the motive with which a prospective claimant crosses a landowner's property, his use derogates from the landowner's rights unless the crossing is by permission, express or legally presumed. Moreover, the state of mind doctrine creates a perverse incentive to offer contrived but virtually unrebuttable testimony. A sophisticated claimant * * * would never admit having thought a road was public; he would simply testify that he used the road because he found it convenient. Accordingly, * * * the adversity of a claimant's use is determined not by his subjective belief but by the nature of the use itself. As the Washington Supreme Court has noted: "[T]here is little persuasive precedent for applying a subjective standard of adverse use in prescriptive easement cases. The gravamen of adversity in such cases is whether the user has occupied the property in a manner which is adverse to the true owner. Although subjective intent may have some relevance in an adverse possession case where the user claims title, the claim in a prescriptive easement case is merely to [a] use which could have been prevented by the rightful owner. We therefore hold that adversity is to be measured by an objective standard; that is, by the objectively observable acts of the user and the rightful owner."

Quoting Dunbar v. Heinrich, 95 Wash.2d 20, 27, 622 P.2d 812, 815–16 (1980). Do you agree with the court's distinction between prescriptive easements and adverse possession? See chapter 3.

5. Note that the *Fischer* court required that the claimant's use be "exclusive" before it would ripen into an easement by prescription. However, the right to exclude the world is inherent in an unencumbered *possessory* interest, but not in an easement. The Nebraska court is really asserting the requirement in order to underscore the fact that the claim is based on the

claimant's own use for the prescriptive period, not on the claimant's shared use with the public in general. This is consistent with the general rule that the *public* cannot acquire an easement by prescription. See Nelson v. Davis, 262 Va. 230, 546 S.E.2d 712 (2001), which concluded that when several persons with no legal relationship used the claimed strip of land as a road, each one who met the requirements could acquire an easement interest, although the general public as a body acquired nothing.

However, many legal entities such as corporations, can act only through their agents. For example, if the various employees of XYZ Corp. all walked across Blackacre in the course of their employment, XYZ Corp. might acquire a prescriptive easement, even though the claim was based on the aggregated activities of dozens of individual employees. A municipality is a corporation. Could a municipality claim an easement by prescription to beachfront property simply because its residents used the beach? See Town of Sparta v. Hamm, 97 N.C.App. 82, 387 S.E.2d 173 (1990), which held that a town could acquire a roadway easement by prescription based on use by mail carriers, school bus drivers and others. There was no discussion of the exclusivity requirement. Contra, Callahan v. White, 238 Va. 10, 381 S.E.2d 1 (1989) (general public could not acquire easement). See also Kornbluth v. Kalur, 577 A.2d 1194 (Me.1990), which held that no prescriptive easement was established when the claimant's guests crossed the defendant's property for a twenty year period, since there was no privity of estate between the claimant and his guests.

In United States on Behalf of Zuni Tribe v. Platt, 730 F.Supp. 318 (D.Ariz.1990), the court held that an Indian tribe could acquire an easement by prescription over a route used for a religious pilgrimage. Although the pilgrimage had occurred since the beginning of the twentieth century, it happened only once every four years.

For several years players at a privately owned golf course hit their golf balls into the yard of a homeowner whose property bordered on the course. Several times daily players walked onto the yard to retrieve them. Has the golf course acquired a prescriptive right for its players to enter the homeowner's land? See MacDonald Properties, Inc. v. Bel–Air Country Club, 72 Cal.App.3d 693, 140 Cal.Rptr. 367 (1977). What result if the municipality owned the golf course?

6. For the first half of the prescriptive period A crossed B's property, entering at point X and exiting at point Y. For the second half A also entered at X and exited at Y, but used a somewhat different course in between. Has A acquired an easement by prescription? See Speight v. Anderson, 226 N.C. 492, 39 S.E.2d 371 (1946). Suppose that A had acquired a prescriptive easement over path X–Y, but now the owner of the servient estate insists that A use an alternative path, X–Z, as the easement? Is A entitled to insist on the same path that he acquired by prescription? See Thomason v. Kern & Co., Inc., 259 Ga. 119, 376 S.E.2d 872 (1989).

7. American courts agree that only "affirmative" easements—i.e., rights to do something on the land of another—can be created by prescription. "Negative" easements, which are rights that an adjoining or nearby landowner *refrain* from doing something on her own land, cannot be. Do you see why?

In Fontainebleau Hotel Corp. v. Forty–Five Twenty–Five, Inc., 114 So.2d 357 (Fla.App.1959), a Florida court refused to grant an easement by prescription for access to sunlight across the defendant's property. Recognition of the easement would have amounted to a requirement that the defendant not build any structure on its own property that would cut off the sunlight to the plaintiff hotel's bathing beach.

In England, the doctrine of "ancient lights" provided that one who had received undisturbed sunlight to his windows for twenty years acquired what amounted to a prescriptive easement across the property through which the sunlight entered. The doctrine has been almost universally rejected in the United States—at least until very recently. See Prah v. Maretti, 108 Wis.2d 223, 321 N.W.2d 182 (1982), and the notes following it, chapter 9.

8. Prescriptive easements are often asserted when the owner of the "servient estate" decides to develop her property in a way that is inconsistent with the existence of the easement. As a result, the loss that the owner of the servient estate experiences is greater at the time that the easement is recognized by the court than it was during the time that it was being acquired by prescription. For example, a landowner of unfenced property may not even notice that a neighbor is driving across his land until he begins to build a building that runs to the edge of his property. Then a dispute arises and the prescriptive easement is claimed.

This raises the possibility, however, that although use of the easement may have been efficient during the time the easement was being created by prescription, it is no longer efficient at the time of litigation. One might ensure that easements created by prescription are efficient when they are created by requiring the claimant of the easement to compensate the servient owner for her loss. If the easement is worth more to the claimant than it is to the servient owner, then the claimant will pay the damages and acquire the easement. If the easement is worth less, then the claimant will choose not to pay and forego the easement. However, see the note in chapter 3 arguing *against* compensation in adverse possession cases. Are there reasons compensation would be appropriate for easements taken by prescription even though it is not appropriate for property interests taken by adverse possession?

In Warsaw v. Chicago Metallic Ceilings, Inc., 35 Cal.3d 564, 199 Cal.Rptr. 773, 676 P.2d 584 (1984), the California Supreme Court refused to change the law of prescriptive easements to require the claimant of the easement to compensate the owner for his loss. Justice Reynoso dissented, arguing that permitting people to take easements by prescription without paying compensation amounted to a "private action akin to eminent domain," except that no just compensation was paid.

9. In Boldt v. Roth, 618 N.W.2d 393 (Minn.2000), the neighbors who built a partially shared driveway were members of a single extended family—one land owner was mother-in-law to the other at the time the driveway was built. However, the mother-in-law subsequently transferred her property. The Minnesota Supreme Court held that the prescriptive period did not begin to run as long as the adjoining landowners were family members; but once the mother-in-law's property was transferred there was sufficient hostility to start the prescriptive period. The court reasoned:

We have recognized that the general rule of presumed hostility is modified in cases in which family members own both the dominant and servient estates. See Wojahn v. Johnson, 297 N.W.2d 298, 306 (Minn. 1980). The reason for this modification is that the nature of close familial relationships is such that mere actual, open, exclusive, and continuous possession is not enough to give notice to a family member that a use is hostile.

The mother-in-law's conveyance of her land to a stranger had occurred more than fifteen years prior to the litigation. Apparently no survey was done and the buyer assumed that the entire driveway was on her property. In recognizing the creation of an easement by prescription the court explained:

> Once the owner of the servient estate is no longer a family member, actual and open use should suffice to notify the owner that the use is hostile. Subsequent servient estate owners who do not have a familial relationship have no reason to presume that a use is not an assertion of a claim of right. They have notice of the boundaries to their property and that the use is actual and open. We now ... hold that, absent evidence of continued permission, the transfer of the servient estate to a stranger renders hostile a use previously considered permissive due to a close familial relationship and such transfer will commence the 15–year prescriptive easement time period....
>
> Regardless of whether Boldt's original use of the driveway was permissive, that use became hostile in 1979 when Boldt's mother-in-law transferred the remaining parcel to nonfamily members.

Other decisions are far more likely than *Fischer* to find uses to be permissive. For example, in Coleman v. Keith, 6 P.3d 145 (Wyo.2000), the claimant owned landlocked property and used a road across adjoining land to reach it. He apparently never asked anyone's permission and spent money improving the roadway. In refusing to find prescription the Wyoming Supreme Court described its law this way:

> In Wyoming, the law requires a manifestation of hostile and adverse intent to use a road, even though it will likely result in revocation of permission to use the road across the neighbor's land. A person claiming a prescriptive easement may not rely on a presumption of adverse use or his subjective intent. Rather, the use is presumed to have been with permission. "To rebut this presumption the claimant must introduce evidence of the facts which demonstrate the manner in which the hostile and adverse nature of his use was brought home to the owner of the adjacent land." [quoting earlier decisions] Finally, the use must be inconsistent with the rights of the owner, such that the use would entitle the owner to a cause of action against the claimant, without permission asked or given.

The court then refused to find adverse use because the claimant was "never denied" permission to use the roadway. Further, "The predecessors in interest to the Keiths did not act to stop the Colemans from using the road, which supports a presumption of permissive use."

So how does one get a prescriptive easement in Wyoming? Apparently by showing that the land owner of the servient estate actually objected or actually denied permission to use the easement, and then neglected to bring a lawsuit for the prescriptive period even though the use continued.

INTERIOR TRAILS PRESERVATION COALITION v. SWOPE

Supreme Court of Alaska (2005).
115 P.3d 527.

BRYNER, C.J.

1. INTRODUCTION

The Interior Trails Preservation Coalition brought an action against Greg and Donna Swope claiming a public prescriptive easement over the Swopes' property for recreational use. The superior court dismissed the action, concluding as a matter of law that the Coalition was incapable of prevailing on its claim because it had not been in existence for ten years-the minimum time required to establish its continuing use of the alleged easement. We reverse, holding that because the Coalition claimed a public easement, it was not required to prove its own continuous use of the land and could instead establish its claim by evidence showing continuous public use.

II. FACTS AND PROCEEDINGS

Greg and Donna Swope bought a parcel of land near the Skyline Ridge Trail in Fairbanks in 1997. After seeing a number of people cross their land, the Swopes posted a "no trespassing" sign and erected a barrier to keep trespassers off. But some people apparently continued to cross over the land.

In 2002 several Fairbanks area residents created the Interior Trails Preservation Coalition, a non-profit corporation established to keep local recreational trails open to the public. The Coalition filed a complaint in the superior court, seeking to establish a public prescriptive easement over the Swopes' property. The complaint alleged that a pathway leading to the Skyline Ridge Trail passes through the Swopes' property and has been used by the public since the 1950s.

The Swopes moved to dismiss the complaint, contending that the Coalition lacked standing to claim a prescriptive easement and that it could not prove its claim in any event, since the Coalition had not been in existence long enough to meet the ten-year period of continuous use necessary to establish a prescription. The superior court granted the Swopes' motion, concluding that the Coalition lacked standing because it had neglected to allege that any of its members could maintain the action on their own and because it had been in existence for less than ten years. The Coalition moved for reconsideration, submitting an affidavit of one of its members who claimed to have used the trail for "many years." The superior court declined to reconsider its ruling, and the Coalition petitioned for review. We granted the petition and now reverse the order of dismissal.

III. DISCUSSION

The main issue presented for our review is whether a corporate organization like the Coalition can maintain an action for a public prescriptive easement even though the organization has not been in existence long enough to engage in the ten-year period of continuous use needed to establish a prescriptive easement. Stated differently, the question is whether the Coalition must establish the prescriptive easement by proof of its own continuous use.

Obtaining rights in another's property by prescription is similar to obtaining rights by adverse possession. "Both doctrines permit acquisition of property rights through the passage of time, if certain conditions are met, but prescription is applied to servitudes while adverse possession is applied to possessory estates." Thus, the focus in a prescriptive easement claim is on "use," whereas the focus in an adverse possession case is on "possession."

The two doctrines differ slightly in other respects as well. To acquire an interest through adverse possession, the claimant ordinarily must prove ten years of adverse and exclusive possession. In contrast, while a prescriptive easement similarly requires ten years of continuous use, "[t]he use need not be, and frequently is not, exclusive" for prescription.

Prescriptive easements may be obtained either by private individuals or by the general public. "The required elements are the same for public and private prescriptive easements. The only difference is that a public prescriptive easement requires qualifying use by the public, while a private prescriptive easement requires qualifying use only by the private party." A prescriptive easement obtained by a private person gives only that person the right to continued use, whereas a prescriptive easement obtained by the general public gives the right of use to the public at large.

Alaska courts have long recognized prescriptive easement claims brought on behalf of the general public as well as private individuals. To succeed on a prescriptive easement claim, a claimant must show that (1) the use was continuous and uninterrupted for the same ten-year period that applies to adverse possession; (2) the claimant acted as an owner and not merely as a person having the permission of the owner; and (3) the use was reasonably visible to the record owner. The claimant must prove each element by clear and convincing evidence.

Here, the Coalition contends that the public has used a pathway that runs through the Swopes' property since the 1950s to gain access to the Skyline Ridge Trail, and that this use established a prescriptive easement in the 1960s that continues today. In dismissing the Coalition's complaint, the court noted that "[t]he association has not as an entity used the trail. . . .

The Coalition argues that the trial court's ruling confuses claims for private prescriptive easements, which seek to establish individual rights of use, with claims for public prescriptive easements, which seek to establish public rights. The Coalition contends that if continuous use by one user were required to establish public prescriptive easements, then public easements could never be obtained, because the individual user could always claim a private easement instead. Because of the settled principle that the scope of a prescriptive easement is limited to the manner in which it was established, the Coalition contends, the court would be obliged to limit the easement to the individual user, thus effectively eliminating any chance of recognizing a public prescriptive use.

The Swopes respond by citing the case relied on by the superior court: our recent opinion in *Price v. Eastham.* In the Swopes' view, *Price* settles this issue by holding that an organization cannot bring a public prescription claim if it has not been in existence for the ten-year period required to establish continuous adverse use. But the Swopes misread *Price.*

* * *

On appeal, the Swopes cite no other authority holding that a plaintiff cannot establish a public prescriptive easement by relying on evidence of continuous use by other members of the general public. We have found no cases that support this conclusion; in fact, case law points to the opposite conclusion. In *Elmer v. Rodgers,* for example, an individual plaintiff brought suit claiming that the public had acquired a prescriptive easement over a church's property. The New Hampshire Supreme Court found that evidence showing twenty years of general public use of the church's land to gain access to a nearby beach was sufficient to establish a public prescriptive easement, even though the individual plaintiff failed to prove sufficient personal use to establish a private easement. In other words, the New Hampshire Supreme Court held, the plaintiff was not precluded "from relying on and asserting the prescriptive right of the general public."

The situation here is analogous to the one at issue in *Elmer v. Rodgers.* To establish a public prescriptive easement, the Coalition was required to prove continuous use by the public in general, not use by the organization itself or by any individual member. Like the individual plaintiff in *Elmer,* the Coalition was not precluded "from relying on and asserting the prescriptive right of the general public."

We thus hold that it was error to dismiss the complaint on the ground that the Coalition had not been in existence for ten or more years.

IV. CONCLUSION

For these reasons, we REVERSE the superior court's order of dismissal.

MATTHEWS, JUSTICE, not participating.

NOTES AND QUESTIONS

1. The *Fisher* case concerned private prescriptive easements. *Interior Trails Preservation Coalition* discusses the law of public prescriptive easements. What are some of the distinctions between public and private prescriptive easements?

2. Can prescriptive rights be obtained across public lands? The general rule is that, absent an enabling statute that provides to the contrary, prescriptive easements cannot be acquired against a state or against the federal government. The same general rule applies to municipal property that is held for use by the public. An exception may exist in the case of another unit of government seeking to obtain a prescriptive easement over municipal property. See The Law of Easements & Licenses in Land § 5:5 (2011). Some states, such as Alaska, have enacted statutes that prohibit prescriptive rights against state lands. E.g., Alaska Stat. § 38.95.010 (2010).

3. What can a property owner do to prevent private or public prescriptive easements from being established on the owner's property? The property owner can bring an action for ejectment prior to the expiration of the statute of limitations for the prescriptive period. As long as the owner interrupts one or more of the elements for prescription before the statute of limitations runs, the owner can prevent the establishment of prescriptive rights. The owner can make the use permissive through a license or lease, for instance. The owner could engage in other acts of dominion and control so as to break the continuity of the adverse user's use. The acts of dominion and control that would be sufficient will vary depending upon the character of the property.

§ 8.2.5 RECOGNITION OF PUBLIC ACCESS RIGHTS: IMPLIED DEDICATION, CUSTOM, AND THE "PUBLIC TRUST"

MATTHEWS v. BAY HEAD IMPROVEMENT ASS'N

Supreme Court of New Jersey (1984).
95 N.J. 306, 471 A.2d 355, cert. denied 469 U.S. 821 (1984).

SCHREIBER, J.

The public trust doctrine acknowledges that the ownership, dominion and sovereignty over land flowed by tidal waters, which extend to the mean high water mark, is vested in the State in trust for the people. The public's right to use the tidal lands and water encompasses navigation, fishing and recreational uses, including bathing, swimming and other shore activities. Borough of Neptune City v. Borough of Avon–by–the–Sea, 61 N.J. 296, 309, 294 A.2d 47 (1972). In *Avon* we held that the public trust applied to the municipally-owned dry sand beach immediately landward of the high water mark.[1] The major issue in this case is whether, ancillary to the public's right to enjoy the tidal lands, the public has a right to gain

---

1. The dry sand area is generally defined as the land west (landward) of the high water mark to the vegetation line or where there is no vegetation to a seawall, road, parking lot or boardwalk.

access through and to use the dry sand area not owned by a municipality but by a quasi-public body.

The Borough of Point Pleasant instituted this suit against the Borough of Bay Head and the Bay Head Improvement Association (Association), generally asserting that the defendants prevented Point Pleasant inhabitants from gaining access to the Atlantic Ocean and the beachfront in Bay Head. The proceeding was dismissed as to the Borough of Bay Head because it did not own or control the beach. Subsequently, Virginia Matthews, a resident of Point Pleasant who desired to swim and bathe at the Bay Head beach, joined as a party plaintiff, and Stanley Van Ness, as Public Advocate, joined as plaintiff-intervenor. When the Borough of Point Pleasant ceased pursuing the litigation, the Public Advocate became the primary moving party. The Public Advocate asserted that the defendants had denied the general public its right of access during the summer bathing season to public trust lands along the beaches in Bay Head and its right to use private property fronting on the ocean incidental to the public's right under the public trust doctrine.

* * *

The Borough of Bay Head (Bay Head) borders the Atlantic Ocean. Adjacent to it on the north is the Borough of Point Pleasant Beach, on the south the Borough of Mantoloking, and on the west Barnegat Bay. Bay Head consists of a fairly narrow strip of land, 6,667 feet long (about 1¼ miles). A beach runs along its entire length adjacent to the Atlantic Ocean. There are 76 separate parcels of land that border the beach. All except six are owned by private individuals. Title to those six is vested in the Association.

The Association was founded in 1910 and incorporated as a nonprofit corporation in 1932. Its certificate of incorporation states that its purposes are

> the improving and beautifying of the Borough of Bay Head, New Jersey, cleaning, policing and otherwise making attractive and safe the bathing beaches in said Borough, and the doing of any act which may be found necessary or desirable for the greater convenience, comfort and enjoyment of the residents.

Its constitution delineates the Association's object to promote the best interests of the Borough and "in so doing to own property, operate bathing beaches, hire life guards, beach cleaners and policemen...."

Nine streets in the Borough, which are perpendicular to the beach, end at the dry sand. The Association owns the land commencing at the end of seven of these streets for the width of each street and extending through the upper dry sand to the mean high water line, the beginning of the wet sand area or foreshore. In addition, the Association owns the fee in six shore front properties, three of which are contiguous and have a

New Jersey Beach Access Study Commission, Public Access to the Oceanfront Beaches: A Report to the Governor and Legislature of New Jersey 2 (1977).

frontage aggregating 310 feet. Many owners of beachfront property executed and delivered to the Association leases of the upper dry sand area. These leases are revocable by either party to the lease on thirty days' notice. Some owners have not executed such leases and have not permitted the Association to use their beaches. Some also have acquired riparian grants from the State extending approximately 1,000 feet east of the high water line.

The Association controls and supervises its beach property between the third week in June and Labor Day. It engages about 40 employees, who serve as lifeguards, beach police and beach cleaners. Lifeguards, stationed at five operating beaches, indicate by use of flags whether the ocean condition is dangerous (red), requires caution (yellow), or is satisfactory (green). In addition to observing and, if need be, assisting those in the water, when called upon lifeguards render first aid. Beach cleaners are engaged to rake and keep the beach clean of debris. Beach police are stationed at the entrances to the beaches where the public streets lead into the beach to ensure that only Association members or their guests enter. Some beach police patrol the beaches to enforce its membership rules.

Membership is generally limited to residents of Bay Head. Class A members are property owners. Class B are non-owners. Large families (six or more) pay $90 per year and small families pay $60 per year. Upon application residents are routinely accepted. Membership is evidenced by badges that signify permission to use the beaches. Members, which include local hotels, motels and inns, can also acquire badges for guests. The charge for each guest badge is $12. Members of the Bay Head Fire Company, Bay Head Borough employees, and teachers in the municipality's school system have been issued beach badges irrespective of residency.

Association membership totals between 4,800 to 5,000. The Association President testified during depositions that its restrictive policy, in existence since 1932, was due to limited parking facilities and to the overcrowding of the beaches. The Association's avowed purpose was to provide the beach for the residents of Bay Head.

The trial court held that the Association was not an arm of the Borough of Bay Head, that the Association was not a municipal agency, and that nothing in the record justified a finding that public privileges could attach to the private properties owned or leased by the Association. A divided Appellate Division affirmed.

* * *

The Public Trust

In Borough of Neptune City v. Borough of Avon–by–the–Sea, 61 N.J. 296, 303, 294 A.2d 47 (1972), Justice Hall alluded to the ancient principle "that land covered by tidal waters belonged to the sovereign, but for the common use of all the people." The genesis of this principle is found in Roman jurisprudence, which held that "[b]y the law of nature" "the air, running water, the sea, and consequently the shores of the sea" were "common to mankind." Justinian, Institutes 2.1.1 (T. Sandars trans. 1st Am. ed. 1876). No one was forbidden access to the sea, and everyone could use the seashore "to dry his nets there, and haul them from the sea...." Id., 2.1.5. The seashore was not private property, but "subject to the same law as the sea itself, and the sand or ground beneath it." Id. This underlying concept was applied in New Jersey in Arnold v. Mundy, 6 N.J.L. 1 (Sup.Ct.1821).

The defendant in *Arnold* tested the plaintiff's claim of an exclusive right to harvest oysters by taking some oysters that the plaintiff had planted in beds in the Raritan River adjacent to his farm in Perth Amboy. The oyster beds extended about 150 feet below the ordinary low water mark. The tide ebbed and flowed over it. The defendant's motion for a nonsuit was granted.

Chief Justice Kirkpatrick, in an extensive opinion, referred to the grant by Charles II of the land comprising New Jersey with "all rivers, harbors, waters, fishings, etc., and of all other royalties, so far as the king had estate, right, title or interest therein" to the Duke of York. 6 N.J.L. at 85 (2d ed. 1875) (emphasis deleted). The duke had been delegated the same power as the king with respect to the land, and by virtue of the charter could divide and grant only those properties and interests that the king could. The Chief Justice's analysis then turned to the power of the English king. According to English law, public property consisted of two classes. Some was necessary for the state's use, and the remainder was common property available to all citizens. Chief Justice Kirkpatrick wrote that "[o]f this latter kind, according to the writers upon the law of nature and of nations, and upon the civil law, are the air, the running water, the sea, the fish and the wild beasts." He argued that "though this title, strictly speaking, is in the sovereign, yet the use is common to all the people."

* * *

In order to exercise these rights guaranteed by the public trust doctrine, the public must have access to municipally-owned dry sand areas as well as the foreshore. The extension of the public trust doctrine to include municipally-owned dry sand areas was necessitated by our conclusion that enjoyment of rights in the foreshore is inseparable from use of dry sand beaches. In *Avon* we struck down a municipal ordinance that required nonresidents to pay a higher fee than residents for the use of the beach. We held that where a municipal beach is dedicated to public use, the public trust doctrine "dictates that the beach and the ocean waters must be open to all on equal terms and without preference and that any contrary state or municipal action is impermissible." The Court was not relying on the legal theory of dedication, although dedication alone would have entitled the public to the full enjoyment of the dry sand. Instead the Court depended on the public trust doctrine, impliedly holding that full enjoyment of the foreshore necessitated some use of the upper sand, so that the latter came under the umbrella of the public trust.

* * *

Public Rights in Privately–Owned Dry Sand Beaches

In *Avon* ... our finding of public rights in dry sand areas was specifically and appropriately limited to those beaches owned by a municipality. We now address the extent of the public's interest in privately-owned dry sand beaches. This interest may take one of two forms. First, the public may have a right to cross privately owned dry sand beaches in order to gain access to the foreshore. Second, this interest may be of the sort enjoyed by the public in municipal beaches under *Avon*—namely, the right to sunbathe and generally enjoy recreational activities.

Beaches are a unique resource and are irreplaceable. The public demand for beaches has increased with the growth of population and improvement of transportation facilities.

* * *

Reasonable enjoyment of the foreshore and the sea cannot be realized unless some enjoyment of the dry sand area is also allowed. The complete pleasure of swimming must be accompanied by intermittent periods of rest and relaxation beyond the water's edge. The unavailability of the physical situs for such rest and relaxation would seriously curtail and in many situations eliminate the right to the recreational use of the ocean. This was a principal reason why in *Avon* ... we held that municipally-owned dry sand beaches "must be open to all on equal terms...." We see no reason why rights under the public trust doctrine to use of the upland dry sand area should be limited to municipally-owned property. It is true that the private owner's interest in the upland dry sand area is not identical to that of a municipality. Nonetheless, where use of dry sand is essential or reasonably necessary for enjoyment of the ocean, the doctrine warrants the public's use of the upland dry sand area subject to an accommodation of the interests of the owner.

* * *

Today, recognizing the increasing demand for our State's beaches and the dynamic nature of the public trust doctrine, we find that the public must be given both access to and use of privately-owned dry sand areas as reasonably necessary. While the public's rights in private beaches are not co-extensive with the rights enjoyed in municipal beaches, private landowners may not in all instances prevent the public from exercising its rights under the public trust doctrine. The public must be afforded reasonable access to the foreshore as well as a suitable area for recreation on the dry sand.

The Beaches of Bay Head

The Bay Head Improvement Association, which services the needs of all residents of the Borough for swimming and bathing in the public trust property, owns the streetwide strip of dry sand area at the foot of seven public streets that extends to the mean high water line. It also owns the fee in six other upland sand properties connected or adjacent to the tracts it owns at the end of two streets. In addition, it holds leases to approximately 42 tracts of upland sand area. The question that we must address is whether the dry sand area that the Association owns or leases should be open to the public to satisfy the public's rights under the public trust doctrine. Our analysis turns upon whether the Association may restrict its membership to Bay Head residents and thereby preclude public use of the dry sand area.

The general rule is that courts will not compel admission to a voluntary association. See Rutledge v. Gulian, 93 N.J. 113, 118, 459 A.2d 680 (1983); Higgins v. American Society of Clinical Pathologists, 51 N.J. 191, 199, 238 A.2d 665 (1968). Ordinarily, a society or association may set its own membership qualifications and restrictions. However, that is not an inexorable rule. Where an organization is quasi-public, its power to exclude must be reasonably and lawfully exercised in furtherance of the public welfare related to its public characteristics.

In Greisman v. Newcomb Hospital, 40 N.J. 389, 192 A.2d 817 (1963), plaintiff, holder of a degree of osteopathy and licensed to practice medicine and surgery, sought to be admitted to the courtesy staff of the defendant hospital. The defendant hospital refused to permit the plaintiff to file an application. The defendant contended that it was a private hospital and that its actions were not reviewable by a court. Justice Jacobs, writing for the Court, responded:

> They are private in the sense that they are nongovernmental but they are hardly private in other senses. Newcomb [Hospital] is a nonprofit organization dedicated by its certificate of incorporation to the vital public use of serving the sick and injured, its funds are in good measure received from public sources and through public solicitation, and its tax benefits are received because of its non-profit and non-private aspects.... It constitutes a virtual monopoly in the area in which it functions and it is in no position to claim immunity from public supervision and control because of its allegedly private nature. Indeed, in the development of the law, activities much less public than the hospital activities of Newcomb, have commonly been subjected to judicial (as well as legislative) supervision and control to the extent necessary to satisfy the felt needs of the times.

* * *

A principle that may be distilled from *Greisman* is that a nonprofit association that is authorized and endeavors to carry out a purpose serving the general welfare of the community and is a quasi-public institution holds in trust its powers of exclusive control in the areas of vital public concern.

* * *

There is no public beach in the Borough of Bay Head. If the residents of every municipality bordering the Jersey shore were to adopt the Bay Head policy, the public would be prevented from exercising its right to enjoy the foreshore. The Bay Head residents may not frustrate the public's right in this manner. By limiting membership only to residents and foreclosing the public, the Association is acting in conflict with the public good and contrary to the strong public policy "in favor of encouraging and expanding public access to and use of shoreline areas."

Accordingly, membership in the Association must be open to the public at large.... Although such membership rights to the use of the beach may be broader than the rights necessary for enjoyment of the public trust, opening the Association's membership to all, nonresidents and residents, should lead to a substantial satisfaction of the public trust doctrine. However, the Association shall also make available a reasonable quantity of daily as well as seasonal badges to the nonresident public. Its decision with respect to the number of daily and seasonal badges to be afforded to nonresidents should take into account all relevant matters, such as the public demand and the number of bathers and swimmers that may be safely and reasonably accommodated on the Association's property, whether owned or leased. The Association may continue to charge reasonable fees to cover its costs of lifeguards, beach cleaners, patrols, equipment, insurance, and administrative expenses. The fees fixed may not discriminate in any respect between residents and nonresidents. The Association may continue to enforce its regulations regarding cleanliness, safety, and other reasonable measures concerning the public use of the beach.

* * *

The judgment of the Appellate Division is reversed in part and affirmed in part. Judgment is entered for the plaintiff against the Association. Judgment of dismissal against the individual property owners is affirmed without prejudice. No costs.

NOTES AND QUESTIONS

1.   The Fifth Amendment's takings clause may limit the ability of states to use the public trust doctrine to reclaim public rights in beachfront or other property that was previously transferred to private entities. Read the *Nollan*, *Dolan* and *Lucas* cases in the takings Chapter (infra, § 10.2), and then the note on Stevens v. City of Cannon Beach, 317 Or. 131, 854 P.2d 449 (1993), cert. denied, 510 U.S. 1207 (1994), following the *Lucas* opinion. Does *Matthews* remain good law? See Leydon v. Town of Greenwich, 57 Conn.App. 712, 750 A.2d 1122 (2000), which followed the *Matthews* reasoning closely, concluding that Connecticut had a public trust doctrine similar to New Jersey's.

How would you argue *Matthews* to the United States Supreme Court? What about the fact that the land made subject to the public trust doctrine in *Matthews* was owned by a homeowner's association, while that in *Nollan* was owned by an individual owner? Does that make *Matthews* more like *Prune-Yard* (reprinted in the takings chapter at § 10.2.1; state may force shopping mall owner to accommodate nonviolent political speech) than it is like *Nollan*? Constitutionally doubtful or not, the New Jersey Supreme Court continues to apply the doctrine so as to create public rights in privately owned beachfront property. See Raleigh Ave. Beach Assn. v. Atlantis Beach Club, 185 N.J. 40, 879 A.2d 112 (2005).

Contrast with *Matthews*, Bell v. Town of Wells, 557 A.2d 168 (Me.1989), where the Supreme Judicial Court of Maine struck down a state law attempting to declare a public trust in intertidal lands (basically, land that is under water during high tide but not at other times) thus permitting the general public to use such lands for bathing, sunbathing, fishing, and other forms of recreation. The court began with the premise that a public trust declaration could be justified only to the extent that the historical common law or legislation had recognized that a conveyance by the state to a private party reserved certain public rights. The court found that colonial statutes governing Massachusetts (of which Maine had been a part) had indeed recognized a public trust easement in intertidal lands for fishing, fowling and navigation. But the new, broader declaration of rights in the general public could not be justified historically:

> The fact that the common law already has reserved to the public an easement in intertidal land for fishing, fowling, and navigation ... does not mean that the State can, without paying compensation to the private landowners, take in addition a public easement for general recreation.... The common law has reserved to the public only a limited easement; the Public Trust in Intertidal Land Act takes a comprehensive easement for "recreation" without limitation. The absence of any compensation to the fee owners renders the Act unconstitutional [under both the Maine and federal constitutions].

Id. at 178–179.

In Summa Corp. v. California ex rel. State Lands Comm'n, 466 U.S. 198 (1984), the United States Supreme Court placed substantial limits on the power of states to claim interests in privately owned lands under the public trust doctrine. California claimed a "public trust easement" in all lands that were tidelands when California became a state. However, in this instance the state was asserting rights to dredge a privately-owned harbor and lagoon, and then construct improvements so substantial that the title holder would remain the owner of nothing more than the "naked fee." Equally problematic, California had never asserted its "public trust" interest when title was settled in favor of the private owner as a result of land title proceedings initiated by the federal government after the Mexican War. The Supreme Court held that:

> The interest claimed by California is one of such substantial magnitude that regardless of the fact that the claim is asserted by the State in its sovereign capacity, this interest ... must have been presented in the

patent proceeding [when the United States quieted the title in the original private owner] or be barred. Id. at 209.

By contrast, in Phillips Petroleum Co. v. Mississippi, 484 U.S. 469 (1988), the Supreme Court held that, since Mississippi had consistently applied its public trust doctrine to recognize a public trust interest in non-navigable waters (in this case, in lands that were under the water only during high tide) the state in fact had retained title to those lands, even though the petitioners claimed under Spanish land grants that antedated Mississippi statehood. As Justice O'Connor pointed out in her dissent, at that time title in the lands had been thought to be established in the private owners for more than 150 years.

For incisive commentary on the public trust doctrine, see Delgado, Our Better Natures: A Revisionist View of Joseph Sax's Public Trust Theory of Environmental Protection and Some Dark Thoughts on the Possibility of Law Reform, 44 Vand.L.Rev. 1209 (1991).

2. Under the theory of implied dedication a private land owner's consent to let the public use his land, coupled with evidence of intent to dedication, can effectively "dedicate" the land to the public. See Gion v. City of Santa Cruz, 2 Cal.3d 29, 84 Cal.Rptr. 162, 465 P.2d 50 (1970) (five years uninterrupted use creates conclusive presumption of intent to dedicate); contra Simmons v. Perkins, 63 Idaho 136, 143, 118 P.2d 740, 744 (1941) (intent is separate from permission to use, which could be a mere license, and must be proven clearly). Under the California rule one who simply permits the public uninterrupted access may find out later that he has "dedicated" his property to the public for that use.

But does aggressive use of a theory of implied dedication to permit the general public access to privately owned land result in more public access or less? Many states have decided that the answer is less. They have passed statutes that permit owners to open their lands to the public without risk of losing the interest to the public. Their reasoning goes like this: if private landowners know that free public access to their property might produce a court ruling that they have given the public a permanent recreational easement, then the private landowners will take elaborate steps, such as fencing and frequent filing of trespass actions, to exclude the public. The landowners do not want to lose future development rights. However, if the landowners can be assured that the public will never acquire a permanent right, then they will be more willing to permit the public to enter land while it remains undeveloped. See Cal.Civ.Code § 1008 (West 1982): "Title by Prescription; Permissive Use":

> No use by any person or persons, no matter how long continued, of any land, shall ever ripen into an easement by prescription, if the owner of such property posts at each entrance to the property or at intervals of not more than 200 feet along the boundary a sign reading substantially as follows: "Right to pass by permission, and subject to control, of owner: Section 1008, Civil Code."

Such signs are common in California on privately owned property that is often entered by the public. In fact, it is not uncommon to see the same property posted with both "No Trespassing" signs and "Section 1008" signs. Why?

3. Under another theory related to prescription or implied dedication, very long use by the public could create a "custom," or common law right of access. See Post v. Pearsall, 22 Wend. 425 (N.Y.1839). For Blackstone the time period had to be very long: as long as the memory of man "runneth not to the contrary." 2 W. Blackstone, Commentaries on the Laws of England 263 (1769). The use "must have continued from time immemorial, without interruption, and as a right; it must be certain as to the place, and as to the persons; and it must be certain and reasonable as to the subject matter or rights created." After nearly a century of nonuse, the doctrine of custom was revitalized by the Oregon Supreme Court in State ex rel. Thornton v. Hay, 254 Or. 584, 462 P.2d 671 (1969). That state has continued to apply the doctrine, as have a few others. However, in Idaho ex rel. Haman v. Fox, 100 Idaho 140, 594 P.2d 1093 (1979), the Idaho Supreme Court concluded that a public use in beachfront property that had continued since 1912—more than 60 years prior to the litigation—was nevertheless an insufficient time because the memory of living witnesses still went that far back.

4. Most states continue to hold that long use of beaches or other recreational property by the general public will not create an easement, implied dedication, custom, or any other legally protected right of entry. However, a few states, notably California, New Jersey, Oregon, Florida, Texas and Hawaii, have created such prescriptive rights under this potpourri of theories.

§ 8.3 SCOPE

FARMER v. KENTUCKY UTILITIES CO.

Supreme Court of Kentucky (1982).
642 S.W.2d 579.

STERNBERG, JUSTICE.

In 1978, Elva Skidmore Farmer, one of the movants, acquired a small tract of land from her mother. In 1923, 55 years prior to the purchase of this property by movant, the respondent, Kentucky Utilities Company, constructed a transmission line which overhangs a portion of this property. The wires are attached to two poles which, themselves, are located on lands adjacent to the subject property but not on it. Since 1976, the premises have been unoccupied. In 1966, Kentucky Utilities Company entered upon this property and cleared out the undergrowth under the wires. The owner filed suit against the utility company claiming that the chemical spray used in clearing the undergrowth had killed some of the lettuce in their garden, killed a grapevine, killed some trees, and had adversely affected the soil. This suit was settled for $700.

In 1980, Kentucky Utilities Company determined that the area beneath the wires again needed to be cleared. It, thereupon, engaged the services of a tree, shrub, and undergrowth removal company who entered upon the subject premises, with men and equipment, and cut and removed trees and other growth of vegetation from beneath the wires and in close proximity thereto. The owners of the land filed a suit against the utility company charging trespass and sought damages by reason thereof.

This case was tried to the court without the intervention of a jury. The trial court assessed the issue as follows:

> "[T]he real question here is the secondary easements or the easements that flow from the main easement, and the Defendant has taken the position that once it establishes its main prescriptive easement, that automatically there are secondary easements that flow from that, including the right to go on the property, the right to maintain the property within a reasonable width which they've shown by proof to be fifty (50) feet on either side of the center line...."

The trial court found that the Kentucky Utilities Company had a prescriptive easement as to the overhanging wires, but did not have any right to enter upon the land over which the wires were hung for the purpose of clearing. The Court of Appeals held that the prescriptive easement to hang lines necessarily includes as an incident thereof a right to enter the property underneath the lines for purposes of maintenance and repairs. This court, on June 29, 1982, granted review.

All counsel agree that the subject issue is one of first impression to this court. Even so, the general principle is so well recognized that it has been enforced in this jurisdiction for decades. The use of the land beneath the overhanging lines is as stated by the trial judge, a secondary easement necessary for the enjoyment of the principal easement. It is ancient law that nothing passes under an easement but what is necessary for its reasonable use and proper enjoyment. The use of the easement must be as reasonable and as little burdensome to the landowner as the nature and purpose of the easement will permit. In Higdon v. Kentucky Gas Transmission Corporation, Ky., 448 S.W.2d 655 (1969), this court was constrained to the view that dominant and servient owners have correlative rights and duties which neither may unreasonably exercise to the injury of the other. In Downey v. Urton, 10 Ky. Opinions 143 (1878), the court wrote that "if there is a passway over a man's land which his neighbor has used, not by his permission merely but under a claim of right for more than twenty years, then such neighbor has a right to continue to use the passway, and it becomes unlawful to obstruct it or hinder his use of it."

It would appear that the Kentucky Utilities Company could not use the primary easement for overhanging wires to the unreasonable detriment of the movants. Conversely, it would appear that the movants cannot use the servient estate to the detriment of the Kentucky Utilities Company. By using the servient estate so as to permit trees, shrubs, and other growth and vegetation to grow to heights as to interfere with the proper enjoyment of the primary easement, the movants inhibited the proper use of the overhanging wire easement.

Insofar as the use of the secondary easement is concerned, this court is of the opinion that the owner of an easement acquired by personal negotiations, by eminent domain, by prescription, or otherwise, for the erection of electric wires may enter upon the premises over which the wires are constructed for the purpose of removing vegetation, or other growth or substance, that interferes with the natural and reasonable use of the easement for the purpose to which the land accommodated by the easement may be naturally and reasonably devoted. It is evident, however, that the Kentucky Utilities Company is limited in the manner and extent of its usage of the servient estate in that only so much thereof may be encroached upon as is necessary to the natural and reasonable use of its primary easement. To this extent, therefore, there is a factual issue to be determined by the factfinder.

We affirm so much of the decision of the Court of Appeals as holds that the Kentucky Utilities Company, by reason of its primary easement, has a right to enter upon the servient property beneath the lines and in the immediate vicinity thereof for the purpose of repairs and maintenance. However, we reverse and remand to the Harlan Circuit Court for a new trial on the issue of whether the Kentucky Utilities Company, in entering upon the servient estate, cut such trees, shrubs, and undergrowth as were necessary for the proper and natural and reasonable use of the primary easement or, if not, to respond in damages.

AKER, JUSTICE, dissenting.

Adverse possession can rest only upon "such open and notorious acts of physical possession as would put the owner upon notice of the assertion of a hostile claim." H.F. Davis & Co. v. Sizemore, 182 Ky. 680, 207 S.W. 16 (1918). In this case, the appellants, and their predecessors in title, were willing to permit the two utility lines to overhang their property. However, on each occasion when Kentucky Utilities came upon the property to clear trees and shrubs, trespass actions were promptly initiated. It is my opinion that the prescriptive right of Kentucky Utilities is thus confined to the right to overhang two lines across the tract of land. As this court has stated, "[a]n easement by prescription is limited by the purpose for which it is acquired and the use to which it is put for the statutory period." Williams v. Slate, Ky., 415 S.W.2d 616 (1966). The easement "... will not ripen into a greater estate after the period of limitation has passed. The right is crystallized as to form during the waiting period and is of the nature of the use during that period."

To now permit Kentucky Utilities to come upon the land and destroy property appears to me an unreasonable expansion of rights incident to the prescriptive easement.

PENN BOWLING RECREATION CENTER
v. HOT SHOPPES, INC.

United States Court of Appeals, D.C. Circuit (1949).
179 F.2d 64.

MCALLISTER, CIRCUIT JUDGE.

In 1938, the Norment Estate conveyed a portion of its real property to appellee, Hot Shoppes, Inc., and subjected a part thereof to a sixteen-foot right of way for ingress and egress. This resulted in an easement for the benefit of the balance of the unconveyed property, adjacent thereto, which was retained by the Estate, and which, by virtue of the easement, became the dominant tenement. A part of this dominant estate came into ownership of appellant, Penn Bowling Recreation Center, Inc., by mesne conveyances, in 1940, two years after the creation of the right of way.

On February 5, 1948, appellee, Hot Shoppes, erected a barrier of iron posts and cement concrete blocks within the right of way and alongside of it, interfering with the full enjoyment of the easement by Penn Bowling; and shortly thereafter, appellant filed its complaint to enjoin appellee from maintaining the structure within the right of way and interfering with the use thereof. Appellee, in its answer denied that appellant was entitled to the use of the right of way, and asked for a permanent injunction against such use by appellant, as well as for a judgment declaring it to be permanently forfeited and extinguished by abandonment. Both parties filed motions for a preliminary injunction, but before a hearing was had on these motions, appellee filed a motion for summary judgment, asking dismissal of the complaint, a permanent injunction against the use by appellant of the right of way, and a declaratory judgment declaring that it had been permanently forfeited and extinguished by abandonment. The district court granted appellee's motion for summary judgment as prayed; and from such judgment, the Penn Bowling Recreation Center appeals.

The arguments that appellee addressed to the district court on the hearing on the motion for summary judgment embraced the contentions that appellant, as owner of the dominant tenement, had forfeited and extinguished the right of way by abandonment, as the result of subjecting the servient tenement to an additional and enlarged use or servitude in connection with other premises to which the easement was not appurtenant; that it had been guilty of the misuse of the easement of the right of way by reason of having used it for the parking of motor vehicles; and that, by certain masonry constructions, appellant had, in any event, made it impossible to use the right of way for egress and ingress.

With regard to the claim that appellant had subjected the servient tenement to a burden in excess of that imposed by the original easement, it appears that after the creation of the right of way for the benefit of the dominant tenement, appellant purchased not only that tenement but other real property adjacent thereto, the latter property not being entitled to the enjoyment of the easement. Appellant then constructed a building occupying a part of the dominant tenement, as well as the additional property adjacent thereto. Not all of the dominant tenement is occupied by the building. In fact, the total of the area of that portion of the dominant tenement, together with the non-dominant property over which the building is constructed, is a smaller area than the area of the original dominant tenement. The building, thus constructed, houses a large bowling alley and restaurant. Appellant in the past has been using the right of way to bring fuel oil, food, equipment, and supplies to the building, and removing trash, garbage, and other material therefrom.

It is contended by appellant that since the area of the dominant and non-dominant land served by the easement is less than the original area of the dominant tenement, the use made by appellant of the right of way to serve the building located on the lesser area is not materially increased or excessive. It is true that where the nature and extent of the use of an easement is, by its terms, unrestricted, the use by the dominant tenement may be increased or enlarged. But the owner of the dominant tenement may not subject the servient tenement to use or servitude in connection with other premises to which the easement is not appurtenant.

* * *

The disposition of the foregoing issue brings us to the principal legal question in the case: whether appellant's use of the right of way resulted in the forfeiture and extinguishment of the easement by abandonment, and thereby entitled appellee, on a motion for summary judgment, to a decree permanently enjoining appellant from using the right of way.

Misuse of an easement right is not sufficient to constitute a forfeiture, waiver, or abandonment of such right. The right to an easement is not lost by using it in an unauthorized manner or to an unauthorized extent, unless it is impossible to sever the increased burden so as to preserve to the owner of the dominant tenement that to which he is entitled, and impose on the servient tenement only that burden which was originally imposed upon it.

* * *

From the record before us, we are unable to ascertain what the total additional burden is that has been cast upon the servient tenement as the result of appellant's use of the right of way for ingress to, and egress from, the building which was located on part of the dominant and the non-dominant property. As has been mentioned, the building houses a bowling alley and restaurant. From affidavits on file, it appears that a soda fountain and luncheonette used in connection with the restaurant are located in that part of the building situate on the non-dominant real estate, which, of course, is not entitled to enjoyment of the easement; and it further appears that the right of way is used for the purpose of bringing supplies for the fountain and luncheonette and removing trash and garbage therefrom. It is not disclosed whether other supplies or materials brought to, or removed from, the building over the right of way are required for the use of that part of the structure located on the dominant estate or on the non-dominant property, or both. Affidavits filed by appellant indicate, however, that oil for heating purposes is delivered to the loading platform over the right of way. Whether the oil furnace is located on the dominant or non-dominant property does not appear.

* * *

But it is declared on the part of Penn Bowling that if the right of way were barred to appellant, a great hardship would result in the operation of the building housing the bowling alley and other facilities, and would necessitate large and expensive alterations of its building. Appellant may well be obliged to remodel its structure in order to operate, but it would appear that this can be done and, consequently, appellee is not entitled to a decree extinguishing the easement or to a permanent injunction on the pleadings and proofs before us. Furthermore, appellant's building fronts on a public thoroughfare and changes conceivably could be made so that the non-dominant property could be served from the street. In any event, appellant can use the right of way only to serve the dominant tenement.

An authorized use and an unauthorized use may be intermingled in such a way as to justify enjoining any use until the circumstances have so changed that the authorized use may be permitted without affording opportunity for the unauthorized use, which it would be difficult to discover or prove. In such a case, the issuance of an injunction may be justified restraining any use until the building is so altered or changed that part of it which is on the dominant tenement may enjoy the easement without permitting its enjoyment by the other part of the building having no right thereto. So where it can not be ascertained whether the easement of a right of way is being used solely for the enjoyment of the dominant tenement, or for additional property also, an injunction may be granted against further use of the easement until such time as it may be shown that only the dominant tenement is served by the easement.

* * *

Appellee further complains that appellant misused the easement by parking motor vehicles on the right of way. The use of the easement for purposes of ingress and egress does not include its use for parking purposes and an injunction may issue to prevent such a use. However, it is to be said that appellant is entitled to a reasonable use and enjoyment of the easement for purposes of ingress and egress. In determining what is a reasonable use, the easement is to be construed in the light of the situation of the property and the surrounding circumstances for the purpose of giving effect to the intention of the parties. The long continued use of the right of way for the purpose of loading or unloading supplies at appellant's premises may indicate an intention of the parties that the easement might be used for that purpose. But appellant would thereby acquire no right to make any use of the easement which would unreasonably interfere with its use by appellee. Appellee has located on the premises in question its central offices and commissary, which is engaged in supplying sixteen restaurants in Washington and vicinity, and requires almost constant use of the driveway by appellee. Appellant's parking of vehicles on the right of way at a time when appellee needs its use would constitute an unlawful interference with the latter's right. The determination of these questions largely depends upon the circumstances of the case and is properly for the district court.

In accordance with the foregoing, the judgment is set aside and the case remanded to the district court for further proceedings consonant with this opinion, with the reservation of right to the appellee to apply for a temporary injunction pending final decision of the court.

Notes and Questions

1. With *Penn Bowling*, compare Koplin v. Hinsdale Hospital, 207 Ill. App.3d 219, 151 Ill.Dec. 685, 564 N.E.2d 1347 (1990), which applied the traditional rule enjoining use of the easement to benefit lands adjacent to the dominant estate. The court rejected the argument that a clause in the easement deed stating that the easement could be used "for all purposes" included the purpose of servicing nondominant lands.

In Brown v. Voss, 105 Wash.2d 366, 715 P.2d 514 (1986) (en banc) the owner of the dominant estate used a driveway easement to benefit both the dominant estate and adjacent lands, but there was no actual injury to the owner of the servient estate. That is, traffic was the same after the expansion as before. The court acknowledged that the expansion constituted "a misuse of the easement," but it affirmed the trial court's denial of an injunction, noting the lack of injury to the defendant's land and the extreme hardship that would result to the plaintiff if the injunction were granted. The court suggested that damages in such a case (where there is no injury to the servient estate) might be the appropriate remedy, noting that the court's award of $1 in nominal damages was not appealed. Query: what should the damage award be if the court adopts this rule? Two possibilities that come to mind are: (a) the injury to the owner of the servient estate, which would support an award of merely nominal damages; or (b) the value of the easement to the plaintiff. If the plaintiff was forced to purchase the additional right, which of these would come closer to the purchase price? Did the *Brown* court effectively give the owner of the dominant estate a power of eminent domain, at least in the no-injury case?

2. How does one measure scope when the easement was acquired by implication and the owner of the dominant estate increases the intensity of use after severance? See Fristoe v. Drapeau, 35 Cal.2d 5, 215 P.2d 729 (1950). When the easement was acquired by prescription and the claimant increases the intensity of use after the prescriptive period has run? Glenn v. Poole, 12 Mass.App.Ct. 292, 423 N.E.2d 1030 (1981). What should the controlling factor be: intensity of the claimant's use, or injury to the servient estate's interest? For example, what if a prescriptive easement is used more intensely than it had been during the prescriptive period, but there is no evidence that the higher intensity use injures the owner of the servient estate? For example, see In re Onarga, Douglas & Danforth Drainage Dist., 179 Ill.App.3d 493, 128 Ill.Dec. 206, 534 N.E.2d 226 (1989), forbidding the owner of a prescriptive drain line easement from installing a line of larger diameter.

3. O grants A an easement appurtenant for a driveway over line x–y. A few years later O grants B an identical driveway easement over x–y. Can A enjoin B's use of the driveway or obtain damages from O? See Sanders v. Roselawn Memorial Gardens, 152 W.Va. 91, 159 S.E.2d 784 (1968). What if O gives a utility company an easement to install a gas line under the driveway? See Rippetoe v. O'Dell, 166 W.Va. 639, 276 S.E.2d 793 (1981). A pipeline

company owns a ten-foot easement for a one-foot diameter pipeline, which has been in place for many years. When the pipeline needs to be replaced may the company locate it in a different portion of the easement? See Scherger v. Northern Natural Gas Co., 575 N.W.2d 578 (Minn.1998).

§ 8.4   TRANSFER OF OBLIGATIONS AND BENEFITS

All easements by grant and most covenants and equitable servitudes are contained in deeds. Nonetheless, the rights and obligations they create often begin as agreements between the original parties. As between the original parties, enforcement of a servitude is frequently a matter of contract law. For example, if A and B promise each other that neither will use his own property for commercial purposes, and A builds a gasoline station, B's action against A to enjoin construction of the building will probably be for breach of contract.

But land is capable of being transferred from one owner to another. The law of servitudes is both important and complex because frequently the party against whom enforcement is sought was not personally a party to the agreement creating the servitude. Rather, she is a successor in interest to one of the parties. To use the above example, suppose that A and B agree that neither will use his property for commercial purposes and one year later A sells his property to X. Now X seeks to build the gasoline station. Whether or not X may do so depends not only on the law of contracts, but also on the law of servitudes.

§ 8.4.1   EASEMENTS APPURTENANT AND IN GROSS

MARTIN v. MUSIC

Court of Appeals of Kentucky (1953).
254 S.W.2d 701.

CULLEN, COMMISSIONER.

This action involves the construction of the following agreement:

"This mutual agreement, made and entered into by and between Marvin Music, of Prestonsburg, Kentucky, party of the first part, and Fred Martin, of Prestonsburg, Kentucky, party of the second part.

"Witnesseth: That for and in consideration of the sum of One ($1.00) Dollar, and other considerations hereinafter set out, parties of the first and second part mutually agree:

"Party of the first part gives and grants to second party the right to construct and maintain a sewer line under and through his property located in the Layne Heirs addition to the City of Prestonsburg, Kentucky, in the Garfield Bottom, and being lots Nos. 17 through 24 inc. of said addition.

"In consideration of said right, second party agrees to lay said sewer line at sufficient depth to not interfere with first party's use and enjoyment of said property; and to place an intake connection in said line for use of said party at a point to be designated by him; and further agrees to pay to first party any damage which may result to his property by reason of the laying, maintaining, repairing and operation of said sewer line.

"Given under our hands, this December 3, 1949."

At the time the agreement was executed, the eight lots owned by Music were unoccupied, except for a garage building used by Music for the vehicles operated by him in his business as a bulk distributor of oil and gasoline. Martin constructed his sewer across the lots, and thereafter Music sold six of the lots to one Moore, who in turn sold three each to the appellees Wells and Allen. Wells and Allen each commenced the construction of a dwelling house on his lots, and prepared to connect with Martin's sewer. Martin then brought this action for a declaration of rights, maintaining that the right to connect with the sewer was personal to Music alone, for the purpose of serving a dwelling house which Music had planned to build, and that the right did not accrue to Wells and Allen. The court adjudged that Music, Wells and Allen each had the right to connect with the sewer, provided that the connection was made through the one intake connection provided for in the written contract. Martin appeals.

Considerable evidence was introduced concerning the circumstances surrounding the execution of the agreement, and the situation that existed at the time the agreement was made. It appears that the lots owned by Music had a depth of 120 feet, from east to west, and a width of 25 feet each, fronting on a street on the west and an alley on the east. Across the alley to the east, Martin owned six lots on which he had his private residence and a motel. Martin's northernmost lot was opposite Music's southernmost lot. The Big Sandy River lies some 600 feet west of Martin's property, and he desired to run the sewer line from his property to the river.

Martin's evidence was that he first proposed to construct his sewer down the alley between his lots and those of Music, but that Music, upon learning of this plan, offered to let the sewer cross his lots, in return for an intake connection privilege. Martin testified that the understanding was that Music was to build a home on his lots, and that the sewer connection was for that purpose.

Music's evidence was that Martin did not want to run his sewer down the alley, for fear that it then would be classified as a public sewer, to which anyone could connect; that Music offered to let the sewer go across his lots in return for a connection privilege; that there was no understanding that the intake was to be limited to one dwelling to be erected by Music, but on the contrary it was clearly understood that the intake was to be available for each of the eight lots.

Martin's sewer is a six-inch main, which the appellees' evidence tends to show is capable of handling the sewage from their buildings, in addition to that from Martin's properties, with no difficulty. On the other hand, Martin testified that the sewer line had a low grade of descent, and that in times of heavy rains, when the river was high, there would be danger of the sewer backing up into his basement. He complains particularly of the proposal of the appellees to connect their eaves and downspouts to the sewer, which he claims will create too great a flow of water for the sewer line to accommodate.

Martin maintains that the agreement provides for an easement in gross, rather than one running with the land. He relies upon Mannin v. Adkins, 199 Ky. 241, 250 S.W. 974, which we do not consider to be in point. In that case, the grantor of a piece of property reserved the right to " 'have, use, and get coal off the lands hereby conveyed for fuel for his own purposes or home consumption as fuel' ". The court held that the reservation was personal to the grantor, and did not run with the adjoining land which he occupied as his home place at the time of the conveyance. There, the reserved privilege was not related to a particular piece of property as a dominant estate, and it necessarily was personal. Here, the sewer connection privilege necessarily is limited to the parcel of land over which the sewer line runs.

If an easement is to be exercised in connection with the occupancy of particular land, then ordinarily it is classified as an easement appurtenant. 28 C.J.S., Easements, § 4(b), p. 635. We think it is clear that the right to connect to Martin's sewer line was to be exercised only in connection with the occupancy of the land through which it ran, and that Music was not granted the right to run a sewer line to the intake point from some parcel of land he might own or acquire in another block. Therefore, the easement must be considered to be an easement appurtenant.

It is the general rule that easements in gross are not favored, and that an easement will never be presumed to be a mere personal right when it can fairly be construed to be appurtenant to some other estate.

* * *

We think the controlling question is whether the use of the sewer by Wells and Allen, as well as by Music, will unduly burden the servient tenement (in this case, the sewer line). It appears to be the general rule that the dominant estate may be divided or partitioned, and the owner of each part may claim the right to enjoy the easement, if no additional burden is placed upon the servient estate. 17 Am.Jur., Easements, sec. 126, p. 1014.

Here, it cannot be ascertained from the written agreement, nor can it be ascertained with certainty from the evidence of the circumstances and conditions surrounding the execution of the agreement, just what burden it was contemplated might be imposed by way of connection with the sewer line. As far as the face of the agreement is concerned, Music could have built an apartment house, a hotel, or even a factory, upon his lots, and connected them with the sewer. Either of these would have required only one intake connection. The agreement does not limit the kind of use that Music was to make of the sewer. Since, under the words of the agreement, Music could have placed a much greater burden upon Martin's sewer we do not believe that two or three dwellings will increase the burden contemplated by the parties as expressed in their agreement.

If we go beyond the words of the agreement, and accept all of the evidence as to what the parties intended, then we find a conflict of evidence, upon which we could not say that the chancellor erred.

The judgment is affirmed.

MILLER v. LUTHERAN CONFERENCE & CAMP ASSOCIATION

Supreme Court of Pennsylvania (1938).
331 Pa. 241, 200 A. 646, 130 A.L.R. 1245.

STERN, JUSTICE.

This litigation is concerned with interesting and somewhat novel legal questions regarding rights of boating, bathing and fishing in an artificial lake.

Frank C. Miller, his brother Rufus W. Miller, and others, who owned lands on Tunkhannock Creek in Tobyhanna Township, Monroe County, organized a corporation known as the Pocono Spring Water Ice Company, to which, in September 1895, they made a lease for a term of ninety-nine years of so much of their lands as would be covered by the backing up of the water as a result of the construction of a 14–foot dam which they proposed to erect across the creek. The company was to have "the exclusive use of the water and its privileges." It was chartered for the purpose of "erecting a dam ..., for pleasure, boating, skating, fishing and the cutting, storing and selling of ice." The dam was built, forming "Lake Naomi," somewhat more than a mile long and about one-third of a mile wide.

By deed dated March 20, 1899, the Pocono Spring Water Ice Company granted to "Frank C. Miller, his heirs and assigns forever, the exclusive right to fish and boat in all the waters of the said corporation at Naomi Pines, Pa." On February 17, 1900, Frank C. Miller (his wife Katherine D. Miller not joining), granted to Rufus W. Miller, his heirs and assigns forever, "all the one-fourth interest in and to the fishing, boating, and bathing rights and privileges at, in, upon and about Lake Naomi ...; which said rights and privileges were granted and conveyed to me by the Pocono Spring Water Ice Company by their indenture of the 20th day of March, A.D. 1899." On the same day Frank C. Miller and Rufus W. Miller executed an agreement of business partnership, the purpose of which was the erection and operation of boat and bath houses on Naomi Lake and the purchase and maintenance of boats for use on the lake, the houses and boats to be rented for hire and the net proceeds to be divided between the parties in proportion to their respective interests in the bathing, boating and fishing privileges, namely, three-fourths to Frank C. Miller and one-fourth to Rufus W. Miller, the capital to be contributed and the losses to be borne in the same proportion. In pursuance of this agreement the brothers erected and maintained boat and bath houses at different points on the lake, purchased and rented out boats, and conducted the business generally, from the spring of 1900 until the death of Rufus W. Miller on October 11, 1925, exercising their control and use of the privileges in an exclusive, uninterrupted and open manner and without challenge on the part of anyone.

Discord began with the death of Rufus W. Miller, which terminated the partnership. Thereafter Frank C. Miller, and the executors and heirs of Rufus W. Miller, went their respective ways, each granting licenses without reference to the other. Under date of July 13, 1929, the executors of the Rufus W. Miller estate granted a license for the year 1929 to defendant, Lutheran Conference and Camp Association, which was the owner of a tract of ground abutting on the lake for a distance of about 100 feet, purporting to grant to defendant, its members, guests and campers, permission to boat, bathe and fish in the lake, a certain percentage of the receipts therefrom to be paid to the estate. Thereupon Frank C. Miller and his wife, Katherine D. Miller, filed the present bill in equity, complaining that defendant was placing diving floats on the lake and "encouraging and instigating visitors and boarders" to bathe in the lake, and was threatening to hire out boats and canoes and in general to license its guests and others to boat, bathe and fish in the lake. The bill prayed for an injunction to prevent defendant from trespassing on the lands covered by the waters of the lake, from erecting or maintaining any structures or other encroachments thereon, and from granting any bathing licenses. The court issued the injunction.

* * *

It is the contention of plaintiffs that, while the privileges of boating and fishing were granted in the deed from the Pocono Spring Water Ice Company to Frank C. Miller, no *bathing* rights were conveyed by that instrument. In 1903 all the property of the company was sold by the sheriff under a writ of fi. fa. on a mortgage bond which the company had executed in 1898. As a result of that sale the Pocono Spring Water Ice Company was entirely extinguished, and the title to its rights and property came into the ownership of the Pocono Pines Ice Company, a corporation chartered for "the supply of ice to the public." In 1928 the title to the property of the Pocono Pines Ice Company became vested in Katherine D. Miller. Plaintiffs therefore maintain that the bathing rights, never having passed to Frank C. Miller, descended in ownership from the Pocono Spring Water Ice Company through the Pocono Pines Ice Company to plaintiff Katherine D. Miller, and that Frank C. Miller could not, and did not, give

Rufus W. Miller any title to them. They further contend that even if such bathing rights ever did vest in Frank C. Miller, all of the boating, bathing and fishing privileges were easements in gross which were inalienable and indivisible, and when Frank C. Miller undertook to convey a one-fourth interest in them to Rufus W. Miller he not only failed to transfer a legal title to the rights but, in attempting to do so, extinguished the rights altogether as against Katherine D. Miller, who was the successor in title of the Pocono Spring Water Ice Company. It is defendant's contention, on the other hand, that the deed of 1899 from the Pocono Spring Water Ice Company to Frank C. Miller should be construed as transferring the bathing as well as the boating and fishing privileges, but that if Frank C. Miller did not obtain them by grant he and Rufus W. Miller acquired them by prescription, and that all of these rights were alienable and divisible even if they be considered as easements in gross, although they might more properly, perhaps, be regarded as licenses which became irrevocable because of the money spent upon their development by Frank C. Miller and Rufus W. Miller.

Coming to the merits of the controversy, * * * [i]t is impossible to construe the deed of 1899 from the Pocono Spring Water Ice Company to Frank C. Miller as conveying to the latter any privileges of bathing. It is clear and unambiguous. It gives to Frank C. Miller the exclusive right to *fish and boat*. Expressio unius est exclusio alterius. No *bathing* rights are mentioned. This omission may have been the result of oversight or it may have been deliberate, but in either event the legal consequence is the same. It is to be noted that the mortgagee to whom the company mortgaged all its property in 1898 executed in 1902 a release of the fishing and boating rights to the company and to Frank C. Miller, thus validating the latter's title to these rights under the company's deed of 1899, but in this release also the bathing rights are omitted.

But, while Frank C. Miller acquired by grant merely boating and fishing privileges, the facts are amply sufficient to establish title to the bathing rights by prescription. True, these rights, not having been granted in connection with, or to be attached to, the ownership of any land, were not easements appurtenant but in gross. There is, however, no inexorable principle of law which forbids an adverse enjoyment of an easement in gross from ripening into a title thereto by prescription. In Tinicum Fishing Co. v. Carter, 61 Pa. 21, 100 Am.Dec. 597, it was questioned whether a fishing right could be created by prescription, although there is an intimation (page 40) that some easements in gross might so arise if there be evidence sufficient to establish them. Certainly the casual use of a lake during a few months each year for boating and fishing could not develop into a title to such privileges by prescription. But here the exercise of the bathing right was not carried on sporadically by Frank C. Miller and his assignee Rufus W. Miller for their personal enjoyment but systematically for commercial purposes in the pursuit of which they conducted an extensive and profitable business enterprise. The circumstances thus presented must be viewed from a realistic standpoint. Naomi Lake is situated in the Pocono Mountains district, has become a summer resort for campers and boarders, and, except for the ice it furnishes, its bathing and boating facilities are the factors which give it its prime importance and value. They were exploited from the time the lake was created, and are recited as among the purposes for which the Pocono Spring Water Ice Company was chartered. From the early part of 1900 down to at least the filing of the present bill in 1929, Frank C. Miller and Rufus W. Miller openly carried on their business of constructing and operating bath houses and licensing individuals and camp associations to use the lake for bathing. This was known to the stockholders of the Pocono Spring Water Ice Company and necessarily also to Katherine D. Miller, the wife of Frank C. Miller; no objection of any kind was made, and Frank C. Miller and Rufus W. Miller were encouraged to expend large sums of money in pursuance of the right of which they considered and asserted themselves to be the owners. Under such circumstances it would be highly unjust to hold that a title by prescription to the bathing rights did not vest in Frank C. Miller and Rufus W. Miller which is just as valid, as far as Katherine D. Miller is concerned, as that to the boating and fishing rights which Frank C. Miller obtained by express grant.

We are ... brought to a consideration of the ... question ... whether the boating, bathing and fishing privileges were assignable by Frank C. Miller to Rufus W. Miller. What is the nature of such rights? In England it has been said that easements in gross do not exist at all, although rights of that kind have been there recognized. In this country such privileges have sometimes been spoken of as licenses, or as contractual in their nature, rather than as easements in gross. These are differences of terminology rather than of substance. We may assume, therefore, that these privileges are easements in gross, and we see no reason to consider them otherwise. It has uniformly been held that a profit in gross—for example, a right of mining or fishing—may be made assignable.

* * *

In regard to easements in gross generally, there has been much controversy in the courts and by textbook writers and law students as to whether they have the attribute of assignability. There are dicta in Pennsylvania that they are non-assignable.

* * *

But there is forcible expression and even definite authority to the contrary. * * * There does not seem to be any reason why the law should prohibit the assignment of an easement in gross if the parties to its creation evidence their intention to make it assignable. Here, * * * the rights of fishing and boating were conveyed to the grantee—in this case Frank C. Miller—"his heirs and assigns," thus showing that the grantor, the Pocono Spring Water Ice Company, intended to attach the attribute of assignability to the privileges granted. Moreover, as a practical matter, there is an obvious difference in this respect between easements for personal enjoyment and those designed for commercial exploitation; while there may be little justification for permitting assignments in the former case, there is every reason for upholding them in the latter.

The question of assignability of the easements in gross in the present case is not as important as that of their divisibility. It is argued by plaintiffs that even if held to be assignable such easements are not divisible, because this might involve an excessive user or "surcharge of the easement" subjecting the servient tenement to a greater burden than originally contemplated. The law does not take that extreme position. It does require, however, that if there be a division, the easements must be used or exercised as an entirety. This rule had its earliest expression in Mountjoy's Case, which is reported in Co. Litt. 164b, 165a. It was there said, in regard to the grant of a right to dig for ore, that the grantee, Lord Mountjoy, "might assign his whole interest to one, two, or more; but then, if there be two or more, they could make no division of it, but work together with one stock." In Caldwell v. Fulton, 31 Pa. 475, 477, 478, 72 Am.Dec. 760, and in Funk v. Haldeman, 53 Pa. 229, that case was followed, and it was held that the right of a grantee to mine coal or to prospect for oil might be assigned, but if to more than one they must hold, enjoy and convey the right as an entirety, and not divide it in severalty. There are cases in other jurisdictions which also approve the doctrine of Mountjoy's Case, and hold that a mining right in gross is essentially integral and not susceptible of apportionment; an assignment of it is valid, but it cannot be alienated in such a way that it may be utilized by grantor and grantee, or by several grantees, separately; there must be a joint user, nor can one of the tenants alone convey a share in the common right.

* * *

These authorities furnish an illuminating guide to the solution of the problem of divisibility of profits or easements in gross. They indicate that much depends upon the nature of the right and the terms of its creation, that "surcharge of the easement" is prevented if assignees exercise the right as "one stock," and that a proper method of enjoyment of the easement by two or more owners of it may usually be worked out in any given instance without insuperable difficulty.

In the present case it seems reasonably clear that in the conveyance of February 17, 1900, it was not the intention of Frank C. Miller to grant, and of Rufus W. Miller to receive, a separate right to subdivide and sub-license the boating, fishing and bathing privileges on and in Lake Naomi, but only that they should together use such rights for commercial purposes, Rufus W. Miller to be entitled to one-fourth and Frank C. Miller to three-fourths of the proceeds resulting from their combined exploitation of the privileges. They were to hold the rights, in the quaint phraseology of Mountjoy's Case, as "one stock." Nor do the technical rules that would be applicable to a tenancy in common of a corporeal hereditament apply to the control of these easements in gross. Defendant contends that, as a tenant in common of the privileges, Rufus W. Miller individually was entitled to their use, benefit and possession and to exercise rights of ownership in regard thereto, including the right to license third persons to use them, subject only to the limitation that he must not thereby interfere with the similar rights of his co-tenant. But the very nature of these easements prevents their being so exercised, inasmuch as it is necessary, because of the legal limitations upon their divisibility, that they should be utilized in common and not by two owners severally, and, as stated, this was evidently the intention of the brothers.

Summarizing our conclusions, we are of [the] opinion (1) that Frank C. Miller acquired title to the boating and fishing privileges by grant; (2) that he made a valid assignment of a one-fourth interest in them to Rufus W. Miller; but (3) that they cannot be commercially used and licenses thereunder granted without the common consent and joinder of the present owners, who with regard to them must act as "one stock." It follows that the executors of the estate of Rufus W. Miller did not have the right, in and by themselves, to grant a license to defendant.

The decree is affirmed; costs to be paid by defendant.

NOTES AND QUESTIONS

1. A owns Blackacre, which adjoins B's land. Blackacre is benefitted by a driveway easement across B's land. A conveys "all my right, title and interest" to X, but the deed fails to mention the easement. Has X acquired the easement? What if the deed simply conveys "Blackacre in fee simple absolute" to X? If X does not get the easement, who does?

2. It is commonly said that easements in gross do not exist under English law. In fact, England recognizes some rights in gross, but does not call them easements. For analysis and criticism of the English rule, see Sturley, Easements in Gross, 96 Law Q.Rev. 557 (1980).

3. Utility easements are generally easements in gross. The burden of the easement runs with the land over which the easement is taken, but the benefit belongs to the utility company itself. In the United States, *commercial* easements in gross are uniformly considered to be assignable. For example, if a utility company is purchased by another utility company or seized by a city under its eminent domain power, ownership of the easements will change.

The status of noncommercial, purely personal easements in gross is more ambiguous. If you deed your grandmother the right to fish in your lake, may she assign it to another? The *Miller* case did not answer that question because the easements there were found to be commercial. Many commentators believe that noncommercial easements in gross are not assignable, unless the language of the grant clearly manifests an intent to permit assignment. However, there are very few cases. See Simes, Assignability of Easements in Gross in American Law, 22 Mich.L.Rev. 521 (1924); Welsh, Assignability of Easements in Gross, 12 U.Chi.L.Rev. 276 (1945). See also Note, The Easement in Gross Revisited: Transferability and Divisibility Since 1945, 39 Vand.L.Rev. 109 (1986).

4. *Mountjoy's Case* (Earl of Huntington v. Lord Mountjoy), 1 And. 307, 123 Eng.Rep. 488, Godb. 17, 78 Eng.Rep. 11 (C.P.1583), discussed in *Miller,* concerned the divisibility of a profit a prendre rather than an easement in gross. A profit a prendre, or more commonly today, "profit," is the right to take something from the burdened land. The concept of the profit is very old, dating back to when a great deal of British land was held in common, and nearby tenants had the right to take certain products—wood, wild game, minerals, etc.—away from the land. The modern profit generally burdens a privately-owned estate, just as an easement does. Unlike easements, profits are generally presumed to be in gross. However, profits appurtenant can be created by express language, for example: "To A, the right to take wood from Blackacre for the purpose of building and maintaining fences on Whiteacre." The profit generally implies an easement in its owner to enter the burdened land to take the subject of the profit. But see Norken Corp. v. McGahan, 823 P.2d 622 (Alaska 1991), which held that a profit to take gravel from land permitted its owner only to have access to a gravel pit that existed when the land was conveyed; it did not permit new excavation for gravel on other parts of the land.

The profit does not explicitly mention the *amount* of the product that may be taken from the burdened land. If it does it is not a profit, but rather ownership of a measured corporeal interest. Easements and profits retained their metaphysical quality of being "incorporeal" as long as the rights they created were not subject to precise measurement. Thus, for example, a conveyance to A of "200 fenceposts per year to be taken away from Blackacre" was not a profit at all, but simply a sale of a corporeal property interest: 200 fenceposts per year. Likewise, a conveyance of "one-third of the coal lying under Blackacre" was not a conveyance of a profit but rather of a one-third undivided interest (a cotenancy) in the rights to a particular mineral. Further, such mineral rights, unlike profits or easements, are generally classified as *estates*, not as incorporeal interests. One still finds grants of *exclusive* rights to take something off the land referred to as "profits," particularly when the amount that the land can produce is incapable of precise measurement. Nevertheless, such a grant does *not* convey a common law "profit." See Stanton v. T.L. Herbert & Sons, 141 Tenn. 440, 447, 211 S.W. 353, 355 (1919):

> If all the minerals are conveyed, or an exclusive right thereto, an interest in the land passes. This is a corporeal interest, which may be assigned, divided, or dealt with as any other interest in land. If, under the grant, there passes only a right to remove minerals in common with the grantor, an incorporeal hereditament results.

This special quality of profits making them incapable of precise quantification has had two effects on the law of profits. First, and most significantly, it has meant that profits a prendre are not nearly as important in the modern economy as they were several centuries ago, although some are still created. Today most natural resources are too scarce to be conveyed away by any measure as imprecise as the profit. Modern profits are usually the product of negotiations between friends rather than arms-length bargains between strangers. Otherwise they concern products that are not very valuable, such as sand and gravel.

Secondly, the law of profits developed relatively elaborate rules for determining how the rights could be assigned. Profits appurtenant did not present a great problem: they ran with the dominant estate just as easements appurtenant. See, e.g., Seven Lakes Development Co., LLC v. Maxson, 144 P.3d 1239 (Wyo. 2006) (deeds that reserved hunting and fishing rights for the benefit of grantor's retained land created profit appurtenant). Personal profits, or profits in gross, were a different matter. They are generally assignable but not divisible. The law's concern was that the grantor of a profit not be subject to an unreasonable burden because far more of a product was being taken from the land than was in the reasonable contemplation of the parties at the time the profit was created. However, the mechanism that the common law used to solve this problem is antiquated, particularly since the rise of the modern business corporation. The rule that profits are freely assignable but not divisible developed in a time when all persons (there were no business corporations) could be expected to have roughly the same needs for a particular product, such as fence posts or coal—or at least the variation in their needs existed in a relatively narrow range. In such an economy it made some sense to rely on the simple rule that a profit can be freely transferred, but a profit originally granted to one person must always be held by one person. This rule helped ensure that the demands on the servient estate would always be more-or-less the same as the profit was transferred from one owner to another.

Today the common law rule no longer serves the function it was designed to serve. However, at least a part of it—the rule that profits are not divisible—is still cited by courts as good law. An assignment of a profit from one legal person to another can have the effect of increasing the demands on a profit twentyfold. For example, see Stanton v. T.L. Herbert & Sons, supra, where a grantor of land who reserved a profit to take sand and gravel transferred it to one of the largest general contractors in the area. The relatively clear rule of *Mountjoy's Case* that a profit is freely transferable but may be divided only if the multiple assignees use it together as "one stock" has gradually yielded to a rule that looks to the intent of the original parties when the profit was created.

The Restatement of Property was particularly hostile toward the concept of profits and tried to destroy them by refusing to distinguish between easements and profits. See Restatement (First) of Property § 450, Special Note (1944). Most courts have ignored the Restatement and continue to treat profits as distinct from easements.

5. Plaintiff granted an easement to a utility, the Ohio Power Company, "its successors, assigns, lessees, and tenants to construct, erect, operate and maintain a line of poles and wires for the purpose of transmitting electric or other power, *including telegraph* or telephone wires...." The power company then licensed a second company, the Hardin Cable Television Co., to run an additional line on its poles. The plaintiff sued to enjoin the second company's use of the easement. What result? Remember, a utility easement is an easement in gross. See Jolliff v. Hardin Cable Television Co., 26 Ohio St.2d 103, 269 N.E.2d 588, 55 O.O.2d 203 (1971). Would it matter that the grant of the easement to the utility said that it was "exclusive"? See Henley v. Continental Cablevision, 692 S.W.2d 825 (Mo.App.1985). The emergent law is

that utility easements in gross are divisible. In addition to Hardin and Henley, see Orange County v. Citgo Pipeline Co., 934 S.W.2d 472 (Tex.App.1996) (permitting pipeline easement in gross to be divided). Indeed, the trend seems to be to permit apportionment of such easements unless the grant manifests an intent not to permit it. See, e.g., Centel Cable Television Co. of Ohio v. Cook, 58 Ohio St.3d 8, 567 N.E.2d 1010 (1991).

§ 8.4.2 REAL COVENANTS AND EQUITABLE SERVITUDES: TRADITIONAL DOCTRINE AND MODERN DEVIATIONS

CANDLEWOOD LAKE ASSOCIATION, INC. v. SCOTT

Ohio Court of Appeals, 2001.
2001 WL 1654288.

BRYANT, P.J.

Defendant-appellant, Kermit E. Scott, appeals from a judgment of the Franklin County Court of Common Pleas awarding plaintiff-appellee, Candlewood Lake Association, Inc. ("the Association"), $29,465.64, plus court costs, in plaintiff's action for collection of unpaid assessments. . . .

The Association is an association of property owners in Candlewood Lake Subdivision in Morrow County, Ohio. Defendant is the record owner of two lots in the Candlewood Lake Subdivision. Defendant's father conveyed the two lots to defendant in a general warranty deed recorded in Morrow County on March 23, 1988. The lots were conveyed subject to "restrictions; conditions reservations and easements of record."

Various deed restrictions were recorded in Morrow County in 1972 in a document entitled the Candlewood Lake Association, Inc. Deed Restrictions (the "deed restrictions") concerning the Candlewood Lake Subdivision. The deed restrictions state the subdivision was established "with a strong recreational orientation." (Paragraph 201 of deed restrictions.) They authorize the Association to assess fees against its property owners for annual operations charges, maintenance services, water and sewer system charges, and various other assessments, including collection costs incurred by the Association to collect overdue fees and assessments. The deed restrictions further provide that "[e]very person who shall become an owner of a lot in the Subdivision will be conclusively held to have covenanted to pay the Association all charges made by the Trustees pursuant to these Restrictions." (Paragraph 605.06 of deed restrictions.)

* * * On May 29, 1997, Elkin filed this lawsuit in Morrow County on the Association's behalf . . . to collect the Association's unpaid assessments arising from the deed restrictions. . . .

* * * [D]efendant asserts the trial court erred in granting summary judgment in favor of the Association and obligating defendant, solely by virtue of his alleged ownership of the two lots in Candlewood Lake

Subdivision, to pay the charges the Association assessed on the two lots.
* * *

[D]efendant argues the covenants of the lot owners to pay those charges expressed in the deed restrictions do not "affect or touch and concern the land" and therefore are not real covenants that "run with the land." Instead, defendant asserts the covenants are merely personal covenants or obligations of individuals who have joined the Association. Because he has not joined the Association, defendant maintains he is not obligated to pay the Association's assessments.

In *Peto v. Korach* (1969), 17 Ohio App.2d 20, the Eighth District Court of Appeals examined a deed restriction that obligated the owner of property to share in the cost of the upkeep, maintenance, and use of water and sewer facilities located on an adjacent parcel of property, reserving to the owner a right to use the water and sewer facilities in common with the owner of the other property. In determining whether the obligation to share in the maintenance cost was a covenant running with the land or a personal covenant, the court summarized the pertinent law as follows:

> The common-law test of a covenant running with the land requires that its performance or nonperformance must affect the nature, quality, value, or mode of enjoyment of the estate demised to which it must relate. The generally-prescribed requisites for a covenant to run with the land are as follows: (1) The intent of the original grantor and grantee must have been that the covenant run with the land; (2) the covenant must either "affect" or "touch and concern" the land in question; (3) there must be privity of estate between the party claiming the benefit of the covenant and the party who is called upon to fulfill it.

Under the first prong of the common-law test, the court in *Peto* held that an obligation to share in the cost of upkeep, maintenance and use of water and sewer facilities is a covenant that runs with the land because the language of the covenant expressed its intent that the owner of the property and his heirs and assigns have rights and duties regarding the water and sewer systems. Moreover, it found the second prong satisfied, as a covenant "touches and concerns the land" where in return for the duty to pay money the property owner has a privilege to use water and sewer facilities that would directly benefit his land. Under the last prong, the court found privity, concluding the owners of the parcels of land were ultimate assignees of the original grantor and grantee, who stood in their predecessors shoes and had "the same rights and obligation as the original owner had in regard to the property." *Peto, supra,* at 25, 244 N.E.2d 502.

Similarly, the covenants at issue, as the covenants in *Peto,* are covenants that run with the land, not personal covenants. First, the deed restrictions affirmatively state a clear intention that "[t]he Restrictions *shall run with the land* and shall be binding upon the Association and upon all parties ('Owners') having or acquiring any right, title or interest in the real property or any part thereof." (Paragraph 203 of deed restrictions; emphasis added.) See, also, paragraph 905 ("The foregoing covenants and restrictions shall run with the land and shall be binding on all parties and all persons claiming under them * * * "). Similar language in a "Membership Covenant" in the by-laws of a resort property association has been held to constitute a covenant running with the land. See *Rome Rock Assoc., Inc. v. Warsing* (Dec. 23, 1999), Ashtabula App. No. 98–A–0051, unreported ("This covenant concerning said real estate and the enjoyment, use and benefit thereof shall be deemed to run with the land and non-payment of the annual charges shall be a lien thereon").

In addition to the express language that the covenants "run with the land," a further intention here that the covenants run with the land is found in language that grantees of deeds subject to the restrictions accept the deed and the restrictions "for themselves, their *heirs, personal representatives, successors, and assigns.*" (Paragraph 901 of deed restrictions; emphasis added.) See *Hughes, supra,* at 384–385 (determining a covenant by a "grantee, his heirs and assigns" to share in the cost of streets is a covenant that runs with the land); *Peto, supra,* at 23, 28 (concluding that although a covenant may run with the land where the original covenant does not use the words "heirs," "assigns," or "successors," use of such words indicates an intent that a covenant run with the land); *LuMac Dev. Corp. v. Buck Point Ltd. Partnership* (1988), 61 Ohio App.3d 558, 563–564 (use of the terms "assigns," "heirs," or "successors" clearly reflects an intent that a covenant runs with the land).

Secondly, as in *Peto,* the covenants here are for maintenance services and access to and use of water and sewer systems. Those benefits inure to defendant's property, not to defendant personally, and increase the value of the property. Therefore, the covenants "touch and concern" the land. *Peto, supra,* at 24.

[Privity of Estate]

* * * Pursuant to his father's conveyance of the property to him in the deed, defendant is an assignee of his father, obtaining not only the rights incident to his father's ownership but also the obligations imposed by the covenants in the deed restrictions. *LuMac Dev., supra,* at 563; *Peto, supra,* at 24–26. On his acceptance of the deed and as an owner of the property, defendant became subject to and bound by the provisions in the Association's deed restrictions, including Paragraph 203 that states "all of the lots located in the various recorded plats * * * are held and shall be held, conveyed, pledged or encumbered, leased, rented, used, occupied and improved, subject to these Restrictions * * *." Paragraph 901 then provides "[t]he grantee of any lot subject to these Restrictions, by acceptance of a deed conveying title thereto * * * acknowledge[s] the rights and powers of the Association with respect to these Restrictions * * * and agree[s] and consent[s] to * * * comply with and perform such Restrictions and agreements." Accordingly, as a grantee of a lot subject to the deed restrictions, defendant agreed to comply with the restrictions.

Defendant's argument that the Association's deed restrictions do not apply to him because he never joined the Association is unavailing. Paragraph 602 of the deed restrictions provides that "[m]embership shall be appurtenant to and required as incidental to ownership to each lot in the Subdivision. * * * [O]ne owner of each lot shall, by reason of such ownership, become a Voting Member of the Association." As the record owner of property in Candlewood Lake Subdivision, defendant automatically became a member of the Association. Privity between defendant and the Association is accordingly established. The evidence thus demonstrates that the covenants at issue run with the land. A person's liability for such covenants arises by virtue of his or her ownership of an interest in land, and it continues at least until he or she is divested of ownership of the land. See *Peto, supra,* at 22.

* * * Accordingly, when defendant became a record owner of lots in Candlewood Lake Subdivision, he became subject to all of the provisions in the recorded Association deed restrictions and liable to pay the charges, fees, and fines the Association assessed on the lots pursuant to the deed restrictions, including attorney fees and costs the Association incurred to collect unpaid charges, fees, and fines. Summary judgment was appropriately granted on behalf of the Association* * *

NOTE: THE COMMON LAW OF REAL COVENANTS

Promises respecting the use of land can be classified as either real covenants or equitable servitudes. A real covenant is a contractual promise that traditionally was enforceable only in courts of law. For breach of a real covenant, the plaintiff was entitled to damages measured by contract principles. Breach of an equitable servitude, by contrast, was addressed by the courts of equity, and the preferred remedy was an injunction.

As a general rule few problems are encountered when the original contracting parties seek to enforce agreements concerning land use. Rather, the difficulty in the law of covenants derives from the fact that such covenants are said to "run with the land"—which means they may be enforced by or against persons who were *not* parties to the original contract. This difficulty has resulted in a number of bizarre and antiquated complexities. One fortunate result of the recording acts (see chapter 16) is that the law of running covenants has been dwarfed in importance and influence by the law of equitable servitudes. Nevertheless, the law of covenants running with the land continues to have vitality.

Before a real covenant would run at law, the following requirements had to be satisfied:

(a) *An Enforceable Contract.* As a general proposition, a real covenant that is not contained in a deed must begin as a valid, enforceable contract between the original parties. This requirement begins to blur when the covenant is contained in a deed, since conveyances are valid whether or not they are contractual. For example, property conveyed as a gift cannot be taken back by the grantor; however, a promise to do something that is not supported by consideration is generally not enforceable.[6] A few decisions deviate from this contract rule in more substantial ways. For example, it now appears to be the law of California that a developer's mere recordation of a subdivision plat listing the covenants effectively "creates" them even if subsequent transactions do not contain them. Citizens for Covenant Compliance v. Anderson, 12 Cal.4th 345, 906 P.2d 1314, 47 Cal.Rptr.2d 898 (1995). One might view the recordation as a "contract" with the government creating the servitudes, but that would be a stretch.

Although real covenants are not "estates," most courts classify them as "interests in land." A real covenant is thus enforceable only if it complies with the real property provisions of the Statute of Frauds. This means that the covenant or deed in which it is contained must describe the affected land with sufficient particularity so that it can be identified, and it must bear the signature of the person against whom enforcement is sought.

(b) *Intent to Bind Successors in Interest.* The parties must have intended their agreement to be binding upon successors in interest to the affected property. See, e.g., Lakewood Racquet Club, Inc. v. Jensen, 156 Wash. App. 215, 232 P.3d 1147, 1151 (2010) (stating that, when interpreting a restrictive covenant, the primary object is to discern the original parties' intent and that doubts should be resolved "in favor of the free use of land"). In most cases intent is manifested by express language, such as: "A hereby covenants that A, her heirs, devisees, or assignees shall never use Blackacre for any commercial or business purpose, but that it shall always be maintained as a single-family residence." However, most courts hold that an intent to bind successors in interest can be inferred from a construction of the instrument as a whole. They generally presume an intent to bind successors when the covenant is clearly a promise to do or refrain from doing something on a particular piece of land, and the promise clearly enhances the value of adjoining land.

See, for example, Rogers v. Watson, 156 Vt. 483, 594 A.2d 409 (1991), in which the grantors placed the following restriction on land that they sold, while retaining adjacent lands:

> No mobile home, trailer, or other similar structure shall be placed or maintained on said premises without the prior approval in writing of the grantor herein or his heirs, executors, administrators or assigns.

The restriction appears to benefit successors in interest to the *grantor*, but does it also bind successors in interest to the *grantee*? The court concluded yes, noting that "intent can be implied as well as expressed," and that it can be shown from "extraneous circumstances." In this case,

> the restriction prohibits the placement of a particular type of structure on defendants' land. This is the sort of restriction "so intimately connected with the land" that we find the "necessary intention . . .

---

6. Easements, it should be noted, do not need to be contracts. See Kuhlman v. Rivera, 216 Mont. 353, 701 P.2d 982 (1985), in which the court held that a hand-written document giving the defendants a right of way as a gift was a valid deed even though it was not an enforceable contract, because there was no consideration.

absent language clearly negating that intent." Extraneous factors also point strongly to the intent to have the burden run with the land. The Bards retained adjoining or nearby land. The inclusion of the restriction in most, if not all, other deeds from the Bards shows an intent to create a common development scheme even if it was implemented imperfectly.

See also Shaff v. Leyland, 154 N.H. 495, 914 A.2d 1240 (2006), where restrictive covenants limiting the number of houses that could be built on the affected land stated that the *burden* of the covenants "shall run with the land," but said nothing about the benefit. In this case the plaintiff had sold the land she formerly owned in the subdivision, but was suing to enforce the covenants. The court noted the common law constructional preference for appurtenant rather than personal interests and concluded that the benefit ran with the plaintiff's formerly owned land rather than herself personally. Once she sold the land she lacked standing to enforce the covenants.

(c) *Mutuality not Required.* Mutuality of burdens or benefits is *not* a prerequisite to the running of a real covenant. To be sure, many covenants do impose equal, reciprocal burdens on all affected land. But covenants that simply burden one parcel for the benefit of another parcel or even a person are generally enforceable. For example, suppose that A, a barber, sells the building containing his shop but intends to build a second shop elsewhere in the same city. A does not want his former customers returning to a shop located in the same place as his old shop. Therefore, he inserts into the deed a restrictive covenant that as long as A personally is engaged in barbering in this city, the grantee, her heirs and assigns will not use the transferred property for a barber shop. In such a case the "burden" of the restrictive covenant—the obligation not to use the old shop location for barbering—is intended to run with the land. The "benefit," however, is purely personal to A and will disappear when A retires, dies or moves to a different city. In the law of real covenants there is a saying that "the burden will not run when the benefit is in gross." Today, however, most courts will enforce such a covenant, provided that the covenant not to compete does not violate legal rules against restraints on trade.

(d) *"Touch and Concern."* At common law a real covenant could not be enforced against a successor to the promisor unless the subject matter of the covenant "touched and concerned" the land. The concept of "touch and concern" is extremely spongy, particularly in the middle. At one extreme it seems clear that promises to do or to refrain from doing some act upon the land which will either enhance or reduce its market value meet the touch and concern requirement. At the other extreme, a promise to do acts that have nothing whatsoever to do with the land generally do not meet it. Assume, for example, that you sell your house to a physician who as part of the purchase price obligates herself by covenant to give you an annual check-up for the rest of your life. Three years later the physician sells the house to an accountant. Now who must give you your annual check-up? A court would almost certainly hold that the physician's contract burdened the physician personally and not the estate she purchased from you. She will have to continue giving you your annual check-up and the accountant will obtain the house free of the requirement.

In between the above extremes are some ambiguous instances that have given courts a great deal of difficulty. Covenants in which a property owner promises to pay money have always been problematic. Courts were generally reluctant to enforce "affirmative" rather than "negative" obligations against successors in interest to the covenantor. See, e.g., Village of Philadelphia v. FortisUS Energy Corp., 48 A.D.3d 1193, 851 N.Y.S.2d 780 (2008) (stating that personal affirmative covenants to pay money usually do not touch and concern).

> However, the overwhelming trend, exhibited in the *Candlewood* decision, is to find that such promises touch and concern the land provided that the payment is for something that enhances the value of the property, its security, or the quality of life on the property. For example, nearly all courts today hold that covenants to purchase insurance touch and concern the land, as well as covenants to pay for maintenance or improvements of the property itself or surrounding common areas. See G. Korngold, Private Land Use Arrangements § 9.10 (1990); Stake, Toward an Economic Understanding of Touch and Concern, 1988 Duke L.J. 925. However, if the obligations are badly distributed, for example, requiring some homeowners to pay while exempting others with no apparent difference in benefits, a court may refuse enforcement. The leading case is Petersen v. Beekmere, 117 N.J.Super. 155, 283 A.2d 911 (Ch.Div.1971). See H. Hovenkamp & S. Kurtz, The Law of Property 396–407 (5th ed. 2001).

> The Restatement (Third) of Property: (Servitudes) (2000) would abolish the touch & concern requirement:

> § 3.2.   Touch-or-Concern Doctrine Superseded

>> Neither the burden nor the benefit of a covenant is required to touch or concern land in order for the covenant to be valid as a servitude.

> The reporter comments that the inquiry more appropriately addressed by the touch and concern requirement is whether the covenant violates public policy. As a result, servitudes formerly invalidated under the touch & concern requirement will now be invalidated "if they impose unreasonable restraints on alienation, undue restraints on trade, or if they are unconscionable or lack a rational justification."

See Touch and Concern, the Restatement (Third) of Property: Servitudes, and a Proposal, 122 Harv. L. Rev. 938 (2009).

> (e) *Privity.* Equally complex is the common law requirement that there be "privity" between the person seeking enforcement of the covenant and the person against whom enforcement is sought. Privity of *contract* exists between the original promisor and the original promisee under a covenant. However, as between either original party and a successor in interest to the other side, or as between two successors in interest, no privity of contract exists. The covenant will be enforced, however, if the court finds both horizontal and vertical privity of estate.

(1) *Horizontal Privity.* Horizontal privity describes a relationship among (a) the original promisor under a covenant; (b) the original promisee under that covenant; and (c) the affected estate in land.

Historically, American states employed three different rules for determining horizontal privity, although the trend is toward unification. The most restrictive definition was the so-called "Massachusetts" rule, under which a promisor and promisee were in privity of estate only if they held simultaneous legal interests in the affected property after the covenant was created. Under this rule privity would exist between a landlord and tenant, or between owners of undivided interests in the same property. Privity could also be found between the owner of an easement and the owner of its servient estate, but generally only if the subject matter of the covenant pertained to the easement. In all these cases the covenantor and covenantee share a simultaneous legal interest in the affected land. However, a grantor and grantee did not meet the privity requirements under this rule, even if the covenant were contained in the deed. Grantors and grantees of a fee simple absolute do not have simultaneous interests in the same piece of land, but only successive interests, because after the conveyance the grantor retains no interest.

The second definition, adopted by nearly all jurisdictions today, expands privity to include a covenant contained in a deed which transfers the grantor's entire estate in the land to the grantee. The creation of the covenant had to be simultaneous with the transfer of the interest, which effectively meant that the covenant had to be contained in the deed. For example, in Wheeler v. Schad, 7 Nev. 204 (1871), the grantor conveyed property to the grantee on June 5, 1862, and the grantor and grantee entered into a contract governing construction and maintenance of a dam on the property on June 11. The court found that there was no horizontal privity because the conveyance and the covenant did not constitute "one instrument or transaction." But contrast Sonoma Development, Inc. v. Miller, 258 Va. 163, 515 S.E.2d 577 (1999). The court found that the horizontal privity requirement had been met even though the real covenant sought to be enforced had been executed in a different piece of paper than the underlying deed. The two pieces of paper were executed on the same day, the declaration of restrictions was recorded, and the deed stated that it was made "subject to easements, restrictive covenants, restrictions and rights-of-way of record." The court said:

> We are not willing to say that, in every situation, only one document can be examined in order to determine if horizontal privity existed between the original covenanting parties. . . .
>
> In order to establish horizontal privity, the party seeking to enforce the real covenant must prove that "the original covenanting parties [made] their covenant in connection with the conveyance of an estate in land from one of the parties to the other." The Restatement of Property § 534(a) (1944), provides that horizontal privity is satisfied when "the transaction of which the promise is a part includes a transfer of an interest either in the land benefitted by or in the land burdened by the performance of the promise." In other words, the

covenant must be part of a transaction that also includes the transfer of an interest in land that is either benefitted or burdened by the covenant.

* * * In the context of the present case, we find that the transaction of which the covenant was a part commenced with the real estate contract between the Schaers and the Millers, and culminated with the deed conveying Lot 38 to the Millers. The "Declaration of Restriction" fulfilled the Schaers' contractual obligation to establish a restriction on Lot 39, which lot was being retained by the Schaers at that time, and was executed in conjunction with the deed to the Millers. Thus, it was part of a transaction that included the transfer of an interest in the land benefitted by the real covenant.

The third, most expansive definition of horizontal privity is really no privity requirement at all. Although few states have expressly abolished all privity requirements, the trend appears to be away from taking horizontal privity very seriously. The Third Restatement would abolish the horizontal privity requirement. "In American law, the horizontal-privity requirement serves no function beyond insuring that most covenants intended to run with the land will be created in conveyances. Formal creation of covenants is desirable because it tends to assure that they will be recorded. However, the horizontal-privity requirement is no longer needed for this purpose. In modern law, the Statute of Frauds and recording acts perform that function." The Restatement (Third) of Property: Servitudes § 2.4 cmt. b (2000).

(2) *Vertical Privity.* Vertical privity describes a relationship that exists among (a) the original promisor or original promisee under a covenant; (b) that particular promisor or promisee's successor in interest; and (c) the affected estate in land. See William B. Stoebuck, *Running Covenants: An Analytical Primer,* 52 Wash.L.Rev. 861, 876 (1977):

The most obvious implication of [the vertical privity obligation] is that the burden of a real covenant may be enforced against remote parties only when they have succeeded to the covenantor's estate in land. Such parties stand in privity of estate with the covenantor. Likewise, the benefit may be enforced by remote parties only when they have succeeded to the covenantee's estate. They are in privity of estate with the covenantee.

See, e.g., Barner v. Chappell, 266 Va. 277, 585 S.E.2d 590 (2003), which held that neighboring landowners whose land was not included within a scheme to which a real covenant applied lacked vertical privity with those against whom enforcement was sought. The neighbors could trace their title to lands owned by the same common owner as the defendants' land, but the neighbors land had been sold off prior to the creation of the covenant.

Historically, before the burden of a real covenant would be imposed upon someone who was not an original party to the agreement creating the obligation, that person must have succeeded to *exactly* the same estate as that held by the original promisor, or else to an estate with precisely the same duration. Thus if the original agreement was between owners in fee and the promisor conveyed a life estate, the promisee in the original agreement could not enforce the covenant against the owner of the life estate. This strict vertical privity rule was commonly relaxed when the running of the benefit, rather than the burden, was being considered. See, e.g., St. Louis, I.M. & S. Ry. v. O'Baugh, 49 Ark. 418, 5 S.W. 711 (1887) (owner of a life estate in the affected land could enforce a promise, even though the original promisee had been the owner of a fee simple absolute).

Many authorities take the position that an adverse possessor cannot meet the vertical privity requirement. See 2 Amer.L.Prop. § 9.20 (A.J. Casner, ed. 1952); French, Toward a Modern Law of Servitudes: Reweaving the Ancient Strands, 55 S.Cal.L.Rev. 1261, 1275 (1982). But even here some distinctions would appear to be in order. Some adverse possessors have no formal legal relationship with the previous possessor (and generally record title holder) of the land. In these cases there is generally no vertical privity. But often the law of adverse possession is used to "correct" legally ineffectual attempts to transfer land. For example, a court might well hold that someone who has occupied land under claim of a written instrument for the statutory period has acquired it by adverse possession, even though the written instrument in question was defective, perhaps because it lacked the grantor's signature. Such a person should be found to be in privity of estate with his predecessor with respect to those covenants contained in the ineffective deed.

One important effect of the requirements of horizontal and vertical privity is that, with the exception of short-term leases, most real covenants that meet the privity requirements are contained in recorded instruments (see chapter 16). Since recordation imparts constructive notice to subsequent grantees, and since constructive notice is generally sufficient to make a covenant enforceable as an equitable servitude, the privity requirement has proved to be the near undoing of covenants at law. Today most promises respecting the use of land that meet the traditional privity requirements are also capable of being enforced as equitable servitudes. The law of real covenants may still be important in these cases, however, if the plaintiff is seeking money damages rather than an injunction against violation of the servitude. Some courts have been reluctant to award damages (a "legal" remedy) in cases involving equitable servitudes, which fall within the court's equity jurisdiction.

The Restatement provides that the benefits of certain affirmative covenants run to adverse possessors who have not yet gained title to the property benefitted by the covenant. These certain covenants include: "(1) the benefit of covenants to repair, maintain, or render services to the property; and (2) covenant benefits that can be enjoyed by the person in possession without diminishing their value to the owner of the property and without materially increasing the burden of performance on the person obligated to perform the covenant." The Restatement (Third) of Property: Servitudes §§ 5.2, 5.5 (2000). The rationale supporting the decision to allow these covenants to run to adverse possessors while the true owner still retains an interest in the property is that the performance of these covenants serves to enhance the property's value thereby protecting the true owner's interests. As for the benefits of restrictive (also called *negative*) covenants, they also run to adverse possessors who have not yet gained title. "[T]he benefit of a restrictive covenant can be enjoyed by both the possessor and the owner ... without diminishing its value to the other, or increasing the costs of performance to the person bound by the restriction." The Restatement (Third) of Property: Servitudes § 5.2 cmt. a (2000).

Under the Restatement view, adverse possessors who have not gained title are liable for the burdens of covenants burdening property. The Restatement (Third) of Property: Servitudes § 5.2 cmt. h (2000).

The Restatement rejects privity of estate and treats adverse possessors who have obtained title just like any other subsequent owner. It states that "the benefits and burdens of ... restrictive covenants run to all subsequent possessors, including lessees, life tenants and adverse possessors, and to all subsequent owners, without regard to the manner in which they acquired title." The Restatement (Third) of Property: Servitudes § 5.2 cmt. a (2000).

(j) *Notice.* Notice is required before a purchaser will be bound by the burden of a real covenant. There are three types of notice: actual, record, and inquiry notice. Actual notice is knowledge and awareness of the existence of the real covenant. Record notice is notice derived from a duly recorded instrument in the chain of title to the burdened estate. One need not have knowledge of the instrument to have record notice if a search of the chain of title would have revealed the recorded instrument. Inquiry notice is constructive notice of all the facts that would be revealed upon a reasonable inquiry and based upon the factual circumstances. For the burden of a real covenant to run, the owner of the burdened estate must have either actual or record notice of the real covenant.

DAVIDSON BROS., INC. v. D. KATZ & SONS, INC.

Supreme Court of New Jersey (1990).
121 N.J. 196, 579 A.2d 288.

GARIBALDI, J.

This case [considers] whether a restrictive covenant in a deed, providing that the property shall not be used as a supermarket or grocery store, is enforceable against the original covenantor's successor, a subsequent purchaser with actual notice of the covenant. * * *

Prior to September 1980 plaintiff, * * * owned certain premises located at 263–271 George Street and 30 Morris Street in New Brunswick (the "George Street" property). Plaintiff operated a supermarket on that property for approximately seven to eight months. The store operated at a loss allegedly because of competing business from plaintiff's other store, located two miles away (the "Elizabeth Street" property). Consequently, plaintiff conveyed, by separate deeds, the George Street property to defendant D. Katz & Sons, Inc., with a restrictive covenant not to operate a supermarket on the premises. Specifically, each deed contained the following covenant: "The lands and premises described herein and conveyed hereby are conveyed subject to the restriction that said lands and premises shall not be used as and for a supermarket or grocery store of a supermarket type, however designated, for a period of forty (40) years from the date of this deed. This restriction shall be a covenant attached to and running with the lands." The deeds were duly recorded in Middlesex County Clerk's office on September 10, 1980. * * *

According to defendants New Brunswick Housing Authority (the "Authority") and City of New Brunswick (the "City"), the closure of the George Street store did not benefit the residents of downtown New Brunswick. Defendants allege that many of the residents who lived two blocks away from the George Street store in multi-family and senior-citizen housing units were forced to take public transportation and taxis to the Elizabeth Street store because there were no other markets in downtown New Brunswick, save for two high-priced convenience stores. The residents requested the aid of the City and the Authority in attracting a new food retailer to this urban-renewal area. For six years, those efforts were unsuccessful. Finally, in 1986, an executive of C–Town, a division of a supermarket chain, approached representatives of New Brunswick about securing financial help from the City to build a supermarket. Despite its actual notice of the covenant the Authority, on October 23, 1986, purchased the George Street property from Katz for $450,000, and agreed to lease from Katz at an annual net rent of $19,800.00, the adjacent land at 263–265 George Street for use as a parking lot. The Authority invited proposals for the lease of the property to use as a supermarket. C–Town was the only party to submit a proposal at a public auction. The proposal provided for an aggregate rent of one dollar per year during the five-year lease term with an agreement to make $10,000 in improvements to the exterior of the building and land. The Authority accepted the proposal in 1987. All the defendants in this case had actual notice of the restrictions contained in the deed and of plaintiff's intent to enforce the same. * * *

Covenants regarding property uses have historical roots in the courts of both law and equity. The English common-law courts first dealt with the issue in Spencer's Case, 5 Co. 16a, 77 Eng.Rep. 72 (Q.B.1583). The court established two criteria for the enforcement of covenants against successors. First, the original covenanting parties must intend that the covenant run with the land. Second, the covenant must "touch and concern" the land. The court explained the concept of "touch and concern" in this manner:

> But although the covenant be for him [an original party to the promise] and his assigns, yet if the thing to be done be merely collateral to the land, and doth not touch and concern the thing demised in any sort, there the assignee shall not be charged. As if the lessee covenants for him and his assignees to build a house upon the land of the lessor which is no parcel of the demise, or to pay any collateral sum to the lessor, or to a stranger, it shall not bind the assignee, because it is merely collateral, and in no manner touches or concerns the thing that was demised, or that is assigned over, and therefore in such case the assignee of the thing demised cannot be charged with it, no more than any other stranger.

The English common-law courts also developed additional requirements of horizontal privity (succession of estate), vertical privity (a landlord-tenant relationship), and that the covenant have "proper form," in order for the covenant to run with the land. C. Clark, Real Covenants and Other Interests Which Run With the Land 94, 95 (2d ed. 1947). Those technical requirements made it difficult, if not impossible, to protect property through the creation of real covenants. To mitigate and to eliminate many of the formalities and privity rules formulated by the common-law courts, the English chancery courts in Tulk v. Moxhay, 2 Phil. 774, 41 Eng.Rep. 1143 (Ch. 1848), created the doctrine of equitable servitudes. In *Tulk*, land was conveyed subject to an agreement that it would be kept open and maintained for park use. A subsequent grantee, with notice of the restriction, acquired the park. The court held that it would be unfair for the original covenantor to rid himself of the burden to maintain the park by simply selling the land. In enjoining the new owner from violating the agreement, the court stated:

> It is said that, the covenant being one which does not run with the land, this court cannot enforce it, but the question is, not whether the covenant runs with the land, but whether a party shall be permitted to use the land in a manner inconsistent with the contract entered into by his vendor, and with notice of which he purchased. Of course, the price would be affected by the covenant, and nothing could be more inequitable than that the original purchaser should be able to sell the property the next day for a greater price, in consideration of the assignee being allowed to escape from the liability which he had himself undertaken.

The court thus enforced the covenant on the basis that the successor had purchased the property with notice of the restriction. Adequate notice obliterated any express requirement of "touch and concern." Reichman, "Toward a Unified Concept of Servitudes," 55 S.Cal.L.Rev. 1177, 1225 (1982); French, "Toward a Modern Law of Servitudes: Reweaving Ancient Strands," 55 S.Cal.L.Rev. 1261, 1276–77 (1982). But see Burger, "A Policy Analysis of Promises Respecting the Use of Land," 55 Minn.L.Rev. 167, 217 (1970) (focusing on language in *Tulk* that refers to "use of land" and "attached to property" as implied recognition of "touch and concern" rule). Some early commentators theorized that the omission of the technical elements of property law such as the "touch and concern" requirement indicated that Tulk was based on a contractual as opposed to a property theory. C. Clark, supra, Real Covenants, at 171–72 nn. 3 and 4. * * * Others contend that "touch and concern" is always, at the very least, an implicit element in any analysis regarding enforcement of covenants because "any restrictive easement necessitates some relation between the restriction and the land itself." McLoone, "Equitable Servitudes—A Recent Case and Its Implications for the Enforcement of Covenants Not to Compete," 9 Ariz.L.Rev. 441, 444, 447 n. 5 (1968). Still others explain the "touch and concern" omission on the theory that equitable servitudes usually involve negative covenants or promises on how the land should not be used. Thus, because those covenants typically do touch and concern the land, the equity courts did not feel the necessity to state "touch and concern" as a separate requirement. Berger, "Integration of the Law of Easements, Real Covenants and Equitable Servitudes," 43 Wash. & Lee L.Rev., 337, 362 (1986). Whatever the explanation, the law of equitable servitudes did generally continue to diminish or omit the "touch and concern" requirement.

Our inquiry of New Jersey law on restrictive property use covenants commences with a re-examination of the rule set forth in Brewer v. Marshall & Cheeseman, 19 N.J.Eq. 537 (E. & A.1868) that a covenant will not run with the land unless it affects the physical use of the land. Hence, the burden side of a noncompetition covenant is personal to the covenantor and is, therefore, not enforceable against a purchaser. In *Brewer* the court objected to all noncompetition covenants on the basis of public policy and refused to consider them in the context of the doctrine of equitable servitudes. Similarly, in National Union Bank at Dover v. Segur, 39 N.J.L. 173 (Sup.Ct.1877), the court held that only the benefit of a noncompetition covenant would run with the land, but the burden would be personal to the covenantor. Because the burden of a noncompetition covenant is deemed to be personal in these cases, enforcement would be possible only against the original covenantor. As soon as the covenantor sold the property, the burden would cease to exist. *Brewer* and *National Union Bank* have been subsequently interpreted as embodying the "unnecessarily strict" position that "while the benefit of [a noncompetition covenant] will run with the land, the burden of the covenant is necessarily personal to the covenantor." This blanket prohibition of noncompetition covenants has been ignored in more recent decisions that have allowed the burden of a noncompetition covenant to run, see Renee Cleaners Inc. v. Good Deal Supermarkets of N.J., 89 N.J.Super. 186, 214 A.2d 437 (App.Div.1965) (enforcing at law covenant not to lease property for dry-cleaning business as against subsequent purchaser of land). Nonetheless, *Brewer* may still retain some vitality, as evidenced by the trial court's reliance on it in this case. The per se prohibition that noncompetition covenants regarding the use of property do not run with the land is not supported by modern real-covenant law, and indeed, appears to have support only in the Restatement of Property section on the running of real covenants, § 537 comment f. Specifically, that approach is rejected in the Restatement's section on equitable servitudes, see Restatement of Property, § 539 comment k (1944); see also Whitinsville Plaza, Inc. v. Kotseas, 378 Mass. 85, 95–96, 390 N.E.2d 243, 249 (1979) (overruling similarly strict approach inasmuch as it was "anachronistic" compared to modern judicial analysis of noncompetition covenants, which focuses on effects of covenant). * * * Accordingly, to the extent that Brewer holds that a noncompetition covenant will not run with the land, it is overruled.

Plaintiff also argues that the "touch and concern" test likewise should be eliminated in determining the enforceability of fully negotiated contracts, in favor of a simpler "reasonableness" standard that has been adopted in most jurisdictions. That argument has some support from commentators, see, e.g., Epstein, "Notice and Freedom of Contract in the Law of Servitudes," 55 S.Cal.L.Rev. 1353, 1359–61 (1982) (contending that "touch and concern" complicates the basic analysis and limits the effectiveness of law of servitudes), including a reporter for the Restatement (Third) of Property, see French, "Servitudes Reform and the New Restatement of Property: Creation Doctrines and Structural Simplification," 73 Cornell L.Rev. 928, 939 (1988) (arguing that "touch and concern" rule should be completely eliminated and that the law should instead directly tackle the "running" issue on public-policy grounds).

New Jersey courts, however, continue to focus on the "touch and concern" requirement as the pivotal inquiry in ascertaining whether a covenant runs with the land. Under New Jersey law, a covenant that "exercise[s][a] direct influence on the occupation, use or enjoyment of the premises" satisfies the "touch and concern" rule. Caullett v. Stanley Stilwell & Sons, Inc., 67 N.J.Super. 111, 116, 170 A.2d 52 (App.Div.1961). The covenant must touch and concern both the burdened and the benefitted property in order to run with the land. Ibid. Because the law frowns on the placing of restrictions on the freedom of alienation of land, New Jersey courts will enforce a covenant only if it produces a countervailing benefit to justify the burden.

Unlike New Jersey, which has continued to rely on the "touch and concern" requirement, most other jurisdictions have omitted "touch and concern" from their analysis and have focused instead on whether the covenant is reasonable. See, e.g., Doo v. Packwood, 265 Cal.App.2d 752, 71 Cal.Rptr. 477 (1968) (covenant not to sell groceries on property conveyed); Natural Prods. Co. v. Dolese & Shepard Co., 309 Ill. 230, 140 N.E. 840 (1923) (covenant not to sell stone on property conveyed); . . . Even the majority of courts that have retained the "touch and concern" test have found that noncompetition covenants meet the test's requirements. [numerous citations omitted]

The "touch and concern" test has, thus, ceased to be, in most jurisdictions, intricate and confounding. Courts have decided as an initial matter that covenants not to compete do touch and concern the land. The courts then have examined explicitly the more important question of whether covenants are reasonable enough to warrant enforcement. The time has come to cut the Gordian knot that binds this state's jurisprudence regarding covenants running with the land. Rigid adherence to the "touch and concern" test as a means of determining the enforceability of a restrictive covenant is not warranted. Reasonableness, not esoteric concepts of property law, should be the guiding inquiry into the validity of covenants at law. We do not abandon the "touch and concern" test, but rather hold that the test is but one of the factors a court should consider in determining the reasonableness of the covenant. A "reasonableness" test allows a court to consider the enforceability of a covenant in view of the realities of today's commercial world and not in the light of out-moded theories developed in a vastly different commercial environment. * * *

Courts today recognize that it is not unreasonable for parties in commercial-property transactions to protect themselves from competition by executing noncompetition covenants. Business persons, either as lessees or purchasers may be hesitant to invest substantial sums if they have no minimal protection from a competitor starting a business in the near vicinity. Hence, rather than limiting trade, in some instances, restrictive covenants may increase business activity.

The pivotal inquiry, therefore, becomes what factors should a court consider in determining whether such a covenant is "reasonable" and hence enforceable. We conclude that the following factors should be considered: *1.* The intention of the parties when the covenant was executed, and whether the parties had a viable purpose which did not at the time interfere with existing commercial laws, such as antitrust laws, or public policy. *2.* Whether the covenant had an impact on the considerations exchanged when the covenant was originally executed. This may provide a measure of the value to the parties of the covenant at the time. *3.* Whether the covenant clearly and expressly sets forth the restrictions. *4.* Whether the covenant was in writing, recorded, and if so, whether the subsequent grantee had actual notice of the covenant. *5.* Whether the covenant is reasonable concerning area, time or duration. Covenants that extend for perpetuity or beyond the terms of a lease may often be unreasonable. Alexander's v. Arnold Constable, 105 N.J.Super. 14, 27, 250 A.2d 792 (Ch.Div.1969). *6.* Whether the covenant imposes an unreasonable restraint on trade or secures a monopoly for the covenantor. This may be the case in areas where there is limited space available to conduct certain business activities and a covenant not to compete burdens all or most available locales to prevent them from competing in such an activity. *7.* Whether the covenant interferes with the public interest. *8.* Whether, even if the covenant was reasonable at the time it was executed, "changed circumstances" now make the covenant unreasonable.

In applying the "reasonableness" factors, trial courts may find useful the analogous standards we have adopted in determining the validity of employee covenants not to compete after termination of employment. Although enforcement of such a covenant is somewhat restricted because of countervailing policy considerations, we generally enforce an employee non-competition covenant as reasonable if it "simply protects the legitimate interests of the employer imposes no undue hardship on the employee, and is not injurious to the public." Solari Indus. v. Malady, 55 N.J. 571, 576, 264 A.2d 53 (1970). We also held in *Solari* that if such a covenant is found to be overbroad, it may be partially enforced to the extent reasonable under the circumstances. That approach to the enforcement of restrictive covenants in deeds offers a mechanism for recognizing and balancing the legitimate concerns of the grantor, the successors in interest, and the public.

[M]any past illogical and contorted applications of the "touch and concern" rules have resulted because courts have been pressed to twist the rules of "touch and concern" in order to achieve a result that comports with public policy and a free market. Most jurisdictions acknowledge the reasonableness factors that affect enforcement of a covenant concerning successors-in-interest, instead of engaging in the subterfuge of twisting the touch and concern test to meet the required result. New Jersey should not remain part of the small minority of States that cling to an anachronistic rule of law.

There is insufficient evidence in this record to determine whether the covenant is reasonable. Nevertheless, we think it instructive to comment briefly on the application of the "reasonableness" factors to this covenant. We consider first the intent of the parties when the covenant was executed. It is undisputed that when plaintiff conveyed the property to Katz, it intended that the George Street store would not be used as a supermarket or grocery store for a period of forty years to protect his existing business at the Elizabeth Street store from competition. Plaintiff alleges that the purchase price negotiated between it and Katz took into account the value of the restrictive covenant and that Katz paid less for the property because of the restriction. There is no evidence, however, of the purchase price. It is also undisputed that the covenant was expressly set forth in a recorded deed, that the Authority took title to the premises with actual notice of the restrictive covenant, and, indeed, that all the defendants, including C–Town, had actual notice of the covenant. The parties do not specifically contest the reasonableness of either the duration or area of the covenant. Aspects of the "touch and concern" test also remain useful in evaluating the reasonableness of a covenant, insofar as it aids the courts in differentiating between promises that were intended to bind only the individual parties to a land conveyance and promises affecting the use and value of the land that was intended to be passed on to subsequent parties. Covenants not to compete typically do touch and concern the land. In noncompetition cases, the "burden" factor of the "touch and concern" test is easily satisfied regardless of the definition chosen because the covenant restricts the actual use of the land. The Appellate Division properly concluded that the George Street store was burdened. However, we disagree with the Appellate Division's conclusion that in view of the covenant's speculative impact, the covenant did not provide a sufficient "benefit" to the Elizabeth Street property because it burdened only a small portion (George Street store) of the "market circle" (less than one-half acre in a market circle of 2000 acres). The size of the burdened property relative to the market area is not a probative measure of whether the Elizabeth store was benefitted. Presumably, the use of the Elizabeth Street store as a supermarket would be enhanced if competition were lessened in its market area. If plaintiff's allegations that the profits of the Elizabeth Street store increased after the sale of the George Street store are true, this would be evidence that a benefit was "conveyed" on the Elizabeth Street store. Likewise, information that the area was so densely populated, that the George Street property was the only unique property available for a supermarket, would show that the Elizabeth Street store property was benefitted by the covenant. In this connection the C–Town executive in his deposition noted that the George Street store location "businesswise was promising because there's no other store in town." Such evidence, however, also should be considered in determining the "reasonableness" of the area covered by the covenant and whether the covenant unduly restrained trade.

Defendants' primary contention is that due to the circumstances of the neighborhood and more particularly the circumstances of the people of the neighborhood, plaintiff's covenant interferes with the public's interest. Whether that claim is essentially that the community has changed since the covenant was enacted or that the circumstances were such that when the covenant was enacted, it interfered with the public interest, we are unable to ascertain from the record. "Public interest" and "changed circumstances" arguments are extremely fact-sensitive. The only evidence that addresses those issues, the three affidavits of Mr. Keefe, Mr. Nero and Ms. Scott, are insufficient to support any finding with respect to those arguments.

The fact-sensitive nature of a "reasonableness" analysis make resolution of this dispute through summary judgment inappropriate. We therefore remand the case to the trial court for a thorough analysis of the "reasonableness" factors delineated herein. The trial court must first determine whether the covenant was reasonable at the time it was enacted. If it was reasonable then, but now adversely affects commercial development and the public welfare of the people of New Brunswick, the trial court may consider whether allowing damages for breach of the covenant is an appropriate remedy. C–Town could then continue to operate but Davidson would get damages for the value of his covenant. On the limited record before us, however, it is impossible to make a determination concerning either reasonableness of the covenant or whether damages, injunctive relief, or any relief is appropriate.

POLLOCK, J., concurring.

* * *

[The] majority's reasonableness test introduces unnecessary uncertainty in the analysis of covenants running with the land. As troublesome as uncertainty is in other areas of the law, it is particularly vexatious in the law of real property. The need for certainty in conveyancing, like that in estate planning, is necessary for people to structure their affairs. Covenants that run with the land can affect the value of real property not only at the time of sale, but for many years thereafter. Consequently, vendors and purchasers, as well as their successors, need to know whether a covenant will run with the land. The majority acknowledges that noncompetition covenants play a positive role in commercial development. Notwithstanding that acknowledgement, the majority's reasonableness test generates confusion that threatens the ability of commercial parties and their lawyers to determine the validity of such covenants. This, in turn, impairs the utility of noncompetition covenants in real estate transactions. As between the vendor and purchaser, a noncompetition covenant generally should be treated as valid if it is reasonable in scope and duration, Irving Inv. Corp. v. Gordon, 3 N.J. 217, 221, 69 A.2d 725 (1949), and neither an unreasonable restraint on trade nor otherwise contrary to public policy. A covenant would contravene public policy if, for example, its purpose were to secure a monopoly, or to carry out an illegal object, such as invidious discrimination. Applying those principles to the validity of the agreement between Davidson and Katz, I find this covenant enforceable against defendants. The majority acknowledges that "[t]he parties do not specifically contest the reasonableness of either the duration or the area of the covenant." I agree. The covenant is limited to one parcel, the George Street property. Defendants do not assert that Davidson has restricted or even owns other property in New Brunswick. Furthermore, they do not allege that other property is not available for a supermarket. In brief, the Authority has not alleged that at the time of the sale from Davidson to Katz, or even at present, the George Street property was the only possible site in New Brunswick for a supermarket. Consequently, the covenant may not be construed to give rise to a monopoly. In all of New Brunswick it restricts a solitary one-half acre tract from use for a single purpose. * * *

Nor does anything indicate that the forty-year length of the restriction between Davidson and Katz is unreasonable in time. * * * Nothing in the record supports the conclusion that when made or at present the subject covenant was an unreasonable restraint on trade or otherwise contrary to public policy. * * *

For me the critical issue is whether the appropriate remedy for enforcing the covenant is damages or an injunction. * * * I would rely on the rule that a court should not grant an equitable remedy when damages are adequate. Here, moreover, the Authority holds a trump card not available to all other property owners burdened by restrictive covenants— the power to condemn. By recourse to that power, the Authority can vitiate the injunction by condemning the covenant and compensating Davidson for its lost benefit. * * *

NOTES AND QUESTIONS

1. The touch and concern requirement has long been criticized for being too indeterminate. Did the list of factors enumerated by the *Davidson Brothers* court increase or decrease the amount of indeterminacy in the law of servitudes? See, BP Products North America, Inc. v. Top Speed Gas, LLC, 2008 WL 4724006, at *4 (D.N.J., 2008) (discussing restrictive covenant limiting the sales of petroleum products to Plaintiff's brand for a ten year period and rejecting "[r]igid adherence to the 'touch and concern' test as a means of determining the enforceability of a restrictive covenant....") The court applied the Davidson factors and upheld the restrictive covenant.

2. What good does it do a grocery store owner who owns property two miles from his store to impose a noncompetition covenant upon the second property? There could be 100 other parcels within the same radius on which

others might be able to build a second grocery store. Is the fact that the plaintiffs had already operated a second grocery store on the burdened land of any significance? Doesn't the dissent make a good point?

3.   What is the purpose of the "touch and concern" requirement? At the very least perhaps, it serves as a guarantee that the original parties *really did intend* successors in interest to be bound and benefitted by the obligations. This is because it is reasonable to expect that a promise not to build a commercial building, or to pay an annual fee for street and park maintenance, would be passed on to successors. It is not reasonable, however, to expect a doctor's promise to perform an annual check-up to be passed on to an accountant who later buys the same land.

If this is the rationale for the "touch and concern" requirement, however, courts have not always used it in deciding whether the requirement was met. Both covenants not to compete and covenants to pay money were widely held not to meet the requirement, even though we can infer that the original parties generally expected the obligations to be passed on to successors in interest.

A somewhat broader, more interventionist view, is that the "touch and concern" requirement is not an attempt to reconstruct the parties' reasonable intent at all. Rather, it is a substantive requirement that is imposed in order that land titles may be encumbered by only a limited variety of obligations. After all, today we think of servitudes as private "land use" devices. The state may want to insist that, no matter what the parties intended, certain promises unrelated to land use should not be permitted to become clogs on title. For an argument supporting this view of the "touch and concern" requirement, see Reichman, Toward a Unified Concept of Servitudes, 55 S.Cal.L.Rev. 1177, 1232–33 (1982); for a critique, see Epstein, Notice and Freedom of Contract in the Law of Servitudes, 55 S.Cal.L.Rev. 1353, 1358–60 (1982). For a decision analyzing "touch and concern" this way, see Cypress Gardens, Ltd. v. Platt, 124 N.M. 472, 952 P.2d 467, 470 (App.1997):

> The requirement that running covenants touch and concern the land is the only one which focuses on an objective analysis of the contents of the covenant itself rather than the intentions of and relationships between the parties.

The court then concluded that a covenant requiring any mobile home to be approved by the developer before it could be placed on a lot met the requirement.

4.   Recall the Restatement's position regarding touch and concern. It abolishes touch and concern in favor of public policy considerations. Servitudes will be invalidated if they unreasonably restrain alienation, unduly restrain trade, are deemed unconscionable, or do not have a rational justification. The Restatement (Third) Property: Servitudes § 3.2 (2000).

5.   Consider the following conveyance: Grantor for good and valuable consideration paid by X and Y, conveys Blackacre to X for as long as he desires to live there and then to Y upon these conditions: [1] if X attempts to use Blackacre for other than residential purposes, without Y's express prior written consent it shall be forfeited to Y; [2] that any attempt by X to transfer

Blackacre by any means including sale, lease, assignment or otherwise without Y's express prior written consent shall be null and void; and [3] X shall, before the 6th day of each month, e-mail Y photographs of Blackacre for the purpose of insuring that Blackacre is not being wasted. How should this conveyance be construed? Is it [1] a defeasible life estate followed by an interest in a 3rd party (present estate = defeasible life estate; future interest = executory interest); or is it [2] a life estate that is subject to a covenant (present estate = life estate; future interest = vested remainder)? See Chapter 4. Why should it matter? If you select the second option, is the covenant "reasonable" based upon the 8 factors discussed in the case? Judge Pollock mentions the power of the Authority to condemn the covenant, thereby terminating it and relieving the property of the restriction. Condemnation is discussed in Chapter 10. It refers to the power of government to take private property by exercising the power of eminent domain and in exchange for the payment to the property owner of just compensation. If this grant is construed as a defeasible life estate followed by an executory interest, who should receive the condemnation award, X? Y? both?

Direct Restraints on Alienation: Restraints on alienation can be direct or indirect. There are three types of direct restraints on alienation: disabling restraints, forfeiture restraints and promissory restraints. See, e.g. Alby v. Banc One Financial, 156 Wash.2d 367, 128 P.3d 81 (2006). Disabling restraints make void any attempt to alienate the property that is the subject of the grant. For example O conveys Blackacre "to X but any attempt by X to convey the property to someone not of the Caucasian race shall be invalid." See, e.g., Shelley v. Kraemer, 334 U.S. 1 (1948), Chapter 12. Forfeiture restraints are conditions that provide that the fee will terminate if there is an attempt to alienate the fee. For example O conveys Blackacre "to X but if X attempts to alienate Blackacre, then Blackacre [shall go to Y or shall revert to O or O shall have a right to enter and take Blackacre]." Lastly, promissory restraints are simply promises by the grantee not to alienate the fee and are enforceable under contract principles if breached. So, O conveys Blackacre "to Y and Y promises not to alienate Blackacre."

Direct restraints on the alienation of a fee simple absolute estate are generally void and unenforceable. There is an exception though for provisions that impose restrictions on the ability of concurrent owners to partition land. Chapter 5 discusses concurrent ownership. Restraints on alienation that are justified by the parties' reasonable expectations and that are reasonable in their terms are valid. If a court finds that a restraint is, in fact, unreasonable, such a finding will not make the entire conveyance void. Rather, the grantee will take the land free of the unreasonable condition.

Jurisdictions are split on the question of whether disabling restraints on the ability to alienate a life estate are enforceable. Many jurisdictions enforce these types of restrictions. In some jurisdictions, forfeiture restraints on life estates are enforceable.

The land sale contract presents another situation in which one must distinguish between restraints on the alienation of a fee simple absolute and restraints on the alienation of the purchaser's interest under the land sale contract during the executory period of the contract. The land sale contract is discussed in Chapter 14.

What about rights of first refusal and purchase options? Generally, courts consider the reasonableness of the duration and price terms and whether there is a legitimate purpose to be achieved other than merely creating a restraint on alienation. "An option to purchase land that is indefinite in length and provides for purchase at a fixed or capped price may be deemed unenforceable as an impermissible restraint on alienation. Similarly, the court may decline to enforce an agreement styled as a right of first refusal that provides for later purchase rights at a fixed amount far below market value. On the other hand, a right of first refusal that merely gives a party the right to purchase land at the price of another bona fide offer is likely to be enforceable." Patton and Palomar on Land Titles § 209 (3d ed. 2011).

Use restraints, including those that provide for the defeasance of the fee upon breach of the restraint, often are indirect restraints on alienability of the fee simple absolute. Consider the following grant: O conveys to X "so long as the property is used as a single-family vacation residence." By limiting the permissible uses of the fee simple absolute, such restrictions can reduce the market for the land and therefore the fair market value. Nevertheless, use restrictions typically are not deemed to be impermissible restraints on alienation.

Finally, courts have enforced prohibitions on leasing condominiums, finding them to be reasonable restraints. See, e.g., Kroop v. The Caravelle Condominium, Inc., 323 So. 2d 307 (1975); Apple II Condominium Assoc. v. Worth Bank and Trust Co., 277 Ill. App. 3d 345, 350 (1995) (declining "to make a blanket pronouncement approving or condemning condominium leasing restrictions"); Patton and Palomar on Land Titles § 209 (3d ed. 2011). Common interest communities are discussed in Chapter 13. But, courts have also held that restrictions on land ownership within a development that are too limited in terms of the permissible possible purchasers are so burdensome as to be unreasonable and unenforceable. See, e.g., Seagate Condominium Ass'n, Inc. v. Duffy, 330 So. 2d 484, 485 (1976) (stating that the validity of restraints on alienation and use will be judged based upon their reasonableness, that is, whether the "leasing restriction is reasonable given the context in which it was promulgated, i.e., the condominium living arrangement").

The Restatement (Third) of Property: Servitudes (2000) states the following regarding servitudes that pose direct and indirect restraints on alienation:

Section 3.4.   Direct Restraints on Alienation

> A servitude that imposes a direct restraint on alienation of the burdened estate is invalid if the restraint is unreasonable.

Reasonableness is determined by weighing the utility of the restraint against the injurious consequences of enforcing the restraint.

Section 3.5.   Indirect Restraints on Alienation and Irrational Servitudes

    (1) An otherwise valid servitude is valid even if it indirectly restrains alienation by limiting the use that can be made of property, by reducing the amount realizable by the owner on sale or other transfer of the property, or by otherwise reducing the value of the property.

    (2) A servitude that lacks a rational justification is invalid.

NEPONSIT PROPERTY OWNERS' ASS'N v. EMIGRANT INDUSTRIAL SAV. BANK

Court of Appeals of New York (1938).
278 N.Y. 248, 15 N.E.2d 793.

LEHMAN, JUDGE.

The plaintiff, as assignee of Neponsit Realty Company, has brought this action to foreclose a lien upon land which the defendant owns. The lien, it is alleged, arises from a covenant, condition or charge contained in a deed of conveyance of the land from Neponsit Realty Company to a predecessor in title of the defendant. The defendant purchased the land at a judicial sale. The referee's deed to the defendant and every deed in the defendant's chain of title since the conveyance of the land by Neponsit Realty Company purports to convey the property subject to the covenant, condition or charge contained in the original deed.

* * *

It appears that in January, 1911, Neponsit Realty Company, as owner of a tract of land in Queens county, caused to be filed in the office of the clerk of the county a map of the land. The tract was developed for a strictly residential community, and Neponsit Realty Company conveyed lots in the tract to purchasers, describing such lots by reference to the filed map and to roads and streets shown thereon. In 1917, Neponsit Realty Company conveyed the land now owned by the defendant to Robert Oldner Deyer and his wife by deed which contained the covenant upon which the plaintiff's cause of action is based.

That covenant provides:

"And the party of the second part for the party of the second part and the heirs, successors and assigns of the party of the second part further covenants that the property conveyed by this deed shall be subject to an annual charge in such an amount as will be fixed by the party of the first part, its successors and assigns, not, however exceeding in any year the sum of four ($4.00) Dollars per lot 20x100 feet. The assigns of the party of the first part may include a Property Owners' Association which may hereafter be organized for the purposes referred to in this paragraph, and in case such association is organized the sums in this paragraph provided for shall be payable to such association. The party of the second part for the party of the second part and the heirs, successors and assigns of the party of the second part covenants that they will pay this charge to the party of the first part, its successors and assigns on the first day of May in each and every year, and further covenants that said charge shall on said date in each year become a lien on the land and shall continue to be such lien until fully paid. Such charge shall be payable to the party of the first part or its successors or assigns, and shall be devoted to the maintenance of the roads, paths, parks, beach, sewers and such other public purposes as shall from time to time be determined by the party of the first part, its successors or assigns. And the party of the second part by the acceptance of this deed hereby expressly vests in the party of the first part, its successors and assigns, the right and power to bring all actions against the owner of the premises hereby conveyed or any part thereof for the collection of such charge and to enforce the aforesaid lien therefor.

"These covenants shall run with the land and shall be construed as real covenants running with the land until January 31st, 1940, when they shall cease and determine."

Every subsequent deed of conveyance of the property in the defendant's chain of title, including the deed from the referee to the defendant, contained, as we have said, a provision that they were made subject to covenants and restrictions of former deeds of record.

* * * The age-old essentials of a real covenant, aside from the form of the covenant, may be summarily formulated as follows: (1) It must appear that grantor and grantee intended that the covenant should run with the land; (2) it must appear that the covenant is one "touching" or "concerning" the land with which it runs; (3) it must appear that there is "privity of estate" between the promisee or party claiming the benefit of the covenant and the right to enforce it, and the promisor or party who rests under the burden of the covenant. Clark on Covenants and Interests Running with Land, p. 74.

* * *

Looking at the problem presented in this case from the same point of view and stressing the intent and substantial effect of the covenant rather than its form, it seems clear that the covenant may properly be said to touch and concern the land of the defendant and its burden should run with the land. True, it calls for payment of a sum of money to be expended for "public purposes" upon land other than the land conveyed by Neponsit Realty Company to plaintiff's predecessor in title. By that conveyance the grantee, however, obtained not only title to particular lots, but an easement or right of common enjoyment with other property owners in roads, beaches, public parks or spaces and improvements in the same tract. For full enjoyment in common by the defendant and other property owners of these easements or rights, the roads and public places must be maintained. In order that the burden of maintaining public improvements should rest upon the land benefitted by the improvements, the grantor exacted from the grantee of the land with its appurtenant easement or right of enjoyment a covenant that the burden of paying the cost should be inseparably attached to the land which enjoys the benefit. It is plain that any distinction or definition which would exclude such a covenant from the classification of covenants which "touch" or "concern" the land would be based on form and not on substance.

Another difficulty remains. Though between the grantor and the grantee there was privity of estate, the covenant provides that its benefit shall run to the assigns of the grantor who "may include a Property Owners' Association which may hereafter be organized for the purposes referred to in this paragraph." The plaintiff has been organized to receive the sums payable by the property owners and to expend them for the benefit of such owners. Various definitions have been formulated of "privity of estate" in connection with covenants that run with the land, but none of such definitions seems to cover the relationship between the plaintiff and the defendant in this case. The plaintiff has not succeeded to the ownership of any property of the grantor. It does not appear that it ever had title to the streets or public places upon which charges which are payable to it must be expended. It does not appear that it owns any other property in the residential tract to which any easement or right of enjoyment in such property is appurtenant. It is created solely to act as the assignee of the benefit of the covenant, and it has no interest of its own in the enforcement of the covenant.

The arguments that under such circumstances the plaintiff has no right of action to enforce a covenant running with the land are all based upon a distinction between the corporate property owners association and the property owners for whose benefit the association has been formed. If that distinction may be ignored, then the basis of the arguments is destroyed. How far privity of estate in technical form is necessary to enforce in equity a restrictive covenant upon the use of land, presents an interesting question. Enforcement of such covenants rests upon equitable principles (Tulk v. Moxhay, 2 Phillips, 774; Trustees of Columbia College v. Lynch, 70 N.Y. 440, 26 Am.Rep. 615), and at times, at least, the violation "of the restrictive covenant may be restrained at the suit of one who owns property or for whose benefit the restriction was established, irrespective of whether there were privity either of estate or of contract between the parties, or whether an action at law were maintainable." Chesebro v. Moers, 233 N.Y. 75, 80, 134 N.E. 842, 843, 21 A.L.R. 1270. The covenant in this case does not fall exactly within any classification of "restrictive" covenants, which have been enforced in this State (Cf. Korn v. Campbell, 192 N.Y. 490, 85 N.E. 687, 37 L.R.A.N.S., 1, 127 Am.St.Rep. 925), and no right to enforce even a restrictive covenant has been sustained in this State where the plaintiff did not own property which would benefit by such enforcement so that some of the elements of an equitable servitude are present. * * * We do not attempt to ... formulate a definite rule as to when, or even whether, covenants in a deed will be enforced, upon equitable principles, against subsequent purchasers with notice, at the suit of a party without privity of contract or estate. * * * There is no need to resort to such a rule if the courts may look behind the corporate form of the plaintiff.

The corporate plaintiff has been formed as a convenient instrument by which the property owners may advance their common interests. We do not ignore the corporate form when we recognize that the Neponsit Property Owners' Association, Inc., is acting as the agent or representative of the Neponsit property owners. As we have said in another case: when Neponsit Property Owners' Association, Inc., "was formed, the property owners were expected to, and have looked to that organization as the medium through which enjoyment of their common right might be preserved equally for all." Matter of City of New York, Public Beach, Borough of Queens, 269 N.Y. 64, 75, 199 N.E. 5, 9. Under the conditions thus presented we said: "It may be difficult, or even impossible, to classify into recognized categories the nature of the interest of the membership corporation and its members in the land. The corporate entity cannot be disregarded, nor can the separate interests of the members of the corporation" (page 73, 199 N.E. page 8). Only blind adherence to an ancient formula devised to meet entirely different conditions could constrain the court to hold that a corporation formed as a medium for the enjoyment of common rights of property owners owns no property which would benefit by enforcement of common rights and has no cause of action in equity to enforce the covenant upon which such common rights depend. Every reason which in other circumstances may justify the ancient formula may be urged in support of the conclusion that the formula should not be applied in this case. In substance if not in form the covenant is a restrictive covenant which touches and concerns the defendant's land, and in substance, if not in form, there is privity of estate between the plaintiff and the defendant.

* * *

The order [denying the defendant's motion for judgment] is affirmed.

NOTE

A landmark American case in the development of the law of equitable servitudes is Trustees of Columbia College v. Lynch, 70 N.Y. 440, 446–453 (1877), noted in *Neponsit*. The decision involved an agreement between adjacent landowners not to permit their lands to be used for commercial purposes. The agreement was recorded and expressly stated that it was binding upon successors in interest. The agreement itself, however, was a simple contract; so there was no privity of estate between the parties. The court held that the agreement could be enforced in equity against a successor in interest to one of the promisors, reasoning as follows:

It is strenuously urged, in behalf of the defendants and respondents, that there was no privity of estate between the mutual covenantors and covenantees, in respect of the premises owned by them respectively, and which were the subjects of the covenants and agreements, and that the covenants did not therefore run with the lands, binding the grantees, and subjecting them to a personal liability thereon. This may be conceded for all the purposes of this action. It is of no importance whether an action at law could be maintained against the grantees of Beers, as upon a covenant running with the land and binding them. Whether it was a covenant running with the land or a collateral covenant, or a covenant in gross, or whether an action at law could be sustained upon it, is not material as affecting the jurisdiction of a court of equity, or the right of the owners of the dominant tenement to relief upon a disturbance of the easements.

* * * An owner may subject his lands to any servitude, and transmit them to others charged with the same; and one taking title to lands, with notice of any equity attached thereto, or any outstanding right or claim affecting the title or the use and enjoyment of the lands, takes subject to such equities, and such right or claim, and stands, in the place of his grantor, bound to do or forbear to do whatever he would have been bound to do or forbear to do. * * *

Here each successive grantee, from Beers, the covenantor, down to and including the defendant Lynch, the present owner, not only had notice of the covenant, and all equities growing out of the same, but took their title in terms subject to it, and impliedly agreeing to observe it. * * * There is no equity or reason for making a servitude of the character of that claimed by the plaintiffs in the lands of the defendant, an exception to the general rule which charges lands in the hands of a purchaser with notice with all existing equities, easements, and servitudes.

* * *

§ 8.4.3 IMPLIED BURDENS

MID–STATE EQUIPMENT CO., INC. v. BELL

Supreme Court of Virginia (1976).
217 Va. 133, 225 S.E.2d 877.

COMPTON, JUSTICE.

We consider in this appeal the equitable doctrine of implied restrictive covenants and its bearing upon the rights of property owners in a residential subdivision. Specifically, the inquiry is whether a restriction for residential use applies to a parcel which appellant Mid–State Equipment Company, Inc., the defendant below, is using for commercial purposes.

The property in controversy, containing about 1.5 acres, is a rectangular parcel of land comprised of two triangular-shaped lots located at the intersection of Waterlick Road and State Route No. 835 (Jefferson Manor Drive) in Campbell County. These lots are designated "James D. & Mary R. Eubank" and "R.N. Clemmons" on the attached sketch, which is a composite of portions of three plat exhibits.

In September 1973 plaintiffs-appellees, property owners in Jefferson Manor, a residential subdivision in Campbell County, filed a bill of complaint seeking to enjoin Mid–State, a corporation engaged in an equipment rental and sale business, from violating certain restrictions, which plaintiffs contended constituted implied reciprocal negative easements or equitable servitudes applicable to Mid–State's property. The plaintiffs sought an order restraining Mid–State from utilizing the property in question "for any other than residential purposes."

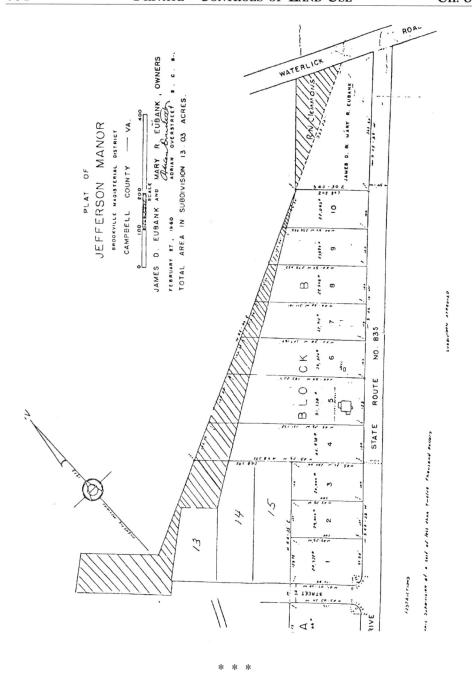

* * *

The property in question is part of a tract of 85 acres purchased in 1945 by James D. Eubank and Mary R. Eubank, his wife. On February 27, 1960 Adrian Overstreet, a certified land surveyor, prepared at the Eubanks'' request a plat (hereinafter Overstreet Plat) for Jefferson Manor Subdivision. A part of the Overstreet Plat is the basis for the foregoing composite sketch. Not shown on the sketch but comprising the remainder of the Overstreet Plat are ... a "vicinity" map, a metes and bounds "Description," and "Restrictions" as follows:

"1. No dwelling shall be erected on any lot in this Subdivision at a cost of less than Twelve Thousand Dollars ($12,000.00) based on 1960 building cost.

"2. No livestock (or poultry) shall be kept on any lot in this Subdivision.

"3. The building set-back line shall be 50' from the road (or street) on which said building fronts and not less than 30' from any side street.

"4. No building shall be erected within 10' of any property line.

"5. *All lots in this Subdivision are restricted to residential use only, house trailers excluded.*" (emphasis supplied).

* * *

The metes and bounds "Description" found on the lower left-hand corner of the Overstreet Plat includes only the numbered lots. * * *

The next significant event of record occurred in 1966 when by deed dated October 6, 1966 and recorded eight days later, the Eubanks conveyed the property in question, that is, the almost rectangular parcel at the northwest corner of Waterlick Road and Route 835, to James R. Hicks and wife.

* * *

The Hickses continued to reside on the disputed property until 1973. In February of that year Hicks authorized Joseph E. Champe, a real estate salesman with Ted Sims Realty of Lynchburg, to seek a buyer for the parcel. During April and June of 1973 the property was advertised for sale in the local newspapers as commercial property. In addition, a "billboard sign" four feet high and eight feet long was placed on the property in an elevated position stating "Ted Sims—Sale—Real Estate—845–2383."

On June 10, 1973 a contract for sale of the property for $20,500 was executed by the Hickses and the president of Mid–State, Robert E. Bankert. The contract provided: "Offer subject to confirmation of commercial zoning and business financing...." Champe testified that he sold the parcel as commercial property after making an independent investigation of the land records and satisfying himself that a commercial use of the property was not prohibited by the restrictions of record. Champe also stated that the frame dwelling on the premises was then in "dilapidated condition" and that the parcel was worth only about $15,000 as residential property.

By deed dated July 3, 1973, drawn on stationery of Mid–State's attorney, and recorded July 9, 1973, the Hickses conveyed the subject property to Mid–State. The deed contained the following provision:

"This land is specifically not subject to subdivision restrictions of record of Jefferson Manor."

* * * Bankert, Mid–State's sole stockholder, testified he instructed Champe "to check the property close, because there were houses bumping up on both sides, and I didn't want any clouds on it". By this time residential subdivisions similar to Jefferson Manor with homes valued from $18,000 to $40,000 had been and were being developed to the north of Jefferson Manor (White Pine Acres, which was platted for Clemmons in 1962), to the east of Jefferson Manor across Waterlick Road (Nottingham Forrest platted in 1971); and to the south of Jefferson Manor across Route 835 adjacent to Waterlick Road (Westwood Manor surveyed in 1964). Bankert stated he agreed to purchase after Champe and Mid–State's attorney reported the parcel was not subject to the residential restrictions.

Mid–State occupied the premises and later made extensive improvements to the dwelling, at a cost of about $14,000, to convert it to an office for the sale and rental of solid waste equipment. The equipment consists of refuse bodies and new "health containers" which are stored on the lot pending delivery to customers. Also maintained on the premises are Mid–State's tractor and trailer, its service truck, and a "boom" for lifting the containers.

Shortly after Mid–State commenced its use of the property, a number of the plaintiffs and other homeowners in the area petitioned the county board of supervisors objecting to the establishment of the "garbage container storage site". Campbell County had no zoning ordinance and the board took no action on the petition. After an effort of several homeowners to buy the property from Mid–State failed, this suit was filed.

* * *

The doctrine of restrictive covenants in equity, distinct from the common law doctrine of covenants running with the land, establishes rights and obligations known as equitable easements and equitable servitudes.... The doctrine is that "when, on a transfer of land, there is a covenant or even an informal contract or understanding that certain restrictions in the use of the land conveyed shall be observed, the restrictions will be enforced by equity, at the suit of the party or parties intended to be benefitted thereby, against any subsequent owner of the land except a purchaser for value without notice of the agreement. The principal purposes of such agreements are to regulate the style and costs of buildings to be erected on a tract that is being sold in parcels for building lots, to restrict their location to certain distances from the street, and to prevent buildings in a locality from being put up or used for any other than residential purposes." The equity which is enforced prevents a third person, who has actual or constructive notice, from violating the equitable rights of another. 148 Va. at 39, 138 S.E. at 549.

The intent of the parties, especially that of the common grantor, determines the existence of the right. In ascertaining the parties' intention, we examine the words used in the restriction, the plats, the deeds, such surrounding circumstances as the parties are presumed to have considered when their minds met, the purpose to be achieved by the covenant, and the use of the property, keeping in mind that such a restriction is not merely for the grantor's benefit but that it assures purchasers that property will be devoted in a specified manner to the intended purpose.

* * *

And where a common grantor develops land for sale in lots and pursues a course of conduct which indicates an intention to execute a general scheme or plan of improvement for the benefit of himself and the purchasers of the various lots, and by numerous conveyances incorporates in the deeds substantially uniform restrictions, conditions and covenants against the use of the property, the grantees acquire by implication the equitable right, sometimes referred to as an implied reciprocal negative easement, to enforce similar restrictions against the residential lot or lots retained by the grantor or subsequently sold without the restrictions to a purchaser with actual or constructive notice of the restrictions and covenants. * * *

When we examine the words of the restriction, the plats, the deeds, and the surrounding circumstances, we think the evidence clearly establishes a course of conduct on the part of the Eubanks which indicates they intended to create and execute a general scheme of residential development of the property within Jefferson Manor for the benefit of themselves and the purchasers of the lots in the subdivision and, further, that the parcel in question was intended to be included within this plan of development, subject to the residential restriction in controversy. The general plan of residential development of the numbered lots is apparent. Indeed, Mid–State does not dispute the fact that all numbered parcels . . . were made expressly subject to the restriction for residential use either by a deed reference to the Overstreet Plat or by inclusion of the restriction in the body of the deeds. So the only real controversy in this branch of the case is whether the parcel in question was included in the plan of development, and we conclude that it was.

First, the Eubanks' home was located on the "James D. & Mary R. Eubank" parcel when the development began in 1960, and it was used for residential purposes by the Eubanks until they sold it in 1966. Second, we have the unchallenged testimony of Overstreet, the surveyor, that he was instructed by Eubank to "leave out" of the platted area sufficient land for two residential lots. * * * It is apparent from this omission of numbered lots 11 and 12 that the "James D. & Mary R. Eubank" parcel was intended to be residential lots 11 and 12. The conclusion is strengthened when we blend the foregoing facts with other circumstances, which standing alone may not be sufficient to establish intent. For example, the property is shown on the Overstreet "Plat of Jefferson Manor" as an unreserved delineated lot; the residential restriction on the face of the plat refers to "[a]ll lots in this subdivision", not all numbered lots; and when the 1966 conveyance to the Hickses took place, . . . the deed made specific reference to the Overstreet Plat containing the restriction. Accordingly the foregoing evidence considered as a whole establishes the equitable right, even though the subject property was not included within the metes and bounds description or within the 13.03–acre reference on the Overstreet Plat.

And we also think Mid–State, through its president and attorney, had notice of the established equitable right. Even if we disregard the effect of the matters of record to which we have just adverted, a view of the property from the ground would have revealed the uniform residential development surrounding the subject parcel and would have been sufficient to put a purchaser on inquiry as to whether there was a general plan to which the restriction applied. Sanborn v. McLean, 233 Mich. 227, 232–33, 206 N.W. 496, 498 (1925); Annot. 4 A.L.R.2d 1364, 1371. Indeed, Bankert ordered a close "check" of the property because "there were houses bumping up on both sides", and the fact that the realtor and Mid–State's attorney concluded the property was not subject to the residential restriction does not establish lack of notice.

We have fully considered Mid–State's other assignments of error dealing with laches (failure of plaintiffs to object until after purchase even though they were placed on notice of pending sale by the newspaper and "billboard" ads); questions of evidence; and a constitutional issue. The constitutional question was not raised below, so we will not notice it on appeal, and we find no merit in the other errors assigned.

For these reasons, the final decree of the trial court is

Affirmed.

Cochran, J., dissenting.

I do not agree that an implied reciprocal negative easement has been established in this case. The property in question was not included in the "Description" found on the Overstreet Plat of Jefferson Manor Subdivision. Therefore, we are not dealing with the omission of restrictive covenants from a deed to a numbered lot in this subdivision, where the intent to apply such covenants to all numbered lots may be implied. The subdivider reserved an unnumbered lot adjoining the subdivision, and there is at least as strong an implication that there was a deliberate exclusion of this property from subdivision restrictions as that there was an intent to make the property subject to the restrictions.

Nor do I find sufficient evidence of notice. A title examiner could no more determine, from the land records, the probability of application of restrictive easements to this property than he could determine title by adverse possession. To hold that implied reciprocal negative easements apply to the subject property is to impose an intolerable burden on the title examiner which, in my view, cannot be justified.

CASH v. GRANITE SPRINGS RETREAT ASS'N, INC.,

Supreme Court of Wyoming (2011).
248 P.3d 614.

KITE, CHIEF JUSTICE.

The district court ruled subdivision covenants recorded before the developer acquired legal title to the property were enforceable as equitable servitudes. * * *

We affirm.

* * *

FACTS

The underlying facts of this case are undisputed. Lorenz Ranch, Inc. owned property off Happy Jack Road, near Curt Gowdy State Park in Laramie County. In the early 1970s, Abraham Lorenz and Deward H. Miller entered into a "handshake" agreement for Mr. Miller to purchase the property with the intention of subdividing it. Because of financing issues, the property was conveyed in two parcels at different times. The first parcel, the property south of Happy Jack Road, was conveyed by warranty deed on August 14, 1972. That property became Granite Springs Retreat, First Filing, and included lots one through eight. The rest of the property, which was north of Happy Jack Road and became Granite Springs Retreat, Second Filing, was conveyed to Mr. Miller in March 1977.

After purchasing the first parcel, Mr. Miller filed a request with Laramie County for a preliminary plat of the Granite Springs Subdivision. Mr. Miller subsequently recorded a preliminary plat dated August 1, 1975, which included the land in both filings. An application for subdivision of land was filed with Laramie County on August 4, 1975, and indicated the subdivision would be known as the Granite Springs Retreat and would include sixty lots. The project scope was also confirmed in an environmental impact report commissioned by Mr. Miller. That report specifically referred to covenants that "would be attached to all tracts to regulate the usage and development of the land."

On October 1, 1976, Mr. Miller filed a plat for Granite Springs Retreat, First Filing. A few days later, on October 4, 1976, Mr. Miller filed a Declaration of Protective Covenants for the Granite Spring Retreat at Happy Jack Road and Curt Gowdy State Park. The declaration did not include a legal description, but referred to the affected property as the Granite Springs Retreat. Mr. Miller obtained legal title to the property included in the second filing approximately five months after he filed the declaration of covenants. He filed the plat for the Granite Springs Retreat, Second Filing, on August 11, 1977.

In a deed recorded September 15, 1977, Mr. Miller conveyed the tracts within the Granite Springs Retreat, both filings, to Happy Jack Stable & Lounge, Inc., a corporation he and Mr. Lorenz formed. On February 23,

1978, Mr. Miller filed an Amended Declaration of Protective Covenants. The amended covenants were identical to the original covenants except that they specifically allowed tracts four and five to be used for commercial purposes. Mr. Miller signed the amended covenants on behalf of the Granite Springs Retreat, but did not, in any way, acknowledge that the Happy Jack Stable & Lounge, Inc. held legal title to the property. On July 29, 1983, Mr. Miller filed an Affidavit of Intention which was recorded against all of the Granite Springs Retreat properties in both filings and stated that he intended the covenants to apply to both filings. Also in 1983, Mr. Miller convened a meeting of the owners of the lots to form a homeowner's association, as contemplated by the covenants. The lot owners agreed to form the Granite Springs Retreat Association (GSRA), for the purposes of administering the common areas and working with the Architectural Control Committee (ACC). The GSRA thereafter filed articles of incorporation with the Wyoming Secretary of State and adopted bylaws.

In 1999, the district court declared the amended covenants invalid in *Millheiser v. Wallace,* Dist. Ct. No. 148–238, because they were signed by Mr. Miller after he had already conveyed the property to Happy Jack Stable & Lounge, Inc. * * *

In *Granite Springs Retreat Association, Inc., v. Manning,* 2006 WY 60, 133 P.3d 1005 (Wyo.2006), the GSRA brought an action against the Mannings in small claims court, seeking recovery of past due association fees. The Mannings defended by arguing the covenants did not encumber their lot in the second filing. The circuit court ruled that the second filing lots were bound by the covenants as equitable servitudes. On appeal, the district court reversed, holding the circuit court did not have subject matter jurisdiction to determine the validity of restrictive covenants. *Id.,* ¶ 3, 133 P.3d at 1009. We affirmed the district court decision. *Id.,* ¶ 13, 133 P.3d at 1012. On remand, the district court conducted a trial *de novo* and, like the circuit court, concluded that the covenants were enforceable against the Mannings' property under the doctrine of equitable servitude.

In February 2009, Cash commenced the present action against the GSRA and other lot owners. Mr. Cash, Mr. Maturi and Mr. and Mrs. McCune own property in Granite Springs Estate, Second Filing. Mr. Nelson and Ms. Hilliker own property in the first filing area. In essence, Cash sought a ruling that the covenants did not encumber Granite Springs Estates, Second Filing lots. Both sides moved for summary judgment and the district court granted summary judgment in favor of the GSRA and against Cash. It ruled that, although Mr. Miller did not have legal title to the second filing property when he recorded the original covenants, he did have an equitable interest and the covenants were enforceable as equitable servitudes against the plaintiffs because they had notice of the restrictions when they purchased their properties. Cash appealed.

* * *

DISCUSSION

Mr. Miller recorded the Declaration of Protective Covenants on October 4, 1976, but he did not receive the deed to the second filing property until March 23, 1977. It is, therefore, undisputed that Mr. Miller did not have legal title to the second filing property when he recorded the covenants. Thus, Mr. Miller could not impose restrictive covenants that would run with the land. *Streets v. JM Land & Developing Co.*, 898 P.2d 377, 379 (Wyo.1995), citing 20 Am. Jur.2d *Covenants, Conditions, and Restrictions* ¶ 33, 604 (1965). Nevertheless, the district court ruled that the second filing landowners were bound by the restrictions contained in the covenants because they were enforceable as equitable servitudes.

The district court relied on our decision in *Streets* in reaching that conclusion. In that case, the developer entered into a contract for deed to purchase property it intended to subdivide. Prior to fully performing the contract and obtaining legal title to the property, the developer recorded restrictive covenants. When the developer brought suit against Streets asserting violation of several provisions of the covenants, she claimed the covenants were not enforceable because the developer did not have legal title to the property when it recorded the covenants. *Id.* at 378–79. We held that, although the developer did not have legal title to the property when it filed the covenants and could not, therefore, impose covenants that run with the land, the restrictions were enforceable as equitable servitudes against purchasers with notice. *Id.* at 380–81.

We explained the legal principles of equitable servitudes as follows:

> The general view is that a restrictive covenant is not strictly an easement and does not run with the land in the true sense of that term. Such agreements are, however, enforceable in equity against all those who take the estate with notice of them, although they may not be, strictly speaking, real covenants so as to run with the land or of a nature to create a technical qualification of the title conveyed by the deed. The question is not whether the covenant runs with the land, but whether a party shall be permitted to use the land in a manner inconsistent with the contract entered into by his vendor, and with notice of which he purchased. It has been noted that the enforcement of restrictive covenants or equitable servitudes is based on the equitable principle of notice; that is, a person taking title to land with notice of a restriction upon it will not, in equity and good conscience, be permitted to violate such restriction.
>
> . . . .
>
> Accordingly, whether such a covenant runs with the land is material only in equity on the question of notice; if the covenant runs with the land, it binds the owner whether or not he had knowledge of it, whereas if it does not run with the land, the owner is bound only if he has taken the land with notice of it. Thus, since ordinarily such a covenant does not run with the land

and since it is not a true easement, it is enforceable against a

purchaser or assignee of the property only if he takes with notice.

One who purchases for value and without notice takes the land

free from the restrictive covenant. (Footnotes omitted, emphasis

20 AM.JUR.2D Covenants, Conditions, and Restrictions § 304, 868 (1965).

Id. at 379 (emphasis in original). See also, Bowers Welding and Hotshot,

Inc. v. Bromley, 699 P.2d 299, 303 (Wyo.1985) (stating that a purchaser

who had notice of an agreement containing restrictions is bound by those

restrictions even if they are not of record).

The Streets decision concluded:

[A] contract theory of restrictive covenants, enforceable through

the courts, makes sense in contemplation of modern land use. It

is not unusual for land, even substantial tracts, to be purchased

by a contract for deed with the intent of creating a subdivision.

Even though the purchaser under the contract for deed is an

owner of an equitable interest, that owner should not be foreclos-

ed from structuring restrictive covenants for the subdivision.

Such a limitation would not comport with logic or valid public

policy in the late Twentieth Century. The only prerequisite to

enforcement should be the notice to the subsequent owner of the

restrictions coupled with the requisite intent on the part of the

seller that those covenants would be binding upon subsequent

purchasers with notice. See Bowers Welding.

Streets, 898 P.2d at 380. Streets identified three elements required for

enforcement of subdivision covenants as equitable servitudes: 1) The

developer had an equitable interest in the property when he imposed the

covenants; 2) the developer intended that the covenants be binding upon

subsequent purchasers; and 3) the purchaser had notice of the covenants

at the time he purchased property within the subdivision. Id. at 380. See

also, Bowers Welding, 699 P.2d at 303.

Applying those elements in the present case, the district court con-

cluded that Mr. Miller held equitable title to the second filing lands by

virtue of the "handshake" agreement with Lorenz Ranch. The general

definition of "equitable title" is "the right to receive legal title upon

performance of an obligation." Merriam–Webster's Dictionary of Law

On appeal, Cash argues that Mr. Miller did not have equitable title

because there was only an oral "handshake" agreement for the purchase

and, as such, the agreement was void under the statute of frauds. The

relevant provision of the statute of frauds provides that an agreement for

the sale of real estate is void unless it is in writing. Wyo. Stat. Ann. § 1–

23–105(a)(v) (LexisNexis 2009). See also, Simek v. Tate, 2010 WY 65, ¶ 19,

231 P.3d 891, 898 (Wyo. 2010). The district court held that Mr. Miller had

an equitable interest in the property when he imposed the restrictive

covenants because the "handshake" agreement was enforceable against

Lorenz Ranch under the doctrine of partial performance. The doctrine of partial performance provides: "an oral agreement for the sale of land that has been partially or wholly performed by one party, to its detriment, may be enforced by that party." *Id.,* ¶ 21, 231 P.3d at 899. The partial performance exception is grounded in equity to prevent a fraud from being perpetrated when a party refuses to perform an oral agreement after the other party has already performed. *Id.,* ¶ 22, 231 P.3d at 899–900.

The evidence in this case unequivocally establishes that Lorenz Ranch and Mr. Miller had entered into an agreement to convey the Granite Springs Retreat property. Herb Lorenz provided an affidavit in which he stated, "I have personal knowledge of the fact that my father, Abraham Lorenz, on behalf of the Lorenz Ranch Corporation, agreed prior to August, 1972 to convey to Deward H. Miller the entirety of the land upon which the Granite Springs Retreat subdivision is currently located." Cash argues that, because the exact terms of the agreement, such as the purchase price, closing date, payment requirements, etc., are not known, the doctrine of partial performance could not save the agreement from application of the statute of frauds. While the exact terms of an agreement are required in a typical case involving the statute of frauds so that the court can require specific performance of said agreement, *see, e.g., Simek,* ¶ 21, 231 P.3d at 899, that is not our concern in this case. Our focus here is on determining whether the record shows the oral agreement had been performed such that a court would have recognized Mr. Miller's equitable right to enforce the agreement.

The record is clear that Lorenz Ranch's and Mr. Miller's agreement pertained to the entire Granite Springs Retreat. At the time Mr. Miller filed the original declaration of restrictive covenants, both parties had partially performed that agreement by completing the transaction involving the first filing property. Because Mr. Miller had partially performed the agreement when he recorded the protective covenants, he had equitable title, i.e., "the right to receive legal title upon performance of an obligation," to the second filing property. *Merriam–Webster's Dictionary of Law* (1996).

As is clear from the preceding discussion, the application of the statute of frauds and the partial performance exception to the facts of this case creates an anomaly. Had Mr. Miller or Lorenz Ranch raised the statute of frauds as a defense and not fully performed the agreement, the Cash plaintiffs would not own any property in the Granite Springs Retreat, Second Filing, and would not have an interest to litigate. It is, therefore, ironic that they are arguing at this point that Mr. Miller did not have an equitable interest in the property by virtue of the oral agreement with Lorenz Ranch.

We addressed a similar situation in *Comet Energy Services, LLC v. Powder River Oil & Gas Ventures, LLC,* 2010 WY 82, 239 P.3d 382 (Wyo.2010). In that case, we recognized that the purpose of the statute of frauds is to "give to the party to a … contract, against whom the enforcement of the contract is sought by the other party, the right to assert the statute as a defense to his or her own liability." *Id.,* ¶ 33, 239 P.3d at 392, quoting 10 Richard A. Lord, *Williston on Contracts* § 27:12 (4th ed. 1999). Neither Lorenz Ranch nor Mr. Miller sought to use the statute of frauds as a defense to liability and, in fact, they fully performed. While generally privies to a contracting party may assert the statute of frauds defense, that is not the case after the contract has been fully performed by the contracting parties. The successors (the Cash plaintiffs) have only the rights which belonged to their predecessor (Miller). *Id.,* ¶ 36, 239 P.3d at 392. Since their predecessor did not raise the statute of frauds as a defense, it is not available to them. *Id.* Using the statute of frauds to disavow an agreement that actually gave rise to the very interest they are seeking to protect would be an improper use of the legal principle.

The second element for an equitable servitude to be imposed is the developer intended that the covenants be binding upon subsequent purchasers of the second filing tracts. Cash argues that, because the declaration of protective covenants does not appear in the chain of title of the second filing properties, the covenants could not encumber the properties. This argument misses the entire point of equitable servitudes. An equitable servitude imposes a restriction on land even though it does not technically encumber or run with the land. The imposition of the restriction is based upon the concept that a purchaser took the property with notice of a common scheme or plan. As we stated in *Bowers Welding,* 699 P.2d at 303, if the purchaser has notice of an agreement containing restrictions, "it is not material that the agreement is not of record." *See also, Hein v. Lee,* 549 P.2d 286, 292 (Wyo.1976) (stating that "[n]either the fact that they [restrictive covenants] do not appear in his deed nor the fact that they are not properly placed on public record relieves the appellant of [his] burden because he had actual notice").

In determining Miller's intent with regard to the subdivision, we start with the language of the covenants. The covenants were titled: "Granite Springs Retreat at Happy Jack Road and Curt Gowdy State Park[,] Cheyenne, Wyoming 82001[,] Declaration of Protective Covenants." The title indicated that the covenants would apply to the entire Granite Springs Retreat development, not just to the first filing property. The actual provisions included in the covenants also contemplated application to both filings. The ACC provision stated that, at first, the developer would appoint the members of the ACC, but once ten dwellings were complete, the ACC members would be elected by the lot owners. The first filing only included eight tracts; consequently, the ACC provision obviously contemplated inclusion of the second filing property when it discussed the ten dwelling requirement. It is also significant that some of the common areas referred to in the covenants, like the green belt streams and lakes, are located on second filing property. In *Bowers Welding,* 699 P.2d at 305, we stated that, because the covenants referenced features within the property that was inadvertently omitted from the description of covered property, the developer obviously intended to impose the restrictions on that property, as well. Thus, the declaration of protective covenants, itself, confirms that Mr. Miller intended for the covenants to apply to the entire Granite Springs Retreat subdivision, including both filings.

The district court also looked to other documents in concluding that Mr. Miller intended the entire Granite Springs Retreat subdivision be developed according to a common plan or scheme. Cash argues that, in searching for the developer's intent, we are restricted to the language of the covenants. If that is true, then as we just pointed out, the intent expressed in the clear language of the covenants was to bind the second filing properties.

However, in *Bowers Welding,* 699 P.2d at 303, we stated: "A common way in which to uphold restrictive covenants is to find a general plan or scheme for the development of a tract of land." The search for a common scheme or plan often involves looking beyond the language of the covenants which were not correctly placed of record. For example, in *Bowers Welding,* 699 P.2d at 305, we considered the "character of use made of all the lots open to a view of the [defendant] when he purchased" his property, *Sanborn v. McLean,* 233 Mich. 227, 206 N.W. 496 (1925) and statements made by the developer to the purchaser, *Hein,* 549 P.2d at 292. We also quoted 20 Am.Jur.2d *Covenants, Conditions, and Restrictions,* § 177 (1965) as indicating that a purchaser will be bound by the common scheme or plan created by the grantor's maps and plans showing the division of the property into tracts so long as the purchaser takes the property with notice of the plan.

In this case, the preliminary plat included all of the Granite Springs Retreat property, both first and second filings, and the application for subdivision filed with Laramie County indicated that the subdivision would be known as Granite Springs Retreat and would include sixty lots. In addition, the environmental impact report stated that the entire development would be burdened by the covenants. The undisputed evidence establishes that Mr. Miller intended that the second filing properties be bound by the protective covenants.

We turn now to the third element required for imposition of equitable servitudes—notice to the subsequent purchasers. Notice is at the heart of the rationale behind enforcement of equitable servitudes. We provided an extensive discussion of the notice requirement in *Bowers Welding,* 699 P.2d at 303:

> "The notice of restrictions sufficient to charge a purchaser may be actual notice or notice of facts sufficient to put him on inquiry. For instance, the notice sufficient to charge a purchaser of a lot in a subdivision with knowledge of restrictions imposed in deeds to other lots as part of a general plan, but inadvertently or otherwise omitted from the deeds in his chain of title, may be actual or constructive, including notice of facts which ought to have put him on inquiry, such as the uniform appearance of the area in which the lot is located. * * * "

"If the purchaser has actual notice of an agreement containing restrictions, it is not material that the agreement is not of record. At least, where it does not appear that the agreement was of record, the purchaser with actual notice has been held bound by the restrictions. Even notice of a parol agreement binds the purchaser to comply with the restrictions." 20 Am.Jur.2d, Covenants, Conditions, and Restrictions, §§ 307–308, pp. 871–872 (1965).

As we discussed in the context of the second equitable servitude element, inquiry notice may be established by a common scheme or plan for development. *Id.* at 303–05.

We will address the plaintiffs separately in determining whether they had notice of the covenants.[2] Mr. Cash purchased his second filing lot in 1992, after the homeowners' association had already been formed. Mr. Cash's chain of title included an affidavit of intention recorded in 1983 in which Mr. Miller stated that he intended for the covenants to apply to the entire Granite Springs Retreat subdivision. That document put him on notice of the covenants.

In addition, Mr. Cash admitted that he looked at several lots before deciding on one, so he obviously knew that he was purchasing in a planned development. He also stated that he received a copy of the amended covenants[3] when he purchased his property; although, in a later affidavit he stated that he did not receive the amended covenants until after he closed on his property.

Mr. Cash participated in numerous activities over the years which indicated he was aware of the covenants. In particular, he sought ACC approval for construction of various improvements on his property, and he even served on the ACC for a time. He did not contest the existence of the restrictions imposed by the covenants for several years after he purchased his property. Without question, Mr. Cash had notice of the existence of the restrictions on his property when he purchased it.

Mr. Maturi also purchased his property after Mr. Miller filed his affidavit indicating that he intended for the covenants to bind the entire Granite Springs Retreat development. Mr. Maturi's real estate agent advised him that there was a homeowners association for the subdivision. As the district court noted, the fact that a homeowners association existed should have alerted Mr. Maturi to the possibility of covenants. Mr. Maturi

---

2. This analysis does not apply to Plaintiffs Nelson and Hilliker. Their property is located in the first filing and they do not argue that the covenants do not bind them. Mr. Nelson and Ms. Hilliker participated in this action because they were concerned that if the second filing properties were found to be bound by the protective covenants, they would be required to help pay for maintenance, etc. in the second filing area. The covenants, plats, etc. gave the first filing property purchasers actual notice that the covenants bound the entire subdivision.

3. The plaintiffs argue that the notice provided by the amended covenants was insufficient because those covenants were later declared to be invalid. We disagree. The amended covenants obviously "amended" a prior version. When the plaintiffs were provided with notice of the amended covenants, together with the other documents in this case, they were certainly put on notice to inquire about other restrictions.

did not contest the existence of the covenants for several years after he purchased his property and, in fact, he served a three year term on the board of the homeowners association. There is simply no question that he was on notice when he purchased the property that it may be subject to land use restrictions.

Mr. and Mrs. McCune purchased their property in 1978, meaning that Mr. Miller's affidavit of intention was not part of their chain of title. They claim they did not receive notice of the covenants until after they purchased their property. However, they were aware they were purchasing a lot in a planned development, as that was clear from their deed and other documents in their chain of title. Mr. and Mrs. McCune were actively involved in forming the homeowners association and other aspects of subdivision governance for many years. Mr. McCune stated that he and Mr. Miller "created" the GSRA. The McCunes also sought ACC approval for the construction of their home. It seems incredible that they would undertake those responsibilities if, as they now argue, they were not aware of the covenants. Under the facts of this case the McCunes were, at the very least, charged with inquiry notice of the existence of restrictions on their land. It would be particularly inequitable to relieve them of the burden of the covenants under the facts of this case. *Streets,* 898 P.2d at 380, citing *Hein,* 549 P.2d at 292.

CONCLUSION

All of the elements for imposition of equitable servitudes upon the Granite Springs Retreat, Second Filing properties are met in this case. The district court properly ruled that Mr. Miller had equitable title to the property when he recorded the declaration of protective covenants, he intended to burden the entire development with the covenants, and the plaintiffs purchased their lots with notice of the covenants. The district court's order granting summary judgment in favor of GSRA and the other defendants is affirmed.

NOTES AND QUESTIONS

1. The elements for an equitable servitude to bind successors are, on the burden side: intent, notice and touch and concern. The elements for the benefit to bind successors are intent and touch and concern. Notice may be actual, record, or inquiry but see Note 2.

2. See Evans v. Pollock, 796 S.W.2d 465, 466 (Tex.1990):

[W]here a common grantor develops a tract of land for sale in lots and pursues a course of conduct which indicates that he intends to inaugurate a general scheme or plan of development for the benefit of himself and the purchasers of the various lots, and by numerous conveyances inserts in the deeds substantially uniform restrictions, conditions and covenants against the use of the property, the grantees acquire by implication an equitable right, variously referred to as an implied reciprocal negative easement or an equitable servitude, to enforce similar restrictions against that part of the tract retained by the grantor or subsequently sold without the restrictions to a purchaser with actual or constructive notice of the restrictions and covenants.

Quoting Minner v. City of Lynchburg, 204 Va. 180, 188, 129 S.E.2d 673, 679 (1963).

Not all jurisdictions are willing to imply equitable servitudes from a "course of conduct." The state that is traditionally most hostile to them is California, whose courts decline enforcement of an equitable servitude unless it is described in a written instrument bearing the signature of the grantor. Werner v. Graham, 181 Cal. 174, 183 P. 945 (1919); Riley v. Bear Creek Planning Committee, 17 Cal.3d 500, 131 Cal.Rptr. 381, 551 P.2d 1213 (1976). One California court has gone so far as to say that equitable servitudes will not be enforced against a grantee who had actual notice of the restrictions and agreed to be bound by them, unless they were created in writing by the grantor. See Murry v. Lovell, 132 Cal.App.2d 30, 281 P.2d 316 (1955) (subdivider orally read the restrictions to each lot buyer, but neglected to have them described in the deeds).

But in Citizens for Covenant Compliance v. Anderson, 12 Cal.4th 345, 906 P.2d 1314, 47 Cal.Rptr.2d 898 (1995), the California Supreme Court held that a set of restrictions that were recorded in a subdivision plat but not included in any subsequent deeds from the developer nevertheless created the restrictions.

> The CC & R's [covenants, conditions, and restrictions] of this case were recorded before any of the properties they purport to govern were sold, thus giving all buyers constructive notice of their existence. They state they are to bind and benefit each parcel of property as part of a planned community. Nevertheless, the Court of Appeal held they are not enforceable because they were not also mentioned in a deed or other document when the property was sold. We disagree, and adopt the following rule: If a declaration establishing a common plan for the ownership of property in a subdivision and containing restrictions upon the use of the property as part of the common plan, is recorded before the execution of the contract of sale, describes the property it is to govern, and states that it is to bind all purchasers and their successors, subsequent purchasers who have constructive notice of the recorded declaration are deemed to intend and agree to be bound by, and to accept the benefits of, the common plan; the restrictions, therefore, are not unenforceable merely because they are not additionally cited in a deed or other document at the time of the sale.

* * *

> In both *Werner* [supra] and *Riley* [supra], we held the property was not bound by the restrictions. It is readily apparent that both are factually distinguishable from this case. In *Werner*, there was no recorded document imposing uniform restrictions on the entire subdivision, only individual deeds imposing restrictions on specific parcels. In *Riley*, the restrictions were recorded after the conveyance at issue.

> * * * We also emphasized the importance of recording the restrictions. "[T]he recording statutes operate to protect the expectations of the

grantee and secure to him the full benefit of the exchange for which he bargained. [Citations.] Where, however, mutually enforceable equitable servitudes are sought to be created outside the recording statutes, the vindication of the expectations of the original grantee, and for that matter succeeding grantees, is hostage not only to the good faith of the grantor but, even assuming good faith, to the vagaries of proof by extrinsic evidence of actual notice on the part of grantees.... The uncertainty thus introduced into subdivision development would in many cases circumvent any plan for the orderly and harmonious development of such properties and result in a crazy-quilt pattern of uses frustrating the bargained-for expectations of lot owners in the tract."

In both *Werner* and *Riley* there was no prior recorded document providing a common plan and stating that the restrictions were to apply to every parcel. The only documents in existence from which the mutual intent and agreement of the parties could be discerned were the deeds themselves, which were silent. No decision by this court invalidating restrictions involves a written plan, like that here, that was applicable to an entire tract and was recorded before conveyancing. However, some intermediate appellate decisions have concluded that for recorded uniform restrictions to take effect, they must at least be referenced in a deed or other instrument at the time of an actual conveyance. ...

The Andersons argue that the CC & R's [in this case] never took effect because they were not mentioned in the deeds to their properties. Under this interpretation, if the developer of a subdivision records a uniform plan of restrictions intended to bind and benefit every parcel alike, implementation of the plan depends upon the vagaries of the actual deeds, and whether they contain at least a ritualistic reference to restrictions of record. When, as may often be the case, some deeds refer to the restrictions, and others do not, the enforceability of the restrictions can hinge upon the sequence of the conveyances, and can vary depending upon what property owner seeks to enforce them and against which property.

* * * The results can be byzantine. One commentator has reviewed some of the possibilities: "If the subdivider fails to insert the agreement in the first deed but remembers to insert it in the fifth deed, for example, the equitable servitude springs into existence from deed five onwards. The restrictions do not apply to the first four lots because the subdivider no longer has any interest in those lots and cannot place a restriction on them in favor of the rest of the tract. If the subdivider inserts the agreement in deeds five and six and then fails again to put them in seven and eight, the courts have held that lot owners five and six can enforce the restrictions against seven and eight, but seven and eight cannot enforce them against each other. When the subdivider put the agreement in the deeds to lots five and six, he agreed to burden the rest of the unsold subdivision. When he sold lots seven and eight, the burden of his agreement passed as an incident to lots seven and eight in favor of lots five and six. There was no agreement between lot owner seven and the subdivider that the subdivider burden the rest of his tract in favor of lot seven. Thus when the subdivider conveyed lot eight, there was no burden

to pass incident to the land in favor of lot seven. Lot seven can enforce the restrictions against lots five and six, however, because just as the burden of the agreement between the subdivider and five and six passed as an incident to lot seven, so should the benefit of that agreement pass. The subdivider had the benefit of enforcing the restrictions against five and six, and that benefit passes to seven.

* * * This situation dramatically complicates title searches. Instead of simply searching for restrictions of record in order to know exactly what is being purchased, a prospective buyer must search the chain of title of all previously sold property in the tract. If the deed to the property in question refers to the restrictions, the search would have to determine which of the earlier deeds, if any, contain a similar reference, for the restrictions would be enforceable only against those and later parcels, and not against earlier parcels whose deeds did not refer to the restrictions. If the deed does not refer to the restrictions, the buyer would nevertheless have to conduct the same search, for any earlier sold property that does refer to them would have a mutual servitude against the later property whether or not the later deed mentioned it.

* * * These uncertainties can be eliminated by adopting the rule stated at the outset. In essence, if the restrictions are recorded before the sale, the later purchaser is deemed to agree to them. The purchase of property knowing of the restrictions evinces the buyer's intent to accept their burdens and benefits. Thus, the mutual servitudes are created at the time of the conveyance even if there is no additional reference to them in the deed.

3. Almost all jurisdictions hold that the "notice" requirement for equitable servitudes can be satisfied by (1) a description of the restriction in a recorded deed or other recorded instrument; or (2) a reference in the grantee's deed to a restriction set out in a plat map or master deed. Most jurisdictions agree with *Mid–State* that the notice requirement can be satisfied by evidence of a "general plan" or scheme which a person could discern from inspecting the property itself. See, for example, Sharts v. Walters, 107 N.M. 414, 759 P.2d 201 (App.1988).

4. In Hiner v. Hoffman, 90 Hawai'i 188, 977 P.2d 878 (1999), the Hawaii Supreme Court held that a covenant restricting a home in a subdivision to "one story" was unenforceable because it was too vague:

Specifically, the ... Declarations, which contain the restrictive covenant at issue, fail to provide a definition or concrete dimensions for the term "story." The failure of the 1966 covenant to prescribe, in feet or by some other numerical measure, the maximum "height" of a "story" renders the language of the covenant ambiguous. As the Hoffmans point out, without such a definition, the "height restriction" of which the plaintiffs-appellees speak is meaningless. Thus, the Hoffmans argue that under the language of the 1966 covenant:

[a] two-story house, with each story being 25 feet tall, would be in compliance with the covenant, [whereas, a] three-story house, with each story being only 10 feet tall would violate the covenant[;] ...

[y]et, the three-story house would have an overall height of only 30 feet while the two-story house would be 50 feet in height.

The court rejected the argument that local building codes, which defined a "story" as floor levels with a vertical distance between them of from six to twelve feet was adequate for purposes of the covenant.

A dissenter complained:

The majority thus saves one story of a single house, but betrays years of reliance by the Hoffmans' neighbors and the larger Pacific Palisades community on the covenant's plain language and increases uncertainty and litigation with respect to other plainly worded covenants. . . .

The phrase "stories in height" is an ordinary, stock expression. The plain reading of "[n]o dwelling shall be erected . . . which exceeds two stories in height," manifests the purpose of limiting structures to two stories or less—without regard or reference to exact "height" in feet and inches. It is undisputed that the Hoffmans' dwelling, built in a three-tiered, terrace-like form and described as "three-stories" by the Hoffmans themselves, is in fact three stories. One need not analyze any further or inquire into the height of the structure in feet and inches to determine that the Hoffmans' house strays from the common and conventional meaning of "two stories in height."

In Fong v. Hashimoto, 92 Hawai'i 568, 994 P.2d 500 (2000) the Hawaii court additionally held that a height restriction imposed on a downslope lot could not be enforced by the upslope lot owner unless the covenant in question expressly named the upslope lot as a beneficiary of the covenant. In this case only three of the lots in the fifteen lot subdivision had height restrictions, so the court was unwilling to find that there was a "general scheme" of height restrictions such that any lot owner in the subdivision could enforce the restriction against any other lot owner. Without the general scheme, that left enforcement to named beneficiaries and the court was unwilling to infer that an upslope lot was an intended beneficiary simply because it was the property whose view would be blocked in the event the burdened property owner built a structure in violation of the restriction.

If a restriction is vague because it fails to describe the affected land with particularity then courts usually rely on the Statute of Frauds requirement that written instruments affecting title to land must describe it sufficiently. See, e.g., Dickson v. Kates, 133 P.3d 498, 132 Wash.App. 724 (2006), which concluded that a height restriction applying to land "immediately to the west" of the benefitted land did not describe the burdened land with sufficient precision. The court noted that there was no way to ascertain from the deed itself precisely what lands were covered by the restriction.

NOTE: IMPLIED SERVITUDES

The Restatement (Third) of Property (Servitudes) (2000) treats implied servitudes and irrevocable licenses (see § 8.2 of this chapter) as siblings. What the two share in common is that both follow upon negotiations sufficient to create some kind of expectancy interest in land, but neither manifests sufficient formality to comply with the requirements of the Statute of Frauds for creating an interest in land. The Restatement begins with the proposition that an easement may be created by a contract as well as a conveyance (§ 2.1). It then provides:

§ 2.8. Failure to Comply with the Statute of Frauds

If a contract or conveyance intended to create a servitude does not comply with the Statute of Frauds, the burden of the servitude is not enforceable and the benefit is terminable at will, unless there is an applicable exemption, or unless the transaction falls within the exception set forth in § 2.9, or § 129 of the Restatement, Second, of Contracts.

§ 2.9. Exception to the Statute of Frauds

The consequences of failure to comply with the Statute of Frauds, set out in § 2.8, do not apply if the beneficiary of the servitude, in justifiable reliance on the existence of the servitude, has so changed position that injustice can be avoided only by giving effect to the parties' intent to create a servitude.

§ 2.10. Servitudes Created by Estoppel

If injustice can be avoided only by establishment of a servitude, the owner or occupier of land is estopped to deny the existence of a servitude burdening the land when:

(1) the owner or occupier permitted another to use that land under circumstances in which it was reasonable to foresee that the user would substantially change position believing that the permission would not be revoked, and the user did substantially change position in reasonable reliance on that belief; or

(2) the owner or occupier represented that the land was burdened by a servitude under circumstances in which it was reasonable to foresee that the person to whom the representation was made would substantially change position on the basis of that representation, and the person did substantially change position in reasonable reliance on that representation.

§ 2.14. Servitudes Implied from General Plan

Unless the facts or circumstances indicate a contrary intent, conveyance of land pursuant to a general plan of development implies the creation of servitudes as follows:

(a) Implied Benefits: Each lot included within the general plan is the implied beneficiary of all express and implied servitudes imposed to carry out the general plan.

(b) Implied Burdens:

(1) Language of condition that creates a restriction or other obligation to implement the general plan creates an implied servitude imposing the same restriction or other obligation.

(2) A conveyance by a developer that imposes a servitude on the land conveyed to implement a general plan creates an implied reciprocal servitude burdening all the developer's remaining land included in the general plan, if injustice can be avoided only by implying the reciprocal servitude.

LALONDE v. RENAUD

Supreme Court of Vermont (1989).
157 Vt. 281, 597 A.2d 305.

PECK, JUSTICE.

Defendants appeal from a trial court judgment declaring that a lot to which defendants claimed title was park area, as designated in the developer's subdivision plans. We affirm. All parties are owners of lots in the so-called Kirk and Fitts development, which was created in 1957 and is adjacent to Lake Champlain in Alburg. Plaintiffs collectively own seven lots in the subdivision, but only plaintiffs Jacques and Therese Lalonde purchased their property from the developers, in 1966. All of the plaintiffs' deeds refer to a map, which the trial court found was recorded and which depicted an area north of lot 10 of the subdivision as a park. The deeds, however, did not expressly refer to a park, nor did the declaration of restrictions in any of the deeds expressly prohibit construction in the area designated as a park. Nevertheless, there was no dispute that the area was used and maintained as a park at least since 1966, and the trial court so found.

* * * Defendants purchased the area in 1982, and in 1984 erected a fence between the beach and the grassy portion of the park. When they made it known that they intended to develop the area, the present action ensued. The trial court concluded that the original lots were sold by reference to a recorded plat indicating a park area and that the purchasers acquired rights in the park. In Clearwater Realty Co. v. Bouchard, 146 Vt. 359, 505 A.2d 1189 (1985), we held that where lots are sold with reference to a recorded plat that indicates a park, "lot purchasers acquire the right to keep open and use roads, streets, highways, and park areas as indicated on the plat."

Defendants contend that the trial court erred in disallowing cross-examination of plaintiff James Ruddy aimed at exploring Ruddy's reliance (or lack of reliance) on the existence of the park in purchasing his lot in 1981. The underlying substantive argument would have been that, absent reliance on the plat denominating the park or reliance on the park itself, plaintiffs were not injured by the subsequent development of the lot denominated "park" in the subdivision plan. Defendants misapprehend the nature of the rights created in lot owners who have purchased by reference to a park in a recorded plat. The holding in *Clearwater* sets forth an objective test, granting lot owners rights as a result of purchasing "with reference to" a plat, without adding a requirement of specific reliance on depictions in the plat. In *Clearwater*, we clearly rejected holdings in some jurisdictions that "lot purchasers only acquire an easement over streets or ways which touch their land or which are necessary for the use and enjoyment of their property." We chose instead what is sometimes called the "broad" or "unity" rule (see generally Annotation, Conveyance with Reference to Plat, 7 A.L.R.2d 607, 612 (1949)) that "lot owners acquire rights in all roads, streets, parks, and other designated ways shown on the plat map unless a contrary intent is affirmatively shown."

Clearwater addressed rights of way, not parks, which might well be considered distinguishable on the basis of a different degree of necessity to the lot owner. We had no occasion in *Clearwater* to consider a third line of cases adopting the "intermediate" or "beneficial enjoyment" rule, under which the extent of the private right is limited to streets, alleys, or parks that are reasonably or materially beneficial to the grantee. See, e.g., Whitton v. Clark, 112 Conn. 28, 151 A. 305 (1930). Even if we were to apply the "reasonable benefit" rule in the present case, an inquiry into whether a lot owner is benefitted involves an objective test, not one that depends on an owner's specific reliance on what was depicted on the plat map. Moreover, in the present case the findings below were ample to support the conclusion that the park benefitted plaintiffs. The court stated: There is no doubt that the character of the neighborhood will be adversely affected should the park be no more.

Defendants' argument that each present owner of a lot must demonstrate reliance on the map filed in 1957 would effectively limit the beneficiaries of the protections contained in *Clearwater* to the original purchasers from a developer since only these persons are likely to have relied directly on the plat. Subsequent purchasers would be unable to prove such reliance and would lose the right to the park. Such a position is clearly inconsistent with our holding in *Clearwater*. Additionally, it would, if adopted, undermine the promises made by developers who seek to attract buyers to a subdivision with dedications of common land. Finally, it would create an undue hardship to subsequent purchasers, whose benefits might depend on proof that they had knowledge of and relied on plats filed at the commencement of the development. There is no reason why purchasers who purchased their properties from someone other than the developer should not enjoy all of their predecessors' rights and interests, unless "a contrary intent is affirmatively shown." Since lack of reliance by plaintiffs on the plat or on the existence of the park would not affect their rights, the court did not err in limiting defendants' cross-examination of plaintiffs on the reliance issue. * * *[2]

Affirmed.

NOTES AND QUESTIONS

1.   Did the plaintiffs acquire an easement by prescription in the park?

---

2. The trial decision did not raise, and we do not consider, the ancillary issues that may persist after this decision, such as responsibility for property taxes and maintenance.

2. A great deal of housing in America is built in subdivisions designed by private developers and usually approved by officials of the city or county in which the subdivision is located. Once such a subdivision is designed it is usually described on a "plat map" like the one that appears in the *Mid–State* case, reprinted supra. The map is generally recorded in the office of the county clerk or recorder, and lots in the subdivision are identified and sold by reference to the plat map. The mechanics of this process are described more fully in chapter 16. If enforcement is being sought against the original developer the plat map need not be recorded since, after all, the developer has actual notice of its own map.

The plat map often serves a twofold function: first, as legal description; second, as promotional or advertising device. When the developer sells lots to individual homeowners in a subdivision which has been platted but not yet developed, the developer will commonly show the buyers the plat map, or perhaps a similar, more graphic map, and point out certain features of the subdivision to the prospective buyer: for example, where the parks and recreational areas will be, how the streets will be developed, which areas will be single family homes and which will be apartments, etc. The map may also describe various restrictions that will be imposed in parts of the subdivision. For example, it may say something like "Lots 1 to 12, section C, single-family residence only, no house trailers, no homes to be built under 1600 square feet of living space, excluding garage."

When the plat map or other statements are ambiguous, courts become reluctant to enforce covenants. For example, see Drye v. Eagle Rock Ranch, 364 S.W.2d 196 (Tex.1962), which refused to imply "easements" in recreational rights that were only ambiguously referred to in the plat maps. Cf., outside of the subdivision context, Estate of Wallis, 276 Ill.App.3d 1053, 659 N.E.2d 423, 213 Ill.Dec. 507 (1995) (oral agreement to maintain fence did not run with the land).

Even more problematic are situations when grantees base their claim against the developer, not on the plat map, but on a promotional map or brochure published by the developer, or else on oral representations made by a sales agent. The court in the *Drye* case, supra, refused such a claim. However, in Haines v. Minnock Constr. Co., 289 Pa.Super. 209, 433 A.2d 30 (1981), the plaintiff bought a condominium unit in reliance on the developer-seller's *oral* promises that a certain area within the development would be left as open, undeveloped space. Four years later the developer began to build more units in this space. The court held that the oral promise did not constitute an easement because the Statute of Frauds required a writing. Furthermore, the sales brochures and maps that were shown to prospective purchasers were too vague and none had been signed by the developer. However, under the law of promissory estoppel an oral promise that land would be used a particular way would be enforced in favor of someone who made expenditures—in this case, purchased the adjoining property—in reliance upon the representations. See also Thisted v. Country Club Tower Corp., 146 Mont. 87, 405 P.2d 432 (1965), rev'd on other grounds, 213 Mont. 6, 689 P.2d 268 (1984), holding that a developer's statement to a prospective purchaser that an entire building would remain "residential" was sufficient to create an "implied equitable servitude." Accord Nicol v. Nelson, 776 P.2d 1144 (Colo.App.1989).

3. The rule that a purchaser whose deed makes explicit reference to a plat map obtains an "easement" or the benefit of an implied servitude in everything described on the map can be carried too far. Subdivisions often take several years to complete, and the market for land can take unexpected turns.

Suppose the subdivision is two miles wide. Half way through its development it becomes apparent that the original design of the subdivision contains too many single family homes, which are relatively expensive, and too little multi-family housing, which is much less expensive. The developer decides to change a half dozen lots from single family housing to multi-family housing. Should a single-family purchaser more than a mile away be able to enjoin the change on the theory that he has an "easement" in the lots requiring that they be maintained as single family homes? The cases generally give the purchaser very broad enforcement power if (1) the plat map unambiguously asserts the restriction or describes the facility that the purchaser is claiming; (2) the plat map is recorded; *and* (3) the purchaser's deed explicitly incorporates the plat map. If any one of these conditions fails, the purchaser's enforcement powers may be considerably less.

One way a developer can retain some flexibility is to create covenants for his own benefit that gives him the right to make changes in the subdivision. If these covenants are both clear and reasonable, they generally will be approved. See Moore v. Megginson, 416 So.2d 993 (Ala.1982). However, if the covenants or reservations are ambiguous, the court may permit affected lot buyers to enjoin any change. See, e.g., Schmidt v. Ladner Constr. Co., 370 So.2d 970 (Ala.1979) (refusing to permit a developer to lower minimum home size restrictions where the reservation that allegedly permitted such a change was unclear); Knight v. City of Albuquerque, 110 N.M. 265, 794 P.2d 739 (App.1990) (developer forbidden from developing land designated as golf course, in spite of developer's reservation of right to build buildings on any tract in the plat). See Reichman, Residential Private Governments: An Introductory Survey, 43 U.Chi.L.Rev. 253 (1976).

4. Should a home owners' association be granted standing to enforce servitudes, not because the creators so intended, but merely because it is a more efficient enforcer of the law? See Westmoreland Assn., Inc. v. West Cutter Estates, Ltd., 174 A.D.2d 144, 579 N.Y.S.2d 413, 416 (1992):

> The individual owner of developed land in the neighborhood ... may not, at the time, realize the impact the proposed change ... will have on his property, or realizing the effect, may not have the financial resources to effectively oppose the proposed change.... Against this background of economic disparity, an individual property owner, who stands only to gain (or prevent the loss of) the maintenance of the status quo as regards the value of his homestead and his peace and quiet, cannot be expected, nor should he be required, to assume by himself the burden and expense of challenging [the violation]. Even if successful, the aggrieved individual will not be able to recoup his expenditures. By granting neighborhood and

civic associations standing in these situations, the expense can be spread out over a number of property owners, putting them on an economic parity with the developer.

(Quoting Matter of Douglaston Civic Assn. v. Galvin, 36 N.Y.2d 1, 364 N.Y.S.2d 830, 324 N.E.2d 317 (1974), which had granted a civic association standing to oppose a variance).

Easements, Covenants, Equitable Servitudes: A Review

	EASEMENT AND PROFIT	REAL COVENANT	EQUITABLE SERVITUDE
FORM AND METHOD OF CREATION	May be created by express grant; however, "affirmative" easements and most profits may also be created by prescription. Easements can also be created by implication or necessity. In form, a property interest, protected under the just compensation clause of the federal constitution.	In form, a contract, not a real property interest. Commonly created in a deed but may be created in another document, provided privity of estate exists between the promisor and promisee (horizontal privity)—for example, a lease, or a contract between cotenants. Not generally capable of creation by implication, necessity or prescription, or adverse possession.	A product of the British courts of equity, historically recognized by the courts whenever equity so required. Today, most commonly created by express grant, but may be created in any binding contract provided that the circumstances are sufficient to give adequate notice to people later alleged to be bound.
HORIZONTAL PRIVITY[10] REQUIRED FOR ASSIGNABILITY	No	In almost all cases privity is required before the burden will run. Many cases suggest that privity is not required before the benefit will run.[11]	No
VERTICAL PRIVITY[12] REQUIRED FOR ASSIGNABILITY	No	Yes, although the requirement of "strict" vertical privity (succession to the same estate as the predecessor) has been weakened.	Generally not. The relevant question is whether there is adequate notice upon the person sought to be bound.
ASSIGNABILITY OF INTERESTS IN GROSS (Personal interests)	In modern American law *commercial* easements in gross are assignable. There is some doubt about the assignability of noncommercial easements in gross.	Yes, although it is sometimes stated that the burden will not run if the benefit is in gross.	Interests in gross are generally assignable. Once again, it is sometimes said that the burden will not run if the benefit is in gross, but there are many exceptions to this rule.
TOUCH AND CONCERN REQUIREMENT	No	Yes. Neither the benefit nor the burden will run if the covenant at issue does not touch and concern the land.	Yes, although many cases state the requirement in a different way—for example, it must be a promise "affecting the use" of real property, or it must be a promise to do or refrain from doing something upon the land.
NOTICE REQUIREMENT	Yes, if the owner of the servient estate is to be bound. The notice may be actual, record, or inquiry notice (as is the case with implied easements).	Yes. Notice is required for the burden to run to successors. Notice may be actual or record. In some cases, notice is not required to burden a successor who is a donee.	Yes. Notice is required for the burden to bind successors. The notice may be actual, record, or inquiry. In some cases, notice is not required to burden a successor who is a donee.

---

10. I.e., privity between the promisor and promisee.

11. I.e., if the person seeking enforcement is an assignee of the original beneficiary of the relevant promise.

12. I.e., privity between the original promisor and the person against whom enforcement of the promise is sought; or privity between the original promisee and the person now seeking enforcement of the promise.

§ 8.5 EASEMENTS, COVENANTS AND EQUITA- BLE SERVITUDES: WHAT IS THE DIFFER- ENCE AND WHEN DOES IT MATTER?

The law has developed three fairly distinctive *legal* mechanisms for analyzing servitudes. However, a tremendous overlap exists between the kinds of *factual* arrangements that are given these three names. Further, the factual distinctions are eroding through time. Is the right to swim in someone else's lake an "easement" or a "covenant"? Is the reciprocal right between neighbors that neither will build a commercial structure a negative easement or an equitable servitude? Clearly, two courts looking at the same factual obligation may call it by two different names. The name a court uses depends a great deal on how the servitude was created and, if it was created by express grant, on the language that the drafter used.

The best explanation for the schizophrenia in the law of servitudes is historical. Originally, most servitudes were created by grant and would today be characterized as easements. In fact, in the United States the concepts of real covenants and equitable servitudes were virtually non-existent before the Civil War. During the second half of the nineteenth century, however, the American law of contracts went through a revolu-tion. While property rights were seen as subject to substantial supervision by the State, contract rights were generally perceived as purely "pri-vate"—that is, as governed exclusively by the parties to the agreement. In an era that placed a high value on individualism and economic *laissez faire,* it was only natural that contract theories of legal rights should take precedence over property theories. See H. Hovenkamp, Enterprise and American law, 1836–1937, chs. 14–17 (1991).

This raises a question worth considering: if the only important differences among "easements", "covenants" and "equitable servitudes" are purely historical, why continue to have the relatively heavy doctrinal baggage and frequent incompatibility of three different analytic ap-proaches? Would it not be much better to have a unified law of servitudes?

The Restatement (Third) of Property: Servitudes (2000) goes very far in unifying the law of servitudes—certainly beyond commonly given descriptions of the law, although perhaps not very much beyond the actual outcomes of cases. Section 2.4 states that "No privity relationship between the parties is necessary to create a servitude." The Reporter's Comment defends the abolition of the privity requirement this way:

> In American law, the horizontal privity requirement serves no func-tion beyond insuring that most covenants intended to run with the

land will be created in conveyances. Formal creation of covenants is desirable because it tends to assure that they will be recorded. However, the horizontal-privity requirement is no longer needed for this purpose. In modern law, the Statute of Frauds and recording acts perform that function.

Application of the horizontal-privity requirement prevents enforcement at law of covenants entered into between neighbors and between other parties who do not transfer or share some other interest in the land. The rule can easily be circumvented by conveyance to a strawperson, who imposes the covenant in the reconveyance. Since the rule serves no necessary purpose and simply acts as a trap for the poorly represented, it has been abandoned.

But can unification be pushed too far? For example, as a general rule an easement can be created by prescription, while a covenant or equitable servitude cannot be. Would we want a unified law of servitudes to destroy this distinction? Suppose that A and B are adjoining landowners and that for twenty years A has been driving daily across B's property on a graded strip that looks like a driveway. If B now decided to interfere with A's use, a court very likely would hold that A had acquired a prescriptive easement across B's property. Suppose, however, that for twenty years A has been farming his property and one day begins building a barn. B sues, claiming that A's twenty-year operation of his farm without a barn created a prescriptive covenant in B's favor that no barns would be built on A's property. No court would adopt such a rule and there is a good reason why none should: it would give everyone a "prescriptive" right that any situation maintained on someone's land for the prescriptive period be maintained indefinitely.

How might a court explain why a right to use a driveway can be acquired prescriptively but not a right to a barnless farm next door? It might say that the former is an "easement" and the second a "servitude" or perhaps a "covenant," and that the doctrine of prescription applies only to the former. Suppose, however, that B claims that for twenty years she has not built a barn on her property either, and as a result A and B have acquired "reciprocal negative easements" by prescription. Do you suppose that would change the court's view of the matter and entitle B to enjoin A's construction of the barn?

Once again the answer is almost certainly no. This time the court would come to the rescue by citing the proposition that only affirmative easements can be created by prescription. Alternatively, it might say that "reciprocal negative easements" are not easements at all. They are equitable servitudes, and prescription does not apply to them. In any case, B would probably not be able to enjoin A's barn by styling her right as an "easement."

Assuming that this outcome is a good one, does society need a distinction between "easements" and "covenants" or "equitable servitudes" in order to maintain it? Probably not. In this particular case there is a solution to the problem that lies outside the law of servitudes. When A was using the driveway across B's property B had a cause of action for trespass against B until the prescriptive period had run. The result was that sufficient legal "hostility" or adverseness existed for the law of prescription to take effect. However, B had no cause of action against A during the time that A was farming without a barn. As a result there was no hostility and no prescription.

In short, the right to cross someone's land can be acquired by prescription, but the right that one's neighbor cannot build a barn on his own land generally cannot be. However, the distinction between "easements" and "covenants" or "equitable servitudes" is not an essential part of that distinction, and to make it so is useless and confusing.

§ 8.6 EQUITABLE SERVITUDES AND THE POWER TO EXCLUDE

HILL v. COMMUNITY OF DAMIEN OF MOLOKAI

Supreme Court of New Mexico (1996).
121 N.M. 353, 911 P.2d 861.

FROST, JUSTICE.

Defendant–Appellant Community of Damien of Molokai (Community) appeals from the district court's ruling in favor of Plaintiffs–Appellees, enjoining the further use of the property at 716 Rio Arriba, S.E., Albuquerque, as a group home for individuals with AIDS. Plaintiffs–Appellees argue that the group home violates a restrictive covenant. The Community contends that the group home is a permitted use under the covenant and, alternatively, that enforcing the restrictive covenant against the group home would violate the Federal Fair Housing Act, 42 U.S.C. §§ 3601–3631 (1988) [hereinafter FHA].

The underlying facts of this case are not in dispute. The Community is a private, nonprofit corporation which provides homes to people with AIDS as well as other terminal illnesses. In December 1992 the Community leased the residence at 716 Rio Arriba, S.E., Albuquerque, located in a planned subdivision called Four Hills Village, for use as a group home for four individuals with AIDS. The four residents who subsequently moved into the Community's group home were unrelated, and each required some degree of in-home nursing care.

Plaintiffs–Appellees, William Hill, III, Derek Head, Charlene Leamons, and Bernard Dueto (hereinafter Neighbors) live in Four Hills Village on the same dead-end street as the group home. Shortly after the group home opened, the Neighbors noticed an increase in traffic on Rio Arriba street, going to and from the group home. The Neighbors believed that the Community's use of its house as a group home for people with AIDS violated one of the restrictive covenants applicable to all the homes in the sixteenth installment of Four Hills Village. Installment sixteen encompasses the Community's group home and the Neighbors' houses. The applicable covenant provides in relevant part:

> No lot shall ever be used for any purpose other than single family residence purposes. No dwelling house located thereon shall ever be used for other than single family residence purposes, nor shall any outbuildings or structure located thereon be used in a manner other than incidental to such family residence purposes. The erection or maintenance or use of any building, or the use of any lot for other purposes, including, but not restricted to such examples as stores, shops, flats, duplex houses, apartment houses, rooming houses, tourist courts, schools, churches, hospitals, and filling stations is hereby expressly prohibited. * * *

On August 12, 1993, the Neighbors filed for an injunction to enforce the covenant and to prevent further use of the Community's house as a group home. The Community defended on the grounds that the covenant did not prohibit the group home and, in the alternative, that enforcement of the covenant would violate the FHA. * * *

The first issue before us is the applicability of the Four Hills restrictive covenant to the Community's group home. As this Court noted in Cain v. Powers, 100 N.M. 184, 186, 668 P.2d 300, 302 (1983), in determining whether to enforce a restrictive covenant, we are guided by certain general rules of construction. First, if the language is unclear or ambiguous, we will resolve the restrictive covenant in favor of the free enjoyment of the property and against restrictions. Second, we will not read restrictions on the use and enjoyment of the land into the covenant by implication. Third, we must interpret the covenant reasonably, but strictly, so as not to create an illogical, unnatural, or strained construction. Fourth, we must give words in the restrictive covenant their ordinary and intended meaning. * * *

At issue here is the proper interpretation of the restriction, "No lot shall ever be used for any purpose other than single family residence purposes." The trial court held that the Community's use of property as a group home for four, unrelated individuals with AIDS violated this restriction. In reaching its conclusion that the group home violated the residential use restriction, the trial court made two specific findings regarding the nature of the current use of the home. The court found that the "Community uses the house ... as a nonprofit hostel for providing services to handicapped individuals" and that the "Community uses of the residence are much closer to the uses commonly associated with health care facilities, apartment houses, and rooming houses than uses which are commonly associated with single family residences." Thus the trial court apparently concluded that the property was being used for commercial purposes rather than residential purposes. However, we find that the trial court's conclusions are incorrect as a matter of law.

It is undisputed that the group home is designed to provide the four individuals who live in the house with a traditional family structure, setting, and atmosphere, and that the individuals who reside there use the home much as would any family with a disabled family member. The four residents share communal meals. They provide support for each other socially, emotionally, and financially. They also receive spiritual guidance together from religious leaders who visit them on Tuesday evenings.

To provide for their health care needs, the residents contract with a private nursing service for health-care workers. These health-care workers do not reside at the home, and they are not affiliated with the Community in any way. * * * The health-care workers do most of the cooking and cleaning. The residents do their own shopping unless they are physically unable to leave the home.

The Community's role in the group home is to provide oversight and administrative assistance. It organizes the health-care workers' schedules to ensure that a nurse is present twenty-four hours per day, and it provides oversight to ensure that the workers are doing their jobs properly. It also receives donations of food and furniture on behalf of the residents. The Community provides additional assistance for the residents at times when they are unable to perform tasks themselves. A Community worker remains at the house during the afternoon and evening but does not reside at the home. The Community, in turn, collects rent from the residents based on the amount of social security income the residents receive, and it enforces a policy of no drinking or drug use in the home.

The Community's activities in providing the group home for the residents do not render the home a nonresidential operation such as a hospice or boarding house. As the South Carolina Supreme Court noted when faced with a similar situation involving a group home for mentally impaired individuals: This Court finds persuasive the reasoning of other jurisdictions which have held that the incident necessities of operating a group home such as maintaining records, filing accounting reports, managing, supervising, and providing care for individuals in exchange for monetary compensation are collateral to the prime purpose and function of a family housekeeping unit. Hence, these activities do not, in and of themselves, change the character of a residence from private to commercial. Rhodes v. Palmetto Pathway Homes, Inc., 303 S.C. 308, 400 S.E.2d 484, 485–86 (1991). In Jackson v. Williams, 714 P.2d 1017, 1022 (Okla. 1985), the Oklahoma Supreme Court similarly concluded: The essential purpose of the group home is to create a normal family atmosphere dissimilar from that found in traditional institutional care for the mentally handicapped. The operation of a group home is thus distinguishable from a use that is commercial—i.e., a boarding house that provides food and lodging only—or is institutional in character. * * * Accordingly, we conclude as a matter of law that, given the undisputed facts regarding how the Community operates the group home and regarding the nature of the family life in the home, the home is used for residential purposes in compliance with the restrictive covenant. * * *

The Neighbors also argue on appeal that the four, unrelated residents of the group home do not constitute a "single family" as required by the restrictive covenant. The Neighbors contend that the restrictive covenant should be interpreted such that the term "family" encompasses only individuals related by blood or by law. We disagree.

The word "family" is not defined in the restrictive covenant and nothing in the covenant suggests that it was the intent of the framers to limit the term to a discrete family unit comprised only of individuals related by blood or by law. Accordingly, the use of the term "family" in the covenant is ambiguous. As we noted above, we must resolve any ambiguity in the restrictive covenant in favor of the free enjoyment of the property. This rule of construction therefore militates in favor of a conclusion that the term "family" encompasses a broader group than just related individuals and against restricting the use of the property solely to a traditional nuclear family.

In addition, there are several other factors that lead us to define the term "family" as including unrelated individuals. First, the Albuquerque municipal zoning ordinance provides a definition of family that is at odds with the restrictive definition suggested by the Neighbors. The Albuquerque zoning ordinance includes within the definition of the term "family," "[a]ny group of not more than five [unrelated] persons living together in a dwelling." Albuquerque, N.M., Rev. Ordinances, art. XIV, § 7–14–5(B)(41) (1974 & Supp.1991). * * *

Second, there is a strong public policy in favor of including small group homes within the definition of the term "family." The federal government has expressed a clear policy in favor of removing barriers preventing individuals with physical and mental disabilities from living in group homes in residential settings and against restrictive definitions of "families" that serve to exclude congregate living arrangements for the disabled. The FHA squarely sets out this important public policy. As the court in United States v. Scott, 788 F.Supp. 1555, 1561 n. 5 (D.Kan.1992), stated, "The legislative history of the amended Fair Housing Act reflects the national policy of deinstitutionalizing disabled individuals and integrating them into the mainstream of society." The Scott court further noted that the Act "is intended to prohibit special restrictive covenants or other terms or conditions, or denials of service because of an individual's handicap and which ... exclud[e], for example, congregate living arrangements for persons with handicaps." * * * It "protects against efforts to 'restrict the ability of individuals with handicaps to live in communities.' " Id. This policy is applicable to the present case because the FHA's protections for handicapped people extend to individuals with AIDS. See Support Ministries for Persons with AIDS, Inc. v. Village of Waterford, 808 F.Supp. 120, 129 (N.D.N.Y.1992) ("The legislative history of the 1988 amendments to the FHA reveals that Congress intended to include among 'handicapped' persons those who are HIV-positive...."). * * *

Furthermore, the state grant of zoning authority to municipalities, NMSA 1978, § 3–21–1(C) (Repl.Pamp.1995), expressly provides: All state-licensed or state-operated community residences for the mentally ill or developmentally disabled serving ten or fewer persons may be considered a residential use of property for purposes of zoning and may be permitted use in all districts in which residential uses are permitted generally, including particularly residential zones for single-family dwellings. Although this section may not necessarily require that municipalities include community residences within single-family residential zones, it clearly indicates a preference for municipalities adopting this inclusionary approach.

Third, other jurisdictions have consistently held that restrictive covenants mandating single-family residences do not bar group homes in which the occupants live as a family unit. For example the Williams court noted, "When ... the restrictive covenant under consideration prohibits occupancy of more than one family unit but does not address itself to the composition of the family, a court is loathe to restrict a family unit to that composed of persons who are related, one to another, by consanguinity or affinity." Williams, 714 P.2d at 1023; see also Welsch v. Goswick, 130 Cal.App.3d 398, 181 Cal.Rptr. 703, 709–10 (1982) (noting that policy considerations mandate that covenant be interpreted to allow residential care facilities of six or fewer people); Maull v. Community Living for the Handicapped, Inc., 813 S.W.2d 90, 92 (Mo.Ct.App.1991) ("[G]roup homes where the residents function in a family setting, interdependent on one another in carrying out the daily operation and routine of the residence meet the single family requirement of the covenant."). * * *

Accordingly, we reject the Neighbors' claim that the term "family" in the restrictive covenants should be read to include only individuals related by blood or by law.

The Neighbors strenuously argue that the covenant should be interpreted to exclude the group home because the group home's operation has an adverse impact on the neighborhood. In support of this claim, the Neighbors point to the trial court's findings that "[t]he amount of vehicular traffic generated by [the] Community's use of the house ... greatly exceeds what is expected in an average residential area" and that, as a result, "the character of [the] residential neighborhood relative to traffic and to parked vehicles has been significantly altered to the detriment of this residential neighborhood and is [sic] residents." The Neighbors contend that these facts are uncontradicted and point out that this Court is bound by the factual findings of the trial court unless the findings are not supported by substantial evidence. * * *

However, the Neighbors fail to appreciate that the amount of traffic generated by the group home simply is not relevant to determining whether the use of the house as a group home violated the covenant in this case. A review of all the provisions in the covenant reveals that the restrictive covenants for the Four Hills Village, sixteenth installment, are not directed at controlling either traffic or on-street parking. The various covenants and restrictions that attach to the neighborhood homes merely regulate the structural appearance and use of the homes. For example, the covenants regulate building architecture, views, frontage, setback, visible fences and walls, signs and billboards, trash and weeds, trailers and campers parked in yards, maintaining livestock, and of course nonresidential uses of homes. However, not one of the fifteen provisions and numerous paragraphs of the covenants attempts to control the number of automobiles that a resident may accommodate on or off the property nor the amount of traffic a resident may generate. * * *

[The Court also concluded that the restriction violated the Federal Fair Housing Act; that statute and its application to the handicapped are discussed in Ch. 12 at § 12.3]

NOTES AND QUESTIONS

1. As the principal case illustrates, the courts have been quite concerned that expansive use of restrictive covenants could effectively deny group homes and similar facilities access to the locations in which they can function most effectively. Most courts have done one of two things. They have either interpreted the restrictions very narrowly so as to tolerate the group homes, or else they have simply declared the restrictions unenforceable under the public policy of the state. Hill is an example of the first approach. Illustrating the second is Crane Neck Association, Inc. v. New York City/Long Island County Services Group, 61 N.Y.2d 154, 472 N.Y.S.2d 901, 460 N.E.2d 1336 (1984), which involved an action against the operators of a leased house used as a residence for eight mentally handicapped adults for violation of a restrictive covenant against the maintenance of other than single-family residences. Rather than construing the covenant so as to permit the use, as the lower court had done, the court held that no such covenant could be enforced, because New York had a long-standing public policy of encouraging the establishment of such homes for the mentally disabled. To the defendants' objection that applying public policy in this fashion impaired the obligation of a pre-existing contract, in violation of Art. I, § 10 of the federal constitution, the court said:

> Although the language of the contract clause is facially absolute, this court has long recognized that the State's interest in protecting the general good of the public through social welfare legislation is paramount to the interests of parties under private contracts, and the State may impair such contracts by subsequent legislation or regulation so long as it is reasonably necessary to further an important public purpose and the measures taken that impair the contract are reasonable and appropriate to effectuate that purpose.

61 N.Y.2d at 167, 460 N.E.2d at 1343. Accord Westwood Homeowners Ass'n v. Tenhoff, 155 Ariz. 229, 745 P.2d 976 (App.1987); Craig v. Bossenbery, 134 Mich.App. 543, 351 N.W.2d 596 (1984).

By contrast, the Indiana Supreme Court found that a statute invalidating covenants restricting group homes violated the state constitution's contract clause, when applied to covenants already in existence at the time the statute was passed. Clem v. Christole, Inc., 582 N.E.2d 780 (Ind.1991). Other decisions have also enforced the restrictions. See Omega Corp. of Chesterfield v. Malloy, 228 Va. 12, 319 S.E.2d 728 (1984), cert. denied, 469 U.S. 1192 (1985), holding that a restrictive covenant providing that "no building shall be erected . . . other than one detached single-family dwelling" prohibited a group home for the mentally disabled from locating within the restricted community. The court held that the use would convert a single-family residence into a "facility," which was precisely what the drafters of the restriction wanted to avoid in their neighborhood.

Decisions such as *Clem* and *Omega* have likely been overruled by the Fair Housing Act Amendments of 1988, insofar as they pertain to group homes for the "handicapped" or some other protected classification. These provisions are discussed in chapter 12. But the Fair Housing Act may not reach group homes for persons falling outside of the "handicapped" classification—such as women who have been physically abused by their partners, or former prison inmates placed into a halfway house as they are in transition to complete release.

2. A few courts have taken the position that servitudes that cover a large enough area, such as a municipality, reflect a sufficient amount of "state action" that the limitations of the Fourteenth Amendment apply to them. The basic problem is addressed more fully in the discussion of private housing discrimination and Shelley v. Kraemer, 334 U.S. 1 (1948), infra, Chapter 12. See Gerber v. Longboat Harbour North Condominium, 757 F.Supp. 1339 (M.D.Fla.1991) (applying *Shelley* to private covenant prohibiting display of the American flag); Park Redlands Covenant Control Committee v. Simon, 181 Cal.App.3d 87, 226 Cal.Rptr. 199 (1986) (covenants restricting occupancy to three persons violated state constitutional right to privacy). Contra, Linn Valley Lakes Property Owners Association v. Brockway, 250 Kan. 169, 824 P.2d 948 (1992) (enforcement of restrictive covenant against signs not unconstitutional state action under Shelley v. Kraemer); Quail Creek Property Owners Ass'n, Inc. v. Hunter, 538 So.2d 1288 (Fla.App.1989) (federal constitution not implicated in private covenants restricting advertising signs). See also Committee for a Better Twin Rivers v. Twin Rivers Homeowners' Assn., 383 N.J.Super. 22, 890 A.2d 947 (App.Div. 2006), which struck down private restrictions on dissenting political speech made by a homeowner's association in a private subdivision. The result was roughly akin to First Amendment protection for political decision making within a completely private association, effectively eliminating the "state action" limitation on free speech rights:

> We reject the notion that a community association's suppression of its own members' campaigns for election to the board of that association or any other expressive exercise relating to life in the community or elsewhere should be regarded as matters of contractual right or business judgment. In the exercise of fundamental rights, we discern no principled basis for distinguishing between the general public at large and the members of a community association. Because of the broadly applicable rights guarantees contained in the New Jersey Constitution, any regulation of a fundamental right engages the public interest by definition,

especially where the regulator is functionally equivalent to a governmental body in its impact upon the affected public.

3.   Several states have enacted statutes that either prevent servitudes to be interpreted so as to exclude group homes, or else require that "single family" restrictions be interpreted in such a way as to permit them. See Sussex Community Services Assn. v. Virginia Society for Mentally Retarded Children, 251 Va. 240, 467 S.E.2d 468 (1996), which approved retroactive application of this state statute:

> A family care home, foster home, or group home in which physically handicapped, mentally ill, mentally retarded, or developmentally disabled persons reside, with one or more resident counselors or other staff persons, shall be considered for all purposes residential occupancy by a single family when construing any restrictive covenant which purports to restrict occupancy or ownership of real or leasehold property to members of a single family or to residential use or structure.

See also California Residential Care Facilities for the Elderly Act, Health & Saf.Code, § 1569:

> For the purposes of any contract, deed, or covenant for the transfer of real property executed on or after January 1, 1979, a residential facility for the elderly which serves six or fewer persons shall be considered a residential use of property and a use of property by a single family, notwithstanding any disclaimers to the contrary.

Hall v. Butte Home Health, 60 Cal.App.4th 308, 70 Cal.Rptr.2d 246 (1997), held that application of the statute to a covenant executed after 1979 but before the statute was passed was not an unconstitutional impairment of an obligation of contract.

§ 8.7   TERMINATION AND AMENDMENT OF SERVITUDES

§ 8.7.1   TERMINATION BY MERGER, ADVERSE POSSESSION AND ABANDONMENT

CASTLE ASSOCIATES v. SCHWARTZ

New York Supreme Court, Appellate Division (1978).
63 A.D.2d 481, 407 N.Y.S.2d 717.

DAMIANI, JUSTICE.

This is an action to compel the location and opening of an easement of ingress and egress across the lands of Irving Schwartz (hereafter defendant), which was granted by deed dated March 26, 1903.

The property involved is situated in the Town of Huntington in Suffolk County. In 1883 some 17 acres of land were acquired by one William Simpson and his wife as shown on the following diagram:

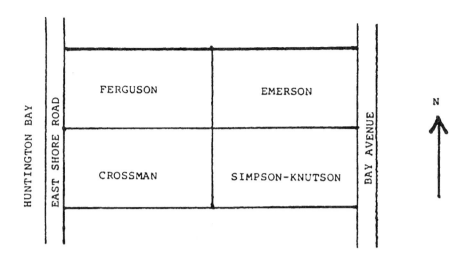

This irregularly shaped tract was longer from east to west, than it was wide from north to south. Two roads adjoin the property. Bay Avenue is a north-south roadway and abuts the eastern edge of the Simpson tract, and East Shore Road runs in the same directions and abuts the western edge. Further to the west lies a body of water known as Huntington Bay. The major portion of the tract is upland, but along its western border the land descends in a steep hill towards East Shore Road and the level of the water. Apparently the existence of this hill makes access to the interior portions of the tract from East Shore Road difficult.

In 1897 Simpson sold a small parcel to Edwin Sweet. The remainder of his land was thereafter divided into four sections. In 1903 Simpson sold the southwest section to Gilbert Crossman. Although the Crossman parcel has frontage on East Shore Road, access to the interior of the parcel is limited by the steep hill. Accordingly, the deed from Simpson to Crossman contained a provision that the land was sold:

> "Together with a right of way for ingress and egress over and along a strip of land 12 feet in width directly adjoining the easterly side of said premises first above described and continuing to Bay Avenue. And the parties of the first part further covenant that when said WILLIAM SIMPSON sells any of his lots fronting on Bay Avenue he will open a road for public use 25 feet in width directly adjoining the said easterly side of said premises first above described and embracing the said 12 feet continuing to Bay Avenue, over which roadway the party of the second part shall have a right of way for ingress and egress to Bay Avenue."

The terms of this grant do not locate the easement and its effect was merely to provide for a right of way running from the eastern border of the Crossman parcel across portions of either the northeast or southeast parcels retained by Simpson to Bay Avenue, depending upon the route chosen for the easement.

In 1907 Simpson sold the northeast parcel to Edward N. Emerson. Since that property fronted on Bay Avenue, the terms of the 1903 deed to Crossman obligated Simpson to open a 25–foot wide roadway from the Crossman parcel to Bay Avenue. The road was never opened and so far as this record shows, no objection to Simpson's failure to do so was ever registered.

Later in 1907 Simpson sold the northwest parcel to Juliana Ferguson and thereafter she purchased the northeast parcel from Emerson and the southwest parcel from mesne grantees of Crossman. Thus, by 1908, Ferguson owned three of the four parcels formerly owned by Simpson, who retained the southeast parcel.

In 1946 John Knutson purchased the southeast parcel from the successors in title to Simpson. When Knutson purchased the property, portions of its boundary were marked by either a barbed wire or wooden picket fence. In 1956 and 1957 Knutson replaced the existing fencing with an anchor chain-link fence on the east, north and west perimeters of his property to protect domestic, farm and game animals which he kept on the land from hunters and wild dogs. Knutson was unaware of the existence of an easement of way across his property.

Eventually, all the Ferguson land was acquired by plaintiff for the purposes of subdivision and development. In preparing a plan for the development of the former Crossman parcel, engineering studies disclosed that because of the contour of the land, it was economically prohibitive to provide for road access to the upland portion of the parcel either from the west or north. Plaintiff attempted to purchase a small triangular corner of the Simpson–Knutson parcel, now owned by defendant, so as to provide it with a route from the rear upland area of the Crossman parcel to Bay Avenue, through the former Emerson parcel that plaintiff already owned. Defendant refused to sell.

In 1976 plaintiff commissioned a title search which disclosed the forgotten easement granted by Simpson for the benefit of the Crossman parcel. Plaintiff demanded that defendant locate and open a right of way across his property, defendant refused, and this suit resulted. Special Term held that in 1908 when Juliana Ferguson acquired both the dominant Crossman parcel and the Emerson parcel which contained a portion of the servient estate and had access to Bay Avenue, a merger of the dominant and servient estates was effected resulting in the extinguishment of the easement.

We hold that the easement was not extinguished or abandoned and that plaintiff is entitled to its right of way across the lands of defendant. It is fundamental that where the title in fee to both the dominant and servient tenements becomes vested in one person, an easement is extinguished.... However, in the case at bar, the easement was granted for the purpose of providing road access to and from the upland portion of the Crossman parcel, which because of the contours of the land, could not be had through the northern or western boundaries of that property. Accordingly, the grant provided that the 12–foot wide right of way was to run from the eastern boundary of the Crossman parcel across the lands then retained by Simpson. Although portions of the Emerson parcel were burdened by and servient to this easement, the western boundary of that parcel is not contiguous to the eastern boundary of the Crossman parcel; they merely touch at their respective southwestern and northeastern corners. This simply means that a portion of the easement was never in the hands of the owner of the dominant estate. In order for an owner of the dominant Crossman parcel to reach Bay Avenue by way of the servient portions of the Emerson parcel he had, by necessity, to cross the Simpson–Knutson parcel. The easement was therefore not extinguished by merger.

Nor do the facts of this case establish that the easement was abandoned. Easements created by grant are not lost by nonuser alone. The owner of the dominant tenement is under no duty to make use of the easement as a condition to retaining his interest therein (Conabeer v. New York Cent. & Hudson Riv. R.R. Co., 156 N.Y. 474, 51 N.E. 402). "[W]here an abandonment of an easement is relied upon, there must be clear and convincing proof of an intention in the owner to abandon it as such", independent of the mere nonuser.

* * *

Defendant contends that the erection of a fence around the Knutson property for more than the prescriptive period extinguished the easement by adverse possession. We disagree.

The established rule is that the maintenance of a fence or structure across an existing right of way which bars its use as such for more than the prescriptive period will terminate the easement by adverse possession.... The key fact is that the fence or obstruction must block an *existing* right of way (see Ann., 1 ALR 884; Ann., 66 ALR 1099; Ann., 25 ALR2d 1265).

* * *

There are five essential elements necessary to constitute an effective adverse possession: first, the possession must be hostile and under a claim of right; second, it must be actual; third, it must be open and notorious; fourth, it must be exclusive; and fifth, it must be continuous. If any of these constituents is wanting, the possession will not effect a bar of the legal title.

* * *

In the instant case, the right of way granted in the deed from Simpson to Crossman has never been "located" and no owner of the Crossman parcel ever requested that a right of way be opened until shortly before the commencement of this action. The upland portion of the Crossman parcel remains unimproved woodland. This fact pattern is similar to Powlowski v. Mohawk Golf Club, 204 App.Div. 200, 198 N.Y.S. 30, in which an owner had divided his property into lots and filed a plat showing the lots and the proposed streets. Powlowski was one of the purchasers of these lots and he had access to an established highway. The Mohawk Golf Club was the purchaser of other lots and it erected a fence across a proposed street which led past the plaintiff's land to the interior of the tract which had been subdivided by the original grantor.

Powlowski sued to restrain the maintenance of the fence across the proposed street by the Mohawk Golf Club upon the ground that the golf club might acquire adverse possession of the land lying in the proposed street and thereby block its use when the entire subdivision was finally opened. The Appellate Division, Third Department, held that the erection of a fence across an unopened right of way could not give rise to an adverse possession stating:

* * *

"We do not approve of the conclusion that 'Unless restrained by the court such continued trespass, continuing for twenty years adversely, will entitle the defendant, its successors and assigns, as a matter of law, to continue the fence permanently and so to deprive the plaintiffs of rights, property and easements.' An adverse possession, under which prescriptive title may ripen, involves an assertion of a right such as exposes the party to an action, unless he has a grant, for it is the fact of his being thus exposed, and the neglect of the opposite party to bring suit, which is seized upon as the ground for presuming a grant in favor of long possession and enjoyment, upon the idea that this adverse possession would not have been submitted to if there had not been a grant. The whole theory of prescription depends upon a presumed grant and upon acquiescence and laches upon the part of the owner.... The construction of the fence does not necessarily assert title in contradiction of the real owner's title."

* * *

There is not here any assertion of a right in conflict with plaintiffs' present right. Plaintiffs have no occasion to assert their right to pass easterly until the streets have been opened, or until demand is made upon the grantor to open them and he fails to do so; no time is fixed when the streets shall be opened. The lot owners have no occasion to pass over or use streets which do not exist.

* * *

We think such possession can never ripen into title as against such right as the plaintiffs may have and choose to assert later."

The rule to be derived ... is that where an easement has been created but no occasion has arisen for its use, the owner of the servient tenement may fence his land and such use will not be deemed adverse to the existence of the easement until such time as (1) the need for the right of way arises, (2) a demand is made by the owner of the dominant tenement that the easement be opened and (3) the owner of the servient tenement refuses to do so. Cases from other jurisdictions support this conclusion (Litchfield v. Boogher, 238 Mo. 472, 142 S.W. 302; Storrow v. Green, 39 Cal.App. 123, 178 P. 339).

Here the upland portion of the Crossman parcel is inaccessible from East Shore Road by reason of the steep hill on the property. This upland portion of the Crossman parcel is woodland and has not been used in all the years since the easement was granted. Now the plaintiff seeks to develop the Crossman parcel and to do so it requires the use of the easement which was specifically granted for the purpose of access. It is our view that the erection of the fence on the defendant's property prior to any demand for an opening of the right of way was not adverse to the existence of the easement and that, in the light of the strong policy against the extinguishment of easements created by specific grant, the plaintiff is entitled to prevail.

CONSOLIDATED RAIL CORP. v. LEWELLEN

Supreme Court of Indiana (1997).
682 N.E.2d 779.

SULLIVAN, JUSTICE.

This case is one of a number of Indiana lawsuits raising issues related to the ownership and use of parcels of land formerly constituting railroad rights-of-way. Here we agree with the trial court and Court of Appeals that the parcels in question are now owned by the owners of the land adjacent to the former right-of-way. * * *

Landowners Pam Lewellen, Jerry Howard, Dale Remley and Cynthia and David Denman brought a class action lawsuit against Consolidated Rail Corporation, Inc. ("Conrail"), to quiet title in segments of land of an abandoned railway corridor. * * * Handwritten deeds more than 100 years old evidence the conveyance of the property to the original railroad. Many of the deeds state: [Grantor], for consideration, "... hereby Conveys and Warrants to the [Railroad] the Land, Right of way and Right of Drainage for its Railway ..."

As activity over the rail line decreased, Conrail elected to discontinue rail service over this corridor. * * *

West Central Indiana Rails to Trails, Inc. ("West Central"), a public interest group concerned with preserving railway corridors, purchased Conrail's interest in the corridor as evidenced by a quitclaim deed recorded July 6, 1994. Landowners filed the present class action lawsuit against Conrail and West Central claiming that Conrail acquired mere easements which upon abandonment of the rail line were extinguished. * * *

Appellants Conrail and West Central argue that the Court of Appeals erred in concluding that the deeds in question conveyed an easement rather than fee simple interest. In support of this argument, appellants point to the statute in place at the time the deeds were executed (still in place today) which provides that any conveyance worded as "A.B. conveys and warrants to C.D." [here describe the premises] "for the sum of" [here insert consideration] "shall be deemed and held to be a conveyance in fee simple to the grantee...." With regard to this argument, we adopt the Court of Appeal's reasoning that the use of the term "right of way" in the deeds in issue in this case conveyed to the railroad only an easement. * * *

In Brown [v. Penn Central Corp., 510 N.E.2d 641 (Ind.1987)], the deed conveyed to the railroad "the Right of Way for the use of the Railroad ..." and "a strip Two hundred feet in width ... for Depot and Rail Road purposes." The dispute was over whether the 200 foot strip used for the depot was an easement. We found that the deed, clearly falling within the general rule articulated above, conveyed only an easement. Here, as in Brown, the handwritten conveyance forms contain, along with the term "right of way," additional language indicating the purpose for which the land was to be used: "Land, Right of way and Right of drainage for its Railway" (emphasis added and differences in capitalization in various deeds ignored). We conclude that the conveyances were merely easements. * * *

Property law in Indiana provides that, upon abandonment by the railroad, a railroad easement terminates and the fee simple interest in the land reverts to the grantor, or the grantor's heirs, assigns or devisees. More precisely, the title of the grantor no longer is subject to the burden of the easement. Lake County Trust Co. v. Lane, 478 N.E.2d 684, 688 (Ind.Ct.App.1985) (where railroad held only an easement "upon abandonment of the railroad, the property passed to the adjoining landowners")* * *

We look to Indiana common law and Indiana statutes in order to determine what constitutes abandonment for purposes of extinguishing a railroad's right-of-way easement. Under the common law of this state, the intent to abandon was a necessary element of abandonment of an easement created by express grant. Seymour Water Company v. Lebline, 195 Ind. 481, 489, 144 N.E. 30, 33 (1924). The question of abandonment was a question of intention to be determined from the facts of the case. Perry v. Carey, 68 Ind.App. 56, 60, 119 N.E. 1010, 1011 (1918). Although an easement acquired by actual grant was not extinguished by mere nonuse, nonuse plus an act indicating an intent to abandon may have had the effect of extinguishing the easement. Id.

* * * [Further,] the common law on whether abandonment has occurred was superseded by the General Assembly. In a statute enacted in 1987, the legislature determined that a railroad abandons its right of way when (1) the ICC issues a certificate relieving the railroad of its common carrier obligation on the right of way and (2) "rails, switches, ties, and other facilities" have been removed from the right of way. Ind. Code § 32–5–12–6(a)(2) (Supp.1996)). The legislature of this state decided that issuance of a certificate of abandonment and removal of railroad "facilities" sufficiently evidence a railroad's intent to abandon. * * *

Conrail and West Central characterize their argument as one promoting the public policy favoring the preservation of railway corridors as recreational trails. In support of its motion for summary judgment before the trial court, Conrail points to the United States National Trails System Act, 16 U.S.C. § 1241 et seq. (Trails System Act), and Ind. Code § 8–3–1– 21.1 (1993) as evidence of the national and state public policy of preserving railroad rights-of-way. We do not disagree that Congress and the Indiana Legislature may have the authority to preserve the right of the public in existing rail corridors. See Preseault v. I.C.C., 494 U.S. 1, 110 S.Ct. 914, 108 L.Ed.2d 1 (1990) (holding the Trails System Act, as amended in 1983, to be a valid exercise of Congressional power under the Commerce Clause). Cf. Preseault v. United States, 100 F.3d 1525 (Fed.Cir. 1996)(in banc) (plurality opinion of Plager, J.) (holding exercise of government authority under Trails System Act to be a compensable taking on facts presented). However, West Central and Conrail do not rely upon any action taken pursuant to such legislative enactments to support the argument urging this Court to reverse the trial court's grant of summary judgment. * * *

* * * [T]he deeds unambiguously convey to the railroad a mere right-of-way easement. * * *

NOTES AND QUESTIONS

1. When the owner of the fee simple in the dominant estate acquires the fee simple in the servient estate the easement is extinguished if both interests are possessory. If the dominant estate is under lease to someone else at the time, the easement continues to exist until the lease expires. If the owner of the two estates sells one of them before the lease expires, the easement will not be extinguished. See Dority v. Dunning, 78 Me. 381, 6 A. 6 (1886).

What if the owner of a fee simple absolute in the dominant estate acquires a life estate in the servient estate? See Crocker v. Cotting, 170 Mass. 68, 48 N.E. 1023 (1898), where the owner of the dominant estate became a tenant in common of the servient estate. The easements were not extinguished. Justice Holmes held that the easements "would not be extinguished so long as any difference in the quality of the title to the dominant and servient estates made it in any degree for the interest of the dominant owners to keep them alive." Id. at 69, 48 N.E. at 1023–1024.

2. Why does the law even recognize a rule that easements can be extinguished by abandonment? After all, possessory interests cannot be extinguished that way. One important difference is that, in the case of possessory interests, there is no one to whom the land will revert, unless it is being possessed by someone else. The common law legal system has never been able to deal with the concept of "unowned" land. In the case of an easement, however, the abandoned right goes to the owner of the servient estate, in the form of a release from the easement.

A few states permit easements to be declared abandoned merely upon proof of non-use for the same period as the statute of limitation for adverse possession or prescription. See, e.g., Owners Assn. of Foxcroft Woods, Inc. v. Foxglen Assocs., 346 Ark. 354, 57 S.W.3d 187 (2001).

§ 8.7.2   CHANGED CONDITIONS WARRANTING TERMINATION

EL DI, INC. v. TOWN OF BETHANY BEACH

Supreme Court of Delaware (1984).
477 A.2d 1066.

HERRMANN, CHIEF JUSTICE, for the majority:

This is an appeal from a permanent injunction granted by the Court of Chancery upon the petition of the plaintiffs. The Town of Bethany Beach, et al., prohibiting the defendant, El Di, Inc. ("El Di") from selling alcoholic beverages at Holiday House, a restaurant in Bethany Beach owned and operated by El Di.

I.

The pertinent facts are as follows:

El Di purchased the Holiday House in 1969. In December 1981, El Di filed an application with the State Alcoholic Beverage Control Commission (the "Commission") for a license to sell alcoholic beverages at the Holiday House. On April 15, 1982, finding "public need and convenience," the Commission granted the Holiday House an on-premises license. The sale of alcoholic beverages at Holiday House began within 10 days of the Commission's approval. Plaintiffs subsequently filed suit to permanently enjoin the sale of alcoholic beverages under the license.

On appeal it is undisputed that the chain of title for the Holiday House lot included restrictive covenants prohibiting both the sale of alcoholic beverages on the property and nonresidential construction.[1] The same restriction was placed on property in Bethany Beach as early as 1900 and 1901 when the area was first under development.

As originally conceived, Bethany Beach was to be a quiet beach community. The site was selected at the end of the nineteenth-century by the Christian Missionary Society of Washington, D.C. In 1900, the Bethany Beach Improvement Company ("BBIC") was formed. The BBIC pur-

---

1. The restrictive covenant stated:

"This covenant is made expressly subject to and upon the following conditions: viz; That no intoxicating liquors shall ever be sold on the said lot, that no other than dwelling or cottage shall be erected thereon and but one to each lot, which must be of full size according to the said plan, excepting, however, suitable and necessary out or back building, which may be erected on the rear of said lot, and no building or buildings shall be erected thereon within ten feet of the front building line of said lot and, if said lot be a corner lot within ten feet of the building line of the side street on which it abuts, and that all buildings erected or to be erected on said lot shall be kept neatly painted; a breach of which said conditions, or any of them, shall cause said lot to revert to and become again the property of the grantor, his heirs and assigns; and upon such breach of said conditions or restrictions, the same may be restrained or enjoined in equity by the grantor, his heirs or assigns, or by any co-lot owner in said plan or other party injured by such breach."

chased lands, laid out a development and began selling lots. To insure the quiet character of the community, the BBIC placed restrictive covenants on many plots, prohibiting the sale of alcohol and restricting construction to residential cottages. Of the original 180 acre development, however, approximately 1/3 was unrestricted.

The Town of Bethany Beach was officially incorporated in 1909. The municipal limits consisted of 750 acres including the original BBIC land (hereafter the original or "old-Town"), but expanded far beyond the 180 acre BBIC development. The expanded acreage of the newly incorporated Town, combined with the unrestricted plots in the original Town, left only 15 percent of the new Town subject to the restrictive covenants.

Despite the restriction prohibiting commercial building ("no other than a dwelling or cottage shall be erected . . ."), commercial development began in the 1920's on property subject to the covenants. This development included numerous inns, restaurants, drug stores, a bank, motels, a town hall, shops selling various items including food, clothing, gifts and novelties and other commercial businesses. Of the 34 commercial buildings presently within the Town limits, 29 are located in the old-Town originally developed by BBIC. Today, Bethany Beach has a permanent population of some 330 residents. In the summer months the population increases to approximately 10,000 people within the corporate limits and to some 48,000 people within a 4 mile radius. In 1952, the Town enacted a zoning ordinance which established a central commercial district designated C–1 located in the old-Town section. Holiday House is located in this district.

Since El Di purchased Holiday House in 1969, patrons have been permitted to carry their own alcoholic beverages with them into the restaurant to consume with their meals. This "brown-bagging" practice occurred at Holiday House prior to El Di's ownership and at other restaurants in the Town. El Di applied for a license to sell liquor at Holiday House in response to the increased number of customers who were engaging in "brown-bagging" and in the belief that the license would permit restaurant management to control excessive use of alcohol and use by minors. Prior to the time El Di sought a license, alcoholic beverages had been and continue to be readily available for sale at nearby licensed establishments including: one restaurant ½ mile outside the Town limits, 3 restaurants within a 4 mile radius of the Town, and a package store some 200–300 yards from the Holiday House.

The Trial Court granted a stay pending the outcome of this appeal.

II.

In granting plaintiffs' motion for a permanent injunction, the Court of Chancery rejected defendant's argument that changed conditions in Bethany Beach rendered the restrictive covenants unreasonable and therefore unenforceable. Citing Restatement of Property, § 564; Welshire, Inc. v. Harbison, Del.Supr., 91 A.2d 404 (1952); and Cruciano v. Ceccarone,

Del.Ch., 133 A.2d 911 (1957). The Chancery Court found that although the evidence showed a considerable growth since 1900 in both population and the number of buildings in Bethany Beach, "the basic nature of Bethany Beach as a quiet, family oriented resort has not changed." The Court also found that there had been development of commercial activity since 1900, but that this "activity is limited to a small area of Bethany Beach and consists mainly of activities for the convenience and patronage of the residents of Bethany Beach."

The Trial Court also rejected defendant's contention that plaintiffs' acquiescence and abandonment rendered the covenants unenforceable. In this connection, the Court concluded that the practice of "brown-bagging" was not a sale of alcoholic beverages and that, therefore, any failure to enforce the restriction as against the practice did not constitute abandonment or waiver of the restriction.

III.

We find that the Trial Court erred in holding that the change of conditions was insufficient to negate the restrictive covenant.

A court will not enforce a restrictive covenant where a fundamental change has occurred in the intended character of the neighborhood that renders the benefits underlying imposition of the restrictions incapable of enjoyment. Welshire v. Harbison, Del.Supr., 91 A.2d 404 (1952); 1.77 Acres of Land v. State, Del.Supr., 241 A.2d 513 (1968); Williams v. Tsiarkezos, Del.Ch., 272 A.2d 722 (1970). Review of all the facts and circumstances convinces us that the change, since 1901, in the character of that area of the old-Town section now zoned C–1 is so substantial as to justify modification of the deed restriction. We need not determine a change in character of the entire restricted area in order to assess the continued applicability of the covenant to a portion thereof.

It is uncontradicted that one of the purposes underlying the covenant prohibiting the sale of intoxicating liquors was to maintain a quiet, residential atmosphere in the restricted area. Each of the additional covenants reinforces this objective, including the covenant restricting construction to residential dwellings. The covenants read as a whole evince an intention on the part of the grantor to maintain the residential, seaside character of the community.

But time has not left Bethany Beach the same community its grantors envisioned in 1901. The Town has changed from a church-affiliated residential community to a summer resort visited annually by thousands of tourists. Nowhere is the resultant change in character more evident than in the C–1 section of the old-Town. Plaintiffs argue that this is a relative change only and that there is sufficient evidence to support the Trial Court's findings that the residential character of the community has been maintained and that the covenants continue to benefit the other lot owners. We cannot agree.

In 1909, the 180 acre restricted old-Town section became part of a 750 acre incorporated municipality. Even prior to the Town's incorporation, the BBIC deeded out lots free of the restrictive covenants. After incorporation and partly due to the unrestricted lots deeded out by the BBIC, 85 percent of the land area within the Town was not subject to the restrictions. Significantly, nonresidential uses quickly appeared in the restricted area and today the old-Town section contains almost all of the commercial businesses within the entire Town. Contrast Whitaker v. Holmes, Ariz. Supr., 74 Ariz. 30, 243 P.2d 462 (1952) (original grantors specifically provided for continued vitality of the covenants in the event a Town was later established). Moreover, these commercial uses have gone unchallenged for 82 years. Contrast Humphreys v. Ibach, N.J.Supr., 110 N.J.Eq. 647, 160 A. 531 (1932).

The change in conditions is also reflected in the Town's decision in 1952 to zone restricted property, including the lot on which the Holiday House is located, specifically for commercial use. Although a change in zoning is not dispositive as against a private covenant, it is additional evidence of changed community conditions. Bard v. Rose, Cal.Dist.Ct.App., 203 Cal.App.2d 232, 21 Cal.Rptr. 382, 384 (1962). See Owens v. Camfield, Ark.Ct.App., 1 Ark.App. 295, 614 S.W.2d 698 (1981).

Time has relaxed not only the strictly residential character of the area, but the pattern of alcohol use and consumption as well. The practice of "brown-bagging" has continued unchallenged for at least twenty years at commercial establishments located on restricted property in the Town. On appeal, plaintiffs rely on the Trial Court finding that the "brown-bagging" practice is irrelevant as evidence of waiver inasmuch as the practice does not involve the sale of intoxicating liquors prohibited by the covenant. We find the "brown-bagging" practice evidence of a significant change in conditions in the community since its inception at the turn of the century. Such consumption of alcohol in public places is now generally tolerated by owners of similarly restricted lots. The license issued to the Holiday House establishment permits the El Di management to better control the availability and consumption of intoxicating liquors on its premises. In view of both the ready availability of alcoholic beverages in the area surrounding the Holiday House and the long-tolerated and increasing use of "brown-bagging," enforcement of the restrictive covenant at this time would only serve to subvert the public interest in the control of the availability and consumption of alcoholic liquors.

Plaintiffs contend that the covenant prohibiting the sale of intoxicating liquors is separate from the other covenants. In the plaintiffs' view, the alcohol sale restriction serves a purpose distinct from the prohibition of nonresidential uses. Plaintiffs argue, therefore, that despite evidence of commercial uses, the alcohol sale restriction provides a substantial benefit to the other lot owners. We find the cases on which plaintiff relies distinguishable:

In Jameson v. Brown, 109 F.2d 830 (D.C.Cir.1939), all of the lots were similarly restricted and there was no evidence of waiver or abandonment of the covenant prohibiting the sale of spiritous liquors. The court found evidence of one isolated violation—in contrast to the long-tolerated practice of "brown-bagging" in Bethany Beach. Compare Alamogordo Improvement Co. v. Prendergast, N.M.Supr., 45 N.M. 40, 109 P.2d 254 (1940). In Brookside Community, Inc. v. Williams, Del.Ch., 290 A.2d 678, aff'd, 306 A.2d 711 (1973), the general rule in Delaware is stated as to the effect of a waiver of a separable covenant. The case is distinguishable because here we consider waiver in conjunction with our assessment of the change of conditions in the community. No such change was alleged or addressed in *Williams*. In Benner v. Tacony Athletic Ass'n, Pa.Supr., 328 Pa. 577, 196 A. 390 (1938), it was found that commercial encroachments were few and that residential properties still closely surrounded the commercial lots. In Bethany Beach commercial uses have not simply crept in, but have been given official sanction through the 1952 Zoning Ordinance.

It is further argued that the commercial uses are restricted to a small area within the old-Town section. But significantly, the section in which Holiday House is located is entirely commercial. The business uses, the availability of alcohol in close proximity to this section, and the repeated use of "brown-bagging" in the C–1 district render the originally intended benefits of the covenants unattainable in what has become an area detached in character from the strictly residential surroundings to the west.

In view of the change in conditions in the C–1 district of Bethany Beach, we find it unreasonable and inequitable now to enforce the restrictive covenant. To permit unlimited "brown-bagging" but to prohibit licensed sales of alcoholic liquor, under the circumstances of this case, is inconsistent with any reasonable application of the restriction and contrary to public policy.

We emphasize that our judgment is confined to the area of the old-Town section zoned C–1. The restrictions in the neighboring residential area are unaffected by the conclusion we reach herein.

* * *

Reversed.

[A dissenting opinion by Justice Christie is omitted.]

NOTES AND QUESTIONS

1. Frequently landowners ask courts to use the doctrine of changed conditions to relieve them of a "residence only" servitude when their land is on the edge of a subdivision and commercial development outside the subdivision has come up against their lots or is right across the street. Most courts decline the invitation. Do you see why? Consider the following from Lebo v. Johnson, 349 S.W.2d 744, 751 (Tex.Civ.App.1961):

In every growing city it is inevitable that sooner or later commercial and business areas must come face to face with residential areas, and it is then that the restrictions are most valuable to the interior lot owners. It is when the outer tier of lots become more valuable for commercial and business purposes that the restrictions come into play and prevent the residential area from being taken over by commercial establishments. * * *

The front tier of lots must bear the brunt of the onslaughts of business and commerce, otherwise there would be started a system of gradual encroachment that might swallow up the entire residential area. The other tiers of lots might fall like ten pins, once the encroachment of commerce and business was begun. One of the best places to hold the encroachment of business and commerce upon a restricted residential area is at a highway or street. Once the building of business houses is allowed to cross Highway 81, and such building begins within the Terrell Hills Subdivision, the halting of it may prove very difficult, and it could continue until this vast residential area was completely destroyed.

2. Was the restriction at issue in *El Di* an equitable servitude or a determinable fee? If the latter, how can you explain the relief given by the court? There is no doctrine of changed conditions for fees simple determinable or fees simple on condition subsequent. Wouldn't the original grantors have been better off had they ended with the words "shall cause said lot to revert to and become again the property of the grantor, his heirs and assigns...."?

3. Most courts recognize two, quite different rationales for deciding that a particular servitude can no longer be enforced. The doctrine of "changed conditions" generally holds that restrictions will no longer be enforced when the general character of the community *outside* the restricted subdivision has changed so much that the owners of the restricted lots can no longer enjoy the benefits for which the restrictions were created. By contrast, the doctrine of "waiver" or "abandonment" applies when for a long time property owners within the subdivision have acquiesced in certain violations of restrictions, with the result that the character of the land *within* the subdivision has changed. In the latter case many courts simply say that once acquiescence in violations becomes widespread, it is no longer equitable to enforce the restrictions in particular instances. See Fink v. Miller, 896 P.2d 649 (Utah App.1995), cert. denied, 910 P.2d 425 (Utah 1995), which concluded that once 23 out of 81 houses in a subdivision failed to comply with a servitude requiring wood shingles, it could no longer be enforced. The party opposing enforcement had, and met, its burden of proving that existing "violations are so great as to lead the mind of the average [person] to reasonably conclude that the restriction in question has been abandoned."

4. One solution to the problem of changed conditions that have made restrictions onerous to some lot owners in a restricted area, while they remain valuable to others, is to grant the plaintiffs damages but not injunctive relief. The case for damages is particularly strong if the defendant's costs are already "sunk" and are grossly out of proportion to the losses suffered by the plaintiffs. In a neighborhood subject to changed conditions, for example, a lot owner's nonconforming commercial use may injure neighboring property

values by only a small amount. However, an injunction requiring the defendant to tear down an illegal structure might impose large losses. Why not permit the person desiring to build the commercial use to do so, provided that he compensates neighbors for their losses? In that case the use will be maintained if it is efficient—that is, if its value exceeds the damage done to the neighbors—but not if it is inefficient.

Since the law of equitable servitudes grew up in courts of equity, the historical development of the law is not conducive to judicial development of damages rules. For example, it is generally not a defense to an action for injunctive relief that the plaintiff's losses are small in comparison to the costs that the relief would impose upon the defendant. Tubbs v. Brandon, 374 So.2d 1358 (Ala.1979); Gladstone v. Gregory, 95 Nev. 474, 596 P.2d 491 (1979). However, some courts have assessed damages as an alternative to injunctive relief. See Lacov v. Ocean Ave. Bldg. Corp., 257 N.Y. 362, 178 N.E. 559 (1931), where the court granted relief from enforcement of a restriction provided that the parties seeking relief compensate the beneficiaries.

The Restatement (Third) of Property: Servitudes, Section 7.10 entitled Modification and Termination of a Servitude Because of Changed Conditions states the following:

> (1) When a change has taken place since the creation of a servitude that makes it impossible as a practical matter to accomplish the purpose for which the servitude was created, a court may modify the servitude to permit the purpose to be accomplished. If modification is not practicable, or would not be effective, a court may terminate the servitude. Compensation for resulting harm to the beneficiaries may be awarded as a condition of modifying or terminating the servitude.

> (2) If the purpose of a servitude can be accomplished, but because of changed conditions the servient estate is no longer suitable for uses permitted by the servitude, a court may modify the servitude to permit other uses under conditions designed to preserve the benefits of the original servitude.

This Restatement section applies to easements which represents a significant shift away from the traditional common law which does not permit the modification or termination of an easement based upon changed conditions. Of course, some jurisdictions have chosen not to adopt the Restatement's approach. See, e.g., Sluyter v. Hale Fireworks Partnership, 370 Ark. 511, 262 S.W.3d 154, 158–59 (2007) (a case involving an express reciprocal easement in which the court expressly chooses to reject the Restatement and the application of Section 7.10).

5. It has been argued that the entire doctrine of changed conditions is misconceived. When the first agreement creating the condition is struck, this argument goes, the parties will try to foresee future changes and bargain for them. Someone who foresees a time when a condition imposed upon his property will become unreasonably onerous will know that the property will be unmarketable, not only in the future, but to current buyers who can also foresee the change. As a result, he will refuse to accept the condition, or else he will insist on additional compensation. Do you agree? See Epstein, Notice

and Freedom of Contract in the Law of Servitudes, 55 S.Cal.L.Rev. 1353, 1364–68 (1982). What about the answer that human foresight is imperfect, and in the case of servitudes imperfect foresight can impose costs on people other than the original bargainers? See Sterk, Foresight and the Law of Servitudes, 73 Cornell L. Rev. 956 (1988).

NOTE: TERMINATION BY EMINENT DOMAIN

Suppose that Blackacre and Whiteacre are nearby lots mutually protected by "residence only" restrictive covenants. The government takes Blackacre under its eminent domain power and builds a sewage treatment plant there, impairing the value of Whiteacre. Is the destruction of the servitude a "property" interest to Whiteacre's owner, entitling her to just compensation?

The compensation question depends on the nature of the servitude. Traditional easements, such as driveways or pipelines, were historically "property" interests conveyed by deed, and both federal and state law require compensation when they are taken. By contrast, real covenants are "contractual" in nature and equitable servitudes are mere rights in equity. With respect to them, federal law is unclear, and states interpreting their own constitutions are divided.

In the leading case, Southern California Edison Co. v. Bourgerie, 9 Cal.3d 169, 107 Cal.Rptr. 76, 507 P.2d 964 (1973), the California Supreme Court held that compensation was due to the owner of Whiteacre as well as Blackacre. The Court said:

> it is difficult to justify affording compensation for the appropriation of an easement, which is unquestionably compensable "property," while denying payment for violation of a[building] restriction. Both easements and building restrictions may be created by agreements between private parties and, therefore, upon condemnation in both situations the financial burden of the condemner is increased solely by virtue of agreements made between private parties. Equally important, the violation of a building restriction could cause far greater damage in monetary value to a property owner than the appropriation of a mere right of way. To establish a substantive distinction by merely labeling one a property interest for which compensation must be made and the other a mere contractual right which may be appropriated by a condemner without any compensation is inequitable and rationally indefensible.

Id. at 172–173, 107 Cal.Rptr. at 78–79, 507 P.2d at 966–967.

But a strongly worded dissent concluded:

> Today's majority opinion is founded upon the tenuous proposition that a building restriction is substantially equivalent to an easement. Since an easement is a compensable property interest, and since both easements and building restrictions bear some similar characteristics, the majority concludes that a violation of a building restriction in a condemnation action is a taking of a property interest, and is likewise compensable. Yet an easement is an affirmative right of use, whereas a building restriction is wholly negative in character, amounting to no more than a promise not to use property in a particular manner. Although the majority character-

izes the distinction between compensability for easements and noncompensability for building restrictions as "inequitable and rationally indefensible," a number of jurisdictions have found the policies underlying the distinction to be reasonable and persuasive. . . .

Id. at 176, 107 Cal.Rptr. at 81, 507 P.2d at 969.

What particularly concerned the dissenter was the fact that servitudes in subdivisions might create interlocking rights among literally hundreds of landowners. If a single lot were taken and a building restriction violated by the government's new use, must all the lot owners then be named in the eminent domain proceeding and perhaps paid compensation:

> . . . If each parcel in a residential subdivision is mutually benefitted and burdened by a building restriction, then upon violation of the restriction by condemnation proceedings and inconsistent use, the problem is raised as to which persons have compensable property interests requiring joinder in the action. The owner of every benefitted parcel should be joined if, as the majority concludes, each has suffered a taking of "property." . . . These are substantial procedural hurdles which, because of the majority's refusal to consider, may return to haunt us in the near future.

Id. at 177, 107 Cal.Rptr. at 82, 507 P.2d at 970.

A substantial minority of jurisdictions continue to hold that a restrictive covenant is not a property interest for which just compensation must be paid. For example, Arkansas State Highway Comm'n v. McNeill, 238 Ark. 244, 381 S.W.2d 425 (1964). Does this mean that a public entity that takes property by eminent domain can simply ignore any restrictions imposed upon the property for the benefit of others and without paying just compensation for the taking of the restrictive covenant? The answer in these states appears to be that when the government acquires property by eminent domain it is free to ignore the restrictive covenant and does not have to pay just compensation to the owners of the benefitted parcel. See, Ryan v. Town of Manalapan, 414 So.2d 193, 196 (Fla.1982) (stating "restrictive covenants are no more enforceable against a governmental body when it acquires land for public purpose by purchase than when it does so by eminent domain"). But see, Leigh v. Village of Los Lunas, 137 N.M. 119, 108 P.3d 525, 529 (2004) (stating that New Mexico covenants are deemed to be property interests and also characterizing the restrictive covenants in the case as equitable easements). Restatement (Third) Property: Servitudes (2000):

Section 7.8. Modification or Extinguishment by Condemnation

> Condemnation of the benefit of a servitude in the exercise of the power of eminent domain modifies or extinguishes the benefit only if that is the purpose of the condemnation. Condemnation of an estate burdened by a servitude modifies or terminates the servitude to the extent that the taking permits a use inconsistent with continuance of the servitude.

§ 8.7.3 AMENDMENTS

WALTON v. JASKIEWICZ

Court of Appeals of Maryland (1989).
317 Md. 264, 563 A.2d 382.

MURPHY, CHIEF JUDGE.

The question presented is whether a majority of property owners in a residential subdivision may amend a Declaration of Covenants to exempt one lot from a restriction against further subdivision or whether the amendment is invalid because it does not apply uniformly to all lots burdened by the restrictive covenants.

The parties in this case are lot owners and residents of the Brock Hall subdivision, located in the Marlboro District of Prince George's County. Plats 1 and 2 of the subdivision consist of forty-five "estate lots" ranging in size from three to seven acres each, all of which are subject to a Declaration of Covenants dated March 18, 1953, recorded among the Land Records of Prince George's County. The introductory paragraphs of the Declaration set forth several purposes for the covenants. They include to protect the lot purchasers from depreciation in value of their lots, to assure them of uniformity of development of the surrounding property, to facilitate the sale of the lots by the original owner, and "to make certain that said restrictions shall apply uniformly to all the lots in said subdivision to the mutual advantage of the present owner of said lots and to all who may in the future claim title through said present owner."

The Declaration's subsequent paragraphs provide in relevant part: "13. RESUBDIVISION. There shall be no further subdivision of lots in this tract. 14. TERM. These covenants are to run with the land and shall be binding on all parties and all persons claiming under them for a period of twenty-five years from the date these covenants are recorded, after which time said covenants shall be automatically extended for successive periods of ten years unless an instrument signed by a majority of the then owners of the lots has been recorded, agreeing to change said covenants in whole or in part."

Samuel and Helen Walton own and reside on lot 26 of Plat 2 of the subdivision. Their lot, containing approximately four acres, is the smallest lot in Plat 2. A ravine runs through the center of the lot, causing a natural separation into two parcels of land, containing approximately two acres each. The Waltons sought to subdivide their lot along the ravine. They obtained the signatures of a majority of the lot owners in the subdivision on an instrument entitled "Amended Declaration of Covenants" which purported to amend paragraph 13 of the original Declaration to read: "Paragraph 13. RESUBDIVISION. Except for Lot 26, Plat Two as shown on the Plat of Subdivision, there shall be no further subdivision of lots in this tract. Lot 26, Plat Two shall not be resubdivided into more than two lots."

The Waltons recorded this instrument, which was dated June 6, 1985, among the Land Records of Prince George's County. Subsequently, Edmund Jaskiewicz and other lot owners in the subdivision, filed a declaratory judgment action in the Circuit Court for Prince George's County; they sought a declaration that the amendment to paragraph 13 was void and an injunction prohibiting the Waltons from pursuing a resubdivision of lot 26. * * *

The parties acknowledge that there is no Maryland case law addressing the specific issue of whether a declaration [amending] restrictive covenants burdening lots in a residential subdivision must apply uniformly to all lots subject to the covenants absent specific authorization in the declaration. * * *

The Waltons ... contend that public policy favors the free and unrestricted use of land, and thus requires that the Declaration of Covenants be construed as permitting the proposed amendment. They note that " 'where the language employed to express a restrictive covenant so far involves a doubt as to require construction, the rule is that such covenants are to "be strictly construed against the person seeking to enforce them," and that "all doubts must be resolved in favor of natural rights and a free use of the property.' " Harbor View Imp. Ass'n. v. Downey, 270 Md. 365, 371, 311 A.2d 422 (1973). While this rule may constitute a correct general statement of law, it is not applicable in the circumstances of this case as the language of the Declaration of Covenants plainly does not permit the amendment here involved. Courts in other jurisdictions, construing similar language, have held that it is not ambiguous and that an amendment must apply uniformly to all lots subject to the restrictions. Thus, these courts have concluded that an attempt to exempt some lots from a restriction while retaining it as to others is invalid. See, e.g., Camelback Del Este Homeowners v. Warner, 156 Ariz. 21, 749 P.2d 930, 936 (1987) (noting that "unless otherwise provided for in the restrictions themselves, any amendment to restrictive covenants must apply to every lot"); Ridge Park Home Owners v. Pena, 88 N.M. 563, 544 P.2d 278 (1975) (holding that "[n]o changes may be made with respect to any one lot without affecting all the others subject to the restrictions"); Zent v. Murrow, 476 S.W.2d 875, 878 (Tex.Civ.App.1972) (rejecting any rule which "would permit the majority of the lot owners to alter or revoke the restrictions as to a few lots only, and to continue the covenants as to all other property in the section" because such a rule would result in uncertainties and possible discrimination). * * *

In Montoya v. Barreras, 81 N.M. 749, 473 P.2d 363 (1970), the Supreme Court of New Mexico examined covenant language almost identical to that used in paragraph 14 of the Brock Hall covenants. The court noted that "the original restrictions were clearly imposed on all of the described property" and that the granting clause declared that "all of the property shall be encumbered by the restrictions." It then stated:

The phrase "in whole or in part" in covenant (X) clearly modifies the words "to change," and the direct object of "to change" is the word "covenants," not the word "lots." Thus, the covenants may be changed in whole or in part, but we cannot construe this language as permitting any such change or changes to apply to only a portion of the lots on which the restrictions were imposed. Nor is there anything in the covenants themselves which can be construed as either expressly or impliedly modifying or changing the granting clause itself, which expresses the intent and purpose that all of the described property is encumbered by the restrictions, whether they remain as originally stated or are subsequently changed in whole or in part. The original restrictions were clearly imposed on all of the described property, and though the restrictions themselves may be changed in whole or in part, the change or changes which might be made must affect all of the described property.

We agree with the principles so well articulated in *Montoya*. Moreover, as a number of courts have noted, property owners expect that covenants will be enforced uniformly and that owners will enjoy a degree of mutuality under the restrictions. See, e.g., Lakeshore [Estates Recreational Area, Inc. v. Turner, 481 S.W.2d 572, 575 (Mo.App.1972)] (noting that "[p]ersons who purchase lots in a subdivision subject to such use and occupancy restrictions do so upon the expectation of a benefit as well as the obvious burden or obligation of compliance"; and that "[t]hey expect the protection that compliance on the part of the rest of the lot owners affords them and absent their consent, they may not continue to be burdened when others are relieved" unless the modification applies uniformly to all lots). * * * Consequently, "[t]o permit individual lots within an area to be relieved of the burden of such covenants, in the absence of a clear expression in the instrument so providing, would destroy the right to rely on restrictive covenants which has traditionally been upheld by our law of real property." [*Montoya*, supra, 473 P.2d] at 365.

In addition, to allow a majority of lot owners to exempt one or more lots from a restrictive covenant, absent explicit language permitting the exemption, could have serious consequences for lot owners in the minority. For example, in *Ridge Park*, supra, a majority of lot owners approved an amendment removing residential restrictions on a few lots within the subdivision, despite the objection of a minority of lot owners whose property was located nearest to the proposed commercial development. The court held the amendment invalid for lack of uniformity noting that "[t]he mutuality of restrictive covenants would be destroyed if we were to allow the majority of owners, who might not be adversely affected because of their insulated location in the subdivision, to authorize offensive consequences for the minority of owners by removing or imposing restrictions only on certain lots within the minority's area." 544 P.2d at 280. * * *

In the present case, the statement of purpose contained in the Declaration of Covenants governing the Brock Hall subdivision expresses an intent that the covenants apply uniformly to all lots within the subdivision. The amendment provision contained in paragraph 14, like the provisions in *Montoya* and the other cases cited above, provides for changing the covenants in whole or in part; it does not indicate that changes can be made selectively to exempt a single lot from a particular restriction, but rather that the amendment must apply uniformly to all lots subject to the covenant. Therefore, the purported amendment in this case to paragraph 13, releasing lot 26 from the restriction against further subdivision, is not authorized by the declaration of covenants and is invalid. Judgment Affirmed.

NOTES AND QUESTIONS

1. The land owner in *Walton* was seeking relief from an existing restriction against subdivision. Suppose that the amendment would increase, rather than decrease, the intensity of restriction imposed on subdivision property. Even if such an amendment were uniform with respect to all lots, it could impose a burden on those who (1) bought in reliance on their ability to do a certain thing on their land; or (2) had already invested in some use or structure that the amendment seeks to condemn. In McMillan v. Iserman, 120 Mich.App. 785, 327 N.W.2d 559 (1982), the court held that such an amendment would not apply to a particular lot if "(1) the lot owner justifiably relied on the existing restrictions (i.e., had no notice of the proposed amendment), and (2) the lot owner will be prejudiced if the amendment is enforced as to his or her lot." The court then held that an amended restriction could not be applied so as to preclude the defendant from using its land for a state licensed facility for the developmentally disabled. See also Armstrong v. Ledges Homeowners Assn., 360 N.C. 547, 633 S.E.2d 78 (2006) where lot owners in a small subdivision initially signed a covenant requiring them to pay only a pro rata share of electricity to light up an entrance sign, which was less than $1.00 per year per lot, but there was also a covenant permitting the home owners association to amend the restrictions. The association then passed amendments increasing assessments 100–fold for all manner of maintenance issues. The court rejected the amendments, holding that the scope of the power to amend must be viewed from the perspective of the owners' reasonable expectations at the time the initial restrictions were created.

States may, by statute, address the issue of amendment of existing covenants, especially in the context of common interest communities, where the conflict between those seeking modification and those opposing it can be highly contested. See, e.g., Charter Club on the River Home Owners Association v. Walker, 301 Ga.App. 898, 689 S.E.2d 344, 346 (2009). "At issue in this case is the construction of OCGA § 44–5–60(d)(4), which provides, in pertinent part, that 'no change in the covenants which imposes a greater restriction on the use or development of the land will be enforced unless agreed to in writing by the owner of the affected property at the time such change is made.'" For a fuller discussion of the issues, see Gerald Korngold, Private Land Use Arrangements, Chs. 6, 11 (1990); 4 & 9 Richard R. Powell, Powell on Real Property §§ 34.18–.19, 677, 679 (1996).

2. Developers often retain the right to make unilateral amendments to a subdivision for a limited period of time, typically so they can make adjustments for unanticipated changes in the market. See, e.g., Raman Chandler Properties, L.C. v. Caldwell's Creek Homeowners Ass'n, Inc., 178 S.W.3d 384 (Tex.App. 2005), which applied a provision that permitted a developer unilaterally to amend servitudes for a specified time period, but thereafter only with the consent of 70% of those who had purchased property in the subdivision. In this case the developer wished to add an access easement across common lands after the time had expired, and the court held that he could not do so without the consent of 70% of existing land owners.

§ 8.8 NOTE: THE (CHAOTIC) MARKET FOR SERVITUDES

Suppose that A and B are adjoining property owners and that A tries to purchase from B an easement appurtenant to do something on B's property—perhaps to use a right of way as a driveway. This transaction will not occur unless A and B are able to agree on a price. If the agreed price is $1000, we know two things: (1) A values the driveway easement across B's property by $1000 or more; (2) B values the interest she surrenders by $1000 or less. Unless both parties value these interests at precisely $1000, the transaction will create a certain amount of "economic surplus." Economic surplus is the difference between the value that a person places on the object or service that she surrenders in a transaction, and the value she places on the object or service that she receives in exchange. For example, if A valued the right to a driveway at $1100, and B valued the loss produced by the burden on her estate at $950, then A is $100 better off as a result of the transaction and B is $50 better off. The transaction yields an economic surplus of $150. If no one else is affected by this transaction, society is $150 richer because the transaction occurred.

The easement in this example is appurtenant. As a result, the economic surplus will show up as a change in the value, and thus the market price, of the two properties. A's property will be worth $1100 more after the easement has been created, and B's property will be worth $950 less.

Importantly, the combined market value of the two properties is greater after the easement is created than it was before. This will always be the case when the easement is created by market transaction. A moment's thought will bear this out. If the injury to B's estate that results from the easement is greater than the benefit that will accrue to A's estate, the two parties will not be able to agree on a price. For example, if the driveway easement across B's property would reduce its value by $1000 but increase the value of A's property by only $900, the two parties would not create the easement: B will not be willing to sell the right for less than $1000, and A will not be willing to pay more than $900.

The fact that the sale of an easement makes both parties to the transaction wealthier (actually, all market transactions do so) suggests that the market for servitudes is a pretty good idea. But there is good reason to believe that the market for servitudes functions poorly in comparison with other markets. In the easement case described above, the relationship between the parties is a bilateral monopoly. A bilateral monopoly exists whenever a monopoly seller and a monopoly buyer (a monopsonist) confront each other. When A tries to purchase a driveway easement he is not indifferent about who will sell it to him, as he would be in a competitive market. He cannot buy an easement from a property owner a mile away, or even from someone two lots away. In all likelihood there is only one property owner from whom he can acquire the easement. As a result B is a monopolist in the market for easements purchased by A.

But B is in precisely the same predicament. B has an easement to sell. However, she cannot sell it to the lot owner a mile away either. In fact, the "market" for B's easement may consist of only one person: A.

A serious problem with bilateral monopolies is that there is no competitive bidding on either the buying side or the selling side of the market that would establish a market price for the easement. One unfortunate result of this situation is that the parties must establish a price by negotiation. A may know how much he is willing to pay for the driveway easement, but he does not know how little B is willing to take. A wants to obtain the lowest possible price. B, by contrast, may know how little she is willing to accept, but she does not know how much A is willing to pay, and she wants the highest possible price. The result may be a great deal of needless negotiation and posturing. Worse yet, many efficient easement transactions may not occur because the parties tire of negotiating before they agree on a price. This suggests that if the market for easements worked better, there would be many more easements than there are now.

Not all servitude markets are bilateral monopolies. Some are better. Some, as it turns out, are far worse. A few easements are transacted in at least nominally competitive markets. For example, if the First Church of Christ, Scientist (see the *Willard* case, supra) wishes to buy a parking lot easement for use on Sunday morning, it may have a choice among lots owned by half a dozen or more sellers within walking distance of the Church; if these behave competitively we would have a well-functioning market in which the Church would obtain the easement at someone's cost of giving it up.

By contrast, the *Walton* case illustrates a situation that is worse than a bilateral monopoly, and calculated to produce chaos. A large group of property owners may each wish some list of servitudes for their subdivision, but they will get what they want only if they can all agree. Further, under a traditional arrangement unanimous consent is required before servitudes can be terminated or changed once they are created. In these cases, any single land owner can hold out against the others for more favorable terms.

The drafter of the servitudes in *Walton* attempted to solve the holdout problem by permitting a mere majority to change the servitudes. But the most likely result of this modification is pure chaos. Suppose the property owners in a ten lot subdivision have a servitude that entitles a majority to change the servitudes. Lot owners #1–#6 might propose a modification that would benefit them by $10 each while injuring owners #7–#10 by $20 each. That proposal would likely pass by majority vote. However, owners #7–#10 might respond with an alternative proposal that would benefit them by $8 each, and also benefit owners #1 and #2 by $12 each, instead of $10 under the first proposal. In that case, lot owners ##1, 2, 7, 8, 9 & 10 would vote for the second proposal. But this proposal could then be defeated by some alternative coalition's proposal. Indeed, any nonunanimous coalition could be defeated by a new coalition, and we could expect an infinite series of votes.

Any consideration of the efficiency of the law of servitudes in subdivisions must deal with this problem. Rules that require unanimous consent for changes permit one owner to frustrate a change that makes everyone else better off. But any rule that requires less than unanimous consent can produce a chaotic market in which irrational changes are made, such as the one in the *Walton* case. See Herbert Hovenkamp, Bargaining in Coasian Markets: Servitudes and Alternative Land Use Controls, 27. J.Corp.L.519 (2002).

CHAPTER 9

"PRIVATE" CONTROLS OF LAND USE: THE LAW OF NUISANCE

■ ■ ■

§ 9.1   INTRODUCTION

The law of nuisance is historically part of the law of torts. Nuisance actions are generally brought where there is no relevant agreement between the parties, by contract or by conveyance, but the plaintiff asserts the right to enjoin the defendant's land use anyway. Because the law of nuisance does not rest on any pre-existing agreement, it represents a larger intrusion by the State into individual land use decisions than does the law of servitudes. The judge necessarily evaluates the social usefulness of the activity being challenged and balances this against the damage to adjoining landowners. Although both the law of servitudes and the law of nuisance contain large infusions of public policy, in nuisance law those infusions are more explicit because the judge cannot purport to base her decision on the four corners of some agreement between the parties. For this reason it is not entirely appropriate to characterize nuisance law as "private" rather than "public."

This chapter deals almost entirely with the law of *private* nuisance, which involves injury to private individuals in their capacity as owners of an interest in land near the nuisance. For the distinction between private and public nuisance, see D. Dobbs, The Law of Torts § 467 (2000). As a general rule, only the government may sue to enjoin a public nuisance, on the theory that such injuries accrue to the public generally, and not to individual members as individuals themselves. An individual may claim relief only if he or she can show some "particularized" injury. 532 Madison Ave. Gourmet Foods, Inc. v. Finlandia Center, Inc., 96 N.Y.2d 280, 750 N.E.2d 1097, 727 N.Y.S.2d 49 (2001). But having made that showing, the injured plaintiff need not be the owner of an interest in land. Thus in Leo v. General Electric Co., 145 A.D.2d 291, 538 N.Y.S.2d 844 (1989), the court permitted fishermen to sue a water polluter on a public nuisance theory after the fish taken from the water were declared unfit for human consumption. In this case the fishermen were "peculiarly aggrieved" and could sue for both damages and injunction.[1]

Contemporary nuisance cases are factually very interesting. For example, the plaintiffs in Gellman v. Seawane Golf & Country Club, Inc., 24 A.D.3d 415, 805 N.Y.S.2d 411 (2005) purchased their home in 1982 which was located across the street from the defendant's golf course and driving range. The defendant's business had been in operation since 1927. The golf balls from the driving range frequently landed on the plaintiff's property causing property damage and the defendant, over a period of more than two decades, failed to prevent the golf balls from continuing to land on the plaintiff's property. The court held that the plaintiffs proved that: [1] the defendant operated its property negligently by failing to take precautions in the operation of its property to prevent reasonably foreseeable injury to the plaintiffs; [2] the defendant's conduct in allowing the golf balls to invade plaintiffs' property with such frequency constituted a trespass and; [3] the "defendant's conduct constitute[d] a private nuisance because the operation of the driving range in a manner that allows golf balls to continuously escape the range produces a tangible and appreciable injury to the plaintiffs' property that renders its enjoyment especially uncomfortable and inconvenient." Id. at 417. Excessively barking dogs can be a "nuisance" in the non-legal as well as in the legal sense of the word. Rae v. Flynn, 690 So.2d 1341 (Fla.App. 1997). In the landlord and tenant context, the court in Acorn Realty LLC affirmed the trial court's determination "that the tenant permitted a nuisance on the premises in failing to take any meaningful steps to curtail the recurrent and well-documented antisocial behavior of her unemancipated teenage children. The disturbing course of conduct included repeated incidents of vandalism of the build-

---

1. An interesting collection of cases applying public nuisance doctrine are several actions brought by the National Organization for Women (NOW) against people interfering with women seeking abortions or other medical services delivered at facilities that also perform abortions. See, for example, NOW v. Operation Rescue, 726 F.Supp. 1483 (E.D.Va.1989) (applying Virginia law), finding a privately actionable public nuisance in Operation Rescue's picketing of NOW-operated abortion clinics so as to impede the entry of those seeking medical services. Accord NOW v. Operation Rescue, 726 F.Supp. 300 (D.D.C.1989) (applying District of Columbia law). In New York State National Organization for Women v. Terry, Operation Rescue, 886 F.2d 1339, 1362 (2d Cir.1989) (applying New York law), the court noted:

[D]efendants state that reliance on the public nuisance doctrine is misplaced because a women's right to obtain an abortion is not a right common to all members of the community. Rather, they assert, it is a wholly private right and interference with it is not actionable as a public nuisance. They claim that the City has not alleged interference with rights common to the community at large. The right shown to be disrupted is not, as defendants suggest, merely the right to obtain an abortion. The City intervened to vindicate the more general right of City residents to obtain medical services—a right common to all residents of New York. Women go to the clinics for a panoply of medical, prenatal and counseling services. Abortion may be the principal focus of defendants' efforts, but their tactics interfere with a broader spectrum of rights. The demonstrations simply pose a special threat to women seeking to obtain abortions because of delays and cancellations caused by the blockades. Moreover, as the district court noted, defendants' chosen tactic of en masse demonstrations has obstructed vehicular and pedestrian traffic in New York's already burdened streets.

See also Cincinnati v. Beretta U.S.A. Corp., 95 Ohio St.3d 416, 418, 768 N.E.2d 1136, 1141 (2002), holding that the distribution of handguns by manufacturers was an actionable public nuisance entitling the city to seek damages for expenses it incurred as a result of law enforcement activities and injuries: "a public-nuisance action can be maintained for injuries caused by a product if the facts establish that the design, manufacturing, marketing, or sale of the product unreasonably interferes with a right common to the general public."

ing's front entrance door and elevator, urinating and marijuana use in the public hallways, and verbal abuse of other residents and actual assaults on building staff." Acorn Realty, L.L.C. v. Torres, 169 Misc.2d 670, 652 N.Y.S.2d 472, 473 (App.Term.1996). In Osborne v. Power, 322 Ark. 229, 908 S.W.2d 340 (1995), the court held that a massive Christmas light display containing some 174,000 lights and attracting an unusually large number of visitors to a residential neighborhood constituted a nuisance and warranted the remedy of injunctive relief. The court stated that massive commercial lighting displays of the nature involved in the case were not appropriate for quiet residential communities.

One historical difference between the law of nuisance and the more explicitly "public" methods of land use regulation, such as zoning, is that zoning was statutory while nuisance was part of the common law. However, today the law of nuisance has become so dominated by statutory solutions that the distinction is beginning to break down.

§ 9.2   WHAT IS A NUISANCE?

Restatement (Second) of Torts (1979):

> § 821D.   Private Nuisance
>
> A private nuisance is a nontrespassory invasion of another's interest in the private use and enjoyment of land.
>
> § 821E.   Who Can Recover for Private Nuisance
>
> For a private nuisance there is liability only to those who have property rights and privileges in respect to the use and enjoyment of the land affected, including
>
>> (a) possessors of the land,
>>
>> (b) owners of easements and profits in the land, and
>>
>> (c) owners of nonpossessory estates in the land that are detrimentally affected by interferences with its use and enjoyment.
>
> § 822.   General Rule
>
> One is subject to liability for a private nuisance if, but only if, his conduct is a legal cause of an invasion of another's interest in the private use and enjoyment of land, and the invasion is either
>
>> (a) intentional and unreasonable, or
>>
>> (b) unintentional and otherwise actionable under the rules controlling liability for negligent or reckless conduct, or for abnormally dangerous conditions or activities.
>
> § 824.   Type of Conduct Essential to Liability
>
> The conduct necessary to make the actor liable for either a public or a private nuisance may consist of
>
>> (a) an act; or

(b) a failure to act under circumstances in which the actor is under a duty to take positive action to prevent or abate the interference with the public interest or the invasion of the private interest.

§ 825. Intentional Invasion—What Constitutes

An invasion of another's interest in the use and enjoyment of land or an interference with the public right, is intentional if the actor

(a) acts for the purpose of causing it, or

(b) knows that it is resulting or is substantially certain to result from his conduct.

§ 826. Unreasonableness of Intentional Invasion

An intentional invasion of another's interest in the use and enjoyment of land is unreasonable if

(a) the gravity of the harm outweighs the utility of the actor's conduct, or

(b) the harm caused by the conduct is serious and the financial burden of compensating for this and similar harm to others would not make the continuation of the conduct not feasible.

§ 827. Gravity of Harm—Factors Involved

In determining the gravity of the harm from an intentional invasion of another's interest in the use and enjoyment of land, the following factors are important:

(a) the extent of the harm involved;

(b) the character of the harm involved;

(c) the social value that the law attaches to the type of use or enjoyment invaded;

(d) the suitability of the particular use or enjoyment invaded to the character of the locality; and

(e) the burden on the person harmed of avoiding the harm.

§ 828. Utility of Conduct—Factors Involved

In determining the utility of conduct that causes an intentional invasion of another's interest in the use and enjoyment of land, the following factors are important:

(a) the social value that the law attaches to the primary purpose of the conduct;

(b) the suitability of the conduct to the character of the locality; and

(c) the impracticability of preventing or avoiding the invasion.

§ 829A. Gravity vs. Utility—Severe Harm

An intentional invasion of another's interest in the use and enjoyment of land is unreasonable if the harm resulting from the invasion is severe and greater than the other should be required to bear without compensation.

§ 830. Gravity vs. Utility—Invasion Avoidable

An intentional invasion of another's interest in the use and enjoyment of land is unreasonable if the harm is significant and it would be practicable for the actor to avoid the harm in whole or in part without undue hardship.

§ 831. Gravity vs. Utility—Conduct Unsuited to Locality

An intentional invasion of another's interest in the use and enjoyment of land is unreasonable if the harm is significant, and

(a) the particular use or enjoyment interfered with is well suited to the character of the locality; and

(b) the actor's conduct is unsuited to the character of that locality.

§ 840D. Coming to the Nuisance

The fact that the plaintiff has acquired or improved his land after a nuisance interfering with it has come into existence is not in itself sufficient to bar his action, but it is a factor to be considered in determining whether the nuisance is actionable.

* * *

PRAH v. MARETTI

Supreme Court of Wisconsin (1982).
108 Wis.2d 223, 321 N.W.2d 182.

ABRAHAMSON, JUSTICE.

This appeal from a judgment of the circuit court for Waukesha county . . . was certified to this court . . . as presenting an issue of first impression, namely, whether an owner of a solar-heated residence states a claim upon which relief can be granted when he asserts that his neighbor's proposed construction of a residence (which conforms to existing deed restrictions and local ordinances) interferes with his access to an unobstructed path for sunlight across the neighbor's property. This case thus involves a conflict between one landowner (Glenn Prah, the plaintiff) interested in unobstructed access to sunlight across adjoining property as a natural source of energy and an adjoining landowner (Richard D. Maretti, the defendant) interested in the development of his land.

According to the complaint, the plaintiff is the owner of a residence which was constructed during the years 1978–1979. The complaint alleges that the residence has a solar system which includes collectors on the roof to supply energy for heat and hot water and that after the plaintiff built his solar-heated house, the defendant purchased the lot adjacent to and immediately to the south of the plaintiff's lot and commenced planning construction of a home. The complaint further states that when the plaintiff learned of defendant's plans to build the house he advised the defendant that if the house were built at the proposed location, defendant's house would substantially and adversely affect the integrity of plaintiff's solar system and could cause plaintiff other damage. Nevertheless, the defendant began construction. The complaint further alleges that the plaintiff is entitled to "unrestricted use of the sun and its solar power" and demands judgment for injunctive relief and damages.

The record * * * reveals the following additional facts: Plaintiff's home was the first residence built in the subdivision, and although plaintiff did not build his house in the center of the lot it was built in accordance with applicable restrictions. Plaintiff advised defendant that if the defendant's home were built at the proposed site it would cause a shadowing effect on the solar collectors which would reduce the efficiency of the system and possibly damage the system. To avoid these adverse effects, plaintiff requested defendant to locate his home an additional several feet away from the plaintiff's lot line, the exact number being disputed. Plaintiff and defendant failed to reach an agreement on the location of defendant's home before defendant started construction. The Architectural Control Committee of the subdivision and the Planning Commission of the City of Muskego approved the defendant's plans for his home, including its location on the lot. After such approval, the defendant apparently changed the grade of the property without prior notice to the Architectural Control Committee. The problem with defendant's proposed construction, as far as the plaintiff's interests are concerned, arises from a combination of the grade and the distance of defendant's home from the defendant's lot line.

The circuit court denied plaintiff's motion for injunctive relief, declared it would entertain a motion for summary judgment and thereafter entered judgment in favor of the defendant.

* * *

We consider first whether the complaint states a claim for relief based on common law private nuisance. This state has long recognized that an owner of land does not have an absolute or unlimited right to use the land in a way which injures the rights of others. The rights of neighboring landowners are relative; the uses by one must not unreasonably impair the uses or enjoyment of the other.[4] VI–A American Law of Property

---

4. In Abdella v. Smith, 34 Wis.2d 393, 399, 149 N.W.2d 537 (1967), this court quoted with approval Dean Prosser's description of the judicial balancing of the reciprocal rights and privileges of neighbors in the use of their land:

"Most of the litigation as to private nuisance has dealt with the conflicting interests of landowners and the question of the reasonableness of the defendant's conduct: The defendant's privilege of making a reasonable use of his own property for his own benefit and conducting his affairs in his own way is no less important than the plaintiff's right to use and enjoy his premises. The two are correlative and interdependent, and neither is entitled to prevail entirely, at the expense of the other. Some balance must be struck between the two. The plaintiff must be expected to endure some inconvenience rather than curtail the defendant's freedom of action, and the defendant must so use his own property that he causes no unreasonable harm to the plaintiff. The law of private nuisance is very largely a series of

§ 28.22, pp. 64–65 (1954). When one landowner's use of his or her property unreasonably interferes with another's enjoyment of his or her property, that use is said to be a private nuisance.

* * *

The private nuisance doctrine has traditionally been employed in this state to balance the conflicting rights of landowners, and this court has recently adopted the analysis of private nuisance set forth in the Restatement (Second) of Torts.

* * *

The Restatement defines private nuisance as "a nontrespassory invasion of another's interest in the private use and enjoyment of land." Restatement (Second) of Torts § 821D (1977). The phrase "interest in the private use and enjoyment of land" as used in § 821D is broadly defined to include any disturbance of the enjoyment of property. The comment in the Restatement describes the landowner's interest protected by private nuisance law as follows:

> "The phrase 'interest in the use and enjoyment of land' is used in this Restatement in a broad sense. It comprehends not only the interests that a person may have in the actual present use of land for residential, agricultural, commercial, industrial and other purposes, but also his interests in having the present use value of the land unimpaired by changes in its physical condition. Thus the destruction of trees on vacant land is as much an invasion of the owner's interest in its use and enjoyment as is the destruction of crops or flowers that he is growing on the land for his present use. 'Interest in use and enjoyment' also comprehends the pleasure, comfort and enjoyment that a person normally derives from the occupancy of land. Freedom from discomfort and annoyance while using land is often as important to a person as freedom from physical interruption with his use or freedom from detrimental change in the physical condition of the land itself."
> Restatement (Second) of Torts, § 821D, Comment *b,* p. 101 (1977).

Although the defendant's obstruction of the plaintiff's access to sunlight appears to fall within the Restatement's broad concept of a private nuisance as a nontrespassory invasion of another's interest in the private use and enjoyment of land, the defendant asserts that he has a right to develop his property in compliance with statutes, ordinances and private covenants without regard to the effect of such development upon the plaintiff's access to sunlight. In essence, the defendant is asking this court to hold that the private nuisance doctrine is not applicable in the instant case and that his right to develop his land is a right which is *per se* superior to his neighbor's interest in access to sunlight. This position is

---

adjustments to limit the reciprocal rights and privileges of both. In every case the court must make a comparative evaluation of the conflicting interests according to objective legal standards, and the gravity of the harm to the plaintiff must be weighed against the utility of the defendant's conduct." Prosser, Law of Torts, sec. 89, p. 596 (2d ed. 1971) (Citations omitted).

expressed in the maxim "cujus est solum, ejus est usque ad coelum et ad infernos," that is, the owner of land owns up to the sky and down to the center of the earth. The rights of the surface owner are, however, not unlimited.

* * *

The defendant is not completely correct in asserting that the common law did not protect a landowner's access to sunlight across adjoining property. At English common law a landowner could acquire a right to receive sunlight across adjoining land by both express agreement and under the judge-made doctrine of "ancient lights." Under the doctrine of ancient lights if the landowner had received sunlight across adjoining property for a specified period of time,[5] the landowner was entitled to continue to receive unobstructed access to sunlight across the adjoining property. Under the doctrine the landowner acquired a negative prescriptive easement and could prevent the adjoining landowner from obstructing access to light.[6]

Although American courts have not been as receptive to protecting a landowner's access to sunlight as the English courts, American courts have afforded some protection to a landowner's interest in access to sunlight. American courts honor express easements to sunlight. American courts initially enforced the English common law doctrine of ancient lights, but later every state which considered the doctrine repudiated it as inconsistent with the needs of a developing country. Indeed, for just that reason this court concluded that an easement to light and air over adjacent property could not be created or acquired by prescription and has been unwilling to recognize such an easement by implication. Depner v. United States National Bank, 202 Wis. 405, 408, 232 N.W. 851 (1930); Miller v. Hoeschler, 126 Wis. 263, 268–69, 105 N.W. 790 (1905).

Many jurisdictions in this country have protected a landowner from malicious obstruction of access to light (the spite fence cases) under the common law private nuisance doctrine.[7] If an activity is motivated by malice it lacks utility and the harm it causes others outweighs any social values.

* * *

---

5. The specified time period of uninterrupted enjoyment required to create a right to receive light across adjoining property varied in English legal history. Thomas, Miller & Robbins, Overcoming Legal Uncertainties About Use of Solar Energy Systems 23 (Am. Bar Foundation 1978).

6. Pfeiffer, Ancient Lights: Legal Protection of Access to Solar Energy, 68 ABAJ 288 (1982). No American common law state recognizes a landowner's right to acquire an easement of light by prescription. Comment, Solar Lights: Guaranteeing a Place in the Sun, 57 Ore.L.Rev. 94, 112 (1977).

7. In several of the spite fence cases, courts have recognized the property owner's interest in sunlight. Hornsby v. Smith, 191 Ga. 491, 500, 13 S.E.2d 20 (1941) ("the air and light no matter from which direction they come are God-given, and are essential to the life, comfort, and happiness of everyone"); Burke v. Smith, 69 Mich. 380, 389, 37 N.W. 838 (1888) ("the right to breathe the air and enjoy the sunshine, is a natural one"); Barger v. Barringer, 151 N.C. 433, 437, 66 S.E. 439 (1909) ("light and air are as much a necessity as water, and all are the common heritage of mankind").

This court's reluctance in the nineteenth and early part of the twentieth century to provide broader protection for a landowner's access to sunlight was premised on three policy considerations. First, the right of landowners to use their property as they wished, as long as they did not cause physical damage to a neighbor, was jealously guarded. Metzger v. Hochrein, 107 Wis. 267, 272, 83 N.W. 308 (1900).

Second, sunlight was valued only for aesthetic enjoyment or as illumination. Since artificial light could be used for illumination, loss of sunlight was at most a personal annoyance which was given little, if any, weight by society.

Third, society had a significant interest in not restricting or impeding land development. Dillman v. Hoffman, 38 Wis. 559, 574 (1875). This court repeatedly emphasized that in the growth period of the nineteenth and early twentieth centuries change is to be expected and is essential to property and that recognition of a right to sunlight would hinder property development. The court expressed this concept as follows:

> "As the city grows, large grounds appurtenant to residences must be cut up to supply more residences. . . . The cistern, the outhouse, the cesspool, and the private drain must disappear in deference to the public waterworks and sewer; the terrace and the garden, to the need for more complete occupancy. . . . Strict limitation [on the recognition of easements of light and air over adjacent premises is] in accord with the popular conception upon which real estate has been and is daily being conveyed in Wisconsin and to be essential to easy and rapid development at least of our municipalities."

* * *

Considering these three policies, this court concluded that in the absence of an express agreement granting access to sunlight, a landowner's obstruction of another's access to sunlight was not actionable. Miller v. Hoeschler, supra, 126 Wis. at 271, 105 N.W. 790.

* * *

These three policies are no longer fully accepted or applicable. They reflect factual circumstances and social priorities that are now obsolete.

First, society has increasingly regulated the use of land by the landowner for the general welfare. Euclid v. Ambler Realty Co., 272 U.S. 365, 47 S.Ct. 114, 71 L.Ed. 303 (1926); Just v. Marinette County, 56 Wis.2d 7, 201 N.W.2d 761 (1972).

Second, access to sunlight has taken on a new significance in recent years. In this case the plaintiff seeks to protect access to sunlight, not for aesthetic reasons or as a source of illumination but as a source of energy. Access to sunlight as an energy source is of significance both to the landowner who invests in solar collectors and to a society which has an interest in developing alternative sources of energy.[8]

---

8. State and federal governments are encouraging the use of the sun as a significant source of energy. In this state the legislature has granted tax benefits to encourage the utilization of solar

Third, the policy of favoring unhindered private development in an expanding economy is no longer in harmony with the realities of our society. State v. Deetz, 66 Wis.2d 1, 224 N.W.2d 407 (1974). The need for easy and rapid development is not as great today as it once was, while our perception of the value of sunlight as a source of energy has increased significantly. * * *

Yet the defendant would have us ignore the flexible private nuisance law as a means of resolving the dispute between the landowners in this case and would have us adopt an approach ... of favoring the unrestricted development of land and of applying a rigid and inflexible rule protecting his right to build on his land and disregarding any interest of the plaintiff in the use and enjoyment of his land. This we refuse to do.[10]

Private nuisance law, the law traditionally used to adjudicate conflicts between private landowners, has the flexibility to protect both a landowner's right of access to sunlight and another landowner's right to develop land. Private nuisance law is better suited to regulate access to sunlight in modern society and is more in harmony with legislative policy and the prior decisions of this court than is an inflexible doctrine of non-recognition of any interest in access to sunlight across adjoining land.

We therefore hold that private nuisance law, that is, the reasonable use doctrine as set forth in the Restatement, is applicable to the instant

energy. See Chs. 349, 350, Laws of 1979. See also Ch. 354, Laws of 1981 (eff. May 7, 1982) enabling legislation providing for local ordinances guaranteeing access to sunlight.

The federal government has also recognized the importance of solar energy and currently encourages its utilization by means of tax benefits, direct subsidies and government loans for solar projects. Energy Tax Act of 1978, Nov. 9, 1978, P.L. 95–618, 92 Stat. 3174, relevant portion codified at 26 U.S.C.A. sec. 44(c) (1982 Supp.); Energy Security Act, June 30, 1980, P.L. 96–294, 94 Stat. 611, relevant portion codified at 12 U.S.C.A. sec. 3610 (1980); Small Business Energy Loan Act, July 4, 1978, P.L. 95 315, 92 Stat. 377, relevant portion codified within 15 U.S.C.A. secs. 631, 633, 636, and 639 (1982 Supp.); National Energy Conservation Policy Act, Nov. 9, 1978, P.L. 95–619, 92 Stat. 3206, relevant portion codified at 42 U.S.C.A. secs. 1451, 1703–45 (1982 Supp.); Energy Conservation and Production Act, Aug. 14, 1976, P.L. 94–385, 90 Stat. 1125, relevant portion codified at 42 U.S.C.A. sec. 6881 (1977).

10. Defendant's position that a landowner's interest in access to sunlight across adjoining land is not "legally enforceable" and is therefore excluded *per se* from private nuisance law was adopted in Fontainebleau Hotel Corp. v. Forty–Five Twenty–Five, Inc., 114 So.2d 357 (Fla.App. 1959), cert. den. 117 So.2d 842 (Fla.1960). The Florida district court of appeals permitted construction of a building which cast a shadow on a neighboring hotel's swimming pool. The court asserted that nuisance law protects only those interests "which [are] recognized and protected by law," and that there is no legally recognized or protected right to access to sunlight. A property owner does not, said the Florida court, in the absence of a contract or statute, acquire a presumptive or implied right to the free flow of light and air across adjoining land. The Florida court then concluded that a lawful structure which causes injury to another by cutting off light and air—whether or not erected partly for spite—does not give rise to a cause of action for damages or for an injunction. See also People ex rel. Hoogasian v. Sears, Roebuck & Co., 52 Ill.2d 301, 287 N.E.2d 677 (1972).

We do not find the reasoning of *Fontainebleau* persuasive. The court leaped from rejecting an easement by prescription (the doctrine of ancient lights) and an easement by implication to the conclusion that there is no right to protection from obstruction of access to sunlight. The court's statement that a landowner has no right to light should be the conclusion, not its initial premise. The court did not explain why an owner's interest in unobstructed light should not be protected or in what manner an owner's interest in unobstructed sunlight differs from an owner's interest in being free from obtrusive noises or smells or differs from an owner's interest in unobstructed use of water. The recognition of a *per se* exception to private nuisance law may invite unreasonable behavior.

case. Recognition of a nuisance claim for unreasonable obstruction of access to sunlight will not prevent land development or unduly hinder the use of adjoining land. It will promote the reasonable use and enjoyment of land in a manner suitable to the 1980s. That obstruction of access to light might be found to constitute a nuisance in certain circumstances does not mean that it will be or must be found to constitute a nuisance under all circumstances. The result in each case depends on whether the conduct complained of is unreasonable.

Accordingly we hold that the plaintiff in this case has stated a claim under which relief can be granted. Nonetheless we do not determine whether the plaintiff in this case is entitled to relief. In order to be entitled to relief the plaintiff must prove the elements required to establish actionable nuisance, and the conduct of the defendant herein must be judged by the reasonable use doctrine.

* * *

The circuit court concluded that because the defendant's proposed house was in conformity with zoning regulations, building codes and deed restrictions, the defendant's use of the land was reasonable. This court has concluded that a landowner's compliance with zoning laws does not automatically bar a nuisance claim. Compliance with the law "is not the controlling factor, though it is, of course, entitled to some weight." Bie v. Ingersoll, 27 Wis.2d 490, 495, 135 N.W.2d 250 (1965). The circuit court also concluded that the plaintiff could have avoided any harm by locating his own house in a better place. Again, plaintiff's ability to avoid the harm is a relevant but not a conclusive factor.

* * *

Furthermore, our examination of the record leads us to conclude that the record does not furnish an adequate basis for the circuit court to apply the proper legal principles on summary judgment. The application of the reasonable use standard in nuisance cases normally requires a full exposition of all underlying facts and circumstances. Too little is known in this case of such matters as the extent of the harm to the plaintiff, the suitability of solar heat in that neighborhood, the availability of remedies to the plaintiff, and the costs to the defendant of avoiding the harm. Summary judgment is not an appropriate procedural vehicle in this case when the circuit court must weigh evidence which has not been presented at trial.

* * *

For the reasons set forth, we reverse the judgment of the circuit court dismissing the complaint and remand the matter to circuit court for further proceedings not inconsistent with this opinion.

* * *

CALLOW, JUSTICE (dissenting).

* * * In the instant case, we are dealing with an action which seeks to restrict the defendant's private right to use his property, notwithstanding a complete lack of notice of restriction to the defendant and the defendant's compliance with applicable ordinances and statutes. The plaintiff who *knew* of the potential problem before the defendant acquired the land seeks to impose such use restriction to accommodate his personal, private benefit—a benefit which could have been accommodated by the plaintiff locating his home in a different place on his property or by acquiring the land in question when it was for sale prior to its acquisition by the defendant. * * *

* * * [T]he majority's conclusion that a cause of action exists in this case thwarts the very foundation of property law. Property law encompasses a system of filing and notice in a place for public records to provide prospective purchasers with any limitations on their use of the property. Such a notice is not alleged by the plaintiff. Only as a result of the majority's decision did Mr. Maretti discover that a legitimate action exists which would require him to defend the design and location of his home against a nuisance suit, notwithstanding the fact that he located and began to build his house within the applicable building, municipal, and deed restrictions.

* * *

I believe the facts of the instant controversy present the classic case of the owner of a solar collector who fails to take any action to protect his investment. There is nothing in the record to indicate that Mr. Prah disclosed his situation to Mr. Maretti prior to Maretti's purchase of the lot or attempted to secure protection for his solar collector prior to Maretti's submission of his building plans to the architectural committee. Such inaction should be considered a significant factor in determining whether a cause of action exists.

The majority's failure to recognize the need for notice may perpetuate a vicious cycle. Maretti may feel compelled to sell his lot because of Prah's solar collector's interference with his plans to build his family home. If so, Maretti will not be obliged to inform prospective purchasers of the problem. Certainly, such information will reduce the value of his land. If the presence of collectors is sufficient notice, it cannot be said that the seller of the lot has a duty to disclose information peculiarly within his knowledge. I do not believe that an adjacent lot owner should be obliged to experience the substantial economic loss resulting from the lot being rendered unbuildable by the contour of the land as it relates to the location and design of the adjoining home using solar collectors.

* * *

Because I do not believe that the facts of the present case give rise to a cause of action for private nuisance, I dissent.

NOTES AND QUESTIONS

1. Is the question of access to sunlight across a neighbor's land fundamentally about the law of nuisance or the law of easements? Plaintiffs using a prescriptive easement theory have lost all their cases. American courts have refused to hold that, in the absence of an express easement or covenant, a person has a right of access to sunlight across adjacent lands held by another. The leading example is Fontainebleau Hotel Corp. v. Forty–Five Twenty–Five, Inc., 114 So.2d 357 (Fla.App.1959), cert. denied 117 So.2d 842 (Fla.1960), discussed in the *Prah* opinions.

The *Prah* majority notes that the English doctrine of "ancient lights," which recognized a prescriptive easement in sunlight, was rejected in the United States as hostile to economic development. See, for example, Morrison v. Marquardt, 24 Iowa 35, 60–67 (1868) ("surely, such an easement, uncertain in its extent and duration, without any written or record evidence of its existence, fettering estates and laying an embargo upon the hand of improvement which carries the trowel and the plane, and, as applied to a subsequent purchaser, against the spirit of our recording acts, ... should not be held to exist by mere implication"); and see L. Friedman, A History of American Law 413 (2d ed. 1985).

However, see P. Karsten, *"Heart" Versus "Head": Judge–Made Law in Nineteenth Century America* (1997), who argues that the English rule may not have been anti-developmental at all. He cites evidence that when relatively wealthy American landowners believed the English rule applied they actually built tall walls or fences designed to block sunlight access immediately, so that the prescriptive period would not run. In other cases, land owners built earlier than they would otherwise have, in order to beat any prescriptive period that might run against them. For example, by racing to build his house only a year or two after Prah's solar system was in place, Maretti would have defeated a prescription claim even under the English rule.

There are some important differences between a prescriptive easement theory of access to sunlight and a nuisance theory. Under the prescriptive easement theory, the person claiming the right must show unobstructed access across the defendant's land for a long period of time. Under the nuisance theory the duration of the use is not important. By contrast, under the nuisance theory but not the prescriptive theory, the court must evaluate the utility, or social value, of the right asserted. Doesn't this make the nuisance approach inherently superior for dealing with such controversial questions of social utility as the right to light across a neighbor's land? For example, in the *Fontainebleau* case, the plaintiff wanted unobstructed solar access to a sun bathing area and swimming pool. The proposed structure that would interfere with the solar access was an addition to a hotel. How would such a case fare under the Restatement's nuisance theory? Is it clear that the "gravity of the harm" as described in Restatement § 826 (the permanent shade over the plaintiff's sunbathing area) outweighs the "utility of the actor's conduct" (the enlarged hotel). How would you measure the "gravity" of the first of these against the "utility" of the second?

Most courts hold that blockage of a view is neither a violation of a prescriptive right to sunlight nor a nuisance. See Kruger v. Shramek, 5 Neb.App. 802, 565 N.W.2d 742 (1997), which declined to apply *Prah* to the plaintiff's complaint that the defendant's fence and other structures blocked the plaintiff's view of a golf course. The court noted that recognition of such a right would amount to a broad restriction on development, all based on interests that did not appear in either statutes or the chain of title. Accord Mohr v. Midas Realty, 431 N.W.2d 380 (Iowa 1988); Collinson v. John L. Scott, Inc., 55 Wash.App. 481, 778 P.2d 534 (1989) (structure that interfered with uphill neighbor's view not a nuisance; distinguishing *Prah* as not involving mere view); and see Sher v. Leiderman, 181 Cal.App.3d 867, 875–79, 226 Cal.Rptr. 698, 701–04 (1986), which found that the construction of a building that obstructed sunlight to the plaintiffs' passive solar home was not a nuisance, generally disagreed with *Prah*, and stated that so radical a change in the American law of nuisance required legislative action. However, in Tenn v. 889 Assoc., Ltd., 127 N.H. 321, 500 A.2d 366 (1985), then State Justice Souter declared that the New Hampshire Supreme Court would follow *Prah* in an appropriate case, perhaps even one involving the mere cutting off of sunlight to light office rooms; but in the case at hand the court found insufficient interference to rise to a nuisance. Should access to beautiful views be treated differently than access to light to service energy-producing solar collectors? Doesn't this bias still reflect the fact that the law favors economic development, *Prah* notwithstanding? Cf. Rattigan v. Wile, 445 Mass. 850, 841 N.E.2d 680 (2006), which found a nuisance when the defendant land owner placed a covered, striped tent on his property so close to a neighbor that it effectively cut off the neighbor's "commanding view of the water." However, the court specifically found that the placement of the tent was intended to harass the neighbor.

Another line of cases condemns so-called "spite fences" where the plaintiff's real grievance is intentional obstruction of a view. For example, in Bordeaux v. Greene, 22 Mont. 254, 56 P. 218 (1899) the Montana Supreme Court held that it was not a nuisance for the defendant to erect a 40–foot high fence less than three feet from the plaintiff's window, concluding that a landowner "has a right to shut off air and light from his neighbor's windows by building on his own lots" even if the motive was "purely malicious." That Court overruled *Bordeaux* in Haugen v. Kottas, 307 Mont. 301, 37 P.3d 672 (2001), but limited its holding to "useless structures" that interfere with another's view. Accord Dowdell v. Bloomquist, 2002 WL 1803933 (R.I.Super. 2002), aff'd 847 A.2d 827 (R.I. 2004) (enjoining trees erected as spite fence to block neighbor's view of Atlantic Ocean); Wilson v. Handley, 97 Cal.App.4th 1301, 119 Cal.Rptr.2d 263 (2002) (same; row of evergreen trees blocking view of mountain).

2. Is it clear that the Restatement sections quoted before the opinion mandate the result in *Prah?* Is it clear that the result is contrary to the position of the Restatement? The leading commentary on the law of nuisance regards the traditional common law of nuisance as a "jungle." D. Dobbs, The Law of Torts § 462 (2000). Does the Restatement make the jungle any easier to penetrate?

3. Nuisance claims frequently arise in the context of zoning regulations which are discussed in Chapter 11. How should the lower court on remand in *Prah* evaluate the fact that the defendant's construction plans conformed to the zoning laws and building codes, as well as all applicable deed restrictions? Zoning ordinances express a legislative judgment that a particular structure or use in a particular place is socially beneficial. See, e.g., Bove v. Donner–Hanna Coke Corp., 236 A.D. 37, 258 N.Y.S. 229 (4th Dept.1932), where the court held that the defendant's operation of a coke plant was not a nuisance, citing the fact that the property was zoned for heavy industry. See generally Note, Zoning Ordinances and Common–Law Nuisance, 16 Syracuse L.Rev. 860 (1965).

Nuisance law is sometimes described as "judicial zoning." See Ellickson, Alternatives to Zoning: Covenants, Nuisance Rules, and Fines as Land Use Controls, 40 U.Chi.L.Rev. 681 (1973), which notes that judges often use nuisance law to prioritize land uses in un-zoned areas or to fill in the "gaps" in existing zoning. They might do this by permitting industrial activity in an area dominated by industry, but forbidding it in an area dominated by residences. The result may not be as systematic as zoning, but it may be more flexible. For historical accounts of the development of nuisance law to "zone" land uses, see M. Horwitz, The Transformation of American Law, 1780–1860 at 74–78 (1977); Brenner, Nuisance Law and the Industrial Revolution, 3 J.Legal Stud. 403 (1974).

Zoning has been described by some as prescient, in contrast with nuisance law which is reactive. Explain this characterization.

4. Prah v. Maretti suggests that the line between nuisance law and the law of easements is not easy to locate. See also Schultz v. Trascher, 249 Wis.2d 722, 640 N.W.2d 130 (2001). Schultz paved an existing driveway that ran between her home and Trascher's home. The existing driveway encroached slightly on Trascher's property (1.2 inches). Schultz's paving extended the encroachment (approximately one foot). Trascher removed the portion of the driveway that encroached on her property and erected a forty-eight inch tall fence within two inches of her own property line. The fence interfered with Schultz's use of her driveway. Schultz sued alleging adverse possession over the disputed area. Later, Schultz amended her complaint to allege that she had obtained a prescriptive easement over the area of the encroachment. The court dismissed the prescriptive easement claim for lack of hostility. Citing Prah v. Maretti, the court concluded that Trascher's fence prevented Schultz from driving on her driveway and constituted a private nuisance. The dissenting judge observed the following:

> If there was ever a case where a plaintiff seeking equity has come into court with dirty hands, this is it. Both parties, Schultz included after she did the survey to which the Majority refers ..., knew that Schultz's driveway encroached on Barbara Trascher's property. Trascher was perfectly willing to permit that, as long as her acquiescence would not lead to a claim of adverse possession. Schultz, however, was adamant that *she* already had Trascher's property by adverse possession and refused to agree to permit Trascher to score in the concrete the survey-validated property line. It was only then,

and on advice of counsel, that Trascher went to the expense and hassle of putting up the fence to cut off the claims of adverse possession that Schultz was admittedly harboring.

5. The line between nuisance and trespass can be even harder to find. Trespass, you will recall, involves the invasion of a physical substance onto the plaintiff's land. In Martin v. Reynolds Metals Co., 221 Or. 86, 342 P.2d 790 (1959), cert. denied 362 U.S. 918 (1960), the court held that the defendant was guilty of a trespass when fluoride gas emitted from its property traveled to the plaintiff's property. As a result the plaintiff was permitted to use a six year statute of limitations that applied to trespass actions, rather than a two year statute that applied to nuisance actions.

6. More recent disputes regarding barriers to solar panels occur in the context of homeowners associations. Restrictive covenants promulgated by homeowners associations often prohibit or restrict the use of solar panels/ solar collectors, citing aesthetic concerns. As a result, some states have enacted statutes that limit restrictions homeowners associations can impose on the use of solar panels. E.g., Vt. Stat. Ann. tit. 27, § 544 (2010); Va. Code Ann. § 67–701, A–B (2009); N.J. Stat. Ann. § 45:22A–48.2(a) (2007); Haw. Rev. Stat. Ann. § 196–7(b) (2010). For a discussion of express solar easements and related covenant agreements, see Troy A. Rule, Renewable Energy and the Neighbors, 4 Utah L. Rev. 1223 (2010); Sara C. Bronin, Solar Rights, 89 Boston L. Rev. 1217 (2009); Kate Galbraith, Solar–Power Incentives Get Results but Are Rare, N.Y., June 3, 2011, at A17A; Kate Galbraith, Home-owners Associations: The Enemy of Solar?, N.Y. Times A Blog About Energy and the Environment (May 15, 2009, 8:15 AM); Catherine Saillant, Solar Panels Causing Some Storms, L.A. Times, Nov. 30, 2009, at A4.

CREST CHEVROLET–OLDSMOBILE–CADILLAC, INC. v. WILLEMSEN

Supreme Court of Wisconsin (1986).
129 Wis.2d 129, 384 N.W.2d 692.

CECI, JUSTICE.

* * * The parties have stipulated to the facts leading up to this litigation. Crest and Bauer Glass [Willemsen] own adjoining parcels of land in Delavan, Wisconsin. The Bauer Glass parcel lies immediately to the west of the Crest parcel. Prior to 1979, the Bauer Glass parcel was at a lower elevation than the Crest parcel. Historically, surface water flowed from the east across the Crest parcel and onto the Bauer Glass parcel, where the water either percolated into the ground or flowed to the north and northwest off the Bauer Glass parcel. In 1979, Roger and Betty Willemsen purchased the undeveloped and unimproved Bauer Glass parcel with knowledge that the land was low in relation to properties to the east and that surface water generally accumulated on the Bauer Glass parcel. They then undertook to develop the parcel and to rectify the surface water problem by adding landfill to the property. When the landfill operation was complete, the Bauer Glass parcel stood at an elevation higher than any portion of the Crest parcel. The development also included installing a

storm sewer system on the Bauer Glass parcel at a cost to Bauer Glass of $68,348.94, which included the cost to Bauer Glass of extending the city of Delavan storm sewer system to its property and to within several feet of the Crest parcel. Bauer Glass invited Crest to participate in the project, specifically, by installing storm sewers on the lower portion of the Crest parcel at a cost to Crest of approximately $9,000, but Crest declined to join. The record reflects that Bauer Glass told Crest of the likelihood of surface water diversion onto the Crest parcel as a result of the Bauer Glass development operation. There had been only minor puddling and no flooding on the Crest property prior to the Bauer Glass development. After completion of the development, however, surface water accumulated on the Crest parcel during periods of heavy precipitation or melting snow. The combination of the higher elevation of the Bauer Glass parcel in relation to the Crest parcel and the absence of a storm sewer serving the Crest parcel resulted in a damming effect on the Crest property of the historical flow of the surface water from the Crest and other east-lying parcels onto the Bauer Glass parcel. Water had to be pumped off the Crest parking lot as a result of the flooding, according to the parties' respective statements of facts. The parties stipulated that Crest sustained damages in the amount of $4,500 to the west portion of its parking lot as a result of the flooding. This amount represents asphalt resurfacing costs incurred by Crest. In addition, Crest was ordered by the circuit court, which issued an alternative writ of mandamus, to connect its parcel to the Bauer Glass storm sewer system in order to avoid further damages to its parking lot. The cost to Crest for such connection was $11,620. The parties stipulated that Crest sustained a total of $16,120 in damages, representing the amount necessary to abate the nuisance and resurface the parking lot. Bauer Glass denied liability for the accumulation of standing water on the Crest parcel caused by the development of its own parcel.

Crest initially filed a complaint on January 12, 1981, seeking damages, and amended its complaint several times thereafter. Bauer Glass answered by asserting eight affirmative defenses, including Crest's failure to mitigate damages, and five counterclaims, all of which were dismissed by Judge Byrnes in an order and partial summary judgment filed March 15, 1982. In a decision filed June 18, 1984, the circuit court denied Crest's request for compensatory damages in the amount of $16,120. The court cited the $68,348.94 sum which Bauer Glass had expended to extend the Delavan storm sewer system to Bauer Glass's property in order to dispose of the surface water on its lot and noted that Bauer Glass had given Crest the opportunity to connect to the system. Bauer Glass was merely developing its property for business purposes as it had a legal right to do, the circuit court reasoned; it had "no duty to maintain its lot in the form of a neighborhood pond or catch basin." The court saw "no reason why Bauer [Glass] should have to stand the expense of Crest hooking up to the storm sewer to dispose of surface waters from the Crest lot." The court believed that each parcel owner should be required to stand the expense of hooking up to the sewer system. [T]he circuit court found that any diversion of surface water from the Bauer Glass property onto the Crest property was neither intentional nor unreasonable conduct.

The court of appeals summarily reversed the judgment of the circuit court. Applying the reasonable use doctrine as adopted by this court in [State v.] Deetz, 66 Wis.2d [1] at 18–19, 224 N.W.2d 407 [1974], and as set forth in the Restatement (Second) of Torts, § 826(b) (1979), the court of appeals held that Bauer Glass was liable for the $16,120 in damages sustained by Crest. It determined that the Bauer Glass landfill project effectively blocked the normal flow of surface waters as the flow existed prior to the landfill project and was a legal cause of Crest's serious water problems. Because the court of appeals deemed the Bauer Glass conduct to be unreasonable, the court reversed and remanded the matter with instructions to award damages to Crest in the stipulated amount. * * *

Bauer Glass first asserts that the court of appeals failed to consider the social utility of the Bauer Glass development in reaching its conclusion that the conduct was unreasonable. Bauer Glass cites State v. Deetz, 66 Wis.2d 1, 224 N.W.2d 407, to support its proposition that the utility of the developer's conduct must be analyzed before a developer's conduct be deemed unreasonable. In *Deetz*, this court discarded the common enemy doctrine and adopted the reasonable use doctrine regarding the flow of surface waters. Under the former doctrine, surface water was viewed as a common enemy which each landowner was privileged to divert, repulse, or retain, even if some injury was thereby caused to surrounding landowners. On the other hand, the reasonable use doctrine essentially states that, " 'each possessor is legally privileged to make a reasonable use of his land, even though the flow of surface waters is altered thereby and causes some harm to others, but incurs liability when his harmful interference with the flow of surface waters is unreasonable.' " Deetz, 66 Wis.2d at 14, 224 N.W.2d 407 (quoting Armstrong v. Francis Corp., 20 N.J. 320, 327, 120 A.2d 4 (1956)). The reasonable use doctrine is substantially embodied in § 822 of the Restatement (Second) of Torts (1979).

The unreasonableness of an intentional invasion is set forth in Restatement (Second) of Torts, § 826 (1979). That section provides: "Section 826. Unreasonableness of Intentional Invasion 'An intentional invasion of another's interest in the use and enjoyment of land is unreasonable if (a) the gravity of the harm outweighs the utility of the actor's conduct, or (b) the harm caused by the conduct is serious and the financial burden of compensating for this and similar harm to others would not make the continuation of the conduct not feasible.' " Section 826(a) was the focus of our application of the reasonable use doctrine in Deetz, 66 Wis.2d at 19, 224 N.W.2d 407. In that case, Deetz, a landowner, sought to develop for residential purposes a large area of land on a bluff overlooking a lake. The development project exacerbated what had previously been only minor erosion and runoff from the bluff into the lake below. The lower-lying property owners brought suit to enjoin the development project, which had rendered the lake unnavigable in several areas because of the increased accumulation of sand and sediment. After determining that the evidence was prima facie proof of the gravity of the harm, we remanded to the circuit court for its consideration of the utility and social value of Deetz's conduct.

Crest and Bauer Glass agree that § 826(a) of the Restatement (Second) of Torts is inapplicable here. Crest does not maintain that the gravity of the harm caused by Bauer Glass's property development outweighs the utility of its conduct. Crest instead asserts under § 826(b) that the harm caused by Bauer Glass's conduct is serious and that the financial burden to Bauer Glass for compensating for such harm would not have rendered infeasible the continuation of the development project. Bauer Glass argues that a correct application of § 826(b) must include an analysis of the social utility of its conduct. * * * We find, however, nothing inherent in the § 826(b) test which dictates that the fact finder must undertake a social utility analysis of an actor's conduct in order to reach a determination of the reasonableness of that conduct.

The first element of the § 826(b) test—whether the harm caused by the conduct is serious—asks the fact finder to consider the quality of the harm sustained by Crest.... [W]e hold that Crest sustained serious harm as a result of the intentional invasion of surface waters caused by Bauer Glass's development project. Regarding the extent of the harm involved, the record includes photographs of the flooding which occurred on the west portion of the Crest parking lot. The parties stipulated that that portion of the lot sustained damages of $4,500, reflecting the cost of resurfacing the lot's asphalt surface, which had cracked from the water accumulation. The character of the harm also suggests its seriousness; the accumulation of surface water constituted a physical invasion to the Crest parcel and rendered the affected portion of the lot difficult if not impossible to utilize during periods of heavy precipitation or melting snow.

There is little doubt that the law does not disfavor the use to which the Crest property was put: a lawful commercial venture. There is significant social value to commercial enterprises such as the one in which Crest engaged. The record does not reflect any lack of suitability of Crest's commercial venture in relation to its location. There is nothing to suggest that the Crest enterprise creates an eyesore, that it causes a zoning difficulty for the city of Delavan, or that the land is inherently unsuitable for the use to which it is being put. Crest has shouldered a significant burden in an attempt to avoid the harm. The parties stipulated that Crest expended $11,620 in response to an alternative writ of mandamus issued by the circuit court to "hook up" to the Bauer Glass storm sewer system. Even if Crest had not been so ordered, Bauer Glass estimates that Crest could have avoided the harm by expending $9,000 at the time when Bauer Glass initially invited Crest to hook up to its system. In either event, Crest faced a significant burden to maintain the status quo of its property, that is, to avoid the harm of the Bauer Glass development.

We also find that the financial burden to Bauer Glass of compensating Crest for the harm it sustained would not have rendered the continuation of Bauer Glass's conduct infeasible. This is the second element of the § 826(b) test. Evidence in the record indicates that Roger and Betty Willemsen paid $201,000 to purchase the Bauer Glass parcel and spent over $68,000 to install a storm sewer system. By its own estimate, Bauer Glass could have avoided the serious harm sustained by Crest by expending $9,000 to hook up a storm sewer system along its common property line with Crest. The stipulated harm sustained by Crest is $16,120, which represents Crest's cost of hooking up to the Bauer Glass storm sewer system and its cost of resurfacing a portion of its parking lot. We agree with the court of appeals that the payment of $16,120 in damages to Crest would not have rendered infeasible a project on which Bauer Glass had previously expended approximately $269,000. Either figure, $9,000 or $16,120, represents only a fraction of the total cost of the Bauer Glass development and would not have kept Bauer Glass from proceeding with the development of its property. Indeed, Bauer Glass does not argue that the financial burden of compensating Crest for the harm it sustained would have been prohibitive in relation to its continuation of the development project. Because we find that Crest suffered serious harm caused by the intentional invasion of surface water stemming from Bauer Glass's conduct and because compensating for the harm sustained would not have rendered completion of the project infeasible, we find that the invasion of surface water caused by Bauer Glass's conduct was unreasonable.

We also find that applying the § 826(b) test does not require a social utility analysis of the developer's conduct. The court of appeals did not err, therefore, in excluding a consideration of the social utility of Bauer Glass's conduct from its § 826(b) analysis. We note that a social utility analysis of a defendant's conduct is expressly undertaken when the § 826(a) test is employed. Section 826(a) compares the gravity of plaintiff's harm with the social value of the actor's conduct and is more properly applied whenever the suit is for an injunction prohibiting the intrusive activity, as in Deetz. See, Restatement (Second) of Torts, § 826, comment f, at 123 (1979). An action for damages concedes that an actor's invasion-causing conduct might have some social utility. But to conclude that an actor's conduct is socially useful does not assist a fact finder in conclusively determining, in an action for damages, whether certain conduct is unreasonable. Even if the development of the Bauer Glass parcel is considered socially useful, an inquiry into the existence of serious harm and the feasibility of continuing certain activity if the harm is compensated must still be undertaken. See, e.g., CEW Mgmt. Corp. v. First Fed. Savings & Loan, 88 Wis.2d 631, 634, 277 N.W.2d 766 (1979). In other words, a fact finder must still determine the reasonableness of an actor's conduct in relation to the plaintiff, even if the conduct has social utility. . . .

* * * Having determined that Bauer Glass's conduct in developing its land was unreasonable insofar as it caused serious harm to Crest and the compensation for the harm was not prohibitive to Bauer Glass's development project, we next consider whether Bauer Glass is liable for the entire

$16,120 in damages sustained by Crest. Bauer Glass asserts that Crest's recovery for damage should be reduced because of Crest's failure to mitigate its damages. Bauer Glass cites Schiro v. Oriental Realty Co., 272 Wis. 537, 76 N.W.2d 355 (1956), to support its proposition. In *Schiro*, a plaintiff-landowner commenced a nuisance action against an adjoining landowner to recover damages for personal injuries sustained as a result of a fall resulting from a deteriorating concrete retaining wall. A primary issue in Schiro was whether contributory negligence principles may act as a defense in a nuisance action in which the underlying conduct was allegedly negligent. But this court also identified a minimization principle applicable to nuisance actions where a plaintiff seeks to recover damages resulting from interference with the use and enjoyment of his land. This principle is that, if the plaintiff by a reasonable expenditure on his part could have remedied the condition or protected his property, or the enjoyable use thereof, from further damage or interference, and he fails so to do, he cannot hold the defendant liable for the subsequent occurring damage. Such failure by a plaintiff to minimize his damages is a defense in cases of nuisance resulting from intentional as well as negligent acts of a defendant....

There is no question that a nuisance victim has an obligation to avoid the consequences of an intentional or negligent nuisance when it is reasonable to do so. Bauer Glass argues in its brief that its liability for Crest's damages, if any, should be reduced to $9,000, representing the stipulated amount which Crest could have expended to connect its parcel with the Bauer Glass storm sewer system when Bauer Glass initially invited Crest to do so. Whether Crest could have avoided any consequences of the nuisance is a function of what reasonable steps Crest could have taken to mitigate its damages. "[A] plaintiff never is required to do more than to act reasonably under the circumstances." W. Prosser, Law of Torts, § 91 at 611 (4th ed. 1971). "If the effort, risk, sacrifice, or expense which the injured person must incur to avoid or minimize the loss or injury is such that a reasonable person under the circumstances might decline to incur it, the injured party's failure to act will not bar recovery of full damages." Kuhlman, Inc. v. G. Heileman Brewing Co., Inc., 83 Wis.2d 749, 752, 266 N.W.2d 382 (1978).

* * * [W]e decline to hold that Crest's initial rejection of the invitation to mitigate its damages by expending $9,000 was unreasonable. Although a nuisance victim is required to mitigate his damages "when with slight labor, expense and inconvenience he might have prevented [some or all of the damages]," W. Prosser, Law of Torts, § 91 at 611 (4th ed. 1971), we do not view an expenditure of $9,000 as being insignificant or slight under the facts and circumstances of this case. While an obligation to mitigate damages must include efforts which are reasonable under the circumstances, the efforts need not be substantial in relation to the damages sustained....

The decision of the court of appeals is affirmed.

HENDRICKS v. STALNAKER

Supreme Court of Appeals of West Virginia (1989).
181 W.Va. 31, 380 S.E.2d 198.

[Stalnaker and Hendricks were neighbors. Local regulations require a distance of at least 100 feet between water wells and septic tank sewage disposal systems. Stalnaker applied for a permit to build a well about the same time that Hendricks applied for a permit to build a septic system, but Stalnaker received approval and built the well first. The properties of the two were configured in such a way that any place suitable for a well on Stalnaker's property would have been within 100 feet of Hendricks' septic system. Hendricks now alleges that the well constitutes a nuisance.—eds.]

NEELY, JUSTICE:

An interference is intentional when the actor knows or should know that the conduct is causing a substantial and unreasonable interference. Restatement (Second) of Torts § 825 (1979). The unreasonableness of an intentional interference must be determined by a balancing of the land-owners' interests. An interference is unreasonable when the gravity of the harm outweighs the social value of the activity alleged to cause the harm.

* * * In the case before us, the Hendrickses' inability to operate a septic system on their property is clearly a substantial interference with the use and enjoyment of their land. The record indicates that the installation of the water well was intentional, but there was no evidence that the installation was done so as maliciously to deprive the Hendrickses of a septic system. Mr. Stalnaker wanted to insure himself of an adequate water supply and found no alternative to the well he dug.

The critical question is whether the interference, the installation of a water well, was unreasonable. Unreasonableness is determined by balancing the competing landholders' interests. We note that either use, well or septic system, burdens the adjacent property. Under Health Department regulations, a water well merely requires non-interference within 100 feet of its location. In the case of a septic system, however, the 100 foot safety zone, extending from the edge of the absorption field, may intrude on adjacent property. Thus, the septic system, with its potential for drainage, places a more invasive burden on adjacent property. Clearly both uses present similar considerations of gravity of harm and social value of the activity alleged to cause the harm. Both a water well and a septic system are necessary to use this land for housing; together they constitute the in and out of many water systems. Neither party has an inexpensive and practical alternative. The site of the water well means quality water for Mr. Stalnaker and the Hendrickses have only one location available for their septic system.

In the case before us, we are asked to determine if the water well is a private nuisance. But if the septic system were operational, the same question could be asked about the septic system. Because of the similar competing interests, the balancing of these landowners' interests is at least equal or, perhaps, slightly in favor of the water well. Thus, the Hendrickses have not shown that the balancing of interests favors their septic system. We find that the evidence presented clearly does not demonstrate that the water well is an unreasonable use of land and, therefore, does not constitute a private nuisance. . . .

ROBIE v. LILLIS

Supreme Court of New Hampshire (1972).
112 N.H. 492, 299 A.2d 155.

KENISON, CHIEF JUSTICE:

Appeal from a denial of a petition for abatement of an alleged nuisance in which the plaintiffs seek a permanent injunction restraining the defendants from maintaining a boat storage shed on a four-acre tract of land belonging to the defendants in the town of Tuftonboro, New Hampshire, near the shore of Lake Winnipesaukee.

Plaintiffs obtained a temporary injunction preventing further construction in December 1968 which was amended on two occasions before the full hearing. Prior to the hearing on the merits, the Judicial Referee (*John H. Leahy*), appointed pursuant to RSA 491:23 and RSA 493–A:1 (supp.), viewed the boat shed, several of plaintiffs' properties and the surrounding area. A full hearing was held before the referee who thereafter issued a decree denying the petition upon a ruling that no nuisance existed since the premises were being used for a reasonable purpose and in a reasonable manner. Plaintiffs seasonably excepted to the decree, to the denial of certain requests for findings and rulings, and to certain findings and rulings made by the referee. All questions of law raised by these exceptions were reserved and transferred to this court without ruling by the Superior Court (*Keller, C.J.*), pursuant to RSA 493–A:3.

Defendants operate a boat repair, rental and storage business about two miles from the boat storage shed in question which was constructed in 1968 to accommodate an increasing number of boats serviced by the defendants which required winter storage. During three months each spring the boats are from time to time taken out of storage and trucked out along a narrow road, and the reverse process occurs over a three-month period in the fall. Plaintiffs claim that the existence and operation of the boathouse constitute a nuisance because the shed is the first and only commercial structure in what is otherwise a quiet, rural and residential area and that it is a blight upon the otherwise unscarred landscape. In particular, plaintiffs allege that the "heavy" trucking in and out of the boats in the spring and fall will cause unreasonable noise and dust and hazards to playing and bicycling children and other persons traveling along the narrow access road. Plaintiffs further contend that the value of their properties will depreciate if the boathouse is allowed to remain and its operation is allowed to continue. Finally, it is claimed that the presence of oil and gasoline in the boats and elsewhere on the premises will create an unreasonable fire hazard to the surrounding properties.

The report of the judicial referee included the following findings and rulings: "The Town of Tuftonboro has no zoning laws or ordinances and the defendants are not in violation of any statutory law or ordinance. The referee finds that the trucking of boats to the boathouse in the Fall and to the corporation marina in the Spring does not of itself constitute an abatable nuisance; that hazard of children playing in the road does not constitute a nuisance in this case. Evidence concerning noise and dust was at a minimum, and it is found that noise and dust, if any, does not exist to a point where it is a nuisance.

"Evidence as to effect on surrounding land values was very scarce. [One witness] bought land in 1971 on Tuftonboro Neck and expects to develop it and 'make a profit.'

"There was evidence from the plaintiffs that the boat storage house constituted a fire hazard because there was always some gasoline around or in the boats, as it was hard to get it all out when storing a boat.

"It is found that the land values near the boathouse have not deteriorated by reason of the boathouse being where it is. The fire hazard complained of appears to be no greater than exists in any storage place where gasoline is present. It is noted that there is a fire department located within one mile of the boat building.

"Upon consideration of all the evidence, it is found that the boat storage building ... does not constitute a public or private nuisance by being where it is or because of its use to store boats. It is further found that the defendants are using the premises involved for a reasonable purpose and in a reasonable manner. It is recommended that the temporary injunction be terminated and the request for a permanent injunction be denied."

Plaintiffs have alleged that the boathouse constitutes both a public and a private nuisance. Prior decisions of this court make it clear that a private nuisance may be defined as an activity which results in an unreasonable interference with the use and enjoyment of another's property. *See Webb v. Rye,* 108 N.H. 147, 230 A.2d 223 (1967); *Urie v. Franconia Paper Co.,* 107 N.H. 131, 218 A.2d 360 (1966); *Proulx v. Keene,* 102 N.H. 427, 158 A.2d 455 (1960); *Lane v. Concord,* 70 N.H. 485, 49 A. 687 (1900). *See generally* 6–A American Law of Propertys. 28.22 (A.J. Casner ed. 1954); Prosser, Tortss. 89 (4th ed. 1971); Restatement (Second) of Torts s. 822, at 22 (Tent. Draft No. 17, 1971). A public nuisance, on the other hand, is "an unreasonable interference with a right common to the general public." Restatement (Second) of Torts, *supra s.* 821B(1), at 3. It is behavior which unreasonably interferes with the health, safety, peace, comfort or convenience of the general community. 6–A American Law of Property, *supra s.* 28.23, at 68; Restatement (Second) of Torts, *supra s.* 821B(2)(a); *see Urie v. Franconia Paper Co.,* 107 N.H. 131, 218 A.2d 360

(1966); *McKinney v. Riley,* 105 N.H. 249, 197 A.2d 218 (1964); *White v. Suncook Mills,* 91 N.H. 92, 13 A.2d 729 (1940). Conduct which unreasonably interferes with the rights of others may be both a public and a private nuisance (*Urie v. Franconia Paper Co. supra;* Restatement (Second) of Torts, *supra s.* 821B, Comment *h* at 9–10), and both actions involve an analysis of similar considerations. Restatement (Second) of Torts, *supra s.* 821B, Comment *e* at 6.

Essential to a finding of either a public or a private nuisance is a determination that the interference complained of is substantial. *Proulx v. Keene, 102 N.H. 427, 158 A.2d 455 (1960); Page v. Brooks, 79 N.H. 70, 104 A. 786 (1918); Lane v. Concord supra; Prosser, supra s. 87, at 577; Restatement (Second) of Torts, supra s. 821B(2) (c), s. 821 (F) at 54 (Tent. Draft No. 16, 1970), and s. 829A at 4 (Tent Draft No. 18, 1972). "Substantial harm is that in excess of the customary interferences a land user suffers in an organized society. It denotes an appreciable and tangible interference with a property interest."* 6–A American Law of Property, *supra s.* 28.25, *at 73. However, "[n]ot every intentional and substantial invasion of a person's interest in the use and enjoyment of land is actionable ... Life in organized society ... involves an unavoidable clash of individual interests. Practically all human activities ... interfere to some extent with others or involve some risk of interference.... [E]ach individual in a community must put up with a certain amount of annoyance, inconvenience and interference, and must take a certain amount of risk in order that all may get on together.... [T]he law of torts does not attempt to impose liability ... in every case where one person's conduct has some detrimental effect on another. Liability is imposed only in those cases where the harm or risk to one is greater than he ought to be required to bear under the circumstances.... [T]he law has developed a ... rule of liability for intentional invasions ... [which] requires that* an intentional invasion be unreasonable before one is liable for causing it." Restatement (Second) of Torts, *s.* 822, Comment g at 27–28 (Tent. Draft No. 17, 1971). This requirement of a finding of unreasonableness is the crux of the law of nuisance. *Webb v. Rye,* 108 N.H. 147, 230 A.2d 223 (1967); *Lane v. Concord supra; Ladd v. Brick Co.,* 68 N.H. 185, 37 A. 1041 (1894); Prosser, *supra s.* 89, at 596.

The proper consideration of all the relevant circumstances involves a balancing of the gravity of the harm to the plaintiff against the utility of the defendant's conduct, both to himself and to the community. *Proulx v. Keene,* 102 N.H. 427, 158 A.2d 455 (1960); 6–A American Law of Property, *supra s.* 28.26, at 75–76; Restatement of Torts ss. 826–31 (1939). *See also Webb v. Rye supra.* "In general, conduct will be unreasonable only when its utility to the actor and to the public is outweighed by the gravity of the harm that results." 6–A American Law of Property, *supra s.* 28.22, at 66. This same weighing process is involved in determining the appropriateness of injunctive relief once a nuisance has been found to exist (*Crocker v. Canaan College,* 110 N.H. 384, 388, 268 A.2d 844, 847 (1970); *Webb v. Rye supra;* 6–A American Law of Property, *supra s.* 28.35, at 97; Restatement of Torts, *supra s.* 941), although the scales must weigh more heavily in the plaintiff's favor because of the extraordinary nature of this form of relief. See *Ferguson v. Keene*, 111 N.H. 222, 225, 279 A.2d 605, 607–08 (1971); *Riter v. Keokuk Electro–Metals Co.*, 248 Iowa 710, 82 N.W.2d 151 (1957); *Boomer v. Atlantic Cement Co.*, 26 N.Y.2d 219, 309 N.Y.S.2d 312, 257 N.E.2d 870 (1970); Restatement of Torts, *supra s.* 941, at 711–12. *See generally* Annot., 40 A.L.R.3d 601 (1971).

It is clear in this case that the judicial referee correctly applied these tests in determining that the defendants' use of the boat shed was reasonable. The record fully supports the conclusion that the harm, if any, inflicted upon the plaintiffs from the existence and operation of the boathouse is neither substantial nor unreasonable.

The only evidence bearing on the claim that the shed would be a fire hazard was an admission by one of the defendants that all gas and oil could never be entirely removed from all of the boats and an assertion from one of the plaintiffs that gasoline can be a potent explosive under certain circumstances. This is plainly insufficient to establish a nuisance.... Even the storage of gasoline and oil in large quantities constitutes a nuisance only when the hazard to adjoining property owners is substantial. *Hilliard v. Shuff, 260 La. 384, 256 So.2d 127 (1971). See also Frazier v. Chambers, 228 Ga. 270, 185 S.E.2d 379 (1971)*; *Erie v. Gulf Oil Corp., 395 Pa. 383, 150 A.2d 351 (1959)*. No substantial hazard was shown in this case.

Evidence on the claim of a depreciation in land values was scarce and conflicting. Furthermore, this argument is ordinarily accorded little weight by the courts in nuisance cases on the ground that the law cannot generally protect landowners from fluctuating land values which is a risk necessarily inherent in all land ownership. *See Nicholson v. Connecticut Half–Way House, Inc., 153 Conn. 507, 218 A.2d 383 (1966)*; *Smith v. Western Wayne County Conservation Ass'n, 380 Mich. 526, 158 N.W.2d 463 (1968)*; *Young v. St. Martin's Church, 361 Pa. 505, 64 A.2d 814 (1949)*; 6–A American Law of Property, *supra s.* 28.22, at 67.

There was similarly insufficient evidence to support a finding of nuisance from increased hazards to children playing in the street, the only evidence on this point being testimony that children lived and played along the road traveled by the defendants' trucks. Nor was there evidence to support a finding that the trucks would create an unreasonable amount of dust or noise. *Stegner v. Bahr & Ledoyen, Inc., 126 Cal. App. 2d 220, 272 P.2d 106 (1954). See generally Note, Noise Nuisances: Commercial Enterprises v. Owners of Residential Property, 7 Vand. L. Rev. 695 (1954)*; Annot., *24 A.L.R.2d 194 (1952)*. The authorities cited by plaintiffs concerning truck noise as a nuisance involve nighttime operations substantially interfering with people's sleep unlike this case where there was undisputed testimony that the trucks only travel during the normal working day. *E.g., Fox v. Ewers, 195 Md. 650, 75 A.2d 357 (1950)*; *cf. Aldridge v. Saxey, 242 Ore. 238, 409 P.2d 184 (1965)*. Increased traffic or trucking generally is not a ground for injunctive relief (*Smith v. Western Wayne County*

Conservation Ass'n supra), and the plaintiffs would have had to prove, as they did not, an unreasonable interference with their use of the road or with their ingress or egress from their properties. *Graves v. Shattuck, 35 N.H. 257 (1857); Stegner v. Bahr & Leyoden, Inc., supra.*

We think that plaintiffs' final and strongest contention that the boat storage shed should be excluded from the otherwise "residential" neighborhood because of its commercial and "unsightly" nature cannot be accepted. A review of the photographs and other evidence in the case indicates that there is no legal basis for the allegation that the shed is unsightly. True, it is not a lovely Georgian edifice of exquisite charm. However, the law has traditionally trod with utmost caution in declaring a structure unsightly, and far greater unattractiveness than was shown here must be established before the law will require its destruction. *See Obrecht v. National Gypsum Co., 361 Mich. 399, 105 N.W.2d 143 (1960)*; 6–A American Law of Property, *supra s.* 28.22, at 67–68. This is not to say, however, that the unaesthetic quality of an activity is not an important consideration in the balancing process involved in the determination of its reasonableness under all the circumstances. *See Gerrish v. Wishbone Farm, 108 N.H. 237, 231 A.2d 622 (1967); Obrecht v. National Gypsum Co., supra, 361 Mich. at 417–18, 105 N.W.2d at 151–52 (1960). See generally Note, Aesthetic Nuisance: An Emerging Cause of Action, 45 N.Y.U.L. Rev. 1075 (1970).*

A nuisance may undoubtedly arise from a land use incompatible with the surrounding neighborhood. Mandelker, The Role of Law in the Planning Process, 30 Law & Contemp. Prob. 26 (1965). "A nuisance may be merely a right thing in the wrong place,—like a pig in the parlor instead of the barnyard." *Euclid v. Ambler Realty Co., 272 U.S. 365, 388, 71 L. Ed. 303, 311, 47 S. Ct. 114, 118 (1926); Catalfo v. Shenton, 102 N.H. 47, 49, 149 A.2d 871, 873 (1959).* A person ordinarily has a valid expectation that an established, closely-settled neighborhood or subdivision will remain exclusively residential. However, the validity of that expectation is substantially weakened where the locality is "pastoral and rural" with large tracts of vacant land as in the instant case. *See Aldridge v. Saxey, 242 Ore. 238, 243–44, 409 P.2d 184, 187–88 (1965); Wade v. Fuller, 12 Utah 2d 299, 365 P.2d 802 (1961)*; Beuscher and Morrison, Judicial Zoning Through Recent Nuisance Cases, 1955 Wis. L. Rev. 440, 444–51.

Plaintiffs urge that in this day of increased ecological concern we should broaden the existing boundaries of the law of nuisance to fill in the gap where environmental and zoning legislation leaves off. We are of the opinion, however, that the traditional nuisance analysis performs just that function admirably well and would be exceptionally difficult to improve upon. We have taken care to outline the basic structure of the law of nuisance to demonstrate that the present rules which resolve conflicting land uses upon an analysis of the unreasonableness and substantiality of a person's interference with another's rights are flexible, equitable and well adapted to the problem. When plaintiffs fail to obtain relief as in the instant case, it is because the interference complained of has not been shown to be substantial or unreasonable under all of the circumstances. It does not appear unreasonable to us to locate a boat storage shed on a four-acre tract of land in a rural albeit "residential" locality which depends in part for its economic livelihood on boating and other recreational activities.

We have reviewed the testimony and examined the exhibits, including photographs of the boat shed and the surrounding area, and we conclude that the findings and rulings of the judicial referee are amply supported by the record and consistent with the law of nuisance as developed and applied in this State.

Exceptions overruled.

NOTES AND QUESTIONS

1. To one degree or another, *Prah, Crest Chevrolet, Hendricks* and *Robie* all stand for the proposition that the subject of nuisance law is not "tortious" land uses, but rather *incompatible* land uses. That is, in many nuisance cases it is neither easy nor helpful to identify one party as a wrongdoer and the other as a victim. Each one wants something which, if done, will injure the property of the other. This was an important insight of Ronald Coase's famous article "The Problem of Social Cost," 3 J.L. & Econ. 1 (1960), discussed below.

Doesn't *Hendricks* suggest that in "close" cases—that is, where the conflicting land uses have about the same amount of social value and cause about the same amount of harm—the court will give preference to the person who got there first? Query: how close must the cases be? Suppose that Stalnaker had built his well before Hendricks had built his septic system, but that Stalnaker could have built his well in a different place, more than 100 feet from Hendricks' system. Should that change the outcome? If so, what should the remedy be? See the *Spur Industries* case, infra this chapter.

2. A private nuisance is a tort action for injury to an interest in the use and enjoyment of land. As a general rule only people who hold some legally recognized interest in property affected by the nuisance may maintain an action. However, the interest need not be large. Should a tenant on an oral tenancy at will be able to maintain an action? See Towaliga Falls Power Co. v. Sims, 6 Ga.App. 749, 65 S.E. 844 (1909). Cf. Lew v. Superior Court, 25 Cal.Rptr.2d 42, 20 Cal.App.4th 866 (1993) (landlord could be liable in nuisance for the mental distress suffered by neighbors as a result of drug dealing outside the apartment). Public nuisances involve unreasonable interferences with rights common to the public that impair the public health, safety, morals or comfort. See, e.g., McMillen Engineering, Inc. v. The Travelers Indemnity Co., 744 F. Supp. 2d 416, 427 (W.D.Pa. 2010) ("Circumstances that constitute a public nuisance are, among other things, conduct that is proscribed by statute or ordinance or conduct that interferes with the public peace, or poses a significant threat to public health."). Unlike private nuisance plaintiffs, public nuisance plaintiffs need not own an interest in land. Public nuisances are discussed further in *Spur Industries, Inc. v. Del E. Webb Development Co.,* infra.

3.   What legal standard do courts use in determining whether the defendants' activity is a nuisance? Clearly, not every activity that injures neighboring land is an actionable nuisance. Most courts as well as the Restatement (Second) of Torts § 825 distinguish between "intentional" and "unintentional" harmful conduct and purport to apply different standards to them. At the same time, they are careful to point out that nuisance is not negligence: an activity can be a nuisance regardless of the actor's level of care. See Justice Cardozo's opinion in McFarlane v. Niagara Falls, 247 N.Y. 340, 343, 160 N.E. 391, 391 (1928):

> One acts sometimes at one's peril. In such circumstances, the duty to desist is absolute whenever conduct, if persisted in, brings damage to another.... Illustrations are abundant. One who emits noxious fumes or gases day by day in the running of his factory may be liable to his neighbor though he has taken all available precautions.... He is not to do such things at all, whether he is negligent or careful.

Both the distinction between intentional and unintentional conduct and the distinction between nuisance and negligence may create as many problems as they solve. First, the meaning of "intentional" is far from clear: obviously, the owner of a coal-burning power plant "intends" to burn coal, but does it "intend" to pollute the air, or does it "intend" to lower the property values of neighboring lands? Perhaps more to the point, why should questions of intent be relevant, except perhaps as one indicator of the social utility of the defendant's conduct? Wouldn't an efficient law of nuisance condemn conduct whose social value was less than its social cost, regardless of the actor's state of mind? Or is evidence of intent a kind of surrogate, to aid the court in measuring social value or cost?

Likewise, should not the care with which an activity is performed *always* be relevant to the court's calculation of its net social utility? Conduct is negligent when the expected social cost of the harm that will result from an untaken precaution is greater than the cost of taking the precaution. As a result, negligence is inefficient. For example, operation of an air-polluting smokestack is negligent if expected injury caused by the pollution is $1000, but a device that would clean the air could be installed and operated for $550. Furthermore, such operation is negligent *even* if the smokestack produces a social value of $1,000,000.[3] A court convinced of such facts in an action for nuisance would probably order installation of the air cleaner. See generally Posner, A Theory of Negligence, 1 J. Legal Stud. 29 (1972); Rabin, Nuisance Law: Rethinking Fundamental Assumptions, 63 Va.L.Rev. 1299 (1977).

4.   *Crest Chevrolet* relied on § 826(b) of the Restatement, which addresses conduct that is socially valuable but nevertheless causes injury to adjoining property. The Restatement provides that in such a case the appropriate remedy is damages rather than an injunction, provided that the damages payment would not render the conduct economically impractical. See also CAE–Link Corp. v. Washington Suburban Sanitary Comm'n, 90 Md.App. 604, 602 A.2d 239 (1992), aff'd, 330 Md. 115, 622 A.2d 745, cert. denied, 510 U.S.

---

3.   That is, the proper remedy in such a case is to permit the smokestack to operate, but to order the defendant to install the air-cleaning device, or else fine the defendant at least $551 for not installing it—in which case the defendant will be better off if he installs it.

907 (1993), holding that a sewage treatment plant could not avoid a nuisance claim by neighboring property owners by showing that the plant used state-of-the-art technology and was operated without negligence. The defendant claimed that even state of the art equipment would cause a certain amount of odor and other pollution. Cf. Vogel v. Grant–Lafayette Electric Cooperative, 201 Wis.2d 416, 548 N.W.2d 829 (1996), holding that stray electrical voltage that injured cattle could be a nuisance to farmers, but that the theory of the complaint was based on negligence, so the doctrine of contributory negligence applied as well.

5.   Some agricultural states have protected certain odor producing activities, such as commercial production of hogs, with statutes that severely limit private nuisance actions. See, e.g., Iowa Code § 657.11 (1995), which creates a rebuttable presumption of legality for a hog confinement lot that is operated with all permits as required by state and federal law. See Goodell v. Humboldt County, 575 N.W.2d 486 (Iowa 1998), holding that a county ordinance that limited a feed lot's hydrogen sulfide emissions (the principal cause of odor from animal waste) was preempted by the state statute. Cf. N.C. Gen. Stat. §§ 106–700–701 (2010), which limits nuisance liability for a broad range of agricultural and forestry operations.

6.   Darryl Drummer is an avid drummer and owns ½ acres of land in Harlem that he allows to be used as a park, Drummer Park. Every Saturday, the park is filled with the scent of blossoming linden trees and the sound of West African drums. Across the street from Drummer Park is Harlem Luxury Co–Op, a new seven-story luxury co-op with $1 million apartments.

The drummers in Drummer Park are there at the invitation of Mr. Drummer. They have played in the park since 1969, when the park was overrun by squatters, drug dealers and addicts and was such a dangerous place that parents were afraid to allow their children to play in the park. The musicians, who play until 10 p.m. every summer Saturday, are widely credited with helping to make the park safer over the years. Drug addicts and dealers do not desire the attention that the drummers bring with their playing. On some days, the musicians would drum for as long as 10 hours, which provided a window of time for the neighborhood's children to play in safety, residents said.

Mr. Drummer acknowledges that the drumbeats can pierce walls and windows, but he regards the musicians as part of the city's vibrant and often noisy cultural mix. But some in Harlem Luxury Co–Op have a different perspective. When the drummers occupy a spot nearby, residents say they are unable to sleep, hear their television sets, speak on the telephone, or even have conversations with their spouses without shouting. Some say they cannot even think straight.

Complaints about the drum circle began long before the co-op was built. In the past, however, if neighbors objected, the drummers simply found a new place in the park without engendering ill will. The residents of Harlem Luxury Co–Op want Mr. Drummer to cease allowing his property to be used as a gathering place for Saturday drumming. Mr. Drummer refuses and says he has the right to use his property as he wishes. Do the residents of Harlem Luxury Co–Op have a viable nuisance claim? See Timothy Williams, An Old

Sound in Harlem Draws New Neighbors' Ire, N.Y. Times (July 6, 2008), http://www.nytimes.com/2008/07/06/nyregion/06drummers.html?emc=eta1.

NOTE: ECONOMIC DEVELOPMENT AND THE LAW OF NUISANCE

The judicial opinions in this chapter should give you some hint of the complex relationship that exists between the law of nuisance and the historical course of economic development in the United States. More than one legal historian has argued that common law judges used the law of nuisance to "meter" the amount of economic development—or, to put it another way, to determine how much economic development neighbors must be willing to tolerate. The strongest version of this argument begins by noting that in eighteenth century England not only was the law of nuisance very strong, but it also was extremely protective of agrarian uses. For example, Blackstone, who wrote shortly before the American Revolution, believed that almost any activity that injured the land of another could be enjoined as a nuisance. 3 W. Blackstone, Commentaries on the Laws of England 217–18 (1765–69).

However, Blackstone's rule made the cost of economic development very high. It effectively forced someone who wanted to build a mill, factory or kiln to "buy out" his neighbors. At the time Blackstone wrote, England was already a densely populated country. Even in the early nineteenth century, however, America was an undeveloped wilderness badly in need of railroads, bridges, dams and factories. Strict adoption of the English law of nuisance as developed by Blackstone would have impeded economic growth substantially.

American judges gradually responded to this difference in physical condition by modifying the English law of nuisance. They replaced the doctrines that permitted a plaintiff to enjoin almost any substantial injury with rules that attempted to balance the social utility of the defendant's conduct against the harm done to the plaintiff. These rules gave courts wide latitude to manipulate the law of nuisance by assigning more or less utility to the defendant's conduct depending on its evaluation of how socially valuable the conduct was. See, e.g., Lexington & Ohio Rail Road v. Applegate, 38 Ky. (8 Dana) 289 (1839), which held that railroads were extremely valuable to society. As a result, they should be permitted to operate even when they caused injury to adjoining lands.

By the late nineteenth century, however, economic development was well under way, the country was more densely populated, and it became apparent that one person's economic development could injure the *developed* property (not merely the undeveloped land) of someone else. As a result, courts began to retreat to older formulations of the law of nuisance. This change can be seen in the law respecting surface waters, outlined in the *Crest Chevrolet* opinion. The "common enemy" rule, which dominated in the nineteenth century, permitted each landowner to rid himself of surface water in any way he pleased without incurring legal liability. Borchsenius v. Chicago, St. P., M. & O. Ry., 96 Wis. 448, 71 N.W. 884 (1897). The common enemy rule minimized the costs of developing land by permitting land owners to build dams or divert streams without concern about economic injury to neighbors. Although that rule may have served a purpose when the United States was economically underdeveloped and land was cheap, it was not a good rule for a much more urbanized America in the twentieth century. In most jurisdictions, the common enemy rule has been replaced by a "reasonable use" rule that attempts to compare the utility of the defendant's conduct and the care with which his conduct was carried out with the injury to the plaintiff; or alternatively, with the Restatement rule that reverts to general nuisance principles whenever the defendant interferes with water's natural flow. See, e.g., Canton v. Graniteville Fire Dist. No. 4, 171 Vt. 551, 762 A.2d 808 (2000) ("An upper property owner creates a nuisance when he or she causes water to flow onto lower lands in a manner or place different from its natural state, harming the lower property owner's interest in the use and enjoyment of that land").

For a more complete account of the relationship between economic development and the common law, see M. Horwitz, The Transformation of American Law, 1780–1860 (1977); H. Hovenkamp, Enterprise and American Law, 1836–1937 (1991).

§ 9.3   REMEDIES

BOOMER v. ATLANTIC CEMENT CO.

Court of Appeals of New York (1970).
26 N.Y.2d 219, 309 N.Y.S.2d 312, 257 N.E.2d 870.

B<small>ERGAN</small>, J<small>UDGE</small>.

Defendant operates a large cement plant near Albany. These are actions for injunction and damages by neighboring land owners alleging injury to property from dirt, smoke and vibration emanating from the plant. A nuisance has been found after trial, temporary damages have been allowed; but an injunction has been denied.

* * * The threshold question raised by the division of view on this appeal is whether the court should resolve the litigation between the parties now before it as equitably as seems possible; or whether, seeking promotion of the general public welfare, it should channel private litigation into broad public objectives.

A court performs its essential function when it decides the rights of parties before it. Its decision of private controversies may sometimes greatly affect public issues. Large questions of law are often resolved by the manner in which private litigation is decided. But this is normally an incident to the court's main function to settle controversy. It is a rare exercise of judicial power to use a decision in private litigation as a purposeful mechanism to achieve direct public objectives greatly beyond the rights and interests before the court.

Effective control of air pollution is a problem presently far from solution even with the full public and financial powers of government. In large measure adequate technical procedures are yet to be developed and some that appear possible may be economically impracticable.

It seems apparent that the amelioration of air pollution will depend on technical research in great depth; on a carefully balanced consideration of the economic impact of close regulation; and of the actual effect on public health. It is likely to require massive public expenditure and to demand more than any local community can accomplish and to depend on regional and interstate controls.

A court should not try to do this on its own as a by-product of private litigation and it seems manifest that the judicial establishment is neither equipped in the limited nature of any judgment it can pronounce nor prepared to lay down and implement an effective policy for the elimination of air pollution. This is an area beyond the circumference of one private lawsuit. It is a direct responsibility for government and should not thus be undertaken as an incident to solving a dispute between property owners and a single cement plant—one of many—in the Hudson River valley.

The cement making operations of defendant have been found by the court at Special Term to have damaged the nearby properties of plaintiffs in these two actions. That court, as it has been noted, accordingly found defendant maintained a nuisance and this has been affirmed at the Appellate Division. The total damage to plaintiffs' properties is, however, relatively small in comparison with the value of defendant's operation and with the consequences of the injunction which plaintiffs seek.

The ground for the denial of injunction, notwithstanding the finding both that there is a nuisance and that plaintiffs have been damaged substantially, is the large disparity in economic consequences of the nuisance and of the injunction. This theory cannot, however, be sustained without overruling a doctrine which has been consistently reaffirmed in several leading cases in this court and which has never been disavowed here, namely that where a nuisance has been found and where there has been any substantial damage shown by the party complaining an injunction will be granted.

The rule in New York has been that such a nuisance will be enjoined although marked disparity be shown in economic consequence between the effect of the injunction and the effect of the nuisance.

The problem of disparity in economic consequence was sharply in focus in Whalen v. Union Bag & Paper Co., 208 N.Y. 1, 101 N.E. 805. A pulp mill entailing an investment of more than a million dollars polluted a stream in which plaintiff, who owned a farm, was "a lower riparian owner". The economic loss to plaintiff from this pollution was small. This court, reversing the Appellate Division, reinstated the injunction granted by the Special Term against the argument of the mill owner that in view of "the slight advantage to plaintiff and the great loss that will be inflicted on defendant" an injunction should not be granted.

> "Such a balancing of injuries cannot be justified by the circumstances of this case", Judge Werner noted (p. 4, 101 N.E. p. 805). He continued: "Although the damage to the plaintiff may be slight as compared with the defendant's expense of abating the condition, that is not a good reason for refusing an injunction" (p. 5, 101 N.E. p. 806).

Thus the unconditional injunction granted at Special Term was reinstated. The rule laid down in that case, then, is that whenever the damage resulting from a nuisance is found not "unsubstantial", viz., $100 a year, injunction would follow. This states a rule that had been followed in this court with marked consistency.

* * *

Although the court at Special Term and the Appellate Division held that injunction should be denied, it was found that plaintiffs had been damaged in various specific amounts up to the time of the trial and damages to the respective plaintiffs were awarded for those amounts. The effect of this was, injunction having been denied, plaintiffs could maintain successive actions at law for damages thereafter as further damage was incurred.

The court at Special Term also found the amount of permanent damage attributable to each plaintiff, for the guidance of the parties in the event both sides stipulated to the payment and acceptance of such permanent damage as a settlement of all the controversies among the parties. The total of permanent damages to all plaintiffs thus found was $185,000. This basis of adjustment has not resulted in any stipulation by the parties.

This result at Special Term and at the Appellate Division is a departure from a rule that has become settled; but to follow the rule literally in these cases would be to close down the plant at once. This court is fully agreed to avoid that immediately drastic remedy; the difference in view is how best to avoid it.[4]

One alternative is to grant the injunction but postpone its effect to a specified future date to give opportunity for technical advances to permit defendant to eliminate the nuisance; another is to grant the injunction conditioned on the payment of permanent damages to plaintiffs which would compensate them for the total economic loss to their property present and future caused by defendant's operations. For reasons which will be developed the court chooses the latter alternative.

If the injunction were to be granted unless within a short period— e.g., 18 months—the nuisance be abated by improved methods, there would be no assurance that any significant technical improvement would occur.

The parties could settle this private litigation at any time if defendant paid enough money and the imminent threat of closing the plant would build up the pressure on defendant. If there were no improved techniques found, there would inevitably be applications to the court at Special Term for extensions of time to perform on showing of good faith efforts to find such techniques.

Moreover, techniques to eliminate dust and other annoying by-products of cement making are unlikely to be developed by any research the

---

4. Respondent's investment in the plant is in excess of $45,000,000. There are over 300 people employed there.

defendant can undertake within any short period, but will depend on the total resources of the cement industry nationwide and throughout the world. The problem is universal wherever cement is made.

For obvious reasons the rate of the research is beyond control of defendant. If at the end of 18 months the whole industry has not found a technical solution a court would be hard put to close down this one cement plant if due regard be given to equitable principles.

On the other hand, to grant the injunction unless defendant pays plaintiffs such permanent damages as may be fixed by the court seems to do justice between the contending parties. All of the attributions of economic loss to the properties on which plaintiffs' complaints are based will have been redressed.

The nuisance complained of by these plaintiffs may have other public or private consequences, but these particular parties are the only ones who have sought remedies and the judgment proposed will fully redress them. The limitation of relief granted is a limitation only within the four corners of these actions and does not foreclose public health or other public agencies from seeking proper relief in a proper court.

It seems reasonable to think that the risk of being required to pay permanent damages to injured property owners by cement plant owners would itself be a reasonable effective spur to research for improved techniques to minimize nuisance.[5]

* * *

The damage base here suggested is consistent with the general rule in those nuisance cases where damages are allowed. "Where a nuisance is of such a permanent and unabatable character that a single recovery can be had, including the whole damage past and future resulting therefrom, there can be but one recovery" (66 C.J.S. Nuisances § 140, p. 947). It has been said that permanent damages are allowed where the loss recoverable would obviously be small as compared with the cost of removal of the nuisance.

* * *

The present cases and the remedy here proposed are in a number of other respects rather similar to Northern Indiana Public Service Co. v. W.J. & M.S. Vesey, 210 Ind. 338, 200 N.E. 620 decided by the Supreme Court of Indiana. The gases, odors, ammonia and smoke from the Northern Indiana company's gas plant damaged the nearby Vesey greenhouse operation. An injunction and damages were sought, but an injunction was denied and the relief granted was limited to permanent damages "present, past, and future" (p. 371, 200 N.E. 620).

Denial of injunction was grounded on a public interest in the operation of the gas plant and on the court's conclusion "that less injury would

---

5. Is the court correct? Suppose that compensating injured neighbors costs $185,000, but developing cleaner technology costs $1,000,000.—Ed.

be occasioned by requiring the appellant [Public Service] to pay the appellee [Vesey] all damages suffered by it ... than by enjoining the operation of the gas plant; and that the maintenance and operation of the gas plant should not be enjoined.''

The Indiana Supreme Court opinion continued: "When the trial court refused injunctive relief to the appellee upon the ground of public interest in the continuance of the gas plant, it properly retained jurisdiction of the case and awarded full compensation to the appellee. This is upon the general equitable principle that equity will give full relief in one action and prevent a multiplicity of suits.''

* * *

Thus it seems fair to both sides to grant permanent damages to plaintiffs which will terminate this private litigation. The theory of damage is the ''servitude on land'' of plaintiffs imposed by defendant's nuisance. (See United States v. Causby, 328 U.S. 256, 261, 262, 267, 66 S.Ct. 1062, 90 L.Ed. 1206, where the term ''servitude'' addressed to the land was used by Justice Douglas relating to the effect of airplane noise on property near an airport.)

The judgment, by allowance of permanent damages imposing a servitude on land, which is the basis of the actions, would preclude future recovery by plaintiffs or their grantees.

* * *

Although the Trial Term has found permanent damages as a possible basis of settlement of the litigation, on remission the court should be entirely free to re-examine this subject. It may again find the permanent damage already found; or make new findings.

The orders should be reversed, without costs, and the cases remitted to Supreme Court, Albany County to grant an injunction which shall be vacated upon payment by defendant of such amounts of permanent damage to the respective plaintiffs as shall for this purpose be determined by the court.

JASEN, JUDGE (dissenting).

I agree with the majority that a reversal is required here, but I do not subscribe to the newly enunciated doctrine of assessment of permanent damages, in lieu of an injunction, where substantial property rights have been impaired by the creation of a nuisance.

It has long been the rule in this State, as the majority acknowledges, that a nuisance which results in substantial continuing damage to neighbors must be enjoined.

* * *

To now change the rule to permit the cement company to continue polluting the air indefinitely upon the payment of permanent damages is, in my opinion, compounding the magnitude of a very serious problem in our State and Nation today.

In recognition of this problem, the Legislature of this State has enacted the Air Pollution Control Act (Public Health Law, Consol.Laws, c. 45, §§ 1264 to 1299–m) declaring that it is the State policy to require the use of all available and reasonable methods to prevent and control air pollution (Public Health Law § 1265).

* * *

It is interesting to note that cement production has recently been identified as a significant source of particulate contamination in the Hudson Valley. This type of pollution, wherein very small particles escape and stay in the atmosphere, has been denominated as the type of air pollution which produces the greatest hazard to human health. We have thus a nuisance which not only is damaging to the plaintiffs, but also is decidedly harmful to the general public.

I see grave dangers in overruling our long-established rule of granting an injunction where a nuisance results in substantial continuing damage. In permitting the injunction to become inoperative upon the payment of permanent damages, the majority is, in effect, licensing a continuing wrong. It is the same as saying to the cement company, you may continue to do harm to your neighbors so long as you pay a fee for it. Furthermore, once such permanent damages are assessed and paid, the incentive to alleviate the wrong would be eliminated, thereby continuing air pollution of an area without abatement. * * *

This kind of inverse condemnation (Ferguson v. Village of Hamburg, 272 N.Y. 234, 5 N.E.2d 801) may not be invoked by a private person or corporation for private gain or advantage. Inverse condemnation should only be permitted when the public is primarily served in the taking or impairment of property.

* * *

This is made clear by the State Constitution (art. I, § 7, subd. [a]) which provides that "[p]rivate property shall not be taken for *public use* without just compensation" (emphasis added). It is, of course, significant that the section makes no mention of taking for a *private* use. * * *

NOTES AND QUESTIONS

1. What does the New York Court of Appeals mean by its statement that "[a] court performs its essential function when it decides the rights of parties before it. . . . It is a rare exercise of judicial power to use a decision in private litigation . . . to achieve direct public objectives greatly beyond the rights and interests before the court." Did the court follow its own advice? Is the Restatement approach to nuisance law consistent with this advice?

2. One difficulty with using the law of nuisance to regulate air pollution is suggested by the facts of the *Boomer* case. The area involved in the

litigation contains many such plants and hundreds of affected landowners. If the plants are in different states, they perhaps cannot even be brought within the jurisdiction of a single state court. This creates the possibility of inconsistent rules being applied to different plants that compete in the same market. For example, suppose that Atlantic Cement Co. is forced to pay an enormous damages award or engage in expensive research and development of pollution control equipment, while a competing cement producer in New Jersey wins its nuisance case and does not have to pay anything. The result will be to put Atlantic at a competitive disadvantage. Its costs will rise and its output may decline as the New Jersey company takes advantage of its own lower costs in order to steal sales from Atlantic. This possibility suggests that not only should air quality be regulated by statutory standards rather than the common law, but that the statutory standards ought to be uniform over a wide geographic area. Thus the federal government is probably a better regulator of air quality than are the individual states.

3. Can a person or firm avoid liability for a nuisance created under its ownership by selling the land containing the nuisance to someone else? The Restatement (Second) of Torts § 840A and comment c say no: "If the vendor or lessor has himself created on the land a condition that results in a nuisance, . . . his responsibility toward those outside of his land is such that he is not free to terminate his liability to them . . . by passing the land itself on to a third person." Suppose that A owns property and contaminates its underground water supply by dumping toxic wastes. A sells the land to B, who subsequently discovers the pollution. Can B maintain a nuisance action against A? See Philadelphia Elec. Co. v. Hercules, Inc., 762 F.2d 303 (3d Cir.1985).

4. Courts sometimes distinguish between "temporary" and "permanent" nuisances, and the difference can be very important for issues such as the running of a statute of limitation. A "temporary" nuisance is activity that occurs a single time, or else recurring activity that re-starts the limitation period each time it occurs. By contrast, a "permanent" nuisance is ongoing activity, and the statute of limitation is generally said to run from the time that neighbors reasonably should have known of the activity or else experienced injury from it. See Schneider National Carriers, Inc. v. Bates, 147 S.W.3d 264 (Tex. 2004), which held that plants producing industrial pollution constituted a permanent nuisance and, since the activity had been going on a long time, the plaintiffs' claim was barred by the statute of limitation. The court observed:

> Generally, if a nuisance occurs at least a few times a year and appears likely to continue, property values will begin to reflect that impact, and jurors should be able to evaluate it with reasonable certainty. Even if a nuisance causes annoyance only during certain weather conditions or certain months, annual experience should provide a sufficient basis for evaluating the nuisance. Absent evidence that current experiences are unrepresentative or about to change, such nuisances should be considered "permanent" as a matter of law.

> Accordingly, we hold that a nuisance should be deemed temporary only if it is so irregular or intermittent over the period leading up to filing and

trial that future injury cannot be estimated with reasonable centrality. Conversely, a nuisance should be deemed permanent if it is sufficiently constant or regular (no matter how long between occurrences) that future impact can be reasonably evaluated. Jurors should be asked to settle the question only to the extent there is a dispute regarding what interference has occurred or whether it is likely to continue.

NOTE: *REMEDIES IN NUISANCE CASES: PROPERTY RULES AND LIABILITY RULES*

Is the right to be free from a nuisance a *property* right? Judge Jasen, the dissenter in *Boomer*, apparently thought so. A property right cannot be taken away from its owner by another private individual merely by payment of compensation. As a long line of courts have observed, that would be tantamount to giving the defendant the power of eminent domain: the right to take an easement or servitude permitting the injurious activity simply by agreeing to pay for it. By reasoning that the right to injure the land of neighbors operates as a servitude upon the neighbors' land, and that the power to take a servitude belongs only to the government, courts from the eighteenth century to the Civil War generally decided that an injunction rather than damages was the only appropriate remedy, regardless of the social utility of the defendant's conduct. Under the literal requirements of the *property* rule virtually any industrial activity that caused measurable injury could be enjoined. See, e.g., American Smelting & Refining Co. v. Godfrey, 158 F. 225 (8th Cir.1907), cert. denied 207 U.S. 597 (1907), which recognized an exception to the injunction rule only for trivial injuries.

In the 1860's, however, several American courts began to deviate from the rule, largely in order to accommodate growing American industry. See, e.g., Richard's Appeal, 57 Pa. 105 (1868), in which the Pennsylvania Supreme Court refused an injunction against the defendant's operation of its air-polluting iron works furnaces, but suggested that an action for damages would lie. Today many courts hold that the ordinary remedy in cases involving a continuing nuisance is "permanent" damages, provided that the activity is socially valuable and cannot reasonably be performed in a less harmful way. This rule compensates the plaintiff for her loss but gives the defendant the right to continue the activity, at least vis-a-vis that particular plaintiff. These courts hold that an injunction ordering abatement of the nuisance is appropriate only where the defendant's activity is performed negligently or recklessly, or where it appears to have no social utility. New York was one of the last jurisdictions to adhere consistently to a strict property rights doctrine. The *Boomer* case illustrates one of the most striking debates about the relative merits of each theory.

In summary, successful plaintiffs in nuisance cases are entitled to the remedy of damages to the extent that plaintiffs can prove losses. But, with the exception of a few jurisdictions, plaintiffs are not entitled to injunctive relief because injunctive relief is an equitable remedy and remains in the discretion of the courts. See, e.g., Lesh v. Chandler, 944 N.E.2d 942, 952 (Ind. Ct. App. 2011) (private nuisance case stating " 'permanent injunction is an extreme remedy and should be carefully limited to preclude only activities which are injuriously interfering with the rights of the parties in whose favor the injunction is granted.' The grant or denial of a permanent injunction lies within the sound discretion of the trial court.'').

The equitable defense raised by defendants most frequently against injunctive relief is the "balancing of the hardship" also called the "balancing of the equities" defense. The *Boomer* case is the classic example of this equitable defense. Observe the court's discussion of the Whalen v. Union Bag & Paper Co. case that laid down the rule "that whenever the damage resulting from a nuisance is found not 'unsubstantial' ... injunction would follow." The majority rejected *Whalen* after weighing the total amount of permanent damages incurred by the plaintiffs against the harm to the defendant if the injunction was granted. This is the essence of balancing the equities. The dissenting judge in *Boomer* objected to "overruling our long-established rule of granting an injunction where a nuisance results in substantial continuing damage." Essentially, the dissenting judge objected to abolishing the plaintiff's *entitlement* to an injunction, as set forth in *Whalen*, when the plaintiff has proven a nuisance and substantial continuing damage as a result of the defendant's conduct.

SPUR INDUSTRIES, INC. v. DEL E. WEBB DEVELOPMENT CO.

Supreme Court of Arizona, In Banc (1972).
108 Ariz. 178, 494 P.2d 700.

CAMERON, VICE CHIEF JUSTICE.

From a judgment permanently enjoining the defendant, Spur Industries, Inc., from operating a cattle feedlot near the plaintiff Del E. Webb Development Company's Sun City, Spur appeals. Webb cross-appeals.

The facts necessary for a determination of this matter on appeal are as follows. The area in question is located in Maricopa County, Arizona, some 14 to 15 miles west of the urban area of Phoenix, on the Phoenix–Wickenburg Highway, also known as Grand Avenue.

Farming started in this area about 1911. In 1929, with the completion of the Carl Pleasant Dam, gravity flow water became available to the property located to the west of the Agua Fria River, though land to the east remained dependent upon well water for irrigation. By 1950, the only urban areas in the vicinity were the agriculturally related communities of Peoria, El Mirage, and Surprise located along Grand Avenue. Along 111th Avenue, approximately one mile south of Grand Avenue and 1½ miles north of Olive Avenue, the community of Youngtown was commenced in 1954. Youngtown is a retirement community appealing primarily to senior citizens.

In 1956, Spur's predecessors in interest, H. Marion Welborn and the Northside Hay Mill and Trading Company, developed feedlots, about ½ mile south of Olive Avenue, in an area between the confluence of the usually dry Agua Fria and New Rivers. The area is well suited for cattle feeding and in 1959, there were 25 cattle feeding pens or dairy operations within a 7 mile radius of the location developed by Spur's predecessors. In April and May of 1959, the Northside Hay Mill was feeding between 6,000 and 7,000 head of cattle and Welborn approximately 1,500 head on a combined area of 35 acres.

In May of 1959, Del Webb began to plan the development of an urban area to be known as Sun City. For this purpose, the Marinette and the Santa Fe Ranches, some 20,000 acres of farmland, were purchased for $15,000,000 or $750.00 per acre. This price was considerably less than the price of land located near the urban area of Phoenix, and along with the success of Youngtown was a factor influencing the decision to purchase the property in question.

By September 1959, Del Webb had started construction of a golf course south of Grand Avenue and Spur's predecessors had started to level ground for more feedlot area. In 1960, Spur purchased the property in question and began a rebuilding and expansion program extending both to the north and south of the original facilities. By 1962, Spur's expansion program was completed and had expanded from approximately 35 acres to 114 acres.

Accompanied by an extensive advertising campaign, homes were first offered by Del Webb in January 1960 and the first unit to be completed was south of Grand Avenue and approximately 2½ miles north of Spur. By 2 May 1960, there were 450 to 500 houses completed or under construction. At this time, Del Webb did not consider odors from the Spur feed pens a problem and Del Webb continued to develop in a southerly direction, until sales resistance became so great that the parcels were difficult if not impossible to sell.

* * *

Del Webb filed its original complaint alleging that in excess of 1,300 lots in the southwest portion were unfit for development for sale as residential lots because of the operation of the Spur feedlot.

Del Webb's suit complained that the Spur feeding operation was a public nuisance because of the flies and the odor which were drifting or being blown by the prevailing south to north wind over the southern portion of Sun City. At the time of the suit, Spur was feeding between 20,000 and 30,000 head of cattle, and the facts amply support the finding of the trial court that the feed pens had become a nuisance to the people who resided in the southern part of Del Webb's development. The testimony indicated that cattle in a commercial feedlot will produce 35 to 40 pounds of wet manure per day, per head, or over a million pounds of wet manure per day for 30,000 head of cattle, and that despite the admittedly good feedlot management and good housekeeping practices by Spur, the resulting odor and flies produced an annoying if not unhealthy situation as far as the senior citizens of southern Sun City were concerned. There is no doubt that some of the citizens of Sun City were unable to enjoy the outdoor living which Del Webb had advertised and that Del Webb was faced with sales resistance from prospective purchasers as well as strong and persistent complaints from the people who had purchased homes in that area.

* * *

May Spur be Enjoined?

The difference between a private nuisance and a public nuisance is generally one of degree. A private nuisance is one affecting a single individual or a definite small number of persons in the enjoyment of private rights not common to the public, while a public nuisance is one affecting the rights enjoyed by citizens as a part of the public. To constitute a public nuisance, the nuisance must affect a considerable number of people or an entire community or neighborhood. City of Phoenix v. Johnson, 51 Ariz. 115, 75 P.2d 30 (1938).

Where the injury is slight, the remedy for minor inconveniences lies in an action for damages rather than in one for an injunction. Kubby v. Hammond, 68 Ariz. 17, 198 P.2d 134 (1948). Moreover, some courts have held, in the "balancing of conveniences" cases, that damages may be the sole remedy. See Boomer v. Atlantic Cement Co.

* * *

We have no difficulty, however, in agreeing with the conclusion of the trial court that Spur's operation was an enjoinable public nuisance as far as the people in the southern portion of Del Webb's Sun City were concerned.

§ 36–601, subsec. A reads as follows:

"§ 36–601. Public nuisances dangerous to public health

"A. The following conditions are specifically declared public nuisances dangerous to the public health:

"1. Any condition or place in populous areas which constitutes a breeding place for flies, rodents, mosquitoes and other insects which are capable of carrying and transmitting disease-causing organisms to any person or persons."

By this statute, before an otherwise lawful (and necessary) business may be declared a public nuisance, there must be a "populous" area in which people are injured:

"... [I]t hardly admits a doubt that, in determining the question as to whether a lawful occupation is so conducted as to constitute a nuisance as a matter of fact, the locality and surroundings are of the first importance. (citations omitted) A business which is not per se a public nuisance may become such by being carried on at a place where the health, comfort, or convenience of a populous neighborhood is affected.... What might amount to a serious nuisance in one locality by reason of the density of the population, or character of the neighborhood affected, may in another place and under different

surroundings be deemed proper and unobjectionable ....." Mac-
Donald v. Perry, 32 Ariz. 39, 49–50, 255 P. 494, 497 (1927).

It is clear that as to the citizens of Sun City, the operation of Spur's
feedlot was both a public and a private nuisance. They could have
successfully maintained an action to abate the nuisance. Del Webb, having
shown a special injury in the loss of sales, had a standing to bring suit to
enjoin the nuisance. Engle v. Clark, 53 Ariz. 472, 90 P.2d 994 (1939); City
of Phoenix v. Johnson, supra. The judgment of the trial court permanently
enjoining the operation of the feedlot is affirmed.

Must Del Webb Indemnify Spur?

A suit to enjoin a nuisance sounds in equity and the courts have long
recognized a special responsibility to the public when acting as a court of
equity. * * *

In addition to protecting the public interest, however, courts of equity
are concerned with protecting the operator of a lawfully, albeit noxious,
business from the result of a knowing and willful encroachment by others
near his business.

In the so-called "coming to the nuisance" cases, the courts have held
that the residential landowner may not have relief if he knowingly came
into a neighborhood reserved for industrial or agricultural endeavors and
has been damaged thereby:

> "Plaintiffs chose to live in an area uncontrolled by zoning laws or
> restrictive covenants and remote from urban development. In such an
> area plaintiffs cannot complain that legitimate agricultural pursuits
> are being carried on in the vicinity, nor can plaintiffs, having chosen
> to build in an agricultural area, complain that the agricultural pur-
> suits carried on in the area depreciate the value of their homes. The
> area being *primarily agricultural,* any opinion reflecting the value of
> such property must take this factor into account. The standards
> affecting the value of residence property in an urban setting, subject
> to zoning controls and controlled planning techniques, cannot be the
> standards by which agricultural properties are judged.

> "People employed in a city who build their homes in suburban areas
> of the county beyond the limits of a city and zoning regulations do so
> for a reason. Some do so to avoid the high taxation rate imposed by
> cities, or to avoid special assessments for street, sewer and water
> projects. They usually build on improved or hard surface highways,
> which have been built either at state or county expense and thereby
> avoid special assessments for these improvements. It may be that they
> desire to get away from the congestion of traffic, smoke, noise, foul air
> and the many other annoyances of city life. But with all these
> advantages in going beyond the area which is zoned and restricted to
> protect them in their homes, they must be prepared to take the

disadvantages." Dill v. Excel Packing Company, 183 Kan. 513, 525, 526, 331 P.2d 539, 548, 549 (1958).

* * *

Were Webb the only party injured, we would feel justified in holding that the doctrine of "coming to the nuisance" would have been a bar to the relief asked by Webb, and, on the other hand, had Spur located the feedlot near the outskirts of a city and had the city grown toward the feedlot, Spur would have to suffer the cost of abating the nuisance as to those people locating within the growth pattern of the expanding city. * * *

There was no indication in the instant case at the time Spur and its predecessors located in western Maricopa County that a new city would spring up, full-blown, alongside the feeding operation and that the developer of that city would ask the court to order Spur to move because of the new city. Spur is required to move not because of any wrongdoing on the part of Spur, but because of a proper and legitimate regard of the courts for the rights and interests of the public.

Del Webb, on the other hand, is entitled to the relief prayed for (a permanent injunction), not because Webb is blameless, but because of the damage to the people who have been encouraged to purchase homes in Sun City. It does not equitably or legally follow, however, that Webb, being entitled to the injunction, is then free of any liability to Spur if Webb has in fact been the cause of the damage Spur has sustained. It does not seem harsh to require a developer, who has taken advantage of the lesser land values in a rural area as well as the availability of large tracts of land on which to build and develop a new town or city in the area, to indemnify those who are forced to leave as a result.

Having brought people to the nuisance to the foreseeable detriment of Spur, Webb must indemnify Spur for a reasonable amount of the cost of moving or shutting down. It should be noted that this relief to Spur is limited to a case wherein a developer has, with foreseeability, brought into a previously agricultural or industrial area the population which makes necessary the granting of an injunction against a lawful business and for which the business has no adequate relief.

It is therefore the decision of this court that the matter be remanded to the trial court for a hearing upon the damages sustained by the defendant Spur as a reasonable and direct result of the granting of the permanent injunction. Since the result of the appeal may appear novel and both sides have obtained a measure of relief, it is ordered that each side will bear its own costs.

NOTES AND QUESTIONS

1. *Spur Industries* is often regarded as an extraordinary opinion, requiring the victim to compensate the tortfeasor. But the decision looks less extraordinary if one considers first that nuisance law is not about tortfeasors and victims, but rather about incompatible land uses; often the nuisance

defendant is no more "guilty" than the nuisance plaintiff. Second, *Spur Industries* is a *public* nuisance case, and the plaintiff, Sun City, is virtually treated by the court as a governmental subdivision, such as a municipality. Isn't the court simply giving Sun City the equivalent of eminent domain power? See Chapter 10.

2. Who was injured by the defendant's nuisance—Del Webb Development Co., which is interested in selling more lots, or Sun City, a residential community filled with people who have already purchased lots? If both Del Webb and Sun City are benefitted by the abatement of the nuisance, why does the court decide that only Del Webb must indemnify Spur for its moving costs and other business losses? Is the court punishing Del Webb for encouraging people to buy property close to Spur's feedlot? Haven't the property owners who already purchased lots in Sun City received a windfall? Suppose Del Webb now offers Spur a settlement: in exchange for a sum of money Del Webb will permit Spur to continue the operation of its feedlot. Would Spur consent to such an agreement?

3. At common law, the doctrine of "coming to the nuisance" generally applied to plaintiffs who *developed* their land so as to create a land use conflict after the defendant's use was in place. Unfortunately, § 840D of the Restatement (Second) of Torts, quoted at the beginning of this Chapter, refers to a plaintiff who "has acquired or improved his land after a nuisance interfering with it has come into existence...." But someone who has merely acquired property after an actionable nuisance exists has not "come to the nuisance." See, e.g., Brooks v. Council of Co–Owners of Stones Throw Horizontal Property Regime I, 315 S.C. 474, 445 S.E.2d 630 (1994), refusing to apply the doctrine of "coming to the nuisance" to someone who purchased a condominium and discovered a pre-existing water leak.

The doctrine of "coming to the nuisance" refers not to the person who owned property first, but rather to the person who acquires its property interest after the activity alleged to constitute a nuisance has already commenced. See Miller v. Rohling, 720 N.W.2d 562 (Iowa 2006), which held that it did not matter that the defendants had owned their property and were operating a grain storage facility before the plaintiffs acquired their interests. In this case the nuisance challenge arose when the defendants expanded their facility, and the expansion occurred after the plaintiffs' rights were established. "Thus, the relevant point in time at which to examine *priority* of location is just prior to the commencement of the nuisance-producing activities."

4. There are essentially four possible outcomes in a nuisance action.

A. The court could rule against the plaintiff and in favor of the defendant by finding that the defendant's conduct does not constitute a nuisance. The plaintiff would be denied all relief and the defendant would be entitled to continue with its conduct. This outcome represents a property rule. See, e.g., Robie v. Lillis and Hendricks v. Stalnaker, supra.

B. The plaintiff could prevail on the nuisance claim and receive an award of damages, a liability rule outcome. See, e.g., Crest Chevrolet–Oldsmobile–Cadillac, Inc. v. Willemsen and Boomer v. Atlantic Cement Co., supra.

C. The plaintiff could prevail on the nuisance claim and the court could enjoin the defendant's conduct, a property rule outcome. See the notes following Prah v. Maretti.

D. The plaintiff could prevail on the nuisance claim and obtain injunctive relief, a property rule outcome, but also be required to pay the defendant damages, a liability rule outcome. See Spur Industries, Inc. v. Del E. Webb Development Co.

§ 9.4 SOCIAL COST, TRANSACTION COSTS, AND THE LAW OF NUISANCE

The remedy given in the *Spur Industries* case—ordering the nuisance abated but requiring the plaintiff to compensate the defendant for its losses—seems quite innovative. However, the remedy is very ordinarily judged by the standards of the marketplace: in effect, one landowner paid another landowner to refrain from engaging in a certain practice. The plaintiffs easily could have purchased the defendant's property and then resold it burdened with a covenant prohibiting the operation of feedlots.

If the remedy was so common in the marketplace, but so unusual for a court, why were the parties unable to resolve their dispute without going to court? Why had they not been able simply to sit down and negotiate a buyout?

In an ideal world, precisely that would have happened. In a famous article written in 1960, Ronald Coase developed what is now called the "Coase Theorem."[1] It says that in a market with no transaction costs two parties will always bargain their way to an efficient solution. An efficient solution in this case is one that maximizes the net total wealth that accrues to all parties affected by the activity. For example, if an activity benefits one person by $1000, injures three people by $200 each and no one else is affected, the net wealth created by the activity is $400.

Suppose that one manufacturer of cement is polluting the air in a community that contains only one landowner, a landlord who owns an apartment complex. The complex contains one hundred units, and if the air were clean each unit would be worth $100. Because the air is polluted, however, the value of the units is only $90 each.[2] The air pollution caused by the cement manufacturer costs the landlord $10 X 100 units, or $1000.

Suppose that two alternatives exist that will clean the air: (1) the manufacturer can shut the plant down, in which case he will forego profits of $1200; or (2) he can install air cleaning devices that will cost $800 and reduce the air pollution to zero. Finally, assume that according to the law of this jurisdiction the operation of the cement plant without the air

---

1. Coase, The Problem of Social Cost, 3 J.L. & Econ. 1 (1960).

2. In this case the air pollution is injuring not only the landlord, but also his 100 tenants. However, the landlord effectively bears their injury because the tenants can avoid it by moving to different communities. The only way the landlord can keep his tenants is by compensating them—i.e., by reducing their rent to the point that they feel just as well off to be living in the polluted neighborhood as in an unpolluted one where the rents are higher.

cleaners is *not* an illegal nuisance. If the landlord sues the cement manufacturer the landlord will lose. Does this mean that the cement manufacturer will continue to pollute the air?

In a well-functioning market the answer is no. The operation of the plant without the air cleaner injures the landlord by $1000. Installation of the air cleaner would cost the cement manufacturer $800. If the landlord paid the manufacturer $900 to install and maintain the air cleaner, both the cement manufacturer and the landlord would be better off by $100. The air cleaner will be installed, in spite of the fact that the cement manufacturer has no legal obligation to install it. Rather, the cement manufacturer will install it because he can make a profit by doing so.

Suppose now that the law of the jurisdiction holds that the operation of the cement plant *is* a nuisance. The landlord can obtain an injunction ordering the cement manufacturer to abate the nuisance. Will the plant close?

Once again the answer is no, provided that the market functions perfectly. The landlord has a right to an injunction that will make him $1000 better off and the cement manufacturer $1200 worse off. The manufacturer might offer the landlord some price between $1000 and $1200 for the right (perhaps an easement) to continue operating the cement plant without the air cleaner. For example, if the manufacturer paid the landlord $1100, both the manufacturer and the landlord would be $100 better off than if the landlord enforced the injunction: the landlord would receive $1100 from the manufacturer but $1000 less in rent; the manufacturer would continue to earn his $1200 in profits but would pay out $1100 to the landlord.

But there is an alternative. The manufacturer could install the air cleaner. In that case the landlord would be just as well off as if the cement plant stopped operating. The cement manufacturer would keep his $1200 in profits by paying $800 for the air cleaner. This illustration suggests that the market will yield the same solution—continued operation of the cement plant, but with the air cleaner—regardless of the liability rule imposed by the courts. The Coase Theorem states this as a general proposition: a well-functioning market will always yield an efficient solution to a particular problem, and that solution will be the same regardless how the court assigns rights and liabilities.[3] In this case, operation of the cement plant with the air cleaner in place is the most efficient solution, because it maximizes the combined wealth of the two parties.

Of course, the court's assignment of liability may have a great deal to do with how wealth is *distributed* between the market participants. In the

---

3. The first of these propositions—that the solution will be efficient—is called the efficiency thesis of the Coase Theorem. The second—that the solution will be the same no matter how liability is assigned—is called the invariance thesis. The second thesis is widely believed to be false to the extent that it fails to take income effects into account. That is, when liability is shifted to cement factories their costs will rise and less cement will be sold. By contrast, the landlord's output will increase as its costs go down. See Hovenkamp, Marginal Utility and the Coase Theorem, 75 Cornell L.Rev. 783 (1990).

first situation above, where there was no nuisance, the cement manufac-turer was relatively well off and the landlord was not well off. In the second situation, where the landlord had the right to stop the plant's production, the landlord was relatively well off and the manufacturer was not.

The Coase Theorem comes with two qualifications. First, the market at issue must be free of all "transaction costs." Second, there must be no "externalities," or "spillovers."

A transaction cost is a cost of using the marketplace. Suppose in the above illustration that there is not a single landlord who owns a 100–unit apartment, but rather 100 individual homeowners, each of whom is injured by $10.00. Assume that the cost of negotiating is $5.00 per contract and the cement manufacturer is not liable. The efficient solution is still for the manufacturer to install the air cleaner. That will benefit each homeowner by $10.00 and cost only $8.00 per owner. However, the negotiation of the 100 agreements will also cost $5.00 each. On average, the homeowners would have to pay $13.00 each to cover both transaction costs and the cost of the air cleaner, which is $3.00 more, per homeowner, than the benefit each homeowner receives from the air cleaner. The cement manufacturer will simply continue to operate without the air cleaner.

Once transaction costs are considered, it becomes impossible to say that the market will yield an efficient solution to the above problem. It is possible to make some generalizations about the effect of transaction costs. If the efficiency improvement that a certain bargain will yield is less than the costs of bargaining, the parties will not bargain for the improve-ment. Once the transaction costs are included, the result will be a net loss. By contrast, if the transaction costs are less than the amount of improve-ment that an agreement would produce, the parties will agree to the improvement. Thus the lower the transaction costs, the more likely that the parties will be able to bargain their way to an efficient solution.

As Coase himself notes, in the real world transaction costs are often high. It then becomes critical that the legal system select the correct legal rule, assuming that the goal is to maximize efficiency:

> If we move from a regime of zero transaction costs to one of positive transaction costs, what becomes immediately clear is the crucial importance of the legal system.... While we can imagine in the hypothetical world of zero transactions costs that the parties to an exchange would negotiate to change any provision of the law which prevents them from taking whatever steps are required to increase the value of production, in the real world of positive transaction costs, such a procedure would be extremely costly.... Because of this, the rights which individuals possess, with their duties and privileges, will be, to a large extent, what the law determines. As a result, the legal system will have a profound effect on the working of the economic system and may in certain respects be said to control it.

Coase, The Institutional Structure of Production 9 (1991 Alfred Nobel Memorial Prize Lecture).

A particularly important transaction cost, undoubtedly contributing to the failure of the parties in *Spur Industries* to reach a negotiated settlement, is information costs—in this case, the costs of being able to predict the legal rule that the court will adopt. Suppose, for example, that the defendant's attorney predicted that the feedlot would not be declared a nuisance because the feedlot was there first; the plaintiffs "came to the nuisance." But suppose the plaintiffs predicted that the feedlot would be declared a nuisance because the defendant's activity was harmful and its value was small in relation to the amount of harm that it caused. In that case the plaintiffs would predict their success in litigation and hold out for a large award. The defendant, however, would predict his own success and would be willing to pay only a very small award or nothing at all. Negotiations would fail and the parties would litigate. All the while, transaction costs would be increasing.

A "market failure" is a situation in which high transaction costs prevent bargaining parties from reaching an efficient solution. A market failure may justify a government-dictated, nonmarket solution to a certain problem. For example, suppose that a legislative committee concludes from a study that operation of cement plants with a certain type of air cleaner is harmless to the air. It might pass a statute requiring cement plants to use the air cleaner and relieve them from any nuisance liability if the air cleaner is working. If the costs of passing this statute are relatively low (perhaps because a single legislative study and statute will apply to dozens of communities containing cement manufacturing plants), then the statute will yield an efficient solution to the problem. The state's cement plants will continue to operate, equipped with the air cleaners, even though the high transaction costs would have prevented the parties from negotiating the same result themselves.

One way to minimize the problem of transaction costs is to eliminate the need for bargaining. The court can do this by assigning rights initially in exactly the same way that they would have been assigned in a cost-free bargaining process. Suppose, for example, that judicial decisions or legislation provided that a cement plant operating without an air cleaner is an enjoinable nuisance, but a plant operating with an air cleaner is not a nuisance at all. In that case the cement manufacturer acting alone, without bargaining with anyone, would install the air cleaner.

Once transaction costs are considered, determining who should have the prevailing right is based, not on the court's concept of fairness, but rather on its prediction of who would buy the right in a perfectly functioning market. The *Spur Industries* court used its novel "reverse compensation" formula to achieve an efficient result that, in its view, was also fair to the parties. The court assigned the prevailing right to the residential developers, who would have acquired it in a properly functioning market, but the court compensated Spur because its feedlot was there first.

One argument in favor of private bargaining as an alternative to various forms of regulation, such as zoning, air and water quality controls, or transportation safety regulation, begins with the observation that Coasian markets produce efficient results. Regulation created by legislation can hardly do better, and will generally do much worse. See generally Richard A. Posner, Economic Analysis of Law 565–586 (5th ed. 1998).

One problem of legislation is that invariably legislators end up not only looking for the optimal regulatory framework, they also redistribute wealth. Wealth distribution games may be inherently unstable. Suppose that $100 is to be divided among A, B & C by majority vote: an agreement by any two will be decisive. A proposes that A and B each take $50 and C takes nothing, and the proposal wins when A and B vote for it. But then C will propose to A that A receive $51 and C $49, and A will be better off; C and A will agree; and so on. This is a division game that has no "core," or equilibrium outcome, and it produces chaos. In the words of Kenneth J. Arrow, one of the developers of this "chaos" theory of legislative decision making, "for any allocation which gives some individual, say 1, a positive amount, there is another, which gives 1 nothing and divides up his share in the first allocation among all the others; the second is preferred to the first by all but one individual." 1 Kenneth J. Arrow, Social Choice and Justice, Collected Papers of Kenneth J. Arrow 87 (1983).

But are "Coasian" markets, aided by private tort law such as nuisance, any more stable? The likely answer is no. Consider the problem of air quality controls that affect many people. Suppose operation of a cement factory is worth $100 to its owners, and imposes $7 in losses on each of ten homeowners. The factory's operation is actionable by any one of the ten homeowners. Now the factory must bargain with the homeowners and obtain a release from all of them, and must be willing to pay them off to make continued operation of the factory possible. There is a $30 surplus to be divided. Presumably the factory and each homeowner will attempt to capture as large a portion of that surplus as possible.

If the factory negotiates with each homeowner separately, there will be holdout problems. It can afford to pay some homeowners, say, $12, but only if it pays others less. There is no obvious reason why the wrangling could not go on indefinitely. Alternatively, the factory might place, say, $90 in an escrow account, and tell the ten homeowners to divide it among themselves. Then the problem has become identical to the legislative wealth transfer problem described above, with the added complication that each homeowner might also threaten to walk away, making the entire pot worthless. No homeowner will accept less than $7, but if the pot were divided equally each would get $9. Homeowners 1 through 8 might agree with each other that they will let homeowners 9 and 10 have only $7.50 each, and keep the remaining $75.00 for themselves, giving them around $9.35 each. But homeowners 9 and 10 might then respond by (1) refusing to bargain at all; or (2) offering owners 1 through 6 a deal that will make them a little better off than under the previous deal, but give homeowners 7 and 8 only slightly more than $7, etc., etc. In short, the chaos problem shows up in exactly the same fashion as it does in the legislative situation. If endless negotiating ("cycling") is indeed costless—and the Coase Theorem assumes costless markets—the parties would engage in endless bargaining for division of the proceeds in a Coasian economic market just as much as in the legislative market.

Indeed, Coasian markets may become quite unstable as soon as they have three or more participants. If that is the case, then private bargaining is no better a solution to land use problems than legislation is—it is just as prone to be unstable and we can never be certain that the solution arrived at is better than alternatives. See the note on chaos in the markets for servitudes at the end of the previous chapter.

Externalities, or "spillovers," are nothing more than a particular kind of transaction cost. An externality is an effect caused by a transaction upon persons who could not be made parties to the transaction. For example, when the cement manufacturer measured the "cost" of entering this business it probably included the cost of the land, the cost of construction, the cost of obtaining an operating permit, and various start-up costs such as obtaining raw materials and labor. If operation of the plant was not an actionable nuisance, however, the firm did not include in its calculations the injuries that its operation would impose on neighboring landowners.

An externality can be either a cost or a benefit. Virtually every use of land creates externalities that either injure or benefit people that cannot practically be made parties to the transaction. If a wealthy art lover commissions a beautiful sculpture to be erected in her front yard, hundreds of people may walk or drive by and benefit from its presence. Although the wealthy buyer may be able to build a fence and exclude these "free riders," she will not easily be able to force them to help pay for the cost of erecting the sculpture. First, the law does not require them to do so. Secondly, even if it did, it would be impossible to identify every such benefitted person.

The economic notions of transaction costs, externalities and market failure can contribute a great deal to our understanding of the value and limitations of the law of nuisance. First and perhaps foremost, nuisance law facilitates efficient solutions by reducing transaction costs. As suggested previously, uncertainty about the state of the law will cause the parties to bargain excessively and eventually to litigate. A clear line of cases, which tell both parties what the law is, will make bargaining much easier.

Secondly, nuisance law may reduce the transaction costs of bargaining by permitting one party to "represent" the interests of other parties and thus reduce the number of people that must be drawn to the bargaining table. This can happen even if the lawsuit is not a class action, in which one party (most often the plaintiff) formally represents the interests of other similarly situated persons. When the judge assesses the costs and benefits of a particular activity alleged to be a nuisance, she will invariably include many costs and benefits experienced by people who are not parties before the court. For example, the judge in the *Boomer* case mentioned the 300 people employed by Atlantic Cement Company even though the employees were not before the court. The fact that these people would lose their jobs if the plant were forced to shut down entered the judge's calculus of the social utility of the cement plant. Likewise, in the *Spur* case the judge took into account both Del Webb's injuries and those that accrued to the adjoining town, even though only Del Webb was a party. If the judge can identify all of these injuries to nonparties (or at least, all the important ones) and measure them properly, she is more likely to reach an efficient solution to the problem.

Finally, the failures of nuisance law can point out serious market failures that require more comprehensive legislative solutions. For example, regulations passed under the Clean Air Act, 42 U.S.C.A. §§ 7401–7626, set out detailed standards for the kinds of particulate emissions that manufacturers can release into the air. See the Revisions to the National Ambient Air Quality Standards for Particulate Matter, 52 Fed.Reg. 24,634 (1987). The development and administration of these rules are generally beyond the capacity of a court.

When market failures are sufficiently substantial so as to prevent the market from reaching efficient solutions, the State may respond by passing "inalienability" rules. An inalienability rule creates a property right that cannot legally be sold. For example, once a lot has been zoned exclusively for residential construction, an entrepreneur bent on building a cement plant will not be able to purchase the right to pollute from his neighbors at any price. In this case, the neighbors not only have a legal right that the entrepreneur not pollute the air, they have a right that they cannot bargain away, even if they should want to. Inalienability rules may be efficient in those cases where transaction costs are so high that any amount of bargaining by the parties will produce an undesirable outcome.

For thoughtful comments on the law and economics of nuisance, see Calabresi & Melamed, Property Rules, Liability Rules, and Inalienability: One View of the Cathedral, 85 Harv.L.Rev. 1089 (1972); Polinsky, Resolving Nuisance Disputes: The Simple Economics of Injunctive and Damage Remedies, 32 Stan.L.Rev. 1075 (1980); Demsetz, When Does the Rule of Liability Matter?, 1 J. Legal Stud. 13 (1972); Ellickson, Order Without Law: How Neighbors Settle Disputes (1991); Cooter, The Cost of Coase, 11 J. Legal Stud. 1 (1982).

NOTE: THE OPTIMUM AMOUNT OF AIR POLLUTION

The amount of air pollution produced by an activity, such as the manufacture of cement could be regulated by the marketplace and the common law of nuisance, or perhaps by a regulator such as the Environmental Protection Agency. If efficiency was the goal of this regulatory agency, it would attempt to reduce the air pollution to a level that would maximize society's wealth. The optimal amount of air pollution—that is, the amount that makes society best off—is probably not zero. For example, society is probably better off with automobiles than without them, even though the cleanest possible automobile pollutes the air to a certain degree. Likewise, the air would be cleaner if people did not heat their homes, but society would probably not have more welfare. To say that society is better off with the automobile or the furnace means that the value society places on these things is greater than the costs that they impose, which include the air pollution that they produce.

The Coase Theorem says that a well-functioning market will produce the optimum amount of air pollution. For example, if an additional quantum of activity produces a value of $50, but creates air pollution injuries of $60, the parties will strike a bargain under which the activity will not occur, regardless of which party bears the cost of the damages that result from the additional activity.

If the market contains externalities, however, certain people injured by the pollution will not be able to bargain with the polluter. In that case, the polluter will not take their losses into account. Figure One illustrates. It shows a demand curve D, which slopes downward to indicate that the more of the manufactured product (cement) that is placed on the market, the lower its price will be. The supply curve S measures the costs that cement plants encounter in manufacturing and distributing the cement. Assume these costs are constant at $1.00 per unit of output.

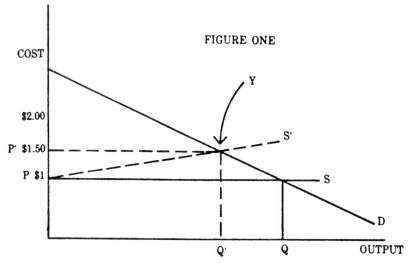

FIGURE ONE

The cement industry will manufacture enough cement to "clear the market" at a price of $1.00. If the industry produces any more than that amount, the large quantity of cement on the market will force its price below $1.00 and the industry will suffer losses. An industry in equilibrium (that is, an industry unaffected by changing market conditions) will produce an output and charge a price determined by the intersection of the supply and demand curves. That is price P and output Q on the graph in Figure One. The supply curve includes all costs that the cement manufacturers actually pay, and thus account for on their profit and loss statements. It does not include costs that the industry's activity may impose on other members of society but for which the industry is not accountable. For example, an industry computing its income and expenses will not regard pollution injuries imposed upon neighbors as an expense unless it is actually forced to compensate the neighbors for their losses. The costs represented by curve S are called "private costs."

By definition, external costs are costs that the market system cannot accommodate, so the industry will not account for them. Assume that the external costs created by air pollution are substantial, and that they increase as the industry's output increase; that is, the greater the output of the cement plants, the larger the pollution injury per unit of cement produced. The "social cost" of producing cement in this case is the sum of all costs that the producers must pay and the costs, such as air pollution, that are borne by other members of society. These are represented on Figure One by dotted line S'.

S' intersects the demand curve at a point equal to price P', or $1.50 per unit of cement. This tells us that when cement is priced at the full social cost of producing it, it will sell for $1.50 per unit. In that case, only people who value cement by $1.50 per unit or more will buy it. When the cement is priced at $1.00 per unit, then someone who values it by only $1.20 will buy it, even though the *total* or "social" cost of producing the cement is $1.50 per unit. In that case society suffers a 30 cents per unit loss. Resources that cost society $1.50 are transferred to someone who values them at only $1.20. The *optimum* price of cement—the price that reflects its full social cost, including the cost of the air pollution—is $1.50 per unit. The optimum output of cement is Q'. The optimum amount of air pollution—that is, the amount that creates at least as much social value as it destroys—is represented by point Y.

How can society best attain this optimum level of pollution (or alternatively, the optimum level of cement production)? The marketplace will not work. Since the difference between S and S' represents external costs, the unregulated market will produce too much cement and create more than the optimal amount of air pollution.

The State could place a quota on cement production, reducing output by law to Q'. In that case air pollution would be reduced to the optimum level. However, if the quota is not accompanied by a higher price shortages will result. At a price of $1.00 the market demands Q cement, but only Q' will be produced. The State might have to intervene on the demand side of the market as well, perhaps by rationing. Furthermore, *some* of the cement will be purchased by people who value it at less than $1.50.

A more efficient way of approximating the optimum level of cement output and air pollution would be to impose a tax of 50 cents per unit on cement production. In that case the price of cement would rise from $1.00 to $1.50, and only people who value cement by $1.50 or more would buy it. Demand would decline from Q to Q'. Furthermore, the proceeds from the tax could finance the development of improved pollution control techniques. The effect of such techniques could bring line S' closer to line S.

Finally, the State might issue regulations that establish the amount of air pollution designated by point Y as the maximum amount that the plants may produce. If the plants merely responded by reducing output to a level sufficient to reduce pollution to that level, the market price of cement would rise to $1.50. However, this third alternative tells the companies how much *pollution* they can produce, not how much cement they can produce. If they can reduce pollution by means other than reducing output, it may be advantageous for them to do so. As a result this alternative has the advantage that it creates a "market"—perhaps even a competitive market—for research and development of pollution control devices. A firm that develops such an efficient device will be able to produce more cement and still stay within the pollution limits.

§ 9.5 SUBJACENT AND LATERAL SUPPORT

At common law, every landowner had a right to lateral and subjacent support from adjacent landowners. (See Chapter 8 and the discussion of negative easements) Lateral support refers to the vertical stability offered to one piece of land by adjacent land. Typically, the common law right to lateral support is violated when the defendant excavates his land too close to the property line, or without taking the necessary support precautions, and the plaintiff's land gives way into the defendant's excavation.

At common law the right to lateral support was absolute, often treated by courts as a property right. Excavators were strictly liable for such injuries to neighboring landowners. Spall v. Janota, 406 N.E.2d 378 (Ind.App.1980). However, generally the common law also provided that the defendant's activity must be such that the plaintiff's land would have subsided even in its undeveloped state. An owner of developed land could recover, but he would have to show that the weight of his own buildings or other artificial structures were not a substantial contributing factor to the subsidence. See Klebs v. Yim, 54 Wash.App. 41, 772 P.2d 523 (1989); Noone v. Price, 171 W.Va. 185, 298 S.E.2d 218 (1982); Simons v. Tri–State Construction Co., 33 Wash.App. 315, 655 P.2d 703 (1982).

The general remedy for breach of the duty to provide lateral support is damages, although an injunction may issue if the damages are incapable of measurement. Today the common law right to lateral support has been modified by statute in many states. In general, the statutes increase the common law right to include structures as well as undeveloped land, and give precise guidelines as to the support requirements for excavations of various depths. See, e.g.:

Mich. Comp. Laws Ann. § 554.251 (West 2005)

> It shall be the duty of every person, partnership or corporation who excavate upon land owned or occupied by them to a depth exceeding 12 feet below the established grade of a street or highway upon which such land abuts or, if there be no such established grade, below the surface of the adjoining land, to furnish sufficient lateral and subjacent support to the adjoining

land to protect said land and all structures thereon from injury due to the removed material in its natural state, or due to the disturbance of other existing conditions caused by such excavation.

765 Ill. Comp. Stat. Ann. 140/1 (West 2011)

§ 1. Each adjacent owner is entitled to the continuous lateral and subjacent support which his land receives from the adjoining land, subject to the right of the owner of the adjoining land to make proper and usual excavations on the same for purposes of construction or improvements, under the following conditions:

1. Any owner or possessor of land intending to make or to permit an excavation to be made on his land shall give due and reasonable notice in writing to the owner or owners of adjoining lands and of adjoining buildings and other structures stating the depth to which the excavation is intended to be made and when the excavation will begin. If the excavation is to be of a depth of not more than the standard depth of foundations, as herein defined, and if it appears that the excavation is to be of a greater depth than the walls or foundations of any adjoining building or other structure and is to be so close as to endanger the building or other structure in any way, then the owner of the building or other structure on the adjoining land shall be allowed a reasonable time, but in no event less than thirty (30) days, in which to take measures to protect the same from any damage or in which to extend the foundations thereof, and he must be given, for the said purpose, a license to enter on the land on which the excavation is to be or is being made.

2. Any owner or possessor of land upon which an excavation is made, who does not comply with the provisions of subparagraph 1, when so required, is liable to the owner of adjacent property for any damage to the land or to any buildings or other structure thereon arising from such excavation, and is also liable to occupants and tenants of the adjoining land or structures for any damage to their property or business, proximately resulting from injury to such land or structures, caused by the failure of such owner or possessor to so comply.

* * * *

Once the guidelines have been given, the standard as to whether they have been complied with is often negligence rather than strict liability. See, for example, Levy v. Schnabel Foundation Co., 584 A.2d 1251 (D.C.App.1991), which applied promulgated standards and used a negligence test.

Subjacent support at common law generally referred to a duty imposed on a property owner to provide support to a property owner *above* him. Most cases involve situations in which the mineral rights of land have been severed from the surface rights, and the mineral owner engages in underground mining in such a way that the land above collapses. The common law of subjacent support closely tracks the common law of lateral support, and generally imposes strict liability. See Gabrielson v. Central Serv. Co., 232 Iowa 483, 5 N.W.2d 834 (1942).

Ambiguously between lateral and subjacent support is the injury caused by one landowner who pumps water or another liquid such as oil out from under a neighbor's land and causes subsidence. The Restatement (Second) of Torts § 818 (1979) treats such injuries as a violation of the right to subjacent support and effectively provides for strict liability. The rule that prevailed in English common law, however, was virtual nonliability. Interestingly, the corresponding section of the First Restatement of Torts, which was published in 1939, followed the English nonliability rule. Most American courts ignore both Restatements and adopt a "reasonable use" rule that requires the plaintiff to show either that the defendant took the water for no good purpose or did so maliciously, or else that the defendant was negligent. See Finley v. Teeter Stone, Inc., 251 Md. 428, 248 A.2d 106 (1968). See also Friendswood Development Co. v. Smith–Southwest Industries, Inc., 576 S.W.2d 21 (Tex. 1978), in which the Texas Supreme Court applied the English rule of nonliability to the case before it, but held that future cases should be governed by a negligence rule. See generally Comment, Controlling Land Surface Subsidence: A Proposal for a Market–Based Regulatory Scheme, 31 U.C.L.A. L.Rev. 1208 (1984).

Closely related to the law of lateral and subjacent support are the rules governing liability of one property owner for injuries caused by movement of physical objects from her land to adjoining land—most commonly such things as falling trees and landslides. At common law the defendant was not liable for any such movement from land in its "natural," or undeveloped, condition. See Cheryl M. Bailey, Annot., Tree or Limb Falls Onto Adjoining Private Property: Personal Injury and Property Damage Liability, 54 A.L.R.4th 530 (1987) (ALR databases are updated weekly with relevant new cases). Already in the nineteenth century, however, courts began to create exceptions to the common law rule for situations where the danger should have been apparent to the defendant and could easily have been averted. See, e.g., Gibson v. Denton, 4 A.D. 198, 38 N.Y.S. 554 (1896), where the court found liability for the fall of an obviously decayed tree which struck the house of the plaintiff. In such a case, the important fact is not that the tree is "natural" but rather that it is an obvious hazard and only the defendant is in a position to remove it.

Many American states apparently still cling to the English nonliability rule. E.g., Schwalbach v. Forest Lawn Memorial Park, 687 S.W.2d 551 (Ky.App.1985). However, a steadily growing minority apply a negligence standard. See Sprecher v. Adamson Cos., 30 Cal.3d 358, 178 Cal.Rptr. 783, 636 P.2d 1121 (1981) (in banc), in which the California Supreme Court adopted the negligence rule for injuries caused by a landslide. Most cases involve falling trees. "The trend is to hold tree owners liable for injuries caused by obviously defective trees or trees known or ought to be known defective." Bailey, supra § 1, at 2a (1987). See Taylor v. Olsen, 282 Or. 343, 578 P.2d 779 (1978). The vast majority of states apply a negligence rule when the falling object is not natural but artificial, such as a dilapidated building or an improperly supported television antenna or other structure.

Should the adoption of a negligence rule for falling trees dictate a negligence rule for landslides as well? A decayed tree is easily removed. But what does a homeowner on the side of a large mountain do when the danger of landslides becomes apparent and it is not of his own making? See the concurring opinion of Justice Richardson in the *Sprecher* case.

CHAPTER 10

TAKINGS, DELIBERATE AND INADVERTENT

■ ■ ■

United States Constitution, Amendment V (1791): "... nor shall private property be taken for public use, without just compensation."

§ 10.1 EMINENT DOMAIN

§ 10.1.1 "PUBLIC USE"

HAWAII HOUSING AUTHORITY v. MIDKIFF

Supreme Court of the United States (1984).
467 U.S. 229.

JUSTICE O'CONNOR delivered the opinion of the Court.

* * * These cases present the question whether the Public Use Clause of [the Fifth] Amendment, made applicable to the States through the Fourteenth Amendment, prohibits the State of Hawaii from taking, with just compensation, title in real property from lessors and transferring it to lessees in order to reduce the concentration of ownership of fees simple in the State. We conclude that it does not.

The Hawaiian Islands were originally settled by Polynesian immigrants from the eastern Pacific. These settlers developed an economy around a feudal land tenure system in which one island high chief, the ali'i nui, controlled the land and assigned it for development to certain subchiefs. The subchiefs would then reassign the land to other lower ranking chiefs, who would administer the land and govern the farmers and other tenants working it. All land was held at the will of the ali'i nui and eventually had to be returned to his trust. There was no private ownership of land.

Beginning in the early 1800's, Hawaiian leaders and American settlers repeatedly attempted to divide the lands of the kingdom among the crown, the chiefs, and the common people. These efforts proved largely unsuccessful, however, and the land remained in the hands of a few. In the mid–1960's, after extensive hearings, the Hawaii Legislature discovered that, while the State and Federal Governments owned almost 49% of the State's land, another 47% was in the hands of only 72 private landowners. The legislature further found that 18 landholders, with tracts of 21,000 acres or more, owned more than 40% of this land and that, on Oahu, the most urbanized of the islands, 22 landowners owned 72.5% of the fee simple titles. Id., at 32–33. The legislature concluded that concentrated land ownership was responsible for skewing the State's residential fee simple market, inflating land prices, and injuring the public tranquility and welfare.

To redress these problems, the legislature decided to compel the large landowners to break up their estates. The legislature considered requiring large landowners to sell lands which they were leasing to homeowners. However, the landowners strongly resisted this scheme, pointing out the significant federal tax liabilities they would incur. Indeed, the landowners claimed that the federal tax laws were the primary reason they previously had chosen to lease, and not sell, their lands. Therefore, to accommodate the needs of both lessors and lessees, the Hawaii Legislature enacted the Land Reform Act of 1967 (Act), Haw.Rev.Stat., ch. 516, which created a mechanism for condemning residential tracts and for transferring ownership of the condemned fees simple to existing lessees. By condemning the land in question, the Hawaii Legislature intended to make the land sales involuntary, thereby making the federal tax consequences less severe while still facilitating the redistribution of fees simple.

Under the Act's condemnation scheme, tenants living on single-family residential lots within developmental tracts at least five acres in size are entitled to ask the Hawaii Housing Authority (HHA) to condemn the property on which they live. Haw.Rev.Stat. §§ 516–1(2), (11), 516–22 (1977). When 25 eligible tenants,[1] or tenants on half the lots in the tract, whichever is less, file appropriate applications, the Act authorizes HHA to hold a public hearing to determine whether acquisition by the State of all or part of the tract will "effectuate the public purposes" of the Act. § 516–22. If HHA finds that these public purposes will be served, it is authorized to designate some or all of the lots in the tract for acquisition. It then acquires, at prices set either by condemnation trial or by negotiation between lessors and lessees, the former fee owners' full "right, title, and interest" in the land. § 516–25.

After compensation has been set, HHA may sell the land titles to tenants who have applied for fee simple ownership. HHA is authorized to lend these tenants up to 90% of the purchase price, and it may condition final transfer on a right of first refusal for the first 10 years following sale. If HHA does not sell the lot to the tenant residing there, it may lease the lot or sell it to someone else, provided that public notice has been given. However, HHA may not sell to any one purchaser, or lease to any one tenant, more than one lot, and it may not operate for profit. In practice, funds to satisfy the condemnation awards have been supplied entirely by

---

1. An eligible tenant is one who, among other things, owns a house on the lot, has a bona fide intent to live on the lot or be a resident of the State, shows proof of ability to pay for a fee interest in it, and does not own residential land elsewhere nearby. Haw.Rev.Stat. § 516–33(3), (4), (7) (1979).

lessees. While the Act authorizes HHA to issue bonds and appropriate funds for acquisition, no bonds have issued and HHA has not supplied any funds for condemned lots.

In April 1977, HHA held a public hearing concerning the proposed acquisition of some of appellees' lands. HHA made the statutorily required finding that acquisition of appellees' lands would effectuate the public purposes of the Act. Then, in October 1978, it directed appellees to negotiate with certain lessees concerning the sale of the designated properties. Those negotiations failed, and HHA subsequently ordered appellees to submit to compulsory arbitration.

Rather than comply with the compulsory arbitration order, appellees filed suit, in February 1979, in United States District Court, asking that the Act be declared unconstitutional and that its enforcement be enjoined.

* * *

The starting point for our analysis of the Act's constitutionality is the Court's decision in Berman v. Parker, 348 U.S. 26, 75 S.Ct. 98, 99 L.Ed. 27 (1954). In *Berman,* the Court held constitutional the District of Columbia Redevelopment Act of 1945. That Act provided both for the comprehensive use of the eminent domain power to redevelop slum areas and for the possible sale or lease of the condemned lands to private interests. In discussing whether the takings authorized by that Act were for a "public use," id., at 31, 75 S.Ct., at 101, the Court stated

> "We deal, in other words, with what traditionally has been known as the police power. An attempt to define its reach or trace its outer limits is fruitless, for each case must turn on its own facts. The definition is essentially the product of legislative determinations addressed to the purposes of government, purposes neither abstractly nor historically capable of complete definition. Subject to specific constitutional limitations, when the legislature has spoken, the public interest has been declared in terms well-nigh conclusive. In such cases the legislature, not the judiciary, is the main guardian of the public needs to be served by social legislation, whether it be Congress legislating concerning the District of Columbia ... or the States legislating concerning local affairs.... This principle admits of no exception merely because the power of eminent domain is involved...."

The Court explicitly recognized the breadth of the principle it was announcing, noting:

> "Once the object is within the authority of Congress, the right to realize it through the exercise of eminent domain is clear. For the power of eminent domain is merely the means to the end.... Once the object is within the authority of Congress, the means by which it will be attained is also for Congress to determine. Here one of the means chosen is the use of private enterprise for redevelopment of the area. Appellants argue that this makes the project a taking from one

businessman for the benefit of another businessman. But the means of executing the project are for Congress and Congress alone to determine, once the public purpose has been established."

The "public use" requirement is thus coterminous with the scope of a sovereign's police powers.

There is, of course, a role for courts to play in reviewing a legislature's judgment of what constitutes a public use, even when the eminent domain power is equated with the police power. But the Court in *Berman* made clear that it is "an extremely narrow" one. [It] emphasized that "[a]ny departure from this judicial restraint would result in courts deciding on what is and is not a governmental function and in their invalidating legislation on the basis of their view on that question at the moment of decision, a practice which has proved impracticable in other fields." In short, the Court has made clear that it will not substitute its judgment for a legislature's judgment as to what constitutes a public use "unless the use be palpably without reasonable foundation."

* * *

[W]here the exercise of the eminent domain power is rationally related to a conceivable public purpose, the Court has never held a compensated taking to be proscribed by the Public Use Clause. * * * On this basis, we have no trouble concluding that the Hawaii Act is constitutional. The people of Hawaii have attempted, much as the settlers of the original 13 Colonies did, to reduce the perceived social and economic evils of a land oligopoly traceable to their monarchs. The land oligopoly has, according to the Hawaii Legislature, created artificial deterrents to the normal functioning of the State's residential land market and forced thousands of individual homeowners to lease, rather than buy, the land underneath their homes. Regulating oligopoly and the evils associated with it is a classic exercise of a State's police powers.

* * *

We cannot disapprove of Hawaii's exercise of this power.

Nor can we condemn as irrational the Act's approach to correcting the land oligopoly problem. The Act presumes that when a sufficiently large number of persons declare that they are willing but unable to buy lots at fair prices the land market is malfunctioning. When such a malfunction is signalled, the Act authorizes HHA to condemn lots in the relevant tract. The Act limits the number of lots any one tenant can purchase and authorizes HHA to use public funds to ensure that the market dilution goals will be achieved. This is a comprehensive and rational approach to identifying and correcting market failure.

Of course, this Act, like any other, may not be successful in achieving its intended goals. But "whether *in fact* the provision will accomplish its objectives is not the question: the [constitutional requirement] is satisfied if ... the ... [state] Legislature *rationally could have believed* that the

[Act] would promote its objective." Western & Southern Life Ins. Co. v. State Bd. of Equalization, 451 U.S. 648, 671–672, 101 S.Ct. 2070, 2084–2085, 68 L.Ed.2d 514 (1981).

* * *

The mere fact that property taken outright by eminent domain is transferred in the first instance to private beneficiaries does not condemn that taking as having only a private purpose. The Court long ago rejected any literal requirement that condemned property be put into use for the general public. "It is not essential that the entire community, nor even any considerable portion, . . . directly enjoy or participate in any improvement in order [for it] to constitute a public use." Rindge Co. v. Los Angeles, 262 U.S., at 707, 43 S.Ct., at 692. As the unique way titles were held in Hawaii skewed the land market, exercise of the power of eminent domain was justified. The Act advances its purposes without the State taking actual possession of the land. In such cases, government does not itself have to use property to legitimate the taking; it is only the taking's purpose, and not its mechanics, that must pass scrutiny under the Public Use Clause.

Similarly, the fact that a state legislature, and not the Congress, made the public use determination does not mean that judicial deference is less appropriate. Judicial deference is required because, in our system of government, legislatures are better able to assess what public purposes should be advanced by an exercise of the taking power. State legislatures are as capable as Congress of making such determinations within their respective spheres of authority. See Berman v. Parker, 348 U.S., at 32, 75 S.Ct., at 102. Thus, if a legislature, state or federal, determines there are substantial reasons for an exercise of the taking power, courts must defer to its determination that the taking will serve a public use.

IV

The State of Hawaii has never denied that the Constitution forbids even a compensated taking of property when executed for no reason other than to confer a private benefit on a particular private party. A purely private taking could not withstand the scrutiny of the public use requirement; it would serve no legitimate purpose of government and would thus be void. But no purely private taking is involved in this case. The Hawaii Legislature enacted its Land Reform Act not to benefit a particular class of identifiable individuals but to attack certain perceived evils of concentrated property ownership in Hawaii—a legitimate public purpose. Use of the condemnation power to achieve this purpose is not irrational. Since we assume for purposes of this appeal that the weighty demand of just compensation has been met, the requirements of the Fifth and Fourteenth Amendments have been satisfied. Accordingly, we reverse the judgment of the Court of Appeals, and remand these cases for further proceedings in conformity with this opinion.

It is so ordered.

NOTES AND QUESTIONS

1. One possible interpretation of the "public use" requirement in the takings clause is that the use of the taken property must somehow inure to the public as a whole, and not merely to some individual members of the public. This principle is most frequently called into question when the taken property is immediately transferred to private owners. In Berman v. Parker, 348 U.S. 26 (1954), the Supreme Court established that the public use requirement may be satisfied even though a substantial part of the land is to be transferred to private parties. The Court upheld a slum clearance statute providing that, after condemnation, the taken lands could be transferred to private owners for re-development. The Court concluded that:

> The public end may be as well or better served through an agency of private enterprise than through a department of government—or so the Congress might conclude. We cannot say that public ownership is the sole method of promoting the public purposes of community redevelopment projects.

2. Justice O'Connor said that Hawaii's identification of a "market failure" in the housing market was a sufficient public purpose to justify the exercise of its eminent domain power. A market failure exists when a market fails to perform efficiently. See the discussion in § 9.4.

Clearly a monopoly or oligopoly is a kind of "market failure." When a market is controlled by one or only a few sellers, they will be tempted to reduce output and charge higher than a competitive price. The result is that less of the product will be available for consumers, and they will pay a higher price for it. A land oligopoly or cartel could charge a monopoly price for residential leases by leaving large areas of land undeveloped.[2]

One difficulty in using the power of eminent domain to eliminate monopoly is that the condemnee is entitled to be paid just compensation, which generally means fair market value determined, if possible, by the market itself. Does this mean that the condemnees are entitled to obtain the prevailing monopoly prices for their fee interests, or may the state pay what the interests would be worth in a competitive market? In Olson v. United States, 292 U.S. 246, 255 (1934), the Supreme Court said that the condemnee is entitled to be placed "in as good a position pecuniarily as if his property had not been taken." Of course, large scale condemnation will increase the supply of fee simple estates on the market. This will eventually drive the price down. In short, a broad program of takings may change conditions in the market, and thus change the market price.

3. Condemnation is also used to avoid the problem of "holdouts"—or people who insist on an unrealistically high price for their land. A problem that often arises when parcels of land are identified as very attractive to a

---

2. Why couldn't a land oligopoly or cartel *sell* the land instead of leasing it? The problem is that land is both very durable and it is incapable of duplication. As the cartel sold parcels, there would be more and more land owners who would eventually resell their parcels in competition with the cartel. Sooner or later the cartel would fall apart. The leases permitted the large landowners to confine ownership to a small number of people. See Coase, Durability and Monopoly, 15 J.L. & Econ. 143 (1972).

certain buyer before purchase is that the owners will be tempted to hold out for a very high price, particularly if the buyer already has substantial "sunk" costs that it will lose if it cannot acquire the parcel. Suppose that a railroad plans a line from point A to point B that will cross 100 consecutive parcels of land. The cost of laying track across each of these parcels is $1000; however, the line is worthless if it does not extend all the way from A to B. Suppose the railroad has already acquired the first 75 parcels of land and laid track across them. It now approaches the owner of the 76th parcel, which has a fair market value of $5000. However, the owner knows that the railroad's "sunk" costs are $75,000, all of which will be wasted if the railroad is unable to acquire the 76th parcel. The owner will hold out for a very high price. This explains why entrepreneurs assembling large tracts of land for development are often very secretive about their activities. If word gets out before all the purchases are made, the price of the remaining parcels may go up substantially. See R. Posner, Economic Analysis of Law 62 (5th ed. 1998). When the buyer is the government or a public utility, that kind of secrecy may not be possible. However, the eminent domain power may enable the government to take the property at the price at which it would have been sold if no development had been planned.

If "just compensation" is intended to mimic the market, and if the market takes all available information into account, have the property owners in such cases received just compensation?

KELO v. CITY OF NEW LONDON, CONNECTICUT

Supreme Court of the United States (2005).
545 U.S. 469.

JUSTICE STEVENS delivered the opinion of the Court.

In 2000, the city of New London approved a development plan that, in the words of the Supreme Court of Connecticut, was "projected to create in excess of 1,000 jobs, to increase tax and other revenues, and to revitalize an economically distressed city, including its downtown and waterfront areas." 268 Conn. 1, 5, 843 A.2d 500, 507 (2004). In assembling the land needed for this project, the city's development agent has purchased property from willing sellers and proposes to use the power of eminent domain to acquire the remainder of the property from unwilling owners in exchange for just compensation. The question presented is whether the city's proposed disposition of this property qualifies as a "public use" within the meaning of the Takings Clause of the Fifth Amendment to the Constitution.

I

The city of New London (hereinafter City) sits at the junction of the Thames River and the Long Island Sound in southeastern Connecticut. Decades of economic decline led a state agency in 1990 to designate the City a "distressed municipality." In 1996, the Federal Government closed the Naval Undersea Warfare Center, which had been located in the Fort Trumbull area of the City and had employed over 1,500 people. In 1998, the City's unemployment rate was nearly double that of the State, and its population of just under 24,000 residents was at its lowest since 1920.

These conditions prompted state and local officials to target New London, and particularly its Fort Trumbull area, for economic revitalization. To this end, respondent New London Development Corporation (NLDC), a private nonprofit entity established some years earlier to assist the City in planning economic development, was reactivated. In January 1998, the State authorized a $5.35 million bond issue to support the NLDC's planning activities and a $10 million bond issue toward the creation of a Fort Trumbull State Park. In February, the pharmaceutical company Pfizer Inc. announced that it would build a $300 million research facility on a site immediately adjacent to Fort Trumbull; local planners hoped that Pfizer would draw new business to the area, thereby serving as a catalyst to the area's rejuvenation. . . . Upon obtaining state-level approval, the NLDC finalized an integrated development plan focused on 90 acres of the Fort Trumbull area.

The Fort Trumbull area is situated on a peninsula that juts into the Thames River. The area comprises approximately 115 privately owned properties, as well as the 32 acres of land formerly occupied by the naval facility (Trumbull State Park now occupies 18 of those 32 acres). The development plan encompasses seven parcels. Parcel 1 is designated for a waterfront conference hotel at the center of a "small urban village" that will include restaurants and shopping. This parcel will also have marinas for both recreational and commercial uses. A pedestrian "riverwalk" will originate here and continue down the coast, connecting the waterfront areas of the development. Parcel 2 will be the site of approximately 80 new residences organized into an urban neighborhood and linked by public walkway to the remainder of the development, including the state park. This parcel also includes space reserved for a new U.S. Coast Guard Museum. Parcel 3, which is located immediately north of the Pfizer facility, will contain at least 90,000 square feet of research and development office space. Parcel 4A is a 2.4–acre site that will be used either to support the adjacent state park, by providing parking or retail services for visitors, or to support the nearby marina. Parcel 4B will include a renovated marina, as well as the final stretch of the riverwalk. . . .

The NLDC intended the development plan to capitalize on the arrival of the Pfizer facility and the new commerce it was expected to attract. In addition to creating jobs, generating tax revenue, and helping to "build momentum for the revitalization of downtown New London," the plan was also designed to make the City more attractive and to create leisure and recreational opportunities on the waterfront and in the park.

The city council approved the plan in January 2000, and designated the NLDC as its development agent in charge of implementation. The city council also authorized the NLDC to purchase property or to acquire property by exercising eminent domain in the City's name. The NLDC successfully negotiated the purchase of most of the real estate in the 90–

acre area, but its negotiations with petitioners failed. As a consequence, in November 2000, the NLDC initiated the condemnation proceedings that gave rise to this case.

II

Petitioner Susette Kelo has lived in the Fort Trumbull area since 1997. She has made extensive improvements to her house, which she prizes for its water view. Petitioner Wilhelmina Dery was born in her Fort Trumbull house in 1918 and has lived there her entire life. Her husband Charles (also a petitioner) has lived in the house since they married some 60 years ago. In all, the nine petitioners own 15 properties in Fort Trumbull—4 in parcel 3 of the development plan and 11 in parcel 4A. Ten of the parcels are occupied by the owner or a family member; the other five are held as investment properties. There is no allegation that any of these properties is blighted or otherwise in poor condition; rather, they were condemned only because they happen to be located in the development area.

In December 2000, petitioners brought this action in the New London Superior Court. They claimed, among other things, that the taking of their properties would violate the "public use" restriction in the Fifth Amendment. . . .

III

Two polar propositions are perfectly clear. On the one hand, it has long been accepted that the sovereign may not take the property of *A* for the sole purpose of transferring it to another private party *B*, even though *A* is paid just compensation. On the other hand, it is equally clear that a State may transfer property from one private party to another if future "use by the public" is the purpose of the taking; the condemnation of land for a railroad with common-carrier duties is a familiar example. Neither of these propositions, however, determines the disposition of this case.

As for the first proposition, the City would no doubt be forbidden from taking petitioners' land for the purpose of conferring a private benefit on a particular private party. See *Midkiff,* 467 U.S. at 245 ("A purely private taking could not withstand the scrutiny of the public use requirement; it would serve no legitimate purpose of government and would thus be void"). . . . Nor would the City be allowed to take property under the mere pretext of a public purpose, when its actual purpose was to bestow a private benefit. The takings before us, however, would be executed pursuant to a "carefully considered" development plan. The trial judge and all the members of the Supreme Court of Connecticut agreed that there was no evidence of an illegitimate purpose in this case. Therefore, as was true of the statute challenged in *Midkiff,* 467 U.S. at 245, the City's development plan was not adopted "to benefit a particular class of identifiable individuals."

On the other hand, this is not a case in which the City is planning to open the condemned land—at least not in its entirety—to use by the general public. Nor will the private lessees of the land in any sense be required to operate like common carriers, making their services available to all comers. But although such a projected use would be sufficient to satisfy the public use requirement, this "Court long ago rejected any literal requirement that condemned property be put into use for the general public." Indeed, while many state courts in the mid–19th century endorsed "use by the public" as the proper definition of public use, that narrow view steadily eroded over time. Not only was the "use by the public" test difficult to administer (*e.g.,* what proportion of the public need have access to the property? at what price?), but it proved to be impractical given the diverse and always evolving needs of society. Accordingly, when this Court began applying the Fifth Amendment to the States at the close of the 19th century, it embraced the broader and more natural interpretation of public use as "public purpose." See, *e.g., Fallbrook Irrigation Dist. v. Bradley,* 164 U.S. 112, 158–164 (1896). Thus, in a case upholding a mining company's use of an aerial bucket line to transport ore over property it did not own, Justice Holmes' opinion for the Court stressed "the inadequacy of use by the general public as a universal test." *Strickley v. Highland Boy Gold Mining Co.,* 200 U.S. 527, 531 (1906).

The disposition of this case therefore turns on the question whether the City's development plan serves a "public purpose." Without exception, our cases have defined that concept broadly, reflecting our longstanding policy of deference to legislative judgments in this field.

In *Berman v. Parker,* 348 U.S. 26 (1954), this Court upheld a redevelopment plan targeting a blighted area of Washington, D. C., in which most of the housing for the area's 5,000 inhabitants was beyond repair. Under the plan, the area would be condemned and part of it utilized for the construction of streets, schools, and other public facilities. The remainder of the land would be leased or sold to private parties for the purpose of redevelopment, including the construction of low-cost housing.

... The public use underlying the taking was unequivocally affirmed:

"We do not sit to determine whether a particular housing project is or is not desirable. The concept of the public welfare is broad and inclusive.... The values it represents are spiritual as well as physical, aesthetic as well as monetary. It is within the power of the legislature to determine that the community should be beautiful as well as healthy, spacious as well as clean, well-balanced as well as carefully patrolled. In the present case, the Congress and its authorized agencies have made determinations that take into account a wide variety of values. It is not for us to reappraise them. If those who govern the District of Columbia decide that the Nation's Capital should be beautiful as well as sanitary, there is nothing in the Fifth Amendment that stands in the way.

In *Hawaii Housing Authority v. Midkiff,* 467 U.S. 229 (1984), the Court considered a Hawaii statute whereby fee title was taken from lessors and transferred to lessees (for just compensation) in order to reduce the concentration of land ownership. We unanimously upheld the statute and rejected the Ninth Circuit's view that it was "a naked attempt on the part of the state of Hawaii to take the property of A and transfer it to B solely for B's private use and benefit." Reaffirming *Berman*'s deferential approach to legislative judgments in this field, we concluded that the State's purpose of eliminating the "social and economic evils of a land oligopoly" qualified as a valid public use. Our opinion also rejected the contention that the mere fact that the State immediately transferred the properties to private individuals upon condemnation somehow diminished the public character of the taking. "[I]t is only the taking's purpose, and not its mechanics," we explained, that matters in determining public use. . . .

Viewed as a whole, our jurisprudence has recognized that the needs of society have varied between different parts of the Nation, just as they have evolved over time in response to changed circumstances. Our earliest cases in particular embodied a strong theme of federalism, emphasizing the "great respect" that we owe to state legislatures and state courts in discerning local public needs. . . . For more than a century, our public use jurisprudence has wisely eschewed rigid formulas and intrusive scrutiny in favor of affording legislatures broad latitude in determining what public needs justify the use of the takings power.

IV

Those who govern the City were not confronted with the need to remove blight in the Fort Trumbull area, but their determination that the area was sufficiently distressed to justify a program of economic rejuvenation is entitled to our deference. The City has carefully formulated an economic development plan that it believes will provide appreciable benefits to the community, including—but by no means limited to—new jobs and increased tax revenue. As with other exercises in urban planning and development, the City is endeavoring to coordinate a variety of commercial, residential, and recreational uses of land, with the hope that they will form a whole greater than the sum of its parts. To effectuate this plan, the City has invoked a state statute that specifically authorizes the use of eminent domain to promote economic development. Given the comprehensive character of the plan, the thorough deliberation that preceded its adoption, and the limited scope of our review, it is appropriate for us, as it was in *Berman,* to resolve the challenges of the individual owners, not on a piecemeal basis, but rather in light of the entire plan. Because that plan unquestionably serves a public purpose, the takings challenged here satisfy the public use requirement of the Fifth Amendment.

To avoid this result, petitioners urge us to adopt a new bright-line rule that economic development does not qualify as a public use. Putting aside the unpersuasive suggestion that the City's plan will provide only purely economic benefits, neither precedent nor logic supports petitioners' proposal. Promoting economic development is a traditional and long accepted function of government. There is, moreover, no principled way of distinguishing economic development from the other public purposes that we have recognized. In our cases upholding takings that facilitated agriculture and mining, for example, we emphasized the importance of those industries to the welfare of the States in question.... [I]n *Berman,* we endorsed the purpose of transforming a blighted area into a "well-balanced" community through redevelopment.... It would be incongruous to hold that the City's interest in the economic benefits to be derived from the development of the Fort Trumbull area has less of a public character than any of those other interests. Clearly, there is no basis for exempting economic development from our traditionally broad understanding of public purpose.

Petitioners contend that using eminent domain for economic development impermissibly blurs the boundary between public and private takings. Again, our cases foreclose this objection. Quite simply, the government's pursuit of a public purpose will often benefit individual private parties. For example, in *Midkiff,* the forced transfer of property conferred a direct and significant benefit on those lessees who were previously unable to purchase their homes.... The owner of the department store in *Berman* objected to "taking from one businessman for the benefit of another businessman," referring to the fact that under the redevelopment plan land would be leased or sold to private developers for redevelopment. Our rejection of that contention has particular relevance to the instant case: "The public end may be as well or better served through an agency of private enterprise than through a department of government—or so the Congress might conclude. We cannot say that public ownership is the sole method of promoting the public purposes of community redevelopment projects."

It is further argued that without a bright-line rule nothing would stop a city from transferring citizen *A*'s property to citizen *B* for the sole reason that citizen *B* will put the property to a more productive use and thus pay more taxes. Such a one-to-one transfer of property, executed outside the confines of an integrated development plan, is not presented in this case. While such an unusual exercise of government power would certainly raise a suspicion that a private purpose was afoot, the hypothetical cases posited by petitioners can be confronted if and when they arise. They do not warrant the crafting of an artificial restriction on the concept of public use.

Alternatively, petitioners maintain that for takings of this kind we should require a "reasonable certainty" that the expected public benefits will actually accrue. Such a rule, however, would represent an even greater departure from our precedent. "When the legislature's purpose is legitimate and its means are not irrational, our cases make clear that empirical debates over the wisdom of takings—no less than debates over the wisdom of other kinds of socioeconomic legislation—are not to be carried out in the federal courts." *Midkiff,* 467 U.S. at 242.... Orderly implementation of a comprehensive redevelopment plan obviously requires that the legal rights of all interested parties be established before new construction can be commenced. A constitutional rule that required postponement of the judicial approval of every condemnation until the likelihood of success of the plan had been assured would unquestionably impose a significant impediment to the successful consummation of many such plans.

Just as we decline to second-guess the City's considered judgments about the efficacy of its development plan, we also decline to second-guess the City's determinations as to what lands it needs to acquire in order to effectuate the project. "It is not for the courts to oversee the choice of the boundary line nor to sit in review on the size of a particular project area. Once the question of the public purpose has been decided, the amount and character of land to be taken for the project and the need for a particular tract to complete the integrated plan rests in the discretion of the legislative branch." *Berman,* 348 U.S. at 35–36.

In affirming the City's authority to take petitioners' properties, we do not minimize the hardship that condemnations may entail, notwithstanding the payment of just compensation. We emphasize that nothing in our opinion precludes any State from placing further restrictions on its exercise of the takings power. Indeed, many States already impose "public use" requirements that are stricter than the federal baseline. Some of these requirements have been established as a matter of state constitutional law, while others are expressed in state eminent domain statutes that carefully limit the grounds upon which takings may be exercised. As the submissions of the parties and their *amici* make clear, the necessity and wisdom of using eminent domain to promote economic development are certainly matters of legitimate public debate. This Court's authority, however, extends only to determining whether the City's proposed condemnations are for a "public use" within the meaning of the Fifth Amendment to the Federal Constitution. Because over a century of our case law interpreting that provision dictates an affirmative answer to that question, we may not grant petitioners the relief that they seek.

The judgment of the Supreme Court of Connecticut is affirmed.

It is so ordered.

JUSTICE KENNEDY, concurring.

I join the opinion for the Court and add these further observations.

This Court has declared that a taking should be upheld as consistent with the Public Use Clause, U.S. Const., Amdt. 5., as long as it is "rationally related to a conceivable public purpose." *Hawaii Housing Authority v. Midkiff,* 467 U.S. 229, 241 (1984).... This deferential standard of review echoes the rational-basis test used to review economic regulation under the Due Process and Equal Protection Clauses.... The determination that a rational-basis standard of review is appropriate does not, however, alter the fact that transfers intended to confer benefits on particular, favored private entities, and with only incidental or pretextual public benefits, are forbidden by the Public Use Clause.

A court applying rational-basis review under the Public Use Clause should strike down a taking that, by a clear showing, is intended to favor a particular private party, with only incidental or pretextual public benefits, just as a court applying rational-basis review under the Equal Protection Clause must strike down a government classification that is clearly intended to injure a particular class of private parties, with only incidental or pretextual public justifications. . . .

A court confronted with a plausible accusation of impermissible favoritism to private parties should treat the objection as a serious one and review the record to see if it has merit, though with the presumption that the government's actions were reasonable and intended to serve a public purpose. Here, the trial court conducted a careful and extensive inquiry into "whether, in fact, the development plan is of primary benefit to . . . the developer . . . and private businesses which may eventually locate in the plan area [*e.g.,* Pfizer], and in that regard, only of incidental benefit to the city." The trial court considered testimony from government officials and corporate officers; documentary evidence of communications between these parties, respondents' awareness of New London's depressed economic condition and evidence corroborating the validity of this concern, the substantial commitment of public funds by the State to the development project before most of the private beneficiaries were known, evidence that respondents reviewed a variety of development plans and chose a private developer from a group of applicants rather than picking out a particular transferee beforehand, and the fact that the other private beneficiaries of the project are still unknown because the office space proposed to be built has not yet been rented. . . .

The trial court concluded, based on these findings, that benefiting Pfizer was not "the primary motivation or effect of this development plan"; instead, "the primary motivation for [respondents] was to take advantage of Pfizer's presence." Likewise, the trial court concluded that "[t]here is nothing in the record to indicate that . . . [respondents] were motivated by a desire to aid [other] particular private entities." Even the dissenting justices on the Connecticut Supreme Court agreed that respondents' development plan was intended to revitalize the local economy, not to serve the interests of Pfizer. . . . This case, then, survives the meaningful rational basis review that in my view is required under the Public Use Clause.

JUSTICE O'CONNOR, with whom THE CHIEF JUSTICE, JUSTICE SCALIA, and JUSTICE THOMAS join, dissenting.

Over two centuries ago, just after the Bill of Rights was ratified, Justice Chase wrote:

"An ACT of the Legislature (for I cannot call it a law) contrary to the great first principles of the social compact, cannot be considered a rightful exercise of legislative authority.... A few instances will suffice to explain what I mean.... [A] law that takes property from A. and gives it to B: It is against all reason and justice, for a people to entrust a Legislature with SUCH powers; and, therefore, it cannot be presumed that they have done it." *Calder v. Bull,* 3 Dall. 386, 388, 1 L.Ed. 648 (1798).

Today the Court abandons this long-held, basic limitation on government power. Under the banner of economic development, all private property is now vulnerable to being taken and transferred to another private owner, so long as it might be upgraded—*i.e.,* given to an owner who will use it in a way that the legislature deems more beneficial to the public—in the process. To reason, as the Court does, that the incidental public benefits resulting from the subsequent ordinary use of private property render economic development takings "for public use" is to wash out any distinction between private and public use of property—and thereby effectively to delete the words "for public use" from the Takings Clause of the Fifth Amendment. Accordingly I respectfully dissent....

.... When interpreting the Constitution, we begin with the unremarkable presumption that every word in the document has independent meaning, "that no word was unnecessarily used, or needlessly added." *Wright v. United States,* 302 U.S. 583, 588 (1938). In keeping with that presumption, we have read the Fifth Amendment's language to impose two distinct conditions on the exercise of eminent domain: "the taking must be for a 'public use' and 'just compensation' must be paid to the owner." *Brown v. Legal Foundation of Wash.,* 538 U.S. 216, 231–232 (2003).

These two limitations serve to protect "the security of Property," which Alexander Hamilton described to the Philadelphia Convention as one of the "great obj[ects] of Gov[ernment]." 1 Records of the Federal Convention of 1787, p. 302 (M. Farrand ed.1934). Together they ensure stable property ownership by providing safeguards against excessive, unpredictable, or unfair use of the government's eminent domain power—particularly against those owners who, for whatever reasons, may be unable to protect themselves in the political process against the majority's will....

Where is the line between "public" and "private" property use? We give considerable deference to legislatures' determinations about what governmental activities will advantage the public. But were the political branches the sole arbiters of the public-private distinction, the Public Use Clause would amount to little more than hortatory fluff. An external, judicial check on how the public use requirement is interpreted, however limited, is necessary if this constraint on government power is to retain any meaning....

Our cases have generally identified three categories of takings that comply with the public use requirement, though it is in the nature of things that the boundaries between these categories are not always firm.

Two are relatively straightforward and uncontroversial. First, the sovereign may transfer private property to public ownership—such as for a road, a hospital, or a military base. . . . Second, the sovereign may transfer private property to private parties, often common carriers, who make the property available for the public's use—such as with a railroad, a public utility, or a stadium. See, *e.g., National Railroad Passenger Corporation v. Boston & Maine Corp.,* 503 U.S. 407 (1992). . . . But "public ownership" and "use-by-the-public" are sometimes too constricting and impractical ways to define the scope of the Public Use Clause. Thus we have allowed that, in certain circumstances and to meet certain exigencies, takings that serve a public purpose also satisfy the Constitution even if the property is destined for subsequent private use. See, *e.g., Berman v. Parker,* 348 U.S. 26 (1954); *Hawaii Housing Authority v. Midkiff,* 467 U.S. 229 (1984).

This case returns us for the first time in over 20 years to the hard question of when a purportedly "public purpose" taking meets the public use requirement. It presents an issue of first impression: Are economic development takings constitutional? I would hold that they are not. We are guided by two precedents about the taking of real property by eminent domain. In *Berman,* we upheld takings within a blighted neighborhood of Washington, D.C. The neighborhood had so deteriorated that, for example, 64.3% of its dwellings were beyond repair. 348 U.S., at 30. It had become burdened with "overcrowding of dwellings," "lack of adequate streets and alleys," and "lack of light and air." Congress had determined that the neighborhood had become "injurious to the public health, safety, morals, and welfare" and that it was necessary to "eliminat[e] all such injurious conditions by employing all means necessary and appropriate for the purpose," including eminent domain. Mr. Berman's department store was not itself blighted. Having approved of Congress' decision to eliminate the harm to the public emanating from the blighted neighborhood, however, we did not second-guess its decision to treat the neighborhood as a whole rather than lot-by-lot. See also *Midkiff,* 467 U.S. at 244 ("it is only the taking's purpose, and not its mechanics, that must pass scrutiny").

In *Midkiff,* we upheld a land condemnation scheme in Hawaii whereby title in real property was taken from lessors and transferred to lessees. At that time, the State and Federal Governments owned nearly 49% of the State's land, and another 47% was in the hands of only 72 private landowners. Concentration of land ownership was so dramatic that on the State's most urbanized island, Oahu, 22 landowners owned 72.5% of the fee simple titles. The Hawaii Legislature had concluded that the oligopoly in land ownership was "skewing the State's residential fee simple market, inflating land prices, and injuring the public tranquility and welfare," and therefore enacted a condemnation scheme for redistributing title.

In those decisions, we emphasized the importance of deferring to legislative judgments about public purpose. . . .

Yet for all the emphasis on deference, *Berman* and *Midkiff* hewed to a bedrock principle without which our public use jurisprudence would collapse: "A purely private taking could not withstand the scrutiny of the public use requirement; it would serve no legitimate purpose of government and would thus be void." *Midkiff,* 467 U.S., at 245; *id.,* at 241 ("[T]he Court's cases have repeatedly stated that 'one person's property may not be taken for the benefit of another private person without a justifying public purpose, even though compensation be paid.' "...)

The Court's holdings in *Berman* and *Midkiff* were true to the principle underlying the Public Use Clause. In both those cases, the extraordinary, precondemnation use of the targeted property inflicted affirmative harm on society—in *Berman* through blight resulting from extreme poverty and in *Midkiff* through oligopoly resulting from extreme wealth. And in both cases, the relevant legislative body had found that eliminating the existing property use was necessary to remedy the harm. Thus a public purpose was realized when the harmful use was eliminated. Because each taking *directly* achieved a public benefit, it did not matter that the property was turned over to private use. Here, in contrast, New London does not claim that Susette Kelo's and Wilhelmina Dery's well-maintained homes are the source of any social harm. Indeed, it could not so claim without adopting the absurd argument that any single-family home that might be razed to make way for an apartment building, or any church that might be replaced with a retail store, or any small business that might be more lucrative if it were instead part of a national franchise, is inherently harmful to society and thus within the government's power to condemn.

In moving away from our decisions sanctioning the condemnation of harmful property use, the Court today significantly expands the meaning of public use. It holds that the sovereign may take private property currently put to ordinary private use, and give it over for new, ordinary private use, so long as the new use is predicted to generate some secondary benefit for the public—such as increased tax revenue, more jobs, maybe even aesthetic pleasure. But nearly any lawful use of real private property can be said to generate some incidental benefit to the public. Thus, if predicted (or even guaranteed) positive side-effects are enough to render transfer from one private party to another constitutional, then the words "for public use" do not realistically exclude *any* takings, and thus do not exert any constraint on the eminent domain power....

Finally, in a coda, the Court suggests that property owners should turn to the States, who may or may not choose to impose appropriate limits on economic development takings. This is an abdication of our responsibility. States play many important functions in our system of dual sovereignty, but compensating for our refusal to enforce properly the Federal Constitution (and a provision meant to curtail state action, no less) is not among them....

I would hold that the takings in both Parcel 3 and Parcel 4A are unconstitutional, reverse the judgment of the Supreme Court of Connecticut, and remand for further proceedings.

JUSTICE THOMAS, dissenting.

Long ago, William Blackstone wrote that "the law of the land ... postpone[s] even public necessity to the sacred and inviolable rights of private property." 1 Commentaries on the Laws of England 134–135 (1765). The Framers embodied that principle in the Constitution, allowing the government to take property not for "public necessity," but instead for "public use." Amdt. 5. Defying this understanding, the Court replaces the Public Use Clause with a " '[P]ublic [P]urpose' " Clause, (or perhaps the "Diverse and Always Evolving Needs of Society" Clause ...), a restriction that is satisfied, the Court instructs, so long as the purpose is "legitimate" and the means "not irrational." This deferential shift in phraseology enables the Court to hold, against all common sense, that a costly urban-renewal project whose stated purpose is a vague promise of new jobs and increased tax revenue, but which is also suspiciously agreeable to the Pfizer Corporation, is for a "public use."

I cannot agree. If such "economic development" takings are for a "public use," any taking is, and the Court has erased the Public Use Clause from our Constitution, as Justice O'Connor powerfully argues in dissent. I do not believe that this Court can eliminate liberties expressly enumerated in the Constitution and therefore join her dissenting opinion. Regrettably, however, the Court's error runs deeper than this. Today's decision is simply the latest in a string of our cases construing the Public Use Clause to be a virtual nullity, without the slightest nod to its original meaning. In my view, the Public Use Clause, originally understood, is a meaningful limit on the government's eminent domain power. Our cases have strayed from the Clause's original meaning, and I would reconsider them. . . .

Though one component of the protection provided by the Takings Clause is that the government can take private property only if it provides "just compensation" for the taking, the Takings Clause also prohibits the government from taking property except "for public use." Were it otherwise, the Takings Clause would either be meaningless or empty. If the Public Use Clause served no function other than to state that the government may take property through its eminent domain power—for public or private uses—then it would be surplusage. See ... *Marbury v. Madison,* 1 Cranch 137, 174, 2 L.Ed. 60 (1803) ("It cannot be presumed that any clause in the constitution is intended to be without effect"). . . . Alternatively, the Clause could distinguish those takings that require compensation from those that do not. That interpretation, however, "would permit private property to be taken or appropriated for private use without any compensation whatever." *Cole v. La Grange,* 113 U.S. 1, 8 (1885) (interpreting same language in the Missouri Public Use Clause). In other words, the Clause would require the government to compensate for takings done "for public use," leaving it free to take property for purely private uses without the payment of compensation. This would contradict a bedrock principle well established by the time of the founding: that all takings required the payment of compensation. 1 Blackstone 135; 2 J.

Kent, Commentaries on American Law 275 (1827) (hereinafter Kent); J. Madison, for the National Property Gazette, (Mar. 27, 1792), in 14 Papers of James Madison 266, 267 (R. Rutland et al. eds.1983) (arguing that no property "shall be taken *directly* even for public use without indemnification to the owner"). The Public Use Clause, like the Just Compensation Clause, is therefore an express limit on the government's power of eminent domain.

The most natural reading of the Clause is that it allows the government to take property only if the government owns, or the public has a legal right to use, the property, as opposed to taking it for any public purpose or necessity whatsoever. At the time of the founding, dictionaries primarily defined the noun "use" as "[t]he act of employing any thing to any purpose." 2 S. Johnson, A Dictionary of the English Language 2194 (4th ed. 1773) (hereinafter Johnson). The term "use," moreover, "is from the Latin *utor,* which means 'to use, make use of, avail one's self of, employ, apply, enjoy, etc." J. Lewis, Law of Eminent Domain § 165, p. 224, n. 4 (1888) (hereinafter Lewis). When the government takes property and gives it to a private individual, and the public has no right to use the property, it strains language to say that the public is "employing" the property, regardless of the incidental benefits that might accrue to the public from the private use. The term "public use," then, means that either the government or its citizens as a whole must actually "employ" the taken property.

Granted, another sense of the word "use" was broader in meaning, extending to "[c]onvenience" or "help," or "[q]ualities that make a thing proper for any purpose." 2 Johnson 2194. Nevertheless, read in context, the term "public use" possesses the narrower meaning. Elsewhere, the Constitution twice employs the word "use," both times in its narrower sense. Claeys, Public–Use Limitations and Natural Property Rights, 2004 Mich. St. L.Rev. 877, 897 (hereinafter Public Use Limitations). Article 1, § 10 provides that "the net Produce of all Duties and Imposts, laid by any State on Imports or Exports, shall be for the Use of the Treasury of the United States," meaning the Treasury itself will control the taxes, not use it to any beneficial end. And Article I, § 8 grants Congress power "[t]o raise and support Armies, but no Appropriation of Money to that Use shall be for a longer Term than two Years." Here again, "use" means "employed to raise and support Armies," not anything directed to achieving any military end. The same word in the Public Use Clause should be interpreted to have the same meaning.

Tellingly, the phrase "public use" contrasts with the very different phrase "general Welfare" used elsewhere in the Constitution. See *ibid.* ("Congress shall have Power To . . . provide for the common Defence and general Welfare of the United States"); preamble (Constitution established "to promote the general Welfare"). The Framers would have used some such broader term if they had meant the Public Use Clause to have a similarly sweeping scope. Other founding-era documents made the contrast between these two usages still more explicit. See Sales, Classical

Republicanism and the Fifth Amendment's "Public Use" Requirement, 49 Duke L.J. 339, 368 (1999) (hereinafter Sales) (noting contrast between, on the one hand, the term "public use" used by 6 of the first 13 States and, on the other, the terms "public exigencies" employed in the Massachusetts Bill of Rights and the Northwest Ordinance, and the term "public necessity" used in the Vermont Constitution of 1786). The Constitution's text, in short, suggests that the Takings Clause authorizes the taking of property only if the public has a right to employ it, not if the public realizes any conceivable benefit from the taking.

The Constitution's common-law background reinforces this understanding. The common law provided an express method of eliminating uses of land that adversely impacted the public welfare: nuisance law. Blackstone and Kent, for instance, both carefully distinguished the law of nuisance from the power of eminent domain. Compare 1 Blackstone 135 (noting government's power to take private property with compensation), with 3 *id.,* at 216 (noting action to remedy "*public* . . . nuisances, which affect the public and are an annoyance to *all* the king's subjects"); see also 2 Kent 274–276 (distinguishing the two). Blackstone rejected the idea that private property could be taken solely for purposes of any public benefit. "So great . . . is the regard of the law for private property," he explained, "that it will not authorize the least violation of it; no, not even for the general good of the whole community." 1 Blackstone 135. He continued: "If a new road . . . were to be made through the grounds of a private person, it might perhaps be extensively beneficial to the public; but the law permits no man, or set of men, to do this without the consent of the owner of the land." Only "by giving [the landowner] full indemnification" could the government take property, and even then "[t]he public [was] now considered as an individual, treating with an individual for an exchange." When the public took property, in other words, it took it as an individual buying property from another typically would: for one's own use. The Public Use Clause, in short, embodied the Framers' understanding that property is a natural, fundamental right, prohibiting the government from "tak[ing] *property* from A. and giv[ing] it to B." *Calder v. Bull,* 3 Dall. 386, 388, 1 L.Ed. 648 (1798). . . .

Early American eminent domain practice largely bears out this understanding of the Public Use Clause. This practice concerns state limits on eminent domain power, not the Fifth Amendment, since it was not until the late 19th century that the Federal Government began to use the power of eminent domain, and since the Takings Clause did not even arguably limit state power until after the passage of the Fourteenth Amendment. See Note, The Public Use Limitation on Eminent Domain: An Advance Requiem, 58 Yale L.J. 599, 599–600, and nn. 3–4 (1949); *Barron ex rel. Tiernan v. Mayor of Baltimore,* 7 Pet. 243, 250–251, 8 L.Ed. 672 (1833) (holding the Takings Clause inapplicable to the States of its own force). Nevertheless, several early state constitutions at the time of the founding likewise limited the power of eminent domain to "public uses." See Sales 367–369, and n. 137 (emphasis deleted). Their practices therefore shed light on the original meaning of the same words contained in the Public Use Clause.

States employed the eminent domain power to provide quintessentially public goods, such as public roads, toll roads, ferries, canals, railroads, and public parks. Lewis §§ 166, 168–171, 175, at 227–228, 234–241, 243. Though use of the eminent domain power was sparse at the time of the founding, many States did have so-called Mill Acts, which authorized the owners of grist mills operated by water power to flood upstream lands with the payment of compensation to the upstream landowner. See, *e.g., id.,* § 178, at 245–246; *Head v. Amoskeag Mfg. Co.,* 113 U.S. 9, 16–19, 5 S.Ct. 441, 28 L.Ed. 889, and n. (1885). Those early grist mills "were regulated by law and compelled to serve the public for a stipulated toll and in regular order," and therefore were actually used by the public. Lewis § 178, at 246, and n. 3; see also *Head, supra,* at 18–19. They were common carriers—quasi-public entities. These were "public uses" in the fullest sense of the word, because the public could legally use and benefit from them equally. See Public Use Limitations 903 (common-carrier status traditionally afforded to "private beneficiaries of a state franchise or another form of state monopoly, or to companies that operated in conditions of natural monopoly").

To be sure, some early state legislatures tested the limits of their state-law eminent domain power. Some States enacted statutes allowing the taking of property for the purpose of building private roads. See Lewis § 167, at 230. These statutes were mixed; some required the private landowner to keep the road open to the public, and others did not. See *id.,* § 167, at 230–234. Later in the 19th century, moreover, the Mill Acts were employed to grant rights to private manufacturing plants, in addition to grist mills that had common-carrier duties. See, *e.g.,* M. Horwitz, The Transformation of American Law 1780–1860, pp. 51–52 (1977).

These early uses of the eminent domain power are often cited as evidence for the broad "public purpose" interpretation of the Public Use Clause, see, *e.g., ante,* at 8, n. 8 (majority opinion); Brief for Respondents 30; Brief for American Planning Assn. et al. as *Amici Curiae* at 6–7, but in fact the constitutionality of these exercises of eminent domain power under state public use restrictions was a hotly contested question in state courts throughout the 19th and into the 20th century. Some courts construed those clauses to authorize takings for public purposes, but others adhered to the natural meaning of "public use." As noted above, the earliest Mill Acts were applied to entities with duties to remain open to the public, and their later extension is not deeply probative of whether that subsequent practice is consistent with the original meaning of the Public Use Clause. At the time of the founding, "[b]usiness corporations were only beginning to upset the old corporate model, in which the raison d'etre of chartered associations was their service to the public," Horwitz, *supra,* at 49–50, so it was natural to those who framed the first Public Use Clauses to think of mills as inherently public entities. The disagreement among state courts, and state legislatures' attempts to circumvent public use limits on their eminent domain power, cannot obscure that the Public Use Clause is most naturally read to authorize takings for public use only if the government or the public actually uses the taken property. . . .

Our current Public Use Clause jurisprudence, as the Court notes, has rejected this natural reading of the Clause. The Court adopted its modern reading blindly, with little discussion of the Clause's history and original meaning, in two distinct lines of cases: first, in cases adopting the "public purpose" interpretation of the Clause, and second, in cases deferring to legislatures' judgments regarding what constitutes a valid public purpose. Those questionable cases converged in the boundlessly broad and deferential conception of "public use" adopted by this Court in *Berman* and *Midkiff*, cases that take center stage in the Court's opinion. The weakness of those two lines of cases, and consequently *Berman* and *Midkiff*, fatally undermines the doctrinal foundations of the Court's decision. Today's questionable application of these cases is further proof that the "public purpose" standard is not susceptible of principled application. This Court's reliance by rote on this standard is ill advised and should be reconsidered. . . .

. . . [T]he "public purpose" interpretation of the Public Use Clause stems from *Fallbrook Irrigation Dist. v. Bradley,* 164 U.S. 112, 161–162 (1896). The issue in *Bradley* was whether a condemnation for purposes of constructing an irrigation ditch was for a public use. This was a public use, Justice Peckham declared for the Court, because "[t]o irrigate and thus to bring into possible cultivation these large masses of otherwise worthless lands would seem to be a public purpose and a matter of public interest, not confined to landowners, or even to any one section of the State." That broad statement was dictum, for the law under review also provided that "[a]ll landowners in the district have the right to a proportionate share of the water." Thus, the "public" did have the right to use the irrigation ditch because all similarly situated members of the public— those who owned lands irrigated by the ditch-had a right to use it. The Court cited no authority for its dictum, and did not discuss either the Public Use Clause's original meaning or the numerous authorities that had adopted the "actual use" test. . . .

A second line of this Court's cases also deviated from the Public Use Clause's original meaning by allowing legislatures to define the scope of valid "public uses." *United States v. Gettysburg Electric R. Co.,* 160 U.S. 668 (1896), involved the question whether Congress' decision to condemn certain private land for the purpose of building battlefield memorials at Gettysburg, Pennsylvania, was for a public use. Since the Federal Government was to use the lands in question, there is no doubt that it was a public use under any reasonable standard. Nonetheless, the Court, speaking through Justice Peckham, declared that "when the legislature has declared the use or purpose to be a public one, its judgment will be respected by the courts, unless the use be palpably without reasonable foundation." As it had with the "public purpose" dictum in *Bradley*, *supra,* the Court quickly incorporated this dictum into its Public Use Clause cases with little discussion.

There is no justification, however, for affording almost insurmountable deference to legislative conclusions that a use serves a "public use." To begin with, a court owes no deference to a legislature's judgment concerning the quintessentially legal question of whether the government owns, or the public has a legal right to use, the taken property. Even under the "public purpose" interpretation, moreover, it is most implausible that the Framers intended to defer to legislatures as to what satisfies the Public Use Clause, uniquely among all the express provisions of the Bill of Rights. We would not defer to a legislature's determination of the various circumstances that establish, for example, when a search of a home would be reasonable, see, *e.g., Payton v. New York,* 445 U.S. 573, 589–590, 100 S.Ct. 1371, 63 L.Ed.2d 639 (1980), or when a convicted double-murderer may be shackled during a sentencing proceeding without on-the-record findings, see *Deck v. Missouri,* 544 U.S. 622 (2005). . . .

Still worse, it is backwards to adopt a searching standard of constitutional review for nontraditional property interests, such as welfare benefits, see, *e.g., Goldberg, supra,* while deferring to the legislature's determination as to what constitutes a public use when it exercises the power of eminent domain, and thereby invades individuals' traditional rights in real property. The Court has elsewhere recognized "the overriding respect for the sanctity of the home that has been embedded in our traditions since the origins of the Republic," *Payton, supra,* at 601, when the issue is only whether the government may search a home. Yet today the Court tells us that we are not to "second-guess the City's considered judgments," when the issue is, instead, whether the government may take the infinitely more intrusive step of tearing down petitioners' homes. Something has gone seriously awry with this Court's interpretation of the Constitution. Though citizens are safe from the government in their homes, the homes themselves are not. . . .

For all these reasons, I would revisit our Public Use Clause cases and consider returning to the original meaning of the Public Use Clause: that the government may take property only if it actually uses or gives the public a legal right to use the property. . . .

The consequences of today's decision are not difficult to predict, and promise to be harmful. So-called "urban renewal" programs provide some compensation for the properties they take, but no compensation is possible for the subjective value of these lands to the individuals displaced and the indignity inflicted by uprooting them from their homes. Allowing the government to take property solely for public purposes is bad enough, but extending the concept of public purpose to encompass any economically beneficial goal guarantees that these losses will fall disproportionately on poor communities. Those communities are not only systematically less likely to put their lands to the highest and best social use, but are also the least politically powerful. If ever there were justification for intrusive judicial review of constitutional provisions that protect "discrete and insular minorities," *United States v. Carolene Products Co.,* 304 U.S. 144, 152, n. 4, (1938), surely that principle would apply with great force to the powerless groups and individuals the Public Use Clause protects. The deferential standard this Court has adopted for the Public Use Clause is therefore deeply perverse. It encourages "those citizens with disproportionate influence and power in the political process, including large corporations and development firms" to victimize the weak. . . .

NOTES AND QUESTIONS

1.   In his concurring opinion Justice Kennedy stated:

> My agreement with the Court that a presumption of invalidity is not warranted for economic development takings in general, or for the particular takings at issue in this case, does not foreclose the possibility that a more stringent standard of review than that announced in *Berman* and *Midkiff* [i.e., *Hawaii Housing*] might be appropriate for a more narrowly drawn category of takings. There may be private transfers in which the risk of undetected impermissible favoritism of private parties is so acute that a presumption (rebuttable or otherwise) of invalidity is warranted under the Public Use Clause. . . . This demanding level of scrutiny, however, is not required simply because the purpose of the taking is economic development.

Justice O'Connor responded:

> For his part, Justice Kennedy suggests that courts may divine illicit purpose by a careful review of the record and the process by which a legislature arrived at the decision to take—without specifying what courts should look for in a case with different facts, how they will know if they have found it, and what to do if they do not. Whatever the details of Justice Kennedy's as-yet-undisclosed test, it is difficult to envision anyone but the "stupid staff[er]" failing it. . . . The trouble with economic development takings is that private benefit and incidental public benefit are, by definition, merged and mutually reinforcing. In this case, for example, any boon for Pfizer or the plan's developer is difficult to disaggregate from the promised public gains in taxes and jobs.

> Even if there were a practical way to isolate the motives behind a given taking, the gesture toward a purpose test is theoretically flawed. If it is true that incidental public benefits from new private use are enough to ensure the "public purpose" in a taking, why should it matter, as far as the Fifth Amendment is concerned, what inspired the taking in the first place? How much the government does or does not desire to benefit a favored private party has no bearing on whether an economic development taking will or will not generate secondary benefit for the public. And whatever the reason for a given condemnation, the effect is the same from the constitutional perspective—private property is forcibly relinquished to new private ownership.

Whatever one thinks of the logic of express judicial analysis of special interest "capture" in determining whether the public use requirement has been met, the fact is that Justice Kennedy was the swing vote in a 5–4 decision. In a case similar to *Kelo* but where special interest capture predominated, the Court would probably rule 5–4 that the public use requirement was not met.

Can you harmonize Justice O'Connor's dissent in *Kelo* with her very forceful opinion for the majority in *Hawaii Housing Authority* that the Court has always found the Public Use requirement to be met when the exercise of the eminent domain power is "rationally related to a conceivable public purpose"?

2.   As a matter of economics is Justice O'Connor correct that a sharp distinction exists between using eminent domain to shut down "blighted" (*Berman v. Parker*) or "oligopoly" (*Hawaii Housing*) uses in order to replace them with more profitable uses, and shutting down otherwise well maintained uses that simply are not contributing as much to society as they could be? "Blighted" property is simply property that is not being used to its full economic potential. And oligopoly property is simply property that is not being priced efficiently. See the discussions of the Coase Theorem in Chapter nine, which note the importance of Coase's observation that, economically speaking, nuisance law is not about wrongdoers but rather about *inconsistent* land uses: one person can do what she wants only by suppressing someone else's wish to do what he wants, and private ordering favors the more valuable use. Doesn't the same analysis apply to takings?

3.   Justice Thomas would apparently permit takings intended to transfer property to private owners if the private owners operated as common carriers (e.g., railroads, toll roads, electric and gas utilities, telephone lines, and the like). By law, common carriers are generally required to serve all paying customers. But does that make the use more "public"? Competitive markets also serve all paying customers, even though individual firms in those markets may turn some customers away.

4.   Wouldn't Justice Thomas' position create a ratchet in private property ownership: once the government decided to sell property to a private individual it could never take it back by paying just compensation unless it actually intended to use the property itself.

5.   Compare Justice Thomas' analysis in *Kelo* with Justice Scalia's analysis in *Lucas*, infra. What justifies an extremely orthodox, history bound reading of the phrase "public use" in the Fifth Amendment, but a broad, non-historical reading of the word "taken" so as to make it refer not only to government acts that seize property or impose a trespass, but also to regulatory acts that cause severe damage? If the framers had meant to protect private property from both wouldn't they have drafted a Fifth Amendment that forbad "taking or damaging" private property? In the last third of the nineteenth century, when rapid growth of railroads led to many instances of private property damage, roughly half of the American states amended their state constitutions so as to reach "damaging" as well as "taking" of private property, but the Federal Constitution was never amended. See Robert Brauneis, The First Constitutional Tort: The Remedial Revolution in Nineteenth–Century Just Compensation Law, 52 Vand.L.Rev. 57, 114 et seq. (1999). For one perspective on Justice Thomas, the jurist, see Jeffrey Toobin,

Partners: Will Clarence and Virginia Thomas Succeed in Killing Obama's Health-care Plan?, The New Yorker, Aug. 29, 2011, at 40.

6. Justice Thomas concludes that there is something "seriously awry" with an interpretation of the Constitution that holds that "[t]hough citizens are safe from the government in their homes, the homes themselves are not." While one might certainly debate whether individual liberty rights are more or less important than property rights, is it absolutely manifest that there is something "seriously awry" with a regime that places liberty rights ahead of property rights?

7. The reaction to *Kelo* has been severe at almost every level. Congress has considered legislation that would deny federal funds to states that permitted eminent domain proceedings except for certain statutorily enumerated "public" purposes.

Kelo still remains controversial. On the fifth anniversary of the Kelo decision, the following resolution was submitted to the United States House of Representatives:

111th CONGRESS, 2nd Session
United States Library of Congress
HRES 1471
Introduced in House

June 23, 2010

H. RES. 1471

Expressing support for the private property rights protections guaranteed by the 5th Amendment to the Constitution on the 5th anniversary of the Supreme Court's decision of Kelo v. City of New London.

IN THE HOUSE OF REPRESENTATIVES

June 23, 2010

Mr. Gingrey of Georgia (for himself, Mr. Kingston, Mr. Graves of Georgia, Mr. Westmoreland, Mr. Price of Georgia, Mr. Broun of Georgia, Mr. Neugebauer, Mr. Pitts, Mrs. Schmidt, Mr. Mack, and Mr. Posey) submitted the following resolution; which was referred to the Committee on the Judiciary

RESOLUTION

Expressing support for the private property rights protections guaranteed by the 5th Amendment to the Constitution on the 5th anniversary of the Supreme Court's decision of Kelo v. City of New London.

Whereas, on June 23, 2005, the Supreme Court issued a 5–4 decision in the case of Kelo v. City of New London;

Whereas the Takings Clause of the 5th Amendment states, 'nor shall private property be taken for public use, without just compensation';

Whereas the majority opinion in Kelo v. City of New London significantly expanded the scope of the public use provision in the Takings Clause of the 5th Amendment;

Whereas the majority opinion in Kelo v. City of New London provided for the taking of a person's private property through eminent domain for the benefit of another private entity;

Whereas the dissenting opinion in Kelo v. City of New London affirmed that 'the public use requirement imposes a more basic limitation upon Government, circumscribing the very scope of the eminent domain power: Government may compel an individual to forfeit her property for the public's use, but not for the benefit of another private person';

Whereas the dissenting opinion in Kelo v. City of New London expressed concern that the beneficiaries of this decision were 'likely to be those citizens with disproportionate influence and power in the political process, including large corporations and development firms' and 'the Government now has license to transfer property from those with fewer resources to those with more'; and

Whereas all levels of government have a constitutional responsibility and a moral obligation to always defend the property rights of individuals and to only execute their power of eminent domain when necessary for public use alone, and with just compensation to the individual property owner: Now, therefore, be it

Resolved, That it is the sense of the House of Representatives that—

(1) State and local governments should only execute the power of eminent domain for those purposes that serve the public good in accordance with the 5th Amendment to the Constitution;

(2) State and local governments must always justly compensate those individuals whose property is taken through eminent domain in accordance with the 5th Amendment to the Constitution;

(3) any execution of eminent domain by State and local governments that does not comply with paragraphs (1) and (2) constitutes an abuse of government power and a usurpation of the individual property rights, as defined in the 5th Amendment to the Constitution;

(4) eminent domain should never be used to advantage one private party over another;

(5) no State or local government should construe the holdings of Kelo v. City of New London as justification to abuse the power of eminent domain; and

(6) Congress maintains the prerogative and reserves the right to address, through legislation, any abuses of eminent domain by State and local governments in light of the ruling in Kelo v. City of New London.

Backlash against the United States Supreme Court's Kelo decision has resulted in a tremendous amount of new state legislation. See, e.g., Harvey M.

Jacobs and Ellen M. Bassett, All Sound, No Fury? The Impacts of State–Based Kelo Laws, American Planning Association, Planning & Environmental Law, Vol. 63 No. 21 pg. 3 (February 2011). At this time, approximately forty-three states have enacted legislation that gives greater protection to private land owners than the federal standard articulated in *Kelo*. Martin E. Gold & Lynne B. Sagalyn, The Use and Abuse of Blight in Eminent Domain, 38 Fordham Urb. L.J. 1119, 1151 (2011).

For example, a Texas statute provides:

... A governmental or private entity may not take private property through the use of eminent domain if the taking:

(1) confers a private benefit on a particular private party through the use of the property;

(2) is for a public use that is merely a pretext to confer a private benefit on a particular private party; or

(3) is for economic development purposes, unless the economic development is a secondary purpose resulting from municipal community development or municipal urban renewal activities to eliminate an existing affirmative harm on society from slum or blighted area[]. . . .

Texas Gov't Code Ann. § 2206.001 (West 2011).

Florida's property rights reforms are among some of the strongest in the nation. See Fla. Stat. Ann. §§ 73.013 & 163.335 (2011).

Chapters 73 and 163 of the Florida General Statutes and Article 10 § 6 of the Florida Constitution contain the state's eminent domain authority. House Bill 1567, signed into law in 2006 and codified in Sections 73 and 163 of the Florida General Statutes, incorporates proposals of a Florida legislative commission organized after *Kelo* to study eminent domain. Section 73.013 narrows transfer of land by eminent domain to private parties, allowing such transfers only in the case of common carriers, utilities, infrastructure provision, or leases of otherwise public space. The law allows transfer to private parties "without restriction" within ten years of the original transfer if the land acquired no longer serves the purpose for which it was condemned and the condemning authority has given the original owner the opportunity to buy back the property for the original price. If ten years have elapsed since the acquisition of the property, the government may freely convey the land to a private party. Section 73.014 also limits the use of eminent domain to abate a public nuisance or cure blight or slum conditions, requiring that a government determine an individual property poses a danger to public health or safety before exercising eminent domain. The statute further specifies that the use of eminent domain for the abatement or clearance of such conditions "does not satisfy the public purpose requirement of [the Florida Constitution]." Further, Section 163 clarifies that "the prevention or elimination of a slum area or blighted area as defined in this part and the preservation or enhancement of the tax base are not public uses or purposes for which private property may be taken by eminent domain and do not satisfy the public purpose requirement of [Section] 6(a), [Article] X of the State Constitution." Florida also passed a constitutional amendment (House Joint Resolution 1569) in 2006 which requires a three fifths majority in both legislative houses to grant exceptions to the general prohibition against taking private property for private use. These efforts "mark ... probably the most restrictive legislation passed by any state."

Marc Mihaly & Turner Smith, The Wake of Kelo Five Years After: A Survey of State and Federal Legislative Action and Judicial Activity, Vermont Law School (Nov. 5, 2010), *http://www.vermontlaw.edu/Documents/2010Takings Conference/20101029_Mihaly.pdf.*

In Mississippi, Initiative #31 appeared on the general election ballot on November 8, 2011. Initiative #31 passed with over seventy percent of voters approving. See Al Ortiz, Election Aftermath: Two Out of Three GOP-backed Measures Approved by Mississippi Voters, Ballot News (Nov. 8, 2011), http:// ballotnews.org/2011/11/08/election-aftermath-two-out-of-three-gop-backed-measures-approved-by-mississippi-voters/. Initiative #31 will amend Mississippi's Constitution to prohibit local and state government from conveying property taken by eminent domain to private businesses or persons for ten years from the date of acquisition. The measure will not apply to public nuisances, abandoned property and structures that are not fit for human habitation. Additionally, ports, utilities, airports, roads, bridges, drainage and levee facilities, and common carriers would be excluded from the prohibition. Business groups and civic leaders that are critics of Initiative #31 argue that it is a "job killer" and that ninety-nine percent of the land that is taken in the state by eminent domain could still be taken under Initiative #31 because of the exceptions to it. A scanned image of the original filing of Initiative #31 can be found online. See 2011 Constitutional Initiatives: Initiative #31– Eminent Domain, Mississippi Secretary of State (Oct. 7, 2009), http://www. sos.ms.gov/Elections/Initiatives/Initiatives/eminent_domain_initiative_ Rvance_E_10–7–2009.pdf.

In addition, at least ten state supreme courts have interpreted their state constitutions so as to impose a stricter "public use" requirement than federal law requires under Kelo. See, e.g., Ilya Somin, The Judicial Reaction to Kelo, 4 Alb. Gov't. L. Rev. 1 (2011). Some of these states had already done so before *Kelo* was decided. See, e.g., County of Wayne v. Hathcock, 471 Mich. 445, 684 N.W.2d 765 (2004) (overruling Poletown Neighborhood Council v. Detroit, 410 Mich. 616, 304 N.W.2d 455 (1981). About a dozen states had "property rights" initiatives on their ballots in the Nov., 2006, election, and most of them passed. For a summary of state legislation, see the website of The National Conference of State Legislatures, *http://www.ncsl.org/default.aspx? tabid=17595.*

In City of Norwood v. Horney, 110 Ohio St.3d 353, 853 N.E.2d 1115 (2006), decided in the wake of *Kelo*, the Ohio Supreme Court held that that state's constitution imposed a higher standard for determining a "public use" than the United States Supreme Court had done. In particular, the Ohio court was concerned with the due process implications of a very vague standard for determining that an area was "blighted," or deteriorating, thus justifying condemnation and subsequent transfer to a private developer for a supposedly superior use. The court wrote:

> In essence, "deteriorating area" is a standardless standard. Rather than affording fair notice to the property owner, the Norwood Code merely recites a host of subjective factors that invite ad hoc and selective enforcement—a danger made more real by the malleable nature of the public-benefit requirement. We must be vigilant in ensuring that so great a power as eminent domain, which historically has been used in areas where the most marginalized groups live, is not abused.
>
> As important, the standard for "deteriorating area" defined in the Norwood Code is satisfied not just upon a finding that a neighborhood *is* deteriorating or *will* deteriorate, but is also satisfied by a finding that it *"is in danger of* deteriorating into a blighted area." The statutory definition, therefore, incorporates not only the existing condition of a neighborhood, but also extends to what that neighborhood might become. But what it *might* become may be no more likely than what *might not* become. Such a speculative standard is inappropriate in the context of eminent domain, even under the modern, broad interpretation of "public use."
>
> A municipality has no authority to appropriate private property for only a contemplated or speculative use in the future....

See also Board of County Commissioners of Muskogee County v. Lowery, 136 P.3d 639, 641 (Okla. 2006), which concluded much more curtly that "economic development alone (not in connection with the removal of blighted property) does not constitute a public use or public purpose to justify the exercise of eminent domain as a matter of Oklahoma constitutional law ..."

8. An Oregon statute passed by public initiative prior to *Kelo* provides:

(1) If a public entity enacts or enforces a new land use regulation or enforces a land use regulation enacted prior to December 2, 2004, that restricts the use of private real property or any interest therein and has the effect of reducing the fair market value of the property, or any interest therein, then the owner of the property shall be paid just compensation.

(2) Just compensation shall be equal to the reduction in the fair market value of the affected property interest resulting from enactment or enforcement of the land use regulation as of the date the owner makes written demand for compensation under this section.

(3) Subsection (1) of this section shall not apply to land use regulations:

(A) Restricting or prohibiting activities commonly and historically recognized as public nuisances under common law. This subsection shall be construed narrowly in favor of a finding of compensation under this section;

(B) Restricting or prohibiting activities for the protection of public health and safety, such as fire and building codes, health and sanitation regulations, solid or hazardous waste regulations, and pollution control regulations;

(C) To the extent the land use regulation is required to comply with federal law;....

The Oregon Supreme Court upheld the statute in *MacPherson v. Department of Administrative Svces.*, 340 Or. 117, 130 P.3d 308 (2006).

9. For good commentary on *Kelo*, see Carol Necole Brown, Private Property, Community Development and Eminent Domain, Ch. 8: Kelo v. City of New London and the Prospects of Development After a Natural Disaster (Robin Paul Malloy ed., 2008); Charles E. Cohen, Eminent Domain After Kelo v. City of New London: An Argument for Banning Economic Development Takings, 29 Harv. J.L. & Pub. Pol'y 491 (2006); Nicole Stelle Garnett, The Neglected Political Economy of Eminent Domain, 105 Mich. L. Rev. 101 (2006); Julia D. Mahoney, Kelo's Legacy: Eminent Domain and the Future of Property Rights, 2005 Sup. Ct. Rev. 103 (2005).

§ 10.1.2 "JUST COMPENSATION"

J.J. NEWBERRY CO. v. CITY OF EAST CHICAGO

Court of Appeals of Indiana (1982).
441 N.E.2d 39.

STATON, JUDGE.

J.J. Newberry Company appeals a condemnation award of $760.00 plus interest for its leasehold interest in property condemned by the City of East Chicago.

Affirmed.

The record reveals that Newberry and the predecessors in interest of the beneficiaries of a land trust held by the Lake County Trust Company (hereinafter "lessor") executed a 25–year written lease agreement on September 30, 1953, for a parcel of real estate and the improvements thereon located in the Indiana Harbor region of the City of East Chicago. The 1953 lease entitled Newberry to continue to operate a variety store which had existed on the premises since 1926. The lease required rental payments of a fixed monthly amount plus a percentage of the gross annual income from the business.

On December 31, 1971, a fire of unknown origin completely destroyed the building and improvements which were the subject of Newberry's lease. Under a "fire clause" in the 1953 lease, the lessor was required to reconstruct the building if the building was damaged or destroyed by fire. The lessor failed to perform its obligations under the "fire clause," and Newberry was unable to operate its retail business on the premises.

On January 4, 1973, Newberry filed a complaint against the lessor and sought either specific performance of the "fire clause," or, in the alternative, an award of compensatory damages for lost profits.... The action culminated on December 16, 1980, with this Court's affirmance of the trial court's award of $116,910.33 as damages sustained by Newberry as a result of the lessor's breach of the "fire clause." See Marcovich Land

Corporation v. J.J. Newberry Company (1980), Ind.App., 413 N.E.2d 935, (trans. denied.)

An event that affected the outcome of Newberry's action on the "fire clause" and generated the subject matter of this appeal was the condemnation of the vacant parcel of property. On June 16, 1976, the City of East Chicago exercised its power of eminent domain. As part of a project to redevelop blighted urban areas, the City of East Chicago condemned the property on which Newberry's variety store stood until the fire in 1971. The decision to condemn the property was made by the representatives of East Chicago with full knowledge of the litigation involving Newberry and the lessor for the breach of the "fire clause."

The condemnation action proceeded to trial without jury on July 26, 1979, on the issue of the amount to be awarded to Newberry and the lessor. . . . Newberry appealed the trial court's award of $760.00 plus interest.

Capitalization of Income Method

Newberry's first assignment of error involves a challenge to the trial court's method of valuing Newberry's leasehold interest in the destroyed premises on June 16, 1976, the date of condemnation. As of that date, Newberry had an unexpired term of approximately 28 months on its lease with the lessor. Newberry contended, and the trial court properly held, that a tenant is entitled to compensation for an unexpired term of lease terminated by a condemnation action. Alamo Land & Cattle Co. v. Arizona (1976), 424 U.S. 295, 303, 96 S.Ct. 910, 916 However, the disputed issue at trial (and now on appeal) involved the method of valuing the unexpired term of Newberry's lease.

In Conclusions of Law 7 and 8, the trial court held that Newberry's leasehold interest "is to be valued as the difference between the fair market rental value of subject premises less the contract rent to be paid over the remainder of the term of the lease" and that Newberry "is not entitled to lost profits as damages for the appropriation and condemnation of subject premises." Based upon the testimony of two qualified real estate appraisers who used the trial court's method of valuation, the trial court determined that Newberry's leasehold interest was worth $760.00. It is this method of valuation which Newberry challenges on appeal.

Newberry contends that the trial court committed reversible error in using the aforementioned method of valuation. Newberry posits that the trial court should have used the "capitalization of income method" of valuing a leasehold interest. Dr. Lesley Singer, an economist, testified on behalf of Newberry and stated that the capitalization of income method was the only feasible method of valuing a leasehold interest that had undergone the calamities suffered by Newberry's interest. According to Dr. Singer's computations, the capitalized value of Newberry's leasehold interest on the date of condemnation was $165,970.42. Newberry asserts that the trial court erred in not setting Newberry's condemnation award at that amount.

The capitalization of income method of valuing condemned property operates as follows:

> "The income approach to valuation usually consists of arriving at an independent value of the land involved and adding to it the value of improvements arrived at by process of capitalization, i.e., converting reasonable or actual income at a reasonable rate of return (capitalization rate) into an indication of value. Land and improvements may be capitalized together in a single process." (Parentheses supplied.)

4 Sackman, Nichols on Eminent Domain § 12.32(3)(c), at 12–577 (3d rev. ed. 1981). Indiana courts permit the valuation of leasehold interests by the capitalization of income method under appropriate circumstances. State v. Nelson (1973), 156 Ind.App. 399, 296 N.E.2d 908. As was observed in State Highway Commission v. Jones (1977), 173 Ind.App. 243, 363 N.E.2d 1018, 1025:

> "It follows that since the 'capitalization approach' is a valid tool for use in evaluating property in the market place, then such technique should be utilized by the courts in valuing property where it is the best means by which 'just compensation' can be afforded."

However, the more traditional method of valuing a leasehold interest for condemnation purposes was enunciated by the Indiana Supreme Court:

> "Generally, the measure of damages where a leasehold interest is taken under eminent domain is the fair market value of the unexpired term of the lease over and above the rent stipulated to be paid."

State v. Heslar, 274 N.E.2d 261, 263 (Ind.1971). The Heslar method of valuation was employed by the trial court in the present case.

Upon reviewing the leading authorities on valuation of leasehold interests, this Court concludes that the trial court did not err in rejecting Newberry's request for use of the capitalization of income method. A proper application of the capitalization of income method requires that "the property is in good condition and capable of producing the income to be capitalized." 29A C.J.S. Eminent Domain § 168(2), at 724–25 (1965). Furthermore, "income cannot be capitalized to produce a residual value where the appropriated land is neither producing income nor equipped to do so...." Id. As such, the trial court properly rejected Newberry's alternate valuation method in light of the incendiary destruction of the building which Newberry used to produce income.

Case law from other jurisdictions support the general proposition of the law stated above. For example, in United States v. Certain Interests in Property (4th Cir.1961), 296 F.2d 264, 269–70, the court held that the "very use of the capitalization-of-income method of evaluation assumes the valuation of the property as a going concern...."

Under the particular circumstances of the present case, the trial court properly applied the *Heslar* method of valuation. The trial court correctly concluded that the capitalization of income method was too speculative to compute the fair market value of the property, regardless of the fact that Newberry had at one time operated a business on the property as a going concern. This Court "will not disturb an award of damages in a condemnation suit where the award is within the bounds of probative evidence introduced at trial." Indiana & Michigan Electric Co. v. Hurm (1981), Ind.App., 422 N.E.2d 371, 381.

Undivided Fee Rule

Newberry's second challenge to the trial court's condemnation award is directed toward the trial court's Conclusion of Law 5, which provided:

"That the sum of the separate interest of each of the Defendants (Newberry and the lessor) in the subject premises cannot exceed the fair market value of subject premises as a whole." (Parentheses supplied.)

The trial court determined that the property was worth $45,000.00 on June 16, 1976. The lessor's interest was valued at $44,240.00, and Newberry's leasehold interest was valued at $760.00. Newberry contends that the superficially appealing truism that the sum of the parts cannot exceed the whole has no application in the law of eminent domain.

Newberry cites several cases from other jurisdictions in support of the proposition that the combined value of a leasehold interest and a reversionary interest may exceed the fair market value of the property as a whole. However, this Court need look no further than the unambiguous directives of the Indiana Supreme Court which stated:

"For the purposes of condemnation proceedings, the value of all the interests or estates in a single parcel of land cannot exceed the value of the property as a whole, and that when the value of the property as a unit is paid to the various owners, or into court for them, the constitutional requirements are fully met, and the fact that the owners of the various interests may not agree as to the apportionment among themselves of the sum awarded does not concern the condemnor."

State v. Montgomery Circuit Court (1959), 239 Ind. 337, 157 N.E.2d 577, 578, n. 1.

* * *

The apportionment of the condemnation award between the tenant and the lessor prescribed by the court is commonly known as the "Undivided Fee Rule" and has wide application in other jurisdictions. See, 4 Sackman, Nichols On Eminent Domain, § 12.42(2), at 12–792 (3d rev.ed. 1981). * * *

Affirmed.

HOFFMAN, P.J., and GARRARD, J., concur.

NOTES AND QUESTIONS

1. The capitalization of income method and the method the court used to evaluate leased business premises often yield different valuations, although theoretically they should be very close. Simply put, "capitalization" is the conversion of income to value. Direct capitalization usually involves analysis of net income for a single year or, alternatively, the average of several years' net income. Under the capitalization of income method, the appraiser tries to predict the income of the business in question for several years, often on the basis of current income. Then he postulates a reasonable rate of return for the type of business in question. After that he determines the fair market value by dividing the predicted income by the postulated reasonable rate of return. For example, if he predicts that over the foreseeable future a business will produce profits of $10,000 per year (after all expenses, including salaries, have been paid), and that 10% is a reasonable rate of return in this particular business, he will conclude that the business is worth $100,000 ($10,000 / .10). However, this figure may have to be adjusted for several factors, such as the replacement costs of depreciable fixtures, and the value of any parts of the business, such as its goodwill, which may not be taken by eminent domain.

But the capitalization of income method can yield serious over-valuation when the expert fails to disaggregate the value of the business itself from the value of the land, as the plaintiff's expert very likely did in *Newberry*. Suppose, for example, that two psychiatrists open a highly innovative and profitable medical practice on the outskirts of a midwestern city. Their business earns $3,000,000 a year, but it resides in a general purpose building on a piece of land that together have a rental value of $2,000.00 per month. In this case simply capitalizing the value of the *business* could produce a sum 50 times larger than capitalizing the rental value of the land and building. Further, the business is ordinarily not what is being taken by the government, but only the property where the business resides. Presumably the psychiatrists will not have their business destroyed by the condemnation; rather, they will find a new location and continue on. See Department of Transp. v. M.M. Fowler, Inc., 361 N.C. 1, 637 S.E.2d 885 (2006) ("with the income approach, the appraisal must differentiate between income directly from the property and profits of the business located on the land"—excluding an expert's testimony that failed to do so).

If the premises are leased, then the landlord's and tenant's separate interests will have to be determined. If there are only four years remaining on the lease and no right of renewal, then how much would someone be willing to pay for the lease? The "salvage value" of a leased business—the amount that the lessee can take with him when the lease expires—may be very low if everything on the land is a fixture that will remain on the land. The question then becomes, what would someone pay for an expected stream of profits of $10,000 per year for four years, with little or no recovery of capital at the end?

The *Newberry* court attempted to determine a fair market value for the lease, probably by comparing the cost of leasing similar properties, and to subtract from that the amount of rent reserved in the lease. Presumably this difference was then (1) discounted to its present value, and (2) increased by any amount necessary to compensate the tenant for fixtures that were placed on the premises at the lessee's expense which will be lost as a result of the eminent domain proceedings.

Why should there very often be a difference between the fair market value of leased premises and the amount of rent reserved in the lease? Wouldn't we normally expect that property would be leased at its fair market value? In such a case the measurement of damages identified by the court, the *difference* between the fair market value of the lease and the rent reserved in the lease, would be zero.

One reason leases may have a higher current value to the tenant than the rent reserved in the lease is that the risk of failure of the tenant's business may have declined substantially since the lease was negotiated. Prospective commercial tenants are either new businesses or else they are new at a particular location. The risk of failure is a cost of doing business, and this risk is generally higher for a business just starting out than for a business that is established. When a firm's other costs are higher, the amount it is willing to pay for a lease will necessarily be lower. As a result, a lease may be more valuable to an established business than it was when the business first started and the lease was negotiated. To look at this from another perspective, if the leasehold is condemned and the tenant forced to move, it may face increased risks all over again. Should the tenant be compensated for these risks?

2. In *Newberry* the entire leasehold was condemned, effectively terminating the lease. In these cases the tenant's obligation to pay rent comes to an end, and the tenant is generally entitled to the fair market value of the lease. Note, however, that the fair market value in most states equals the *difference* between the amount of rent the tenant is paying and the rental value of the property. Suppose, for example, that T is leasing property for $1,000/month and that the market value of this property today is also $1,000/month. In that case the tenant loses a leasehold valued at $1,000, but she also loses the obligation to pay $1,000 in rent. The two cancel each other out and the amount of compensation is zero. See Lil Champ Food Stores, Inc. v. Department of Transp., 230 Ga.App. 715, 498 S.E.2d 94 (1998), cert. denied, (June 5, 1998), which produced this result. However, when only part of the leased property is taken *and* the remainder is still usable, most courts require the tenant to continue to pay the entire rent reserved for the duration of the lease. However, the tenant is entitled to share in the condemnation award for the loss of the property that was condemned. Once again, this will ordinarily be a single lump sum. See Elliott v. Joseph, 163 Tex. 71, 351 S.W.2d 879 (1961). If the lease provides that it will terminate upon an assertion of eminent domain power or if the lessee expressly assigns to the landlord all of the lessee's rights to compensation for a taking under the power of eminent domain, then the lessee is generally not entitled to part of the award. Fibreglas Fabricators v. Kylberg, 799 P.2d 371 (Colo.1990) (en banc); Village of Palatine v. Palatine Associates, LLC, 406 Ill.App.3d 973, 347 Ill.Dec. 177, 942 N.E.2d 10 (2010).

3. The undivided fee rule is followed in a majority of states. It consists of two steps. First, a jury or court ascertains the total compensation to be paid

as if one person owns all rights in the fee. Second, the jury or court apportions the compensation award among all of those with an ownership interest in the fee. In County of Clark v. Sun State Properties, Ltd., 119 Nev. 329, 72 P.3d 954 (2003), a divided Nevada Supreme Court found that the undivided fee rule was compelled by Nevada law rather than the alternative "aggregate of interests" test that a minority of states applied. Under the "aggregate of interests" test one places a value on each "division" of the fee individually, and the compensation award is equal to the sum of these individual interests. The dissenter noted that the undivided fee rule might overcompensate the landowners when an assembled parcel of land is worth more than its individual components, or undercompensate them when the assembled parcel is worth less.

Is the "undivided fee" rule a more economically sound basis for measuring just compensation than the "aggregate of interests" approach, or some other approach that simply values each condemnee's interests separately? For example, will the value of a lease plus the reversion held by the landlord always equal the total value of the same land with both interests merged into a single owner? The undivided fee rule assumes that the value of a leasehold estate to a tenant is exactly the same as the value given up by the landlord when the lease is executed. In fact, the value that a tenant places on the leasehold is always equal to *or greater* than the value placed on it by the landlord, or else the landlord and tenant would not be able to agree on a price. The tenant generally places a greater value on what it receives when a lease is executed than the landlord places on what it gives up. In that case, the undivided fee rule would seem to undercompensate at least one of the parties to the lease. The other side of the coin, of course, is that the fair market value of the undivided fee should be equal to its value when the property is used for its optimal purpose. To be sure, the lease increases value to the extent that the lessee values what she gets by more than the lessor values what he gives up. However, a purchase by someone for the same purpose should reflect exactly the same value. See V. Goldberg, T. Merrill and D. Unumb, Bargaining in the Shadow of Eminent Domain: Valuing and Apportioning Condemnation Awards Between Landlord and Tenant, 34 UCLA L. Rev. 1083 (1987); Mark S. Dennison, 96 Am. Jur. Trials 211 Condemnation of Leasehold Interests (2005).

One dubious application of the undivided fee rule arises when property has decreased in value since the lease was negotiated. Suppose, for example, that when a long-term lease was negotiated the property had a fair market value of $100,000 and had a lease value of $1,000 per month, which was the rent reserved in the tenant's lease. When it is condemned a few years later, the property is worth only $80,000 and has a rental value of $750 per month. Now the lessee will actually benefit from the condemnation of the property. The lease will be terminated and the lessee relieved of the burden of lease terms that have become unattractive. (The lessee will be able to find a similar piece of property in the same area for $750 per month.) The landlord, however, is in a somewhat different position: she owns a reversion in property worth $80,000, but she also owns a lease which promises a continuing stream of payments $200 *greater* than the fair market rental value of the property. The combined value of these two interests held by the landlord is clearly greater than $80,000. However, under the undivided fee rule the landlord will be entitled to no more than the $80,000. See 4 Nichols on Eminent Domain § 12D.01 (J. Sackman, ed., rev. 3d ed. 2000).

4. Suppose that a lessee's interest is taken by eminent domain, and the lease contains an option to renew or an option to purchase the property at a particular price. This option can have a substantial value. For example, an option to renew a ten-year lease at a rental of $800 per month is worth a substantial amount if the fair rental value at the time the option is exercised is $1,000 per month. In this case, the option is worth the present value of $200 per month payable for ten years. (The option is generally worth nothing, however, if the rental value of the land is $800 per month or less.) Likewise an option to purchase for $75,000 land which is now worth $90,000 is worth as much as $15,000. Often if the tenant has made improvements on the property the current lease value will be greater than the option price, and the option will have a positive value. In that case, compensation is required. See State v. Jan–Mar, Inc., 236 N.J.Super. 28, 563 A.2d 1153 (App.Div.1989).

Most courts hold that the tenant is entitled to be compensated for the condemned option. What if a lease does not contain an option to renew, but the tenant has a reasonable expectation that the lease will be renewed— perhaps because the landlord has in fact renewed the lease a half dozen times in the past? Nearly all courts hold that this expectation, no matter how reasonable, is not a "property interest" for which compensation is due. In Emery v. Boston Terminal Co., 178 Mass. 172, 185, 59 N.E. 763, 765 (1901), Justice Holmes reasoned:

> Changeable intentions are not an interest in land, and although no doubt such intentions may have added practically to the value of the petitioners' holding, they could not be taken into account in determining what the respondent should pay. They added nothing to the tenants' legal rights, and legal rights are all that must be paid for. Even if such intentions added to the salable value of the lease, the addition would represent a speculation on a chance, not a legal right.

Should it matter whether the tenant has built buildings or other fixtures on the leasehold? In that case the prospect of renewal could be quite valuable, simply because the consequence of nonrenewal—loss of the buildings—is so expensive. In Almota Farmers Elevator & Warehouse Co. v. United States, 409 U.S. 470 (1973), the Supreme Court held that a lessee who had a lease with seven years remaining, but who owned highly specialized buildings on the land, which had virtually no salvage value, was entitled to be compensated for the reasonable life expectancy of the buildings, in spite of the fact that the lease itself contained no renewal rights.

Did the court in *Almota* give the compensation to the wrong person? Once the lease expired the valuable buildings would belong to the landlord—that is, the value of the buildings remaining at the time the lease expired was part of the landlord's reversion, not of the tenant's present interest. Even if the tenant could have renewed the lease, we could expect the landlord to charge a higher rent, since the remaining interest in the buildings then belonged to the landlord rather than the tenant. In short, the Court in *Almota* compensated the tenant for something that belonged to the landlord. See R. Epstein, Takings: Private Property and the Power of Eminent Domain 77–79 (1985).

5. Problems of valuation can be substantial when the duration of the present estate is unknown. Suppose a thirty-year old person has a life estate, with a reversion or remainder in another. There is no telling how long the owner of the life estate will live. When property owned in this way is condemned, courts frequently use mortality tables to predict life expectancy, and give both the life tenant and the remainderman a lump sum immediately. Typically, the owner of the life estate will be entitled to the present value of the fair rental value of the property for a period equal to his life expectancy. Under the undivided fee rule the owner of the reversion or remainder will get the difference.

The problem becomes more complex when the future estate is made subject to some condition which may or may not ever occur. Consider a grant of land "To A so long as the premises are used for a school, but whenever they are not so used, to revert to O and his heirs." Absent condemnation, such land may be used for a school indefinitely and O's possibility of reverter will never become possessory. Many courts address the problem by holding that possibilities of reverter and rights of entry are not qualifying "property" at all for condemnation purposes, and no just compensation is due for their taking.

Doesn't a rule that treats a possibility of reverter as valueless because it may never become possessory ignore one very important element of value: namely, market exchange value? Suppose that you own land in fee simple determinable as long as the premises are used for a residence. I own the possibility of reverter. Because of recent development the property is now worth $100,000 if it can be used for commercial development, but only $30,000 if it must be used for a residence. Clearly, you will be willing to pay me some amount of money up to $70,000 for my possibility of reverter, so that you can merge the two interests into a fee simple absolute. My possibility of reverter has a very large market value even though the condition that will permit it to become possessory may never occur. (That is, if I refuse to sell you my possibility of reverter you are unlikely to use the land for commercial purposes, for then you would lose even your $30,000.) If this land is taken by eminent domain, isn't the owner of the fee simple determinable entitled to $30,000 and the owner of the possibility of reverter to $70,000?

In Leeco Gas & Oil Co. v. County of Nueces, 736 S.W.2d 629 (Tex.1987), the Texas Supreme Court objected when a private property owner gave land to the county in fee simple determinable so long as a public park was maintained on the property. Wishing to do something else, the County then filed a condemnation action against the donor's possibility of reverter and cited the rule that the damages for taking of a possibility of reverter are zero. The court began with the general proposition that "a mere possibility of reverter has no ascertainable value when the event upon which the possessory estate in fee simple defeasible is to end is not probable within a reasonably short period of time." However,

> [t]o allow a governmental entity, as grantee in a gift deed, to condemn the grantor's reversionary interest by paying only nominal damages would have a negative impact on gifts of real property to charities and govern-

mental entities. It would discourage these types of gifts in the future. This is not in the best interests of the citizens of this State.

The court remanded for compensation, to be measured as "the amount by which the value of the unrestricted fee exceeds the value of the restricted fee." See also City of Palm Springs v. Living Desert Reserve, 70 Cal.App.4th 613, 82 Cal.Rptr.2d 859 (1999) (following *Leeco*).

6. Suppose a city "downzones" property in order to reduce its market value shortly before condemning the property under its eminent domain power. In City of Baltimore v. Kelso Corp., 281 Md. 514, 380 A.2d 216 (1977), the plaintiff alleged that the city rezoned the plaintiff's property from commercial to residential, substantially reducing its value on the market. Seven months later the city began condemnation proceedings. Worse yet, the city intended to rezone the property for commercial use once again, after it had been condemned. As a general rule, just compensation is measured by the fair market value of land for the best *legal* use, within the limits of the zoning ordinances. However, the court held that if the plaintiff's allegations were true it was entitled to the value of the property under the commercial zoning. Accord Riggs v. Long Beach Twp., 109 N.J. 601, 538 A.2d 808 (1988).

§ 10.2   INVERSE CONDEMNATION

§ 10.2.1   TAKING BY TRESPASS

PRUNEYARD SHOPPING CENTER v. ROBINS

Supreme Court of the United States (1980).
447 U.S. 74.

MR. JUSTICE REHNQUIST delivered the opinion of the Court.

* * *

Appellant PruneYard is a privately owned shopping center in the city of Campbell, Cal. It covers approximately 21 acres—5 devoted to parking and 16 occupied by walkways, plazas, sidewalks, and buildings that contain more than 65 specialty shops, 10 restaurants, and a movie theater. The PruneYard is open to the public for the purpose of encouraging the patronizing of its commercial establishments. It has a policy not to permit any visitor or tenant to engage in any publicly expressive activity, including the circulation of petitions, that is not directly related to its commercial purposes. This policy has been strictly enforced in a nondiscriminatory fashion. The PruneYard is owned by appellant Fred Sahadi.

Appellees are high school students who sought to solicit support for their opposition to a United Nations resolution against "Zionism." On a Saturday afternoon they set up a card table in a corner of PruneYard's central courtyard. They distributed pamphlets and asked passersby to sign petitions, which were to be sent to the President and Members of Congress. Their activity was peaceful and orderly and so far as the record indicates was not objected to by PruneYard's patrons.

Soon after appellees had begun soliciting signatures, a security guard informed them that they would have to leave because their activity violated PruneYard regulations. The guard suggested that they move to the public sidewalk at the PruneYard's perimeter. Appellees immediately left the premises and later filed this lawsuit. . . .

The California Supreme Court [held] that the California Constitution protects "speech and petitioning, reasonably exercised, in shopping centers even when the centers are privately owned." 23 Cal.3d 899, 910, 153 Cal.Rptr. 854, 860, 592 P.2d 341, 347 (1979). It concluded that appellees were entitled to conduct their activity on PruneYard property. In rejecting appellants' contention that such a result infringed property rights protected by the Federal Constitution, the California Supreme Court observed:

> " 'It bears repeated emphasis that we do not have under consideration the property or privacy rights of an individual homeowner or the proprietor of a modest retail establishment. As a result of advertising and the lure of a congenial environment, 25,000 persons are induced to congregate daily to take advantage of the numerous amenities offered by the [shopping center there]. A handful of additional orderly persons soliciting signatures and distributing handbills in connection therewith, under reasonable regulations adopted by defendant to assure that these activities do not interfere with normal business operations ... would not markedly dilute defendant's property rights.' "

Before this Court, appellants contend that their constitutionally established rights under the Fourteenth Amendment to exclude appellees from adverse use of appellants' private property cannot be denied by invocation of a state constitutional provision or by judicial reconstruction of a State's laws of private property.

* * *

Here the California Supreme Court decided that Art. 1, §§ 2 and 3, of the California Constitution gave appellees the right to solicit signatures on appellants' property in exercising their state rights of free expression and petition.[1] In so doing, the California Supreme Court rejected appellants' claim that recognition of such a right violated appellants' "right to exclude others," which is a fundamental component of their federally protected property rights. Appeal is thus the proper method of review.

* * *

Appellants contend that a right to exclude others underlies the Fifth Amendment guarantee against the taking of property without just com-

---

1. Article 1, § 2, of the California Constitution provides:

"Every person may freely speak, write and publish his or her sentiments on all subjects, being responsible for the abuse of this right. A law may not restrain or abridge liberty of speech or press."

Article 1, § 3, of the California Constitution provides:

"[P]eople have the right to ... petition government for redress of grievances."

pensation and the Fourteenth Amendment guarantee against the deprivation of property without due process of law.

It is true that one of the essential sticks in the bundle of property rights is the right to exclude others. Kaiser Aetna v. United States, 444 U.S. 164, 179–180, 100 S.Ct. 383, 392–393, 62 L.Ed.2d 332 (1979). And here there has literally been a "taking" of that right to the extent that the California Supreme Court has interpreted the State Constitution to entitle its citizens to exercise free expression and petition rights on shopping center property. But it is well established that "not every destruction or injury to property by governmental action has been held to be a 'taking' in the constitutional sense." Armstrong v. United States, 364 U.S. 40, 48, 80 S.Ct. 1563, 1568, 4 L.Ed.2d 1554 (1960). Rather, the determination whether a state law unlawfully infringes a landowner's property in violation of the Taking Clause requires an examination of whether the restriction on private property "forc[es] some people alone to bear public burdens which, in all fairness and justice, should be borne by the public as a whole." This examination entails inquiry into such factors as the character of the governmental action, its economic impact, and its interference with reasonable investment-backed expectations. Kaiser Aetna v. United States, supra, at 175, 100 S.Ct., at 390.

Here the requirement that appellants permit appellees to exercise state-protected rights of free expression and petition on shopping center property clearly does not amount to an unconstitutional infringement of appellants' property rights under the Taking Clause. There is nothing to suggest that preventing appellants from prohibiting this sort of activity will unreasonably impair the value or use of their property as a shopping center. The PruneYard is a large commercial complex that covers several city blocks, contains numerous separate business establishments, and is open to the public at large. The decision of the California Supreme Court makes it clear that the PruneYard may restrict expressive activity by adopting time, place, and manner regulations that will minimize any interference with its commercial functions. Appellees were orderly, and they limited their activity to the common areas of the shopping center. In these circumstances, the fact that they may have "physically invaded" appellants' property cannot be viewed as determinative.

* * *

Affirmed.

MR. JUSTICE BLACKMUN joins the opinion of the Court except that sentence thereof, *ante,* at 2042, which reads: "Nor as a general proposition is the United States, as opposed to the several States, possessed of residual authority that enables it to define 'property' in the first instance."

NOTES AND QUESTIONS

1. For the definition of "inverse condemnation," see Justice Brennan's dissenting opinion in San Diego Gas & Elec. Co. v. San Diego, 450 U.S. 621, 638 n. 2 (1981):

The phrase "inverse condemnation" generally describes a cause of action against a government defendant in which a landowner may recover ... for a "taking" of his property under the Fifth Amendment, even though formal condemnation proceedings in exercise of the sovereign's power of eminent domain have not been instituted by the government entity. ... In an "inverse condemnation" action, the condemnation is "inverse" because it is the landowner, not the government entity, who institutes the proceeding.

2.　A few states have followed California's lead and given petitioners in a private shopping mall the equivalent of First Amendment protections under their state constitutions. Green Party of New Jersey v. Hartz Mountain Industries, Inc., 164 N.J. 127, 752 A.2d 315 (2000) (state constitution protects right to distribute leaflets at regional shopping center); Bock v. Westminster Mall, 819 P.2d 55 (Colo.1991) (en banc). But in People v. Yutt, 231 Ill.App.3d 718, 173 Ill.Dec. 500, 597 N.E.2d 208 (1992), the court held that although Illinois' constitutional protection for speech was broader than the Federal Constitution gave, anti-abortion protestors had no right to operate on the property of a privately owned clinic, since the clinic had not opened itself as a forum to the public generally.

But most state supreme courts that have addressed the issue conclude that the speech clauses of their constitutions extend no further than that of the Federal Constitution. Stranahan v. Fred Meyer, Inc., 331 Or. 38, 11 P.3d 228 (2000); Cahill v. Cobb Place Associates, 271 Ga. 322, 519 S.E.2d 449 (1999); State v. Wicklund, 589 N.W.2d 793 (Minn.1999); Citizens for Ethical Government v. Gwinnett Place, 260 Ga. 245, 392 S.E.2d 8 (1990); Fiesta Mall Venture v. Mecham Recall Committee, 159 Ariz. 371, 767 P.2d 719 (App. 1988); Estes v. Kapiolani Women's & Children's Medical Center, 71 Haw. 190, 787 P.2d 216 (1990) (hospital); SHAD Alliance v. Smith Haven Mall, 66 N.Y.2d 496, 498 N.Y.S.2d 99, 488 N.E.2d 1211 (1985); Cologne v. Westfarms Assoc., 192 Conn. 48, 469 A.2d 1201 (1984).

Finally, the California Supreme Court has limited its own *PruneYard* holding: see Golden Gateway Center v. Golden Gateway Tenants Assn., 26 Cal.4th 1013, 29 P.3d 797, 111 Cal.Rptr.2d 336 (2001), which refused to extend *PruneYard* to create a right in residential tenants to distribute a newsletter in their building in violation of their landlord's nondistribution policies.

Suppose a business owner has granted the city an easement for a sidewalk in front of his property; so the business owns the land but the public has a right of way. Do the First Amendment's protections apply to the sidewalk? See S.O.C., Inc. v. Mirage Casino–Hotel, 117 Nev. 403, 23 P.3d 243 (2001) (status of the property as "private" or "public" depended on construction of easement grant under state law; in this case the land owner did not create a right to picket when it gave up a right to use the sidewalk for passage).

3.　The *PruneYard* case should give you some idea about the complex relationship between state and federal law respecting property rights. The appellant was arguing that *state* recognition of a liberty right (freedom of speech under the California Constitution) was itself a violation of a *federal* property right. If a conflict had been found, the state right would have to yield to the federal right. Under the Supremacy Clause of the United States Constitution, Art. 6, *any* state law, even a state constitution, must yield to *any* valid federal law, even if the federal law is only a statute or administrative ruling.

PruneYard also contains an interesting debate about whether common law property rights contain a "federal" element. Clearly, the Federal Constitution protects property rights, but does it *define* them? Justice Rehnquist's ambiguous but loaded statement that the United States is not "possessed of residual authority that enables it to define 'property' in the first instance" prompted disagreement by two Justices.

Under the prevailing view, there is no federal content to substantive, common law property rights—provided that the definition of those rights or the way they are enforced does not conflict with federal law. Under this view of the relationship between the takings clause and state property law, the states have broad latitude to define their substantive property rights, but property owners have a right to stability in the state's chosen scheme. A taking may then occur if historically based expectations are frustrated. The takings clause effectively says to the states, once you have established a property law scheme, you must follow it with sufficient stability that you do not undermine people's reasonable expectations. The *Lucas* decision, reprinted infra, returns to this debate.

LORETTO v. TELEPROMPTER MANHATTAN CATV CORP.

Supreme Court of the United States (1982).
458 U.S. 419.

JUSTICE MARSHALL delivered the opinion of the Court.

This case presents the question whether a minor but permanent physical occupation of an owner's property authorized by government constitutes a "taking" of property for which just compensation is due under the Fifth and Fourteenth Amendments of the Constitution. New York law provides that a landlord must permit a cable television company to install its cable facilities upon his property. N.Y.Exec.Law § 828(1) (McKinney Supp. 1981–1982). In this case, the cable installation occupied portions of appellant's roof and the side of her building. The New York Court of Appeals ruled that this appropriation does not amount to a taking. 53 N.Y.2d 124, 423 N.E.2d 320 (1981). Because we conclude that such a physical occupation of property is a taking, we reverse.

I

Appellant Jean Loretto purchased a five-story apartment building located at 303 West 105th Street, New York City, in 1971. The previous owner had granted appellees Teleprompter Corporation and Teleprompter Manhattan CATV (collectively Teleprompter) permission to install a cable on the building and the exclusive privilege of furnishing cable television

(CATV) services to the tenants. The New York Court of Appeals described the installation as follows:

> "On June 1, 1970 TelePrompter installed a cable slightly less than one-half inch in diameter and of approximately 30 feet in length along the length of the building about 18 inches above the roof top, and directional taps, approximately 4 inches by 4 inches by 4 inches, on the front and rear of the roof. By June 8, 1970 the cable had been extended another 4 to 6 feet and cable had been run from the directional taps to the adjoining building at 305 West 105th Street." Id., at 135, 423 N.E.2d, at 324.

Teleprompter also installed two large silver boxes along the roof cables. The cables are attached by screws or nails penetrating the masonry at approximately two-foot intervals, and other equipment is installed by bolts.

* * *

Prior to 1973, Teleprompter routinely obtained authorization for its installations from property owners along the cable's route, compensating the owners at the standard rate of 5% of the gross revenues that Teleprompter realized from the particular property. To facilitate tenant access to CATV, the State of New York enacted § 828 of the Executive Law, effective January 1, 1973. Section 828 provides that a landlord may not "interfere with the installation of cable television facilities upon his property or premises," and may not demand payment from any tenant for permitting CATV, or demand payment from any CATV company "in excess of any amount which the [State Commission on Cable Television] shall, by regulation, determine to be reasonable." The landlord may, however, require the CATV company or the tenant to bear the cost of installation and to indemnify for any damage caused by the installation. Pursuant to § 828(1)(b), the State Commission has ruled that a one-time $1 payment is the normal fee to which a landlord is entitled.

* * *

The Commission ruled that this nominal fee, which the Commission concluded was equivalent to what the landlord would receive if the property were condemned pursuant to New York's Transportation Corporations Law, satisfied constitutional requirements "in the absence of a special showing of greater damages attributable to the taking."

Appellant did not discover the existence of the cable until after she had purchased the building. She brought a class action against Teleprompter in 1976 on behalf of all owners of real property in the State on which Teleprompter has placed CATV components, alleging that Teleprompter's installation was a trespass and, insofar as it relied on § 828, a taking without just compensation. She requested damages and injunctive relief. Appellee the City of New York, which has granted Teleprompter an exclusive franchise to provide CATV within certain areas of Manhattan, intervened. The Supreme Court, Special Term, granted summary judgment to Teleprompter and the city, upholding the constitutionality of § 828 in both crossover and noncrossover situations. The Appellate Division affirmed without opinion.

On appeal, the Court of Appeals, over dissent, upheld the statute. 53 N.Y.2d 124, 423 N.E.2d 320 (1981).

* * *

II

The Court of Appeals determined that § 828 serves the legitimate public purpose of "rapid development of and maximum penetration by a means of communication which has important educational and community aspects," and thus is within the State's police power. We have no reason to question that determination. It is a separate question, however, whether an otherwise valid regulation so frustrates property rights that compensation must be paid. See Penn Central Transportation Co. v. New York City. We conclude that a permanent physical occupation authorized by government is a taking without regard to the public interests that it may serve. Our constitutional history confirms the rule, recent cases do not question it, and the purposes of the Takings Clause compel its retention.

* * * [This] Court has often upheld substantial regulation of an owner's use of his own property where deemed necessary to promote the public interest. At the same time, we have long considered a physical intrusion by government to be a property restriction of an unusually serious character for purposes of the Takings Clause. Our cases further establish that when the physical intrusion reaches the extreme form of a permanent physical occupation, a taking has occurred. In such a case, "the character of the government action" not only is an important factor in resolving whether the action works a taking but also is determinative.

When faced with a constitutional challenge to a permanent physical occupation of real property, this Court has invariably found a taking.[1] As early as 1872, in Pumpelly v. Green Bay Co., 13 Wall. 166, this Court held that the defendant's construction, pursuant to state authority, of a dam which permanently flooded plaintiff's property constituted a taking. A unanimous Court stated, without qualification, that "where real estate is actually invaded by superinduced additions of water, earth, sand, or other material, or by having any artificial structure placed on it, so as to

---

1. Professor Michelman has accurately summarized the case law concerning the role of the concept of physical invasions in the development of takings jurisprudence:

"At one time it was commonly held that, in the absence of explicit expropriation, a compensable 'taking' could occur *only* through physical encroachment and occupation. The modern significance of physical occupation is that courts, while they sometimes do hold nontrespassory injuries compensable, *never* deny compensation for a physical takeover. The one incontestable case for compensation (short of formal expropriation) seems to occur when the government deliberately brings it about that its agents, or the public at large, 'regularly' use, or 'permanently' occupy, space or a thing which theretofore was understood to be under private ownership." Michelman, Property, Utility, and Fairness: Comments on the Ethical Foundations of "Just Compensation" Law, 80 Harv.L.Rev. 1165, 1184 (1967) (emphasis in original; footnotes omitted).

effectually destroy or impair its usefulness, it is a taking, within the meaning of the Constitution."

* * *

In St. Louis v. Western Union Telegraph Co., 148 U.S. 92 (1893), the Court applied the principles enunciated in *Pumpelly* to a situation closely analogous to the one presented today. In that case, the Court held that the city of St. Louis could exact reasonable compensation for a telegraph company's placement of telegraph poles on the city's public streets. The Court reasoned:

> The use which the [company] makes of the streets is an exclusive and permanent one, and not one temporary, shifting and in common with the general public. The ordinary traveler, whether on foot or in a vehicle, passes to and fro along the streets, and his use and occupation thereof are temporary and shifting. The space he occupies one moment he abandons the next to be occupied by any other traveller.... *But the use made by the telegraph company is, in respect to so much of the space as it occupies with its poles, permanent and exclusive.* It as effectually and permanently dispossesses the general public as if it had destroyed that amount of ground. Whatever benefit the public may receive in the way of transportation of messages, that space is, so far as respects its actual use for purposes of highway and personal travel, wholly lost to the public....

* * *

The historical rule that a permanent physical occupation of another's property is a taking has more than tradition to commend it. Such an appropriation is perhaps the most serious form of invasion of an owner's property interests. To borrow a metaphor, cf. Andrus v. Allard, 444 U.S. 51, 65–66 (1979), the government does not simply take a single "strand" from the "bundle" of property rights: it chops through the bundle, taking a slice of every strand.

* * *

Moreover, an owner suffers a special kind of injury when a *stranger* directly invades and occupies the owner's property. As Part II–A, supra, indicates, property law has long protected an owner's expectation that he will be relatively undisturbed at least in the possession of his property. To require, as well, that the owner permit another to exercise complete dominion literally adds insult to injury. See Michelman, Property, Utility, and Fairness: Comments on the Ethical Foundations of "Just Compensation" Law, 80 Harv.L.Rev. 1165, 1228, and n. 110 (1967). Furthermore, such an occupation is qualitatively more severe than a regulation of the *use* of property, even a regulation that imposes affirmative duties on the owner, since the owner may have no control over the timing, extent, or nature of the invasion.

The traditional rule also avoids otherwise difficult line-drawing problems. Few would disagree that if the State required landlords to permit third parties to install swimming pools on the landlords' rooftops for the convenience of the tenants, the requirement would be a taking. If the cable installation here occupied as much space, again, few would disagree that the occupation would be a taking. But constitutional protection for the rights of private property cannot be made to depend on the size of the area permanently occupied. Indeed, it is possible that in the future, additional cable installations that more significantly restrict a landlord's use of the roof of his building will be made. Section 828 requires a landlord to permit such multiple installations.

Finally, whether a permanent physical occupation has occurred presents relatively few problems of proof. The placement of a fixed structure on land or real property is an obvious fact that will rarely be subject to dispute. Once the fact of occupation is shown, of course, a court should consider the *extent* of the occupation as one relevant factor in determining the compensation due. For that reason, moreover, there is less need to consider the extent of the occupation in determining whether there is a taking in the first instance.

Teleprompter's cable installation on appellant's building constitutes a taking under the traditional test. The installation involved a direct physical attachment of plates, boxes, wires, bolts, and screws to the building, completely occupying space immediately above and upon the roof and along the building's exterior wall.

* * *

III

Our holding today is very narrow. We affirm the traditional rule that a permanent physical occupation of property is a taking. In such a case, the property owner entertains a historically rooted expectation of compensation, and the character of the invasion is qualitatively more intrusive than perhaps any other category of property regulation. We do not, however, question the equally substantial authority upholding a State's broad power to impose appropriate restrictions upon an owner's *use* of his property.

Furthermore, our conclusion that § 828 works a taking of a portion of appellant's property does not presuppose that the fee which many landlords had obtained from Teleprompter prior to the law's enactment is a proper measure of the value of the property taken. The issue of the amount of compensation that is due, on which we express no opinion, is a matter for the state courts to consider on remand.

The judgment of the New York Court of Appeals is reversed, and the case is remanded for further proceedings not inconsistent with this opinion.

It is so ordered.

JUSTICE BLACKMUN, with whom JUSTICE BRENNAN and JUSTICE WHITE join, dissenting.

In a curiously anachronistic decision, the Court today acknowledges its historical disavowal of set formulae in almost the same breath as it constructs a rigid *per se* takings rule: "a permanent physical occupation authorized by government is a taking without regard to the public interests that it may serve." To sustain its rule against our recent precedents, the Court erects a strained and untenable distinction between "temporary physical invasions," whose constitutionality concededly "is subject to a balancing process," and "permanent physical occupations," which are "taking[s] without regard to other factors that a court might ordinarily examine."

In my view, the Court's approach "reduces the constitutional issue to a formalistic quibble" over whether property has been "permanently occupied" or "temporarily invaded." Sax, Takings and the Police Power, 74 Yale L.J. 36, 37 (1964). The Court's application of its formula to the facts of this case vividly illustrates that its approach is potentially dangerous as well as misguided. Despite its concession that "States have broad power to regulate ... the landlord-tenant relationship ... without paying compensation for all economic injuries that such regulation entails," ante, at 440, the Court uses its rule to undercut a carefully considered legislative judgment concerning landlord-tenant relationships. I therefore respectfully dissent.

I

Before examining the Court's new takings rule, it is worth reviewing what was "taken" in this case. At issue are about 36 feet of cable one-half inch in diameter and two 4″ x 4″ x 4″ metal boxes. Jointly, the cable and boxes occupy only about one-eighth of a cubic foot of space on the roof of appellant's Manhattan apartment building.

* * *

In any event, § 828 differs little from the numerous other New York statutory provisions that require landlords to install physical facilities "permanently occupying" common spaces in or on their buildings. As the Court acknowledges, the States traditionally—and constitutionally—have exercised their police power "to require landlords to ... provide utility connections, mailboxes, smoke detectors, fire extinguishers, and the like in the common area of a building." Like § 828, these provisions merely ensure tenants access to services the legislature deems important, such as water, electricity, natural light, telephones, inter-communication systems, and mail service. A landlord's dispositional rights are affected no more adversely when he sells a building to another landlord subject to § 828, than when he sells that building subject only to these other New York statutory provisions.

The Court also suggests that § 828 unconstitutionally alters appellant's right to control the *use* of her one-eighth cubic foot of roof space.

But other New York multiple dwelling statutes not only oblige landlords to surrender significantly larger portions of common space for their tenants' use, but also compel the *landlord*—rather than the tenants or the private installers—to pay for and to maintain the equipment. For example, New York landlords are required by law to provide and pay for mailboxes that occupy more than five times the volume that Teleprompter's cable occupies on appellant's building. If the State constitutionally can insist that appellant make this sacrifice so that her tenants may receive mail, it is hard to understand why the State may not require her to surrender less space, *filled at another's expense*, so that those same tenants can receive television signals.

* * *

In the end, what troubles me most about today's decision is that it represents an archaic judicial response to a modern social problem. Cable television is a new and growing, but somewhat controversial, communications medium.... The New York Legislature not only recognized, but also responded to, this technological advance by enacting a statute that sought carefully to balance the interests of all private parties.

* * * I would affirm the judgment and uphold the reasoning of the New York Court of Appeals.

NOTES AND QUESTIONS

1. Are the *PruneYard* and *Loretto* decisions consistent? Both involve a "physical" intrusion. Is the chief difference between them the nature of the intruder, or the nature of the property being intruded upon? In City of Los Angeles v. Preferred Communications, 476 U.S. 488 (1986), the Supreme Court held that cable television companies also have First Amendment rights to reach their audiences. Should that be relevant in *Loretto*?

2. Closely related to the trespassory taking is the uncompensated transfer of a legally recognized incident of ownership from a private citizen to the government. In Hodel v. Irving, 481 U.S. 704 (1987), the Supreme Court struck down the "escheat" provisions of the federal Indian Land Consolidation Act of 1983 as an unconstitutional taking. Under earlier treaty arrangements, many tribal lands were held in trust and the rentals of the lands were paid to individual tribe members proportionate to their shares. Over several generations the number of interest holders had grown very large, and some proportional shares very small. In some cases the rentals amounted to less than one cent per individual, only a tiny fraction of the administrative cost of making the payments. In response, Congress passed a statute that provided, in part:

> "No undivided fractional interest in any tract of trust or restricted land within a tribe's reservation or otherwise subjected to a tribe's jurisdiction shall descend by intestacy or devise but shall escheat to that tribe if such interest represents 2 per centum or less of the total acreage in such tract and has earned to its owner less than $100 in the preceding year before it

is due to escheat." Indian Land Consolidation Act, Pub. L. No. 97–459, § 207, 96 Stat. 2515, 2519.

The statute made no provision for payment of compensation to owners of small fractional interests taken under this statute.

In finding an unconstitutional taking, the Court noted first that in some cases the fair market value of the escheated lands was as high as $2,700, even though the annual rentals earned on such fractional interests was less than $100 per year. Thus it was not true that the statute merely caused land with a de minimis value to escheat. The Court then noted:

> [T]he regulation here amounts to virtually the abrogation of the right to pass on a certain type of property—the small undivided interest—to one's heirs. In one form or another, the right to pass on property—to one's family in particular—has been part of the Anglo–American legal system since feudal times. The fact that it may be possible for the owners of these interests to effectively control disposition upon death through complex inter vivos transactions such as revocable trusts, is simply not an adequate substitute for the rights taken given the nature of the property. Even the United States concedes that total abrogation of the right to pass property is unprecedented and likely unconstitutional. Moreover, this statute effectively abolishes both descent and devise of these property interests even when the passing of the property to the heir might result in consolidation of property—as for instance when the heir already owns another undivided interest in the property.

481 U.S. at 716. Congress then amended the Indian Land Consolidation Act so as to encourage the tribes themselves to consolidate very small interests, but the Supreme Court once again found that a taking had occurred when a devisee chose to keep his interests separate without consolidating them. Babbitt v. Youpee, 519 U.S. 234 (1997).

3. Hundreds of jurisdictions in the United States require by statute or local ordinance that buildings rented for human occupancy be equipped with electricity. What is the difference between a statute that requires a landlord to permit a CATV installation on her building and one requiring her to permit the installation of an electric utility box and electric meter? Is the difference that CATV for tenants is a luxury, while electricity is a necessity? What if New York's housing code simply listed the presence of CATV connections as a habitability standard, and required that all buildings rented to tenants be equipped with them, at the owner's expense?

See Building Owners and Managers Ass'n Intern. v. F.C.C., 254 F.3d 89 (D.C.Cir.2001), which upheld a federal regulation requiring landlords to permit tenants to install satellite dishes on leased property. The court distinguished *Loretto* because in this case the placement of the reception dish was done at the tenant's request, and the tenant has possession of the property.

Contrast with *Loretto* the decision of the Texas Supreme Court in City of Austin v. Travis County Landfill Co., 73 S.W.3d 234 (Tex.2002), which held that overflights by planes taking off and landing at a nearby airport did not constitute a trespassory taking unless the flights "directly, immediately, and substantially" interfered with the land's "use and enjoyment." Are the two decisions distinguishable? Recall that it is commonly said that the landowner's right extends to the "highest heavens," not merely to her rooftop. How important is it that we have to accept overflying aircraft as a fact of life? Cf. McCarran Int'l Airport v. Sisolak, 122 Nev. 645, 137 P.3d 1110 (2006), which held that severe *height* restrictions on land adjacent to an airport in order to accommodate air traffic amounted to a taking because they actually did deprive the land owners of beneficial use of their land.

> [U]nder the United States and Nevada Constitutions, the ordinances authorize the permanent physical invasion of [the landowner's] airspace. The ordinances exclude the owners from using their property and, instead, allow aircraft to exclusively use the airspace as a critical departure area within an airport approach zone. The essential purpose of the ordinances adopted to facilitate flights through private property is to compel landowner acquiescence.

137 P.3d at 1116. See also United States v. Causby, 328 U.S. 256 (1946) (analogizing the air space above private property to a river). "The airplane is part of the modern environment of life, and the inconveniences which it causes are normally not compensable under the Fifth Amendment. The airspace, apart from the immediate reaches above the land, is part of the public domain. We need not determine at this time what those precise limits are. Flights over private land are not a taking, unless they are so low and so frequent as to be a direct and immediate interference with the enjoyment and use of the land." Id. at 266. In this case, the Court found that the frequency and the path of the flights resulted in a taking of an easement in the property owners' airspace.

4. In *Loretto* the Supreme Court did not reach the issue of compensation. Assume that New York decided to proceed against Loretto by condemnation. If the government must pay the difference in the fair market value of Loretto's building before and after the CATV system was installed, is it likely that Loretto is entitled to any compensation? Suppose Loretto's tenants cannot receive cable television unless the CATV box is installed. Is her building worth more or less as a result of this "taking?"

On remand, the New York Court of Appeals held that the Supreme Court's decision entitled Loretto and other New York apartment building owners to apply to the Commission on Cable Television for just compensation, but suggested that the actual injury would probably not exceed the $1.00 provided for in the original statute. Loretto v. Teleprompter Manhattan CATV Corp., 58 N.Y.2d 143, 459 N.Y.S.2d 743, 446 N.E.2d 428 (1983). Loretto and the other plaintiffs never bothered to apply for compensation. See Loretto v. Group W. Cable, 135 A.D.2d 444, 522 N.Y.S.2d 543, 522 N.Y.S.2d 543 (1987).

NOLLAN v. CALIFORNIA COASTAL COMMISSION
Supreme Court of the United States (1987).
483 U.S. 825.

JUSTICE SCALIA delivered the opinion of the Court.

James and Marilyn Nollan appeal from a decision of the California Court of Appeal ruling that the California Coastal Commission could condition its grant of permission to rebuild their house on their transfer to the public of an easement across their beachfront property. The California Court rejected their claim that imposition of that condition violates the Takings Clause of the Fifth Amendment, as incorporated against the States by the Fourteenth Amendment. We noted probable jurisdiction.

I

The Nollans own a beachfront lot in Ventura County, California. A quarter-mile north of their property is Faria County Park, an oceanside public park with a public beach and recreation area. Another public beach area, known locally as "the Cove," lies 1,800 feet south of their lot. A concrete seawall approximately eight feet high separates the beach portion of the Nollans' property from the rest of the lot. The historic mean high tide line determines the lot's oceanside boundary.

The Nollans originally leased their property with an option to buy. The building on the lot was a small bungalow, totaling 504 square feet, which for a time they rented to summer vacationers. After years of rental use, however, the building had fallen into disrepair, and could no longer be rented out. The Nollans' option to purchase was conditioned on their promise to demolish the bungalow and replace it. In order to do so, under California Public Resources Code §§ 30106, 30212, and 30600 (West 1986), they were required to obtain a coastal development permit from the California Coastal Commission. On February 25, 1982, they submitted a permit application to the Commission in which they proposed to demolish the existing structure and replace it with a three-bedroom house in keeping with the rest of the neighborhood.

The Nollans were informed that their application had been placed on the administrative calendar, and that the Commission staff had recommended that the permit be granted subject to the condition that they allow the public an easement to pass across a portion of their property bounded by the mean high tide line on one side, and their seawall on the other side. This would make it easier for the public to get to Faria County Park and the Cove. The Nollans protested imposition of the condition, but the Commission overruled their objections and granted the permit subject to their recordation of a deed restriction granting the easement. * * *

[The Commission] found that the new house would increase blockage of the view of the ocean, thus contributing to the development of "a 'wall' of residential structures" that would prevent the public "psychologically

... from realizing a stretch of coastline exists nearby that they have every right to visit." The new house would also increase private use of the shorefront. These effects of construction of the house, along with other area development, would cumulatively "burden the public's ability to traverse to and along the shorefront." Therefore the Commission could properly require the Nollans to offset that burden by providing additional lateral access to the public beaches in the form of an easement across their property. * * *

II

Had California simply required the Nollans to make an easement across their beachfront available to the public on a permanent basis in order to increase public access to the beach, rather than conditioning their permit to rebuild their house on their agreeing to do so, we have no doubt there would have been a taking. To say that the appropriation of a public easement across a landowner's premises does not constitute the taking of a property interest but rather, (as Justice Brennan contends) "a mere restriction on its use," is to use words in a manner that deprives them of all their ordinary meaning. Indeed, one of the principal uses of the eminent domain power is to assure that the government be able to require conveyance of just such interests, so long as it pays for them.... In Loretto [v. Teleprompter Manhattan CATV Corp.] we observed that where governmental action results in "[a] permanent physical occupation" of the property, by the government itself or by others, "our cases uniformly have found a taking to the extent of the occupation, without regard to whether the action achieves an important public benefit or has only minimal economic impact on the owner." We think a "permanent physical occupation" has occurred, for purposes of that rule, where individuals are given a permanent and continuous right to pass to and fro, so that the real property may continuously be traversed, even though no particular individual is permitted to station himself permanently upon the premises.

Given, then, that requiring uncompensated conveyance of the easement outright would violate the Fourteenth Amendment, the question becomes whether requiring it to be conveyed as a condition for issuing a land use permit alters the outcome. * * *

The Commission argues that a permit condition that serves the same legitimate police-power purpose as a refusal to issue the permit should not be found to be a taking if the refusal to issue the permit would not constitute a taking. We agree. Thus, if the Commission attached to the permit some condition that would have protected the public's ability to see the beach notwithstanding construction of the new house—for example, a height limitation, a width restriction, or a ban on fences—so long as the Commission could have exercised its police power (as we have assumed it could) to forbid construction of the house altogether, imposition of the condition would also be constitutional. Moreover (and here we come closer to the facts of the present case), the condition would be constitutional even if it consisted of the requirement that the Nollans provide a viewing spot on their property for passersby with whose sighting of the ocean their new house would interfere. Although such a requirement, constituting a permanent grant of continuous access to the property, would have to be considered a taking if it were not attached to a development permit, the Commission's assumed power to forbid construction of the house in order to protect the public's view of the beach must surely include the power to condition construction upon some concession by the owner, even a concession of property rights, that serves the same end. If a prohibition designed to accomplish that purpose would be a legitimate exercise of the police power rather than a taking, it would be strange to conclude that providing the owner an alternative to that prohibition which accomplishes the same purpose is not.

The evident constitutional propriety disappears, however, if the condition substituted for the prohibition utterly fails to further the end advanced as the justification for the prohibition. When that essential nexus is eliminated, the situation becomes the same as if California law forbade shouting fire in a crowded theater, but granted dispensations to those willing to contribute $100 to the state treasury. While a ban on shouting fire can be a core exercise of the State's police power to protect the public safety, and can thus meet even our stringent standards for regulation of speech, adding the unrelated condition alters the purpose to one which, while it may be legitimate, is inadequate to sustain the ban. Therefore, even though, in a sense, requiring a $100 tax contribution in order to shout fire is a lesser restriction on speech than an outright ban, it would not pass constitutional muster. Similarly here, the lack of nexus between the condition and the original purpose of the building restriction converts that purpose to something other than what it was. The purpose then becomes, quite simply, the obtaining of an easement to serve some valid governmental purpose, but without payment of compensation.

Reversed.

JUSTICE BRENNAN, with whom JUSTICE MARSHALL joins, dissenting.

* * * The Coastal Commission, if it had so chosen, could have denied the Nollans' request for a development permit, since the property would have remained economically viable without the requested new development. Instead, the State sought to accommodate the Nollans' desire for new development, on the condition that the development not diminish the overall amount of public access to the coastline. Appellants' proposed development would reduce public access by restricting visual access to the beach, by contributing to an increased need for community facilities, and by moving private development closer to public beach property. The Commission sought to offset this diminution in access, and thereby preserve the overall balance of access, by requesting a deed restriction that would ensure "lateral" access: the right of the public to pass and repass along the dry sand parallel to the shoreline in order to reach the tidelands and the ocean. In the expert opinion of the Coastal Commission,

development conditioned on such a restriction would fairly attend to both public and private interests.

The Court finds fault with this measure because it regards the condition as insufficiently tailored to address the precise type of reduction in access produced by the new development. The Nollans' development blocks visual access, the Court tells us, while the Commission seeks to preserve lateral access along the coastline. Thus, it concludes, the State acted irrationally. Such a narrow conception of rationality, however, has long since been discredited as a judicial arrogation of legislative authority. * * *

B

Even if we accept the Court's unusual demand for a precise match between the condition imposed and the specific type of burden on access created by the appellants, the State's action easily satisfies this requirement. First, the lateral access condition serves to dissipate the impression that the beach that lies behind the wall of homes along the shore is for private use only. It requires no exceptional imaginative powers to find plausible the Commission's point that the average person passing along the road in front of a phalanx of imposing permanent residences, including the appellants' new home, is likely to conclude that this particular portion of the shore is not open to the public. If, however, that person can see that numerous people are passing and repassing along the dry sand, this conveys the message that the beach is in fact open for use by the public. Furthermore, those persons who go down to the public beach a quarter-mile away will be able to look down the coastline and see that persons have continuous access to the tidelands, and will observe signs that proclaim the public's right of access over the dry sand. The burden produced by the diminution in visual access—the impression that the beach is not open to the public—is thus directly alleviated by the provision for public access over the dry sand. The Court therefore has an unrealistically limited conception of what measures could reasonably be chosen to mitigate the burden produced by a diminution of visual access.

The second flaw in the Court's analysis of the fit between burden and exaction is more fundamental. The Court assumes that the only burden with which the Coastal Commission was concerned was blockage of visual access to the beach. This is incorrect. The Commission specifically stated in its report in support of the permit condition that "[t]he Commission finds that the applicants' proposed development would present an increase in view blockage, an increase in private use of the shorefront, and that this impact would burden the public's ability to traverse to and along the shorefront." It declared that the possibility that "the public may get the impression that the beachfront is no longer available for public use" would be "due to the encroaching nature of private use immediately adjacent to the public use, as well as the visual 'block' of increased residential build-out impacting the visual quality of the beachfront."

The record prepared by the Commission is replete with references to the threat to public access along the coastline resulting from the seaward encroachment of private development along a beach whose mean high tide line is constantly shifting. * * * As the Commission explained:

"The placement of more private use adjacent to public tidelands has the potential of creating conflicts between the applicants and the public. The results of new private use encroachment into boundary/buffer areas between private and public property can create situations in which landowners intimidate the public and seek to prevent them from using public tidelands because of disputes between the two parties over where the exact boundary between private and public ownership is located. If the applicants' project would result in further seaward encroachment of private use into an area of clouded title, new private use in the subject encroachment area could result in use conflict between private and public entities on the subject shorefront."

* * * The Court is therefore simply wrong that there is no reasonable relationship between the permit condition and the specific type of burden on public access created by the appellants' proposed development. Even were the Court desirous of assuming the added responsibility of closely monitoring the regulation of development along the California coast, this record reveals rational public action by any conceivable standard.

II

* * * Examination of the economic impact of the Commission's action reinforces the conclusion that no taking has occurred. Allowing appellants to intensify development along the coast in exchange for ensuring public access to the ocean is a classic instance of government action that produces a "reciprocity of advantage." *Pennsylvania Coal [v. Mahon]*, 260 U.S. [393], at 415, 43 S.Ct., at 160 [1922]. Appellants have been allowed to replace a one-story 521–square–foot beach home with a two-story 1,674–square–foot residence and an attached two-car garage, resulting in development covering 2,464 square feet of the lot. Such development obviously significantly increases the value of appellants' property; appellants make no contention that this increase is offset by any diminution in value resulting from the deed restriction, much less that the restriction made the property less valuable than it would have been without the new construction. Furthermore, appellants gain an additional benefit from the Commission's permit condition program. They are able to walk along the beach beyond the confines of their own property only because the Commission has required deed restrictions as a condition of approving other new beach developments. Thus, appellants benefit both as private landowners and as members of the public from the fact that new development permit requests are conditioned on preservation of public access.

JUSTICE BLACKMUN, dissenting.

I do not understand the Court's opinion in this case to implicate in any way the Public Trust doctrine. The Court certainly had no reason to address the issue, for the Court of Appeal of California did not rest its decision on Art. X, § 4, of the California Constitution. Nor did the parties base their arguments before this Court on the doctrine.

DOLAN v. CITY OF TIGARD
Supreme Court of the United States (1994).
512 U.S. 374.

REHNQUIST, C.J., delivered the opinion of the Court.

Petitioner challenges the decision of the Oregon Supreme Court which held that the city of Tigard could condition the approval of her building permit on the dedication of a portion of her property for flood control and traffic improvements. * * * We granted certiorari to resolve a question left open by our decision in Nollan v. California Coastal Comm'n, 483 U.S. 825 (1987), of what is the required degree of connection between the exactions imposed by the city and the projected impacts of the proposed development.

I

The State of Oregon enacted a comprehensive land use management program in 1973. Ore.Rev.Stat. §§ 197.005–197.860 (1991). The program required all Oregon cities and counties to adopt new comprehensive land use plans that were consistent with the statewide planning goals. §§ 197.175(1), 197.250. The plans are implemented by land use regulations which are part of an integrated hierarchy of legally binding goals, plans, and regulations. §§ 197.175, 197.175(2)(b). Pursuant to the State's requirements, the city of Tigard, a community of some 30,000 residents on the southwest edge of Portland, developed a comprehensive plan and codified it in its Community Development Code (CDC). The CDC requires property owners in the area zoned Central Business District to comply with a 15% open space and landscaping requirement, which limits total site coverage, including all structures and paved parking, to 85% of the parcel. After the completion of a transportation study that identified congestion in the Central Business District as a particular problem, the city adopted a plan for a pedestrian/bicycle pathway intended to encourage alternatives to automobile transportation for short trips. The CDC requires that new development facilitate this plan by dedicating land for pedestrian pathways where provided for in the pedestrian/bicycle pathway plan. * * *

Petitioner Florence Dolan owns a plumbing and electric supply store located on Main Street in the Central Business District of the city. The store covers approximately 9,700 square feet on the eastern side of a 1.67–acre parcel, which includes a gravel parking lot. Fanno Creek flows through the southwestern corner of the lot and along its western boundary. The year-round flow of the creek renders the area within the creek's

100–year floodplain virtually unusable for commercial development. The city's comprehensive plan includes the Fanno Creek floodplain as part of the city's greenway system.

Petitioner applied to the city for a permit to redevelop the site. Her proposed plans called for nearly doubling the size of the store to 17,600 square feet, and paving a 39–space parking lot. The existing store, located on the opposite side of the parcel, would be razed in sections as construction progressed on the new building. In the second phase of the project, petitioner proposed to build an additional structure on the northeast side of the site for complementary businesses, and to provide more parking. The proposed expansion and intensified use are consistent with the city's zoning scheme in the Central Business District.

The City Planning Commission granted petitioner's permit application subject to conditions imposed by the city's CDC. The CDC establishes the following standard for site development review approval: "Where landfill and/or development is allowed within and adjacent to the 100–year floodplain, the city shall require the dedication of sufficient open land area for greenway adjoining and within the floodplain. This area shall include portions at a suitable elevation for the construction of a pedestrian/bicycle pathway within the floodplain in accordance with the adopted pedestrian/bicycle plan." CDC § 18.120.180.A.8. Thus the Commission required that petitioner dedicate the portion of her property lying within the 100–year floodplain for improvement of a storm drainage system along Fanno Creek and that she dedicate an additional 15–foot strip of land adjacent to the floodplain as a pedestrian/bicycle pathway.[2] The dedication required by that condition encompasses approximately 7,000 square feet, or roughly 10% of the property. In accordance with city practice, petitioner could rely on the dedicated property to meet the 15% open space and landscaping requirement mandated by the city's zoning scheme. The city would bear the cost of maintaining a landscaped buffer between the dedicated area and the new store. * * *

The Commission made a series of findings concerning the relationship between the dedicated conditions and the projected impacts of petitioner's project. First, the Commission noted that "[i]t is reasonable to assume that customers and employees of the future uses of this site could utilize a pedestrian/bicycle pathway adjacent to this development for their transportation and recreational needs." The Commission noted that the site plan has provided for bicycle parking in a rack in front of the proposed building and "[i]t is reasonable to expect that some of the users of the bicycle parking provided for by the site plan will use the pathway adjacent to Fanno Creek if it is constructed." In addition, the Commission found that creation of a convenient, safe pedestrian/bicycle pathway system as

---

2. The city's decision includes the following relevant conditions: "1. The applicant shall dedicate to the City as Greenway all portions of the site that fall within the existing 100–year floodplain [of Fanno Creek] (i.e., all portions of the property below elevation 150.0) and all property 15 feet above (to the east of) the 150.0 foot floodplain boundary. The building shall be designed so as not to intrude into the greenway area."

an alternative means of transportation "could offset some of the traffic demand on [nearby] streets and lessen the increase in traffic congestion."

The Commission went on to note that the required floodplain dedication would be reasonably related to petitioner's request to intensify the use of the site given the increase in the impervious surface. The Commission stated that the "anticipated increased storm water flow from the subject property to an already strained creek and drainage basin can only add to the public need to manage the stream channel and floodplain for drainage purposes." Based on this anticipated increased storm water flow, the Commission concluded that "the requirement of dedication of the floodplain area on the site is related to the applicant's plan to intensify development on the site." * * *

II

* * * One of the principal purposes of the Takings Clause is "to bar Government from forcing some people alone to bear public burdens which, in all fairness and justice, should be borne by the public as a whole." Armstrong v. United States, 364 U.S. 40, 49 (1960). Without question, had the city simply required petitioner to dedicate a strip of land along Fanno Creek for public use, rather than conditioning the grant of her permit to redevelop her property on such a dedication, a taking would have occurred. *Nollan*, supra. Such public access would deprive petitioner of the right to exclude others, "one of the most essential sticks in the bundle of rights that are commonly characterized as property." Kaiser Aetna v. United States, 444 U.S. 164, 176 (1979).

On the other side of the ledger, the authority of state and local governments to engage in land use planning has been sustained against constitutional challenge as long ago as our decision in Euclid v. Ambler Realty Co., 272 U.S. 365 (1926). "Government hardly could go on if to some extent values incident to property could not be diminished without paying for every such change in the general law." Pennsylvania Coal Co. v. Mahon, 260 U.S. 393, 413 (1922). A land use regulation does not effect a taking if it "substantially advance[s] legitimate state interests" and does not "den[y] an owner economically viable use of his land." Agins v. Tiburon, 447 U.S. 255, 260 (1980).

The sort of land use regulations discussed in the cases just cited, however, differ in two relevant particulars from the present case. First, they involved essentially legislative determinations classifying entire areas of the city, whereas here the city made an adjudicative decision to condition petitioner's application for a building permit on an individual parcel. Second, the conditions imposed were not simply a limitation on the use petitioner might make of her own parcel, but a requirement that she deed portions of the property to the city. In *Nollan*, we held that governmental authority to exact such a condition was circumscribed by the Fifth and Fourteenth Amendments. Under the well-settled doctrine of "unconstitutional conditions," the government may not require a person to give up a constitutional right—here the right to receive just compensation when property is taken for a public use—in exchange for a discretionary benefit conferred by the government where the property sought has little or no relationship to the benefit. See Perry v. Sindermann, 408 U.S. 593 (1972); Pickering v. Board of Ed. of Township High School Dist., 391 U.S. 563, 568 (1968).

Petitioner contends that the city has forced her to choose between the building permit and her right under the Fifth Amendment to just compensation for the public easements. Petitioner does not quarrel with the city's authority to exact some forms of dedication as a condition for the grant of a building permit, but challenges the showing made by the city to justify these exactions. She argues that the city has identified "no special benefits" conferred on her, and has not identified any "special quantifiable burdens" created by her new store that would justify the particular dedications required from her which are not required from the public at large.

III

In evaluating petitioner's claim, we must first determine whether the "essential nexus" exists between the "legitimate state interest" and the permit condition exacted by the city. *Nollan*, 483 U.S., at 837, 107 S.Ct., at 3148. If we find that a nexus exists, we must then decide the required degree of connection between the exactions and the projected impact of the proposed development. We were not required to reach this question in *Nollan*, because we concluded that the connection did not meet even the loosest standard. Here, however, we must decide this question.

A

* * * Undoubtedly, the prevention of flooding along Fanno Creek and the reduction of traffic congestion in the Central Business District qualify as the type of legitimate public purposes we have upheld. It seems equally obvious that a nexus exists between preventing flooding along Fanno Creek and limiting development within the creek's 100–year floodplain. Petitioner proposes to double the size of her retail store and to pave her now-gravel parking lot, thereby expanding the impervious surface on the property and increasing the amount of stormwater run-off into Fanno Creek.

The same may be said for the city's attempt to reduce traffic congestion by providing for alternative means of transportation. In theory, a pedestrian/bicycle pathway provides a useful alternative means of transportation for workers and shoppers: "Pedestrians and bicyclists occupying dedicated spaces for walking and/or bicycling ... remove potential vehicles from streets, resulting in an overall improvement in total transportation system flow."

B

The second part of our analysis requires us to determine whether the degree of the exactions demanded by the city's permit conditions bear the required relationship to the projected impact of petitioner's proposed development. *Nollan*, supra, 483 U.S., at 834 (" '[A] use restriction may constitute a taking if not reasonably necessary to the effectuation of a substantial government purpose' "). Here the Oregon Supreme Court deferred to what it termed the "city's unchallenged factual findings" supporting the dedication conditions and found them to be reasonably related to the impact of the expansion of petitioner's business.

The city required that petitioner dedicate "to the city as Greenway all portions of the site that fall within the existing 100–year floodplain [of Fanno Creek] ... and all property 15 feet above [the floodplain] boundary." In addition, the city demanded that the retail store be designed so as not to intrude into the greenway area. The city relies on the Commission's rather tentative findings that increased stormwater flow from petitioner's property "can only add to the public need to manage the [floodplain] for drainage purposes" to support its conclusion that the "requirement of dedication of the floodplain area on the site is related to the applicant's plan to intensify development on the site."

The city made the following specific findings relevant to the pedestrian/bicycle pathway: "In addition, the proposed expanded use of this site is anticipated to generate additional vehicular traffic thereby increasing congestion on nearby collector and arterial streets. Creation of a convenient, safe pedestrian/bicycle pathway system as an alternative means of transportation could offset some of the traffic demand on these nearby streets and lessen the increase in traffic congestion."

The question for us is whether these findings are constitutionally sufficient to justify the conditions imposed by the city on petitioner's building permit. Since state courts have been dealing with this question a good deal longer than we have, we turn to representative decisions made by them. In some States, very generalized statements as to the necessary connection between the required dedication and the proposed development seem to suffice.

We think this standard is too lax to adequately protect petitioner's right to just compensation if her property is taken for a public purpose. Other state courts require a very exacting correspondence, described as the "specifi[c] and uniquely attributable" test. The Supreme Court of Illinois first developed this test in Pioneer Trust & Savings Bank v. Mount Prospect, 22 Ill.2d 375, 380, 176 N.E.2d 799, 802 (1961).[3] Under this standard, if the local government cannot demonstrate that its exaction is directly proportional to the specifically created need, the exaction becomes "a veiled exercise of the power of eminent domain and a confiscation of private property behind the defense of police regulations." We do not

3. The "specifically and uniquely attributable" test has now been adopted by a minority of other courts. See, e.g., J.E.D. Associates., Inc. v. Atkinson, 121 N.H. 581, 585, 432 A.2d 12, 15 (1981); Divan Builders, Inc. v. Planning Bd. of Twp. of Wayne, 66 N.J. 582, 600–601, 334 A.2d 30, 40 (1975); McKain v. Toledo City Plan Comm'n, 26 Ohio App.2d 171, 176, 270 N.E.2d 370, 374 (1971); Frank Ansuini, Inc. v. Cranston, 107 R.I. 63, 69, 264 A.2d 910, 913 (1970).

think the Federal Constitution requires such exacting scrutiny, given the nature of the interests involved.

A number of state courts have taken an intermediate position, requiring the municipality to show a "reasonable relationship" between the required dedication and the impact of the proposed development. Typical is the Supreme Court of Nebraska's opinion in Simpson v. North Platte, 206 Neb. 240, 245, 292 N.W.2d 297, 301 (1980), where that court stated: "The distinction, therefore, which must be made between an appropriate exercise of the police power and an improper exercise of eminent domain is whether the requirement has some reasonable relationship or nexus to the use to which the property is being made or is merely being used as an excuse for taking property simply because at that particular moment the landowner is asking the city for some license or permit." Thus, the court held that a city may not require a property owner to dedicate private property for some future public use as a condition of obtaining a building permit when such future use is not "occasioned by the construction sought to be permitted."

Some form of the reasonable relationship test has been adopted in many other jurisdictions. See, e.g., Jordan v. Menomonee Falls, 28 Wis.2d 608, 137 N.W.2d 442 (1965); Collis v. Bloomington, 310 Minn. 5, 246 N.W.2d 19 (1976) (requiring a showing of a reasonable relationship between the planned subdivision and the municipality's need for land).…

We think the "reasonable relationship" test adopted by a majority of the state courts is closer to the federal constitutional norm than either of those previously discussed. But we do not adopt it as such, partly because the term "reasonable relationship" seems confusingly similar to the term "rational basis" which describes the minimal level of scrutiny under the Equal Protection Clause of the Fourteenth Amendment. We think a term such as "rough proportionality" best encapsulates what we hold to be the requirement of the Fifth Amendment. No precise mathematical calculation is required, but the city must make some sort of individualized determination that the required dedication is related both in nature and extent to the impact of the proposed development. * * *

It is axiomatic that increasing the amount of impervious surface will increase the quantity and rate of storm-water flow from petitioner's property. Therefore, keeping the floodplain open and free from development would likely confine the pressures on Fanno Creek created by petitioner's development. In fact, because petitioner's property lies within the Central Business District, the Community Development Code already required that petitioner leave 15% of it as open space and the undeveloped floodplain would have nearly satisfied that requirement. But the city demanded more—it not only wanted petitioner not to build in the floodplain, but it also wanted petitioner's property along Fanno Creek for its Greenway system. The city has never said why a public greenway, as opposed to a private one, was required in the interest of flood control.

The difference to petitioner, of course, is the loss of her ability to exclude others. As we have noted, this right to exclude others is "one of the most essential sticks in the bundle of rights that are commonly characterized as property." *Kaiser Aetna*, 444 U.S., at 176. It is difficult to see why recreational visitors trampling along petitioner's floodplain easement are sufficiently related to the city's legitimate interest in reducing flooding problems along Fanno Creek, and the city has not attempted to make any individualized determination to support this part of its request.

The city contends that the recreational easement along the Greenway is only ancillary to the city's chief purpose in controlling flood hazards. It further asserts that unlike the residential property at issue in Nollan, petitioner's property is commercial in character and therefore, her right to exclude others is compromised. * * * The city maintains that "[t]here is nothing to suggest that preventing [petitioner] from prohibiting [the easements] will unreasonably impair the value of [her] property as a [retail store]." *PruneYard*, 447 U.S. 74, 83 (1980).

Admittedly, petitioner wants to build a bigger store to attract members of the public to her property. She also wants, however, to be able to control the time and manner in which they enter. The recreational easement on the Greenway is different in character from the exercise of state-protected rights of free expression and petition that we permitted in *PruneYard*. In *PruneYard*, we held that a major private shopping center that attracted more than 25,000 daily patrons had to provide access to persons exercising their state constitutional rights to distribute pamphlets and ask passersby to sign their petitions. We based our decision, in part, on the fact that the shopping center "may restrict expressive activity by adopting time, place, and manner regulations that will minimize any interference with its commercial functions." By contrast, the city wants to impose a permanent recreational easement upon petitioner's property that borders Fanno Creek. Petitioner would lose all rights to regulate the time in which the public entered onto the Greenway, regardless of any interference it might pose with her retail store. Her right to exclude would not be regulated, it would be eviscerated.

If petitioner's proposed development had somehow encroached on existing greenway space in the city, it would have been reasonable to require petitioner to provide some alternative greenway space for the public either on her property or elsewhere. See *Nollan*, 483 U.S. at 836 ("Although such a requirement, constituting a permanent grant of continuous access to the property, would have to be considered a taking if it were not attached to a development permit, the Commission's assumed power to forbid construction of the house in order to protect the public's view of the beach must surely include the power to condition construction upon some concession by the owner, even a concession of property rights, that serves the same end"). But that is not the case here. We conclude that the findings upon which the city relies do not show the required reasonable relationship between the floodplain easement and the petitioner's proposed new building.

With respect to the pedestrian/bicycle pathway, we have no doubt that the city was correct in finding that the larger retail sales facility proposed by petitioner will increase traffic on the streets of the Central Business District. The city estimates that the proposed development would generate roughly 435 additional trips per day. Dedications for streets, sidewalks, and other public ways are generally reasonable exactions to avoid excessive congestion from a proposed property use. But on the record before us, the city has not met its burden of demonstrating that the additional number of vehicle and bicycle trips generated by the petitioner's development reasonably relate to the city's requirement for a dedication of the pedestrian/bicycle pathway easement. The city simply found that the creation of the pathway "could offset some of the traffic demand . . . and lessen the increase in traffic congestion." * * *

IV

Cities have long engaged in the commendable task of land use planning, made necessary by increasing urbanization particularly in metropolitan areas such as Portland. The city's goals of reducing flooding hazards and traffic congestion, and providing for public greenways, are laudable, but there are outer limits to how this may be done. "A strong public desire to improve the public condition [will not] warrant achieving the desire by a shorter cut than the constitutional way of paying for the change." *Pennsylvania Coal*, 260 U.S., at 416.

The judgment of the Supreme Court of Oregon is reversed, and the case is remanded for further proceedings consistent with this opinion.

[*A dissenting opinion by Justice Stevens, joined by Justices Blackmun and Ginsburg, is omitted.*]

NOTES AND QUESTIONS

1. Ever since the decision in Lochner v. New York, 198 U.S. 45 (1905) was repudiated in 1937, the Supreme Court has stated that it would defer to legislative findings of facts pertaining to the public interest. Do *Nollan* and *Dolan* undermine that tradition, or does the tradition simply not apply in takings cases? Lower court decisions subsequent to *Nollan* generally conclude that facts determined by the legislative body are subject to full review by the court. For example, see William J. Jones Ins. Trust v. City of Fort Smith, 731 F.Supp. 912 (W.D.Ark.1990), which applied *Nollan* to condemn a city's refusal to permit the plaintiff to add a convenience store to his gasoline station unless he dedicated an easement to the city for purposes of widening the street. The court rejected the city's fact finding that the business would increase traffic along the street, and that this fact satisfied *Nollan*'s requirement of a nexus between the government's demand and any increased public burden caused by the landowner's request. Rather, *Nollan* required the City to show:

> that plaintiff's planned expansion of its business will create additional burdens on the present public right-of-way along Phoenix Avenue. In other words, *Nollan* teaches that the City may constitutionally "tax"

plaintiff to recoup the costs of the negative externalities that its increased business activities cause: Without a showing of such externalities, the condition which the City attaches to building permits is simple extortion. Perhaps it is not necessary for the City to show an exact, mathematical, one-to-one correspondence between increased burden and tax, though it is plain that any clearly disproportionate tax would run afoul of the Fifth Amendment.

From that point on, however, the federal court weighed and balanced the evidence for itself, finding that the testimony was conflicting but that a "reasonable fact finder could conclude" that the city's exaction was excessive. 731 F.Supp. at 914.

2. In Sparks v. Douglas County, 127 Wash.2d 901, 904 P.2d 738 (1995), the Washington Supreme Court applied the *Dolan* test and concluded that no taking had occurred. In this case, the government conditioned a development permit on the land owner's dedication of some strips of land for road improvements. Although the road improvements were not going to be undertaken immediately, it was thought that they would be required in the future. The court observed:

It is not clear whether, under *Dolan*, municipalities may take into account future developments and their anticipated cumulative impacts.... At any rate, the determinative issue in this case is not future use, but the degree of connection between the County's exaction and the impact of the developments.

While *Dolan* disregarded precise calculations in analyzing development impacts, it ruled that local government must make some effort to quantify its findings to support its permit conditions. In this case, the findings made by the County were more than mere conclusory statements of general impact. They were the result of the kind of individualized analysis required under *Dolan*. The report prepared by the Planning Office for each of the short plats documented the deficiencies in right of way width and surfacing of the adjoining streets. Douglas County's records also reflect calculation of increase in traffic and the specific need for dedication of rights-of-way based upon the individual and cumulative impacts of the series of short subdivisions.

The findings upon which the County relies reflect the required rough proportionality between the exactions and the impact of the Respondents' proposed developments. It is undisputed that the developments would generate increased traffic on adjacent roads which are not adequate for safe access under county standards. The County has, in the process of individualized analysis, satisfied the final step of the *Dolan* test.

Respondents argue that the substandard conditions of the roads existed even prior to the Sparkses' plat applications and cannot therefore be caused by their proposed developments. But it has been established that the increase in traffic generated by those plats on already unsafe roads would require additional right-of-way and reconstruction to accommodate the overflow. The adverse impact created by the plats on adjacent roads was concluded by the trial court upon substantial evidence and need not be re-examined by this Court.

127 Wash.2d at 915–916, 904 P.2d at 745–746. See also Hallmark Inns & Resorts, Inc. v. City of Lake Oswego, 193 Or.App. 24, 88 P.3d 284 (2004), which found that both the nexus and "rough proportionality" requirements were met when the City insisted on a pedestrian walkway across the landowner's property as a condition of permitting it to enlarge the property for use as a corporate headquarters. The court credited the City's fact findings that there would be both increased vehicular and pedestrian traffic after the enlargement, and that the landowner's own employees needed access to local shops.

3. In Yee v. City of Escondido, 503 U.S. 519, 520 (1992), the Supreme Court refused to find a trespassory taking on the following facts. A state statute prohibited landlords from terminating mobile home lot tenancies (except for enumerated reasons, such as nonpayment of rent) unless the landlords were taking the land off the market altogether. The statute also required landlords to permit mobile homes sitting on these lots to be transferred to others. The City then passed an ordinance regulating the maximum rents that could be charged for mobile home lots. The combination of the two statutes created the bizarre and perhaps unintended consequence that the benefits of the rent control often accrued to the *sellers* of the mobile home rather than the actual tenants. For example, suppose Sandra has a lease on a mobile home lot which has a market value of $250 per month, but under the rent control ordinance she pays only $100. She also has a mobile home on this lot and Randall wishes to buy it. Under the statutory scheme Randall is entitled to a transfer of Sandra's lease on the lot and may not be charged higher rent. As a result, Randall will pay a premium for Sandra's mobile home—for example, if the mobile home alone has a value of $10,000, Randall might be willing to pay $12,000 because the home is accompanied by a leasehold on the lot at a $150 per month discount.

The petitioner lot owners argued that this scheme amounted to a forced physical invasion of their lots, since they could not terminate the tenancies except by going out of business altogether. In rejecting that claim, the Court noted that

> Petitioners voluntarily rented their land to mobile home owners. At least on the face of the regulatory scheme, neither the City nor the State compels petitioners, once they have rented their property to tenants, to continue doing so. To the contrary, the Mobilehome Residency Law provides that a park owner who wishes to change the use of his land may evict his tenants, albeit with six or twelve months notice. Cal. Civ. Code Ann. § 798.56(g). Put bluntly, no government has required any physical invasion of petitioners' property. Petitioners' tenants were invited by petitioners, not forced upon them by the government.

The Court then suggested that the California courts decide whether the statutory scheme constituted a *regulatory* taking, under standards developed *infra*.

§ 10.2.2   TAKING BY REGULATION

Consider this statement from the Supreme Court's decision in Tahoe–Sierra Preservation Council, Inc. v. Tahoe Regional Planning Agency (TRPA), 535 U.S. 302 (2002):

> The text of the Fifth Amendment itself provides a basis for drawing a distinction between physical takings and regulatory takings. Its plain language requires the payment of compensation whenever the government acquires private property for a public purpose, whether the acquisition is the result of a condemnation proceeding or a physical appropriation. But the Constitution contains no comparable reference to regulations that prohibit a property owner from making certain uses of her private property. Our jurisprudence involving condemnations and physical takings is as old as the Republic and, for the most part, involves the straightforward application of per se rules. Our regulatory takings jurisprudence, in contrast, is of more recent vintage and is characterized by "essentially ad hoc, factual inquiries. . . ."

Historically, the Fifth Amendment was intended to cover explicit exercises of the eminent domain power, governmental trespasses, and forcible transfers of title. According to St. George Tucker, Blackstone's first American editor and one of the earliest historians of the Amendment, its only real purpose was "to restrain the arbitrary and oppressive mode of obtaining supplies for the army, and other public uses, by impressment, as was too frequently practiced during the revolutionary war." 1 W. Blackstone, Commentaries on the Laws of England *139 (Tucker ed., 1803). The Continental Army was notoriously underpaid and under-supplied, and the soldiers were frequently forced to take what they needed from local farmers and other property owners. See Respublica v. Sparhawk, 1 U.S. 357 (1788), concluding that in times of war the army was entitled to help itself to privately owned provisions without paying compensation.

Because the Fifth Amendment was not made applicable to the states until the 1890s, there are few nineteenth century Supreme Court decisions interpreting the takings clause. However, there are a couple, and there are several others interpreting similar clauses in state constitutions. Without exception, they conclude that the government need not pay compensation for merely regulating or reducing the value of property. See Smith v. Washington, 61 U.S. 135 (1857) (no compensation for "consequential damage" when federal municipality graded and landscaped in front of, but not on, plaintiff's land); Northern Transportation Co. v. Chicago, 99 U.S. 635 (1878) (no compensation when municipality's excavation along dock denied land owner access to his primary entrance, making the property commercially useless); Mugler v. Kansas, 123 U.S. 623 (1887) (no compensation due when state statute closed liquor stills that were legal when built, and property was much less valuable as a result of still's closure); Gibson v. United States, 166 U.S. 269 (1897) (if government actually floods plaintiff's land there is a taking; but here the flooding was adjacent to the land and merely destroyed access, reducing its value from $600/acre to $200/acre; no compensation due); Hadacheck v. Sebastian, 239 U.S. 394 (1915) (no compensation due when city closes down brick kiln that was lawful when built). However, the Court awarded compensation when a government act imposed a trespass on the land owner's property: Pumpelly v. Green Bay Co., 80 U.S. 166 (1871) (compensation due when government's dam project actually flooded plaintiff's land)

The following decision is often cited as the first time the Supreme Court condemned a purely regulatory taking. Does it qualify for that distinction?

PENNSYLVANIA COAL CO. v. MAHON

Supreme Court of the United States (1922).
260 U.S. 393.

MR. JUSTICE HOLMES delivered the opinion of the Court.

This is a bill in equity brought by the defendants in error to prevent the Pennsylvania Coal Company from mining under their property in such way as to remove the supports and cause a subsidence of the surface and of their house. The bill sets out a deed executed by the Coal Company in 1878, under which the plaintiffs claim. The deed conveys the surface but in express terms reserves the right to remove all the coal under the same and the grantee takes the premises with the risk and waives all claim for damages that may arise from mining out the coal. But the plaintiffs say that whatever may have been the Coal Company's rights, they were taken away by an Act of Pennsylvania, approved May 27, 1921 (P. L. 1198), commonly known there as the Kohler Act. * * *

The statute forbids the mining of anthracite coal in such way as to cause the subsidence of, among other things, any structure used as a human habitation, with certain exceptions, including among them land where the surface is owned by the owner of the underlying coal and is distant more than one hundred and fifty feet from any improved property belonging to any other person. As applied to this case the statute is admitted to destroy previously existing rights of property and contract. The question is whether the police power can be stretched so far.

Government hardly could go on if to some extent values incident to property could not be diminished without paying for every such change in the general law. As long recognized some values are enjoyed under an implied limitation and must yield to the police power. But obviously the implied limitation must have its limits or the contract and due process clauses are gone. One fact for consideration in determining such limits is the extent of the diminution. When it reaches a certain magnitude, in most if not in all cases there must be an exercise of eminent domain and compensation to sustain the act. So the question depends upon the particular facts. The greatest weight is given to the judgment of the legislature but it always is open to interested parties to contend that the legislature has gone beyond its constitutional power.

This is the case of a single private house. No doubt there is a public interest even in this, as there is in every purchase and sale and in all that happens within the commonwealth. Some existing rights may be modified even in such a case. * * * But usually in ordinary private affairs the public interest does not warrant much of this kind of interference. A source of damage to such a house is not a public nuisance even if similar damage is inflicted on others in different places. The damage is not common or public. * * * The extent of the public interest is shown by the statute to be limited, since the statute ordinarily does not apply to land when the surface is owned by the owner of the coal. Furthermore, it is not justified as a protection of personal safety. That could be provided for by notice. Indeed the very foundation of this bill is that the defendant gave timely notice of its intent to mine under the house. On the other hand the extent of the taking is great. It purports to abolish what is recognized in Pennsylvania as an estate in land—a very valuable estate—and what is declared by the Court below to be a contract hitherto binding the plaintiffs. If we were called upon to deal with the plaintiffs' position alone we should think it clear that the statute does not disclose a public interest sufficient to warrant so extensive a destruction of the defendant's constitutionally protected rights. * * *

It is our opinion that the act cannot be sustained as an exercise of the police power, so far as it affects the mining of coal under streets or cities in places where the right to mine such coal has been reserved. As said in a Pennsylvania case, "For practical purposes, the right to coal consists in the right to mine it." Commonwealth v. Clearview Coal Co., 256 Pa. 328, 331, 100 Atl. 820, L. R. A. 1917E, 672. What makes the right to mine coal valuable is that it can be exercised with profit. To make it commercially impracticable to mine certain coal has very nearly the same effect for constitutional purposes as appropriating or destroying it. This we think that we are warranted in assuming that the statute does.

It is true that in Plymouth Coal Co. v. Pennsylvania, 232 U. S. 531, 34 Sup. Ct. 359, 58 L. Ed. 713, it was held competent for the legislature to require a pillar of coal to the left along the line of adjoining property, that with the pillar on the other side of the line would be a barrier sufficient for the safety of the employees of either mine in case the other should be abandoned and allowed to fill with water. But that was a requirement for the safety of employees invited into the mine, and secured an average reciprocity of advantage that has been recognized as a justification of various laws.

The rights of the public in a street purchased or laid out by eminent domain are those that it has paid for. If in any case its representatives have been so short sighted as to acquire only surface rights without the right of support we see no more authority for supplying the latter without compensation than there was for taking the right of way in the first place and refusing to pay for it because the public wanted it very much. The protection of private property in the Fifth Amendment presupposes that it is wanted for public use, but provides that it shall not be taken for such use without compensation. A similar assumption is made in the decisions upon the Fourteenth Amendment. Hairston v. Danville & Western Ry. Co., 208 U.S. 598, 605, 28 Sup.Ct. 331, 52 L.Ed. 637, 13 Ann. Cas. 1008. When this seemingly absolute protection is found to be qualified by the police power, the natural tendency of human nature is to extend the qualification more and more until at last private property disappears. But that cannot be accomplished in this way under the Constitution of the United States.

The general rule at least is that while property may be regulated to a certain extent, if regulation goes too far it will be recognized as a taking. It may be doubted how far exceptional cases, like the blowing up of a house to stop a conflagration, go—and if they go beyond the general rule, whether they do not stand as much upon tradition as upon principle. * * * In general it is not plain that a man's misfortunes or necessities will justify his shifting the damages to his neighbor's shoulders. We are in danger of forgetting that a strong public desire to improve the public condition is not enough to warrant achieving the desire by a shorter cut than the constitutional way of paying for the change. As we already have said this is a question of degree—and therefore cannot be disposed of by general propositions. But we regard this as going beyond any of the cases decided by this Court. The late decisions upon laws dealing with the congestion of Washington and New York, caused by the war, dealt with laws intended to meet a temporary emergency and providing for compensation determined to be reasonable by an impartial board. They were to the verge of the law but fell far short of the present act. Block & Hirsh, 256 U.S. 135, 41 Sup.Ct. 458, 65 L. Ed. 865, 16 A. L. R. 165; Marcus Brown Holding Co. v. Feldman, 256 U.S. 170, 41 Sup.Ct. 465, 65 L. Ed. 877; Levy Leasing Co. v. Siegel, 258 U.S. 242, 42 Sup.Ct. 289, 66 L. Ed. 595, March 20, 1922.

We assume, of course, that the statute was passed upon the conviction that an exigency existed that would warrant it, and we assume that an exigency exists that would warrant the exercise of eminent domain. But the question at bottom is upon whom the loss of the changes desired should fall. So far as private persons or communities have seen fit to take the risk of acquiring only surface rights, we cannot see that the fact that their risk has become a danger warrants the giving to them greater rights than they bought.

Decree reversed.

Mr. Justice Brandeis dissenting.

The Kohler Act prohibits, under certain conditions, the mining of anthracite coal within the limits of a city in such a manner or to such an extent "as to cause the * * * subsidence of * * * any dwelling or other structure used as a human habitation, or any factory, store, or other industrial or mercantile establishment in which human labor is employed." Coal in place is land, and the right of the owner to use his land is not absolute. He may not so use it as to create a public nuisance, and uses, once harmless, may, owing to changed conditions, seriously threaten the public welfare. Whenever they do, the Legislature has power to prohibit such uses without paying compensation; and the power to prohibit extends alike to the manner, the character and the purpose of the use. Are we justified in declaring that the Legislature of Pennsylvania has, in restricting the right to mine anthracite, exercised this power so arbitrarily as to violate the Fourteenth Amendment?

Every restriction upon the use of property imposed in the exercise of the police power deprives the owner of some right theretofore enjoyed, and is, in that sense, an abridgment by the state of rights in property without making compensation. But restriction imposed to protect the public health, safety or morals from dangers threatened is not a taking. The restriction here in question is merely the prohibition of a noxious use. The property so restricted remains in the possession of its owner. The state does not appropriate it or make any use of it. The state merely prevents the owner from making a use which interferes with paramount rights of the public. Whenever the use prohibited ceases to be noxious—as it may because of further change in local or social conditions—the restriction will have to be removed and the owner will again be free to enjoy his property as heretofore.

The restriction upon the use of this property cannot, of course, be lawfully imposed, unless its purpose is to protect the public. But the purpose of a restriction does not cease to be public, because incidentally some private persons may thereby receive gratuitously valuable special benefits. Thus, owners of low buildings may obtain, through statutory restrictions upon the height of neighboring structures, benefits equivalent to an easement of light and air. Welch v. Swasey, 214 U.S. 91. * * * Furthermore, a restriction, though imposed for a public purpose, will not be lawful, unless the restriction is an appropriate means to the public end. But to keep coal in place is surely an appropriate means of preventing subsidence of the surface; and ordinarily it is the only available means. Restriction upon use does not become inappropriate as a means, merely because it deprives the owner of the only use to which the property can then be profitably put. The liquor and the oleomargarine cases settled that. Mugler v. Kansas, 123 U.S. 623; Powell v. Pennsylvania, 127 U.S. 678. * * * Nor is a restriction imposed through exercise of the police power inappropriate as a means, merely because the same end might be effected through exercise of the power of eminent domain, or otherwise at public expense. Every restriction upon the height of buildings might be secured through acquiring by eminent domain the right of each owner to build above the limiting height; but it is settled that the state need not resort to that power. * * * If by mining anthracite coal the owner would necessarily unloose poisonous gases, I suppose no one would doubt the power of the state to prevent the mining, without buying his coal fields.

And why may not the state, likewise, without paying compensation, prohibit one from digging so deep or excavating so near the surface, as to expose the community to like dangers? In the latter case, as in the former, carrying on the business would be a public nuisance.

It is said that one fact for consideration in determining whether the limits of the police power have been exceeded is the extent of the resulting diminution in value, and that here the restriction destroys existing rights of property and contract. But values are relative. If we are to consider the value of the coal kept in place by the restriction, we should compare it with the value of all other parts of the land. That is, with the value not of the coal alone, but with the value of the whole property. The rights of an owner as against the public are not increased by dividing the interests in his property into surface and subsoil. The sum of the rights in the parts can not be greater than the rights in the whole. The estate of an owner in land is grandiloquently described as extending ab orco usque ad coelum. But I suppose no one would contend that by selling his interest above 100 feet from the surface he could prevent the state from limiting, by the police power, the height of structures in a city. And why should a sale of underground rights bar the state's power? For aught that appears the value of the coal kept in place by the restriction may be negligible as compared with the value of the whole property, or even as compared with that part of it which is represented by the coal remaining in place and which may be extracted despite the statute. Ordinarily a police regulation, general in operation, will not be held void as to a particular property, although proof is offered that owing to conditions peculiar to it the restriction could not reasonably be applied. * * * Where the surface and the coal belong to the same person, self-interest would ordinarily prevent mining to such an extent as to cause a subsidence. It was, doubtless, for this reason that the Legislature, estimating the degrees of danger, deemed statutory restriction unnecessary for the public safety under such conditions.

It is said that this is a case of a single dwelling house, that the restriction upon mining abolishes a valuable estate hitherto secured by a contract with the plaintiffs, and that the restriction upon mining cannot be justified as a protection of personal safety, since that could be provided for by notice. * * * May we say that notice would afford adequate protection of the public safety where the Legislature and the highest court of the state, with greater knowledge of local conditions, have declared, in effect, that it would not? If the public safety is imperiled, surely neither grant, nor contract, can prevail against the exercise of the police power. * * *

A prohibition of mining which causes subsidence of such structures and facilities is obviously enacted for a public purpose; and it seems, likewise, clear that mere notice of intention to mine would not in this connection secure the public safety. Yet it is said that these provisions of the act cannot be sustained as an exercise of the police power where the right to mine such coal has been reserved. The conclusion seems to rest upon the assumption that in order to justify such exercise of the police power there must be "an average reciprocity of advantage" as between the owner of the property restricted and the rest of the community; and that here such reciprocity is absent. Reciprocity of advantage is an important consideration, and may even be an essential, where the state's power is exercised for the purpose of conferring benefits upon the property of a neighborhood. * * * But where the police power is exercised not to confer benefits upon property owners but to protect the public from detriment and danger, there is, in my opinion, no room for considering reciprocity of advantage. There was no reciprocal advantage to the owner prohibited from using his oil tanks in 248 U.S. 498; his brickyard, in 239 U.S. 394; his livery stable, in 237 U.S. 171; his billiard hall, in 225 U.S. 623; his oleomargarine factory, in 127 U.S. 678; his brewery, in 123 U.S. 623; unless it be the advantage of living and doing business in a civilized community. That reciprocal advantage is given by the act to the coal operators.

NOTES AND QUESTIONS

1. Did *Pennsylvania Coal* involve a purely "regulatory" taking, or something more? Pennsylvania law differed from that of all other states in recognizing three, rather than two, common law estates in mining property: the surface, the minerals, and a unique "third estate" which consisted of support rights for the surface. If one owner held both the surface estate and the third estate, the owner of the mineral rights was liable for any damage caused by sinking of the surface. Generally, the mining company could avoid such subsidence by leaving columns of unmined rock and minerals in the mine to hold up the surface. By contrast, if the owner of the minerals owned the third estate, then any problems of subsidence belonged to the owner of the surface. This made the surface far less valuable for development, although it might still be used for farming.

The Kohler Act effectively transferred the entire support estate from the coal company to the Mahons, by forcing the company to take the same precautions that would be necessary if the Mahons had owned the third estate. As Justice Holmes noted, the Act "purports to abolish what is recognized in Pennsylvania as an estate in land—a very valuable estate...." While the Takings Clause provides that "private property" may not be taken, it does not come with a glossary telling us what "private property" is. Further, most of the law of private property originates with the states. Holmes, the greatest historian of the common law who ever sat on the Supreme Court, adhered religiously to the position noted previously that in deciding whether a taking occurs under federal law one must first determine what the relevant state law is. In that case, the Kohler Act was a forcible transfer of an entire estate in land from one party to another, without compensation.

In very sharp contrast, *Keystone Bituminous Coal Assn. v. DeBenedictis*, 480 U.S. 470 (1987), looked at a very similar statute and proclaimed no taking. Pennsylvania still had its unique tripartite system of surface, mineral and "support" estates, but the Court concluded:

> Pennsylvania property law is apparently unique in regarding the support estate as a separate interest in land that can be conveyed apart from either the mineral estate or the surface estate. Petitioners therefore argue that even if comparable legislation in another State would not constitute a taking, the Subsidence Act has that consequence because it entirely destroys the value of their unique support estate. It is clear, however, that our takings jurisprudence forecloses reliance on such legalistic distinctions within a bundle of property rights.

But if the property rights in question do not come from state law, then where do they come from? More recently, in the *Lucas* decision, infra, the Supreme Court returned with a vengeance to Holmes' position that a person's "settled expectations" under the prevailing state law property regime must be the background for determining whether a taking has occurred.

2. The Denominator Problem: The *Pennsylvania Coal* decision discussed a "diminution in value" test for inverse condemnation, which is still used today. But diminution of what? If the support estate is worth $100,000 and the mineral estate is worth $1,000,000, then requiring the coal mining company to provide support takes 100 percent if the support estate is the denominator in the fraction, but only some nine percent if the entire value of the coal is the denominator. *Mahon* would make the support estate the denominator, while *Keystone, supra,* looked entirely at the value of the coal to be mined. Determining the proper denominator is critical. The larger the denominator, the less likely it is that a regulation will be found to result in a taking. The smaller the denominator, the more likely it is that a regulation will be found to result in a taking. The majority in *Pennsylvania Coal* segmented the estates, thereby reducing the size of the denominator, as discussed above. Justice Brandeis, dissenting, would not have segmented the estates. Fifty-six years later in Penn Central Transportation Co. v. New York City, 438 U.S. 104 (1978), infra, the Supreme Court revisited the denominator question. The Court adopted a non-segmentation approach, similar to the *Pennsylvania Coal* dissent. As you read *Penn Central*, next, see if you can find this important language in the decision.

Estates can be segmented: (1) vertically, see, e.g., *Pennsylvania Coal* and *Penn Central*; (2) horizontally, see, e.g., Palazzolo v. Rhode Island, discussed in the notes following the *Lucas* opinion, infra; or (3) temporarily, see, e.g., the discussion of development moratoria in Tahoe–Sierra Preservation Council, Inc. v. Tahoe Regional Planning Agency following the *Lucas* opinion, infra.

Trace the evolution of the denominator problem from *Pennsylvania Coal, Penn Central, Lucas, Palazzolo,* and *Tahoe–Sierra Preservation Council, Inc..* See Rose, *Mahon* Reconstructed: Why the Takings issue is Still A Muddle, 57 S.Cal.L.Rev. 561 (1984); see the discussion following the *Lucas* opinion, infra, of the Supreme Court's decisions in Palazzolo v. Rhode Island, 533 U.S. 606 (2001); and Tahoe–Sierra Preservation Council, Inc. v. Tahoe Regional Planning Agency (TRPA), 535 U.S. 302 (2002).

3. For other interesting historical and economic commentary on *Pennsylvania Coal,* see W. Fischel, Regulatory Takings: Law, Economics, and

Politics (Cambridge: Harv. Univ. Press, 1995); Brauneis, The Foundation of Our "Regulatory Takings" Jurisprudence: the Myth and Meaning of Justice Holmes's Opinion in *Pennsylvania Coal Co. v. Mahon*, 106 Yale L.J. 613 (1996); DiMento, Mining the Archives of *Pennsylvania Coal*: Heaps of Constitutional Mischief, 11 J. Legal Hist. 396 (1990).

4. What is the "average reciprocity of advantage" that the Court discusses? The average reciprocity of advantage concept has been most famously articulated in *Pennsylvania Coal*. Simply put, the concept describes an analysis of whether a regulatory restriction simultaneously burdens a property owner but also indirectly benefits the owner by imposing similar restrictions upon other property owners who are similarly situated. The classic example is residential zoning which requires all property owners to forego commercial uses of their property by imposing residential only zoning restrictions. Thus, everyone is burdened by the restriction because each individual's ability to use her property for commercial purposes is restricted. But, simultaneously, each property owner is benefited by the same restrictions that are imposed upon others and ensure each property owner that offensive, commercial enterprises will not be constructed next door. The dissent in *Pennsylvania Coal* states that the average reciprocity of advantage concept is applicable when the state exercises its power in order to confer benefits upon property owners. But, according to the dissent, it is not appropriate to apply the concept in a case such as the one before the Court in which the state is exercising its power "to protect the public from detriment and danger...." Is this distinction appropriate? Average reciprocity of advantage is raised again in *Penn Central,* infra.

5. The value of property is a function of the market. The ability to sell something is an important determinant of its value. Suppose that the government does nothing to acquire or to reduce the "intrinsic" value of an object but instead eliminates the *market* for that object, perhaps by making it illegal to buy it and sell it. Has a taking occurred? See Andrus v. Allard, 444 U.S. 51 (1979), which involved a challenge to the federal Eagle Protection Act, 16 U.S.C.A. § 668(a). The Act made it illegal for private owners to buy and sell objects containing eagle feathers, even if the feathers had previously been acquired legally.

PENN CENTRAL TRANSPORTATION CO. v. NEW YORK CITY

Supreme Court of the United States (1978).
438 U.S. 104.

MR. JUSTICE BRENNAN delivered the opinion of the Court.

The question presented is whether a city may, as part of a comprehensive program to preserve historic landmarks and historic districts, place restrictions on the development of individual historic landmarks—in addition to those imposed by applicable zoning ordinances—without effecting a "taking" requiring the payment of "just compensation." Specifically, we must decide whether the application of New York City's Landmarks Preservation Law to the parcel of land occupied by Grand Central Terminal has "taken" its owners' property in violation of the Fifth and Fourteenth Amendments.

I

Over the past 50 years, all 50 States and over 500 municipalities have enacted laws to encourage or require the preservation of buildings and areas with historic or aesthetic importance. These nationwide legislative efforts have been precipitated by two concerns. The first is recognition that, in recent years, large numbers of historic structures, landmarks, and areas have been destroyed without adequate consideration of either the values represented therein or the possibility of preserving the destroyed properties for use in economically productive ways. The second is a widely shared belief that structures with special historic, cultural, or architectural significance enhance the quality of life for all. Not only do these buildings and their workmanship represent the lessons of the past and embody precious features of our heritage, they serve as examples of quality for today. * * *

The New York City law is typical of many urban landmark laws in that its primary method of achieving its goals is not by acquisitions of historic properties, but rather by involving public entities in land-use decisions affecting these properties and providing services, standards, controls, and incentives that will encourage preservation by private owners and users. While the law does place special restrictions on landmark properties as a necessary feature to the attainment of its larger objectives, the major theme of the law is to ensure the owners of any such properties both a "reasonable return" on their investments and maximum latitude to use their parcels for purposes not inconsistent with the preservation goals.

The operation of the law can be briefly summarized. The primary responsibility for administering the law is vested in the Landmarks Preservation Commission (Commission), a broad based, 11–member agency assisted by a technical staff. The Commission first performs the function, critical to any landmark preservation effort, of identifying properties and areas that have "a special character or special historical or aesthetic interest or value as part of the development, heritage or cultural characteristics of the city, state or nation." If the Commission determines, after giving all interested parties an opportunity to be heard, that a building or area satisfies the ordinance's criteria, it will designate a building to be a "landmark," situated on a particular "landmark site," or will designate an area to be a "historic district," § 207–1.0(h). After the Commission makes a designation, New York City's Board of Estimate, after considering the relationship of the designated property "to the master plan, the zoning resolution, projected public improvements and any plans for the renewal of the area involved," may modify or disapprove the designation, and the owner may seek judicial review of the final designation decision. Thus far, 31 historic districts and over 400 individual landmarks have been finally designated, and the process is a continuing one.

Final designation as a landmark results in restrictions upon the property owner's options concerning use of the landmark site. First, the law imposes a duty upon the owner to keep the exterior features of the building "in good repair" to assure that the law's objectives not be defeated by the landmark's falling into a state of irremediable disrepair. Second, the Commission must approve in advance any proposal to alter the exterior architectural features of the landmark or to construct any exterior improvement on the landmark site, thus ensuring that decisions concerning construction on the landmark site are made with due consideration of both the public interest in the maintenance of the structure and the landowner's interest in use of the property. * * *

Although the designation of a landmark and landmark site restricts the owner's control over the parcel, designation also enhances the economic position of the landmark owner in one significant respect. Under New York City's zoning laws, owners of real property who have not developed their property to the full extent permitted by the applicable zoning laws are allowed to transfer development rights to contiguous parcels on the same city block. See New York City, Zoning Resolution Art. I, ch. 2, § 12–10 (1978) (definition of "zoning lot"). A 1968 ordinance gave the owners of landmark sites additional opportunities to transfer development rights to other parcels. Subject to a restriction that the floor area of the transferee lot may not be increased by more than 20% above its authorized level, the ordinance permitted transfers from a landmark parcel to property across the street or across a street intersection. In 1969, the law governing the conditions under which transfers from landmark parcels could occur was liberalized, see New York City Zoning Resolutions 74–79 to 74–793, apparently to ensure that the Landmarks Law would not unduly restrict the development options of the owners of Grand Central Terminal. See Marcus, Air Rights Transfers in New York City, 36 Law & Contemp.Prob. 372, 375 (1971). The class of recipient lots was expanded to include lots "across a street and opposite to another lot or lots which except for the intervention of streets or street intersections f[or]m a series extending to the lot occupied by the landmark building[, provided that] all lots [are] in the same ownership." In addition, the 1969 amendment permits, in highly commercialized areas like midtown Manhattan, the transfer of all unused development rights to a single parcel.

This case involves the application of New York City's Landmarks Preservation Law to Grand Central Terminal (Terminal). The Terminal, which is owned by the Penn Central Transportation Co. and its affiliates (Penn Central), is one of New York City's most famous buildings. Opened in 1913, it is regarded not only as providing an ingenious engineering solution to the problems presented by urban railroad stations, but also as a magnificent example of the French beaux-arts style.

The Terminal is located in midtown Manhattan. Its south facade faces 42d Street and that street's intersection with Park Avenue. At street level, the Terminal is bounded on the west by Vanderbilt Avenue, on the east by the Commodore Hotel, and on the north by the Pan–American Building.

Although a 20–story office tower, to have been located above the Terminal, was part of the original design, the planned tower was never constructed. The Terminal itself is an eight-story structure which Penn Central uses as a railroad station and in which it rents space not needed for railroad purposes to a variety of commercial interests. The Terminal is one of a number of properties owned by appellant Penn Central in this area of midtown Manhattan. The others include the Barclay, Biltmore, Commodore, Roosevelt, and Waldorf–Astoria Hotels, the Pan–American Building and other office buildings along Park Avenue, and the Yale Club. At least eight of these are eligible to be recipients of development rights afforded the Terminal by virtue of landmark designation.

* * *

Penn Central * * * applied to the Commission for permission to construct an office building atop the Terminal. Two separate plans, both designed by architect Marcel Breuer and both apparently satisfying the terms of the applicable zoning ordinance, were submitted to the Commission for approval. The first, Breuer I, provided for the construction of a 55–story office building, to be cantilevered above the existing facade and to rest on the roof of the Terminal. The second, Breuer II Revised, called for tearing down a portion of the Terminal that included the 42d Street facade, stripping off some of the remaining features of the Terminal's facade, and constructing a 53–story office building. The Commission denied [the request] on September 20, 1968.

* * *

The Commission's reasons for rejecting certificates are summarized in the following statement: "To protect a Landmark, one does not tear it down. To perpetuate its architectural features, one does not strip them off."

* * *

Appellants sought a declaratory judgment [and] injunctive relief. . . .

II

The issues presented by appellants are (1) whether the restrictions imposed by New York City's law upon appellants' exploitation of the Terminal site effect a "taking" of appellants' property for a public use within the meaning of the Fifth Amendment, which of course is made applicable to the States through the Fourteenth Amendment, and, (2), if so, whether the transferable development rights afforded appellants constitute "just compensation" within the meaning of the Fifth Amendment. We need only address the question whether a "taking" has occurred.

A

Before considering appellants' specific contentions, it will be useful to review the factors that have shaped the jurisprudence of the Fifth Amendment injunction "nor shall private property be taken for public use, without just compensation." The question of what constitutes a "taking" for purposes of the Fifth Amendment has proved to be a problem of considerable difficulty. While this Court has recognized that the "Fifth Amendment's guarantee . . . [is] designed to bar Government from forcing some people alone to bear public burdens which, in all fairness and justice, should be borne by the public as a whole," Armstrong v. United States, 364 U.S. 40, 49, 80 S.Ct. 1563, 1569, 4 L.Ed.2d 1554 (1960), this Court, quite simply, has been unable to develop any "set formula" for determining when "justice and fairness" require that economic injuries caused by public action be compensated by the government, rather than remain disproportionately concentrated on a few persons. See Goldblatt v. Hempstead, 369 U.S. 590, 594, 82 S.Ct. 987, 990, 8 L.Ed.2d 130 (1962). Indeed, we have frequently observed that whether a particular restriction will be rendered invalid by the government's failure to pay for any losses proximately caused by it depends largely "upon the particular circumstances [in that] case." United States v. Central Eureka Mining Co., 357 U.S. 155, 168, 78 S.Ct. 1097, 1104, 2 L.Ed.2d 1228 (1958).

In engaging in these essentially ad hoc, factual inquiries, the Court's decisions have identified several factors that have particular significance. The economic impact of the regulation on the claimant and, particularly, the extent to which the regulation has interfered with distinct investment-backed expectations are, of course, relevant considerations. So, too, is the character of the governmental action. A "taking" may more readily be found when the interference with property can be characterized as a physical invasion by government, see, e.g., United States v. Causby, 328 U.S. 256, 66 S.Ct. 1062, 90 L.Ed. 1206 (1946), than when interference arises from some public program adjusting the benefits and burdens of economic life to promote the common good.

* * *

Zoning laws generally do not affect existing uses of real property, but "taking" challenges have also been held to be without merit in a wide variety of situations when the challenged governmental actions prohibited a beneficial use to which individual parcels had previously been devoted and thus caused substantial individualized harm. Miller v. Schoene, 276 U.S. 272, 48 S.Ct. 246, 72 L.Ed. 568 (1928), is illustrative. In that case, a state entomologist, acting pursuant to a state statute, ordered the claimants to cut down a large number of ornamental red cedar trees because they produced cedar rust fatal to apple trees cultivated nearby. Although the statute provided for recovery of any expense incurred in removing the cedars, and permitted claimants to use the felled trees, it did not provide compensation for the value of the standing trees or for the resulting decrease in market value of the properties as a whole. A unanimous Court held that this latter omission did not render the statute invalid. The Court held that the State might properly make "a choice between the preservation of one class of property and that of the other" and since the apple industry was important in the State involved, concluded that the State had not exceeded "its constitutional powers by deciding upon the destruction of one class of property [without compensation] in order to save another which, in the judgment of the legislature, is of greater value to the public."

* * *

B

In contending that the New York City law has "taken" their property in violation of the Fifth and Fourteenth Amendments, appellants make a series of arguments, which, while tailored to the facts of this case, essentially urge that any substantial restriction imposed pursuant to a landmark law must be accompanied by just compensation if it is to be constitutional.

* * *

They first observe that the airspace above the Terminal is a valuable property interest, citing United States v. Causby, supra. They urge that the Landmarks Law has deprived them of any gainful use of their "air rights" above the Terminal and that, irrespective of the value of the remainder of their parcel, the city has "taken" their right to this superadjacent airspace, thus entitling them to "just compensation" measured by the fair market value of these air rights.

Apart from our own disagreement with appellants' characterization of the effect of the New York City law, the submission that appellants may establish a "taking" simply by showing that they have been denied the ability to exploit a property interest that they heretofore had believed was available for development is quite simply untenable. Were this the rule, this Court would have erred not only in upholding laws restricting the development of air rights, but also in approving those prohibiting both the subjacent, see Goldblatt v. Hempstead, 369 U.S. 590, 82 S.Ct. 987, 8 L.Ed.2d 130 (1962), and the lateral, see Gorieb v. Fox, 274 U.S. 603, 47 S.Ct. 675, 71 L.Ed. 1228 (1927), development of particular parcels. "Taking" jurisprudence does not divide a single parcel into discrete segments and attempt to determine whether rights in a particular segment have been entirely abrogated. In deciding whether a particular governmental action has effected a taking, this Court focuses rather both on the character of the action and on the nature and extent of the interference with rights in the parcel as a whole—here, the city tax block designated as the "landmark site."

Secondly, appellants, focusing on the character and impact of the New York City law, argue that it effects a "taking" because its operation has significantly diminished the value of the Terminal site. Appellants concede that the decisions sustaining other land use regulations, which, like the New York City law, are reasonably related to the promotion of the general welfare, uniformly reject the proposition that diminution in property value, standing alone, can establish a "taking," see Euclid v. Ambler

Realty Co., 272 U.S. 365, 47 S.Ct. 114, 71 L.Ed. 303 (1926) (75% diminution in value caused by zoning law); Hadacheck v. Sebastian, 239 U.S. 394, 36 S.Ct. 143, 60 L.Ed. 348 (1915) (87½% diminution in value).

* * *

Appellants, moreover, also do not dispute that a showing of diminution in property value would not establish a taking if the restriction had been imposed as a result of historic-district legislation, but appellants argue that New York City's regulation of individual landmarks is fundamentally different from zoning or from historic-district legislation because the controls imposed by New York City's law apply only to individuals who own selected properties.

Stated baldly, appellants' position appears to be that the only means of ensuring that selected owners are not singled out to endure financial hardship for no reason is to hold that any restriction imposed on individual landmarks pursuant to the New York City scheme is a "taking" requiring the payment of "just compensation." Agreement with this argument would, of course, invalidate not just New York City's law, but all comparable landmark legislation in the Nation. We find no merit in it.

It is true, as appellants emphasize, that both historic-district legislation and zoning laws regulate all properties within given physical communities whereas landmark laws apply only to selected parcels. But, contrary to appellants' suggestions, landmark laws are not like discriminatory, or "reverse spot," zoning: that is, a land-use decision which arbitrarily singles out a particular parcel for different, less favorable treatment than the neighboring ones. See 2 A. Rathkopf, The Law of Zoning and Planning 26–4, and n. 6 (4th ed. 1978). In contrast to discriminatory zoning, which is the antithesis of land-use control as part of some comprehensive plan, the New York City law embodies a comprehensive plan to preserve structures of historic or aesthetic interest wherever they might be found in the city, and as noted, over 400 landmarks and 31 historic districts have been designated pursuant to this plan.

* * *

Next, appellants observe that New York City's law differs from zoning laws and historic-district ordinances in that the Landmarks Law does not impose identical or similar restrictions on all structures located in particular physical communities. It follows, they argue, that New York City's law is inherently incapable of producing the fair and equitable distribution of benefits and burdens of governmental action which is characteristic of zoning laws and historic-district legislation and which they maintain is a constitutional requirement if "just compensation" is not to be afforded. It is, of course, true that the Landmarks Law has a more severe impact on some landowners than on others, but that in itself does not mean that the law effects a "taking." Legislation designed to promote the general welfare commonly burdens some more than others. The owners of the brickyard in *Hadacheck,* of the cedar trees in Miller v. Schoene, and of the gravel and sand mine in Goldblatt v. Hempstead, were uniquely burdened by the legislation sustained in those cases. Similarly, zoning laws often affect some property owners more severely than others but have not been held to be invalid on that account. For example, the property owner in *Euclid* who wished to use its property for industrial purposes was affected far more severely by the ordinance than its neighbors who wished to use their land for residences.

* * *

Appellants' final broad-based attack would have us treat the law as an instance, like that in United States v. Causby, in which government, acting in an enterprise capacity, has appropriated part of their property for some strictly governmental purpose. Apart from the fact that *Causby* was a case of invasion of airspace that destroyed the use of the farm beneath and this New York City law has in nowise impaired the present use of the Terminal, the Landmarks Law neither exploits appellants' parcel for city purposes nor facilitates nor arises from any entrepreneurial operations of the city. The situation is not remotely like that in *Causby* where the airspace above the property was in the flight pattern for military aircraft. The Landmarks Law's effect is simply to prohibit appellants or anyone else from occupying portions of the airspace above the Terminal, while permitting appellants to use the remainder of the parcel in a gainful fashion.

C

Rejection of appellants' broad arguments is not, however, the end of our inquiry, for all we thus far have established is that the New York City law is not rendered invalid by its failure to provide "just compensation" whenever a landmark owner is restricted in the exploitation of property interests, such as air rights, to a greater extent than provided for under applicable zoning laws. We now must consider whether the interference with appellants' property is of such a magnitude that "there must be an exercise of eminent domain and compensation to sustain [it]." Pennsylvania Coal Co. v. Mahon, 260 U.S., at 413, 43 S.Ct., at 159. That inquiry may be narrowed to the question of the severity of the impact of the law on appellants' parcel, and its resolution in turn requires a careful assessment of the impact of the regulation on the Terminal site.

[T]he New York City law does not interfere in any way with the present uses of the Terminal. Its designation as a landmark not only permits but contemplates that appellants may continue to use the property precisely as it has been used for the past 65 years: as a railroad terminal containing office space and concessions. So the law does not interfere with what must be regarded as Penn Central's primary expectation concerning the use of the parcel. More importantly, on this record, we must regard the New York City law as permitting Penn Central not only to profit from the Terminal but also to obtain a "reasonable return" on its investment.

Appellants, moreover, exaggerate the effect of the law on their ability to make use of the air rights above the Terminal in two respects. First, it simply cannot be maintained, on this record, that appellants have been prohibited from occupying *any* portion of the airspace above the Terminal. While the Commission's actions in denying applications to construct an office building in excess of 50 stories above the Terminal may indicate that it will refuse to issue a certificate of appropriateness for any comparably sized structure, nothing the Commission has said or done suggests an intention to prohibit *any* construction above the Terminal. The Commission's report emphasized that whether any construction would be allowed depended upon whether the proposed addition "would harmonize in scale, material and character with [the Terminal]." Since appellants have not sought approval for the construction of a smaller structure, we do not know that appellants will be denied any use of any portion of the airspace above the Terminal.

Second, to the extent appellants have been denied the right to build above the Terminal, it is not literally accurate to say that they have been denied *all* use of even those pre-existing air rights. Their ability to use these rights has not been abrogated; they are made transferable to at least eight parcels in the vicinity of the Terminal, one or two of which have been found suitable for the construction of new office buildings. Although appellants and others have argued that New York City's transferable development-rights program is far from ideal, the New York courts here supportably found that, at least in the case of the Terminal, the rights afforded are valuable. While these rights may well not have constituted "just compensation" if a "taking" had occurred, the rights nevertheless undoubtedly mitigate whatever financial burdens the law has imposed on appellants and, for that reason, are to be taken into account in considering the impact of regulation. Cf. Goldblatt v. Hempstead, 369 U.S., at 594 n. 3, 82 S.Ct., at 990 n. 3.

On this record, we conclude that the application of New York City's Landmarks Law has not effected a "taking" of appellants' property. The restrictions imposed are substantially related to the promotion of the general welfare and not only permit reasonable beneficial use of the landmark site but also afford appellants opportunities further to enhance not only the Terminal site proper but also other properties.

Affirmed.

MR. JUSTICE REHNQUIST, with whom THE CHIEF JUSTICE [BURGER] and MR. JUSTICE STEVENS join, dissenting.

* * *

Only in the most superficial sense of the word can this case be said to involve "zoning." Typical zoning restrictions may, it is true, so limit the prospective uses of a piece of property as to diminish the value of that property in the abstract because it may not be used for the forbidden purposes. But any such abstract decrease in value will more than likely be at least partially offset by an increase in value which flows from similar restrictions as to use on neighboring properties. All property owners in a designated area are placed under the same restrictions, not only for the benefit of the municipality as a whole but also for the common benefit of one another. In the words of Mr. Justice Holmes, speaking for the Court in Pennsylvania Coal Co. v. Mahon, 260 U.S. 393, 415, 43 S.Ct. 158, 160, 67 L.Ed. 322 (1922), there is "an average reciprocity of advantage."

Where a relatively few individual buildings, all separated from one another, are singled out and treated differently from surrounding buildings, no such reciprocity exists. The cost to the property owner which results from the imposition of restrictions applicable only to his property and not that of his neighbors may be substantial—in this case, several million dollars—with no comparable reciprocal benefits. And the cost associated with landmark legislation is likely to be of a completely different order of magnitude than that which results from the imposition of normal zoning restrictions. * * * Under the historic-landmark preservation scheme adopted by New York, the property owner is under an affirmative duty to *preserve* his property *as a landmark* at his own expense. To suggest that because traditional zoning results in some limitation of use of the property zoned, the New York City landmark preservation scheme should likewise be upheld, represents the ultimate in treating as alike things which are different. The rubric of "zoning" has not yet sufficed to avoid the well-established proposition that the Fifth Amendment bars the "Government from forcing some people alone to bear public burdens which, in all fairness and justice, should be borne by the public as a whole." Armstrong v. United States, 364 U.S. 40, 49, 80 S.Ct. 1563, 1569, 4 L.Ed.2d 1554 (1960).

* * *

It is exactly this imposition of general costs on a few individuals at which the "taking" protection is directed. The Fifth Amendment "prevents the public from loading upon one individual more than his just share of the burdens of government, and says that when he surrenders to the public something more and different from that which is exacted from other members of the public, a full and just equivalent shall be returned to him." Monongahela Navigation Co. v. United States, 148 U.S. 312, 325, 13 S.Ct. 622, 626, 37 L.Ed. 463 (1893).

NOTES AND QUESTIONS

1. An historic preservation ordinance like the one in *Penn Central* can be very expensive for the owner of a designated building, even if the building can be adopted for some modern business purpose. In most cases this economic loss results from the fact that historic buildings are much smaller than modern buildings. Grand Central Terminal, for example, was dwarfed by the proposed skyscraper that would have hovered above it but for the ordinance. Congress has reduced the burden for the owners of religious

buildings such as churches, synagogues or mosques with the Religious Land Use and Institutionalized Persons Act of 2000, 42 U.S.C.A. § 2000cc (2000). The statute prohibits any state or local government from imposing or implementing a land use regulation that places a "substantial burden" on religious exercise unless the government shows a compelling interest. See R. Storzer & A. Picarello, Jr., The Religious Land Use and Institutionalized Persons Act of 2000: A Constitutional Response to Unconstitutional Zoning Practices, 9 Geo. Mason L.Rev. 929 (2001).

Under the New York zoning law, building density was regulated by the maximum Floor Area Ratio (FAR), which is a ratio between the maximum allowable square feet of building floor space and lot size. A FAR of one is a floor area equal to the size of the lot. Thus, if the FAR for a particular lot is ten, a builder could build a ten-story building that filled the entire lot, a twenty-story building that filled one half the lot, or a fifty-story building that filled one-fifth of the lot, provided that the building did not violate an independent building height limitation or setback requirement. A builder who promised to include a plaza open to the public could increase the permissible FAR by 20%. The FAR for the area in which Grand Central Station was located was 18. However, the actual FAR used by the Grand Central Station was 1.5. More than 90% of the legal development potential of the site was unused, and the historic preservation ordinance prevented it from being used.

Suppose, however, that Penn Central were permitted to transfer the unused development potential from the Grand Central site to a different location. If the right to develop one unit of building space is fungible, then Penn Central would be precisely compensated for its loss. Alternatively, if it had no other site, suppose it could sell these development rights to the highest bidder. In effect, Penn Central would be compensated for the "taking" even though no money was paid from the city's treasury.

However, many problems restrict the practical use of TDRs by those who have them. Perhaps most obviously, land and the right to develop it are not fungible: development of one block may be worth much more than development of another. If TDRs could be transferred to any parcel of land within the jurisdiction that created them, the owner of an historic landmark could actually be overcompensated for the "taking." In a market in which TDRs are sold to the highest bidder, they would ordinarily go to the owner of the parcel upon which the development was most valuable. If the land whose development is restricted is not the parcel upon which development is worth the most, we could expect that the TDRs would actually command a price greater than their value on the restricted parcel.

In most cases TDRs are not freely assignable anywhere. In *Penn Central* they could be transferred only to an adjacent lot or a lot across the street from the restricted site. Furthermore, the transferee lot must be one upon which further development is economically practicable. Adding extra space to existing urban buildings is not often feasible. Ideally, the transferee lot will be vacant, or its owners will be contemplating further development.

The use of TDRs has been criticized for yielding *over* development on the transferee parcel. A TDR is valuable to the owner of the transferee parcel only because that parcel is burdened with density restrictions. A "right to develop" would be worthless on unzoned property where the owner has the unrestrained right to develop as much as she wants. In the process of zoning, however, the sovereign makes a judgment about how much development is appropriate for a particular parcel. Acquisition of the TDR will result in more than the optimal amount of development, assuming that the original amount permitted by the zoning ordinance was correct. New York initially attempted to ameliorate this problem by providing that the TDR could not be used to increase density more than 20% above the amount originally permitted by the zoning ordinance. That created the likelihood that Penn Central's TDR would have to be divided and transferred to a number of different parcels. However, the 20% limitation was subsequently abandoned because it made the TDRs too difficult to transfer.

2. *Penn Central* articulated a three part balancing test to be applied to takings claims other than those claims that benefit from the categorical takings rules of *Lucas* and *Loretto*. The *Penn Central* Court describes the three parts of the "essentially ad hoc, factual inquiries" as considering the following significant factors: (1) the regulation's economic impact; (2) whether the regulation has interfered with the landowner's distinct investment-backed expectations, and (3) the character of the government action, whether the regulation resembles a physical invasion. The Court provided very little guidance regarding how the factors should be applied. For instance, should they be weighted equally? If there is compelling evidence regarding two of the three factors and no evidence providing the third, does the claimant lose? If the property in question was received by gift or devise, does the claimant lack an *investment-backed* expectation?

3. The *Lucas* case, reprinted next, seemed to some commentators to cast doubt on the continuing viability of *Penn Central*. However, *Penn Central* came roaring back with a vengeance in Palazzolo v. Rhode Island, 533 U.S. 606 (2001); and Tahoe–Sierra Preservation Council, Inc. v. Tahoe Regional Planning Agency (TRPA), 535 U.S. 302 (2002). Both decisions are discussed in the notes following *Lucas*.

LUCAS v. SOUTH CAROLINA COASTAL COUNCIL

Supreme Court of the United States (1992).
505 U.S. 1003.

JUSTICE SCALIA delivered the opinion of the Court.[1]

In 1986, petitioner David H. Lucas paid $975,000 for two residential lots on the Isle of Palms in Charleston County, South Carolina, on which he intended to build single family homes. In 1988, however, the South Carolina Legislature enacted the Beachfront Management Act, S.C. Code § 48–39–250 et seq. (Supp. 1990) (Act), which had the direct effect of barring petitioner from erecting any permanent habitable structures on his two parcels. See § 48–39290(A). A state trial court found that this prohibition rendered Lucas's parcels "valueless." This case requires us to

---

1. Joined by Chief Justice Rehnquist, and Justices White, O'Connor and Thomas. Justice Kennedy concurred; Justices Blackmun and Stevens dissented in separate opinions; Justice Souter filed a separate statement, which is omitted.—*ed.*

decide whether the Act's dramatic effect on the economic value of Lucas's lots accomplished a taking of private property under the Fifth and Fourteenth Amendments requiring the payment of "just compensation."

... In its original form, the South Carolina Act required owners of coastal zone land that qualified as a "critical area" (defined in the legislation to include beaches and immediately adjacent sand dunes) to obtain a permit from the newly created South Carolina Coastal Council (respondent here) prior to committing the land to a "use other than the use the critical area was devoted to on [September 28, 1977]." In the late 1970s, Lucas and others began extensive residential development of the Isle of Palms, a barrier island situated eastward of the City of Charleston. Toward the close of the development cycle for one residential subdivision known as "Beachwood East," Lucas in 1986 purchased the two lots at issue in this litigation for his own account. No portion of the lots, which were located approximately 300 feet from the beach, qualified as a "critical area" under the 1977 Act; accordingly, at the time Lucas acquired these parcels, he was not legally obliged to obtain a permit from the Council in advance of any development activity. His intention with respect to the lots was to do what the owners of the immediately adjacent parcels had already done: erect single-family residences. He commissioned architectural drawings for this purpose.

The Beachfront Management Act brought Lucas's plans to an abrupt end. Under that 1988 legislation, the Council was directed to establish a "baseline" connecting the landward-most "point[s] of erosion ... during the past forty years" in the region of the Isle of Palms that includes Lucas's lots. § 48–39–280(A)(2) (Supp. 1988). In an action not challenged here, the Council fixed this baseline landward of Lucas's parcels. That was significant, for under the Act construction of occupiable improvements[2] was flatly prohibited seaward of a line drawn 20 feet landward of, and parallel to, the baseline. The Act provided no exceptions.

Lucas promptly filed suit in the South Carolina Court of Common Pleas, contending that the Beachfront Management Act's construction bar effected a taking of his property without just compensation. Lucas did not take issue with the validity of the Act as a lawful exercise of South Carolina's police power, but contended that the Act's complete extinguishment of his property's value entitled him to compensation regardless of whether the legislature had acted in furtherance of legitimate police power objectives. Following a bench trial, the court agreed. Among its factual determinations was the finding that "at the time Lucas purchased the two lots, both were zoned for single-family residential construction and ... there were no restrictions imposed upon such use of the property by either the State of South Carolina, the County of Charleston, or the Town of the Isle of Palms." The trial court further found that the Beachfront Management Act decreed a permanent ban on construction insofar as Lucas's lots

---

2. The Act did allow the construction of certain nonhabitable improvements, e.g., "wooden walkways no larger in width than six feet," and "small wooden decks no larger than one hundred forty-four square feet."

were concerned, and that this prohibition "deprive[d] Lucas of any reasonable economic use of the lots, . . . eliminated the unrestricted right of use, and render[ed] them valueless." The court thus concluded that Lucas's properties had been "taken" by operation of the Act, and it ordered respondent to pay "just compensation" in the amount of $1,232,387.50. The Supreme Court of South Carolina reversed. It found dispositive what it described as Lucas's concession "that the Beachfront Management Act [was] properly and validly designed to preserve . . . South Carolina's beaches." 304 S.C. 376, 379, 404 S.E.2d 895, 896 (1991). Failing an attack on the validity of the statute as such, the court believed itself bound to accept the "uncontested . . . findings" of the South Carolina legislature that new construction in the coastal zone—such as petitioner intended— threatened this public resource. The court ruled that when a regulation respecting the use of property is designed "to prevent serious public harm," no compensation is owing under the Takings Clause regardless of the regulation's effect on the property's value (citing, inter alia, Mugler v. Kansas, 123 U.S. 623 (1887).

Prior to Justice Holmes' exposition in Pennsylvania Coal Co. v. Mahon, 260 U.S. 393 (1922), it was generally thought that the Takings Clause reached only a "direct appropriation" of property, Legal Tender Cases, 12 Wall. 457, 551 (1871), or the functional equivalent of a "practical ouster of [the owner's] possession." Transportation Co. v. Chicago, 99 U.S. 635, 642 (1879).

Justice Holmes recognized in *Mahon*, however, that if the protection against physical appropriations of private property was to be meaningfully enforced, the government's power to redefine the range of interests included in the ownership of property was necessarily constrained by constitutional limits. * * * These considerations gave birth in that case to the oft-cited maxim that, "while property may be regulated to a certain extent, if regulation goes too far it will be recognized as a taking."

Nevertheless, our decision in *Mahon* offered little insight into when, and under what circumstances, a given regulation would be seen as going "too far" for purposes of the Fifth Amendment. In 70–odd years of succeeding "regulatory takings" jurisprudence, we have generally eschewed any "set formula" for determining how far is too far, preferring to "engag[e] in . . . essentially ad hoc, factual inquiries," *Penn Central*. See Epstein, Takings: Descent and Resurrection, 1987 Sup. Ct. Rev. 1, 4.

We have, however, described at least two discrete categories of regulatory action as compensable without case-specific inquiry into the public interest advanced in support of the restraint. The first encompasses regulations that compel the property owner to suffer a physical "invasion" of his property. In general (at least with regard to permanent invasions), no matter how minute the intrusion, and no matter how weighty the public purpose behind it, we have required compensation. * * *

The second situation in which we have found categorical treatment appropriate is where regulation denies all economically beneficial or productive use of land. See ... Nollan v. California Coastal Comm'n, 483 U.S. 825, 834 (1987); Keystone Bituminous Coal Assn. v. DeBenedictis, 480 U.S. 470, 495 (1987). As we have said on numerous occasions, the Fifth Amendment is violated when land-use regulation "does not substantially advance legitimate state interests or denies an owner all economically viable use of his land."[3]

We have never set forth the justification for this rule. Perhaps it is simply, as Justice Brennan suggested, that total deprivation of beneficial use is, from the landowner's point of view, the equivalent of a physical appropriation. See San Diego Gas & Electric Co. v. San Diego, 450 U.S., at 652 (Brennan, J., dissenting). "[F]or what is the land but the profits thereof[?]" 1 E. Coke, Institutes ch. 1, § 1 (1st Am. ed. 1812). Surely, at least, in the extraordinary circumstance when no productive or economically beneficial use of land is permitted, it is less realistic to indulge our usual assumption that the legislature is simply "adjusting the benefits and burdens of economic life," *Penn Central*, in a manner that secures an "average reciprocity of advantage" to everyone concerned. Pennsylvania Coal Co. v. Mahon, 260 U.S., at 415. And the functional basis for permitting the government, by regulation, to affect property values without compensation—that "Government hardly could go on if to some extent values incident to property could not be diminished without paying for every such change in the general law"—does not apply to the relatively rare situations where the government has deprived a landowner of all economically beneficial uses.

On the other side of the balance, affirmatively supporting a compensation requirement, is the fact that regulations that leave the owner of land without economically beneficial or productive options for its use—

---

3. Regrettably, the rhetorical force of our "deprivation of all economically feasible use" rule is greater than its precision, since the rule does not make clear the "property interest" against which the loss of value is to be measured. When, for example, a regulation requires a developer to leave 90% of a rural tract in its natural state, it is unclear whether we would analyze the situation as one in which the owner has been deprived of all economically beneficial use of the burdened portion of the tract, or as one in which the owner has suffered a mere diminution in value of the tract as a whole. (For an extreme—and, we think, unsupportable—view of the relevant calculus, see Penn Central Transportation Co. v. New York City, 42 N.Y.2d 324, 333–334, 366 N.E.2d 1271, 1276–1277 (1977), aff'd, 438 U.S. 104 (1978), where the state court examined the diminution in a particular parcel's value produced by a municipal ordinance in light of total value of the taking claimant's other holdings in the vicinity.) Unsurprisingly, this uncertainty regarding the composition of the denominator in our "deprivation" fraction has produced inconsistent pronouncements by the Court. Compare Pennsylvania Coal Co. v. Mahon, 260 U.S. 393, 414 (1922) (law restricting subsurface extraction of coal held to effect a taking), with Keystone Bituminous Coal Assn. v. DeBenedictis, 480 U.S. 470, 497–502 (1987) (nearly identical law held not to effect a taking); see also id., at 515–520 (Rehnquist, C.J., dissenting); Rose, Mahon Reconstructed: Why the Takings Issue is Still a Muddle, 57 S. Cal. L. Rev. 561, 566–569 (1984).

The answer to this difficult question may lie in how the owner's reasonable expectations have been shaped by the State's law of property—i.e., whether and to what degree the State's law has accorded legal recognition and protection to the particular interest in land with respect to which the takings claimant alleges a diminution in (or elimination of) value. In any event, we avoid this difficulty in the present case, since the "interest in land" that Lucas has pleaded (a fee simple interest) is an estate with a rich tradition of protection at common law, and since the South Carolina Court of Common Pleas found that the Beachfront Management Act left each of Lucas's beachfront lots without economic value.

typically, as here, by requiring land to be left substantially in its natural state—carry with them a heightened risk that private property is being pressed into some form of public service under the guise of mitigating serious public harm. * * * The many statutes on the books, both state and federal, that provide for the use of eminent domain to impose servitudes on private scenic lands preventing developmental uses, or to acquire such lands altogether, suggest the practical equivalence in this setting of negative regulation and appropriation. See, e.g., 16 U.S.C. § 410ff–1(a) (authorizing acquisition of "lands, waters, or interests [within Channel Islands National Park] (including but not limited to scenic easements)"); § 460aa–2(a) (authorizing acquisition of "any lands, or lesser interests therein, including mineral interests and scenic easements" within Saw-tooth National Recreation Area); §§ 3921–3923 (authorizing acquisition of wetlands); N.C. Gen. Stat. § 113A–38 (1990) (authorizing acquisition of, inter alia, "scenic easements" within the North Carolina natural and scenic rivers system). * * *

We think, in short, that there are good reasons for our frequently expressed belief that when the owner of real property has been called upon to sacrifice all economically beneficial uses in the name of the common good, that is, to leave his property economically idle, he has suffered a taking.

The trial court found Lucas's two beachfront lots to have been rendered valueless by respondent's enforcement of the coastal-zone construction ban. Under Lucas's theory of the case, which rested upon our "no economically viable use" statements, that finding entitled him to compensation. Lucas believed it unnecessary to take issue with either the purposes behind the Beachfront Management Act, or the means chosen by the South Carolina Legislature to effectuate those purposes.

The South Carolina Supreme Court, however, thought otherwise. In its view, the Beachfront Management Act was no ordinary enactment, but involved an exercise of South Carolina's "police powers" to mitigate the harm to the public interest that petitioner's use of his land might occasion. By neglecting to ... challenge the legislature's purposes, petitioner "concede[d] that the beach/dune area of South Carolina's shores is an extremely valuable public resource; that the erection of new construction, inter alia, contributes to the erosion and destruction of this public resource; and that discouraging new construction in close proximity to the beach/dune area is necessary to prevent a great public harm." In the [state] court's view, these concessions brought petitioner's challenge within a long line of this Court's cases sustaining against Due Process and Takings Clause challenges the State's use of its "police powers" to enjoin a property owner from activities akin to public nuisances. See Mugler v. Kansas, 123 U. S. 623 (1887) (law prohibiting manufacture of alcoholic beverages); Hadacheck v. Sebastian, 239 U.S. 394 (1915) (law barring operation of brick mill in residential area). * * *

It is correct that many of our prior opinions have suggested that "harmful or noxious uses" of property may be proscribed by government regulation without the requirement of compensation. For a number of reasons, however, we think the South Carolina Supreme Court was too quick to conclude that that principle decides the present case. The "harmful or noxious uses" principle was the Court's early attempt to describe in theoretical terms why government may, consistent with the Takings Clause, affect property values by regulation without incurring an obligation to compensate—a reality we nowadays acknowledge explicitly with respect to the full scope of the State's police power. See, e.g., Penn Central Transportation Co., 438 U.S., at 125 (where State "reasonably conclude[s] that 'the health, safety, morals, or general welfare' would be promoted by prohibiting particular contemplated uses of land," compensation need not accompany prohibition). * * *

The transition from our early focus on control of "noxious" uses to our contemporary understanding of the broad realm within which government may regulate without compensation was an easy one, since the distinction between "harm-preventing" and "benefit-conferring" regulation is often in the eye of the beholder. It is quite possible, for example, to describe in either fashion the ecological, economic, and aesthetic concerns that inspired the South Carolina legislature in the present case. One could say that imposing a servitude on Lucas's land is necessary in order to prevent his use of it from "harming" South Carolina's ecological resources; or, instead, in order to achieve the "benefits" of an ecological preserve. . . . Whether one or the other of the competing characterizations will come to one's lips in a particular case depends primarily upon one's evaluation of the worth of competing uses of real estate. See Restatement (Second) of Torts § 822, Comment g, p. 112 (1979) ("'[p]ractically all human activities unless carried on in a wilderness interfere to some extent with others or involve some risk of interference'"). A given restraint will be seen as mitigating "harm" to the adjacent parcels or securing a "benefit" for them, depending upon the observer's evaluation of the relative importance of the use that the restraint favors. See Sax, Takings and the Police Power, 74 Yale L. J. 36, 49 (1964) ("'[T]he problem [in this area] is not one of noxiousness or harm-creating activity at all; rather it is a problem of inconsistency between perfectly innocent and independently desirable uses'").

Whether Lucas's construction of single-family residences on his parcels should be described as bringing "harm" to South Carolina's adjacent ecological resources thus depends principally upon whether the describer believes that the State's use interest in nurturing those resources is so important that any competing adjacent use must yield. When it is understood that "prevention of harmful use" was merely our early formulation of the police power justification necessary to sustain (without compensation) any regulatory diminution in value; and that the distinction between regulation that "prevents harmful use" and that which "confers benefits" is difficult, if not impossible, to discern on an objective, value-free basis; it becomes self-evident that noxious-use logic cannot serve as a touchstone to distinguish regulatory "takings"—which require compensation—from regulatory deprivations that do not require compensation. A fortiori the legislature's recitation of a noxious-use justification cannot be the basis for departing from our categorical rule that total regulatory takings must be compensated. If it were, departure would virtually always be allowed. The South Carolina Supreme Court's approach would essentially nullify *Mahon*'s affirmation of limits to the noncompensable exercise of the police power. * * *

Where the State seeks to sustain regulation that deprives land of all economically beneficial use, we think it may resist compensation only if the logically antecedent inquiry into the nature of the owner's estate shows that the proscribed use interests were not part of his title to begin with. This accords, we think, with our "takings" jurisprudence, which has traditionally been guided by the understandings of our citizens regarding the content of, and the State's power over, the "bundle of rights" that they acquire when they obtain title to property. It seems to us that the property owner necessarily expects the uses of his property to be restricted, from time to time, by various measures newly enacted by the State in legitimate exercise of its police powers; "[a]s long recognized, some values are enjoyed under an implied limitation and must yield to the police power." *Pennsylvania Coal*, . . .

[W]e think the notion pressed by the Council that title is somehow held subject to the "implied limitation" that the State may subsequently eliminate all economically valuable use is inconsistent with the historical compact recorded in the Takings Clause that has become part of our constitutional culture. Where "permanent physical occupation" of land is concerned, we have refused to allow the government to decree it anew (without compensation), no matter how weighty the asserted "public interests" involved—*Loretto*. * * *

We believe similar treatment must be accorded confiscatory regulations, i.e., regulations that prohibit all economically beneficial use of land: Any limitation so severe cannot be newly legislated or decreed (without compensation), but must inhere in the title itself, in the restrictions that background principles of the State's law of property and nuisance already place upon land ownership. A law or decree with such an effect must, in other words, do no more than duplicate the result that could have been achieved in the courts—by adjacent landowners (or other uniquely affected persons) under the State's law of private nuisance, or by the State under its complementary power to abate nuisances that affect the public generally, or otherwise.

On this analysis, the owner of a lake bed, for example, would not be entitled to compensation when he is denied the requisite permit to engage in a landfilling operation that would have the effect of flooding others' land. Nor the corporate owner of a nuclear generating plant, when it is directed to remove all improvements from its land upon discovery that the plant sits astride an earthquake fault. Such regulatory action may well have the effect of eliminating the land's only economically productive use, but it does not proscribe a productive use that was previously permissible under relevant property and nuisance principles. The use of these properties for what are now expressly prohibited purposes was always unlawful, and (subject to other constitutional limitations) it was open to the State at any point to make the implication of those background principles of nuisance and property law explicit. See Michelman, Property, Utility, and Fairness, Comments on the Ethical Foundations of "Just Compensation" Law, 80 Harv. L. Rev. 1165, 1239–1241 (1967).

In light of our traditional resort to "existing rules or understandings that stem from an independent source such as state law" to define the range of interests that qualify for protection as "property" under the Fifth (and Fourteenth) amendments, Board of Regents of State Colleges v. Roth, 408 U.S. 564, 577 (1972), . . . this recognition that the Takings Clause does not require compensation when an owner is barred from putting land to a use that is proscribed by those "existing rules or understandings" is surely unexceptional.

When, however, a regulation that declares "off-limits" all economically productive or beneficial uses of land goes beyond what the relevant background principles would dictate, compensation must be paid to sustain it. The "total taking" inquiry we require today will ordinarily entail (as the application of state nuisance law ordinarily entails) analysis of, among other things, the degree of harm to public lands and resources, or adjacent private property, posed by the claimant's proposed activities, see, e.g., Restatement (Second) of Torts §§ 826, 827, the social value of the claimant's activities and their suitability to the locality in question, see, e.g., id., §§ 828(a) and (b), 831, and the relative ease with which the alleged harm can be avoided through measures taken by the claimant and the government (or adjacent private landowners) alike, see, e.g., id., §§ 827(e), 828(c), 830.

The fact that a particular use has long been engaged in by similarly situated owners ordinarily imports a lack of any common-law prohibition (though changed circumstances or new knowledge may make what was previously permissible no longer so, see Restatement (Second) of Torts, supra, § 827, comment g). So also does the fact that other landowners, similarly situated, are permitted to continue the use denied to the claimant. It seems unlikely that common-law principles would have prevented the erection of any habitable or productive improvements on petitioner's land; they rarely support prohibition of the "essential use" of land.

The question, however, is one of state law to be dealt with on remand. We emphasize that to win its case South Carolina must do more than proffer the legislature's declaration that the uses Lucas desires are inconsistent with the public interest, or the conclusory assertion that they violate a common-law maxim such as *sic utere tuo ut alienum non laedas*. As we have said, a "State, by *ipse dixit*, may not transform private property into public property without compensation...." Webb's Fabulous Pharmacies, Inc. v. Beckwith, 449 U.S. 155, 164 (1980). Instead, as it would be required to do if it sought to restrain Lucas in a common-law action for public nuisance, South Carolina must identify background principles of nuisance and property law that prohibit the uses he now intends in the circumstances in which the property is presently found. Only on this showing can the State fairly claim that, in proscribing all such beneficial uses, the Beachfront Management Act is taking nothing.[4]

The judgment is reversed and the cause remanded for proceedings not inconsistent with this opinion. So ordered.

[JUSTICE KENNEDY'S concurring opinion is omitted.]

JUSTICE BLACKMUN, dissenting.

* * * This Court repeatedly has recognized the ability of government, in certain circumstances, to regulate property without compensation no matter how adverse the financial effect on the owner may be. More than a century ago, the Court explicitly upheld the right of States to prohibit uses of property injurious to public health, safety, or welfare without paying compensation: "A prohibition simply upon the use of property for purposes that are declared, by valid legislation, to be injurious to the health, morals, or safety of the community, cannot, in any just sense, be deemed a taking or an appropriation of property." Mugler v. Kansas, 123 U.S. 623, 668–669 (1887). On this basis, the Court upheld an ordinance effectively prohibiting operation of a previously lawful brewery, although the "establishments will become of no value as property." Mugler was only the beginning in a long line of cases [discussing other decisions]....

Until today, the Court explicitly had rejected the contention that the government's power to act without paying compensation turns on whether the prohibited activity is a common-law nuisance. The brewery closed in *Mugler* itself was not a common-law nuisance, and the Court specifically stated that it was the role of the legislature to determine what measures would be appropriate for the protection of public health and safety.... Instead the Court has relied in the past, as the South Carolina Court has done here, on legislative judgments of what constitutes a harm. The Court rejects the notion that the State always can prohibit uses it deems a harm to the public without granting compensation because "the distinction between 'harm-preventing' and 'benefit-conferring' regulation is often in the eye of the beholder." Since the characterization will depend "primarily upon one's evaluation of the worth of competing uses of real estate," the Court decides a legislative judgment of this kind no longer can provide the desired "objective, value-free basis" for upholding a regulation.

The Court, however, fails to explain how its proposed common law alternative escapes the same trap. The threshold inquiry for imposition of the Court's new rule, "deprivation of all economically valuable use," itself

---

4. ... We stress that an affirmative decree eliminating all economically beneficial uses may be defended only if an objectively reasonable application of relevant precedents would exclude those beneficial uses in the circumstances in which the land is presently found.

cannot be determined objectively. As the Court admits, whether the owner has been deprived of all economic value of his property will depend on how "property" is defined. The "composition of the denominator in our 'deprivation' fraction," is the dispositive inquiry. Yet there is no "objective" way to define what that denominator should be. "We have long understood that any land-use regulation can be characterized as the 'total' deprivation of an aptly defined entitlement...."

Common-law public and private nuisance law is simply a determination whether a particular use causes harm. There is nothing magical in the reasoning of judges long dead. They determined a harm in the same way as state judges and legislatures do today. If judges in the 18th and 19th centuries can distinguish a harm from a benefit, why not judges in the 20th century, and if judges can, why not legislators? There simply is no reason to believe that new interpretations of the hoary common law nuisance doctrine will be particularly "objective" or "value-free." ...

Even into the 19th century, state governments often felt free to take property for roads and other public projects without paying compensation to the owners. See M. Horwitz, *The Transformation of American Law, 1780–1860*, pp. 63–64 (1977). As one court declared in 1802, citizens "were bound to contribute as much of [land], as by the laws of the country, were deemed necessary for the public convenience." M'Clenachan v. Curwen, 3 Yeates 362, 373 (Pa.1802). There was an obvious movement toward establishing the just compensation principle during the 19th century, but "there continued to be a strong current in American legal thought that regarded compensation simply as a 'bounty given ... by the State' out of 'kindness' and not out of justice." Horwitz 65 (quoting Commonwealth v. Fisher, 1 Pen. & W. 462, 465 (Pa.1830)). Although, prior to the adoption of the Bill of Rights, America was replete with land use regulations describing which activities were considered noxious and forbidden, see Bender, The Takings Clause: Principles or Politics?, 34 Buffalo L. Rev. 735, 751 (1985); L. Friedman, A History of American Law 66–68 (1973), the Fifth Amendment's Taking Clause originally did not extend to regulations of property, whatever the effect.[5]

Most state courts agreed with this narrow interpretation of a taking. "Until the end of the nineteenth century ... jurists held that the constitution protected possession only, and not value." Siegel, Understanding the Nineteenth Century Contract Clause: The Role of the Property–Privilege Distinction and "Takings" Clause Jurisprudence, 60 S.Cal. L. Rev. 1, 76 (1986).... Even indirect and consequential injuries to property resulting from regulations were excluded from the definition of a taking. Callender v. Marsh, 1 Pick. 418, 430 (Mass.1823). * * *

---

5. James Madison, author of the Taking Clause, apparently intended it to apply only to direct, physical takings of property by the Federal Government. See Treanor, The Origins and Original Significance of the Just Compensation Clause of the Fifth Amendment, 94 Yale L.J., 694, 711 (1985). Professor Sax argues that although "contemporaneous commentary upon the meaning of the compensation clause is in very short supply," 74 Yale L.J., at 58, the "few authorities that are available" indicate that the clause was "designed to prevent arbitrary government action," not to protect economic value.

JUSTICE STEVENS, dissenting.

. . . . In addition to lacking support in past decisions, the Court's new rule is wholly arbitrary. A landowner whose property is diminished in value 95% recovers nothing, while an owner whose property is diminished 100% recovers the land's full value. . . . The arbitrariness of such a rule is palpable. Moreover, because of the elastic nature of property rights, the Court's new rule will also prove unsound in practice. In response to the rule, courts may define "property" broadly and only rarely find regulations to effect total takings. This is the approach the Court itself adopts in its revisionist reading of venerable precedents. We are told that-notwithstanding the Court's findings to the contrary in each case-the brewery in *Mugler*, the brickyard in *Hadacheck*, and the gravel pit in *Goldblatt* all could be put to "other uses" and that, therefore, those cases did not involve total regulatory takings. On the other hand, developers and investors may market specialized estates to take advantage of the Court's new rule. The smaller the estate, the more likely that a regulatory change will effect a total taking. Thus, an investor may, for example, purchase the right to build a multi-family home on a specific lot, with the result that a zoning regulation that allows only single-family homes would render the investor's property interest "valueless."

In short, the categorical rule will likely have one of two effects: Either courts will alter the definition of the "denominator" in the takings "fraction," rendering the Court's categorical rule meaningless, or investors will manipulate the relevant property interests, giving the Court's rule sweeping effect. To my mind, neither of these results is desirable or appropriate, and both are distortions of our takings jurisprudence. * * *

. . . The Court's categorical approach rule will, I fear, greatly hamper the efforts of local officials and planners who must deal with increasingly complex problems in land-use and environmental regulation. As this case—in which the claims of an individual property owner exceed $1 million—well demonstrates, these officials face both substantial uncertainty because of the ad hoc nature of takings law and unacceptable penalties if they guess incorrectly about that law. . . .

NOTES AND QUESTIONS

1. Note the majority's reliance on the nuisance section of the Restatement (Second) of Torts. (See Chapter 9). Is the Court suggesting a kind of cost-benefit analysis for determining whether a regulation that makes property valueless is an unconstitutional taking? The Restatement, § 826, condemns activities as nuisances when the "gravity of the harm outweighs the utility of the actor's conduct." The Court adopts a distinctly "Coasian" approach to property rights, which does not view one owner as tortfeasor and the other as victim; rather the uses are seen as merely incompatible. See the note on the Coase Theorem in chapter 9. In a purely Coasian world, if Lucas could previously build without liability he would *always* be able to obtain compensation, because the transaction is purely voluntary.

2. Note that Justice Scalia regards Pennsylvania Coal v. Mahon, reprinted supra, as a purely regulatory taking. See our critique of that position in the notes following the decision. In any event, Justice Scalia believed the decision should be accorded stare decisis and that it necessitated a search through South Carolina's legal heritage to see if Lucas could reasonably have expected the state to regulate as it did. Note also that prior to *Pennsylvania Coal* purely regulatory takings were held to be noncompensable.

3. What do you make of Justice Stevens' dissenting statement that "[a] landowner whose property is diminished in value 95% recovers nothing, while an owner whose property is diminished 100% recovers the land's full value.... "? Is it more accurate to state that in the first instance, the landowner would have to prove a taking under the *Penn Central* balancing test in order to receive compensation, while in the latter the landowner would be entitled to compensation under the *Lucas* categorical rule?

4. In Stevens v. City of Cannon Beach, 317 Or. 131, 854 P.2d 449 (1993), cert. denied, 510 U.S. 1207 (1994), the Supreme Court of Oregon held that the state's doctrine of "custom" was historically part of the law of the state of Oregon, and thus *Lucas* permitted a local government to prevent a land owner from creating a seawall that would have excluded the public from the dry sand area of property located along the Pacific Ocean. The doctrine of custom (described briefly in § 8.2.5, supra) recognizes as permanent various usages and practices that have existed "from time immemorial, without interruption."

The Oregon Supreme Court noted that its own previous decision in State ex rel. Thornton v. Hay, 254 Or. 584, 462 P.2d 671 (1969), had concluded that the doctrine of custom was part of the law of Oregon and could be applied so as to give the public a right of access to privately owned beachfront land. Throughout Oregon's history, the dry sand area customarily had been used by the public:

"The dry-sand area in Oregon has been enjoyed by the general public as a recreational adjunct of the wet-sand or foreshore area since the beginning of the state's political history. The first European settlers on these shores found the aboriginal inhabitants using the foreshore for clam digging and the dry-sand area for their cooking fires. The newcomers continued these customs after statehood. Thus, from the time of the earliest settlement to the present day, the general public has assumed that the dry-sand area was a part of the public beach, and the public has used the dry-sand area for picnics, gathering wood, building warming fires, and generally as a headquarters from which to supervise children or to range out over the foreshore as the tides advance and recede. In the Cannon Beach vicinity, state and local officers have policed the dry sand, and municipal sanitary crews have attempted to keep the area reasonably free from man-made litter. 'Perhaps one explanation for the evolution of the custom of the public to use the dry-sand area for recreational purposes is that the area could not be used conveniently by its owners for any other purpose. The dry-sand area is unstable in its seaward boundaries, unsafe during winter storms, and for the most part unfit for the construction of permanent structures.' "

Stevens, 854 P.2d at 453–454, quoting *Thornton*, 254 Or. at 588–589, 462 P.2d 673–674.

The court concluded that "the record shows that the custom of the inhabitants of Oregon and of visitors in the state to use the dry sand as a public recreation area is so notorious that notice of the custom on the part of persons buying land along the shore must be presumed." Responding specifically to *Lucas'* requirement that a state regulatory action that reduces property values to zero must be sufficiently justified historically so as to be part of the landowner's "title," the *Stevens* court said:

> When plaintiffs took title to their land, they were on notice that exclusive use of the dry sand areas was not a part of the "bundle of rights" that they acquired, because public use of dry sand areas "is so notorious that notice of the custom on the part of persons buying land along the shore must be presumed." ... We, therefore, hold that the doctrine of custom as applied to public use of Oregon's dry sand areas is one of "the restrictions that background principles of the State's law of property * * * already place upon land ownership." Lucas, 112 S.Ct. at 2900. We hold that plaintiffs have never had the property interests that they claim were taken by defendants' decision and regulations.

The United States Supreme Court denied certiorari, with Justice Scalia, the author of *Lucas*, dissenting (joined by Justice O'Connor). He wrote:

> As a general matter, the Constitution leaves the law of real property to the States. But [o]ur opinion in *Lucas* ... would be a nullity if anything that a State court chooses to denominate "background law"—regardless of whether it is really such—could eliminate property rights. "[A] State cannot be permitted to defeat the constitutional prohibition against taking property without due process of law by the simple device of asserting retroactively that the property it has taken never existed at all." ... Since opening private property to public use constitutes a taking [citing *Nollan*], ... if it cannot fairly be said that an Oregon doctrine of custom deprived Cannon Beach property owners of their rights to exclude others from the dry sand, then the decision now before us has effected an uncompensated taking.

* * *

It is by no means clear that the facts—either as to the entire Oregon coast, or as to the small segment at issue here—meet the requirements for the English doctrine of custom. The requirements set forth by Blackstone included, inter alia, that the public right of access be exercised without interruption, and that the custom be obligatory, i.e., in the present context that it not be left to the option of each landowner whether he will recognize the public's right to go on the dry-sand area for recreational purposes. In *Thornton*, however, the Supreme Court of Oregon determined the historical existence of these fact-intensive criteria (as well as five others) in a discussion that took less than one full page of the Pacific Reporter. That is all the more remarkable a feat since the Supreme Court of Oregon was investigating these criteria in the first instance; the trial court had not rested its decision on the basis of custom and the state did not argue that theory to the Supreme Court.

510 U.S. 1207 (1994).

Query: Under *Lucas*, who gets to decide whether a historical rule—particularly, a common law rule such as custom—is a part of the state's own legal traditions so that it can be said to be a part of the land owner's title? Particularly in common law adjudication, it is quite common for a state court facing an issue for the first time first to declare the rule and second to state that the rule has always been part of the common law of that state. Suppose (1) Blackstone describes the doctrine of custom in the 1760's; (2) no case presenting the issue arises in Oregon until the *Thornton* case in 1969; and (3) in *Thornton* the Oregon Supreme Court declares that the state of Oregon has always followed the doctrine of custom. Does (or should) *Lucas* require more?

And what of the dissenting protests by Justices Blackmun and Stevens in the *Lucas* case, that the Court's rule will freeze traditional legal policy in time? If a use could be condemned as a nuisance (or other well established legal violation) under well settled legal principles, regulation prohibiting the use is noncompensable even if it makes the property worthless. Does this rule accommodate no legal change whatsoever? Could it accommodate creeping change? Does the Court's rule dictate a preference for common law decisions affecting property rights over legislative decisions? If so, what justifies that preference?

A once-common error in the writing of legal history was the assumption that the past contains some objective or politically neutral set of "baseline" legal rules, and that ever since society has been deviating to one degree or another from these rules. Does the majority opinion commit this error, as Justice Blackmun's dissent suggests? Or is the majority simply saying that people are entitled to rely on legal rules that have been around for a long time.

5. When is a state law or recognized environmental problem one of the "background" principles that are a part of a landowner's reasonable expectation, and when are they just an example of state interference that can be challenged as a taking? In *Good v. United States*, 189 F.3d 1355 (Fed.Cir. 1999), the court concluded that no *Lucas*-style taking occurred because the land owner clearly contemplated when he purchased the property twenty-five years earlier that environmental problems were significant and severe regulation was likely. The sale contract had stated that "Buyers recognize that . . . as of today there are certain problems in connection with the obtaining of State and Federal permission for dredging and filling operations." As a result the land owner "lacked a reasonable, investment-backed expectation that he would obtain the regulatory approval needed to develop the property at issue here."

Compare the Supreme Court's decision in Palazzolo v. Rhode Island, 533 U.S. 606 (2001), which held that the simple "passage of title" did not transform the challenged regulation into a "background" principle. The State had argued that the landowner could not assert a takings claim because the challenged restriction on development had already been present when he purchased the property:

It is asserted here that *Lucas* stands for the proposition that any new regulation, once enacted, becomes a background principle of property law which cannot be challenged by those who acquire title after the enactment.

* * * [A] regulation that otherwise would be unconstitutional absent compensation is not transformed into a background principle of the state's law by mere virtue of the passage of title. This relative standard would be incompatible with our description of the concept in *Lucas,* which is explained in terms of those common, shared understandings of permissible limitations derived from a state's legal tradition. A regulation or common-law rule cannot be a background principle for some owners but not for others. The determination whether an existing, general law can limit all economic use of property must turn on objective factors, such as the nature of the land use proscribed.

But query: in a well-functioning market a rational buyer would pay no more than value of the property under the then-existing regulatory regime. In *Palazzolo* the property was worth $3,150,000 prior to the regulation but only $200,000 under the regulation. In that setting the new buyer would have paid only the latter figure. In that case, shouldn't the Takings claim belong to the seller of the property rather than the current owner? Suppose the purchaser had paid $1,000,000—$200,000 for the property and $800,000 for assignment of the Taking claim? Was the Court effectively assuming that the purchaser had bought an assignment of the taking claim, even if there was no evidence that he did so in the purchase contract? For additional discussion of the notice rule, see Carol Necole Brown, Taking the Takings Claim: A Policy and Economic Analysis of the Survival of Takings Claims After Property Transfers, 36 Conn. L. Rev. 7 (2003).

6. Suppose that on reconsideration the state court corrects its earlier fact finding and concludes that Lucas' property was not made worthless by the regulation after all, but is still worth $300,000, or about thirty percent of the price Lucas paid for it. Has a taking occurred under the Supreme Court's analysis? If not, isn't *Lucas* an extremely narrow decision? On remand, the South Carolina Supreme Court held that the Coastal Council did not possess "the ability under the common law to prohibit Lucas from constructing a habitable structure on his land." Lucas v. South Carolina Coastal Council, 309 S.C. 424, 424 S.E.2d 484, 484 (1992). Further, the Court held that Lucas "suffered a temporary taking deserving of compensation commencing with enactment of the 1988 Act and continuing through date of this Order." Lucas, supra, at 486. The parties eventually settled the case. Although Lucas's actual damages amounted to more than three million dollars, Lucas agreed to the state's offer of $1,575,000 for the title to the lots. After paying his creditors and lawyers, Lucas realized less than $10,000 of that settlement. Shortly after the settlement, the state decided to auction the lots and issue the highest bidders building permits to develop the property. The lots were sold to a private developer for $730,000 in late 1993. Pictures of two homes currently located on the lots formerly owned by Lucas can be accessed at *Voices of American Law: Lucas v. SC Coastal Council*, Duke University School of Law,

http://www.law.duke.edu/voices/gallery?id=156. David Lucas wrote a book in 1995 telling the story of the litigation from his perspective. See David Lucas, *Lucas vs. The Green Machine: The Landmark Supreme Court Property Rights Decisions by the Man Who Won It Against All Odds, and His continuing Fight to Protect YOUR Property Rights!* (1995).

7.　In Monterey v. Del Monte Dunes, Ltd., 526 U.S. 687 (1999), the City repeatedly delayed and rejected the landowner's development proposals plus revisions made to satisfy various concerns. When it appeared that the City was not acting in good faith, the landowner claimed a taking. As the Supreme Court said:

> [T]he District Court instructed the jury it should find for Del Monte Dunes if it found either that Del Monte Dunes had been denied all economically viable use of its property or that "the city's decision to reject the plaintiff's 190 unit development proposal did not substantially advance a legitimate public purpose." With respect to the first inquiry, the jury was instructed, in relevant part, as follows: "For the purpose of a taking claim, you will find that the plaintiff has been denied all economically viable use of its property, if, as the result of the city's regulatory decision there remains no permissible or beneficial use for that property. In proving whether the plaintiff has been denied all economically viable use of its property, it is not enough that the plaintiff show that after the challenged action by the city the property diminished in value or that it would suffer a serious economic loss as the result of the city's actions."

> With respect to the second inquiry, the jury received the following instruction: "Public bodies, such as the city, have the authority to take actions which substantially advance legitimate public interest[s] and legitimate public interest[s] can include protecting the environment, preserving open space agriculture, protecting the health and safety of its citizens, and regulating the quality of the community by looking at development. So one of your jobs as jurors is to decide if the city's decision here substantially advanced any such legitimate public purpose. The regulatory actions of the city or any agency substantially advance a legitimate public purpose if the action bears a reasonable relationship to that objective. Now, if the preponderance of the evidence establishes that there was no reasonable relationship between the city's denial of the ... proposal and legitimate public purpose, you should find in favor of the plaintiff. * * * "

The Supreme Court approved the verdict but added this qualifier:

> As the city itself proposed the essence of the instructions given to the jury, it cannot now contend that the instructions did not provide an accurate statement of the law. In any event, although this Court has provided neither a definitive statement of the elements of a claim for a temporary regulatory taking nor a thorough explanation of the nature or applicability of the requirement that a regulation substantially advance legitimate public interests outside the context of required dedications or exactions, we note that the trial court's instructions are consistent with our previous general discussions of regulatory takings liability.

Then, in *Lingle v. Chevron U.S.A. Inc.*, 544 U.S. 528 (2005), the Supreme Court clarified the relationship between *Lucas*, *Penn Central*, and other possible Takings tests, such as the one articulated in *Monterey*. The Court held that *Monterey's* language suggesting that a regulatory act could be a taking if it does not "substantially advance" a legitimate state interest was misplaced, and really described a Due Process test rather than a Takings Clause test.

At issue was a price regulation statute that limited the rent that oil companies could charge dealers for the lease of company-owned facilities. In *Agins v. City of Tiburon*, 447 U.S. 255, 260 (1980), the Court had first suggested that a government regulation "effects a taking if [such regulation] does not substantially advance legitimate state interests...." The Court repeated that formulation in *Monterey v. Del Monte Dunes at Monterey, Ltd.*, 526 U.S. 687, 704 (1999) and had alluded to it in other decisions.

However, in *Lingle* the Court stated that:

> Our precedents stake out two categories of regulatory action that generally will be deemed *per se* takings for Fifth Amendment purposes. First, where government requires an owner to suffer a permanent physical invasion of her property—however minor—it must provide just compensation. See *Loretto v. Teleprompter Manhattan CATV Corp.*, 458 U.S. 419 (1982).... A second categorical rule applies to regulations that completely deprive an owner of "*all* economically beneficial us[e]" of her property....

> Outside these two relatively narrow categories (and the special context of land-use exactions discussed below), regulatory takings challenges are governed by the standards set forth in *Penn Central*.... The Court in *Penn Central* acknowledged that it had hitherto been "unable to develop any 'set formula' " for evaluating regulatory takings claims, but identified "several factors that have particular significance." Primary among those factors are "[t]he economic impact of the regulation on the claimant and, particularly, the extent to which the regulation has interfered with distinct investment-backed expectations." In addition, the "character of the governmental action"—for instance whether it amounts to a physical invasion or instead merely affects property interests through "some public program adjusting the benefits and burdens of economic life to promote the common good"—may be relevant in discerning whether a taking has occurred. The *Penn Central* factors—though each has given rise to vexing subsidiary questions—have served as the principal guidelines for resolving regulatory takings claims that do not fall within the physical takings or *Lucas* rules. See, *e.g., Palazzolo v. Rhode Island*, 533 U.S. 606, 617–618, 121 S.Ct. 2448 (2001).

> Although our regulatory takings jurisprudence cannot be characterized as unified, these three inquiries (reflected in *Loretto*, *Lucas*, and *Penn Central*) share a common touchstone. Each aims to identify regulatory actions that are functionally equivalent to the classic taking in which government directly appropriates private property or ousts the owner from his domain. Accordingly, each of these tests focuses directly upon the severity of the burden that government imposes upon private proper-

ty rights. The Court has held that physical takings require compensation because of the unique burden they impose: A permanent physical invasion, however minimal the economic cost it entails, eviscerates the owner's right to exclude others from entering and using her property—perhaps the most fundamental of all property interests. See *Dolan v. City of Tigard,* 512 U.S. 374, 384, 114 S.Ct. 2309 (1994); *Nollan v. California Coastal Comm'n,* 483 U.S. 825, 831–832, 107 S.Ct. 3141 (1987); *Loretto.* . . . In the *Lucas* context, of course, the complete elimination of a property's value is the determinative factor. . . . And the *Penn Central* inquiry turns in large part, albeit not exclusively, upon the magnitude of a regulation's economic impact and the degree to which it interferes with legitimate property interests.

In *Agins v. City of Tiburon,* a case involving a facial takings challenge to certain municipal zoning ordinances, the Court declared that "[t]he application of a general zoning law to particular property effects a taking if the ordinance does not substantially advance legitimate state interests . . . or denies an owner economically viable use of his land. . . ." Because this statement is phrased in the disjunctive, *Agins'* "substantially advances" language has been read to announce a stand-alone regulatory takings test that is wholly independent of *Penn Central* or any other test. Indeed, the lower courts in this case struck down Hawaii's rent control statute as an "unconstitutional regulatory taking," based solely upon a finding that it does not substantially advance the State's asserted interest in controlling retail gasoline prices. Although a number of our takings precedents have recited the "substantially advances" formula minted in *Agins,* this is our first opportunity to consider its validity as a freestanding takings test. We conclude that this formula prescribes an inquiry in the nature of a due process, not a takings, test, and that it has no proper place in our takings jurisprudence.

There is no question that the "substantially advances" formula was derived from due process, not takings, precedents. In support of this new language, *Agins* cited *Nectow v. Cambridge,* 277 U.S. 183, 48 S.Ct. 447, a 1928 case in which the plaintiff claimed that a city zoning ordinance "deprived him of his property without due process of law in contravention of the Fourteenth Amendment," *Agins* then went on to discuss *Village of Euclid v. Ambler Realty Co.,* 272 U.S. 365, 47 S.Ct. 114 (1926), a historic decision holding that a municipal zoning ordinance would survive a substantive due process challenge so long as it was not "clearly arbitrary and unreasonable, having no *substantial relation to the public health, safety, morals, or general welfare.*"

When viewed in historical context, the Court's reliance on *Nectow* and *Euclid* is understandable. *Agins* was the Court's first case involving a challenge to zoning regulations in many decades, so it was natural to turn to these seminal zoning precedents for guidance. Moreover, *Agins'* apparent commingling of due process and takings inquiries had some precedent in the Court's then-recent decision in *Penn Central.* See 438 U.S., at 127, 98 S.Ct. 2646 (stating in dicta that "[i]t is . . . implicit in *Goldblatt [v. Hempstead,* 369 U.S. 590 (1962),] that a use restriction on real property may constitute a 'taking' if not reasonably necessary to the effectuation of a substantial public purpose....") Finally, when *Agins* was decided, there had been some history of referring to deprivations of property without due process of law as "takings," see, *e.g., Rowan v. Post Office Dept.,* 397 U.S. 728, 740, 90 S.Ct. 1484 (1970), and the Court had yet to clarify whether "regulatory takings" claims were properly cognizable under the Takings Clause or the Due Process Clause, see *Williamson County Regional Planning Comm'n v. Hamilton Bank of Johnson City,* 473 U.S. 172, 197–199, 105 S.Ct. 3108, 87 L.Ed.2d 126 (1985).

Although *Agins'* reliance on due process precedents is understandable, the language the Court selected was regrettably imprecise. The "substantially advances" formula suggests a means-ends test: It asks, in essence, whether a regulation of private property is *effective* in achieving some legitimate public purpose. An inquiry of this nature has some logic in the context of a due process challenge, for a regulation that fails to serve any legitimate governmental objective may be so arbitrary or irrational that it runs afoul of the Due Process Clause.

In stark contrast to the three regulatory takings tests discussed above, the "substantially advances" inquiry reveals nothing about the *magnitude or character of the burden* a particular regulation imposes upon private property rights. Nor does it provide any information about how any regulatory burden is *distributed* among property owners. In consequence, this test does not help to identify those regulations whose effects are functionally comparable to government appropriation or invasion of private property; it is tethered neither to the text of the Takings Clause nor to the basic justification for allowing regulatory actions to be challenged under the Clause.

Chevron appeals to the general principle that the Takings Clause is meant " 'to bar Government from forcing some people alone to bear public burdens which, in all fairness and justice, should be borne by the public as a whole.' " But that appeal is clearly misplaced, for the reasons just indicated. A test that tells us nothing about the actual burden imposed on property rights, or how that burden is allocated cannot tell us when justice might require that the burden be spread among taxpayers through the payment of compensation. The owner of a property subject to a regulation that *effectively* serves a legitimate state interest may be just as singled out and just as burdened as the owner of a property subject to an *ineffective* regulation. It would make little sense to say that the second owner has suffered a taking while the first has not. Likewise, an ineffective regulation may not significantly burden property rights at all, and it may distribute any burden broadly and evenly among property owners. The notion that such a regulation nevertheless "takes" private property for public use merely by virtue of its ineffectiveness or foolishness is untenable.

Instead of addressing a challenged regulation's effect on private property, the "substantially advances" inquiry probes the regulation's underlying validity. But such an inquiry is logically prior to and distinct from the question whether a regulation effects a taking, for the Takings Clause presupposes that the government has acted in pursuit of a valid public purpose. The Clause expressly requires compensation where government takes private property *"for public use."* It does not bar government from interfering with property rights, but rather requires compensation "in the event of *otherwise proper interference* amounting to a taking." *First English Evangelical Lutheran Church,* 482 U.S., at 315, 107 S.Ct. 2378 (emphasis added). Conversely, if a government action is found to be impermissible—for instance because it fails to meet the "public use" requirement or is so arbitrary as to violate due process— that is the end of the inquiry. No amount of compensation can authorize such action.

Chevron's challenge to the Hawaii statute in this case illustrates the flaws in the "substantially advances" theory. To begin with, it is unclear how significantly Hawaii's rent cap actually burdens Chevron's property rights. The parties stipulated below that the cap would reduce Chevron's aggregate rental income on 11 of its 64 lessee-dealer stations by about $207,000 per year, but that Chevron nevertheless expects to receive a return on its investment in these stations that satisfies any constitutional standard. Moreover, Chevron asserted below, and the District Court found, that Chevron would recoup any reductions in its rental income by raising wholesale gasoline prices. In short, Chevron has not clearly argued—let alone established—that it has been singled out to bear any particularly severe regulatory burden. Rather, the gravamen of Chevron's claim is simply that Hawaii's rent cap will not actually serve the State's legitimate interest in protecting consumers against high gasoline prices. Whatever the merits of that claim, it does not sound under the Takings Clause. Chevron plainly does not seek compensation for a taking of its property for a legitimate public use, but rather an injunction against the enforcement of a regulation that it alleges to be fundamentally arbitrary and irrational.

Finally, the "substantially advances" formula is not only *doctrinally* untenable as a takings test—its application as such would also present serious practical difficulties. The *Agins* formula can be read to demand heightened means-ends review of virtually any regulation of private property. If so interpreted, it would require courts to scrutinize the efficacy of a vast array of state and federal regulations—a task for which courts are not well suited. Moreover, it would empower—and might often require—courts to substitute their predictive judgments for those of elected legislatures and expert agencies.

Although the instant case is only the tip of the proverbial iceberg, it foreshadows the hazards of placing courts in this role. To resolve Chevron's takings claim, the District Court was required to choose between the views of two opposing economists as to whether Hawaii's rent control statute would help to prevent concentration and supracompetitive prices in the State's retail gasoline market. Finding one expert to be "more persuasive" than the other, the court concluded that the Hawaii Legislature's chosen regulatory strategy would not actually achieve its objectives. Along the way, the court determined that the State was not entitled to enact a prophylactic rent cap without actual evidence that oil companies had charged, or would charge, excessive rents. Based on these findings, the District Court enjoined further enforcement of Act 257's rent cap provision against Chevron. We find the proceedings below remarkable, to say the least, given that we have long eschewed such heightened scrutiny when addressing substantive due process challenges to government regulation. . . .

For the foregoing reasons, we conclude that the "substantially advances" formula . . . is not a valid method of identifying regulatory takings for which the Fifth Amendment requires just compensation. Since Chevron argued only a "substantially advances" theory in support of its takings claim, it was not entitled to summary judgment on that claim.

We emphasize that our holding today—that the "substantially advances" formula is not a valid takings test—does not require us to disturb any of our prior holdings. To be sure, we applied a "substantially advances" inquiry in *Agins* itself, . . . and arguably also in *Keystone Bituminous Coal Assn. v. DeBenedictis,* 480 U.S. 470, 485–492, 107 S.Ct. 1232, 94 L.Ed.2d 472 (1987) (quoting " 'substantially advance[s]' " language and then finding that the challenged statute was intended to further a substantial public interest). But in no case have we found a compensable taking based on such an inquiry. . . .

Although *Nollan* and *Dolan* [also] quoted *Agins'* language, see *Dolan, supra,* at 385, 114 S.Ct. 2309; *Nollan, supra,* at 834, 107 S.Ct. 3141, the rule those decisions established is entirely distinct from the "substantially advances" test we address today. Whereas the "substantially advances" inquiry before us now is unconcerned with the degree or type of burden a regulation places upon property, *Nollan* and *Dolan* both involved dedications of property so onerous that, outside the exactions context, they would be deemed *per se* physical takings. In neither case did the Court question whether the exaction would substantially advance *some* legitimate state interest. See *Dolan, supra,* at 387–388, 114 S.Ct. 2309; *Nollan, supra,* at 841, 107 S.Ct. 3141. Rather, the issue was whether the exactions substantially advanced the *same* interests that land-use authorities asserted would allow them to deny the permit altogether. As the Court explained in *Dolan,* these cases involve a special application of the "doctrine of 'unconstitutional conditions,'" which provides that "the government may not require a person to give up a constitutional right—here the right to receive just compensation when property is taken for a public use—in exchange for a discretionary benefit conferred by the government where the benefit has little or no relationship to the property." That is worlds apart from a rule that says a regulation affecting property constitutes a taking on its face solely because it does not substantially advance a legitimate government interest. In short, *Nollan* and *Dolan* cannot be characterized as applying the "substantially advances" test we address today, and our decision should not be read to disturb these precedents.

* * *

Twenty-five years ago, the Court posited that a regulation of private property "effects a taking if [it] does not substantially advance [a] legitimate state interes[t]." *Agins, supra.* The lower courts in this case took that statement to its logical conclusion, and in so doing, revealed its imprecision. Today we correct course. We hold that the "substantially advances" formula is not a valid takings test, and indeed conclude that it has no proper place in our takings jurisprudence. In so doing, we reaffirm that a plaintiff seeking to challenge a government regulation as an uncompensated taking of private property may proceed under one of the other theories discussed above—by alleging a "physical" taking, a *Lucas*-type "total regulatory taking," a *Penn Central* taking, or a land-use exaction violating the standards set forth in *Nollan* and *Dolan*. Because Chevron argued only a "substantially advances" theory in support of its takings claim, it was not entitled to summary judgment on that claim. Accordingly, we reverse the judgment of the Ninth Circuit and remand the case for further proceedings consistent with this opinion.

8.   In Palazzolo v. Rhode Island, 533 U.S. 606 (2001) the Supreme Court addressed a situation where most but not all of the landowner's property was subjected to a coastal wetlands regulation that made most construction impossible. An appraisal had valued the entire parcel at $3,150,000; however, the portion of the landowner's property on which development remained lawful was still worth $200,000. The Court held that a *Lucas* style takings claim would not apply to these facts:

> Assuming a taking is otherwise established, a State may not evade the duty to compensate on the premise that the landowner is left with a token interest. This is not the situation of the landowner in this case, however. A regulation permitting a landowner to build a substantial residence on an 18–acre parcel does not leave the property "economically idle." [quoting *Lucas*]

> In his brief submitted to us petitioner attempts to revive this part of his claim by reframing it. He argues, for the first time, that the upland parcel is distinct from the wetlands portions, so he should be permitted to assert a deprivation limited to the latter. This contention asks us to examine the difficult, persisting question of what is the proper denominator in the takings fraction. See Michelman, Property, Utility, and Fairness: Comments on the Ethical Foundations of "Just Compensation Law," 80 Harv. L.Rev. 1165, 1192 (1967). Some of our cases indicate that the extent of deprivation effected by a regulatory action is measured against the value of the parcel as a whole, see, *e.g., Keystone Bituminous Coal Assn. v. DeBenedictis,* 480 U.S. 470, 497, 107 S.Ct. 1232 (1987); but we have at times expressed discomfort with the logic of this rule, see *Lucas, supra,* at 1016–1017, n. 7, 112 S.Ct. 2886, a sentiment echoed by some commentators, see, *e.g.,* Epstein, Takings: Descent and Resurrection, 1987 Sup.Ct. Rev. 1, 16–17 (1987); Fee, Unearthing the Denominator in Regulatory Takings Claims, 61 U. Chi. L.Rev. 1535 (1994). Whatever the merits of these criticisms, we will not explore the point here. Petitioner did not press the argument in the state courts, and the issue was not presented in the petition for certiorari. The case comes to us on the premise that petitioner's entire parcel serves as the basis for his takings claim, and, so framed, the total deprivation argument fails.

Rather, the Court held, the taking claim should be remanded for examination under the principles of *Penn Central*, reprinted supra.

For a good discussion of the denominator problem, see City of Coeur D'Alene v. Simpson, 142 Idaho 839, 136 P.3d 310 (2006), where one parcel of land was owned by two natural persons and the other by a corporation they had created. The court noted that the mere fact of separate ownership could not establish that there are separate parcels. If that were the case land owners could manipulate the parcels in order to reduce the size of the denominator. In this case the landowners stated that the purpose of the transfer was not manipulation of the takings rule, but rather to limit the land owners' liability and to facilitate estate planning. However, the transfer occurred after the takings litigation had commenced, but before it terminated. Given this latter fact, the court remanded so that the City could present evidence that the real purpose of the transfer had been to create an "advantageous denominator" for the landowners. The court also noted as relevant such factors as whether the two parcels of land were subject to different sets of zoning restrictions, and whether it was contemplated that they would be developed together or separately.

In Tahoe–Sierra Preservation Council, Inc. v. Tahoe Regional Planning Agency (TRPA), 535 U.S. 302 (2002), the Supreme Court concluded that a government agency's 32–month moratorium on development pending study of the environmental impact on Lake Tahoe did not constitute a "categorical" taking. Significantly, the action was a facial challenge to the moratorium as a whole, not an "as applied" challenge to the impact on any particular parcel of land. The landowners had argued that the *Lucas* test should apply because, while the moratorium was only temporary, during that period it did in fact prevent all economically viable use of the affected land. In rejecting that proposition the majority stated:

> The categorical rule that we applied in *Lucas* states that compensation is required when a regulation deprives an owner of "*all* economically beneficial uses" of his land. Under that rule, a statute that "wholly eliminated the value" of Lucas' fee simple title clearly qualified as a taking. But our holding was limited to "the extraordinary circumstance when *no* productive or economically beneficial use of land is permitted." The emphasis on the word "no" in the text of the opinion was, in effect, reiterated in a footnote explaining that the categorical rule would not apply if the diminution in value were 95% instead of 100%. Anything less than a "complete elimination of value," or a "total loss," the Court acknowledged, would require the kind of analysis applied in *Penn Central*. *Lucas*, 505 U.S. at 1019–1020, n. 8, 112 S.Ct. 2886, 505 U.S. 1003.

> Certainly, our holding that the permanent "obliteration of the value" of a fee simple estate constitutes a categorical taking does not answer the question whether a regulation prohibiting any economic use of land for a 32–month period has the same legal effect. Petitioners seek to bring this case under the rule announced in *Lucas* by arguing that we can effectively sever a 32–month segment from the remainder of each landowner's fee simple estate, and then ask whether that segment has been taken in its entirety by the moratoria. Of course, defining the property interest taken

in terms of the very regulation being challenged is circular. With property so divided, every delay would become a total ban; the moratorium and the normal permit process alike would constitute categorical takings. Petitioners' "conceptual severance" argument is unavailing because it ignores *Penn Central's* admonition that in regulatory takings cases we must focus on "the parcel as a whole." 438 U.S., at 130–131, 98 S.Ct. 2646. We have consistently rejected such an approach to the "denominator" question. See *Keystone,* 480 U.S., at 497, 107 S.Ct. 1232.... Thus, the District Court erred when it disaggregated petitioners' property into temporal segments corresponding to the regulations at issue and then analyzed whether petitioners were deprived of all economically viable use during each period.

An interest in real property is defined by the metes and bounds that describe its geographic dimensions and the term of years that describes the temporal aspect of the owner's interest. See Restatement of Property §§ 7–9 (1936). Both dimensions must be considered if the interest is to be viewed in its entirety. Hence, a permanent deprivation of the owner's use of the entire area is a taking of "the parcel as a whole," whereas a temporary restriction that merely causes a diminution in value is not. Logically, a fee simple estate cannot be rendered valueless by a temporary prohibition on economic use, because the property will recover value as soon as the prohibition is lifted. Cf. *Agins v. City of Tiburon,* 447 U.S., at 263, n. 9, 100 S.Ct. 2138 ("Even if the appellants' ability to sell their property was limited during the pendency of the condemnation proceeding, the appellants were free to sell or develop their property when the proceedings ended. Mere fluctuations in value during the process of governmental decisionmaking, absent extraordinary delay, are 'incidents of ownership. They cannot be considered as a "taking" in the constitutional sense' ")

* * * [Our] cases make clear that the categorical rule in *Lucas* was carved out for the "extraordinary case" in which a regulation permanently deprives property of all value; the default rule remains that, in the regulatory taking context, we require a more fact specific inquiry. * * *

* * * [T]he extreme categorical rule that any deprivation of all economic use, no matter how brief, constitutes a compensable taking surely cannot be sustained. Petitioners' broad submission would apply to numerous "normal delays in obtaining building permits, changes in zoning ordinances, variances, and the like," [citing *First English*, 482 U.S. at 321, 107 S.Ct. 2378,] as well as to orders temporarily prohibiting access to crime scenes, businesses that violate health codes, fire-damaged buildings, or other areas that we cannot now foresee. Such a rule would undoubtedly require changes in numerous practices that have long been considered permissible exercises of the police power. As Justice Holmes warned in *Mahon,* "[g]overnment hardly could go on if to some extent values incident to property could not be diminished without paying for every such change in the general law." 260 U.S. at 413, 43 S.Ct. 158. A rule that required compensation for every delay in the use of property would render routine government processes prohibitively expensive or encour-

age hasty decisionmaking. Such an important change in the law should be the product of legislative rulemaking rather than adjudication.

The Court rejected any categorical rule that a moratorium on development lasting longer than a specified number of years should be treated as a taking, and in particular, Chief Justice Rehnquist's dissenting suggestion that a six year delay should be regarded as automatically excessive. As Justice Rehnquist noted in his dissent, a taking of a leasehold requires compensation even though the taking, as far as the tenant is concerned, is only "temporary." Is that argument persuasive?

In a separate dissent Justice Thomas argued that even a temporary moratorium should be treated as a taking under the *Lucas* rule. The issue of duration and amount of future value remaining after the moratorium is lifted should go to the amount of compensation to be paid, not to whether a taking has occurred at all.

The *Tahoe–Sierra* opinion also contrasted the situation in that case, where the government agency was acting "diligently and in good" faith, with the *Monterey* situation, limiting the *Monterey* argument that a taking could occur when the government's action "did not substantially advance a legitimate state interest" to situations where the government was merely "stalling" or not engaging in "a proportional response to a serious risk of harm...." And the *Palazzolo* opinion added: "Government authorities, of course, may not burden property by imposition of repetitive or unfair land-use procedures in order to avoid a final decision." (citing *Monterey v. Del Monte Dunes*).

Thus the post-*Lucas* law seems consistent with two propositions. *First*, as to substantive, policy-grounded limitations on development, *Palazzolo* and *Tahoe–Sierra* appear to limit *Lucas* to situations where the landowner's entire parcel is valueless or nearly so, although uncertainty remains about whether the land owner might be able to "divide" the parcel and show that the portion affected by the regulation is indeed valueless. One possible way of doing so is if the regulation applies to a specific geographic proportion of the land in question, but not to another portion. However, under *Tahoe–Sierra* the land owner cannot come within *Lucas* by showing that all economic use of a parcel was prohibited during a temporary moratorium period; so the "denominator" in the taking fraction may not be sliced temporally.

Second, as to unreasonable delays, failure to act in good faith, or other government actions that impair a lands value significantly and cannot be justified, *Monterey* permits a jury to find a taking even when the *Lucas* requirements cannot be met.

9. In Bormann v. Board of Supervisors in and for Kossuth County, 584 N.W.2d 309 (Iowa 1998), the Iowa Supreme Court considered a state statute providing that once a hog production facility had been built in a designated agricultural area and received regulatory approval from the county, it would thereafter be immune from all common law nuisance suits, provided that it was operated in compliance with all relevant federal and state laws.

In a facial challenge to the statute by nearby land owners, the court held that the deprivation of the nuisance action was an unconstitutional taking.

The challenge was to the statute "on its face" rather than "as applied" because the plaintiffs had not proven that a nuisance actually existed in their case. The court reasoned:

> The property interest at stake here is that of an easement, which is an interest in land. Over one hundred years ago, this court held that the right to maintain a nuisance is an easement. Churchill v. Burlington Water Co., 94 Iowa 89, 93, 62 N.W. 646, 647 (1895). * * *

> *Churchill's* holding that the right to maintain a nuisance is an easement and its definition of an easement are consistent with the Restatement of Property: An easement is an interest in land which entitles the owner of the easement to use or enjoy land in the possession of another. . . . It may entitle him to do acts which he would otherwise not be privileged to do, or it may merely entitle him to prevent the owner of the land subject to the easement from doing acts which he would otherwise be privileged to do. An easement which entitles the owner to do acts which, were it not for the easement, he would not be privileged to do, is an affirmative easement. . . . [The easement] may entitle [its] owner to do acts on his own land which, were it not for the easement, would constitute a nuisance. Restatement of Property § 451 comment. a, at 2911–12 (1944) (emphasis added). * * *

For example, in their farming operations the applicants would be allowed to generate "offensive smells" on their property which without the easement would permit affected property owners to sue the applicants for nuisances. See Iowa Code § 352.2(6); see also Buchanan v. Simplot Feeders Ltd. Partnership, 134 Wash.2d 673, 952 P.2d 610, 615 (Wash. 1998) (holding that Washington's Right-to-Farm Act gives farms a quasi easement, against urban developments that subsequently locate next to farm, to continue nuisance activities) (dictum).

[Under the Takings clause there] are two categories of state action that must be compensated without any further inquiry into additional factors, such as the economic impact of the governmental conduct on the land-owner or whether the regulation substantially advances a legitimate state interest. The two categories include regulations that (1) involve a perma-nent physical invasion of the property or (2) deny the owner all economi-cally beneficial or productive use of the land.

The neighbors do not contend the record supports a finding that the challenged statute denies them all economically beneficial or productive use of their property. * * *

Generally, when the government has physically invaded property in carrying out a public project and has not compensated the landowner, the United States Supreme Court will find that a per se taking has occurred. * * * For example, in Pumpelly v. Green Bay & Mississippi Canal Co., the Court held there was a taking where the defendant's construction of a dam, pursuant to state authority, permanently flooded the plaintiff's property. 13 Wall. 166, 80 U.S. 166, 181, 20 L.Ed. 557, 561 (1871). In so holding, the Court enunciated the following rule: "[W]here real estate is actually invaded by superinduced additions of water, earth, sand, or other material, or by having any artificial structure placed on it, so as to effectually destroy or impair its usefulness, it is a taking, within the meaning of the constitution."

Richards v. Washington Terminal Co. presents a factual scenario closer to the facts in this case. 233 U.S. 546, 34 S.Ct. 654, 58 L.Ed. 1088 (1914). In Richards, the plaintiff owned residential property along the tracks of a railroad that had the power of eminent domain. The property lay near the mouth of a tunnel. The Court recognized that two kinds of the railroad's activities had partially destroyed the plaintiff's interest in the enjoyment of his property. The first kind involved smoke, dust, cinders, and vibrations invading the plaintiff's property at all points at which the property abutted the tracks. The second kind involved gases and smoke emitted from engines in the tunnel that contaminated the air and invaded the plaintiff's property. A fanning system inside the tunnel forced the emission of the gases and smoke from the tunnel. As to the first activity, the Court denied compensation because it was the kind of harm normally incident to railroading operations. Id. at 554–55, 34 S.Ct. at 657–58. As to the second activity—gases and smoke from the tunnel— the Court concluded the plaintiff was entitled to compensation for the "special and peculiar damage" resulting in diminution of the value of the plaintiff's property.

Richards is viewed as recognizing the taking of a property interest or right "to be free from 'special and peculiar' governmental interference with enjoyment." The taking involved "no kind of physical taking or touching—none whatever." [citing William B. Stoebuck, Condemnation by Nuisance: The Airport Cases in Retrospect and Prospect, 71 Dick. L.Rev. 207 (1967)]

Thus, the state cannot regulate property so as to insulate the users from potential private nuisance claims without providing just compensation to persons injured by the nuisance. The Supreme Court firmly established this principle in *Richards*, holding that "while the legislature may legalize what otherwise would be a public nuisance, it may not confer immunity from action for a private nuisance of such a character as to amount in effect to a taking." *Richards*, 233 U.S. at 553, 34 S.Ct. at 657.

A number of state courts have decided takings cases on the basis that the government entity operated a nuisance-producing enterprise. See, e.g., Thornburg v. Port of Portland, 233 Or. 178, 376 P.2d 100, 106 (Or.1962) ("[A] taking occurs whenever government acts in such a way as substantially to deprive an owner of the useful possession of that which he owns, either by repeated trespasses or by repeated nontrespassory invasions called 'nuisance.' "). Significantly, a large number of these cases deal with smoke and odors from sewage disposal plants and city dumps. One commentator describes the cases this way: Typically, a city sewage plant or dump in the vicinity of, but not necessarily directly adjacent to, the plaintiff's land has wafted its noxious smoke, odors, dust, or ashes, usually combinations of these, over the plaintiff's land, with the obvious result of lessening its enjoyment. No physical touching is present, nor do the courts try to equate the municipal acts with touchings. [Several states] have allowed eminent domain compensation in cases of this kind.... More significant than a court's language is the result it announces, and in this respect all the decisions stand for the proposition that nuisance-type activities are a taking.... Stoebuck, at 226–27 * * * "[G]overnmental activity by an entity having the power of eminent domain, which activity constitutes a nuisance according to the law of torts, is a taking of property for public use, even though such activity may be authorized by legislation." Id. at 208–09. * * *

We reverse and remand for an order declaring that portion of Iowa Code section 352.11(1)(a) that provides for immunity against nuisances unconstitutional and without any force or effect.

The Iowa Supreme Court based its holding on both the United States and Iowa Constitutions, probably insulating it from federal review. Would the United States Supreme Court, following *Lucas*, come out the same way? To what extent does the decision blur the line between trespassory takings and regulatory takings?

STOP THE BEACH RENOURISHMENT, INC. v. FLORIDA DEPARTMENT OF ENVIRONMENTAL PROTECTION

Supreme Court of the United States (2010).
560 U.S. ___, 130 S.Ct. 2592.

Opinion

JUSTICE SCALIA announced the judgment of the Court and delivered the opinion of the Court with respect to Parts I, IV, and V, and an opinion with respect to Parts II and III, in which THE CHIEF JUSTICE, JUSTICE THOMAS, and JUSTICE ALITO join.

We consider a claim that the decision of a State's court of last resort took property without just compensation in violation of the Takings Clause of the Fifth Amendment, as applied against the States through the Fourteenth....

I

A

Generally speaking, state law defines property interests, *Phillips v. Washington Legal Foundation,* 524 U.S. 156, 164, 118 S.Ct. 1925, 141 L.Ed.2d 174 (1998), including property rights in navigable waters and the lands underneath them.... In Florida, the State owns in trust for the public the land permanently submerged beneath navigable waters and the foreshore (the land between the low-tide line and the mean high-water line). Fla. Const., Art. X, § 11; *Broward v. Mabry,* 58 Fla. 398, 407–409, 50 So. 826, 829–830 (1909). Thus, the mean high-water line (the average reach of high tide over the preceding 19 years) is the ordinary boundary between private beachfront, or littoral[1] property, and state-owned land.

---

1. Many cases and statutes use "riparian" to mean abutting any body of water. The Florida Supreme Court, however, has adopted a more precise usage whereby "riparian" means abutting a river or stream and "littoral" means abutting an ocean, sea, or lake. *Walton Cty. v. Stop the*

See *Miller v. Bay–To–Gulf, Inc.*, 141 Fla. 452, 458–460, 193 So. 425, 427–428 (1940) *(per curiam);* Fla. Stat. §§ 177.27(14)–(15), 177.28(1) (2007).

Littoral owners have, in addition to the rights of the public, certain "special rights" with regard to the water and the foreshore, *Broward,* 58 Fla., at 410, 50 So., at 830, rights which Florida considers to be property, generally akin to easements, see ibid.; *Thiesen v. Gulf, Florida & Alabama R. Co.,* 75 Fla. 28, 57, 78, 78 So. 491, 500, 507 (1918) (on rehearing). These include the right of access to the water, the right to use the water for certain purposes, the right to an unobstructed view of the water, and the right to receive accretions and relictions to the littoral property. . . . This is generally in accord with well-established common law, although the precise property rights vary among jurisdictions. . . .

At the center of this case is the right to accretions and relictions. Accretions are additions of alluvion (sand, sediment, or other deposits) to waterfront land; relictions are lands once covered by water that become dry when the water recedes. . . . (For simplicity's sake, we shall refer to accretions and relictions collectively as accretions, and the process whereby they occur as accretion.) In order for an addition to dry land to qualify as an accretion, it must have occurred gradually and imperceptibly-that is, so slowly that one could not see the change occurring, though over time the difference became apparent. Sand Key, supra, at 936; *County of St. Clair v. Lovingston,* 23 Wall. 46, 66–67, 23 L.Ed. 59 (1874). When, on the other hand, there is a "sudden or perceptible loss of or addition to land by the action of the water or a sudden change in the bed of a lake or the course of a stream," the change is called an avulsion. *Sand Key, supra,* at 936; see also 1 Farnham § 69, at 320.

In Florida, as at common law, the littoral owner automatically takes title to dry land added to his property by accretion; but formerly submerged land that has become dry land by avulsion continues to belong to the owner of the seabed (usually the State). . . . Thus, regardless of whether an avulsive event exposes land previously submerged or submerges land previously exposed, the boundary between littoral property and sovereign land does not change; it remains (ordinarily) what was the mean high-water line before the event. See *Bryant v. Peppe,* 238 So.2d 836, 838–839 (Fla.1970); J. Gould, Law of Waters § 158, p. 290 (1883). It follows from this that, when a new strip of land has been added to the shore by avulsion, the littoral owner has no right to subsequent accretions. Those accretions no longer add to *his* property, since the property abutting the water belongs not to him but to the State. See Maloney § 126.6, at 393; 1 Farnham § 71a, at 328.

B

In 1961, Florida's Legislature passed the Beach and Shore Preservation Act, 1961 Fla. Laws ch. 61–246, as amended, Fla. Stat. §§ 161.011–

Beach Renourishment, Inc., 998 So.2d 1102, 1105, n. 3 (2008). When speaking of the Florida law applicable to this case, we follow the Florida Supreme Court's terminology.

161.45 (2007). The Act establishes procedures for "beach restoration and nourishment projects," § 161.088, designed to deposit sand on eroded beaches (restoration) and to maintain the deposited sand (nourishment). §§ 161.021(3), (4). A local government may apply to the Department of Environmental Protection for the funds and the necessary permits to restore a beach, see §§ 161.101(1), 161.041(1). When the project involves placing fill on the State's submerged lands, authorization is required from the Board of Trustees of the Internal Improvement Trust Fund, see § 253.77(1), which holds title to those lands, § 253.12(1).

Once a beach restoration "is determined to be undertaken," the Board sets what is called "an erosion control line." §§ 161.161(3)–(5). It must be set by reference to the existing mean high-water line, though in theory it can be located seaward or landward of that. See § 161.161(5). Much of the project work occurs seaward of the erosion-control line, as sand is dumped on what was once submerged land. See App. 87–88. The fixed erosion-control line replaces the fluctuating mean high-water line as the boundary between privately owned littoral property and state property. § 161.191(1). Once the erosion-control line is recorded, the common law ceases to increase upland property by accretion (or decrease it by erosion). § 161.191(2). Thus, when accretion to the shore moves the mean high-water line seaward, the property of beachfront landowners is not extended to that line (as the prior law provided), but remains bounded by the permanent erosion-control line. Those landowners "continue to be entitled," however, "to all common-law riparian rights" other than the right to accretions. § 161.201. If the beach erodes back landward of the erosion-control line over a substantial portion of the shoreline covered by the project, the Board may, on its own initiative, or must, if asked by the owners or lessees of a majority of the property affected, direct the agency responsible for maintaining the beach to return the beach to the condition contemplated by the project. If that is not done within a year, the project is canceled and the erosion-control line is null and void. § 161.211(2), (3). Finally, by regulation, if the use of submerged land would "unreasonably infringe on riparian rights," the project cannot proceed unless the local governments show that they own or have a property interest in the upland property adjacent to the project site. Fla. Admin. Code Rule 18–21.004(3)(b) (2009).

C

In 2003, the city of Destin and Walton County applied for the necessary permits to restore 6.9 miles of beach within their jurisdictions that had been eroded by several hurricanes. The project envisioned depositing along that shore sand dredged from further out. See *Walton Cty. v. Stop the Beach Renourishment, Inc.,* 998 So.2d 1102, 1106 (Fla. 2008). It would add about 75 feet of dry sand seaward of the mean high-water line (to be denominated the erosion-control line). The Department issued a notice of intent to award the permits, App. 27–41, and the Board approved the erosion-control line, *id.,* at 49–50.

The petitioner here, Stop the Beach Renourishment, Inc., is a non-profit corporation formed by people who own beachfront property bordering the project area (we shall refer to them as the Members). It brought an administrative challenge to the proposed project, see *id.,* at 10–26, which was unsuccessful; the Department approved the permits. Petitioner then challenged that action in state court under the Florida Administrative Procedure Act, Fla. Stat. § 120.68 (2007). The District Court of Appeal for the First District concluded that, contrary to the Act's preservation of "all common-law riparian rights," the order had eliminated two of the Members' littoral rights: (1) the right to receive accretions to their property; and (2) the right to have the contact of their property with the water remain intact. *Save Our Beaches, Inc. v. Florida Dept. of Environmental Protection,* 27 So.3d 48, 57 (2006). This, it believed, would be an unconstitutional taking, which would "unreasonably infringe on riparian rights," and therefore require the showing under Fla. Admin. Code Rule 18–21.004(3)(b) that the local governments owned or had a property interest in the upland property. It set aside the Department's final order approving the permits and remanded for that showing to be made. 27 So.3d, at 60. It also certified to the Florida Supreme Court the following question (as rephrased by the latter court):

> "On its face, does the Beach and Shore Preservation Act unconstitutionally deprive upland owners of littoral rights without just compensation?" 998 So.2d, at 1105 (footnotes omitted).

The Florida Supreme Court answered the certified question in the negative, and quashed the First District's remand. *Id.,* at 1121. It faulted the Court of Appeal for not considering the doctrine of avulsion, which it concluded permitted the State to reclaim the restored beach on behalf of the public. *Id.,* at 1116–1118. It described the right to accretions as a future contingent interest, not a vested property right, and held that there is no littoral right to contact with the water independent of the littoral right of access, which the Act does not infringe. *Id.,* at 1112, 1119–1120. Petitioner sought rehearing on the ground that the Florida Supreme Court's decision itself effected a taking of the Members' littoral rights contrary to the Fifth and Fourteenth Amendments to the Federal Constitution. The request for rehearing was denied. We granted certiorari, 557 U.S. ___, 129 S.Ct. 2792, 174 L.Ed.2d 290 (2009).

II

A

Before coming to the parties' arguments in the present case, we discuss some general principles of our takings jurisprudence. The Takings Clause-"nor shall private property be taken for public use, without just compensation," U.S. Const., Amdt. 5–applies as fully to the taking of a landowner's riparian rights as it does to the taking of an estate in land. See *Yates v. Milwaukee,* 10 Wall. 497, 504, 19 L.Ed. 984 (1871). Moreover, though the classic taking is a transfer of property to the State or to another private party by eminent domain, the Takings Clause applies to other state actions that achieve the same thing. Thus, when the government uses its own property in such a way that it destroys private property, it has taken that property. See *United States v. Causby,* 328 U.S. 256, 261–262, 66 S.Ct. 1062, 90 L.Ed. 1206 (1946); *Pumpelly v. Green Bay Co.,* 13 Wall. 166, 177–178, 20 L.Ed. 557 (1872). Similarly, our doctrine of regulatory takings "aims to identify regulatory actions that are functionally equivalent to the classic taking." *Lingle v. Chevron U.S.A. Inc.,* 544 U.S. 528, 539, 125 S.Ct. 2074, 161 L.Ed.2d 876 (2005). Thus, it is a taking when a state regulation forces a property owner to submit to a permanent physical occupation, *Loretto v. Teleprompter Manhattan CATV Corp.,* 458 U.S. 419, 425–426, 102 S.Ct. 3164, 73 L.Ed.2d 868 (1982), or deprives him of all economically beneficial use of his property, *Lucas v. South Carolina Coastal Council,* 505 U.S. 1003, 1019, 112 S.Ct. 2886, 120 L.Ed.2d 798 (1992). Finally (and here we approach the situation before us), States effect a taking if they recharacterize as public property what was previously private property. See *Webb's Fabulous Pharmacies, Inc. v. Beckwith,* 449 U.S. 155, 163–165, 101 S.Ct. 446, 66 L.Ed.2d 358 (1980).

The Takings Clause (unlike, for instance, the Ex Post Facto Clauses, see Art. I, § 9, cl. 3; § 10, cl. 1) is not addressed to the action of a specific branch or branches. It is concerned simply with the act, and not with the governmental actor ("nor shall private property *be taken*" (emphasis added)). There is no textual justification for saying that the existence or the scope of a State's power to expropriate private property without just compensation varies according to the branch of government effecting the expropriation. Nor does common sense recommend such a principle. It would be absurd to allow a State to do by judicial decree what the Takings Clause forbids it to do by legislative fiat. See *Stevens v. Cannon Beach,* 510 U.S. 1207, 1211–1212, 114 S.Ct. 1332, 127 L.Ed.2d 679 (1994) (SCALIA, J., dissenting from denial of certiorari).

Our precedents provide no support for the proposition that takings effected by the judicial branch are entitled to special treatment, and in fact suggest the contrary. *PruneYard Shopping Center v. Robins,* 447 U.S. 74, 100 S.Ct. 2035, 64 L.Ed.2d 741 (1980), involved a decision of the California Supreme Court overruling one of its prior decisions which had held that the California Constitution's guarantees of freedom of speech and of the press, and of the right to petition the government, did not require the owner of private property to accord those rights on his premises. The appellants, owners of a shopping center, contended that their private property rights could not "be denied by invocation of a state constitutional provision *or by judicial reconstruction of a State's laws of private property,*" *id.,* at 79, 100 S.Ct. 2035 (emphasis added). We held that there had been no taking, citing cases involving legislative and executive takings, and applying standard Takings Clause analysis. See *id.,* at 82–84, 100 S.Ct. 2035. We treated the California Supreme Court's application of the constitutional provisions as a regulation of the use of private property, and evaluated whether that regulation violated the property owners' "right to exclude others," *id.,* at 80, 100 S.Ct. 2035 (internal quotation marks omitted). Our opinion addressed only the claimed taking by the constitutional provision. Its failure to speak separately to the claimed taking by "judicial reconstruction of a State's laws of private property" certainly does not suggest that a taking by judicial action cannot occur, and arguably suggests that the same analysis applicable to taking by constitutional provision would apply.

Webb's Fabulous Pharmacies, supra, is even closer in point. There the purchaser of an insolvent corporation had interpleaded the corporation's creditors, placing the purchase price in an interest-bearing account in the registry of the Circuit Court of Seminole County, to be distributed in satisfaction of claims approved by a receiver. The Florida Supreme Court construed an applicable statute to mean that the interest on the account belonged to the county, because the account was "considered 'public money,' " *Beckwith v. Webb's Fabulous Pharmacies,* 374 So.2d 951, 952–953 (1979) *(per curiam).* We held this to be a taking. We noted that "[t]he usual and general rule is that any interest on an interpleaded and deposited fund follows the principal and is to be allocated to those who are ultimately to be the owners of that principal," 449 U.S., at 162, 101 S.Ct. 446. "Neither the Florida Legislature by statute, nor the Florida courts by judicial decree," we said, "may accomplish the result the county seeks simply by recharacterizing the principal as 'public money.' " *Id.,* at 164, 101 S.Ct. 446.

In sum, the Takings Clause bars *the State* from taking private property without paying for it, no matter which branch is the instrument of the taking. To be sure, the manner of state action may matter: Condemnation by eminent domain, for example, is always a taking, while a legislative, executive, or judicial restriction of property use may or may not be, depending on its nature and extent. But the particular state *actor* is irrelevant. If a legislature *or a court* declares that what was once an established right of private property no longer exists, it has taken that property, no less than if the State had physically appropriated it or destroyed its value by regulation. "[A] State, by *ipse dixit,* may not transform private property into public property without compensation." *Ibid.*

* * *

C

* * *

We do not grasp the relevance of Justice KENNEDY's speculation, *post,* at 2616, that the Framers did not envision the Takings Clause would apply to judicial action. They doubtless did not, since the Constitution was adopted in an era when courts had no power to "change" the common law. See 1 Blackstone 69–70 (1765); *Rogers v. Tennessee,* 532 U.S. 451, 472–478, 121 S.Ct. 1693, 149 L.Ed.2d 697 (2001) (SCALIA, J., dissenting). Where the text they adopted is clear, however ("nor shall private property be taken for public use"), what counts is not what they envisioned but what they wrote. Of course even after courts, in the 19th century, did assume the power to change the common law, it is not true that the new "common-law tradition ... allows for incremental modifications to property law," *post,* at 2615, so that "owners may reasonably expect or anticipate courts to make certain changes in property law," *post,* at 2615. In the only sense in which this could be relevant to what we are discussing, that is an astounding statement. We are talking here about judicial elimination of established private property rights. If that is indeed a "common-law tradition," Justice KENNEDY ought to be able to provide a more solid example for it than the only one he cites, *post,* at 2615, a state-court change (from "noxious" to "harmful") of the test for determining whether a neighbor's vegetation is a tortious nuisance. *Fancher v. Fagella,* 274 Va. 549, 555–556, 650 S.E.2d 519, 522 (2007). But perhaps he does not really mean that it is a common-law tradition to eliminate property rights, since he immediately follows his statement that "owners may reasonably expect or anticipate courts to make certain changes in property law" with the contradictory statement that "courts cannot abandon settled principles," *post,* at 2615. If no "settled principl[e]" has been abandoned, it is hard to see how property law could have been "change[d]," rather than merely clarified.

Justice KENNEDY has added "two additional practical considerations that the Court would need to address before recognizing judicial takings," *post,* at 2616. One of them is simple and simply answered: the assertion that "it is unclear what remedy a reviewing court could enter after finding a judicial taking," *post,* at 2617. Justice KENNEDY worries that we may only be able to mandate compensation. That remedy is even rare for a legislative or executive taking, and we see no reason why it would be the exclusive remedy for a judicial taking. If we were to hold that the Florida Supreme Court had effected an uncompensated taking in the present case, we would simply reverse the Florida Supreme Court's judgment that the Beach and Shore Preservation Act can be applied to the property in question. Justice KENNEDY's other point, *post,* at 2616–2617—that we will have to decide when the claim of a judicial taking must be asserted-hardly presents an awe-inspiring prospect. These, and all the other "difficulties," *post,* at 2613, "difficult questions," *post,* at 2615, and "practical considerations" *post,* at 2616–2617, that Justice KENNEDY worries *may perhaps* stand in the way of recognizing a judicial taking, are either nonexistent or insignificant.

Finally, we cannot avoid comment upon Justice KENNEDY's donning of the mantle of judicial restraint-his assertion that it is we, and not he, who would empower the courts and encourage their expropriation of private property. He warns that if judges know that their action is covered by the Takings Clause, they will issue "sweeping new rule[s] to adjust the rights of property owners," comfortable in the knowledge that their innovations will be preserved upon payment by the State. *Post,* at 2616. That is quite impossible. As we have said, if we were to hold that the Florida Supreme Court had effected an uncompensated taking in this case, we would not validate the taking by ordering Florida to pay compensation. We would simply reverse the Florida Supreme Court's judgment that the Beach and Shore Preservation Act can be applied to the Members' property. The power to effect a *compensated* taking would then reside, where it has always resided, not in the Florida Supreme Court but in the Florida Legislature—which could either provide compensation or acquiesce in the invalidity of the offending features of the Act. Cf. *Davis v. Michigan Dept. of Treasury,* 489 U.S. 803, 817–818, 109 S.Ct. 1500, 103 L.Ed.2d 891 (1989). The only realistic incentive that subjection to the Takings Clause might provide to any court would be the incentive to get reversed, which in our experience few judges value.

* * *

<h2 style="text-align:center">III</h2>

Respondents put forward a number of arguments which contradict, to a greater or lesser degree, the principle discussed above, that the existence of a taking does not depend upon the branch of government that effects it. First, in a case claiming a judicial taking they would add to our normal takings inquiry a requirement that the court's decision have no "fair and substantial basis." This is taken from our jurisprudence dealing with the question whether a state-court decision rests upon adequate and independent state grounds, placing it beyond our jurisdiction to review. See E. Gressman, K. Geller, S. Shapiro, T. Bishop, & E. Hartnett, Supreme Court Practice, ch. 3.26, p. 222 (9th ed.2007). To assure that there is no "evasion" of our authority to review federal questions, we insist that the nonfederal ground of decision have "fair support." *Broad River Power Co. v. South Carolina ex rel. Daniel,* 281 U.S. 537, 540, 50 S.Ct. 401, 74 L.Ed. 1023 (1930); see also *Ward v. Board of Comm'rs of Love Cty.,* 253 U.S. 17, 22–23, 40 S.Ct. 419, 64 L.Ed. 751 (1920). A test designed to determine whether there has been an evasion is not obviously appropriate for determining whether there has been a taking of property. But if it is to be extended there it must mean (in the present context) that there is a "fair and substantial basis" for believing that petitioner's Members did not have a property right to future accretions which the Act would take away. This is no different, we think, from our requirement that petitioners' Members must prove the elimination of an established property right.

Next, respondents argue that federal courts lack the knowledge of state law required to decide whether a judicial decision that purports merely to clarify property rights has instead taken them. But federal courts must often decide what state property rights exist in nontakings contexts, see, *e.g., Board of Regents of State Colleges v. Roth,* 408 U.S. 564, 577–578, 92 S.Ct. 2701, 33 L.Ed.2d 548 (1972) (Due Process Clause). And indeed they must decide it to resolve claims that legislative or executive action has effected a taking. For example, a regulation that deprives a property owner of all economically beneficial use of his property is not a taking if the restriction "inhere[s] in the title itself, in the restrictions that background principles of the State's law of property and nuisance already place upon land ownership." *Lucas,* 505 U.S., at 1029, 112 S.Ct. 2886. A constitutional provision that forbids the uncompensated taking of property is quite simply insusceptible of enforcement by federal courts unless they have the power to decide what property rights exist under state law.

Respondents also warn us against depriving common-law judging of needed flexibility. That argument has little appeal when directed against the enforcement of a constitutional guarantee adopted in an era when, as we said *supra,* at 2606, courts had no power to "change" the common law. But in any case, courts have no peculiar need of flexibility. It is no more essential that judges be free to overrule prior cases that establish property entitlements than that state legislators be free to revise pre-existing statutes that confer property entitlements, or agency-heads pre-existing regulations that do so. And insofar as courts merely clarify and elaborate property entitlements that were previously unclear, they cannot be said to have taken an established property right.

* * *

For its part, petitioner proposes an unpredictability test. Quoting Justice Stewart's concurrence in *Hughes v. Washington,* 389 U.S. 290, 296, 88 S.Ct. 438, 19 L.Ed.2d 530 (1967), petitioner argues that a judicial taking consists of a decision that " 'constitutes a sudden change in state law, unpredictable in terms of relevant precedents.' " See Brief for Petitioner 17, 34–50. The focus of petitioner's test is misdirected. What counts is not whether there is precedent for the allegedly confiscatory decision, but whether the property right allegedly taken was established. A "predictability of change" test would cover both too much and too little. Too much, because a judicial property decision need not be predictable, so long as it does not declare that what had been private property under established law no longer is. A decision that clarifies property entitlements (or the lack thereof) that were previously unclear might be difficult to predict, but it does not eliminate established property rights. And the predictability test covers too little, because a judicial elimination of established private-property rights that is foreshadowed by dicta or even by holdings years in advance is nonetheless a taking. If, for example, a state court held in one case, to which the complaining property owner was not a party, that it had the power to limit the acreage of privately owned real estate to 100 acres, and then, in a second case, applied that principle to declare the complainant's 101st acre to be public property, the State would have taken an acre from the complainant even though the decision was predictable.

IV

* * *

Petitioner argues that the Florida Supreme Court took two of the property rights of the Members by declaring that those rights did not exist: the right to accretions, and the right to have littoral property touch the water (which petitioner distinguishes from the mere right of access to the water). Under petitioner's theory, because no prior Florida decision had said that the State's filling of submerged tidal lands could have the effect of depriving a littoral owner of contact with the water and denying him future accretions, the Florida Supreme Court's judgment in the present case abolished those two easements to which littoral property owners had been entitled. This puts the burden on the wrong party. There is no taking unless petitioner can show that, before the Florida Supreme Court's decision, littoral-property owners had rights to future accretions and contact with the water superior to the State's right to fill in its submerged land. Though some may think the question close, in our view the showing cannot be made.

Two core principles of Florida property law intersect in this case. First, the State as owner of the submerged land adjacent to littoral property has the right to fill that land, so long as it does not interfere with the rights of the public and the rights of littoral landowners.... Second, as we described *supra,* at 2598–2599, if an avulsion exposes land seaward of littoral property that had previously been submerged, that land belongs to the State even if it interrupts the littoral owner's contact with the water. See *Bryant,* 238 So.2d, at 837, 838–839. The issue here is whether there is an exception to this rule when the State is the cause of the avulsion. Prior law suggests there is not. In *Martin v. Busch,* 93 Fla. 535, 112 So. 274 (1927), the Florida Supreme Court held that when the State drained water from a lakebed belonging to the State, causing land that was formerly below the mean high-water line to become dry land, that land continued to belong to the State. *Id.,* at 574, 112 So., at 287; see also *Bryant, supra,* at 838–839 (analogizing the situation in *Martin* to an avulsion). "'The riparian rights doctrine of accretion and reliction,'" the Florida Supreme Court later explained, "'does not apply to such lands.'" *Bryant, supra,* at 839 (quoting *Martin, supra,* at 578, 112 So., at 288 (Brown, J., concurring)). This is not surprising, as there can be no accretions to land that no longer abuts the water.

Thus, Florida law as it stood before the decision below allowed the State to fill in its own seabed, and the resulting sudden exposure of previously submerged land was treated like an avulsion for purposes of ownership. The right to accretions was therefore subordinate to the State's right to fill. *Thiesen v. Gulf, Florida & Alabama R. Co.* suggests the same result. That case involved a claim by a riparian landowner that a railroad's state-authorized filling of submerged land and construction of tracks upon it interfered with the riparian landowners' rights to access and to wharf out to a shipping channel. The Florida Supreme Court determined that the claimed right to wharf out did not exist in Florida, and that therefore only the right of access was compensable. 75 Fla., at 58–65, 78 So., at 501–503. Significantly, although the court recognized that the riparian-property owners had rights to accretion, see *id.,* at 64–65, 78 So., at 502–503, the only rights it even suggested would be infringed by the railroad were the right of access (which the plaintiff had claimed) and the rights of view and use of the water (which it seems the plaintiff had not claimed), see *id.,* at 58–59, 78, 78 So., at 501, 507.

The Florida Supreme Court decision before us is consistent with these background principles of state property law. Cf. *Lucas,* 505 U.S., at 1028–1029, 112 S.Ct. 2886; *Scranton v. Wheeler,* 179 U.S. 141, 163, 21 S.Ct. 48, 45 L.Ed. 126 (1900). It did not abolish the Members' right to future accretions, but merely held that the right was not implicated by the beach-restoration project, because the doctrine of avulsion applied. See 998 So.2d, at 1117, 1120–1121. The Florida Supreme Court's opinion describes beach restoration as the reclamation by the State of the public's land, just as *Martin* had described the lake drainage in that case. Although the opinion does not cite *Martin* and is not always clear on this point, it suffices that its characterization of the littoral right to accretion is consistent with *Martin* and the other relevant principles of Florida law we have discussed.

What we have said shows that the rule of *Sand Key,* which petitioner repeatedly invokes, is inapposite. There the Florida Supreme Court held that an artificial accretion does not change the right of a littoral-property owner to claim the accreted land as his own (as long as the owner did not cause the accretion himself). 512 So.2d, at 937–938. The reason *Martin* did not apply, *Sand Key* explained, is that the drainage that had occurred in *Martin* did not lower the water level by " 'imperceptible degrees,' " and so did not qualify as an accretion. 512 So.2d, at 940–941.

The result under Florida law may seem counter-intuitive. After all, the Members' property has been deprived of its character (and value) as oceanfront property by the State's artificial creation of an avulsion. Perhaps state-created avulsions ought to be treated differently from other avulsions insofar as the property right to accretion is concerned. But nothing in prior Florida law makes such a distinction, and *Martin* suggests, if it does not indeed hold, the contrary. Even if there might be different interpretations of *Martin* and other Florida property-law cases that would prevent this arguably odd result, we are not free to adopt them. The Takings Clause only protects property rights as they are established under state law, not as they might have been established or ought to have been established. We cannot say that the Florida Supreme Court's decision eliminated a right of accretion established under Florida law.

Petitioner also contends that the State took the Members' littoral right to have their property continually maintain contact with the water. To be clear, petitioner does not allege that the State relocated the property line, as would have happened if the erosion-control line were *landward* of the old mean high-water line (instead of identical to it). Petitioner argues instead that the Members have a separate right for the boundary of their property to be always the mean high-water line. Petitioner points to dicta in *Sand Key* that refers to "the right to have the property's contact with the water remain intact," 512 So.2d, at 936. Even there, the right was included in the definition of the right to access, *ibid.,* which is consistent with the Florida Supreme Court's later description that "there is no independent right of contact with the water" but it "exists to preserve the upland owner's core littoral right of access to the water," 998 So.2d, at 1119. Petitioner's expansive interpretation of the dictum in *Sand Key* would cause it to contradict the clear Florida law governing avulsion. One cannot say that the Florida Supreme Court contravened established property law by rejecting it.

V

Because the Florida Supreme Court's decision did not contravene the established property rights of petitioner's Members, Florida has not violated the Fifth and Fourteenth Amendments. The judgment of the Florida Supreme Court is therefore affirmed.

It is so ordered.

JUSTICE STEVENS took no part in the decision of this case.

JUSTICE KENNEDY, with whom JUSTICE SOTOMAYOR joins, concurring in part and concurring in the judgment.

The Court's analysis of the principles that control ownership of the land in question, and of the rights of petitioner's members as adjacent owners, is correct in my view, leading to my joining Parts I, IV, and V of the Court's opinion. As Justice BREYER observes, however, this case does not require the Court to determine whether, or when, a judicial decision determining the rights of property owners can violate the Takings Clause of the Fifth Amendment of the United States Constitution. This separate opinion notes certain difficulties that should be considered before accepting the theory that a judicial decision that eliminates an "established property right," *ante,* at 2608, constitutes a violation of the Takings Clause.

The Takings Clause is an essential part of the constitutional structure, for it protects private property from expropriation without just compensation; and the right to own and hold property is necessary to the exercise and preservation of freedom. The right to retain property without the fact or even the threat of that sort of expropriation is, of course, applicable to the States under the Due Process Clause of the Fourteenth Amendment. *Chicago, B. & Q. R. Co. v. Chicago,* 166 U.S. 226, 239, 17 S.Ct. 581, 41 L.Ed. 979 (1897).

* * *

If a judicial decision, as opposed to an act of the executive or the legislature, eliminates an established property right, the judgment could be set aside as a deprivation of property without due process of law. The Due Process Clause, in both its substantive and procedural aspects, is a central limitation upon the exercise of judicial power. And this Court has long recognized that property regulations can be invalidated under the Due Process Clause. See, *e.g., Lingle v. Chevron U.S.A. Inc.,* 544 U.S. 528,

542, 125 S.Ct. 2074, 161 L.Ed.2d 876 (2005); *Goldblatt v. Hempstead,* 369 U.S. 590, 591, 592–593, 82 S.Ct. 987, 8 L.Ed.2d 130 (1962); *Demorest v. City Bank Farmers Trust Co.,* 321 U.S. 36, 42–43, 64 S.Ct. 384, 88 L.Ed. 526 (1944); *Broad River Power Co. v. South Carolina ex rel. Daniel,* 281 U.S. 537, 539, 540–541, 50 S.Ct. 401, 74 L.Ed. 1023 (1930); *Washington ex rel. Seattle Title Trust Co. v. Roberge,* 278 U.S. 116, 121, 49 S.Ct. 50, 73 L.Ed. 210 (1928); *Nectow v. Cambridge,* 277 U.S. 183, 188, 48 S.Ct. 447, 72 L.Ed. 842 (1928); *Village of Euclid v. Ambler Realty Co.,* 272 U.S. 365, 395, 47 S.Ct. 114, 71 L.Ed. 303 (1926); see also *Pennsylvania Coal Co. v. Mahon,* 260 U.S. 393, 413, 43 S.Ct. 158, 67 L.Ed. 322 (1922) (there must be limits on government's ability to diminish property values by regulation "or the contract and due process clauses are gone"). It is thus natural to read the Due Process Clause as limiting the power of courts to eliminate or change established property rights.

The Takings Clause also protects property rights, and it "operates as a conditional limitation, permitting the government to do what it wants so long as it pays the charge." *Eastern Enterprises v. Apfel,* 524 U.S. 498, 545, 118 S.Ct. 2131, 141 L.Ed.2d 451 (1998) (KENNEDY, J., concurring in judgment and dissenting in part). Unlike the Due Process Clause, therefore, the Takings Clause implicitly recognizes a governmental power while placing limits upon that power. Thus, if the Court were to hold that a judicial taking exists, it would presuppose that a judicial decision eliminating established property rights is "otherwise constitutional" so long as the State compensates the aggrieved property owners. *Ibid.* There is no clear authority for this proposition.

When courts act without direction from the executive or legislature, they may not have the power to eliminate established property rights by judicial decision. "Given that the constitutionality" of a judicial decision altering property rights "appears to turn on the legitimacy" of whether the court's judgment eliminates or changes established property rights "rather than on the availability of compensation, . . . the more appropriate constitutional analysis arises under general due process principles rather than under the Takings Clause." *Ibid.* Courts, unlike the executive or legislature, are not designed to make policy decisions about "the need for, and likely effectiveness of, regulatory actions." *Lingle,supra,* at 545, 125 S.Ct. 2074. State courts generally operate under a common-law tradition that allows for incremental modifications to property law, but "this tradition cannot justify a *carte blanch* judicial authority to change property definitions wholly free of constitutional limitations." Walston, The Constitution and Property: Due Process, Regulatory Takings, and Judicial Takings, 2001 Utah L.Rev. 379, 435.

The Court would be on strong footing in ruling that a judicial decision that eliminates or substantially changes established property rights, which are a legitimate expectation of the owner, is "arbitrary or irrational" under the Due Process Clause. * * *

To announce that courts too can effect a taking when they decide cases involving property rights, would raise certain difficult questions. Since this case does not require those questions to be addressed, in my respectful view, the Court should not reach beyond the necessities of the case to announce a sweeping rule that court decisions can be takings, as that phrase is used in the Takings Clause. The evident reason for recognizing a judicial takings doctrine would be to constrain the power of the judicial branch. Of course, the judiciary must respect private ownership. But were this Court to say that judicial decisions become takings when they overreach, this might give more power to courts, not less.

* * *

Indeed, it is unclear whether the Takings Clause was understood, as a historical matter, to apply to judicial decisions. The Framers most likely viewed this Clause as applying only to physical appropriation pursuant to the power of eminent domain. See *Lucas v. South Carolina Coastal Council,* 505 U.S. 1003, 1028, n. 15, 112 S.Ct. 2886, 120 L.Ed.2d 798 (1992). And it appears these physical appropriations were traditionally made by legislatures. See 3 J. Story, Commentaries on the Constitution of the United States § 1784, p. 661 (1833). Courts, on the other hand, lacked the power of eminent domain. See 1 W. Blackstone, Commentaries 135 (W. Lewis ed. 1897). The Court's Takings Clause jurisprudence has expanded beyond the Framers' understanding, as it now applies to certain regulations that are not physical appropriations. See *Lucas, supra,* at 1014, 112 S.Ct. 2886 (citing *Mahon,* 260 U.S. 393, 43 S.Ct. 158, 67 L.Ed. 322). But the Court should consider with care the decision to extend the Takings Clause in a manner that might be inconsistent with historical practice.

* * *

JUSTICE BREYER, with whom JUSTICE GINSBURG joins, concurring in part and concurring in the judgment.

I agree that no unconstitutional taking of property occurred in this case, and I therefore join Parts I, IV, and V of today's opinion. I cannot join Parts II and III, however, for in those Parts the plurality unnecessarily addresses questions of constitutional law that are better left for another day.

* * *

NOTES AND QUESTIONS

1. After reading *Stop the Beach Renourishment, Inc.,* can you think of a set of facts that might give rise to a successful judicial takings claim?

2. Can there be a judicial taking? This is the fundamental question and it was not definitively answered by the Court's decision. Noted scholar John D. Echeverria stated the following in his article, *Stop the Beach Renourishment: Why the Judiciary is Different,* 35 Vt. L. Rev. 475 (2010):

> All of the justices participating in the case agreed on one point: that the Florida Supreme Court applied an interpretation of Florida property law consistent with Florida precedent defining the rights of coastal property owners. Thus, the Court rejected the claim that the Florida court, in the course of rejecting a takings challenge to a beach renourishment project, itself effected a taking by changing Florida property rules. But the Court split 4 to 4 on the fundamental question of whether a judicial ruling that does change property rules can constitute a taking. Justice Scalia's plurality opinion, joined by three other justices, embraced the judicial takings concept, while the other four justices declined to adopt it.

What do you think of the merits of the claim that judicial decisions, just like legislative actions, can constitute takings? Does Justice Scalia make the most persuasive argument? Or, has *Stop the Beach Renourishment, Inc.* simply added to the "muddle" that is regulatory takings, see the discussion, supra, following *Pennsylvania Coal*.

3.   Fifth Amendment Takings and Due Process Violations. The Court distinguishes between takings and due process violations under the Federal Constitution. It is important to keep these concepts separate and distinct. The Takings Clause permits government to intentionally deprive private citizens of private property for public use (which is broadly understood to include public purposes, see the *Kelo* decision, supra) upon the payment of just compensation. Thus, property owners whose property is taken are entitled to be compensated; they are not entitled to enjoin the government and retain their property. In contrast, the Due Process Clause prohibits government from treating property owners in an "arbitrary or irrational" manner. The relief for government action that violates the due process clause is to enjoin the government action. For additional discussion of the distinction between the Takings and Due Process Clauses in the context of *Stop the Beach Renourishment, Inc.*, see Eduardo Moises Penalver and Lior Strahilevitz, Judicial Takings or Due Process? The University of Chicago Law School John M. Olin Law & Economics Working Paper No. 549 (2011); D. Benjamin Barros, The Complexities of Judicial Takings, Widener Law School Legal Studies Research Paper No. 10–32 (2010).

4.   Why should the government have to compensate private property owners when the state intervenes, at great expense to the public, to protect the beachfront homes of these property owners from rising sea levels and storms?

5.   After *Stop the Beach Renourishment, Inc.*, how would you advise local governments to proceed when addressing beachfront preservation? Does your answer depend primarily upon what the relevant state property law says?

NOTE: IMPACT FEES AND MONETARY EXACTIONS

In both *Nollan* and *Dolan* the Supreme Court assessed a quid pro quo requirement and found a taking when the government insisted on a dedication of land in exchange for the right to develop. Suppose the sovereign requires instead that the land owner make a major monetary contribution. In

Benchmark Land Co. v. City of Battle Ground, 103 Wash.App. 721, 14 P.3d 172 (2000), the plaintiff received a permit to enlarge and improve its business site on the condition that it expend substantial monies to improve its side of a city street adjoining the parcel. However, no land was to be taken from the plaintiff and no easement was to be dedicated to the public. Nevertheless, the court held, the *Nollan/Dolan* proportionality test applied:

> [T]he City required the developer to address a problem that existed outside the development property—an adjoining street in need of improvement. And the development did not cause this problem, at most it only aggravated it.

> * * * If the government in *Nollan* and *Dolan* had exacted money rather than land and then purchased land to solve the problems, the same questions would arise: was the money exacted for and used to solve a problem connected to the proposed development? (*Nollan.*) And was the amount of money exacted roughly proportional to the development's impact on the problem? (*Dolan.*) Surely if the issues for an exaction of money are the same as for an exaction of land, the test must be the same: a showing of "nexus" and "proportionality." * * *

> Further, if the *Dolan* proportionality test does not apply, the government can exact conditions such as the one here with few limits. The condition advances a legitimate state interest-improving the public roads. And the condition does not deny the developer all economically viable use of its land. But the condition also seeks to force "some people alone to bear public burdens which, in all fairness and justice, should be borne by the public as a whole." *Armstrong,* 364 U.S. at 49, 80 S.Ct. 1563. It is this attempted transfer of a public burden that calls for a *Dolan* proportionality test.

By contrast, in San Remo Hotel v. San Francisco, 27 Cal.4th 643, 117 Cal.Rptr.2d 269, 41 P.3d 87 (2002), the land owner wished to convert their its used as a permanent residence for low income tenants into a tourist hotel. The City conditioned the conversion on the owner's contribution of money to help replace the lost low income housing with similar housing elsewhere in the City. The Court, adhering to and expanding on its own decisions, refused to apply a *Nollan/Dolan* proportionality test, but distinguished between "ad hoc" fees imposed by agencies on specific requests for development, with more general legislatively created fees that were uniform across similarly situated prospective developers:

> [T]he taking of money is different, under the Fifth Amendment, from the taking of real or personal property. The imposition of various monetary exactions—taxes, special assessments, and user fees—has been accorded substantial judicial deference. [Quoting *Ehrlich v. City of Culver City*, 12 Cal.4th 854, 892, 50 Cal.Rptr.2d 242, 911 P.2d 429 (1996)] "There is no question that the takings clause is specially protective of property against *physical occupation* or invasion. . . . It is also true . . . that government generally has greater leeway with respect to noninvasive forms of land-use regulation, where the courts have for the most part given greater deference to its power to impose broadly applicable fees, whether in the form of taxes, assessments, user or development fees."

> In *Ehrlich,* we * * * recogniz[ed] an exception to the general rule of
> deference on distribution of monetary burdens, because the ad hoc,
> discretionary fee imposed in that case bore special potential for govern-
> ment abuse. We continue to believe heightened scrutiny should be limited
> to such fees. * * * Extending *Nollan* and *Dolan* generally to all govern-
> ment fees affecting property value or development would open to search-
> ing judicial scrutiny the wisdom of myriad government economic regula-
> tions, a task the courts have been loath to undertake pursuant to either
> the takings or due process clause.

Even so, the California Court concluded that there must be a "reasonable
relationship" between the social cost of the proposed development and the
particular monetary payment that was required. In this case:

> the housing replacement fees bear a reasonable relationship to loss of
> housing. Under the ordinance, the amount of the in lieu fee is based on
> the number of rooms being converted from residential to tourist designa-
> tion; the number of rooms designated residential is, in turn, based on the
> self-reported use as of September 23, 1979, shortly before a City moratori-
> um on residential hotel conversion first came into force. On its face, the
> use of a defined historical measurement point is reasonably related to the
> HCO's housing preservation goals. * * *

See also Home Builders Assn. of Dayton v. City of Beavercreek, 89 Ohio St.3d
121, 729 N.E.2d 349 (2000) (*Nollan/Dolan* test applied to a city's insistence on
a cash payment, or "impact fee," in exchange for a right to develop, but in
this case the proportionality requirement was satisfied). See A. Carlson & D.
Pollak, Takings on the Ground: How the Supreme Court's Takings Jurisprudence Affects Local Land Use Decisions, 35 U.C.Davis L.Rev. 103 (2001).

NOTE: THE CONTRACTARIAN VISION OF TAKINGS

One libertarian view of the takings clause is that its fundamental concern
is not merely with regulation that makes property less valuable, but with any
kind of governmental intervention that transfers wealth from one person for
the benefit of others. So, for example, progressive income taxation amounts to
an unconstitutional taking.

Richard A. Epstein uses the following illustration:

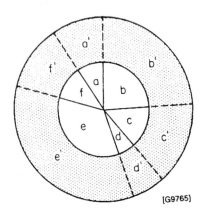

[G9765]

The inner circle represents the value of different individuals' starting wealth. The shaded outer circle represents the gains that are possible from law & government, which can make property rights more valuable by adding security, correcting market failure, and the like. Presumably, no one would enter into a social contract—or a contract for the provision of governmental services—if he believed that government would diminish rather than enlarge his starting wealth.

For Epstein, government regulation can be justified only if it makes *every* person's piece of the pie proportionately larger. Anything that gives some people a larger portion by making others' smaller is impermissible. If, in the process of making total social wealth greater, that state must make one person's property less valuable, then that person is entitled to compensation before the newly created surplus is divided among the others:

> The boundaries of the slices in the first [inner] pie are the limits of the private rights to be protected by the state; they identify the private property that cannot be taken without just compensation.... The requirement of just compensation assures that the state will give to each person a fair equivalent to what has been taken.... Finally, the public use requirement conditions the use of the coercive power by demanding that any surplus generated by the action, here the outer ring, is divided among individuals in accordance with the size of their original contributions.

Richard A. Epstein, Takings: Private Property and the Power of Eminent Domain 4–5 (1985).

What effect would Epstein's approach have on historical preservation zoning? On land use planning? On regulation generally? Is the transfer of wealth a legitimate purpose of land use planning? Or is planning justified only if it makes the community as a whole wealthier? One problem with many land use regulations is that the loss to affected landowners (such as Lucas, Penn Central or Ambler Realty) is quite easily documented. By contrast, the gains to the community as a whole are difficult to quantify. For example, how does one measure the gains that result from landmark preservation ordinances?

Would Epstein's approach add needed rigor to land use planning, or would it simply make most such planning impossible?

NOTE: TAKINGS, COMPENSATION AND RISK

Whenever an entrepreneur develops a parcel of land he faces certain risks—risks that there will not be a sufficient market for what he has to sell (whether homes in a subdivision or clothing in a department store); risks of natural disasters such as fires, tornadoes or floods; and risks that he will be the victim of government regulation or condemnation of his property. The entrepreneur himself must bear the cost of most of these risks—either by taking a chance that the event will not occur, or else by purchasing insurance.[1]

A very good argument can be made that forcing entrepreneurs to bear these risks results in an efficient amount of development. For example, if a developer would be fully compensated if he built homes that no one wanted to buy, he would not have much incentive to take care that his homes were attractive to customers. If people could costlessly be compensated in full for all natural disasters, they would have little incentive to avoid them. (For this reason, insurance companies must assess risks and charge risk premiums for high risk enterprises.)

Should a risk of loss as a result of government action, such as condemnation or intensive regulation, be treated any differently? For example, if an entrepreneur builds an "adult" movie theater, there is clearly some risk that in the future the government will respond with a statute that forces him to shut down. If the Fifth Amendment requires that he be paid full compensation, he will go ahead and build regardless of this risk. However, if he would have to bear the loss himself, he would be much more careful about what he built and where he built it. In short, a rule requiring compensation when the government shuts down "adult" theaters will result in more than the optimal number of adult theaters. See Kaplow, An Economic Analysis of Legal Transitions, 99 Harv.L.Rev. 511 (1986).

However, the other side of a rule that a developer is not entitled to receive compensation for a government action is that the government is not obliged to pay it. Just as the private developer will overinvest when he does not have to bear all relevant risks, so we can expect that the government will "overinvest" when it does not have to pay all the costs of what it does. If the government were free to regulate or condemn property without paying any compensation we could expect a significantly greater number of takings. The government would have an incentive, for example, to seize a private office building for its own use, fail to maintain it, and when the building became unfit for use abandon it and seize another one. In short, the just compensation rule requires the government to mimic market behavior just as the private developer would, and thus to make the appropriate amount of invest-

---

1. The insurance premium will always be at least as high as the expected cost of the risk. For example, if a fire could be expected to cause $100,000 in damage and the chance that a fire will occur in any given year is .001, then the insurance premium must be at least $100 annually, or the insurer will lose money. As a result, even by purchasing insurance the entrepreneur bears the entire cost of the risk.

ment. One important difference between the risk of a natural disaster such as fire, and a risk of loss through government takings is that the consequence of assigning the risk to the property owner (by not providing compensation) is to *reduce* the number of fires (by making the property owner more careful), but to *increase* the number of takings (by making them cheaper for the government).

The question has recently arisen with regard to deregulation, particularly of electric and telephone utilities. Regulation, it turns out, was quite inefficient and required firms to build a great many more plants and installations than they needed. Under deregulation many of these investments have proven to be excessive, creating the problem of "stranded" costs—or investments in a plant that can no longer be recovered. On the one hand, deregulation is a government action; on the other, most of these plants were built at the initiative of the utilities themselves. Are the utilities constitutionally entitled to compensation? For conflicting views see, Sidak & Spulber, Deregulatory Takings and the Regulatory Contract: the Competitive Transformation of Network Industries in the United States (Cambridge, UK: Cambridge Univ. Press 1997) (compensation due); Williamson, Deregulatory Takings and Breach of the Regulatory Contract: Some Precautions, 71 N.Y.U. L. Rev. 1007, 1013 (1996) (doubting that compensation is due); Hovenkamp, The Takings Clause and Improvident Regulatory Bargains, 108 Yale L.J. 801 (1999) (compensation not due except where state has made explicit commitment or compelled the construction of the plant).

There is a healthy economic literature on the impact of possible eminent domain proceedings on incentives to develop. To the extent that undercompensation is systematic and predictable, one would expect that the possibility of condemnation would lead to underdevelopment. But suppose the government biases its eminent domain choices in favor of undeveloped land, since condemnation of such land is less costly. Then landowners might develop in order to reduce the likelihood of condemnation, thus leading to overdevelopment. See Hart, Takings and Compensation in Early America: the Colonial Highway Acts in Social Context, 40 Am. J. Legal Hist. 253 (1996), noting that colonial governments often provided no compensation at all when they took undeveloped land for purposes of highway construction. On the economic relationship between takings and developmental incentives, see Innes, Takings, Compensation, and Equal Treatment for Owners of Developed and Undeveloped Property, 40 J. L. & Econ. 403 (1997); Blume and Rubinfeld, Compensation for Takings: an Economic Analysis, 72 Cal. L. Rev. 569 (1984).

§ 10.2.3 REMEDIES FOR UNCONSTITUTIONAL TAKINGS

Someone whose property interest is subjected to an unconstitutional taking can always obtain an injunction against the offending statute, ordinance or government regulation. See, e.g., *Stop the Beach Renourishment, Inc., supra,* and the discussion following the case. A few states had interpreted their own constitutions to require damages payments as well. See, e.g., Martin v. Port of Seattle, 64 Wash.2d 309, 391 P.2d 540 (1964), cert. denied 379 U.S. 989 (1965). But until 1987 federal courts had not generally awarded damages for regulatory takings.

All that changed with the Supreme Court's decision in First English Evangelical Lutheran Church v. County of Los Angeles, 482 U.S. 304 (1987). The appellant owned flood plain land, and after it was submerged several times the County of Los Angeles responded with an ordinance forbidding all construction. It sought not merely an injunction, but also damages for deprivation of its use of the affected land. In denying the compensation claim the California Supreme Court concluded that:

> [T]he need for preserving a degree of freedom in the land-use planning function, and the inhibiting financial force which inheres in the inverse condemnation remedy, persuade us that on balance mandamus or declaratory relief rather than inverse condemnation is the appropriate relief under the circumstances.

The Supreme Court reversed, stating:

> "[T]emporary" takings which, as here, deny a landowner all use of his property, are not different in kind from permanent takings, for which the Constitution clearly requires compensation. . . . It is axiomatic that the Fifth Amendment's just compensation provision is "designed to bar Government from forcing some people alone to bear public burdens which, in all fairness and justice, should be borne by the public as a whole." Armstrong v. United States, 364 U.S., at 49, 80 S.Ct., at 1569. * * * In the present case the interim ordinance was adopted by the County of Los Angeles in January 1979, and became effective immediately. Appellant filed suit within a month after the effective date of the ordinance and yet when the Supreme Court of California denied a hearing in the case on October 17, 1985, the merits of appellant's claim had yet to be determined. The United States has been required to pay compensation for leasehold interests of shorter duration than this. The value of a leasehold interest in property for a period of years may be substantial, and the burden on the property owner in extinguishing such an interest for a period of years may be great indeed. Where this burden results from governmental action that amounted to a taking, the Just Compensation Clause of the Fifth Amendment requires that the government pay the landowner for the value of the use of the land during this period.
>
> * * * We also point out that the allegation of the complaint which we treat as true for purposes of our decision was that the ordinance in question denied appellant all use of its property. We limit our holding to the facts presented, and of course do not deal with the quite different questions that would arise in the case of normal delays in obtaining building permits, changes in zoning ordinances, variances, and the like which are not before us. We realize that even our present holding will undoubtedly lessen to some extent the freedom and flexibility of land-use planners and governing bodies of municipal corporations when enacting land-use regulations. But

such consequences necessarily flow from any decision upholding a claim of constitutional right; many of the provisions of the Constitution are designed to limit the flexibility and freedom of governmental authorities and the Just Compensation Clause of the Fifth Amendment is one of them.

JUSTICE STEVENS (joined by JUSTICE BLACKMUN and O'CONNOR) dissented:

> The policy implications of today's decision are obvious and, I fear, far reaching. Cautious local officials and land-use planners may avoid taking any action that might later be challenged and thus give rise to a damage action. Much important regulation will never be enacted, even perhaps in the health and safety area. Were this result mandated by the Constitution, these serious implications would have to be ignored. But the loose cannon the Court fires today is not only unattached to the Constitution, but it also takes aim at a long line of precedents in the regulatory takings area. It would be the better part of valor simply to decide the case at hand instead of igniting the kind of litigation explosion that this decision will undoubtedly touch off.

On remand, the state court found that no taking had occurred. 210 Cal.App.3d 1353, 258 Cal.Rptr. 893 (1989), cert. denied 493 U.S. 1056 (1990). Even assuming that the flood control ordinance denied a property owner any possible use of his property, the court reasoned, a taking would not necessarily result:

> It would not be remarkable at all to allow government to deny a private owner "all uses" of his property where there is no use of that property which does not threaten lives and health. So it makes perfect sense to deny compensation for the denial of "all uses" where health and safety are at stake but require compensation for the denial of "all uses" where the land use regulation advances lesser public purposes. Indeed it would be extraordinary to construe the Constitution to require a government to compensate private landowners because it denied them "the right" to use property which cannot be used without risking injury and death.

210 Cal.App.3d at 1366, 258 Cal.Rptr. at 901–901. Is that holding consistent with the *Lucas* decision, reprinted supra? Suppose the only risk of injury or death is to the property owner himself?

The prophecy in Justice Steven's dissent has some support. The 300 members of the National Association of County Planning Directors were presented with this hypothetical:

> A municipality, concerned that a water-filled gravel pit might prove a dangerous attraction to children attending schools in the vicinity, enacts an ordinance requiring the owner to fill in the pit and to construct a high fence around the site. The effect is to shut down a functioning quarry that opened more than thirty years ago when the area was still rural. Can the town use its land use regulatory powers

to shut down the quarry, in effect destroying the landowner's business, without violating the takings clause?

Forty-eight of the planners said they would risk adopting the ordinance provided that the risk was only invalidation, should it prove unconstitutional. But if the risk was a damage award to the landowner only twenty-four were willing to adopt it.

How expensive can the loss from a temporary taking be? Consider the damages analysis in Wheeler v. City of Pleasant Grove, 896 F.2d 1347 (11th Cir.1990), which found that a municipality's refusal to permit development of an apartment building was an unconstitutional taking. The unconstitutional denial applied to a relatively small apartment building and for the relatively short period of fourteen months. The court predicated damages on the difference in rate of return on the land with the right to develop and its return while the right was denied, for as many months as the unconstitutional regulation was in force:

> [T]he landowner should be awarded the market rate of return computed over the period of the temporary taking on the difference between the property's fair market value without the regulatory restriction and its fair market value with the restriction. The complex which appellants had the right to construct had an undisputed appraised fair market value of $2.3 million in 1978. After the City prohibited appellants from constructing apartments, appellants retained only the land, appraised at $200,000. Experts at the damages hearing testified that the loan-to-value ratio was seventy-five percent in 1978, so that appellants would have held a twenty-five percent equity interest. The investment on which appellants could have expected a return, then, was twenty-five percent of the project's value, or $575,000. After the City withdrew the permit, appellants held a twenty-five percent equity in the land, a value of $50,000. The difference in fair market value lost as a result of the regulatory restrictions was $525,000. The City withdrew appellants' building permit on September 6, 1978. The district court enjoined the City from enforcing Ordinance No. 216 against appellants on November 9, 1979. The period of temporary taking spans fourteen months and three days. According to the experts, the market rate of return for that period was 9.77 percent. When we compute the return on $525,000 over fourteen months at 9.77 percent, we arrive at a figure of $59,841.23. This is the correct amount of damages sustained by appellants.

896 F.2d at 1351–1352. But isn't the court assuming that the plaintiff's money earned nothing during the period that development was prohibited? Suppose the government unconstitutionally delays the starting date of my project by one year. The investment in the project is $1,000,000 and the court predicts it would have earned a 12% return. But during the one year delay my $1,000,000 is in the bank earning 9%. Is my injury $120,000 or $30,000?

In A.A. Profiles, Inc. v. City of Fort Lauderdale, 253 F.3d 576 (11th Cir.2001), the Eleventh Circuit distinguished *Wheeler* and divided takings damages recoveries into two classes. First, in a case such as *Wheeler* where the taking is temporary and amounts to a loss of projected income, the correct measure is the lost income itself. *Second*, in cases where the taking is permanent, damages are measured by the difference in the market value of the property as unencumbered and its value when subject to the offending regulation. In this case a regulation that prevented the land owners use of his property for a wood chipping operation permanently reduced its value.

NOTE: TAKINGS AND PUBLIC CHOICE

During the 1960s and 1970s the Supreme Court articulated the view that the law forbidding uncompensated takings was designed to protect isolated minorities who might not be well represented in the political process from unfair treatment by a legislative majority. For example, in Armstrong v. United States, 364 U.S. 40, 49 (1960) the Supreme Court suggested that the takings clause was "designed to bar Government from forcing some people alone to bear public burdens which, in all fairness and justice, should be borne by the public as a whole." See also Richard Ely, *Democracy and Distrust* (1980); Michelman, Property, Utility and Fairness: Comments on the Ethical Foundations of "Just Compensation" Law, 80 Harv. L. Rev. 1165, 1218–1224 (1967).

Under this theory a court might consider whether the group victimized by a statute challenged under the takings clause (such as the owners of land-marked buildings or of underground coal mines) were relatively unique, isolated, and not well represented in the political process. If so, they might be branded as the victims of an unconstitutional attempt to transfer wealth away from them for the benefit of the public at large, or at least of some larger and more powerful interest group. This view of takings jurisprudence followed closely after the Warren Court's development of the Equal Protection clause to protect "discrete and insular" minorities from unjust discrimination at the hands of the majority. The purpose of the takings clause is to "spread the cost of operating the governmental apparatus throughout the society rather than imposing it upon some small segment of it." Sax, Takings and the Police Power, 74 Yale L.J. 36, 75 (1964).

But the intellectual landscape has changed since the 1960's. Today a more frequently heard theory is that small, homogeneous interest groups are actually much more effective at carrying their message to legislatures than larger, more diffuse groups. In particular, the larger groups are plagued by "free rider" problems; each member of the larger group knows that there are plenty of others who are able to lobby the legislature, and so the tendency to shirk is very high. Further, the larger group tends to be less homogeneous and may have more poorly articulated goals. This scholarship, which goes under the name of "public choice" theory, argues that the small, homogeneous special interest groups will often succeed in obtaining the legislation they want at the expense of the public in general. The Public Choice classic is James Buchanan & Gordon Tullock, *The Calculus of Consent* (1962).

The implications of public choice for takings law are quite different from the implications of the older, liberal view. Under the public choice approach, the court would look for instances of legislative "capture" by homogeneous special interest groups. However, if the beneficiaries of legislation are diffuse, while the victims are discrete and homogeneous, then no taking should be found. Thus in *Keystone Bituminous Coal* there should *not* be a taking "because the burdened class [coal mining companies] is far more compact than the beneficiaries of the regulation." See Daniel A. Farber & Philip P. Frickey, *Law and Public Choice* 72 (1991). In short, the same facts that tend to prove a taking under the liberal theory, tend to disprove it under the public choice theory.

Which theory is the better fit between the takings clause and the legislation to which it applies? Suppose a city council representing 10,000 people passes an ordinance preventing any development on the land of a half dozen adjoining property owners, in order to protect the view from a public park across those property owners' land. Would the liberal view (taking) or the public choice view (no taking) be more sensible? Suppose the only three apartment building owners in a town lobbied for and obtained an ordinance preventing any further apartment buildings from being built. Would the liberal view (no taking) or the public choice view (taking) be more sensible? Do all forms of legislation fall into one category or another? Would a court be able to distinguish one kind of "legislative failure" from the other?

Incidentally, how does public choice theory fare empirically? That remains an open question, but property law seems to be filled with anomalous situations. Consider rent control, housing codes and the implied warranty of habitability, all discussed in Chapter 7 on landlord-tenant law. By and large this set of legal rules protects tenants at the expense of landlords, and these are the two classes seriously affected. In fact, rent control is the one form of price regulation that regulated firms consistently object to because it leaves the entire competitive market intact; that is, (1) landlords are free to charge a lower price than the controlled price, so price competition remains; (2) the number of landlords in the market remains the same—that is, there are no restrictions on new entry or other effort to protect landlords from competition with one another or with newcomers.

But landlords should be a much more effective interest group than tenants. First of all, the landlords' interest group is smaller—every landlord has at least one tenant and many have several tenants. As a result, tenants should be more plagued by free rider problems than landlords are. Second, landlords as a general matter probably have more resources to commit to the lobbying process—this is certainly the case with respect to that portion of the residential market where housing codes and implied warranties of habitability are a factor. Nevertheless, most states and many municipalities have relatively extensive legislation governing implied warranties of habitability, housing codes, municipal rent control, and the like.

Indeed, most of the takings cases in this chapter involve regulatory regimes that are more consistent with the traditional liberal theory than with public choice. In *Hawaii Housing Authority*, the large landowners should have been the more efficient interest group, but the highly diffuse individual home owners obtained the regulation they wanted; *Pennsylvania Coal* and *Keystone* victimized coal mining companies, that were small and presumably homogeneous, for the benefit of a much larger and more varied set of surface owners; both *Nollan* and *Lucas* injured coastal developers to protect a larger, more diverse collection of interior land owners or the public generally. What about *Penn Central*? The historic preservation statute victimized a relatively small group of owners of historic buildings. But should the beneficiaries be seen as the general public? The tourist industry? Historic preservationists? The one regulatory regime that seems most consistent with public choice is the CATV statute in *Loretto*, which benefitted cable television companies, a small and highly effective interest group, at the expense of building owners.

NOTE: TAKINGS AND TORTS

When the government exercises its eminent domain power a taking has occurred. Likewise, it can "take" property by forcing entry by persons or objects that the owner would prefer to exclude, or by regulating the use of property so as to substantially destroy its value. But suppose the government commits a tort, such as a trespass or a nuisance, which injures private property. Is such a tort a taking? The issue is particularly important because many governmental subdivisions have immunity from tort damages; however, they cannot immunize themselves from damages for unconstitutional takings. The other side of the coin is that governmental tort immunity statutes would be meaningless if every tort suit against the government involving property damage could constitute a taking. Given the long pedigree of governmental immunity, clearly the framers of the Fifth Amendment did not have such a result in mind. The problem, then, is how to reconcile the two kinds of actions.

In addition to the immunity problem is the fact that many projects built by governmental subdivisions are authorized by state statute. To the extent those statutes are inconsistent with the common law, the common law is generally abrogated. The common law action will survive only if the project is negligently built or operated in a manner that was not authorized by the statute. See Harding v. Department of Transportation, 159 Cal.App.3d 359, 205 Cal.Rptr. 561 (1984). Many states have statutes such as Cal.Civ.Code § 3482, which provides that: "Nothing which is done or maintained under express authority of a statute can be deemed a nuisance." However, once again, the state statute cannot abrogate the governmental entity's Fifth Amendment obligation not to take private property without paying just compensation. Therefore, the inverse condemnation action may survive. See, for example, Wegner v. Milwaukee Mut. Ins. Co., 479 N.W.2d 38 (Minn.1991), which interpreted the state constitution's takings clause to hold a municipality liable to pay just compensation for damage to a home caused by police who apprehended a felony suspect there.

What if the "tort" at issue is not intentional, such as nuisance or trespass, but is based on negligence? Does the takings clause prevent the government from claiming sovereign immunity for torts alleging the government's negligence? For example, suppose the government is building a highway and it negligently destroys a fence and crops on adjoining land. Has it "taken" the property?

The first problem is the "public use" clause. The highway itself is presumably a public use. But the action for negligence does not attack the building of the highway. Rather, it attacks the negligent way in which the work was done, and the negligence itself was certainly not for a public use. See Robinson v. City of Ashdown, 301 Ark. 226, 783 S.W.2d 53, 56–57 (1990), where a municipality's sewage treatment plant constantly overflowed raw sewage into the plaintiff landowner's property, but the state had a statute that exempted the city from tort damages. The municipality argued there could be no taking, because the overflowing sewage was not a public use, but merely the result of poor construction. The court responded that:

> The benefit to the public in this case has been [the municipality's] use of the Robinsons' home as an overflow dump for sewage. While it might have been less expensive for the city to have seen to it that the overflow did not occur by installing pumps that worked automatically or by hiring more employees to see that they were working when they should have been, it is our view that by failing to remedy the problem the city effectively chose to purchase the Robinsons' property to the extent the value of that property was diminished by its actions. The public benefitted by not having to spend the money it would have taken to prevent the sewage overflow.

Accord, Aetna Life & Casualty Co. v. Los Angeles, 170 Cal.App.3d 865, 216 Cal.Rptr. 831 (1985), holding that an action for inverse condemnation was appropriate for a fire negligently caused by a municipality, because "the doctrine of inverse condemnation has subsumed the principles of negligence and in effect rendered it unnecessary for a property owner who has suffered property damage at the hands of a government agency . . . to proceed in tort."

Do decisions such as *Robinson* and *Aetna* effectively eliminate tort law immunity for negligent injuries to property? Perhaps yes, if the injury is "trespassory," such as flooding sewage. If the injury is merely a nuisance, however, such as loud noise, odor or air pollution, then the taking would be analyzed as "regulatory" rather than trespassory, and the likely scope of liability would be much less. For example, a regulatory action that reduced property's value by thirty percent, but permitted it to remain profitable, would likely not constitute a taking (applying the *Penn Central* balancing test, discussed supra); but the same action could almost certainly be a nuisance if it were committed by a private party.

CHAPTER 11

"PUBLIC" CONTROLS OF LAND USE: AN INTRODUCTION TO ZONING AND LAND USE PLANNING

■ ■ ■

This chapter deals with land use restrictions that are strictly "public," in the sense that they are the product of government initiative and are given effect by means of statutes and local ordinances. The government has the power to control land uses in ways that are not available to private persons. However, the government's power to control land uses also is subject to limitations that do not constrain private persons, most notably those imposed by federal and state constitutions.

The word "zoning" is sometimes used as a catch-all to describe a variety of public land use controls. In fact, public controls include statutory restrictions on (1) the uses to which people can put their land; (2) the relationship of the occupants; (3) the kinds of structures that can be erected on land and the way in which those structures are built; (4) the "density" of development on a particular parcel; (5) the rate of growth in a particular community; and (6) the ability of landowners to interfere with the environment through construction, emission of polluting substances, and noise. A wide variety of statutes passed by every level of government addresses these problems.

Zoning has always been a highly political process. The first comprehensive land use statute in the United States was passed in New York City. That ordinance was the outcome of a political dispute between factory owners in New York's garment district and the owners of fashionable shops on Fifth Avenue and nearby. Historically, the garment district lay in the southern part of the City, south of 14th St. However, by the turn of the century, garment manufacturing had become one of New York City's most productive growth industries, and factories began to expand. As they encroached on the more fashionable areas of mid-Manhattan, shop owners and residents began to organize lobbying groups such as the Fifth Avenue Association, whose purpose was to seek legislation that would confine the factories to the south.

The event that turned the tide in favor of the Fifth Avenue Association was the great Triangle Shirt Waist Company fire, March 25, 1911, which killed 146 workers, almost all women. An investigation revealed that not only was the factory very poorly constructed, but all means of escape had been locked from the outside in order to prevent employees from sneaking out to take unauthorized breaks. Soon thereafter, the New York legislature amended New York City's charter to give it the authority to zone and the zoning ordinance itself followed in 1916. See Behrens, The Triangle Shirtwaist Company Fire of 1911: A Lesson in Legislative Manipulation, 62 Tex. L. Rev. 361 (1983). For more on the history of zoning and land use planning in the United States, see S. Toll, Zoned American (1969); Zoning and the American Dream: Promises Still to Keep (C. Haar, et al., eds., 1989); R. Chused, *Euclid*'s Historical Imagery, 51 Case Western Reserve L.Rev. 597 (2001).

Is Zoning a Socially Useful Activity?

Since the first comprehensive zoning statutes were passed in the 1910s they have become extraordinarily popular. Nearly every large city and most smaller ones have enacted some form of land use planning legislation. Legislatures do not always make good choices, but could such a large number of legislative bodies be wrong on such a fundamental choice?

In order to determine whether zoning is socially beneficial we must consider two different questions. First, is the set of land uses that results better than the set of land uses created by some alternative system, such as servitudes, nuisance or other common law rules such as adverse possession and prescription? Secondly, do the costs of operating the zoning system justify the improvement in the outcome? For example, if a zoning system makes total property values in a zoned community $1,000,000 higher than they would be under common law regulation, but the operation of the zoning system costs $1,500,000 more than the administration of the common law, then the community is better off without the zoning. We are assuming that the community itself bears all the costs and realizes all the benefits of each system (that is, there are no externalities).

The Coase theorem (see § 9.4, supra) suggests that an unregulated community could negotiate its way to an efficient, or wealth maximizing, set of land uses. Any time someone planned a use that injured neighbors more than it benefitted the developer; the neighbors would pay the developer not to engage in the use.

The fact that a perfectly functioning market would yield optimal land uses has suggested to some that private bargaining and common law rules are inherently better regulators of land uses than zoning. See Siegan, Non–Zoning is the Best Zoning, 31 Cal. W. L. Rev. 127 (1994); Ellickson, Alternatives to Zoning: Covenants, Nuisance Rules, and Fines as Land Use Controls, 40 U.Chi.L.Rev. 681 (1973). Three arguments support this conclusion. First of all, the common law determines optimal land uses on a case-by-case basis. This approximates market behavior, in which transactions (particularly of non-fungibles such as land) are very different from one another. By contrast, zoning generally "bundles" land parcels into large groups and places them into a single use district. Invariably, some parcels do not fit into the scheme.

Second, common law rules generally create "alienable" entitlements. The fact that I obtain an injunction ordering you to stop using your land for a junkyard does not necessarily mean that you will stop. You might "settle" with me—that is, you might buy from me the right to continue operating, if you valued your junkyard by more than I valued the right to stop you. By contrast, the rights created by zoning laws generally are *inalienable,* subject to a few exceptions. Once your land has been zoned exclusively for residential occupancy you cannot purchase from your neighbors the right to operate a junkyard even if they are willing to sell the right.

Third, just like all legislative processes, zoning is susceptible to "capture" by interest groups. Those who control the political processes, or those who have the best access to them, can use these processes in ways that are anticompetitive, racist, or contrary to the public interest in other ways. See the note on takings and public choice theory in the preceding chapter; and see Frug, The Geography of a Community, 48 Stan. L. Rev. 1047 (1996).

Zoning, it would appear, is an inferior alternative to the common law *if* the unregulated market is the optimal assignor of land uses. In the case of land use, however, there is considerable evidence of substantial, expensive market failures. For example, the costs of assembling all parties affected by a land use decision and forcing them to bargain with each other could be very high. It might be far more efficient to bundle transactions into large numbers—e.g., by a zoning process that classifies an entire area into a particular use district. This would particularly be true if we were fairly confident about our ability to predict what kinds of land uses a bargaining process would yield in a properly functioning market. Critics of zoning often observe that the zoning process is cumbersome and expensive. That should be conceded. However, any system of private land use controls based on individual transactions that actually accounted for the interests of every affected party would be extremely cumbersome and expensive as well.

Zoning—or at least certain parts of it—may be preferred for reasons that have nothing to do with zoning's efficiency. Many questions of distributive justice—such as what constitutes fair treatment to people of color or those who are poor—may not have an "efficient" answer that society finds acceptable. A community in which all property rights are assigned to the highest bidder may be a community substantially of Anglo–European descent. Our own cultural and constitutional values may force us to accept a solution that is less efficient, in the sense that it fails to maximize the market value of a community's property. For example, a racially integrated neighborhood may be a neighborhood in which property values are lower than a segregated neighborhood; deciding which is better is fundamentally a noneconomic judgment.

There is one other problem of comparative advantage. As the note on the Coase theorem and the law of nuisance, § 9.4, suggests, land use markets can cease to function effectively when the number of bargainers becomes large. In fact, most servitude agreements are *bi*lateral, even though the number of affected landowners is large. For example, when a 100–lot subdivision is planned, the developer generally drafts a set of covenants and places them in the recorded plat documents. Then the lots are sold to one buyer at a time; so each individual transaction involves only two parties. Further, the purchaser of the first lot has a right to object to any changes made in at least some of the servitudes in sales to later purchasers. What this means is that although the series of transactions by which the subdivision is sold make the parties better off, there might be alternative outcomes that would make everyone better off but which the structure of the transactions prevents.[1] In this respect, the efficiency case for servitudes over zoning is not very strong. See H. Hovenkamp, Bargaining in Coasian Markets: Servitudes and Alternative Land Use Controls, 27 J. Corp. L. 519 (2002).

The unfortunate fact is that we have not even come close to developing a practical mechanism for comparing the costs and benefits of zoning with the costs and benefits of a purely market, or common law, solution to land use problems. Both, it must be conceded, are quite imperfect, because the market for land is highly imperfect.

§ 11.1   THE POWER TO ZONE

VILLAGE OF EUCLID v. AMBLER REALTY CO.

Supreme Court of the United States (1926).
272 U.S. 365.

MR. JUSTICE SUTHERLAND delivered the opinion of the Court.

The village of Euclid is an Ohio municipal corporation. It adjoins and practically is a suburb of the city of Cleveland. Its estimated population is between 5,000 and 10,000, and its area from 12 to 14 square miles, the greater part of which is farm lands or unimproved acreage. It lies, roughly, in the form of a parallelogram measuring approximately $3\frac{1}{2}$ miles each way. East and west it is traversed by three principal highways: Euclid Avenue, through the southerly border, St. Clair Avenue, through the central portion, and Lake Shore boulevard, through the northerly border, in close proximity to the shore of Lake Erie. The Nickel Plate Railroad lies from 1,500 to 1,800 feet north of Euclid Avenue, and the Lake Shore Railroad 1,600 feet farther to the north. The three highways and the two railroads are substantially parallel.

---

1. Economically speaking, the servitudes are Pareto-superior in the sense that the parties are better off than if they had not purchased at all. But they are not necessarily Pareto-optimal, because there may be alternative arrangements that would make everyone better off without injuring anyone. Of course, the parties can always modify the servitudes by unanimous consent.

Appellee is the owner of a tract of land containing 68 acres, situated in the westerly end of the village, abutting on Euclid Avenue to the south and the Nickel Plate Railroad to the north. Adjoining this tract, both on the east and on the west, there have been laid out restricted residential plats upon which residences have been erected.

On November 13, 1922, an ordinance was adopted by the village council, establishing a comprehensive zoning plan for regulating and restricting the location of trades, industries, apartment houses, two-family houses, single family houses, etc., the lot area to be built upon, the size and height of buildings, etc.

The entire area of the village is divided by the ordinance into six classes of use districts, denominated U–1 to U–6, inclusive; three classes of height districts, denominated H–1 to H–3, inclusive; and four classes of area districts, denominated A–1 to A–4, inclusive. The use districts are classified in respect of the buildings which may be erected within their respective limits, as follows: U–1 is restricted to single family dwellings, public parks, water towers and reservoirs, suburban and interurban electric railway passenger stations and rights of way, and farming, non-commercial greenhouse nurseries, and truck gardening; U–2 is extended to include two-family dwellings; U–3 is further extended to include apart-ment houses, hotels, churches, schools, public libraries, museums, private clubs, community center buildings, hospitals, sanitariums, public play-grounds and recreation buildings, and a city hall and courthouse; U–4 is further extended to include banks, offices, studios, telephone exchanges, fire and police stations, restaurants, theaters and moving picture shows, retail stores and shops, sales offices, sample rooms, wholesale stores for hardware, drugs, and groceries, stations for gasoline and oil (not exceeding 1,000 gallons storage) and for ice delivery, skating rinks and dance halls, electric substations, job and newspaper printing, public garages for motor vehicles, stables and wagon sheds (not exceeding five horses, wagons or motor trucks), and distributing stations for central store and commercial enterprises; U–5 is further extended to include billboards and advertising signs (if permitted), warehouses, ice and ice cream manufacturing and cold storage plants, bottling works, milk bottling and central distribution stations, laundries, carpet cleaning, dry cleaning, and dyeing establish-ments, blacksmith, horseshoeing, wagon and motor vehicle repair shops, freight stations, street car barns, stables and wagon sheds (for more than five horses, wagons or motor trucks), and wholesale produce markets and salesrooms; U–6 is further extended to include plants for sewage disposal and for producing gas, garbage and refuse incineration, scrap iron, junk, scrap paper, and rag storage, aviation fields, cemeteries, crematories, penal and correctional institutions, insane and feeble-minded institutions, storage of oil and gasoline (not to exceed 25,000 gallons), and manufactur-ing and industrial operations of any kind other than, and any public utility not included in, a class U–1, U–2, U–3, U–4, or U–5 use. There is a seventh class of uses which is prohibited altogether.

Class U–1 is the only district in which buildings are restricted to those enumerated. In the other classes the uses are cumulative—that is to say, uses in class U–2 include those enumerated in the preceding class U–1; class U–3 includes uses enumerated in the preceding classes, U–2 and U–1; and so on. In addition to the enumerated uses, the ordinance provides for accessory uses; that is, for uses customarily incident to the principal use, such as private garages. Many regulations are provided in respect of such accessory uses.

The height districts are classified as follows: In class H–1, buildings are limited to a height of 2½ stories, or 35 feet; in class H–2, to 4 stories, or 50 feet; in class H–3, to 80 feet. To all of these, certain exceptions are made, as in the case of church spires, water tanks, etc.

The classification of area districts is: In A–1 districts, dwellings or apartment houses to accommodate more than one family must have at least 5,000 square feet for interior lots and at least 4,000 square feet for corner lots; in A–2 districts, the area must be at least 2,500 square feet for interior lots, and 2,000 square feet for corner lots; in A–3 districts, the limits are 1,250 and 1,000 square feet, respectively; in A–4 districts, the limits are 900 and 700 square feet, respectively. The ordinance contains, in great variety and detail, provisions in respect of width of lots, front, side, and rear yards, and other matters, including restrictions and regulations as to the use of billboards, signboards, and advertising signs. * * *

Appellee's tract of land comes under U–2, U–3 and U–6. The first strip of 620 feet immediately north of Euclid Avenue falls in class U–2, the next 130 feet to the north, in U–3, and the remainder in U–6. The uses of the first 620 feet, therefore, do not include apartment houses, hotels, churches, schools, or other public and semipublic buildings, or other uses enumerated in respect of U–3 to U–6, inclusive. The uses of the next 130 feet include all of these, but exclude industries, theaters, banks, shops, and the various other uses set forth in respect of U–4 to U–6, inclusive.

Annexed to the ordinance, and made a part of it, is a zone map, showing the location and limits of the various use, height, and area districts, from which it appears that the three classes overlap one another; that is to say, for example, both U–5 and U–6 use districts are in A–4 area districts, but the former is in H–2 and the latter in H–3 height districts.

* * *

The enforcement of the ordinance is entrusted to the inspector of buildings, under rules and regulations of the board of zoning appeals. Meetings of the board are public, and minutes of its proceedings are kept. It is authorized to adopt rules and regulations to carry into effect provisions of the ordinance. Decisions of the inspector of buildings may be appealed to the board by any person claiming to be adversely affected by any such decision. The board is given power in specific cases of practical difficulty or unnecessary hardship to interpret the ordinance in harmony with its general purpose and intent, so that the public health, safety and general welfare may be secure and substantial justice done. * * *

The ordinance is assailed on the grounds that it is in derogation of section 1 of the Fourteenth Amendment to the Federal Constitution in that it deprives appellee of liberty and property without due process of law and denies it the equal protection of the law, and that it offends against certain provisions of the Constitution of the state of Ohio. The prayer of the bill is for an injunction restraining the enforcement of the ordinance and all attempts to impose or maintain as to appellee's property any of the restrictions, limitations or conditions. The court below held the ordinance to be unconstitutional and void, and enjoined its enforcement, 297 F. 307.

Before proceeding to a consideration of the case, it is necessary to determine the scope of the inquiry. The bill alleges that the tract of land in question is vacant and has been held for years for the purpose of selling and developing it for industrial uses, for which it is especially adapted, being immediately in the path of progressive industrial development; that for such uses it has a market value of about $10,000 per acre, but if the use be limited to residential purposes the market value is not in excess of $2,500 per acre; that the first 200 feet of the parcel back from Euclid avenue, if unrestricted in respect of use, has a value of $150 per front foot, but if limited to residential uses, and ordinary mercantile business be excluded therefrom, its value is not in excess of $50 per front foot. * * *

The record goes no farther than to show, as the lower court found, that the normal and reasonably to be expected use and development of that part of appellee's land adjoining Euclid Avenue is for general trade and commercial purposes, particularly retail stores and like establishments, and that the normal and reasonably to be expected use and development of the residue of the land is for industrial and trade purposes. * * *

Building zone laws are of modern origin. They began in this country about 25 years ago. Until recent years, urban life was comparatively simple; but, with the great increase and concentration of population, problems have developed, and constantly are developing, which require, and will continue to require, additional restrictions in respect of the use and occupation of private lands in urban communities. Regulations, the wisdom, necessity, and validity of which, as applied to existing conditions, are so apparent that they are now uniformly sustained, a century ago, or even half a century ago, probably would have been rejected as arbitrary and oppressive. Such regulations are sustained, under the complex conditions of our day, for reasons analogous to those which justify traffic regulations, which, before the advent of automobiles and rapid transit street railways, would have been condemned as fatally arbitrary and unreasonable. And in this there is no inconsistency, for, while the meaning of constitutional guaranties never varies, the scope of their application must expand or contract to meet the new and different conditions which are constantly coming within the field of their operation. In a changing world it is impossible that it should be otherwise. But although a degree of elasticity is thus imparted, not to the *meaning,* but to the *application* of constitutional principles, statutes and ordinances, which, after giving due weight to the new conditions, are found clearly not to conform to the Constitution, of course, must fall.

The ordinance now under review, and all similar laws and regulations, must find their justification in some aspect of the police power, asserted for the public welfare. The line which in this field separates the legitimate from the illegitimate assumption of power is not capable of precise delimitation. It varies with circumstances and conditions. A regulatory zoning ordinance, which would be clearly valid as applied to the great cities, might be clearly invalid as applied to rural communities. In solving doubts, the maxim "sic utere tuo ut alienum non laedas," which lies at the foundation of so much of the common law of nuisances, ordinarily will furnish a fairly helpful clew. And the law of nuisances, likewise, may be consulted, not for the purpose of controlling, but for the helpful aid of its analogies in the process of ascertaining the scope of, the power. Thus the question whether the power exists to forbid the erection of a building of a particular kind or for a particular use, like the question whether a particular thing is a nuisance, is to be determined, not by an abstract consideration of the building or of the thing considered apart, but by considering it in connection with the circumstances and the locality. A nuisance may be merely a right thing in the wrong place, like a pig in the parlor instead of the barnyard. If the validity of the legislative classification for zoning purposes be fairly debatable, the legislative judgment must be allowed to control.

There is no serious difference of opinion in respect of the validity of laws and regulations fixing the height of buildings within reasonable limits, the character of materials and methods of construction, and the adjoining area which must be left open, in order to minimize the danger of fire or collapse, the evils of overcrowding and the like, and excluding from residential sections offensive trades, industries and structures likely to create nuisances. See Welch v. Swasey, 214 U.S. 91, 29 S.Ct. 567, 53 L.Ed. 923 [1909].

* * *

Here, however, the exclusion is in general terms of all industrial establishments, and it may thereby happen that not only offensive or dangerous industries will be excluded, but those which are neither offensive nor dangerous will share the same fate. But this is no more than happens in respect of many practice-forbidding laws which this court has upheld, although drawn in general terms so as to include individual cases that may turn out to be innocuous in themselves. The inclusion of a reasonable margin, to insure effective enforcement, will not put upon a law, otherwise valid, the stamp of invalidity. * * * It cannot be said that the ordinance in this respect "passes the bounds of reason and assumes the character of a merely arbitrary fiat." Purity Extract Co. v. Lynch, 226

U.S. 192, 204, 33 S.Ct. 44, 47 (57 L.Ed. 184). Moreover, the restrictive provisions of the ordinance in this particular may be sustained upon the principles applicable to the broader exclusion from residential districts of all business and trade structures, presently to be discussed.

It is said that the village of Euclid is a mere suburb of the city of Cleveland; that the industrial development of that city has now reached and in some degree extended into the village, and in the obvious course of things will soon absorb the entire area for industrial enterprises; that the effect of the ordinance is to divert this natural development elsewhere, with the consequent loss of increased values to the owners of the lands within the village borders. But the village, though physically a suburb of Cleveland, is politically a separate municipality, with powers of its own and authority to govern itself as it sees fit, within the limits of the organic law of its creation and the state and federal Constitutions. Its governing authorities, presumably representing a majority of its inhabitants and voicing their will, have determined, not that industrial development shall cease at its boundaries, but that the course of such development shall proceed within definitely fixed lines. If it be a proper exercise of the police power to relegate industrial establishments to localities separated from residential sections, it is not easy to find a sufficient reason for denying the power because the effect of its exercise is to divert an industrial flow from the course which it would follow, to the injury of the residential public, if left alone, to another course where such injury will be obviated. It is not meant by this, however, to exclude the possibility of cases where the general public interest would so far outweigh the interest of the municipality that the municipality would not be allowed to stand in the way.

We find no difficulty in sustaining restrictions of the kind thus far reviewed. The serious question in the case arises over the provisions of the ordinance excluding from residential districts apartment houses, business houses, retail stores and shops, and other like establishments. This question involves the validity of what is really the crux of the more recent zoning legislation, namely, the creation and maintenance of residential districts, from which business and trade of every sort, including hotels and apartment houses, are excluded. Upon that question this court has not thus far spoken. The decisions of the state courts are numerous and conflicting; but those which broadly sustain the power greatly outnumber those which deny it altogether or narrowly limit it, and it is very apparent that there is a constantly increasing tendency in the direction of the broader view.

* * *

The matter of zoning has received much attention at the hands of commissions and experts, and the results of their investigations have been set forth in comprehensive reports. These reports, which bear every evidence of painstaking consideration, concur in the view that the segregation of residential, business and industrial buildings will make it easier to provide fire apparatus suitable for the character and intensity of the development in each section; that it will increase the safety and security of home life, greatly tend to prevent street accidents, especially to children, by reducing the traffic and resulting confusion in residential sections, decrease noise and other conditions which produce or intensify nervous disorders, preserve a more favorable environment in which to rear children, etc. With particular reference to apartment houses, it is pointed out that the development of detached house sections is greatly retarded by the coming of apartment houses, which has sometimes resulted in destroying the entire section for private house purposes; that in such sections very often the apartment house is a mere parasite, constructed in order to take advantage of the open spaces and attractive surroundings created by the residential character of the district. Moreover, the coming of one apartment house is followed by others, interfering by their height and bulk with the free circulation of air and monopolizing the rays of the sun which otherwise would fall upon the smaller homes, and bringing, as their necessary accompaniments, the disturbing noises incident to increased traffic and business, and the occupation, by means of moving and parked automobiles, of larger portions of the streets, thus detracting from their safety and depriving children of the privilege of quiet and open spaces for play, enjoyed by those in more favored localities—until, finally, the residential character of the neighborhood and its desirability as a place of detached residences are utterly destroyed. Under these circumstances, apartment houses, which in a different environment would be not only entirely unobjectionable but highly desirable, come very near to being nuisances.

* * *

It is true that when, if ever, the provisions set forth in the ordinance in tedious and minute detail, come to be concretely applied to particular premises, including those of the appellee, or to particular conditions, or to be considered in connection with specific complaints, some of them, or even many of them, may be found to be clearly arbitrary and unreasonable. But where the equitable remedy of injunction is sought, as it is here, not upon the ground of a present infringement or denial of a specific right, or of a particular injury in process of actual execution, but upon the broad ground that the mere existence and threatened enforcement of the ordinance, by materially and adversely affecting values and curtailing the opportunities of the market, constitute a present and irreparable injury, the court will not scrutinize its provisions, sentence by sentence, to ascertain by a process of piecemeal dissection whether there may be, here and there, provisions of a minor character, or relating to matters of administration, or not shown to contribute to the injury complained of, which, if attacked separately, might not withstand the test of constitutionality. In respect of such provisions, of which specific complaint is not made, it cannot be said that the landowner has suffered or is threatened with an injury which entitles him to challenge their constitutionality.

* * *

The gravamen of the complaint is that a portion of the land of the appellee cannot be sold for certain enumerated uses because of the general and broad restraints of the ordinance. What would be the effect of a restraint imposed by one or more of the innumerable provisions of the ordinance, considered apart, upon the value or marketability of the lands, is neither disclosed by the bill nor by the evidence, and we are afforded no basis, apart from mere speculation, upon which to rest a conclusion that it or they would have any appreciable effect upon those matters. Under these circumstances, therefore, it is enough for us to determine, as we do, that the ordinance in its general scope and dominant features, so far as its provisions are here involved, is a valid exercise of authority, leaving other provisions to be dealt with as cases arise directly involving them. * * *

Decree reversed.

MR. JUSTICE VAN DEVANTER, MR. JUSTICE MCREYNOLDS, and MR. JUSTICE BUTLER dissent.

NOTES AND QUESTIONS

1. The *Euclid* case was one of the hardest fought battles on the Supreme Court during a time when the Due Process clause of the Fourteenth Amendment had been interpreted to create a "liberty of contract" that permitted people to bargain freely, with relatively little state intrusion. The leading case was Lochner v. New York, 198 U.S. 45 (1905), which struck down a state law regulating the number of hours bakers could work, on the theory that bakers had the constitutional right to bargain freely for their own working conditions. In 1923, Justice Sutherland, *Euclid*'s author, had written an opinion striking down a minimum wage law for women under the same theory. Adkins v. Childrens' Hospital, 261 U.S. 525 (1923). In fact, Justice Sutherland himself had initially voted against the statute in *Euclid* and was asked to write the majority opinion striking it down. The four original dissenters, however, were able to change Justice Sutherland's mind, and the result was the decision upholding the statute. McCormack, A Law Clerk's Recollections, 46 Colum. L. Rev. 710, 712 (1946).

One of the great unexplained mysteries of the "liberty of contract" era is why the Supreme Court so often used the doctrine to strike down relatively modest state regulation of employment relations, but fairly consistently upheld extensive regulation of land use. For example, Justice Peckham was the author of *Lochner*. Only a few years later, he wrote an opinion upholding a statute that regulated the maximum heights of buildings in Boston Welch v. Swasey, 214 U.S. 91 (1909). This statute interfered substantially with people's right to bargain for what they wanted to build, just as the *Euclid* ordinance interfered with nearly every property owner's independent decision about how best to use his property.

Is it possible that the members of the Supreme Court relied on an economic theory of "externalities" in distinguishing between employment contracts and land use contracts? (See § 9.4 supra.) They may have believed that an employment agreement was a contract that affected only the two parties to the agreement, thus giving them a constitutional right to contract for whatever they pleased. By contrast, a contract to build a building of a certain height or for a certain use necessarily affected the property values of many neighboring people who could not be made parties to the agreement. These external effects justified more intensive state regulation. See H. Hovenkamp, Enterprise and American Law: 1836–1937 at Ch. 17 (1991).

Economic theories of external costs and benefits were well-developed by the time *Euclid* was decided. For example, in 1920 economist Arthur Cecil Pigou observed that certain transactions create a "divergence" between the bargained for result and the socially optimal result. This occurs when "A, in the course of rendering some service, for which payment is made, to a second person B, incidentally also renders services or disservices to other persons . . . of such a sort that payment cannot be exacted from the benefitted parties or compensation enforced on behalf of the injured parties." Pigou went on to suggest one externality pertaining to land use: when someone builds a tall building neighbors are injured when their access to light and air circulation are cut off; however they are usually not in a good position to negotiate with the builder or the purchaser. A. Pigou, The Economics of Welfare 183, 192 (London, 1920; reprint edition, 1962). More than a half century earlier John Stuart Mill said almost the same thing in his Principles of Political Economy, Book V, Chap. XI, § 14 (1848).

The *Euclid* opinion mentions some externalities that might justify a zoning statute. For example, it cited the fact that apartment builders might want to take advantage of the open space in areas occupied by single family homes, and thus take a "free ride" by imposing their own high density structures on areas of lower density. Assuming an apartment building is not an actionable nuisance, the home owners could do nothing to stop this except buy up all vacant land.

In 1926, the members of the Supreme Court had no modern, conceptual theory of externalities. The observation about apartment buildings was just plain common sense. No member of the Supreme Court likely read Pigou. Some, certainly Holmes, had read Mill, but nothing suggests that they knew about his theory of externalities. See Olken, Justice George Sutherland and Economic Liberty: Constitutional Conservatism and the Problem of Factions, 6 William & Mary Bill of Rights J. 1 (1997).

More likely, the Supreme Court distinguished the land use cases by relying upon the historical fact that the sovereign had always engaged in a certain amount of regulation of land use while state regulation of the terms of employment contracts was somewhat novel. In England, you will recall from chapter 4, only the King "owned" land. Everyone else held an estate in land *under* the King. This model of land ownership justified a certain amount of land use regulation.

2.   The activities of Ambler Realty Company in the Village of Euclid were one of the best arguments in favor of the zoning ordinance. During the fifteen years preceding the ordinance, Ambler Realty had bought and sold dozens of parcels in Euclid, many of them located along Euclid Avenue, where most of the Village's economic activity took place. Every time it sold a parcel for residential purposes, however, it had inserted into the deed a restrictive covenant limiting the land to residential use. Meanwhile, Ambler Realty had

been saving an island of land that was unrestricted, but surrounded by the restricted land it had sold to others. Apparently, Ambler's intent had been to obtain a monopoly of land that could be used for commercial or industrial purposes.

Ambler's plan backfired when the ordinance zoned most of Ambler's island residential as well. As the Village argued, if Ambler Realty's property "were to be permitted to be used . . . for factory and industrial purposes . . . , it would result in each and all of the dwellings . . . built upon the restricted lots which were sold by the complainant itself being subjected to the noise, the smoke, the inconvenience, and the unhealthful resulting effects arising from an unlimited . . . industrial use." *Record,* p. 33, Village of Euclid v. Ambler Realty Co.

3. Did you note the stark distinction that the Court makes between single-family, detached residences and multi-family housing? In fact, the Court says that "[t]he serious question in the case arises over the provision of the ordinance excluding from residential districts apartment houses. . . ." The Court upholds preferences favoring single-family, detached residences over multi-family housing. Part of *Euclid*'s prescience is that it anticipates the debate that would later surround the exclusion of multi-family residences from single-family districts. In fact, would it be fair to say that, the emphasis on the "ownership society" and the climate that eventually led to the modern mortgage crisis might find their origins, at least in small part, in the *Euclid* decision? In October 2004, George W. Bush said: " 'We're creating . . . an ownership society in this country, where more Americans than ever will be able to open up their door where they live and say, welcome to my house, welcome to my piece of property.' " Naomi Klein, Disowned by the Ownership Society, Nation, Feb. 18, 2008, at 10 (quoting President George W. Bush, Remarks to the National Association of Home Builders (Oct. 2, 2004), http://georgewbush-whitehouse.archives.gov/news/releases/2004/10/20041002–7.html). See also Carol Necole Brown, Intent and Empirics: Race to the Subprime, 93 Marq. L. Rev. 907 (2010) (discussing the implications of the ownership society in the context of the subprime mortgage crisis). "President Bush is taking advantage of the positive associations we have with ownership, of the perception that owners have it better than non-owners." Joseph William Singer, The Ownership Society and Takings of Property: Castles, Investments, and Just Obligations, 30 Harv. Envtl. L. Rev. 309, 311 (2006).

Nuisance law is the precursor to zoning as a method of regulating the use of land. Recall the discussion of nuisance law in Chapter 9. In contrast with zoning's rational and forward-looking comprehensive planning (discussed supra) nuisance law is piece-meal and reactive. But, nuisance law can be useful in defining and ascertaining the police power's scope. For instance, when determining if government can exercise its police power to prohibit a particular use, the proposed use will be considered in connection with the surrounding circumstances and with the locality. Also, recall the role of nuisance in the *Lucas* case. The Court analogizes apartments to nuisances stating that apartments come close to constituting nuisances when they are built in single-family, detached neighborhoods. Do you see the remnants of this perception of multi-family housing today when you observe where apartments tend to be located in relationship to single-family houses, commercial and industrial areas?

4.   As discussed below, the zoning scheme in *Euclid* is cumulative. How do the mentally handicapped fare under this particular scheme; are they unduly "discriminated" against? Note, that the handicapped ("insane and feeble-minded institutions") are confined to use district U–6 along with cemeteries, crematories, places for garbage and refuse incineration, penal and correctional institutions, gas production and sewage disposal plants, and other manufacturing and industrial operations. Single-family dwellings are placed in U–1, two-family dwellings are in U–2, and apartments are in U–3. Does *Euclid* foretell or even condone the type of discrimination against the handicapped that necessitated the protections later afforded to the handicapped under the Federal Fair Housing Act, for instance? The Federal Fair Housing Act is discussed in Chapter 12.

5.   Variances are discussed in § 11.4.2 infra. The *Euclid* Court adopts a "practical difficulty or unnecessary hardship" standard for granting variances. The Standard State Zoning Act is the dominant model used by most states in fashioning their zoning enabling legislation. Section 7 reflects the concern that zoning could result in a compensable taking without a variance procedure. The variance process allows government the flexibility to change zoning restrictions when application of the restrictions, as written, in particular circumstances, might trigger a taking. This concern was wise. Just as an example, in *Lucas* (discussed in Chapter 10), the granting of a variance could have allowed the owner enough development potential to avoid a per se taking; however, the law in *Lucas* did not initially contain a variance provision.

6.   The standard of judicial review in zoning cases is generally the fairly debatable test. "If the validity of the legislative classification for zoning purposes be fairly debatable, the legislative judgment must be allowed to control" according to the *Euclid* Court. This is a highly deferential test, analogous to the rational basis test under the Equal Protection Clause. Just two years after deciding the facial challenge in *Euclid*, the Court decided Nectow v. Cambridge, 277 U.S. 183 (1928), an as applied zoning challenge, discussed below. *Nectow* tempered *Euclid* by applying closer scrutiny and not the deferential, "fairly debatable" review applied in *Euclid*. Though in some states the presumption of validity is not as strong as that in *Euclid*, the scrutiny of *Euclid* is more the norm and that of *Nectow* is more the anomaly.

The fairly debatable standard of review only applies in "bread and butter" land use cases. In those instances when fundamental rights or suspect classes are implicated, less deferential standards of review apply (see, e.g., City of Los Angeles v. Alameda Books, below, and its discussion of intermediate and strict scrutiny review in the context of zoning that affects First Amendment rights).

NOTE: FACIAL AND "AS APPLIED" CONSTITUTIONAL REVIEW: NECTOW

In *Euclid*, Justice Sutherland made it quite clear that the Court was upholding the zoning ordinance on its face, "as a package," so to speak. As a result, the Court did not need to scrutinize each minute detail of the ordinance. The Justices reserved for another day the possibility that a *particular application* of such an ordinance might be unconstitutional. In Nectow v. Cambridge, 277 U.S. 183 (1928), the Supreme Court, once again speaking through Justice Sutherland, found such a case. The statute itself was similar to the one at issue in *Euclid*, and the parties agreed that the ordinance, on its face, was constitutional. The plaintiff's land was a strip less than 100 feet wide zoned exclusively for residences, but wedged among a Ford Motor Company assembly plant, a soap factory, and the Boston & Albany Railroad. A special master to whom the case had been referred found that no economic residential use could be made of the strip. Zoned as it was, the strip was worthless. The Supreme Court concluded:

> The governmental power to interfere by zoning regulations with the general rights of the land owner by restricting the character of his use, is not unlimited, and other questions aside, such restriction cannot be imposed if it does not bear a substantial relation to the public health, safety, morals, or general welfare.... Here, the express finding of the master, ... confirmed by the court below, is that the health, safety, convenience, and general welfare of the inhabitants of the part of the city affected will not be promoted by the disposition made by the ordinance of the locus in question. This finding of the master, after a hearing and an inspection of the entire area affected, supported, as we think it is, by other findings of fact, is determinative of the case. That the invasion of the property of plaintiff in error was serious and highly injurious is clearly established; and, since a necessary basis for the support of that invasion is wanting, the action of the zoning authorities comes within the ban of the Fourteenth Amendment and cannot be sustained.

277 U.S. at 188–189.

NOTE: MUNICIPAL POWER TO ZONE AND THE ZONING ORDINANCE

Ever since *Euclid*, courts have held that zoning is within the regulatory or police power of the state. The term "police power" refers to government's authority to engage in regulation to provide for the health, safety, morals or economic welfare of its citizens. Statutory price regulation of utilities, licensing of plumbers or taxicab drivers, prohibitions of commercial sex, and legal restrictions on entry for doctors and lawyers are only a few examples of a government's exercise of its police power. As a basic premise, the federal government is a government of "enumerated powers," which means that it may regulate only in ways that are authorized by the Federal Constitution. The states are governments of "residual powers," which means that they can regulate in any way that is not forbidden them by the Federal Constitution, or preempted by federal law. Most regulation of land use falls upon the state.

Unlike states, municipalities have no *inherent* police power, but only the regulatory power that the state gives them. Before a governmental subdivision (i.e., a municipality, county, borough, township or other unit of government smaller than a state) may zone it must have state enabling legislation. See Frug, The City As a Legal Concept, 93 Harv.L.Rev. 1057, 1062–66 (1980); 1A

C. Antieau, Municipal Corporation Law §§ 2, 7.01 (1991). Authority from the state may take the form of a zoning enabling act, which is a limited authorization from the state to a local government to zone. However, some cities zone under constitutional or statutory "home rule" provisions that give them a wide range of regulatory powers within their territories.

The zoning process generally starts with a map of the area to be zoned and the development of a "comprehensive plan" for the area's development. Ideally, the comprehensive plan is a rational plan for both predicting and guiding the development of the area. Most state zoning enabling acts require governmental subdivisions to develop a comprehensive plan that takes into account the community's anticipated economic needs. Although future deviations from the plan are permitted, the deviations must be reasonable and must not favor one person too strongly at the expense of others. The Standard State Zoning Enabling Act, published by the U.S. Department of Commerce in 1923 and still the model for most state zoning enabling acts, requires that all such deviations be "in accordance with a comprehensive plan." See Udell v. Haas, 21 N.Y.2d 463, 288 N.Y.S.2d 888, 235 N.E.2d 897 (1968); Haar, "In Accordance With a Comprehensive Plan," 68 Harv.L.Rev. 1154 (1955); Mandelker, The Role of the Local Comprehensive Plan in Land Use Regulation, 74 Mich.L.Rev. 899 (1976). See the discussion of "spot" zoning infra at § 11.4.1.

Zoning restrictions can be broadly classified as height, bulk and density limitations, which fall into one category, and use restrictions which fall into another. Height restrictions establish a maximum height for buildings within a given zone. Bulk and density restrictions attempt to control both population and structural density by fixing ratios of land area to maximum building area, or by establishing setback requirements, which specify a minimum distance that a building may be located from the lot boundary. Sometimes height and density are regulated together in a formula. For example, some zoning ordinances use a "floor area ratio" (FAR) restriction that establishes the maximum permissible floor space that a building can contain, usually as a fraction of lot size. The FAR is discussed in § 10.2 above.

The oldest form of use regulation is the "cumulative" restriction at issue in *Euclid*. One effect of the Supreme Court decision approving the ordinance was that many municipalities copied the ordinance with little or no variation, in order to avoid legal problems of their own. Under such an ordinance single-family homes are designated as the "highest" use, multiple-family dwellings second highest, and so on down to the heaviest and most offensive industries, assigned to the "lowest" districts. (Actually, under many ordinances the "lowest" use is a restriction forbidding all development whatsoever.) The zoning is "cumulative" because any land designated for a particular use permits all "higher" uses, but no "lower" ones. Effectively, under these ordinances it is legal to build a house in an area zoned for smokestack industries, but illegal to build a factory in an area zoned for residences.

The clear trend today is away from cumulative zoning. In the 1920's urban planners commonly believed that residential neighborhoods needed protection from nonresidential uses. Today we are inclined to believe that the reverse is true as well. For example, residential neighborhoods frequently produce a great deal more congestion and traffic than is optimal for industry.

Most new zoning today is "exclusive" rather than cumulative. In exclusive zoning, areas are designated for certain activities, and all other uses are prohibited. Some states are even beginning to classify industrial districts based on "industrial performance." An industrial performance zoning plan classifies manufacturing districts by the amount of noise, smoke, or other pollutants that the industry emits. A permit for a particular industrial use will be denied if it does not meet the pollution requirements for the particular district. See DeCoals, Inc. v. Board of Zoning Appeals, 168 W.Va. 339, 284 S.E.2d 856 (1981), which upheld the creation of a municipal "no dust" district and its application so as to exclude the plaintiff. Any person seeking to open a business in the area had to show that its activities would produce no dust that crossed its own property lines. See also Jones v. Zoning Hearing Board of McCandless, 134 Pa.Cmwlth. 435, 578 A.2d 1369 (1990), which upheld such zoning against a takings challenge.

Today courts generally look upon exclusive zoning with approval, provided that a community does not use it to exclude some uses altogether. For example, under cumulative zoning apartment buildings could be built in a district zoned for retailing or light industry, because multifamily housing was considered to be a "higher" use than any nonresidential use. By contrast, exclusive zoning can make it possible for a community to exclude *all* multi-family housing, while permitting both single-family housing and various forms of retailing and industry; when that happens the courts can become far more critical.

§ 11.2 LEGITIMATE RATIONALES OF ZONING LAW

One of the most important federal limitations on state and local power to zone is, of course, the takings clause, see Chapter 10. This section deals with Federal Constitutional limitations on the power to zone *other* than takings law. An additional important set of federal limitations originate with federal statutes, such as laws designed to protect the environment. These federal statutes are generally not treated here, but Chapter 12 addresses the relationship between state and local zoning and the federal civil rights laws.

§ 11.2.1 FEDERAL LAW: ZONING LIMITING EXPRESSION, OR REGULATING INDECENCY AND EXCESS?

CITY OF LOS ANGELES v. ALAMEDA BOOKS
Supreme Court of the United States (2002).
535 U.S. 425.

O'CONNOR, J., announced the judgment of the Court and delivered an opinion, in which REHNQUIST, C.J., and SCALIA and THOMAS, JJ., joined.

Los Angeles Municipal Code § 12.70(C) (1983), as amended, prohibits "the establishment or maintenance of more than one adult entertainment business in the same building, structure or portion thereof." Respondents, two adult establishments that each operated an adult bookstore and an adult video arcade in the same building, filed a suit ... alleging that § 12.70(C) violates the First Amendment and seeking declaratory and injunctive relief....

* * *

In 1977, the city of Los Angeles conducted a comprehensive study of adult establishments and concluded that concentrations of adult businesses are associated with higher rates of prostitution, robbery, assaults, and thefts in surrounding communities.... Accordingly, the city enacted an ordinance prohibiting the establishment, substantial enlargement, or transfer of ownership of an adult arcade, bookstore, cabaret, motel, theater, or massage parlor or a place for sexual encounters within 1,000 feet of another such enterprise or within 500 feet of any religious institution, school, or public park.... [This statute was later amended to additionally prohibit two such businesses from being conducted in the same building].

... An "Adult Bookstore" is an operation that "has as a substantial portion of its stock-in-trade and offers for sale" printed matter and videocassettes that emphasize the depiction of specified sexual activities. § 12.70(B)(2)(a). An adult arcade is an operation where, "for any form of consideration," five or fewer patrons together may view films or videocassettes that emphasize the depiction of specified sexual activities. § 12.70(B)(1).

* * *

In *Renton v. Playtime Theatres, Inc., supra,* this Court considered the validity of a municipal ordinance that prohibited any adult movie theater from locating within 1,000 feet of any residential zone, family dwelling, church, park, or school. Our analysis of the ordinance proceeded in three steps. First, we found that the ordinance did not ban adult theaters altogether, but merely required that they be distanced from certain sensitive locations. The ordinance was properly analyzed, therefore, as a time, place, and manner regulation. We next considered whether the ordinance was content neutral or content based. If the regulation were content based, it would be considered presumptively invalid and subject to strict scrutiny. *Simon & Schuster, Inc. v. Members of N.Y. State Crime Victims Bd.,* 502 U.S. 105, 115, 118, 112 S.Ct. 501, 116 L.Ed.2d 476 (1991); *Arkansas Writers' Project, Inc. v. Ragland,* 481 U.S. 221, 230–231, 107 S.Ct. 1722, 95 L.Ed.2d 209 (1987). We held, however, that the Renton ordinance was aimed not at the content of the films shown at adult theaters, but rather at the secondary effects of such theaters on the surrounding community, namely at crime rates, property values, and the quality of the city's neighborhoods. Therefore, the ordinance was deemed content neutral. Finally, given this finding, we stated that the ordinance would be upheld so long as the city of Renton showed that its ordinance was designed to serve a substantial government interest and that reasonable alternative avenues of communication remained available. We concluded that Renton had met this burden, and we upheld its ordinance.

The Court of Appeals applied the same analysis to evaluate the Los Angeles ordinance challenged in this case. First, the Court of Appeals found that the Los Angeles ordinance was not a complete ban on adult entertainment establishments, but rather a sort of adult zoning regulation, which *Renton* considered a time, place, and manner regulation. The Court of Appeals turned to the second step of the *Renton* analysis, but did not draw any conclusions about whether the Los Angeles ordinance was content based. It explained that, even if the Los Angeles ordinance were content neutral, the city had failed to demonstrate, as required by the third step of the *Renton* analysis, that its prohibition on multiple-use adult establishments was designed to serve its substantial interest in reducing crime. The Court of Appeals noted that the primary evidence relied upon by Los Angeles to demonstrate a link between combination adult businesses and harmful secondary effects was the 1977 study conducted by the city's planning department. The Court of Appeals found, however, that the city could not rely on that study because it did not " 'suppor[t] a reasonable belief that [the] combination [of] businesses ... produced harmful secondary effects of the type asserted.' "

The central component of the 1977 study is a report on city crime patterns provided by the Los Angeles Police Department. That report indicated that, during the period from 1965 to 1975, certain crime rates grew much faster in Hollywood, which had the largest concentration of adult establishments in the city, than in the city of Los Angeles as a whole. For example, robberies increased 3 times faster and prostitution 15 times faster in Hollywood than citywide.

* * *

The Court of Appeals found that the 1977 study did not reasonably support the inference that a concentration of adult operations within a single adult establishment produced greater levels of criminal activity because the study focused on the effect that a concentration of establishments—not a concentration of operations within a single establishment—had on crime rates. The Court of Appeals pointed out that the study treated combination adult bookstore/arcades as single establishments and did not study the effect of any separate-standing adult bookstore or arcade.

The Court of Appeals misunderstood the implications of the 1977 study. While the study reveals that areas with high concentrations of adult establishments are associated with high crime rates, areas with high concentrations of adult establishments are also areas with high concentrations of adult operations, albeit each in separate establishments. It was therefore consistent with the findings of the 1977 study, and thus reasonable, for Los Angeles to suppose that a concentration of adult establishments is correlated with high crime rates because a concentration of operations in one locale draws, for example, a greater concentration of adult consumers to the neighborhood, and a high density of such consumers either attracts or generates criminal activity. The assumption behind this theory is that having a number of adult operations in one single adult establishment draws the same dense foot traffic as having a number of distinct adult establishments in close proximity, much as minimalls and department stores similarly attract the crowds of consumers. Brief for Petitioner 28. Under this view, it is rational for the city to infer that reducing the concentration of adult operations in a neighborhood, whether within separate establishments or in one large establishment, will reduce crime rates.

* * *

The error that the Court of Appeals made is that it required the city to prove that its theory about a concentration of adult operations attracting crowds of customers, much like a minimall or department store does, is a necessary consequence of the 1977 study. For example, the Court of Appeals refused to allow the city to draw the inference that "the expansion of an adult bookstore to include an adult arcade would increase" business activity and "produce the harmful secondary effects identified in the Study." It reasoned that such an inference would justify limits on the inventory of an adult bookstore, not a ban on the combination of an adult bookstore and an adult arcade. The Court of Appeals simply replaced the city's theory—that having many different operations in close proximity attracts crowds—with its own—that the size of an operation attracts crowds. If the Court of Appeals' theory is correct, then inventory limits make more sense. If the city's theory is correct, then a prohibition on the combination of businesses makes more sense. Both theories are consistent with the data in the 1977 study. The Court of Appeals' analysis, however, implicitly requires the city to prove that its theory is the only one that can plausibly explain the data because only in this manner can the city refute the Court of Appeals' logic.

* * *

In *Renton,* we specifically refused to set such a high bar for municipalities that want to address merely the secondary effects of protected speech. We held that a municipality may rely on any evidence that is "reasonably believed to be relevant" for demonstrating a connection between speech and a substantial, independent government interest. 475 U.S., at 51–52, 106 S.Ct. 925; see also, *e.g., Barnes v. Glen Theatre, Inc.,* 501 U.S. 560, 584, 111 S.Ct. 2456 (1991) (SOUTER, J., concurring in judgment) (permitting municipality to use evidence that adult theaters are correlated with harmful secondary effects to support its claim that nude dancing is likely to produce the same effects). This is not to say that a municipality can get away with shoddy data or reasoning. The municipality's evidence must fairly support the municipality's rationale for its ordinance. If plaintiffs fail to cast direct doubt on this rationale, either by demonstrating that the municipality's evidence does not support its rationale or by furnishing evidence that disputes the municipality's factual findings, the municipality meets the standard set forth in *Renton*. If plaintiffs succeed in casting doubt on a municipality's rationale in either manner, the burden shifts back to the municipality to supplement the record with evidence renewing support for a theory that justifies its ordinance. See, *e.g., Erie v. Pap's A.M.,* 529 U.S. 277, 298, 120 S.Ct. 1382, 146 L.Ed.2d 265 (2000) (plurality opinion). This case is at a very early stage in this process. It arrives on a summary judgment motion by respondents defended only by complaints that the 1977 study fails to prove that the city's justification for its ordinance is necessarily correct. Therefore, we conclude that the city, at this stage of the litigation, has complied with the evidentiary requirement in *Renton*.

Justice Souter faults the city for relying on the 1977 study not because the study fails to support the city's theory that adult department stores, like adult minimalls, attract customers and thus crime, but because the city does not demonstrate that free-standing single-use adult establishments reduce crime. In effect, Justice Souter asks the city to demonstrate, not merely by appeal to common sense, but also with empirical data, that its ordinance will successfully lower crime. Our cases have never required that municipalities make such a showing, certainly not without actual and convincing evidence from plaintiffs to the contrary. See, *e.g., Barnes, supra,* at 583–584, 111 S.Ct. 2456 (Souter, J., concurring in judgment). Such a requirement would go too far in undermining our settled position that municipalities must be given a " 'reasonable opportunity to experiment with solutions' " to address the secondary effects of protected speech. *Renton, supra,* at 52, 106 S.Ct. 925 (quoting *Young v. American Mini Theatres, Inc.,* 427 U.S. 50, 71, 96 S.Ct. 2440, 49 L.Ed.2d 310 (1976) (plurality opinion)). A municipality considering an innovative solution may not have data that could demonstrate the efficacy of its proposal because the solution would, by definition, not have been implemented previously. The city's ordinance banning multiple-use adult establishments is such a solution. Respondents contend that there are no adult video arcades in Los Angeles County that operate independently of adult bookstores. But without such arcades, the city does not have a treatment group to compare with the control group of multiple-use adult establishments, and without such a comparison Justice Souter would strike down the city's ordinance. This leaves the city with no means to address the secondary effects with which it is concerned.

Our deference to the evidence presented by the city of Los Angeles is the product of a careful balance between competing interests. One the one hand, we have an "obligation to exercise independent judgment when First Amendment rights are implicated." *Turner Broadcasting System, Inc. v. FCC,* 512 U.S. 622, 666, 114 S.Ct. 2445, 129 L.Ed.2d 497 (1994) (plurality opinion); see also *Landmark Communications, Inc. v. Virginia,* 435 U.S. 829, 843–844, 98 S.Ct. 1535, 56 L.Ed.2d 1 (1978). On the other hand, we must acknowledge that the Los Angeles City Council is in a better position than the Judiciary to gather and evaluate data on local problems. See *Turner, supra,* at 665–666, 114 S.Ct. 2445; *Erie v. Pap's A.M., supra,* at 297–298, 120 S.Ct. 1382 (plurality opinion). We are also guided by the fact that *Renton* requires that municipal ordinances receive only intermediate scrutiny if they are content neutral. *Renton, supra,* at 48–50, 106 S.Ct. 925. There is less reason to be concerned that municipalities will use these ordinances to discriminate against unpopular speech.

* * *

Accordingly, we reverse the court of appeals' judgment granting summary judgment to respondents and remand the case for further proceedings.

* * *

Justice Souter, with whom Justice Stevens and Justice Ginsburg join, and with whom Justice Breyer joins as to Part II, dissenting.

* * *

This ordinance stands or falls on the results of what our cases speak of as intermediate scrutiny, generally contrasted with the demanding standard applied under the First Amendment to a content-based regulation of expression. The variants of middle-tier tests cover a grab-bag of restrictive statutes, with a corresponding variety of justifications. While spoken of as content neutral, these regulations are not uniformly distinct from the content-based regulations calling for scrutiny that is strict, and zoning of businesses based on their sales of expressive adult material receives mid-level scrutiny, even though it raises a risk of content-based restriction. It is worth being clear, then, on how close to a content basis adult business zoning can get, and why the application of a middle-tier standard to zoning regulation of adult bookstores calls for particular care.

Because content-based regulation applies to expression by very reason of what is said, it carries a high risk that expressive limits are imposed for the sake of suppressing a message that is disagreeable to listeners or readers, or the government.... A restriction based on content survives only on a showing of necessity to serve a legitimate and compelling governmental interest, combined with least-restrictive narrow tailoring to serve it, see *United States v. Playboy Entertainment Group, Inc.,* 529 U.S. 803, 813, 120 S.Ct. 1878, 146 L.Ed.2d 865 (2000); since merely protecting listeners from offense at the message is not a legitimate interest of the government, see *Cohen v. California,* 403 U.S. 15, 24–25, 91 S.Ct. 1780, 29 L.Ed.2d 284 (1971), strict scrutiny leaves few survivors.

The comparatively softer intermediate scrutiny is reserved for regulations justified by something other than content of the message, such as a straightforward restriction going only to the time, place, or manner of speech or other expression. It is easy to see why review of such a regulation may be relatively relaxed. No one has to disagree with any message to find something wrong with a loudspeaker at three in the morning, see *Kovacs v. Cooper,* 336 U.S. 77, 69 S.Ct. 448, 93 L.Ed. 513

(1949); the sentiment may not provoke, but being blasted out of a sound sleep does. In such a case, we ask simply whether the regulation is "narrowly tailored to serve a significant governmental interest, and . . . leave[s] open ample alternative channels for communication of the information." *Clark v. Community for Creative Non–Violence,* 468 U.S. 288, 293, 104 S.Ct. 3065, 82 L.Ed.2d 221 (1984). . . .

Although this type of land-use restriction has even been called a variety of time, place, or manner regulation, *id.,* at 46, 106 S.Ct. 925, equating a secondary-effects zoning regulation with a mere regulation of time, place, or manner jumps over an important difference between them. A restriction on loudspeakers has no obvious relationship to the substance of what is broadcast, while a zoning regulation of businesses in adult expression just as obviously does. And while it may be true that an adult business is burdened only because of its secondary effects, it is clearly burdened only if its expressive products have adult content. Thus, the Court has recognized that this kind of regulation, though called content neutral, occupies a kind of limbo between full-blown, content-based restrictions and regulations that apply without any reference to the substance of what is said. *Id.,* at 47, 106 S.Ct. 925.

It would in fact make sense to give this kind of zoning regulation a First Amendment label of its own, and if we called it content correlated, we would not only describe it for what it is, but keep alert to a risk of content-based regulation that it poses. The risk lies in the fact that when a law applies selectively only to speech of particular content, the more precisely the content is identified, the greater is the opportunity for government censorship. Adult speech refers not merely to sexually explicit content, but to speech reflecting a favorable view of being explicit about sex and a favorable view of the practices it depicts; a restriction on adult content is thus also a restriction turning on a particular viewpoint, of which the government may disapprove.

This risk of viewpoint discrimination is subject to a relatively simple safeguard, however. If combating secondary effects of property devaluation and crime is truly the reason for the regulation, it is possible to show by empirical evidence that the effects exist, that they are caused by the expressive activity subject to the zoning, and that the zoning can be expected either to ameliorate them or to enhance the capacity of the government to combat them (say, by concentrating them in one area), without suppressing the expressive activity itself. This capacity of zoning regulation to address the practical problems without eliminating the speech is, after all, the only possible excuse for speaking of secondary-effects zoning as akin to time, place, or manner regulations.

. . . The weaker the demonstration of facts distinct from disapproval of the "adult" viewpoint, the greater the likelihood that nothing more than condemnation of the viewpoint drives the regulation.

Equal stress should be placed on the point that requiring empirical justification of claims about property value or crime is not demanding anything Herculean. Increased crime, like prostitution and muggings, and declining property values in areas surrounding adult businesses, are all readily observable, often to the untrained eye and certainly to the police officer and urban planner. These harms can be shown by police reports, crime statistics, and studies of market value, all of which are within a municipality's capacity or available from the distilled experiences of comparable communities.

And precisely because this sort of evidence is readily available, reviewing courts need to be wary when the government appeals, not to evidence, but to an uncritical common sense in an effort to justify such a zoning restriction. It is not that common sense is always illegitimate in First Amendment demonstration. The need for independent proof varies with the point that has to be established, and zoning can be supported by common experience when there is no reason to question it. * * *

The lesson is that the lesser scrutiny applied to content-correlated zoning restrictions is no excuse for a government's failure to provide a factual demonstration for claims it makes about secondary effects; on the contrary, this is what demands the demonstration.... In this case, however, the government has not shown that bookstores containing viewing booths, isolated from other adult establishments, increase crime or produce other negative secondary effects in surrounding neighborhoods, and we are thus left without substantial justification for viewing the city's First Amendment restriction as content correlated but not simply content based. By the same token, the city has failed to show any causal relationship between the breakup policy and elimination or regulation of secondary effects.

* * *

[concurring opinions by Justices Scalia and Kennedy are omitted]

NOTES AND QUESTIONS

1. The plurality opinion concludes that a city may "consider[ ] an innovative solution" to crime problems even when the solution has never been attempted before and studies do not specifically suggest the proposed solution as a remedy. As a result, "novel" property regulations that limit freedom of expression are permissible. Compare the position in the Supreme Court's *Lucas* decision, reprinted supra, § 10.2.2., holding that novel regulations limiting the value of property can be takings precisely because the land owner could not reasonably anticipate them. Are the two positions consistent?

2. In City of Erie v. Pap's A.M. tdba "Kandyland," 529 U.S. 277 (2000), a divided Supreme Court also upheld a municipal ordinance cast as an anti-nudity provision, which required live female dancers in adult entertainment places to wear at least a G-string and pasties. Pap's had previously featured nude dancers and challenged the ordinance on First Amendment grounds. Once again the Court majority treated the ordinance as "content neutral"— that is, as not regulating expression because of its content. In this case,

Justice O'Connor wrote, the ordinance merely prohibited "being in a state of nudity," and nudity itself is not an "inherently expressive" activity. As in *Alameda Books* this finding of content neutrality justified a lower level of First Amendment scrutiny. To the argument that nude dancing conveyed an erotic message, which is clearly a form of expression, the Court wrote:

> * * * [E]ven if Erie's public nudity ban has some minimal effect on the erotic message by muting that portion of the expression that occurs when the last stitch is dropped, the dancers at Kandyland and other such establishments are free to perform wearing pasties and G-strings. Any effect on the overall expression is de minimis. And as Justice Stevens eloquently stated for the plurality in Young v. American Mini Theatres, Inc., 427 U.S. 50, 70, 96 S.Ct. 2440, 49 L.Ed.2d 310 (1976), "even though we recognize that the First Amendment will not tolerate the total suppression of erotic materials that have some arguably artistic value, it is manifest that society's interest in protecting this type of expression is of a wholly different, and lesser, magnitude than the interest in untrammeled political debate," and "few of us would march our sons or daughters off to war to preserve the citizen's right to see" specified anatomical areas exhibited at establishments like Kandyland. If States are to be able to regulate secondary effects, then *de minimis* intrusions on expression such as those at issue here cannot be sufficient to render the ordinance content based. . . .

The *Erie* case represents a highly successful trend in municipal zoning ordinances controlling adult entertainment to focus on nudity rather than the various forms of expression that are inherent in sexually explicit entertainment. See also Buzzetti v. City of New York, 140 F.3d 134 (2d Cir.), cert. denied, 525 U.S. 816 (1998), upholding a somewhat similar New York provision that had been highly successful in eliminating sexually oriented adult entertainment from such tourist areas as Times Square. In part, the court rejected an Equal Protection challenge to a provision that forbade women, but not men, from appearing topless in public.

An earlier generation of ordinances directed at such things as "live dancing" or "erotic behavior" were struck down by the court as attacking expression itself when they sought to exclude these activities from all parts of the municipality. See, e.g., Schad v. Borough of Mount Ephraim, 452 U.S. 61 (1981) (striking down ordinance that banned live entertainment in all parts of the Borough). See also Erznoznik v. Jacksonville, 422 U.S. 205 (1975), which struck down an ordinance that prohibited drive-in movie theaters from showing films containing nudity when the screen was visible from a public area outside the theater:

> "The ordinance is not directed against sexually explicit nudity, nor is it otherwise limited. Rather, it sweepingly forbids display of all films containing any uncovered buttocks or breasts, irrespective of context or pervasiveness. Thus it would bar a film containing a picture of a baby's buttocks, the nude body of a war victim, . . . scenes from a culture in which nudity is indigenous [or] shots of bathers on a beach. . . . Clearly all nudity cannot be deemed obscene even as to minors."

Id. at 213.

In Young v. American Mini Theatres, Inc., 427 U.S. 50 (1976), the Supreme Court upheld a Detroit "Anti–Skid Row" ordinance forbidding the operation of "adult" theatres or bookstores within 1000 feet of any two other "regulated uses," which included other similar establishments, liquor stores, pool halls, and pawn shops. Thus, although the Detroit ordinance limited the number of locations where such theatres and bookstores could operate, it did not ban them entirely. The Court relied on a long line of cases that generally prohibited the sovereign from suppressing constitutionally protected speech, but permitted it to regulate the "time, place and manner" of speech.

In City of Renton v. Playtime Theatres, 475 U.S. 41 (1986), the Supreme Court upheld an ordinance prohibiting "adult" theatres within 1000 feet of a residential dwelling, church, park, or school. As a result of the ordinance 95% of the land area of Renton, Washington, could not be used for such theaters. The Court held that free access to the remaining 5% was adequate to comply with the standard articulated in the *American Mini Theatres* case, even though nearly all this land was fully developed and virtually none of it was for sale or lease at the time of the litigation. In dissent, Justices Brennan and Marshall argued that the practical effect of the ordinance was to exclude all adult theatres, thus bringing it within the rule adopted in *Schad*.

The important point about *Renton* is that First Amendment issues are very prominent in the zoning game and the Court permitted the city of Renton to, in effect, zone out adult uses by permitting the city to isolate the adult theatres into a warehouse district where no one would ever go, assuming they could locate it. Those who disagree with *Renton* and *Alameda* argue that these cases are examples of the Court disregarding the First Amendment. In the case of *Alameda*, the Court allowed the city to rely on an outdated study. And, in *Renton*, the Court allowed the city to use a study regarding secondary effects that was developed for Seattle and other cities. The Court stated: "We hold that Renton was entitled to rely on the experiences of Seattle and other cities ... in enacting its adult theater zoning ordinance. The First Amendment does not require a city, before enacting such an ordinance, to conduct new studies or produce evidence independent of that already generated by other cities, so long as whatever evidence the city relies upon is reasonably believed to be relevant to the problem that the city addresses." Renton, 475 U.S. at 51–52.

In the context of zoning adult uses, there are basically two models, the concentration model in which cities concentrate adult uses into what some call a "ghetto", i.e. *Renton*, and the dispersion model in which adult uses are spread out, i.e. *Alameda* and *American Mini Theatres*.

Note, that state constitutional law may prescribe greater protection than the United States Constitution does. See Mendoza v. Licensing Board of Fall River, 444 Mass. 188, 827 N.E.2d 180 (2005), where the Supreme Judicial Court of Massachusetts held that a municipal prohibition on nude dancing that was very likely constitutional under the Supreme Court's *Erie* decision, supra, nevertheless conflicted with the free speech provision of the Massachusetts constitution.

3. In Linmark Associates, Inc. v. Willingboro, 431 U.S. 85 (1977), the Supreme Court struck down a city ordinance forbidding "for sale" signs, even

though the manifested purpose of the ordinance was to encourage integration by discouraging panic selling. The First Amendment "prevented the township from achieving its goal by restricting the free flow of truthful information." In Metromedia, Inc. v. San Diego, 453 U.S. 490 (1981), a bitterly divided Supreme Court struck down a municipal ordinance that prohibited most outdoor advertising signs unless they were located on the premises of the business being advertised. The stated purpose of the ordinance was "to eliminate hazards to pedestrians and motorists brought about by distracting sign displays" and "to preserve and improve the appearance of the City...." A plurality of four justices held that the ordinance improperly limited non-commercial as well as commercial advertising, but suggested that substantial restrictions on billboards containing commercial advertising would be permissible.

Then, in City of Ladue v. Gilleo, 512 U.S. 43 (1994), the Supreme Court struck down an ordinance that applied to homeowners and forbad all signs except address designations, for sale signs, and signs warning of hazardous materials. The Court said:

> In *Linmark* we held that the city's interest in maintaining a stable, racially integrated neighborhood was not sufficient to support a prohibition of residential "For Sale" signs. We recognized that even such a narrow sign prohibition would have a deleterious effect on residents' ability to convey important information because alternatives were "far from satisfactory." Ladue's sign ordinance is supported principally by the City's interest in minimizing the visual clutter associated with signs, an interest that is concededly valid but certainly no more compelling than the interests at stake in *Linmark*. Moreover, whereas the ordinance in *Linmark* applied only to a form of commercial speech, Ladue's ordinance covers even such absolutely pivotal speech as a sign protesting an imminent governmental decision to go to war. * * *

> * * * Ladue contends, however, that its ordinance is a mere regulation of the "time, place, or manner" of speech because residents remain free to convey their desired messages by other means, such as hand-held signs, "letters, handbills, flyers, telephone calls, newspaper advertisements, bumper stickers, speeches, and neighborhood or community meetings." However, even regulations that do not foreclose an entire medium of expression, but merely shift the time, place, or manner of its use, must "leave open ample alternative channels for communication." In this case, we are not persuaded that adequate substitutes exist for the important medium of speech that Ladue has closed off.

> Displaying a sign from one's own residence often carries a message quite distinct from placing the same sign someplace else, or conveying the same text or picture by other means. Precisely because of their location, such signs provide information about the identity of the "speaker." As an early and eminent student of rhetoric observed, the identity of the speaker is an important component of many attempts to persuade. A sign advocating "Peace in the Gulf" in the front lawn of a retired general or decorated war veteran may provoke a different reaction than the same sign in a 10–year–old child's bedroom window or the same message on a bumper

sticker of a passing automobile. An espousal of socialism may carry different implications when displayed on the grounds of a stately mansion than when pasted on a factory wall or an ambulatory sandwich board. * * *

Residential signs are an unusually cheap and convenient form of communication. Especially for persons of modest means or limited mobility, a yard or window sign may have no practical substitute. * * * Even for the affluent, the added costs in money or time of taking out a newspaper advertisement, handing out leaflets on the street, or standing in front of one's house with a hand held sign may make the difference between participating and not participating in some public debate. Furthermore, a person who puts up a sign at her residence often intends to reach neighbors, an audience that could not be reached nearly as well by other means.

A special respect for individual liberty in the home has long been part of our culture and our law; that principle has special resonance when the government seeks to constrain a person's ability to speak there. Most Americans would be understandably dismayed, given that tradition, to learn that it was illegal to display from their window an 8–by–11 inch sign expressing their political views.

See also Beaulieu v. City of Alabaster, 454 F.3d 1219 (11th Cir. 2006), holding that an ordinance limiting signs with political messages to residential areas was an unconstitutional, content based limitation on speech.

Restrictions on the size or appearance of signs are generally lawful, provided that the restrictions are not based on the content of the sign's message. See e.g., La Tour v. City of Fayetteville, 442 F.3d 1094 (8th Cir. 2006), which upheld an ordinance against signs bearing blinking or flashing lights. The court rejected the plaintiff's contention that the ordinance had been interpreted so as to allow "time and temperature" signs with blinking lights, and that the only way one could determine whether a sign contained only time and temperature information was by looking at its content. In this case the stated purpose of the sign restriction was traffic safety, and the court agreed that the city could reasonably conclude that a "short" and "rudimentary" blinking message showing the time and temperature posed no traffic risk.

4. May a landlord or homeowners association restrict residents by prohibiting them from displaying signs outside of their dwelling units such as for sale signs, political signs, religious artifacts, decorations, etc.? Yes. The First Amendment does not apply to private citizens and organizations. It applies to government to protect individuals from censorship by the government. "Congress shall make no law respecting an establishment of *religion*, or prohibiting the free exercise thereof; or abridging the freedom of *speech*, or of the *press*; or the right of the people peaceably to *assemble*, and to *petition* the Government for a redress of grievances." U.S. Const. amend. I. Such restrictions may violate other state or federal laws such as the federal Fair Housing Act if they are discriminatorily enforced.

Bloch v. Frischholz, 587 F.3d 771 (7th Cir. 2009), is an interesting and recent example of private restrictions that violate the federal Fair Housing

Act but that were not actionable under the First Amendment. The Blochs lived in a Chicago condominium building for approximately thirty years. They were observant Jews and during this entire time, they displayed a mezuzot on the doorpost on the outside of their condominium unit, without protest or objection from the Condominium Association (the Association). In 2001, the Association enacted a new set of " 'Hallway Rules.' " In relevant part, Hallway Rule 1 stated that " '[m]ats, boots, shoes, carts or objects of any sort are prohibited outside Unit entrance doors.' " *Id.* at 773. For three years, the Association did not remove the mezuzot; it primarily relied on Hallway Rule 1 to clear the hallways of clutter. The Association renovated its building's hallways in May 2004, after which the Association began removing the mezuzot. The Association also removed and confiscated political posters, crucifixes, Christmas ornaments, wreaths, and Chicago Bears pennants. The Blochs voiced their concerns and received no relief.

The Blochs sued seeking injunctive relief and damages for distress, humiliation, and embarrassment on federal and state grounds. Their federal claims alleged violation of various provisions of the Fair Housing Act. A magistrate judge enjoined the Defendants from removing the mezuzot, which was consistent with a rule change that was under consideration by the Association's board of managers. Subsequently, the board of managers modified Hallway Rule 1, creating an exception for religious objects. *Id.* at 774. The City of Chicago later amended its code to prohibit condominiums and rental properties from placing restrictions on affixing religious symbols or signs to the exterior of doorposts. The legislative claims mooted the Blochs' claim for injunctive relief but not for damages.

The Seventh Circuit Court of Appeals considered the Section 3604(a) claim under the Fair Housing Act which states that it is unlawful " '[t]o refuse to sell or rent after the making of a bona fide offer, or to refuse to negotiate for the sale or rental of, or otherwise make unavailable or deny, a dwelling to any person because of race, color, religion, sex, familial status, or national origin.' " *Id.* 776. The court observed that housing availability is the heart of this Section and that the language of the statute could be construed to reach instances of constructive eviction. *Id.* at 77. Though the court held that Section 3604(a) reached *post-acquisition* discrimination that makes housing unavailable, similar to a constructive eviction, the court held that a reasonable jury could not find that the Defendant's conduct rendered the condominium " 'unavailable' " to the Blochs. *Id.* at 778. The Blochs compared their plight to constructive eviction; however, they never vacated their condominium. Moreover, the Blochs' argument that Hallway Rule 1 made their unit unavailable to observant Jews was unavailing as the court found no evidence that the Blochs intended to sell their units. *Id.* at 778–779.

Second, the court considered the Blochs' claim that the Defendants violated Section 3604(b) of the Fair Housing Act which states that it is unlawful " '[t]o discriminate against any person in the terms, conditions, or privileges of sale or rental of a dwelling, or in the provision of services or facilities in connection therewith, because of race, color, religion, sex, familial status, or national origin.' " *Id.* at 779. The court held that the Blochs' action was within Section 3604(b). The Blochs alleged discrimination by the Association in the enforcement of the Association's rules and agreed to be governed by the Association at the time of the purchase. According to the court, this agreement by the Blochs constituted a "term or condition of sale" which made Section 3604(b) applicable. *Id.* at 779–780.

The Blochs' final Fair Housing Act challenge arose under Section 3617 which states that it is unlawful " 'to coerce, intimidate, threaten, or interfere with any person in the exercise or enjoyment of, or on account of his having exercised or enjoyed, or on account of his having aided or encouraged any other person in the exercise of enjoyment of, any right granted or protected by section 3603, 3604, 3605, or 3606 of this title.' " The court held that Section 3617 applies to post acquisition discrimination and that, with sufficient evidence, the Blochs could proceed under Section 3617 based upon the Defendant's interference with their Section 3604 rights. According to the court, Section 3617's prohibition on interference with the exercise or enjoyment of fair housing rights "reach[ed] a broader range of post-acquisition conduct" than Section 3604. *Id.* at 782. And, a Section 3617 claim of interference with Section 3604 rights did not require the Blochs to vacate. *Id.*

5. The United States Supreme Court's decision in Roe v. Wade, 410 U.S. 113 (1973) recognized a woman's constitutional right to have an abortion, at least during the first six months of pregnancy. Suppose that a city zones property in such a way as to make it almost impossible to operate an abortion clinic. Haskell v. Washington Tp., 864 F.2d 1266 (6th Cir.1988) struck down an ordinance that zoned all abortion clinics into one classification and all other medical services into a different classification. As a result, no building in the city could be used for both abortions and the delivery of other kinds of medical services. The economics of abortion services are such that as a practical matter the clinics have to perform a variety of services in order to be profitable. See also P.L.S. Partners, Women's Medical Center of R.I. v. City of Cranston, 696 F.Supp. 788 (D.R.I.1988) (striking down a zoning requirement that an abortion clinic be required to obtain the same special use permit that a hospital would need); and see Note, Exclusionary Zoning of Abortion Facilities, 32 Wash. U.J. Urb. & Contemp. L. 361 (1987).

§ 11.2.2 THE ROLE OF STATE LAW: REGULATING RELATIONSHIPS AND AESTHETICS

CHARTER TOWNSHIP OF DELTA v. DINOLFO

Supreme Court of Michigan (1984).
419 Mich. 253, 351 N.W.2d 831.

BRICKLEY, JUSTICE.

This case requires us to consider the constitutionality of a township zoning ordinance which limits the occupation of single-family residences to an individual, or a group of two or more persons related by blood, marriage, or adoption, and not more than one other unrelated person. We conclude that this ordinance, which prohibits the defendants from including in their households six unrelated persons, is unreasonable and arbitrary and, accordingly, in violation of the Due Process Clause of the Michigan Constitution.

In July and September of 1977, the Sierawski and Dinolfo "families" moved into homes in plaintiff township. The defendants' homes are located in an R 3, Moderate Density Residential District, which allows for single-family dwellings, duplexes, and quadruplexes. The defendants' homes qualify only as single-family dwellings. Each household consists of a husband and wife, that couple's several children, and six unrelated single adults. All members of these households are members of The Work of Christ Community, a nonprofit and federally tax-exempt organization chartered by the State of Michigan. Each of these households functions as a family in a single housekeeping unit and members intend to reside in their respective households permanently. All of the members of these "families" have adopted their lifestyle as a means of living out the Christian commitment that they stress is an important part of their lives.

Over a year after defendants occupied these residences with their "families", plaintiff's planning department sent violation notices citing them for having more than one unrelated individual residing in their homes in violation of the plaintiff's zoning ordinance. Plaintiff's zoning ordinance limits those groups which can live in single-family dwellings to an individual, or a group of two or more persons related by blood, adoption, or marriage, and not more than one unrelated person, excluding servants.[2] It is undisputed that the space requirements of the township building ordinance were not violated by the number of persons in each of the defendant's households. Indeed, that ordinance would allow for three more persons to live in homes the size of those owned by defendants.

Defendants jointly filed an application for a variance from the family definition section of the plaintiff's zoning ordinance, which was denied by the Zoning Board of Appeals. The minutes of the meeting at which the application was considered reflect no complaints about the defendants or the members of their households by any of their neighbors who attended that meeting. To the contrary, all present found them to be good neighbors. The variance was denied by the board because the defendants did not fall under the four general outlines for the granting of variances in the zoning ordinance.

Defendant Dinolfo then petitioned the Board of Trustees of Delta Township to overrule the decision of the Zoning Board of Appeals, and also formally presented a petition, supported by the signatures of twenty-seven neighbors, for a change in the language of the family definition section of the ordinance. Both of these efforts were unsuccessful. Plaintiff set a deadline for defendants to bring their households into compliance with the ordinance definition of a family.

After that time had expired, plaintiff filed separate complaints for injunctive relief against defendants in Eaton Circuit Court. The com-

---

2. Delta Township zoning ordinance, § 2.2.0(28) provides:

"Family: An individual or a group of two or more persons related by blood, marriage, or adoption, including foster children and servants, together with not more than one additional person not related by blood, marriage, or adoption, living together as a single housekeeping unit in a dwelling unit."

plaints were consolidated on order of the circuit court upon stipulation of counsel.

The trial court ultimately ruled in favor of the plaintiff on cross-motions for summary judgment under GCR 1963, 117.2(3). It found that plaintiff had the power under the Township Rural Zoning Act, M.C.L. § 125.271 et seq.; M.S.A. § 5.2963(1) et seq., to define the word "family", that its definition was reasonable, and that the governmental effort to promote the traditional notion of a family was a legitimate exercise of its authority. The court justified the allowance of one unrelated adult in a household as a way to allow for some flexibility. The court relied on Village of Belle Terre v. Boraas, 416 U.S. 1, 94 S.Ct. 1536, 39 L.Ed.2d 797 (1974), to state that simply because the Legislature drew the line at one unrelated adult did not mean the ordinance was arbitrary. The court also found that defendants' intended land use was not entirely excluded from the township by the ordinance in violation of M.C.L. § 125.297a; M.S.A. § 5.2963(27a), since they could still request conditional use permits. The court entered an order permanently enjoining defendants from occupying their residences in violation of the ordinance.

The Court of Appeals affirmed, 106 Mich.App. 1, 3, 308 N.W.2d 437 (1981), and this Court granted defendants' application for leave to appeal. 417 Mich. 887 (1983).

The defendants argue here, as below, that the plaintiff has no authority to define the word family and that the word "family", as it appears in the Township Rural Zoning Act, is intended to be interpreted as referring to a functional family rather than a traditional biological family. Defendants contend that they constitute functional families within that broad definition. Defendants also argue that the net effect of plaintiff's enforcement of this ordinance is to totally exclude them from the township in violation of their constitutional rights and their rights under M.C.L. § 125.297a; M.S.A. § 5.2963(27a). Defendants further contend that the definition of family in the ordinance both prohibits and allows property uses in an unreasonable, arbitrary, and capricious manner in violation of the Due Process and Equal Protection Clauses of the United States and Michigan Constitutions. Finally, defendants argue that the ordinance, by interfering with their chosen lifestyle and religious needs, is an impairment of their fundamental rights of privacy, association, and free exercise of religion in violation of the United States and Michigan Constitutions.

I

We first consider whether plaintiff had the power to define a family at all. The Township Rural Zoning Act is, on its face, a broad grant of power, providing in part:

> "The township board of an organized township in this state may provide by zoning ordinance for the regulation of land development and the establishment of districts in the portions of the township outside the limits of cities and villages which regulate the use of land

and structures; to meet the needs of the state's citizens for food, fiber, energy, and other natural resources, places of residence, recreation, industry, trade, service, and other uses of land; *to insure that use of the land shall be situated in appropriate locations and relationships; to limit the inappropriate overcrowding of land and congestion of population, transportation systems, and other public facilities * * *.* Ordinances regulating ... *the maximum number of families which may be housed in buildings,* dwellings, and structures, including tents and trailer coaches, erected or altered." (emphasis added.) M.C.L. § 125.271; M.S.A. § 5.2963(1).

* * *

The Township Rural Zoning Act is a broad grant of authority to townships to zone for the "public health, safety, and welfare". Included within this broad grant is the power to zone for the purpose of density control. We do not suggest that the act delegates to townships the unfettered authority to define the term family because any definition by a political subdivision must be within the intendment of the Legislature. We do find, however, that the definition of "family" in the ordinance is consistent with the enabling legislation.

At the time of the adoption of the Township Rural Zoning Act the traditional family was the most prevalent living pattern. The literal meaning of the word "family", particularly in the context of a statute dealing with living arrangements, could lead to the conclusion that the Legislature was considering only the existence of the biological family. Such an interpretation, however, would leave a void in the act, allowing townships to consider only traditional families in their zoning ordinances, legislatively precluding an individual living alone or a family from ever having an unrelated person in the household. On the other hand, to interpret "family" as being so fluid that each homeowner could define his own family would preclude townships from giving any consideration to the composition of a household. We do not think the Legislature intended either result. Nothing in the act precludes a township from considering the legal relationships between persons and nothing in the act forbids considering other kinds of relationships.

II

* * *

[I]n Village of Belle Terre v. Boraas, 416 U.S. 1 (1974), the Supreme Court confronted the constitutionality of a local zoning ordinance that is in all significant respects identical to the ordinance in question here. The Village of Belle Terre ordinance limited residential occupancy to a biological family plus no more than two unrelated persons. The case arose when the house in question was leased to eight college students. In upholding the constitutionality of the ordinance, Justice Douglas, writing for the majority, held that there were no fundamental rights involved which would require a scrutiny higher than determining if the ordinance was arbitrary. The Court found that distinguishing between a biological family and an unrelated group was not unreasonable or arbitrary under the Due Process and Equal Protection Clauses of the United States Constitution. It was argued in *Belle Terre,* 416 U.S. p. 8, as it is here, that "if two unmarried people can constitute a 'family' there is no reason why three or four may not". To that argument the Supreme Court responded "[b]ut every line drawn by a legislature leaves some out that might well have been included. That exercise of discretion, however, is a legislative, not a judicial, function."

* * * [W]e find *Belle Terre* to be clear authority for the proposition that to limit residentially zoned property to a traditional family and a number of non-related persons is permissible under the United States Constitution.

Our conclusion is not altered by *Moore v. East Cleveland,* 431 U.S. 494 (1977), notwithstanding defendants' contention that *Moore* modifies *Belle Terre.* In *Moore,* the Court held unconstitutional an ordinance which allowed only nuclear families to reside in single-family dwellings. On the facts of the case, the ordinance prohibited a grandchild from living with his grandmother. The Supreme Court came to a quick and strong defense of the traditional extended family, stating:

> "Ours is by no means a tradition limited to respect for the bonds uniting the members of the nuclear family. The tradition of uncles, aunts, cousins, and especially grandparents sharing a household along with parents and children has roots equally venerable and equally deserving of constitutional recognition. Over the years millions of our citizens have grown up in just such an environment, and most, surely, have profited from it. Even if conditions of modern society have brought about a decline in extended family households, they have not erased the accumulated wisdom of civilization, gained over the centuries and honored throughout our history, that supports a large conception of the family. Out of choice, necessity, or a sense of family responsibility, it has been common for close relatives to draw together and participate in the duties and the satisfactions of a common home." Id., pp. 504–505, 97 S.Ct. pp. 1938–1939.

We view *Moore* not as a limitation of *Belle Terre,* but, instead, as dealing with the other side of the *Belle Terre* coin—that while the state can restrict residential occupancy to the family, it cannot dissect the family. Having so found, we, therefore, must conclude that plaintiff's ordinance is constitutional as a matter of federal law. We must then accept the defendants' challenge that we examine the Delta Township ordinance in light of Michigan's Constitution. * * *

We think the appropriate standard ... is that due process standard generally used to evaluate the normal use of the police power. Of course, we still presume the constitutionality of the ordinance. But, extraordinary deference given to the line drawing in traditional zoning matters is not appropriate here.

* * *

Plaintiff lists the objectives of this ordinance: preservation of traditional family values, maintenance of property values and population and density control.[3] We cannot disagree that those are not only rational but laudable goals. Where the difficulty arises, however, is when plaintiff attempts to convince us that the classification at hand—limiting to two the number of unrelated persons who may occupy a residential dwelling together or with a biological family—is reasonably related to the achievement of those goals. It is precisely this rational relationship between the means used to achieve the legislative goals that must exist in order for this deprivation of the defendants' use of their property to pass the due process test.

Running through plaintiff's arguments is the assumption that unrelated persons will manifest a behavior pattern different from the biological family. They see

> "the potential for occupancy by one 'nuclear family' together with any number of unrelated and *unruly* individuals who view regular late night parties as a common bond and a proper function of child rearing."

If defendants succeed here, plaintiff fears that the next group taking advantage of the opportunity might not be of defendants' character. Plaintiff suggests that the "common bond of the group . . . [might be] not the Work of Christ, but the Work of Satan".

Amicus curiae, Michigan Townships Association, is even more direct in its perception of the evils that will result if non-related persons are allowed to live as a functional family.

> "The purpose of such regulations is to prohibit the influx of informal residential groups of people whose primary inclination is toward the enjoyment of a licentious style of living.

---

3. We note with interest that neither the Legislature in the enabling legislation nor the township in its zoning ordinance make any mention of the goal of "preserving traditional family values". The Township Rural Zoning Act lists as the statute's goals:

"to ensure that the use of the land shall be situated in appropriate locations and relationships; to limit the inappropriate overcrowding of land and congestion of population, transportation systems, and other public facilities". M.C.L. § 125.271; M.S.A. § 5.2963(1).

The Delta Township ordinance cites as its purposes:

"1) Promoting and protecting the public health, safety, and general welfare; 2) Protecting the character and stability of the recreational, agricultural, residential, commercial, and industrial areas within the unincorporated portions of Delta Charter Township; 3) Regulating growth of Delta Charter Township to obtain orderly and beneficial development; 4) Preventing the overcrowding of land and undue concentration of buildings and structures so far as is possible and appropriate in each zoning district by regulating the use and size of buildings in relation to the land surrounding them; 5) Pursue all township responsibilities set forth in [the enabling legislation]."

"While it seems apparent that defendants are not of this character, it would seem equally apparent that allowing in excess of six unrelated individuals to occupy a single-family dwelling unit would allow college fraternities, 'hippie' communes, motorcycle clubs, and assorted loosely structured groups of people associating for the purpose of enjoying a purely licentious style of living to locate at will in settled, low density residential neighborhoods and, perhaps even worse in duplexes, quadruplexes, and even in high-density apartment buildings. No somber recitations of anthropologists and sociologists are required to make one visualize the problems of noise, nuisance, vehicular traffic, and general disruption of orderly and peaceful living that could be brought about by permitting such arrangements."

* * * But we fail to see how plaintiff's ordinance furthers these goals. We, therefore, must part company with the United States Supreme Court. In *Belle Terre,* the Supreme Court made no attempt to suggest how a line drawn between the related and the unrelated advances these goals. It merely said that the line drawing was a "legislative, not a judicial, function". We agree that line drawing is a legislative function, but certainly there can be no argument against the well-understood rule of law that the task of deciding whether the line itself is reasonably related to the object of the line drawing is a judicial function.

Here, plaintiff attempts to have us accept its assumption that different and undesirable behavior can be expected from a functional family. Yet, we have been given not a single argument in support of such an assumption, only the assumption. Defendants, on the other hand, relying on decisions from other jurisdictions construing their own state constitutions, present a compelling argument that the means are not rationally related to the end sought.

Those states that have rejected *Belle Terre* have stressed that a line drawn near the limit of the traditional family is both over- and under-inclusive. See *New Jersey v. Baker,* 81 N.J. 99, 405 A.2d 368 (1979); *Santa Barbara v. Adamson,* 27 Cal.3d 123, 164 Cal.Rptr. 539, 610 P.2d 436 (1980) (finding over- and under-inclusiveness in the context of a right to privacy challenge). Unrelated persons are artificially limited to as few as two, while related families may expand without limit. Under the instant ordinance, twenty male cousins could live together, motorcycles, noise, and all, while three unrelated clerics could not. A greater example of over- and under-inclusiveness we cannot imagine. The ordinance indiscriminately regulates where no regulation is needed and fails to regulate where regulation is most needed.

* * * Plaintiff brings to our attention cases from those jurisdictions that have adopted the *Belle Terre* rationale. One in particular, *Town of Durham v. White Enterprises, Inc.,* 115 N.H. 645, 649, 348 A.2d 706 (1975), is typical of that point of view. There the court said:

"*The State has no particular interest in keeping together a certain group of unrelated persons.* The State has a clear interest, however, in preserving the integrity of the biological or legal family. The promotion of this legitimate government purpose justifies the exclusion of a blood related family from the density requirements of the ordinance which applies to an unrelated household.... Hence this classification is not invidious or arbitrary and is constitutional."

Indeed, "the state has no particular interest in keeping together a certain group of unrelated persons", but, most certainly, it has no business keeping them apart, absent a valid reason for doing so. We have found no such reason in the facts or arguments of this case. We agree with the conclusion of the Pennsylvania appellate court in Hopkins v. Zoning Hearing Board of Abington Twp., 55 Pa.Commw.Ct. 365, 370, 423 A.2d 1082 (1980). In holding that three retarded children could not be excluded from living with a married couple under a zoning family definition similar to the instant case, the court found

"no rational relationship between the restrictive definition of family in the Township ordinance and the state interest to preserve the residential character of the neighborhood".

We know from common experience that, while the motorcycle gang argument is a threatening one, it is more a symbol, one that is not by any stretch of the imagination representative of the life style of the countless people who seek residential living in something other than the biological family setting. As to the specter of a "Work of Satan" group that could slip in if defendants succeed here, we note that if this ordinance were upheld it would not keep out Ma Barker and her sons.

We agree that it would be easier for the plaintiff, with one broad stroke of its legislative brush, to sweep out of its residential neighborhoods a whole class of persons desiring residential accommodations than to have to legislate and enforce against the specific behavior it finds offensive and finds associated with the unrelated class. But protecting the constitutional rights of citizens comes before making life easy for government.

There has been no evidence presented nor do we know of any that unrelated persons, as such, have any less a need for the advantages of residential living or that they have as a group behavior patterns that are more opprobrious than the population at large. In the absence of such demonstration to justify this kind of classification, the ordinance can only be termed arbitrary and capricious under the Due Process Clause of the Michigan Constitution. * * *

Reversed.

[The dissenting opinion of Chief Justice Williams is omitted.]

NOTES AND QUESTIONS

1. Several states agree with Michigan and give greater protection to the family than the Federal Constitution does. See Baer v. Town of Brookhaven, 73 N.Y.2d 942, 540 N.Y.S.2d 234, 537 N.E.2d 619 (1989) (striking down

ordinance forbidding four unrelated persons from living together); City of
Santa Barbara v. Adamson, 27 Cal.3d 123, 164 Cal.Rptr. 539, 610 P.2d 436
(1980). Through a long line of cases the New Jersey courts have struck down
numerous attempts to define "family" and have apparently concluded that
the only reasonable limitations on occupancy are those that relate the *number*
of persons to a given amount of space. Thus, under New Jersey, law the
zoning authority can dictate that a house of 1000 square feet can accommodate only four people, but it can say nothing about their blood or marital
relationship to one another. The cases are summarized in Ocean County Bd.
of Realtors v. Township of Long Beach, 252 N.J.Super. 443, 599 A.2d 1309
(Law Div.1991). Likewise, Genesis of Mount Vernon v. Zoning Board of
Appeals, 152 Misc.2d 997, 579 N.Y.S.2d 968 (1991) interpreted New York
decisions to require that if a group of people operated as a single housekeeping unit they constituted a "family" under state law and could not be
forbidden from living together by local zoning regulations. This is consistent
with the New York decision in the *Braschi* case, supra Chapter 6, that two gay
men could constitute a "family" protected by a rent control ordinance.

However several states offer no more than the federal level of protection.
See State v. Champoux, 252 Neb. 769, 566 N.W.2d 763 (1997) (adhering to
Belle Terre standard); City of Brookings v. Winker, 554 N.W.2d 827 (S.D.
1996) (noting that state's zoning enabling legislation empowered municipalities to zone "[f]or the purpose of promoting health, safety, morals, or the
general welfare of the community," and this was broad enough to encompass
regulation of content of "family"); Dinan v. Board of Zoning Appeals of Town
of Stratford, 220 Conn. 61, 595 A.2d 864 (1991) (town could legitimately
conclude that unrelated individuals would not develop friendly relations with
neighbors that traditional families usually developed); Penobscot Area Housing Development Corp. v. Brewer, 434 A.2d 14 (Me.1981).

2. The *Dinolfo* court found that the Township's *stated* goal (preserving
family values) was permissible, but that the means used to achieve it were
irrational. Did the court disapprove the statute because the means were inept,
or because the court suspected that the Township really had other, hidden
motives?

3. Even federal tolerance has its limits. In Moore v. East Cleveland, 431
U.S. 494 (1977), a divided (5–4) Supreme Court restricted *Belle Terre* by
striking down an ordinance that confined occupancy of certain housing to a
single family, and defined "family" so narrowly that it included only one set
of grandchildren. Mrs. Moore was sentenced to jail for the crime of living with
her son and two grandsons who were cousins instead of brothers. The Court
noted that "freedom of personal choice in matters of marriage and family life
is one of the liberties protected by the Due Process Clause of the Fourteenth
Amendment."

4. The Michigan Supreme Court is careful to clarify that its decision is
based on the Michigan Constitution, not on the Federal Constitution. Only a
year earlier, the United States Supreme Court held in Michigan v. Long, 463
U.S. 1032 (1983), that if a state court did not explicitly say that its holding
was based on state law rather than federal law, the Supreme Court would

presume that the holding was based on federal law. In that case, the United States Supreme Court can review the decision.

ANDERSON v. CITY OF ISSAQUAH

Court of Appeals of Washington (1993).
70 Wash.App. 64, 851 P.2d 744.

KENNEDY, JUDGE.

Appellants M. Bruce Anderson, Gary D. LaChance, and M. Bruce Anderson, Inc. (hereinafter referred to as "Anderson"), challenge the denial of their application for a land use certification, arguing, inter alia, that the building design requirements contained in Issaquah Municipal Code (IMC) 16.16.060 are unconstitutionally vague. * * *

Anderson owns property located at 145 N.W. Gilman Boulevard in the City of Issaquah (City). In 1988, Anderson applied to the City for a land use certification to develop the property. The property is zoned for general commercial use. Anderson desired to build a 6800 square foot commercial building for several retail tenants. After obtaining architectural plans, Anderson submitted the project to various City departments for the necessary approvals. The process went smoothly until the approval of the Issaquah Development Commission (Development Commission) was sought. This commission was created to administer and enforce the City's land use regulations. It has the authority to approve or deny applications for land use certification.

Chapter 16.16.060 of the IMC enumerates various building design objectives which the Development Commission is required to administer and enforce. Insofar as is relevant to this appeal, the Development Commission is to be guided by the following criteria:

IMC 16.16.060(B). Relationship of building and site to adjoining area. 1. Buildings and structures shall be made compatible with adjacent buildings of conflicting architectural styles by such means as screens and site breaks, or other suitable methods and materials. 2. Harmony in texture, lines, and masses shall be encouraged....

IMC 16.16.060(D). Building Design. 1. Evaluation of a project shall be based on quality of its design and relationship to the natural setting of the valley and surrounding mountains. 2. Building components, such as windows, doors, eaves and parapets, shall have appropriate proportions and relationship to each other, expressing themselves as a part of the overall design. 3. Colors shall be harmonious, with bright or brilliant colors used only for minimal accent. 4. Design attention shall be given to screening from public view all mechanical equipment, including refuse enclosures, electrical transformer pads and vaults, communication equipment, and other utility hardware on roofs, grounds or buildings. 5. Exterior lighting shall be part of the architectural concept. Fixtures, standards and all exposed accessories shall be harmonious with the building design. 6. Monotony of design in single or multiple building projects shall be avoided. Efforts should be made to create an interesting project by use of complimentary details, functional orientation of buildings, parking and access provisions and relating the development to the site. In multiple building projects, variable siting of individual buildings, heights of buildings, or other methods shall be used to prevent a monotonous design.

As initially designed, Anderson's proposed structure was to be faced with off-white stucco and was to have a blue metal roof. It was designed in a "modern" style with an unbroken "warehouse" appearance in the rear, and large retail style windows in the front. The City moved a Victorian era residence, the "Alexander House," onto the neighboring property to serve as a visitors' center. Across the street from the Anderson site is a gasoline station that looks like a gasoline station. Located nearby and within view from the proposed building site are two more gasoline stations, the First Mutual Bank Building built in the "Issaquah territorial style," an Elk's hall which is described in the record by the Mayor of Issaquah as a "box building", an auto repair shop, and a veterinary clinic with a cyclone fenced dog run. The area is described in the record as "a natural transition area between old downtown Issaquah and the new village style construction of Gilman [Boulevard]."

The Development Commission reviewed Anderson's application for the first time at a public hearing on December 21, 1988. Commissioner Nash commented that "the facade did not fit with the concept of the surrounding area." Commissioner McGinnis agreed. Commissioner Nash expressed concern about the building color and stated that he did not think the building was compatible with the image of Issaquah. Commissioner Larson said that he would like to see more depth to the building facade. Commissioner Nash said there should be some interest created along the blank back wall. Commissioner Garrison suggested that the rear facade needed to be redesigned.

* * * On February 15, 1989, Anderson came back before the Development Commission. In the meantime, Anderson's architects had added a 5–foot overhang and a 7–foot accent overhang to the plans for the front of the building. More brick had been added to the front of the building. Wood trim and accent colors had been added to the back of the building and trees were added to the landscaping to further break up the rear facade.

Anderson explained the plans still called for large, floor to ceiling windows as this was to be a retail premises: "[A] glass front is necessary to rent the space . . ." Commissioner Steinwachs stated that he had driven Gilman Boulevard and taken notes. The following verbatim statements by Steinwachs was placed into the minutes: "My General Observation From Driving Up and Down Gilman Boulevard". I see certain design elements and techniques used in various combinations in various locations to achieve a visual effect that is sensitive to the unique character of our Signature Street. I see heavy use of brick, wood, and tile. I see minimal use of stucco. I see colors that are mostly earthtones, avoiding extreme contrasts. I see various methods used to provide modulation in both horizontal and vertical lines, such as gables, bay windows, recesses in front faces, porches, rails, many vertical columns, and breaks in roof lines. I see long, sloping, conspicuous roofs with large overhangs. I see windows with panels above and below windows. I see no windows that extend down to floor level. This is the impression I have of Gilman Boulevard as it relates to building design.

At that point, the Development Commission denied Anderson's application, giving four reasons: 1. * * * [T]he applicant has not been sufficiently responsive to concerns expressed by the Commission to warrant approval or an additional continuance of the review. 2. The primary concerns expressed relate to the building architecture as it relates to Gilman Boulevard in general, and the immediate neighborhood in particular. 3. The Development Commission is charged with protecting, preserving and enhancing the aesthetic values that have established the desirable quality and unique character of Issaquah, reference IMC 16.16.010C. 4. We see certain design elements and techniques used in various combinations in various locations to achieve a visual effect that is sensitive to the unique character of our Signature Street. On Gilman Boulevard we see heavy use of brick, wood and tile. We see minimal use of stucco. We see various methods used to provide both horizontal and vertical modulation, including gables, breaks in rooflines, bay windows, recesses and protrusions in front face. We see long, sloping, conspicuous roofs with large overhangs. We see no windows that extend to ground level. We see brick and wood panels at intervals between windows. We see earthtone colors avoiding extreme contrast.

* * * Anderson filed a complaint in King County Superior Court.

A statute which either forbids or requires the doing of an act in terms so vague that men [and women] of common intelligence must necessarily guess at its meaning and differ as to its application, violates the first essential of due process of law. * * * The purpose of the void for vagueness doctrine is to limit arbitrary and discretionary enforcements of the law. Burien Bark Supply, 106 Wash.2d at 871, 725 P.2d 994.

Looking first at the face of the building design sections of IMC 16.16.060, we note that an ordinary citizen reading these sections would learn only that a given building project should bear a good relationship with the Issaquah Valley and surrounding mountains; its windows, doors, eaves and parapets should be of "appropriate proportions", its colors should be "harmonious" and seldom "bright" or "brilliant"; its mechanical equipment should be screened from public view; its exterior lighting should be "harmonious" with the building design and "monotony should be avoided." The project should also be "interesting". If the building is not "compatible" with adjacent buildings, it should be "made compatible" by the use of screens and site breaks "or other suitable methods and materials." "Harmony in texture, lines, and masses [is] encouraged." The landscaping should provide an "attractive ... transition" to adjoining properties.

* * * [W]e conclude that these code sections "do not give effective or meaningful guidance" to applicants, to design professionals, or to the public officials of Issaquah who are responsible for enforcing the code. Although it is clear from the code sections here at issue that mechanical equipment must be screened from public view and that, probably, earth tones or pastels located within the cool and muted ranges of the color wheel are going to be preferred, there is nothing in the code from which an applicant can determine whether his or her project is going to be seen by the Development Commission as "interesting" versus "monotonous" and as "harmonious" with the valley and the mountains. Neither is it clear from the code just what else, besides the valley and the mountains, a particular project is supposed to be harmonious with, although "[h]armony in texture, lines, and masses" is certainly encouraged. * * *

In attempting to interpret and apply this code, the commissioners charged with that task were left with only their own individual, subjective "feelings" about the "image of Issaquah" and as to whether this project was "compatible" or "interesting". The commissioners stated that the City was "making a statement" on its "signature street" and invited Anderson to take a drive up and down Gilman Boulevard and "look at good and bad examples of what has been done with flat facades." One commissioner drove up and down Gilman, taking notes, in a no doubt sincere effort to define that which is left undefined in the code.

* * * [N]either Anderson nor the commissioners may constitutionally be required or allowed to guess at the meaning of the code's building design requirements by driving up and down Gilman Boulevard looking at "good and bad" examples of what has been done with other buildings, recently or in the past. We hold that the code sections here at issue are unconstitutionally vague on their face. The words employed are not technical words which are commonly understood within the professional building design industry. Neither do these words have a settled common law meaning.

* * * A design review ordinance must contain workable guidelines. Too broad a discretion permits determinations based upon whim, caprice, or subjective considerations. * * *

Clearly, however, aesthetic standards are an appropriate component of land use governance. Whenever a community adopts such standards they can and must be drafted to give clear guidance to all parties concerned. Applicants must have an understandable statement of what is expected from new construction. Design professionals need to know in advance what standards will be acceptable in a given community. It is unreasonable to expect applicants to pay for repetitive revisions of plans in an effort to comply with the unarticulated, unpublished "statements" a given community may wish to make on or off its "signature street". It is equally unreasonable, and a deprivation of due process, to expect or allow a design review board such as the Issaquah Development Commission to create standards on an ad hoc basis, during the design review process.

It is not disputed that Anderson's project meets all of the City's land use requirements except for those unwritten and therefore unenforceable requirements relating to building design which the Development Commission unsuccessfully tried to articulate during the course of several hearings. We order that Anderson's land use certification be issued, provided however, that those changes which Anderson agreed to through the hearing before the City Council may validly be imposed.

Notes and Questions

1. With the principal case, compare Rolling Pines Limited Partnership v. City of Little Rock, 73 Ark.App. 97, 40 S.W.3d 828 (2001), upholding an ordinance that required a developer to show that a manufactured home (often similar to large mobile homes in design, but usually placed on permanent foundations) satisfy a standard that it be "compatible with and will not adversely affect other property in the area where it is proposed to be located." The ordinance then specified eight "minimum standards" for compatibility, namely, that such houses have:

> (1) a pitched roof of three (3) in twelve (12) or fourteen (14) degrees or greater; (2) removal of all transport elements; (3) permanent foundation; (4) exterior wall finished so as to be compatible with the neighborhood; (5) orientation compatible with placement of adjacent structures; (6) underpinning with permanent materials; (7) all homes shall be multisectional; and (8) off-street parking per single-family dwelling standard.

The plaintiff's housing proposal met the eight "minimum" standards but the defendant nevertheless concluded that this was insufficient to show compatibility under the circumstances. The court rejected the argument that a standard that measured compatibility by an unspecified standard in addition to the eight articulated requirements was void for vagueness, distinguishing *Anderson*:

> *Anderson* [v. City of Issaquah] involved an ordinance with phrases such as "harmonious," and "interesting," as well as "compatible," and the case was marked by numerous attempts on the part of the applicant to meet the board members' subjective concepts of acceptability. Because the board had to draw upon its own subjective "feelings" due to the absence of objective guidelines, the court held that the ordinance failed to pass constitutional muster.

> More on point is the decision in *Anderson v. Peden*, 569 P.2d 633 (Or.App.1977). As in the instant case, the municipal code designated mobile homes as a conditional use and included a "compatibility with the established neighborhood" standard. The court found that the phrase was not unconstitutionally vague. Also in *Life Concepts, Inc. v. Harden*, 562 So.2d 726 (Fla.Ct.App.1990), the court addressed a challenge to the term "compatible" and found that it was not impermissibly vague because it has a plain and ordinary meaning that could be readily understood by reference to a dictionary. We agree that the term has a well-defined

meaning and is not so vague as to leave an applicant guessing as to its import or meaning. Moreover, there is no indication that appellant was laboring under any misconception of what the ordinance required in order to obtain a permit. We conclude that appellant has not established that the ordinance is unconstitutional.

Are you convinced? See also Saurer v. Board of Zoning Appeals, 629 N.E.2d 893 (Ind.App.1994), which refused to imply the power to regulate for aesthetics from an ordinance whose declared purpose was "to promote public health, safety, comfort, morals, convenience, and general welfare...." Contrast Parking Assn. of Georgia v. City of Atlanta, 264 Ga. 764, 450 S.E.2d 200 (1994), cert. denied, 515 U.S. 1116 (1995), upholding an ordinance requiring commercial parking lots to plant trees and shrubs around the periphery, at their own expense. The landscaped areas had to be at least ten percent of the total lot area, provided that this did not reduce the number of parking spaces by more than three percent. Justice Thomas, joined by Justice O'Connor, dissented from the denial of certiorari. See also Kucera v. Lizza, 59 Cal.App.4th 1141, 69 Cal.Rptr.2d 582 (1997), rev. denied, which approved a Tiburon, California, ordinance designed to protect views by limiting the growth of trees and shrubs, and permitted one landowner to sue her neighbor directly for violations. The court noted that some 70 California communities had similar ordinances. See Bobrowski, Scenic Landscape Protection under the Police Power, 22 Boston Coll. Environmental Affairs L. Rev. 697 (1995).

In fact, most decisions addressing the issue conclude that regulation of aesthetics is a permissible purpose of zoning law. See, e.g., Carpenter v. City of Snohomish, 2007 WL 1742161 at 7 (W.D. Wash. 2007) (stating that "[a]esthetic considerations are a substantial government interest"); R.H. Gump Revocable Trust v. City of Wichita, 35 Kan.App.2d 501, 131 P.3d 1268 (2006), which upheld a restriction that prevented the plaintiffs from constructing a cellular phone antenna disguised as a flagpole when there were no similar flagpoles in the area. Problems frequently arise when either the zoning enabling act or the municipal ordinance's own declaration of purpose fails to include aesthetics, as in the *Saurer* case cited above. Nevertheless, the courts tend to view aesthetic regulation somewhat more closely than regulation clearly related to health or safety, and find arbitrariness more quickly. See, e.g., City of Nichols Hills v. Richardson, 939 P.2d 17 (Okla.Crim.App. 1997) (aesthetic ordinance that permitted parking of cars but not pickup trucks in front of houses on occupant's own driveway was unconstitutionally arbitrary).

2.   While Anderson did not raise the First Amendment as a defense to his design, others have noted the possibility that architectural design is a form of protected speech. See Nivala. Constitutional Architecture: The First Amendment and the Single Family House, 33 San Diego L. Rev. 291 (1996).

§ 11.3   RACIAL AND ECONOMIC EXCLUSION

Exclusionary zoning refers to the use of zoning ordinances to exclude certain types of housing, often from suburban municipalities. The type of housing that is frequently the object of exclusionary zoning is housing that is affordable and housing for those who need assistance with daily living activities. Thus, exclusionary zoning practices often implicate other types of discrimination such as discrimination based upon race and discrimination against the handicapped.

§ 11.3.1   EXCLUSIONARY ZONING UNDER FEDERAL LAW

VILLAGE OF ARLINGTON HEIGHTS v. METROPOLITAN HOUSING DEVELOPMENT CORP.

Supreme Court of the United States (1977).
429 U.S. 252.

Mr. JUSTICE POWELL delivered the opinion of the Court.

In 1971 respondent Metropolitan Housing Development Corporation (MHDC) applied to petitioner, the Village of Arlington Heights, Ill., for the rezoning of a 15–acre parcel from single-family to multiple-family classification. Using federal financial assistance, MHDC planned to build 190 clustered townhouse units for low- and moderate-income tenants. The Village denied the rezoning request. MHDC, joined by other plaintiffs who are also respondents here, brought suit in the United States District Court for the Northern District of Illinois. They alleged that the denial was racially discriminatory and that it violated, inter alia, the Fourteenth Amendment and the Fair Housing Act of 1968, 82 Stat. 81, 42 U.S.C. § 3601 et seq.

* * *

I

Arlington Heights is a suburb of Chicago, located about 26 miles northwest of the downtown Loop area. Most of the land in Arlington Heights is zoned for detached single-family homes, and this is in fact the prevailing land use. The Village experienced substantial growth during the 1960's, but, like other communities in northwest Cook County, its population of racial minority groups remained quite low. According to the 1970 census, only 27 of the Village's 64,000 residents were black.

The Clerics of St. Viator, a religious order (Order), own an 80–acre parcel just east of the center of Arlington Heights. Part of the site is occupied by the Viatorian high school, and part by the Order's three-story novitiate building, which houses dormitories and a Montessori school. Much of the site, however, remains vacant. Since 1959, when the Village first adopted a zoning ordinance, all the land surrounding the Viatorian property has been zoned R–3, a single-family specification with relatively small minimum lot-size requirements.

* * *

MHDC * * * was organized in 1968 by several prominent Chicago citizens for the purpose of building low- and moderate-income housing throughout the Chicago area. In 1970 MHDC was in the process of building one § 236 development near Arlington Heights and already had provided some federally assisted housing on a smaller scale in other parts of the Chicago area.

After some negotiation, MHDC and the Order entered into a 99–year lease and an accompanying agreement of sale covering a 15–acre site in the southeast corner of the Viatorian property. MHDC became the lessee immediately, but the sale agreement was contingent upon MHDC's securing zoning clearances from the Village and § 236 housing assistance from the Federal Government.

* * *

The planned development did not conform to the Village's zoning ordinance and could not be built unless Arlington Heights rezoned the parcel to R–5, its multiple-family housing classification. Accordingly, MHDC filed with the Village Plan Commission a petition for rezoning, accompanied by supporting materials describing the development and specifying that it would be subsidized under § 236. The materials made clear that one requirement under § 236 is an affirmative marketing plan designed to assure that a subsidized development is racially integrated.

* * *

During the spring of 1971, the Plan Commission considered the proposal at a series of three public meetings, which drew large crowds. Although many of those attending were quite vocal and demonstrative in opposition to [MHDC's proposed project,] Lincoln Green, a number of individuals and representatives of community groups spoke in support of rezoning. Some of the comments, both from opponents and supporters, addressed what was referred to as the "social issue"—the desirability or undesirability of introducing at this location in Arlington Heights low- and moderate-income housing, housing that would probably be racially integrated.

Many of the opponents, however, focused on the zoning aspects of the petition, stressing two arguments. First, the area always had been zoned single-family, and the neighboring citizens had built or purchased there in reliance on that classification. Rezoning threatened to cause a measurable drop in property value for neighboring sites. Second, the Village's apartment policy, adopted by the Village Board in 1962 and amended in 1970, called for R–5 zoning primarily to serve as a buffer between single-family development and land uses thought incompatible, such as commercial or manufacturing districts. Lincoln Green did not meet this requirement, as it adjoined no commercial or manufacturing district.

At the close of the third meeting, the Plan Commission adopted a motion to recommend to the Village's Board of Trustees that it deny the request. The motion stated: "While the need for low and moderate income housing may exist in Arlington Heights or its environs, the Plan Commission would be derelict in recommending it at the proposed location." Two members voted against the motion and submitted a minority report, stressing that in their view the change to accommodate Lincoln Green represented "good zoning." The Village Board met on September 28, 1971, to consider MHDC's request and the recommendation of the Plan Commission. After a public hearing, the Board denied the rezoning by a 6–1 vote.

The following June MHDC and three Negro individuals filed this lawsuit against the Village, seeking declaratory and injunctive relief. [T]he District Court held that the petitioners were not motivated by racial discrimination or intent to discriminate against low-income groups when they denied rezoning, but rather by a desire "to protect property values and the integrity of the Village's zoning plan." 373 F.Supp., at 211. The District Court concluded also that the denial would not have a racially discriminatory effect.

A divided Court of Appeals reversed.

* * *

III

Our decision last Term in *Washington v. Davis,* 426 U.S. 229, 96 S.Ct. 2040, 48 L.Ed.2d 597 (1976), made it clear that official action will not be held unconstitutional solely because it results in a racially disproportionate impact. "Disproportionate impact is not irrelevant, but it is not the sole touchstone of an invidious racial discrimination." Id., at 242, 96 S.Ct., at 2049. Proof of racially discriminatory intent or purpose is required to show a violation of the Equal Protection Clause.

* * *

Davis does not require a plaintiff to prove that the challenged action rested solely on racially discriminatory purposes. Rarely can it be said that a legislature or administrative body operating under a broad mandate made a decision motivated solely by a single concern, or even that a particular purpose was the "dominant" or "primary" one. In fact, it is because legislators and administrators are properly concerned with balancing numerous competing considerations that courts refrain from reviewing the merits of their decisions, absent a showing of arbitrariness or irrationality. But racial discrimination is not just another competing consideration. When there is a proof that a discriminatory purpose has been a motivating factor in the decision, this judicial deference is no longer justified.

Determining whether invidious discriminatory purpose was a motivating factor demands a sensitive inquiry into such circumstantial and direct evidence of intent as may be available. The impact of the official action— whether it "bears more heavily on one race than another," *Washington v. Davis, supra,* 426 U.S., at 242, 96 S.Ct., at 2049—may provide an important starting point. Sometimes a clear pattern, unexplainable on grounds other than race, emerges from the effect of the state action even when the governing legislation appears neutral on its face. *Yick Wo v. Hopkins,* 118 U.S. 356, 6 S.Ct. 1064, 30 L.Ed. 220 (1886).

* * *

The evidentiary inquiry is then relatively easy. But such cases are rare. Absent a pattern as stark as that in *Yick Wo,* impact alone is not determinative, and the Court must look to other evidence.

The historical background of the decision is one evidentiary source, particularly if it reveals a series of official actions taken for invidious purposes. . . . The specific sequence of events leading up the challenged decision also may shed some light on the decisionmaker's purposes. . . . For example, if the property involved here always had been zoned R–5 but suddenly was changed to R–3 when the town learned of MHDC's plans to erect integrated housing, we would have a far different case. Departures from the normal procedural sequence also might afford evidence that improper purposes are playing a role. Substantive departures too may be relevant, particularly if the factors usually considered important by the decisionmaker strongly favor a decision contrary to the one reached.

The legislative or administrative history may be highly relevant, especially where there are contemporary statements by members of the decisionmaking body, minutes of its meetings, or reports.

* * *

This case was tried in the District Court and reviewed in the Court of Appeals before our decision in *Washington v. Davis, supra.* The respondents proceeded on the erroneous theory that the Village's refusal to rezone carried a racially discriminatory effect and was, without more, unconstitutional. But both courts below understood that at least part of their function was to examine the purpose underlying the decision. In making its findings on this issue, the District Court noted that some of the opponents of Lincoln Green who spoke at the various hearings might have been motivated by opposition to minority groups. The court held, however, that the evidence "does not warrant the conclusion that this motivated the defendants." 373 F.Supp., at 211.

On appeal the Court of Appeals focused primarily on respondents' claim that the Village's buffer policy had not been consistently applied and was being invoked with a strictness here that could only demonstrate some other underlying motive. The court concluded that the buffer policy, though not always applied with perfect consistency, had on several occasions formed the basis for the Board's decision to deny other rezoning proposals. "The evidence does not necessitate a finding that Arlington Heights administered this policy in a discriminatory manner." The Court of Appeals therefore approved the District Court's findings concerning the Village's purposes in denying rezoning to MHDC.

We also have reviewed the evidence. The impact of the Village's decision does arguably bear more heavily on racial minorities. Minorities constitute 18% of the Chicago area population, and 40% of the income groups said to be eligible for Lincoln Green. But there is little about the sequence of events leading up to the decision that would spark suspicion. The area around the Viatorian property has been zoned R–3 since 1959, the year when Arlington Heights first adopted a zoning map. Single-family homes surround the 80–acre site, and the Village is undeniably committed to single-family homes as its dominant residential land use. The rezoning request progressed according to the usual procedures. The Plan Commission even scheduled two additional hearings, at least in part to accommodate MHDC and permit it to supplement its presentation with answers to questions generated at the first hearing.

The statements by the Plan Commission and Village Board members, as reflected in the official minutes, focused almost exclusively on the zoning aspects of the MHDC petition, and the zoning factors on which they relied are not novel criteria in the Village's rezoning decisions. There is no reason to doubt that there has been reliance by some neighboring property owners on the maintenance of single-family zoning in the vicinity. The Village originally adopted its buffer policy long before MHDC entered the picture and has applied the policy too consistently for us to infer discriminatory purpose from its application in this case. Finally, MHDC called one member of the Village Board to the stand at trial. Nothing in her testimony supports an inference of invidious purpose.

In sum, the evidence does not warrant overturning the concurrent findings of both courts below. Respondents simply failed to carry their burden of proving that discriminatory purpose was a motivating factor in the Village's decision. This conclusion ends the constitutional inquiry. The Court of Appeals' further finding that the Village's decision carried a discriminatory "ultimate effect" is without independent constitutional significance.

V

Respondents' complaint also alleged that the refusal to rezone violated the Fair Housing Act of 1968, 42 U.S.C. § 3601 et seq. They continue to urge here that a zoning decision made by a public body may, and that petitioners' action did, violate § 3604 or § 3617. The Court of Appeals, however, proceeding in a somewhat unorthodox fashion, did not decide the statutory question. We remand the case for further consideration of respondents' statutory claims.

Reversed and remanded.

NOTES AND QUESTIONS

1. On remand, the Seventh Circuit concluded that Arlington Heights' refusal to rezone *did* violate the federal Fair Housing Act (FHA), holding that under the appropriate circumstances the FHA, unlike the Fourteenth Amend-

ment, required only proof of a discriminatory *effect,* not necessarily of discriminatory intent. 558 F.2d 1283 (7th Cir.1977), cert. denied 434 U.S. 1025 (1978). A few years later, the Seventh Circuit affirmed a district court's approval of a consent decree between the parties. 616 F.2d 1006 (7th Cir. 1980). The parties agreed that low income housing would not be built on the site near the center of Arlington Heights that was involved in the original litigation. Rather, the Village promised to annex some vacant land for construction of a large development that included substantial low income housing.

For more on FHA violations by local governments, see the note on that subject in Chapter 12.

2. In City of Cleburne v. Cleburne Living Center, 473 U.S. 432 (1985), the Supreme Court struck down a city's denial of a special permit for construction of a home for the mentally handicapped. The lower court found that the city's decision was motivated primarily by the fact that the residents would be mentally disabled, and that the city's declared motives—protection of students in a nearby junior high school, which already contained many mentally handicapped students, and reduction of street congestion—were questionable. The Supreme Court held that the city's acts were invidious discrimination motivated by "an irrational prejudice against the mentally retarded," and thus violated the Equal Protection clause. Amendments to the Fair Housing Act passed three years later and identifying "handicap" as a protected status would compel the same result. See Chapter 12.

3. What do you think of the Village's buffer policy? Recall, the Court stated noted that "the Village's apartment policy ... called for R–5 zoning primarily to serve as a buffer between single-family development and land uses thought incompatible, such as commercial or manufacturing districts. Lincoln Green did not meet this requirement, as it adjoined no commercial or manufacturing district." Does this type of policy seem familiar after considering *Euclid*?

§ 11.3.2   EXCLUSIONARY ZONING UNDER STATE LAW

SOUTHERN BURLINGTON COUNTY N.A.A.C.P. v. TOWNSHIP OF MOUNT LAUREL

Supreme Court of New Jersey (1975).
67 N.J. 151, 336 A.2d 713.

HALL, J.

This case attacks the system of land use regulation by defendant Township of Mount Laurel on the ground that low and moderate income families are thereby unlawfully excluded from the municipality. The trial court so found, 119 N.J.Super. 164, 290 A.2d 465 (Law Div.1972), and declared the township zoning ordinance totally invalid.

* * *

Plaintiffs represent the minority group poor (black and Hispanic) seeking such quarters. But they are not the only category of persons barred from so many municipalities by reason of restrictive land use regulations. We have reference to young and elderly couples, single persons and large, growing families not in the poverty class, but who still cannot afford the only kinds of housing realistically permitted in most places—relatively high-priced, single-family detached dwellings on sizeable lots and, in some municipalities, expensive apartments. We will, therefore, consider the case from the wider viewpoint that the effect of Mount Laurel's land use regulation has been to prevent various categories of persons from living in the township because of the limited extent of their income and resources. * * *

The location and nature of development has been, as usual, controlled by the local zoning enactments. * * * Under the present ordinance, 29.2% of all the land in the township, or 4,121 acres, is zoned for industry. * * * Only industry meeting specified performance standards is permitted. The effect is to limit the use substantially to light manufacturing, research, distribution of goods, offices and the like. Some nonindustrial uses, such as agriculture, farm dwellings, motels, a harness racetrack, and certain retail sales and service establishments, are permitted in this zone. At the time of trial no more than 100 acres, mostly in the southwesterly corner along route 73 adjacent to the turnpike and I–295 interchanges, were actually occupied by industrial uses. The rest of the land so zoned has remained undeveloped. * * * [H]owever, the land cannot be used for residential development under the general ordinance.

The amount of land zoned for retail business use under the general ordinance is relatively small—169 acres, or 1.2% of the total. While the greater part of the land so zoned appears to be in use, there is no major shopping center or concentrated retail commercial area—"downtown"—in the township.

The balance of the land area, almost 10,000 acres, has been developed until recently in the conventional form of major subdivisions. The general ordinance provides for four residential zones, designated R–1, R–1D, R–2 and R–3. All permit only single-family, detached dwellings, one house per lot—the usual form of grid development. Attached townhouses, apartments (except on farms for agricultural workers) and mobile homes are not allowed anywhere in the township under the general ordinance. * * *

* * *

The record thoroughly substantiates the findings of the trial court that over the years Mount Laurel "has acted affirmatively to control development and to attract a selective type of growth" and that "through its zoning ordinances has exhibited economic discrimination in that the poor have been deprived of adequate housing and the opportunity to secure the construction of subsidized housing, and has used federal, state, county and local finances and resources solely for the betterment of middle and upper-income persons." (119 N.J.Super. at 178, 290 A.2d at 473).

There cannot be the slightest doubt that the reason for this course of conduct has been to keep down local taxes on *property* (Mount Laurel is not a high tax municipality) and that the policy was carried out without regard for non-fiscal considerations with respect to *people,* either within or without its boundaries. This conclusion is demonstrated not only by what was done and what happened, as we have related, but also by innumerable direct statements of municipal officials at public meetings over the years which are found in the exhibits. The trial court referred to a number of them. No official testified to the contrary.

This policy of land use regulation for a fiscal end derives from New Jersey's tax structure, which has imposed on local real estate most of the cost of municipal and county government and of the primary and secondary education of the municipality's children. The latter expense is much the largest, so, basically, the fewer the school children, the lower the tax rate.

* * *

One incongruous result is the picture of developing municipalities rendering it impossible for lower paid employees of industries they have eagerly sought and welcomed with open arms (and, in Mount Laurel's case, even some of its own lower paid municipal employees) to live in the community where they work.

The legal question before us, as earlier indicated, is whether a developing municipality like Mount Laurel may validly, by a system of land use regulation, make it physically and economically impossible to provide low and moderate income housing in the municipality for the various categories of persons who need and want it and thereby, as Mount Laurel has, exclude such people from living within its confines because of the limited extent of their income and resources. Necessarily implicated are the broader questions of the right of such municipalities to limit the kinds of available housing and of any obligation to make possible a variety and choice of types of living accommodations.

We conclude that every such municipality must, by its land use regulations, presumptively make realistically possible an appropriate variety and choice of housing. More specifically, presumptively it cannot foreclose the opportunity of the classes of people mentioned for low and moderate income housing and in its regulations must affirmatively afford that opportunity, at least to the extent of the municipality's fair share of the present and prospective regional need therefor. These obligations must be met unless the particular municipality can sustain the heavy burden of demonstrating peculiar circumstances which dictate that it should not be required so to do.

We reach this conclusion under state law and so do not find it necessary to consider federal constitutional grounds urged by plaintiffs.

We begin with some fundamental principles as applied to the scene before us.

* * *

It is elementary theory that all police power enactments, no matter at what level of government, must conform to the basic state constitutional requirements of substantive due process and equal protection of the laws. These are inherent in Art. I, par. 1 of our Constitution, the requirements of which may be more demanding than those of the federal Constitution.

* * *

It is required that, affirmatively, a zoning regulation, like any police power enactment, must promote public health, safety, morals or the general welfare. (The last term seems broad enough to encompass the others.) Conversely, a zoning enactment which is contrary to the general welfare is invalid.

* * *

Indeed these considerations are specifically set forth in the zoning enabling act as among the various purposes of zoning for which regulations must be designed. N.J.S.A. 40:55–32. Their inclusion therein really adds little; the same requirement would exist even if they were omitted. If a zoning regulation violates the enabling act in this respect, it is also theoretically invalid under the state constitution.

* * * [I]t is fundamental and not to be forgotten that the zoning power is a police power of the state, and the local authority is acting only as a delegate of that power and is restricted in the same manner as is the state. So, when regulation does have a substantial external impact, the welfare of the state's citizens beyond the borders of the particular municipality cannot be disregarded and must be recognized and served.

* * *

It is plain beyond dispute that proper provision for adequate housing of all categories of people is certainly an absolute essential in promotion of the general welfare required in all local land use regulation. Further the universal and constant need for such housing is so important and of such broad public interest that the general welfare which developing municipalities like Mount Laurel must consider extends beyond their boundaries and cannot be parochially confined to the claimed good of the particular municipality. It has to follow that, broadly speaking, the presumptive obligation arises for each such municipality affirmatively to plan and provide, by its land use regulations, the reasonable opportunity for an appropriate variety and choice of housing, including, of course, low and moderate cost housing, to meet the needs, desires and resources of all categories of people who may desire to live within its boundaries. Negatively, it may not adopt regulations or policies which thwart or preclude that opportunity.

* * *

The township's general zoning ordinance * * * permits * * * only one type of housing—single-family detached dwellings. This means that all other types—multifamily including garden apartments and other kinds housing more than one family, town (row) houses, mobile home parks— are prohibited. Concededly, low and moderate income housing has been intentionally excluded. * * *

Mount Laurel's zoning ordinance is also so restrictive in its minimum lot area, lot frontage and building size requirements, earlier detailed, as to preclude single-family housing for even moderate income families. * * * The conclusion is irresistible that Mount Laurel permits only such middle and upper income housing as it believes will have sufficient taxable value to come close to paying its own governmental way.

* * * Without further elaboration at this point, our opinion is that Mount Laurel's zoning ordinance is presumptively contrary to the general welfare and outside the intended scope of the zoning power in the particulars mentioned. A facial showing of invalidity is thus established, shifting to the municipality the burden of establishing valid superseding reasons for its action and non-action. We now examine the reasons it advances.

The township's principal reason in support of its zoning plan and ordinance housing provisions, advanced especially strongly at oral argument, is the fiscal one previously adverted to, i.e., that by reason of New Jersey's tax structure which substantially finances municipal governmental and educational costs from taxes on local real property, every municipality may, by the exercise of the zoning power, allow only such uses and to such extent as will be beneficial to the local tax rate. In other words, the position is that any municipality may zone extensively to seek and encourage the "good" tax ratables of industry and commerce and limit the permissible types of housing to those having the fewest school children or to those providing sufficient value to attain or approach paying their own way taxwise.

We have previously held that a developing municipality may properly zone for and seek industrial ratables to create a better economic balance for the community *vis-a-vis* educational and governmental costs engendered by residential development, provided that such was "... done reasonably as part of and in furtherance of a legitimate comprehensive plan for the zoning of the entire municipality." Gruber v. Mayor and Township Committee of Raritan Township, 39 N.J. 1, 9–11, 186 A.2d 489, 493 (1962). We adhere to that view today. But we were not there concerned with, and did not pass upon, the validity of municipal exclusion by zoning of types of housing and kinds of people for the same local financial end. We have no hesitancy in now saying, and do so emphatically, that, considering the basic importance of the opportunity for appropriate housing for all classes of our citizenry, no municipality may exclude or limit categories of housing for that reason or purpose. While we fully recognize the increasingly heavy burden of local taxes for municipal governmental and school costs on homeowners, relief from the consequences of this tax system will have to be furnished by other branches of government. It cannot legitimately be accomplished by restricting types of housing through the zoning process in developing municipalities.

* * *

By way of summary, what we have said comes down to this. As a developing municipality, Mount Laurel must, by its land use regulations, make realistically possible the opportunity for an appropriate variety and choice of housing for all categories of people who may desire to live there, of course including those of low and moderate income. It must permit multifamily housing, without bedroom or similar restrictions, as well as small dwellings on very small lots, low cost housing of other types and, in general, high density zoning, without artificial and unjustifiable minimum requirements as to lot size, building size and the like, to meet the full panoply of these needs. Certainly when a municipality zones for industry and commerce for local tax benefit purposes, it without question must zone to permit adequate housing within the means of the employees involved in such uses. (If planned unit developments are authorized, one would assume that each must include a reasonable amount of low and moderate income housing in its residential "mix," unless opportunity for such housing has already been realistically provided for elsewhere in the municipality.) The amount of land removed from residential use by allocation to industrial and commercial purposes must be reasonably related to the present and future potential for such purposes. In other words, such municipalities must zone primarily for the living welfare of people and not for the benefit of the local tax rate.

We have earlier stated that a developing municipality's obligation to afford the opportunity for decent and adequate low and moderate income housing extends at least to ". . . the municipality's fair share of the present and prospective regional need therefore." Some comment on that conclusion is in order at this point. Frequently it might be sounder to have more of such housing, like some specialized land uses, in one municipality in a region than in another, because of greater availability of suitable land, location of employment, accessibility of public transportation or some other significant reason. But, under present New Jersey legislation, zoning must be on an individual municipal basis, rather than regionally. So long as that situation persists under the present tax structure, or in the absence of some kind of binding agreement among all the municipalities of a region, we feel that every municipality therein must bear its fair share of the regional burden. (In this respect our holding is broader than that of the trial court, which was limited to Mount Laurel-related low and moderate income housing needs.)

The composition of the applicable "region" will necessarily vary from situation to situation and probably no hard and fast rule will serve to furnish the answer in every case. Confinement to or within a certain county appears not to be realistic, but restriction within the boundaries of the state seem practical and advisable. (This is not to say that a developing municipality can ignore a demand for housing within its boundaries on the part of people who commute to work in another state.) Here we have already defined the region at present as "those portions of Camden, Burlington and Gloucester Counties within a semicircle having a radius of 20 miles or so from the heart of Camden City." The concept of "fair share" is coming into more general use and, through the expertise of the municipal planning adviser, the county planning boards and the state planning agency, a reasonable figure for Mount Laurel can be determined, which can then be translated to the allocation of sufficient land therefor on the zoning map.

* * *

The Remedy

* * * The township is granted 90 days from the date hereof, or such additional time as the trial court may find it reasonable and necessary to allow, to adopt amendments to correct the deficiencies herein specified. It is the local function and responsibility, in the first instance at least, rather than the court's, to decide on the details of the same within the guidelines we have laid down. If plaintiffs desire to attack such amendments, they may do so by supplemental complaint filed in this cause within 30 days of the final adoption of the amendments.

We are not at all sure what the trial judge had in mind as ultimate action with reference to the approval of a plan for affirmative public action concerning the satisfaction of indicated housing needs and the entry of a final order requiring implementation thereof. Courts do not build housing nor do municipalities. That function is performed by private builders, various kinds of associations, or, for public housing, by special agencies created for that purpose at various levels of government. The municipal function is initially to provide the opportunity through appropriate land use regulations and we have spelled out what Mount Laurel must do in that regard. It is not appropriate at this time, particularly in view of the advanced view of zoning law as applied to housing laid down by this opinion, to deal with the matter of the further extent of judicial power in the field or to exercise any such power. The municipality should first have full opportunity to itself act without judicial supervision. We trust it will do so in the spirit we have suggested, both by appropriate zoning ordinance amendments and whatever additional action encouraging the fulfillment of its fair share of the regional need for low and moderate income housing may be indicated as necessary and advisable.
* * *

The judgment of the Law Division is modified as set forth herein. No costs.

NOTES AND QUESTIONS

1. A decade after *Mt. Laurel* the New Jersey Supreme Court found that the township still had not complied with the 1975 order. Southern Burlington County N.A.A.C.P. v. Mt. Laurel, 92 N.J. 158, 456 A.2d 390 (1983) (*Mt. Laurel II*). The township had zoned 20 acres, less than one-fourth of one per cent of its land area, for low-income housing. Further, not a single unit of low income housing had actually been built. The court concluded that "Mt. Laurel remains afflicted with a blatantly exclusionary ordinance" because of its "determination to exclude the poor" from its communities.

The court then provided that all future *Mt. Laurel* housing litigation should be assigned to three judges selected by the Chief Justice, that the municipality cooperate in helping developers obtain federal housing construction subsidies, and that the communities could no longer prohibit mobile homes "unless there is solid proof that sound planning in a particular municipality requires such prohibition." The court also created a "builder's remedy": judicial permission to build to a developer of low income housing even though the village's grant of a permit had not been forthcoming. See Toll Bros. v. Township of West Windsor, 173 N.J. 502, 803 A.2d 53 (2002) (granting such a remedy where the city had zoned for types of lower income housing for which there was very little market demand, with the result that little actual development occurred); Van Dalen v. Washington Township, 120 N.J. 234, 576 A.2d 819 (1990) (builder not entitled to builder's remedy unless he can show that the local government at issue would not be able to meet its "fair share" obligation without the builder's proposed project).

The *Mt. Laurel* litigation is discussed in Tarr and Harrison, Legitimacy and Capacity in State Supreme Court Policymaking: the New Jersey Court and Exclusionary Zoning, 15 Rutgers L.J. 513 (1984), a symposium in 14 Seton Hall L.Rev. 829–1086 (1984), and in R. Babcock & C. Siemon, The Zoning Game Revisited (1985).

2. In response to the *Mt. Laurel* litigation the New Jersey legislature passed its own Fair Housing Act of 1985, N.J.Stat.Annot. 52:27D–301 et seq. The statute permits New Jersey municipalities operating under a *Mount Laurel* injunction to adopt "phasing schedules for meeting their fair share" (suggested by the *Mt. Laurel* court) provided that the schedules are consistent with the "timely achievement" of *Mount Laurel*'s goals. The statute also provides that a "municipality may propose the transfer of up to 50% of its fair share to another municipality within its housing region by means of a contractual agreement into which two municipalities voluntarily enter." Such agreements require the approval of the New Jersey Council on Affordable Housing (COAH), a state agency created by the Act. In Hills Development Co. v. Township of Bernards, 103 N.J. 1, 510 A.2d 621 (1986), the court upheld the statute against charges that it was an attempt to undermine, rather than effectuate, the goals articulated in *Mount Laurel I*. In Tocco v. New Jersey Council on Affordable Housing, 242 N.J.Super. 218, 576 A.2d 328 (App.Div.

1990), cert. denied, 499 U.S. 937 (1991), the court held that the Council had the power to order a community not to issue any construction permits at all for an eighteen month period because the community was not fulfilling its fair share requirement; further, the delay did not constitute a taking of the complainant's property. In re Township of Warren, 247 N.J.Super. 146, 588 A.2d 1227 (App.Div.1991), initially upheld a transfer agreement between relatively affluent Warren and less affluent New Brunswick. The COAH had previously determined that Warren had a "fair share" obligation to provide 367 units of low cost housing. Warren satisfied this obligation by rehabilitating 34 substandard units within Warren and constructing 134 new ones, and then by providing $4.4 million dollars to the City of New Brunswick to be used for the construction of 166 low income housing units there, as well as for rent subsidies that would make up for the shortfall in its fair share obligation. However, the New Jersey Supreme Court later found the transfer invalid, concluding that it was inconsistent with sound planning policy and each municipality's obligation to provide a fair share of regional housing needs. In re Township of Warren, 132 N.J. 1, 622 A.2d 1257 (1993). The court also suggested that permitting cities to contract out of their obligation to serve less affluent people could violate the 1968 federal Fair Housing Act. Id. at 28, 622 A.2d at 1271.

On the workings of the COAH, see Payne, Rethinking Fair Share: Enforcement of Affordable Housing Policies, 16 Real Est.L.J. 20 (1987).For historical background on the Mt. Laurel litigation, see Williams & Yates, The Background of *Mt. Laurel I*, 20 Vt. L. Rev. 687 (1996).

3. The United States Constitution does not guarantee citizens a right to housing. Does the Supreme Court of New Jersey say that housing is a fundamental right or that citizens of New Jersey have a fundamental right to housing under New Jersey state law? Remember, states can afford citizens greater rights and protections than the federal government but not less.

States and localities have taken various approaches to providing affordable housing. According to the American Planning Association, only twenty-five states have enacted legislation that requires their comprehensive plans to contain a housing element. See American Planning Association, Growing Smart Legislative Guidebook: Model Statutes for Planning and Management of Change pp. 7–278 (S. Meck, gen. ed., 2002). The guidebook can be accessed on-line at http://www.planning.org/growingsmart/guidebook/print/index.htm. Professor Daniel Mandelker discusses the housing element in modern state comprehensive plans in his article, The Affordable Housing Element in Comprehensive Plans, 30 B.C. Envtl. Aff. L. Rev. 555 (2003). He states, in part:

> To carry out the comprehensive plan, statutes always require what we call "elements" to be included in the comprehensive plan document. All states require a land use element and a transportation element. The housing element is a newer idea.... What is different about the housing element, as compared with the other comprehensive plan elements, is that the other elements the statutes prescribe must include a policy on a particular issue, such as transportation, but the statute does not tell municipalities what that policy should

be. The housing element tells municipalities what their housing policy should be, and so it is what we call a "substantive planning element" and not an element that simply requires a planning process. For that reason, there can be a conflict between what the housing element requires for housing and what the rest of the comprehensive plan requires for other problems in the community.

* * *

The role of affordable housing policy in comprehensive plans should be rethought. I would personally abandon any attempt to make numerical assignments of affordable housing need. I don't think that's a realistic way of approaching the problem, partly because of the land availability issue in older suburbs and partly because I think it becomes a holy grail that's never found or never achieved. Instead of that, I think there should be a focus on land-based policies, such as mixed-use and transit-oriented development, which can bring affordable housing to places where affordable housing is needed in communities.

Id. at 555, 557–58, 565 (2003).

BRITTON v. TOWN OF CHESTER

Supreme Court of New Hampshire (1991).
134 N.H. 434, 595 A.2d 492.

BATCHELDER, JUSTICE.

The plaintiffs brought a petition in 1985, for declaratory and injunctive relief, challenging the validity of the multi-family housing provisions of the Chester Zoning Ordinance. * * *

The plaintiffs in this case are a group of low- and moderate-income people who have been unsuccessful in finding affordable, adequate housing in the town, and a builder who, the master found, is committed to the construction of such housing. At trial, two plaintiffs testified as representative members of the group of low- and moderate-income people. Plaintiff George Edwards is a woodcutter who grew up in the town. He lives in Chester with his wife and three minor children in a one-bedroom, thirty-foot by eight-foot camper trailer with no running water. Their annual income is $14,040, which places them in the low-income category. Roger McFarland grew up and works in the town. He lives in Derry with his wife and three teenage children in a two-bedroom apartment which is too small to meet their needs. He and his wife both work, and their combined annual income is $24,000. Under the area standards, the McFarlands are a moderate-income family. Raymond Remillard is the plaintiff home builder. A long-time resident of the town, he owns an undeveloped twenty-three-acre parcel of land on Route 102 in the town's eastern section. Since 1979, he has attempted to obtain permission from the town to build a moderate-sized multi-family housing development on his land.

The zoning ordinance in effect at the beginning of this action in 1985 provided for a single-family home on a two-acre lot or a duplex on a three-acre lot, and it excluded multi-family housing from all five zoning districts in the town. In July, 1986, the town amended its zoning ordinance to allow multi-family housing. Article six of the amended ordinance now permits multi-family housing as part of a "planned residential development" (PRD), a form of multi-family housing required to include a variety of housing types, such as single-family homes, duplexes, and multi-family structures.

After a hearing, the master recommended that judgment be ordered for the plaintiffs; that the town's land use ordinances, including the zoning ordinance, be ruled invalid; and that plaintiff Remillard be awarded a "builder's remedy." * * *

* * * The master found * * * that the ordinance placed an unreasonable barrier to the development of affordable housing for low- and moderate-income families. Under the ordinance, PRDs are allowed on tracts of not less than twenty acres in two designated "R–2" (medium-density residential) zoning districts. Due to existing home construction and environmental considerations, such as wetlands and steep slopes, only slightly more than half of all the land in the two R–2 districts could reasonably be used for multi-family development. This constitutes only 1.73% of the land in the town. This fact standing alone does not, in the confines of this case, give rise to an entitlement to a legal remedy for those who seek to provide multi-family housing. However, it does serve to point out that the two R–2 districts are, in reality, less likely to be developed than would appear from a reading of the ordinance. A reviewing court must read the entire ordinance in the light of these facts.

Article six of the ordinance also imposes several subjective requirements and restrictions on the developer of a PRD. Any project must first receive the approval of the town planning board as to "whether in its judgment the proposal meets the objectives and purposes set forth [in the ordinance] in which event the Administrator [i.e., the planning board] may grant approval to [the] proposal subject to reasonable conditions and limitations." Consequently, the ordinance allows the planning board to control various aspects of a PRD without reference to any objective criteria. One potentially onerous section permits the planning board to "retain, at the applicant's expense, a registered professional engineer, hydrologist, and any other applicable professional to represent the [planning board] and assist the [planning board] in determining compliance with [the] ordinance and other applicable regulations." The master found such subjective review for developing multi-family housing to be a substantial disincentive to the creation of such units, because it would escalate the economic risks of developing affordable housing to the point where these projects would not be realistically feasible. In addition, we question the availability of bank financing for such projects, where the developer is required to submit a "blank check" to the planning board along with his proposal, and where to do so could halt, change the character of, or even bankrupt the project.

The defendant first argues that the trial court erred in ruling that the zoning ordinance exceeds the powers delegated to the town by the zoning enabling legislation. In support of this argument, the town asserts that the zoning enabling act does not require it to zone for the low-income housing needs of the region beyond its boundaries. Further, the town maintains that even if it were required to consider regional housing needs when enacting its zoning ordinance, the Chester Zoning Ordinance is valid because it provides for an adequate range of housing types. These arguments fail to persuade us of any error in the master's proposed order. RSA 674:16 authorizes the local legislative body of any city or town to adopt or amend a zoning ordinance "[f]or the purpose of promoting the health, safety, or the general welfare of the community." The defendant asserts that the term "community" as used in the statute refers only to the municipality itself and not to some broader region in which the municipality is situated. We disagree.

The possibility that a municipality might be obligated to consider the needs of the region outside its boundaries was addressed early on in our land use jurisprudence by the United States Supreme Court, paving the way for the term "community" to be used in the broader sense. In Village of Euclid v. Ambler Realty Co., 272 U.S. 365 (1926), the Court recognized "the possibility of cases where the general public interest would so far outweigh the interest of the municipality that the municipality would not be allowed to stand in the way." When an ordinance will have an impact beyond the boundaries of the municipality, the welfare of the entire affected region must be considered in determining the ordinance's validity.

In Beck v. Town of Raymond, 118 N.H. 793, 394 A.2d 847 (1978), we held that "[growth] controls must not be imposed simply to exclude outsiders, * * * especially outsiders of any disadvantaged social or economic group." [citing Mount Laurel] We reasoned that "each municipality [should] bear its fair share of the burden of increased growth." Today, we pursue the logical extension of the reasoning in Beck and apply its rationale and high purpose to zoning regulations which wrongfully exclude persons of low- or moderate-income from the zoning municipality.

In Beck, this court sent a message to zoning bodies that "[t]owns may not refuse to confront the future by building a moat around themselves and pulling up the drawbridge." The town of Chester appears willing to lower that bridge only for people who can afford a single-family home on a two-acre lot or a duplex on a three-acre lot. Others are realistically prohibited from crossing.

Municipalities are not isolated enclaves, far removed from the concerns of the area in which they are situated. As subdivisions of the State, they do not exist solely to serve their own residents, and their regulations should promote the general welfare, both within and without their boundaries. Therefore, we interpret the general welfare provision of the zoning enabling statute to include the welfare of the "community", as defined in this case, in which a municipality is located and of which it forms a part.

A municipality's power to zone property to promote the health, safety, and general welfare of the community is delegated to it by the State, and the municipality must, therefore, exercise this power in conformance with the enabling legislation. Because the Chester Zoning Ordinance does not provide for the lawful needs of the community, in that it flies in the face of the general welfare provision of RSA 674:16 and is, therefore, at odds with the statute upon which it is grounded, we hold that, as applied to the facts of this case, the ordinance is an invalid exercise of the power delegated to the town pursuant to RSA 674:16–30. We so hold because of the master's finding that "there are no substantial and compelling reasons that would warrant the Town of Chester, through its land use ordinances, from fulfilling its obligation to provide low[-] and moderate[-]income families within the community and a proportionate share of same within its region from a realistic opportunity to obtain affordable housing." * * *

Although we determine that the "builder's remedy" is appropriate in this case, we do not adopt the *Mt. Laurel* analysis for determining whether such a remedy will be granted. Instead, we find the rule developed in Sinclair Pipe Line Co. v. Richton Park, 19 Ill.2d 370, 167 N.E.2d 406 (1960), is the better rule as it eliminates the calculation of arbitrary mathematical quotas which *Mt. Laurel* requires. * * * Once an existing zoning ordinance is found invalid in whole or in part, whether on constitutional grounds or, as here, on grounds of statutory construction and application, the court may provide relief in the form of a declaration that the plaintiff builder's proposed use is reasonable, and the municipality may not interfere with it. The plaintiff must bear the burden of proving reasonable use by a preponderance of the evidence. Id. Once the plaintiff's burden has been met, he will be permitted to proceed with the proposed development, provided he complies with all other applicable regulations. * * *

The zoning ordinance evolved as an innovative means to counter the problems of uncontrolled growth. It was never conceived to be a device to facilitate the use of governmental power to prevent access to a municipality by "outsiders of any disadvantaged social or economic group." Beck, 118 N.H. at 801, 394 A.2d at 852. The town of Chester has adopted a zoning ordinance which is blatantly exclusionary. This court will not condone the town's conduct.

Affirmed in part and reversed in part.

NOTES AND QUESTIONS

1. *Mount Laurel* has had considerable influence in both New Jersey and, as the *Britton* case suggests, on the courts of other states:

Minimum Home Size

In Home Builders League of South Jersey, Inc. v. Berlin, 81 N.J. 127, 405 A.2d 381 (1979), the Supreme Court of New Jersey struck down an ordinance that imposed minimum floor area requirements on homes regardless of the number of people living in them or the size of the lots upon which the homes sat. The court relied heavily on *Mt. Laurel*. The court was clearly unimpressed with any defense that the home size ordinance had been designed to prevent unhealthy overcrowding. First, the requirements at issue were limitations on absolute size, not on the number of square feet of floor space per occupant. Second, the ordinance imposed different size requirements in different areas, and it was "ridiculous to suggest that a 1,100 square foot house may be 'healthful' in one part of town and not another." Finally, the court cited several studies to the effect that limitations on minimum house size did not improve property values or improve the aesthetic quality of a neighborhood. There was also substantial evidence that the minimum home size requirements excluded lower income families from housing in the area subject to the controls. The court concluded that the ordinance "appears to be directed solely toward economic segregation" and declared it invalid. To the same effect is Suffolk Housing Services v. Town of Brookhaven, 70 N.Y.2d 122, 517 N.Y.S.2d 924, 511 N.E.2d 67 (1987).

Minimum Lot Size

Minimum lot size restrictions have generally been viewed as less suspicious than minimum home size restrictions, largely because the lot size restrictions serve the obvious function of keeping the neighborhood open and free from congestion. (Congestion outside the home is more apparent than congestion inside.) Most minimum lot size restrictions have been upheld. See, e.g., Robert E. Kurzius, Inc. v. Incorporated Village of Upper Brookville, 51 N.Y.2d 338, 434 N.Y.S.2d 180, 414 N.E.2d 680 (1980). But see Bailes v. Township of East Brunswick, 380 N.J.Super. 336, 882 A.2d 395 (App.Div. 2005), which struck down an ultra low density zoning ordinance (one house per six acres) applied to undeveloped land, when the restriction seemed unreasonable given that the area in question had more than adequate support for much higher density construction.

Restrictions on Apartment Buildings

Most comprehensive plans zone certain areas exclusively for single family homes, and perhaps others exclusively for duplexes or triplexes. Such restrictions are generally legal. In Appeal of Girsh, 437 Pa. 237, 263 A.2d 395 (1970), however, the Pennsylvania Supreme Court struck down an ordinance that prohibited apartment buildings from being constructed anywhere in the township. See also Berenson v. New Castle, 38 N.Y.2d 102, 378 N.Y.S.2d 672, 341 N.E.2d 236 (1975), on remand 67 A.D.2d 506, 415 N.Y.S.2d 669 (1979), which disapproved an ordinance that excluded multifamily housing.

Restrictions Limiting Mobile Homes

Many comprehensive plans prohibit mobile homes or house trailers from being set up in areas zoned for single-family or multi-family housing. The plan can be disapproved by the court, however, if it does not make adequate provision for mobile homes anywhere in the community. See Robinson Township v. Knoll, 410 Mich. 293, 302 N.W.2d 146 (1981).

2. *Growth controls.* The *Britton* opinion, supra, referred to the town's zoning ordinance as a growth control. However, other municipalities regulate

growth in far more explicit ways than the Town of Chester did. Some municipalities have enacted so-called "quota" plans, because they put an absolute limit on the number of new residences that can be constructed within the city each year. See, e.g., Boulder Builders Group v. City of Boulder, 759 P.2d 752 (Colo.App.1988), whose ordinance limited the number of building permits so as to maintain a population growth rate not exceeding two percent per year. In contrast with Britton, the court concluded that the ordinance was of local interest only and that Boulder had no duty to accommodate people from elsewhere. Accord Sustainable Growth Initiative Committee v. Jumpers, LLC, 122 Nev. 53, 128 P.3d 452 (2006) (approving growth control provision in principle, but remanding to consider whether it was consistent with the county's master plan).

Somewhat different was the "phasing" system at issue in Golden v. Planning Board of the Town of Ramapo, 30 N.Y.2d 359, 334 N.Y.S.2d 138, 285 N.E.2d 291 (1972), appeal dism'd 409 U.S. 1003 (1972). The *Ramapo* plan provided no fixed quota; however, developers were required to accumulate a certain number of "points" before a proposed development would be approved. The award of points was based on the availability of adequate sewage systems, parks, public schools, public roads, firehouses, etc. Someone who wanted to develop before these support systems were available in the area proposed for development could hasten the process by providing the improvements himself. The New York Court of Appeals approved the plan.

Growth controls may make communities more attractive. They also increase housing prices by limiting the supply, although they may decrease the value of undeveloped land by making it more difficult for the owner to get a development permit. Further, neighboring communities complain that the impact of a growth control is to put increasing pressure on them to accommodate people who cannot move into the growth controlled community. In Zuckerman v. Town of Hadley, 442 Mass. 511, 813 N.E.2d 843 (2004), the Supreme Judicial Court of Massachusetts held that while a municipality could channel its growth by means of temporary growth controls, it could not impose indefinite restraints on the number of new people who could come in. Such restraints would simply force these people to go to neighboring communities and increase the population pressure on them:

> Rate of development bylaws such as the one at issue here are restrictions not on how land ultimately may be used, but on when certain classes of property owners may use their land. Where classic zoning bylaws keep the pig out of the parlor, ... rate of development bylaws tell the farmer how many new pigs may be in the barnyard each year. In their intent and in their effect, rate of development bylaws reallocate population growth from one town to another, and impose on other communities the increased burdens that one community seeks to avoid. Through zoning bylaws, a town may allow itself breathing room to plan for the channeling of normal growth; it may not turn that breathing room into a choke hold against further growth.... Despite the perceived benefits that enforced isolation may bring to a town facing a new wave of permanent home seekers, it does not serve the general welfare of the Commonwealth to permit one particular town to deflect that wave onto its neighbors.... "[P]revent[ing] the entrance of newcomers in order to avoid burdens

upon the public services and facilities . . . is not a valid public purpose."
Beck v. Raymond, 118 N.H. 793, 801, 394 A.2d 847 (1978).

See generally Growth Management: The Planning Challenge of the 1990s
(J. Stein, ed. 1993); Ellickson, Suburban Growth Controls: an Economic and
Legal Analysis, 86 Yale L.J. 385 (1977). They have been extremely popular
items for public initiatives and referenda. See Glickfeld, Graymer & Morrison,
Trends in Local Growth Control Ballot Measures in California, 6 UCLA J.
Envtl. L. & Pol'y 111 (1987) (counting some 112 such referenda between 1971
and 1986, with well over half passing).

3. New Hampshire enacted legislation that was intended to clarify
Britton's requirements. See N.H. Rev. Stat. Ann. §§ 674:58–674:61 (2011).
The New Hampshire Housing Authority published the following statement
regarding this important housing legislation in New Hampshire:

> Seventeen years ago, the New Hampshire Supreme Court issued
> a resounding decision in favor of affordable housing. In the case
> Britton v. Town of Chester, the Court determined that the state's
> planning and zoning statutes called for every municipality to provide
> a reasonable and realistic opportunity for the development of housing
> that is affordable to low- and moderate-income households, and
> particularly for the development of multi-family structures. Although
> that case generated great interest and discussion among local plan-
> ning boards and in the development community, that interest was
> not accompanied by action at the local level to provide the sort of
> opportunity that Britton seemed to promise. Despite the economic
> and housing growth in the later 1990s, regulatory barriers remained
> in many municipalities making it difficult for developers to create the
> amount of affordable housing the market demanded.

* * *

> SB 342 (codified as Chapter 299, Laws of 2008) amends the
> planning and zoning statues of the state by including the Court's
> holding from Britton that all municipalities must provide reasonable
> and realistic opportunities for the development of workforce housing,
> including rental and multi-family housing. To determine if such
> opportunities exist, the collective impact of all local land use regula-
> tions must be considered, and workforce housing of some type must
> be allowed in a majority of land area where residential uses are
> permitted (but not necessarily multi-family in a majority of such
> areas). Recognizing that some municipalities have already done what
> is necessary under this law, the existing housing stock of a communi-
> ty is to be accounted for to determine if a municipality is providing
> its "fair share" of current and reasonably foreseeable regional need
> for workforce housing. Importantly, reasonable restrictions may still
> be imposed for environmental protection, water supply, sanitary
> disposal, traffic safety, and fire and life safety protection.

> This new law also significantly mitigates the cost of litigation by
> providing an accelerated appeals mechanism. If a developer proposes
> to create workforce housing that meets the statute's definitions and

requirements and the local board reviewing the proposal either denies the application or imposes conditions on it that would have an unreasonable financial burden, the developer can petition the superior court for review. This is not new—what is changed is that for workforce housing proposals, the court must conduct a hearing on the merits within six months. As a means of addressing exclusionary municipal land use regulations, the court will be able to order the "builder's remedy," allowing the developer to proceed without further local review in situations that call for such an award.

SB 342 provides a series of definitions, including ones for "affordability" (30% cost burden), "workforce housing" (affordable for renters at 60% area median income or owners at 100% area median income), multi-family housing (five or more units per structure), and "reasonable and realistic opportunities" (addressing the economic viability of a proposal).

* * *

New Hampshire Legislature Passes Important Housing Laws: Workforce Housing, New Hampshire Housing Finance Authority, http://www.nhhfa.org/abt_docs/newsletter/Summer08/legislation.htm. The law became effective in 2009 (last visited Nov. 8, 2011).

NOTE: ZONING BY SMALL GOVERNMENTS

Municipalities create most exclusionary zoning. However, as the *Mount Laurel* and *Britton* opinions point out, the market for housing in a given area may be much larger than a single municipality. The automobile and modern public transportation have made work commutes of twenty or thirty miles quite common. Often the sovereign that enacts a particular zoning ordinance is smaller than the market that is being regulated. The result can be inefficient regulation.

The decision concerning *who* should regulate a market is often just as important as the decision concerning the manner of regulation. For example, no one would suggest that the city of Berkeley, California, should be given the responsibility of regulating interstate trucking or international air travel. The reason is fairly simple: when the regulator is smaller than the market being regulated, substantial opportunities for self-dealing arise. For example, Berkeley could make its own trucking firms the beneficiaries of high rates, or its own businesses and citizens the beneficiaries of very low rates on shipments into Berkeley.

At the same time, it would seem that the United States Government or the United Nations would not be a very efficient regulator of Berkeley taxicab fares. The kind of information needed to create such fares—the costs of operating a cab in Berkeley and the transportation needs of Berkeley residents—is information that Berkeley can obtain more efficiently than the United States government can.

As a general rule, the optimal regulatory sovereign for any market is the smallest sovereign that is large enough to encompass the entire market. If most taxicab trips in Berkeley are confined to the city, and if the operation of Berkeley taxicabs does not have any important effects on people outside of Berkeley, then the optimal regulatory sovereign for this market is Berkeley itself. Likewise, the optimal regulatory sovereign for interstate trucking is probably the United States government. (In this case, it is a federal agency: the Interstate Commerce Commission.)

As *Mount Laurel* suggests, a great deal of zoning is undertaken by sovereigns that are too small. The result may be self-dealing at the expense of outsiders. For example, suppose that a certain region (a market within which people are willing to commute to their jobs) has an unemployment rate of 10%. A village within that region could reduce its own unemployment rate by refusing to zone for the kinds of housing typically occupied by the unemployed. Likewise, it could ensure itself of adequate taxes to fund schools and other municipal services by "zoning out" the kinds of housing occupied by people who are unlikely to pay much in taxes, or who have more children who need schooling. This necessarily means that other communities in the same area must accommodate a disproportionately large number of unemployed or low income people. Effectively, the community can force low income people who work within its limits to live and send their children to school elsewhere.

By contrast, if a governmental entity large enough to encompass an entire market for municipal services is given the responsibility to zone, it will more likely feel a responsibility to *all* constituencies, including the poor and the unemployed, for all are within its territory. Most likely it would attempt to distribute different income groups in the most efficient way, which generally means a mixture of low income, middle class, and expensive housing.

The *Mount Laurel* opinion deals with this problem by the clever observation that a municipality has the power to regulate land use only if the state legislature has given it that power through a zoning enabling act or equivalent legislation. Since the power to regulate land use belongs in the first instance to the state, the municipality is obligated to consider the state's overall housing needs in deciding on its own mixture of uses.

The problem of self-dealing when zoning is undertaken by a sovereign that is too small has been noticed by several states. Some have passed legislation forcing communities to zone in such a way as to accept their "fair share" of all population groups. For example, California legislation requires that governmental subdivisions' determination of housing requirements "include the locality's share of the regional housing need...." Cal. Gov't Code § 65583(a)(1) (West 2011). Other states have adopted rules that facilitate state-based, rather than community-based, comprehensive plans. For example, legislation in Florida creates a State Land Planning Agency, which in turn designates Regional Planning Agencies to coordinate land use planning on a statewide basis. Fla.Stat.Ann. § 380.

§ 11.4   SETTLED EXPECTATIONS AND THE ZONING PROCESS

§ 11.4.1   THE COMPREHENSIVE PLAN, THE ZONING AMENDMENT AND "SPOT" ZONING

LITTLE v. WINBORN

Supreme Court of Iowa (1994).
518 N.W.2d 384.

TERNUS, JUSTICE.

The Scott County Board of Supervisors rezoned a 223–acre parcel of agricultural land. Neighboring landowners filed a petition for writ of certiorari challenging the rezoning. The district court found the rezoning ordinance invalid and the owner of the rezoned property appealed. Because we think the rezoning constituted illegal spot zoning, we affirm.

In September 1991, the Davenport Shooting Association (Association) petitioned the Scott County Zoning and Planning Commission (Commission) to consider rezoning a 223–acre parcel of land. The land was zoned Agricultural One—agricultural protection district (A–1) and the Association wanted it rezoned Agricultural Two—agricultural district (A–2). The 223–acre parcel was surrounded by land zoned A–1. In its rezoning petition the Association stated that it intended to build two uninhabited structures on the land for recreational club use, the balance of the land to remain in its agricultural state.

The Commission held two public hearings to consider the petition. The Association explained that rezoning the property was necessary because the Association planned to build a shooting house and a target house on the property.

Several adjacent property owners addressed the Commission and expressed their opposition to the rezoning. They feared the shooting range would be loud, the noise would bother their livestock, and the shooting range would cause more activity in the area. They argued that the land should stay in tillage and that the two structures proposed to be built on the parcel posed a fire hazard. The Association responded that the two buildings would take less than five acres of land out of agricultural production and would create a minimum fire hazard.

* * * [T]hree members of the Commission voted in favor of rezoning and three members voted against. The Commission forwarded its report to the Board of Supervisors. The Board of Supervisors held a public hearing on the rezoning petition and received comments similar to those made at the hearings before the Commission. The Board voted 3 to 2 to approve the petition.

The neighboring landowners * * * contended that the rezoning constituted illegal spot zoning.

"Spot zoning results when a zoning ordinance creates a small island of property with restrictions on its use different from those imposed on the surrounding property." Jaffe v. City of Davenport, 179 N.W.2d 554, 556 (Iowa 1970). Spot zoning is not automatically invalid. 8 E. McQuillen, Municipal Corporations s 25.84, at 319 (3rd ed. rev.1991). If it is germane to an object within the police power and there is a reasonable basis to treat the spot-zoned property differently from the surrounding property, the spot zoning is valid. * * * In determining whether there is a reasonable basis for spot zoning, we consider the size of the spot zoned, the uses of the surrounding property, the changing conditions of the area, the use to which the subject property has been put and its suitability and adaptability for various uses. In rural county zoning, the size of the tract is not very important. The factor of primary importance is whether the rezoned tract has a peculiar adaptability to the new classification as compared to the surrounding property. Spot zoning for the benefit of the owner and contrary to the comprehensive plan is unreasonable. *Jaffe*, 179 N.W.2d at 556.

We conclude that the rezoning of the farmland here is spot zoning. This property is surrounded by land zoned A–1. Rezoning this parcel to A–2 would create an island of property with restrictions on its use different from those imposed on surrounding property.

The next question is whether this spot zoning is valid. We consider (1) whether the new zoning is germane to an object within the police power, (2) whether there is a reasonable basis for making a distinction between the spot-zoned land and the surrounding property, and (3) whether the rezoning is consistent with the comprehensive plan.

We discern no object within the police power that would justify rezoning this property. The rezoning of this parcel is not related to the public health, safety, morals or general welfare designed to serve the best interests of the community as a whole. Only the owner of the property and its members would receive any benefit from rezoning this land.

Nor do we find a reasonable basis for distinguishing this property from the surrounding property. The 223–acre parcel contains farm ground and timber. It has no unique quality that makes it more suitable than the property surrounding it to be zoned A–2.

More important, we do not believe the rezoning is pursuant to the Scott County Comprehensive Zoning Plan or the County's zoning district classifications. One of the main thrusts of the comprehensive plan is to "identify and seek means to protect prime agricultural land from scattered development." To carve out a parcel of land in an A–1 district and zone it A–2 would result in the type of scattered development the comprehensive plan seeks to avoid. Moreover, half of the rezoned property qualifies as "prime" agricultural land. Although the Association says that it will remove only five acres from production, there is nothing in the zoning classification or the rezoning ordinance that would limit the property owner's attempts to use the land in a manner other than farming and yet within the A–2 district restrictions. Uses permitted in an A–2 district include schools, parks, government buildings, golf courses, churches, cemeteries, and solid waste disposal sites. Thus, rezoning provides less, not more, protection for the prime agricultural land in this parcel.

The A–1 agricultural protection district is designed to "protect agricultural land from encroachment of urban development." The A–2 agricultural district is intended to "act as a holding zone until a compatible urban development proposal is approved."

According to the county's zoning policies, new urban development in the rural areas should, among other factors, (1) be on marginal or poor farmland, (2) have access to adequately constructed paved roads, (3) have present or planned water and sanitary sewer systems, and (4) be near existing employment and commercial areas. The proposed rezoning does not meet these criteria. There are no plans to develop this rural area for urban uses. As previously noted, half the land is prime farmland. Access to the property is by a dirt road and the County does not intend to improve this road. In fact, the county engineer disapproved of the rezoning request unless the Association would agree to maintain the road itself. There is no private or public sanitary sewer system on the property. The property is not located near existing employment centers or commercial areas. The zoning commissioners who voted against the rezoning petition were aware of such problems. They opposed the rezoning because they thought it was improper spot zoning and represented a change in the County's policies to preserve agricultural land and check urban encroachment on farmland.

Basically, the Association argues that a change from A–1 to A–2 is not very great and will not really change the use of the property. However, as noted above, many uses are allowed in an A–2 district that are incompatible with the preservation of the property in its present form. Consequently, the Association's argument that rezoning will not change the use of the property is not necessarily true. Even if it were true, however, this argument fails to address why this property should be rezoned to A–2 and the surrounding similar property remain in an A–1 district. * * *

In summary, * * * we believe the Board's enactment of the ordinance rezoning this parcel of land to an A–2 district was invalid spot zoning. Therefore, we affirm the district court's ruling sustaining the writ of certiorari.

AFFIRMED.

NOTES AND QUESTIONS

1. The entire notion that future zoning decisions must be consistent with the original comprehensive plan has been subjected to a great deal of criticism. *First,* no one believes that a comprehensive plan should freeze in perpetuity all initially assigned land uses: even the best planners are unable to predict a community's future development that well. *Second,* no standard capable of articulation exists for determining which changes are "in accor-

dance with" the initial comprehensive plan and which ones are not. To be sure, easy cases do exist. For example, zoning amendments procured by bribery or corruption and that appear completely irrational on their face are undoubtedly not pursuant to the plan. But most cases are far more ambiguous. See, e.g., Greater Yellowstone Coalition, Inc. v. Board of County Com'rs of Gallatin County, 305 Mont. 232, 25 P.3d 168 (2001) (change of classification of undeveloped property from single family residence to planned unit development, with some multifamily housing and nonresidential uses, constituted illegal spot zoning). As a result, some scholars have urged that the traditional comprehensive plan be abolished and some more workable alternative—such as an annual series of planning reports produced by the appropriate legislative body—be put in their place. Krasnowiecki, Abolish Zoning, 31 Syracuse L.Rev. 719, 747–48 (1980); and see Tarlock, Consistency with Adopted Land Use Plans as a Standard of Judicial Review: The Case Against, 9 Urb.L.Ann. 69 (1975).

Many courts hold that a city's failure to follow its comprehensive plan is not forbidden by the state's constitution. See Quinn v. Dodgeville, 120 Wis.2d 304, 354 N.W.2d 747 (App.1984). Other courts have taken a "process" rather than a "substance" approach to the entire question of spot zoning and consistency with the comprehensive plan. This approach proceeds on the theory that the primary goal of the amendment process is to achieve a result that is fair to all the affected parties, not necessarily to achieve some poorly defined "consistency" with a plan that was written many years before. This means that hearings considering zoning amendments must be well publicized and all interested parties must be permitted to participate and give their views. It may also mean that the decision maker must make fact findings and articulate reasons for the decision. See the *Eastlake* and *Snyder* decisions below.

The extreme in such approaches is to permit *everyone* to have a voice in the amendment process. When that happens, any notion that zoning changes are "in accordance" with the original comprehensive plan disappears. At the same time, the process undeniably permits everyone affected by a change (and probably many who are not affected) to have a voice in the decision. In the following case the Supreme Court considered just such an approach.

2. The *Little* court noted that, by definition, spot zoning is the singling out of "a small island of property" and placing restrictions on that property that are different from the restrictions on surrounding property. Thus, in spot zoning cases, the size of the proposed tract to be rezoned is an important fact that most courts consider; however, it is not dispositive. In Childress v. Yadkin County, 186 N.C. App. 30, 650 S.E.2d 55, 59–60 (2007), the court held that the rezoning of approximately fifty-one acres from rural agricultural to restricted residential did not constitute spot zoning and that even if it did constitute spot zoning, it was not illegal or unreasonable spot zoning. The court listed four factors to consider when determining whether a rezoning is reasonable: "(1) 'the size of the tract in question'; (2) 'the compatibility of the disputed zoning action with an existing comprehensive zoning plan'; (3) 'the benefits and detriments resulting from the zoning action for the owner of the newly zoned property, his neighbors, and the surrounding community; and' (4) 'the relationship between the uses envisioned under the new zoning and

the uses currently present in adjacent tracts.' " *Id.* at 61. Though fifty-one acres could be considered a small tract, the court found that the rezoning was consistent with Yadkin County's comprehensive plan, that the weighing of the detriments and benefits of the rezoning led to a conclusion that the county had a reasonable basis for rezoning the property, and that the two zoning classifications were similar in substantial ways. The very same day, the court in McDowell v. Randolph County, 186 N.C. App. 17, 649 S.E.2d 920, 920–28 (2007) held that Randolph County did engage in illegal spot zoning when it rezoned 29.95 acres of a 120.30 acre property owned by a lumber company from light industrial and residential agricultural to heavy industrial/conditional use. The court found, in part, that the acreage fell within the range of cases where the court had found illegal spot zoning in the past, that the rezoning violated the county's comprehensive plan, and that the rezoning would be very detrimental for the community.

CITY OF EASTLAKE v. FOREST CITY ENTERPRISES, INC.

Supreme Court of the United States (1976).
426 U.S. 668.

MR. CHIEF JUSTICE BURGER delivered the opinion of the Court.

The question in this case is whether a city charter provision requiring proposed land use changes to be ratified by 55% of the votes cast violates the due process rights of a landowner who applies for a zoning change.

The city of Eastlake, Ohio, a suburb of Cleveland, has a comprehensive zoning plan codified in a municipal ordinance. Respondent, a real estate developer, acquired an eight-acre parcel of real estate in Eastlake zoned for "light industrial" uses at the time of purchase.

In May 1971, respondent applied to the City Planning Commission for a zoning change to permit construction of a multifamily, high-rise apartment building. The Planning Commission recommended the proposed change to the City Council, which under Eastlake's procedures could either accept or reject the Planning Commission's recommendation. Meanwhile, by popular vote, the voters of Eastlake amended the city charter to require that any changes in land use agreed to by the Council be approved by a 55% vote in a referendum. The City Council approved the Planning Commission's recommendation for reclassification of respondent's property to permit the proposed project. Respondent then applied to the Planning Commission for "parking and yard" approval for the proposed building. The Commission rejected the application, on the ground that the City Council's rezoning action had not yet been submitted to the voters for ratification.

Respondent then filed an action in state court, seeking a judgment declaring the charter provision invalid as an unconstitutional delegation of legislative power to the people. While the case was pending, the City Council's action was submitted to a referendum, but the proposed zoning change was not approved by the requisite 55% margin. Following the election, the Court of Common Pleas and the Ohio Court of Appeals sustained the charter provision.

The Ohio Supreme Court reversed.

* * *

The conclusion that Eastlake's procedure violates federal constitutional guarantees rests upon the proposition that a zoning referendum involves a delegation of legislative power. A referendum cannot, however, be characterized as a delegation of power. Under our constitutional assumptions, all power derives from the people, who can delegate it to representative instruments which they create. See, e.g., The Federalist No. 39 (Madison). In establishing legislative bodies, the people can reserve to themselves power to deal directly with matters which might otherwise be assigned to the legislature. *Hunter v. Erickson,* 393 U.S. 385, 392, 89 S.Ct. 557, 561, 21 L.Ed.2d 616 (1969).

The reservation of such power is the basis for the town meeting, a tradition which continues to this day in some States as both a practical and symbolic part of our democratic processes. The referendum, similarly, is a means for direct political participation, allowing the people the final decision, amounting to a veto power, over enactments of representative bodies. The practice is designed to "give citizens a voice on questions of public policy." *James v. Valtierra, supra,* 402 U.S., at 141, 91 S.Ct., at 1333.

In framing a state constitution, the people of Ohio specifically reserved the power of referendum to the people of each municipality within the State.

> "The initiative and referendum powers are hereby reserved to the people of each municipality on all questions which such municipalities may now or hereafter be authorized by law to control by legislative action...." Ohio Const., Art. II, § 1f.

To be subject to Ohio's referendum procedure, the question must be one within the scope of legislative power. The Ohio Supreme Court expressly found that the City Council's action in rezoning respondent's eight acres from light industrial to high-density residential use was legislative in nature. Distinguishing between administrative and legislative acts, the court separated the power to zone or rezone, by passage or amendment of a zoning ordinance, from the power to grant relief from unnecessary hardship. The former function was found to be legislative in nature.

* * *

The Ohio Supreme Court further concluded that the amendment to the city charter constituted a "delegation" of power violative of federal constitutional guarantees because the voters were given no standards to guide their decision. Under Eastlake's procedure, the Ohio Supreme Court reasoned, no mechanism existed, nor indeed could exist, to assure that the voters would act rationally in passing upon a proposed zoning change. This meant that "appropriate legislative action [would] be made dependent upon the potentially arbitrary and unreasonable whims of the voting public." The potential for arbitrariness in the process, the court concluded, violated due process.

Courts have frequently held in other contexts that a congressional delegation of power to a regulatory entity must be accompanied by discernible standards, so that the delegate's action can be measured for its fidelity to the legislative will.

* * *

Assuming, *arguendo,* their relevance to state governmental functions, these cases involved a delegation of power by the legislature to regulatory bodies, which are not directly responsible to the people; this doctrine is inapplicable where, as here, rather than dealing with a delegation of power, we deal with a power reserved by the people to themselves.

In basing its claim on federal due process requirements, respondent also invokes *Euclid v. Ambler Realty Co.,* 272 U.S. 365, 47 S.Ct. 114, 71 L.Ed. 303 (1926), but it does not rely on the direct teaching of that case. Under *Euclid,* a property owner can challenge a zoning restriction if the measure is "clearly arbitrary and unreasonable, having no substantial relation to the public health, safety, morals, or general welfare." If the substantive result of the referendum is arbitrary and capricious, bearing no relation to the police power, then the fact that the voters of Eastlake wish it so would not save the restriction. As this Court held in invalidating a charter amendment enacted by referendum:

> "The sovereignty of the people is itself subject to those constitutional limitations which have been duly adopted and remain unrepealed." *Hunter v. Erickson,* 393 U.S., at 392, 89 S.Ct., at 561.

But no challenge of the sort contemplated in *Euclid v. Ambler Realty* is before us. The Ohio Supreme Court did not hold, and respondent does not argue, that the present zoning classification under Eastlake's comprehensive ordinance violates the principles established in *Euclid v. Ambler Realty.* If respondent considers the referendum result itself to be unreasonable, the zoning restriction is open to challenge in state court, where the scope of the state remedy available to respondent would be determined as a matter of state law, as well as under Fourteenth Amendment standards. That being so, nothing more is required by the Constitution.

Nothing in our cases is inconsistent with this conclusion. Two decisions of this Court were relied on by the Ohio Supreme Court in invalidating Eastlake's procedure. The thread common to both decisions is the delegation of legislative power, originally given by the people to a legislative body, and in turn delegated by the legislature to a *narrow segment* of the community, not to the people at large. In *Eubank v. Richmond,* 226 U.S. 137, 33 S.Ct. 76, 57 L.Ed. 156 (1912), the Court invalidated a city ordinance which conferred the power to establish building setback lines upon the owners of two-thirds of the property abutting any street. Similarly, in *Washington ex rel. Seattle Title Trust Co. v. Roberge*, 278 U.S. 116, 49 S.Ct. 50, 73 L.Ed. 210 (1928), the Court struck down an ordinance which permitted the establishment of philanthropic homes for the aged in residential areas, but only upon the written consent of the owners of two-third of the property within 400 feet of the proposed facility.

Neither *Eubank* nor *Roberge* involved a referendum procedure such as we have in this case; the standardless delegation of power to a limited group of property owners condemned by the Court in *Eubank* and *Roberge* is not to be equated with decisionmaking by the people through the referendum process. The Court of Appeals for the Ninth Circuit put it this way:

> "A referendum, however, is far more than an expression of ambiguously founded neighborhood preference. It is the city itself legislating through its voters—an exercise by the voters of their traditional right through direct legislation to override the views of their elected representatives as to what serves the public interest." *Southern Alameda Spanish Speaking Organization v. Union City, California*, 424 F.2d 291, 294 (1970).

Our decision in *James v. Valtierra*, upholding California's mandatory referendum requirement, confirms this view. Mr. Justice Black, speaking for the Court in that case, said:

> "This procedure ensures that *all the people* of a community will have a voice in a decision which may lead to large expenditures of local governmental funds for increased public services...." 402 U.S., at 143, 91 S.Ct., at 1334 (emphasis added).

Mr. Justice Black went on to say that a referendum procedure, such as the one at issue here, is a classic demonstration of "devotion to democracy...." Id., at 141, 91 S.Ct., at 1333. As a basic instrument of democratic government, the referendum process does not, in itself, violate the Due Process Clause of the Fourteenth Amendment when applied to a rezoning ordinance. Since the rezoning decision in this case was properly reserved to the People of Eastlake under the Ohio Constitution, the Ohio Supreme Court erred in holding invalid, on federal constitutional grounds, the charter amendment permitting the voters to decide whether the zoned use of respondent's property could be altered.

Reversed and remanded.

MR. JUSTICE POWELL, dissenting.

There can be no doubt as to the propriety and legality of submitting generally applicable legislative questions, including zoning provisions, to a popular referendum. But here the only issue concerned the status of a single small parcel owned by a single "person." This procedure, affording no realistic opportunity for the affected person to be heard, even by the electorate, is fundamentally unfair. The "spot" referendum technique appears to open disquieting opportunities for local government bodies to bypass normal protective procedures for resolving issues affecting individual rights.

MR. JUSTICE STEVENS, with whom MR. JUSTICE BRENNAN joins, dissenting.

* * *

The fact that an individual owner (like any other petitioner or plaintiff) may not have a legal right to the relief he seeks does not mean that he has no right to fair procedure in the consideration of the merits of his application. The fact that codes regularly provide a procedure for granting individual exceptions or changes, the fact that such changes are granted in individual cases with great frequency, and the fact that the particular code in the record before us contemplates that changes consistent with the basic plan will be allowed, all support my opinion that the opportunity to apply for an amendment is an aspect of property ownership protected by the Due Process Clause of the Fourteenth Amendment.

* * *

The essence of fair procedure is that the interested parties be given a reasonable opportunity to have their dispute resolved on the merits by reference to articulable rules. If a dispute involves only the conflicting rights of private litigants, it is elementary that the decision-maker must be impartial and qualified to understand and to apply the controlling rules.

I have no doubt about the validity of the initiative or the referendum as an appropriate method of deciding questions of community policy. I think it is equally clear that the popular vote is not an acceptable method of adjudicating the rights of individual litigants.

BOARD OF COUNTY COMMISSIONERS OF BREVARD COUNTY v. SNYDER

Supreme Court of Florida (1993).
627 So.2d 469.

GRIMES, JUSTICE.

* * * Jack and Gail Snyder owned a one-half acre parcel of property on Merritt Island in the unincorporated area of Brevard County. The property is zoned GU (general use) which allows construction of a single-family residence. The Snyders filed an application to rezone their property to the RU–2–15 zoning classification which allows the construction of fifteen units per acre. * * *

After the application for rezoning was filed, the Brevard County Planning and Zoning staff reviewed the application and completed the county's standard "rezoning review worksheet." The worksheet indicated that the proposed multifamily use of the Snyders' property was consistent with all aspects of the comprehensive plan. * * *

When the matter came before the board, * * * a number of citizens spoke in opposition to the rezoning request. Their primary concern was the increase in traffic which would be caused by the development. Ultimately, the commission voted to deny the rezoning request without stating a reason for the denial.

The district court of appeal acknowledged that zoning decisions have traditionally been considered legislative in nature. Therefore, courts were required to uphold them if they could be justified as being "fairly debatable." Drawing heavily on Fasano v. Board of County Commissioners, 264 Or. 574, 507 P.2d 23 (1973), however, the court concluded that, unlike initial zoning enactments and comprehensive rezonings or rezonings affecting a large portion of the public, a rezoning action which entails the application of a general rule or policy to specific individuals, interests, or activities is quasi-judicial in nature. Under the latter circumstances, the court reasoned that a stricter standard of judicial review of the rezoning decision was required. The court went on to hold:

> (4) Since a property owner's right to own and use his property is constitutionally protected, review of any governmental action denying or abridging that right is subject to close judicial scrutiny. Effective judicial review, constitutional due process and other essential requirements of law, all necessitate that the governmental agency (by whatever name it may be characterized) applying legislated land use restrictions to particular parcels of privately owned lands, must state reasons for action that denies the owner the use of his land and must make findings of fact and a record of its proceedings, sufficient for judicial review of: the legal sufficiency of the evidence to support the findings of fact made, the legal sufficiency of the findings of fact supporting the reasons given and the legal adequacy, under applicable law (i.e., under general comprehensive zoning ordinances, applicable state and case law and state and federal constitutional provisions) of the reasons given for the result of the action taken.

> (5) The initial burden is upon the landowner to demonstrate that his petition or application for use of privately owned lands, (rezoning, special exception, conditional use permit, variance, site plan approval, etc.) complies with the reasonable procedural requirements of the ordinance and that the use sought is consistent with the applicable comprehensive zoning plan. Upon such a showing the landowner is presumptively entitled to use his property in the manner he seeks unless the opposing governmental agency asserts and proves by clear and convincing evidence that a specifically stated public necessity requires a specified, more restrictive, use. After such a showing the burden shifts to the landowner to assert and prove that such specified more restrictive land use constitutes a taking of his property for public use for which he is entitled to compensation under the taking provisions of the state or federal constitutions.

Applying these principles to the facts of the case, the court found (1) that the Snyders' petition for rezoning was consistent with the comprehensive plan; (2) that there was no assertion or evidence that a more restrictive zoning classification was necessary to protect the health, safety, morals, or welfare of the general public; and (3) that the denial of the requested zoning classification without reasons supported by facts was, as a matter of law, arbitrary and unreasonable. The court granted the petition for certiorari.

Before this Court, the county contends * * * that the opinion below eliminates a local government's ability to operate in a legislative context and impairs its ability to respond to public comment. * * *

Historically, local governments have exercised the zoning power pursuant to a broad delegation of state legislative power subject only to constitutional limitations. Both federal and state courts adopted a highly deferential standard of judicial review early in the history of local zoning.

Inhibited only by the loose judicial scrutiny afforded by the fairly debatable rule, local zoning systems developed in a markedly inconsistent manner. Many land use experts and practitioners have been critical of the local zoning system. Richard Babcock deplored the effect of "neighborhood-ism" and rank political influence on the local decision-making process. Richard F. Babcock, The Zoning Game (1966). Mandelker and Tarlock recently stated that "zoning decisions are too often ad hoc, sloppy and self-serving decisions with well-defined adverse consequences without off-setting benefits." Daniel R. Mandelker and A. Dan Tarlock, Shifting the Presumption of Constitutionality in Land–Use Law, 24 Urb.Law. 1, 2 (1992).

Professor Charles Harr, a leading proponent of zoning reform, was an early advocate of requiring that local land use regulation be consistent with a legally binding comprehensive plan which would serve long range goals, counteract local pressures for preferential treatment, and provide courts with a meaningful standard of review. Charles M. Harr, "In Accordance With A Comprehensive Plan," 68 Harv.L.Rev. 1154 (1955). In 1975, the American Law Institute adopted the Model Land Development Code, which provided for procedural and planning reforms at the local level and increased state participation in land use decision-making for developments of regional impact and areas of critical state concern.

Reacting to the increasing calls for reform, numerous states have adopted legislation to change the local land use decision-making process. As one of the leaders of this national reform, Florida adopted the Local Government Comprehensive Planning Act of 1975. Ch. 75–257, Laws of Fla. This law was substantially strengthened in 1985 by the Growth Management Act. Ch. 85–55, Laws of Fla.

Pursuant to the Growth Management Act, each county and municipality is required to prepare a comprehensive plan for approval by the Department of Community Affairs. The adopted local plan must include "principles, guidelines, and standards for the orderly and balanced future economic, social, physical, environmental, and fiscal development" of the local government's jurisdictional area. * * *

The first issue we must decide is whether the Board's action on Snyder's rezoning application was legislative or quasi-judicial. A board's legislative action is subject to attack in circuit court. * * * However, in deference to the policy-making function of a board when acting in a legislative capacity, its actions will be sustained as long as they are fairly debatable. Nance v. Town of Indialantic, 419 So.2d 1041 (Fla.1982). On the other hand, the rulings of a board acting in its quasi-judicial capacity are subject to review by certiorari and will be upheld only if they are supported by substantial competent evidence.

Enactments of original zoning ordinances have always been considered legislative. * * * In Schauer v. City of Miami Beach, this Court held that the passage of an amending zoning ordinance was the exercise of a legislative function. 112 So.2d at 839. However, the amendment in that case was comprehensive in nature in that it effected a change in the zoning of a large area so as to permit it to be used as locations for multiple family buildings and hotels. Id. In City of Jacksonville Beach v. Grubbs and Palm Beach County v. Tinnerman, the district courts of appeal went further and held that board action on specific rezoning applications of individual property owners was also legislative.

* * * [I]t is evident that comprehensive rezonings affecting a large portion of the public are legislative in nature. However, we agree with the court below when it said: [R]ezoning actions which have an impact on a limited number of persons or property owners, on identifiable parties and interests, where the decision is contingent on a fact or facts arrived at from distinct alternatives presented at a hearing, and where the decision can be functionally viewed as policy application, rather than policy setting, are in the nature of ... quasi-judicial action.... Therefore, the board's action on Snyder's application was in the nature of a quasi-judicial proceeding and properly reviewable by petition for certiorari. * * *

At this point, we depart from the rationale of the court below. * * * [W]e cannot accept the proposition that once the landowner demonstrates that the proposed use is consistent with the comprehensive plan, he is presumptively entitled to this use unless the opposing governmental agency proves by clear and convincing evidence that specifically stated public necessity requires a more restricted use. [A]bsent the assertion of some enforceable property right, an application for rezoning appeals at least in part to local officials' discretion to accept or reject the applicant's argument that change is desirable. The right of judicial review does not ipso facto ease the burden on a party seeking to overturn a decision made by a local government, and certainly does not confer any property-based right upon the owner where none previously existed ..... Moreover, when it is the zoning classification that is challenged, the comprehensive plan is relevant only when the suggested use is inconsistent with that plan. Where any of several zoning classifications is consistent with the plan, the applicant seeking a change from one to the other is not entitled to judicial relief absent proof the status quo is no longer reasonable. * * *

[W]e hold that a landowner seeking to rezone property has the burden of proving that the proposal is consistent with the comprehensive plan and complies with all procedural requirements of the zoning ordinance. At this point, the burden shifts to the governmental board to demonstrate that maintaining the existing zoning classification with respect to the property accomplishes a legitimate public purpose. In effect, the landowners' traditional remedies will be subsumed within this rule, and the board will now have the burden of showing that the refusal to rezone the property is not arbitrary, discriminatory, or unreasonable. If the board carries its burden, the application should be denied.

While they may be useful, the board will not be required to make findings of fact. However, in order to sustain the board's action, upon review by certiorari in the circuit court it must be shown that there was competent substantial evidence presented to the board to support its ruling. * * *

NOTES AND QUESTIONS

1. Is too much democracy ever a bad thing? According to the dissenters in *Eastlake*, sometimes it is. What would you think about a procedure that did not require the electorate to attend a trial in a well-publicized murder case, but permitted all of them to vote on the guilt or innocence of the defendant? On the other hand, any suggestion by the *Eastlake* dissenters that decision making by a commission can exempt the zoning process from politics must be taken with several wheelbarrows of salt.

The Supreme Court returned to the *Eastlake* issue in City of Cuyahoga Falls v. Buckeye Community Hope Foundation, 538 U.S. 188 (2003), upholding a process by which the government delayed construction of a low income housing project until voters acted by referendum to repeal the ordinance that authorized the project. The ordinance in question, although not the public comment, was facially neutral. The Supreme Court rejected the Sixth Circuit's view that for the government to stop the project pending the referendum process "gave effect to the racial bias reflected in the public's opposition to the project." The Court reiterated that *Eastlake* had made clear that:

> because all power stems from the people, "[a] referendum cannot ... be characterized as a delegation of power," unlawful unless accompanied by "discernible standards." The people retain the power to govern through referendum " 'with respect to any matter, legislative or administrative, within the realm of local affairs.' " Though the "substantive result" of a referendum may be invalid if it is "arbitrary and capricious," respondents do not challenge the referendum itself.

(citations omitted)

2. The *Snyder* decision is a recent example of the so-called *Fasano* doctrine: Fasano v. Board of County Commissioners of Washington County, 264 Or. 574, 507 P.2d 23 (1973) (en banc), held that zoning amendments of single tracts should be treated as "quasi-judicial," or adjudicative, rather than "legislative" acts. The result was a much stricter state standard of judicial

review. When an act is considered legislative, a court's inquiry on review is merely whether the agency or commission had a rational basis for what it did. However, if an action is judicial, it can generally be fully reviewed as to both law and findings of fact. In *Eastlake* the United States Supreme Court effectively held that nothing in the Federal Constitution required that zoning amendments be treated as adjudicative acts; therefore no federal right was violated by the referendum approving a zoning amendment.

After *Fasano*, Oregon passed a comprehensive statewide land use planning statute that substantially overruled *Fasano*. However, a few states in addition to Florida have followed *Fasano* and treat local zoning changes affecting single parcels as adjudicative actions subject to substantial court review. Fleming v. City of Tacoma, 81 Wash.2d 292, 502 P.2d 327 (1972) (en banc), followed *Fasano*, but was subsequently overruled by Raynes v. City of Leavenworth, 118 Wash.2d 237, 821 P.2d 1204 (1992) (en banc); Cooper v. Board of County Comm'rs, 101 Idaho 407, 614 P.2d 947 (1980), adhered to in, Chambers v. Kootenai County Board of Commissioners, 125 Idaho 115, 867 P.2d 989 (1994); Golden v. City of Overland Park, 224 Kan. 591, 584 P.2d 130 (1978).

In Kaiser Hawaii Kai Development Co. v. City of Honolulu, 70 Haw. 480, 777 P.2d 244 (1989), the Hawaii Supreme Court condemned a procedure using an initiative, or public vote, to downzone property. The court concluded that "[z]oning by initiative is inconsistent with the goal of long range comprehensive planning." It continued:

> Zoning is intended to be accomplished in accordance with a comprehensive plan and should reflect both present and prospective needs of the community. Among other things, the social, economic, and physical characteristics of the community should be considered. The achievement of these goals might well be jeopardized by piecemeal attacks on the zoning ordinances if referenda were permissible for review of any amendment. Sporadic attacks on a municipality's comprehensive plan would tend to fragment zoning without any overriding concept. That concept should not be discarded because planning boards and governing bodies may not always have acted in the best interest of the public and may not, in every case, have demonstrated the expertise which they might be expected to develop....
>
> A single decision by electors in a referendum could well destroy the very purpose of zoning where such decision was in conflict with the general scheme fixing the uses of property in designated areas.... It would permit the electors by referendum to change, delay, and defeat the real purposes of the comprehensive zoning ordinance by creating the chaotic situation such ordinance was designed to prevent.

777 P.2d at 247. Other state courts hold that, as a matter of state law, zoning amendments by referendum are inconsistent with state law requirements of notice and opportunity to be heard. See L.A. Ray Realty v. Town Council of the Town of Cumberland, 603 A.2d 311 (R.I.1992); Westgate Families v. County Clerk of the Incorporated County of Los Alamos, 100 N.M. 146, 667 P.2d 453 (1983). And see Idaho Historic Preservation Council, Inc. v. City Council of City of Boise, 134 Idaho 651, 8 P.3d 646 (2000) (when city council

passes judgment on requests for demolishing buildings in historic preservation zone it is acting in quasi-judicial capacity and must avoid such things as *ex parte* communications with interested persons).

3. Clearly, a popular referendum does not meet the *Fasano* test for review of an adjudicative act. When a zoning change is effected by popular referendum, no "facts" or "law" are reviewed, nor is there any formal opportunity to be heard on the part of those opposing the change. The voters simply do what they want. As a result, following *Eastlake*, the federal standard is in fairly sharp contrast to that of many states. For example, in Shelton v. College Station, 780 F.2d 475 (5th Cir.1986), a divided court held that a municipality's refusal to grant a variance would, for Federal Constitutional purposes, be treated as a "legislative" rather than an "adjudicative" act. The "most obvious difference" between the two standards of review, the court noted, was:

> how the judiciary reviews the facts behind the decision at issue. In the adjudicative model, historical facts are determined by judge or jury and thereafter are to be accepted *unless unsupported by adequate evidence found within a defined record.* ...
>
> Review of legislative facts is quite different.... "[T]hose challenging the legislative judgment must convince the court that the legislative facts on which the classification is apparently based *could not reasonably be conceived to be true by the governmental decisionmaker.*"

780 F.2d at 479 (emphasis added, citations omitted). Accord Sameric Corp. of Delaware, Inc. v. City of Philadelphia, 142 F.3d 582 (3d Cir.1998).

4. *Eastlake* shows a high degree of federal tolerance for the process under which zoning changes are made; but zoning changes can still be challenged as substantive violations of federal law. For example, if an ordinance violated the First Amendment by prohibiting all live performing arts in the city, it would not be a defense that the ordinance had been passed by referendum. See Poirier v. Grand Blanc Township, 192 Mich.App. 539, 481 N.W.2d 762 (1992), app. denied, 441 Mich. 931, 498 N.W.2d 737 (1993), which held that the disapproval of rezoning by popular referendum amounted to an unconstitutional taking.

§ 11.4.2 THE VARIANCE

ROWE v. CITY OF SOUTH PORTLAND

Supreme Judicial Court of Maine (1999).
730 A.2d 673.

WATHEN, C.J.

Edward Rowe appeals from a judgment entered in the Superior Court (Cumberland County, *Cole, J.*) affirming the decision of the City of South Portland Zoning Board of Appeals' granting a setback variance to Nancy Buck. Because we agree with Rowe's contention that Buck failed to show that the property could not yield a reasonable return without the variance, we vacate the judgment.

The facts may be summarized as follows: Buck built a home on a lot in South Portland in 1996. The home and the lot are irregular in shape. The area of the lot is approximately 28,000 square feet, and the area of the house is 4,600 square feet. Buck hired a designer and a contractor to design, locate, and build the house. In building the house, because of his concern for sea erosion, the contractor set the house back 20 feet from the ocean instead of 12.6 feet as indicated in the plan by the designer. In so doing, because of the irregular shape of the house and the lot, the house encroached upon the 20–foot front yard setback requirement by 1.26 feet and the 25–foot rear yard setback requirement in three places by 1.56 feet, 2.05 feet, and .79 feet. The home was substantially completed when Rowe, the abutting neighbor on the front side, undertook a survey for other reasons and discovered the encroachments. As a result, the certificate of occupancy was denied. Buck sought a zoning variance. After holding a hearing, the Board of Appeals granted the variance. Rowe appealed the Board's decision to the Superior Court pursuant to M.R. Civ. P. 80B, and the court affirmed. Rowe now appeals to this Court.

* * *

The issues in this case are complicated by the fact that the building was substantially completed at the time the error was discovered. We apply, however, the same requirements and analysis to post-construction cases. *See Pepperman v. Town of Rangeley,* 659 A.2d 280 (Me.1995) (upheld denial of variance for applicant who built a lean-to that violated a setback requirement on the ground that applicant failed to meet the reasonable return prong). Failure to yield a "reasonable return" means "the practical loss of all beneficial use of the land." *Twigg v. Town of Kennebunk,* 662 A.2d 914, 918 (Me.1995) (citation omitted). We have often stated that reasonable return does not mean maximum return. *See id.* at 919.

In this case, if Buck had approached the zoning board for a variance prior to building the house, it could not have been granted because Buck could have constructed a house smaller than 4,600 square feet and still had a beneficial use. Moreover, Buck could still enjoy a beneficial use as a residence if she moves the house or rebuilds the part of the house that encroaches upon the front setback requirement. Buck argues that it would cost tens of thousands of dollars to move or rebuild the parts of the house that encroach upon the setback, and, without doing so, she is unable to get a certificate of occupancy to use the house as her residence. We determine that those arguments are insufficient to meet the reasonable return prong. The costs, even if prohibitive, were not construction costs caused by restrictions in the ordinance. They are reconstruction costs caused by human error in the construction of a building that could have conformed to the zoning requirements. Accordingly, the record does not rationally permit the conclusion that denial of the variance would result in the practical loss of all beneficial use of the land. * * *

Notwithstanding Buck's failure to meet the reasonable return prong of the undue hardship test, both the City of South Portland and Buck ask us to allow the variance. The City asks that we adopt a "practical difficulty" test for determining an area variance request, arguing that the reasonable return prong is difficult to apply to area variances. Buck argues that we should apply a *de minimis* test to the facts of this case.

We note that in 1991 the Legislature expressly authorized municipalities to adopt a more relaxed, less rigid test for single-family residences. *See* 30–A M.R.S.A. § 4353(4–B) (1996). In addition, in 1997 the Legislature also enacted an exception to the "undue hardship" requirement for variances from dimensional standards. *See* 30–A M.R.S.A. § 4353(4–C) (Supp.1998).

The history behind these two subsections is as follows: In 1991 "An Act Allowing Zoning Boards of Appeal to Grant Dimensional Variances Based on Practical Difficulty" was introduced. L.D. 1832 (115th Legis.1991). The Statement of Fact read as follows:

> Current law strictly limits the authority of a municipal zoning board of appeals to grant variances. A zoning board may grant a variance only if strict application of an ordinance causes undue hardship to the property owner. To prove undue hardship, a property owner must show that the ordinance prevents the property owner from realizing any reasonable return on the property.

> This bill allows municipal zoning boards of appeals to grant dimensional variances if the petitioner can demonstrate "practical difficulty." To meet the practical difficulty standard in the bill, the property owner must show that strict application of an ordinance prevents the owner from using the property for a purpose otherwise allowed. The property owner must also show that granting the variance does not reduce the value or impair the use of abutting property in the zone and does not conflict with the general purpose of the ordinance, that the public safety and welfare is protected and that the variance does not conflict with the municipality's comprehensive plan.

L.D. 1832, Statement of Fact (115th Legis.1991). The bill was amended to replace the dimensional language with the single-family dwellings language that was eventually adopted in 1991. In 1997, a new "Act to Establish Practical Difficulty Standards for a Variance from the Dimensional Standards of a Municipal Zoning Ordinance" was introduced. The Statement of Fact stated:

> This bill amends the zoning adjustment statute to adopt "practical difficulty" standards for variances from dimensional standards in zoning ordinances. The bill allows a petitioner to obtain a variance from a dimensional standard, such as a yard setback, lot area, lot width or a frontage provision, upon a showing that is less stringent than must be made under "undue hardship" conditions in the Maine Revised Statutes, Title 30–A, section 4353, subsection 4. This bill requires a petitioner for use variances to prove undue hardship under

section 4353, subsection 4; a petitioner for dimensional, or area variances may utilize the less stringent practical difficulty standards under section 4353, subsection 4–C. Although there now are less stringent undue hardship conditions for set-back variances under section 4353, subsection 4–B, which is limited to a single-family dwelling and which is the petitioner's primary year-round residence, these conditions do not afford relief from lot area, lot width or frontage requirements, and is only available if a municipality affirmatively adopts the standard by ordinance. This bill makes all petitioners for dimensional variances, whether by residential, commercial or industrial property owners, subject to the practical difficulty standards and does not require municipal adoption of these standards.

* * * Thus, the Legislature has taken action and the City has the option to adopt the less stringent ordinances allowed by the Legislature. We decline to circumvent the legislative and municipal authority and adopt a "practical difficulty" test for all area variances when the Legislature has expressly granted authority to municipalities to adopt such a test and the City of South Portland has chosen not to take such action. For similar reasons, we decline to adopt a *de minimis* test.

Judgment vacated. Remanded to the Superior Court for entry of judgment in favor of plaintiff.

NOTES AND QUESTIONS

1. As the principal case suggests, state law often distinguishes between "use" variances and "area" variances. The former is relevant when someone wishes to engage in a use that the zoning ordinance disapproves for that parcel, such as operating a business on a residential lot. An area variance, which is typically considered less obtrusive, deals mainly with deviations from minimum setback requirements. If area variances are minor they may not even be observed except by someone who has a measuring tape. Other area variances are for deviations from minimum lot size requirements, minimum floor area requirements, or height restrictions. As *Rowe* indicates, legislatures or judicial decisions typically require a strict "undue hardship" test for a use variance, but a less strict "practical difficulties" test for an area variance. Some states prohibit use variances altogether. See, e.g., Topanga Assn. for a Scenic Community v. County of Los Angeles, 11 Cal.3d 506, 511 n. 5, 113 Cal.Rptr. 836, 522 P.2d 12 (1974); Lee v. Board of Adjustment of City of Rocky Mount, 226 N.C. 107, 37 S.E.2d 128, 133 (1946). On area variances, see Sciacca v. Caruso, 769 A.2d 578 (R.I. 2001), holding that someone who first petitioned to have her lots subdivided and then requested an area variance because one of the resulting lots was too small was precluded because her hardship was "self-created." See also the divided decision of the Supreme Court of Wisconsin in State v. Waushara County Board of Adjustment, 271 Wis.2d 547, 679 N.W.2d 514 (2004), which overruled the state's traditional, strict "no reasonable use" test for area variances and instead adopted a more flexible test that permitted the Board to consider the variance request in light of the historical purpose of the zoning regulation in question. The property

owner wanted to replace a nonconforming house with a new house that would have violated applicable setback requirements. A dissenter complained that the property owner was in fact requesting a variance, the effect of which was to limit public access to the shoreline.

See City of Dallas v. Vanesko, 189 S.W.3d 769 (Tex. 2006), which followed the principal case and declined to approve a variance where the landowner had already completed a structure whose roof was higher than the relevant ordinance permitted. Further, in this case the city inspector had caught the violation much earlier and had advised the landowner to go ahead and complete construction while seeking a variance. Finally, a plan reviewer in the City's office had issued a conditional approval, after mistakenly concluding that the site was in a different place with a more permissive height limitation.

There is widespread agreement that zoning boards of adjustment are much too quick to grant variances, whether or not the request is justified. Most requests for variances are unopposed, and governmental officials do not do themselves any good by making enemies; so they look for reasons to grant the variance. See Dukeminier and Stapleton, The Zoning Board of Adjustment: A Case Study in Misrule, 50 Ky.L.J. 273 (1952).

2. Why is the standard for obtaining a use variance more stringent than the standard for obtaining an area variance? Because use variances allow uses or activities that would otherwise be prohibited under the zoning ordinance, use variances are much broader in impact and in scope than are area (dimensional) variances. Use variances are also potentially more damaging to the zoning ordinance's integrity because the aggressive application of use variances virtually amounts to rezoning property piecemeal, one lot at a time, and without going through the normal rezoning process.

3. The cases also make clear that a variance is a *land use* device, designed to ensure that a city's zoning policies are consistently administered without excessive effect on a particular property. That is, it must be attached to the land and not to a particular occupant. For example a municipality is typically not permitted to grant a variance to someone to operate, say, a day care center in a residential neighborhood, but only for the period that the applicant owns the house.

4. Historically, the variance developed as a device to save zoning ordinances from unconstitutionality. See, e.g., Nectow v. Cambridge, 277 U.S. 183 (1928), which struck down a municipality's zoning ordinance because of its adverse effect on a single landowner and see the notes following *Euclid* discussing variances in the context of the *Euclid* and *Lucas* cases. The purpose of the variance was to save the ordinance from unconstitutionality by giving land owners such as Nectow relief that did not require rewriting the entire zoning ordinance.

5. Variances run with the land once granted and are not generally treated as personal to the property owner. See e.g., Campus Associates L.L.C. v. Zoning Bd. of Adjustment of Twp. of Hillsborough, 413 N.J. Super. 527, 534–35, 996 A.2d 1054, 1058 (App. Div. 2010). "A variance is not a personal right granted by a board to an applicant, but rather it is a right that attaches to the land and successive owners take subject to the benefits of the vari-

ance.... This principle is consistent with land use law throughout the country."

6. The *variance* should be distinguished from the *special exception (special use permit)*. The special exception is a permit to do something that the sovereign regards as *permissible* within the zoned area, but which nevertheless must be regulated as to location and intensity. For example, the zoning authority may regard gasoline stations or small grocery stores as appropriate in an area generally zoned for single- and multi-family housing. However, it does not want the unregulated market to determine the number, location, or spacing of such businesses. Therefore it requires people who want to build them in the zoned area to apply for a special exception. At the time of application the authority can consider the needs of the community, the number and distribution of existing uses of the same kind, the impact on traffic patterns, and any other relevant factors. See Tullo v. Millburn Twp., 54 N.J.Super. 483, 490–491, 149 A.2d 620, 624–625 (App.Div.1959):

> The theory [of the special exception] is that certain uses, considered by the local legislative body to be essential or desirable for the welfare of the community and its citizenry or substantial segments of it, are entirely appropriate and not essentially incompatible with the basic uses in any zone (or in certain particular zones), but not at every location therein or without restrictions or conditions being imposed by reason of special problems the use or its particular location in relation to neighboring properties presents from a zoning standpoint, such as traffic congestion, safety, health, noise, and the like. The enabling act therefore permits the local ordinance to require approval of the local administrative agency as to the location of such use within the zone.... The point is that such special uses are permissive in the particular zone under the ordinance and neither non-conforming nor akin to a variance.

The standard for acquiring a special exception often is much easier to meet than the standard for acquiring a variance. The applicant does not need to show extreme hardship, or that the property cannot be used profitably as it is currently zoned. See Value Oil Co. v. Irvington, 152 N.J.Super. 354, 364, 377 A.2d 1225, 1230 (Law Div.1977):

> To obtain a special exception permit an applicant must satisfy three requirements. He must produce proof that the requested exception can be granted without substantial detriment to the public good, that it will not substantially impair the intent and purpose of the zone plan and zoning ordinance of the municipality, and that he has complied with all the specifically enumerated criteria of the ordinance.

This statement suggests that the board of adjustment has little discretion in granting special exceptions: the applicant either meets the test or he does not. In fact, the statutes authorizing special exceptions and the local ordinances passed under them vary considerably among the states. In some cases the board will be entitled to grant or withhold a special exception depending on its judgment whether the use applied for "is reasonably necessary for the convenience and welfare of the public." Barbone v. Zoning Board of Review of City of Warwick, 107 R.I. 74, 264 A.2d 921, 923 (1970) (cited in the notes and decisions of R.I. Gen. Laws Ann. § 45–24–41 (West 2011)). Likewise, the "enumerated criteria" contained in the typical ordinance often contain very general requirements that effectively give the board substantial latitude in evaluating the applicant's proposal.

Other ordinances are very specific about the criteria that an applicant must meet, and generally provide that an applicant who meets them is entitled to a special exception. In the *Value Oil* case, supra, the court overruled the board's refusal to grant a special exception. The applicant had qualified under the "enumerated criteria" established in the ordinance. The board rejected the application, however, because the applicant intended to operate its service station 24 hours per day. The town had no ordinance forbidding such operation. Since the board had no legislative power, its only duty was to determine whether the applicant complied with the specific criteria enumerated in the ordinance. If it found that the applicant complied, it was obliged to grant the special exception.

NOTE: ZONING AND COMPETITION

Zoning unquestionably affects competition. From the time the master plan is drafted and throughout every application for a variance or special exception, the zoning authorities will be invited to consider such questions as whether an area already has "too many" gasoline stations or restaurants or department stores. An unregulated, competitive market will generally produce the competitive number of sellers. As long as high profits can be earned, new entrepreneurs will seek to enter. If the supply already exceeds the demand, however, new entry will be unprofitable. If an applicant seeks a variance or special exception for, say, a gasoline station at a certain location and the board of adjustment denies it, the number of gasoline stations is likely being restricted to fewer than the number that would exist in an unregulated, competitive market. However, there may be externalities, such as increased traffic, that justify a nonmarket solution to this particular problem of competition.

Frequently the opposition to an application for a variance or special exception for business use comes from people who are already operating similar businesses nearby. Often these opponents are established members of the community or occasionally even members of the adjustment board or other relevant government body. By contrast, the applicant is often a newcomer and a stranger. As a result, restrictions on competition can often be either an explicit or implicit factor in zoning decisions. The established businesses stand to make less money if new competitors are permitted to come in.

Courts have been hostile toward zoning regulations or actions that clearly serve no purpose except to reduce competition. For example, in Mobil Oil Corp. v. Board of Adjustment of the Town of Newport, 283 A.2d 837 (Del.Super.1971), the court invalidated an ordinance that prohibited the construction of any gasoline station within 200 feet of an existing station. The court could discern no purpose in the ordinance except the protection of existing gasoline station operators from competition.

Most anticompetitive zoning decisions are more subtle than the statute at issue in *Mobil Oil,* however. For example, in Lucky Stores, Inc. v. Board of

Appeals of Montgomery County, 270 Md. 513, 312 A.2d 758 (1973), the court upheld a zoning board's refusal to grant a special exception to an applicant who wished to build a discount gasoline station. Most of the testimony opposing the special exception came from operators of nearby gasoline stations. They complained about the increased competition from an additional discount station, but they also voiced other concerns, such as increased traffic and risk of fire. The court held that the board was entitled to consider all these factors, including the complaints about the increased competition.

Municipalities whose refusal to zone affects competition have also confronted another problem: the federal antitrust laws. Section 1 of the Sherman Act prohibits contracts, combinations, or conspiracies in restraint of trade. Typically, plaintiffs were frustrated entrepreneurs who used the antitrust laws to claim that a city illegally conspired with established business persons to deny the plaintiffs a permit for their proposed new business. In 1984 Congress passed the Local Government Antitrust Act, which provides that cities found to be in violation of the federal antitrust laws may face a federal injunction, but they are no longer liable for damages. Further, in City of Columbia & Columbia Outdoor Advertising v. Omni Outdoor Advertising, 499 U.S. 365 (1991), the Supreme Court effectively rejected conspiracy theories of municipal antitrust liability, finding that a private person's request to the government for favorable legislation and the government's affirmative response cannot be considered an antitrust conspiracy. Further, said the Court, all such municipal actions were immune from federal antitrust prosecution, provided that they were authorized by state law.

§ 11.4.3 NONCONFORMING USES

VILLAGE OF VALATIE v. SMITH

Court of Appeals of New York (1994).
83 N.Y.2d 396, 632 N.E.2d 1264, 610 N.Y.S.2d 941.

SIMONS, JUDGE.

This appeal challenges the facial validity of chapter 85 of the Village Code of the Village of Valatie, a local law that terminates the nonconforming use of a mobile home upon the transfer of ownership of either the mobile home or the land upon which it sits. Defendant argues that it is unconstitutional for the Village to use a change in ownership as the termination date for a nonconforming use. We conclude, however, that defendant has failed to carry her burden of showing that the local law is unreasonable on its face. * * *

In 1968, the Village enacted chapter 85 to prohibit the placement of mobile homes outside mobile home parks. Under the law, any existing mobile home located outside a park which met certain health standards was allowed to remain as a nonconforming use until either ownership of the land or ownership of the mobile home changed. * * *

In 1989, defendant inherited the mobile home from her father and the Village instituted this action to enforce the law and have the unit removed. Both the Village and defendant moved before the Supreme Court for summary judgment. The court granted defendant's motion and denied the Village's. The court characterized defendant's mobile home as a lawful nonconforming use—i.e., a use that was legally in place at the time the municipality enacted legislation prohibiting the use. Reasoning that the right to continue a nonconforming use runs with the land, the court held that the portion of the ordinance setting termination at the transfer of ownership was unconstitutional. The Appellate Division affirmed. The Court acknowledged that a municipality had the authority to phase out a nonconforming use with an "amortization period", but it concluded that this particular law was unreasonable, and therefore unconstitutional, because the period of time allowed "bears no relationship to the use of the land or the investment in that use".

Preliminarily, it is important to note that the question presented is the facial validity of the local law. The Court is not called upon to decide whether the local law as applied so deprived defendant of the value of her property as to constitute a governmental taking under the Fifth Amendment. * * * [T]here is no question that municipalities may enact laws reasonably limiting the duration of nonconforming uses.[4] * * * Thus, the narrow issue is whether the Village acted unreasonably by establishing an amortization period that uses the transfer of ownership as an end point.

The policy of allowing nonconforming uses to continue originated in concerns that the application of land use regulations to uses existing prior to the regulations' enactment might be construed as confiscatory and unconstitutional (4 Rathkopf, Zoning and Planning § 51.01[2][b], at 51–6 [Ziegler 4th ed.]). While it was initially assumed that nonconforming uses would disappear with time, just the opposite proved to be true in many instances, with the nonconforming use thriving in the absence of any new lawful competition (Matter of Harbison v. City of Buffalo, 4 N.Y.2d 553, 560, 176 N.Y.S.2d 598, 152 N.E.2d 42). In light of the problems presented by continuing nonconforming uses, this Court has characterized the law's allowance of such uses as a "grudging tolerance", and we have recognized the right of municipalities to take reasonable measures to eliminate them. * * *

Most often, elimination has been effected by establishing amortization periods, at the conclusion of which the nonconforming use must end. As commentators have noted, the term "amortization period" is somewhat misleading. "Amortization" properly refers to a liquidation, but in this context the owner is not required to take any particular financial step. "Amortization period" simply designates a period of time granted to owners of nonconforming uses during which they may phase out their operations as they see fit and make other arrangements. * * * It is, in effect, a grace period, putting owners on fair notice of the law and giving them a fair opportunity to recoup their investment. * * * Though the amortization period is typically discussed in terms of protecting the

---

4. Though the difference between a nonconforming use and a nonconforming structure will at times be relevant, our reasoning in this case applies equally whether the mobile home is characterized as a use or a structure.

owners' financial interests, it serves more generally to protect "an individual's interest in maintaining the present use" of the property (Modjeska Sign Studios v. Berle, supra, 43 N.Y.2d at 479, 402 N.Y.S.2d 359, 373 N.E.2d 255).

The validity of an amortization period depends on its reasonableness (*Harbison*, supra). We have avoided any fixed formula for determining what constitutes a reasonable period. Instead, we have held that an amortization period is presumed valid, and the owner must carry the heavy burden of overcoming that presumption by demonstrating that the loss suffered is so substantial that it outweighs the public benefit to be gained by the exercise of the police power. * * * Using this approach, courts have declared valid a variety of amortization periods. * * * Indeed, in some circumstances, no amortization period at all is required (see, New York State Thruway Auth. v. Ashley Motor Ct., 10 N.Y.2d 151, 218 N.Y.S.2d 640, 176 N.E.2d 566; People v. Miller, 304 N.Y. 105, 106 N.E.2d 34). In other circumstances, the amortization period may vary in duration among the affected properties. * * * We have also held that an amortization period may validly come to an end at the occurrence of an event as unpredictable as the destruction of the nonconforming use by fire (see, Matter of Pelham Esplanade v. Board of Trustees, 77 N.Y.2d 66, 563 N.Y.S.2d 759, 565 N.E.2d 508, supra).

Defendant here does not challenge the local law's constitutionality under our established balancing test for amortization periods—i.e., whether the individual loss outweighs the public benefit. Instead, the challenge is a more basic due process claim: that the means of eliminating nonconforming uses is not reasonably related to the Village's legitimate interest in land use planning. More particularly, defendant makes two arguments: first, that the length of an amortization period must be related either to land use objectives or to the financial recoupment needs of the owner and, second, that the local law violates the principle that zoning is to regulate land use rather than ownership. * * * Neither argument withstands analysis.

We have never required that the length of the amortization period be based on a municipality's land use objectives. To the contrary, the periods are routinely calculated to protect the rights of individual owners at the temporary expense of public land use objectives. Typically, the period of time allowed has been measured for reasonableness by considering whether the owners had adequate time to recoup their investment in the use. * * * Patently, such protection of an individual's interest is unrelated to land use objectives. Indeed, were land use objectives the only permissible criteria for scheduling amortization, the law would require immediate elimination of nonconforming uses in all instances. Instead, the setting of the amortization period involves balancing the interests of the individual and those of the public. Thus, the real issue here is whether it was irrational for the Village, in striking that balance, to consider a nonfinancial interest of the individual owners—specifically, the individual's interest in not being displaced involuntarily.

It is significant that the * * * properties involved here are residential. In our previous cases dealing with amortization, we have focused almost exclusively on commercial properties, where the owner's interest is easily reduced to financial considerations. The same may not be true for the owners of residential properties, especially in instances where the property is the primary residence of the owner. Simply being able to recoup one's financial investment may be a secondary concern to staying in a neighborhood or remaining on a particular piece of land. Indeed, when mobile homes are involved, there may actually be little or no financial loss, given that the owner often will be able to relocate the structure and sell the land for legal development. Here, rather than focusing solely on financial recoupment, the Village apparently took a broader view of "an individual's interest in maintaining the present use" of the property. * * * It enacted a law that allowed owners to keep their mobile homes in place until they decided to sell, even though they may have recouped their investment long ago. By doing so, it saved the owners from a forced relocation at the end of a predetermined amortization period set by the Village. Defendant has not demonstrated why such an approach is irrational or explained why a municipality should be barred constitutionally from considering the nonfinancial interests of the owners in setting an amortization schedule. Thus, on this motion for summary judgment and the present record, defendant has failed to overcome the presumption of the law's validity and prove, as she must, unconstitutionality beyond a reasonable doubt. * * *

Equally unavailing on this facial challenge is defendant's contention that the law might prevent some owners from recouping their investment. Defendant raises the hypothetical concern that in some circumstances owners might not have adequate time to recoup—for instance, if a sale took place shortly after the law's enactment. Whatever the validity of that concern, it is not relevant to this facial challenge to the law. Defendant has not claimed that she was so injured, and her argument must fall to the general principle that a litigant cannot sustain a facial challenge to a law when that law is constitutional in its application to that litigant. * * *

It is true that, in the absence of amortization legislation, the right to continue a nonconforming use runs with the land. * * * However, once a valid amortization scheme is enacted, the right ends at the termination of the amortization period. As a practical matter, that means the owner of record during the amortization period will enjoy a right that cannot be transferred to a subsequent owner once the period passes. In such circumstances, the law is not rendered invalid because the original owner no longer has a right to transfer or because the original owner and subsequent owners have received disparate treatment under the land use regulations. * * *

Nor can we subscribe to the Appellate Division's theory that the amortization period here is unreasonable because it may be too long. In the Appellate Division's view, an open-ended amortization schedule does not reasonably advance land use objectives. The Appellate Division noted that if a corporation owned one of the mobile homes here, the amortization period would be limitless in theory. The Village answers by stating that all six mobile homes were owned by individuals, and thus amortization would end, at the latest, upon their deaths. Because the class of nonconforming users became closed at the law's enactment and will never contain more than those six, the concern about corporate ownership is unfounded, the Village argues. At this point in the litigation, defendant has not demonstrated that the Village is factually in error as to the ownership of the six units.

Of greater concern to us, the Appellate Division's rationale would seriously undermine the law of nonconforming uses. Amortization periods are the exceptions; in the absence of such schemes, owners of nonconforming uses are free to continue the uses indefinitely and transfer them to successor owners. Were the Appellate Division's rationale accepted, amortization periods would be required to avoid the problem of indefinite continuation of nonconforming uses. Amortization periods have never been mandatory as a matter of constitutional law, and consequently we must reject the Appellate Division's reasoning.

Thus, we conclude that defendant has failed to prevail on her facial challenge to the Village law. * * *

NOTES AND QUESTIONS

1. In contrast with the holding in *Village of Valatie*, nonconforming uses are generally treated as running with the land and therefore are not affected by changes in ownership. See The Lamar Co., LLC v. City of Fremont, 278 Neb. 485, 771 N.W.2d 894, 902 (2009) stating:

> While this court has not previously addressed the issue, upon review of the jurisprudence of other jurisdictions and the treatises addressing nonconforming use rights, we are persuaded that the right to maintain a legal nonconforming use "runs with the land," meaning it is an incident of ownership of the land, and is not a personal right. Therefore, a change in the ownership or tenancy of a nonconforming business or structure which takes advantage of the nonconforming rights does not affect the current landowner's right to continue the nonconforming use.... The rationale for this rule is amply explained in 4 Rathkopf's The Law of Zoning and Planning § 72:20 at 72–56 (Edward H. Ziegler, Jr., ed. 2005), which states:
>
> > It is obvious that if the right to continue a nonconforming use were not considered one of the "bundle of rights" which together constitute the attributes of ownership of the land, exercisable by [a landowner who] had the possessory interest therein, it would prevent a purchaser [of the land] from using the land for any purpose other than one permitted by the ordinance in effect at the time of transfer. The owner of the land would be unable to sell all of his rights in the land and in the use thereof, and, being out of possession of the land, could not exercise the right to the nonconforming use.

There are four types of nonconformities: (1) nonconforming uses of land, (2) nonconforming buildings, (3) nonconforming uses of conforming buildings, and (4) conforming uses of nonconforming buildings. What type/types of nonconformities were involved in *Village of Valatie*?

2.   As the principal opinion indicates, most states uphold zoning ordinances that require the amortization and eventual retirement of nonconforming uses, provided that the amortization period is reasonable and reasonably applied. In Modjeska Sign Studios, Inc. v. Berle, 43 N.Y.2d 468, 402 N.Y.S.2d 359, 373 N.E.2d 255 (1977), the court held that a statute requiring removal of nonconforming outdoor advertising signs without compensation was not unconstitutional if it was reasonable. Then it remanded to the lower court for a determination whether the statute, which included a six and one-half year amortization period, was reasonable under the following criteria:

> Certainly, a critical factor to be considered is the length of the amortization period in relation to the investment.... Similarly, another factor ... is the nature of the nonconforming activity prohibited. Generally a shorter amortization period may be provided for a nonconforming use as opposed to a nonconforming structure.... [T]he critical question which must be asked is whether the public gain achieved by the exercise of the police power outweighs the private loss suffered by the owners of the nonconforming uses. [citation omitted] While an owner need not be given that period of time necessary to recoup his investment entirely, ... the amortization period should not be so short as to result in a substantial loss of his investment [citation omitted]....

> In determining what constitutes a substantial loss, a court ... should look to, for example, such factors as: initial capital investment, investment realization to date, life expectancy of the investment, the existence or nonexistence of a lease obligation, as well as a contingency clause permitting termination of the lease. As a general rule, most regulations requiring the removal of nonconforming billboards and providing a reasonable amortization period should pass constitutional muster.

Id. at 480, 402 N.Y.S.2d at 367, 373 N.E.2d at 262.

3.   As the principal case notes, the early proponents of zoning did not propose legislation phasing out nonconforming uses because they believed these laws would be declared unconstitutional unless they provided for compensation to the owners. They also apparently believed that nonconforming uses would eventually disappear of their own accord. Is this belief plausible? It depends on the use. The owner of a nonconforming use obtains a monopoly in a local area, and protection from new entry by competitors. For example, a nonconforming gasoline station in an area subsequently zoned residential might end up being the only gasoline station in the subdivision. Furthermore, the zoning ordinance prevents any new gasoline stations from being built in the area. This gasoline station is not likely to go out of business as a result of the zoning ordinance.

4.   Courts that approve "amortization" ordinances generally apply a stricter constitutional standard to nonconforming *structures* than they do to nonconforming uses. Indeed, some cases suggest that the amortization period for structures must approximate their useful lives. See Harbison v. Buffalo, 4

N.Y.2d 553, 176 N.Y.S.2d 598, 152 N.E.2d 42 (1958). See also Note, A Suggested Means of Determining the Proper Amortization Period for Nonconforming Structures, 27 Stan.L.Rev. 1325 (1975). What justifies the difference? Most of the investment in a nonconforming structure is "sunk." A sunk cost is a cost that a firm will not be able to recover when it goes out of business. When a building is torn down its salvage value is often close to zero. A nonconforming business *use,* by contrast, can often be moved with loss of little more than some goodwill attached to the old address.

5.   Some jurisdictions have statutes that permit the owner of a nonconforming use or structure to continue indefinitely, but forbid her from enlarging upon the use or structure or substantially changing its character. See Town of Belleville v. Parrillo's, Inc., 83 N.J. 309, 416 A.2d 388 (1980), where the court decided that the defendant violated such an ordinance by changing a nonconforming restaurant into a discotheque. See also Rotter v. Coconino County, 169 Ariz. 269, 818 P.2d 704 (1991) (en banc), which interpreted an ordinance that permitted a nonconforming business to expand its operations by up to 100 percent. The court held that the ordinance did not permit the plaintiffs to acquire an adjacent parcel of land, also subject to the zoning restriction, and expand their business by moving it onto the new parcel as well. Some courts recognize a "diminishing assets" exception that permits certain uses such as mines or quarries to expand, because in the process of operating they use up their reserves in one place and must move to another. E.g., City of University Place v. McGuire, 144 Wash.2d 640, 30 P.3d 453 (2001); Town of West Greenwich v. A. Cardi Realty, 786 A.2d 354 (R.I.2001).

Other ordinances permit nonconforming structures to exist indefinitely, but forbid the owner from making repairs to them, on the theory that eventually the structure will have to be torn down. See People v. Tahoe Regional Planning Agency, 766 F.2d 1319 (9th Cir.1985). Yet others hold that once nonconforming uses have been abandoned they cannot be resumed. See Spicer v. Holihan, 158 A.D.2d 459, 550 N.Y.S.2d 943 (1990), interpreting an ordinance to say that once a use had been ceased for twelve months it could not be re-started. Likewise, CG & T Corp. v. Board of Adjustment, 105 N.C.App. 32, 411 S.E.2d 655 (1992) interpreted such an ordinance to mean that once a use had ceased for a year or more, the land owner could not re-start it without obtaining a special use permit. See also Mayberry v. Town of Old Orchard Beach, 599 A.2d 1153 (Me.1991) (nonconforming use of building lapsed when it became unoccupied for two years).

Finally, many municipalities simply grant variances liberally for nonconforming uses, effectively giving these uses a perpetual right to operate. In some cases, of course, such a liberal variance policy may be motivated by a concern that any forced retirement of non-conforming uses will be struck down. See, for example, Burbridge v. Governing Body of Township of Mine Hill, 117 N.J. 376, 568 A.2d 527 (1990), which permitted such a variance.

6.   In Balough v. Fairbanks North Star Borough, 995 P.2d 245 (Alaska 2000), the Alaska Supreme Court upheld an ordinance that granted nonconforming use status to junkyards only if the yards had been in compliance with all other building and use regulations prior to the zoning. In this case the

plaintiffs' junkyard had not been properly fenced prior to the re-zoning and the effect was to deny it any nonconforming use status whatsoever.

§ 11.5 ADDING FLEXIBILITY TO ZONING: CONDITIONAL ZONING, FLOATING ZONES AND THE PLANNED UNIT DEVELOPMENT (PUD)

ST. ONGE v. DONOVAN; DRIESBAUGH v. GAGNON

Court of Appeals of New York (1988).
71 N.Y.2d 507, 527 N.Y.S.2d 721, 522 N.E.2d 1019.

ALEXANDER, JUDGE.

* * * In St. Onge v. Donovan, petitioners contracted to purchase a two-story house in the Town of Colonie for the purpose of operating a real estate business. Operation of such a business is not a permitted use in the residential district where the property is located. This property had been used exclusively for that purpose, however, by the previous owners pursuant to a variance granted by the local zoning board in 1977. The record demonstrates that the variance was granted on the basis of evidence showing that the applicants would suffer unnecessary hardship if they were not permitted to convert the property to commercial use. The variance contained a restrictive condition, however, that provided that the building was "to be used solely by the applicants and may be used only in connection with their existing real estate business". When petitioners sought site plan approval from the Town Planning Board in 1985 for the continued use of the property as a real estate office, the Planning Board denied approval, citing the fact that the variance granted in 1977 was only temporary, and that under the terms of the restrictive condition a transfer of the property would terminate the variance. Petitioners appealed that determination to the Zoning Board of Appeals (Board), contending that the previous variance continued to be valid. * * *

The [trial] court held that a variance runs with the land and cannot be a right personal to the landowner, concluding that the restrictive condition in the 1977 variance is void, and that the variance thus is unconditional with no time limitation. * * *

In Driesbaugh v. Gagnon, petitioner owns and operates two automobile body repair shops in the Town of Fenton, both of which are located in agricultural-residential districts in violation of the local zoning ordinance. One of the repair shops, located along Route 369 in the Village of Port Crane, is a lawful prior nonconforming use; the other shop, located on Route 7, was purchased by petitioner in 1984, after the enactment of the zoning ordinance, and therefore is not a protected nonconforming use. In February 1985, petitioner was served with a "Notice of Violation" requesting that he cease operations at the Route 7 location. He then applied to the Town Zoning Board of Appeals (Board) for a use variance that would permit him to continue operation of the Route 7 shop.

* * * [T]he Board resolved to grant a variance, but imposed six conditions designed to prevent expansion of the nonconforming use.

Petitioner instituted [this] proceeding seeking to annul ... the sixth condition, [which] required petitioner to phase out his operations at the Port Crane location by July 10, 1986. Petitioner contended that the former condition placed a limitation on the number of cars he could recondition in a given week, and thus threatened the economic viability of his business. He further contended that the latter requirement that he phase out his Port Crane business improperly interfered with a lawful nonconforming use.

In Matter of Dexter v. Town Bd., 36 N.Y.2d 102, 365 N.Y.S.2d 506, 324 N.E.2d 870, a corporation sought to have the Zoning Board of the Town of Gates rezone 12 acres of land from a residential to a commercial classification so as to permit the development of a retail shopping center. Although the zoning board granted the reclassification, it imposed several conditions, one of which provided that the " 'application for the construction of a retail supermarket by [the corporation] and related commercial structures, shall inure to the benefit of [the corporation] only, and for that specific purpose only' " * * * We invalidated the condition, holding that although a local zoning board may impose "appropriate conditions and safeguards in conjunction with a change of zone or a grant of a variance or special permit", those conditions "must be reasonable and relate only to the real estate involved without regard to the person who owns or occupies it." We recognized that where a zoning change such as a variance or special permit is sought, there is ordinarily a specific project sponsored by a particular developer that is the subject of the application and that, as a consequence, attention generally focuses on the reputation of the applicant, the applicant's relationship to the community and the particular intended use, so that "all too often the administrative or legislative determination seems to turn on the identity of the applicant or intended user, rather than upon neutral planning and zoning principles." We characterized this approach as error, however, and a "lack of adherence to the fundamental rule that zoning deals basically with land use and not with the person who owns or occupies it." * * *

Our holding in Dexter did not, nor was it intended to, divest zoning boards of their discretionary power to impose reasonable conditions in connection with a zoning decision; it merely established limitations on the exercise of that power. A zoning board may, where appropriate, impose "reasonable conditions and restrictions as are directly related to and incidental to the proposed use of the property", and aimed at minimizing the adverse impact to an area that might result from the grant of a variance or special permit. Such conditions might properly relate "to fences, safety devices, landscaping, screening and access roads relating to period of use, screening, outdoor lighting and noises, and enclosure of buildings and relating to emission of odors, dust, smoke, refuse matter, vibration noise and other factors incidental to comfort, peace, enjoyment, health or safety of the surrounding area." Similarly, we have upheld, as a condition of rezoning property for commercial use, the imposition of a requirement that the owners of the property execute and record restrictive covenants relating to the maximum area to be occupied by buildings, the erection of a fence, and the planting of shrubbery (see, Church v. Town of Islip, 8 N.Y.2d 254, 259, 203 N.Y.S.2d 866, 168 N.E.2d 680). Such conditions are proper because they relate directly to the use of the land in question, and are corrective measures designed to protect neighboring properties against the possible adverse effects of that use. Conditions imposed to protect the surrounding area from a particular land use are consistent with the purposes of zoning, which seeks to harmonize the various land uses within a community (see generally, Collard v. Incorporated Vil. of Flower Hill, 52 N.Y.2d 594, 602, 439 N.Y.S.2d 326, 421 N.E.2d 818).

On the other hand, zoning boards may not impose conditions which are unrelated to the purposes of zoning. Thus, a zoning board may not condition a variance upon a property owner's agreement to dedicate land that is not the subject of the variance application (see, e.g., Gordon v. Zoning Bd. of Appeals, 126 Misc.2d 75, 481 N.Y.S.2d 275 [condition requiring dedication of portion of front yard invalid where variance sought related to side yard requirements]; Matter of Allen v. Hattrick, 87 A.D.2d 575, 447 N.Y.S.2d 741 [conditions unrelated to relief requested in variance invalid]). Nor may a zoning board impose a condition that seeks to regulate the details of the operation of an enterprise, rather than the use of the land on which the enterprise is located (see, e.g., Matter of Summit School v. Neugent, 82 A.D.2d 463, 442 N.Y.S.2d 73 [conditions regulating details of the operation of a private school invalid]; Matter of Schlosser v. Michaelis, 18 A.D.2d 940, 238 N.Y.S.2d 433[conditions regulating details of a wholesale florist business invalid]). Such conditions are invalid because they do not seek to ameliorate the effects of the land use at issue, and are thus unrelated to the legitimate purposes of zoning.

In *St. Onge*, the condition imposed on the variance granted by the Town Zoning Board in 1977 clearly relates to the landowner rather than the use of the land. By its terms, the condition purports to terminate the variance automatically if any persons other than the original applicants use the property as a real estate office. This is precisely the type of personal condition proscribed by Matter of Dexter v. Town Bd., 36 N.Y.2d 102, 365 N.Y.S.2d 506, 324 N.E.2d 870, supra, for it focuses on the persons occupying the property rather than the use of the land or the possible effects of that use on the surrounding area. As this condition bears no relation to the proper purposes of zoning, therefore, it was properly ruled invalid. Similarly in *Driesbaugh*, the Zoning Board of the Town of Fenton improperly conditioned its grant of the variance on the phasing out of petitioner's Port Crane operation. The variance requested by petitioner related only to the business located on Route 7 and, therefore, any conditions imposed on the variance must relate solely to that property (Matter of Dexter v. Town Bd., 36 N.Y.2d, at 105, 365 N.Y.S.2d 506, 324 N.E.2d 870, supra). By conditioning the variance on the elimination of the Port Crane operation, the Board has imposed a requirement completely unrelated either to the use of the land at issue or to the potential impact of that use on neighboring properties.

The Town's contention in Driesbaugh, that the sixth condition is justified by the close relationship between the two properties and, generally, by the interrelated nature of land in the community must be rejected. We acknowledge that, in exercising their zoning powers, local authorities must consider the needs of the community as a whole. * * * Indeed, it is for this reason that zoning decisions must be made "in accordance with a comprehensive plan. * * *" The zoning power is not without limits, however, and its mere invocation does not excuse the arbitrary infringement of property rights. In seeking a variance for a specific parcel petitioner should not have been required to forfeit valuable property rights merely because he happened to own other property in the same community. The fact that the two separate parcels here are held in common ownership is purely a matter of personal circumstance, and does not furnish a basis for regulating the parcel which is not the subject of the variance.

NOTES AND QUESTIONS

1. Variances, it is sometimes said, must "run with the land," just as real covenants, see discussion supra. Must they also "touch and concern" the land?

2. Many cases distinguish "conditional" zoning, in which the land owner makes "unilateral" promises to the zoning authority before the authority grants the land owner's wishes, from "contract zoning," in which there is a bilateral agreement between land owner and sovereign. The former is said to be legal while the latter is not. See Chrismon v. Guilford County, 322 N.C. 611, 635–636, 370 S.E.2d 579, 593 (1988):

> Illegal contract zoning properly connotes a transaction wherein both the landowner who is seeking a certain zoning action and the zoning authority itself undertake reciprocal obligations in the context of a bilateral contract. One commentator provides as illustration the following example:
>
>> A Council enters into an agreement with the landowner and then enacts a zoning amendment. The agreement, however, includes not merely the promise of the owner to subject his property to deed restrictions; the Council also binds itself to enact the amendment and not to alter the zoning change for a specified period of time. Most courts will conclude that by agreeing to curtail its legislative power, the Council acted ultra vires. Such contract zoning is illegal and the rezoning is therefore a nullity.

Shapiro, The Case for Conditional Zoning, 41 Temp. L.Q. 267, 269 (1968). As the excerpted illustration suggests, contract zoning of this type is objectionable primarily because it represents an abandonment on the part of the zoning authority of its duty to exercise independent judgment in making zoning decisions.

[V]alid conditional use zoning, on the other hand, is * * * an outgrowth of the need for a compromise between the interests of the developer who is seeking appropriate rezoning for his tract and the community * * * and the interests of the neighboring landowners who will suffer if the most intensive use permitted by the new classification is instituted. One commentator has described its mechanics as follows:

> An orthodox conditional zoning situation occurs when a zoning authority, without committing its own power, secures a property owner's agreement to subject his tract to certain restrictions as a prerequisite to rezoning. These restrictions may require that the rezoned property be limited to just one of the uses permitted in the new classification; or particular physical improvements and mainte- nance requirements may be imposed.

[Shapiro, Id. at 270–71 (emphasis added).]

Are you convinced by the court's unilateral-bilateral distinction?

NOTE: THE PLANNED UNIT DEVELOPMENT

The Planned Unit Development, or PUD, is a flexibility device that permits the developer to design a subdivision by selecting his own mixture of lot sizes and shapes, inserting common areas, and even mixing in some multifamily housing. A good way to think of the PUD is as a form of zoning deregulation. Traditional zoning regulated intensely at the micro level, right to the point of designating individual lot sizes, setback requirements, alloca- tions of single- and multi-family houses, and the like. In a PUD the developer may be required to produce an overall allocation of single- and multi-family, but he will have considerably more discretion in determining what the precise distribution and configuration will be. After all, the developer must work in the market, and has an incentive to produce a commercially successful package that the regulator does not have. In Cheney v. Village 2 at New Hope, Inc., 429 Pa. 626, 241 A.2d 81 (1968), the Pennsylvania Supreme Court upheld an ordinance that permitted developers to create PUDs against a charge of unlawful "spot" zoning. The court observed:

> Under traditional concepts of zoning the task of determining the type, density and placement of buildings which should exist within any given zoning district devolves upon the local legislative body. In order that this body might have to speak only infrequently on the issue of municipal planning and zoning, the local legislature usually enacts detailed require- ments for the type, size and location of buildings within each given zoning district, and leaves the ministerial task of enforcing these regula- tions to an appointed zoning administrator, with another administrative body, the zoning board of adjustment, passing on individual deviations from the strict district requirements, deviations known commonly as

variances and special exceptions. At the same time, the overall rules governing the dimensions, placement, etc. of primarily public additions to ground, e.g., streets, sewers, playgrounds, are formulated by the local legislature through the passage of subdivision regulations. These regulations are enforced and applied to individual lots by an administrative body usually known as the planning commission.

This general approach to zoning fares reasonably well so long as development takes place on a lot-by-lot basis, and so long as no one cares that the overall appearance of the municipality resembles the design achieved by using a cookie cutter on a sheet of dough. However, with the increasing popularity of large scale residential developments, particularly in suburban areas, it has become apparent to many local municipalities that land can be more efficiently used, and developments more aesthetically pleasing, if zoning regulations focus on density requirements rather than on specific rules for each individual lot. * * *

Admittedly the range of permissible uses within the PUD district is greater than that normally found in a traditional zoning district. Within a New Hope PUD district there may be: single family attached or detached dwellings; apartments; accessory private garages; public or private parks and recreation areas including golf courses, swimming pools, ski slopes, etc. (so long as these facilities do not produce noise, glare, odor, air pollution, etc., detrimental to existing or prospective adjacent structures); a municipal building; a school; churches; art galleries; professional offices; certain types of signs; a theater (but not a drive-in); motels and hotels; and a restaurant. The ordinance then sets certain overall density requirements. The PUD district may have a maximum of 80% of the land devoted to residential uses, a maximum of 20% for the permitted commercial uses and enclosed recreational facilities, and must have a minimum of 20% for open spaces. The residential density shall not exceed 10 units per acre, nor shall any such unit contain more than two bedrooms. All structures within the district must not exceed maximum height standards set out in the ordinance. Finally, although there are no traditional "set back" and "side yard" requirements, ordinance 160 does require that there be 24 feet between structures, and that no townhouse structure contain more than 12 dwelling units.

The procedure to be followed by the aspiring developer reduces itself to presenting a detailed plan for his planned unit development to the planning commission, obtaining that body's approval and then securing building permits. Of course, the planning commission may not approve any development that fails to meet the requirements set forth in the ordinance as outlined above. * * *

The primary reason that planning commissions have not traditionally interpreted this type of ordinance is that such regulations do not usually come into play until the landowner wishes to begin the actual construction of a particular building. By this time, the relevant subdivision plan has already been approved by the commission; thus the task of examining the plans for a particular structure to see whether it conforms to the regulations for the zoning district in which it will be erected devolves upon the local building inspector who issues the building permit.

However, in the case of PUD the entire development (including specific structures) is mapped out and submitted to the administrative agency at once.

Today the PUD is typically more regulated by statute than it was when *Cheney* was decided in 1968. The Pennsylvania court upheld the ordinance there in spite of the fact that the municipality had not obtained any enabling legislation from the state. Since then, many states have passed PUD enabling acts that prescribe the standards that governmental subdivisions must employ in creating PUD zones and approving specific applications. Some courts have also required that there be a local ordinance that authorizes the creation of PUDs. See Tri–State Generation & Transmission Co. v. Thornton, 647 P.2d 670 (Colo.1982) (en banc). The existence of PUD enabling legislation generally undermines any claim that the creation of PUDs is illegal *per se* as spot zoning and not in accordance with a comprehensive plan.

In general, however, the courts have been kind to PUDs, even in the absence of special enabling legislation, and it has become a quite conventional and even preferred part of the planning process. See, e.g., Board of County Commissioners v. Bainbridge, Inc., 929 P.2d 691 (Colo.1996) (describing and applying Colorado Planned Unit Development Act, which both authorizes and regulates PUDS); Sheridan Planning Assn. v. Board of Sheridan County Commissioners, 924 P.2d 988 (Wyo.1996) (county's approval of PUD was a legislative act, and thus not subject to appellate-style judicial review). See 2 R. Anderson, American Law of Zoning, Ch. 11 (Young, ed. 4th ed. 1996).

CHAPTER 12

THE LAW OF HOUSING DISCRIMINATION

■ ■ ■

§ 12.1 INTRODUCTION: THE RIGHT TO FAIR TREATMENT IN THE PROVISION OF HOUSING SERVICES

Someone who has a house to sell or an apartment to rent is free to select among competing prospects. For example, no one is required by law to rent an apartment to someone who has left a trail of unpaid bills. In fact, people do not need a particularly good reason to refuse to sell or rent their property to someone. At common law, a seller was free to deal or refuse to deal with anyone for any reason, as he or she pleased. Even today that rule generally applies to housing.

However, the government has recognized various protected classifications of people who have a legal right not to be denied a housing opportunity *because* of their membership in that particular classification. Today housing discrimination is regulated by federal, state and local governments. The result is a complex system of tenant's and purchaser's rights that every property and civil rights lawyer must understand.

One important distinction among federal, state and local antidiscrimination laws is in the protected classes that they recognize. Since federal law applies throughout the United States, state legislation is generally meaningful only if it creates more protection, in some way, than federal law does. Likewise, since state legislation applies everywhere within the state, meaningful local legislation must generally give more protection than state legislation. The federal antidiscrimination laws recognize race, color, religion, gender, national origin, familial status and handicap as protected classes, although some cases have gone further. State and local legislation typically protects all these classifications as well as some additional ones, such as age or in a few instances sexual orientation.

An equally important difference among the statutory schemes is the enforcement mechanisms that they create. Most antidiscrimination statutes permit lawsuits by private parties. Most also provide for public enforcement through an agency or officer of the sovereign that passed the statute. Funding for such enforcement is not unlimited, however. For example, although the Department of Housing and Urban Development (HUD) and the Attorney General enforce the federal Fair Housing Act (FHA), they do not receive sufficient funding to challenge every discovered instance of housing discrimination. They must set priorities. Furthermore, the enforcement position of any agency is a function of the political principles of the current administration, and some have been much more aggressive than others about enforcing antidiscrimination laws.

The effect of a multi-level enforcement scheme is that the victim of discrimination may be able to seek help from more than one governmental enforcement agency. An inhabitant of a large city protected by federal, state and local enforcement agencies may have a threefold choice. People in cities or states that have no applicable antidiscrimination legislation, however, may be limited to the federal legislation.

§ 12.2　"STATE ACTION" AND RACE DISCRIMINATION

SHELLEY v. KRAEMER

Supreme Court of the United States (1948).
334 U.S. 1.

MR. CHIEF JUSTICE VINSON delivered the opinion of the Court.

These cases present for our consideration questions relating to the validity of court enforcement of private agreements, generally described as restrictive covenants, which have as their purpose the exclusion of persons of designated race or color from the ownership or occupancy of real property. Basic constitutional issues of obvious importance have been raised.

On February 16, 1911, thirty out of a total of thirty-nine owners of property fronting both sides of Labadie Avenue between Taylor Avenue and Cora Avenue in the city of St. Louis, signed an agreement, which was subsequently recorded, providing in part:

"... the said property is hereby restricted to the use and occupancy for the term of Fifty (50) years from this date, so that it shall be a condition all the time and whether recited and referred to as [sic] not in subsequent conveyances and shall attach to the land, as a condition precedent to the sale of the same, that hereafter no part of said property or any portion thereof shall be, for said term of Fifty-years, occupied by any person not of the Caucasian race, it being intended hereby to restrict the use of said property for said period of time against the occupancy as owners or tenants of any portion of said property for resident or other purpose by people of the Negro or Mongolian Race."

* * * At the time this action was brought, four of the premises were occupied by Negroes, and had been so occupied for periods ranging from

twenty-three to sixty-three years. A fifth parcel had been occupied by Negroes until a year before this suit was instituted.

On August 11, 1945, pursuant to a contract of sale, petitioners Shelley, who are Negroes, for valuable consideration received from one Fitzgerald a warranty deed to the parcel in question. The trial court found that petitioners had no actual knowledge of the restrictive agreement at the time of the purchase.

On October 9, 1945, respondents, as owners of other property subject to the terms of the restrictive covenant, brought suit in the Circuit Court of the city of St. Louis praying that petitioners Shelley be restrained from taking possession of the property and that judgment be entered divesting title out of petitioners Shelley and revesting title in the immediate grantor or in such other person as the court should direct. The trial court denied the requested relief on the ground that the restrictive agreement, upon which respondents based their action, had never become final and complete because it was the intention of the parties to that agreement that it was not to become effective until signed by all property owners in the district, and signatures of all the owners had never been obtained.

The Supreme Court of Missouri sitting *en banc* reversed and directed the trial court to grant the relief for which respondents had prayed. That court held the agreement effective and concluded that enforcement of its provisions violated no rights guaranteed to petitioners by the Federal Constitution.

* * *

Petitioners have placed primary reliance on their contentions, first raised in the state courts, that judicial enforcement of the restrictive agreements in these cases has violated rights guaranteed to petitioners by the Fourteenth Amendment of the Federal Constitution and Acts of Congress passed pursuant to that Amendment. Specifically, petitioners urge that they have been denied the equal protection of the laws, deprived of property without due process of law, and have been denied privileges and immunities of citizens of the United States. We pass to a consideration of those issues.

* * *

[T]he covenant declares that no part of the affected property shall be ... "occupied by any person not of the Caucasian race, it being intended hereby to restrict the use of said property ... against the occupancy as owners or tenants of any portion of said property for resident or other purpose by people of the Negro or Mongolian Race." Not only does the restriction seek to proscribe use and occupancy of the affected properties by members of the excluded class, but as construed by the Missouri courts, the agreement requires that title of any person who uses his property in violation of the restriction shall be divested.

It should be observed that these covenants do not seek to proscribe any particular use of the affected properties. Use of the properties for residential occupancy, as such, is not forbidden. The restrictions of these agreements, rather, are directed toward a designated class of persons and seek to determine who may and who may not own or make use of the properties for residential purposes. The excluded class is defined wholly in terms of race or color; "simply that and nothing more."

It cannot be doubted that among the civil rights intended to be protected from discriminatory state action by the Fourteenth Amendment are the rights to acquire, enjoy, own and dispose of property. Equality in the enjoyment of property rights was regarded by the framers of that Amendment as an essential pre-condition to the realization of other basic civil rights and liberties which the Amendment was intended to guarantee. Thus, § 1978 of the Revised Statutes, derived from § 1 of the Civil Rights Act of 1866 which was enacted by Congress while the Fourteenth Amendment was also under consideration, provides:

> "All citizens of the United States shall have the same right, in every State and Territory, as is enjoyed by white citizens thereof to inherit, purchase, lease, sell, hold, and convey real and personal property."

* * *

It is likewise clear that restrictions on the right of occupancy of the sort sought to be created by the private agreements in these cases could not be squared with the requirements of the Fourteenth Amendment if imposed by state statute or local ordinance. We do not understand respondents to urge the contrary. In the case of Buchanan v. Warley a unanimous Court declared unconstitutional the provisions of a city ordinance which denied to colored persons the right to occupy houses in blocks in which the greater number of houses were occupied by white persons, and imposed similar restrictions on white persons with respect to blocks in which the greater number of houses were occupied by colored persons. During the course of the opinion in that case, this Court stated: "The Fourteenth Amendment and these statutes enacted in furtherance of its purpose operate to qualify and entitle a colored man to acquire property without state legislation discriminating against him solely because of color."

* * *

But the present cases, unlike those just discussed, do not involve action by state legislatures or city councils. Here the particular patterns of discrimination and the areas in which the restrictions are to operate, are determined, in the first instance, by the terms of agreements among private individuals. Participation of the State consists in the enforcement of the restrictions so defined. The crucial issue with which we are here confronted is whether this distinction removes these cases from the operation of the prohibitory provisions of the Fourteenth Amendment.

Since the decision of this Court in the Civil Rights Cases, 1883, 109 U.S. 3, 3 S.Ct. 18, the principle has become firmly embedded in our constitutional law that the action inhibited by the first section of the Fourteenth Amendment is only such action as may fairly be said to be that of the States. That Amendment erects no shield against merely private conduct, however discriminatory or wrongful.

We conclude, therefore, that the restrictive agreements standing alone cannot be regarded as a violation of any rights guaranteed to petitioners by the Fourteenth Amendment. So long as the purposes of those agreements are effectuated by voluntary adherence to their terms, it would appear clear that there has been no action by the State and the provisions of the Amendment have not been violated.

But here there was more. [T]he purposes of the agreements were secured only by judicial enforcement by state courts of the restrictive terms of the agreements. The respondents urge that judicial enforcement of private agreements does not amount to state action; or, in any event, the participation of the State is so attenuated in character as not to amount to state action within the meaning of the Fourteenth Amendment. Finally, it is suggested, even if the States in these cases may be deemed to have acted in the constitutional sense, their action did not deprive petitioners of rights guaranteed by the Fourteenth Amendment. We move to a consideration of these matters.

That the action of state courts and of judicial officers in their official capacities is to be regarded as action of the State within the meaning of the Fourteenth Amendment, is a proposition which has long been established by decisions of this Court. That principle was given expression in the earliest cases involving the construction of the terms of the Fourteenth Amendment. Thus, in Commonwealth of Virginia v. Rives, 1880, 100 U.S. 313, 318, 25 L.Ed. 667, this Court stated: "It is doubtless true that a State may act through different agencies,—either by its legislative, its executive, or its judicial authorities; and the prohibitions of the amendment extend to all action of the State denying equal protection of the laws, whether it be action by one of these agencies or by another."

* * *

One of the earliest applications of the prohibitions contained in the Fourteenth Amendment to action of state judicial officials occurred in cases in which Negroes had been excluded from jury service in criminal prosecutions by reason of their race or color. These cases demonstrate, also, the early recognition by this Court that state action in violation of the Amendment's provisions is equally repugnant to the constitutional commands whether directed by state statute or taken by a judicial official in the absence of statute.

* * *

The short of the matter is that from the time of the adoption of the Fourteenth Amendment until the present, it has been the consistent ruling of this Court that the action of the States to which the Amendment has reference, includes action of state courts and state judicial officials. Although, in construing the terms of the Fourteenth Amendment, differences have from time to time been expressed as to whether particular types of state action may be said to offend the Amendment's prohibitory provisions, it has never been suggested that state court action is immunized from the operation of those provisions simply because the act is that of the judicial branch of the state government.

* * * We have no doubt that there has been state action in these cases in the full and complete sense of the phrase. The undisputed facts disclose that petitioners were willing purchasers of properties upon which they desired to establish homes. The owners of the properties were willing sellers; and contracts of sale were accordingly consummated. It is clear that but for the active intervention of the state courts, supported by the full panoply of state power, petitioners would have been free to occupy the properties in question without restraint.

These are not cases, as has been suggested, in which the States have merely abstained from action, leaving private individuals free to impose such discriminations as they see fit. Rather, these are cases in which the States have made available to such individuals the full coercive power of government to deny to petitioners, on the grounds of race or color, the enjoyment of property rights in premises which petitioners are willing and financially able to acquire and which the grantors are willing to sell. The difference between judicial enforcement and nonenforcement of the restrictive covenants is the difference to petitioners between being denied rights of property available to other members of the community and being accorded full enjoyment of those rights on an equal footing.

* * * We hold that in granting judicial enforcement of the restrictive agreements in these cases, the States have denied petitioners the equal protection of the laws and that, therefore, the action of the state courts cannot stand. * * *

Reversed.

NOTES AND QUESTIONS

1. The Court's reasoning that judicial enforcement of a restrictive covenant is "state action" has the potential to destroy the ancient distinction between "private" and "public" law: even a contract between two people involves "state action" if it must be enforced in a court. The result was an increasing erosion between the "public-private" distinction in American law. See M. Horwitz, The Transformation of American Law, 1870–1960: the Crisis of Legal Orthodoxy 206–209 (1992). With respect to this question, however, Shelley v. Kraemer has generally been limited to its facts. See, e.g., Casa Marie v. Superior Court of Puerto Rico, 988 F.2d 252 (1st Cir.1993) (judicial enforcement of private "single-family only" restrictive covenant so as to exclude elder-care facility was not unconstitutional "state action" under *Shelley*).

2.   Enforcement of a restrictive covenant requires help from a court and thus falls within the Fourteenth Amendment's state action doctrine. However, the fee simple determinable, as you will recall from Chapter 4, "automatically" terminates an estate upon the occurrence of a specified limitation. Could someone make an end run around *Shelley* by creating a racially restrictive fee simple determinable? In Charlotte Park & Recreation Commission v. Barringer, 242 N.C. 311, 88 S.E.2d 114 (1955), cert. denied 350 U.S. 983 (1956), the court opined that no state action was involved in mere judicial "recognition" that a fee simple determinable had been terminated.

However, the Supreme Court of Colorado squarely disagreed in Capitol Federal Savings & Loan Assoc. v. Smith, 136 Colo. 265, 316 P.2d 252 (1957) (en banc), involving racially restrictive agreements that provided for automatic forfeiture of title in the case of violation. Those defending the restrictions argued that they created executory interests which "vested automatically in the defendants upon the happening of the events specified in the original instrument of grant, and the validity of the vesting did not in any way depend upon judicial action by the courts." The Colorado Supreme Court replied:

> Covenants such as the one here considered, whether denominated "executory interests" or "future interests" . . . cannot change the character of what was here attempted.

* * *

No matter by what ariose terms the covenant under consideration may be classified by astute counsel, it is still a racial restriction in violation of the Fourteenth Amendment of the Federal Constitution. Id. at 269–270, 316 P.2d at 254–255.

LEGISLATED RESIDENTIAL SEGREGATION: A NOTE ON BUCHANAN V. WARLEY

Shelley v. Kraemer represented a major turning point in the Supreme Court's treatment of racial segregation. Earlier it had not only upheld various "private" arrangements for enforcing segregation, it had even approved some statutes that mandated segregation. For example, in Berea College v. Kentucky, 211 U.S. 45 (1908), it upheld a state statute that mandated racial segregation of schools.

One of the most tragic episodes in American racial history occurred in the second decade of the twentieth century and, ironically, was a product of the newly developed social sciences, especially sociology and educational psychology. Early in the twentieth century the social sciences were dominated by a genetic determinism which held that racial intermarriage would produce inferior children. The result of this thinking in many cities was a response that can only be described as hysterical. Several municipalities passed "racial zoning" ordinances designed to prevent black and white people from living in too close contact. For example, the Louisville, Kentucky, ordinance prevented any black person from moving into "any house upon any block upon which a greater number of houses are occupied . . . by white people than are occupied . . . by colored people." The ordinance contained a similar provision that applied to white people. The intent of the statute was that eventually every block in the city would be segregated as between black and white residents.

In Buchanan v. Warley, 245 U.S. 60 (1917), the Supreme Court declared the Louisville ordinance unconstitutional, not because it discriminated by race, but because it interfered with every person's "liberty of contract" to sell his home to whomever he pleased. (The constitutional right of liberty of contract, which came to an end in 1937, basically gave private persons the right to enter into legal contracts free of state regulation.) The case was a major triumph for the newly organized National Association for the Advancement of Colored People (NAACP). See Hovenkamp, Social Science and Segregation Before Brown, 1985 Duke L.J. 624; and the very good colloquium on Buchanan, including a variety of perspectives, in 51 Vand.L.Rev. 787 (1998).

One reaction to *Buchanan* was that white people who wanted to assure themselves of perpetually segregated neighborhoods began to look for alternatives to segregation ordinances. The doctrine of "liberty of contract" applied only to *governmental* interference with each person's right to purchase or sell property. Many people hit upon the idea of using private, racially restrictive covenants to ensure that a house, once so encumbered, would never again be occupied by someone who was black. In Corrigan v. Buckley, 271 U.S. 323 (1926), the Supreme Court found that such covenants raised no federal questions because they were not forbidden by the Thirteenth Amendment, which abolished slavery, and they were not prohibited by the Fourteenth Amendment, which reached only state action. As a result, racially restrictive covenants were in widespread use until Shelley v. Kraemer.

§ 12.3 HOUSING DISCRIMINATION AND FEDERAL LAW: THE 1866 CIVIL RIGHTS ACT AND THE 1968 FAIR HOUSING ACT

The Civil Rights Act of 1866, 42 U.S.C.A. § 1982 provides that:

All citizens of the United States shall have the same right, in every State and Territory, as is enjoyed by white citizens thereof to inherit, purchase, lease, sell, hold, and convey real and personal property.

The Civil Rights Act of 1968, Title VIII ("The Fair Housing Act," or FHA), 42 U.S.C.A. §§ 3601–3631 provides in part as follows:

§ 3601. *Declaration of policy*

It is the policy of the United States to provide, within constitutional limitations, for fair housing throughout the United States.

* * *

§ 3603. *Effective dates of certain prohibitions*

(a) Application to certain described dwellings

* * *

(b) Exemptions

Nothing in section 3604 of this title (other than subsection (c)) shall apply to—

(1) any single-family house sold or rented by an owner: *Provided,* That such private individual owner does not own more than three such single-family houses at any one time: *Provided further,* That in the case of the sale of any such single-family house by a private individual owner not residing in such house at the time of such sale or who was not the most recent resident of such house prior to such sale, the exemption granted by this subsection shall apply only with respect to one such sale within any twenty-four month period: *Provided further,* That such bona fide private individual owner does not own any interest in, nor is there owned or reserved on his behalf, under any express or voluntary agreement, title to or any right to all or a portion of the proceeds from the sale or rental of, more than three such single-family houses at any one time: *Provided further,* That after December 31, 1969, the sale or rental of any such single-family house shall be excepted from the application of this subchapter only if such house is sold or rented (A) without the use in any manner of the sales or rental facilities or the sales or rental services of any real estate broker, agent, or salesman, or of such facilities or services of any person in the business of selling or renting dwellings, or of any employee or agent of any such broker, agent, salesman, or person and (B) without the publication, posting or mailing, after notice, of any advertisement or written notice in violation of section 3604(c) of this title; but nothing in this proviso shall prohibit the use of attorneys, escrow agents, abstractors, title companies, and other such professional assistance as necessary to perfect or transfer the title, or

(2) rooms or units in dwellings containing living quarters occupied or intended to be occupied by no more than four families living independently of each other, if the owner actually maintains and occupies one of such living quarters as his residence.

* * *

§ 3604. *Discrimination in the sale or rental of housing and other prohibited practices*

As made applicable by section 3603 of this title and except as exempted by sections 3603(b) and 3607 of this title, it shall be unlawful—

(a) To refuse to sell or rent after the making of a bona fide offer, or to refuse to negotiate for the sale or rental of, or otherwise make unavailable or deny, a dwelling to any person because of race, color, religion, sex, familial status, or national origin.

(b) To discriminate against any person in the terms, conditions, or privileges of sale or rental of a dwelling, or in the provision of services or facilities in connection therewith, because of race, color, religion, sex, familial status, or national origin.

(c) To make, print, or publish, or cause to be made, printed, or published any notice, statement, or advertisement, with respect to the sale or rental of a dwelling that indicates any preference, limitation, or discrimination based on race, color, religion, sex, handicap, familial status, or national origin, or an intention to make any such preference, limitation, or discrimination.

(d) To represent to any person because of race, color, religion, sex, handicap, familial status, or national origin that any dwelling is not available for inspection, sale, or rental when such dwelling is in fact so available.

(e) For profit, to induce or attempt to induce any person to sell or rent any dwelling by representations regarding the entry or prospective entry into the neighborhood of a person or persons of a particular race, color, religion, sex, handicap, familial status, or national origin.

(f)(1) To discriminate in the sale or rental, or to otherwise make unavailable or deny, a dwelling to any buyer or renter because of a handicap of—

    (A) that buyer or renter;

    (B) a person residing in or intending to reside in that dwelling after it is so sold, rented, or made available; or

    (C) any person associated with that buyer or renter.

(2) To discriminate against any person in the terms, conditions, or privileges of sale or rental of a dwelling, or in the provision of services or facilities in connection with such dwelling, because of a handicap of—

    (A) that person; or

    (B) a person residing in or intending to reside in that dwelling after it is so sold, rented, or made available; or

    (C) any person associated with that person.

(3) For purposes of this subsection, discrimination includes—

    (A) a refusal to permit, at the expense of the handicapped person, reasonable modifications of existing premises occupied or to be occupied by such person if such modifications may be necessary to afford such person full enjoyment of the premises except that, in the case of a rental, the landlord may where it is reasonable to do so condition permission for a modification on the renter agreeing to restore the interior of the premises to the condition that existed before the modification, reasonable wear and tear excepted;

    (B) a refusal to make reasonable accommodations in rules, policies, practices, or services, when such accommodations may be necessary to afford such person equal opportunity to use and enjoy a dwelling; or

(C) in connection with the design and construction of covered multifamily dwellings for first occupancy after the date that is 30 months after September 13, 1988, a failure to design and construct those dwellings in such a manner that—

(i) the public use and common use portions of such dwellings are readily accessible to and usable by handicapped persons;

(ii) all the doors designed to allow passage into and within all premises within such dwellings are sufficiently wide to allow passage by handicapped persons in wheelchairs; and

(iii) all premises within such dwellings contain the following features of adaptive design:

(I) an accessible route into and through the dwelling;

(II) light switches, electrical outlets, thermostats, and other environmental controls in accessible locations;

(III) reinforcements in bathroom walls to allow later installation of grab bars; and

(IV) usable kitchens and bathrooms such that an individual in a wheelchair can maneuver about the space.

(4) Compliance with the appropriate requirements of the American National Standard for buildings and facilities providing accessibility and usability for physically handicapped people (commonly cited as "ANSI A117.1") suffices to satisfy the requirements of paragraph (3)(C)(iii).

* * *

(9) Nothing in this subsection requires that a dwelling be made available to an individual whose tenancy would constitute a direct threat to the health or safety of other individuals or whose tenancy would result in substantial physical damage to the property of others.

* * *

§ 3607. *Exemptions*

(a) Religious organizations and private clubs

Nothing in this subchapter shall prohibit a religious organization, association, or society, or any nonprofit institution or organization operated, supervised or controlled by or in conjunction with a religious organization, association, or society, from limiting the sale, rental or occupancy of dwellings which it owns or operates for other than a commercial purpose to persons of the same religion, or from giving preference to such persons, unless membership in such religion is restricted on account of race, color, or national origin....

(b) Numbers of occupants; housing for older persons; ...

(1) Nothing in this subchapter limits the applicability of any reasonable local, State, or Federal restrictions regarding the maximum number of occupants permitted to occupy a dwelling. Nor does any provision in this subchapter regarding familial status apply with respect to housing for older persons. (2) As used in this section, "housing for older persons" means housing—(A) provided under any State or Federal program that the Secretary determines is specifically designed and operated to assist elderly persons (as defined in the State or Federal program); or (B) intended for, and solely occupied by, persons 62 years of age or older; or (C) intended and operated for occupancy by at least one person 55 years of age or older, and—

(i) at least 80 percent of the occupied units are occupied by at least one person who is 55 years of age or older;

(ii) the housing facility or community publishes and adheres to policies and procedures that demonstrate the intent required under this subparagraph; and

(iii) the housing facility or community complies with rules issued by the Secretary for verification of occupancy, ...

§ 3613. Enforcement by Private Persons

(a) Civil Action

(1)(A) An aggrieved person may commence a civil action in an appropriate United States district court or State court not later than 2 years after the occurrence or the termination of an alleged discriminatory housing practice....

(c) Relief Which May be Granted

(1) In a civil action under subsection (a) of this section, if the court finds that a discriminatory housing practice has occurred or is about to occur, the court may award to the plaintiff actual and punitive damages, and.... [a] permanent or temporary injunction....

(2) ... the court, in its discretion, may allow the prevailing party, other than the United States, a reasonable attorney's fee and costs.

Notes and Questions

1. Does § 1982 of the Civil Rights Act of 1866 strike you as a complete fair housing law? What rights does it actually confer and to whom? The statute purports to cover all "citizens of the United States." What does this mean? Are white people protected from adverse discrimination by others? Could a landlord refuse to rent an apartment to a recently arrived Polish

immigrant? See Vietnamese Fishermen's Assn. v. Knights of the Ku Klux Klan, 518 F.Supp. 993 (S.D.Tex.1981) (statute protects only citizens of the United States, but issuing injunction under other civil rights laws).

In Jones v. Alfred H. Mayer Co., 392 U.S. 409, 413–16 (1968), the Supreme Court concluded:

> Whatever else it may be, 42 U.S.C.A. § 1982 is not a comprehensive open housing law. In sharp contrast to the Fair Housing Title (Title VIII) of the Civil Rights Act of 1968 ... the statute in this case deals only with racial discrimination and does not address itself to discrimination on grounds of religion or national origin. It does not deal specifically with discrimination in the provision of services or facilities in connection with the sale or rental of a dwelling. It does not prohibit advertising or other representations that indicate discriminatory preferences. It does not refer explicitly to discrimination in financing arrangements or in the provision of brokerage services. It does not empower a federal administrative agency to assist aggrieved parties. It makes no provision for intervention by the Attorney General. And, although it can be enforced by injunction, it contains no provision expressly authorizing a federal court to order the payment of damages.

> Thus, although § 1982 contains none of the exemptions that Congress included in the Civil Rights Act of 1968, it would be a serious mistake to suppose that § 1982 in any way diminishes the significance of the law recently enacted by Congress. Indeed, the Senate Subcommittee on Housing and Urban Affairs was informed in hearings held after the Court of Appeals had rendered its decision in this case that § 1982 might well be "a presently valid federal statutory ban against discrimination by private persons in the sale or lease of real property." The Subcommittee was told, however, that even if this Court should so construe § 1982, the existence of that statute would not "eliminate the need for congressional action" to spell out the "responsibility on the part of the federal government to enforce the rights it protects." The point was made that, in light of the many difficulties confronted by private litigants seeking to enforce such rights on their own, "legislation is needed to establish federal machinery for enforcement of the rights guaranteed under Section 1982 of Title 42...."

In other ways, however, § 1982 may actually be broader than the FHA. For example, the FHA contains an exemption from parts of its coverage for single family homes or apartment buildings of four units or less if the owner lives in one of them. The Civil War era statute contains no such exemptions. See Johnson v. Zaremba, 381 F.Supp. 165 (N.D.Il.1973) (defendant who was exempt under FHA because he lived in one of the units in building that he rented was not exempt from 1866 Civil Rights Act).

2. The FHA was originally passed in 1968. A 1974 amendment added gender ("sex") as a protected classification. In 1988 familial status and handicap were added as protected classifications.

Sections 3610, 3612 and 3613 of the FHA set forth the principal remedies available to aggrieved persons. A person who has been the subject of impermissible discrimination has a cause of action against the violator for damages and injunctive relief. The court may award a prevailing party, whether plaintiff or defendant, costs and attorneys' fees. 42 U.S.C.A. §§ 3612(a) & (c). An aggrieved person may also file a complaint with the Secretary of Housing and Urban Development. 42 U.S.C.A. § 3610. Lastly, the Attorney General is empowered to bring suits against any person who is engaged in a pattern or practice of discrimination. 42 U.S.C.A. § 3613.

3. An elderly man places the following advertisement in the local paper: "Furnished apartment located in a high rise apartment building, well located, clean, quiet. Gentlemen only. $34 a week. Call JO3–5493." Does the "gentlemen only" language constitute impermissible sex discrimination? See Braunstein v. Dwelling Managers, Inc., 476 F.Supp. 1323 (S.D.N.Y.1979). See generally, Karst, The Freedom of Intimate Association, 89 Yale L.J. 624 (1980).

Do you suppose any member of the Congresses that passed or amended the FHA believed it should prevent gender based selection of one's roommate? How about race-based selections? Does the FHA exempt such choices? Note that the exemption stated in § 3603 for landlords who live themselves in small buildings containing four or fewer units applies only when there are four or fewer "families living independently of each other. . . ." Further, the only person exempted is the "owner." Is it clear that a person renting a two bedroom apartment and seeking a roommate qualifies for the exemption? Further, note that the "make, print, or publish" provision of § 3604(c) is excluded from the exemption. Thus an advertisement stating "female roommate wanted" violates the statute. Nevertheless such statements appear thousands of times in newspapers across the country. In 1986, the U.S. Department of Justice made this informal statement of its enforcement policy:

> The Department will not take legal action where sexual preferences are stated in ads involving shared living facilities, but such ads cannot legally include a preference or limitation based on race, religion, or national origin.

Of course, that statement does not limit the rights of private plaintiffs. See Wilson v. Glenwood Intermountain Properties, Inc., 98 F.3d 590 (10th Cir. 1996) (denying standing to nonstudents to challenge advertising and some provision of gender segregated housing to BYU students).

4. Suppose L places the following advertisement in the local newspaper: "Apartment for rent. Tenant may not be an attorney." Or how about "Tenants must not be housing activists." Any violations of the FHA? See Kramarsky v. Stahl Management, 92 Misc.2d 1030, 401 N.Y.S.2d 943 (1977).

5. Suppose a clerk in the registry of deeds accepts for recordation a deed containing a racially restrictive covenant. Has he violated the "make, print, or publish" provision of § 3604 of the FHA, reprinted supra? Does it matter that racially restrictive covenants are unenforceable under Shelley v. Kraemer, supra? Or does it matter even more that the average layperson examining a deed containing such a covenant would not know that they are unenforceable? Compare Woodward v. Bowers, 630 F.Supp. 1205 (M.D.Pa.1986), with Mayers v. Ridley, 465 F.2d 630 (D.C.Cir.1972).

When now Chief Justice Rehnquist was being questioned by the Senate prior to his confirmation, he was accused of racial insensitivity because in 1974 he had purchased a house subject to a racially restrictive covenant. His answer was that virtually everyone knew that such covenants were unenforceable. See 12A The Supreme Court of the United States: Hearings and Reports on Successful and Unsuccessful Nominations of Supreme Court Justices 1510–1511 (Mersky & Jacobstein eds., 1989). Was that an appropriate question, or did Justice Rehnquist get a bum rap? Liberal former San Francisco mayor and now U.S. Senator Diane Feinstein once did the same thing. See Roisman, The Lessons of American Apartheid: the Necessity and Means of Promoting Residential Racial Integration, 81 Iowa L. Rev. 471, 525 (1995). Suppose you did a title search of a house you were about to purchase and found such a covenant. What could you do about it?

6. Jancik v. Department of Housing and Urban Development, 44 F.3d 553 (7th Cir.1995), concluded that a landlord's advertisement stating "mature person preferred" violated the FHA under the "ordinary reader" test. An ordinary reader might interpret the statement as reflecting a preference based on familial status. The court found this statement alone to be discriminatory, although it also relied on evidence that when a "tester" telephoned he was told by the landlord that the landlord wanted someone without children and did not want teenagers in the building. Under the familial status provision a landlord may still refuse to rent to a large family because, in his judgment, the number is to large for an apartment of a given size. But he had better make clear that that is the reason. See Sams v. HUD, 76 F.3d 375 (4th Cir.1996) (landlord's ambiguous refusal to rent to a family with five children violated the statute).

See also Campbell v. Robb, 162 Fed.Appx. 460 (6th Cir. 2006, unpublished) (prospective landlord who told prospective tenant that she would rent to her even though her fiancé was Afro–American, but she did not want "black people hanging around in my parking lot" violated 3604(c) because the statement was "related to the decisional process" of renting the dwelling).

7. New York State Assn. of Realtors v. Shaffer, 27 F.3d 834 (2d Cir.), cert. denied, 513 U.S. 1000 (1994), held that regulations forbidding real estate brokers from making representations about the entry of minorities into a certain neighborhood ("blockbusting"—see FHA at § 3604e) did not violate the First Amendment even when the statements were truthful and not misleading.

HARRIS v. ITZHAKI
United States Court of Appeals, Ninth Circuit (1999).
183 F.3d 1043.

HUG, CHIEF JUDGE:

Anna Harris was a tenant of an apartment complex owned by the defendants at the time she filed an action under the Fair Housing Act for racial discrimination....

Rafael and Edna Itzhaki (the "Itzhakis") own the property located at 1123 South Shenandoah Street in Los Angeles, California (the "Shenandoah Apartments"). Leah Waldman, an elderly tenant, has assisted the Itzhakis in the operation of the Shenandoah Apartments since they purchased the property. Ms. Waldman's assistance includes keeping spare keys of all the units, receiving rent checks, and showing vacant apartments to prospective tenants.

Generally, Mr. Itzhaki would instruct prospective tenants to contact Ms. Waldman in order to inspect a vacant unit available for rent at the Shenandoah Apartments. Mr. Itzhaki would then notify Ms. Waldman that prospective tenants would be visiting. Ms. Waldman would give the unit keys to prospective tenants to inspect units, and then give the prospective tenants rental applications along with the Itzhakis' telephone number for application submission. Finally, Ms. Waldman would call Mr. Itzhaki to inform him when prospective tenants visited the property.

Ms. Waldman also collected the rent checks for the Itzhakis. The tenants were instructed to pay their rent to Ms. Waldman or to leave it under her doormat. Ms. Waldman would then communicate to the Itzhakis who has paid rent and who has not.

Anna Harris became a resident of the Shenandoah Apartments in October 1994. Ms. Harris is the only African–American that the Itzhakis have ever rented to at this property. On December 6, 1995, Ms. Harris overheard a conversation between Ms. Waldman and the repairman/gardener regarding a recent vacancy in the building, in which Ms. Waldman stated, "The owners don't want to rent to Blacks." Ms. Harris immediately informed Ms. Waldman that her comments were "illegal and racist."

Ms. Harris complained to the Westside Fair Housing Council based on Ms. Waldman's statement. In response to that complaint, Westside Fair Housing Council tested the Shenandoah Apartments for racial discrimination through the use of black and white fair housing testers.

On December 21, 1995, Faith Bautista, a white fair housing tester posing as a prospective tenant, called Mr. Itzhaki and spoke with him regarding the vacancy at the Shenandoah Apartments. Mr. Itzhaki told Ms. Bautista that the rent was $700 per month. He did not inquire into Ms. Bautista's marital status or her current residence. He also made no negative remarks about the rental premises or area. Instead, he told Ms. Bautista how to go about seeing the unit.

Approximately four hours later on that same day, Karla Ford, a black fair housing tester posing as a prospective tenant, called Mr. Itzhaki and spoke with him regarding the same vacancy at the Shenandoah Apartments. Mr. Itzhaki initially told Ms. Ford that the unit rented for $700 per month, but after inquiring about Ms. Ford's marital status, indicated that there would be an extra charge of $50 per month for two persons in a one-bedroom. Mr. Itzhaki told her that the place was small and that they usually preferred to rent to singles. He also stated that there was only one parking space with the unit and that since she was married she would need two spaces. Mr. Itzhaki then asked Ms. Ford where she was currently residing. When she said Culver City, Mr. Itzhaki commented that Culver

City was a better area for safety reasons and questioned Ms. Ford why she would want the available unit, reiterating that the unit was small. Mr. Itzhaki then asked Ms. Ford where she and her husband worked, and closed with telling her how to inspect the unit and repeating that the unit was really small.

The following day, Karla Ford contacted Leah Waldman at the Shenandoah Apartments to inspect the vacant unit. Ms. Waldman gave her the key to the unit. After viewing the apartment, Ms. Ford told Ms. Waldman that she liked the unit. Ms. Waldman gave Ms. Ford two applications (one "just in case") and instructed her to copy down the owner's telephone number from the rental sign posted outside. When Ms. Ford asked about the rental price, application fee and security deposit, Ms. Waldman told her that she would have to speak to the owner because Ms. Waldman "didn't know anything." This conversation took place in Ms. Waldman's doorway.

Twenty minutes after Ms. Ford left the Shenandoah Apartments, Faith Bautista arrived and contacted Ms. Waldman to inspect the vacant unit. After viewing the unit, Ms. Bautista asked Ms. Waldman about the rent and security deposit. Ms. Waldman said that the apartment rented for $700, with a $700 security deposit for a $1,400 move-in requirement. When Ms. Bautista indicated that she liked the unit, Ms. Waldman invited Ms. Bautista into her apartment and called the owner so that Ms. Bautista could discuss the details with the owner. Ms. Waldman introduced Ms. Bautista as "a beautiful girl who I'd love to have as my neighbor here, who would like to talk to you." During Ms. Bautista's conversation with Ms. Itzhaki, she was not told of any "extra charge" for two persons in a one-bedroom, despite informing Ms. Itzhaki that she was married. At the conclusion of the conversation, Ms. Waldman gave Ms. Bautista an application and the owner's fax number.

After Ms. Harris made the complaint to Westside Fair Housing Council she received two notices to pay rent or quit (for April 1996 and May 1996). Ms. Harris maintains that she left her rent checks under her doormat, pursuant to the accepted practice at the apartment. Mr. Itzhaki claimed that the rent checks were not there on time. Although the Itzhakis have no formal policy on issuing three-day notices, they followed an informal procedure where Ms. Itzhaki would call the tenant whose rent had not been received by the tenth of the month. If the tenant failed to respond to the demand for payment, then the Itzhakis would proceed with a three-day notice. Ms. Harris maintains that she was not called or given any warning prior to receiving the three-day notices.... Thereafter, Ms. Harris paid her rent by certified mail.

On June 12, 1996, Ms. Harris filed a complaint in the United States District Court for the Central District of California alleging that the Itzhakis discriminated against African–Americans on the basis of race or color in the operation of their apartment complex, in violation of the federal Fair Housing Act ("FHA"), 42 U.S.C. §§ 3601, *et seq*....

I. Standing

* * * The Supreme Court has long held that claims brought under the Fair Housing Act are to be judged under a very liberal standing requirement. Unlike actions brought under other provisions of civil rights law, under the FHA the plaintiff need not allege that he or she was a victim of discrimination. *See Gladstone Realtors v. Village of Bellwood,* 441 U.S. 91, 115, 99 S.Ct. 1601 (1979) (holding that Caucasian residents have standing under the Act to challenge racial discrimination against African–Americans in their neighborhood). Rather, the sole requirement for standing under the Act is the "Article III minima of injury in fact." *Havens Realty Corp. v. Coleman,* 455 U.S. 363, 372, 102 S.Ct. 1114, 71 L.Ed.2d 214 (1982). To meet this requirement, a plaintiff need only allege "that as a result of the defendant's [discriminatory conduct] he has suffered a distinct and palpable injury."

Under the Act, any person harmed by discrimination, *whether or not the target of the discrimination,* can sue to recover for his or her own injury. *See Trafficante v. Metropolitan Life Ins. Co.,* 409 U.S. 205, 212, 93 S.Ct. 364, 34 L.Ed.2d 415 (1972).

* * * The district court limited its analysis to Ms. Harris' claim of an indirect injury for alleged differential treatment of the rental testers. Following *Trafficante* . . ., we conclude that Ms. Harris can maintain an action based solely on such an indirect injury because she has alleged that she suffered "a distinct and palpable injury" resulting from the differential treatment. . . . Furthermore, Ms. Harris also claims that she has been injured directly by the eviction notices given contrary to established policy and claims injury from Ms. Waldman's discriminatory statement, both independent violations under the Fair Housing Act. Consequently, we conclude the evidence establishes that Ms. Harris is an "aggrieved person" and entitled to maintain an action under the Fair Housing Act.

* * *

II. Discrimination Claims Under the Fair Housing Act

"We apply Title VII discrimination analysis in examining Fair Housing Act discrimination claims." *Gamble v. City of Escondido,* 104 F.3d 300, 304 (9th Cir.1997). A plaintiff can establish a FHA discrimination claim under a theory of disparate treatment or disparate impact. To bring a disparate treatment claim, the plaintiff must first establish a prima facie case. Adapted to this situation, the prima facie case elements are: (1) plaintiff's rights are protected under the FHA; and (2) as a result of the defendant's discriminatory conduct, plaintiff has suffered a distinct and palpable injury. Establishing the prima facie case affords the plaintiff a presumption of discrimination. This test does not permit the court to consider rebuttal evidence at the prima facie case stage. *Lowe,* 775 F.2d at 1006.

After the plaintiff has established the prima facie case, the burden then must shift to the defendant to articulate some legitimate, nondiscriminatory reason for the action. *See McDonnell Douglas Corp. v. Green,* 411 U.S. 792, 802, 93 S.Ct. 1817 (1973). To accomplish this, the defendant is only required to set forth a legally sufficient explanation. *Texas Dept. of Community Affairs v. Burdine,* 450 U.S. 248, 255, 101 S.Ct. 1089 (1981).

Assuming the defendant can successfully rebut the presumption of discrimination, the burden shifts back to the plaintiff to raise a genuine factual question as to whether the proffered reason is pretextual. *Id.* at 255–56, 101 S.Ct. 1089. A plaintiff may succeed in persuading the court that she has been a victim of intentional discrimination, "either directly by persuading the court that a discriminatory reason more likely motivated the [defendant] or indirectly by showing that the [defendant's] proffered explanation is unworthy of credence." The trier of fact may consider the same evidence that the plaintiff introduced to establish a prima facie case in determining whether the defendant's explanation is merely pretext. "Once a prima facie case is established ... summary judgment for the defendant will ordinarily not be appropriate on any ground relating to the merits because the crux of a [discrimination claim] is the elusive factual question of intentional discrimination." *Lowe,* 775 F.2d at 1009.

* * *

Ms. Harris raises three independent claims under the FHA: (1) for eviction notices contrary to established policy; (2) for disparate treatment of rental testers; and (3) for the discriminatory statement by Ms. Waldman. Central to this analysis is the characterization of evidence by the parties. Appellees seek to consider and justify each piece of evidence separately. In contrast, Ms. Harris asks this court to look at the evidence as components of a larger whole.

The FHA makes it unlawful to: (1) deny a dwelling to any person because of race (42 U.S.C. § 3604(a); 24 C.F.R. § 100.50(b)(1)); (2) discriminate against any person in the *terms, conditions* or privileges of rental of a dwelling because of race (42 U.S.C. § 3604(b); 24 C.F.R. § 100.50(b)(2)); and (3) coerce, intimidate, threaten, or interfere with any person in the exercise or enjoyment of any right granted or protected by §§ 3603–06 of this title (42 U.S.C. § 3617). Additionally, HUD regulations state that it is unlawful to use different provisions in leases or contracts of sale, such as those relating to rental charges because of race. (24 C.F.R. § 100.65(b)(1)).

Ms. Harris confronted Ms. Waldman regarding her discriminatory statement in December 1995. Four months later, the Itzhakis contend they did not find her check under Ms. Harris' doormat, the previously agreed method of payment. The accepted practice was for Mrs. Itzhaki to call the tenant before sending a three-day notice. The following month, the same incident occurred, causing Ms. Harris to send all subsequent payments by certified mail. Ms. Harris presented evidence that she suffered emotional distress as a result of the notices and feared a racially motivated eviction in the future. Under these facts, we conclude that Ms.

Harris has established a prima facie disparate treatment claim under the FHA....

The Itzhakis contend that the check wasn't there. They assert that the check could have been stolen or lost within the unsecured building. Furthermore, while the Itzhakis don't remember calling Ms. Harris, they contend that this is merely a courtesy and consequently should not implicate FHA liability. Here the Itzhakis have provided a nondiscriminatory reason for their action—that they simply didn't get the check and that the phone call is merely a courtesy to the tenant.

Ms. Harris contends that the Itzhakis' explanation is merely pretext, citing circumstantial and direct evidence from her other claims, including the discriminatory statement by Ms. Waldman and the treatment of the rental testers. Under these facts, applying the shifting burden analysis of *McDonnell Douglas* and *Burdine,* we conclude that there is genuine factual question as to whether the Itzhakis' nondiscriminatory reason is pretextual, thereby making summary judgment inappropriate. *See also Lowe,* 775 F.2d at 1009; *Smith v. Town of Clarkton,* 682 F.2d 1055, 1066 (4th Cir.1982) (holding that deviations from a procedural norm are suspect when they lead to results impacting more harshly on one race than on another). We reverse the district court's dismissal of Harris' eviction notice claim to the extent that retrospective relief is available.

Disparate Treatment of Rental Testers

The FHA makes it unlawful to represent to any person because of race that any dwelling is not available for inspection or rental when such dwelling is in fact so available. 42 U.S.C. § 3604(d). Additionally, HUD regulations state that it is unlawful to: (1) provide false or inaccurate information regarding the availability of a dwelling for rental to any person, including testers, regardless of whether such person is actually seeking housing, because of race (24 C.F.R. § 100.80(b)(5)); (2) discourage any person from inspecting or renting a dwelling because of race (24 C.F.R. § 100.70(c)(1)); (3) discourage the rental of a dwelling because of race by exaggerating drawbacks or failing to inform any person of desirable features of a dwelling or of a community, neighborhood or development (24 C.F.R. § 100.70(c)(2)); and (4) deny or delay the processing of an application made by a renter because of race (24 C.F.R. § 100.70(d)(3)).

The rental testers were treated differently by Mr. Itzhaki with regard to: (1) the owner's rental preferences (no preference told to white tester; black tester told that owner prefers singles); (2) the rent charged ($700 for white tester; black tester told that owner may charge an additional $50 for two people); (3) description of the unit (a one bedroom for the white tester; black tester told unit is really small); and (4) safety of the neighborhood (safety not discussed with white tester; black tester told area unsafe).

The testers were also treated differently by Ms. Waldman with regard to: (1) the terms of the rental (white tester told rent, deposit & total move-in cost; black tester told to contact owner); (2) encouragement to pursue the property (white tester invited into Ms. Waldman's home to call owner; black tester told to get owner's telephone number from sign outside); (3) endorsement to the owner (white tester introduced as "a beautiful girl who I'd love to have as my neighbor"; black tester was not endorsed to the owner). Under these facts, we conclude that Ms. Harris has established a prima facie disparate treatment claim under the FHA—that the black tester as a protected class member was discouraged from renting the apartment, while the white tester was given preferential treatment, and as a result of these actions, Ms. Harris was deprived of the opportunity to live in an apartment free of housing discrimination.

Again, the Itzhakis provide a nondiscriminatory reason—that the distinctions between these conversations are the consequence of bad timing and differing personality types, rather than discriminatory intent. Ms. Harris again contends that the Itzhakis' explanation is merely pretext. A reasonable inference can be drawn from these facts that Mr. Itzhaki sought to discourage the black tester, citing safety and size. Ms. Harris argues that these actions are inconsistent with an interest to fill a rental vacancy. Furthermore, Ms. Harris contends that Ms. Waldman serves as a filter, where Blacks are screened out for the owner. Under these facts, applying the shifting burden analysis of *McDonnell Douglas* and *Burdine,* we conclude that there is a genuine factual question as to whether the Itzhakis' nondiscriminatory reason is pretextual, thereby making summary judgment inappropriate. *See also Lowe,* 775 F.2d at 1009; *Gresham v. Windrush Partners, Ltd.,* 730 F.2d 1417, 1422 (11th Cir.1984) (upholding an injunction against landlords who offered "prospective white tenants encouragement that had not been given to blacks . . ."); *McDonald v. Verble,* 622 F.2d 1227, 1234 (6th Cir.1980) ("[D]isparity of treatment between whites and blacks, burdensome application procedures, and tactics of delay, hindrance, and special treatment must receive short shrift from the courts."). We reverse the district court's dismissal of Ms. Harris' rental tester claim to the extent that retrospective relief is available.

Ms. Waldman's Discriminatory Statement

The FHA makes it unlawful for owners or their agents to make any statement with respect to the sale or rental of a dwelling that indicates any preference, limitation, or discrimination based on color or an intention to make any such preference, limitation or discrimination. 42 U.S.C. § 3604(c); 24 C.F.R. 100.50(b)(4). Furthermore, HUD states that 42 U.S.C. § 3604(c) applies to all oral notices or statements by a person engaged in the rental of a dwelling. 24 C.F.R. 100.75(b). *See also Soules v. HUD,* 967 F.2d 817, 824 (2d Cir.1992) ("Openly discriminatory oral statements merit . . . straightforward treatment."). Ms. Harris has asserted a prima facie case of discrimination under the FHA—that Ms. Waldman's discriminatory statement caused Ms. Harris emotional distress and disruption in the quiet enjoyment of her apartment.

The Itzhakis do not contest that Ms. Waldman made the statement; rather they contend that Ms. Waldman is not an agent or employee, thereby making any statements inadmissible. We disagree. The question whether an agency relationship exists for purposes of the Fair Housing Act is determined under federal law, not state law. *Cabrera v. Jakabovitz,* 24 F.3d 372, 386 n. 13 (2d Cir.1994). The policy reason underlying the application of federal law is to avoid predicating liability for Fair Housing Act violations on the vagaries of state law. *Id.* * * *

Ms. Waldman has assisted the Itzhakis by collecting rent checks and showing vacant units to prospective tenants. Ms. Harris points to these facts supporting her contention that Ms. Waldman is an agent or employee of the Itzhakis. The Itzhakis, however, point to the fact that they don't pay Ms. Waldman or offer her any discount on rent, supporting their contention that Ms. Waldman is not their agent or employee.

HUD regulations define an agent under the FHA as "*any person authorized to perform an action* on behalf of another person *regarding any matter related* to the ... rental of dwellings, including offers, solicitations or contracts *and the administration of matters* regarding such offers, solicitations or contracts or any residential real estate-related transactions." 24 C.F.R. § 100.20 (emphasis added). Under HUD's definition, which is afforded deference, there are facts from which a jury could reasonably find that Ms. Waldman is an agent of the Itzhakis. * * *

The Itzhakis contend that Ms. Waldman's statement should be treated as a "stray" remark, insufficient to establish discrimination. If the remark is unrelated to the decisional process, then it is insufficient to show discrimination. *Merrick v. Farmers Ins. Group,* 892 F.2d 1434, 1438 (9th Cir.1990); *Smith v. Firestone Tire and Rubber Co.,* 875 F.2d 1325, 1330 (7th Cir.1989). Ms. Harris contends that Ms. Waldman acts as a filter for the Itzhakis, thereby making her comments related to her decision to recommend tenants. Viewing the evidence in the light most favorable to Harris, we cannot hold that Ms. Waldman's statement is a stray remark as a matter of law. Consequently, we reverse the district court's dismissal of Harris' discriminatory statement claim to the extent that retrospective relief is available.

* * * The district court's order dismissing Harris' claims under the Fair Housing Act for insufficient evidence is reversed.

NOTES AND QUESTIONS

1. See Meyer v. Holley, 537 U.S. 280 (2003), where the Supreme Court held that a real estate corporation could be held liable for the race discrimination of one of its employees, but that liability did not extend to the president, even though he was the only shareholder of the corporation:

> This Court has noted that an action brought for compensation by a victim of housing discrimination is, in effect, a tort action. And the Court has assumed that, when Congress creates a tort action, it legislates against a

legal background of ordinary tort-related vicarious liability rules and consequently intends its legislation to incorporate those rules. . . .

It is well established that traditional vicarious liability rules ordinarily make principals or employers vicariously liable for acts of their agents or employees in the scope of their authority or employment. "The principal is liable for the acts and negligence of the agent in the course of his employment, although he did not authorize or did not know of the acts complained of"; . . . And in the absence of special circumstances it is the corporation, not its owner or officer, who is the principal or employer, and thus subject to vicarious liability for torts committed by its employees or agents. . . .

The Ninth Circuit held that the Fair Housing Act imposed more extensive vicarious liability—that the Act went well beyond traditional principles. The Court of Appeals held that the Act made corporate owners and officers liable for the unlawful acts of a corporate employee simply on the basis that the owner or officer controlled (or had the right to control) the actions of that employee. We do not agree with the Ninth Circuit that the Act extended traditional vicarious liability rules in this way.

For one thing, Congress said nothing in the statute or in the legislative history about extending vicarious liability in this manner. And Congress' silence, while permitting an inference that Congress intended to apply *ordinary* background tort principles, cannot show that it intended to apply an unusual modification of those rules.

See also Cleveland v. Caplaw Enterp., 448 F.3d 518 (2d Cir. 2006) (manager who engaged in race discrimination was agent for landlord even though the contract specified that all tenant contacts should be made through the landlord; court noted that much race discrimination lies in the way managers deal with tenants prior to the formation of any lease); City of Chicago v. Matchmaker Real Estate Sales Center, Inc., 982 F.2d 1086, 1096–98 (7th Cir.1992), which held that the brokerage firm could be liable even though the firm had expressly instructed its agents that race discrimination was unlawful. Cf. Cabrera v. Jakabovitz, 24 F.3d 372 (2d Cir.), cert. denied, 513 U.S. 876 (1994) holding that under the doctrine of respondeat superior a landlord is liable for a real estate agency's race discrimination. Liability did not require a showing that the landlord had authorized the discrimination. Does this mean that the landlord must explicitly instruct the real estate agent not to engage in race discrimination? Why should a layperson have to instruct a real estate professional not to disobey the law? Suppose the seller or landlord does give such an instruction and the agency engages in discrimination anyway? Suppose an employee of the landlord refuses to rent to a prospective tenant on racial grounds. Has the landlord violated the statute? The answer generally is yes, for the employee is an agent of the landlord. Suppose, that a tenant of the landlord refuses to sublet an apartment to a black couple on racial grounds. Has the landlord violated the Act? Walker v. Fox, 395 F.Supp. 1303 (S.D.Ohio 1975). Should it matter whether the landlord reserved the right to approve assignments or sublets? See also Alexander v. Riga, 208 F.3d 419 (3d Cir.2000), cert. denied, 531 U.S. 1069 (2001) (husband could be held liable for race discrimination in building that he co-owned, but which his wife's company managed);

2.   In Gladstone Realtors v. Village of Bellwood, 441 U.S. 91 (1979), the Supreme Court decided that a municipality had standing to challenge racial steering by realtors as a violation of the FHA. The Court concluded that one result of steering could be depressed housing prices in certain areas, leading to a reduction in the tax base, "threatening [the city's] ability to bear the costs of local government and to provide services."

3.   Damage measurement in FHA cases can pose a problem when a defendant with a limited amount of housing discriminates against a large number of applicants. For example, if a lessor of a single residential unit turns away ten applicants because of their race, all ten have been victims of racial discrimination. However, only one could have obtained the housing. Should all ten be entitled to damages? The Sixth Circuit addressed this problem in Jordan v. Dellway Villa of Tenn., 661 F.2d 588 (6th Cir.1981), cert. denied 455 U.S. 1008 (1982). The lower court had found that the defendant apartment complex had rejected many applications from prospective residents because they were black. During the violation period the defendant had 100 vacancies, but it had received some 1200 applications from prospective black tenants. Even if the defendant had accepted applications from blacks to the exclusion of everyone else, 1100 of the black applicants would have been turned away. Furthermore, after the fact there was no way of determining which 100 would have been accepted.

Who was a "victim" of discrimination in this instance? The case was brought as a class action in behalf of all 1200 applicants. The district court held that the size of the class should be reduced to the maximum number that could have obtained an apartment had the defendant not been engaged in unlawful discrimination, holding that Congress did not intend to create a damages action for "solely intellectual discrimination." The Sixth Circuit reversed, holding that even an applicant who could not show that she would have been accepted absent the discrimination could obtain damages for emotional suffering, as well as nominal damages.

One problem with civil rights violations is that measuring the injury caused by discrimination is extraordinarily difficult. To be sure, courts can compensate for moving expenses, loss of the opportunity to rent, and so on. But how do they compensate for the "hurt" caused by the discrimination itself? In Woods v. Beavers, 922 F.2d 842 (6th Cir.) (unpublished), cert. denied, 500 U.S. 943 (1991), the trial court found that the defendant had violated the FHA by refusing to rent to an interracially married couple. The Sixth Circuit then approved this jury instruction:

> [On] the value of the loss of the plaintiffs' right not to be discriminated against. In the eyes of the law, this right is so valuable that damages are presumed from the wrongful deprivation of it without evidence of actual loss of money, property, or any other valuable thing, and the amount of damages is a question peculiarly appropriate for the determination of a jury because each member of you has personal knowledge of the value of the right.

... [C]ivil rights are so valuable that actual damages, not nominal damages such as one cent or one dollar, that is, actual compensatory damages are presumed from the wrongful deprivation of civil rights.... [I]f you find that the plaintiffs were wrongfully deprived of their rights not be discriminated against in the rental of property, you must compensate them for that loss in an amount which you consider to be the value you would place on your own rights, the amount that you would consider necessary to make each of you whole if you were deprived of your right not to be discriminated against in this particular respect.

In defending this instruction the Sixth Circuit noted that:

No physical or mental injuries need be shown under the Act to justify a recovery. Under the facts of this case, an actual injury occurred merely by committing discriminatory acts in violation of the Fair Housing Act. Furthermore, a discriminatory act in violation of the Fair Housing Act is a type of injury that is likely to have occurred but "impossible to measure."

In a later decision that court upheld a damage award of $35,000 and an attorney fee award of $40,000. Woods v. Beavers, 961 F.2d 1580 (6th Cir.1992) (unpublished).

One argument against "golden rule" damages such as these is that willingness to accept compensation is directly related to a person's existing wealth. A poor person will often be willing to subject himself to pain, ridicule or some other unpleasant experience for a relatively small amount of money. A wealthy person would typically set a much higher price. As a result, a wealthy jury would, other circumstances being the same, produce a higher damages award than a poorer jury.

UNITED STATES v. STARRETT CITY ASSOCIATES

United States Court of Appeals, Second Circuit (1988).
840 F.2d 1096, cert. denied 488 U.S. 946.

M INER , C IRCUIT J UDGE .

Appellants ... own and operate "Starrett City," the largest housing development in the nation, consisting of 46 high-rise buildings containing 5,881 apartments in Brooklyn, New York * * *

Starrett has sought to maintain a racial distribution by apartment of 64% white, 22% black and 8% hispanic.... Starrett claims that these racial quotas are necessary to prevent the loss of white tenants, which would transform Starrett City into a predominantly minority complex. Starrett points to the difficulty it has had in attracting an integrated applicant pool from the time Starrett City opened, despite extensive advertising and promotional efforts. Because of these purported difficulties, Starrett adopted a tenanting procedure to promote and maintain the desired racial balance. This procedure has resulted in relatively stable percentages of whites and minorities living at Starrett City between 1975 and the present. * * *

The government commenced the present action against Starrett in June 1984.... The complaint alleged that Starrett, through its tenanting policies, discriminated in violation of the Fair Housing Act. Specifically, the government maintained that Starrett violated the Act by making apartments unavailable to blacks solely because of race, 42 U.S.C. § 3604(a); by forcing black applicants to wait significantly longer for apartments than whites solely because of race, id. § 3604(b); by enforcing a policy that prefers white applicants while limiting the numbers of minority applicants accepted, id. § 3604(c); and by representing in an acknowledgement letter that no apartments are available for rental when in fact units are available, id. § 3604(d).

Starrett maintained that the tenanting procedures "were adopted ... solely to achieve and maintain integration and were not motivated by racial animus." To support their position, appellants submitted the written testimony of three housing experts. They described the "white flight" and "tipping" phenomena, in which white residents migrate out of a community as the community becomes poor and the minority population increases, resulting in the transition to a predominantly minority community. Acknowledging that " 'the tipping point for a particular housing development, depending as it does on numerous factors and the uncertainties of human behavior, is difficult to predict with precision,' " one expert stated that the point at which tipping occurs has been estimated at from 1% to 60% minority population, but that the consensus ranged between 10% and 20%. Another expert, who had prepared a report in 1980 on integration at Starrett City for the New York State Division of Housing and Community Renewal, estimated the complex's tipping point at approximately 40% black on a population basis. A third expert, who had been involved in integrated housing ventures since the 1950's, found that a 2:1 white-minority ratio produced successful integration.

The court, however, accepted the government's contention that Starrett's practices of making apartments unavailable for blacks, while reserving them for whites, and conditioning rental to minorities based on a "tipping formula" derived only from race or national origin are clear violations of the Fair Housing Act. The district court found that apartment opportunities for blacks and hispanics were far fewer "than would be expected if race and national origin were not taken into account," while opportunities for whites were substantially greater than what their application rates projected. Minority applicants waited up to ten times longer than the average white applicant before they were offered an apartment.
* * *

The court concluded that Starrett's obligation was "simply and solely to comply with the Fair Housing Act" by treating "black and other minority applicants ... on the same basis as whites in seeking available housing at Starrett City." ... Accordingly, Judge Neaher granted summary judgment for the government, enjoining Starrett from discriminating against applicants on the basis of race and "[r]equiring [them] to adopt written, objective, uniform, nondiscriminatory tenant selection standards and procedures" subject to the court's approval. * * *

[P]rograms designed to maintain integration by limiting minority participation, such as ceiling quotas ... are of doubtful validity.... First, Starrett City's practices have only the goal of integration maintenance. The quotas already have been in effect for ten years. Appellants predict that their race-conscious tenanting practices must continue for at least fifteen more years, but fail to explain adequately how that approximation was reached. In any event, these practices are far from temporary. Since the goal of integration maintenance is purportedly threatened by the potential for "white flight" on a continuing basis, no definite termination date for Starrett's quotas is perceivable. Second, appellants do not assert, and there is no evidence to show, the existence of prior racial discrimination or discriminatory imbalance adversely affecting whites within Starrett City or appellants' other complexes. On the contrary, Starrett City was initiated as an integrated complex, and Starrett's avowed purpose for employing race-based tenanting practices is to maintain that initial integration.

Finally, Starrett's quotas do not provide minorities with access to Starrett City, but rather act as a ceiling to their access. Thus, the impact of appellants' practices falls squarely on minorities, for whom Title VIII was intended to open up housing opportunities. Starrett claims that its use of quotas serves to keep the numbers of minorities entering Starrett City low enough to avoid setting off a wave of "white flight."

Although the "white flight" phenomenon may be a factor "take[n] into account in the integration equation," Parent Ass'n of Andrew Jackson High School v. Ambach, 598 F.2d 705, 720 (2d Cir.1979), it cannot serve to justify attempts to maintain integration at Starrett City through inflexible racial quotas that are neither temporary in nature nor used to remedy past racial discrimination or imbalance within the complex.

NEWMAN, CIRCUIT JUDGE (dissenting)

Congress enacted the Fair Housing Act to prohibit racial segregation in housing. Starrett City is one of the most successful examples in the nation of racial integration in housing. I respectfully dissent because I do not believe that Congress intended the Fair Housing Act to prohibit the maintenance of racial integration in private housing. * * *

Though the terms of the statute literally encompass the defendants' actions, the statute was never intended to apply to such actions. This statute was intended to bar perpetuation of segregation. To apply it to bar maintenance of integration is precisely contrary to the congressional policy "to provide, within constitutional limitations, for fair housing throughout the United States." 42 U.S.C. § 3601.

Title VIII bars discriminatory housing practices in order to end segregated housing. Starrett City is not promoting segregated housing. On the contrary, it is maintaining integrated housing. It is surely not within the spirit of the Fair Housing Act to enlist the Act to bar integrated housing. Nor is there any indication that application of the statute toward such a perverse end was within the intent of those who enacted the statute. It is true that there are some statements in the legislative history that broadly condemn discrimination for "any" reason. Senator Mondale, the principal sponsor of Title VIII, said that "we do not see any good reason or justification, in the first place, for permitting discrimination in the sale or rental of housing." 114 Cong.Rec. 5642 (1968). But his context, like that in which the entire debate occurred, concerned maintenance of segregation, not integration. His point was that there was no reason for discriminating against a Black who wished to live in a previously all-White housing project. He explicitly decried the prospect that "we are going to live separately in white ghettos and Negro ghettos." The purpose of Title VIII, he said, was to replace the ghettos "by truly integrated and balanced living patterns." As he pointed out, "[O]ne of the biggest problems we face is the lack of experience in actually living next to Negroes." Starrett City is committed to the proposition that Blacks and Whites shall live next to each other. A law enacted to enhance the opportunity for people of all races to live next to each other should not be interpreted to prevent a landlord from maintaining one of the most successful integrated housing projects in America.

NOTES AND QUESTIONS

1.   What is the evil that the FHA was designed to correct: discrimination or segregation? Do you suppose it occurred to Congress that these could be conflicting, rather than harmonious, goals? Would *Starrett* have come out the other way if white persons rather than people of color were forced to be on the longer waiting list?

United States v. Charlottesville Redevelopment and Housing Authority, 718 F.Supp. 461 (W.D.Va.1989) also condemned a tenant selection policy that gave preferential treatment to white applicants for public housing, where the defendant's intention was to achieve a "50/50 mix of black and white residents." The court identified a conflict between the FHA's twin purposes of nondiscrimination and integration:

> In the present conflict between these two legal principles, nondiscrimination and integration, the obligation of [the defendant] to avoid discrimination must "trump" [its] obligation to promote integration, as regards the promotion of integration through the specific policy mechanism and controversy before this court. It is not that this court ascribes to integration a status inferior to nondiscrimination in the pantheon of legal values. It is, rather, that the duty to avoid discrimination must circumscribe the specific particular ways in which a party under the duty to integrate can seek to fulfill that second duty.

718 F.Supp. at 468.

By contrast South–Suburban Housing Center v. Greater South Suburban Board of Realtors, 935 F.2d 868 (7th Cir.1991), cert. denied, 502 U.S. 1074

(1992), found no such conflict in the defendant's practice of making special efforts to interest whites in a predominantly black housing development, where no black applicants were being turned away or wait-listed. The court noted the lower court's conclusion that "The SSHC's stated purpose in entering into and implementing the Apache Street listings was to add some 'white traffic to the properties in addition to the black traffic,' not to decrease or restrict the black traffic."

2. Suppose a newspaper routinely accepts display advertising for apartments or condominiums and the advertisers use only white models in the photographs in the advertising. No verbal statements in the advertisements suggests that the advertisers discriminate on the basis of race, and the advertisers in fact do not discriminate in their sales. Has the FHA been violated? See Ragin v. New York Times Co., 923 F.2d 995 (2d Cir.), cert. denied 502 U.S. 821 (1991), which said yes. The *Ragin* court relied on a Department of Housing and Urban Development (HUD) Regulation which at that time read:

> Human models in photographs, drawings, or other graphic techniques may not be used to indicate exclusiveness because of race, color, religion, sex, handicap, familial status, or national origin.

24 C.F.R. § 109.30(b). In related litigation against one of the real estate brokers who had used white models exclusively, the court noted that the broker's advertisements had been pitched to high income white people. The photographs had all been selected from stock photograph books provided by ad agencies, which contained photographs of models from all races, but the defendant broker had selected only white models. The court's award included $2500 to each member of a group of plaintiffs whose injury was based on the fact that they had read the advertisements and suffered from emotional distress. Ragin v. Harry Macklowe Real Estate Co., 6 F.3d 898 (2d Cir.1993).

3. Suppose a male landlord conditions a female tenant's lease renewal on her having sexual relations with him, or engages in a pattern of harassing women tenants. Has the landlord violated the FHA? Has he denied someone a housing opportunity on the basis of sex? The Supreme Court has never applied the FHA to sexual harassment; however, it has applied similar language in Title VII, which involves employment discrimination, to such situations. Meritor Savings Bank v. Vinson, 477 U.S. 57 (1986). Taking their cue from *Meritor*, several lower courts have held that sexual harassment can violate the FHA if it interferes with the victim's right to obtain housing, or amounts to threats or intimidation against someone in the exercise of housing privileges. See Quigley v. Winter, 598 F.3d 938 (8th Cir. 2010) (landlord conditioned Section 8 housing vouchers on unwelcome sexual harassment); Krueger v. Cuomo, 115 F.3d 487 (7th Cir.1997) (landlord who suggested that single mother could "fool around or something" in order to avoid $100 rent increase, then touched her inappropriately and came repeatedly to her apartment, violated FHA); Shellhammer v. Lewallen, 770 F.2d 167 (6th Cir.1985) (landlord's sexual harassment of tenant violates FHA). The law recognizes so-called "hostile environment" sexual harassment which generally refers to such actions as inappropriate comments or touching, or similar actions by men reasonably likely to humiliate or intimidate women on the basis of

gender. However, a single incident is usually insufficient to state a hostile environment claim. See DiCenso v. Cisneros, 96 F.3d 1004 (7th Cir.1996) (single incident in which landlord fondled arm of 18–year old woman and said that if she could not pay rent they could take care of it "another way" insufficient to state harassment claim). However, the law also recognizes quid-pro-quo claims in which the defendant conditions a certain opportunity on sex—such as availability of a new or larger apartment, lease renewal, etc. See Krueger v. Cuomo, 115 F.3d 487 (7th Cir.1997) (landlord's eviction notice in response to tenant's rejection of his sexual advance constituted quid-pro-quo harassment).

BLOCH v. FRISCHHOLZ

United States Court of Appeals, Seventh Circuit (2009) (en banc).
587 F.3d 771.

TINDER, CIRCUIT JUDGE.

In this case, we consider whether condominium owners can sue their condo association under the Fair Housing Act (FHA), 42 U.S.C. §§ 3601 et seq., for alleged religious and racial discrimination that took place after the owners bought their condo unit. We highlight the word "after" because based on a prior opinion from this court, Halprin v. Prairie Single Family Homes of Dearborn Park Ass'n, 388 F.3d 327 (7th Cir.2004), the district court concluded that condo owners couldn't rely on the FHA to safeguard their rights from any post-acquisition discrimination. We took this case to the full court to consider this important question. Upon careful review of the FHA and our prior opinion in Halprin, we conclude that in some circumstances homeowners have an FHA cause of action for discrimination that occurred after they moved in. . . .

At the center of this case is a little rectangular box, about six inches tall, one inch wide, and one inch deep, which houses a small scroll of parchment inscribed with passages from the Torah, the holiest of texts in Judaism. The scroll is called a mezuzah (or in the plural form, mezuzot or mezuzoh). Though small in size, the mezuzah is a central aspect of the Jewish religious tradition-many Jews believe they are commanded by God to affix mezuzot on the exterior doorposts of their dwelling (specifically, on the right doorpost when facing into the home, one-third of the way down from the top of the doorway, within about three inches of the doorway opening). Many Jews touch and kiss the mezuzah and pray when entering a home with a mezuzah on the doorpost.

The Blochs, long-time residents of three units in the Shoreline Towers condominium building, are Jewish. As residents, the Blochs are subject to the rules and regulations enacted by the Condo Association's Board of Managers. For approximately three decades, the Blochs displayed mezuzot on the doorposts outside of their condo units without objection. In 2001, the Association's rules and regulations committee enacted a set of rules to govern certain activities taking place outside the units in the common hallways. Lynne chaired that committee at that time and voted in favor of the rules. The "Hallway Rules," as they have come to be called, stated [in relevant part]: . . .

Mats, boots, shoes, carts or objects of any sort are prohibited outside Unit entrance doors.

. . . From the Rules' enactment until mid–2004, the Association did not remove mezuzot or any other object affixed to the outside of unit doors or doorposts, with the exception of a few pictures, depicting a swastika, a marijuana plant, and the Playboy bunny. Instead, the Association ordinarily relied on Rule 1 to remove clutter from the hallways.

In May 2004, the Association began renovating the building's hallways and repainted the walls and doors. The Association asked residents to remove everything from their doors to prepare for the work. The Blochs obliged and took down their mezuzot. When the work was finished, they put their mezuzot back up. But then, without notice to the Blochs, the Association began removing and confiscating the mezuzot. The Association said that mezuzot on doorposts violated Hallway Rule 1, because "objects of any sort" included mezuzot. It included more than that, though, as the Association also confiscated crucifixes, wreaths, Christmas ornaments, political posters, and Chicago Bears pennants.

The Blochs voiced their concerns to the Association and provided the Association with information explaining the religious significance of the mezuzah. For example, a letter from the Chicago Rabbinical Council explained that Jewish law requires mezuzot to be displayed on the exterior doorpost, rather than indoors. Another letter explained that observant Jews could not live in a place that prohibited them from affixing mezuzot to their doorposts. But the Blochs received no relief from Frischholz [the condominium association president] or the Association.

. . . The mezuzah removals persisted even during the funeral of Marvin Bloch, Lynne's husband and Helen and Nathan's father, despite the Blochs' request that the mezuzot be left up for the seven-day Shivah, the Jewish period of mourning. Frischholz had agreed to allow the mezuzah to stay up during Shivah. The Association also provided a coat rack and a card table, both of which were placed in the hall outside the Blochs' condo unit. A jug of water was placed on the table so visitors could wash their hands when returning from the cemetery. Upon their return from the burial, though, the Blochs and their guests, including a rabbi, were shocked to find the doorpost empty once again. The Blochs were humiliated having to explain to the rabbi why, on the day of the funeral, their mezuzah was not on the doorpost. The coat rack and the table, however, were still sitting in the hallway. . . .

This case presents essentially two questions. First, under which federal theories, if any, can the Blochs seek relief? We focus exclusively on the three FHA provisions to determine whether any of them supports a claim for post-sale discrimination. Second, did the Blochs offer sufficient evidence of discrimination to proceed to trial on one or more of their federal theories? . . .

Section 3604(a) makes it unlawful "[t]o refuse to sell or rent after the making of a bona fide offer, or to refuse to negotiate for the sale or rental of, or otherwise make unavailable or deny, a dwelling to any person because of race, color, religion, sex, familial status, or national origin." The issue is whether this text prohibits any form of discrimination after the buyer or renter signs on the dotted line. (We recognize that the plaintiffs in this case are owners rather than renters, but there is no reason that there would be a distinction under the relevant provisions of the FHA.) Our opinion in *Halprin* left little room for a post-acquisition discrimination claim. *Halprin* also involved allegations of anti-Semitic harassment; members of the homeowners' association allegedly graffitied and vandalized the plaintiff's property and thwarted the plaintiff's attempts to investigate this conduct. This harassment did not give rise to an FHA claim, we concluded in *Halprin*, because the FHA by and large concerned only "access to housing."

Nonetheless, *Halprin* noted that "[a]s a purely semantic matter the statutory language might be stretched far enough to reach a case of 'constructive eviction.' " Id. That statutory language is the "otherwise make unavailable or deny" part, which is not tethered to the words "sale or rental" that constrain the other two § 3604(a) clauses. Availability of housing is at the heart of § 3604(a). "Section 3604(a) is designed to ensure that no one is denied the right to live where they choose for discriminatory reasons...." There could be situations where a person is denied that right after he or she moves in. Prohibiting discrimination at the point of sale or rental but not at the moment of eviction would only go halfway toward ensuring availability of housing. A landlord would be required to rent to an African–American but then, the day after he moves in, could change all the locks and put up signs that said, "No blacks allowed." That clearly could not be what Congress had in mind when it sought to create "truly integrated and balanced living patterns." Trafficante v. Metro. Life Ins. Co., 409 U.S. 205, 211, 93 S.Ct. 364 (1972)....

The question here is whether the defendants have made the Blochs' units "unavailable" because of their religion (or their race). Proving constructive eviction is a tall order, but it's the best analogy the Blochs give to support their argument. Ordinarily, the plaintiff in such a case must show her residence is "unfit for occupancy," often to the point that she is "compelled to leave." BLACK'S LAW DICTIONARY 594 (8th ed. 2004). Plaintiffs must show more than a mere diminution in property values, see Southend Neighborhood, 743 F.2d at 1210; Cox v. City of Dallas, Tex., 430 F.3d 734, 742–43 & n. 21 (5th Cir.2005), more than just that their properties would be less desirable to a certain group, see Tenafly Eruv Ass'n v. Tenafly, 309 F.3d 144, 157 n. 13 (3d Cir.2002). Even in Halprin, the allegations of the defendants' blatantly discriminatory acts, including spraying the plaintiff's yard with harmful chemicals, were insufficient to give rise to a § 3604(a) claim. Availability, not simply habitability, is the right that § 3604(a) protects....

Still, despite the analogy to constructive eviction, nothing in § 3604(a) suggests that "unavailability" refers only to the physical condition of the premises. . . .

The Blochs argue that the defendants' reinterpretation of Hallway Rule 1 rendered Shoreline Towers unavailable to them and other observant Jews because their religion requires that they be able to affix mezuzot to their doorposts. Letters from the Mezuzah Division of Chicago Mitzvah Campaigns, the Rabbinical Council of Chicago, and the Decalogue Society of Lawyers state that Jewish law requires observant Jews to place mezuzot on the exterior of their entrance doorposts. One went so far as to explain that, "A Jew who is not permitted to affix mezuzohs as aforesaid to all of the doorposts of his dwelling would therefore be required by Jewish Law not to live there." We think this evidence is sufficient to establish a dispute about whether Shoreline Towers was unavailable to observant Jews.

But was it ever unavailable to the Blochs? Though our interpretation of unavailability under the FHA is undoubtedly a matter of federal law, an analogy to the common law property concept of constructive eviction is useful. The defendants argue that the Blochs were never evicted, actually or constructively, because they never vacated the premises. . . .

Though the Blochs compare their plight to constructive eviction, they give no reason why they failed to vacate. Instead, they stayed put and resisted (by repeatedly replacing their mezuzot) the defendants' allegedly discriminatory enforcement of Hallway Rule 1 for over a year before a court enjoined the Rule's enforcement and the Association amended the Rules. Whether "unavailability" means that a plaintiff must, in every case, vacate the premises to have a § 3604(a) claim is an issue we refrain from reaching. But based on these facts, we see no possibility that a reasonable jury could conclude that the defendants' conduct rendered Shoreline Towers "unavailable" to the Blochs, which is what § 3604(a) requires. . . .

Turning to the second of the three FHA theories, § 3604(b) makes it unlawful "[t]o discriminate against any person in the terms, conditions, or privileges of sale or rental of a dwelling, or in the provision of services or facilities in connection therewith, because of race, color, religion, sex, familial status, or national origin." . . . Subsection (b)'s language is broad, mirroring Title VII, which we have held reaches both pre-and post-hiring discrimination. See Kyles v. J.K. Guardian Sec. Servs., Inc., 222 F.3d 289, 295 (7th Cir.2000) ("Courts have recognized that Title VIII is the functional equivalent of Title VII, and so the provisions of these two statutes are given like construction and application." . . .

Like subsection (a), constructive eviction is an option under § 3604(b) as well. . . . However, as we just discussed, the Blochs have no constructive eviction claim. So this § 3604(b) avenue is closed to them.

But the "privilege" to inhabit the condo is not the only aspect of § 3604(b) that this case implicates. The Blochs alleged discrimination by their condo association, an entity by which the Blochs agreed to be governed when they bought their units. This agreement, though contemplating future, post-sale governance by the Association, was nonetheless a term or condition of sale that brings this case within § 3604(b). See Woods–Drake v. Lundy, 667 F.2d 1198, 1201 (5th Cir.1982) ("'[W]hen a landlord imposes on white tenants the condition that they may lease his apartment only if they agree not to receive blacks as guests, the landlord has discriminated against the tenants in the 'terms, conditions and privileges of rental' on the grounds of 'race.'").

. . . [T]he Blochs' agreement to subject their rights to the restrictions imposed by the Board was a "condition" of the Blochs' purchase; the Board's power to restrict unit owners' rights flows from the terms of the sale. And the Blochs alleged that the Board discriminated against them in wielding that power. Consequently, because the Blochs purchased dwellings subject to the condition that the Condo Association can enact rules that restrict the buyer's rights in the future, § 3604(b) prohibits the Association from discriminating against the Blochs through its enforcement of the rules, even facially neutral rules. . . . Accordingly, if the Blochs produced sufficient evidence of discrimination, we conclude that § 3604(b) could support the Blochs' claim.

The Blochs' third and final FHA theory arises under § 3617, which makes it unlawful "to coerce, intimidate, threaten, or interfere with any person in the exercise or enjoyment of, or on account of his having exercised or enjoyed, or on account of his having aided or encouraged any other person in the exercise or enjoyment of, any right granted or protected by section 3603, 3604, 3605, or 3606 of this title." The Blochs argue that § 3617 supports a post-acquisition discrimination claim independent of any allowed under § 3604. "Interference" with the enjoyment of fair housing rights, they argue, encompasses a broader swath of conduct than an outright deprivation of those rights. Supporting the Blochs' position is a HUD regulation, 24 C.F.R. § 100.400(c)(2), which prohibits "[t]hreatening, intimidating or interfering with persons in their enjoyment of a dwelling because of the race [or] . . . religion . . . of such persons, or of visitors or associates of such persons." Interference with the "enjoyment of a dwelling" could only occur post-sale.

Whether a violation of § 3617 can exist without a violation of § 3604 or any other FHA provision is a question we have routinely reserved. . . . We know that the Association's enforcement of the Hallway Rule did not constructively evict the Blochs in violation of § 3604(a) or (b). But that does not foreclose the possibility that the defendants "interfered" with the Blochs' enjoyment of their § 3604 rights or "coerced" or "intimidated" the Blochs on account of their having exercised those rights. To hold otherwise would make § 3617 entirely duplicative of the other FHA provisions. . . . For instance, if a landlord rents to a white tenant but then threatens to evict him upon learning that he is married to a black woman, the landlord has plainly violated § 3617, whether he actually evicts the tenant or not. That §§ 3604 and 3617 might overlap in some circumstances is "neither unusual nor unfortunate." See United States v. Naftalin, 441 U.S. 768, 778 (1979).

Despite the fact that a § 3617 claim might stand on its own, *Halprin* seems to cut the legs out from under it in a case like this. Because § 3604 covers pre-sale conduct, Halprin goes, § 3617 is likewise limited to pre-sale "interference" with § 3604 rights. But, as we've discussed above, even Halprin recognized that § 3604 might not be constrained to purely pre-sale discrimination. Sections 3604(a) and (b) prohibit discriminatory evictions. Eviction, actual or constructive, can only occur after the sale or rental is complete. Therefore, "interference" with certain rights protected by § 3604—rights that prohibit discriminatory evictions-may also occur post-acquisition. We recognize this interpretation effectively overrules Halprin as far as § 3617 is concerned. . . .

We find this construction of § 3617 consistent with Congress' intent in enacting the FHA-"the reach of the proposed law was to replace the ghettos by truly integrated and balanced living patterns." *Trafficante*, 409 U.S. at 211. Requiring the Blochs to vacate their homes before they can sue undoubtedly stifles that purpose. Moreover, our view is consistent with HUD's interpretation of § 3617. HUD's regulations prohibit "interfering with persons in their enjoyment of a dwelling because of the race [or] religion ... of such persons." 24 C.F.R. § 100.400(c)(2) (emphasis added).

So the § 3617 question in this case becomes whether the defendants coerced, intimidated, threatened, or interfered with the Blochs' exercise or enjoyment of their right to inhabit their condo units because of their race or religion. To prevail on a § 3617 claim, a plaintiff must show that (1) she is a protected individual under the FHA, (2) she was engaged in the exercise or enjoyment of her fair housing rights, (3) the defendants coerced, threatened, intimidated, or interfered with the plaintiff on account of her protected activity under the FHA, and (4) the defendants were motivated by an intent to discriminate.

Discriminatory intent is the pivotal element in this case. The Blochs clearly meet the first two elements: they are Jewish and they lived in the condo units they purchased at Shoreline Towers. The defendants also engaged in a pattern of conduct, repeatedly ripping down the Blochs' mezuzot for over a year's time. This conduct would constitute "interference" if it was invidiously motivated-that is, if it was intentionally discriminatory. Thus, like their § 3604(b) claim for discrimination in the terms or conditions of sale and their § 1982 claim, if the Blochs produced sufficient evidence of discrimination, they can proceed under § 3617 for interference with their § 3604 rights.

Whether the Blochs demonstrated a triable issue as to discrimination is the central question that divided the panel of this court that previously considered this case. Not seeing any evidence of discriminatory animus, the panel majority viewed the Blochs' claim as one seeking a religious exception to a neutral rule of general applicability because the Hallway

Rules applied to all objects, not just mezuzot. Under the Supreme Court's reasoning in Employment Division v. Smith, 494 U.S. 872, 110 S.Ct. 1595 (1990), the Association's failure to grant a "mezuzah exception" is not tantamount to intentional discrimination. That the Blochs' claim arose under the FHA (unlike the Free Exercise Clause of the First Amendment, at issue in *Smith*) doesn't change matters; the FHA requires accommodations only for handicaps, 42 U.S.C. § 3604(f)(3)(B), not for religion.

We agree with the panel dissent that the Blochs are not seeking an exception to a neutral rule. Hallway Rule 1 might have been neutral when adopted; indeed, Lynne Bloch voted for the Rule when she was on the Board of Managers. But the Blochs' principal argument is that the Rule isn't neutral anymore. As the dissent put it, "The whole point of the Blochs' case, however, is that the Association, under the guise of 'interpreting' the rule in 2004, transformed it from a neutral one to one that was targeted exclusively at observant Jewish residents." In essence, the Blochs claim that, after the 2004 hallway repainting project, the Board, by its reinterpretation of Rule 1, effectively enacted a new rule to deprive Jews of an important religious practice.

. . . Although the Blochs' case is no slam dunk, we think the record contains sufficient evidence, with reasonable inferences drawn in the Blochs' favor, that there are genuine issues for trial on intentional discrimination.

To begin with, the Blochs produced evidence to show that the Association reinterpreted the Hallway Rules in 2004 to apply to mezuzot, and other objects, which the Rules were never designed to reach. In addition to statements from past Board members and evidence that the Blochs' mezuzot were never removed prior to 2004, a common canon of construction supports the Blochs' argument. See Corley v. United States, 556 U.S. 303, 129 S.Ct. 1558, 1566 (2009) ("'[O]ne of the most basic interpretive canons'" is "'that [a] statute should be construed so that effect is given to all its provisions, so that no part will be inoperative or superfluous, void or insignificant'" (quotation omitted)). Hallway Rule 1 prohibits "objects of any sort . . . outside Unit entrance doors." After the 2004 hallway painting project, the Association construed that language to reach doors and doorposts. But Hallway Rule 2 prohibits "signs or name plates . . . placed on Unit doors." So if Rule 1 were originally intended to cover doors and doorposts, Rule 2 would have been superfluous. As such, a trier of fact could conclude that when the Association adopted the Hallway Rules (with Lynne Bloch voting for their adoption), it never intended them to prohibit objects on the doorposts like mezuzot. . . .

As the panel majority correctly observed, though, this evidence alone is insufficient to create a triable issue as to discriminatory intent. The Hallway Rules were applied neutrally after 2004. The Association cleared the doors and doorposts of everything from mezuzot to crucifixes to Christmas decorations to Chicago Bears' pennants. Even if we were to assume that Judaism was the only religion affected by the reinterpretation of the Rules, the reasoning in *Smith* would put the kibosh on the plaintiff's case. *Smith* requires more than just evidence of an adverse impact on observant Jews. Even the evidence of the Blochs' attempt to amend the Hallway Rules is insufficient standing alone. Under *Smith*, the denial of a religious exception is not intentional discrimination.

This makes the Blochs' task more difficult, but not impossible. They must show that the Association reinterpreted the Hallway Rules to apply to mezuzot "because of" and not merely "in spite of" the Blochs' religion. ... So, to side with the defendants, we must assume that the "design, construction, or enforcement" of Hallway Rule 1 does not target observant Jews.

That's an assumption we just can't make on this record. "A finding of discriminatory intent is usually based on circumstantial evidence and the district court must exercise extreme caution in granting summary judgment in such a context." Gomez, 867 F.2d at 402. We think the district court was too hasty here....

The Blochs also produced evidence of animus between Frischholz and Lynne Bloch. In some circumstances, evidence of animus might detract from an intentional discrimination claim-one could assume that the harasser acted out of personal spite instead of improper prejudice. But in this case, the evidence shows more than just a petty spat between neighbors. As early as 2001, Frischholz knew that Lynne Bloch would be offended by removing mezuzot from her doorposts. Still, he approved of their repeated removal from 2004 on. When she confronted him about it, he retaliated. He accused Lynne of being a racist, called her a liar, encouraged other tenants not to elect her to the Board, and told her that if she didn't like the Association's taking down her mezuzot, she should "get out." ...

Perhaps the strongest evidence of anti-Semitic motives, though, occurred during the Shivah after Marvin Bloch's death. Despite the Blochs' request, and the Association's agreement, to keep their mezuzah up during the mourning period, the defendants repeatedly removed it. In fact, as the panel dissent put it, "the defendants waited until the family literally was attending Dr. Bloch's funeral and then removed the mezuzot while everyone was away." Not only that, but the record shows that the defendants selectively enforced the Hallway Rule only against the mezuzah. The coat rack and the table remained in the hallway outside the unit even after the mezuzah was stripped away. Instead of clearing the hallway of these obstacles, the Association's maintenance person pulled down only a six-inch-by-one-inch religious item. Selectively interpreting "objects of any sort" to apply only to the mezuzah but not to secular objects creates an inference of discriminatory intent.

It is the combination of all of these facts and inferences, rather than any single one, that pushes this case beyond summary judgment. A trier of fact could conclude that the Association's reinterpretation of the Hallway Rule and clearing of all objects from doorposts was intended to target the only group of residents for which the prohibited practice was religiously required.

NOTES AND QUESTIONS

1.   In Bachman v. St. Monica's Congregation, 902 F.2d 1259 (7th Cir. 1990), the court held that a Catholic Church's policy of giving its own members preferred access to housing did not violate the FHA even though the policy subjected the Jewish plaintiffs to unequal treatment. To be sure, concluded the court, the action probably constituted discrimination on the basis of religion under the terms of the FHA, but the Act contains a provision permitting a religious organization to "limit ... the sale ... of dwellings which it owns or operates for other than a commercial purpose to persons of the same religion," and to "giv[e] preference to such persons." 42 U.S.C.A. § 3607. Although the older Civil Rights statutes, 42 U.S.C.A. §§ 1981 & 1982, contained no such defense, they applied only to discrimination on the basis of race. And

> while for this purpose Jews constitute a race, it is not the case that every preference based on religion is a discrimination against a race. Suppose a Bahai organization refused to sell property to persons not of the Bahai faith. It would be extremely odd to describe such a policy as anti-Semitic. The policy would cut across racial grounds, however broadly or narrowly the term "race" was construed.... A preference for Bahais hurts all non-Bahais, a preference for Catholics all non-Catholics; it is not a harm to a particular group of non-Bahais, or of non-Catholics, such as Jews.

902 F.2d at 1261–1262. Accord Intermountain Fair Housing Council v. Boise Rescue Mission Ministries, 657 F.3d 988 (9th Cir. 2011). Compare United States v. Columbus Country Club, 915 F.2d 877 (3d Cir.1990), cert. denied, 501 U.S. 1205 (1991), holding that a country club affiliated with the Catholic Church could not discriminate against non-Catholics. Although the club was affiliated with the Church, it was not itself a "religious organization," and on this point the FHA should be narrowly construed.

2.   Suppose a realtor advertises housing in a newspaper and, without stating an explicit religious preference, adds a Christian cross or the statement "Jesus Saves" to the advertisement. Does the use of such symbols constitute discrimination on the basis of religious belief? See Virginia v. Lotz Realty Co., 237 Va. 1, 376 S.E.2d 54 (1989).

CITY OF EDMONDS v. OXFORD HOUSE, INC.

Supreme Court of the United States (1925).
514 U.S. 725.

GINSBURG, J., delivered the opinion of the Court.

The Fair Housing Act (FHA or Act) prohibits discrimination in housing against, inter alios, persons with handicaps. Section 3607(b)(1) of the Act entirely exempts from the FHA's compass "any reasonable local, State, or Federal restrictions regarding the maximum number of occupants permitted to occupy a dwelling." 42 U.S.C. § 3607(b)(1). This case presents the question whether a provision in petitioner City of Edmonds' zoning code qualifies for § 3607(b)(1)'s complete exemption from FHA scrutiny. The provision, governing areas zoned for single-family dwelling units, defines "family" as "persons [without regard to number] related by genetics, adoption, or marriage, or a group of five or fewer [unrelated] persons." Edmonds Community Development Code (ECDC) § 21.30.010 (1991).

The defining provision at issue describes who may compose a family unit; it does not prescribe "the maximum number of occupants" a dwelling unit may house. We hold that § 3607(b)(1) does not exempt prescriptions of the family-defining kind, i.e., provisions designed to foster the family character of a neighborhood. Instead, § 3607(b)(1)'s absolute exemption removes from the FHA's scope only total occupancy limits, i.e., numerical ceilings that serve to prevent overcrowding in living quarters.

In the summer of 1990, respondent Oxford House opened a group home in the City of Edmonds, Washington for 10 to 12 adults recovering from alcoholism and drug addiction. The group home, called Oxford House–Edmonds, is located in a neighborhood zoned for single-family residences. Upon learning that Oxford House had leased and was operating a home in Edmonds, the City issued criminal citations to the owner and a resident of the house. The citations charged violation of the zoning code rule that defines who may live in single-family dwelling units. The occupants of such units must compose a "family," and family, under the City's defining rule, "means an individual or two or more persons related by genetics, adoption, or marriage, or a group of five or fewer persons who are not related by genetics, adoption, or marriage." Edmonds Community Development Code (ECDC) § 21.30.010. * * * The parties have stipulated, for purposes of this litigation, that the residents of Oxford House–Edmonds "are recovering alcoholics and drug addicts and are handicapped persons within the meaning" of the Act.

Discrimination covered by the FHA includes "a refusal to make reasonable accommodations in rules, policies, practices, or services, when such accommodations may be necessary to afford [handicapped] person[s] equal opportunity to use and enjoy a dwelling." § 3604(f)(3)(B). Oxford House asked Edmonds to make a "reasonable accommodation" by allowing it to remain in the single-family dwelling it had leased. Group homes for recovering substance abusers, Oxford urged, need 8 to 12 residents to be financially and therapeutically viable. Edmonds declined to permit Oxford House to stay in a single-family residential zone, but passed an ordinance listing group homes as permitted uses in multifamily and general commercial zones.

* * * [T]he District Court held that ECDC § 21.30.010, defining "family," is exempt from the FHA under § 3607(b)(1) as a "reasonable . . . restrictio[n] regarding the maximum number of occupants permitted to occupy a dwelling." The United States Court of Appeals for the Ninth

Circuit reversed; holding § 3607(b)(1)'s absolute exemption inapplicable. . . .

Congress enacted § 3607(b)(1) against the backdrop of an evident distinction between municipal land use restrictions and maximum occupancy restrictions.

Land use restrictions designate "districts in which only compatible uses are allowed and incompatible uses are excluded." D. Mandelker, Land Use Law § 4.16, pp. 113–114 (3d ed.1993). These restrictions typically categorize uses as single-family residential, multiple-family residential, commercial, or industrial. * * *

Maximum occupancy restrictions, in contradistinction, cap the number of occupants per dwelling, typically in relation to available floor space or the number and type of rooms. See, e.g., Uniform Housing Code § 503(b) (1988); * * * These restrictions ordinarily apply uniformly to all residents of all dwelling units. Their purpose is to protect health and safety by preventing dwelling overcrowding.

We recognized this distinction between maximum occupancy restrictions and land use restrictions in Moore v. City of East Cleveland, 431 U.S. 494 (1977). In *Moore*, the Court held unconstitutional the constricted definition of "family" contained in East Cleveland's housing ordinance. East Cleveland's ordinance "select[ed] certain categories of relatives who may live together and declare[d] that others may not"; in particular, East Cleveland's definition of "family" made "a crime of a grandmother's choice to live with her grandson." In response to East Cleveland's argument that its aim was to prevent overcrowded dwellings, streets, and schools, we observed that the municipality's restrictive definition of family served the asserted, and undeniably legitimate, goals "marginally, at best." Another East Cleveland ordinance, we noted, "specifically addressed . . . the problem of overcrowding"; that ordinance tied "the maximum permissible occupancy of a dwelling to the habitable floor area." * * *

Section § 3607(b)(1)'s language—"restrictions regarding the maximum number of occupants permitted to occupy a dwelling"—surely encompasses maximum occupancy restrictions. But the formulation does not fit family composition rules typically tied to land use restrictions. In sum, rules that cap the total number of occupants in order to prevent overcrowding of a dwelling "plainly and unmistakably," see A.H. Phillips, Inc. v. Walling, 324 U.S. 490, 493 (1945), fall within § 3607(b)(1)'s absolute exemption from the FHA's governance; rules designed to preserve the family character of a neighborhood, fastening on the composition of households rather than on the total number of occupants living quarters can contain, do not.

Turning specifically to the City's Community Development Code, we note that the provisions Edmonds invoked against Oxford House, ECDC §§ 16.20.010 and 21.30.010, are classic examples of a use restriction and complementing family composition rule. These provisions do not cap the number of people who may live in a dwelling. In plain terms, they direct that dwellings be used only to house families. Captioned "USES," ECDC § 16.20.010 provides that the sole "Permitted Primary Us[e]" in a single-family residential zone is "[s]ingle-family dwelling units." Edmonds itself recognizes that this provision simply "defines those uses permitted in a single family residential zone." Pet. for Cert. 3. A separate provision caps the number of occupants a dwelling may house, based on floor area: "Floor Area. Every dwelling unit shall have at least one room which shall have not less than 120 square feet of floor area. Other habitable rooms, except kitchens, shall have an area of not less than 70 square feet. Where more than two persons occupy a room used for sleeping purposes, the required floor area shall be increased at the rate of 50 square feet for each occupant in excess of two." * * *

Family living, not living space per occupant, is what ECDC § 21.30.010 describes. Defining family primarily by biological and legal relationships, the provision also accommodates another group association: five or fewer unrelated people are allowed to live together as though they were family. This accommodation is the peg on which Edmonds rests its plea for § 3607(b)(1) exemption. Had the City defined a family solely by biological and legal links, § 3607(b)(1) would not have been the ground on which Edmonds staked its case. It is curious reasoning indeed that converts a family values preserver into a maximum occupancy restriction once a town adds to a related persons prescription "and also two unrelated persons."

Edmonds additionally contends that subjecting single-family zoning to FHA scrutiny will "overturn Euclidian zoning" and "destroy the effectiveness and purpose of single-family zoning." This contention both ignores the limited scope of the issue before us and exaggerates the force of the FHA's antidiscrimination provisions. We address only whether Edmonds' family composition rule qualifies for § 3607(b)(1) exemption. Moreover, the FHA antidiscrimination provisions, when applicable, require only "reasonable" accommodations to afford persons with handicaps "equal opportunity to use and enjoy" housing. * * *

The parties have presented, and we have decided, only a threshold question: Edmonds' zoning code provision describing who may compose a "family" is not a maximum occupancy restriction exempt from the FHA under § 3607(b)(1). It remains for the lower courts to decide whether Edmonds' actions against Oxford House violate the FHA's prohibitions against discrimination.... [T]he judgment of the United States Court of Appeals for the Ninth Circuit is Affirmed.

JUSTICE THOMAS, with whom JUSTICE SCALIA and JUSTICE KENNEDY join, dissenting.

* * * The majority does not ask whether petitioner's zoning code imposes any restrictions regarding the maximum number of occupants permitted to occupy a dwelling. Instead, observing that pursuant to ECDC § 21.30.010, "any number of people can live in a house," so long as they

are "related 'by genetics, adoption, or marriage.' " The majority concludes that § 21.30.010 does not qualify for § 3607(b)(1)'s exemption because it "surely does not answer the question: 'What is the maximum number of occupants permitted to occupy a house?' " The majority's question, however, does not accord with the text of the statute. To take advantage of the exemption, a local, state, or federal law need not impose a restriction establishing an absolute maximum number of occupants; under § 3607(b)(1), it is necessary only that such law impose a restriction "regarding" the maximum number of occupants. Surely, a restriction can "regar[d]"—or "concern," "relate to," or "bear on"—the maximum number of occupants without establishing an absolute maximum number in all cases.

* * *

I turn now to the substance of the majority's analysis, the focus of which is "maximum occupancy restrictions" and "family composition rules." The first of these two terms has the sole function of serving as a label for a category of zoning rules simply invented by the majority: rules that "cap the number of occupants per dwelling, typically in relation to available floor space or the number and type of rooms," that "ordinarily apply uniformly to all residents of all dwelling units," and that have the "purpose ... to protect health and safety by preventing dwelling overcrowding." The majority's term does bear a familial resemblance to the statutory term "restrictions regarding the maximum number of occupants permitted to occupy a dwelling," but it should be readily apparent that the category of zoning rules the majority labels "maximum occupancy restrictions" does not exhaust the category of restrictions exempted from the FHA by § 3607(b)(1). The plain words of the statute do not refer to "available floor space or the number and type of rooms"; they embrace no requirement that the exempted restrictions "apply uniformly to all residents of all dwelling units"; and they give no indication that such restrictions must have the "purpose ... to protect health and safety by preventing dwelling overcrowding." Ibid.

* * *

The majority fares no better in its treatment of "family composition rules," a term employed by the majority to describe yet another invented category of zoning restrictions. Although today's decision seems to hinge on the majority's judgment that ECDC § 21.30.010 is a "classic exampl[e] of a ... family composition rule," the majority says virtually nothing about this crucial category. * * *

Although the majority does not say so explicitly, one might infer from its belated definition of "family composition rules" that § 3607(b)(1) does not encompass zoning rules that have one particular purpose ("to preserve the family character of a neighborhood") or those that refer to the qualitative as well as the quantitative character of a dwelling (by "fastening on the composition of households rather than on the total number of occupants living quarters can contain"). Ibid. Yet terms like "family character," "composition of households," "total [that is, absolute] number of occupants," and "living quarters" are noticeably absent from the text of the statute. Section 3607(b)(1) limits neither the permissible purposes of a qualifying zoning restriction nor the ways in which such a restriction may accomplish its purposes. Rather, the exemption encompasses "any" zoning restriction—whatever its purpose and by whatever means it accomplishes that purpose—so long as the restriction "regard[s]" the maximum number of occupants. * * *

In sum, it does not matter that ECDC § 21.030.010 describes "[f]amily living, not living space per occupant," because it is immaterial under § 3607(b)(1) whether § 21.030.010 constitutes a "family composition rule" but not a "maximum occupancy restriction." The sole relevant question is whether petitioner's zoning code imposes "any . . . restrictions regarding the maximum number of occupants permitted to occupy a dwelling." Because I believe it does, I respectfully dissent.

NOTES AND QUESTIONS

1. The FHA's prohibition of discrimination against the handicapped has raised unique questions of interpretation. First, the handicapped are also protected by a "reasonable accommodation" provision (§ 3604(f)) that can operate as a kind of "affirmative action" obligation. See, e.g., Astralis Condominium Ass'n v. Secretary, HUD, 620 F.3d 62 (1st Cir. 2010) (reasonable accommodations extended to provision of convenient reserved parking spaces).

Second, municipalities are often involved in the provision of services to the handicapped, or else they become involved in policy making respecting treatment of the handicapped. This may lead to actions that would clearly be unlawful if the protected classification were race. One example is the debate among experts over the appropriate degree of institutionalization or "mainstreaming" for the mentally handicapped. Several decades ago many classes of mentally handicapped people were simply committed to mental institutions, which were quite distinctive and segregated facilities. Today, the mentally handicapped are often placed into group homes, on the theory that it is far better for them to be integrated into the social and economic structure of the community. A municipality might become involved in such policy making if, following the recommendations of experts, it makes a land use policy forbidding the clustering of residential facilities. In Familystyle v. St. Paul, 923 F.2d 91 (8th Cir.1991), the court concluded that a zoning provision requiring the dispersal of group homes did not violate the FHA:

> The district court found that although local and state dispersal requirements for group homes on their face limit housing choices for the mentally ill, the government's interest in deinstitutionalization sufficiently rebutted any discriminatory effect of the laws.... [W]e agree with the district court that the government's interests are valid. The state aims to integrate the mentally ill into the mainstream of society. One method to achieve that goal is to license group homes which advance the process of deinstitutionalization. * * * The state's group home dispersal require-

ments are designed to ensure that mentally handicapped persons needing residential treatment will not be forced into enclaves of treatment facilities that would replicate and thus perpetuate the isolation resulting from institutionalization. * * *

Subsequent to *Familystyle,* the Supreme Court decided International Union, United Auto. Aerospace & Agricultural Implement Workers v. Johnson Controls, Inc., 499 U.S. 187 (1991), a labor discrimination case in which the court condemned an employer's policy of barring women from working in areas of high lead exposure as long as it was still possible for them to have children. The Court concluded that the statute bars all discrimination not justified as a bona fide occupational qualification, even if there is some scientific basis for it (in this case, a fear of birth defects). Subsequently, Larkin v. Michigan Dept. of Social Services, 89 F.3d 285 (6th Cir.1996), concluded that *Johnson Controls* "implicitly overruled" *Familystyle,* and thus put a municipality out of the business of making policy respecting dispersal of group care facilities. Problematically, that holding would appear to apply to any state agency as well as a municipality. For example, suppose the state's mental health agency, acting under the advice of its psychologist and social worker experts, adopted a policy of refusing to license "clustered" group facilities. See also United States v. City of Chicago Heights, 161 F.Supp.2d 819 (N.D.Ill.2001) (also rejecting *Familystyle*).

2.   Marbrunak v. City of Stow, Ohio, 974 F.2d 43 (6th Cir.1992), held that a city's zoning regulations that required a home for the developmentally disabled to be equipped with a whole house sprinkler system for fires, fire retardant wall and floor coverings, lighted exit signs, smoke alarms and numerous fire extinguishers violated the Fair Housing Act Amendments. Why? See also, Bangerter v. Orem City Corporation, 46 F.3d 1491 (10th Cir.1995) (municipal requirement of 24–hour supervision in group home for mentally handicapped stated prima facie claim of FHA violation).

Suppose a landlord makes some units in its apartment complex available for the handicapped, as the Fair Housing Act amendments mandate, but refuses to do so with other units that a handicapped person might prefer; further, the reason he does so is bias against handicapped persons. Any violation? See Growth Horizons v. Delaware County, 983 F.2d 1277 (3d Cir.1993) (no violation; compliance requires making a reasonable number of units available, but not giving the tenant a complete choice).

3.   Suppose a city closes its shelters for the homeless, and that a substantial number of homeless are (1) people of color; (2) women, and (3) handicapped. Does the closure violate the FHA? Does the statute even apply to people who are not buying or renting, but are simply staying as short-term guests? See Johnson v. Dixon, 786 F.Supp. 1 (D.D.C.1991).

4.   In Doe v. City of Butler, 892 F.2d 315 (3d Cir.1989), the court held that a zoning ordinance that limited group homes to six persons did not violate the gender discrimination provision of the FHA when applied to a home for women who had been physically abused by their husbands. The court noted that the provision was "nondiscriminatory" in that it applied equally to group homes for men, such as recovering male alcoholics. Further, it could find no intent to discriminate against women. However, the court

remanded the case for a determination whether the limitation violated the "familial status" provision of the 1988 FHA Amendments. The plaintiffs alleged that the six-person limitation made it impossible to permit battered women to bring their children with them to the group home.

One problem with some group homes is that the average duration of stay is quite short, and the Fair Housing Act applies only to "dwellings." See Lakeside Resort Enterp., L.P. v. Board of Supervisors, 455 F.3d 154 (3d Cir. 2006) (drug/alcohol treatment facility qualified as "dwelling" under FHA even though the average length of stay was slightly more than two weeks). Cf. Schwarz v. City of Treasure Island, 544 F.3d 1201 (11th Cir. 2008) (halfway house for recovering substance abusers is a dwelling); Patel v. Holley House Motels, 483 F.Supp. 374, 381 (S.D.Ala.1979) (motel not a dwelling); Baxter v. City of Belleville, 720 F.Supp. 720, 731 (S.D.Ill.1989) (hospice for terminally ill AIDS patients a dwelling).

In Gorski v. Troy, 929 F.2d 1183 (7th Cir.1991) the court held that the "familial status" provisions of the FHA could protect parents from being evicted by their landlords because they desired to take in foster children, where the parents had been licensed by the state to take in such children. In Seniors Civil Liberties Ass'n v. Kemp, 965 F.2d 1030 (11th Cir.1992) the court held that the "familial status" provision did not violate the constitutional rights of senior citizens to freedom of association in a challenge to a traditional condominium's age restriction. As the court noted, freedom of association in the housing context refers to a person's right to determine whom he wishes to live with; it does not protect a person's right to determine who will live next door or in the apartment across the hall. Nothing in the statute compelled senior citizens to share their own apartments with children.

7. The FHA protects people from discrimination on account of race, color, religion, sex, familial status, handicap or national origin. The majority of cases brought under the Act have involved alleged discrimination on the basis of race, color or national origin. Although gender discrimination is a common problem in American society, it is much more pervasive in employment than in the provision of housing. Nevertheless, some gender discrimination cases have been brought under the Act. See United States v. Reece, 457 F.Supp. 43 (D.Mont.1978), where the court found that a landlord violated the FHA by (1) refusing to consider alimony and child support payments in determining whether a divorced woman would be capable of paying the rent; and (2) refusing to rent to women without cars, although he would rent to men without cars, on the theory that the local streets were unsafe for women to be walking alone at night. "Benign" discrimination is no exception under the FHA.

NOTE: FAIR HOUSING ACT VIOLATIONS BY LOCAL GOVERNMENTS

Municipalities and other local governments, just as private actors, can violate the federal Fair Housing Act. For some time the Justice Department has used the Act to challenge racially discriminatory governmental decisions affecting land use and related practices. See Selig, The Justice Department and Racially Exclusionary Municipal Practices: Creative Ventures in Fair

Housing Act Enforcement, 17 U.C.D.L.Rev. 445 (1984); Blaesser & Stansell, Municipal Liability Under the Fair Housing Act: an Update, 40 Land Use L. & Zoning Digest 3 (1988). See also Jonathan T. Rothwell, Racial Enclaves and Density Zoning: the Institutionalized Segregation of Racial Minorities in the United States, 13 Am.L. & Econ. Rev. 290 (2011) (empirical evidence indicating strong link between low density zoning and racial segregation).

Most FHA violations by local governments have been somewhat different in character than private violations. For example, most municipalities are not accused of intentionally excluding a particular member of a racial minority from publicly owned or subsidized housing. Rather, most governmental violations involve practices such as zoning or other restrictions on development that have a disproportionately adverse impact on racial minorities. The lower courts agree that a zoning restriction or refusal to permit development that has an unreasonable exclusionary impact on members of racial minorities can violate the FHA even if those responsible had no discriminatory motive. In Huntington Branch, NAACP v. Town of Huntington, 844 F.2d 926 (2d Cir.), aff'd per curiam, 488 U.S. 15 (1988) the court held that a municipality violated the Fair Housing Act by limiting multifamily housing to a designated "urban renewal" area and denying a permit to someone wishing to build subsidized multifamily housing outside that area. The Supreme Court's per curiam affirmance approved the lower court's decision, but did not necessarily approve the disparate impact test that the lower court employed. Except for *Huntington*, the Supreme Court has never decided whether discriminatory intent is essential to an FHA violation. However, in Griggs v. Duke Power Co., 401 U.S. 424 (1971), the Supreme Court did create an "effects" test for employment discrimination under federal civil rights laws. Circuit courts that have created an "effects" test for the FHA have generally analogized housing discrimination to discrimination in employment.

At this writing the Supreme Court has agreed to review the question whether the FHA can be violated by a showing of disparate impact, or whether a showing of disparate treatment is required. See Gallagher v. Magner, 619 F.3d 823 (8th Cir. 2010), cert. granted ___ U.S. ___, 132 S.Ct. 548 (2011). The Eighth Circuit that the City of Saint Paul's enforcement of housing code provisions had not been properly alleged to result from disparate treatment but could be challenged for disparate impact. Under current law the government or private plaintiff challenging a municipal action under the FHA generally makes out a *prima facie* case by showing that the action perpetuates racial segregation or makes it more difficult for racial minorities than for white people to obtain housing in a particular community. However, the municipality or other unit of local government can rebut by showing a legitimate interest substantial enough to outweigh this discriminatory effect which could not have been achieved by some alternate means. See United States v. Yonkers Board of Education, 837 F.2d 1181, 1217 (2d Cir.1987); Resident Advisory Bd. v. Rizzo, 564 F.2d 126, 149 (3d Cir.1977), cert. denied 435 U.S. 908 (1978). On the relationship between zoning that is not facially discriminatory and segregation, see David Ray Papke, Keeping the Underclass in its Place: Zoning, the Poor, and Residential Segregation, 41 Urban Law. 787 (2009).

How does one make out a prima facie showing of disparate impact under the FHA? In Metropolitan Housing Dev. Corp. v. Village of Arlington Heights, 558 F.2d 1283, 1287–90 (7th Cir.1977), cert. denied 434 U.S. 1025 (1978), the court found the following four factors to be relevant: (1) the strength of the showing of discriminatory effect; (2) whether there was some evidence of discriminatory intent, although not enough to warrant finding an Equal Protection Clause violation; (3) the nature of the defendant's interest in taking the action being challenged; (4) whether the defendant is being asked to affirmatively provide housing, or merely to refrain from interfering with private owners or developers who wish to provide such housing. Thus, for example, under *Arlington*'s fourth factor, disparate impact would be found more readily if the city intervened (by rezoning) in order to prevent low income housing from being built than if it merely refused to rezone in order to permit such housing.

The *Huntington* court found the *Arlington Heights* test too difficult for plaintiffs. Rather, a prima facie case could be established without any evidence of discriminatory intent, but merely by a showing of segregative effects. 844 F.2d at 935. In so holding, the *Huntington* court found that Congress' intent in passing the FHA was to abolish housing segregation, whether or not the segregation was intentionally produced.

The *Huntington* court then found that this test was met by a showing that, although seven percent of all families in Huntington needed subsidized housing, 24 percent of black families needed such housing. Further, a far larger percentage of nonwhites than whites currently occupied subsidized housing. Thus any decision to block the construction of additional subsidized housing would likely satisfy the disparate impact test for a prima facie case.

Then, "[o]nce a plaintiff has made a prima facie showing of discriminatory effect, a defendant must present bona fide and legitimate justifications for its action with no less discriminatory alternatives available." This required the court to consider "(1) whether the reasons [for the city's refusal to permit the housing] are bona fide and legitimate; and (2) whether any less discriminatory alternative can serve those ends." On these questions, the court noted a distinction between "plan specific" and "site specific" objections. If the municipality's basis for refusal to permit the subsidized development were "plan specific," then less restrictive alternatives are likely to be available because the city's objections should be removed after the promoters make suitable design changes. However, if the municipality's objection is to the site itself, then more intense judicial scrutiny is needed because the city is in effect objecting to the very idea of building this particular project at this particular site.

The city's main objection in *Huntington* was site specific, since it had effectively forbad all such projects outside of its designated urban renewal area. On this the court said,

> The Town asserts that limiting multi-family development to the urban renewal area will encourage restoration of the neighborhood because, otherwise, developers will choose to build in the outlying areas and will bypass the zone. The Town's goal, however, can be achieved by less discriminatory means, by encouraging development in the urban renewal

area with tax incentives or abatements. The Town may assert that this is less effective, but it may actually be more so. Developers are not wed to building in Huntington; they are filling a perceived economic void. Developments inside the urban renewal area and outside it are not fungible. Rather, developers prevented from building outside the urban renewal area will more likely build in another town, not the urban renewal area. Huntington incorrectly assumes that developers limit their area of interest by political subdivision. In fact, the decision where to build is much more complex. Hence, if the Town wishes to encourage growth in the urban renewal area, it should do so directly through incentives which would have a less discriminatory impact on the Town.

844 F.2d at 939.

Query: isn't the court merely speculating that a rather vaguely defined tax incentive scheme would be effective and also less discriminatory than Huntington's actual policy? How can a municipality show that no less restrictive alternative is available if the plaintiffs or the court are entitled to offer hypothetical alternatives that may be less restrictive but are not proven to work? Or is this simply a way of saying that the burden of showing that there are no less restrictive alternatives is a very difficult one for municipalities to meet?

The 1988 Amendments to the FHA have produced a new wave of litigation against municipalities, mainly for enforcement of zoning provisions alleged to discriminate against the handicapped. See *City of Edmonds* case, supra, as well as the *Familystyle* and *Larkin* cases cited previously. See also Smith & Lee Associates, Inc. v. City of Taylor, Mich., 102 F.3d 781 (6th Cir.1996) (municipality violated FHA by refusing to amend zoning ordinance so as to permit adult foster care facility); Bangerter v. Orem City Corp., 46 F.3d 1491 (10th Cir.1995) (municipality's requirement of 24–hour supervision for group home for mentally handicapped was prima facie violation of FHA; remanded to determine if requirement was reasonable under the circumstances). See also Regional Economic Community Action Program, Inc. v. City of Middletown, 294 F.3d 35 (2d Cir.2002), cert. denied, 537 U.S. 813 (2002) (municipality's refusal to grant special use permit for halfway house for recovering alcoholics may have violated amended FHA).

§ 12.4 HOUSING DISCRIMINATION AND STATE LAW

STATE v. FRENCH

Supreme Court of Minnesota (1990).
460 N.W.2d 2.

YETKA, JUSTICE.

Appellant was found guilty of discrimination by an administrative law judge to whom a complaint filed with the Department of Human Rights was referred for hearing. Appellant had refused to rent his property to one Susan Parsons because she planned to live there with her fiance. French was ordered to pay $368.50 in compensatory damages to Parsons, $400 for mental anguish and suffering, and $300 civil penalties. We reverse. * * *

French owned and occupied a two-bedroom house ("subject property") in Marshall, Minnesota, until moving to a house he purchased in the country. While attempting to sell the subject property, French rented it to both single individuals and married couples. From January to March 1988, French advertised the subject property as being available for rent. On February 22, 1988, French agreed to rent the property to Parsons and accepted a $250 check as a security deposit.

Shortly thereafter, French decided that Parsons had a romantic relationship with her fiance, Wesley Jenson, and that the two would likely engage in sexual relations outside of marriage on the subject property. On February 24, 1988, French told Parsons that he had changed his mind and would not rent the property to her because unmarried adults of the opposite sex living together were inconsistent with his religious beliefs. French is a member of the Evangelical Free Church in Marshall, and his beliefs include that an unmarried couple living together or having sexual relations outside of marriage is sinful. Despite being questioned by French, neither Parsons nor Jenson told French whether they were planning to have sexual relations on the subject property. The record is in dispute as to whether appellant had knowledge of Parsons' intended sexual activity with her fiance, but Parsons did not deny such an intent when queried by French. Even if they would not have had sexual relations on the property, French believes that living together constitutes the "appearance of evil" and would not have rented to them on that basis. French admits that if Parsons had been married to Jenson, he would not have objected renting to them. * * *

We must examine whether appellant's refusal to rent to Parsons constituted a prima facie violation of the Human Rights Act's prohibition of marital status discrimination. The act provides in relevant part:

It is an unfair discriminatory practice:

(1) For an owner, lessee * * *

(a) to refuse to sell, rent, or lease ... any real property because of race, color, creed, religion, national origin, sex, marital status, status with regard to public assistance, disability, or familial status.

Minn.Stat. § 363.03, subd. 2.

I. The Definition of "Marital Status"

The administrative law judge (ALJ) found that appellant refused to rent to Parsons because she "was single and planned to cohabit with another person of the opposite sex." The version of the MHRA in effect at the time the alleged discrimination occurred and when the charge was filed did not contain a definition of the term "marital status."

It is well settled that, in the interpretation of ambiguous statutes, this court is required to discover and effectuate legislative intent. The term "marital status" is ambiguous because it is susceptible to more than one meaning, namely, a meaning which includes cohabiting couples and one which does not. In order to show that construing "marital status" to include unmarried cohabiting couples is inconsistent with public policy, legislative intent, and previous decisions of this court, it is necessary to examine the history of the MHRA and our cases interpreting it. * * *

This court, in construing the term "marital status" has consistently looked to the legislature's policy of discouraging the practice of fornication and protecting the institution of marriage. See Kraft, Inc. v. State ex rel. Wilson, 284 N.W.2d 386, 388 (Minn.1979). *Kraft* presented the question of whether an employer's anti-nepotism policy constituted marital status discrimination within the meaning of the MHRA. In answering this question in the affirmative, Chief Justice Sheran stated:

> Endorsing a narrow definition of marital status and uncritically upholding an employment policy such as respondent's could discourage similarly situated employees from marrying. In a locale where a predominant employer enforced such a policy, economic pressures might lead two similarly situated individuals to forsake the marital union and live together in violation of Minn.Stat. § 609.34 [fornication statute]. Such an employment policy would thus undermine the preferred status enjoyed by the institution of marriage.

* * * The *Kraft* court unanimously concluded that the fornication statute was a valid expression of Minnesota public policy. Moreover, the *Kraft* court did not ignore the destructive practical effect of a contrary ruling simply because there was no direct evidence of fornication. It is easy to see that, but for these important public policies, the *Kraft* decision would have been different. * * *

Kraft [as well as other cases] stand for the proposition that, absent express legislative guidance, the term "marital status" will not be construed in a manner inconsistent with this state's policy against fornication and in favor of the institution of marriage. [Recent legislative amendments in the employment discrimination act] also demonstrate that the legislature did not intend to expand the definition of "marital status" in order to penalize landlords for refusing to rent to unmarried, cohabiting couples. Minn.Stat. § 363.01, subd. 40 (1988) defines "marital status" as follows:

> "Marital status" means whether a person is single, married, remarried, divorced, separated, or a surviving spouse and, in employment cases, includes protection against discrimination on the basis of the identity, situation, actions, or beliefs of a spouse or former spouse.

The plain language of this new definition shows that, in non-employment cases, the legislature intended to address only the status of an individual, not an individual's relationship with a spouse, fiance, fiancee, or other domestic partner. The extremely broad language following the phrase "and, in employment cases" constitutes legislative recognition that employment cases are fundamentally different from housing cases such as the case at bar. The legislative history of this subdivision indicates that the legislature did not intend to extend the protection of the MHRA to unmarried, cohabiting couples in the area of housing. * * *

Plaintiffs' interpretation of the Act would have us conclude that the legislature intended to protect from discrimination those individuals who choose to cohabit with a person of the opposite sex without entering into marriage. The fornication statute, as it existed when plaintiffs attempted to rent the apartments, evidenced this State's policy against such a practice. We believe plaintiffs' interpretation of the Act is in conflict with the longstanding policy reflected by the fornication statute. Statutory provisions relating to the same subject matter should be construed harmoniously where possible. * * *

II. Minnesota Constitution

The pertinent language in the Minnesota Constitution addressing religious liberty is as follows:

> The right of every man to worship God according to the dictates of his own conscience shall never be infringed . . . nor shall any control of or interference with the rights of conscience be permitted, or any preference be given by law to any religious establishment or mode of worship; but the liberty of conscience hereby secured shall not be so construed as to excuse acts of licentiousness or justify practices inconsistent with the peace or safety of the state * * *.

Minn. Const. art. I, § 16 (emphasis added). The plain language of this section commands this court to weigh the competing interests at stake whenever rights of conscience are burdened. Under this section, the state may interfere with the rights of conscience only if it can show that the religious practice in question is "licentious" or "inconsistent with the peace or safety of the state."

In view of the above considerations . . . we are compelled to conclude that French must be granted an exemption from the MHRA unless the state can demonstrate compelling and overriding state interest, not only in the state's general statutory purpose, but in refusing to grant an exemption to French.

In short, we interpret the Minnesota Constitution as requiring a more stringent burden on the state in our opinion and grants far more protection of religious freedom than the broad language of the United States Constitution. Pursuant to this analysis, we conclude that the state has failed to sustain its burden in demonstrating a sufficiently compelling interest. It appears that we have now reached the stage in Minnesota constitutional law where the religious views of a probable majority of the Minnesota citizens are being alleged by a state agency to violate state law. Today we have a department of state government proposing that, while French has sincere religious beliefs and those beliefs are being infringed on by the Human Rights Act, the state, nevertheless, has an interest in promoting access to housing for cohabiting couples which overrides French's right to exercise his religion. Respondent characterizes the state's interest as "eliminating pernicious discrimination, including marital status discrimination." We are not told what is so pernicious about refusing to treat unmarried, cohabiting couples as if they were legally married. * * *

How can there be a compelling state interest in promoting fornication when there is a state statute on the books prohibiting it? See Minn.Stat. § 609.34 (1988). Moreover, if the state has a duty to enforce a statute in the least restrictive way to accommodate religious beliefs, surely it is less restrictive to require Parsons to abide by the law prohibiting fornication than to compel French to cooperate in breaking it. Rather than grant French an exemption from the MHRA, the state would rather grant everyone an exemption from the fornication statute. Such a result is absurd. * * *

[A strenuous dissent by CHIEF JUSTICE POPOVICH is omitted.]

NOTES AND QUESTIONS

1.   Suppose *French* had been decided under the federal FHA, whose 1988 Amendments include "familial status" as a protected classification. What outcome? Suppose French's refusal to rent had been challenged under the "sex" provision of the federal fair housing act? Could one argue that French refused to rent to Susan Parsons because her roommate was a male? Federal courts have routinely applied the race discrimination provision to those who discriminate against interracially married couples. See Woods v. Beavers, 922 F.2d 842 (6th Cir.) (unpublished), cert. denied, 500 U.S. 943 (1991), noted supra. Is the analogy sufficiently close?

2.   The courts are having an extraordinarily difficult time with the question of landlords who claim a religion-based right to exclude unmarried heterosexual couples from their housing. In North Dakota Fair Housing Council, Inc. v. Peterson, 625 N.W.2d 551, 2001 N.D. 81 (2001), a divided state supreme court followed *French* and held that the state fair housing law did not prohibit the discrimination. By contrast, in McCready v. Hoffius, 459 Mich. 131, 586 N.W.2d 723 (1998), the Michigan Supreme Court held that the landlord violated Michigan law by refusing to rent to unmarried couples. Further, the Michigan statute did not violate the landlords' right to the free exercise of their religious beliefs, under either the Federal or Michigan Constitutions. Subsequently, however, the court vacated that portion of its order holding that the Michigan statute did not violate the landlords' free exercise rights, and remanded to the lower court for further consideration of the question. McCready v. Hoffius, 459 Mich. 1235, 593 N.W.2d 545 (1999). In Thomas v. Anchorage Equal Rights Comm., 165 F.3d 692 (9th Cir.1999), a Ninth Circuit panel held that a similar housing ordinance violated the landlords' rights of free exercise of their religion. However, the Ninth Circuit en banc then vacated that decision, holding that because the ordinance had not yet been enforced the question was not ripe for review. Thomas v. Anchorage Equal Rights Com'n, 220 F.3d 1134 (9th Cir.2000), cert. denied, 531 U.S. 1143 (2001). And in Smith v. Fair Employment and Housing Comm'n, 12 Cal.4th 1143, 913 P.2d 909, 51 Cal.Rptr.2d 700 (1996), cert.

denied, 521 U.S. 1129 (1997), the California Supreme Court disagreed with both parts of *French*, finding that the California civil rights statute prohibited a landlord from refusing to rent to an unmarried cohabiting couple, and concluding that neither federal nor state constitutional provisions respecting religious freedom provided the landlord with a defense. On the religious freedom claim, the court did not dispute the defendant's assertion that she had a sincere religious belief that cohabitation by unmarried persons was wrong. But it noted that nothing in her religious belief compelled her to invest her capital in residential real property rather than some alternative. "[O]ne who earns a living through the return on capital invested in rental properties can, if she does not wish to comply with an antidiscrimination law that conflicts with her religious beliefs, avoid the conflict, without threatening her livelihood, by selling her units and redeploying the capital in other investments." See also Swanner v. Anchorage Equal Rights Com'n, 874 P.2d 274, 278 (Alaska), cert. denied, 513 U.S. 979 (1994) (landlord's policy of not renting to unmarried, cohabitating couples violated Anchorage municipal code, and landlord's religious belief not a defense where the law itself was facially neutral and of general application); cf. Attorney General v. Desilets, 418 Mass. 316, 320, 636 N.E.2d 233 (1994) (landlord's refusal to rent to cohabiting unmarried adults violated state antidiscrimination statute, but Massachusetts has stronger state constitutional provision respecting religious freedom than federal law does; remanding for determination whether compelling state interest justified applying statute to landlord with unquestionably sincere religious beliefs).

3. In Lepar Realty Corp. v. Griffin, 151 Misc.2d 579, 581 N.Y.S.2d 521 (1991), the court extended *Braschi* to a case involving an unmarried heterosexual couple who had held themselves out as a family, including having a child. Thus New York seems well on the way to extending the concept of "family status," at least for rent control purposes, to couples who are not legally married. See also 119–121 East 97th Street Corp. v. New York City Comm'n on Human Rights, 220 A.D.2d 79, 642 N.Y.S.2d 638 (1996) (modifying and approving a damage award against a tenant harassed by his landlord because he was gay and HIV-positive).

In State ex rel. Sprague v. City of Madison, 205 Wis.2d 110, 555 N.W.2d 409 (App.1996, unpublished), rev. denied, 207 Wis.2d 284, 560 N.W.2d 273 (1996), cert. denied, 520 U.S. 1212 (1997), the court held that a tenant violated a municipal antidiscrimination provision by refusing to accept a lesbian who responded to her advertisement for a housemate. The defendant cited several Supreme Court right of privacy cases she claimed protected her right to select a housemate, but the court replied that the transaction was "commercial," and that no right of privacy applied to a commercial transaction. However, the court's use of the term "commercial" apparently meant nothing more than that the housemate was to share rental expenses. While the action was pending the City of Madison amended its ordinance to declare that "Nothing in this ordinance shall affect any person's decision to share occupancy of a lodging room, apartment or dwelling unit with another person or persons." Cf. Levin v. Yeshiva University, 96 N.Y.2d 484, 754 N.E.2d 1099, 730 N.Y.S.2d 15 (2001), in which the New York Court of Appeals held that Yeshiva University may have violated New York City's civil rights law, which protects from discrimination based on sexual orientation, when it restricted its medical school housing to traditional married students and their spouses.

4. In Harris v. Capital Growth Investors XIV, 52 Cal.3d 1142, 278 Cal.Rptr. 614, 805 P.2d 873 (1991) (in bank) the California Supreme Court held that a landlord's requirement that prospective tenants have a monthly income equal to three times the rent did not violate that state's Unruh civil rights statute. Most significantly, the court held that the Unruh act contains no separate coverage for practices that are not intentionally discriminatory but that have a "disparate impact" on a particular class of people—in this case, the income requirement was alleged to have an adverse disparate impact on women applicants.

CHAPTER 13

PUBLIC REGULATION OF COMMUNITY OWNERSHIP: CONDOMINIUMS AND COOPERATIVES

■ ■ ■

The condominium is a form of shared ownership that has been popular in the United States since the middle of the twentieth century. Condominiums are unique in two important respects. First, part of the condominium development, generally referred to as the common areas, is owned by all condominium owners as tenants in common. Other parts of the condominium, generally called the individual units, are owned individually by each member. The individual units usually consist of an individual housing unit (which could be either "apartments" in a larger building or free standing independent units), plus perhaps a garage, a small yard or garden, and perhaps private storage facilities. The common areas generally include the exterior walls of a building, shared hallways, laundry and recreational facilities, and the like; the individual units generally include the living space up to and including the interior walls.

The second important difference is that property in a condominium development is usually divided "horizontally" as well as vertically; that is, the owner does not necessarily own the space above her land to the highest heavens or below it to the center of the earth. In fact, many condominium statutes are called "horizontal property acts," to distinguish this kind of ownership from the more traditional kind.

§ 13.1 EXTERNAL RELATIONS

BERISH v. BORNSTEIN

Supreme Judicial Court of Massachusetts (2002).
437 Mass. 252, 770 N.E.2d 961.

CORDY, J.

The plaintiff trustees of the Trust of the Cotuit Bay Condominium (unit owners' association), commenced an action against the developer of the Cotuit Bay Condominium (condominium development), Stuart Born-

1116

stein (Bornstein); the original trustees of the unit owners' association, including Jamila, Morris, and Paul Bornstein (Bornstein trustees); and the general contractor of the condominium development, Cotuit Bay Condominium, Inc. (CBC). In their complaint, the trustees alleged inter alia that Bornstein breached the implied warranty of habitability by improperly constructing the condominium development, and that he and the Bornstein trustees breached various duties by failing properly to manage the unit owners' association and care for the common areas while they were original trustees.

* * *

* * * Construction of the condominium development began in 1981, and as the units were completed and sold between 1981 and 1985, Bornstein amended the master deed to expand the condominium development from the thirty-two original units to a total of sixty-two units.

On October 30, 1981, the unit owners' association was created. The declaration of trust, which sets out the trustees' rights and responsibilities, conveyed "[a]ll rights and powers in and with respect to the common areas and facilities of [the condominium development]" to the trustees "to exercise, manage, administer and dispose of the same and to receive the income therefrom for the benefit of the owners of record." It also required that the trustees set and assess common expenses for the upkeep of the common areas. . . .

Between 1982 and May, 1985, serious problems were identified in the common areas of the condominium development, including problems with the sliding doors, chimneys, skylights, decks, and roofs. None of the skylights, chimneys, or sliding doors had been installed with flashing, as required by the State building code (code), resulting in water leakage and damage to the sheet rock and other materials on the inside of the individual units. In addition, none of the outside decks was constructed in accordance with the code, causing their supporting columns to deteriorate prematurely and rot. No action was undertaken by Bornstein and the other original trustees of the unit owners' association to cure these and other problems. . . .

In October, 1988, the [current] trustees filed their third amended complaint, which set forth the following claims against Bornstein:

(1) negligence, individually and as a trustee of the unit owners' association, based on his failure to exercise due care in the design and construction of the condominium;

(2) misrepresentation, individually, based on statements about the condominium that the unit owners relied on to their detriment;

(3) breach of the implied warranty of habitability. . . .

The complaint also included one count against CBC for negligence based on its failure to exercise due care in the design and construction of the condominiums. . . .

The judge . . . dismissed the claim for breach of implied warranty of habitability against Bornstein because Massachusetts did not recognize a cause of action for breach of implied warranty of habitability arising out of the purchase of a house or condominium unit. . . .

This case raises issues similar to those raised in *Albrecht v. Clifford,* 436 Mass. 706, 767 N.E.2d 42 (2002). There we held that an implied warranty of habitability attaches to the sale of new homes by builder-vendors in the Commonwealth. Here, the judge allowed Bornstein's motion to dismiss because "[u]nder the current state of the law in this Commonwealth, such a cause of action arises only in situations involving the rental of residential property, and does not extend to the purchase of a house or condominium." We now consider whether the implied warranty of habitability attaches to the sale of residential condominium units by a builder-vendor.

Ownership of a residential condominium involves a form of property ownership different from ownership of a house. "Ownership of a condominium unit is a hybrid form of interest in real estate, entitling the owner to both 'exclusive ownership and possession of his unit, G.L. c. 183A, § 4, and . . . an undivided interest [as tenant in common together with all the other unit owners] in the common areas. . . .' " *Noble v. Murphy,* 34 Mass.App.Ct. 452, 455–456, 612 N.E.2d 266 (1993), quoting *Kaplan v. Boudreaux,* 410 Mass. 435, 438, 573 N.E.2d 495 (1991).[1] "This division between individual and common rights is basic to the theory of condominium ownership." *Golub v. Milpo, Inc.,* 402 Mass. 397, 401–402, 522 N.E.2d 954 (1988), citing Rohan, The "Model Condominium Code"—A Blueprint for Modernizing Condominium Legislation, 78 Colum. L.Rev. 587, 587 n.3 (1978), and Schwartz, Condominium: A Hybrid Castle in the Sky, 44 B.U. L.Rev. 137, 139 (1964). "It affords an opportunity to combine the legal benefits of fee simple ownership with the economic advantages of joint acquisition and operation of various amenities including recreational facilities, contracted caretaking, and security safeguards" (footnote omitted). *Noble v. Murphy, supra* at 456, 612 N.E.2d 266. In keeping with this division of property ownership, condominium unit owners cede the management and control of the common areas to the organization of unit owners, which is the only party that may bring litigation relating to the common areas of the condominium development on their behalf. G.L. c. 183A, § 10(*b*)(4). See *Strauss v. Oyster River Condominium Trust,* 417 Mass. 442, 445, 631 N.E.2d 979 (1994) ("Only the trustees have the right to conduct litigation concerning 'common areas and facilities' "). The division in property ownership, however, does not mean that a condominium unit owner has "relinquish[ed] to the condominium association all

---

1. See *Golub v. Milpo, Inc.,* 402 Mass. 397, 400, 522 N.E.2d 954 (1988) ("The condominium is a form of property ownership in which the unit owner retains an exclusive fee interest in his individual unit in addition to an undivided interest with all other unit owners in the condominium's common areas and facilities"); *McEneaney v. Chestnut Hill Realty Corp.,* 38 Mass.App.Ct. 573, 577, 650 N.E.2d 93 (1995) ("Ownership of a condominium is a dual form of interest in real estate, entitling the owner both to exclusive ownership and possession of his unit and to an undivided interest together with other unit owners in the common areas").

actions against the developer for failure to deliver what was promised." *Cigal v. Leader Dev. Corp.,* 408 Mass. 212, 215, 557 N.E.2d 1119 (1990). For example, "[n]othing ... divests the purchaser of a condominium unit of the right to sue in breach of contract." *Id.* ("a breach of contract claim has an 'individual character' and is the sort of action that we have ruled may be brought or settled only by an individual unit owner").

The policy reasons that led us to adopt an implied warranty of habitability in the purchase of a new home apply equally to the purchase of a new condominium unit. See *Albrecht v. Clifford, supra* at 710–712, 767 N.E.2d 42 (implied warranty protects purchasers from structural defects which are nearly impossible to ascertain by inspection after home is built and imposes burden of repairing latent defects on person who has opportunity to notice, avoid, or correct them during construction process). The legal differences between the purchase and ownership of a condominium unit and the purchase and ownership of a house are inconsequential when compared to the similarity of purpose underlying both transactions, i.e., the acquisition of a habitable home. We therefore decide that an implied warranty of habitability attaches to the sale of new residential condominium units by builder-vendors in the Commonwealth, just as it now applies to the sale of new houses. See *Gable v. Silver,* 258 So.2d 11, 18 (Fla.Dist.Ct.App.1972) ("implied warranties of fitness and merchantability extend to the purchase of new condominiums in Florida from builders"); *Pontiere v. James Dinert, Inc.,* 426 Pa.Super. 576, 627 A.2d 1204 (1993) (original purchasers of condominium units may bring suit for breach of implied warranty of habitability and workmanlike construction).

A claim for breach of this implied warranty may be brought by an individual unit owner who can establish that (1) he purchased a new residential condominium unit from the builder-vendor; (2) the condominium unit contained a latent defect; (3) the defect manifested itself to the purchaser only after its purchase; (4) the defect was caused by the builder's improper design, material, or workmanship; and (5) the defect created a substantial question of safety or made the condominium unit unfit for human habitation. *Albrecht v. Clifford, supra* at 711–712, 767 N.E.2d 42. . . .

Because of the distinctive ownership divisions between units and common areas that characterize condominiums, the protections afforded purchasers of newly constructed condominium units by this implied warranty against latent defects in their own units may not be adequate to ensure the habitability of those units. Therefore, we next consider whether an organization of unit owners may bring a claim for breach of an implied warranty of habitability against a vendor-builder for defects in the common areas of a condominium development that implicate the habitability of the individual units.

In Massachusetts, condominium unit owners own the common areas as tenants in common in proportion to their respective undivided interests. See *Kaplan v. Boudreaux, supra* at 438, 573 N.E.2d 495; *Noble v.*

Murphy, supra at 456, 612 N.E.2d 266. However, the management and control of the common areas of a condominium development is vested in the organization of unit owners, G.L. c. 183A, § 10, which is defined as "the corporation, trust or association owned by the unit owners and used by them to manage and regulate the condominium." G.L. c. 183A, § 1. The trustees or other members of the organization of unit owners may act only on behalf of all of the unit owners. *Golub v. Milpo, Inc., supra* at 401, 522 N.E.2d 954. Here, the organization of unit owners is a trust, and the trustees are empowered by G.L. c. 183A, § 10(*b*)(4), to "conduct litigation and to be subject to suit as to any course of action involving the common areas and facilities."

When there are defects or other problems in the common areas, the organization of unit owners has the exclusive right to seek a remedy. G.L. ch. 183A, § 10(*b*)(4). See *Strauss v. Oyster River Condominium Trust, supra.* This exclusive right, combined with a unit owner's virtually nonexistent control over the common areas, may result in an incomplete remedy for unit owners against a builder whose improper design, material, or workmanship is responsible for a defect in a common area that causes units to be unhabitable or unsafe. To ensure that there is a complete remedy for a breach of habitability in the sale of condominium units, we conclude that an organization of unit owners may bring a claim for breach of the implied warranty of habitability when there are latent defects in the common areas that implicate the habitability of individual units.

To establish such a claim, the organization of unit owners must demonstrate that (1) it is an organization of unit owners as defined by G.L. c. 183A, § 1; (2) the common area of the condominium development contains a latent defect; (3) the latent defect manifested itself after construction of the common areas was substantially completed; (4) the defect was caused by the builder's improper design, material, or workmanship; and (5) the defect created a substantial question of safety as to one or more individual units, or made such units unfit for human habitation. . . .

We vacate the dismissal of the claim for breach of the implied warranty of habitability. . . .

NOTES AND QUESTIONS

1. In Dutcher v. Owens, 647 S.W.2d 948 (Tex.1983), the Texas Supreme Court considered the extent of a landlord's tort liability to a tenant who had rented a condominium from the unit owner. The injury resulted from the negligence of the condominium owners' association, not the landlord, when the association failed to insulate an electrical box. As a result, a fire began in a common area and destroyed most of the tenant's property in the adjacent unit. The landlord's liability was assessed at $1,087, which the trial court computed by taking the plaintiff's loss and multiplying it by the defendant landlord's ownership interest in the common elements: in this case 1.572%. The Texas Supreme Court affirmed, holding that a condominium owner was

not jointly and severally liable—that is, liable for the tenant's entire loss—but rather was liable only in proportion to his ownership interest in the property as a whole. The court based its conclusion on the fact that the individual owner of a condominium unit had no "control" over negligence with respect to common elements; rather, such negligence was within the control of the owners' association, which represented the interests and responsibilities of all unit owners. The decision was expressly restricted to injuries caused by negligent conditions existing in the common areas and not within the area controlled exclusively by the landlord. Accord Luchejko v. City of Hoboken, 207 N.J. 191, 23 A.3d 912 (2011) (condominium association, not individual unit owner, liable for slip and fall accident on icy public sidewalk in front of unit owner's unit).

2. Suppose an owner of a single unit suffers an injury from a defect in the sidewalk in front of his unit, which is part of the common areas. Under the *Berish* reasoning, could the unit owner unilaterally sue the contractor, or must he rely on the owners' association to bring the action? See Rouse v. Glascam Builders, Inc., 101 Wash.2d 127, 677 P.2d 125 (1984) (en banc) (permitting individual unit owner to proceed).

3. Suppose a developer acquires an easement for something like beach access across adjoining land. At the time of the acquisition the dominant estate is undeveloped, but the owner than develops a 50–unit condominium and claims that each of the 250 tenants has beach access rights. See Perdido Place Condominium Owners Assoc. v. Bella Luna Condominium Owners Assoc., 43 So.3d 1201 (Ala. 2009), following the usual rule that a dominant estate can be divided and that each portion then becomes a dominant estate as to the easement.

§ 13.2   INTERNAL DISPUTES

PENNEY v. ASSOCIATION OF APARTMENT OWNERS OF HALE KAANAPALI

Supreme Court of Hawaii (1989).
70 Haw. 469, 776 P.2d 393.

WAKATSUKI, JUSTICE.

Robert C. Penney and P. Jean Penney (Plaintiffs–Appellants) are owners of an apartment in Hale Kaanapali, a condominium project which has both residential/hotel apartments and apartments used as commercial spaces. Hale Kaanapali Hotel Associates, a Hawaii Limited Partnership, (Defendant–Appellee) is the owner of an apartment designated in the Declaration of the horizontal property regime as Building F constituting a snack bar containing 625 square feet except for the two bathrooms which are common elements within the Building. When a special meeting was called for the purpose of amending the Declaration, Defendant–Appellee had approximately 72.3% of the common interest of the condominium project and controlled another 4.53% interest by proxies. The amendment proposed to change a common area of approximately 2,664 square feet which was used as the Association clubhouse area including the restrooms from a common element to a limited common element for Defendant–Appellee's exclusive use. The proposed amendment was approved by a vote of 76.83% of the interest of all the apartment owners.

Plaintiffs–Appellants contended in the circuit court that the amendment is invalid because approval of 100 percent of the ownership interest is required to change a common element to a limited common area for the exclusive use by an apartment owner. * * *

Hawaii Revised Statutes (HRS) § 514A–13(b) (1985) provides:

The common interest appurtenant to each apartment as expressed in the declaration shall have a permanent character and shall not be altered without the consent of all the apartment owners affected[.]

In contrast, HRS § 514A–13(d)(1) (1985) permits the board of directors of the association of apartment owners "upon the approval of the owners of seventy-five per cent of the common interests, to change the use of the common elements."

Defendant–Appellee contends that the amendment to the Declaration is merely a change in the use of the common elements, and therefore, § 514–13(d)(1) applies. This would require an approval of only 75 percent of the common interests.

The change of use of a common element (e.g., changing from shuffleboard to tennis court, or erecting a maintenance shed on what was open space), and conversion of a common element to a limited common element are significantly different. In the former, the benefit to all the apartment owners is not diminished. In the latter, however, the benefit to all the apartment owners is significantly diminished by the restricted and exclusive use of the limited common area to one or fewer than all of the apartment owners. "In effect, then, the common elements as to all other tenants have thereby been diminished." Stuewe v. Lauletta, 93 Ill.App.3d 1029, 1031, 49 Ill.Dec. 494, 496, 418 N.E.2d 138, 140 (1981).

Defendant–Appellee further contends that although there may be an alteration to the common elements, § 514A–13(b) requires unanimous consent only when the common interest is altered.

"Common interest" is defined as the percentage of undivided interest in the common elements appertaining to each apartment. HRS § 514A–3 (1985). Since the percentage of undivided interest in the common elements owned by each apartment owner will remain the same, Defendant–Appellee reasons that § 514–13(b) is inapplicable. We disagree.

We agree with the Florida appellate court which stated: "An undivided interest [in the common elements] is an undivided interest in the whole and when that whole changes, that interest, if not the percent, also changes." Tower House Condominium, Inc. v. Millman, 410 So.2d 926, 930 (Fla.Dist.Ct.App., 3d Dist.1981). See also Grimes v. Moreland, 41 Ohio Misc. 69, 74, 322 N.E.2d 699, 703 (1974) ("Fencing-in of one area for almost exclusive use of one unit owner will not alter the percentage interest of the other unit owners (each will still have this approximately

6% interest) but it will mean that each unit owner will have 6% of the smaller remaining common area.")

For all intents and purposes, converting a common element to a limited common element diminishes the common interest appurtenant to each apartment. Under HRS § 514A–13(b), we hold that such conversion requires the consent of all the apartment owners.

NOTES AND QUESTIONS

1. Suppose the owner of an individual condominium unit wishes merely to enlarge his unit by taking advantage of "unused" common space—for example, suppose the tenant in a single story condominium complex wishes to add a second story. The great majority of courts say that an owner may not do so unless the condominium declarations or bylaws specifically permit it, or he obtains unanimous consent from other owners. See, for example, Makeever v. Lyle, 125 Ariz. 384, 609 P.2d 1084 (App.1980), which forbad the plaintiff from erecting a second story on his single story unit after he had received the permission of ten out of sixteen of the unit owners. Accord Lake v. Woodcreek Homeowners Assn., 169 Wash.2d 516, 243 P.3d 1283 (2010) (en banc).

2. Condominium owners are generally subject to numerous provisions concerning their rights in both common elements and individual units. These provisions generally take the form of servitudes (see Chapter 8), whether they are express in the deed or listed in a separate document (often called a master deed or declaration of restrictions) and incorporated by reference.

Most condominium agreements contain a servitude that permits the home owners' association to make or amend by-laws that govern owners and occupants. However, some courts say that subsequent by-laws passed by the association are subject to a weaker presumption of reasonableness than declarations in the original condominium documents. Do you see why? Board of Directors of 175 East Delaware Place Homeowners Assn. v. Hinojosa, 287 Ill.App.3d 886, 223 Ill.Dec. 222, 679 N.E.2d 407, app. denied, 174 Ill.2d 555, 686 N.E.2d 1158, 227 Ill.Dec. 2 (1997).

Nevertheless, courts generally approve such by-law amendments even if they did not receive unanimous support, provided that (1) the amendments do not reduce the size of the common area; and (2) they are not made to apply retroactively to people who have already relied substantially on the status quo. For example, see Constellation Condominium Ass'n, Inc. v. Harrington, 467 So.2d 378 (Fla.App.1985) (age restriction amendment could not be applied retroactively to people who owned their units previous to the amendment); Chateau Village North Condominium Ass'n v. Jordan, 643 P.2d 791 (Colo. App.1982) (pet regulation upheld respecting new pets, but not for pets acquired before regulation was passed). Cf. Granby Heights Assn. v. Dean, 38 Mass.App.Ct. 266, 647 N.E.2d 75 (1995) (striking down rule preventing dogs from being exercised in common areas because it effectively made it impossible to maintain large pets even though condominium rules permitted them). California has recently passed a statute requiring that any owner occupant of a residential condominium be entitled to keep at least one pet. Cal.Civ.Code § 1360.5. See Villa De Las Palmas Homeowners Ass'n v. Terifaj, 99 Cal.

App.4th 1202, 121 Cal.Rptr.2d 780 (2002), which held that the statute was not retroactive). For a thoughtful attempt to identify the boundary between private right and community concern in shared residential communities such as condominiums, see Lee Anne Fennell, The Unbounded Home: Property Values Beyond Property Lines (2009). See also Paul Boudreaux, Homes, Rights, and Private Communities, 20 U.Fla. J.L. & Pub. Pol'y 479 (2009).

In considering the validity of subsequent by-law amendments that receive less than unanimous support, the courts generally distinguish between general policy changes affecting everyone and rules that explicitly enlarge or diminish the property interest of a single owner. In Kaplan v. Boudreaux, 410 Mass. 435, 573 N.E.2d 495 (1991), the court held that a non-unanimous vote of owners was insufficient to give one unit holder an "easement" or "license" for the purpose of landscaping a part of the common area in front of that owner's unit. The court held that any grant of a superior right in common areas to one unit owner over and above that given to others required a unanimous vote. It might also have noted that the access to the common area created by the by-law amendment was *exclusive*, thus casting doubt on the assertion that it was merely an easement or license. On by-law amendments taking rights away from unit owners, see Ridgely Condominium Assn. v. Smyrnioudis, 343 Md. 357, 681 A.2d 494 (1996) (rule change limiting commercial unit owner's right to receive clients required unanimous consent, not merely the 2/3 vote needed for by-law amendment).

Compare Buckingham v. Weston Village Homeowners Assn., 571 N.W.2d 842 (N.D.1997). The plaintiffs owned seven new units recently added to the defendant condominium. The streets in the older part of the development needed significant repair and the association passed a by-law assessing owners in proportion to value. This resulted in higher payments for the new owners than the existing ones who benefitted most from the repairs. More importantly, the condominium declaration required that all assessments be divided equally among the unit owners. The court concluded that the Association's action was manifestly unreasonable.

3.   Needless to say, the Fair Housing Act applies to condominiums, and thus may condemn various restrictions on age and familial status, whether or not they were put into place before the relevant Fair Housing Act amendment was enacted. See Chapter Twelve, and in particular, Bloch v. Frischholz, 587 F.3d 771 (7th Cir. 2009) (en banc), reprinted there.

NOTE: RESTRAINTS ON ALIENATION IN THE CONDOMINIUM AGREEMENT

Condominiums and cooperatives frequently try to exercise some control over the sale of units by individual members. Their motive is generally apparent: the remaining owners must share the building with whoever buys the unit that is for sale. However, restrictions on the resale of a condominium unit can run afoul of the legal rules prohibiting direct restraints on alienation (see chap. 4). Courts are divided in their treatment of these restraints. In Gale v. York Center Community Cooperative, 21 Ill.2d 86, 171 N.E.2d 30 (1960), the Illinois Supreme Court upheld a set of rules that gave the association the first right to purchase any unit which its owner wanted to sell, and permitted the association twelve months in which to exercise that right. Cf. Woodside Village Condominium Assn. v. Jahren, 806 So.2d 452 (Fla.2002) (upholding restriction limiting owners' right to lease condominium unit).

Restraints on alienation, including the association's right of first refusal, can also violate the Rule against Perpetuities. See ch. 4, supra. However, the trend is to uphold reasonable restraints, in spite of their indefinite duration. Some states have statutes or provisions in condominium enabling acts that exempt them from the Rule. See 4B Powell on Real Property ¶ 633.14[2], n. 10. Other states have dealt with the problem judicially. For example, in Franklin v. Spadafora, 388 Mass. 764, 447 N.E.2d 1244 (1983), the Supreme Judicial Court of Massachusetts upheld a condominium by-law that limited to two the number of condominiums that could be owned by any one person, against a charge that the rule was an unreasonable restraint on alienation. Even though the by-law had a potentially infinite duration, the court found it to be a "reasonable adjustment to the demands of condominium management...." The court acknowledged earlier Massachusetts decisions that struck down similar restraints, if they could extend "for a period beyond that fixed by the rule against perpetuities...." However, it noted that those decisions dated from a time when condominium ownership was "little known," and declined to apply them in this case.

A BRIEF NOTE ON HOUSING COOPERATIVES

The housing cooperative is another form of "shared but separate" home ownership. It differs from the condominium in several important respects. In a stock-cooperative, the most common kind of cooperative, a non-profit corporation is created which owns a residential building containing multiple units. The individual "owners" actually own one or more shares in the corporation and *rent* their individual units from the cooperative. Effectively, in a building containing ten identical units, each resident is both a tenant of the corporate landlord and an owner of 10% of the corporation's shares. However, the shares of the corporation are *personal* property, not real property.

The economic and financial differences between the condominium and the cooperative can be substantial, although some of the traditional disadvantages of cooperative ownership have been ameliorated by statute. For example, the owner's income tax deductions for such items as property taxes were not available to owners of cooperatives until Congress provided for them in the Internal Revenue Code. Internal Revenue Code of 1986, § 216(a).

Today the most severe financial disadvantage of the cooperative results from its corporate status. The individual members do not own a separate piece of real property, but only a share in a corporation. Since the security for a mortgage on real property is the real property itself, this can mean that only the cooperative as a unit will be able to obtain mortgage financing. In that case, however, all the cooperative residents end up sharing the obligation of a single mortgage loan with an outside lender. A default in rental payment by one resident can throw the entire cooperative into default, unless they have sufficient reserves to make up the defaulter's payment. As a practical matter, it is often very difficult for a single purchaser or owner of an interest in a cooperative building to obtain separate financing for purchase of the unit or rehabilitation of an existing unit. Furthermore, because the fortunes of the entire cooperative depend so heavily on the creditworthiness of each member, the cooperative association is likely to be much more cautious about approving prospective buyers. This can make shares of stock in the cooperative difficult to sell. A result of these disadvantages is that cooperative housing, which was once very popular, has given way in most places to the condominium form of communal ownership. Cooperative housing is common only in New York City and a few other large urban areas. See P. Rohan & M. Reskin, Cooperative Housing Law and Practice (1986).

CHAPTER 14

VOLUNTARY TRANSFERS OF INTERESTS IN REAL PROPERTY: THE REAL ESTATE TRANSACTION

■ ■ ■

§ 14.1 INTRODUCTION: THE MARKET FOR REAL PROPERTY AND THE LAND SALE CONTRACT

Most transfers of ownership in real property are voluntary, arms-length exchanges. Until the parties reach a binding agreement they are not legally obligated to make the transaction and presumably will not make it unless they receive terms that are mutually agreeable to them. Two characteristics of real property make the market relatively complex. First, real property is expensive compared to most things that people buy and sell. As a general rule the amount of bargaining people are willing to undergo in making an exchange varies with the purchase price.

Second, real property has traditionally been considered not to be "fungible." A product is fungible when all sellers have more-or-less identical offerings and buyers are more-or-less indifferent from whom they purchase, as long as the price is the same. For example, if ten farmers are offering wheat for sale and a prospective customer cannot distinguish one farmer's wheat from another's, she will buy from the farmer who offers the lowest price. However, if ten sellers are offering a house for sale, a purchaser will not necessarily take the one offered at the lowest price, because she will be able to distinguish the house offered by one seller from that offered by another. She will take the house that gives the most that she wants for the money she can pay. That may be the least expensive house; but it may also be the biggest house, the house with the swimming pool, the one that will be available earliest, the one that needs the smallest amount of repair, etc.

Price-setting in real estate markets is complicated. The farmer about to sell wheat may look in the *Wall Street Journal* to see what the going price is that day. Although housing in a particular community certainly has a "going price," the price is far more ambiguous. The seller or broker establishing an asking price will not be able to find a house that is absolutely identical to the one he is preparing to sell. Rather, he will find a number of houses of approximately the same size and quality which are currently on the market or which have sold in the previous few weeks and attempt to establish some base price. Then he may adjust the price to account for unusual features that make this particular house desirable or undesirable. Is it across the street from a park or a gasoline station? Is it on a secluded street or a busy boulevard? Does it have a low interest "assumable" loan whose terms will not be changed, or must it be refinanced? Inevitably, price setting will involve some guesswork. If the price is set too low, the house may sell quickly, but the seller will not obtain the highest amount she could obtain. If it is set too high, no offers may be forthcoming. An experienced broker will generally establish an asking price slightly higher than the amount he feels the house will likely bring, and leave a little room for negotiating. Likewise, the experienced agent working for a buyer knows that most asking prices are "soft," and will probably advise the client to submit an offer somewhat lower than the asking price.

At that point negotiation begins in earnest. The parties will negotiate not only to find a price about which they can agree, but also to establish certain other terms. Will the seller leave the draperies or take them out? Will the seller pay to have the roof fixed before the sale is completed? Will the seller help the buyer obtain financing, perhaps by loaning the buyer part of the purchase price? All these terms affect the "price" of the house at the same time that they disguise it. A seller might be absolutely unwilling to take a penny less than $89,000, but may agree to leave the draperies or the refrigerator behind, even though both have a replacement value. The bargaining mind is a complex thing.

Today most sales of a home begin with a listing agreement between the prospective seller and a licensed real estate broker. After the house has been shown, often for several weeks and to many prospective purchasers, an interested customer will make an offer. Negotiations for a single-family home or condominium may involve several offers and counteroffers. When the parties have agreed on most of the important terms of the sale, they will execute a written land sale contract. Sometimes the contract is called an "earnest money contract," because by its terms the buyer deposits a sum of money to guarantee the seriousness of her intentions. If the buyer later changes her mind the earnest money may be forfeited as liquidated damages. See Lynch v. Andrew, 20 Mass.App.Ct. 623, 481 N.E.2d 1383 (1985), infra.

In most areas land sale contracts are written on preprinted forms provided by the local real estate board or bar association. Up to this point, lawyers are typically not involved in the ordinary residential transaction. Later, when the title has to be searched and deeds drafted, there is at least some lawyer involvement in most states. Of course, a complex transaction, including most commercial sales, may involve lawyers much more. This is particularly true if the property is being sold in conjunction with other legal proceedings, such as a divorce, bankruptcy, or the settlement of a decedent's estate.

§ 14.2   THE ROLE OF REAL ESTATE BROKERS, LAWYERS AND OTHER PROFESSIONALS

DWORAK v. MICHALS

Supreme Court of Nebraska (1982).
211 Neb. 716, 320 N.W.2d 485.

BUCKLEY, DISTRICT JUDGE.

This is an action brought by plaintiff, Douglas J. Dworak, a licensed real estate broker, against defendants, F.R. Michals, Sr., and Nebraska Real Estate Corporation, for the sum of $5,376, the same representing the amount of commission plaintiff claimed he was entitled to for having produced ready, willing, and able buyers to purchase an apartment complex owned by Michals and listed for sale with defendant Nebraska Real Estate Corporation, of which he was president.

The action was tried to the court, which determined that plaintiff was not entitled to a commission but was entitled to $250, which was one-half of the earnest money deposit, and entered judgment for that amount against both defendants. From this judgment plaintiff appeals.

The material facts are not disputed. The listing contract between Michals and Nebraska Real Estate Corporation was executed on April 6, 1977. It provided for a 6 percent commission in the event a purchaser was found "who is ready, willing and able to purchase the property before the expiration of this listing." It was a Multiple Listing Service contract, which meant that the listing was promulgated to all member realtors of the Multiple Listing Service in the Lincoln, Nebraska, area. This was accomplished by distribution of a Multiple Listing "sheet" or "ticket" which contained a photograph of the building and information concerning the property, which included an "income estimate" and "expense estimate." The income estimate specified 12 five-room apartments at $215 per month rent and 10 garages renting for $15 monthly.

Plaintiff, at that time a self-employed realtor and a member of the Lincoln Multiple Listing Service, received the listing on April 12, 1977. He contacted Michael Johanns and A.J. Swanson, whom he knew were interested in buying an apartment building for investment purposes. He gave them a copy of the listing sheet and took them through the property. Johanns and Swanson used the income and expense information on the listing sheet to calculate the cash flow, i.e., whether or not the rental income would be sufficient to cover all expenses, including the projected mortgage payment. They relied on the information on the listing sheet in making their cash flow calculations, which they determined would meet their requirements.

They then submitted an offer to purchase the property for $256,000 on April 14, 1977, which offer was accepted by Michals on the same day. The offer was accompanied by a $500 deposit, which was held by defendant Nebraska Real Estate Corporation.

While the buyers were in the process of securing a mortgage loan, the appraiser for the mortgage lender called Johanns on May 3 and told him that while he was at the property many tenants expressed extreme concern over the increase in rents planned for June 1, and that many of them threatened to move. Johanns relayed this to Swanson. Since both buyers were totally unaware of any planned increase in rents, Swanson immediately called Michals, who admitted that at about the same time the property was listed for sale the tenants were sent notices of an increase in rent, averaging about $15 per unit, effective June 1. He also admitted that the rents as shown on the listing sheet were not the rents currently in effect but in fact were the rents to be charged on June 1. When Swanson demanded that some form of action be taken over the situation, Michals immediately agreed to release the buyers from the purchase contract, which they elected to do, and the release was executed on the following day, with the $500 deposit returned to the buyers. The plaintiff Dworak first learned of the release later and, after his demand for a commission was refused, brought this suit.

The parties agree that if plaintiff is entitled to a commission it would be in the sum of $5,376, which is 2.1 percent of the sales price and his share as a nonlisting broker of the total commission due. Plaintiff contends he is entitled to the commission because he produced buyers who were ready, willing, and able to purchase the property when the contract to purchase was signed, notwithstanding that the sale was never closed. Defendants contend that plaintiff's commission would not be earned until the sale is consummated, unless the failure to consummate is the fault of the seller. They then contend that in fact the sale did not close because the buyers became unwilling and backed out of the agreement.

As to the applicable law, the defendants are correct. In the case of *Cornett v. Nathan,* 196 Neb. 277, 242 N.W.2d 855 (1976), we analyzed the law in this area. First, we noted that "[t]his court has consistently held that a broker has not earned his commission unless he produces a buyer who is ready, able, and willing to buy on terms satisfactory to the seller." Id. at 279, 242 N.W.2d at 857. In *Wisnieski v. Coufal,* 188 Neb. 200, 204, 195 N.W.2d 750, 753 (1972), we said: "A broker earns his commission and becomes entitled thereto when he produces a purchaser who is ready, able, and willing to purchase at a price and upon terms specified by the principal or satisfactory to him." * * *

In *Cornett,* however, the buyer was financially unable to consummate the sale. It is not clear whether this condition existed when he signed the agreement to purchase. We recognized that the intent of the parties in the usual listing agreement is that the seller expects to pay a commission only if the sale is completed, because, in most cases, the only source capable of paying the commission is the proceeds from the sale of the property. We further recognized that the reason for the payment of substantial commission fees is the requirement placed upon the real estate broker that he produce not just a person who will sign an agreement to purchase on hopes and expectation, but one who is ready, willing, and able to pay.

We then went on in *Cornett* to disapprove any notion that the commission is earned as soon as the seller accepts an offer to purchase, noting that to do this would place an unreasonable and unrealistic burden on the seller to determine the buyer's readiness, willingness, and ability to complete the purchase at the time the offer to purchase is made. Rather, we placed this burden and the risk involved on the broker, since this would be his most important function in earning his commission.

We then concluded in *Cornett* that where the buyer is financially unable to close the sale, the broker has not earned his commission. In support of this conclusion, we cited the following language from *Ellsworth Dobbs, Inc. v. Johnson,* 50 N.J. 528, 551, 236 A.2d 843, 855 (1967): "When a broker is engaged by an owner of property to find a purchaser for it, the broker earns his commission when (a) he produces a purchaser ready, willing and able to buy on the terms fixed by the owner, (b) the purchaser enters into a binding contract with the owner to do so, and (c) the purchaser completes the transaction by closing the title in accordance with the provisions of the contract." This three-part test, as generally stated, would apply to the unwilling as well as the financially unable buyer. Since the rationale previously stated for requiring consummation of the sale for the broker to earn the commission would be just as applicable to the buyer who becomes unwilling as it would to the buyer who becomes unable, we adopt the three-part test set out in *Ellsworth Dobbs* as the general rule to determine when a real estate broker earns his commission.

The adoption of this rule, however, does not alter the obligation of the seller to pay a commission if the sale is not completed due to the fault or refusal of the seller. We have always held that, in such event, the broker has a right to the commission called for.

This is also recognized in *Ellsworth Dobbs, Inc. v. Johnson,* supra, where the court, after setting out the three-part test, went on to say: "If the contract is not consummated because of lack of financial ability of the buyer to perform or because of any other default of his . . . there is no right to commission against the seller. On the other hand, if the failure of completion of the contract results from a wrongful act or interference of the seller, the broker's claim is valid and must be paid. In short, *in the absence of default by the seller*, the broker's right to commission against the seller comes into existence only when his buyer performs in accordance with the contract of sale." (Emphasis supplied.) Id. at 551, 236 A.2d at 855.

This case, then, turns on the question of whether the buyers Johanns and Swanson had a legal right to refuse to go further with the sale. If not, they become unwilling buyers and plaintiff is not entitled to a commission.

If they did, the failure to close the sale is attributable to Michals and plaintiff has earned his commission.

The trial court found that the buyers backed out of a valid purchase contract. We feel the evidence is insufficient to support that finding. The decision of Johanns and Swanson not to complete the sale was based on the representation of the rents on the listing sheet and their discovery that those rents were not the current rents but new rent increases effective almost immediately after they would become the new landlord. They faced the risk of tenants leaving, with resultant vacant units and an insufficient cash flow, the very thing they relied on in their purchase offer. It would also lock them in from June 1 as to future rent adjustments. And, as Johanns put it, "there was a general pervasive fear of whether I could trust this seller."

The buyers could have defended an action by Michals for specific performance on the ground of misrepresentation. The facts support the essential elements, namely, a representation as a statement of fact, untrue when made, known to be untrue by the maker, with the intention that it be acted upon, and acted upon with resulting detriment. *Moser v. Jeffrey,* 194 Neb. 132, 231 N.W.2d 106 (1975).

* * *

The judgment of the District Court is reversed and the cause remanded with directions to enter judgment for the plaintiff against defendant Michals in the sum of $5,376 plus interest from May 15, 1977, that being the date of the scheduled closing of the sale, and to dismiss the action as to defendant Nebraska Real Estate Corporation.

NOTES AND QUESTIONS

1. Courts commonly state the traditional rule to be that unless the broker-seller contract provides to the contrary, a broker earns her commission when she produces a buyer ready, willing and able to complete the purchase. Bennett Realty, Inc. v. Muller, 100 N.C.App. 446, 396 S.E.2d 630 (1990) (broker gets commission even though seller refuses to perform). However, many courts refused to award the commission unless the ready, willing and able purchaser actually got as far as signing a binding agreement to purchase. In practice this means that the broker is entitled to her commission whenever the buyer is entitled to specific performance. Hallmark & Johnson Properties, Ltd. v. Taylor, 201 Ill.App.3d 512, 147 Ill.Dec. 141, 559 N.E.2d 141 (1990). Under the traditional rule, once the agent produces a ready, willing and able buyer, the agent can collect the commission from the *buyer* if the buyer defaults, even if there was no listing or brokerage agreement between broker and buyer. Kuga v. Chang, 241 Va. 179, 399 S.E.2d 816 (1991).

The broker's entitlement to a commission can be varied by contract. For example, if the contract provides that the commission is to be paid from the "proceeds at closing," then the commission will not be due unless the closing actually occurs. Chamberlain v. Porter, 562 A.2d 675 (Me.1989).

Ellsworth Dobbs, Inc. v. Johnson, 50 N.J. 528, 236 A.2d 843 (1967), first deviated from the traditional "ready, willing and able" rule, and held that a broker is entitled to her commission only out of the proceeds of a completed sale. Although Nebraska follows *Ellsworth Dobbs*, the *Dworak* rule illustrates an important exception: the broker is entitled to her commission even if the transaction fails, if failure results from the unjustified actions of the seller rather than the buyer. See also Hildebrandt v. Anderson, 180 Or.App. 192, 42 P.3d 355 (2002) (creating an exception when the commission is for a rental rather than a sale and the lessee stops making lease payments after the closing has occurred; broker entitled to commission).

2.   In *Dworak* the seller's failure was voluntary. What if it were involuntary? What if both parties entered the contract, but the seller turned out to be legally incapable of producing a marketable title? For example, Leo Johnson contracted with broker Hugh McHugh to sell some property that Leo purported to own. McHugh found a ready, willing and able purchaser. However, later it turned out that Leo actually owned the property jointly with his wife Darline who refused to sell. Is the commission due? See McHugh v. Johnson, 268 N.W.2d 225 (Iowa 1978), applying the traditional "ready, willing and able" rule and concluding that the commission was due. Would the case come out the same way under the *Ellsworth Dobbs* rule? Should it matter whether the seller knew when he entered the brokerage agreement that the title was defective? Compare Mayberry v. Davis, 288 Minn. 73, 178 N.W.2d 911 (1970) with Blau v. Friedman, 26 N.J. 397, 140 A.2d 193 (1958).

3.   Broker finds a buyer ready, willing, and able to purchase the property. However, before the closing day a fire totally destroys the property. The contract is rescinded. Is the commission due? See Hecht v. Meller, 23 N.Y.2d 301, 296 N.Y.S.2d 561, 244 N.E.2d 77 (1968), which applied the traditional "ready, willing, and able" rule to hold that the broker was entitled to the commission.

4.   Suppose the listing agreement requires that a commission be paid if the property is sold during the listing period. During that period the government condemns the property and just compensation is paid. Is a commission due? See Lundstrom, Inc. v. Nikkei Concerns, Inc., 52 Wash.App. 250, 758 P.2d 561 (1988), saying no. Suppose that when the listing is about to expire the owner transfers the property to a corporation in which he owns 100 percent of the shares. Is the commission due? See Hagan v. Adams Property Assocs., 253 Va. 217, 482 S.E.2d 805 (1997).

5.   The typical brokerage commission on the sale of residential property ranges from 5 percent to 7 percent of the purchase price. This does not include all the other substantial costs of closing a housing transaction: title appraisal and insurance, loan appraisal and loan origination fees, escrow fees, fees for various inspections of the premises for structural defects or infestation, lawyer's fees, and perhaps a transfer tax. The costs of using the housing market can easily run to 10 percent to 15 percent of the purchase price.

Several writers have tried to explain the high transaction costs of the real estate market. Their explanations range from price fixing among real estate professionals to plain incompetence. Their proposals for reform include governmental regulation and assumption of settlement costs by lending institutions. See Erxleben, In Search of Price and Service Competition in Residential Real Estate Brokerage: Breaking the Cartel, 56 Wash.L.Rev. 179 (1981); Owen, Kickbacks, Specialization, Price Fixing, and Efficiency in Residential Real Estate Markets, 29 Stan.L.Rev. 931 (1977); Whitman, Home Transfer Costs: An Economic and Legal Analysis, 62 Geo.L.J. 1311 (1974).

The Real Estate Settlement Procedures Act (RESPA), 12 U.S.C.A. §§ 2601–2617 et seq. was passed by Congress in 1974. It requires lenders to provide purchasers with full information about closing costs before closing occurs, forbids rebates from one real estate professional to another, and directs the U.S. Department of Housing and Urban Development (HUD) to investigate the causes of high real estate transaction costs. See Field, RESPA In a Nutshell, 11 Real Prop., Prob. & Tr.J. 447 (1976).

KUBINSKY v. VAN ZANDT REALTORS

Court of Appeals of Texas (1991).
811 S.W.2d 711.

WEAVER, CHIEF JUSTICE.

This case involves a claim by the purchasers of a house, with a defective foundation, against the listing agent and her broker. In June, 1987, Ralph and Christine Bane (the Sellers) retained Lynn Neathery to list their home. In August of that year, appellants, John and Janice Kubinsky, purchased this house from the Sellers. Two or three weeks after the appellants moved into the house, they noticed cracks above doors, around windows, and in the slab. As a result, appellants filed suit against the Sellers, the company who inspected the house, and appellees, Lynn Neathery and her broker, Van Zandt Realtors. * * * [The trial court issued judgment for the defendants.]

The record indicates that appellants had retained their own real estate agent, Pam Homer of Henry S. Miller Real Estate Agency, to aid them in the purchase of a new home. The Sellers and appellants executed a contract to purchase the Sellers' house, which permitted the appellants to have the foundation and other components of the home inspected by an inspector of their choice prior to closing the purchase. Appellants did have the house inspected by Meruss Inspection Company, which noted in its inspection report: "Evidence of minor [foundation] movement noted on East side of House. No major movement noted at this time." Appellant John Kubinsky was present during the inspection and, concerned over the notation that the house showed minor foundation movement, went outside with the inspector to see what the inspector had found. Appellants' agent, Pam Homer, was also present during the inspection, as well as Christine Bane, one of the sellers, but neither appellant nor Homer nor the inspector questioned Christine Bane about the foundation movement or whether any repairs had been performed. * * *

Both appellees and appellants agree that the main issue on this appeal is whether a listing real estate agent has a legal duty to inspect the listed property for defects over and above asking the sellers if such defects exist.

Appellants claim under their first point of error that such a duty does exist in Texas and that appellees breached this duty. Specifically, appellants assert two major points: 1) that appellees had a duty to take reasonable measures to determine whether the property was defective, including inspection of the home for signs of foundation problems and to explain to the Sellers the need to disclose prior foundation problems to a prospective purchaser; and 2) that upon receiving a copy of the inspection report indicating that foundation movement had occurred, appellees should have made sufficient and adequate inquiries of the Sellers concerning the foundation movement. However, appellants concede that they have found no Texas cases supporting their contentions. In support of their argument, appellants rely primarily upon interpretations of provisions of The Real Estate License Act (TRELA) and upon a case out of the California Court of Appeals, Easton v. Strassburger, 152 Cal.App.3d 90, 199 Cal.Rptr. 383 (1984).

Appellants begin their argument by looking to section 15(a)(6)(A) of TRELA which provides that the Texas Real Estate Commission may suspend or revoke a license if a licensing agent makes a "material misrepresentation" or fails "to disclose to a potential purchaser any latent structural defect or any other defect known to the broker or salesman." Under this point of error, appellants do not contend that appellees had knowledge of the foundation damages, and we do not read this section as imposing a duty to inspect listed properties or to make an affirmative investigation for possible defects. Further, section 18C of TRELA provides detailed criteria for licensing of real estate inspectors. This section, entitled Real Estate Inspectors; Licensing; Violations; Penalties; Real Estate Inspection Recovery Fund, defines a real estate inspector as a person who holds himself out to the public as "being trained and qualified to inspect improvements to real property, including structural items and/or equipment and systems, and who accepts employment for the purpose of performing such an inspection for a buyer or seller of real property." TEX.REV.CIV.STAT.ANN. art. 6573a, § 18C(a)(1) (Vernon Supp.1991). Subsection (a)(2) of section 18C defines a real estate inspection as a "written or oral opinion as to the condition of improvements to real property, including structural items and/or equipment and systems." Subsection (c) provides: "A person may not act or attempt to act as a real estate inspector in this state for a buyer or seller of real property unless the person possesses a real estate inspector license issued under this section." Subsection (c) further provides that in order to be eligible for a license as a real estate inspector, an applicant must successfully complete at least ninety classroom hours of "core real estate inspection courses" and satisfactorily complete an examination thereon. Under subsection (i)(5), a licensed real estate inspector may not "act in the dual capacity of real estate inspector and real estate broker or salesman." Finally, subsection (j) provides: "A person commits an offense if the person knowingly or intentionally engages in the business of real estate inspecting without a license...."

Referring back to the definition of real estate inspection, the business of real estate inspecting under subsection (j) can be defined to be the giving of a written or oral opinion as to the condition of improvements to real property, including structural items. Appellants next point to section 15(a)(6)(W) of TRELA, which provides that a licensee is subject to suspension or revocation of his license if he has been guilty of "acting negligently or incompetently in performing an act for which a person is required to hold a real estate license." Listing, selling, and offering to sell real estate are acts for which a real estate broker's or salesman's license is required under section 2(2) of TRELA. However, inspection of real estate for defects is not included in the list of acts contained in section 2(2). Inspection of real estate requires a separate license under section 18C of TRELA, which specifically prohibits blending the functions of broker or salesman and inspector.

In the Canons of Professional Ethics and Conduct for Real Estate Licensees, the Texas Real Estate Commission promulgated a section entitled "Fidelity," and it provides, in part, "that the primary duty of the real estate agent is to represent the interests of his clients, ... however, the agent, in performing his duties to his client, shall treat other parties to a transaction fairly." Tex. Real Estate Comm'n, 22 TEX.ADMIN.CODE s 531.1 (West January 1, 1976) (Fidelity). Appellees' fiduciary duties in this case ran to the Sellers of the home, although appellees were also required to treat appellants fairly in the transaction. That duty is adequately protected by the provisions of section 15(a)(6)(A) requiring disclosure to a potential purchaser of any latent structural defect or other defect known to the broker or salesman. Further, we note that appellants engaged the services of their own real estate agent, Pam Homer of Henry S. Miller Real Estate Agency, who assisted them throughout the transaction and that appellants and their real estate agent engaged the services of Meruss Inspection Company to inspect the property to assure its structural integrity and condition prior to contracting for purchase of the home.

Appellants further point to the California case Easton v. Strassburger, which imposed a duty on the listing agent to inspect the listed residential property and to disclose to prospective purchasers all facts materially affecting the value or desirability of the property that such an investigation would reveal. However, in light of our discussion of TRELA, we decline to follow the California Court of Appeals. We believe that the imposition of such liability in this situation should be left to the Texas Legislature. * * *

The trial court's judgment is affirmed.

NOTES AND QUESTIONS

1. Under the traditional common-law rule, the real estate broker represents the seller who hired her, and owes no duties to the buyer. This generally means that the buyer can sue the broker only for fraud, which generally requires a showing that the broker made statements that she knew were not

true. See, e.g., Herbert v. Saffell, 877 F.2d 267 (4th Cir.1989). See also Harkala v. Wildwood Realty, Inc., 200 Ill.App.3d 447, 146 Ill.Dec. 232, 558 N.E.2d 195 (1990) (broker not liable for innocent misrepresentation concerning termites where there was no evidence he knew or should have known about them); Hoffman v. Connall, 108 Wash.2d 69, 736 P.2d 242 (1987) (no broker's liability for innocent misrepresentation or failure to verify the seller's statements). In any event, brokers can be held liable for things they actually knew but failed to disclose. See Strawn v. Canuso, 140 N.J. 43, 657 A.2d 420 (1995) (broker knew of nearby toxic waste but failed to disclose).

2. A few cases have either expanded the common law or relied on special statutes regulating brokers to impose a higher duty upon brokers than the common law requires. These decisions require brokers not merely to disclose known defects to buyers, but also to make reasonable inquiry concerning suspected defects. See Easton v. Strassburger, 152 Cal.App.3d 90, 199 Cal. Rptr. 383 (1984), which the Texas court in the principal case refused to follow, holding that a broker can be guilty of negligence for failing to inquire about basement cracks that suggested structural instability. The *Easton* rule was later codified by the California legislature, but was limited to residential properties of four or fewer units. See also Lombardo v. Albu, 199 Ariz. 97, 14 P.3d 288 (2000), where the Arizona Supreme Court held that the broker had an obligation to inform the seller of the buyer's shaky financial condition that might make him unable to perform.

In Johnson v. Geer Real Estate Co., 239 Kan. 324, 720 P.2d 660 (1986), the Kansas Supreme Court interpreted Kansas' Real Estate Brokers' and Salespersons' License Act, K.S.A. 58–3034 et seq. (1980), both to impose a duty to inspect on listing brokers and also to give injured buyers a private cause of action. The Kansas legislature later amended the statute to provide that "[n]othing in this act shall be construed to grant any person a private right of action for damages...." The court later interpreted this provision to mean that the affirmative obligations that the statute imposed on brokers could be enforced through self-regulation by the brokerage industry, but not by private plaintiffs. The court said:

> By amending the Real Estate Brokers' and Salespersons' License Act, the legislature made it regulatory in nature and intended the Act to benefit the public rather than a special class of individuals—those who purchase or sell property through real estate brokers.

Brunett v. Albrecht, 248 Kan. 634, 810 P.2d 276, 278 (1991).

Do you agree with the court? Or is this just another instance of regulatory "capture" of the state legislature, in this case, by the realtors' and brokers' lobby?

IN RE LANZA

Supreme Court of New Jersey (1974).
65 N.J. 347, 322 A.2d 445.

PER CURIAM.

The Bergen County Ethics Committee filed a presentment with this Court against respondent, Guy J. Lanza, who has been a practicing member of the bar of this State since 1954.

The Committee specifically found that respondent's conduct violated DR5–105. This Disciplinary Rule forbids an attorney to represent adverse interests, except under certain very carefully circumscribed conditions.

In April or May of 1971, Elizabeth F. Greene consulted respondent with respect to the sale of her residence property in Palisades Park, New Jersey. Mr. Lanza agreed to act for her. In due course a contract, apparently prepared by a broker, was signed by Mrs. Greene as seller as well as by the prospective purchasers, James and Joan Connolly. The execution and delivery of the contract took place in Mr. Lanza's office, although he seems to have played little or no part in the negotiation of its terms. By this time he had agreed with the Connollys that he would represent them, as well as Mrs. Greene, in completing the transaction. The testimony is conflicting as to whether or not Mrs. Greene had been told of this dual representation at the time she signed the contract. Mr. Lanza says that she had been told, but according to her recollection she only learned of this at a later date from Mrs. Connolly. In any event it is quite clear that respondent agreed to act for the purchasers before discussing the question of such additional representation with Mrs. Greene.

The contract as originally drawn provided for a closing date in late July, 1971. At Mrs. Greene's request this date was postponed to September 1. A short time later, circumstances having again changed, Mrs. Greene found that she would now prefer the original date. This proved satisfactory to the purchasers but Mr. Connolly told Mrs. Greene that at this earlier date he would not have in hand funds sufficient to make up the full purchase price of $36,000. Of this sum he would lack $1,000. He suggested, however, that the parties might close title upon the earlier date if Mrs. Greene would accept, as part of the purchase price, a check for $1,000 postdated approximately 30 days. Mrs. Greene was personally agreeable to this. She consulted respondent who advised her that he saw no reason why she should not follow this course.

The closing accordingly took place late in July and in accordance with the foregoing arrangement, Mrs. Greene received, as part of the purchase price, Mr. Connolly's check in the sum of $1,000 dated August 31, 1971. Shortly after this latter date she deposited the check for collection and it was returned because of insufficient funds. When questioned, Mr. Connolly said that after he and his wife had taken possession of the property they discovered a serious water condition in the cellar. He added that Mrs. Greene had made an explicit representation that the cellar was at all times dry. For this reason he refused to make good the check, saying that it would cost him $1,000 to rectify the condition in the cellar. Mrs. Greene denied that she had ever made any representation whatsoever. She immediately got in touch with respondent who did nothing effective on her behalf. She then retained other counsel and has subsequently initiated legal proceedings against the Connollys.

We find respondent's conduct to have been unprofessional in two respects. In the first place, the way in which he undertook the dual representation failed to meet the standards imposed upon an attorney who elects to follow such a course. In the second place, after the latent conflict of interests of the two clients had become acute, he nevertheless continued to represent both parties. At that point, rather than going forward with the matter as he did, he should have withdrawn altogether.

Mr. Lanza first undertook to act for the seller, Mrs. Greene. This immediately placed upon him an obligation to represent her with undivided fidelity. Despite this obligation, he later agreed, without prior consultation with Mrs. Greene, to represent Mr. and Mrs. Connolly, whose interest in the matter was of course potentially adverse to that of his client. He should not have undertaken to represent the purchasers until he had initially conferred with Mrs. Greene. He should have first explained to her all the facts and indicated in specific detail all the areas of potential conflict that foreseeably might arise. He should also have made her aware that if indeed any of these contingencies should thereafter eventuate and not prove susceptible of ready solution in a manner fair and agreeable to all concerned, it would then become his professional duty immediately to cease acting for all parties. Only after such a conference with his client, and following her informed consent, would he have been at liberty to consider representing the purchasers. They, too, were entitled to the same explanation as is set forth above, as well as being told of respondent's existing attorney-client relationship with the seller.

The second instance of misconduct arose after respondent learned that the purchasers would not be able to pay the full purchase price in cash at the time of closing title. At that point adequate representation of the seller required that her attorney first strongly insist on her behalf that cash be forthcoming. Failing this, and if the seller persisted in her wish to close upon the earlier date, her attorney should have vigorously urged the execution and delivery to her of a mortgage from the purchasers in the amount of $1,000, or of other adequate security, in order to protect her interest pending receipt of the full cash payment. We think it fair to assume that had respondent not found himself in a position of conflicting loyalties, his representation of the seller would have taken some such course. Had the purchasers persisted in their unwillingness to pay the full amount in cash at the time of closing and had they also refused to execute and deliver a mortgage or other security, respondent should have immediately withdrawn from the matter, advising both parties to secure independent counsel of their respective choosing. At that point in time it would have clearly been impossible for any single attorney adequately and fairly to represent both sides.

This case serves to emphasize the pitfalls that await an attorney representing both buyer and seller in a real estate transaction. The Advisory Committee on Professional Ethics, in its Opinion 243, 95 N.J.L.J. 1145 (1972), has ruled that in all circumstances it is unethical for the same attorney to represent buyer and seller in negotiating the terms of a contract of sale. Here the respondent did not enter into these negotiations so he does not come under the ban of this rule. Canon 6 declared, however, that "[i]t is unprofessional to represent conflicting interests, except by express consent of all concerned given after a full disclosure of the facts." DR 5–105 is at least as strict in the requirements it lays down and in subparagraph (C) carries forward the injunction quoted above by prohibiting multiple representation unless "each [party] consents to the representation after full disclosure of the facts and of the possible effect of such representation on the exercise of his [the attorney's] independent professional judgment on behalf of each."

The extent of the necessary disclosure is what is important. As Opinion 243, supra, makes clear, this is a question that must be conscientiously resolved by each attorney in the light of the particular facts and circumstances that a given case presents. It is utterly insufficient simply to advise a client that he, the attorney, foresees no conflict of interest and then to ask the client whether the latter will consent to the multiple representation. This is no more than an empty form of words. A client cannot foresee and cannot be expected to foresee the great variety of potential areas of disagreement that may arise in a real estate transaction of this sort. The attorney is or should be familiar with at least the more common of these and they should be stated and laid before the client at some length and with considerable specificity. Of course all eventualities cannot be foreseen, but a great many can. Here respondent was representing Mrs. Greene, a seller of property. Generally a seller who has entered into a mutually binding contract of sale is principally interested in securing the full purchase price to which he or she is entitled. As counsel experienced in this field of practice well know, to allow a purchaser to take possession of the premises in question before the entire consideration has been received, either in the form of cash or purchase money mortgage, will often prove contrary to the seller's best interests. So it was here.

For the reasons set forth above, we deem respondent's conduct to merit censure. He is hereby reprimanded.

NOTES AND QUESTIONS

1. Many lawyers believe that every real estate transaction should involve at least two lawyers, one representing the buyer and one representing the seller. If there are more than one buyer or seller and they have potentially conflicting interests, then perhaps there should be even more lawyers. This view is expressed in Yzenbaard, Drafting the Residential Contract of Sale, 9 Wm. Mitchell L.Rev. 37 (1983); see also A.B.A. Special Committee on Residential Real Estate Transactions, Residential Real Estate Transactions: the Lawyer's Proper Role—Services—Compensation, 14 Real Prop., Prob. & Tr.J. 581 (1978). Real estate brokers, by contrast, appear to be quite confident that a lawyer is unnecessary, at least for routine purchases. Needless to say, a lawyer costs money, and two lawyers cost more than one. However, a non-attorney broker or real estate agent who gives his client too much legal advice runs a risk of being cited for the unauthorized practice of law.

One argument in favor of using an attorney in even routine home purchases is that brokers may have a conflict of interest that has nothing to do with the opposing needs of buyer and seller: a broker can generally expect to be paid *only* if the transaction is completed. The lawyer, by contrast, generally charges by the hour or task, and will be paid whether or not the sale is consummated. As a result some brokers are quick to advise clients to go ahead with transactions that lawyers might regard as questionable. For example, the broker may tell the client not to worry about easements of record that do not appear on the surface, or apparent violations of building codes or restrictive covenants.

2. In Goldfarb v. Virginia State Bar, 421 U.S. 773 (1975), the United States Supreme Court held that a county bar association violated the federal antitrust laws when it created a fee schedule for title searches and disciplined attorneys who deviated from the schedule. Today it is illegal for lawyers to agree about or "standardize" professional fees. The same rule generally applies to real estate brokers and other real estate professionals.

BOWERS v. TRANSAMERICA TITLE INSURANCE CO.

Supreme Court of Washington, en banc (1983).
100 Wash.2d 581, 675 P.2d 193.

PEARSON, JUSTICE.

Defendant Transamerica Title Insurance Company (Transamerica) appeals a summary judgment holding it liable to a vendor of real estate for failing to meet the standard of care required of an attorney, and an award of $42,805 in attorney fees.

* * *

Plaintiffs Mr. and Mrs. Bowers, and Mr. Bowers' brother Robert, purchased a parcel of real estate in 1971 as an investment. In 1978, plaintiffs advertised the property for sale at a price of $45,000. They received a response to the advertisement from one Dan Brown, president of Quantum Construction, Inc. (Quantum). Brown expressed interest in buying the property, and after some discussion presented Mr. and Mrs. Bowers with an earnest money agreement, in which Quantum agreed to buy the property for $45,000, payable $10,000 at closing, with the balance to be paid "by purchaser executing a note in favor of the seller." The earnest money agreement designated Transamerica as the closing agent for the transaction. Mr. and Mrs. Bowers signed the earnest money agreement.

* * * The sale from the Bowerses to Quantum was closed by Bonniejean Evans, an escrow closer employed by Transamerica. Mrs. Evans is not an attorney. She prepared the closing documents from the earnest money agreement drawn up by Quantum and signed by Mr. and Mrs. Bowers. Mrs. Evans prepared the seller's escrow instructions and the buyer's escrow instructions, both of which specified that the note representing the unpaid portion of the purchase price was to be unsecured. In the course of preparing the papers, Mrs. Evans asked Dan Brown of Quantum whether the note was to be unsecured. Brown replied "The earnest money [agreement] does not say secured by a deed of trust. It says a note." Mrs. Evans accordingly prepared an unsecured promissory note. Mrs. Bowers signed these and the other closing documents.

After closing, the deed to the property was delivered to Quantum. Quantum borrowed in excess of $30,000, using the property as security. In May 1979 a petition in bankruptcy was filed against Quantum. It was subsequently discovered that the shareholders of Quantum had departed the jurisdiction for places unknown. Plaintiffs consulted an attorney upon learning of the bankruptcy petition and the present litigation was commenced in May 1979.

Plaintiffs alleged that Transamerica had engaged in the unauthorized practice of law and in so doing had caused the plaintiffs to lose $35,000. Plaintiffs sought damages, attorney fees, and costs pursuant to RCW 19.86 (Consumer Protection Act). Transamerica denied it was practicing law, and claimed that plaintiffs were negligent in not seeking legal advice and that any loss suffered by plaintiffs was the result of fraud perpetrated by Quantum. Cross motions for summary judgment came before the Spokane County Superior Court in March 1981. The court decided that Transamerica had engaged in the unauthorized practice of law and was therefore held to the standard of an attorney. Transamerica fell below this standard by failing either to advise plaintiffs to seek independent counsel if they did not understand the transaction, or to explain to plaintiffs the hazards of an unsecured sale of real property. Transamerica was, therefore, liable to plaintiffs for the loss caused by this breach of duty.

* * *

It is not disputed that defendant's escrow closer, Mrs. Evans, engaged in the unauthorized practice of law. Mrs. Evans, who is not an attorney, prepared, in accordance with the earnest money agreement, escrow instructions, a promissory note, a statutory warranty deed, and a modification of the promissory note.

The selection and drafting of such documents is the work of lawyers and is not to be performed by laymen. We recognized in *In re Droker & Mulholland*, 59 Wash.2d 707, 719, 370 P.2d 242 (1962), that preparation of legal forms is the practice of law. We explained our position at greater length in *Washington State Bar Ass'n v. Great Western Union Federal Sav. & Loan Ass'n*, 91 Wash.2d 48, 55, 586 P.2d 870 (1978), where we held that

> the selection and completion of form legal documents, or the drafting of such documents, including deeds, mortgages, deeds of trust, promissory notes and agreements modifying these documents constitutes the practice of law.

More recently, we reaffirmed our commitment " 'to protect the public from the activity of those who, because of lack of professional skills, may cause injury whether they are members of the bar or persons never qualified for or admitted to the bar' ". *Hagan & Van Camp, P.S. v.*

Kassler Escrow, Inc., 96 Wash.2d 443, 447, 635 P.2d 730 (1981), quoting *Great Western,* 91 Wash.2d at 60, 586 P.2d 870. We invalidated in *Hagan* legislation (RCW 19.62) by which the Legislature sought to authorize laymen to perform legal tasks relating to real estate transactions.

If any explanation of our position were needed on this matter, this case surely provides it. Plaintiffs were exploited by a less than scrupulous businessman who contrived to obtain clear title to plaintiffs' property and proceeded immediately to encumber it. Plaintiffs did not understand that, because the sale was unsecured, they would have no recourse against the property if the purchaser defaulted. They proceeded blindly into the transaction, unaware of the pitfalls which awaited them. An attorney, trained to be aware of such pitfalls, could have restructured the transaction to avoid them. The lay escrow closer, lacking a lawyer's training, did not do so.

This court has held that a layman who attempts to practice law is liable for negligence. *Mattieligh v. Poe,* 57 Wash.2d 203, 204, 356 P.2d 328 (1960). The duties of an attorney practicing law are also the duties of one who without a license attempts to practice law.

* * * Transamerica seeks to avoid such liability in the present case by relying on the principle that an escrow agent is limited to the terms of his instructions and therefore has no duty to advise a party to a closing of any attendant risks. The leading authority for this proposition in Washington is *National Bank of Washington v. Equity Investors,* 81 Wash.2d 886, 506 P.2d 20 (1973). In that case, an escrow agent prepared a subordination agreement which subordinated the vendor's security interest in the realty to that of another party. The vendor claimed that the escrow agent breached its duty to him by failing to advise of the effects of the subordination agreement. This court held otherwise. We stated the general rule that an escrow agent or holder becomes liable to his principals for damage proximately resulting from his breach of the instructions, or from his exceeding the authority conferred on him by the instructions.

The court then proceeded to the conclusion that the escrow agent "was not authorized to practice law nor under any duty to advise [the principal] to consult further with his own lawyer."

A similar result was reached in respect of an escrow agent in *Wegg v. Henry Broderick, Inc.,* 16 Wash.App. 589, 557 P.2d 861 (1976). In that case, a real estate broker was held liable for failing to inform his clients of a provision prohibiting forfeiture in a real estate contract. The broker had selected the form of the contract, but it had been drawn up by an escrow agent. . . . The Court of Appeals noted without discussion or authority that the escrow agent had no liability because "he had a duty to obey the escrow instructions and the duty not to interfere with the transaction between the parties."

In neither case, however, was it argued that preparation of documents by the escrow agent constituted the practice of law. Therefore neither *Equity Investors* nor *Wegg* dealt with the implications of holding an escrow agent to the standard of an attorney. In the case before us, where this issue is squarely presented, we must consider the duties of an attorney who acts as an escrow agent.

In addition to the duty to follow the escrow instructions, a duty which applies to all escrow agents whether attorneys or lay persons, an attorney escrow agent must also meet the standards of the legal profession, including those standards set forth in the Code of Professional Responsibility. Among the duties imposed by this code is the duty to refuse to accept or to continue employment if the interests of another client may impair the independent professional judgment of the lawyer. CPR DR 5–105.

* * * As the case before us dramatically illustrates, an attorney who acts as an escrow agent for the parties to a real estate transaction is placed in the position of representing differing interests. The buyer's interest in obtaining an unsecured sale was diametrically opposed to the seller's interest in securing full payment of the purchase price. The potential for such adversity of interests exists in every real estate transaction. Therefore, while the attorney's duty as an escrow agent requires him to exercise strict impartiality between the parties, his duties as an attorney require him to provide each client "the opportunity to evaluate his need for representation free of any potential conflict and to obtain other counsel if he so desires." CPR EC 5–16. Accordingly, an attorney acting as an escrow agent has a duty to inform the parties to the real estate closing of the advisability of obtaining independent counsel. This duty to inform, which extends equally to both parties to the closing, in no way conflicts with the attorney escrow agent's duty of impartiality.

The standards that govern attorneys also apply to lay escrow agents who engage in the unauthorized practice of law. In the present case, the lay escrow agent employed by Transamerica breached the duty by failing to inform plaintiffs of the advisability of obtaining legal representation. The trial court was therefore correct in granting plaintiffs' motion for summary judgment on the issue of liability.

NOTES AND QUESTIONS

1. In Duncan & Hill Realty, Inc. v. Department of State, 62 A.D.2d 690, 405 N.Y.S.2d 339, appeal denied 45 N.Y.2d 821, 409 N.Y.S.2d 210, 381 N.E.2d 608 (1978), the court observed that a large number of states permit brokers and agents to help buyers and sellers prepare purchase contracts. The court went on to hold, however, that it was the unauthorized practice of law for a realtor to aid a client in preparing and negotiating a purchase contract unless the realtor advised the client (in this case, by a statement printed on the form contract in boldface type) that the contract was a legally binding document and that anyone who did not fully understand it should consult a lawyer. Second, the court observed that whenever a contract achieved a certain level of complexity, preparation by a non-lawyer broker automatically amounted to unauthorized practice of law. The court did not specify just how complex the

contract could be before it stepped over this line, but it held that a contract containing detailed requirements for a purchase money mortgage to be taken back by the sellers was too complex to be prepared without an attorney. Accord Opinion No. 26 of the Committee on Unauthorized Practice of Law, 139 N.J. 323, 654 A.2d 1344 (1995). See Corgel, Occupational Boundary Setting and the Unauthorized Practice of Law by Real Estate Brokers, 10 Research in L. & Econ. 161 (1987), concluding that brokers generally do about as well as lawyers in the preparation of legal documents attending a routine real estate transaction.

2.   One disconcerting implication of *Bowers* is that, once the real estate broker has crossed the line and is preparing legal documents, he can be held liable for *failing* to give legal advice, even though giving it would constitute the unauthorized practice of law. See Norman I. Krug Real Estate Invest., Inc. v. Praszker, 220 Cal.App.3d 35, 269 Cal.Rptr. 228 (1990), which found a broker at fault for failing to advise a creditor that his mortgage instrument should be recorded.

§ 14.3   THE LAND SALE CONTRACT AND THE STATUTE OF FRAUDS

The following contract form has been approved by the National Conference of Lawyers and Realtors, which is a joint committee of the American Bar Association and the National Association of Real Estate Boards. It is reprinted from Duncan & Hill Realty v. Department of State of New York, 62 A.D.2d 690, 405 N.Y.S.2d 339, appeal denied 45 N.Y.2d 821, 409 N.Y.S.2d 210, 381 N.E.2d 608 (1978).

THIS IS A LEGALLY BINDING CONTRACT:
IF NOT FULLY UNDERSTOOD, SEEK COMPETENT ADVICE!
CONTRACT OF SALE

PARTIES: _____, hereinafter called Seller (whether one or more, male, female, or corporate), agrees to sell to _____ hereinafter called Buyer (whether one or more, male, female, or corporate), who agrees to buy from Seller the property hereinafter described upon the terms and conditions hereinafter set forth.

1. **LEGAL DESCRIPTION** of real estate in _____ County. _____.

   Personal property included: _____.
   Street Address: _____. Said property fronts _____ feet on said street and runs back _____ feet.
   Seller represents that the property can be used for the following purposes: _____.

2. **PURCHASE PRICE:** $_____, payable as follows:
   $_____ earned money deposited with _____ as escrow agent.
   $_____ approximate balance of first mortgage, which Buyer assumes. Mortgage holder _____
   Interest _____% per annum, payable _____
   $_____ purchase money note and mortgage to Seller. Interest _____%, payable _____
   $_____ cash or cashier's check on closing (or such greater or lesser amount as may be required after credits, adjustments and prorations).

3. **ACCEPTANCE:** If this contract shall not have been signed by both parties on or before _____ the party having signed may declare it void, and if Buyer, he shall receive back his earnest deposit. The date of the last signature shall be the date of this contract.

4. **LOAN COMMITMENT:** This contract is conditioned upon Buyer's obtaining within 30 days from its date a commitment for a loan of $_____ with interest at _____% or less, and principal and interest payable together in _____ installments.

5. **DAMAGE BY FIRE, ETC.:** This contract is further conditioned upon delivery of the improvements in their present condition, and in event of material damage by fire or otherwise before closing. Buyer may declare the contract void and shall be entitled to return of his escrow deposit.

6. **CONVEYANCE:** The conveyance shall be by general warranty deed, signed by _____ and shall describe the grantee(s) as follows:
   _____

7. Seller shall furnish marketable title and shall convey the property free from encumbrances other than those named herein. Seller shall have the option of furnishing either a complete abstract of title or an Owner's Title Insurance Policy, insuring the title in the amount of the purchase price, issued by _____
   If Seller elects to furnish title insurance, he shall place an order therefor within five days from the date of this contract. If he furnishes abstract, Buyer shall have ten days within which to submit in writing any objections to the title. In the event of title objections, either by Buyer's attorney or by the title company, Seller shall have a reasonable time within which to cure them.
   On Seller's failure to furnish marketable title within a reasonable time, Buyer may either cancel the contract and receive back his escrow deposit or enforce specific performance.

8. **SURVEY:** If a survey be required, the cost shall be paid by _____.

9. **PRORATIONS:** Taxes, insurance, rents, and interest shall be prorated to the date of closing, and Buyer shall assume taxes for the current year and shall take over the unexpired fire and other casualty insurance, except _____.

10. **CLOSING:** The transaction shall be closed at _____ when title objections have been met; and Seller shall have _____ days after closing within which to deliver possession.

11. **COMMISSION:** Seller agrees to pay _____, the Broker who negotiated this sale, a commission of $_____; if Buyer shall default, said Broker shall be entitled to half the escrow deposit, or his full commission, whichever shall be smaller.

12. **DEFAULT:** On default by Buyer, Seller may retain the escrow as liquidated damages or enforce specific performance. On default by Seller, Buyer may reclaim his escrow deposit, sue for damages, or enforce specific performance.

EXECUTED IN QUADRUPLICATE on the dates shown.

_____Date _____Date
_____Date _____Date

[D10144]

WILEY v. TOM HOWELL & ASSOC., INC.

Court of Appeals of Georgia (1980).
154 Ga.App. 235, 267 S.E.2d 816.

QUILLIAN, PRESIDING JUDGE.

This is an appeal from the grant of a motion for summary judgment to the defendant—Tom Howell & Associates, Inc. (Howell). Plaintiff—Wiley, signed an "exclusive listing contract" with defendant Howell for the sale of his home. Included within the "special stipulations" section of the listing contract was the phrase: "w/option to accept appraised in 60 days." The testimony of the plaintiff—Wiley, and Mr. Wood, an employee of the defendant realty firm established that Wiley gave Howell the exclusive listing contract to sell his house within 60 days, and if the house was not sold to a third party, Howell would purchase the house—at an undetermined price—the "appraised" value. Wiley would then have the option of accepting or rejecting the tendered "appraised" price. The house was not sold and no offer was forthcoming from Howell to purchase the house. Wiley had moved to Texas, was unable to continue to make payments upon his former home, and foreclosure was made upon the house and it was sold. Wiley brought this action. Howell moved for summary judgment, substantially alleging that the Statute of Frauds precluded enforcement of that portion of the sales contract relating to the "sales option" of Wiley. Wiley appeals from the grant of summary judgment to Howell.

An option contract for the sale of realty comes within the Statute of Frauds and "writings ... relied on to take the transaction out of the Statute of Frauds ... 'must (a) identify the buyer and seller, (b) describe the subject matter of the contract, and (c) name the consideration.' "

* * *

Thus, the crucial issue is whether the cryptic phrase—"w/option to accept appraised in 60 days" embodies all of the essentials of an option contract for realty. We are of the opinion that it does not.

The document sufficiently identified the buyer and seller, and subject matter of the contract. However, we do not find the consideration stated with sufficient certainty.

Option contracts for the sale of realty require the same degree of definiteness as general contracts. "The required definiteness includes such matters as ... the price, and the terms of payment."

"The contract must either state the price to be paid for the property or set forth criteria by which it may be calculated."

* * *

"The offer must be complete and definite in all respects, since it becomes a contract on acceptance."

* * *

Although this is an action for damages, cases grounded in equity may be considered. "A court of equity will not decree the specific performance of a contract for the sale of land unless there is a definite and specific statement of the terms of the contract. The requirement of certainty extends not only to the subject matter and purpose of the contract, but also to the parties, consideration, and even the time and place of performance, where these are essential. Its terms must be such that neither party can reasonably misunderstand them. It would be inequitable to carry a contract into effect where the court is left to ascertain the intention of the parties by mere guess or conjecture, because it might be guilty of erroneously decreeing what the parties never intended or contemplated."

* * *

"In an action for specific performance of a contract to convey realty, the consideration must either be expressly stated by the writing itself or it must furnish a key by which the amount of the purchase-price can be ascertained. If its ascertainment becomes impossible, there is no sale. Such a key cannot however afford a basis to add by parol an essential element to the validity of a contract, or to in anywise contradict the terms of the written agreement." *Sturdivant v. Walker,* 202 Ga. 585(4), 43 S.E.2d 527. "A contract cannot be enforced in any form of action if its terms are incomplete or incomprehensible. There are instances when certain deficiencies or ambiguities may be explained by facts aliunde the instrument itself. However, information of such extrinsic nature may not be utilized to supply that which is essential to constitute a valid contract." *West v. Downer,* 218 Ga. 235, 241, 127 S.E.2d 359, 364.

"Option agreements have generally been held or recognized to be sufficiently definite as to price to justify their enforcement if either a specific price is provided for in the agreement or a practicable mode is provided by which the price can be determined by the court *without any new expression by the parties themselves.*" (Emphasis supplied.) 2 A.L.R.3d 703, § 3. Accordingly, from the foregoing criteria, we conclude that the agreement must be complete within itself as to the essential elements or a "key" or "practical mode" provided within the contract by which a definite price may be ascertained, and if there is such a deficiency, parol evidence is not admissible to add to, take away from, or vary the written contract ... but would be admissible to explain ambiguities.

We do not find the term "appraised" to be ambiguous but conclude that it does not provide sufficient certainty—standing alone—to provide a "key" or "mode" by which a sale price could be determined by a court without any new expression of the parties.... The basic deficiency of this term lies not in the designation of the method, but the incompleteness of the manner by which the property was to be appraised. Was it to be appraised by a "banker" as the defendant stated? Or—was it to be a person "picked from the Yellow Pages" as related by Wiley? Was the omission of the word "appraiser" intentional—as stated by the defendant, or was it inadvertent as it was understood by the plaintiff? Was the defendant to select the appraiser—because he was going to select a "banker," or were the parties jointly to select an appraiser—as stated by the plaintiff? The appraisal method could have been made certain by designating by whom or how the appraisal was to be conducted.

* * *

Parol or extrinsic evidence cannot supply the deficiency of the missing essential element. " 'A contract involving the purchase and sale of land, that has been partly reduced to writing and partly rests in parol, does not meet the requirement of the statute [of frauds] and is incapable of enforcement.' " *McKee v. Cartledge,* 79 Ga.App. 629(2), 54 S.E.2d 665. "There is a difference between ambiguity, which imports doubleness and uncertainty of meaning, and that degree of indefiniteness which imports no meaning at all. The former can be explained by parol. The latter cannot be merely explained, but a deficiency must be supplied."

* * *

In the instant case where the parties differ as to the method of appraisal—or determining the amount of the consideration, this deficiency cannot be supplied by parol.

We find the contract incomplete, indefinite and unenforceable. The trial court did not err in granting summary judgment to defendant.

Judgment affirmed.

SMITH, JUDGE, dissenting.

* * * The provisions of the following option for the sale of real estate were at issue in *Pearson v. Horne,* 139 Ga. 453, 77 S.E. 387 (1913): "In consideration of an advance of $1,000 to me by H. Horne, I hereby agree if I should decide to sell my half interest in the property corner of Second and Cherry Streets, Macon, Ga., to give to him the option of purchasing same for his clients, *at any price that may be offered for the property by other parties.*" (Emphasis supplied.) The Georgia Supreme Court held: "The price to be paid was sufficiently stated. Reasonably construed, the contract means that, if any price should be offered the defendant which she would be willing to accept, she should give to the plaintiff the option of purchasing at that price."

The majority does not attempt to distinguish *Pearson* from the case at bar. In neither case can the purchase price be ascertained from the contract itself. To essentially the same extent as the contract in *Pearson,* the contract in the instant case "furnishes the key by which [the purchase price] can be ascertained...." *Baker v. Lilienthal,* 176 Ga. 802, 806, 169 S.E. 28, 31 (1933). Certainly, the price term at issue in this case is no less specific than the price term upheld by the Georgia Supreme Court in *Pearson.* I do not believe the statement of consideration is insufficient merely because it speaks in terms of an "appraised" value rather than a specific dollar amount.

* * *

NOTES AND QUESTIONS

1. Who drafted the contract in the *Wiley* case? Should it matter that the person seeking to avoid enforcement under the Statute of Frauds is also the party who prepared the agreement, particularly if that person is a real estate professional while the other is a babe in the woods?

2. Since 1677 the English Statute of Frauds (29 Car. II, ch. 3) has required certain kinds of contracts to be in writing before courts can enforce

them. Under the original statute, all creations or transfers of interests in land except for leases of less than three years must be evidenced by a writing signed by the person against whom enforcement is sought. Some form of the Statute of Frauds has been adopted by all fifty states, although there are significant variations in the technical coverage of the statutes. Most commonly, the exception for leases of less than three years has been shortened to two years or even one year. In addition, the statutes have been covered with substantial judicial gloss concerning such questions as exactly what a qualifying "writing" must say. Most statutes invalidate a written contract for the sale of land unless it either contains or else refers to other written documents that contain: (a) the names of the buyer and seller; (b) a description of the land being sold; (c) other "essential" terms of sale; and (d) the signature of the party against whom enforcement is sought. The meaning of an "essential" term of sale varies from one jurisdiction to another. The *Wiley* case reflects the dominant trend, which is to insist on a fair amount of specificity as to either the price or the mechanism by which the price will be determined. See, e.g., Heinzel v. Backstrom, 310 Or. 89, 794 P.2d 775 (1990) (refusing to enforce document containing no words of promise to purchase); Booth v. Flanagan, 23 Conn.App. 579, 583 A.2d 148 (1990). Significantly, this provision in the Statute of Frauds typically refers to "land" or "real estate." As a result it typically does not cover mobile homes, factory built houses or related structures when they are sold apart from any land. See Pardoe & Graham Real Estate v. Schulz Homes Corp., 259 Va. 398, 525 S.E.2d 284 (2000).

For example, suppose A promises to sell B "forty acres of my 180 acre farm, as the buyer may select it." Does the contract describe the land to be sold with sufficient particularity? See Barker v. Francis, 741 P.2d 548 (Utah App.1987). Suppose land is owned by tenants in common and one signs the sale agreement while the other does not. Can the buyer obtain specific performance? Does he have any rights at all against the non-signing owner? Against the signing owner? See Turnipseed v. Jaje, 267 Ga. 320, 477 S.E.2d 101 (1996); see also Sanders v. Knapp, reprinted infra, § 14.4.3.

3. The Statute of Frauds does not apply to contracts that have been partially performed. Although most courts recognize this, judges have not found this doctrine to apply nearly as often in sales of land as in sales of goods. Nevertheless, courts have considered whether three broad categories of partial performance might take land sale contracts out of the Statute. These include: (1) partial or full payment of the purchase price; (2) delivery of possession *pursuant* to the contract; and (3) the making of improvements by the purchaser.

Today the majority of American jurisdictions hold that the buyer's payment of all or part of the purchase price, standing alone, is not sufficient to take an oral agreement out of the Statute of Frauds. See Bradshaw v. Ewing, 297 S.C. 242, 376 S.E.2d 264 (1989). A few states recognize delivery of possession, standing alone, as sufficient. However, the delivery of possession must be "exclusively referable" to the contract of purchase. See Coleman v. Dillman, 624 P.2d 713 (Utah 1981). For example, if the purchaser under an oral agreement was already a month-to-month tenant of the seller under an oral lease, then the purchaser is in possession, but not in possession "exclusively referable" to the sale agreement. The possession is as consistent with the existence of the lease as with the sale. Klein v. Klein, 79 N.Y.2d 876, 581 N.Y.S.2d 159, 589 N.E.2d 382 (1992) (ex-wife's possession of former marital residence was not "unequivocally referable" to alleged oral promise to convey).

Several states hold that delivery of possession pursuant to the agreement *plus* payment of all or part of the purchase price takes an oral land sale contract out of the Statute. Several states also hold that delivery of possession plus the purchaser's making of valuable and permanent improvements takes the contract out of the Statute. Once again, however, the improvements must be referable exclusively to the possessor's belief that he is acquiring the property by purchase. See 2 A. Corbin, Contracts, Ch. 18 (1950). Finally, four states—Kentucky, Mississippi, North Carolina and Tennessee—appear not to recognize the doctrine of partial performance at all.

4.   Note Judge Smith's observation in dissent that the preemption (the right to purchase property by matching another offeror's price) in the *Pearson* case did not violate the Statute of Frauds. As a result, Judge Smith reasoned, the option in the principal case must be valid under the Statute of Frauds as well. Is the Judge's reasoning correct? When do you determine whether a contract violates the Statute of Frauds? At the time of its making, or at the time enforcement is sought?

5.   The development of the Statute and its relation to land conveyancing and recording is traced in Hamburger, The Conveyancing Purposes of the Statute of Frauds, 27 Am.J.Leg.History 354 (1983).

§ 14.4   CONSTRUCTION AND PERFORMANCE OF THE LAND SALE CONTRACT

§ 14.4.1   CONDITIONS AND LIQUIDATED DAMAGES

LYNCH v. ANDREW

Appeals Court of Massachusetts (1985).
20 Mass.App.Ct. 623, 481 N.E.2d 1383.

KASS, JUSTICE.

At the behest of the buyers' lawyer, a mortgage financing condition was added to a purchase and sale agreement prepared on a printed form published by the Greater Boston Real Estate Board. Claiming inability to secure mortgage financing, the buyers, the plaintiffs in this action, say they were excused from performance and demand recovery of the $25,400 deposit which they made under that agreement.

The text of the financing clause is as follows: "Buyer shall apply to a conventional bank or other mortgage loan institution for a loan of [$155,-000] payable in not less than thirty ... years at prevailing interest rates.

"If, despite Buyer's diligent efforts, a commitment for such a loan is not obtained on or before April 26, 1982, the Buyer may terminate this Agreement by written notice to Seller or the brokers as agent for the

Seller prior to the expiration of such time, whereupon all deposits made under this Agreement shall be [returned and this agreement shall be] void and without recourse to the parties hereto."

On the deadline date, April 26, 1982, the buyers notified the seller that they were unable to secure financing and, therefore, exercised their rights of termination under the agreement. The seller thought the buyers' effort to obtain mortgage financing had been less than diligent and refused to return the buyers' $25,400 deposit, thus provoking this action. A judge of the Probate Court, sitting by statutory designation in the Superior Court, heard the case without a jury. The judge determined that the buyers' efforts to secure financing lacked diligence, but that the liquidated damages clause in the purchase and sale agreement, which provided for retention by the seller of the entire deposit, was punitive. Actual damages, he found, were $8,400, and he reduced the amount which the seller could retain accordingly. Both sides have appealed from the resulting judgment.

1. *Diligence of the buyers' efforts to obtaining financing.* The judge found that the buyers' efforts to obtain a mortgage loan consisted chiefly of inquiries about interest rates and lending options at various banks and the making of loan applications with two lenders, BayBank Middlesex and Old Stone Bank of Providence, Rhode Island. On the calculation that a loan from BayBank Middlesex was likely, the buyers withdrew the loan application to Old Stone to avoid a $275 application fee. As the deadline for obtaining a loan commitment grew nearer, the buyers flirted with a third lending source, but it looked as if consideration of the loan would take them past the date of decision and the buyers made no further loan application. Only one application, to BayBank Middlesex for a loan of $130,000, was perfected.

There was evidence that BayBank informed the buyers that it was ready to lend the $130,000 requested, if the buyers would show the bank where the rest of the purchase money (the balance was $98,600) was coming from. The buyers responded that proceeds of sale of a house they owned in Wellesley would provide the money above the mortgage. No agreement to sell that house had yet been made, however. To accommodate its customer, the bank offered a "bridge loan," i.e., a loan for the balance figure which the borrowers would repay when they sold the house they already owned, and which the bank asked to secure with a mortgage on the buyers' existing house and a property they owned in Chatham.

Those loan terms struck the buyers as "getting a little more complicated." The bank offered a blanket mortgage but that, similarly, was not to the liking of the borrowers. On April 26th John Lynch called the loan officer he had been dealing with at the bank and told her he had "decided not to go through with the transaction," and requested that she send him a rejection letter. She did so.

In deciding that the buyers had not made diligent efforts to obtain a mortgage loan, the judge thought that the buyers could reasonably refuse to encumber other of their properties but that making only one loan application unreasonably staked the game on a single roll of the dice. Whether the buyers acted diligently is a factual question, the determination of which is entitled to the customary appellate deference. What constitutes diligent effort presents a question of law. We affirm the judge's conclusion that the buyers did not make diligent efforts to obtain mortgage financing, but do so on a different ground.

Unless otherwise qualified by express language, a financing condition clause presupposes that the buyers will accept commercially reasonable loan terms. Cf. *Stabile v. McCarthy,* 336 Mass. 399, 404, 145 N.E.2d 821 (1957) and *Sechrest v. Safiol,* 383 Mass. 568, 571, 419 N.E.2d 1384 (1981), which require, to trigger a contingency in an agreement, conduct reasonably calculated to fulfill the condition by action or expenditure proportionate to the circumstances. If less is required, the condition becomes an option. It was reasonable for the bank to be concerned about, and make some provision for, the funds required above the mortgage.... See generally, annot., Purchaser's Efforts to Secure Financing, 78 A.L.R.3d 880 (1977 with 1984 supp.).

In the instant case, a single bridge loan involving property which the buyers soon intended to sell, in any event, would not have been unduly onerous. The standard of reasonableness is objective at least to the degree that it cannot be satisfied by the buyers with their flat statement that the various loan propositions made by the bank were "too complicated." See *Phillipe v. Thomas,* 3 Conn.App. 471, 472–476, 489 A.2d 1056 (1985) (in contract with mortgage contingency, court implies a promise to exert objectively reasonable efforts). Compare *Fry v. George Elkins Co.,* 162 Cal.App.2d 256, 260, 327 P.2d 905 (1958) (rejection of two percent prepayment penalty in loan terms from mortgage company, when lenders not requiring such terms had refused to make loan, did not constitute a good faith attempt to obtain financing). When buyers, through their actions, bring about a failure to satisfy a condition, they may not claim the benefit of that failure.

2. *Liquidated damages.* The option of the seller to retain the buyers' deposit as liquidated damages (as an alternative to specific performance) is, as buyers' counsel conceded, the common practice in Massachusetts conveyancing. See also Mendler, Massachusetts Conveyancer's Handbook § 1:17 (3d ed. 1984). We are disinclined to tamper with a well established solution to the problems of expense and uncertainty in litigating the precise damages in cases of this kind. It is appropriate to recall the observation of Justice Holmes, that "so far as precedent permits the proper course is ... not to undertake to be wiser than the parties." *Guerin v. Stacey,* 175 Mass. 595, 597, 56 N.E. 892 (1900).

It has been the rule in Massachusetts that contract provisions which clearly and reasonably establish liquidated damages should be enforced, if "not so disproportionate to the losses and expenses caused by the defendant's breach" as to constitute a penalty. *Warner v. Wilkey,* 2 Mass.App.

Ct. 798, 799, 307 N.E.2d 847 (1974). *Kaplan v. Gray,* 215 Mass. 269, 270–273, 102 N.E. 421 (1913). There is nothing to suggest that the liquidated damages provision in this case was negotiated at other than an arm's length basis between adequately represented parties. If there was any advantage in experience or sophistication, it was on the side of the buyers.

Under paragraph 19 of the purchase and sale agreement, if the buyers defaulted, half of the deposit was to be paid to the broker, who was a party to the agreement. The funds left to the seller, therefore, are $12,700. When the seller managed to sell her property in October, 1982, she received $5,000 less for it than her price with the buyers in the instant case. She also claimed loss of the opportunity to purchase a house she had placed under agreement on the strength of her agreement with the plaintiffs. That house was larger, required less upkeep, and generally was a better investment than the house she bought the following autumn. The delay in the sale, the seller claimed, also cost her payments which her ex-husband had been prepared to make and put her to extra moving expenses.

This was not a case in which the house sold within days of the first buyer's default, at about the same price, and without complicating factors which make the actual damages difficult to calculate with precision. It is not a case in which the liquidated damages provision is grossly disproportionate to a reasonable estimate of actual damages. When losses are difficult to quantify, considerable deference is due the parties' reasonable agreement as to liquidated damages. *Kroeger v. Stop & Shop Cos.,* 13 Mass.App.Ct. 310, 322 (1982).

The judgment is vacated and judgment shall be entered for the defendant.

NOTES AND QUESTIONS

1. Many purchasers of homes are unable to complete the purchase unless they can obtain financing. As a result, many real estate contracts make completion of the sale contingent on the buyer's ability to obtain financing on specified terms by a certain date. If the contract simply states that it is contingent on the buyer's obtaining financing, then the court will generally assess a good faith requirement against the buyer. As the principal case notes, good faith is generally measured by an objective standard.

Likewise, many buyers who already own a home cannot afford to buy a larger or more attractive home until they sell the first one. Many land sale contracts also are made contingent on the buyer's ability to sell the first home by a certain date.

Both contingency clauses entail some likelihood that the contract will never result in a completed sale. The frequent result of nonsale is a hard look at the document for any ambiguity that a frustrated seller might use against the buyer—if not to force the sale, which may be impossible, then at least to justify retaining the earnest money.

2. Most courts permit liquidated damages clauses to be enforced if: (1) actual damages are very difficult to measure; and (2) the amount of liquidated damages appears to be reasonable in proportion to the amount of actual harm. The First Restatement of Contracts placed the emphasis on the reasonableness of the liquidated damages clause in relation to the range of *anticipated* damages, looking from the viewpoint of the time that the contract was formed. Restatement of Contracts § 339 (1933). The Second Restatement of Contracts permits the court to look at the reasonableness of the damages at the time enforcement is sought as well. Restatement (Second) of Contracts § 356 (1981). Thus, under the Second Restatement a court might hold that liquidated damages are excessive if they clearly would provide a windfall to the seller, even if the amount of liquidated damages was a reasonable estimate of actual damages at the time the contract was negotiated. See Colonial at Lynnfield v. Sloan, 870 F.2d 761 (1st Cir.1989).

Suppose the seller suffers no damages whatsoever. For example, suppose he finds a second buyer willing to pay even more than the defaulting buyer had agreed to pay. May the seller nonetheless keep the defaulting buyer's deposit as liquidated damages? See Stabenau v. Cairelli, 22 Conn.App. 578, 577 A.2d 1130 (1990).

§ 14.4.2   MARKETABLE TITLE

BETHUREM v. HAMMETT

Supreme Court of Wyoming (1987).
736 P.2d 1128.

URBIGKIT, JUSTICE.

In 1983, appellants, the Bethurems (Buyers), contracted to purchase a residence in Sheridan, Wyoming from appellees, the Hammetts (Sellers). In exchange for the realty, Buyers made a cash down payment and agreed to monthly installment payments for the purchase-price balance. In 1985, a dispute arose from encroachment of the residence structure, the garage and the cemented-in fence into the dedicated city street, as then confirmed by surveys by both parties. After unsatisfactory negotiations, Buyers sued to rescind the sales agreement, claiming that Sellers had materially misrepresented the property in failing to apprise Buyers of known encroachments.

At trial, Buyers relied on provisions of the executed Offer, Acceptance & Receipt (Specific Performance Contract), a pre-printed document which stated:

"8.   Title shall be merchantable in the Seller, except as stated in this paragraph. Subject to payment or tender as above provided and compliance with the other terms and conditions hereunder by Purchaser, the Seller shall execute and deliver a good and sufficient statutory warranty deed in favor of those persons named in Paragraph 7 above, including the release and waiver of all homestead rights, if any, and a good and sufficient bill of sale, and deliver the same to said Purchaser

at closing, which shall occur on or before April 29, 1983, conveying said real and personal properties free and clear of all liens and encumbrances, except: '(a) The general taxes for 1983; '(b) Liens for special improvements, if any; '(c) Easements for utilities; '(d) Subject to building and zoning regulations; '(e) City, state and county subdivision laws; '(f) Reservations, restrictions and easements of record, if any;'" * * * and "10. The Seller covenants that upon execution of this Contract: '(a) The above-described property is in substantial compliance with applicable city, county and state subdivision laws, requirements and regulations in force and effect as of that date, '(b) There are no known defects, EXCEPT: '(1) Those which are readily visible upon inspection; * * * "

[A] typed sales agreement, which also included a nonpayment provision, in part provided:

"Sellers shall, at their expense, furnish Buyers with an Abstract or Title or Commitment for Title Insurance covering the above described premises. Said Abstract of Title or Commitment for Title Insurance shall be of recent date and shall show good merchantable title in Edward L. Hammett and Elsie Mae K. Hammett, husband and wife, free and clear of all encumbrances. Buyers shall have ten (10) days within which to cause said Abstract or Commitment to be examined by an Attorney of their choice. Any defects in title shall be forthwith corrected by Sellers."

Contrary to the covenant in Paragraph 10(a) of the standard Offer, Acceptance & Receipt that the property was in substantial compliance with all applicable city, county, and state subdivision laws, requirements and regulations, those street line encroachments also violated Section 23–22 of the Sheridan City Code, which provides that "[n]o person shall erect, build, set up or maintain in whole or in part any fence, sign, shop, post, building or obstruction whatsoever in or upon any street, avenue, alley, sidewalk or public ground within the city." The property was repossessed by Sellers, and is presently in their possession. * * *

Buyers contended that the breach of the sales agreement covenants was a misrepresentation entitling them to rescission, also asserting that encroachment onto the public street was a defect which renders title unmarketable in violation of Sellers' covenants in Paragraphs 8 and 10 of the standard offer document and Section IV of the typed sales agreement. At trial, the parties took opposite positions regarding Buyers' knowledge of the encroachment. Buyers claimed that Sellers led them to believe that there were no defects, that the transferred realty included all the land and improvements enclosed by the fence, and that the enclosed property was marketable. Sellers contended that they had orally discussed the encroachments and that Buyers assured them that the defect would not pose a problem. . . .

This court set forth the general rule regarding a seller's misrepresentation of boundaries in Meeker v. Lanham, Wyo., 604 P.2d 556, 559

(1979), stating: "With regard to the boundary lines, the rule regarding misrepresentations concerning the boundaries of property, is correctly pointed out to us by the appellant: 'A purchaser has the right to rely upon the representations of the seller as to the boundaries of the land, and if the seller misrepresents the true boundary of the land, whether innocently or intentionally, it is ground for rescission by the purchaser.' "From Buyers' contentions we discern their three claims of false representations to have been made by Sellers as covenants in the contractual documents: first, that title was merchantable (marketable); second, that property was in compliance with the relevant city ordinance; and third, that there were no known defects in title or condition.

* * * [T]he uniform rule regarding marketability has been explained in an Oregon decision: "A purchaser is not required to accept title which might reasonably be expected to involve litigation. '[I]f there is doubt and uncertainty about the title sufficient to form the basis for litigation, * * * it cannot be thrown upon the purchaser to contest that doubt * * *.' " Cameron v. Benson, 57 Or.App. 169, 643 P.2d 1360, 1363 (1982), rev'd on other grounds, 295 Or. 98, 664 P.2d 412 (1983). * * *

Whether title to real estate is marketable is a question of law for the court. In this case, the fence encroached approximately 17 feet into the city street, the garage encroached approximately eight feet, and the actual residence encroached approximately four feet. Clearly, such substantial encroachments subjected Buyer to potential litigation involving the purchased property. Furthermore, a reasonably prudent person familiar with the nature and extent of these encroachments would decline to purchase at an otherwise reasonable market price. Accordingly, we find that the title was unmarketable. In analogous situations numerous courts in other jurisdictions have found title unmarketable, and have granted buyers of realty the right to rescind their purchase agreements. In Zatzkis v. Fuselier, La.App., 398 So.2d 1284, writ denied 405 So.2d 533 (1981), the conveyed property encroached onto neighboring property. The gutter encroached six inches; the roof encroached two feet; and the step and fence encroached eight-tenths of a foot. That court held that the encroachments rendered title to the property unmarketable, and allowed the purchaser to rescind. Likewise, in Morrison v. Fineran, La.App., 397 So.2d 838 (1981), it was held that a fence which encroached onto neighboring property for a distance at the front of 0.31 feet gradually increasing to 1.24 feet at the rear rendered title unmarketable, and the prospective purchaser was permitted to reject the sale. * * * In Young v. Stevens, 252 La. 69, 209 So.2d 25 (1967), where a fence encroached ten inches, tapering down to three inches onto the adjoining lot to the rear of the property, and encroached six inches onto the adjoining property on the side, the Louisiana Supreme Court concluded that the title was not merchantable, and permitted the purchaser to rescind the contract. That court stated: " * * * [A] person buying property whose improvements encroach upon his neighbor is likely to sustain a law suit to defend his right to possession of the property sold to him beyond his title. [Citations.] * * * What makes the title unmerchantable * * * is not necessarily the extent of the encroachment, but the fact that it suggests litigation.''

* * * Sellers contend that, lacking misrepresentation, Buyers are not entitled to rescind the agreement because Buyers accepted title with full knowledge that the encroachments existed. In order to substantiate these contentions, Mr. Hammett, Seller, testified at trial that he orally informed Buyers of the encroachments, and, furthermore, that the encroachments were readily visible upon inspection because the boundary between the parcel and the street was marked by two pieces of string tied to a fence. Buyers denied that the statement was made, and objected to its introduction, arguing that any testimony about the oral representations which communicated the existence of the encroachment violates the parol evidence rule. They claim that this evidence, extrinsic to the parties' written agreements, contradicts the parties' clear intentions as expressed by the specific terms of the written and mutually signed documents. One of the covenants states: "There are no known defects, EXCEPT: Those which are readily visible upon inspection." From this, Sellers contend that trial testimony is not precluded by the parol evidence rule because it did not contradict, alter, add to, or vary their agreement, but merely explained which defects were readily visible upon inspection. A piece of string on a fence, which basic fact was controverted in this case, does not prove more than its existence without explanatory oral testimony to communicate purpose. * * * An unexplained piece of string on a fence is just that, and is not determinative as an encroachment readily visible upon inspection. * * *

"[I]f a vendor wishes to convey subject to an encumbrance affecting title the contract should include the appropriate exception [citation], and the Court may not impose an agreement other than that which was arrived at between the parties [citation]." Atlas Realty of East Meadow, Inc. v. Ostrofsky, 56 Misc.2d 787, 289 N.Y.S.2d 784, 786 (1967). * * *

Reversed and remanded.

CARDINE, J., filed a dissenting opinion in which GRANT, DISTRICT JUDGE, joined.

I would affirm the decision of the trial judge who observed the witnesses, listened to their live testimony, judged their credibility, and accorded such evidence the weight to which he determined it was entitled. When, as in this case, the parties' written agreement specifically provides "[t]here are no known defects, except: Those which are readily visible upon inspection," it is patently clear that the parties were properly allowed to testify orally as to what was readily visible upon inspection. It was the function of the trial court to accept or reject that testimony and to resolve the disputed statements of fact that were present.

NOTES AND QUESTIONS

1. The contract at issue in *Bethurem* was an installment sale contract, under which the vendor promised to convey title after the buyer paid for the property in a series of installment payments. The marketable title requirement is the same for installment contracts as for the land sale contract contemplating a cash transaction or third party financing, with the title transfer to occur within a reasonable or other specified time after the execution of the contract.

One important factual difference, however, is that under the installment contract the seller may not have to produce good title until many years after the contract is executed, unless the contract itself provides to the contrary. For example, installment contracts might contemplate monthly or annual payments stretched out over ten or even twenty years, with the seller obliged to convey a warranty deed only after the last payment has been made. More importantly, the seller under an installment contract may not have to produce good title until after the property has been fully paid for.

Most courts agree that a seller is not obliged to produce marketable title until the date specified in the contract for delivery of the deed or provision of evidence of title. As a result, a buyer generally cannot refuse to go ahead with her contractual obligations simply because the seller does not have marketable title at the time the contract is executed. See, e.g., Seligman v. First National Investments, Inc., 184 Ill.App.3d 1053, 133 Ill.Dec. 191, 540 N.E.2d 1057 (1989). This is generally the rule even when the contract at issue is an installment sale contract, and the buyer will have tendered the entire purchase price by the time delivery of the seller's title is due. See Liddle v. Petty, 249 Mont. 442, 816 P.2d 1066 (1991). *Bethurem* illustrates an important exception: the buyer need not proceed with the contract if it becomes clear that the seller will never be able to acquire marketable title.

2. Did *Bethurem* deal correctly with the problem of visible encumbrances? Contracts to sell land are often rather informally drafted in the sense that they are done before any title search; they often include informal descriptions, etc. Suppose that property is subject to an obvious driveway easement but the contract to sell says nothing about the easement's existence. Should the buyer later be able to avoid the contract by claiming that the title is unmarketable? In Alcan Aluminum Corp. v. Carlsberg Financial Corp., 689 F.2d 815, 817 (9th Cir.1982) the court concluded that a land sale contract could be enforced notwithstanding that it failed to except a utility easement, where the utility lines were visible on the property. In this case, the land sale contract specified that the buyer "acknowledges that it is not and will not act in reliance upon any representations made by Seller to Buyer or upon any information supplied by Seller. Buyer is acting, and will act only upon information obtained by it directly from its inspection of the purchased property and from public records or from independent third parties." The court concluded, "An intending purchaser who undertakes to make his own examination of the property and who goes upon it for that purpose, and with a free opportunity to make a thorough examination without interference by the seller or anyone acting in his behalf, will be conclusively presumed to have

acquired all of the information which would be disclosed to him if his inquiry should be pursued with ordinary diligence." Id. at 817.

But this still does not mean that Justice Cardine's dissent in the *Bethurem* case is correct, does it? An exception in a written contract for visible encroachments is not the same thing as permitting oral testimony to the effect that, at the time of inspection, the sellers informed the buyers that a particular object was an encroachment. The difference between a visible driveway and a visible piece of string is that a prudent person seeing the driveway would be on notice simply from viewing the land that an encroachment existed. By contrast, a piece of string on a fence is no evidence of an encroachment at all, except to the extent it is supplemented with oral statements.

What if the contract makes the deed subject to a restrictive covenant, and inspection of the property shows a violation of the covenant? Is the title marketable? See Staley v. Stephens, 404 N.E.2d 633 (Ind.Ct.App.1980).

3. Wallach v. Riverside Bank, 206 N.Y. 434, 437, 100 N.E. 50, 51 (1912) held that a seller who promises to convey a certain parcel of land by quitclaim deed must, absent a contrary indication in the sale contract, produce a marketable title. A quitclaim deed contains no warranties of title whatsoever. In fact, quitclaim deeds are often used when it is doubtful that the grantor has anything to convey. (See the note on quitclaim deeds as market facilitators in Chapter 16 infra). Does this mean that the deed itself ends up conveying less than the contract impliedly requires? The court in *Wallach* reasoned that:

> Even if the conveyance is to be made without warranties, still the land itself is to be conveyed, and as the grantor can convey only that which he has, unless he has title to the land he cannot convey the land. Id.

In short, regardless of the type of deed to be used, the contract stated the seller would convey "the land" and thus implied that the seller would produce a marketable title at the time of conveyance. A seller who is uncertain of his title and wants to convey land by quitclaim deed is well advised to make the language of the contract track the language of the quitclaim deed. Rather than promising to convey "the land," which implies that the seller must produce marketable title, the contract should promise that the seller will convey "all my right, title, and interest," or "whatever interest I may have," in the land.

4. In Dwight v. Cutler, 3 Mich. 566 (1855), the court stated that "in every contract for the sale of land, unless the contrary intention is expressed, there is an implied undertaking on the part of the vendor ... while the contract remains executory, to make out a good title clear of all defects and encumbrances." As *Dwight* notes, the parties may give effect to a "contrary intention" by means of an express contract term. For example, Campbell v. Hart, 256 S.W.2d 255 (Tex.Civ.App.1953), held that a land sale contract requiring the seller to produce "satisfactory" title meant a title that was subjectively satisfactory to the purchaser, not a title that would have been objectively satisfactory to a reasonable and prudent purchaser. Other courts disagree and assess an objective requirement. See Annotation, "Marketable Title," 57 A.L.R. 1253, 1314–22 (1928).

Suppose the parties expressly agree that the seller will provide an "insurable" title. An insurable title can be less than a marketable title for two different reasons. First, the insurance company may willingly undertake a risk that a reasonable buyer would not, because the insurance company is in the business of calculating the odds. If the risk that a title is bad is relatively high, the title insurer can simply increase the premium. Theoretically, *any* title is "insurable," provided that the premium is high enough.

Second, the title company will normally except from coverage any defects that it discovers during its title search. For example, suppose that A agrees to sell Blackacre to B and provide B with "insurable" title by a certain date. The title insurer searches the title and finds evidence of an outstanding lien that has never been released, even though it has probably been paid off. The title insurer may insure the title but create an exception from the insurance coverage for any claims arising out of the outstanding lien. Subject to the exception, the title is "insurable," but will the seller be able to force the buyer's performance? Probably not. Most courts hold that any exception from coverage required by the title insurer must be an exception contemplated by the parties to the contract. If the contract contemplated that A would furnish a title free and clear of all outstanding liens or other encumbrances, the title insurer must be willing to insure such a title. See Gilchrest–Great Neck, Inc. v. Byers, 210 N.Y.S.2d 881 (1960). See generally Comment, Title Insurance and Marketable Title, 31 Fordham L.Rev. 559 (1963).

5. The contractual requirement of a marketable *record* title also can work against the seller. What if the seller claims part of the land conveyed by adverse possession—as might happen if the conveyed parcel is larger than the parcel described in the seller's chain of title, but the seller has satisfactorily occupied the larger parcel for the statutory period? See Conklin v. Davi, 76 N.J. 468, 472–73, 388 A.2d 598, 601 (1978), where the court reasoned:

> When a prospective seller's title is grounded upon adverse possession, or contains some apparent flaw of record, he has a choice of options. He may at once take whatever steps are necessary to perfect the record title, including resort to an action to quiet title, an action to cancel an outstanding encumbrance, or whatever other appropriate step may be necessary to accomplish the purpose. In the alternative he may, believing his title to be marketable despite the fact that it rests on adverse possession or is otherwise imperfect of record, choose to enter into a contract of sale, hoping to convince the purchaser or, if necessary, a court, that his estimate of the marketability of his title is justified.... It must be borne in mind that this latter course is available only where the contract of sale does not require the vendor to give a title valid of record, but provides for a less stringent requirement, such as marketability or insurability.

As the *Conklin* opinion indicates, if the contract provides that the seller must provide marketable *record* title—i.e., title affirmatively shown on the record to be good—then title established by adverse possession probably will not suffice. Good title will not appear on the record until after there has been a judicial determination that the seller in fact acquired the property by adverse possession and evidence of the court's judgment is recorded. See Tri–

State Hotel Co. v. Sphinx Investment Co., 212 Kan. 234, 510 P.2d 1223 (1973); Escher v. Bender, 338 Mich. 1, 61 N.W.2d 143 (1953).

Although virtually all title standards conclude that titles based strictly on adverse possession are unmarketable, a few courts have found marketable titles based on adverse possession and ordered specific performance. See Taccone v. DiRenzi, 92 Misc.2d 786, 793, 401 N.Y.S.2d 722, 727 (1978), which concluded:

> [T]he passage of a sufficient period of time may operate to transform even a defective title into a good and marketable one. * * * It is undisputed that decedent was in continuous possession of the property for over fifteen years. The possession was open and notorious and the land was held under claim of right. Conceding the validity of defendant's argument that plaintiff has the burden of proving the marketability of title the plaintiff's sworn and unrebutted statements in his pleadings and motion papers are sufficient to meet that burden. * * * Policy and common sense also dictate this conclusion. Plaintiff's decedent has held recorded title to the land for a substantial period of time and no one has asserted any claims against it. * * * No individual, such as a prior owner contesting title, is being divested of or is forfeiting any right. Indeed, the holding here will have just the opposite effect and prevent a future forfeiture by quieting title. Whenever, possible, in situations such as this, title should be held good and marketable so that land transactions may be freely transferable in the open real estate market. Accordingly, plaintiff's motion for summary judgment and for specific performance is granted.

Do you agree that "policy and common sense" dictate this result? If so, why do we not simply abolish title searches as mechanisms for establishing marketability and permit sellers to provide a sworn affidavit to the effect that "I have marketable title?" Often the litigation in which marketability is established involves only the adverse possessor/vendor and the vendee; the owner of record is not a party. What impact does this have on the decision? Suppose the record owner shows up later and proves that he has been under a legal disability that tolled the statute of limitations. Should a court require that the owner of record be made a party to any dispute over the marketability of title claimed by adverse possession?

§ 14.4.3   REMEDIES FOR NONPERFORMANCE

A.   Specific Performance

SANDERS v. KNAPP

Colorado Court of Appeals (1983).
674 P.2d 385.

TURSI, JUDGE.

Plaintiff, Ronald Sanders, appeals the trial court's denial of specific performance on a contract to purchase a condominium owned by defendants, Robert and Barbara Knapp. We reverse in part and affirm in part.

On July 1, 1978, Robert Knapp entered into a listing agreement with the Romero Corporation (Broker), listing his condominium at the Val

D'Isere Condominiums in Breckenridge at $19,750. Through Broker, Sanders executed a "receipt and option contract" on July 28, 1978, counter-offering to buy the Knapp condominium for $19,000. * * *

Sanders performed all the conditions under the contract and tendered the purchase price to Broker on October 16, 1978, even though Broker did not have Robert's deed and closing papers. Sanders immediately began to treat the condominium as his own by making mortgage payments and improvements. It was not until on or about October 25, 1978, that Broker discovered that Robert had not received the closing documents purportedly sent to him October 2, and a duplicate set was sent in November. Only then did Robert determine that he held the condominium in joint tenancy with his estranged wife, and when he suggested selling the condominium, she refused to sign the documents.

In January 1979, Sanders filed suit against Robert, requesting specific performance. On learning of Barbara's interest, he joined her as a co-defendant in the action and requested a declaration of tenancy in common with her. His motion for partial summary judgment on the validity of the contract was denied and the matter was tried to the court. The court found that mutual mistake as to ownership of the condominium prevented formation of a binding contract, and therefore denied Sanders' claim for specific performance and liquidated damages. * * *

Sanders first claims that he is entitled to specific performance of his contract with Robert to the extent Robert's interest, despite the court's finding that Robert and Sanders were mutually mistaken in their belief that Robert could tender complete title to the condominium. We agree.

* * *

When a seller of land is unable to convey the full title which he or she contracted to sell, and the seller has any interest in the property, the purchaser may exercise the option of enforcing the contract with respect to whatever interest the seller possesses. The seller may not defend an action for specific performance on the ground that his title is not as complete as the one he had agreed would be conveyed.

It is presumed that the shares of co-tenants are equal, whether they be tenants in common or joint tenants. Absent rebuttal, it is therefore presumed that Barbara has an outstanding one-half interest in the property.

We therefore find the contract enforceable to the extent of Robert's interest, and we remand to the trial court for entry of judgment ordering specific performance of the contract, with an abatement of one-half of the contract price.

NOTES AND QUESTIONS

1.   What do you suppose Ronald Sanders will do next? He may have to live with the ex-spouse of the seller. See the discussion of joint ownership in Chapter 5.

2. Needless to say, specific performance is an appropriate remedy only when the defendant is legally capable of performing. Robert Knapp had title to only one half the property that he had agreed to convey, so the court could award specific performance only with respect to that half. Someone in Sanders' position may still be entitled to damages for any losses he suffers because he is unable to acquire the other half, or able to acquire it only at a higher price.

3. The problem raised by *Sanders* is more complex in a community property state, where marital property is held by the marital "community" rather than in a common law joint tenancy or tenancy in common. One important difference between the community estate and the common law co-tenancy is that in the former there may not be a unilateral right to sever the estate. In Andrade Development Co. v. Martin, 138 Cal.App.3d 330, 334, 187 Cal.Rptr. 863, 866 (1982) the California court refused specific performance to a plaintiff on facts nearly identical to those in *Sanders*. The court held:

> We believe the nonconsenting spouse should be fully protected in such efforts to dispose of community real property and hold the contract is subject to a timely action during the marriage to avoid it, a corollary of which is no specific performance or damages are recoverable as to any part of the effort to dispose of the community real property. Any effort to dispose of this property will adversely affect the spouses' interests.

Andrade resulted in a split among California courts, finally resolved by the California Supreme Court in Droeger v. Friedman, Sloan & Ross, 54 Cal.3d 26, 283 Cal.Rptr. 584, 812 P.2d 931 (1991) (en banc), which agreed with Andrade and held that a nonconsenting spouse may invalidate entirely an attempted unilateral transfer made during the marriage.

4. Specific performance is an equitable remedy and, as such, its availability is subject to equitable defenses. For example, in Landers v. Biwer, 714 N.W.2d 476 (N.D. 2006) the court refused to grant specific performance because the buyers had misrepresented the nature of the contract and, therefore, had unclean hands.

CENTEX HOMES CORP. v. BOAG

Superior Court of New Jersey, Chancery Division (1974).
128 N.J.Super. 385, 320 A.2d 194.

GELMAN, J.S.C.

Plaintiff Centex Homes Corporation (Centex) is engaged in the development and construction of a luxury high-rise condominium project in the Boroughs of Cliffside Park and Fort Lee. The project when completed will consist of six 31–story buildings containing in excess of 3600 condominium apartment units, together with recreational buildings and facilities, parking garages and other common elements associated with this form of residential development. As sponsor of the project Centex offers the condominium apartment units for sale to the public and has filed an offering plan covering such sales with the appropriate regulatory agencies of the States of New Jersey and New York.

On September 13, 1972 defendants Mr. & Mrs. Eugene Boag executed a contract for the purchase of apartment unit No. 2019 in the building under construction and known as "Winston Towers 200." The contract purchase price was $73,700, and prior to signing the contract defendants had given Centex a deposit in the amount of $525. At or shortly after signing the contract defendants delivered to Centex a check in the amount of $6,870 which, together with the deposit, represented approximately 10% of the total purchase of the apartment unit. Shortly thereafter Boag was notified by his employer that he was to be transferred to the Chicago, Illinois, area. Under date of September 27, 1972 he advised Centex that he "would be unable to complete the purchase" agreement and stopped payment on the $6,870 check. Centex deposited the check for collection approximately two weeks after receiving notice from defendant, but the check was not honored by defendants' bank. On August 8, 1973 Centex instituted this action in Chancery Division for specific performance of the purchase agreement or, in the alternative, for liquidated damages in the amount of $6,870. The matter is presently before this court on the motion of Centex for summary judgment.

Both parties acknowledge, and our research has confirmed, that no court in this State or in the United States has determined in any reported decision whether the equitable remedy of specific performance will lie for the enforcement of a contract for the sale of a condominium apartment. The closest decision on point is Silverman v. Alcoa Plaza Associates, 37 A.D.2d 166, 323 N.Y.S.2d 39 (App.Div.1971), which involved a default by a contract-purchaser of shares of stock and a proprietary lease in a cooperative apartment building. The seller, who was also the sponsor of the project, retained the deposit and sold the stock and the lease to a third party for the same purchase price. The original purchaser thereafter brought suit to recover his deposit, and on appeal the court held that the sale of shares of stock in a cooperative apartment building, even though associated with a proprietary lease, was a sale of personalty and not of an interest in real estate. Hence, the seller was not entitled to retain the contract deposit as liquidated damages.

As distinguished from a cooperative plan of ownership such as involved in *Silverman,* under a condominium housing scheme each condominium apartment unit constitutes a separate parcel of real property which may be dealt with in the same manner as any real estate. Upon closing of title the apartment unit owner receives a recordable deed which confers upon him the same rights and subjects him to the same obligations as in the case of traditional forms of real estate ownership, the only difference being that the condominium owner receives in addition an undivided interest in the common elements associated with the building and assigned to each unit.

* * *

Centex urges that since the subject matter of the contract is the transfer of a fee interest in real estate, the remedy of specific performance is available to enforce the agreement under principles of equity which are well-settled in this state.

* * *

The principle underlying the specific performance remedy is equity's jurisdiction to grant relief where the damage remedy at law is inadequate. The text writers generally agree that at the time this branch of equity jurisdiction was evolving in England, the presumed uniqueness of land as well as its importance to the social order of that era led to the conclusion that damages at law could never be adequate to compensate for the breach of a contract to transfer an interest in land. Hence specific performance became a fixed remedy in this class of transactions. The judicial attitude has remained substantially unchanged and is expressed in *Pomeroy* as follows:

> ... in applying this doctrine the courts of equity have established the further rule that in general the legal remedy of damages is inadequate in all agreements for the sale or letting of land, or of any estate therein; and therefore in such class of contracts the jurisdiction is always exercised, and a specific performance granted, unless prevented by other and independent equitable considerations which directly affect the remedial right of the complaining party ... [1 Pomeroy, Equity Jurisprudence (5th ed. 1941), § 221(b)].

While the inadequacy of the damage remedy suffices to explain the origin of the vendee's right to obtain specific performance in equity, it does not provide a *rationale* for the availability of the remedy at the instance of the vendor of real estate. Except upon a showing of unusual circumstances or a change in the vendor's position, such as where the vendee has entered into possession, the vendor's damages are usually measurable, his remedy at law is adequate and there is no jurisdictional basis for equitable relief.

* * *

So far as can be determined from our decisional law, the mutuality of remedy concept has been the prop which has supported equitable jurisdiction to grant specific performance in actions by vendors of real estate. * * * The first reported discussion of the question occurs in Hopper v. Hopper, 16 N.J.Eq. 147 (Ch.1863), which was an action by a vendor to compel specific performance of a contract for the sale of land. In answer to the contention that equity lacked jurisdiction because the vendor had an adequate legal remedy, Chancellor Green said (at p. 148);

> "It constitutes no objection to the relief prayed for, that the application is made by the vendor to enforce the payment of the purchase money, and not by the vendee to compel a delivery of the title. The vendor has not a complete remedy at law. Pecuniary damages for the breach of the contract is not what the complainant asks, or is entitled to receive at the hands of a court of equity. He asks to receive the price stipulated to be paid in lieu of the land. The doctrine is well

established that the remedy is mutual, and that the vendor may maintain his bill in all cases where the purchaser could sue for a specific performance of the agreement.''

* * *

Our present Supreme Court has squarely held, however, that mutuality of remedy is not an appropriate basis for granting or denying specific performance.

* * *

The disappearance of the mutuality of remedy doctrine from our law dictates the conclusion that specific performance relief should no longer be automatically available to a vendor of real estate, but should be confined to those special instances where a vendor will otherwise suffer an economic injury for which his damage remedy at law will not be adequate, or where other equitable considerations require that the relief be granted.

* * *

Here the subject matter of the real estate transaction—a condominium apartment unit—has no unique quality but is one of hundreds of virtually identical units being offered by a developer for sale to the public. The units are sold by means of sample, in this case model apartments, in much the same manner as items of personal property are sold in the market place. The sales prices for the units are fixed in accordance with schedule filed by Centex as part of its offering plan, and the only variance as between apartments having the same floor plan (of which six plans are available) is the floor level or the building location within the project. In actuality, the condominium apartment units, regardless of their realty label, share the same characteristics as personal property.

From the foregoing one must conclude that the damages sustained by a condominium sponsor resulting from the breach of the sales agreement are readily measurable and the damage remedy at law is wholly adequate. No compelling reasons have been shown by Centex for the granting of specific performance relief and its complaint is therefore dismissed as to the first count.

Centex also seeks money damages pursuant to a liquidated damage clause in its contract with the defendants. It is sufficient to note only that under the language of that clause (which was authored by Centex) liquidated damages are limited to such moneys as were paid by defendant at the time the default occurred. Since the default here consisted of the defendant's stopping payment of his check for the balance of the downpayment, Centex's liquidated damages are limited to the retention of the ''moneys paid'' prior to that date, or the initial $525 deposit. Accordingly, the second count of the complaint for damage relief will also be dismissed.

NOTES AND QUESTIONS

1. The Uniform Land Transactions Act § 2–506(b) grants specific performance only when "the seller is unable after a reasonable effort to resell [the property] at a reasonable price or the circumstances reasonably indicate the effort will be unavailing." In practice, specific performance is a more unique remedy for buyers than it is for sellers. An award of specific performance against a defaulting seller is tantamount to a judicial transfer of title up to the limits of the seller's legal capacity to make the transfer. By contrast, an award of specific performance against a defaulting buyer, generally entitles the seller to the consideration stated in the land sale contract. Most commonly, this is the balance of the purchase price. A seller who sold the property to someone else and then sued the defaulting buyer for any shortfall in a common law damages action would often end up in about the same position. In Wolf v. Anderson, 334 N.W.2d 212 (N.D. 1983), the court held that the doctrine of mutuality of remedies was not sufficient to support a vendor's action for specific performance. Rather, the vendor would have to make the traditional showing required by courts of equity that it had an inadequate remedy at law. Many other courts adhere to the traditional rule entitling a seller to specific performance "irrespective of any special proof" of the "uniqueness" of the property in question. Pruitt v. Graziano, 215 N.J.Super. 330, 521 A.2d 1313 (App.Div.1987).

2. Suppose that a land sale contract provides that if the buyer defaults the seller will be entitled to keep the buyer's deposit as liquidated damages. The buyer defaults. However, instead of keeping the deposit the seller brings suit for specific performance. Does the liquidated damages clause in the contract preclude specific performance? See Kohrs v. Barth, 212 Ill.App.3d 468, 156 Ill.Dec. 551, 570 N.E.2d 1273 (1991); cf. Seabaugh v. Keele, 775 S.W.2d 205 (Mo.Ct.App.1989).

NOTE: SPECIFIC PERFORMANCE AND THE MARKET FOR REAL PROPERTY

Actions for breach of land sale contracts are unique in that specific performance is the presumed remedy, while an award of damages is the exception. The doctrine of specific performance for breach of land sale contracts, an equitable remedy, had its origin in the doctrine of equitable conversion. As described by the Supreme Court:

> The principle upon which the whole of this doctrine [of equitable conversion] is founded is, that a court of equity, regarding the substance, and not the mere forms and circumstances of agreements and other instruments, considered things directed or agreed to be done, as having been actually performed, where nothing has intervened which ought to prevent a performance.... Thus, where the whole beneficial interest in the money, in the one case, or in the land, in the other, belongs to the person for whose use it is given, a court of equity ... will permit him to take the money, o[r] the land, if he elect to do so, before the conversion has actually been made; ...

Craig v. Leslie, 16 U.S. (3 Wheat.) 563, 578 (1818).

The doctrine of equitable conversion rests on the fiction that the instant a binding land sale contract comes into existence the seller's interest in real property changes into an interest in personal property (the purchase price), and the buyer's interest in personal property changes into an interest in real property. The doctrine has had a wide influence, not only on the right of specific performance, but also on questions of conflict of laws, inheritance taxation, statutory construction (e.g., does a statute which applies only to real property cover the property at issue in this case?) and, as the following section illustrates, questions concerning the assignment of loss when something happens to property during the interval after the formation of a contract of sale but before title is transferred. The doctrine is also used to support a buyer's right of specific performance against the seller's estate, heirs or devisees if the seller dies after the contract was made but before execution and delivery of the deed.

The doctrine of equitable conversion does nothing to explain *why* contracts for the sale of land should be treated differently from other kinds of contracts in which damages are the preferred remedy. The reason that is given most frequently is that land is unique, and as a result damages are harder to measure in contract actions involving land sales than in those involving the sale of, say, wheat or lumber.

Even more important is the fact that different buyers place much different values on a particular piece of property. As a result, "objective" measures of damages (the amount that a reasonable person would pay) are much less reliable. To be sure, different purchasers place different values on fungibles as well. The orthodontist who purchases steel in order to make braces may be willing to pay $200 a pound for it, while the bridge builder will pay only $2 a pound. That is, if the price of steel rises above $2 per pound, the bridge builder will find a substitute product, such as wood. The orthodontist would not look for a substitute product until the price of steel exceeded $200 per pound. But if the market price for steel is $1.50 per pound, both the orthodontist and the bridge builder will be able to find substitute steel for $1.50 per pound. As a result, both the orthodontist and the bridge builder can be fairly compensated by damages actions. In fact, their damages will be the same per unit of steel lost by the default, *in spite of* the fact that the orthodontist values the steel one hundred times higher than the bridge builder does.

The market for real property is different. Different buyers may place widely different values on a particular parcel *and* the parcel may have no close substitutes. As a result, a purely objective estimate of the property's market value will often fall short of covering the buyer's loss.

Does this theory tell us anything about the wisdom of preserving the right of specific performance by sellers against defaulting buyers? Perhaps a little. If the seller is entitled to the full benefit of his bargain, he must receive the difference between the amount he agreed to accept from the defaulting buyer and the amount he actually receives in a substitute transaction. If a substitute transaction is available, then computation of damages is not difficult: they equal the difference between the sale price in the unperformed contract and the purchase price obtained in the substitute transaction.

Specific performance is not necessary. In fact, if a substitute transaction is available, specific performance may be inefficient. It may force someone who no longer wants the property (the defaulting buyer) to take it and pay for it, while it deprives someone else who wants it from the opportunity to purchase it.

When no substitute transaction is available, then the case for specific performance against defaulting buyers may be a little stronger. Suppose that after a buyer's default a seller attempts to sell his property for an additional year, but no one makes a bid. Now, under established damages rules the seller would be entitled to the difference between the price established in the contract with the defaulting buyer and the "market" price. Once again, however, an objective market price will be difficult to establish.

B. Damages

BEARD v. S/E JOINT VENTURE

Court of Appeals of Maryland (1990).
321 Md. 126, 581 A.2d 1275.

RODOWSKY, JUDGE.

This case involves the measure of damages for the breach by vendors of a contract to construct a residence and then to convey the improved realty. The real estate market for the subject property was escalating during the potentially relevant period.... We shall hold that the purchasers' damages are not limited to certain out-of-pocket losses, as held by the courts below, but that the purchasers may also recover damages for loss of the benefit of their bargain. * * *

The purchasers are the petitioners, DeLawrence and Lillian M. Beard (the Beards), who were plaintiffs in the circuit court. The vendors, respondents here and defendants in the circuit court, are Diana C. Etheridge (Etheridge) and Gene Stull (Stull), joint venturers in S/E Joint Venture. Etheridge is a licensed real estate agent and Stull is a home builder. S/E Joint Venture had acquired an unimproved lot in Piney Glen Farms subdivision in the Potomac section of Montgomery County for the purpose of building a home for speculation.

Protracted negotiations between the Beards and S/E Joint Venture led to a contract formed on March 17, 1986, under which S/E Joint Venture would construct a house on the lot and convey the improved premises to the Beards for $785,000. The contract in part provided "that the PURCHASER is purchasing a completed dwelling [and] that the SELLER is not acting as a contractor for the PURCHASER in the construction of the dwelling[.]" The contract recited that "the approximate date of completion of the improvements now scheduled by the SELLER is November 30, 1986." For a period of ninety days the contract was contingent on the sale of two residences, one the then residence of the Beards and the other that of Mrs. Beard's mother, who also was to occupy the home to be built.

Matters did not proceed smoothly. On March 16, 1987, the vendors, through counsel, terminated the contract. The letter declaring the contract terminated invoked a provision under which "the SELLER shall have the right to return the PURCHASER'S deposit and to declare this Contract null and void if, in the SELLER'S sole discretion, it determines that ... performance within 365 days from the date hereof will not be possible."

In May 1987 the Beards filed a ... complaint against respondents. * * *

In a written opinion the circuit judge found, on conflicting evidence, that the vendors had breached the contract by the purported termination of March 16, 1987. The trial judge concluded "that it is implicit that before the right of termination can be exercised the defendants must have acted in good faith to try to complete construction of the house within the stated time period; this, in the court's judgment, they did not do." The circuit court found that Stull "knew some two months after the inception of the contract that he would be unable to meet the time deadline." This was found to be "significant because defendants were aware that the plaintiffs and [Mrs. Beard's mother] had to sell their homes in order to meet their financial commitment[.]" The trial court also found undue delay in the performance of plumbing work, which "had a ripple effect on the subsequent course of construction." * * *

Itemizing claimed damages in their post trial memorandum, the Beards included $100,000 for "loss of bargain." Factually, the $100,000 figure is said to represent the excess of the value of the property, with the home completed in accordance with the contract, as of March 16, 1987, over the contract price. * * *

Legally to support their loss of the bargain claim, the plaintiffs relied on Horner v. Beasley, 105 Md. 193, 65 A. 820 (1907). *Horner* was a purchaser's action against a vendor for breach of a contract to convey, for $1,200, improved realty worth $1,800.... This Court ... approved a jury instruction that if "the defendant acted in good faith in failing to perform the contract of sale, the plaintiff was entitled to recover only the amount of his deposit with interest and the expense if any incurred in the investigation of the title; but if they found that the defendant did not act in good faith then in addition to the amounts aforesaid the plaintiff could recover the excess, if any, of the market value of the property, at the time of the sale, over the contract price."

The Beards, also citing Charles County Broadcasting Co. v. Meares, 270 Md. 321, 311 A.2d 27 (1973), argued that, because the respondents were able to perform, their breach was in "bad faith," so that benefit of the bargain damages should be awarded. The trial court did not accept this contention, explaining that it did "not award any damages for loss of the benefit of the bargain[,] finding no evidence of bad faith in the sense that the termination was activated by malice, fraud or the like." * * *

Damages for breach of a contract ordinarily are that sum which would place the plaintiff in as good a position as that in which the plaintiff would have been, had the contract been performed. These expectation interest damages embrace both losses incurred and gains prevented. See Restatement (Second) of Contracts § 347 (1981); Restatement of Contracts § 329 (1932). Here the circuit court undertook to apply an exception to the ordinary rule. The exception traces to Flureau v. Thornhill, 2 W. Black. 1078, 96 Eng.Rep. 635 (K.B.1776). In England, and in the diminishing number of American states that recognize *Flureau*, the exception applies only where, due to no fault on the part of the seller, there is an inability to convey good title. In the case at hand respondents' breach had nothing to do with title to the property. Further, under the trial court's findings, the inability timely to deliver a completed house, which motivated the wrongful termination of March 16, 1987, is not a "good faith" failure to perform within the meaning of the *Flureau* exception. In any event, "good faith," per the *Flureau* rule, is not so all inclusive as to embrace any breach which was not "activated by malice, fraud or the like," as the trial judge said. Thus, the trial court applied an erroneous legal standard when it refused to consider benefit of the bargain damages.

In *Flureau*, the plaintiff had purchased at auction a property that paid an advantageous rent in relation to the purchase price. The seller, however, could not produce good title. In the ensuing suit the court's instructions limited the jury to awarding the return of the deposit paid, plus interest; but the jury allowed an additional twenty pounds. A new trial was ordered. The report of the judgment of De Grey, C.J., reads in full: "I think the verdict wrong in point of law. Upon a contract for a purchase, if the title proves bad, and the vendor is (without fraud) incapable of making a good one, I do not think that the purchaser can be entitled to any damages for the fancied goodness of the bargain, which he supposes he has lost." *Flureau*, 2 W. Black. 1078, 96 Eng.Rep. 635. * * *

It has been recognized in England that the *Flureau* exception was an "anomalous rule" brought about by the difficulties in that country, as late as 1899 (if not later), "in shewing a good title to real property" and that the exception "ought not be extended to cases in which the reasons on which it is based do not apply." Day v. Singleton, [1899] 2 Ch. 320, 329 (C.A.).[1]

Although English courts have struggled over the scope of the *Flureau* exception, the English cases considering *Flureau* have all concerned some aspect of title. See Hopkins v. Grazebrook, 6 B. & C. 31 (K.B.1826) (vendor who knows he has no title, but expects to be able to procure it

---

1. The difficulties included the absence of a land register. The deeds evidencing the chain of title were delivered by the solicitor for the vendor to the solicitor for the purchaser. "Neither possession of the land nor possession of the deeds was a sufficient guarantee of a good title. Deeds might be suppressed intentionally, or as the result of mistake or accident." 15 W. Holdsworth, A History of English Law 173 (A. Goodhart & H. Hanbury ed. 1965) (footnote omitted). In Donovan v. Bachstadt, 91 N.J. 434, 441, 453 A.2d 160, 164 (1982), the court attributes to Lord Westbury, a mid-nineteenth century Lord Chancellor, the description of a bundle of documents evidencing title as "difficult to read, disgusting to touch, and impossible to understand."

prior to sale cannot rely on *Flureau* exception); Engell v. Fitch, [1869] L.R. 4 Q.B. 659 (Ex.Ch.) (*Flureau* limitation on damages not available where failure to convey results from vendor's refusal to oust a tenant); Bain v. Fothergill, [1874] L.R. 7 H.L. 158 (1873–74) (*Flureau* applies when inability to convey interest in mining royalty results from inability to get permission from lessor); Day v. Singleton, [1899] 2 Ch. 320 (C.A.) (*Flureau* limitation on damages unavailable in sale of leasehold, where vendor fails to use best efforts to obtain lessor's consent to sale); In re Daniel, [1917] 2 Ch. 405 (*Flureau* not applicable where difficulty in conveyance results from inability to obtain partial release of mortgage); Braybrooks v. Whaley, [1919] 1 K.B. 435 (*Flureau* not applicable where failure to convey relates to noncompliance with Emergency Powers Act, rather than title defect).

More recently, *Flureau* has been given a very narrow reading in England. In Malhotra v. Choudhury, [1979] 1 All E.R. 186 (C.A.), a partner in a medical practice, Malhotra, conveyed the medical office to the junior partner, Choudhury, and the latter's wife. The partnership agreement provided that, if Choudhury left the practice, Malhotra would have the option to buy back the property at fair market value. The next year Malhotra gave notice of dissolution of the partnership, exercised the option, and later brought an action for specific performance, which was denied. Two years later Malhotra sought damages. The trial court found that Choudhury could not convey good title because of his wife's refusal to join and, applying *Flureau*, limited the recovery to reliance damages. The Court of Appeal reversed, holding that the *Flureau* rule was an exception to be applied only where the vendor showed best efforts to make a good title. The court reasoned that the origin of the exception virtually required that bad faith be defined as a failure to make best efforts, with no requirement for fraud, and that failure of the vendor to demonstrate good faith precluded the *Flureau* exception.

With respect to this country, Professor Corbin summarizes: "A great many courts in the United States have not been inclined to follow the English courts or to differentiate land contracts from other contracts. The rule they adopt is that, if the seller fails to convey the title that he contracted to convey, the buyer has a right to damages measured by the value of the land at the time it should have been conveyed, less the contract price as yet unpaid." 5 A. Corbin, Corbin on Contracts § 1098, at 525 (1964) (footnote omitted). "Some of the courts, however, have recognized the English rule. . . ." Id. at 525–28 (footnote omitted). But even among American courts applying *Flureau*, "[i]f the seller in fact has title and refuses to perform his contract without excuse, the buyer has a right to damages." * * *

Respondents have no basis for invoking the *Flureau* exception because they do not even assert that inability to convey title produced their breach of the contract to convey. * * *

Thus, the trial court erred in failing to consider breach of the bargain damages.

NOTES AND QUESTIONS

1. The leading American case rejecting benefit of the bargain damages is *Kramer v. Mobley*, 309 Ky. 143, 216 S.W.2d 930 (1949). This is sometimes called the "English" rule. By contrast, other states award full benefit of the bargain damages even when the seller acted in good faith. For example, *Smith v. Warr*, 564 P.2d 771 (Utah 1977).

2. A vendee of *personal* property is generally entitled to full benefit of the bargain damages against a defaulting vendor, regardless of the vendor's good faith or failure of title. What is the justification for the different treatment of real property in the states that follow the so-called English rule? The uniqueness of land? Perhaps, if the court is highly conscious of the difficulty of measuring benefit-of-the-bargain damages when the transaction involves land. A buyer who suffers a default on a contract to sell wheat at $1.00 per unit and who makes a substitute purchase at $1.10 per unit can quite easily show the amount of his damages—10¢ per unit. But what about the buyer who has agreed to buy Blackacre for $100,000 and later discovers that the seller has a defective title? He buys Whiteacre instead for $110,000. Before we know whether the buyer has been injured by $10,000 we have to obtain some information about the differences between Blackacre and Whiteacre (or perhaps, the differences in his preferences as between the two). The buyer may be better off purchasing Whiteacre at $110,000 than he was purchasing Blackacre at $100,000.

This analysis suggests, however, that the justification for the English rule rests, not on the distinction between real property and personal property, but rather on the distinction between fungible property and unique property.

STAMBOVSKY v. ACKLEY

Supreme Court, Appellate Division, First Department, New York (1991).
169 A.D.2d 254, 572 N.Y.S.2d 672.

RUBIN, JUSTICE.

Plaintiff, to his horror, discovered that the house he had recently contracted to purchase was widely reputed to be possessed by poltergeists, reportedly seen by defendant seller and members of her family on numerous occasions over the last nine years. Plaintiff promptly commenced this action seeking rescission of the contract of sale. Supreme Court reluctantly dismissed the complaint, holding that plaintiff has no remedy at law in this jurisdiction.

The unusual facts of this case, as disclosed by the record, clearly warrant a grant of equitable relief to the buyer who, as a resident of New York City, cannot be expected to have any familiarity with the folklore of the Village of Nyack. Not being a "local," plaintiff could not readily learn that the home he had contracted to purchase is haunted. Whether the source of the spectral apparitions seen by defendant seller are parapsychic or psychogenic, having reported their presence in both a national publication ("Readers' Digest") and the local press (in 1977 and 1982, respectively), defendant is estopped to deny their existence and, as a matter of law, the house is haunted. More to the point, however, no divination is required to conclude that it is defendant's promotional efforts in publicizing her close encounters with these spirits which fostered the home's reputation in the community. In 1989, the house was included in a five-home walking tour of Nyack and described in a November 27th newspaper article as "a riverfront Victorian (with ghost)." The impact of the reputation thus created goes to the very essence of the bargain between the parties, greatly impairing both the value of the property and its potential for resale. The extent of this impairment may be presumed for the purpose of reviewing the disposition of this motion to dismiss the cause of action for rescission (*Harris v. City of New York*, 147 A.D.2d 186, 188–189, 542 N.Y.S.2d 550) and represents merely an issue of fact for resolution at trial.

While I agree with Supreme Court that the real estate broker, as agent for the seller, is under no duty to disclose to a potential buyer the phantasmal reputation of the premises and that, in his pursuit of a legal remedy for fraudulent misrepresentation against the seller, plaintiff hasn't a ghost of a chance, I am nevertheless moved by the spirit of equity to allow the buyer to seek rescission of the contract of sale and recovery of his downpayment. New York law fails to recognize any remedy for damages incurred as a result of the seller's mere silence, applying instead the strict rule of caveat emptor. Therefore, the theoretical basis for granting relief, even under the extraordinary facts of this case, is elusive if not ephemeral.

"Pity me not but lend thy serious hearing to what I shall unfold" (William Shakespeare, Hamlet, Act I, Scene V [Ghost]).

From the perspective of a person in the position of plaintiff herein, a very practical problem arises with respect to the discovery of a paranormal phenomenon: "Who you gonna' call?" as the title song to the movie "Ghostbusters" asks. Applying the strict rule of caveat emptor to a contract involving a house possessed by poltergeists conjures up visions of a psychic or medium routinely accompanying the structural engineer and Terminix man on an inspection of every home subject to a contract of sale. It portends that the prudent attorney will establish an escrow account lest the subject of the transaction come back to haunt him and his client—or pray that his malpractice insurance coverage extends to supernatural disasters. In the interest of avoiding such untenable consequences, the notion that a haunting is a condition which can and should be ascertained upon reasonable inspection of the premises is a hobgoblin which should be exorcised from the body of legal precedent and laid quietly to rest.

It has been suggested by a leading authority that the ancient rule which holds that mere non-disclosure does not constitute actionable misrepresentation "finds proper application in cases where the fact undisclosed is patent, or the plaintiff has equal opportunities for obtaining information which he may be expected to utilize, or the defendant has no reason to think that he is acting under any misapprehension" (Prosser, Law of Torts § 106, at 696 [4th ed., 1971]). However, with respect to transactions in real estate, New York adheres to the doctrine of caveat emptor and imposes no duty upon the vendor to disclose any information concerning the premises . . .

Caveat emptor is not so all-encompassing a doctrine of common law as to render every act of non-disclosure immune from redress, whether legal or equitable. "In regard to the necessity of giving information which has not been asked, the rule differs somewhat at law and in equity, and while the law courts would permit no recovery of *damages* against a vendor, because of mere concealment of facts *under certain circumstances,* yet if the vendee refused to complete the contract because of the concealment of a material fact on the part of the other, equity would refuse to compel him so to do, because equity only compels the specific performance of a contract which is fair and open, and in regard to which all material matters known to each have been communicated to the other" (*Rothmiller v. Stein,* 143 N.Y. 581, 591–592, 38 N.E. 718 [emphasis added]). Even as a principle of law, long before exceptions were embodied in statute law (*see, e.g.,* UCC 2–312, 2–313, 2–314, 2–315; 3–417[2][e]), the doctrine was held inapplicable to contagion among animals, adulteration of food, and insolvency of a maker of a promissory note and of a tenant substituted for another under a lease (*see, Rothmiller v. Stein, supra,* at 592–593, 38 N.E. 718 and cases cited therein). Common law is not moribund. *Ex facto jus oritur* (law arises out of facts). Where fairness and common sense dictate that an exception should be created, the evolution of the law should not be stifled by rigid application of a legal maxim.

The doctrine of caveat emptor requires that a buyer act prudently to assess the fitness and value of his purchase and operates to bar the purchaser who fails to exercise due care from seeking the equitable remedy of rescission (*see, e.g., Rodas v. Manitaras,* 159 A.D.2d 341, 552 N.Y.S.2d 618). For the purposes of the instant motion to dismiss the action pursuant to CPLR 3211(a)(7), plaintiff is entitled to every favorable inference which may reasonably be drawn from the pleadings (*Arrington v. New York Times Co.,* 55 N.Y.2d 433, 442, 449 N.Y.S.2d 941, 434 N.E.2d 1319; *Rovello v. Orofino Realty Co.,* 40 N.Y.2d 633, 634, 389 N.Y.S.2d 314, 357 N.E.2d 970), specifically, in this instance, that he met his obligation to conduct an inspection of the premises and a search of available public records with respect to title. It should be apparent, however, that the most meticulous inspection and the search would not reveal the presence of poltergeists at the premises or unearth the property's ghoulish reputation in the community. Therefore, there is no sound policy reason to deny plaintiff relief for failing to discover a state of affairs which the most prudent purchaser would not be expected to even contemplate.

The case law in this jurisdiction dealing with the duty of a vendor of real property to disclose information to the buyer is distinguishable from the matter under review. The most salient distinction is that existing cases invariably deal with the physical condition of the premises (*e.g., London v. Courduff, supra* [use as a landfill]; *Perin v. Mardine Realty Co.,* 5 A.D.2d 685, 168 N.Y.S.2d 647 *affd.* 6 N.Y.2d 920, 190 N.Y.S.2d 995, 161 N.E.2d 210 [sewer line crossing adjoining property without owner's consent]), defects in title (*e.g., Sands v. Kissane,* 282 App.Div. 140, 121 N.Y.S.2d 634 [remainderman]), liens against the property (*e.g., Noved Realty Corp. v. A.A.P. Co., supra*), expenses or income (*e.g., Rodas v. Manitaras, supra* [gross receipts]) and other factors affecting its operation. No case has been brought to this court's attention in which the property value was impaired as the result of the reputation created by information disseminated to the public by the seller (or, for that matter, as a result of possession by poltergeists).

Where a condition which has been created by the seller materially impairs the value of the contract and is peculiarly within the knowledge of the seller or unlikely to be discovered by a prudent purchaser exercising due care with respect to the subject transaction, nondisclosure constitutes a basis for rescission as a matter of equity. Any other outcome places upon the buyer not merely the obligation to exercise care in his purchase but rather to be omniscient with respect to any fact which may affect the bargain. No practical purpose is served by imposing such a burden upon a purchaser. To the contrary, it encourages predatory business practice and offends the principle that equity will suffer no wrong to be without a remedy.

Defendant's contention that the contract of sale, particularly the merger or "as is" clause, bars recovery of the buyer's deposit is unavailing. Even an express disclaimer will not be given effect where the facts are peculiarly within the knowledge of the party invoking it (*Danann Realty Corp. v. Harris,* 5 N.Y.2d 317, 322, 184 N.Y.S.2d 599, 157 N.E.2d 597; *Tahini Invs., Ltd. v. Bobrowsky, supra*). Moreover, a fair reading of the merger clause reveals that it expressly disclaims only representations made with respect to the physical condition of the premises and merely makes general reference to representations concerning "any other matter or things affecting or relating to the aforesaid premises". As broad as this language may be, a reasonable interpretation is that its effect is limited to tangible or physical matters and does not extend to paranormal phenomena. Finally, if the language of the contract is to be construed as broadly as defendant urges to encompass the presence of poltergeists in the house, it cannot be said that she has delivered the premises "vacant" in accordance with her obligation under the provisions of the contract rider.

To the extent New York law may be said to require something more than "mere concealment" to apply even the equitable remedy of rescission, the case of *Junius Construction Corporation v. Cohen,* 257 N.Y. 393, 178 N.E. 672, *supra,* while not precisely on point, provides some guidance. In that case, the seller disclosed that an official map indicated two as yet unopened streets which were planned for construction at the edges of the parcel. What was not disclosed was that the same map indicated a third street which, if opened, would divide the plot in half. The court held that, while the seller was under no duty to mention the planned streets at all, having undertaken to disclose two of them, he was obliged to reveal the third (*see also, Rosenschein v. McNally*, 17 A.D.2d 834, 233 N.Y.S.2d 254).

In the case at bar, defendant seller deliberately fostered the public belief that her home was possessed. Having undertaken to inform the public at large, to whom she has no legal relationship, about the supernatural occurrences on her property, she may be said to owe no less a duty to her contract vendee. It has been remarked that the occasional modern cases which permit a seller to take unfair advantage of a buyer's ignorance so long as he is not actively misled are "singularly unappetizing" (Prosser, Law of Torts § 106, at 696 [4th ed. 1971]). Where, as here, the seller not only takes unfair advantage of the buyer's ignorance but has created and perpetuated a condition about which he is unlikely to even inquire, enforcement of the contract (in whole or in part) is offensive to the court's sense of equity. Application of the remedy of rescission, within the bounds of the narrow exception to the doctrine of caveat emptor set forth herein, is entirely appropriate to relieve the unwitting purchaser from the consequences of a most unnatural bargain.

Accordingly, the judgment of the Supreme Court, New York County ... which dismissed the complaint ... should be modified, on the law and the facts and in the exercise of discretion, and the first cause of action seeking rescission of the contract reinstated, without costs.

Judgment, Supreme Court, New York County (Edward H. Lehner, J.), entered on April 9, 1990, modified, on the law and the facts and in the exercise of discretion, and the first cause of action seeking rescission of the contract reinstated, without costs.

All concur except MILONAS, J.P. and SMITH, J., who dissent in an opinion by SMITH, J.

SMITH, JUSTICE (dissenting).

I would affirm the dismissal of the complaint by the motion court.

Plaintiff seeks to rescind his contract to purchase defendant Ackley's residential property and recover his down payment. Plaintiff alleges that Ackley and her real estate broker, defendant Ellis Realty, made material misrepresentations of the property in that they failed to disclose that Ackley believed that the house was haunted by poltergeists. Moreover, Ackley shared this belief with her community and the general public through articles published in *Reader's Digest* (1977) and the local newspaper (1982). In November 1989, approximately two months after the parties entered into the contract of sale but subsequent to the scheduled October 2, 1989 closing, the house was included in a five-house walking tour and again described in the local newspaper as being haunted.

Prior to closing, plaintiff learned of this reputation and unsuccessfully sought to rescind the $650,000 contract of sale and obtain return of his $32,500 down payment without resort to litigation. The plaintiff then commenced this action for that relief and alleged that he would not have entered into the contract had he been so advised and that as a result of the alleged poltergeist activity, the market value and resaleability of the property was greatly diminished. Defendant Ackley has counterclaimed for specific performance.

> "It is settled law in New York that the seller of real property is under no duty to speak when the parties deal at arm's length. The mere silence of the seller, without some act or conduct which deceived the purchaser, does not amount to a concealment that is actionable as a fraud (*see Perin v. Mardine Realty Co., Inc.,* 5 A.D.2d 685, 168 N.Y.S.2d 647, *aff'd.,* 6 N.Y.2d 920, 190 N.Y.S.2d 995, 161 N.E.2d 210; *Moser v. Spizzirro,* 31 A.D.2d 537, 295 N.Y.S.2d 188, *aff'd.,* 25 N.Y.2d 941, 305 N.Y.S.2d 153, 252 N.E.2d 632). The buyer has the duty to satisfy himself as to the quality of his bargain pursuant to the doctrine of caveat emptor, which in New York State still applies to real estate transactions." *London v. Courduff,* 141 A.D.2d 803, 804, 529 N.Y.S.2d 874, *app. dism'd.,* 73 N.Y.2d 809, 537 N.Y.S.2d 494, 534 N.E.2d 332 (1988).

The parties herein were represented by counsel and dealt at arm's length. This is evidenced by the contract of sale which, *inter alia,* contained various riders and a specific provision that all prior understandings and agreements between the parties were merged into the contract, that the contract completely expressed their full agreement and that neither had relied upon any statement by anyone else not set forth in the contract. There is no allegation that defendants, by some specific act, other than the failure to speak, deceived the plaintiff. Nevertheless, a cause of action may be sufficiently stated where there is a confidential or fiduciary relationship creating a duty to disclose and there was a failure to disclose a material fact, calculated to induce a false belief. *County of Westchester v. Welton Becket Assoc.,* 102 A.D.2d 34, 50–51, 478 N.Y.S.2d 305, *aff'd.,* 66 N.Y.2d 642, 495 N.Y.S.2d 364, 485 N.E.2d 1029 (1985). However, plaintiff herein has not alleged and there is no basis for concluding that a confidential or fiduciary relationship existed between these parties to an arm's length transaction such as to give rise to a duty to disclose. In addition, there is no allegation that defendants thwarted plaintiff's efforts to fulfill his responsibilities fixed by the doctrine of caveat emptor. See *London v. Courduff, supra,* 141 A.D.2d at 804, 529 N.Y.S.2d 874.

Finally, if the doctrine of caveat emptor is to be discarded, it should be for a reason more substantive than a poltergeist. The existence of a poltergeist is no more binding upon the defendants than it is upon this court.

Based upon the foregoing, the motion court properly dismissed the complaint.

§ 14.4.4 RISK OF LOSS

BRUSH GROCERY KART, INC. v. SURE FIRE MARKET, INC.

Supreme Court of Colorado (2002).
47 P.3d 680.

JUSTICE COATS delivered the Opinion of the Court.

In October 1992 Brush Grocery Kart, Inc. and Sure Fine Market, Inc. entered into a five-year "Lease with Renewal Provisions and Option to Purchase" for real property, including a building to be operated by Brush as a grocery store. Under the contract's purchase option provision, any time during the last six months of the lease, Brush could elect to purchase the property at a price equal to the average of the appraisals of an expert designated by each party.

Shortly before expiration of the lease, Brush notified Sure Fine of its desire to purchase the property and begin the process of determining a sale price. Although each party offered an appraisal, the parties were unable to agree on a final price by the time the lease expired. Brush then vacated the premises, returned all keys to Sure Fine, and advised Sure Fine that it would discontinue its casualty insurance covering the property during the lease. Brush also filed suit, alleging that Sure Fine failed to negotiate the price term in good faith and asking for the appointment of a special master to determine the purchase price. Sure Fine agreed to the appointment of a special master and counterclaimed, alleging that Brush negotiated the price term in bad faith and was therefore the breaching party.

During litigation over the price term, the property was substantially damaged during a hail storm. With neither party carrying casualty insurance, each asserted that the other was liable for the damage. The issue was added to the litigation at a stipulated amount of $60,000. The court appointed a special master ... and accepted his appraised value of $375,000. The court then found that under the doctrine of equitable conversion, Brush was the equitable owner of the property and bore the risk of loss. It therefore declined to abate the purchase price or award damages to Brush for the loss.

Brush appealed the loss allocation, and the court of appeals affirmed on similar grounds. It considered the prior holdings of this court acknowledging the doctrine of equitable conversion and found that in *Wiley v. Lininger,* 119 Colo. 497, 204 P.2d 1083 (1949), that doctrine was applied to allocate the risk of casualty loss occurring during the executory period of a contract for the purchase of real property. Relying heavily on language from the opinion purporting to adopt the "majority rule," the court of appeals found that our characterization of the rule as placing the risk of casualty loss on a vendee who "is in possession," *id.* at 502, 204 P.2d at 1086, reflected merely the facts of that case rather than any intent to limit the rule to vendees who are actually in possession. Noting that allocation of the risk of loss in circumstances where the vendee is not in possession had not previously been addressed by an appellate court in this jurisdiction, the court of appeals went on to conclude that a "bright line rule" allocating the risk of loss to the vendee, without regard to possession, would best inform the parties of their rights and obligations under a contract for the sale of land.

Brush petitioned for a writ of certiorari to determine the proper allocation of the risk of loss and the appropriate remedy under these circumstances. . . .

In the absence of statutory authority, the rights, powers, duties, and liabilities arising out of a contract for the sale of land have frequently been derived by reference to the theory of equitable conversion. . . . This theory or doctrine, which has been described as a legal fiction. . . . is based on equitable principles that permit the vendee to be considered the equitable owner of the land and debtor for the purchase money and the vendor to be regarded as a secured creditor. . . . The changes in rights and liabilities that occur upon the making of the contract result from the equitable right to specific performance . . . Even with regard to third parties, the theory has been relied on to determine, for example, the devolution, upon death, of the rights and liabilities of each party with respect to the land . . . and to ascertain the powers of creditors of each party to reach the land in payment of their claims. . . .

The assignment of the risk of casualty loss in the executory period of contracts for the sale of real property varies greatly throughout the jurisdictions of this country. What appears to yet be a slim majority of states . . . places the risk of loss on the vendee from the moment of contracting, on the rationale that once an equitable conversion takes place, the vendee must be treated as owner for all purposes. See *Skelly Oil v. Ashmore,* 365 S.W.2d 582, 588 (Mo.1963) (criticizing this approach). Once the vendee becomes the equitable owner, he therefore becomes responsible for the condition of the property, despite not having a present right of occupancy or control. In sharp contrast, a handful of other states reject the allocation of casualty loss risk as a consequence of the theory of equitable conversion and follow the equally rigid "Massachusetts Rule," under which the seller continues to bear the risk until actual transfer of the title, absent an express agreement to the contrary. *See, e.g., Skelly Oil,* 365 S.W.2d at 588–89. A substantial and growing number of jurisdictions, however, base the legal consequences of no-fault casualty loss on the right to possession of the property at the time the loss occurs. . . . This view has found expression in the Uniform Vendor and Purchaser Risk Act, [ed. note: See Note 1 following] and while a number of states have adopted some variation of the Uniform Act, others have arrived at a similar position through the interpretations of their courts . . .

This court has applied the theory of equitable conversion in limited circumstances affecting title, see *Konecny v. von Gunten,* 151 Colo. 376, 379 P.2d 158 (1963)(finding vendors incapable of unilaterally changing their tenancy in common to joint tenancy during the executory period of the contract because their interest had been equitably converted into a mere security interest and the vendee's interest into realty), and refused to apply it in some circumstances, see *Chain O'Mines,* 101 Colo. 231, 72 P.2d 265 (holding that even if the doctrine applies to option contracts, no conversion would take place until the option were exercised by the party having the right of election). It has also characterized the theory as affording significant protections to purchasers of realty in Colorado. See *Dwyer v. Dist. Court,* 188 Colo. 41, 532 P.2d 725 (1975) (finding personal jurisdiction over out-of-state vendee in part because of the protections afforded vendees of land in this jurisdiction during the executory period of the contract). It has never before, however, expressly relied on the theory of equitable conversion alone as allocating the risk of casualty loss to a vendee.

In *Wiley v. Lininger,* 119 Colo. 497, 204 P.2d 1083, where fire destroyed improvements on land occupied by the vendee during the multi-year executory period of an installment land contract, we held, according to the generally accepted rule, that neither the buyer nor the seller, each of whom had an insurable interest in the property, had an obligation to insure the property for the benefit of the other.... We also adopted a rule, which we characterized as "the majority rule," that "the vendee under a contract for the sale of land, being regarded as the equitable owner, assumes the risk of destruction of or injury to the property *where he is in possession,* and the destruction or loss is not proximately caused by the negligence of the vendor." *Id.* (emphasis added). The vendee in possession was therefore not relieved of his obligation to continue making payments according to the terms of the contract, despite material loss by fire to some of the improvements on the property.

Largely because we included a citation, preceded by the introductory signal, "see," to an A.L.R. annotation, describing a "majority rule" without reference to possession, see 101 A.L.R. 1241 ..., the court of appeals found our characterization of the rule, as imposing the risk on vendees who are in possession, to be uncontrolling. While it may have been unnecessary to determine more than the obligations of a vendee in possession in that case, rather than limit the holding to that situation, this court pointedly announced a broader rule. The rule expressly articulated by this court limited the transfer of the risk of loss to vendees who are already in possession. Had this not been the court's deliberate intention, there would have been no need to mention possession at all because a rule governing all vendees would necessarily include vendees in possession. Whether or not a majority of jurisdictions would actually limit the transfer of risk in precisely the same way, the rule as clearly stated and adopted by this court was supported by strong policy and theoretical considerations at the time, and those considerations apply equally today.

Those jurisdictions that indiscriminately include the risk of casualty loss among the incidents or "attributes" of equitable ownership do so largely in reliance on ancient authority or by considering it necessary for consistent application of the theory of equitable conversion. See *Skelly Oil,* 365 S.W.2d at 592 (Stockman, J. dissenting)(quoting 4 Williston, *Contracts,* § 929, at 2607: "Only the hoary age and frequent repetition of the maxim prevents a general recognition of its absurdity."); see *also Paine v. Meller,* (1801) 6 Ves. Jr. 349, 31 Eng. Reprint 1088. Under virtually any accepted understanding of the theory, however, equitable conversion is not viewed as entitling the purchaser to every significant right of ownership, and particularly not the right of possession. As a matter of both logic and equity, the obligation to maintain property in its physical condition follows the right to have actual possession and control rather than a legal right to force conveyance of the property through specific performance at some future date. See 17 Samuel Williston, *A Treatise On the Law of Contracts* § 50:46, at 457–58 (Richard A. Lord ed., 4th ed. 1990) ("[I]t is wiser to have the party in possession of the property care for it at his peril, rather than at the peril of another.").

The equitable conversion theory is literally stood on its head by imposing on a vendee, solely because of his right to specific performance, the risk that the vendor will be unable to specifically perform when the time comes because of an accidental casualty loss. It is counterintuitive, at the very least, that merely contracting for the sale of real property should not only relieve the vendor of his responsibility to maintain the property until execution but also impose a duty on the vendee to perform despite the intervention of a material, no-fault casualty loss preventing him from ever receiving the benefit of his bargain. Such an extension of the theory of equitable conversion to casualty loss has never been recognized by this jurisdiction, and it is neither necessary nor justified solely for the sake of consistency.

By contrast, there is substantial justification, both as a matter of law and policy, for not relieving a vendee who is entitled to possession before transfer of title, like the vendee in *Wiley,* of his duty to pay the full contract price, notwithstanding an accidental loss. In addition to having control over the property and being entitled to the benefits of its use, an equitable owner who also has the right of possession has already acquired virtually all of the rights of ownership and almost invariably will have already paid at least some portion of the contract price to exercise those rights. By expressly including in the contract for sale the right of possession, which otherwise generally accompanies transfer of title ... the vendor has for all practical purposes already transferred the property as promised, and the parties have in effect expressed their joint intention that the vendee pay the purchase price as promised. . . .

In *Wiley,* rather than adopting a rule to the effect that a vendee assumes the risk of casualty loss as an incident of equitable ownership, our holding stands for virtually the opposite proposition. Despite being the equitable owner, the vendee in that case was prohibited from rescinding only because he was already rightfully in possession at the time of the loss. While *Wiley* could be read to have merely resolved the situation under an installment contract for the sale of land that gave the vendee a right of immediate possession, the rule we adopted foreshadowed the resolution of this case as well. In the absence of a right of possession, a vendee of real property that suffers a material casualty loss during the executory period of the contract, through no fault of his own, must be permitted to rescind and recover any payments he had already made. *Cf.* Uniform Vendor and Purchaser Risk Act § 1.

Furthermore, where a vendee is entitled to rescind as a result of casualty loss, the vendee should generally also be entitled to partial specific performance of the contract with an abatement in the purchase price reflecting the loss. Where the damage is ascertainable, permitting partial specific performance with a price abatement allows courts as nearly as possible to fulfill the expectations of the parties expressed in the contract, while leaving each in a position that is equitable relative to the other. . . . Partial specific performance with a price abatement has long been recognized in this jurisdiction as an alternative to rescission in the analogous situation in which a vendor of real property is unable to convey marketable title to all of the land described in the contract. . . .

Here, Brush was clearly not in possession of the property as the equitable owner. Even if the doctrine of equitable conversion applies to the option contract between Brush and Sure Fine and could be said to have converted Brush's interest to an equitable ownership of the property at the time Brush exercised its option to purchase . . . neither party considered the contract for sale to entitle Brush to possession. Brush was, in fact, not in possession of the property, and the record indicates that Sure Fine considered itself to hold the right of use and occupancy and gave notice that it would consider Brush a holdover tenant if it continued to occupy the premises other than by continuing to lease the property. The casualty loss was ascertainable and in fact stipulated by the parties, and neither party challenged the district court's enforcement of the contract except with regard to its allocation of the casualty loss. Both the court of appeals and the district court therefore erred in finding that the doctrine of equitable conversion required Brush to bear the loss caused by hail damage . . .

Where Brush was not an equitable owner in possession at the time of the casualty loss, it was entitled to rescind its contract with Sure Fine. At least under the circumstances of this case, where Brush chose to go forward with the contract under a stipulation as to loss from the hail damage, it was also entitled to specific performance with an abatement of the purchase price equal to the casualty loss. The judgment of the court of appeals is therefore reversed and the case is remanded for further proceedings consistent with this opinion. . . .

NOTES AND QUESTIONS

1.   The Uniform Vendor and Purchaser Risk Act, 14 U.L.A. § 1, strongly advocated by contracts theorist Samuel Williston, provides that in cases where the parties have not explicitly provided for risk of loss, the loss shall be assigned as follows:

> (a) If, when neither the legal title nor the possession of the subject matter of the contract has been transferred, all or a material part thereof is destroyed without fault of the purchaser or is taken by eminent domain, the vendor cannot enforce the contract, and the purchaser is entitled to recover any portion of the price that he has paid;

> (b) If, when either the legal title or the possession of the subject matter of the contract has been transferred, all or any part thereof is destroyed without fault of the vendor or is taken by eminent domain, the purchaser is not thereby relieved from a duty to pay the price, nor is he entitled to recover any portion thereof that he has paid.

Thirteen states have adopted the Uniform Vendor and Purchaser Risk Act. The traditional rule of Paine v. Meller, discussed in *Brush* as placing risk of loss on the buyer from the instant the contract becomes binding, is probably the majority rule in the United States. See M. Friedman, Contracts and Conveyances of Real Property § 4.11 (5th ed. 1998).

2.   The traditional allocation of risk of loss is subject to several exceptions. If the loss was caused by the seller's negligence, then the seller will not be able to obtain specific performance from the buyer. Marks v. Tichenor, 85 Ky. 536, 4 S.W. 225 (1887). Likewise, if any defect that would otherwise have prevented the seller from obtaining specific performance is apparent on the settlement date, then the risk of loss will ordinarily stay with the seller. For example, if the seller could not have delivered good title anyway, then the buyer will have no duty to perform and will not suffer the loss, even if the loss is unrelated to the failure of title.

Most of the states that follow the traditional rule that the risk of loss remains on the buyer give the buyer the benefit of any casualty insurance held by the seller—that is, the buyer will still have to assume the loss, but the insurance payment to the seller will operate as a credit in favor of the buyer. In Hanson v. Hamnes, 460 N.W.2d 647 (Minn.Ct.App.1990), however, the Minnesota Supreme Court distinguished such decisions, and held that where (1) the contract required the buyer to carry his own fire insurance; and in fact (2) both parties carried fire insurance, the seller could keep the proceeds from his own policy even though the buyer's policy was inadequate to cover the entire loss.

In Skelly Oil Co. v. Ashmore, 365 S.W.2d 582 (Mo. 1963), the court adopted the Massachusetts rule. Under this rule, the risk of loss remains on vendor and if the vendor "has not protected himself by insurance, he can have no reimbursement of this loss; but the contract is no longer binding upon either party." Id. at 589. In Skelly, the buyer sought specific performance of the contract and a reduction in the purchase price as a result of the partial destruction of the property where the vendor had been reimbursed for the loss by the vendor's casualty insurance company. The vendor argued that it alone was entitled to the insurance proceeds. In rejecting the vendor's claim, the court stated: "[T]he issue in this case is not whether the vendee can be compelled to take the property without the building but whether the vendee is entitled to enforce the contract of sale, with the insurance proceeds substituted for the destroyed building. We see no inequity to defendants in such enforcement since they will receive the full amount ($20,000.00) for which they contracted to sell the property.... The short of the matter is that defendants will get all they bargained for; but without the building or its value plaintiff will not." Id.

In a case like *Skelly Oil* where the $10,000 insurance proceeds will be a windfall to either party, why doesn't the court merely split the difference? Common law courts have traditionally been extraordinarily reluctant to do so, at least explicitly. Considered *ex post*, that may seem unwise; but considered *ex ante*, all or nothing rules give parties such as Ashmore and Skelly Oil an incentive to settle, particularly if they are averse to taking risks. An out-of-court settlement likely would have resulted in a division of some sort. If the court was likely to divide the insurance proceeds the parties' incentives to settle out of court would be reduced, because the outcome would be less of a gamble.

3. Courts generally permit the vendor and purchaser to assign risk of loss in the contract. Today most preprinted contracts for the sale of homes assign the risk of loss to the seller until possession is delivered to the buyer. Otherwise they specify that the improvements in the land must be delivered to the buyer in their present condition, which is virtually the same thing as assigning the risk of loss to the seller. See the contract printed in the first section of this chapter.

NOTE: THE RISK OF LOSS RULE

An efficient risk of loss rule for transfers of interests in real property would try to minimize the social cost of these losses. First, and perhaps most importantly, it would try to minimize the total number of losses. This suggests that in cases involving negligence by either vendor or purchaser, the loss should fall upon the negligent party. This would encourage people to be less negligent, and less negligence should result in fewer losses.

The number of losses would also be reduced if the losses in each case were assigned to the person capable of taking precautions against them at the lowest cost. Suppose that the expected loss from a certain casualty is $100. The buyer can prevent the loss for $150 and the seller can prevent it for $50. In that case an efficient risk of loss rule would assign the risk of loss to the seller. The buyer would not take the precaution, for the cost of the precaution for him would exceed its expected value. The seller, by contrast, would take the precaution, for it costs less than the expected loss. This analysis suggests that there is a great deal of wisdom in Professor Samuel Williston's proposed rule, embodied in the Uniform Vendor and Purchaser Risk Act, that risk of loss should change when *possession* changes. In most cases a possessor is in a better position to take precautions against casualty losses than a non-possessor.

The efficient rule in cases involving certain non-casualty losses is more difficult to identify. For example, who should bear the loss if part of the property is taken by eminent domain during the executory period, or if a zoning or building code change makes the property far less valuable to the purchaser? The traditional equitable conversion doctrine places these losses on the buyer. See Hauben v. Harmon, 605 F.2d 920 (5th Cir.1979), which applied the traditional rule to a loss caused by eminent domain proceedings. However, the court noted the existence of two exceptions. First, if the action for eminent domain was already filed before the contract was executed, then the pending condemnation would be a defect in the title that would prevent specific enforcement by the seller. Second, if a seller had specific information about a future eminent domain action and failed to disclose it to the buyer, the seller might be guilty of fraud.

There is one argument for following the traditional rule when the loss is caused by government intervention. First of all, the party in possession is not generally in any position to minimize such losses, as he would be, for example, with respect to losses by fire. Secondly, assuming that any adverse government action is foreseeable, that risk is already reflected in a discounted purchase price,[2] which is determined when the contract is negotiated, not when the deed is delivered. As a result, the market has already assigned the risk of this particular kind of loss to the purchaser.

§ 14.5 CONTRACTUAL PROMISES (EXPRESS AND IMPLIED) AND THE DOCTRINE OF MERGER

MALLIN v. GOOD

Appellate Court of Illinois (1981).
93 Ill.App.3d 843, 49 Ill.Dec. 168, 417 N.E.2d 858.

NASH, JUSTICE:

Plaintiffs, Paul and Gila Mallin, brought this action in the Circuit Court of Lake County against defendant Arline Good seeking to enforce certain covenants in a contract for the sale of real estate. They appeal from an order which granted summary judgment to defendant on the grounds that all of the terms of the contract merged into the deed....

On February 5, 1977, the parties entered into a contract for the purchase by plaintiffs of defendant's single family dwelling in River Woods, Illinois. It provided that the purchase price was $165,000 and closing was to occur on July 1, 1977, or sooner by mutual agreement. The following type-written language was inserted into the printed form contract:

"All heating, plumbing, electrical and air conditioning to be in working order at the time of closing...."

---

2. This assumes, of course, that the loss will not be compensated. If the property is taken by eminent domain, the owner will be entitled to compensation. However, many governmental regulations can injure property values without creating any right to compensation. See Chapters 10 & 11.

The word "reasonable" was handwritten above "working" and the words "or adjustment at closing" were also appended by hand. Also inserted in the contract was another typewritten provision which read:

"Roof to be inspected when weather permits (no later than May 1) any damage to roof to be repaired by sellerz...."

The original contract language "to buyer's satisfaction at that time" was deleted and replaced with "in a good and workmanlike manner".

Examination of the discovery deposition of Paul Mallin, offered in support of defendant's motion for summary judgment, reveals plaintiffs had inspected the house three or four times prior to executing the contract and observed water marks on the ceiling. Mr. Mallin had the roof inspected on April 30, 1977, and was informed that there were "a lot of problems with this roof". On advice of his attorney, Mr. Mallin then obtained three written estimates of the cost of the needed repairs, but had no work done prior to closing. He stated that at the closing on June 23, 1977, defendant's attorney told plaintiff "they had a roofer that was willing to fix it for $200", but defendant's attorney would not guarantee the work.

According to the affidavit of plaintiff's attorney offered in response to defendant's motion, a list of other repairs which defendant was purportedly required to make under the contract was given orally to defendant's attorney at the closing which he then wrote down. Plaintiffs had complained that a faucet was not working, the dryer would not start, water was leaking into a closet, there was an odor permeating throughout the house, and there were problems with the septic tank. No "adjustment" was made for these items at the closing, however. Although plaintiffs considered defendant to be in breach of the contract, their attorney informed defendant's attorney that they would pay the agreed upon purchase price and accept the title, but would enforce their rights under the covenants of repair in the contract.... While an escrow account was set up to withhold funds pending clearance of title, no agreement was made to set aside funds for any repairs to the house.

* * *

We consider first plaintiffs' contention that their action is not barred by the doctrine of merger by deed. While plaintiffs agree that the provisions of the contract governing the conveyance of title were merged into the deed, they argue that the covenant to repair the roof and the purported warranty of condition of the designated house equipment survived since they are collateral undertakings which were not fulfilled by delivery of the deed.

The doctrine of merger by deed evolved solely to protect the security of land titles.... In general, if the terms of a contract for the sale of real estate are fulfilled by delivery of the deed there is a merger of the two instruments and, unless a reservation is made in the deed it supersedes all contract provisions. . . . Where there are provisions in a contract which are not fulfilled by delivery of the deed, the contract is not merged, but remains open for performance of such terms.

Whether and to what extent the contract merges into the deed is also a matter of the intention of the parties as evidenced by the language of their agreement and the surrounding circumstances. . . .

Here the roof was to be inspected no later than May 1, and defendant agreed she would repair any damage. Delivery of the deed would not constitute performance of this portion of the contract as it was incidental to the main purpose of the contract, that is, the conveyance of real estate. Accordingly, we conclude the doctrine of merger does not apply to the covenant to repair the roof. Neither are we persuaded by defendant's contention that the roof was to be repaired no later than May 1 and that this provision was not intended to survive the closing. The reference in the contract to May 1 clearly was only a time limit on inspection of the roof and the contract did not purport to obligate the seller to repair the roof by then. Defendant's contention would have more merit were it not for the fact that the words "to buyer's satisfaction *at that time*" (emphasis supplied) were deleted from the contract and the words "in a good and workmanlike manner" were substituted in their stead.

Plaintiffs construe the provision in the contract relating to the plumbing, heating and other home systems as a warranty of quality similar to that involved in *Rouse v. Brooks* (1978), 66 Ill.App.3d 107, 22 Ill.Dec. 858, 383 N.E.2d 666. In that case, an express warranty that all of the equipment in the house was in "good, proper, satisfactory and functional working order . . ." was held not to merge into the subsequent deed. The court characterized such language as warranties of quality and reasoned that:

> "the better rule [is] that quality warranties are independent of and collateral to the conveyance of title and, therefore, are not satisfied by the acceptance of the deed. Most of the provisions in a land sales contract deal with the mechanics and requirements of conveyancing which the deed conclusively settles. Warranties as to quality, in comparison, touch upon aspects other than the conveyance itself and are incidental to the main purpose of the deed, which is to transfer good title."

* * * Referring to *Petersen v. Hubschman Construction Co.* (1979), 76 Ill.2d 31, 27 Ill.Dec. 746, 389 N.E.2d 1154, defendant also contends that the doctrine of merger should be relaxed only in the case of latent defects and that plaintiffs discovered, or should have discovered, any defects when they inspected the home before the closing. Defendant's reliance on *Petersen* is misplaced; in that case the court did limit the application of an implied warranty of habitability to latent defects, but it did not hold that

the scope of the implied warranty was coextensive with the concept of collateral agreements which do not merge in the deed.

We conclude that the trial court erroneously applied the doctrine of merger and summary judgment should not have been granted on this basis.

* * *

Reversed and remanded.

NOTES AND QUESTIONS

1. The *Mallin* case states the merger rule quite clearly: contractual obligations that would normally be considered to become part of the deed are merged into the deed. See, e.g., Summit Lake Assocs. v. Johnson, 158 A.D.2d 764, 551 N.Y.S.2d 357 (1990). However, a deed would not ordinarily contain language that "the roof is in good shape," or "grantor warrants that she has fixed the roof." Such contractual promises are considered to be "collateral" to the deed, and an action for breach of one of them survives the buyer's acceptance of the deed. The doctrine is discussed more fully in 6A R. Powell, Powell on Real Property ¶ 893.

2. What is the purpose of the doctrine of merger by deed? It is relatively easy to justify the doctrine of contract merger that the *oral* negotiations of the parties become merged into the written instrument: the policy of both the Statute of Frauds and the parol evidence rule is to encourage people to use writings and to avoid the uncertainty and increased litigation that would occur if people were permitted to use oral testimony to avoid the consequences of their written agreements. However, the doctrine of merger by deed holds that one *written* instrument (the Statute of Frauds also requires written land sale contracts) is merged into another written instrument. Clearly, these same policies do not apply. The Uniform Land Transactions Act would repeal the doctrine, although few states have followed it. ULTA § 1–309.

3. Suppose that a seller promises in the contract to give the buyer an easement over adjoining land that the seller owns but which is not part of the conveyance. The subsequent deed fails to include the easement. If the contractual obligation was fulfilled at all, it would have been fulfilled in the deed. Does the doctrine of merger prevent the buyer, who has accepted the deed without the easement, from bringing an action on the contract to have the easement granted? See Eubanks v. Pine Plaza Joint Venture, 562 So.2d 220 (Ala.1990). Suppose the seller promises to convey the land free of an existing easement. However, after the buyer accepts the deed she discovers that the easement still exists. Does she have an action under the contract? Suppose the contract subjects land to a restrictive covenant but the subsequent deed does not. Is the land free of the covenant? See Hammerquist v. Warburton, 458 N.W.2d 773 (S.D.1990), saying no, because the restrictive covenant (against using single family homes as duplexes) was not an "integral part of the conveyance of title" and did not affect the "quantity of land." Do you agree?

REDAROWICZ v. OHLENDORF

Supreme Court of Illinois (1982).
92 Ill.2d 171, 65 Ill.Dec. 411, 441 N.E.2d 324.

CLARK, JUSTICE:

Plaintiff, Donald J. Redarowicz, filed a four-count complaint against Ohlendorf Builders, Inc., on December 14, 1978, in the circuit court of McLean County. The complaint asserts that the defendant was responsible for faulty construction of the plaintiff's residence. The original complaint sought relief on contract, tort, fraud, and implied warranty of habitability theories.

* * *

The complaint alleges that the defendant builder completed the house in early 1976. The plaintiff purchased the premises from the original owners in April of 1977. At the time the plaintiff purchased the house none of the defects complained of were apparent. Soon thereafter the plaintiff discovered that the chimney and adjoining brick wall were beginning to pull away from the rest of the house. Upon further inspection the plaintiff found that the wall and chimney were set in loose soil and that the supporting lintel was set only 24 inches deep. The plaintiff complains that the basement wall was cracked and there was water leakage in the basement as well as leakage in the roof area around the chimney.

. . . Counts I and V of the plaintiff's complaint are based in negligence and seek recovery for the costs of repair or replacement of the defectively constructed chimney, wall and patio. The defendant concedes that privity is not a necessary element of a tort action brought in negligence.

The measure of liability in a tort action is based rather on the scope of the duty owed to the plaintiff. *Rozny v. Marnul* (1969), 43 Ill.2d 54, 250 N.E.2d 656.

While it is foreseeable that a house will be sold more than once, and that substandard construction that results in structural defects could harm a subsequent purchaser, we need not discuss in detail the scope of the duty owed to this plaintiff. For it is now clear in view of our decision in *Moorman Manufacturing Co. v. National Tank Co.* (1982), 91 Ill.2d 69, 61 Ill.Dec. 746, 435 N.E.2d 443, that a plaintiff cannot recover solely economic losses in tort.

* * *

To recover in negligence there must be a showing of harm above and beyond disappointed expectations. A buyer's desire to enjoy the benefit of his bargain is not an interest that tort law traditionally protects. (See Prosser, Torts sec. 92, at 613 (4th ed. 1971).) In *Crowder v. Vandendeale* (Mo.1978), 564 S.W.2d 879, the front porch and steps of the plaintiff's home began to settle and proceeded to separate from the foundation of the house. While the Supreme Court of Missouri recognized an implied warranty of habitability in the new house, the court concluded that recovery for deterioration alone, caused by latent structural defects, was not actionable in negligence. We concur in our sister court's statement:

> "A duty to use ordinary care and skill is not imposed in the abstract. It results from a conclusion that an interest entitled to protection will be damaged if such care is not exercised. Traditionally, interests which have been deemed entitled to protection in negligence have been related to *safety* or freedom from physical harm. Thus, where personal injury is threatened, a duty in negligence has been readily found. Property interests also have generally been found to merit protection from physical harm. However, where mere deterioration or loss of bargain is claimed, the concern is with a failure to meet some standard of *quality*. This standard of quality must be defined by reference to that which the parties have agreed upon." (564 S.W.2d 879, 882.)

* * *

Count III of the plaintiff's amended complaint alleges that the home was not fit for its residential purpose when constructed. The plaintiff asserts that the defendant builder breached the implied warranty of habitability and asks that the warranty be extended to the plaintiff as a subsequent purchaser.

Buyers of homes have traditionally assumed the burden of inequitable transactions, as the doctrine of *caveat emptor* dominated sales of real property well into the 20th century. Purchasers of dwellings that proved to be defective looked for a breach of contract based upon the failure of the builder to do the job in a workmanlike manner. The notion that the builder was an artisan who was amenable to constant supervision by the owner of the homesite came under severe attack as mass production of homes came to be a common practice in the post-World War II building boom. Roberts, *The Case of the Unwary Home Buyer: The Housing Merchant Did It*, 52 Cornell L.Q. 835, 837 (1967).

The implied warranty of habitability was first recognized in the English case of *Miller v. Cannon Hill Estates, Ltd.* (1931), 2 K.B. 113. The court said that in the purchase of an unfinished house the builder was aware that his buyer intended to live in the house and therefore impliedly warranted that it would be suitable for that purpose. (2 K.B. 113.) In 1957 an Ohio court in *Vanderschrier v. Aaron* (1957), 103 Ohio App. 340, 140 N.E.2d 819, applied the *Miller* rule for the first time in the United States. In 1964 the Colorado Supreme Court extended the implied warranty to a completed house. *Carpenter v. Donohoe* (1964), 154 Colo. 78, 388 P.2d 399.

. . . This court addressed the issue of an implied warranty of habitability in the sale of new homes by the builder-vendor in *Petersen v. Hubschman Construction Co.* (1979), 76 Ill.2d 31, 27 Ill.Dec. 746, 389 N.E.2d 1154. The court reasoned that the skill and integrity of the builder-vendor is relied upon by the purchaser who is not capable of making a meaningful inspection of the house. The court recognized that the purchaser does not stand on equal footing with the builder-vendor and that the doctrine of *caveat emptor* was based "on reasons founded in antiquity." . . .

In defining the scope of the warranty the court found that the house must be reasonably suited for its intended use and not simply inhabitable.

By 1980 at least 35 State courts had afforded some measure of protection for purchasers of new homes by implying some form of a warranty of habitability. Sheed, *The Implied Warranty of Habitability: New Implications, New Applications,* 8 Real Estate L.J. 291, 308, 316 (1980) . . .

The warranty of habitability is a creature of public policy. (*Petersen v. Hubschman Construction Co.* (1979), 76 Ill.2d 31, 41, 43, 27 Ill.Dec. 746, 389 N.E.2d 1154.) It is a judicial innovation that has evolved to protect purchasers of new houses upon discovery of latent defects in their homes. While the warranty of habitability has roots in the execution of the contract for sale (76 Ill.2d 31, 43, 27 Ill.Dec. 746, 389 N.E.2d 1154), we emphasize that it exists independently (76 Ill.2d 31, 41, 27 Ill.Dec. 746, 389 N.E.2d 1154). Privity of contract is not required. Like the initial purchaser, the subsequent purchaser has little opportunity to inspect the construction methods used in building the home. Like the initial purchaser, the subsequent purchaser is usually not knowledgeable in construction practices and must, to a substantial degree, rely upon the expertise of the person who built the home. If construction of a new house is defective, its repair costs should be borne by the responsible builder-vendor who created the latent defect. The compelling public policies underlying the implied warranty of habitability should not be frustrated because of the short intervening ownership of the first purchaser; in these circumstances the implied warranty of habitability survives a change of hands in the ownership. . . .

In extending the implied warranty the Supreme Court of South Carolina aptly observed:

"Common experience teaches that latent defects in a house will not manifest themselves for a considerable period of time, likely as alleged in this case, after the original purchaser has sold the property to a subsequent unsuspecting buyer. Furthermore, the character of society has changed such that the ordinary buyer is not in a position to discover hidden defects in a structure. . . . The fact that the subsequent purchaser did not know the home builder, as did the original purchaser, does not negate the reality of the 'holding out' of the builder's expertise and reliance which occurs in the market place." *Terlinde v. Neely* (1980), 275 S.C. 395, 398, 271 S.E.2d 768, 769.

Extending the implied warranty to subsequent buyers is also consistent with the Uniform Land Transactions Act, which was adopted by the National Conference of Commissioners on Uniform State Laws on August 7, 1975 (13 Unif.Laws Ann. 615 (1980)). Section 2–312 of the Act provides that a subsequent purchase carries with it an assignment of the seller's warranty of quality rights to the buyer. It states in pertinent part:

"Section 2–312. (*Third Party Beneficiaries and Assignment of Warranty*)

(a) A seller's warranty of title extends to the buyer's successors in title.

(b) Notwithstanding any agreement that only the immediate buyer has the benefit of warranties of quality with respect to the real estate, or that warranties received from a prior seller do not pass to the buyer, a conveyance of real estate transfers to the buyer all warranties of quality made by prior sellers. However, any rights the seller has against a prior seller for loss incurred before the conveyance may be reserved by the seller expressly or by implication from the circumstances." 13 Unif.Laws Ann. 615 (1980).

We agree with the Supreme Court of Wyoming that the purpose of the implied warranty is to protect innocent purchasers and "any reasoning which would arbitrarily interpose a first buyer as an obstruction to someone equally as deserving of recovery is incomprehensible." *Moxley v. Laramie Builders, Inc.* (Wyo.1979), 600 P.2d 733, 736.

Our holding today in extending the implied warranty of habitability from builder-vendors to subsequent purchasers is limited to latent defects which manifest themselves within a reasonable time after the purchase of the house. The subsequent purchaser should not be denied the protection of the warranty of habitability because he happened to purchase the home about one year after the original buyer. We are an increasingly mobile people; a builder-vendor should know that a house he builds might be resold within a relatively short period of time and should not expect that the warranty will be limited by the number of days that the original owner chooses to hold onto the property. The purpose of the warranty is to protect purchasers' expectations by holding builder-vendors accountable; we do not believe it is logical to arbitrarily limit that protection to the first purchaser of a new house. Count III of the plaintiff's complaint, based upon an implied warranty of habitability, should not have been dismissed.

NOTES AND QUESTIONS

1. Although many states have implied a warranty of fitness of new construction in favor of the first purchaser, there has been less agreement with respect to second and subsequent purchasers. The traditional obstacle to such actions has been privity of contract. Some courts have avoided this obstacle by permitting indirect purchasers to sue builders for negligence. Most, however, have permitted the action to proceed under a warranty theory by abandoning the requirement of privity of contract. See Lempke v. Dagenais, 130 N.H. 782, 547 A.2d 290 (1988) (following *Redarowicz*); Speight v. Walters Dev. Co. Ltd., 744 N.W.2d 108, 114 (Iowa 2008) (removing privity

requirement as consistent with products liability law and holding that the "subsequent purchaser is in no better position to discover ... defects than the original purchaser"). But see Boris v. Hill, 237 Va. 160, 375 S.E.2d 716 (1989) (clinging to caveat emptor, at least where a reasonable inspection would uncover the defects). Accord Sewell v. Gregory, 179 W.Va. 585, 371 S.E.2d 82 (1988). See also Hansen v. Residential Dev., Ltd., 128 Wash.App. 1066 (2005) (declining to extend the implied warranty of habitability to subsequent purchasers).

2. One important difference between a tort theory and a contract theory is that under the former the traditional basis of liability is negligence, while under the latter there may be strict liability, depending on the content of the implied warranty. Should home builders be held to a negligence standard or a strict liability standard for economic injuries caused by latent defects? What is the practical difference between the two standards in this context? Should there be one standard for the mass producer of prefabricated homes and another standard for the small builder who produces two or three homes per year?

3. The court in *Redarowicz* was troubled by the fact that contract recoveries are confined to those in privity of contract with the defendant, while tort theories go to the opposite extreme and give a cause of action to almost every injured person. However, isn't there a third alternative that the court did not consider—namely, privity of estate? Could not the court have found that the builder's sale contract contained an implied warranty of fitness, and that this warranty was a covenant that ran with the land? Do you see any obstacles to such a view? See Chapter 8.

4. In G–W–L, Inc. v. Robichaux, 643 S.W.2d 392 (Tex.1982), the court gave effect to a builder's disclaimer of all warranties, express or implied, in its sale contract. However, in Melody Home Mfg. Co. v. Barnes, 741 S.W.2d 349 (Tex.1987), the court changed its mind and declared such disclaimer's unenforceable. See also Caceci v. Di Canio Construction Corp., 72 N.Y.2d 52, 530 N.Y.S.2d 771, 526 N.E.2d 266 (1988) (refusing to recognize contractual limitation of liability).

It has been argued that judicial regulation of the contents of contracts makes it easier for buyers to understand what they are receiving because contracts by different providers become more-or-less alike. This permits the buyers to negotiate more effectively on price. See Goldberg, Institutional Change and the Quasi–Invisible Hand, 17 J.L. & Econ. 461 (1974).

§ 14.6 A BRIEF LOOK AT REAL ESTATE FINANCING

Today the great majority of real estate purchasers are either unwilling or unable to pay for their purchases out of their own savings. They must borrow a substantial part of the money, either from the seller, who might agree to "take back" part of the purchase price in the form of a loan (often called a purchase money mortgage), or else from a third-party lending institution.[1] Sometimes the buyer will obtain financing from both of these sources by giving a mortgage to a bank or savings & loan association and agreeing to a "second lien" from the seller. The seller's lien in this case is described as "second" because it ranks in priority below that of the bank, or primary mortgagee. If there is a default and foreclosure, the bank's claim against the borrower will be fully satisfied first, and the second lien holder thereafter. The risk of loss is generally higher for lenders who are lower on the priority scale. As a result, interests rates are usually higher for second loans than they are for primary loans, and even higher for third loans.

Most loans to facilitate purchases of real estate are "secured" by the purchased real estate itself. To say that a loan is secured means that the borrower has given the lender certain rights that the lender can assert directly against the property should the borrower default on his payments. This is important to the lender for two reasons. First, the lender can acquire the borrower's secured property more easily in case of default than it could if the property were not secured. Second, once the secured loan is attached to the real property and recorded in the registry of deeds, any subsequent purchaser of the property takes subject to the loan at the same time that she acquires the property. (See the discussion of the recording acts in Chapter 16.) Even if the borrower is forced into bankruptcy, the lender generally will be able to keep its security interest in the real property. However, some recent decisions have imposed close scrutiny on mortgagees who foreclose when bankruptcy of the mortgagor is imminent. See Durrett v. Washington National Insurance Co., 621 F.2d 201 (5th Cir.1980), holding that a foreclosure that yielded too low a price could be construed as an attempt to defraud creditors by reducing the fund available to them from the bankruptcy proceeding.

The three instruments most widely used to facilitate the financing of real estate purchases are the mortgage, the deed of trust, and the installment sale contract.

The traditional common law mortgage is in form a deed that purports to convey the secured property from the mortgagor (the borrower) to the mortgagee (the lender). The grant generally provides that it is for the "use and benefit" of the mortgagee—largely a relic of a time when the mortgagee took possession of the property during the period that it was covered by the mortgage. Within the mortgage instrument the mortgagor will likely make certain covenants to the mortgagee—to keep the premises in good repair, to insure them against loss, and perhaps to pay the mortgagee's attorney's fees in case of foreclosure. Then the language imposes a condition on the grant, generally by referring to a certain promissory note that describes a loan from the mortgagee to the mortgagor, and providing that if the loan is fully paid in accordance with its terms the "mortgage grant and everything herein contained shall cease and be void." The

---

1. In some states a mortgage taken by a third party lender is also called a "purchase money" mortgage.

promissory note itself, which contains the mortgagor's promise to pay a particular debt according to specified terms, is usually a separate instrument.

At common law the mortgage grant transferred legal title from the mortgagor to the mortgagee during the period the property was mortgaged. By the nineteenth century the mortgage was primarily a device for securing a loan, however. The mortgagor almost always remained in possession of the property and retained certain important rights, such as the right to make improvements and to lease the property to someone else. Nevertheless, the prevailing view in most states was that the mortgage transferred title from the borrower to the lender until the condition established in the mortgage (generally full payment of the note) was satisfied. In an era heavily inclined toward formalism, this rule had unforeseen consequences that served no useful policy ends. For example, many courts held that if one joint tenant mortgaged her interest in the property, the effect was to sever the interest and create a tenancy in common which lasted even after the mortgage had been satisfied. Today most states have abandoned this "title" theory of mortgages in favor of the more modern "lien" theory that treats the mortgage above all as a security device rather than a transfer of an "ownership" or title interest. See, e.g., Oryx Energy Co. v. Union National Bank of Texas, 895 S.W.2d 409 (Tex.App.1995) (under lien theory, when mortgage is in default mortgagee nevertheless not entitled to rents until it actually takes possession).

The deed of trust differs from the traditional mortgage in that it is a three party transaction. Once again, the borrower (called the "trustor") gives away a deed to the property, but this time the deed goes to a "trustee," who is instructed to hold the deed until it has been notified by the lender (called the "beneficiary") that one of two different conditions has occurred. One condition is the full satisfaction of the debt by the borrower. In that case, the trustee is instructed to give to the borrower a deed free and clear of that particular encumbrance. The other condition occurs if the borrower defaults on the loan payments and foreclosure is due. In that case, the trustee is instructed to proceed with a foreclosure sale, as prescribed by state law.

Historically, if foreclosure was necessary the mortgage operated much like a conditional fee: title and all other indicia of ownership passed to the mortgagee when he established the right to foreclosure. Today this process is called "strict" foreclosure, and most states greatly restrict the opportunities for its use. See, e.g., 91st St. Joint Venture v. Goldstein, 114 Md.App. 561, 691 A.2d 272 (1997) (strict foreclosure proceeding inapplicable to judgment lien). Most foreclosures today are by sale. In such a foreclosure the property is sold to the highest bidder at a public auction. If the property brings a price greater than the amount of indebtedness plus the mortgagee's expenses, and if there are no other liens on the property, the mortgagor will be able to retain the excess.

Foreclosures by sale have traditionally been administered by a court, which generally holds a hearing to determine whether a foreclosure is appropriate. The court also supervises the sale. However, most states authorize nonjudicial foreclosures, in which the sale is made by a public official such as the sheriff or clerk of court, or sometimes by a private party named in the deed of trust. The courts become actively involved in such foreclosures only if a dispute arises. Today nonjudicial foreclosures are conceded to be much faster and less expensive than judicial foreclosures. Since the mortgagor is entitled to retain what is left over when both the debt and the expenses of foreclosure have been paid, the nonjudicial foreclosure theoretically leaves the defaulting mortgagor better off than if he had to pay for a judicial foreclosure.[2] Nevertheless, the nonjudicial foreclosure has been treated with some skepticism and hostility by consumer groups. To be sure, the nonjudicial foreclosure procedure can create substantial opportunities for abuse.

Clearly, in the case of the judicial foreclosure, which is administered by the court, the borrower is entitled to notice of any proceedings against him or her, and also to notice of the sale. When the foreclosure is nonjudicial, there might be some doubt about whether the "state action" requirements of the Fourteenth Amendment apply, and so perhaps such notice is unnecessary. But most decisions are to the contrary. See, e.g., Turner v. Blackburn, 389 F.Supp. 1250 (W.D.N.C.1975), holding that the mortgagor was entitled to notice of a foreclosure sale even in the case of a nonjudicial foreclosure; and further, a boilerplate waiver of such rights in the mortgage instrument was unenforceable. Likewise, in Mennonite Board of Missions v. Adams, 462 U.S. 791 (1983) a divided Supreme Court held that a mortgage lender also is entitled to notice by personal service or mail when the mortgaged property is sold by the state because the mortgagor failed to pay property taxes. The court held that the mortgagee, just as much as the mortgagor, had a constitutionally recognized property interest that could not be taken away without notice, and that notice by publication was insufficient, where the mortgagee and its address were known.

States generally treat mortgages and deeds of trust as identical for most purposes. The installment sale contract, however, is quite different. The installment contract, sometimes called a land contract, is a contract between the buyer and seller under which the buyer promises to pay the purchase price in installments as described in the contract, and the seller promises to convey the property by deed *after* the buyer has performed. For the entire period during which the buyer is indebted to the seller— often ten or more years—legal title to the property remains with the seller, while the buyer has only an equitable interest. Traditionally, installment sale contracts created the opportunity for outrageous abuses. For example, because the seller retained legal title to the property he might mortgage it and even convey it away. If the buyer neglected to

---

2. Even if there is nothing left over, the lower cost of nonjudicial foreclosure may leave the defaulting property owner with less personal indebtedness after the sale.

record the contract (and many do) he might lose the entire interest. Likewise many states that have abolished strict foreclosure of mortgages in favor of foreclosure by sale continue to permit the equivalent of strict foreclosure on the contract of sale: in case of default, the seller no longer has an obligation to perform the contract, and he already has legal title to the property. See, e.g., Harris v. Griffin, 109 Or.App. 253, 818 P.2d 1289 (1991) (permitting strict foreclosure of installment contract). A simple foreclosure action might be sufficient to give him possession; in the process the buyer loses her entire investment, which may be several years of monthly payments. See Jensen v. Schreck, 275 N.W.2d 374 (Iowa 1979). The trend in both case law and legislation, however, is to give buyers under installment contracts protection analogous to that offered to buyers under mortgages or deeds of trust. See, e.g., Parise v. Citizens National Bank, 438 So.2d 1020 (Fla.App.1983).

Today every state gives the defaulting mortgagor the right to perform fully her obligations under the mortgage and receive a clear title. The right, traditionally known as an "equity of redemption," generally lasts only until the foreclosure sale has occurred. The development of the doctrine, which originated in the British courts of equity, is discussed in G. Nelson & D. Whitman, supra, § 3.1.

Several states have gone further than the courts of equity, however, and have given mortgagors a right to redeem even *after* foreclosure has occurred. These statutes generally permit the mortgagor to redeem the property within a certain specified time period after the foreclosure sale, by tendering the foreclosure sale price, plus interest and costs, to the foreclosure sale purchaser. The time period during which statutory redemption may be made is typically six months or a year after the foreclosure sale. The political impetus for statutory redemption has come from various debtor groups. Institutions that lend money to finance real estate purchases generally have opposed the legislation.

The statutory right of post-foreclosure redemption may injure *both* borrowers and lenders, however, perhaps the former more than the latter. As a practical matter, very few mortgagors whose property is foreclosed are able to redeem the property within a year after foreclosure. Redemption generally involves not merely the payment of the mortgage debt, but also of all costs incurred during the foreclosure, and these can be substantial. By contrast, every prospective purchaser at a foreclosure sale knows that there is some possibility that the property can be repurchased by the previous owner—generally at the sale price plus a statutory rate of interest that is frequently lower than the market rate. Furthermore, many states give the mortgagor the right to possession during the redemption period. This makes foreclosed property far less attractive to buyers, so it often brings a lower price at the foreclosure sale than it would in the absence of the statutory right to redeem. Since the defaulting mortgagor is entitled to have any surplus from the foreclosure sale (i.e., any proceeds left after all liens and expenses have been paid), it is likely that the most common effect of the statutory right of post-foreclosure redemption is to reduce or eliminate any equity that might otherwise go to the mortgagor. In this case, the "right" of statutory redemption probably injures defaulting mortgagors more often than it benefits them.

In the complex world of home financing, today few loans granted by a bank remain with that bank until fully paid. Rather, the bank that loans the money to the borrower sells off that loan on what is known as the secondary mortgage market. Before the 1970s, a bank issuing a mortgage "would keep the loan on its balance sheet until the loan was repaid."[3] Because the bank retained the loan—barring default or other calamity prematurely extinguishing the mortgage or property—the bank would have to wait several years before it recovered its initial capital outlay. Depending on its liquidity, a bank's subsequent business ventures, including issuing additional loans, could be contingent on the bank replenishing its coffers.[4] Until the loan was repaid the bank's cash inflow from the loan would be the monthly principal and interest payments accruing under the terms of the mortgage. With its borrowed funds frozen until the loan was repaid, the bank would miss out on other opportunities to capitalize on higher yield spreads as market interest rates climbed.[5] Over the long haul, this strategy, while favorable to the borrower, proved unsustainable both to banks and to the housing market. Combined with the fact that a mortgage is an "inflexible and illiquid debt instrument," and is often "subject to default and prepayment risk,"[6] economic conditions of this time promulgated the need for a more liquid and responsive market. Congress answered with the creation of the secondary mortgage market.

At the core of the secondary mortgage market is Fannie Mae, Freddie Mac, and Ginnie Mae, all created by Congress. Each of them, along with private players in the secondary mortgage market, plays a critical role in promoting the availability and efficiency of credit on the open market.[7] Fannie Mae does so by buying conforming loans issued by banks and other institutions and then packaging or pooling these loans into mortgage-backed securities that it then sells or passes through to investors on the open market.[8] Freddie Mac operates in an almost identical manner by purchasing guaranteed "first lien, fixed-rate conventional residential

---

3. Richard J. Rosen, *The Role of Securitization in Mortgage Lending, in* 244 Chi. Fed. Letter 1 (Nov. 2007), *available at* http://www.chicagofed.org/webpages/publications/chicago_fed_letter/ 2007/november_244.cfm.

4. As an example, if Bank X loans M $100,000 for a mortgage on M's home, and if the terms of the mortgage require a 6% monthly interest payment for 30 years, then Bank X will recapture its original $100,000 investment in the 167th month—almost 14 years after the initial loan. At this time, Bank X's return on investment is 0%.

5. *See* Robin Paul Malloy, The Secondary Mortgage Market: A Catalyst for Change in Real *Estate Transactions*, 39 Sw. L.J. 991, 996 (1986).

6. Kenneth G. Lore & Cameron L. Cowan, Mortgage–Backed Securities § 1:2 (2010).

7. Id. at § 2:2.

8. Id. at § 2:3. "The sale of a . . . mortgage-backed security is said to be a pass-through security when the monthly payments of principal and interest on each of the underlying mortgages merely passes from the party serving the loans [such as Fannie Mae], less a fee for serving, to the investor." Malloy, supra, at 1004.

mortgage loans" and reselling these loans to investors.[9] However, "[u]nlike Fannie Mae and Freddie Mac, Ginnie Mae does not originate or purchase mortgage loans; rather, it *guarantees* securities backed by mortgages issued by certain federal agencies, such as the [FHA]."[10] By insuring and guaranteeing mortgage-derived securities, Ginnie Mae infuses the market with liquid capital.[11] Additionally, it utilizes the "full faith and credit of the United State government [to guarantee] the timely payment of principal and interest on [investor's] securities."[12]

The theoretical workings of the secondary mortgage market might appear straightforward; however, as may be expected, its intricacies and processes can often become confusing. To illustrate the secondary mortgage market's dynamics, it is helpful to illustrate the process from a practical perspective, start to finish.

Suppose a woman wants to buy a home but lacks sufficient funds to pay the seller the entire purchase price. In this case the woman will need to finance the purchase of a home. To do so, typically she contacts her bank or other mortgage lender to inquire about financing (i.e. how much of a loan does she qualify for, what interest rate will she have to pay, how long will she have over which to repay the loan).[13] If the loan terms are satisfactory to her, then at the closing she'll pay the seller a portion of the purchase price with her own funds and a portion (typically a substantially larger portion) with the borrowed funds. She will also sign a note, secured by a mortgage on the newly purchased home. By the note the woman promises to repay the loan according to its terms; by the mortgage she grants the bank the right to foreclose on her home should she default on the payment of the note. The bank, however, will not want to wait until the woman—now a mortgagor—repays the loan; it will want to continue issuing additional loans to other customers. To do so the bank needs to replace the funds the woman borrowed with new funds. It can do so by selling the woman's mortgage on the secondary market.[14] If the mortgage is conforming, meaning it is consistent with the requirements of Freddie Mac or Fannie Mae, the bank can sell the loan off to Fannie Mae or Freddie Mac; if the loan is not conforming it can sell the loan off to a private financial institution.[15]

---

9. Lore & Cowan, supra, at § 2:7.

10. Id. at § 2:4.

11. Id.

12. Adam J. Levitin & Tara Twomey, *Mortgage Servicing*, 28 Yale J. on Reg. 1, 19 (2011).

13. *See* Lore & Cowan, supra, at § 3:2. Unless, of course, she is paying in cash and does not need a mortgage.

14. *See* Raymond H. Brescia, *Capital in Chaos: The Subprime Mortgage Crisis and the Social Capital Response*, 56 Clev. St. L. Rev. 271, 290 (2008).

15. *See* Lore & Cowan, supra, at §§ 2:3, 2:7, 2:14.

"Private sector issuers include commercial banks, mortgage companies, investment banking firms, private mortgage conduits, and thrifts." Lore & Cowan, supra, at § 2:14. These entities deal with non-conforming loans. Id. Additionally, the private sector represents a significant part of the secondary mortgage market. Malloy, supra, at 1004.

After acquiring the original loan, the intermediary financial institution which purchased the loan from the bank can either resell the mortgage to others or service the mortgage. Under either scenario, the intermediary will package or pool this loan with similar mortgages and then offer it on the secondary market as a so-called mortgage backed security.[16] If the intermediary sells the pool, it receives capital from investors that it can then use to purchase additional mortgages from the primary market. If the intermediary decides to service the pool, it collects the principal and interest paid by the mortgagor and passes this capital through to investors who purchased the rights to the pool (the intermediary will charge a servicing fee for the collection of mortgage payments).[17]

The law of real estate financing is a complex and highly technical field. This discussion has done no more than give you a little glimpse. If you want to know more, see G. Nelson, & D. Whitman, Real Estate Finance Law (5th ed. 2007).

---

16. Malloy, supra, at 1004. "At the simplest level, a MBS is an obligation secured by, or representing an interest in, mortgages or other debt instruments ... that have been pooled to secure payment of [an] obligation." Lore & Cowan, supra, at § 3:9 (citation omitted).

17. Malloy, supra, at 1004.

CHAPTER 15

VOLUNTARY TRANSFERS OF INTERESTS IN REAL PROPERTY: CONVEYANCING BY DEED

■ ■ ■

§ 15.1 INTRODUCTION: THE RISE OF THE DEED

2 SIR WM. BLACKSTONE, COMMENTARIES ON THE LAWS OF ENGLAND 315–16 (1765–69)

Livery of seisin is either in *deed* or in *law*. Livery in *deed* is thus performed. The feoffor, lessor, or his attorney, together with the feoffee, lessee, or his attorney (for this may as effectually be done by deputy or attorney, as by the principals themselves in person), come to the land, or to the house; and there, in the presence of witnesses, declare the contents of the feoffment or lease, on which livery is to be made. And then the feoffor, if it be of land, doth deliver to the feoffee, all other persons being out of the ground, a clod or turf, or a twig or bough there growing, with words to this effect: "I deliver these to you in the name of seisin of all the lands and tenements contained in this deed." But if it be of a house, the feoffor must take the ring or latch of the door, the house being quite empty, and deliver it to the feoffee in the same form; and then the feoffee must enter alone, and shut-to the door, and then open it, and let in the others. If the conveyance or feoffment be of divers lands, lying scattered in one and the same county, then in the feoffor's possession, livery of seisin of any parcel, in the name of the rest, sufficeth for all; but if they be in several counties, there must be as many liveries as there are counties. For if the title in these lands comes to be disputed, there must be as many trials as there are counties, and the jury of one county are no judges of the notoriety of a fact in another. Besides, anciently this seisin was obliged to be delivered *coram paribus de vicineto,* before the peers or freeholders of the neighborhood, who attested such delivery in the body or on the back of the deed; according to the rule of the feudal law (y) *pares debent interesse investituros feudi, et non alii:* for which this reason is expressly given:

because the peers or vassals of the lord, being bound by their oath of fealty, will take care that no fraud be committed to his prejudice, which strangers might be apt to connive at. And though afterwards the ocular attestation of the *pares* was held unnecessary, and livery might be made before any credible witnesses, yet the trial, in case it was disputed (like that of all other attestations), was still reserved to the *pares* or jury of the county. * * *

———

The term "feoffment" properly applied only to the creation of a fee simple estate. Estates in fee tail were said to be created by "gift," and life estates were created by "lease." At common law a freehold estate could be conveyed only by livery of seisin. The origins of this method of conveyance described by Blackstone remain mysterious. Suffice it to say that the method was a product of times when few people could read or write. As a result the best testimony to the fact of a conveyance was often the memory of witnesses who had seen a solemn ceremony. See S. Thorne, Livery of Seisin, 52 L.Q.Rev. 345 (1936).

The Statute of Uses, passed in 1536, made the modern conveyance by written instrument possible as an alternative to feoffment by livery of seisin. Not until after the Statute of Frauds was passed in 1677, however, did courts begin to hold that a writing was *required* to effect a conveyance of a freehold. Finally in 1845 Parliament expressly provided that a feoffment should be void unless it were evidenced by a written deed. 8 & 9 Vict. ch. 3, § 1 (1845). See Frank Goodwin, Before the Statute of Frauds, Must an Agreement to Stand Seised Have Been in Writing? 7 Harv. L. Rev. 464 (1894).

The ceremony of feoffment with livery of seisin was used in Colonial America in the seventeenth century, but was quickly abandoned in favor of written conveyances. For a good, brief history of the law and forms of conveyancing up to Blackstone's time, see T. Plucknett, A Concise History of the Common Law 610–623 (1956).

§ 15.2 THE FORM OF THE MODERN DEED

METZGER v. MILLER
Dist. Court, N.D. California (1923).
291 F. 780.

VAN FLEET, DISTRICT JUDGE. This is an action in equity against the defendant as Alien Property Custodian to have it declared that certain property, seized by the latter under the supposed protection of the Trading with the Enemy Act of October 6, 1917 (Comp.St.1918, Comp.St. Ann.Supp.1919, §§ 3115 ½a–3115 ½j), is the property of the plaintiff, and for an accounting of the income and profits thereof.

In 1914, one Mathilde Graf died in Sacramento, in this state, leaving an estate, the bulk of which she devised to her sister, Karoline Schwab, living in Germany and a subject of the then German Emperor. Her will was in due course admitted to probate, the estate administered, and the devised property regularly distributed to the devisee by decree entered in 1916. The money or cash distributed to Mrs. Schwab, something over $63,000, was duly transmitted to her in Germany; but the property in suit, consisting of two parcels of real estate in the city of Sacramento and certain notes secured by trust deeds on real estate, were left standing in her name on the records under the decree of distribution and so remained at the time of the passage of the Trading with the Enemy Act, and was thereafter seized and taken into the custody of the defendant Miller as the property of an alien enemy and is still so held by him.

Plaintiff, a son of Karoline Schwab, who has lived in this country for many years and is now a naturalized citizen, brings the action based upon the claim that prior to the seizure of the property in suit, the same had been for a good and valuable consideration conveyed and assigned to him by his mother, and for that reason was not subject to seizure by the defendant under the act in question as the property of the latter. The plaintiff's alleged deraignment of title is a series of letters written to him by his mother and a daughter at her direction, and the sole question upon which the cause has been submitted is whether the declarations in these letters are of a character to constitute a conveyance of the property to plaintiff.

The evidence in behalf of plaintiff is wholly uncontroverted and discloses in a general way these facts: The plaintiff, at the death of his mother's sister, was living in Idaho and employed in earning his livelihood—receiving a salary of $100 per month. Upon learning of her sister's death and of the devise made to her, his mother wrote the plaintiff asking and urging upon him that he leave Idaho and go to Sacramento to look after her interests in the sister's estate, stating that she would pay his expenses and, moreover, intended that the property left to her, except the ready money, should be his; that all she wanted was the money. Plaintiff, it seems, was an illegitimate son, and his mother took occasion to refer to the fact and that he had never gotten anything from her husband's estate, which she felt was an injustice, and that now she proposed to provide for him and make up for the wrong done him.

After the receipt of several letters and repeated assurances of his mother's intention to give him a portion of the estate left to her by her sister, plaintiff abandoned his employment and home in Idaho, and went to live in Sacramento, and has resided there since; aiding in looking after the property of his aunt's estate during the administration, and being permitted by his mother to occupy with his family the dwelling of his late aunt (one of the parcels of real estate involved) without rent, and to enjoy the rent of the other and smaller parcel. During this time and prior to the time of the seizure of the property by the defendant, plaintiff had many letters from his mother with reference to her purpose to give him the property. At first the statements took the form more of a future purpose than a present intent to give him the property, but later her expressions assumed a more definite form indicating a present intention that the property, excepting the cash, was to be then regarded by him as his own. The following extracts from the letters will illustrate their character:

In one of her early letters addressed to him in Idaho she wrote, "Now you go to Sacramento and I will give you what my sister left me," stating that her intention to do this was because he was an illegitimate son and she had not been able to do as much for him as she had for the other children. In a letter of March 13, 1915, the sister wrote him:

"You worry so much about the inheritance. All you want to know I have already often written you. The house on Ninth street mother has written you already long since; you shall have it."

In January, 1916, the mother wrote:

"The house which Marcus built shall belong to you. You need no lawyer for that. I have already written Reverend Oehler to this effect. You are now living there and are to stay there and nobody can ever send you out."

In another letter written in 1916 she wrote plaintiff:

"I am giving you that property and you now send me the remainder of the cash and then you have a nice share. I could not have done so much for you as I have for the other children. They got their share from the father so this is now yours."

On February 11, 1916, the mother wrote plaintiff:

"I am grateful to you for looking after the matter and hope it will soon be settled finally"—referring to the administration of the estate.

On March 16, 1916, she wrote plaintiff:

"Now dear August, you repeatedly write of the house in which you are living. I have on several occasions written to you and the Reverend (Reverend Oehler, one of the executors) that the house and the little place with the garden are your property. It is surely a nice large share of aunt's property. And also Uncle John's watch. I have already written you. I do not know whether you received the letter."

On June 8, 1916, she wrote:

"How often have you not written about our dear aunt's house on Ninth street? I have written to you many times and also to the Reverend Oehler that the small place also, as well as all the mortgages are your property. On account of the wicked war some letters are lost."

Do these expressions sufficiently disclose a present intention and purpose on the part of the mother to pass the title to constitute in law a grant or transfer of the property in question? I was left somewhat in doubt on the question at the hearing, but a more mature consideration of the material features of the correspondence in the light of the authorities has tended to remove that doubt. The mother's expressions of her purpose are to be considered in the light of the circumstances surrounding the parties at the time. As to the later of the letters, written after plaintiff's removal to Sacramento and the abandonment of his employment in Idaho, they show that the mother knew that plaintiff had no means of support for himself and family other than this property. She had authorized his occupation with his family of one piece of the real estate and the enjoyment of the rent coming from the other, while the notes and mortgages were evidently not yet surrendered by the executors because of the administration of the estate being still incomplete. This course on the part of the mother would seem to have an important bearing upon the question whether her intention was to presently vest title of the property in her son or was only intended as expressing a future purpose to do so.

* * *

A contract concerning real property need not be in any particular form. A letter is a sufficient memorandum of an agreement relating to such property to avoid the statute of frauds. Moss v. Atkinson, 44 Cal. 3. The California Civil Code defines a "transfer" as an act of the parties by which title to property is conveyed from one person to another. Civil Code, § 1039. When in writing it is called a grant (Civil Code, § 1053), and a grant is to be interpreted in like manner as contracts in general (Id. § 1066), and may be explained by the circumstances under which they are made and the matters to which they relate (Id. § 1647).

Words of inheritance or succession are not necessary to transfer a fee (C.C. § 1072), and a fee-simple title is presumed to pass by a grant unless it appears a lesser estate was intended (C.C. § 1105). These provisions of the California Code were intended to modify the common-law rule in this state with respect to transfers of real property. Painter v. Pasadena, 91 Cal. 74, 27 Pac. 539.

In Devlin on Deeds (2d Ed.) 211, it is said:

"The word 'grant' has become a generic term of transfer. But no particular formula of words is necessary to effect a valid conveyance of land. If the words used show an intent to convey they are sufficient for the purpose."

And in a note to the text it is said:

"Precise technical words, however, are unnecessary, any language equivalent to a present contract of bargain and sale being sufficient. If the courts can discover an intention to pass title they will give effect to the deed, although the expression may be inaccurate."

See, also, Ball v. Wallace, 32 Ga. 170.

Tested by the foregoing rules of interpretation, I am constrained to the view that when considered in the light of the circumstances as they existed when the letters were written, the language employed must be regarded as sufficient to show a present purpose to convey and to sustain the contention that it operated as a conveyance by the mother of the real property involved; and there is no question made that it was sufficient to pass title to the chattels described in the bill.

* * *

Plaintiff should have a decree directing a surrender by defendant of the property described in his bill, and for an accounting of the income derived therefrom since its seizure.

It is so ordered.

NOTES AND QUESTIONS

1.   The Trading With the Enemy Act of 1917, 50 U.S.C.A.App. § 1, et seq., prohibits certain commercial transactions with governments or citizens of governments that have been declared to be enemies of the United States. Section 16 of the Act provides that property involved in such transactions may be seized by the United States and forfeited. The Alien Property Custodian is a federal official, whose chief duty is to hold property within the United States that might belong to an enemy or to the citizen of an enemy state, pending cessation of hostilities and a decision as to how the property should be disposed of. If the property at issue in *Metzger* still belonged to Karoline Schwab, a German Citizen during World War I when the United States and Germany went to war, then the property was within the jurisdiction of the Alien Property Custodian. On the other hand, if she had effectively "deeded" the property to the plaintiff, an American citizen at that time, then it was not subject to the Custodian's control.

2.   Did the letters in the *Metzger* case constitute a "deed," or should they more properly be considered a contract that entitled the plaintiff to specific performance? If the latter, what was the consideration? As a general matter, an effective deed minimally must be a writing that includes: (1) an identifiable grantor; (2) an identifiable grantee; (3) operative words of conveyance; (4) identification of the property being conveyed; and (5) the grantor's signature. See R. Natelson, Modern Law of Deeds to Real Property § 3.2 (1992).

3.   Cal.Civ.Code § 1092 (West 2002) provides:

A grant of an estate in real property may be made in substance as follows:

> "I, A B grant to C D all that real property situated in (insert name of county) county, State of California, bounded (or described) as follows: (here insert description, or if the land sought to be conveyed has a descriptive name, it may be described by the name, as for instance, 'The Norris Ranch.')
>
> "Witness my hand this (insert day) day of (insert month), 20___."

"A B"

4.   The Burns' owed Mrs. McGurl $2000, but were unable to pay it back. They wrote the following document, which they acknowledged in front of a notary public:

$_____ Nov. 1st, 1935 _____ after Date _____ Promise to Pay to the Order of Mrs. Owen McGurl Senior _____

We resign any further claim to property at 9009 Ft. H. Pway, Brooklyn. Value Received in payment of the $2,000 we borrowed & will never be able to pay.

In concluding that this writing constituted a deed, the court noted:

Concededly, the instrument in question is not in recordable form (it is to remedy this latter deficiency that this action is brought), but * * * it seems to me that the words "Mrs. Owen McGurl Senior" indicate the specific grantee; the words "property at 9009 Ft. H. Pway, Brooklyn" sufficiently identify the property; the words "in payment of the $2,000 we borrowed & will never be able to pay back in cash" set forth the consideration for the grant; the words "We resign any further claim to property etc." are sufficient to indicate a "surrender" of any claim to the property by the signers, Margaret McGrath Burns and Philip Burns, as grantors.

McGurl v. Burns, 192 Misc. 1045, 81 N.Y.S.2d 51, 52 (1948).

5. As the *Metzger* opinion and the previous notes suggest, the modern written deed can be quite an informal document. In the vast majority of cases, however, it is not. The chief reason for the formality is not that the law prescribes certain elaborate statements. Most states are quite flexible about the legal requirements of the deed *form*. The formality results in large part from the fact that most deeds are written on pre-printed forms in which the conveyancer simply fills in several blank spaces. Warranty deed forms like the following are widely used today:

WARRANTY DEED

THE STATE OF _____

COUNTY OF _____

KNOW ALL MEN BY THESE PRESENTS:

That _____, of the County of _____, the State of _____, for and in consideration of the sum of _____ dollars and other valuable consideration to the undersigned paid by the grantee herein named, the receipt of which is hereby acknowledged, and the further consideration of _____, has GRANTED, SOLD AND CONVEYED, and by these presents does GRANT, SELL AND CONVEY unto _____ of the County of _____ and State of _____, all the following described real property in _____ County, State of _____, to wit:

TO HAVE AND TO HOLD the above described premises, together with all and singular the rights and appurtenances thereto in anywise belonging unto the said grantee, her heirs and assigns forever. And the grantor HEREBY COVENANTS with the said grantee, and successors in interest, that said grantor holds said real estate by title in fee simple; that he has good and lawful authority to sell and convey the same; that said premises are FREE AND CLEAR OF ALL LIENS AND ENCUMBRANCES WHATSOEVER except as may be above stated; and said grantor binds himself, his heirs, executors and administrators to WARRANT AND

Cov. Quiet. enj.

FOREVER DEFEND all and singular the said premises unto the said grantee, her heirs and assigns, against every person whomsoever lawfully claiming or to claim the same or any part thereof, except as may be above stated.

EXECUTED this the ___ day of _____, 20___.

_____

Grantor

ACKNOWLEDGED

THE STATE OF _____

COUNTY OF _____

Before me, the undersigned authority, on this day personally appeared _____, Known to me to be the person whose name is subscribed to the foregoing instrument and acknowledged to me that he executed the same for the purposes and consideration therein expressed.

Given under my hand and seal of office on the ___ day of _____, 20___.

_____

Notary Public in and for _____
County, _____

* * *

6. Historically, the general warranty deed contained six explicit covenants of warranty respecting the quality of the vendor's title. The legal meaning of the covenants is explored more fully in chapter 16. The six covenants may not be explicit in every "warranty deed" form, however, because most states have prescribed "short forms" that imply the existence of some or all of the six warranties. For example, in Texas the word "grant" implies that the estate is free from encumbrances not described in the deed, and that the grantor has not previously conveyed the same or a conflicting interest. An Arkansas statute provides that the words "grant, bargain and sell" in a deed presumptively connote covenants of seisin, freedom from encumbrances created by the conveyor, quiet enjoyment and general warranty. In Illinois and Pennsylvania, the words "grant," "bargain," and "convey" or "sell," or any combination of them imply covenants of seisin, freedom from encumbrances created by the conveyor, and quiet enjoyment. These statutes and many others are discussed in 6A R. Powell, Powell on Real Property ¶ 885.

7. Traditionally all deeds contained four, quite distinct parts. While the distinctiveness of the parts has tended to blur in modern deed forms, in most the parts can still be picked out:

(a) The *Premises* names the grantor and grantee, recites the consideration, explains the transaction (if an explanation is necessary), gives the operative words of conveyance, and describes the land.

(b) The *Habendum,* or *Habendum and Tenendum,* clause traditionally began with the words "to have and to hold" and then described the kind of estate being granted, as well as any conditions that might be imposed and the explicit covenants of title.

(c) The *Execution* historically contained the signature of the grantor, the signatures of witnesses, and a seal. The signature of all grantors is still required. Most states no longer require witnesses or a seal.

(d) The *Acknowledgement* is the signature and seal of a notary public who witnessed the signature on the deed and attests to its authenticity. In most states an acknowledgement is not necessary to make a deed *valid,* but it is necessary before a deed can be properly recorded.

§ 15.3 DESCRIPTIONS

The Statute of Frauds requires a deed to describe the land to be conveyed with sufficient precision that the land can be properly identified and its boundaries demarcated. Over the years three methods of land description have developed: (1) metes and bounds, (2) government survey, and (3) plat. All three are still used today, although different types prevail in different places. Today most residential land in subdivisions and most urban property is described by plat. Much farm land is still described by government survey, metes and bounds, or a combination of the two.

§ 15.3.1 DESCRIPTION BY METES AND BOUNDS

Description by metes and bounds is the oldest method of property description used today. A description by metes and bounds generally begins at some identifiable "corner" of the conveyed property and then describes its boundaries, one line at a time, by referring either to "monuments," which are physical objects that can be seen on the land itself, or to "courses and distances," which give compass headings and lengths of boundary lines, commencing from a certain point.

A simple description by metes and bounds might look like this:

All that land lying in Section 8, Township 16 North, Range 4 West of the Gila and Salt River Base and Meridian, Yavapai County, Arizona, being that portion of the tract lying North of Cutler Road and West of Butler road, beginning at the intersection of same and extending 300′ in a northeasterly direction along Butler Road, thence North 80 degrees West for 350′, thence South 5 degrees East about 350′ to Cutler Road, thence in an easterly direction along Cutler Road to the intersection with Butler Road.

To plot this description on a map is relatively easy. First ignore the words Section, Township, Range, Base and Meridian. These words are references to a survey and help in finding the general area in which the property is located, but not in delineating its precise boundaries. These terms are explained later in the discussion of the government survey.

Second, you need a map showing the intersection of Cutler Road and Butler Road and several hundred feet north and west. Then begin at point A, which is the northwest corner of the intersection. Go along the west side of Butler Road north from A for a distance of 300′. Mark that point B. That completes the eastern boundary of the property.

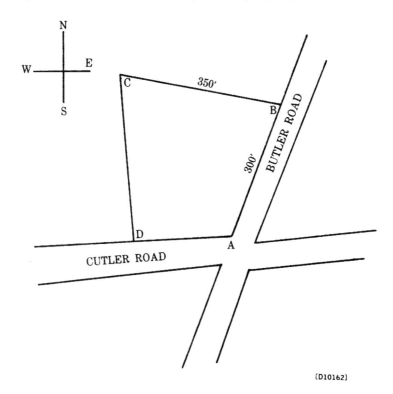

[D10162]

The next line, beginning at point B, is a little more difficult to determine. When measuring by courses and distances, it is common to describe courses in terms of their deviation from either north or south. For example, a line that runs "North 10 degrees West" runs in a generally northerly direction but deviates ten degrees to the west from true north. The entire compass is divided into 360 degrees, with each degree divided into 60 minutes, and each minute divided into 60 seconds. Our description refers only to degrees, so we will not worry about minutes or seconds. Starting from point B we must strike a line that runs "North 80 degrees West" for 350 feet. That line will look like this on the compass:

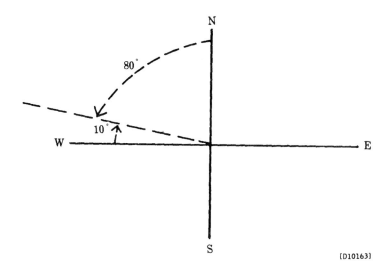

[D10163]

Now we can draw a line in the same direction on the map, beginning at point B, and extend the line 350′ to point C. From C we must strike a line that runs "South 5 degrees East" (or slightly east of due south) back to Cutler Road. Finally, the description tells us that we should strike a line back in an easterly direction to the intersection of Cutler Road and Butler Road, point A. Once we end where we started, which a complete metes and bounds description must always do, we have successfully described the property. With the proper equipment (a compass, transit, and a set of measuring chains or a tape) we could do the same thing on the land itself.

You will note that the deed description said two things about line C–D. First it describes the line as going back to Cutler Road South 5 degrees East. Secondly, however, it says that that line, properly struck, will be about 350′ long. What if we struck that line at the proper angle but then discovered that the distance along the line to Cutler Road was 450′, or only 250′

§ 15.3.2   DESCRIPTION BY GOVERNMENT SURVEY

Shortly after the American Revolution the United States government began to survey undeveloped land held in public domain in order to facilitate its settlement by private grantees. As new American lands were acquired, they were included in the survey. Although the thirteen original states were not surveyed, the survey eventually included almost all territory west of the Mississippi except for Texas, all states east of the Mississippi River and north of the Ohio River, and Alabama, Florida and Mississippi south of the Ohio River. The survey is described in 3 Amer.L.Prop. § 12.100 (J. Casner, ed. 1952); Fegtly, Historical Development of Land Surveys, 38 Ill.L.Rev. 270 (1944).

The survey is notable for its lack of flexibility. Its goal was to facilitate the quick sale and settlement of land. This meant the survey had to be relatively simple. It established a checkerboard pattern of rectangular parcels six miles square, regardless of the terrain. Needless to say, the squares are not perfect, but they are certainly quite regular and yield a surprising uniformity in the shape of landholdings, particularly in the midwest.

In each area to be surveyed the surveyors began by running a line that ran north and south, called the principal or prime meridian. Parallel to the principal meridian, running at six mile intervals, are range lines. Each six-mile wide strip demarcated by the lines is called a range. Each principal meridian is intersected by a perpendicular line called a base line, running east and west. Parallel to the base lines at six mile intervals are township lines. The result is a checkerboard of squares with six-mile sides. Each square is called a township. Incidentally, the surveyors' "township" bears no necessary relationship to the political subdivision called by the same name. Some governmental "townships" are coterminous with the surveyor's township; others are not.

Townships themselves are identified by their relationship to the principal meridian and the baseline. The first row of townships north of the baseline are referred to as "Township One North." The second row of townships north of the baseline are referred to as "Township Two North." The first row of townships south of the baseline are referred to as "Township One South," etc. Likewise, the first row of townships east of the principal meridian are referred to as "Range One East." The second row of townships east of the principal meridian are referred to as "Range Two East," etc. Each individual township can be identified by a particular township and range number. Thus the township three townships north of the baseline and two townships east the principal meridian would be identified as "Township Three North, Range Two East," or in surveyors parlance, "T3N, R2E," or "T3N/R2E."

A standard township is itself divided into 36 sections numbered like this:

6	5	4	3	2	1
7	8	9	10	11	12
18	17	16	15	14	13
19	20	21	22	23	24
30	29	28	27	26	25
31	32	33	34	35	36

[D10143]

Because the township is six miles on a side, each of the above squares, or "sections," is one mile on a side, or one square mile, which is also 640 acres. A section has been a basic unit of ranch and farm ownership in the United States ever since the completion of the survey.

Finally, each section is divided into halves and quarters, and each quarter is itself divided into quarters, like this:

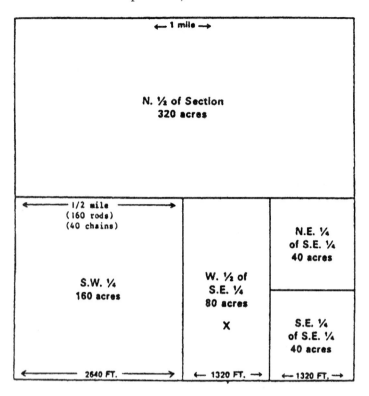

A simple property description based on the government survey might look like this:

> All that property located in the County of Contra Costa, State of California, being the Northeast one quarter of the Southeast one quarter of section 16, T3N, R2E, Mount Diablo Base and Meridian, being forty acres more or less.

Most descriptions based on government surveys are more complex than this one. Furthermore, many sales involve parcels that are too small or irregular to be described entirely in terms of the government survey. Such descriptions commonly contain a combination of references to the government survey as well as to metes and bounds, including both monuments and courses and distances.

§ 15.3.3 DESCRIPTIONS BY REFERENCE TO PLAT

Generally, the easiest kind of description to use is one that simply refers to a more elaborate "plat map" of a particular subdivision or area. Plat maps are usually developed by surveyors who work for private developers or governmental entities. The plat map itself contains detailed descriptions of all individual lots by metes and bounds, or perhaps by reference to the governmental survey. Each individual lot on the map is then assigned a number and the plat map is recorded. A conveyance of a particular lot within the plat need identify only the appropriate plat and the number of the block and the lot being conveyed. Such a description might look like this:

> Lot 9, Block C, University Hills Section 4, Phase 1 Addition to the City of Austin, Travis County, Texas, according to the plat of record in Vol. 32, Page 48, Plat Records of Travis County, Texas.

See the plat map in Mid–State Equipment Co., Inc. v. Bell, 217 Va. 133, 225 S.E.2d 877 (1976), printed in chapter 8.

§ 15.3.4 PROBLEMS INVOLVING DEED DESCRIPTIONS

DOMAN v. BROGAN

Superior Court of Pennsylvania (1991).
405 Pa.Super. 254, 592 A.2d 104.

POPOVICH, JUDGE:

. . .

George and Donna Doman (appellees), and Bertha Brogan (appellant), are owners of adjacent lots in a double-block dwelling—lots 34 and 36 Old Boston Road, respectively. Both parties claim title under Ada Doman, a/k/a Ada Maxwell, (appellant's mother, appellee George's grandmother) as common grantor, said grantor having first acquired title to the full residence (lots 34 & 36) in 1955. Appellant, in 1968, began renting from Ada Doman that portion of the dwelling known as 36 Old Boston Road. In 1972 she purchased lot 36 and has since resided there. Her deed recites:

> THE SAID PREMISES ARE SITUATE, BOUNDED AND DE-SCRIBED AS FOLLOWS: BEGINNING at a nail in pave corner, being of the intersection of what was formally an approximate right angle turn on the Old Boston Road leading from Plymouth to Kingston, said corner being located . . . (N. 62 degrees 34′ E.) . . . (242.82) feet from the intersection of the Southerly line of Old Boston Road and the Northerly line of State Highway Route 11, No. 4 Spur; THENCE along the Westerly line of Old Boston Road, . . . (S. 29 degrees 45′ E.) . . . (60.13) feet to a corner; THENCE along land of Robert E. Doman, et ux., . . . (S. 21 degrees 30′ W.) . . . (86.81) feet to the corner on the Northerly right-of-way line of State Highway Route 11; THENCE along said right-of-way by a curve to the left by a chord having a course of . . . (N. 76 degrees 18′ W.) for a distance of (40.32) feet to a corner; BEING also the point of intersection of a line running through the center wall of a double dwelling; THENCE along the line running through the center wall of the double dwelling . . . (N. 18 degrees 24′ E.) . . . (130) feet to a nail corner, the place of beginning. . . .

* * * Apparent from a literal interpretation of the parties' respective deeds is that the lots were to be divided according to "the center wall" as further described by metes and bounds ("M & B") figures. At trial, plaintiffs offered into evidence ... schematic diagrams[1] [confirming] that there exists no one "center" wall forming an unbroken vertical plane from the basement to the second floor. Moreover, the projected M & B property line used to demarcate the mutual boundary between the lots forms one vertical plane not consistent with any wall located in the basement, first or second floor of the dwelling.[2]

* * * Appellees assert title to, and the right to immediate possession of, a second floor bedroom, basement steps and landing occupied by appellant. More generally, and at variance with their specific claim for the bedroom, etc., appellees contend that their title extends laterally (on all floors) up to the M & B division line as heretofore described.

* * * [T]he trial court * * * "abandoned the [M & B] division line" because it found that the deeds supported an "intention to divide the double dwelling along the central walls." Indeed, Judge O'Malley observed that to divide the dwelling pursuant to the M & B line would create the

---

1. In an ejectment action to resolve a disputed boundary, parol evidence is admissible to establish the existence of monuments. See, e.g., Baker v. Roslyn Swim Club, 206 Pa.Super. 192, 213 A.2d 145, 148 (1965); Will v. Piper, 184 Pa.Super. 313, 134 A.2d 41, 44 (1957); see generally, 5 P.L.E., Boundaries, § 28 (1958).

2. Although the record alludes to the fact that there may have been one center wall consistent with the M & B line prior to appellant's and appellees' purchases, this point was not developed by the parties. Mrs. Brogan testified that she could recall George Doman's parents remodeling sometime "in the '50's, 59, in the '60's, early '60's." * * * Also, appellant in her brief implies the former existence of a center wall: "However a number of years previous to the Deed, a number of renovations had taken place with regard to the property, and the center wall no longer exists."

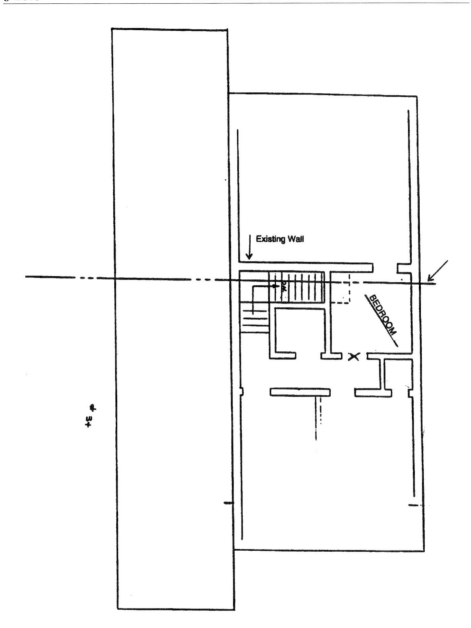

absurd result of "divid[ing] rooms on [a] particular side of the center wall." Hence, in locating the disputed boundary line the court opted against strict reliance on the M & B figures choosing, rather, to divide the dwelling by "extend[ing] the vertical plane established by the central walls on the first and second floors from the center of the earth to the heavens...."

* * * [L]egal title to real property, and the precise location of boundaries thereon, is not always clear from a plain reading of a written deed. See Stewart v. Chernicky, 439 Pa. 43, 266 A.2d 259 (1970); * * * Consequently, within an action in ejectment a court of law often must employ established principles of deed "construction" to assist in arriving at the parties' intentions by artificial means.[3] Where there exists an uncertainty due to the use of vague or ambiguous language, resort may be had to extrinsic or parol evidence to explain—but not vary—the written word.[4] See Flaherty v. DeHaven, 302 Pa.Super. 412, 448 A.2d 1108, 1111 (1982) ("where the deed is not clear and the intentions of the parties cannot be construed from the instrument itself, the parties' intentions are to be ascertained from the language of the entire instrument, from a consideration of the subject matter and from conditions existing when it was executed"). * * *

We have often repeated that the primary function of a court faced with a boundary dispute is to ascertain and effectuate the intentions of the parties' at the time of the original subdivision. See, e.g., Plott v. Cole, 377 Pa.Super. 585, 547 A.2d 1216 (1988); ... To achieve this result, our courts have employed certain rules of construction that are commonly thought to provide the best indication of that intent. Among such rules are the following: (1) the nature and quantity of the interest conveyed must be ascertained from the instrument itself and cannot be orally shown in the absence of fraud, accident or mistake and we seek to ascertain not what the parties may have intended by the language but what is the meaning of the words; (2) effect must be given to all the language of the instrument and-no part shall be rejected if it can be given a meaning; (3)[to ascertain the intention of the parties,] the language of a deed shall be interpreted in the light of the subject matter, the apparent object or purpose of the parties and the conditions existing when it was executed. Yuscavage v. Hamlin, 391 Pa. 13, 137 A.2d 242, 244 (1958).

---

3. Deed "construction" should not be confused with deed "reformation", whereby a Court of Equity might rewrite the written word based on clear, precise and indubitable evidence of mutual mistake or fraud. See Easton v. Wash. County Ins. Co., 391 Pa. 28, 137 A.2d 332, 337 (1957). In cases of deed "reformation", the claim is that the words used do not represent the "true" agreement of the parties. The two processes must be kept distinct since an action for reformation lies solely in equity. * * * Trexler v. Fisher, 130 Pa. 275, 18 A. 733 (1889) (per curiam) ("Where there is a plain mistake or fraud the courts of Pennsylvania, through the intervention of a jury, may reform the agreement to make it agree with the deed and make the deed agree with the real title of the parties.")

4. Thus, in an ejectment action parol evidence is competent to explain ambiguities, but not to vary or contradict a boundary description contained within a deed; such latter usage is limited to an action in equity to reform a deed where accident, mistake or fraud is shown.

More particularly, certain general principles of preference are followed when the calls of a deed are found to be inconsistent: Where the calls for the location of the boundaries to land are inconsistent, other things being equal, resort is to be had first to natural objects or landmarks, next to artificial monuments, then to adjacent boundaries (which are considered a sort of monument), and thereafter to courses and distances. Baker v. Roslyn Swim Club, 206 Pa.Super. 192, 213 A.2d 145, 148 (1965) (citing 12 Am.Jur.2d, Boundaries, s 65 at 603 (1964)). Hence, "[a]s a general rule, where there is a conflict between courses and distances or quantity of land and natural or artificial monuments, the monuments prevail." Roth v. Halberstadt, 258 Pa.Super. at 405, 392 A.2d at 857 (citing Appeals of Borough of Dallas, 169 Pa.Super. 129, 82 A.2d 676 (1951)). The rationale for this rule has been explained thusly: If titles were to depend upon the fluctuations of the compass, or errors of the chain or rod-pole, upon the measurement or angles or of distances, instead of the lines monuments, or marks upon the ground, it would open a door to a flood of litigation, every new artist furnishing fresh cause of a new suit. Lodge v. Barnett, 46 Pa. 477, 485 (1864). Thus, it is generally believed that erroneous descriptions are more probably found in calls for measurements and distances than in calls for fixed landmarks either natural or artificial. See Pittsburgh Outdoor Advertising Co. v. Surowski, 164 Pa.Super. 383, 64 A.2d 854, 856 (1949).

The preference for monuments is not, however, imperative nor mutually exclusive in the sense that to rely on a monument prevents any reference to other measurements, distances, etc., that are proximate, and thus supportive, but not coexistent with the monument. The parties' intentions are not so narrowly confined. * * * Lastly, where the terms of a deed will admit of two reasonable interpretations (patent ambiguity), or where the calls conflict when applied to the ground whereby admitting of different reasonable bases for division (latent ambiguity), their construction, as a rule, should be submitted to the jury as a question of fact. Where the trial court sits as trier of fact, an appellate court will not reverse on appeal unless the judge's findings are not supported by competent evidence.

Initially, a thorough review of the parties' respective deeds reveals an intent to divide the dwelling into easterly and westerly portions according to "the center wall" as further described by M & B figures. This call for an artificial monument, however, apparently conflicts with the call described by M & B figures which, as projected by plaintiffs' surveyor, form a single vertical plane consistent with no wall in the dwelling. Obviously, more than one M & B line would have been necessary to describe accurately the various central walls [on the basement, first and second floors of the building.] Hence, as applied to the ground, the calls in appellant's and appellees' deeds conflict and presented Judge O'Malley with a latent ambiguity. * * *

Where the calls in a deed conflict to present a latent ambiguity, before the issue of the true location of the boundary line is submitted to the jury, the court first must ask whether the conflicting boundary descriptions admit of more than one reasonable division. In making this determination the court should consider all evidence of the parties' intentions, extrinsic or otherwise, offered in support of the conflicting boundary descriptions, including a consideration of the instrument as a whole, its subject matter and the circumstances attending its execution. Instantly, neither party has offered any evidence—apart from the projected M & B figures—to suggest that the original grantor intended to divide the dwelling according to a nonexistent "center wall" and, thereby, intended to convey property extending both beyond, and short of, the existing dividing walls. No evidence, extrinsic or otherwise, was offered to explain the ambiguity or to suggest that the conflicting boundary descriptions would admit of more than one reasonable division. As such, we feel that the question of conflicting calls should be resolved by the court as a matter of law through application of established rules of construction. Instantly, as between the choice of dividing the dwelling according to a nonexistent "center" wall coextensive with the projected M & B figures, versus dividing the dwelling according to the then-existing "central" walls, with no evidence to support the former, the only proper inference is that the call for latter was the intended result and that the call for the former was a mistake. Accordingly, we defer to the well-established rule that monuments on the ground, if referred to in the deed, must prevail over measurements, see Medara v. DuBois, 187 Pa. 431, 41 A. 322 (1898), as well as to the "general principle that ordinarily the center of a party wall, extended the entire length of the lots between which it has been erected, is the true dividing line between those lots, though it varies from the line indicated in the description in the deed." Ross v. Golden, 146 Pa.Super. 417, 22 A.2d 310, 312 (1941), aff'd, 344 Pa. 487, 25 A.2d 700 (1942). Furthermore, the M & B line supports this interpretation. While it is coextensive with neither wall, nonetheless, it is proximate with both and roughly forms an east-west median between the central walls.

Accordingly, Judge O'Malley's construction of the parties' respective deeds does not divide the dwelling in accordance with a nonexistent "center" wall nor rely exclusively on the M & B figures, as alleged by appellant. We affirm the judgment below which locates the boundary line by "extend[ing] the vertical plane established by the central walls on the first and second floors from the center of the earth to the heavens...."

NOTES AND QUESTIONS

1. Most states have adopted a "hierarchy" of methods of property description. In cases of inconsistency, any higher method on the hierarchy takes precedence over any lower one. The following is the most commonly used hierarchy:

   a) Natural Monuments

   b) Artificial Monuments (usually including surveyor's marks)

   c) References to Adjacent Tracts or Boundaries

d) Courses/Directions

e) Distances

f) Area or Quantity

g) Place Names (such as "the Norris Ranch")

Suppose a deed describes a farm by courses and distances and also says that the conveyed land is sixty acres in size. In fact, however, the courses and distances describe an enclosure seventy acres in size. Based upon the above hierarchy, the grantee will receive the full seventy acres described by the courses and distances.

2. As the hierarchy notes, monuments generally take precedence over inconsistent courses and distances. But this preference produces a strain on the requirement of the Statute of Frauds that the terms of a deed be completely contained in a written instrument. Given an agreed starting point, metes and bounds descriptions identify land solely by reference to the language of the deed. By contrast, one must view the land in order to locate monuments. As the *Doman* case suggests, the rule that monuments trump inconsistent metes and bounds descriptions produces difficulties when the monuments cannot be located readily. Should oral testimony, photographs or other collateral evidence be permitted to prove where the monuments had been located at the time the description was drafted? For example, nineteenth century surveyors commonly marked rural land by "blazing," or placing hatchet marks, on trees. Suppose the trees are later removed. In Riley v. Griffin, 16 Ga. 141 (1854), the court permitted the son of a previous owner to testify as to where such trees had been located, and this testimony was then used to establish the boundary line as following the trees rather than an inconsistent course and distance description. The son was an old man when the testimony was given and the trees had been removed when he was a child. See also Theriault v. Murray, 588 A.2d 720 (Me.1991), where the deed had a metes and bounds description that was apparently inconsistent with a call to a surveyor's stakes, driven into the ground but apparently later removed. The court held that the trial court was obliged to make a fact finding concerning where the stakes had been, assuming that such evidence was available. Accord, Lloyd v. Benson, 910 A.2d 1048 (Maine 2006). See also, Sledge v. Peach County, 276 Ga.App. 780, 624 S.E.2d 288 (2005). Contrast Sun Valley Shamrock Resources, Inc. v. Travelers Leasing Corp., 118 Idaho 116, 794 P.2d 1389 (1990), which held that a deed call to the boundary of a road would not trump a conflicting metes and bounds description when the boundary of the road could not be precisely ascertained.

One possibility that the *Doman* court refers to in footnote 2 but did not consider further is that although the metes and bounds (M & B) line did not correspond to the *current* center wall, it did describe accurately the center wall as it existed before renovation done in the 1950s. In that case there was no inconsistency, and the deed did in fact divide the house as remodeled in the center of rooms rather than down the center wall. In other words, the current walls were not monuments at all; they were not even in existence when the deed was drafted. What is the court's obligation in that case? Perhaps we should modify the list of priorities given above to say that *currently existing* monuments trump courses, distances or other methods of description, but that testimony about monuments that have disappeared should be given little weight. Or would that create an incentive to obliterate monuments? Is the court's obligation to "fix" the deed so as to minimize hardship on the owners, or to determine what the grantor's intent had been?

3. Cullen v. Sprigg, 83 Cal. 56, 23 P. 222 (1890), involved a deed which conveyed "60 acres lying in Block Hill." However, Block Hill contained 107 acres, and the deed did not identify the particular 60 acres to be conveyed. What should the judge do: (1) hold the deed void for failure to describe the land with sufficient particularity? (2) Permit the grantor to select the 60 acres? (3) Permit the grantee to select the 60 acres; or (4) hold that the deed conveys a 60/107 undivided interest in the whole, with grantor and grantee as tenants in common? The answer might surprise you.

4. Many jurisdictions hold that if adjoining landowners are uncertain or in dispute about the precise location of a boundary they may establish it by agreement or acquiescence. Once they have agreed on the location of the boundary and taken certain acts pursuant to the agreement, such as the building of fences or other structures, the boundary line they have agreed to will prevail over any line subsequently proven to be the true line. The technical requirements for such a boundary by agreement vary from one state to another. For example, some require that the boundary by agreement must have been established for a long period of time before it will trump the true line. See Seddon v. Edmondson, 411 So.2d 995 (Fla.App. 1982). See generally Browder, The Practical Location of Boundaries, 56 Mich.L.Rev. 487 (1958).

A good discussion of these doctrines is contained in Halladay v. Cluff, 685 P.2d 500 (Utah 1984), where the court noted that the common law distinguished the doctrines of boundary by acquiescence and boundary by parol agreement. To establish a boundary by acquiescence required a long period of *tacit* acquiescence by neighbors in a particular boundary location; however, it did not require evidence of an express oral agreement between the parties that the boundary should be in a particular place. By contrast, the doctrine of boundary by parol agreement required evidence of an express agreement, but not the long period of acquiescence.

The court in *Halladay* noted that historically the requirement that the parties be uncertain or "in dispute" over the location of their common boundary applied to the doctrine of boundary by parol agreement, but not to the doctrine of boundary by acquiescence. However, this court followed the modern trend by requiring either uncertainty or dispute under both doctrines. Finally, the *Halladay* court appeared to apply an objective test to the uncertainty or "in dispute" requirement. That is, before the doctrines would apply, there must be

> some objectively measurable circumstance in the record title or in the reasonably available survey information ... that would have prevented a landowner, as a practical matter, from being reasonably certain about the true location of the boundary. Id. at 505.

A few years later the same court retreated from this position in Staker v. Ainsworth, 785 P.2d 417 (Utah 1990), which refused to require objective uncertainty evidenced from the record and found subjective uncertainty to be sufficient. Which rule is better?

§ 15.4   DELIVERY

§ 15.4.1   DELIVERY TO THE GRANTEE

LEMEHAUTE v. LEMEHAUTE

Missouri Court of Appeals (1979).
585 S.W.2d 276.

SHANGLER, PRESIDING JUDGE.

The court determined that the deed of realty by plaintiff Vincent LeMehaute jointly to himself, his present wife and defendant Renee LeMehaute [daughter by a previous marriage] was not a present conveyance of interest to daughter Renee and decreed that the instrument be reformed so as to nullify the recital of grant to her.

The plaintiff LeMehaute and the former wife [mother of the defendant Renee LeMehaute] acquired the real estate now in contention. The property served as the residence until her death and continued as the place of residence after she died and the husband remarried. Two children were born of the first marriage, Renee and Lorna. No child was born to the remarriage, but the successor wife brought a son, Bruce Perkins.

On September 18, 1975, after remarriage, the plaintiff LeMehaute consulted with attorney Colley to draft a deed of grant of the premises to himself, his wife and his children, as joint tenants in order to avoid probate procedure should an event befall him. The attorney counselled that, to avoid the undue difficulty from tenure by one under age or absent from the state, LeMehaute designate one child, local and of age, to trust to hold title for all the children. It thus came about that daughter Renee was designated as a joint grantee along with father LeMehaute and the new wife—and that daughter Lorna, then a minor, was not made a party to the grant. The plaintiff LeMehaute read the instrument prepared by counsel and signed it. The deed was recorded and some days later the plaintiff retrieved the instrument from the abstract company. He placed the deed under lock and key in a cabinet at home where it has remained.

In November of 1975, some two months after the deed was executed and recorded, the plaintiff LeMehaute disclosed to daughter Renee for the first time that she, himself and the new wife were joint grantees to the home premises. The plaintiff took the occasion to ask for her signature at the office of attorney Colley to a conveyance which added daughter Lorna and step-son Bruce Perkins as other grantees of the premises. After consultation with her own lawyer, daughter Renee refused the request as ill-advised because of the nonage of the two children. About a year later, father LeMehaute asked daughter Renee to subscribe a mortgage against the premises for a loan of $5,000 to pay bills. She refused to put the premises, only lately free from debt, under obligation again. That mortgage had been paid by the father LeMehaute without request for contribution from daughter Renee. Nor was she asked to contribute to the maintenance of the property, nor did she. On one occasion [presumably after she was designated a joint grantee by deed] she was asked to endorse the insurance check which issued for damage to the roof.

In January of 1977, some year and one-half after the execution of the deed of joint tenancy, the father LeMehaute and new wife sued to reform the deed of conveyance so as to nullify the recital of grant of any estate in the realty to daughter Renee on the ground that the deed was not delivered to her. The court rendered judgment of reformation for want of present intention by the grantor to convey any interest in the land to the daughter Renee.

The delivery of the deed is the act of consummation essential to give effect to the instrument as a conveyance of estate to realty. The delivery signifies that dominion and control over the deed passes from the grantor to the grantee with the intention to transfer the present ownership or interest in the land from the one to the other.... Delivery may be by word or act, without formula or ceremony or manual tradition of the instrument.... There may be delivery notwithstanding the deed remains with the grantor.... It is sufficient in law for delivery that the grantor by act or word manifest that he relinquishes dominion and control over the deed and that the instrument operate presently as a transfer of title, and acceptance by the grantee.

Thus, whether there has been valid delivery is controlled by no fixed rule but presents a mixed question of fact and law determined by the concrete case. This case stands altogether on the written instrument of grant, the signature of the grantor, formal acknowledgment of signature, registry of the instrument in the office of the recorder of deeds and the intention of the grantor LeMehaute at the moment of his act.

The deed with acknowledgment of signature was recorded by the grantor. The effect of the registry act is to displace the solemn common law ceremony of livery of seisin as notice to the world that there has been a transfer of title from the grantor to the grantee. The registry act accomplishes that announcement of delivery by means of a public record rather than by the twig, clod, or key symbolic of enfeoffment at common law. A recorded deed " 'is evidence of a most cogent character tending to show delivery, for it is tantamount to a public proclamation by the grantor at a public place, intended for the world to act upon, that the grantor had in apt and due form transferred his title [and thereby his land] to another.' "

The registry act operates to create a presumption of delivery, and although the recordation of a deed—even by the grantor—does not have the effect of delivery, that fact proves a prima facie case of delivery.

The plaintiff LeMehaute disputes that the recorded deed may bear to prove delivery because he neither registered the deed nor authorized the act. The evidence was that attorney Colley—called as his witness—did not recall who recorded the deed. The testimony of plaintiff LeMehaute shows, merely, that in response to inquiry by counsel for daughter Renee: "Did you record this deed?", LeMehaute answered: "No." He then testified that three or four days after he signed the deed he retrieved the instrument, fully recorded, from the abstract company. While the evidence shows that LeMehaute did not himself present the deed to the recorder, the scant testimony gives inference that he [or attorney Colley for him in the normal course of such a transaction] empowered the abstract company for that purpose, caused acknowledgment of his signature on the deed to that end, awaited the lapse of time necessary for that procedure, and thereafter picked up the instrument from the abstract company, fully recorded—with all expectation and without demur.

The efficacy of delivery to recited grantee Renee is enhanced by her relationship as a daughter of grantor LeMehaute for where a parent makes a voluntary settlement of lands upon a child, the presumption of delivery is more insistent than in a case of bargain and sale ... The plaintiffs contend, however, that whatever formal presumptions may favor the defendant Renee the evidence that grantor retained possession of the deed, never disclosed the transaction to Renee nor had delivery accepted by her, and that the grantor never intended a present conveyance of estate, all rebut the technical inference of delivery and establish the cause of action for reformation.

The retention of the deed by the grantor does not hinder the passage of title where delivery is intended.... In the circumstances of this case, however, grantor LeMehaute was also a grantee and the rule applies with logic that a deed delivered to one of the several grantees operates as a delivery to all of them, in the absence of a disclaimer. The absence of an overt acceptance by the grantee at the moment of execution does not mar the completion of delivery where, by the circumstances, the intention of the grantor to convey title was not known. Acceptance by the grantee is presumed, however, where the grant is beneficial.... Acceptance, as delivery, may be by word or act without formula or ceremony—according to the circumstances.

The refusal by Renee to reconvey, her execution of the insurance claim check for damage to the premises, and her refusal to subject the property to a mortgage, were tantamount to an assent to acceptance of delivery once the conveyance was disclosed to her. In these circumstances, the acceptance, although accomplished later related back to the time the deed was delivered by registration by the plaintiff LeMehaute with intention that title should pass to the grantee Renee.

The question remains of the intention of the parties, especially that of the grantor, essential to delivery. The contentions of the plaintiffs reduce to the proposition that, the full evidence considered, LeMehaute did not intend to pass a present estate to daughter Renee—that he was unaware of the legal implications of the deed of joint tenancy and that the deed was recorded without authority.

The evidence on this issue derives altogether from the plaintiff LeMehaute and his attorney witness.... Although there was no discussion of "the legal import of the deed as such," the lawyer explained "as part of the discussion that he would have to be able to trust this child, because *if he ever wanted to do anything with the property it was going to require her signature.*" [Emphasis added]. Only then did LeMehaute sign the deed prepared according to his instructions. LeMehaute was not informed, as such, that the effect of the deed was to pass a present interest to Renee, but the testimony of his lawyer-witness unmistakably conveys that import in the practical and colloquial terms best suited to his understanding. It was with that awareness that the deed was signed, acknowledged and recorded.[1]

The contention for reformation does not rest on any evidence that the instrument of conveyance did not conform to the directions of the grantor or was fraudulent or mistaken. The initial inclination of plaintiff LeMehaute for a deed of joint tenancy to himself, his new wife and *his* children was modified on the advice of counsel to join only the adult daughter as a grantee. The plaintiff was prompted to the suit for reformation not to redress any oversight as to *his* children but by the petulance of the new wife that *her* son Bruce was not on the deed. * * *

The burden to prove nondelivery of a deed rests on the party who asserts the affirmative of the issue—in this case, the plaintiffs LeMehaute.... The reformation of a deed is a remedy not easily gained. Equity will not divest title on less than clear and convincing proof of mistake or fraud—and will not overturn a deed, put of record by the grantor, for nondelivery on evidence any less cogent.... The plaintiff LeMehaute has not overcome the presumptions of delivery which favor the grantee from the registry of an acknowledged deed, the grant to a family member, and the retention of the instrument thereafter by the plaintiff LeMehaute as a joint grantee.

The discovery of intention of the grantor to make delivery of a deed refers to "the very time those acts [which consummated delivery] sprang into existence."

An afterthought of regret does not nullify the passage of title by a delivery and made by the grantor. The admissible evidence shows an intention by LeMehaute to make the joint grant and delivery to daughter Renee, thoughtfully considered and effected with full understanding of the consequences of that conduct. This intention to part with dominion over

---

1. The trial court excluded from evidence, as a "legal conclusion," this vital testimony from the cross-examination of the plaintiff LeMehaute:

Q. And you understood at the time you signed the deed, since Mr. Colley told you, Renee would have to sign papers in the future. That you, by signing the deed, were passing title—conveying title of the property to yourself and Ruth and Renee?

A. Yes.

The state of mind, as well as the words and acts, of the grantor bear relevantly on the issue of intent to deliver a deed. Since delivery is a mixed question of fact and law what the grantor understood—and so, intended—as the effect of his signature on the deed is also directly relevant on that issue despite the evidence may at once prove a fact and assume a legal proposition. The evidence was admissible, and though rejected by the trial court, was preserved and must be considered on appeal.

the instrument and to pass dominion and control over the conveyance as a present grant of joint title to the land was not overcome by sufficient proof. . . . Rather, the evidence by the plaintiff that he sought the consent and concurrence of his daughter to make additional grants to the other children, to encumber the land and to endorse the check which issued from the insurance coverage on the premises tends to prove that he considered he had delivered a present estate in that property to Renee.

The argument made to extricate the deed from the recordation as done without the authority of the grantor, we have shown, does not rest on any substantial proof. The full evidence refutes the contention: the plaintiff LeMehaute made no effort to expunge the record of the deed but rather went to the abstract office with every expectation to receive a recorded instrument. In all events, whatever the intimations of the testimony by the plaintiff, that he did not record the deed, there was *no* evidence that he did not intend the deed to be put of record. In such circumstances, the argument falls without force of proof.

* * * The judgment is reversed and remanded with direction to enter judgment for the defendant.

NOTES AND QUESTIONS

1. What the Statute of Frauds gives, the traditional law of delivery in substantial part takes away. An undelivered deed conveys nothing and is as worthless to a grantee as an oral deed. However, the fact of delivery must be established by physical acts that are "dehors the instrument;" that is, delivery must be established without reference to the language of the deed itself. As a result, the law of delivery preserves a certain amount of the witnessed ceremony of feoffment with livery of seisin.

But not all courts require delivery to be established without reference to the language of the instrument itself. See, e.g., State, by Pai v. Thom, 58 Haw. 8, 563 P.2d 982 (1977), which found that a deed had been delivered, in part because the court found the language of the deed to be "absolute and unconditional." Specifically the court found that the words of the deed— "grant, bargain, sell, transfer and deliver unto Grantee"—clearly showed "the present intention of the appellants to grant their interest or estate in the lands described in the deed. We find no clauses or conditions in the deed limiting or qualifying the estate conveyed. . . ." Query: don't almost all warranty deeds contain words such as these? Should a deed be found to be delivered simply because it is a warranty deed? Under this reasoning, wasn't the deed "delivered" the instant the grantor signed it? Suppose the deed says "by her signature hereto affixed the grantor irrevocably delivers this deed to the grantee." When the grantor dies a few days later the deed is still in his possession, has never been recorded, and the grantee, who lives many miles away does not even know about the deed. Has it been delivered?

Compare the Hawaii court's analysis with that of the Supreme Court of Wisconsin in Erbach v. Brauer, 188 Wis. 312, 206 N.W. 62 (1925), finding non-delivery because "the deed itself contains no language expressive of a delivery or of an intention of delivery." By this reasoning this deed could *never* be delivered, regardless of the grantor's acts or intentions.

2.   One particularly troublesome set of cases concerns deeds that contain language entitling the grantor to revoke the conveyance at some future time. Courts have taken three different positions respecting these deeds. First some have held that the deed is not capable of being delivered, because there is no manifested intention by the grantor to part with dominion and control; or alternatively, that such deeds are in fact testamentary and are invalid unless they meet the legal prerequisites for wills. See Peebles v. Rodgers, 211 Miss. 8, 50 So.2d 632 (1951). See also Chapter 4, supra.

Second, other courts have held that the grant is valid, assuming there have been proper manifestations of delivery, but that the reservation of the power to revoke is void. The result is to make the conveyance absolute. See Newell v. McMillan, 139 Kan. 94, 30 P.2d 126 (1934).

Third, most courts hold that both the grant and the reservation of the power to revoke are valid. For example, St. Louis County National Bank v. Fielder, 364 Mo. 207, 260 S.W.2d 483 (1953) (en banc), involved a deed that reserved to the grantor a life estate with the "power to sell, rent, lease, mortgage or otherwise dispose of said property during his natural lifetime." As the court observed, the power to sell the life estate meant that the grantor in effect had the power to revoke the grant in which the reservation of the life estate was contained. Nevertheless, it found the "modern trend" of cases to be in favor of upholding the grant, reasoning that "modern statutes for the transfer of lands by deed and the recording thereof have removed all the reasons on which the rule of the common law (holding void the reservation of such a power) was founded...." The court found that the principal reason for the common law rule was that conveyances with reservation of a power to revoke might be used to defraud creditors. However, under the recording acts creditors have notice not only of the deed, but also of the reservation. The court then concluded that the deed "created a defeasible fee subject to a life estate and, since the life estate has terminated [by the death of the grantor], defendant [the grantee] is now the absolute owner." Id. at 486.

Revocable deeds often function as will substitutes. The revocable deed permits the grantor to give the grantee something unless the grantor changes his mind before his death. During the grantor's lifetime, the grantee has a contingent interest or estate rather than, as is the case with a will, no estate at all. There are other significant differences. For one thing, the revocable deed is an inter vivos transfer of property that passes title at the time of delivery, just as any other deed. As a result the property does not pass through the grantor's probate estate, and this may have important tax consequences.[2] Secondly, once the revocable deed is delivered, the grantee has a title that is good against all the world except the grantor. Virtually all states that have a death tax provide by statute, however, that if a grantor retains an absolute right to revoke, the grantor is considered to be the true owner with

---

2. However, Internal Revenue Code § 2038 (West 1985) provides that if a deed is revocable it will be treated as if the grantor retained the property in fee. Therefore, the property will be subject to the estate tax when the grantor dies. State law determines whether the deed is revocable.

respect to subsequent creditors and purchasers. See Garvey, Revocable Gifts of Legal Interests in Land, 54 Ky.L.Rev. 19 (1965).

3.   The problem of establishing delivery or nondelivery of a deed has generally been simplified by the use of a set of rebuttable presumptions, some of which are discussed in the *LeMehaute* case. Many states hold that recordation of the deed by the grantor or his agent creates a rebuttable presumption that the deed has been delivered. See, Rausch v. Devine, 80 P.3d 733 (Alaska 2003). Some states additionally hold that recordation by the grantee or by unknown persons creates the same presumption. As the *LeMehaute* opinion suggests, recordation of a deed is often done more-or-less "automatically" by the attorney, title company or escrow company that participates in the transaction. Often the parties, who are laypersons, know little about the significance of recordation. Should the presumption apply in cases where the real estate professional records the deed without specifically asking the grantor whether he wants it recorded?

Possession of a deed by the grantee generally creates a presumption of delivery. Continued possession of the deed by the grantor generally creates a presumption of non-delivery. In all cases, the presumptions should be regarded as rebuttable. That is, if the opposing party comes forward with no conflicting evidence, the presumption controls; however, credible conflicting evidence will defeat the presumption. See 6A R. Powell, Powell on Real Property ¶ 891.

The court in *LeMehaute* employed the presumption of delivery when the deed was in the possession of a grantee. However, it relied on an argument that went something like this: (1) the grantor (Vincent) and one of the three grantees were the same person; (2) possession by one of the three grantees implies possession by all of them; (3) thus the deed was in the possession of the grantees and should be presumed to have been delivered. Isn't there a bit of bootstrapping in this argument? Since the possessor of the deed was both grantor and grantee, didn't the two conflicting presumptions cancel each other out?

4.   Given the fact that the deed was recorded, is the fact that Vincent LeMehaute asked Renee to cosign a mortgage particularly good evidence that the deed was delivered? Can you think of another reason why Renee's signature might be necessary? How about the fact that Renee was asked to endorse the insurance check? Presumably, she was asked to endorse the check, not because Vincent thought she owned an interest in the property but because the check was made out to her as well as to Vincent and his present wife. Does that indicate that the deed was delivered?

5.   Suppose a deed reserves a present possessory interest, such as a life estate in the grantor. Some courts hold that if both (a) possession of the property and (b) possession of the deed stay with the grantor, delivery can be established on much weaker evidence than is usually required. Indeed, some courts go so far as to state that if the grantor merely shows the grantee the executed deed, a presumption of delivery arises. See, e.g., Barker v. Nelson, 306 Ark. 204, 812 S.W.2d 477 (1991).

§ 15.4.2   ACCEPTANCE OF THE DEED

UNDERWOOD v. GILLESPIE

Missouri Court of Appeals, Southern District, Div. III (1980).
594 S.W.2d 372.

PREWITT, JUDGE.

Plaintiff brought an action for partition contending that she and defendants were co-owners as tenants in common of 100 acres in Stoddard County, Missouri. Defendants denied that plaintiff had any interest in the property and asked the court to quiet title in them. The trial court found that plaintiff owned an undivided one-third of the property and decreed partition.

Plaintiff claims that she and defendants acquired their interests in the property as residuary devisees under the will of Zella Bacon. Mrs. Bacon died February 10, 1974. Defendants claim they alone own the land under a deed from her dated March 9, 1966. That deed provided a life estate to her brother, Gus Gillespie, with the remainder in fee to defendants-appellants, his sons. The deed was taken to her house on that date by her attorney. She signed and acknowledged it there. Gus Gillespie then arrived and Mrs. Bacon handed him the deed. He looked at it and said "Damn it, sister, you can't do this, you can't treat my children this way, you can't give part of my children something and not give them all something." Mrs. Bacon replied, "Well, honey, I've given the girls something in my will." Gus then said something to the effect of "You can tear it up", or "You can revoke the will". The attorney left while they were still talking. Later that day Mrs. Bacon called him and he went back to her house. Gus was gone. She told him that Gus had torn up the deed. The attorney saw the torn up deed in the wastebasket. She asked the attorney what happens to the land, and was advised, "Well, he just doesn't get it." In September of 1969, she had her attorney prepare an additional will, devising this and other property to plaintiff for life, with the remainder to plaintiff's children. That will was never executed. Gus Gillespie died October 20, 1968, and half of the deed (ed. the one torn up) was then found in his papers. Apparently this was the first defendants knew of the deed. Whether he retained this part from the time he first received the deed and why he kept it is not known. It was never recorded. Following the deed, Mrs. Bacon continued to collect rent on the 100 acres until a guardian was appointed for her in early 1972. Then it was paid to the guardian, and after she died, to her estate. From 1966 through 1975 the property was assessed for tax purposes in Mrs. Bacon's name. She paid the taxes on the land herself until 1971. Thereafter, her guardian, and executor, paid the taxes. The property was inventoried in both her guardianship and decedent estates and record title was in her name at her death. The trial court found the deed to be invalid "for want of proper delivery and acceptance".

The defendants contend that the trial court erred ... in determining that the refusal of a life tenant to accept a deed defeats the remainder interests.

The delivery of a deed is necessary to pass title, and in order to have delivery there must be an acceptance. Fritz v. Fritz, 479 S.W.2d 198, 200 (Mo.App.1972). Whether there was delivery depends upon the facts of each case and all relevant facts and circumstances should be considered in determining the question. Carr v. Lincoln, 293 S.W.2d 396, 401 (Mo.1956). Had Gus accepted the deed, defendants would have received their interest, as delivery of a deed to a life tenant is a sufficient delivery for the benefit of the remaindermen. 26 C.J.S. Deeds s 49, p. 707. His actions justified the trial court's finding that the deed was not accepted. Having rejected the deed, did that action prevent the defendants from receiving the fee? ... Appellants' counsel cite Maynard v. Hustead, 185 Okl. 20, 90 P.2d 30 (1939), and Miller v. Miller, 91 Kan. 1, 136 P. 953 (1913), holding in similar situations that it does not. Our research has found Martin v. Adams, 216 Miss. 270, 62 So.2d 328 (1953), which holds that such conduct does prevent defendants from acquiring any interest. While these cases are similar on their facts, we do not find the basis for their holdings persuasive.

The Maynard and Miller decisions state, and defendants acknowledge, that at common law remainder interests are dependent upon a life estate and that the refusal of the life tenant to accept the life estate defeats the remainder. Based on a Kansas statute like § 442.020, RSMo 1959, Miller holds that this rule no longer applies. Maynard was decided upon an Oklahoma statute which specifically removes the necessity for an estate prior to a remainder. Even if we construe ... [that statute] as changing this common law rule, we do not think that it necessarily follows that defendants are granted an interest in the property. This section provides that "conveyances of lands, ... may be made by deed ... without any other act or ceremony whatever." What she could have done and what she attempted here may be two different things. She may have been able to grant the remainders without the life estate, but she did not try to do that. She tried to grant a life estate with a remainder. We do not think that removing the common law rule, if that is the effect of applying § 442.020 here, necessarily requires that when the life estate fails the remainder is still valid nor do we believe it does away with the necessity for acceptance of the deed....

Smith v. Smith, 289 Mo. 405, 233 S.W. 183, 186 (1921) states that although some of the grantees refuse their interest under a deed, the deed is still valid as to those grantees which accept unless the validity of the deed was conditioned on all accepting. However, it does not appear that the case was decided on that basis. We also believe that even if this statement in the case is correct it does not determine this case because of the different situation. In Smith the deed was delivered to one of the accepting grantees, all of which were granted a present possessory interest. When a grantor delivers it to one, for that one to retain it and normally record it, it can be presumed that the grantor intended it to be effective to all that accept, absent some condition. It is different where there is no actual acceptance, and where the remainder may not become effective for many years, pending the death of the life tenant.

The controlling element in determining delivery is the intention of the parties, particularly that of the grantor. Cartmill v. Evans, supra, 498 S.W.2d at 545. Acceptance is a part of delivery and we feel her intentions as to who might accept the deed and the conditions under which it could be accepted must be considered. Under these circumstances only inferences as to her intentions can be made. Mrs. Bacon apparently intended to deliver the deed when she gave it to Gus. Saying that she still intended that title pass to his sons, if Gus rejected it, might be speculation. With Gus's rejection of the deed, Mrs. Bacon may not have wished that the remainder interest pass to his sons. Had she wanted it to go directly to them, she could have done so at the time of this deed. For whatever reason, she wanted Gus to first have a life estate in the property. When that was rejected, we cannot say that she still wanted title to eventually vest in defendants. She would likely assume that this unrecorded, torn deed would not pass any interest. She thereafter could have made a deed directly to the defendants but did not. Later she instructed her attorney to prepare a will, which she never signed, devising the land to plaintiff for life, with remainder in plaintiff's children. She apparently assumed that Gus had a right of approval and could accept or reject the entire deed. The deed was rejected because Gus did not want the boys alone to take under the deed. She appears to have acquiesced in that decision. Following his death, when the remainders would have taken effect, she continued to treat the land as hers. While it can be presumed that defendants would have accepted the property, (See Bailey v. Williams, 326 S.W.2d 115, 122 (Mo.1959); 26A C.J.S. Deeds s 186) we cannot assume that Mrs. Bacon wanted them to have it or any right of acceptance of it under circumstances different than she contemplated. Were we to say that the deed was valid without a life estate, we may be in effect creating a new instrument contrary to her wishes. If we presume acceptance, it may be an acceptance not intended by Mrs. Bacon.

In Miller v. McCaleb, 208 Mo. 562, 106 S.W. 655 (1907), the grantor made a deed to his wife and to his "lawful heirs". The deed was recorded but there was no evidence that it was delivered to or accepted by her or the heirs. The court noted that while the recording of a deed may raise a presumption of delivery, this may be rebutted. As there was evidence that she did not accept the deed, it had no effect, and the heirs received no interest in the property. While the facts are much different than here, the decision indicates the necessity for acceptance of the deed.

Before giving the deed to Gus, Mrs. Bacon likely had no intention as to what should occur to the remainder in the event of rejection. If a future interest passed as a matter of law when the deed was handed to Gus, it may have been against her wishes and intentions, but it would thereafter be out of her control to change. If nothing passes by such a deed, the grantor can make such other disposition as he or she may wish. We believe the better rule is to hold that the entire deed is invalid in such a situation rather than to hold it is partly binding. It would be a simple matter to transfer an interest by a new deed in such event and it would not necessitate a result not likely contemplated and perhaps not desired. Upon its rejection, no further efforts were made to deliver the deed or record it. The inferences from her conduct are that Mrs. Bacon then viewed the deed as invalid. She did not indicate that she was still intending to transfer an interest to the remaindermen. Acceptance is a necessary part of delivery and as the person to whom the deed was given rejected it, it was not accepted. The grantor did not indicate that acceptance by the remaindermen was thereafter available to them. The presumption that they would have accepted does not apply, as it appears that acceptance was not considered by the grantor to be a decision for the remaindermen, unless their father agreed to the disposition and accepted the deed. We hold that the deed was not accepted in the manner apparently contemplated by the grantor and passed no interest to defendants . . .

The judgment is affirmed.

NOTES AND QUESTIONS

1. Would the remaindermen have had a cause of action against their father for not accepting the deed on their behalf?

§ 15.4.3   THE DEATH ESCROW

ROSENGRANT v. ROSENGRANT

Court of Appeals of Oklahoma (1981).
629 P.2d 800.

BOYDSTON, JUDGE.

This is an appeal by J.W. (Jay) Rosengrant from the trial court's decision to cancel and set aside a warranty deed which attempted to vest title in him to certain property owned by his aunt and uncle, Mildred and Harold Rosengrant. The trial court held the deed was invalid for want of legal delivery. We affirm that decision.

Harold and Mildred were a retired couple living on a farm southeast of Tecumseh, Oklahoma. They had no children of their own but had six nieces and nephews through Harold's deceased brother. One of these nephews was Jay Rosengrant. He and his wife lived a short distance from Harold and Mildred and helped the elderly couple from time to time with their chores.

In 1971, it was discovered that Mildred had cancer. In July, 1972 Mildred and Harold went to Mexico to obtain laetrile treatments accompanied by Jay's wife. Jay remained behind to care for the farm.

Shortly before this trip, on June 23, 1972, Mildred had called Jay and asked him to meet her and Harold at Farmers and Merchants Bank in

Tecumseh. Upon arriving at the bank, Harold introduced Jay to his banker J.E. Vanlandengham who presented Harold and Mildred with a deed to their farm which he had prepared according to their instructions. Both Harold and Mildred signed the deed and informed Jay that they were going to give him "the place," but that they wanted Jay to leave the deed at the bank with Mr. Vanlandengham and when "something happened" to them,[1] he was to take it to Shawnee and record it and "it" would be theirs. Harold personally handed the deed to Jay to "make this legal." Jay accepted the deed and then handed it back to the banker who told him he would put it in an envelope and keep it in the vault until he called for it.

In July, 1974, when Mildred's death was imminent, Jay and Harold conferred with an attorney concerning the legality of the transaction. The attorney advised them it should be sufficient but if Harold anticipated problems he should draw up a will.

In 1976, Harold discovered he had lung cancer. In August and December 1977, Harold put $10,000 into two certificates of deposit in joint tenancy with Jay.

Harold died January 28, 1978. On February 2, Jay and his wife went to the bank to inventory the contents of the safety deposit box. They also requested the envelope containing the deed which was retrieved from the collection file of the bank.

Jay went to Shawnee the next day and recorded the deed.

The petition to cancel and set aside the deed was filed February 22, 1978, alleging that the deed was void in that it was never legally delivered and alternatively that since it was to be operative only upon recordation after the death of the grantors it was a testamentary instrument and was void for failure to comply with the Statute of Wills.

The trial court found the deed was null and void for failure of legal delivery. The dispositive issue raised on appeal is whether the trial court erred in so ruling. We hold it did not and affirm the judgment.

* * * In cases involving attempted transfers such as this, it is the grantor's intent *at the time the deed is delivered* which is of primary and controlling importance. It is the function of this court to weigh the evidence presented at trial as to grantor's intent and unless the trial court's decision is clearly against the weight of the evidence, to uphold that finding. . . .

When the deed was retrieved, it was contained in an envelope on which was typed: "J.W. Rosengrant—or Harold H. Rosengrant."

The import of the writing on the envelope is clear. It creates an inescapable conclusion that the deed was, in fact, retrievable at any time by Harold before his death. The bank teller's testimony as to the custom and usage of the bank leaves no other conclusion but that at any time Harold was free to retrieve the deed. There was, if not an expressed, an

---

1. Common euphemism meaning their deaths.

implied agreement between the banker and Harold that the grant was not to take effect until two conditions occurred—the death of both grantors and the recordation of the deed.

In support of this conclusion conduct relative to the property is significant and was correctly considered by the court. Evidence was presented to show that after the deed was filed Harold continued to farm, use and control the property. Further, he continued to pay taxes on it until his death and claimed it as his homestead.

Grantee confuses the issues involved herein by relying upon grantors' goodwill toward him and his wife as if it were a controlling factor. From a fair review of the record it is apparent Jay and his wife were very attentive, kind and helpful to this elderly couple. The donative intent on the part of grantors is undeniable. We believe they fully intended to reward Jay and his wife for their kindness. Nevertheless, where a grantor delivers a deed under which he reserves a right of retrieval and attaches to that delivery the condition that the deed is to become operative only after the death of grantors and further continues to use the property as if no transfer had occurred, grantor's actions are nothing more than an attempt to employ the deed as if it were a will. Under Oklahoma law this cannot be done. The ritualistic "delivery of the deed" to the grantee and his redelivery of it to the third party for safe keeping created under these circumstances only a symbolic delivery. It amounted to a pro forma attempt to comply with the legal aspects of delivery. Based on all the facts and circumstances the true intent of the parties is expressed by the notation on the envelope and by the later conduct of the parties in relation to the land. Legal delivery is not just a symbolic gesture. It necessarily carries all the force and consequence of absolute, outright ownership at the time of delivery or it is no delivery at all.[2]

From a complete review of the record and weighing of the evidence we find the trial court's judgment is not clearly against the weight of the evidence. * * *

NOTES AND QUESTIONS

1. Not all states agree that Harold's delivery had no legal effect. For example, in Osborn v. Osborn, 42 Cal.2d 358, 362–63, 267 P.2d 333, 335 (1954) the court stated:

> It has long been established in this state that the deposit of a deed granting an estate in fee simple, with instructions that it be transmitted to the grantee upon the death of the grantor, conveys a remainder

---

2. In *Anderson v. Mauk*, Okl., 67 P.2d 429 (1937), the court stated:

[I]t is the established law in this jurisdiction that when the owner of land executes a deed during his lifetime and delivers the same to a third party (who acts as a depository rather than an agent of the property owner) with instructions to deliver the deed to the grantee therein named upon his death, *intending at the time of delivery to forever part with all lawful right and power to retake or repossess the deed,* or to thereafter control the same, the delivery to the third party thus made is sufficient to operate as a valid conveyance of real estate.

interest in fee simple with a life estate reserved in the grantor, if the grantor intended the deposit to be irrevocable.... The result is the same as if the grantor delivered to the grantee a deed reserving a life estate and granting a remainder in fee.

2. Who typed "J.W. Rosengrant—or Harold H. Rosengrant" on the envelope that contained the deed held by the bank? The court emphasizes that the "custom and usage" of the bank was that the grantor could have retrieved the deed anytime he wished. However, the *grantor's* intent to pass title, not the escrow agent's intent, determines delivery. See Hutchinson v. Colvin, 9 Cal.2d 91, 69 P.2d 416 (1937), where the grantor put two deeds in an envelope and gave them to a bank with instructions that they be delivered after both he and his wife were dead. Later the grantor wrote the bank and asked that deed #1 be returned to him, which the bank did. Deed #2 stayed in the envelope until after the grantor's death, and was then given to the named grantee. The court held that the second deed was properly delivered, even though the grantor withdrew the first deed from the envelope. In explaining this decision the California Supreme Court suggested that the withdrawal of the first deed could have been a "wrongful or idle act" that had no bearing on the grantor's intent with respect to the second deed. Cf. Estate of Dittus, 497 N.W.2d 415 (N.D.1993), where the grantor gave the grantee one key to a safe deposit box containing the deed but retained the other. The court indicated that delivery of *both* keys would have been sufficient evidence of delivery, but the grantor's retention of one key was sufficient to suggest that he did not intend immediately to give up control.

3. When a layperson has a deed prepared, places it in escrow for a gratuitous grantee, and says to the grantee "this will become operative when I die," what do you suppose he means by the words "become operative?" He could mean that the grantor will relinquish the title at the time of his death. In that case, the prevailing opinion is that there has not been a complete delivery, because the grantor has not parted with dominion or control. By contrast, if the grantor regards title as already having passed and means merely that the grantee may take possession at the time of the grantor's death, then the delivery through the escrow is valid because the grantee's interest is irrevocable. More often than not, the distinction between transfer of title and transfer of possession does not mean much to a layperson unless it is explained. Is the grantor's intention in the *Rosengrant* case clear?

4. What was the meaning of the little "feoffment" ceremony that took place in the banker's office? The court held that it had no legal consequence. Clearly, however, if it had any consequence whatsoever, it would have been to effect an *immediate* delivery of the deed to Jay—clearly not what Uncle Harold had in mind. The banker was practicing law without a license, and he was doing so ineptly.

5. Suppose the grantor leaves the deed with the escrow with instructions to deliver the deed to the grantee upon the grantor's death, or to return it to the grantor whenever the grantor asks to have it returned. Is the effect of this conveyance any different than that of a deed containing a power to revoke? Courts uniformly hold that a delivery to an escrow agent expressly revocable by the grantor is invalid. See Brandt v. Schucha, 250 Iowa 679, 96

N.W.2d 179 (1959). What justifies a rule upholding deeds that explicitly contain powers to revoke, but disapproving revocable escrows? One obvious difference is that in the ordinary course of things the revocable deed is delivered and recorded. However, the deed subject to a revocable escrow is not likely to be recorded until after the grantor's death. This yields the possibility for fraud upon the grantor's creditors. Cf. Walls v. Click, 209 W.Va. 627, 550 S.E.2d 605 (2001) (father gave son acknowledged deeds with instructions to place them in safe deposit box and not record them until after father's death; instruction not to record until after father's death did not turn transaction into an attempted conditional delivery).

6. Death escrows, like revocable deeds, can also be used as will substitutes. Like revocable deeds, they may have the effect of keeping the deeded property out of the probate system.

7. Some courts require a grantor to satisfy two conditions before recognizing delivery through an escrow created by the grantor alone: (1) the grantor must give up all control of the title (although generally not the possession) of the deeded property; *and* (2) the condition necessary for delivery must be certain to occur. A properly executed death escrow satisfies both conditions. Suppose, however, that the grantor clearly gives up all control over the title, but she states the death condition in such a way that it is not certain to occur. For example, suppose O deeds Blackacre to A, and the escrow agent's instructions are to deliver the deed to A *if* O dies before A. If O dies before A and the agent delivers the deed to A, does A own Blackacre? Compare Atchison v. Atchison, 198 Okla. 98, 175 P.2d 309 (1946) with Videon v. Cowart, 241 So.2d 434 (Fla.Dist. Ct. App.1970).

8. Under the Uniform Real Property Transfer on Death Act (2009), an owner of real property may transfer real property to one or more beneficiaries by a deed executed with sufficient formalities of a recordable deed. The deed must expressly state that the transfer to the beneficiaries occurs at the transferor's death and, to be effective, the deed must be recorded before the transferor's death in the office of the recorder for the county where the real estate is located. The transfer is effective at the transferor's death and is revocable throughout the transferor's lifetime. No interest is created in the beneficiaries named in the deed during the transferor's lifetime and during life the transferor is free to transfer the land in fee simple to another.

§ 15.4.4 THE COMMERCIAL ESCROW

FERGUSON v. CASPAR

District of Columbia Court of Appeals (1976).
359 A.2d 17.

REILLY, CHIEF JUDGE:

One of the most formal transactions known to the law is the transfer of title to real estate. In order to insure finality to such transactions, the practice in this jurisdiction is for the contracting parties, including the lienors and lienees, after they are satisfied with the report on title search, to meet with one another in the office of a title company, agree on the apportionment of outstanding taxes and other charges, and execute and deliver the conveyances (deeds) necessary to close the transaction. Such a meeting, popularly called a "closing" or a "settlement", precedes the transmission by the title company of the conveyancing instruments to the Recorder of Deeds for permanent entry into the official land records.

Although hundreds of such settlements occur every year in the District of Columbia, it is seldom indeed that the parties conduct themselves in such a way as to taint the finality of the "closing." The case before us stems from one of these uncommon situations and raises the question as to what point in a settlement proceeding finality attaches.

* * *

Appellee Mrs. Ida Caspar was the owner of an unrestored row house in the Capitol Hill area. On November 18, 1972, she entered into a contract for the sale of the premises to the appellants for the sum of $23,000.00, payment of the purchase price to be made in cash at the time of settlement. Settlement was to be made at the office of the Lawyers Title Insurance Corporation on or before February 1, 1973. The contract of sale included a provision that the seller would convey the premises free of all notices of municipal violations existing at the date of the contract, such provision to survive the delivery of the deed.[1] On October 13, 1972, Mrs. Caspar had been personally served with a deficiency notice by a District of Columbia housing inspector informing her that there existed 126 Housing Code violations upon the premises and calling for their correction within 60 days. Subsequently, Mrs. Caspar, upon her written request, obtained an extension of time for compliance to January 25, 1973.

Early in January, 1973, the appellants became aware of the existence of the Housing Code violations but did not bring this matter to the attention of the seller. Instead, they obtained an estimate of $6,125.00 from a housing contractor as the cost of correcting the deficiencies. The notice of violations was still outstanding at the time of settlement.

By agreement, the parties met at the office of the Lawyers Title Insurance Corporation for settlement on the afternoon of February 1, 1973. Mrs. Caspar was attended by her son and daughter who assisted their mother in business matters. The appellants were present with their attorney. The settlement officer, an employee of the title company, prepared settlement statements for the respective parties which each of them signed. In addition, the parties signed the requisite District of Columbia tax recordation forms. Mrs. Caspar executed and delivered her deed to the property to the settlement officer. The purchasers delivered to the settlement officer the personal check of Mr. Ferguson in the sum of $12,924.42

---

1. The printed clause in the contract provided:

All notices of violations of Municipal orders or requirements noted or issued by any department of the District of Columbia, or prosecutions in any of the courts of the District of Columbia on account thereof against or affecting the property at the date of this contract shall be complied with by the seller and the property conveyed free thereof. This provision shall survive the delivery of the deed hereunder.

payable to the order of the title company, representing the balance due as set forth in the settlement statement.

After the documents had been delivered to the settlement officer and as the parties were rising to leave, the attorney for the appellants handed separate letters to the settlement officer and to Mrs. Caspar's son. The letter addressed to the title company, after referring to the clause in the contract of sale requiring Mrs. Caspar to convey the premises free of any municipal violation notices, advised the title company that as of January 26, 1973, the outstanding Housing Code violations had not been corrected and that the purchasers had obtained an estimate in the amount of $6,125.00 to bring the premises into compliance. The letter concluded by stating:

> This is to put you on notice that purchasers are paying $6,125.00 of the purchase price to you as escrow agent to hold until seller has complied with the outstanding violation notices on this property. Written notice signed by the purchaser shall be sufficient to discharge you from any further obligations with respect to this sum.

The letter directed to Mrs. Caspar informed her of the existence of the notice of the Housing Code violations and her obligation under the agreement to comply with the notice. It went on to state that the Fergusons had obtained an estimate of approximately $6,125.00 as the cost of repairing the premises and concluded as follows:

> This is to advise you that Fergusons intend to enforce the requirement that these violations be corrected. Accordingly, I have written Lawyers Title requesting that they withhold the above amount from the purchase price in an escrow account until you and the Fergusons have reached a final understanding as to the cost of making these corrections.

Upon receiving the letter directed to the title company, the settlement officer advised the parties that the company could not record the deed or withhold any funds without formal authority to hold any funds in escrow. He informed the parties that he could not proceed with the settlement since the contract of sale provided for payment in cash and there was no provision for withholding any funds in escrow. Mrs. Caspar's son suggested that the parties complete the settlement, have the deed recorded, and thereafter "work out or litigate" the question of the Housing Code violations. The attorney for the appellants recommended that Mrs. Caspar seek the advice of an attorney. The parties then dispersed without the matter being resolved.

On February 13, 1973, not having received any further word or instructions from the parties, the settlement officer wrote to the Fergusons, returning the personal check which had been presented at the settlement and informing them that the deed could not be recorded in view of their attorney's letter directing the title company to withhold certain monies in escrow. Two days later, the Fergusons' attorney replied, returning the personal check to the settlement officer and insisting that the deed be recorded. This letter was received by the title company on February 16 and on the same day, the deed executed by Mrs. Caspar was returned to her son. On February 17, Mrs. Caspar signed a contract of sale for the premises to the appellees, John and Mary McAteer, and her deed to them was executed and recorded on February 23.

On February 21, 1973, appellants filed a complaint against Mrs. Caspar seeking a declaratory judgment and specific performance of the contract of sale entered into between the parties. Subsequently, the complaint was amended to include the McAteers as parties-defendant. In her answer to the amended complaint, Mrs. Caspar alleged inter alia that the appellants had breached the contract of sale and were not entitled to specific performance. The case was tried before the court without a jury. At the close of all the evidence, the court granted appellees' motion to dismiss the complaint on the ground that the plaintiffs, by imposing conditions on their tender of payment of the purchase price, had failed to make an unconditional tender of full performance of the contract on their part and had forfeited their right to specific performance. On June 15, 1973, the trial court entered its Judgment and Order of Dismissal setting forth its Findings of Fact and Conclusions of Law.

On this appeal, appellants' principal contentions are that legal title to the property in question passed to them upon the settlement between the seller and purchasers and that the trial court erred in concluding that the appellants were not entitled to specific performance of the contract of sale by reason of their failure to tender the full purchase price for the property as required by the contract. We agree with the determination of the trial court and affirm.

The initial contention of appellants is based upon the erroneous conclusion that legal title to the property in question passed to them when the settlement statements were signed by the respective parties, the seller's deed delivered to the settlement officer, and the personal check of the purchasers for the balance due delivered to the settlement officer. In this conclusion, appellants misconstrue the nature and effect of the settlement proceedings engaged in between the various parties at the meeting. In their briefs on appeal, the appellants and appellees both infer that under the circumstances of this case the title company's position in the transaction was that of an escrow agent. Our study of the contract of sale and the proceedings which ensued at the settlement meeting confirms our understanding that, as is the usual and customary practice in real estate transactions in the District of Columbia where the parties employ a third party to accept their respective tenders of performance under the contract, a valid escrow arrangement is created and the title company serves in the capacity of an escrow agent in the transaction.

Generally, an escrow agreement is created in a formal contract between the parties, setting forth the conditions and contingencies under which the instruments deposited in escrow are to be delivered and to take effect. However, no precise form of words is necessary to create an escrow but it must appear from all the facts and circumstances surrounding the execution and delivery of the instruments that they were not to take effect until certain conditions are performed.

A valid escrow agreement is a triangular arrangement. First there must be a contract between the seller and the buyer agreeing to the conditions of a deposit, then there must be delivery of the items on deposit to the escrow agent, and he must agree to perform the function of receiving and dispersing the items. The agreement by the seller and buyer to all the terms of the escrow instructions and the acceptance by the escrow agent of the position of depository create the escrow.

In the case at bar, the seller and the purchasers agreed to make full settlement in accordance with the terms of the contract of sale at the office of Lawyers Title Insurance Corporation, the title company searching the title, and that "... deposit with the Title Company ... of the purchase money, the deed of conveyance for execution and such other papers as are required of either party by the terms of this contract shall be considered good and sufficient tender of performance of the terms hereof." Significantly, the deed executed by the seller was delivered to the settlement officer. The purchasers' personal check, which included the balance of the purchase price, was made payable to the title company and delivered to the settlement officer. The deed was deposited with the settlement officer as an escrow agent with the implied understanding that delivery to the purchasers was not to be effected until the purchasers had complied with their obligation under the contract of sale to pay the amount due the seller as purchase money. On the other hand, the settlement officer was not free to disburse any of the funds deposited by the purchasers until the title company was assured that the seller's deed conveyed title "good of record and in fact". Thus, the settlement meeting was only the initial step in the transaction and until all the conditions of the contract had been fulfilled, the settlement was not complete.[2] Where a deed is deposited as an escrow, title does not pass to the grantee unless and until the condition of its delivery is performed. Although the purchasers tendered their personal check for the balance due from them at the settlement in ostensible payment of the purchase price, their subsequent direction to the title company to withhold from the seller a substantial portion of the purchase money to which she was entitled created a deviation from the condition upon which delivery of the deed to them could be effected. The settlement officer informed the purchasers that the settlement could not be completed and the deed could not be recorded. Since the condition precedent to the delivery of the deed had not been fulfilled, legal title to the property did not pass to the purchasers.

---

2. The customary practice in settlements of this nature is for the title company to deposit the purchaser's check to assure that the check is honored. After the check clears and before recording the deed, the title company brings the title down to date by making a continuation title search from the date of its initial search to the date of recordation of the deed to assure that no liens or encumbrances have been filed against the property in the interim.

Appellants point to the fact that settlement statements were signed by the respective parties as indicative that settlement between the parties had been completed. Each of these statements was a separate and distinct document, one being the seller's statement establishing the "AMOUNT TO BE PAID SELLER" and the other, the purchasers' statement indicating the "BALANCE REQUIRED TO COMPLETE SETTLEMENT." The seller's statement contained an itemization of charges to be borne by the seller, including a charge for the apportionment of unpaid taxes, the brokerage fee to be paid to the real estate broker, disbursements to be paid to the broker for the costs of evicting the tenants, one-half of the recordation tax, and a charge of $50 to be held for water charges. These charges and anticipated disbursements were applied against the purchase price of the property and a balance struck, establishing the net amount which would be paid to the seller by the title company as the proceeds of the sale after the disbursements had been made and the settlement completed. The seller's signature on the statement noted her approval and acceptance of the statement as correct.

The purchasers' statement itemized the credits to their account, consisting of a credit for apportionment of unpaid taxes, the amount deposited with the broker as earnest money, and a credit to the purchasers of the sum to be received by the title company as the proceeds of the refinancing of other property owned by the purchasers. Against these credits, the purchasers were charged with the purchase price of the property and miscellaneous closing costs to be paid by them, including examination of title, title insurance, settlement fee, conveyancing fees, recording fees, and their share of the recordation tax. Offsetting the credits against the charges established a balance to be paid by the purchasers to the title company at settlement.

We do not attribute to these documents the significance which appellants attach to them. In effect, the seller's statement merely indicated what the seller would receive as the net proceeds of the sale after the settlement had been fully completed. The purchasers' statement was a statement of account of what remained to be paid by the purchasers to the title company, including the closing costs to be paid to the title company, after crediting the purchasers for the earnest money paid to the real estate broker and the sum anticipated to be received from the refinancing settlement. The incidental charges set forth on each statement were the concern solely of the party charged. Neither party bound himself to the settlement statement of the other. Neither statement constituted an acknowledgment that either the seller or the title company had received the purchase money which the purchasers were obligated to pay. The individual settlement statements were in effect an account stated separately between the title company and the seller and between the title company and the purchasers. Thus we reject the contention that the signing of the individual settlement statements by each of the parties signified that the transaction had been completed.

The appellants, contending that the settlement proceeding was completed, argue further that when the legal title to the premises passed to them the title to the purchase money vested in the seller and the subsequent demand by the purchasers that the title company withhold a portion of the seller's money was a "legal nullity" and "obviously unenforceable". In an escrow arrangement, the escrow holder is the dual agent of both parties until the performance of the conditions of the escrow agreement, whereupon he becomes the agent of each of the parties to the transaction in respect to those things placed in escrow to which each party has thus become entitled. Thus, when the conditions specified in the escrow agreement have been fully performed, the title to the premises passes to the purchaser and title to the purchase money passes to the seller. Thereupon, the escrow holder becomes the agent of the purchaser as to the deed and of the seller as to the money. However, as we have pointed out supra, the settlement was not completed and since the conditions upon which the seller's deed was to be delivered to the purchasers had not been performed, legal title to the property did not pass to the purchasers and title to the purchase money deposited with the settlement officer did not vest in the seller.

Furthermore, we find it difficult to comprehend appellants' present contention that their written demand upon the title company was a "legal nullity" in view of their contrary position at the settlement meeting. Upon receipt of the written demand from appellants' attorney, the settlement officer notified the parties that under the circumstances he could not proceed with the settlement. At the same time, Mrs. Caspar's son suggested that the appellants permit the settlement to proceed and that thereafter the parties "work out" the question of the Housing Code violations. Nevertheless, the appellants persisted in their demand that a portion of the purchase money be retained in escrow by the title company. The impasse was not resolved and the meeting broke up. By making the demand upon the title company, appellants placed the company in the difficult position of having to determine the rights of the respective parties. If the company honored appellants' demand, the seller could complain that the company had breached its duty to her. If the company refused to comply with the demand, the appellants would charge the title company with having disbursed the purchase money contrary to their express direction. In either event, the title company would have risked being subject to legal action by the party aggrieved. After waiting a reasonable period for the parties to adjust their differences and not having received any further word from either of them, the title company terminated its escrow agency and returned the escrow instruments to the respective parties. This turn of events was brought about by appellants' actions in serving the demand upon the title company and in persisting in their position. They cannot escape the consequences of their action by now claiming that their demand was a "nullity."

There is no dispute that a substantial number of violations of Housing Code regulations were duly noted against the premises and were in existence at the time the contract of sale was executed. Nor is there any dispute that Mrs. Caspar, as record owner of the property, was officially notified of the violations. Prior to the time for settlement, none of these violations had been corrected. Under these circumstances, the purchasers could have refused to consummate settlement and then have brought an action at law against the seller for such damages as they may have sustained. Alternatively, the purchasers could have elected to complete the settlement, and under the survival provisions of the contract, could have sued to recover from the seller such damages as they may have sustained by reason of her failure to correct the outstanding violations. The appellants here made no effort to rescind the contract but instead gave every indication of their intention to go forward with the transaction. Thus, despite the breach of the contract by the seller, the purchasers elected to proceed with the contract and obligated themselves to continue their performance of its terms.

* * * The conclusion that appellants were not ready or willing to perform their obligation under the contract to pay the purchase price in cash is adequately supported by the record. By their own conduct, the appellants precluded their right to obtain specific performance of the contract.

Affirmed.

NOTES AND QUESTIONS

1. The commercial escrow created pursuant to a land sale contract has given rise to far less litigation than the death escrow, which is unilateral. Under a typical commercial escrow arrangement the buyer and seller enter a contract that provides that by a given date the seller will execute a deed and deliver it to the escrow agent (often a title company, commercial bank or attorney). The buyer agrees to place the purchase price or agreed-upon obligations with the escrow by the same date. If everyone performs properly, then on the specified date—sometimes called "closing," and sometimes "law day" (that is, the day the parties' equitable rights change into legal rights)—the escrow agent gives each party what he is entitled to under the contract.

2. Suppose the grantor dies after placing the deed with the escrow agent, but before closing day. Has the deed been delivered? The general rule is that the escrow agent's delivery to the grantee on closing day "relates back" to the grantor's delivery to the escrow agent, provided that the grantee has performed his part of the contract. Fuqua v. Fuqua, 528 S.W.2d 896 (Tex.Civ. App.1975), writ refused n.r.e. See R. Natelson, Modern Law of Deeds to Real Property § 17.10 (1992).

CHAPTER 16

ASSURING GOOD TITLE

■ ■ ■

§ 16.1 INFORMATION COSTS AND THE MARKET FOR REAL PROPERTY

Two attributes of real property make assurance of good title particularly difficult. First, real property is particularly durable—in fact, almost every parcel bought and sold today has been around for as long as there have been markets. Second, possession (or lack of it) is not always conclusive evidence of ownership. Many people have nonpossessory ownership interests in real property. Conversely, many people in possession of real property have only very small ownership interests in it (such as month-to-month tenancies).

For our purposes, information costs are the costs that a buyer incurs in determining the value to him of a certain piece of property, and therefore what he is willing to pay for it. Suppose that a prospective buyer places a value of $10,000 on a fee simple absolute in Blackacre, but believes there is a 50% chance that Blackacre's title is so defective that if he bought it he would have no rights in it whatsoever. Because of this uncertainty, the prospective buyer values Blackacre at $5,000. Suppose, further, that the prospective buyer intends to erect a $90,000 building on Blackacre. If he builds this building his total investment in Blackacre would be $100,000, but there would *still* be a 50% chance that he would lose Blackacre, and we presume his investment in the building as well. In that case, the prospective buyer will place a *negative* value on investment in Blackacre and its development; that is, even if Blackacre were free, an investment of $90,000 would give him a value of only $45,000. The prospective buyer will not risk development on Blackacre.

The illustration suggests why land for which title is questionable is worth much less than land for which title is relatively good. The owner of property with a questionable title must discount not only the value of what he already has, but also of any future investment. Considering the fact that most purchasers of land intend to invest *something*—even if nothing more than their time—it should be clear that assurance of title is absolutely essential to the effective functioning of any real estate market.

The other side of the coin is that there is no such thing as "perfect" title. The quality of land titles exists on a continuum, running from the very good to the very bad. Furthermore, establishing good title is hardly costless. In one of the original thirteen states a title search that went back thirty years might provide moderate assurance of good title and cost $250. A search that went back sixty years would provide better assurance of good title but might cost $400. A search that went back to the "root of title"—that is, to the original grant from the sovereign—might provide highly reliable evidence of good title but cost $800. Which should you buy? The question is complicated, because the quality of a title search is a function not only of its "depth" into the past, but also of its "breadth"— the number of related chains of title that it covers, and the number of collateral questions that must be pursued.

A prospective purchaser can obtain "assurance" of good title—or, alternatively, protection from the consequences of having a bad title—by three different mechanisms. None of them is foolproof. First, the buyer can obtain a promise from the immediate seller that title is good. This promise takes the form of one or more warranties contained in the deed from the seller. Most, but not all, deeds contain such warranties.

Deed warranties are not particularly good assurances for the buyer in the modern era. If a defect surfaces that can be remedied by the grantor, a court will often award specific performance and force the grantor to make the title good. However, many subsequently discovered title defects are not within the ability of the grantor to remedy; otherwise they may be technically in the legal control of the grantor but can be remedied only by the grantor's payment of money that he does not have. A warranty in a deed often amounts to nothing more than a cause of action against a grantor, and the value of such claims is no greater than the grantor's solvency.

Second, by doing a title search the purchaser can evaluate the risk for herself. Title searches range from very expensive to quite inexpensive, depending on the condition of the local land records, the complexity of the title being searched, and the amount of assurance one wants to obtain. The seller may agree in the sales contract to pay for the title search by promising to furnish an abstract or other evidence of good title. Nevertheless, a title search is part of the transaction costs of the real property market, and will be reflected in the purchase price. Ultimately, buyers pay. Traditionally a title search plus the seller's warranties respecting title have been the only available methods of title assurance.

At this point title insurance, the third method of title assurance, comes in and at least potentially prevents a great deal of grief. The title insurance policy itself provides, not further evidence that title is good, but rather a promise to compensate the owner if title should happen to be bad. Title insurance makes it possible for someone to do a less than perfect title search, and still have protection from defective title.

§ 16.2 COMMON LAW MECHANISMS OF TITLE ASSURANCE

§ 16.2.1 COMMON LAW PRIORITIES

Questions of title "assurance" are meaningful only after some rules have been established for distinguishing good title from bad. More precisely, there must be a basis for determining which of two conflicting claimants to the same property interest wins. One rule established at common law centuries ago is still followed today, at least to the extent it is not superseded by the recording acts: *first in time is first in right*. If O deeds Blackacre to A today and to B tomorrow, A owns Blackacre and B owns nothing except perhaps a cause of action against O. That basic rule still governs transactions in both real and personal property.

The vast majority of disputes over priorities and the title established by them do not involve anything quite as outrageous as a seller conveying the same fee simple interest to two different people on two consecutive days—although even that happens more often than you might think. Most conflicts involve nonpossessory interests in land—mortgages, mechanics liens, easements or restrictive covenants, mineral rights, and the like. Many other controversies involve leasehold estates for years. The basic common law rule for all these interests is the same. If today O, the owner of Blackacre, should give his neighbor A an easement across Blackacre, then any sale of Blackacre to B tomorrow will be "subject to" the easement. B's subsequent grant—regardless of what it says—is in fact a grant of Blackacre *minus* A's easement.

The common law rule of first in time was the simplest when both the first and second grantees acquired a legal interest, such as a conveyance by deed, in the disputed property. The rule was the same for successive equitable interests. If on March 1 O contracts to sell an easement across Blackacre to A, and on March 2, while the contract with A is still executory, O contracts to sell Blackacre to B, unencumbered by any easements, A will obtain the easement and B will obtain Blackacre subject to the easement (or have the right to rescind the contract because of O's inability to produce an unencumbered marketable title). A was first in time, and is therefore first in right.

The common law rule of priorities veered from this course only when the first interest created was equitable and the second legal. Suppose, for example, that on March 1 O contracts to sell an easement across Blackacre to A. On March 2, while this contract is still executory, O gives a warranty deed to Blackacre showing no encumbrances to B. In this situation the common law held that if B was a bona fide purchaser with no notice of A's prior claim, and if B paid value for the interest, then B's *legal* interest would prevail over A's earlier *equitable* interest. In that case, A would be relegated to a cause of action against O for damages for breach of contract. However, if B either had knowledge of A's earlier contract with O, or if the deed from O to B was gratuitous, then A's former equitable interest would prevail. These distinctions have been incorporated into the recording acts of most states and apply even when both claimants hold legal interests. However, the recording acts, which are discussed later in this chapter, generally use the date of recordation, rather than the date of creation of the interest, in determining priority as between conflicting claims.

§ 16.2.2   DEED COVENANTS FOR TITLE

LEACH v. GUNNARSON

Supreme Court of Oregon, en banc (1980).
290 Or. 31, 619 P.2d 263.

HOWELL, JUSTICE.

This action involves the question whether an irrevocable license to use a spring on a grantee's land is a breach of the grantor's covenant against encumbrances if the license is an open, notorious and visible physical encumbrance. * * *

Defendant and her husband (who died prior to trial) were the original owners of a 20–acre parcel of land in Douglas County on which was located a spring. Around 1954, they sold a small piece of an adjoining parcel, which they also owned, to defendant's brother-in-law and his wife, Henry and Betty Leach. Defendant and her husband also orally granted the Leaches the right to locate, construct and maintain a facility to draw water from the spring on defendants' land. The Leaches built a concrete dam one foot high by three feet long and installed a 370–gallon storage tank with a plastic pipe running for 175 feet across defendants' land to convey the water to the Leaches' homesite.

In May, 1975, defendant and her husband sold their 20–acre parcel to plaintiffs. Plaintiff Ove Gunnarson admitted that he knew the Leaches were using the spring, but he also testified that defendant's husband had assured him that the Leaches had no right to use the spring. The warranty deed from defendant and her husband to plaintiffs, after describing the parcel of property, states that the grantors "... covenant to and with the grantees that [the parcel] is free and clear of all encumbrances, and that grantors will warrant and defend the same against all persons who may lawfully claim the same."

In June of 1977, the Leaches filed a suit in circuit court seeking a decree that they own in fee simple an easement for installing and maintaining a domestic water supply line and water basin and tank located at the spring on plaintiffs' land. Plaintiffs filed an answer denying that the Leaches have a right to use the spring. Plaintiffs also filed a third-party complaint against defendant alleging that, if the Leaches do establish a right to use the spring, then defendant is in breach of her covenant in the warranty deed that the parcel was free and clear of all encumbrances. Defendant denied any breach of warranty.

* * * Plaintiffs requested jury instructions to the effect that their knowledge of the Leaches' use of the spring does not relieve the defendant of her liability under her covenant against encumbrances in her warranty deed. The trial court failed to give plaintiffs' requested instructions and, instead, gave the following instructions:

"A covenant in a deed conveying real property that the same is free from encumbrances except those listed therein is not breached by the existence upon the property described in said deed by an open, notorious and visible, physical encumbrance.

* * * The jury returned a verdict for defendant, and the circuit court entered a judgment dismissing plaintiffs' complaint.

Historically, a warranty deed would include covenants of title, which typically are the covenant of seisin, the covenant of good right to convey, the covenant of quiet enjoyment, and the covenant against encumbrances. See generally Powell, Real Property ¶ 904; Tiffany, Real Property § 999 (1975). If the warranty deed contains the grantor's covenant that the real property is free and clear of all encumbrances, that covenant protects the grantee against all encumbrances that exist as of the date of the delivery of the deed, whether the encumbrance was known or unknown to the grantee at that time.

Because the deed is a document containing the grantor's covenants, courts generally construe the deed against the grantor and in favor of the grantee.

When a grantor covenants against encumbrances, the grantor is expected to clearly state in his deed what, if any, encumbrances are accepted by the grantee, will continue in existence and are therefore excluded from the scope of his covenant against encumbrances.

* * * The warranty deed used by defendant to convey the real property to plaintiffs reads, in pertinent part, as follows:

"KNOW ALL MEN BY THESE PRESENTS, that CLIFFORD LEACH and WILMA LEACH, husband and wife, grantors, convey to OVE K. GUNNARSON and INGA–LILL GUNNARSON, husband and wife, grantees, for and in consideration of the sum of THIRTY THOUSAND DOLLARS ($30,000) to them in hand paid, all that real property situated in the County of Douglas, State of Oregon, described as:

[Legal description omitted]

and covenant to and with the grantees that it is free and clear of all encumbrances, and that grantors will warrant and defend the same against all persons who may lawfully claim the same.

"DATED this 12 day of May, 1975.

"/s/ Clifford A. Leach"

* * * ORS 93.850(3) requires a grantor who uses a warranty deed and covenants against encumbrances to expressly exclude any encumbrance or other interests from the scope of the covenant against encumbrance.[1] Otherwise, ORS 93.850(2)(b) has the effect of estopping the grantor, her heirs, successors and assigns, from asserting that the grantor had an estate or interest in the land less than that estate or interest which the deed purported to convey. Thus ORS 93.850 and the prior case law of this state require a grantor who covenants against encumbrances in a warranty deed to be liable to the grantee if the real property, as of the date of the deed, is encumbered by any interest not expressly excluded from the scope of the covenant against encumbrances.

* * * Turning now to plaintiffs' argument for reversal, plaintiffs assign as error the failure of the trial court to strike defendant's affirmative answer, alleging that (1) the irrevocable license did not constitute an encumbrance; (2) the plaintiffs knew of the Leaches' rights in the spring; and (3) the license was open, notorious and visible.

ORS 93.850 does not define the term "encumbrance" but our prior cases have done so. An "encumbrance," as the term is used in a grantor's covenant that the premises are free and clear of all encumbrances, generally means "any right to or interest in the land, subsisting in a third person, to the diminution of the value of the land, though consistent with the passing of the fee by conveyance."

* * * ORS 93.850 does not distinguish between types of encumbrances and does not state a rule regarding a grantee's knowledge of the encumbrance. Our prior decisions, however, clearly state that a grantor's covenant against encumbrances in a warranty deed protects the grantee against all encumbrances existing at the time of the delivery of the deed even if the grantee knew about the encumbrance.

In some jurisdictions, however, a different rule applies with respect to encumbrances that affect the physical condition of the real property and that are open, notorious and visible.

With respect to known easements for a public highway or a railroad right-of-way, courts are in conflict, and some have held that such an easement does not constitute a breach of the covenant against encumbrances. This court has previously considered this rule with respect to physical encumbrances in two cases: Ford v. White, [179 Or. 490, 172 P.2d 822 (1946)], and Barnum v. Lockhart, 75 Or. 528, 146 P. 975 (1915).

In *Barnum* a vendor of real property, in an installment contract, promised to provide his purchaser with a deed covenanting against encumbrances. The vendor provided the purchaser with an abstract of title which showed that the Coos Bay Roseburg Eastern Railway & Navigation Company owned a railroad right-of-way across the property. The purchas-

---

1. Oregon Revised Statutes § 93.850(3), which prescribes a statutory form for warranty deeds, provides that the covenant against encumbrances implies the following:

"(2) ... (B) That at the time of the delivery of the deed the property is free from encumbrances except as specifically set forth on the deed.

"(3) If the grantor desires to exclude any encumbrances or other interests from the scope of his covenants, such exclusions must be expressly set forth on the deed."—ed.

er refused to continue making the installment payments on the contract, claiming that the vendor's abstract did not show marketable title free and clear of encumbrances. This court held that the vendor's title was not unmarketable because the railroad right-of-way was an encumbrance of such a character that the parties could not have contemplated that the vendor would remove the encumbrance prior to conveying the deed.

The *Barnum* court relied on a rule of law stated in Maupin on Marketable Title 197 (2d ed. 1889):

> "As a general rule, the existence of an open, notorious, and visible physical encumbrance upon the estate, such as a public highway, forms no objection to the title, because it is presumed that the purchaser was to take subject to such encumbrance. Neither does such encumbrance entitle the purchaser to ... a conveyance with a covenant against the encumbrance, because it is presumed that in fixing the purchase price the existence of the encumbrance was taken into consideration." 75 Or. at 540, 146 P. 975.

* * * In Ford v. White, supra, the purchasers of real property sought to rescind their executory contract because the vendor, who had promised to convey the premises free and clear of encumbrances, furnished an abstract of title that showed that the California Oregon Power Company owned an easement on the land. The easement affected the real property only to the extent that two guy wires, attached to a pole not on the property, extended about 20 feet onto the property where they were anchored. The trial court found that the purchasers had observed the power line and the two guy wires prior to entering into the contract. Citing *Barnum,* this court held that

> "[a] covenant to convey real property free from incumbrances is not breached by the existence upon the property of an open, notorious, and visible physical incumbrance, as it is presumed that, in fixing the purchase price, the existence of the incumbrance was taken into consideration." 179 Or. at 495–96, 172 P.2d 822.

The court then concluded that the encumbrance, known to the purchasers, did not render the vendor's title unmarketable.

It is unnecessary for us to decide whether the decisions in *Barnum* and *Ford* are correct today, especially in light of ORS 93.850, because we hold that the Leaches' use of the spring on plaintiffs' property is not the type of an open and notorious encumbrance to which the *Barnum* and *Ford* decisions apply. The exception carved out in those decisions is limited to known easements for public highways, powerlines, railroads and the like. An irrevocable license to use a spring is neither so palpable nor so physically permanent as to come within the exception.

We therefore hold that the trial court erred in not striking from defendant's answer her affirmative defense alleging that the Leaches' irrevocable license was an open, notorious and visible encumbrance. We also hold that the trial court erred in not striking from defendant's answer her allegation that plaintiffs knew of the Leaches' irrevocable license.

* * * Reversed and remanded.

NOTES AND QUESTIONS

1. Historically, there were six covenants in a general warranty deed, although some states recognize less. The six covenants are:

a) The covenant of *Seisin* is the grantor's covenant that he is in fact seised of the interest the deed purports to convey.

b) The covenant of *Power to Convey* is the grantor's promise that he has the legal right to convey the land in question. Today most courts regard the covenants of seisin and power to convey as identical. One exception occurs when the grantor is seised of land subject to a valid restraint on alienation, but there are few such cases.

c) The covenant *Against Encumbrances* promises that the property is subject to no interests in third parties other than those explicitly excepted in the deed. These encumbrances might include easements, profits, real covenants, equitable servitudes, mortgages, liens, or leases. Once the court in *Leach* had determined that the property was subject to an irrevocable license, that license became an encumbrance. Courts disagree whether a violation of a building code, which is not a servitude at all, qualifies as an "encumbrance." See Monti v. Tangora, 99 Ill.App.3d 575, 54 Ill.Dec. 732, 425 N.E.2d 597 (1981), which summarizes authority for both sides. And see Bianchi v. Lorenz, 166 Vt. 555, 701 A.2d 1037 (1997), concluding that failure to obtain a certificate of occupancy as a result of the property's defective septic tank system amounted to a breach of the covenant.

d) The covenant of *Quiet Enjoyment* promises that the title conveyed is equal to that which the deed describes. The chief difference between the covenant of quiet enjoyment and the covenant of seisin is that the covenant of seisin applies to the status of the title at the time the land is conveyed and is violated, if at all, at the instant of conveyance. By contrast, the covenant of quiet enjoyment promises that the grantee will not be ousted from the land or have a successful claim asserted against her at some future time.

e) The covenant of *Warranty* is generally considered to be identical with quiet enjoyment.

f) The covenant of *Further Assurances* is the grantor's promise to execute any documents necessary to perfect the title which the deed purports to convey. Only this covenant can be enforced by specific performance as well as damages. However, the doctrine of after-acquired title, discussed in the next principal case, has rendered most applications of the covenant of further assurances superfluous.

2. Modern decisions disagree whether a purchaser who takes with actual or constructive notice of a particular encumbrance can later maintain an action for violation of the covenant against encumbrances. But the common

law rule was relatively clear: a purchaser is entitled to rely upon the covenants in a deed, and "if open, visible and notorious easements are to be excepted from the operation of the covenants, it should be the duty of the grantor to except them, and the burden should not be cast upon the grantee to show that he was not aware of them." Huyck v. Andrews, 113 N.Y. 81, 20 N.E. 581 (1889). The more recent rule not protecting purchasers with actual knowledge of an encumbrance, or where the encumbrance is clearly visible, is largely a product of attitudes that have been changed by the recording acts, which place a premium on notice.

Which rule is better? A good case can be made for the traditional rule maintained in *Leach,* particularly under the facts of that case. Many encumbrances are not on the record—such as orally created irrevocable licenses or those created by adverse possession or prescription. Perhaps both buyer and seller can see the activity on the property being conveyed. However, the seller is usually in a better position than the buyer to know what the legal status of the actors is—that is, whether they have a license and can be removed at the owner's will, a short-term lease or periodic tenancy, or have a legal right to permanent occupancy. For example, the seller in *Leach* was in a much better position than the buyer to know the facts that might indicate that the Leaches had an irrevocable license.

3. The ordinary remedy for violation of any deed covenant except the covenant of further assurances is damages. However, the majority of courts limit recovery to the purchase price or the cost of clearing the title, whichever is less. See Holmes Development v. Cook, 48 P.3d 895 (Utah 2002); MGIC Financial Corp. v. H.A. Briggs Co., 24 Wash.App. 1, 600 P.2d 573 (1979); McClure v. Turner, 165 Ga.App. 380, 301 S.E.2d 304 (1983). For more on the measurement of damages for breach of covenant of title, see R. Natelson, Modern Law of Deeds to Real Property, ch. 12 (1992).

4. Suppose that a title search shows properly recorded encumbrances that were not excepted in a general warranty deed. The general rule is that the fact of recordation and constructive notice to the purchaser does not relieve the seller from making good on the covenant. See Blissett v. Riley, 667 So.2d 1335 (Ala.1995). But suppose the grantor claims that the encumbrances have been cleared, and no one is around to assert a conflicting interest. For example, the grantor claims that a loan secured by a recorded mortgage has in fact been paid off, even though no release was ever recorded and the whereabouts of the mortgagee are unknown. Has any deed covenant been broken? At common law, a mere inconsistency or apparent defect in the record title is not a breach of the covenant against encumbrances. There must be an *actual* claimant who is determined by the court to hold an interest inconsistent with the interest granted in the warranty deed. See Colonial Capital Corp. v. Smith, 367 So.2d 490 (Ala.Civ.App.1979), which held that an unreleased mortgage in the chain of title was not a violation of any deed covenant. The covenant was not broken "unless the alleged outstanding encumbrance is valid, legal and subsisting.... A paid mortgage, although unsatisfied of record, is not an encumbrance within the meaning of the covenant."

One implication of this common law rule was that a lawsuit by a third party attempting to assert an encumbrance covered by the covenant must be defended by the grantee at its own expense. Not until it has actually been established that the warranted title was defective does the grantee have a cause of action against the grantor who gave the warranty. This rule contrasts sharply with the rule governing title insurers, which requires them to defend the insured's title against all claims arguably covered by the policy.

The same rule generally applies to the covenant of quiet enjoyment, which is breached not merely by a failure of title, but by an actual "ouster under a paramount title." Moore v. Vail, 17 Ill. 185 (1855). By contrast, the covenants of seisin and power to convey are breached any time a grantor warrants that he holds a particular title when in fact he does not, even if no one is around to claim the remaining interest. Thus the covenant is breached, if at all, at the instant of the conveyance. In Brown v. Lober, 75 Ill.2d 547, 27 Ill.Dec. 780, 389 N.E.2d 1188 (1979), the Illinois Supreme Court held that a grantor who purported to convey all the rights to the property by a warranty deed, but who in fact did not own part of the mineral rights, may have breached the covenant of seisin at the time of the conveyance. However, the covenant of quiet enjoyment and the covenant against encumbrances had not been violated, because no one had asserted a claim to the outstanding mineral rights. The court then held, however, that any action on the covenant of seisin was barred by a ten-year statute of limitations, for it had been more than ten years since the conveyance had occurred. A breach of the covenants of quiet enjoyment and against encumbrances would occur only when someone successfully asserted a paramount title.

5.   To this point you have seen two different kinds of deeds, the general warranty deed, which contains as many as six common law covenants, and the quitclaim deed, which contains no warranties whatsoever. Both the laws of most states and common real estate practice involve a variety of deed forms that fall between these two extremes. The deeds are called by various names in various places, but "grant deed" and "special warranty deed" are probably the most common.[1] The meaning of these terms varies from one state to another. In some states a "grant" deed warrants against the grantor's own acts, although not those of a grantor's predecessors. See, e.g., Cal.Civ.Code Ann. § 1113 (West 2002). Under this deed, if a grantee receives property later found to be subject to an unexcepted encumbrance, he has an action against the immediate grantor *if* that grantor had been responsible for creating the encumbrance. However, if the grantor himself received the land subject to the encumbrance it would not be covered by the warranty. Other states have statutes or judicial decisions that give the term "special warranty deed" a similar meaning. See Erlewine v. Happ, 39 Md.App. 106, 383 A.2d 82 (1978). These grant deeds, or special warranty deeds, have become common conveyancing practice in many areas, particularly where title insurance is widely used. Do you see why?

NOTE: THE QUITCLAIM DEED AS A MARKET FACILITATOR

A quitclaim deed contains no covenants for title, but it is hardly useless or unimportant. To be sure, there are many circumstances when a buyer

---

1. You will also come across "bargain and sale" deeds, which in most jurisdictions are deeds given without warranties. In a few jurisdictions a deed of bargain and sale implies a covenant against the grantor's own acts, but not against the acts of the grantor's predecessors in interest.

would be foolish to take a quitclaim deed. Someone buying vacant land in order to develop a large shopping center would be well advised to obtain every possible assurance of good title, including, if possible, a general warranty deed.

The great value of the quitclaim deed is its usefulness as a claim-settling or transaction-facilitating device. For example, suppose that a title search of Y's land reveals an outstanding easement held by X, a neighbor. X has not used the easement for many years, however, and it has been obstructed for most of that time. Chances are very good that the easement has been extinguished by abandonment or adverse possession. Nevertheless, the reference to the easement in Y's chain of title is a cloud that may affect marketability. If X conveyed the easement to Y the easement would be extinguished by merger. However, X would not want to give a warranty deed to the easement, for there is every chance that X has nothing left to convey. One way the title can be cleared is if X will quitclaim any interest she has in the easement to Y. If X is a friendly neighbor who concedes abandonment, she may do this for free, or she may have to be bribed with a small sum. In any case, clearing the title by this mechanism could be far cheaper than bringing an action to try title. Quitclaim deeds are frequently used to resolve uncertainties created by questionable claims.

§ 16.2.3 ESTOPPEL BY DEED

SCHWENN v. KAYE

California Court of Appeals (1984).
155 Cal.App.3d 949, 202 Cal.Rptr. 374.

COMPTON, ASSOCIATE JUSTICE.

Plaintiff Lillian Schwenn acquired real property in Long Beach in 1965. The property was generating oil and gas royalties pursuant to a lease with Atlantic Richfield Company (not a party to this appeal).

In 1969, plaintiff conveyed the oil and gas royalties as a gift to her daughter and son-in-law by grant deed which was duly recorded.

In 1974, plaintiff sold the real property to defendants Richard and Johanna Kaye. Neither the written offer to purchase nor the original escrow instructions made any mention of oil and gas rights, royalties or leases.

During the escrow, the preliminary title report revealed that the property was subject to the oil and gas lease, but for unexplained reasons did not reveal the 1969 conveyance of the rights in the oil and gas lease. As a result of the indication regarding the lease, an amendment to escrow was signed by plaintiff's agent to the effect that such lease would be "assigned, if assignable," (presumptively to the Kayes) after the close of escrow.

After escrow closed, Atlantic Richfield was notified of the sale and thereafter sent royalty payments to the defendants. When plaintiff complained to Atlantic Richfield that the payments belonged to her daughter and son-in-law, she was told that no further royalties would be paid without a court order determining who was entitled to the royalty payments.

In anticipation of litigation, plaintiff asked her daughter and son-in-law to reconvey the oil and gas rights to her. Plaintiff's explanation for this request was that she did not want them to be involved in litigation over a gift she had made to them.

After a court trial, title was quieted in favor of defendants Kaye on the basis of the doctrine of after-acquired title. This common law doctrine was codified in Civil Code section 1106 which provides: Where a person purports by proper instrument to grant real property in fee simple, and subsequently acquires any title, or claim of title thereto, the same passes by operation of law to the grantee, or his successors.

The thrust of plaintiff's argument on appeal is that she mistakenly allowed the doctrine of after-acquired title to govern this case when she asked her daughter to reconvey the oil and gas rights to her. Plaintiff contends that she never intended such a result and therefore, her true intent ought to have been considered by the court and equitable principles applied in order to preserve her family's interest in the royalties. We disagree. Such a result would be contrary to the law and to the policy underlying the doctrine of after-acquired title.

Civil Code section 1106 has as its genesis the common law doctrine of estoppel by deed. That doctrine generally precludes a grantor of real property from asserting, as against the grantee, any right or title in derogation of the deed. (6A Powell, The Law of Real Property, ¶ 927). The policy behind the doctrine is to protect an unwitting grantee who relies upon the good title of the grantor when the latter does not possess legal or perfect title to the property.

* * * In the case at bench, plaintiff delivered a grant deed into escrow. The operative language was typical of fee simple grant deeds: "LILLIAN SCHWENN, A WIDOW hereby GRANTS to RICHARD KAYE AND JOHANNA KAYE, HUSBAND AND WIFE AS JOINT TENANTS the following described real property...." No reservation of rights or other limiting language appeared in the deed. A fee simple title is presumed to pass by a grant of real property, unless it appears *from the grant* that a lesser estate, was intended.

* * *

Application of these general principles to the facts of the instant case make it clear that plaintiff granted defendants' fee simple title to the property including any oil and gas rights and the royalties attendant thereto. The fact that she had previously deeded away the oil and gas rights did not invalidate the subsequent grant deed, but probably would have subjected her to liability for breach of an implied covenant had she not later reacquired the rights.

When plaintiff subsequently acquired title to the oil and gas rights, the title passed to the defendants by operation of law, thereby obviating the need for bringing an action for breach of covenant.

Plaintiff's argument that the trial court erred in excluding parol evidence of her intent is none too clear. It is patently clear, however, that any reason she had for re-acquiring the oil and gas rights is simply irrelevant. The applicability of the common law doctrine or Civil Code section 1106 does not depend on the grantor's motive in re-acquiring the property. Moreover, parol evidence is not admissible to add to, detract from or vary the terms of a deed.

* * * [Plaintiff also argues] because defendants were aware of the lease from the title report and the above mentioned amendment to the escrow instructions and because defendants had constructive notice of the assignment of the lease by plaintiff to her children, defendants had no reasonable expectation of receiving the oil and gas rights.

* * * The trial court's finding that defendants, because of the recordation, had constructive notice of plaintiff's prior transfer is of no consequence since the doctrine of after-acquired title applies even if the grantee had knowledge of the deficiency.

* * *

Defendants gained the royalty rights in a perfectly legal manner. They secured title to those rights by virtue of a law designed for cases just like this. The fact that plaintiff would not have re-acquired the oil and gas rights had she known the legal consequences thereof, does not alter the fact that the parties entitled to those rights under the grant deed were defendants.

The judgment is affirmed.

NOTES AND QUESTIONS

1. Suppose that Ms. Schwenn had conveyed the property to the Kayes by a quitclaim rather than a grant deed. Would the doctrine of after-acquired title apply? The traditional answer is no. A quitclaim deed conveys whatever the grantor may happen to own on the date the quitclaim is delivered, not whatever the grantor may happen to acquire in the future. See Webster Oil Co. v. McLean Hotels, 878 S.W.2d 892 (Mo.App.1994). However, several courts have held that the doctrine of estoppel by deed *does* apply to a quitclaim deed if the language of the deed purports to convey a title that is later acquired by the grantor. For example, a deed purporting to "quitclaim any and all rights, including all mineral rights" would probably be sufficient to give the grantee the mineral rights if they were acquired by the grantor after the conveyance was made. Likewise, statutes in many states provide that a deed purporting to "quitclaim in fee simple absolute" will be sufficient to give the grantee any

after-acquired title tending to perfect a fee simple absolute. The modern trend in the cases is not to draw a hard line between quitclaim deeds and warranty deeds, but rather to look at the language of the quitclaim deed to see if it purports to give only the grantor's interest as of the moment of quitclaim, or instead gives some more "substantive" estate. See H. Hovenkamp & S. Kurtz, The Law of Property, ch. 17 (5th ed. 2000).

2.   In 1996, O granted a lease of mineral rights under Blackacre to T for a 10–year term, terminating in 2006. In 1999, O granted a lease of mineral rights under Blackacre to T–1 for a 10–year term, terminating in 2009. In 2000, O and T settled a dispute. Under the terms of the settlement agreement T surrendered all of T's rights in the mineral lease. O and T–1 now dispute who is entitled to the mineral rights through 2006 when T's lease would have terminated. See Kennedy Oil v. Lance Oil & Gas Co., Inc., 126 P.3d 875 (Wyo. 2006).

3.   The doctrine of estoppel by deed can create some complex problems for the determination of priorities under the recording acts. Some of these are discussed below.

§ 16.3   THE RECORDING ACTS

§ 16.3.1   "RECORD TITLE"—THE RECORDING ACTS AND THEIR INTERPRETATION

The common law first-in-time-first-in-right priority rule applies whenever a state's recording act is inapplicable. States have enacted one of three types of recording statutes—the notice statute, the race-notice statute, and the race statutes. For example,

Notice Statute. Mass.Gen.Ann. Laws ch. 183, § 4 (West 2002):

A conveyance of an estate in fee simple ... or a lease for a term of more than seven years from the making thereof ... shall not be valid as against any person, except the grantor or lessor, his heirs and devisees and persons having actual notice of it, unless it ... is recorded in the registry of deeds for the county or district in which the land to which it relates lies.

Race–Notice Statute. Utah Code Ann. § 57–3–103:

Each document not recorded as provided in this title is *void as against any subsequent purchaser* of the same real property, or any portion of it, if:

(1) the subsequent purchaser purchased the property *in good faith* and for a valuable consideration; and

(2) the subsequent purchaser's document is *first duly recorded.*

Race Statute. N.C.Gen.Stat. § 47–18(a) (2002):

No ... conveyance of land ... or ... lease of land for more than three years shall be valid to pass any property interest as against lien creditors or purchasers for a valuable consideration from the donor, bargainor or lessor but from the time of registration thereof in the county where the land lies, or if the land is located in more than one county, then in each county where any portion of the land lies to be effective as to land in that county. . . .

PROBLEMS

1. On May 1, 1995, O conveys Blackacre to A; A fails to record the deed.

On Sept. 3, 1995, O conveys Blackacre to B; B records on Sept. 9, 1995. B had no notice of the earlier grant to A.

On Oct. 1, 1995, A records.

Who would prevail in a title dispute between A and B in a race jurisdiction? A race-notice jurisdiction? A notice jurisdiction?

2. On May 1, 1995, O conveys Blackacre to A; A fails to record the deed.

On Sept. 3, 1995, O conveys Blackacre to B. B fails to record. B has no notice of the earlier grant to A.

On Oct. 1, 1995, A records.

On Oct. 5, 1995, B records.

Who would prevail in a title dispute between A and B in a race jurisdiction? A race-notice jurisdiction? A notice jurisdiction?

Some more challenging problems are presented later in this chapter.

HAIK v. SANDY CITY

Supreme Court of Utah (2011)
254 P.3d 171

JUSTICE NEHRING, opinion of the Court:

This case illustrates the importance of promptly recording a deed to a property right. Sandy City and the Plaintiffs ("Haik Parties") each hold deeds to the same water right. Sandy City recorded an "Agreement of Sale" for the water right in 1977, but did not record the deed until 2004. The Haik Parties purchased the same water right in 2003 and recorded their deed that year. We are asked to determine whether the district court erred when it quieted title in favor of the Haik Parties after concluding that the Haik Parties had first recorded their deed to the water right in good faith. The district court reasoned that the Agreement of Sale did not put the Haik Parties on notice of Sandy City's interest in the water right because it was an executory contract, i.e., there was no way to determine whether the contract was performed and whether the deed to the water right was delivered to Sandy City.

We conclude that the Agreement of Sale put the Haik Parties on record notice that Sandy City had an equitable interest in the water right. Whether record notice of an equitable interest in property defeats another's claim of having subsequently purchased the same property in good faith is a question of first impression. Although record notice of an equitable interest in a water right can, in some circumstances, subvert a claim of having subsequently purchased the same water right in good faith, those circumstances are not present in this case. Accordingly, we hold that the Haik Parties first recorded their deed to the disputed water right in good faith and affirm the decision of the district court.

Sandy City and the Haik Parties hold deeds to the same water right. Sandy City's chain of title is relatively straightforward. In 1974, Harold Bentley conveyed certain property, to which the disputed water right is appurtenant, to Saunders–Sweeney, Inc. About two years later, both Mr. Bentley and Saunders–Sweeney, as grantors, each signed quitclaim deeds that named Sandy City as grantee of the water right. Shortly thereafter, Mr. Bentley, Saunders–Sweeney, and the mayor of Sandy City Corporation signed an "Agreement of Sale" for the water right. The Agreement of Sale was recorded on January 14, 1977, in the Salt Lake County Recorder's Office. Sandy City thereafter received a quitclaim deed conveying the water right, but that deed was not recorded. It was simply kept in a separate file in the Sandy City Recorder's Office.

The Haik Parties' chain of title is a bit more circuitous. In 1978, Saunders–Sweeney designated the property to which the water right is appurtenant as Lot 31 of the Little Cottonwood Subdivision. That same year, Saunders–Sweeney conveyed Lot 31 to Judith Saunders. The deed was recorded. Lot 31 was subsequently conveyed, through intermediate owners, to Lynn Biddulph in 1983. The water right was not reserved in any of these conveyances.

In 1999, Saunders–Sweeney separately conveyed "all of its right, title and interest" in the water right to Ms. Biddulph by quitclaim deed, which was recorded. Shortly thereafter, Ms. Biddulph filed an application with the Utah State Engineer for a permanent change of water, which was approved. In response to the change application, Sandy City wrote a letter to the State Engineer expressing concern "if any activity to expand or further change the water right were to take place," but Sandy City did not claim ownership of the water right or otherwise contest Ms. Biddulph's ownership of the water right. Ms. Biddulph then expended money and effort to maintain the water right and related facilities.

In 2003, Ms. Biddulph conveyed the water right by quitclaim deed to LWC, L.L.C. Shortly thereafter, LWC conveyed the water right by quitclaim deed to Kevin Tolton (one of the Haik Parties). In October 2003, Kevin Tolton then conveyed the water right by quitclaim deed to the Haik Parties as tenants in common. The Haik Parties recorded the deed on December 10, 2003.

Before the water right was conveyed to the Haik Parties, Mark Haik, a professional title examiner, searched the Salt Lake County Recorder's records concerning the water right. Mr. Haik did not locate the 1977 Agreement of Sale because his search started with records beginning in 1983 or 1984. Had Mr. Haik searched back to 1977, he likely would have found the [recorded] Agreement of Sale.

In 2004, the Haik Parties filed an application with the Utah Division of Water Rights to change the diversion point of the water right. In an effort to oppose the application, Sandy City investigated the water right and located the Agreement of Sale from 1977. Sandy City then asked the Sandy City Recorder to find the referenced water right deed. The city recorder quickly located the original deed in the Sandy City Recorder's Office. At Sandy City's request, the city recorder recorded the deed in April 2004. But when Sandy City sought to update title with the Division of Water Rights, its request was rejected.

The Haik Parties filed an action to quiet title to the water right. Both parties moved for summary judgment. The district court granted the Haik Parties' motion for summary judgment and denied Sandy City's cross-motion for summary judgment. The district court found that the Haik Parties (1) recorded their deed before Sandy City and (2) purchased the water right in good faith because they did not have notice of Sandy City's unrecorded deed to the water right. The court reasoned that even though the Agreement of Sale referenced the disputed water right, the Agreement of Sale did not put the Haik Parties on record notice of Sandy City's interest in the water right because it was merely an executory contract with "no way to determine whether performance under the agreement actually occurred." Sandy City now appeals . . .

The issue in this case is whether the Agreement of Sale put the Haik Parties on record notice of Sandy City's unrecorded interest in the disputed water right. The Haik Parties contend that the Agreement of Sale did not impart record notice because it is merely an executory contract, i.e., it is impossible to know from the text of the Agreement of Sale whether it was executed and whether the deed was actually delivered. Sandy City contends that the Agreement of Sale imparted record notice because it unambiguously describes a conveyance of the water right to Sandy City. Alternatively, Sandy City contends that even if the Agreement of Sale is an executory contract, it nevertheless put the Haik Parties on record notice that Sandy City possessed an equitable interest in the water right.

It is unclear whether the Agreement of Sale was an executory contract or whether it was fully performed. Nevertheless, we conclude that the Agreement of Sale put the Haik Parties on record notice that Sandy City had an equitable interest in the water right. There are circumstances where record notice of an equitable interest in property may subvert a subsequent purchaser's claim of having purchased the same property in good faith. But those circumstances are not present here for three reasons: (1) the Haik Parties reasonably believed they had a clear and inviolate chain of title to the disputed water right; (2) nearly twenty-seven years had passed since the Agreement of Sale was recorded and Sandy City had still not recorded its deed to the water right; and (3) the Haik Parties' predecessors-in-interest maintained the water right and filed a change application in 1999, yet Sandy City never contested ownership to the water right. Accordingly, we hold that the Haik Parties purchased their deed to the water right in good faith. We therefore affirm the district court's grant of summary judgment in favor of the Haik Parties on these alternative grounds ...

Utah is a race-notice jurisdiction. Under Utah's Recording Act and Utah's Water and Irrigation Act,[2] a subsequent purchaser for value prevails over a previous purchaser if the subsequent purchaser (1) takes title in good faith and (2) records before the previous purchaser. There is no dispute that the Haik Parties were the first to record their deed to the disputed water right. Thus, the only issue is whether the Haik Parties took title to the water right in good faith.

"To be in good faith, a subsequent purchaser must take [title to] the property without notice of a prior, unrecorded interest in the property." This court recognizes two types of notice: (1) actual notice and (2) constructive notice. Actual notice arises from actual knowledge "of an unrecorded interest or infirmity in the grantor's title." Constructive notice can be either inquiry or record notice. To be on inquiry notice, a person must have "[actual] knowledge of certain facts and circumstances that are sufficient to give rise to a duty to inquire further." But inquiry notice "does not arise from a record." Record notice "results from a record or ... is imputed by the recording statutes." Thus, purchasers of real property are charged with having record notice of the contents of recorded documents.

Because it is undisputed that the Haik Parties had neither actual nor constructive inquiry notice of Sandy City's interest in the water right,[3] the only question is whether the Agreement of Sale put the Haik Parties on constructive record notice that Sandy City possessed an unrecorded deed to the water right ...

In Utah, real estate documents filed with the county recorder "impart notice to all persons *of their contents.*" A real estate "document" is defined as "every instrument in writing, including every conveyance, affecting, purporting to affect, describing, or otherwise concerning any right, title, or interest in real property." Thus, the Agreement of Sale imparted to the Haik Parties notice of its contents....

Where a party has record notice of a contract but the degree to which the contract has been performed is ambiguous, we will treat that contract

2. Utah's Water and Irrigation Act § 73–1–12 (Supp. 2010) provides:

Every deed of a water right which shall not be recorded as provided in this title shall be *void as against any subsequent purchaser, in good faith* and for a valuable consideration, of the same water right, or any portion thereof, where his own deed shall be *first duly recorded.*

3. Inquiry notice is not at issue in this case because the Haik Parties did not have actual knowledge of any facts, such as the existence of the Agreement of Sale, giving rise to a duty to inquire further. *See J.B. Ranch,* 966 P.2d at 838 ("[I]nquiry notice arises from knowledge of certain facts and circumstances, not from records."). Had the Haik Parties known of the Agreement of Sale, they would have had actual knowledge about the possible defect in title and would have been on inquiry notice to inquire further. And upon further inquiry, it is likely that the Haik Parties would have discovered Sandy City's deed to the water right. But because the Haik Parties did not have any knowledge of the Agreement of Sale, our inquiry is limited to whether the *contents of the Agreement of Sale* would have imparted notice to the Haik Parties of Sandy City's unrecorded deed to the water right.

as executory. Here, Sandy City recorded the Agreement of Sale in 1977. However, ... nothing in the recorded Agreement of Sale sufficiently specified whether Sandy City had performed its agreement. Moreover, the degree of any such performance could not be ascertained by the Haik Parties due to Sandy City's failure to record the deed to the water right. Nonetheless, the recorded Agreement of Sale put the Haik Parties on record notice that Sandy City had agreed to purchase the water right at one time—regardless of whether the agreement was fully performed or remained executory. Thus, at the very least, the Haik Parties had record notice of an executory contract regarding the water rights. Therefore, for purposes of record notice, we must treat a contract as executory if it is ambiguous whether it is executory or has been fully performed. This conclusion, however, does not end our inquiry.

Sandy City contends that even if the Agreement of Sale is an executory contract, it nevertheless put the Haik Parties on record notice that Sandy City possessed an equitable interest in the water right. Sandy City argues that under the doctrine of equitable conversion, "the vendee of an executory land sale contract holds equitable ownership of the property but not legal title." Thus, "[e]ven though the vendor may retain title to the property, that title is effectively held for the benefit of the vendee, to whom it will pass if the contract is carried out."[4] And the vendee "acquires the equitable interest in the property at the moment the contract is created and is thereafter treated as the owner of the [property]."[5] Sandy City argues that like other instruments affecting an interest in real property—such as an option contract, mechanics lien, or mortgage—the Agreement of Sale put the Haik Parties on notice that Sandy City had an equitable interest in the water right, and that notice of this equitable interest defeats the Haik Parties' claim to having purchased the water right in good faith.

We agree that the Agreement of Sale put the Haik Parties on record notice that Sandy City had equitable interest in the water right *at the time the Agreement of Sale was recorded.* But we have not previously addressed whether notice of an equitable interest in property will defeat a subsequent purchaser's claim of having obtained title to the property in good faith. Assuming without deciding that there are circumstances under which record notice of an equitable interest in property may subvert a subsequent purchaser's claim to having purchased the property in good faith, those circumstances are not present here. Thus, we hold that the Haik Parties took title to the water right in good faith.

First, we find it telling that Sandy City recorded the Agreement of Sale in 1977 but failed to record the deed to the water right for nearly twenty-seven years. This fact is particularly relevant given the statutory requirement that water rights be recorded by deed. Utah Code section 73–1–10 provides that "[a] water right ... shall be transferred *by deed* in

---

4. *Cannefax v. Clement,* 818 P.2d 546, 549–550 (Utah 1991).

5. *Lach v. Deseret Bank,* 746 P.2d 802, 805 (Utah Ct.App.1987).

substantially the same manner as is real estate," and clearly states that "*[t]he deed must be recorded* in the office of the recorder of the county where the point of diversion of the water is located and in the county where the water is used." Moreover, section 73–1–12 warns that "*[e]very deed of a water right which shall not be recorded* . . . shall be void as against any subsequent purchaser, in good faith and for a valuable consideration, of the same water right, or any portion thereof, where his own *deed* shall be first duly recorded." This statutory language, combined with the fact that Sandy City had not recorded its deed to the water right more than twenty-seven years after the Agreement of Sale was recorded, weighs heavily in favor of concluding that the Agreement of Sale was never executed and the deed never delivered to Sandy City. That a recorded deed will destroy a subsequent purchaser's claim of having purchased the same property in good faith could not be more clear. It falls, therefore, to the grantee of the water right to take responsibility for protecting its legal interests by recording the deed.

Second, we find it important that both the Salt Lake County Recorder's Office and the Utah Division of Water Rights (or "UDWR") showed that the Haik Parties had a clear and inviolate chain of title to the water right. As to the Salt Lake County Recorder's Office, the records show a complete chain of title from Lot 31—the land to which the Haik water right was appurtenant—to the Haik Parties. The records show the following: In 1974, the land that would eventually become Lot 31 was conveyed to Saunders–Sweeney and the deed was recorded. In 1978, the land was conveyed to Judith Saunders and the deed was recorded. In 1983, the land was conveyed to Lynn Biddulph and the deed was recorded. Importantly, the water right was not reserved in any of these conveyances. Utah Code section 73–1–11 states in relevant part:

> A water right appurtenant to land shall pass to the grantee of the land unless the grantor:
>
> (a) specifically reserves the water right or any part of the water right in the land conveyance document;
>
> (b) conveys a part of the water right in the land conveyance document; or
>
> (c) conveys the water right in a separate conveyance document prior to or contemporaneously with *the execution of the land conveyance document.*

And in 1999, Saunders–Sweeney separately conveyed "all of its right, title and interest" in the water right to Lynn Biddulph (the Haik Parties' predecessor-in-interest) and the deed was recorded. Thus, under Utah Code section 73–1–11, the Haik Parties had a clear chain of title to the water right unless the right was "convey[ed] . . . in a separate conveyance document prior to or contemporaneously with the execution of the land conveyance document. [citation omitted]. And the only possible conveyance was the Agreement of Sale. But as we explained above, it is ambiguous whether the Agreement of Sale was performed or was merely an executory contract, particularly since twenty-seven years had passed since the Agreement of Sale was recorded and no deed to the water right had yet been recorded. Thus, it would have been reasonable for the Haik Parties to conclude that the Agreement of Sale was never executed and, therefore, the water right passed to the Haik Parties' predecessor-in-interest as an appurtenance to the land conveyed by Saunders–Sweeney in 1978.

This conclusion is particularly compelling considering that Saunders–Sweeney, a named grantor on the Agreement of Sale, separately conveyed "all of its right, title and interest" in the water right in 1999. Had the Agreement of Sale been performed and the deed to the water right been delivered to Sandy City, it would be reasonable to conclude that Saunders–Sweeney would not have transferred the water right again in 1999. In other words, it would be reasonable to conclude that Saunders–Sweeney did not twice convey the same water right. Likewise, even assuming Saunders–Sweeney did twice convey the same water right—once in the 1977 Agreement of Sale and once in the 1999 conveyance—it would be reasonable to conclude that Sandy City would have contested the 1999 conveyance. Yet when Lynn Biddulph filed a change application for the water right in 1999, Sandy City wrote a letter to the State Engineer that merely expressed concern "if any activity to expand or further change the water right were to take place," but did not claim ownership of the water right or otherwise contest Ms. Biddulph's ownership of the water right.

Likewise, the records from the Utah Division of Water Rights showed a complete chain of title to the water right. Although UDWR records do not impart record notice or warrant or guarantee title to water rights, the fact that the UDWR records corroborate the official Salt Lake County Recorder's Office records weighs in favor of finding that the Haik Parties would have been justified in believing they had a clear and inviolate chain of title to the disputed water right.

Third, we find it persuasive that the Haik Parties and their predecessor-in-interest, Ms. Biddulph, expended money and effort to maintain the water right, and that Sandy City knew Ms. Biddulph filed a change application for the water right, yet Sandy City never asserted its own interest in the water right. Again, if Sandy City had obtained a deed to the water right under the Agreement of Sale, it would be reasonable to conclude that Sandy City would have contested such efforts to maintain the water right. Instead, when Ms. Biddulph filed the change application, Sandy City did not assert ownership of the right, but stated in a letter to the State Engineer that it did "not have any concerns" if the change application "is merely a correction in the point of diversion to reflect historical water use practices." Thus, even with record notice of the Agreement of Sale, it would have been reasonable for the Haik Parties to conclude that Sandy City no longer had an equitable interest in the water right . . .

We hold that under the facts presented in this case, the Haik Parties were the first to record their deed to the disputed water right in good faith. We therefore affirm the district court's entry of summary judgment quieting title to the water right in favor of the Haik Parties.

NOTES AND QUESTION

1. The *Haik* court holds that even though the recorded agreement of sale gives constructive record notice of the Sandy City claim, the Haik Parties are still bona fide purchasers who first duly recorded. Make sure you fully understand why that is true?

2. In a notice-race state (and presumably race states as well), the question arises whether the subsequent bona fide purchaser for value first duly records when that purchaser does not have his or her entire chain of title on the record first. For example, suppose:

    a. On May 1, O deeds Blackacre to A who does not record.

    b. On June 1, O deeds Blackacre to B, a bona fide purchaser for value, who does not record.

    c. On August 1, B deeds Blackacre to C, a bona fide purchase for value, who immediately records the B–C deed.

    d. On September 1, A records the O–A deed.

    e. Thereafter the O–B deed is recorded.

In this sequence, both B and C are bona fide purchasers for value but the O–B deed (which is in C's chain of title) was not recorded prior to the O–A deed being recorded. If a dispute arises between A and C, can C win when A recorded the O–A deed before the O–B deed was recorded? In Messersmith v. Smith, 60 N.W.2d 276 (ND 1953), the court held that C did not satisfy the "first recording" requirement in a notice-race statute because C's entire chain of title was not recorded before A recorded the O–A deed. The court did so even though in fact an improperly notarized deed from O–B had been recorded. Under North Dakota law the recorder was not entitled to record an improperly notarized deed. Thus, even though the O–B deed was filed with the land records offices it was treated as if it were not part of the public land records.

Some states have attempted to solve the problem of hidden defects in a recorded deed by statutes such as this one:

Cal.Civ.Code § 1207 (West 2002). *Defectively executed instruments; validity.*

> Any instrument affecting the title to real property, one year after the same has been copied into the proper book of record, kept in the office of any county recorder, imparts notice of its contents to subsequent purchasers and encumbrancers, notwithstanding any defect, omission, or informality in the execution of the instrument, or in the certificate of acknowledgement thereof, or the absence of any such certificate....

Would this statute have changed the result in *Messersmith?* The North Dakota legislature responded to *Messersmith* by passing a similar statute, but

without the one-year waiting period. See N.D.Cent.Code § 47–19–41 (2001), providing that the "record of all instruments whether or not the same were entitled to be recorded shall be deemed valid and sufficient as the legal record thereof."

Not even statutes such as that cited above solves the problem of a recorded deed that was never delivered to the grantee. In this case, of course, the deed itself conveys no property interest and is invalid even as between the original grantor and grantee. Again, however, the problem is the same: the absence of delivery does not appear on the face of the recorded document. The courts help out a bit by creating a presumption that a recorded instrument has been delivered. See Chapter 15 supra. The Uniform Simplification of Land Transfers Act, § 3–402(c), goes one step further and makes the presumption conclusive if it has been recorded more than three years.

3.   Suppose O conveys Blackacre to A by a warranty deed. Thereafter O conveys Blackacre to B by a quitclaim deed and B records. Is B on notice of a defect in O's title by virtue of taking by quitclaim rather than warranty deed? The answer is no in the overwhelming majority of states, although there are a few outliers decided generally on the grounds that by O's giving and B's accepting a quitclaim deed, neither shows great confidence in the quality of O's title. See generally, Amer. Law Prop. § 17.16.

Assuming B will prevail as against A, can A in turn claim damages from O for breach of any warranty under the warranty deed? The most likely deed covenants on which A might sue would be the covenant of quiet enjoyment and the covenant of warranty. But, according to American Law of Property § 12.129 at 467, these covenants are only violated when the paramount title that interferes with the grantee existed *on the date of the conveyance to the grantee*. Here B's claim, based upon O's wrongful act, arises after the conveyance from O–A. This would suggest A cannot recover from O. And, arguably, she shouldn't, because A's title would have been good against B had A done what was expected of her, namely record the O–A deed. Can you make an argument that courts today should ignore the American Law of Property position?

§ 16.3.2   THE TITLE SEARCH AND THE ABSTRACT OF TITLE

In the nineteenth and early twentieth centuries searching title was almost exclusively the job of lawyers—in fact, in many areas it was the prerogative of a special group of lawyers called conveyancers. Today, the lawyer's role has been greatly reduced by the title company or abstract company and its specialists. However, lawyers still search titles in many states. In others, title or abstract companies hire lawyers to supervise title searching. Furthermore, in most states only lawyers may give legal opinions about the quality of a particular title.

The traditional grantor-grantee index that is described in the following paragraphs has given way in many states to the publicly prepared tract index, which is organized by parcel of land rather than by the names

of grantors and grantees. More significantly, the *privately* prepared land records kept by title and abstract companies are usually organized by tract. These private "title plants" are generally not official.[6] The private records generally also take advantage of modern data retrieval systems such as microfilm or computers that make the title searcher's job much easier.

The title search begins in the office of the registry of deeds, sometimes called the office of the recorder, county recorder, or clerk. The registry is a governmental office, generally operated by the county. It contains a complete copy of every document affecting title to real property that has been recorded there. Note, it does *not* necessarily contain a copy of every document affecting title to real property in that county. As a general rule, the only penalty for failure to record is possible subsequent loss of the interest. Most states prescribe by statute the documents that are *entitled* to be recorded. These typically include deeds, wills, contracts affecting the use or sale of land, leases, mortgages, deeds of trust, and other financial instruments, mechanics' liens, powers of attorney, lis pendens, or other documents alerting people to the fact that title to a particular piece of property is in dispute, and court judgments affecting title.[7]

As documents come into the registry office they are assigned a number and stamped with the date and time of their recordation. Then they are copied (formerly by hand, now by photocopy machine) and the originals are returned to their owners. The copies are then collected and eventually bound into a volume. In many offices, particularly, the larger ones, different types of documents may be bound in different volumes—for example, mortgages and other financial instruments may be in one set of volumes and deeds in another. Each volume is given a number, and the documents within each volume are paginated throughout the volume.

The documents are also indexed, optimistically, within a day or two after they are submitted for recordation. The delay between recording and indexing may be longer. However, most registry offices maintain a "daily sheet" or "current entries" sheet which describes recently recorded documents that have not yet been indexed. A traditional recording system indexes each document twice—once alphabetically by the last name of the grantor, and once by the last name of the grantee.

The title search in a registry having a grantor-grantee index system begins with the grantee index, which in most offices looks something like this:

---

6. There is one important exception. After the Cook County Records were destroyed in the great Chicago fire of 1871, the records of the Chicago Title Company were legislatively declared to be the official records of the county.

7. In many jurisdictions, particularly large metropolitan areas, wills may be recorded in offices other than the registry of deeds, such as the probate or surrogates courts. Further, federal tax liens are generally recorded in the regional office of the district directors of the Internal Revenue Service. A complete title search generally includes an examination of these collateral records.

Grantee Index Years 1960–1969

Grantee's Names beginning with Na

Grantee	Grantor	No.	Date Filed	Book & Page	Instrmnt.	Brief Legal Descrip.
Nagle, Ralph	ABC Homes, Inc.	3342	4–4–60	467/p. 1134	Deed	Meadowlane Subd., Block G, lot 12
Nathanson, Nate	Brandeis, Louie	3671	5–3–61	467/p. 1430	Deed	S½ of NE¼ Sec. 16, R3W, T2N
Nagler, Damir	Steiger, Stephanie	4490	8–27–64	470/p. 113	Deed	Rolling Hills Subd., Block 5, Phase 3, Lot 16
Nalo, Audrie	Bird, Gail	4990	5–5–65	471/p. 546	Lease	Cherokee Acre Subd., Block 3, Lot 3
Naomi, Stephen	Honeychuck Plmb. & Htg.	5123	5–5–65	471/p. 549	Easement Deed	Dwntwn., Block 9, Lot 3, 234 Congress

The top of this index page shows that it covers documents that were recorded during the years 1960–1969. Indexes are started over periodically, or else they become unwieldy. In large urban areas they may be started over annually, in more rural areas perhaps every five or ten years. In the grantee index, the grantee's names are in roughly alphabetical order. They are not alphabetized precisely, because the entries are made manually as new documents are recorded, and sometimes there is no room for a new entry to be wedged between existing entries. The indexes commonly assign a page or two to all grantees whose names begin with the same two letters—one page for Ha, another page for He, etc.

Suppose that your client is buying a parcel of land and you must investigate whether the grantor has good title. The grantor's name is Damir Nagler and the property your client is purchasing is lot 16, Block 5, phase 3, Rolling Hills Subdivision, Van Buren County. When you arrive at the registry office you will begin with the most recent grantee index and look under Na for Nagler. If you don't find the grantor's name in the most recent index, you will go to the previous index and continue back until you find the name. Remember, although your client is the buyer and Damir Nagler is the grantor, you want to find when Nagler was a grantee—every grantor was once a grantee, or else something is wrong!

In this case Damir Nagler acquired the land in 1964 by deed, from someone named Stephanie Steiger. The column entitled ''book and page'' tells you where you can find a copy of that deed. The column entitled ''Brief Legal Description'' gives you sufficient information to determine that this particular deed covers the same property that your client is buying. Not all grantor-grantee indexes contain a column describing the land. In that case the only way you can be sure that the parcel acquired by Nagler in 1964 is the same parcel your client wants is to examine the full copy of the 1964 deed. If Nagler was a real wheeler and dealer who acquired ten pieces of property in the 1960's, you may have to look at ten documents before you find the right one.

In order to do a complete title search you will have to go back through the grantee index earlier than 1964. In most jurisdictions title searchers go back 40 to 60 years in order to investigate the title, and in some they go all the way back to the original patent from the sovereign. Now you will repeat the process, using Ms. Steiger's name as grantee. You will begin with the 1960–1969 index to ascertain whether Ms. Steiger acquired the property during 1960–1964. If not, you will look at the 1950–1959 index, then at the 1940–1949 index, etc.

You repeat this process again and again, and finally find a grantor named Fred Smith, who acquired the property in 1906. Since you are searching in the late 1980's, that is long enough. Now the easiest part of your search is over. You have ascertained that every grantor in the chain of title was in fact someone else's grantee. However you have not yet determined whether any of those grantors conveyed away interests inconsistent with the interest your client thinks he is acquiring. Now you must examine the grantor index:

Grantor Index Years 1930–1939

Grantor's Names beginning with Sm

Grantor	Grantee	No.	Date Filed	Book & Page	Instrmnt.	Brief Legal Descrip.
Smathers, Henry	Smathers, Irene	856	1–16–30	59/p. 349	Deed	N½ of NE¼ Sec. 3, R2E, T3N
Smith, Arthur	Wiliams, Sheldon	902	2–3–31	59/p. 440	Lease	Dwntwn. Pine & Rockridge
Smythe, Francis	VanKamp, Lillie	959	5–5–31	60/p. 12	Mech's Lien	Westwood Subd., Block G, Lot 2
Smith, Fred	Anderson, Bruce	1015	2–13–32	61/p. 330	Mtge. to Sec. $10,000 note	Rolling Hills Subd., Block 5, Phase 3, Lot 16

The grantor index looks much like the grantee index, except that it is indexed alphabetically by grantors. Now you will search forward in time instead of backwards. You will begin with Smith, who acquired his interest in 1906. You will look through the 1900–1909 index first to see if Smith conveyed away any interest inconsistent with the interest your client is acquiring. If you find none, you will look in the 1910–1919 index, then in the 1920–29 index, etc.

Suppose you find that in 1932 Smith borrowed $10,000 secured by a mortgage on the property in question to someone named Anderson. Since your client does not believe he is acquiring the property subject to a $10,000 mortgage, you must now find evidence that this mortgage has been released. In order to find that evidence you will look for a release in the grantor index under Anderson's name, beginning in 1932. (Some grantor-grantee index systems index releases by both the grantor's and grantee's names, while others list them only under the names of the grantors.) If you don't find the release in the 1930–1939 index, you will look under Anderson's name in the 1940–1949 index. Suppose there you find a full release recorded in 1948. In that case, the 1932 mortgage and the 1948 release cancel each other out. As you proceed up through the list of grantors to the present you must find a release to offset each inconsistent interest created. If an interest appears that has no offsetting release, you may have discovered a cloud on the title, unless your client's deed makes the property subject to that particular interest.

Your title search is still not complete. Now you must carefully examine every document in the record chain of title. You will look for inconsistencies in the property descriptions, faulty signatures, acknowledgements or other legally required formalities, and references to possible inconsistent interests that are not recorded. See the *Guerin* case below.

Title searching is generally much easier in those offices and private title plants that have tract or parcel indexes. The tract index assigns one page (or a series of pages) to each tract of land in the county. For example, the top of a page may read "Meadowlark Subdivision, Block D, lot 16." Then on that page in chronological order will be listed all recorded documents affecting the title to that particular lot. The next page in the book will cover lot 17 in the same block of the same subdivision, and so on. It is theoretically possible to do the preliminary title search under a tract index simply by examining a single page, although the individual documents must still be inspected. Tract index searching becomes a little more complicated when land is subdivided or sold in different configurations than it had been previously. It is also a little harder from the recording officer's point of view, for occasionally he will have to interpret a property description in order to identify the parcel to which it applies. Most of these problems have been worked out, however, and the superiority of the tract index system seems to be established.

In an attempt to rectify some of the perceived deficiencies in the grantor/grantee system and the tract index system, another system—the parcel identifier ("PIN") system—has been proposed. Under a PIN system, the county recorder assigns each parcel of land a unique identifying parcel number, say 12345678. Utilization of a unique identifying number eliminates the need for describing land by grantor/grantee. By referencing the location of a parcel though a unique number, the PIN system replaces the metes and bounds legal description used in the tract system. Furthermore, the unique number allows a "parcel to be searched, conveyed, mortgaged, or otherwise affected" as in the existing methods.[8] Additionally, the unique identifying number carries the history of the parcel's chain of title, and in so doing, eliminates the need to rely upon names of predecessors in title. Despite its straightforwardness and efficient means

---

8. Arthur Gaudio, Electronic Real Estate Records: A Model for Action, 24 W. New Eng. L. Rev. 271, 296 (2002).

to improve upon the existing methods, the majority of states have yet to adopt the PIN system relying instead on old indexing practices.[9] Resistance to the PIN system stems from recording being a localized, political process.[10] Furthermore, conversion to a PIN system can be daunting and financially challenging.

In many states, particularly where the use of title insurance is not universal, the lawyer may be called upon to examine an "abstract of title." The abstract is a document that gives the title history of a particular parcel of land and therefore furnishes the buyer with evidence concerning the quality of the title.

The abstract generally begins with a legal description of the property, usually including a map that identifies the property's shape and location. Then in chronological order it gives a detailed description of every recorded document affecting the title, usually beginning with the original grant from the sovereign. If the abstract is stored in a safe place by the buyer and can be produced when the property is resold, it can facilitate the subsequent title search, for the searcher can use the existing abstract as a guide and perhaps simply bring it up to date.

For fuller discussions of the mechanics of searching title and some of the problems that can arise, see H. Hovenkamp & S. Kurtz, The Law of Property § 17.3 (5th ed. 2000); Stroup, The Unreliable Record Title, 60 N.Dak.L.Rev. 203 (1984); Cross, The Record "Chain of Title" Hypocrisy, 57 Colum.L.Rev. 787 (1957).

§ 16.3.3 PERSONS PROTECTED BY THE RECORDING ACTS, AND THE CONSEQUENCES OF BEING UNPROTECTED

Almost every state's recording statutes limit the classes of people who are protected by them. In general, the statutes protect "bona fide purchasers." The concept of the bona fide purchaser involves two things: 1) the purchaser must have given something of value in exchange for the interest; and 2) the purchaser must not have had notice, whether actual or constructive, of prior claims.

A. Bona Fide Purchasers for Value

Two extremes are relatively easy to identify. The purchaser who pays the fair market value of the property he receives is clearly protected by the statutes. By contrast, the gratuitous donee, who receives property as a gift, is not protected.[11] Neither are heirs or devisees. In between are many ambiguous situations.

---

9. Id.

10. Id. at 284.

11. One exception is Colorado, whose recording act protects subsequent donees as well as purchasers. See Eastwood v. Shedd, 166 Colo. 136, 442 P.2d 423 (1968), interpreting Colo.Rev. Stat. § 38–35–109.

Courts do not frequently inquire into the substantive sufficiency of the consideration. For example, it has been widely held that a person can be a bona fide purchaser protected by the recording acts even though he paid less than the fair market value of the property that he received, as long as the consideration was not outrageously inadequate. See Phillips v. Latham, 523 S.W.2d 19 (Tex.Civ.App.1975). By contrast, merely nominal consideration or consideration recited as "my love and affection" is inadequate. Does this mean that deeds, which do not need consideration to be binding, must nevertheless recite that consideration has been paid?

The more problematic cases involve various kinds of creditors who acquire an interest in property either as security for, or in satisfaction of, a debt. Once again, the creditor who takes a mortgage as security for a loan has clearly given value and is protected under the recording acts. But suppose a mortgagee takes his interest as security for a *pre-existing* debt. Suppose, for example, that Smith owes Jones $1000 and is seriously in default on his payments. Although Jones would be entitled to obtain a judgment against Smith immediately, he and Smith instead work out an arrangement under which Smith will pay off the loan in several monthly installments. In exchange for this forbearance from suit Smith gives Jones a mortgage on certain real property that Smith owns. If Smith defaults on this new agreement Jones will be able to foreclose on the mortgage. Assuming it is properly recorded, Jones's mortgage will probably be protected under the recording acts. Most courts hold that if Jones actually gives up a valuable right—for example, if Smith and Jones prepare a new agreement which replaces the old one and postpones the date of payment—then the acquisition of the mortgage was "for value," and Jones will be protected under the recording acts. But see Gabel v. Drewrys Limited, U.S.A., Inc., 68 So.2d 372 (Fla.1953), holding that if the creditor merely gave an indefinite promise to postpone suit "for the time being," there was no legally enforceable forbearance by the creditor. As a result, he could not be treated as a "purchaser" under the recording act.

B. Bona Fide Purchasers Without Notice

GUERIN v. SUNBURST OIL & GAS CO.

Supreme Court of Montana (1923).
68 Mont. 365, 218 P. 949.

HOLLOWAY, J.

* * *

In 1921 Mrs. Mary T. Thornton owned 320 acres of land in Toole county. On August 26 of that year she gave to Gordon Campbell a lease upon the land, by the terms of which the lessee was, or his successors and assigns were, authorized to go upon the premises and explore for oil, gas, hydrocarbons, and other minerals, and, if any such minerals were discovered, to extract and market the same, paying to the lessor a specified royalty. The lessee agreed that, within 3 months from the date of the lease, he would commence drilling operations in the northeast part of the Rocky Ridge dome—a territory which embraced the Thornton land—and within 24 months from the date of the lease would commence sinking a well upon the leased premises. That lease was not recorded. On December 8, 1921, Mrs. Thornton gave to James L. Rock an option to purchase her land, but the option was made subject to the Campbell lease. The option was duly recorded on December 9 in the Miscellaneous Record Book of Toole county. In May, 1922, Campbell assigned his lease to L.C. Stevenson, and Stevenson in turn assigned it to the Sunburst Oil & Gas Company. Each of the assignments was duly recorded. On June 6, 1922, Mrs. Thornton conveyed her land to Mrs. M.M. Guerin by warranty deed. In August following the Sunburst Oil & Gas Company went upon the land and commenced to explore for oil and gas, when this action was commenced by Mrs. Guerin to secure an injunction restraining the company from continuing its operations. In its answer to the complaint, the defendant set forth the foregoing matters, and alleged that it was carrying forward its explorations pursuant to the terms of the Campbell lease, and that Mrs. Guerin had purchased the land with notice of the existence of that lease. After a hearing the trial court denied the application for an injunction, and caused a judgment to be entered dismissing the complaint. From that judgment, and from the order denying an injunction, plaintiff appealed.

The ultimate question for determination is: Did plaintiff purchase the Thornton land with notice of the outstanding Campbell lease? As observed heretofore, that lease was not recorded; but section 6938, Revised Codes 1921, provides, "An unrecorded instrument is valid as between the parties and those who have notice thereof," and that notice may be either actual or constructive. The trial court concluded from the evidence before it that Mrs. Guerin "purchased with constructive notice," at least, "of the outstanding rights in defendant under said lease," and it is the correctness of that conclusion which is challenged by counsel for plaintiff. The trial court relied upon the record of the Rock option and the assignments of the Campbell lease, and the immediate question is: Did the record of those instruments, or the record of any of them, impart constructive notice to Mrs. Guerin of the existence and contents of the lease itself?

* * *

Since the option was an instrument entitled to be recorded, and was recorded as prescribed by law, it imparted constructive notice of its contents to Mrs. Guerin, who was a subsequent purchaser of the property affected by the option, from the time it was filed with the county clerk of Toole county on December 9, 1921. One who purchases land from the owner, after the recording of an option given by the owner to another person to purchase the same land, takes with constructive notice of the option, and cannot claim to be an innocent purchaser.

The option recited that the right to purchase given to Rock was "subject, however, to one certain oil and gas lease given in favor of Gordon Campbell," and that recital constituted a part of the contents of the option.... Mrs. Guerin was chargeable, not merely with notice that such a recital was contained in the option; she was chargeable also with notice of all material facts which an inquiry suggested by that recital would have disclosed. She was bound to make inquiry of the owner of the lease, and, if she failed to do so, she is chargeable with notice of all that she would have learned, if she had pursued the inquiry to the full extent to which it led.

In other words, she was chargeable with notice of the contents of the Campbell lease, though it was not recorded, and she could not rely upon the representation by Mrs. Thornton that there was not any outstanding lease upon the property. If Mrs. Guerin had caused proper search of the records to be made before she purchased, she would have known of the defendant's right to prospect the property for oil and gas. If she did not cause such search to be made, she cannot invoke the aid of a court of equity to relieve her from the consequences of her own want of ordinary care and prudence.

* * *

The judgment and order are affirmed.

NOTES AND QUESTIONS

1. Long before the passage of the recording acts, the law of both real and personal property had developed mechanisms for protecting bona fide purchasers without notice of a former infirmity in a legal transaction. As Chief Justice Marshall explained in Fletcher v. Peck, 10 U.S. (6 Cranch) 87, 133–34 (1810):

> If a suit be brought to set aside a conveyance obtained by fraud, and the fraud be clearly proved, the conveyance will be set aside, as between the parties; but the rights of third persons, who are purchasers without notice, for a valuable consideration, cannot be disregarded. Titles which, according to every legal test, are perfect, are acquired with that confidence which is inspired by the opinion that the purchaser is safe. If there be any concealed defect, arising from the conduct of those who had held the property long before he acquired it, of which he had no notice, that concealed defect cannot be set up against him. He has paid his money for a title good at law, he is innocent, whatever may be the guilt of others, and equity will not subject him to the penalties attached to that guilt. All titles would be insecure, and the intercourse between man and man would be very seriously obstructed, if this principle be overturned.

The famous case of Swift v. Tyson, 41 U.S. (16 Pet.) 1 (1842) involved this principle. Justice Story adopted the eminently sensible federal rule that a bona fide purchaser without notice of earlier title defects takes clear of the defects, rather than the much less sensible rule of some states that failed to protect purchasers without notice. The fact that the adopted rule was *federal* turned out to be much more significant than the fact that it was better. See Hovenkamp, Enterprise and American Law: 1836–1937, ch. 8 (1991).

2. The *Guerin* case is an example of constructive notice from muniments (documentary evidence) of title. The lesson to be learned: a title searcher should not merely look to see *that* particular documents have been recorded, she must also read the recorded documents. A recorded document that refers to an unrecorded document imparts constructive notice of the unrecorded document and its contents.

But how far should this rule be carried? Suppose that a grant recorded twenty years earlier simply refers to an oil and gas lease. The apparent lessor is dead, the identity of the lessee is uncertain, and the reference in the grant says nothing about the terms or duration of the lease. Furthermore, there is no evidence on the property itself of petroleum exploration or pumping. A rule that any subsequent purchaser takes subject to such an outstanding lease could substantially reduce the market value of the property, even though the lease itself, were it ever found, might be invalid or expired. Prominent scholars have criticized a broad doctrine of muniments of title. For example, L. Simes & C. Taylor, The Improvement of Conveyancing by Legislation 101–02 (1985), conclude that the doctrine places an unreasonable burden upon title searchers.

Under a few state statutes, a reference to a secondary document in the document being examined imparts notice of the secondary document only if it is recorded and the reference indicates where it is recorded. See L.C. Stroh & Sons, Inc. v. Batavia Homes & Development Corp., 17 A.D.2d 385, 234 N.Y.S.2d 401 (1962). Other state statutes provide that unrecorded instruments referred to in recorded instruments are binding only on the parties to the second instrument and do not impart notice of their contents to anyone else. See, e.g., Colo.Rev.Stat. § 38–35–108 (2002). See also Gilpin Investment Co. v. Blake, 712 P.2d 1051 (Colo.App.1985). Does such a statute undermine the doctrine of muniments of title?

3. Suppose that a deed is properly recorded but improperly indexed as a result of a clerk's negligence. As a practical matter, a misindexed deed is a lost deed if the records use a grantor-grantee index. Most courts hold that someone who has recorded his instrument has fulfilled his obligation, and the instrument imparts constructive notice to subsequent grantees even if it is "lost" because improperly indexed. See Maddox v. Astro Investments, 45 Ohio App.2d 203, 343 N.E.2d 133 (1975); Jones v. Folks, 149 Va. 140, 140 S.E. 126 (1927). Others have held that a misindexed deed does not impart constructive notice; therefore a subsequent grantee takes clear of the earlier deed. See Mortensen v. Lingo, 13 Alaska 419, 99 F.Supp. 585 (1951), in which the court decided that it "seems unreasonable to require each person interested in ascertaining the status of the title to any piece of property to examine every page of a great number of volumes."

The question of notice and the misindexed deed may have an economic answer: the loss should be assigned to the person who can avoid it most cheaply. In the *Mortensen* case, supra, the judge characterized both the first purchaser, whose deed was improperly indexed, and the defendant, the subsequent purchaser, as equally "innocent." However, the first purchaser could have returned to the recording office a week or two after his deed was deposited with the recorder and made sure that it was entered and indexed properly. If he had found that the deed was not indexed where it should have been, he could have had the index corrected. The subsequent purchaser, by contrast, could discover the defect only by examining every recorded conveyance. The better rule is the one expressed in the *Mortensen* case. See also Greenpoint Mortgage Funding, Inc. v. Schlossberg, 390 Md. 211, 888 A.2d 297 (2005).

4. Similar analysis applies when the chain of title contains an after-acquired interest. Suppose these facts:

> On July 1, 1998, O conveys Blackacre to A by a general warranty deed, and A records; however at the time O has no title.

> On July 15, 1998, O acquires title to Blackacre, which immediately "shoots through" to A under the doctrine of estoppel by deed, or after-acquired title (See Schwenn v. Kaye in § 16.2.3, supra).

> On July 18, 1998, O conveys Blackacre to B, whose title search reveals that O acquired title on July 15, but does not reveal the previous conveyance to A, because a grantor-grantee index search does not ordinarily anticipate that someone conveyed property away before they acquired it.

In a dispute between A and B, who wins? Early cases tended to favor A, on the theory that the deed was in fact recorded and could be discovered by a diligent, although somewhat expansive title search. Ayer v. Philadelphia & Boston Face Brick Co., 159 Mass. 84, 34 N.E. 177 (1893).

But once again, a rule that assigns the loss to the lowest cost avoider is easy to develop. B's title search in the above example will not uncover the July 1 conveyance from O to A unless B and all other searchers in B's position search every grantor for pre-acquisition conveyances—a procedure that would add greatly to the search's cost and uncover relatively few instances of premature conveyances.

By contrast, A should know from her own title search at the time of the July 1 conveyance that O did not have title at that time. At relatively little cost, A can re-record his title after O actually receives it. The best rule is to place the burden of perfecting the chain of title on A. See Sabo v. Horvath, 559 P.2d 1038 (Alaska 1976), which follows this reasoning; and see Johanson, Estoppel by Deed and the Recording System: the "Ayer Rule" Re-examined, 43 B.U.L.Rev. 441 (1963) (discussing Ayer v. Philadelphia & Boston Face Brick Co., 159 Mass. 84, 34 N.E. 177 (1893)). For an exhaustive discussion of the problem, see Philbrick, Limits of Record Search and Therefore Notice, 93 U.Pa.L.Rev. 125, 391–440 (1944). An analogous situation arises when the earlier deed to an encumbrance such as a servitude is recorded, but only in one of the affected chains of title. See Witter v. Taggart, reprinted infra in § 16.3.5.

COHEN v. THOMAS & SON TRANSFER LINE, INC.

Supreme Court of Colorado, en banc (1978).
196 Colo. 386, 586 P.2d 39.

Groves, Justice.

Parties to this appeal are Thomas & Son Transfer Line, Inc., the lessee, and the Cohens who purchased the leased premises from the lessors. The district court denied the lessee's claim for specific performance of a right of first refusal against the Cohens. The Colorado Court of Appeals reversed. Colo.App., 574 P.2d 107 (1977). We granted certiorari, and now affirm.

The question is whether the Cohens, who had constructive notice of the lessee's tenancy, had a duty to inquire of the lessee concerning the lessee's rights in the leased property.

In 1968, the lessors, who are not parties to this appeal, leased 10 contiguous lots to the lessee for five years at a monthly rental of $400. The lease contained provisions regarding holding over, a right of first refusal and an option to renew. The latter two provisions were typewritten below other printed provisions of the lease. It was never recorded.

After the lease expired on May 1, 1973, the lessee retained possession and continued to pay rent. No discussion occurred concerning any extension or renewal of the lease, but the lessee agreed to pay $550 per month beginning November 1, 1973. Throughout, the entire property was used by the occupant as a truck terminal.

On July 26, 1974, the lessors sold the leased property, together with four additional lots, to the Cohens. The lessee first learned of the sale on August 5, 1974, and protested both to the lessors and the Cohens.

Prior to their purchase of the property, the Cohens were aware of the lessee's tenancy and questioned the lessors about the existence of a lease. The lessors responded that the written lease had expired and that the lessee had a month-to-month tenancy. The Cohens did not ask to see the expired lease, nor did they question the lessee directly.

The trial court concluded that, since the lease did not require notice to the lessor, the lessee had exercised its option to renew by remaining in possession and continuing to pay rent after May 1, 1973. The court of appeals agreed.

The parties disputed whether the right of first refusal provision was part of the renewed leasing agreement. The district court held that, since the first refusal option was embodied in a typewritten provision set off by parentheses which was separate from the rest of the lease terms, it consequently was not renewed along with the other terms of the tenancy. The court of appeals reversed, stating that where a lease provides that its extension or renewal is to be on the same terms and conditions as were in the original lease, the renewal extends a right of first refusal option.

Since the parties have not appealed the decision that the lease was renewed in its entirety, the only remaining question is whether the Cohens took title subject to the lessee's right of first refusal. The notice provisions of the Colorado recording statute provide:

> "All ... instruments ... affecting the title to real property, ... may be recorded in the office of the county clerk and recorder ... and no such instrument or document shall be valid as against any class of persons with any kind of rights, except between the parties thereto and such as have notice thereof...." Section 38–35–109, C.R.S.1973.

Both courts below correctly determined that the lessee's possession put the Cohens on constructive notice of the terms of the lessee's tenancy.

Having such notice, the Cohens took title subject to any rights of the lessee which reasonable inquiry would have revealed.

* * *

Under these circumstances, we conclude that reasonable inquiry would have included inquiry of the lessee who was the sole tenant in possession. *Keck v. Brookfield*, 2 Ariz.App. 424, 409 P.2d 583 (1965). We do not agree with the Cohens' contention that the prospective purchaser with constructive notice has a duty to inquire concerning only possessory rights.

The rule that prospective purchasers must inquire of lessees in possession as to their rights does not have universal application. Exceptions typically have been applied in cases where possession was consistent with record title; where the tenant occupied only part of the leased property or the tenant's possession was not sufficiently visible to put a prospective purchaser on inquiry notice; and where various equitable defenses were pertinent.

The exceptions pertain to issues not presented by this case. We note them to show that the proper parties and the scope of inquiry may vary according to circumstances.

Neither do we have a situation involving multiple tenants. Here, the lessee as the sole tenant was the proper party of whom to inquire. The Cohens had actual knowledge of the lessee's possession for 13 years and did not avail themselves of an opportunity for inquiry when they inspected the leased premises shortly before they purchased the property.

We conclude that, having notice of the tenancy by virtue of the lessee's possession, the Cohens had a duty to inquire of the lessee concerning its rights in the leased property. They take subject to all rights which would have been revealed by reasonable inquiry, including the lessee's right of first refusal.

Judgment affirmed.

PRINGLE, J., does not participate.

Notes and Questions

1. Gates Rubber Co. v. Ulman, 214 Cal.App.3d 356, 262 Cal.Rptr. 630 (1989), held that where a lease was recorded and was consistent with the tenant's possession, the buyer did not have constructive notice of an *un*recorded option to purchase. This is a sensible exception to the *Cohen* rule, isn't it? When the lease is recorded, notice from the tenant's possession should extend only to those things inconsistent with the recorded lease.

2. In most jurisdictions, leases do not need to be recorded unless they exceed a statutorily specified number of years, generally three to seven. For example, see the Massachusetts recording statute, reprinted supra at § 16.3.1, which applies only to leases of seven years or longer. A purchaser of the landlord's interest takes subject to a shorter lease even though it is unrecorded and the purchaser has no knowledge of the lease. As the *Cohen* case illustrates, this can become a major problem if the lease contains an option to purchase or a preemption, which effectively gives the lessee the right to buy the property out from under a prospective purchaser by matching his offer. One solution to the problem is to require that options to purchase—even those contained in short term leases—be recorded. After all, even though the option or preemption can be exercised only during the lease term, once exercised it creates an interest of potentially indefinite duration. In the *Cohen* case the court took the alternate route: it placed on the subsequent purchaser a duty to inspect the contents of the lease. Perhaps this rule will work when the subsequent purchaser has actual notice of an unrecorded lease; but what will happen when the purchaser has no such notice?

3. The title searcher, whether lawyer, abstract company, or title insurance company, can be held liable for a negligently conducted search that fails to uncover an imperfection in the title. Traditionally, this liability was contractual, and only the purchaser of the title searcher's services could recover, for only he met the requirement of privity of contract. See Sickler v. Indian River Abstract & Guaranty Co., 142 Fla. 528, 195 So. 195 (1940). The more recent trend has been to permit a broader class of plaintiffs to recover. Some courts confine recovery to persons known by the title searcher to be relying on the quality of the abstract. For example, if a seller hires the title searcher to produce evidence of marketable title, the searcher should know that the *buyer* will rely on the report, and the buyer should be able to recover for negligence. First Amer. Title Ins. Co. v. First Title Serv. Co. of the Florida Keys, 457 So.2d 467 (Fla.1984). Likewise, mortgage lenders will almost certainly rely on title reports before making a loan. See Westport Bank and Trust Co. v. Corcoran, Mallin and Aresco, 221 Conn. 490, 605 A.2d 862 (1992), which held that a law firm could be liable to a lender for a negligent title search where the search was solicited by the borrower who directed that a copy of the results be supplied to the prospective lender. Other courts have gone further, and permitted all persons who foreseeably might be injured—including future purchasers—to recover. Williams v. Polgar, 391 Mich. 6, 215 N.W.2d 149 (1974).

§ 16.3.4 RECORD CHAIN OF TITLE PROBLEMS

(Refer to the sample statutes at the beginning of this section)

1. In 2000, O, who owns Blackacre in fee simple absolute, conveys an easement for an underground pipeline across Blackacre to A who does not immediately record.

In March, 2003, O conveys Blackacre to B in fee simple absolute by a deed which says nothing about the easement. B does not immediately record.

In April, 2003, A records the O–A easement.

In May, 2003, B records the O–B deed.

Does B acquire Blackacre free and clear of the easement or subject to the easement in a notice jurisdiction? In a race-notice jurisdiction? In a race jurisdiction?

2. In January, 2006, O, not having any title, conveys Blackacre to A who fails to record.

In March, 2006, O, still not having any title, conveys Blackacre to B who immediately records.

In June, 2006, X, the record owner of Blackacre, conveys Blackacre to O.

In August, 2006, A records the O–A deed.

Who owns Blackacre? What would a title search in a grantor-grantee index reveal?

3. In 2001, J, the owner of Blackacre, grants R a mortgage on Blackacre. R does not immediately record.

In 2002, J sells Blackacre to E, a bona fide purchaser, by a deed that makes no mention of the J–R mortgage. E does not record.

In 2003, E conveys to M, another bona fide purchaser, who immediately records.

In March, 2004, R records the J–R mortgage.

In April, 2004, E records the J–E deed.

In a dispute between R and M, who wins in a race-notice jurisdiction? A notice jurisdiction?

4. In 2002, T, who owns Blackacre, sells Blackacre to C, who fails to record.

In 2004, T sells Blackacre again to W, a bona fide purchaser who immediately records.

In March, 2005, C learns about the T–W deed, raises a loud fuss and files a lawsuit against T and W. News about the lawsuit is published in all the papers.

In June, 2005, W sells Blackacre to F, who knows about the controversy.

In September, 2005, C sues F as well, claiming that C has paramount title because F had actual knowledge of the 2002 conveyance to C. Who prevails? See Corey v. United Savings Bank, Mutual, 52 Or.App. 263, 628 P.2d 739 (1981).

5. In 2004, B, who is record owner in fee simple absolute of Blackacre, gives Blackacre to A, but reserves a life estate for herself. A fails to record his interest.

In 2005, B sells Blackacre to E, who has actual knowledge of the gift to A. E records the B–E deed promptly.

In 2006, E sells Blackacre to S, a bona fide purchaser without notice.

Who owns Blackacre?

6. On January 5, 2005, O executes a deed conveying Blackacre to B. On the same date B executes a mortgage to Bank. The B–Bank mortgage is immediately recorded.

On March 1, 2005, the O–B deed is recorded.

On April 1, 2005, B conveys Blackacre to B–1 who claims to take free of the B–Bank mortgage. Is B–1 correct? See Bank of New York v. Nally, 820 N.E.2d 644 (Ind.2005).

§ 16.3.5 THE DUTY TO RECORD AND THE DUTY TO SEARCH

WITTER v. TAGGART

Court of Appeals of New York (1991).
78 N.Y.2d 234, 573 N.Y.S.2d 146, 577 N.E.2d 338.

BELLACOSA, JUDGE.

Plaintiff Witter and defendants Taggarts are East Islip neighboring property owners. Their homes are on opposite sides of a canal on the south shore of Long Island. Witter's home is north of the canal and the Taggarts' home and dock are across the canal on the south side. The Winganhauppauge or Champlin's Creek lies immediately west of both parcels. Their property dispute arose when the Taggarts erected a 70–foot long dock on their canal-side frontage. This was done after a title search revealed that their deed expressly permitted building the dock and reflected no recorded restrictions in their direct property chain against doing so. Witter complained of a violation of his scenic easement to an unobstructed view of the creek and an adjacent nature preserve, which he claims is protected by a restrictive covenant contained in his chain of title. He sued to compel the Taggarts to dismantle and remove the dock and to permanently enjoin any such building in the future.

We * * * decide whether the covenant recited in Witter's chain of title to his purported "dominant" land, which appears nowhere in the direct chain of title to the Taggarts' purported "servient" land, burdens the Taggarts' property. We agree with the lower courts that it does not. * * * The homes of these neighbors are located on lots which have been separately deeded through a series of conveyances, originally severed and conveyed out by a common grantor, Lawrance. Lawrance conveyed one parcel of his land to Witter's predecessor in title in 1951. The deed contained the restrictive covenant providing that "no docks, buildings, or other structures [or trees or plants] shall be erected [or grown]" on the grantor's (Lawrance's) retained servient lands to the north "which shall obstruct or interfere with the outlook or view from the [dominant] premises" over the Winganhauppauge Creek. That deed provided that the covenant expressly ran with the dominant land. William and Susan Witter purchased the dominant parcel in 1963 by deed granting them all the rights of their grantor, which included the restrictive covenant. In 1984, Susan Witter transferred her interest to William Witter alone. After common grantor Lawrance died, his heirs in 1962 conveyed his retained, allegedly servient, land to the Taggarts' predecessor in title. Lawrance's deed made no reference to the restrictive covenant benefiting the Witter property and neither did the heirs' deed to the Taggarts' predecessors. The restrictive covenant was also not included or referenced in any of the several subsequent mesne conveyances of that allegedly servient parcel or in the deed ultimately to the Taggarts in 1984. Quite to the contrary, the Taggarts' deed specifically permitted them to build a dock on their parcel.

* * * [T]he law has long favored free and unencumbered use of real property, and covenants restricting use are strictly construed against those seeking to enforce them. Courts will enforce restraints only where their existence has been established with clear and convincing proof by the dominant landowner (Huggins v. Castle Estates, 36 N.Y.2d at 430, 369 N.Y.S.2d 80, 330 N.E.2d 48).

The guiding principle for determining the ultimate binding effect of a restrictive covenant is that "[i]n the absence of actual notice before or at the time of * * * purchase or of other exceptional circumstances, an owner of land is only bound by restrictions if they appear in some deed of record in the conveyance to [that owner] or [that owner's] direct predecessors in title." (Buffalo Academy of Sacred Heart v. Boehm Bros., 267 N.Y. 242 at 250, 196 N.E. 42). Courts have consistently recognized and applied this principle, which provides reliability and certainty in land ownership and use (see, Doyle v. Lazarro, 33 A.D.2d 142, 144, 306 N.Y.S.2d 268, aff'd without opn. 33 N.Y.2d 981, 353 N.Y.S.2d 740, 309 N.E.2d 138).

In *Buffalo Academy*, we held that a restrictive covenant did not run with the dominant land, but added that even if it did, the servient landowners were not bound because the deed to the servient land did not reflect the covenant. We noted that this rule is "implicit in the acts providing for the recording of conveyances." The recording act (Real Property Law art. 9) was enacted to accomplish a twofold purpose: to protect the rights of innocent purchasers who acquire an interest in property without knowledge of prior encumbrances, and to establish a public record which will furnish potential purchasers with actual or at least constructive notice of previous conveyances and encumbrances that might affect their interests and uses (see, Andy Assocs. v. Bankers Trust Co., 49 N.Y.2d, supra, at 20, 424 N.Y.S.2d 139, 399 N.E.2d 1160).

The recording statutes in a grantor-grantee indexing system charge a purchaser with notice of matters only in the record of the purchased land's chain of title back to the original grantor. *Buffalo Academy* recognized that a "purchaser is not normally required to search outside the chain of title," and is not chargeable with constructive notice of conveyances recorded outside of that purchaser's direct chain of title where, as in Suffolk County (see, Real Property Law § 316–a), the grantor-grantee system of indexing is used. This is true even if covenants are included in a deed to another lot conveyed by the same grantor (Doyle v. Lazarro, 33 A.D.2d at 144, 306 N.Y.S.2d 268; 5A Warren's Weed, Title Examination, § 5.18, at 67).

To impute legal notice for failing to search each chain of title or "deed out" from a common grantor "would seem to negative the beneficent purposes of the recording acts" and would place too great a burden on prospective purchasers (Buffalo Academy of Sacred Heart v. Boehm Bros., 267 N.Y., supra, at 250, 196 N.E. 42). Therefore, purchasers like the Taggarts should not be penalized for failing to search every chain of title branching out from a common grantor's roots in order to unearth potential restrictive covenants. They are legally bound to search only within their own tree trunk line and are bound by constructive or inquiry notice only of restrictions which appear in deeds or other instruments of conveyance in that primary stem. Property law principles and practice have long established that a deed conveyed by a common grantor to a dominant landowner does not form part of the chain of title to the servient land retained by the common grantor. A grantor may effectively extinguish or terminate a covenant when, as here, the grantor conveys retained servient land to a bona fide purchaser who takes title without actual or constructive notice of the covenant because the grantor and dominant owner failed to record the covenant in the servient land's chain of title. One way the dominant landowner or grantor can prevent this result is by recording in the servient chain the conveyance creating the covenant rights so as to impose notice on subsequent purchasers of the servient land (see, 3 Powell, Real Property ¶ 424, at 34–271—34–272). It goes almost without repeating that definiteness, certainty, alienability and unencumbered use of property are highly desirable objectives of property law. To restrict the Taggarts because of Lawrance's failure to include the covenant in the deed to his retained servient land, or for the failure by Witter's predecessors to insist that it be protected and recorded so as to be enforceable against the burdened property, would seriously undermine these paramount values, as well as the recording acts.

Affirmed.

N<small>OTES AND</small> Q<small>UESTIONS</small>

1. It is sensible to impose an obligation to record an easement or restrictive covenant on the owner of the benefit (dominant estate) rather than the burden (servient estate). The owner of the benefit has an economic incentive to have the covenant recorded, while the owner of the burden may have an incentive that it not be recorded. Nevertheless, many courts disagree with the *Witter* holding. See, e.g., Guillette v. Daly Dry Wall, Inc., 367 Mass. 355, 325 N.E.2d 572 (1975); Stegall v. Robinson, 81 N.C.App. 617, 344 S.E.2d 803 (1986).

2. O, who owns Blackacre, conveys an easement appurtenant across Blackacre to A, who owns adjacent Whiteacre. A records the easement in Whiteacre's chain of title but not Blackacre. A few years later O conveys a possessory interest in Blackacre to B, by a deed that makes no reference to the easement. Has the easement been extinguished? See Puchalski v. Wedemeyer, 185 A.D.2d 563, 586 N.Y.S.2d 387 (1992).

§ 16.4   TITLE INSURANCE

DAVID HAPGOOD, THE SCREWING OF THE AVERAGE MAN 90–94 (1974)

Life and health insurance as businesses must cope with the fact that the risks they insure against are real: certain in one case, likely in the other. Everyone dies, and many get sick. Title insurance avoids this problem by insuring against a risk that, with exceedingly rare exceptions, does not exist at all. It is the perfect kind of insurance to sell. It is also . . . the expert's dream: he charges for his services, then he charges a second time for insurance against his possible incompetence.

The average man confronts title insurance only rarely—which helps account for the industry's survival. Their only encounter occurs when the average man buys a home and thereby submits himself to that remarkable ceremony known as the closing. As the buyer is led to the closing table for the ritual sacrifice, he sees half a dozen experts eyeing him with friendly appetite as they finger their carving knives. He may identify the title expert, but as they all fall upon him to slice off their respective hunks of closing costs, he is hardly likely to remember among all his other losses the cut of his flesh that went to title insurance. Probably he will lump them all together in his mind and console himself that it won't happen again soon, if ever.

Title insurance derives from the title search. The purpose of the search is to find out whether the seller really owns the property free and clear of any claims against it. Someone has to go and leaf through the records down at the county courthouse. In theory, the search may go back to the original colonial charter or land grant (pre-colonial owners' rights not being recognized) in order to ward off the insurer's favorite nightmare: the person who bursts through your door, waving a valid title dating from 1756, and shouts: "Get off my property!" Now that just about never happens, although Vincent Price did once claim about half the Southwest on a phony Spanish land grant—but that was in a movie, *Baron of Arizona,* and even on film Price wasn't able to make his claim stick. In the real world, the title search is usually limited to recent years, and often goes back no further than the last time the property was sold, when of course the title was also searched. Already at this stage, even before title insurance has appeared, the search can generate considerable make-work for the experts. Take, for example, the developer who buys a hundred acres, pays to have its title searched, and eventually sells it off in 400 quarter-acre lots. Each of the 400 buyers will have to pay for his own title search, though all their lots are part of the property that was just searched, and, if the referral system is working properly, all 400 will be steered to the same experts who did the original search—and who now can charge for it 400 times over.

The job of title searching can be tedious in some cases because the records are scattered around in a disorder guaranteed to keep a few more county employees on the payroll. (A centralized standard record-keeping system could easily be installed and would wipe out the entire title industry.) Still, the skill required is not great; you can learn the basics of title searching in a day or two. But experts have to eat too, and so the business is monopolized by lawyers and title companies. The companies often keep their own set of efficient property records, but they still charge from $100 to $500 as if they were groping around the original land grants down at the courthouse.

The work is easy and the searchers are experts—but evidently their product cannot be counted upon. That's why the buyer also needs title insurance to protect him in case there's something wrong with his title. Of course, the buyer thought he had paid the title searchers to do just that. But now he finds out he has to buy more protection, often from the same people who did the search: the kind of double exaction that is frowned on by the more ethical members of the Mafia. He may say, if he has faith in experts or if he figures he can sue the title searchers if something goes wrong, that he doesn't want the insurance, he'll take his chances on just the search. But no: the bank says if he wants a mortgage he has to buy the title insurance. The reason given is that the insurance is required to enable the bank to resell the mortgage on the national market, where— here we close another circle—it will most likely be bought by a life insurance company. If the buyer says, since he has to take the insurance he doesn't want to buy the title search, and if he can make that stick, then he will be issued a policy that exempts from coverage any title defect that would have been uncovered by a search—a policy, in other words, that fails to cover the only danger for which the insurance was needed in the first place.

The amount of the title insurance screwing can be calculated from the industry's figures. The average cost of title insurance, a one-shot payment, is $129. Title insurers pay out 2.5 per cent of their income in claims. That gives us $3.22 as the average value of that $129 policy. The rest, just short of $126, minus a bit for overhead, is expert make-work. Although not a major screwing for the average man because it happens so seldom, from the industry's point of view it comes fairly close to the ideal of selling a service and providing nothing at all in return.

* * *

ANOTHER VIEW OF TITLE INSURANCE

Would the title insurance industry survive if it did no more good than Hapgood says? Why would banks and other mortgage companies, who make money selling real property financing, insist on title insurance if it is worthless? That would mean that title insurance simply raises the price of buying a house and fewer people would buy houses. The banks would earn less.

Title insurers are professional risk takers. Furthermore, they are informed risk takers. The title insurance company more often than not combines a title-searching service with a title-insuring service. For example, the title insurance company may look at a large number of conveyances in which a twenty-year title search was done and conclude that in only .1% of those situations did the grantee end up having a defective title. From this information it may decide that the expected loss to a piece of property due to failure of title when there has been a twenty-year search is $150. If the twenty-year title search itself costs $200, the company will be able to perform the twenty-year search and insure any remaining risk for a total cost of $350. Importantly, if a sixty-year search costs $500, it is not a good investment *even* if it provides 100% assurance of good title (in fact the assurance would almost certainly be less than 100%). In this case a little knowledge about the costs of obtaining information tells us that bearing the risk of some uncertainty is more efficient than acquiring the information. For her $350 premium the purchaser will get a twenty-year title search and the title insurer's assumption of the remaining risk, as long as the loss is covered by the policy.

Several courts have held that—contrary to popular belief—the title company has no independent duty to do a title search; it is an *insurer*. The question comes up when the company creates an exception to its coverage for a particular defect in title, but a reasonable search would have uncovered such a defect. In that case the insurer has liability, if at all, for negligence, not for breach of the insurance contract. Among the decisions refusing to impose such liability are Brown's Tie & Lumber v. Chicago Title, 115 Idaho 56, 764 P.2d 423 (1988); Walker Rogge v. Chelsea Title & Guaranty Co., 116 N.J. 517, 562 A.2d 208 (1989).

§ 16.4.1   THE TITLE POLICY

OWNER TITLE INSURANCE POLICY
American Land Title Association Owner Policy—amended 10-21-1987

ATTORNEYS' TITLE GUARANTY FUND, INC.

CHAMPAIGN, ILLINOIS

SUBJECT TO THE EXCLUSIONS FROM COVERAGE, THE EXCEPTIONS FROM COVERAGE CONTAINED IN SCHEDULE B AND THE CONDITIONS AND STIPULATIONS, **Attorneys' Title Guaranty Fund, Inc.**, an Illinois corporation, herein called The Fund, insures, as of Date of Policy shown in Schedule A, against loss or damage, not exceeding the Amount of Insurance stated in Schedule A, sustained or incurred by the insured by reason of:

1. Title to the estate or interest described in Schedule A being vested other than as stated therein;

2. Any defect in or lien or encumbrance on the title;

3. Unmarketability of the title;

4. Lack of a right of access to and from the land.

The Fund will also pay the costs, attorneys' fees and expenses incurred in defense of the title, as insured, but only to the extent provided in the Conditions and Stipulations.   [G9766]

EXCLUSIONS FROM COVERAGE

The following matters are expressly excluded from the coverage of this policy, and The Fund will not pay loss or damage, costs, attorneys' fees or expenses which arise by reason of:

1. (a) Any law, ordinance, or governmental regulation (including but not limited to building and zoning laws, ordinances or regulations) restricting, regulating, prohibiting or relating to (i) the occupancy, use or enjoyment of the land; (ii) the character, dimensions or location of any improvement now or hereafter erected on the land; (iii) a separation in ownership or a change in the dimensions or area of the land or any parcel of which the land is or was a part; or (iv) environmental protection, or the effect of any violation of these laws, ordinances or governmental regulations, except to the extent that a notice of the enforcement thereof or a notice of a defect, lien or encumbrance resulting from a violation or alleged violation affecting the land has been recorded in the public records at Date of Policy.

   (b) Any governmental police power not excluded by (a) above, except to the extent that a notice of the exercise thereof or a notice of a defect, lien or encumbrance resulting from a violation or alleged violation affecting the land has been recorded in the public records at Date of Policy.

2. Rights of eminent domain unless notice of the exercise thereof has been recorded in the public records at Date of Policy, but not excluding from coverage any taking which has occurred prior to Date of Policy which would be binding on the rights of a purchaser for value without knowledge.

3. Defects, liens, encumbrances, adverse claims or other matters:

   (a) created, suffered, assumed or agreed to by the insured claimant;

   (b) not known to The Fund, not recorded in the public records at Date of Policy, but known to the insured claimant and not disclosed in writing to The Fund by the insured claimant prior to the date the insured claimant became an insured under this policy;

   (c) resulting in no loss or damage to the insured claimant;

   (d) attaching or created subsequent to Date of Policy; or

   (e) resulting in loss or damage which would not have been sustained if the insured claimant had paid value for the estate or interest insured by this policy.

CONDITIONS AND STIPULATIONS

1. DEFINITION OF TERMS.

The following terms when used in this policy mean:

(a) "insured": the insured named in Schedule A, and, subject to any rights or defenses The Fund would have had against the named insured, those who succeed to the interest of the named insured by operation of law as distinguished from purchase including, but not limited to, heirs, distributees, devisees, survivors, personal representatives, next of kin or corporate or fiduciary successors.

(b) "insured claimant": an insured claiming loss or damage.

(c) "knowledge" or "known": actual knowledge, not constructive knowledge or notice which may be imputed to an insured by reason of the public records as defined in this policy or any other records which impart constructive notice of matters affecting the land.

(d) "land": the land described or referred to in Schedule A, and improvements affixed thereto which by law constitute real property. The term "land" does not include any property beyond the lines of the area described or referred to in Schedule A, nor any right, title, interest, estate or easement in abutting streets, roads, avenues, alleys, lanes, ways or waterways, but nothing herein shall modify or limit the extent to which a right of access to and from the land is insured by this policy.

(e) "mortgage": mortgage, deed of trust, trust deed or other security instrument.

(f) "public records": records established under state statutes at Date of Policy for the purpose of imparting constructive notice of matters relating to real property to purchasers for value and without knowledge. With respect to Section 1(a) (iv) of the Exclusions From Coverage, "public records" shall also include environmental protection liens filed in the records of the clerk of the United States district court for the district in which the land is located.

(g) "unmarketability of the title": an alleged or apparent matter affecting the title to the land, not excluded or excepted from coverage, which would entitle a purchaser of the estate or interest described in Schedule A to be released from the obligation to purchase by virtue of a contractual condition requiring the delivery of marketable title.

2. CONTINUATION OF INSURANCE AFTER CONVEYANCE OF TITLE.

The coverage of this policy shall continue in force as of Date of Policy in favor of an insured only so long as the insured retains an estate or interest in the land, or holds an indebtedness secured by a purchase money mortgage given by a purchaser from the insured, or only so long as the insured shall have liability by reason of covenants of warranty made by the insured in any transfer or conveyance of the estate or interest. This policy shall not continue in force in favor of any purchaser from the insured of either (i) an estate or interest in the land, or (ii) an indebtedness secured by a purchase money mortgage given to the insured.

3. NOTICE OF CLAIM TO BE GIVEN BY INSURED CLAIMANT.

The insured shall notify The Fund promptly in writing (i) in case of any litigation as set forth in Section 4(a) below; (ii) in case knowledge shall come to an insured hereunder of any claim of title or interest which is adverse to the title to the estate or interest, as insured, and which might cause loss or damage for which The Fund may be liable by virtue of this policy; or (iii) if title to the estate or interest, as insured, is rejected as unmarketable. If prompt notice shall not be given to The Fund, then as to the insured all liability of The Fund shall terminate with regard to the matter or matters for which prompt notice is required; provided, however, that failure to notify The Fund shall in no case prejudice the rights of any insured under this policy unless The Fund shall be prejudiced by the failure and then only to the extent of the prejudice.   [G9767]

4. DEFENSE AND PROSECUTION OF ACTIONS; DUTY OF INSURED CLAIMANT TO COOPERATE.

(a) Upon written request by the insured and subject to the options contained in Section 6 of these Conditions and Stipulations, The Fund, at its own cost and without unreasonable delay, shall provide for the defense of an insured in litigation in which any third party asserts a claim adverse to the title or interest as insured, but only as to those stated causes of action alleging a defect, lien or encumbrance or other matter insured against by this policy. The Fund shall have the right to select counsel of its choice (subject to the right of the insured to object for reasonable cause) to represent the insured as to those stated causes of action and shall not be liable for and will not pay the fees of any other counsel. The Fund will not pay any fees, costs or expenses incurred by the insured in the defense of those causes of action which allege matters not insured against by this policy.

(b) The Fund shall have the right, at its own cost, to institute and prosecute any action or proceeding or to do any other act which in its opinion may be necessary or desirable to establish the title to the estate or interest, as insured, or to prevent or reduce loss or damage to the insured. The Fund may take any appropriate action under the terms of this policy, whether or not it shall be liable hereunder, and shall not thereby concede liability or waive any provision of this policy. If The Fund shall exercise its rights under this paragraph, it shall do so diligently.

(c) Whenever The Fund shall have brought an action or interposed a defense as required or permitted by the provisions of this policy, The Fund may pursue any litigation to final determination by a court of competent jurisdiction and expressly reserves the right, in its sole discretion, to appeal from any adverse judgment or order.

(d) In all cases where this policy permits or requires The Fund to prosecute or provide for the defense of any action or proceeding, the insured shall secure to The Fund the right to so prosecute or provide defense in the action or proceeding, and all appeals therein, and permit The Fund to use, at its option, the name of the insured for this purpose. Whenever requested by The Fund, the insured, at The Fund's expense, shall give The Fund all reasonable aid (i) in any action or proceeding, securing evidence, obtaining witnesses, prosecuting or defending the action or proceeding, or effecting settlement; and (ii) in any other lawful act which in the opinion of The Fund may be necessary or desirable to establish the title to the estate or interest as insured. If The Fund is prejudiced by the failure of the insured to furnish the required cooperation, The Fund's obligations to the insured under the policy shall terminate, including any liability or obligation to defend, prosecute or continue any litigation, with regard to the matter or matters requiring such cooperation.

5. PROOF OF LOSS OR DAMAGE.

In addition to and after the notices required under Section 3 of these Conditions and Stipulations have been provided The Fund, a proof of loss or damage signed and sworn to by the insured claimant shall be furnished to The Fund within 90 days after the insured claimant shall ascertain the facts giving rise to the loss or damage. The proof of loss or damage shall describe the defect in, or lien or encumbrance on the title, or other matter insured against by this policy which constitutes the basis of loss or damage and shall state, to the extent possible, the basis of calculating the amount of the loss or damage. If The Fund is prejudiced by the failure of the insured claimant to provide the required proof of loss or damage, The Fund's obligations to the insured under the policy shall terminate, including any liability or obligation to defend, prosecute or continue any litigation, with regard to the matter or matters requiring such proof of loss or damage.

In addition, the insured claimant may reasonably be required to submit to examination under oath by any authorized representative of The Fund and shall produce for examination, inspection and copying, at such reasonable times and places as may be designated by any authorized representative of The Fund, all records, books, ledgers, checks, correspondence and memoranda, whether bearing a date before or after Date of Policy, which reasonably pertain to the loss or damage. Further, if requested by any authorized representative of The Fund, the insured claimant shall grant its permission, in writing, for any authorized representative of The Fund to examine, inspect and copy all records, books, ledgers, checks, correspondence and memoranda in the custody or control of a third party, which reasonably pertain to the loss or damage. All information designated as confidential by the insured claimant provided to The Fund pursuant to this Section shall not be disclosed to others unless, in the reasonable judgment of The Fund, it is necessary in the administration of the claim. Failure of the insured claimant to submit for examination under oath, produce other reasonably requested information or grant permission to secure reasonably necessary information from third parties as required in this paragraph shall terminate any liability of The Fund under this policy as to that claim.

6. OPTIONS TO PAY OR OTHERWISE SETTLE CLAIMS; TERMINATION OF LIABILITY.

In case of a claim under this policy, The Fund shall have the following additional options:

(a) To Pay or Tender Payment of the Amount of Insurance.

To pay or tender payment of the amount of insurance under this policy together with any costs, attorneys' fees and expenses incurred by the insured claimant, which were authorized by The Fund, up to the time of payment or tender of payment and which The Fund is obligated to pay.

Upon the exercise by The Fund of this option, all liability and obligations to the insured under this policy, other than to make the payment required, shall terminate, including any liability or obligation to defend, prosecute or continue any litigation, and the policy shall be surrendered to The Fund for cancellation.

(b) To Pay or Otherwise Settle with Parties Other than the Insured or with the Insured Claimant.

(i) To pay or otherwise settle with other parties for or in the name of an insured claimant any claim insured against under this policy, together with any costs, attorneys' fees and expenses incurred by the insured claimant which were authorized by The Fund up to the time of payment and which The Fund is obligated to pay; or

(ii) to pay or otherwise settle with the insured claimant the loss or damage provided for under this policy, together with any costs, attorneys' fees and expenses incurred by the insured claimant which were authorized by The Fund up to the time of payment and which The Fund is obligated to pay.

Upon the exercise by The Fund of either of the options provided for in paragraphs (b)(i) or (ii), The Fund's obligations to the insured under this policy for the claimed loss or damage, other than the payments required to be made, shall terminate, including any liability or obligation to defend, prosecute or continue any litigation.

7. DETERMINATION, EXTENT OF LIABILITY AND COINSURANCE.

This policy is a contract of indemnity against actual monetary loss or damage sustained or incurred by

the insured claimant who has suffered loss or damage by reason of matters insured against by this policy and only to the extent herein described.

(a) The liability of The Fund under this policy shall not exceed the least of:

(i) the Amount of Insurance stated in Schedule A; or,

(ii) the difference between the value of the insured estate or interest as insured and the value of the insured estate or interest subject to the defect, lien or encumbrance insured against by this policy.

(b) In the event the Amount of Insurance stated in Schedule A at the Date of Policy is less than 80 percent of the value of the insured estate or interest or the full consideration paid for the land, whichever is less, or if subsequent to the Date of Policy an improvement is erected on the land which increases the value of the insured estate or interest by at least 20 percent over the Amount of Insurance stated in Schedule A, then this policy is subject to the following:

(i) where no subsequent improvement has been made, as to any partial loss, The Fund shall only pay the loss pro rata in the proportion that the Amount of Insurance at Date of Policy bears to the total value of the insured estate or interest at Date of Policy; or

(ii) where a subsequent improvement has been made, as to any partial loss, The Fund shall only pay the loss pro rata in the proportion that 120 percent of the Amount of Insurance stated in Schedule A bears to the sum of the Amount of Insurance stated in Schedule A and the amount expended for the improvement.

The provisions of this paragraph shall not apply to costs, attorneys' fees and expenses for which The Fund is liable under this policy, and shall only apply to that portion of any loss which exceeds, in the aggregate, 10 percent of the Amount of Insurance stated in Schedule A.

(c) The Fund will pay only those costs, attorneys' fees and expenses incurred in accordance with Section 4 of these Conditions and Stipulations.

8. APPORTIONMENT.

If the land described in Schedule A consists of two or more parcels which are not used as a single site, and a loss is established affecting one or more of the parcels but not all, the loss shall be computed and settled on a pro rata basis as if the amount of insurance under this policy was divided pro rata as to the value on Date of Policy of each separate parcel to the whole, exclusive of any improvements made subsequent to Date of Policy, unless a liability or value has otherwise been agreed upon as to each parcel by The Fund and the insured at the time of the issuance of this policy and shown by an express statement or by an endorsement attached to this policy.

9. LIMITATION OF LIABILITY.

(a) If The Fund establishes the title, or removes the alleged defect, lien or encumbrance, or cures the lack of a right of access to or from the land, or cures the claim of unmarketability of title, all as insured, in a reasonably diligent manner by any method, including litigation and the completion of any appeals therefrom, it shall have fully performed its obligations with respect to that matter and shall not be liable for any loss or damage caused thereby.

(b) In the event of any litigation, including litigation by The Fund or with The Fund's consent, The Fund shall have no liability for loss or damage until there has been a final determination by a court of competent jurisdiction, and disposition of all appeals therefrom, adverse to the title as insured.

(c) The Fund shall not be liable for loss or damage to any insured for liability voluntarily assumed by the insured in settling any claim or suit without the prior written consent of The Fund. [G9786]

10. REDUCTION OF INSURANCE; REDUCTION OR TERMINATION OF LIABILITY.

All payments under this policy, except payments made for costs, attorneys' fees and expenses, shall reduce the amount of the insurance pro tanto.

11. LIABILITY NONCUMULATIVE.

It is expressly understood that the amount of insurance under this policy shall be reduced by any amount The Fund may pay under any policy insuring a mortgage to which exception is taken in Schedule B or to which the insured has agreed, assumed or taken subject, or which is hereafter executed by an insured and which is a charge or lien on the estate or interest described or referred to in Schedule A, and the amount so paid shall be deemed a payment under this policy to the insured owner.

12. PAYMENT OF LOSS.

(a) No payment shall be made without producing this policy for endorsement of the payment unless the policy has been lost or destroyed, in which case proof of loss or destruction shall be furnished to the satisfaction of The Fund.

(b) When liability and the extent of loss or damage has been definitely fixed in accordance with these Conditions and Stipulations, the loss or damage shall be payable within 30 days thereafter.

13. SUBROGATION UPON PAYMENT OR SETTLEMENT.

(a) The Fund's Right of Subrogation.

Whenever The Fund shall have settled and paid a claim under this policy, all right of subrogation shall vest in The Fund unaffected by any act of the insured claimant.

The Fund shall be subrogated to and be entitled to all rights and remedies which the insured claimant would have had against any person or property in respect to the claim had this policy not been issued. If requested by The Fund, the insured claimant shall transfer to The Fund all rights and remedies against any person or property necessary in order to perfect this right of subrogation. The insured claimant shall permit The Fund to sue, compromise or settle in the name of the insured claimant and to use the name of the insured claimant in any transaction or litigation involving these rights or remedies.

If a payment on account of a claim does not fully cover the loss of the insured claimant, The Fund shall be subrogated to these rights and remedies in the proportion which The Fund's payment bears to the whole amount of the loss.

If loss should result from any act of the insured claimant, as stated above, that act shall not void this policy, but The Fund, in that event, shall be required to pay only that part of any losses insured against by this policy which shall exceed the amount, if any, lost to The Fund by reason of the impairment by the insured claimant of The Fund's right of subrogation.

(b) The Fund's Rights Against Non-insured Obligors.

The Fund's right of subrogation against non-insured obligors shall exist and shall include, without limitation, the rights of the insured to indemnities, guaranties, other policies of insurance or bonds, notwithstanding any terms or conditions contained in those instruments which provide for subrogation rights by reason of this policy.

14. ARBITRATION.

Unless prohibited by applicable law, either The Fund or the insured may demand arbitration pursuant to the Title Insurance Arbitration Rules of the American Arbitration Association. Arbitrable matters may include, but are not limited to, any controversy or claim between The Fund and the insured arising out of or relating to this policy, any service of The Fund in connection with its issuance or the breach of a policy provision or other obligation. All arbitrable matters when the Amount of Insurance is $1,000,000 or less shall be arbitrated at the option of either The Fund or the insured. All arbitrable matters when the Amount of Insurance is in excess of $1,000,000 shall be arbitrated only when agreed to by both The Fund and the insured. Arbitration pursuant to this policy and under the Rules in effect on the date the demand for arbitration is made or, at the option of the insured, the Rules in effect at Date of Policy shall be binding upon the parties. The award may include attorneys' fees only if the laws of the state in which the land is located permit a court to award attorneys' fees to a prevailing party. Judgment upon the award rendered by the arbitrator(s) may be entered in any court having jurisdiction thereof.

The law of the situs of the land shall apply to an arbitration under the Title Insurance Arbitration Rules.

A copy of the Rules may be obtained from The Fund upon request.

15. LIABILITY LIMITED TO THIS POLICY; POLICY ENTIRE CONTRACT.

(a) This policy together with all endorsements, if any, attached hereto by The Fund is the entire policy and contract between the insured and The Fund. In interpreting any provision of this policy, this policy shall be construed as a whole.

(b) Any claim of loss or damage, whether or not based on negligence, and which arises out of the status of the title to the estate or interest covered hereby or by any action asserting such claim, shall be restricted to this policy.

(c) No amendment of or endorsement to this policy can be made except by a writing endorsed hereon or attached hereto signed by either the President, a Vice President, the Secretary, an Assistant Secretary, or validating officer or authorized signatory of The Fund.

16. SEVERABILITY.

In the event any provision of the policy is held invalid or unenforceable under applicable law, the policy shall be deemed not to include that provision and all other provisions shall remain in full force and effect.

17. NOTICES, WHERE SENT.

All notices required to be given The Fund and any statement in writing required to be furnished The Fund shall include the number of this policy and shall be addressed to The Fund at 2408 Windsor Place, P.O. Box 3036, Champaign, Illinois 61826-3036. [G3769]

Schedule A

Policy No.:   2286283   Effective Date: May 22, 1991 at 04:00 PM

Amount of Insurance: $111,500.00

1. Name of Insured:

_____

2. The estate or interest in the land described herein and which is covered by this policy is, at the effective date hereof, vested in the named insured and is a fee simple (if other specify same):

_____

3. The land referred to in this policy is described as follows:

_____

Schedule B

OPA No.:   2286283

This Policy does not insure against loss or damage (and The Fund will not pay costs, attorneys' fees or expenses) that arise by reason of the following exceptions:

STANDARD EXCEPTIONS

1. Rights or claims of parties in possession not shown by the public records.

2. Encroachments, overlaps, boundary line disputes, and any matters that would be disclosed by an accurate survey and inspection of the premises.

3. Easements, or claims of easements, not shown by the public records.

4. Any lien, or right to a lien, for services, labor, or material heretofore or hereafter furnished, imposed by law and not shown by the public records.

5. Taxes or special assessments that are not shown as existing liens by the public records.

NOTES AND QUESTIONS

1. Title insurance is generally purchased at the time of a land transfer and generally insures either the principal purchasers, the institution financing the transaction, or both. The policy is not periodic, as casualty or life insurance, but insures title as long as the named insured holds her interest. Any new transferee will have to purchase a new policy. The policy printed above is approved by the American Land Title Association (ALTA), and is in widespread use.

2. Suppose Smith or Seale in Messersmith v. Smith, 60 N.W.2d 276 (N.D.1953), supra, had obtained title insurance when they purchased their interests. Would their loss be covered by the title policy?

3. In comparison to other forms of insurance, title insurers pay out an extraordinarily low percentage of their collected premiums in claims. See U.S. Dept. of Justice, The Pricing and Marketing of Insurance 253 (1977) (suggesting a ratio of claims to premiums of 5% to 10%); Payne, Conveyancing Practice and the Feds: Some Thoughts About RESPA, 29 Ala.L.Rev. 339, 380 (1978) (suggesting 3%–10%). Does this mean that title insurance is overpriced? The title insurance companies are quick to answer no. They point out that the title insurance premium covers not only the assumption of the risk of loss (which is the only thing most other kinds of insurers do), but also the cost of the title search itself.

The title insurance industry also has been subject to repeated charges of price fixing. In fact, there is evidence suggesting that, at least in some states, title insurers have fixed the prices of title searches and escrow fees, but have continued to compete with one another by giving "commissions" or "rebates" to banks or brokers who direct their clients to that company. Commonly the banker or broker is an expert, while the home seller or purchaser is inexperienced and inclined to follow the expert's recommendation. As a result, the decision about whether to purchase title insurance and from whom often is made by the professional, who does not pay for it. Rather, he earns more if he convinces a client to purchase and earns a "commission" from the title company. He will likely select the title company that pays the highest "commission." In this situation, title companies bid against each other for the business of a particular bank or broker. This theory is consistent with information suggesting that price fixing is common among title insurers, but that they nevertheless earn only a competitive rate of return. See Roussel & Rosenberg, Lawyer–Controlled Title Insurance Companies: Legal Ethics and the Need for Insurance Department Regulation, 48 Fordham L.Rev. 25 (1979); Quiner, Title Insurance and the Title Insurance Industry, 22 Drake L.Rev. 711 (1973). The Supreme Court has held that the fact of state insurance regulation did not give title insurers an immunity from federal antitrust liability. The defendants were ordered to cease and desist from fixing prices for title search and examination services. Federal Trade Comm'n v. Ticor Title Ins. Co., 504 U.S. 621 (1992).

One state, Iowa, has made the sale of title insurance illegal in the state. Iowa Code Ann. § 515.48(10). The constitutionality of that statute was upheld in Chicago Title Ins. Co. v. Huff, 256 N.W.2d 17 (Iowa 1977). The evidence indicated that during the relevant period the plaintiff had collected $370,000 in title insurance premiums on Iowa real estate but had paid out nothing in claims. The court stated: "Obviously, a loss ratio of zero per cent presents a potentially lucrative source of revenue to an insurer of titles and this court cannot say the general assembly overstepped its power in barring a costly form of 'insurance' for which plaintiff's own testimony demonstrates there is little need." Id. at 27–28. See Note, Iowa's Prohibition of Title Insurance— Leadership or Folly, 33 Drake L.Rev. 683 (1984).

4. Buyers are not required by law to purchase title insurance. However, many mortgage companies require that the buyer obtain a mortgagee's policy, which is a policy that covers the amount of the loan made by the mortgagee and makes the mortgagee the beneficiary to the extent of the balance due on the loan.

Good discussions of title insurance are Uri, The Title Insurance Industry: A Reexamination, 17 Real Est. L.J. 313 (1989); Taub, Rights and Remedies Under a Title Policy, 15 Real Prop., Prob. & Tr. J. 422 (1980).

§ 16.4.2 JUDICIAL CONSTRUCTION OF THE TITLE POLICY

RYCZKOWSKI v. CHELSEA TITLE & GUARANTY CO.

Supreme Court of Nevada (1969).
85 Nev. 37, 449 P.2d 261.

THOMPSON, JUSTICE.

This is an action for damages by the record owners of land against the title insurance company for its failure to list on the policy of title insurance a recorded easement as an encumbrance upon the owners' title. The controlling issue is whether that recorded easement, granted by a predecessor in interest while the equitable owner of state land and before his acquisition of patent thereto, falls within the coverage of a policy of title insurance written for the present owners who are successors in interest of the patentee. The title insurance policy does not insure against loss or damage by reason of "easements, claims of easement, or encumbrances which are not shown by the public records."

* * * In 1946 one J. J. Cleary entered into a land sale contract with the State of Nevada (N.R.S. 321.240) and, in 1952, acquired title from the state by patent (N.R.S. 321.310). The patent contained the land sale contract number in the upper right-hand corner of the document. The land sale contract, however, was not recorded. In 1949, while enjoying his equitable interest in the land, and before acquiring legal title thereto by patent, Cleary granted a power line easement over a portion of the property to the Sierra Pacific Power Company, which document the company caused to be recorded. The easement embraced about 2.1 acres upon which the company placed its poles and power lines. Title to the patented land thereafter passed from Cleary to various persons and finally, in 1964, to the present owners. Title Guaranty (now defunct) was engaged to search the record for defects in title, and Chelsea Title to insure title to the land. The title search by Title Guaranty stopped with the 1952 recorded patent from the state. Consequently, the 1949 power company easement was not discovered, and was not listed in the title insurance policy issued by Chelsea as an encumbrance upon the owners' title. Hence, this litigation.

Snow v. Pioneer Title Insurance Company, [444 P.2d 125 (1968)], established the rule for Nevada that an instrument executed by an owner which is recorded before acquisition or after relinquishment of title is outside the chain of title. Consequently, the title searcher is not liable for its failure to discover such an instrument, and the title insurer is not liable since such an instrument falls within the exclusion of the insurance policy of "easements, liens or encumbrances not shown by the public records." We there noted that such rule is preferred in the states which use the grantor-grantee indexing system, and is justified by the practical considerations which attend title record searching.

The 1952 patent from the state to Cleary was the original source of title and the first link in the chain of title for the purposes of title searching. Thompson, Abstracts and Titles, 2d ed., §§ 817, 125. A patent is the first instrument by which title passes from the sovereign to an individual. Accordingly, the power company easement which was executed and recorded before the issuance of patent by the state was a "wild" document, not within the chain of title, and not "shown by the public records."

Affirmed.

NOTES AND QUESTIONS

1. A rule stated almost universally is that title policies, which are drafted by the insurer, must be construed against the insurer and in favor of the insured: "... Doubts, ambiguities, and uncertainties arising out of the language used must be resolved in [the insured's] favor." Coast Mut. Bldg.–Loan Ass'n v. Security Title Ins. & Guar. Co., 14 Cal.App.2d 225, 57 P.2d 1392 (1936). Did the insured in *Ryczkowski* receive the benefit of this construction? Contrast the decision in New England Federal Credit Union v. Stewart Title Guarantee Co., 171 Vt. 326, 765 A.2d 450 (2000), holding that the title insurer's obligation to cover any encumbrance contained in the "public records" included a state public health regulation that the land's sewage system violated. The court rejected the lower court's interpretation of "public records" as limited to "public land records."

2. The Nevada Supreme Court followed the modern rule defended in § 16.3.3.B, supra, that a deed recorded before the grantor acquired and recorded his own legal title does not give notice to subsequent purchasers. As *Ryczkowski* observes, this rule makes sense when the title search is made from a grantor-grantee index. However, if a recording office uses a *tract* index, in which all conveyances respecting a given tract are recorded in one place, then a deed which is recorded early is usually quite easy to find: one must simply take care to look back through the tract index for several years.

Most title insurance companies search, not through the public land records in the county clerk's office, but through their own private copy of the records. These private records are almost always organized by tract rather than by grantor-grantee, regardless of how the records in the local public office are organized. If that were the case in *Ryczkowski,* then Chelsea Title Company was simply negligent in its title search.

3. If the Nevada Court consistently applies the rule that a deed recorded prematurely must be considered as unrecorded, then did Cleary's grantees and their successors obtain Cleary's title free and clear of the power line easement as bona fide purchasers without notice of a previously created but unrecorded instrument? No. In this case, the power company not only acquired the easement but actually built the power line. As a result the

subsequent purchasers probably had notice of the easement. Likewise, many title policies exclude from their coverage defects that are known to the claimant on the date the policy issues.

Many title insurance policies exclude from their coverage any claims asserted by parties who were "in possession" at the time the policy was issued and whose claims were not recorded. Thus a loss of the insured's interest through adverse possession is generally not covered by the policy. See Bothin v. California Title Ins. & Trust Co., 153 Cal. 718, 96 P. 500 (1908).

4. In 1996 A purchases Blackacre, correctly described in the deed as a forty-acre parcel. A also purchases a title policy that contains a promise to defend against claims, but has an exception for any losses from boundary disputes if a "correct" survey showed that the disputed land was not within A's deed. A then has a professional survey performed, but the surveyor makes an error and A ends up building a fence that encroaches some twenty feet onto Whiteacre next door. A few years later the owner of Whiteacre files an ejectment claim to oust A from the encroaching strip of land. Does the title insurer have a duty to defend? Does it matter if the correctness of the survey is an issue to be established in the litigation? American Title Ins. Co. v. Carter, 670 So.2d 1115 (Fla.App.1996).

5. Most title insurance policies provide that the insurer will defend the insured's title in any litigation that attacks the insured's title and is arguably covered by the policy. Furthermore, if the insurer refuses to defend and its refusal later is found to have been in breach of the policy provision, the general contract rule respecting insurance policies applies: the liability of the title insurer will not necessarily be limited to the face amount of the policy, and the insured is entitled to recover attorneys' fees and other reasonable litigation expenses. See Ticor Title Ins. Co. of California v. American Resources, Ltd., 859 F.2d 772 (9th Cir.1988). One alternative generally available to title insurers may greatly weaken the duty to defend: insurers generally have the right simply to pay their maximum liability under the policy, and then all further duties cease to exist. Suppose, for example, that A purchases a $10,000 lot, takes out a $10,000 title insurance policy, and builds a $200,000 house on the lot. Then a plaintiff alleges that the house violates a restriction against development that the title insurer neglected to find. Under such facts the insurer generally has the right to pay A $10,000, its maximum contractual liability, and leave A to finance the lawsuit herself. See D. Burke, Law of Title Insurance § 9.3.2. (1991).

§ 16.5   THE SPECIAL ROLE OF STATUTES OF LIMITATION IN CLEARING LAND TITLES

Cal.Civ.Code § 885.020 (West 2002):

> Fees simple determinable and possibilities of reverter are abolished. Every estate that would be at common law a fee simple determinable is deemed to be a fee simple subject to a restriction in the form of a condition subsequent. Every interest that would be at common law a possibility of reverter is deemed to be and is enforceable as a power of termination.

§ 885.030 (West 2002):

(a) A power of termination of record expires at the later of the following times:

(1) Thirty years after the date the instrument reserving, transferring, or otherwise evidencing the power of termination is recorded.

(2) Thirty years after the date a notice of intent to preserve the power of termination is recorded, if the notice is recorded within the time prescribed in paragraph (1).

* * *

(b) This section applies notwithstanding any provision to the contrary in the instrument reserving, transferring, or otherwise evidencing the power of termination. . . .

§ 885.060 (West 2002):

(a) Expiration of a power of termination pursuant to this chapter makes the power unenforceable and is equivalent for all purposes to a termination of the power of record and a quitclaim of the power to the owner of the fee simple estate, and execution and recording of a termination and quitclaim is not necessary to terminate or evidence the termination of the power.

(b) Expiration of a power of termination pursuant to this chapter terminates the restriction to which the fee simple estate is subject and makes the restriction unenforceable by any other means, including, but not limited to, injunction and damages.

Notes and Questions

1. The California statute printed above applies to future interests that were created before the statute was passed. The grace period in the California statute is five years. Cal.Civ.Code § 885.070 (West 2002). Is retroactive application of a statute so as to extinguish already-existing future interests constitutional? The Supreme Court said yes in Texaco, Inc. v. Short, 454 U.S. 516 (1982), a 5–4 decision upholding an Indiana statute that extinguished "dormant," or unused, mineral interests that were not re-recorded for a period of twenty years.

Traditionally, the statutes of limitation most widely used to clear real property titles are the statutes governing actions for title or for recovery of land—that is, the adverse possession statutes. However, adverse possession statutes are frequently unreliable mechanisms for clearing titles because they are subject to many exceptions. They may not run against minors, incompetents, or other people having a legally recognized disability. Furthermore, the statutes have been the subject of such an elaborate judicial gloss that it is often difficult to determine whether an interest has actually been acquired (or lost) by adverse possession, in spite of the fact that the possession has lasted for more than the prescribed statutory period. See generally Chapter 3 supra. The modern "re-recording" statutes, such as those discussed in this section, are designed to solve some problems of clearing title by eliminating this uncertainty.

But don't statutes that require re-recording of nonpossessory interests go substantially further than an adverse possession statute? The Indiana Supreme Court thought not in its own opinion in the *Short* case, which the Supreme Court, supra, affirmed:

> Study of this Act reveals that its outstanding feature is its declaration that mineral interests are terminable. Whatever may be the exact legal dimensions of such interests, they are not greater than fee simple titles. Under the statute of limitations and the law of adverse possession a fee simple title to land is terminable. The Mineral Lapse Act can be viewed as vesting legal title in the owner of the surface rights which is free of the mineral servitude when the conditions required by it exist. A statute of limitations vests legal title in an adverse possessor as against the true legal owner when the conditions required by it exist.... Statutes of limitation are statutes of repose founded upon a rule of necessity and convenience and the well-being of society. [Citations omitted.] This act is also based upon the same rule. We do not disregard the distinctions between the two types of statutes. The element of possession is different. No cause of action has arisen in the owner of the mineral interest which is required to be prosecuted. Given these differences and aforementioned similarities, we believe that this Act is, according to its principal intent and effect, and for the purpose of constitutional analysis, analogous to acts of limitation which vests title to real and personal property.

Short v. Texaco, Inc., 273 Ind. 518, 524, 406 N.E.2d 625, 629 (1980).

§ 16.6   MARKETABLE TITLE ACTS

The traditional recording and title insurance systems discussed above attempt to give buyers assurance of good title by (1) supplying evidence of title all the way back through the title chain to the original patent from the sovereign; and (2) compensating the buyer if a defect should be successfully asserted against him. By this time you should be quite aware of the infirmities in both parts of this system.

Statutes of limitation, such as the statutes for adverse possession and the special statutes discussed in the previous section go a step further. They are designed not merely to provide evidence of the quality of a title or to compensate those who receive a defective title, but actually to *make* the title good by cutting off potentially conflicting interests that have not been asserted for a long time.

The most comprehensive statutory attempts to solve marketability problems by making title good, rather than merely by providing evidence that it is good, are the marketable record title acts, which have been passed in about one-third of the American states.[1] Marketable title acts

---

1. Connecticut, Florida, Illinois, Indiana, Iowa, Kansas, Michigan, Minnesota, Nebraska, North Carolina, North Dakota, Ohio, Oklahoma, South Dakota, Utah, Vermont, Wisconsin, and Wyoming.

accomplish this by defining a "root of title" as the most recent conveyance of the property in question older than a specified number of years—most commonly, twenty to forty—and cutting off any interest pre-existing the root that is not recorded subsequent to the root.

The concept of "root of title" is an old one: a traditional title search to the "root" of title goes all the way back to the time the land was originally conveyed to the first grantee from the sovereign who held it. In the United States, that original conveyance usually occurred more than a century ago, and in many cases it occurred more than two centuries ago. A 200 year title search would often be prohibitively expensive. The marketable record title act is designed to permit searches that go all the way back to the root of title by giving the concept of "root of title" a new meaning. Suppose that you are investigating the title to Blackacre in 1992, in a state whose marketable title act provides that the root of title predates the search date by thirty years. Suppose that Blackacre was conveyed by deed in 1940, 1952, 1959, and 1968. The root of title under the Act in this case would be the 1959 deed, for that is the most recent deed that predates the search date by at least thirty years. Suppose that the 1940 deed stated that the property was subject to an unpaid lien and that no release of the lien appears in the chain of title. However, neither the 1959 deed nor any document recorded later than that deed refers to the lien. By definition, the lien has become unenforceable and is no longer a cloud on the title. If the creditor who holds that lien wants to keep it alive in this marketable title act state, she would have to re-record it every thirty years.

The following example of a marketable record title act is taken from the Uniform Simplification of Land Transfers Act. It is printed here together with some comments written by its authors, who also discuss the statute at length in L. Simes & C. Taylor, The Improvement of Conveyancing by Legislation 3–6 (1985).

Marketable Record Title

Introductory Comment

* * * The basic idea of the marketable title act is to codify the venerable New England tradition of conducting title searches back not to the original creation of title, but for a reasonable period only. The Model Act is designed to assure a title searcher who has found a chain of title starting with a document at least 30 years old that he need search no further back in the record.

Provisions for rerecording and for protection of persons using or occupying land are designed to prevent the possibility of fraudulent use of the marketable record title rules to oust true owners of property.

Section 3–301. [Definitions]

In this Part, unless the context otherwise requires:

(1) "Marketable record title" means a title of record, as indicated in Section 3–302, which operates to extinguish interests and claims, existing before the effective date of the root of title, as stated in Section 3–304.

(2) "Records" includes probate and other official records available in the recording office.

(3) "Person dealing with real estate" includes a purchaser of real estate, the taker of a security interest, a levying or attaching creditor, a real estate contract vendee, or another person seeking to acquire an estate or interest therein, or impose a lien thereon.

(4) "Root of title" means a conveyance or other title transaction, whether or not it is a nullity, in the record chain of title of a person, purporting to create or containing language sufficient to transfer the interest claimed by him, upon which he relies as a basis for the marketability of his title, and which was the most recent to be recorded as of a date 30 years before the time marketability is being determined. The effective date of the "root of title" is the date on which it is recorded.

(5) "Title transaction" means any transaction purporting to affect title to real estate, including title by will or descent, title by tax deed, or by trustee's, referee's, guardian's, executor's, administrator's, master in chancery's, or sheriff's deed, or decree of a court, as well as warranty deed, quitclaim deed, or security interest.

Comment

The definition of root of title has been expanded to make it clear that a quitclaim deed or a forgery can be a root of title.

Section 3–302. [Marketable Record Title]

A person who has an unbroken chain of title of record to real estate for 30 years or more has a marketable record title to the real estate, subject only to the matters stated in Section 3–303. A person has an unbroken chain of title when the official public records disclose a conveyance or other title transaction, of record not less than 30 years at the time the marketability is to be determined, and the conveyance or other title transaction, whether or not it was a nullity, purports to create the interest in or contains language sufficient to transfer the interest to either:

(1) the person claiming the interest, or

(2) some other person from whom, by one or more conveyances or other title transactions of record, the purported interest has become vested in the person claiming the interest; with nothing appearing of record, in either case, purporting to divest the claimant of the purported interest.

Comment

This is the basic section which frees the holder of marketable record title from adverse claims antedating his root of title, even if the root of title is a forgery. See Marshall v. Hollywood, 224 So.2d 743 (Fla.App. 1969), affirmed 236 So.2d 114 (Fla.1970).

Section 3–303. [Matters to Which Marketable Record Title is Subject]

The marketable record title is subject to:

(1) all interests and defects which are apparent in the root of title or inherent in the other muniments of which the chain of record title is formed; however, general reference in a muniment to easements, use restrictions, encumbrances or other interests created prior to the root of title is not sufficient to preserve them (Section 3–207) unless a reference by record location is made therein to a recorded title transaction which creates the easement, use, restriction, encumbrance or other interests;

(2) all interests preserved by the recording of proper notice of intent to preserve an interest (Section 3–305);

(3) an interest arising out of a title transaction recorded after the root of title, but recording does not revive an interest previously extinguished (Section 3–304); [and]

(4) the exceptions stated in Section 3–306[; and] [.]

[(5) interests preserved by the [Torrens Title Act.]]

Comment

This section states the types of claims to which a marketable record title is subject. As mentioned in the introductory comment, any extension of this list may defeat the whole purpose of marketable title legislation.

Section 3–304. [Interests Extinguished by Marketable Record Title]

Subject to the matters stated in Section 3–303, the marketable record title is held by its owner and is taken by a person dealing with the real estate free and clear of all interests, claims, or charges whatsoever, the existence of which depends upon an act, transaction, event, or omission that occurred before the effective date of the root of title. All interests, claims, or charges, however denominated, whether legal or equitable, present or future, whether the interests, claims or charges are asserted by a person who is or is not under a disability, whether the person is within or without the state, whether the person is an individual or an organization, or is private or governmental, are null and void.

Comment

This section is designed to make absolutely clear what has already been indicated in Section 3–302, that all interests except those indicated in Section 3–303 are extinguished by marketable record title.

Section 3–305. [Effect Upon Marketable Record Title of Recording Notice of Intent to Preserve an Interest]

A person claiming an interest in real estate may preserve and keep the interest, if any, effective by recording during the 30–year period immediately following the effective date of the root of title of the person who would otherwise obtain marketable record title, a notice of intent to preserve the interest (Section 2–308). No disability or lack of knowledge of any kind on the part of anyone suspends the running of the 30–year period. The notice may be recorded by the claimant or by another person acting on behalf of a claimant who is:

(1) under a disability;

(2) unable to assert a claim on his own behalf; or

(3) one of a class, but whose identity cannot be established or is uncertain at the time of recording the notice of intent to preserve the interest.

Comment

A simple method is provided for persons whose title depends solely upon documents which have been of record for more than 30 years to prevent a later recorded document from cutting off the effect of the documents upon which they rely. Suppose real estate was owned by A in 1930 and that he conveyed to B in 1940, to C in 1950, and to D in 1960. If this Act became effective in 1977, then in 1981 C has a marketable record title free of all claims of A and B and superior to that of D. If C does not record a notice of intent to preserve his interest by 1990, D will obtain a marketable record title and C's interest will be extinguished.

Section 3–306. [Interests Not Barred by Part]

This Part does not bar:

(1) a restriction, the existence of which is clearly observable by physical evidence of its use;

(2) interests of a person using or occupying the real estate, whose use or occupancy is inconsistent with the marketable record title, to the extent that the use or occupancy would have been revealed by reasonable inspection or inquiry;

(3) rights of a person in whose name the real estate or an interest therein was carried on the real property tax rolls within 3 years of the time when marketability is to be determined, if the relevant tax rolls are accessible to the public at the time marketability is to be determined;

(4) a claim of the United States not subjected by federal law to the recording requirements of this State and which has not terminated under federal law;

[(5) mineral interests including oil, gas, sulphur, coal, and all other mineral interests of any kind, whether similar or dissimilar to those minerals specifically named.]

Comment

This list of exceptions is designed to be as limited as possible, given the restrictions imposed by federal law and the need to avoid use of marketable record title for fraudulent purposes. The provisions on use or occupancy and on tax assessment should virtually eliminate situations in which more than one person can claim marketable record title to the same property.

STATE v. HESS

Supreme Court of Minnesota (2004).
684 N.W.2d 414.

ANDERSON, PAUL H., JUSTICE.

Appellant State of Minnesota, through its Department of Natural Resources (DNR), brought this quiet title action to determine ownership of a strip of land formerly used as a railroad corridor and currently used as part of the Paul Bunyan State Trail. Respondents Duwayne Hess, Brian M. Sandberg, and Amelia A. Sandberg claim ownership of parts of the old railroad corridor, which corridor passes through and borders their real property in Hubbard County. The issue before us is whether an 1898 deed, which purports to convey the land used for the railroad corridor to a railroad company for right of way and for railway purposes, conveys an easement or a fee simple determinable. The district court granted summary judgment for the state, concluding that the 1898 deed conveyed a fee simple determinable and that the Marketable Title Act, Minn.Stat. § 541.023 (2002), extinguished any subsequent limitation on the conveyance. The court of appeals reversed, holding that the 1898 deed conveyed only an easement. We reverse the court of appeals.

On April 1, 1898, Thomas B. Walker and his wife Harriet G. Walker, and W.T. Joyce and Clotilde G. Joyce, conveyed their interests in the real property in question to the Brainerd and Northern Minnesota Railway Company "for and in consideration of" one dollar. The signed deed, written by hand, states that the grantors hereby grant, bargain, sell and convey unto the said company, its successors and assigns, a strip, belt or piece of land, one hundred feet, wide, extending across the following lands in Cass and Hubbard Counties, State of Minnesota, described as follows to wit[:] . . .

> Following a detailed description of the property conveyed and also following language conveying the right to erect snow fences up to 150 feet from the center line of the railway, the deed states that the grantors
>
> hereby release all damages and claims thereto, to all _____ lands, by reason of or occasioned by the Location, construction, or operation of a Railway over and upon the premises hereby conveyed. And the said Harriet G. Walker and _____ hereby _____ their rights of dower in the tracts hereby conveyed . . .

Provided that this Grant or Conveyance shall continue in force *[, so] long as the said strips of land shall be used for Right of Way and for Railway purposes; but to cease and terminate if the Railway is removed from the said strips.* [Ed. Note: Emphasis added].

Now, more than a century after this deed was executed, we must determine the meaning of the foregoing language as used by the grantors and grantees.

[By subsequent conveyances, title to the land passed to the Burlington Northern Railway Company (BNRC)] . . .

In 1985, BNRC discontinued service on 193.12 miles of its railroad line between Brainerd and Bemidji and between Bemidji and International Falls. . . .

[Thereafter,] the Minnesota Legislature authorized the DNR to purchase the corridor between Baxter and Bemidji in order to create the Paul Bunyan State Trail. BNRC subsequently conveyed the corridor to the DNR by a quitclaim deed dated September 13, 1991, which deed was recorded December 31, 1991. . . . The DNR opened the Paul Bunyan State Trail for public use in December 1991. The trail extends approximately 90 miles from Baxter to Bemidji, passing through Crow Wing, Cass, Hubbard, and Beltrami Counties. Residents and tourists presently use the trail for hiking, bicycling, horseback riding, and snowmobile riding.

On August 10, 1977, respondents Brian and Amelia Sandberg acquired a parcel of land in Hubbard County lying east of and bordering the railroad corridor at issue here. At the time of this acquisition, the railroad line was still operational. On July 29, 1993, the Sandbergs acquired an adjoining parcel of land that is bisected by the Paul Bunyan State Trail. On October 11, 1995, the Sandbergs acquired a third parcel of land east of and bordering the trail. The trail was visible and open for public use at the time of the Sandbergs' second and third acquisitions.

On December 8, 1992, respondent Duwayne Hess acquired approximately 210 acres of real property in Hubbard County that is partially adjacent to and is partially bisected by the Paul Bunyan State Trail. The trail was visible and open for public use at the time that Hess acquired his property.

In October 1998, the Sandbergs and Hess began blockading the Paul Bunyan State Trail where it crossed their respective properties. . . .

In February 2002, appellant . . . initiated this quiet title action, seeking a declaration that the DNR owns the parts of the Paul Bunyan State Trail being blockaded by the Sandbergs and Hess. . . . [The trial court granted the state] . . . summary judgment . . . On July 29, 2003, the court of appeals reversed the district court . . . The DNR petitioned for review and we granted that petition. . . .

The DNR urges us to reverse the court of appeals and adopt the district court's conclusions of law. The district court concluded that the 1898 Walker/Joyce deed conveyed a fee simple determinable, subject to the limitation "so long as the said strips of land shall be used for Right of Way and for Railway purposes; but to cease and terminate if the Railway is removed from the said strips." Having concluded that the interest conveyed in 1898 was a fee simple determinable, the court went on to conclude that the DNR owns the subject property in fee simple. It did so because notice of a claim to the contrary was not given within 40 years of the 1898 deed; thus, all limitations on the conveyance were extinguished in accordance with the Marketable Title Act, Minn.Stat. § 541.023 (2002).

Hess and the Sandbergs urge us to affirm the court of appeals, which concluded that the 1898 Walker/Joyce deed created an easement for a right of way rather than a fee simple determinable. After concluding that the 1898 deed conveyed an easement ... Based on these conclusions, the court of appeals held that the district court erred in its interpretation of the law and Hess and the Sandbergs were the fee owners of the land in question. . . .

A fee simple determinable is an interest in real property subject to the limitation that the property reverts to the grantor upon the occurrence of a specified event. . . . A fee simple determinable is typically conveyed through language with the operative words "until," "so long as," or "during," which indicate that the grantor retains a possibility of reverter upon the occurrence of the stated event or condition. . . . An easement, in contrast, is an entitlement to the use or enjoyment of the land rather than an interest in the real property itself. . . . An easement does not convey an estate; rather, it passes only a right of use. . . .

We have considered deeds that convey an interest in a strip of land to a railroad company before. In *Chambers v. Great Northern Power Co.,* 100 Minn. 214, 219, 110 N.W. 1128, 1129–30 (1907), we held that title to land acquired in condemnation proceedings for right of way purposes was in the nature of either an easement or a fee simple determinable. We concluded in *Chambers* that "a mere easement was granted," rather than a fee simple absolute. *Id.* at 219, 110 N.W. at 1129–30. We recognized, however, that the distinction between an easement and a fee simple determinable was immaterial to the resolution of the case.

> It [is] immaterial whether the title amounted to a mere easement, or a qualified or terminable fee. Whatever the nature of the title, it would terminate whenever the company failed to perform the very function which it was created to perform, viz., operate a railroad over the land.

Id. at 219, 110 N.W. at 1130.

In *Norton v. Duluth Transfer Ry.,* 129 Minn. 126, 131, 151 N.W. 907, 908 (1915), we again considered the nature of the conveyance to a railroad company by a deed purporting to convey land for right of way purposes. In *Norton,* the appellants argued that the deed at issue "conveyed an absolute fee title limited only as to use, namely, railroad right of way purposes, and that a failure to use it for that purpose or at all would not terminate the absolute title thus granted." *Id.* at 129, 151 N.W. at 908.

We held that the conveyance of a strip of land to a railroad company for a right of way conveyed an easement rather than the absolute title for which the appellants in *Norton* argued. 129 Minn. at 131, 151 N.W. at 908.

Five years later, in *Chicago Great W. R.R. v. Zahner,* 145 Minn. 312, 314, 177 N.W. 350, 350 (1920), we held that a warranty deed conveying portions of two lots to a railroad conveyed an easement. As in *Norton,* we reasoned that the intent of the parties was to "limit the grant" and held that the interest conveyed was an easement rather than a "fee." *Zahner,* 145 Minn. at 314, 177 N.W. 350. In *Norton* and *Zahner,* we did not discuss whether the conveyances at issue could have been fees simple determinable. Presumably, we did not discuss the distinction between an easement and a fee simple determinable because, as we had recognized in *Chambers,* the interests at issue would have reverted to the grantors upon the termination of their use regardless of the distinction. Although we referred to the conveyances as easements in *Norton* and *Zahner,* the distinction between an easement and a fee simple determinable was not material to the outcome of the cases. For this reason, we conclude that *Norton* and *Zahner* provide limited guidance to us in determining whether the interest conveyed by the 1898 Walker/Joyce deed was an easement or a fee simple determinable.[2]

---

2. The dissent disagrees with our analysis of our prior cases. This is a crucial point and one in which we have major disagreement. The dissent argues that *Norton* did distinguish between an easement and a fee simple determinable: "[a]n 'absolute fee title limited only as to use' *is* a fee simple determinable." It is clear from the discussion in *Norton,* however, that the appellants had argued that the deed at issue conveyed a fee simple absolute, limited only by the restriction that it could be used only for railroad purposes. *Norton,* 129 Minn. at 129, 151 N.W. at 908. This is *not* a fee simple determinable, i.e., not an interest in real property subject to the limitation that the property reverts to the grantor upon the occurrence of a specified event. *See Cons. Sch. Dist. No. 102,* 243 Minn. at 163, 66 N.W.2d at 884. There was no reason for the appellants in *Norton* to argue, or for us to discuss, whether the conveyance at issue in *Norton* was a fee simple determinable. As in *Chambers,* the distinction between an easement and a fee simple determinable was not material to the case.

For similar reasons, it is also clear from our analysis in *Zahner* that the issue before us was only whether the conveyance was an easement or a fee simple absolute. Our analysis in *Zahner* was minimal. *Zahner* states that the conveyance was not a "fee" and does not discuss whether the conveyance could have been a fee simple determinable because the distinction between an easement and a fee simple determinable was not material to resolution of the case. 145 Minn. at 314, 177 N.W. at 350.

Moreover, even if in *Norton* and *Zahner* we had discussed the possibility that the conveyance was a fee simple determinable, the analysis would not be binding on us. This is so because when *Norton* was decided in 1915, it *would not have made any difference to the outcome of the case whether the conveyance was labeled an easement or a fee simple determinable.* The dissent is suggesting that an issue that is irrelevant to the outcome of a case is part of the holding of the case. We do not believe this is compelling. Considerations made in a judicial opinion that are unnecessary to the decision in the case are dicta. *See State v. Rainer,* 258 Minn. 168, 178, 103 N.W.2d 389, 396 (1960).

Our conclusion that *Norton* and *Zahner* provide limited guidance to the issue before us is also buttressed by the following commentary:

Throughout most of the 19th century, courts made fine distinctions among the various types of property rights the railroads could acquire. But by 1900, anti-railroad animus caused many courts to hold that all ambiguities and presumptions were to be resolved in favor of the grantor landowners. *The result was that many courts simply imposed a binary structure on railroad title disputes: either the railroad acquired fee simple absolute title, allowing it to do virtually anything it wanted with its land, even if it had discontinued services and abandoned certain parcels, or the railroad merely acquired an easement or a right-of-way over the original*

The Marketable Title Act

Chambers, Norton, and *Zahner* were decided before the adoption of the Marketable Title Act, Minn.Stat. § 541.023, in 1943, which now makes it material whether a limited interest conveyed is an easement or a fee simple determinable ... The declared policy of the Marketable Title Act is to prevent restrictions on uses that have not been reasserted as a matter of record within the last 40 years from "fetter[ing] the marketability of title." Minn.Stat. § 541.023, subd. 5 (2002). We have recognized that the passage of the Marketable Title Act was "a marked departure from the policy and operation underlying our land transfer system." *Hersh Properties, LLC v. McDonald's Corp.,* 588 N.W.2d 728, 734 (Minn.1999). The Act represents "a new point of departure for the process of judicial reasoning" in real estate law. *Wichelman,* 250 Minn. at 99, 83 N.W.2d at 812 (internal quotation marks omitted).

The adoption of the Marketable Title Act is important to our analysis for two reasons. First, the Marketable Title Act now makes the difference between an easement and a fee simple determinable material to the issue before us because, as we later discuss, an interest in fee simple determinable may be subject to the Act's conclusive presumption of abandonment. Second, public policy reasons behind the Marketable Title Act, such as finality of conveyances and enforcing settled expectations, should be considered in our framework for analyzing the intent of the parties in a conveyance of land for right of way purposes in a deed.[3]

---

landowner's land, extinguishable under principles of abandonment. This binary structure elides important differences among the different property interests and their methods of acquisition.

* * * *

Judges who believe they are making things simpler by consistently finding that railroad corridor instruments always convey easements are mistaken. * * * The nature of railroad use demands that the servient fee owner has something less than a fee subject to an easement, and the easement owner has something closely approaching fee title. Fitting the interests into common-law categories is counter productive.

Danaya C. Wright & Jeffrey M. Hester, *Pipes, Wires, and Bicycles: Rails-to-Trails, Utility Licenses, and the Shifting Scope of Railroad Easements from the Nineteenth Century to the Twenty–First Centuries,* 27 Ecology L.Q. 351, 377, 384–85 (2000) (citations omitted) (emphasis added).

3. The public policy interests that underlie this issue are well described by Wright and Hester as follows.

Rural farms, bisected by a corridor, are now residential subdivisions with an undeveloped greenbelt providing recreational and utility services. When the trains did not discontinue operations until the past decade or so, the land rights of the railroads and the adjacent landowners had coexisted, in most cases, for over 100 years. Many landowners may have come and gone in that time and successive deeds may have dropped references to the railroad corridor. Quieting the interest in the long-term user makes sense on many different levels.

Property law doctrines, first and foremost, try to prevent upsetting settled expectations. Finding fee title in the railroad would further the public policy of quieting title that underlies our doctrines of adverse possession, the rule against forfeitures, marketable title acts, the rule against perpetuities, and rules against transfers of future interests. This is especially true when there is little, if any, expectation on the part of adjoining landowners to receive the windfall of a rail corridor.

Moreover, a strong public interest exists in preserving these corridors for trails and utilities. Perhaps the strongest policy motive in favor of the railroads is that evidenced by federal regulations concerning railroad services and the abandonment of rail corridors. * * * To the extent that deed construction can further protect the public's interest, especially when the cost

Following the passage of the Marketable Title Act, we considered in *Walter* whether the conveyance of a small tract of a larger parcel of real property used as a schoolhouse site was an easement or a fee simple determinable. 243 Minn. at 161–62, 66 N.W.2d at 883–84. In *Walter,* the deed at issue conveyed the premises "In Trust * * * for the use, intent and purpose of a site for a School House for the use of the Inhabitants of said School District." *Id.* at 160, 66 N.W.2d at 882. The deed also provided that "whenever said School House ceases to be used as the Public School House for the use of the Inhabitants of said School District then the said Trust shall cease and determine and the said land shall revert to [the grantors]." *Id.* Importantly, the deed did not use the word "forever" in the conveying language.

We held in *Walter* that the deed conveyed a fee simple determinable with a possibility of reverter because "the intent of the grantor, as expressed in the deed and in light of the surrounding circumstances, was to convey the land to the school district in fee for so long as it was needed for the purpose given." *Id.* at 162, 66 N.W.2d at 883. We concluded that *Norton* and *Zahner* did not apply "[b]ecause of the particular factual situations in those cases." *Id.* at 161–62, 66 N.W.2d at 883 . . .

With our prior cases and the effect of the Marketable Title Act as background, we turn now to an analysis of the 1898 Walker/Joyce deed. To determine the nature of the conveyance at issue, we look to the deed to ascertain and give effect to the intention of the parties to the instrument. *Walter,* 243 Minn. at 162, 66 N.W.2d at 883; *Lawton v. Joesting,* 96 Minn. 163, 166–67, 104 N.W. 830, 831–32 (1905). In construing the deed, we "must consider all parts of it, and the construction must be upon the entire deed, and not upon disjointed parts." *Id.* at 167, 104 N.W. at 832. If the deed's language is ambiguous, we may look to evidence of the surrounding circumstances and the situation of the parties to cast light upon their intention. *Id.*

A review of cases from other jurisdictions reveals that there is considerable conflict in the way courts construe the nature of deeds purporting to convey land where there is also a reference to a right of way or a reference to the purpose of the conveyance. . . . The decisions usually turn on a case-by-case examination of each deed. *See id.*

For the foregoing reasons, we must begin our examination of the 1898 Walker/Joyce deed by looking to the granting language to determine the intent of the parties as to the nature of the conveyance. The deed's granting clause expressly conveys land rather than mere use of the land, stating that the grantors "hereby grant, bargain, sell and convey unto the said company, its successors and assigns, a strip, belt or piece of land."

to landowners is minimal, the courts have an obligation to realize that the public is a party to these cases as well. When landowners do not have title to the corridor land, heirs of the grantor are long gone, and the corridor can continue to provide vital public utility, recreational, environmental, and transportation services, there is no reason to continue the century-old anti-railroad animus that prevailed in the days of frontier expansion.

Wright & Hester, *supra* n. 6, at 385–86 (citations omitted).

The deed also contains a habendum clause, which is a provision in a deed that traditionally could "explain, enlarge, or qualify, but [could not] contradict or defeat, the estate granted." *New York Indians v. United States,* 170 U.S. 1, 20, 18 S.Ct. 531, 42 L.Ed. 927 (1898). We must, however, read the granting and habendum clauses together "in order to arrive at the true intention, even to the extent of allowing the habendum to qualify or control the granting clause where it was manifestly intended that it should do so." *Youngers v. Schafer,* 196 Minn. 147, 153, 264 N.W. 794, 798 (1936) (internal quotation marks omitted). In the 1898 deed, the habendum clause states:

> Provided that this Grant or Conveyance shall continue in force[, so] long as the said strips of land shall be used for Right of Way and for Railway purposes; but to cease and terminate if the Railway is removed from the said strips.

Here, we conclude that the use of the phrase "so long as" in the habendum clause provides clear evidence of the grantors' intent to convey a determinable fee because the phrase "so long as" is typically used in a conveyance of a fee simple determinable. . . .

The habendum clause also states that the land shall be used "for Right of Way and for Railway Purposes." Courts have long recognized that use of the phrase "right of way" is ambiguous because the phrase may be used to describe either (1) " 'a right belonging to a party, a right of passage over any tract' " or (2) the physical " 'strip of land which railroad companies take upon which to construct their road-bed.' " *Bosell v. Rannestad,* 226 Minn. 413, 418, 33 N.W.2d 40, 43–44 (1948) (quoting *Joy v. City of St. Louis,* 138 U.S. 1, 44, 11 S.Ct. 243, 34 L.Ed. 843 (1891)). Reference to a "right of way" in a conveyance has been frequently cited as evidence that a conveyance is an easement, but use of the phrase does not necessarily mean that a conveyance is an easement. *See, e.g., Grill v. West Virginia R.R. Maint. Auth.,* 188 W.Va. 284, 423 S.E.2d 893, 896–97 (W.Va.1992); *Maberry v. Gueths,* 238 Mont. 304, 777 P.2d 1285, 1287–88 (1989). Moreover, Minnesota law does not presume that a conveyance of land to a railroad for "right of way" purposes is an easement.[4]

---

4. Subdivision 6 of the Marketable Title Act, which provides exceptions for persons in possession of real estate from the requirement of filing notice of their interests, refers specifically to "reservations or exceptions of land for right-of-way or other railroad purposes contained in deeds of conveyance" as exceptions to the subdivision. Minn.Stat. § 541.023, subd. 6 (2002). While this reference to reservations of land for right of way or other railroad purposes does not help us in determining the parties' intent as to the nature of the 1898 Walker/Joyce deed, it casts substantial doubt on respondents' argument that *Norton* and *Zahner* represent a clearly established presumption that a grant to a railroad company that limits the use of the property granted in some fashion, such as by using the phrase "right of way," conveys an easement. The Marketable Title Act protects "claim[s] of title based upon a source of title," Minn.Stat. § 541.023, subd. 1 (2002), which means that the Act protects only titles in fee simple. *Wichelman,* 250 Minn. at 105, 83 N.W.2d at 815. The Marketable Title Act itself thus presumes that "reservations or exceptions of land for right-of-way or other railroad purposes contained in deeds of conveyance" are *not necessarily* easements. To the extent that *Norton* and *Zahner* could be read to suggest that *any* conveyance of a right of way to a railroad is an easement, they are no longer good law.

The phrase "right of way" is used in the 1898 deed to indicate its purpose, which, even if we were to interpret the phrase as being used to indicate a mere right of passage, does not provide much evidence of the parties' intent as to the nature of the conveyance. As the Iowa Supreme Court has recognized:

> Determining the nature of the interest conveyed by reference to the intended use by the grantee seems frivolous in matters involving narrow tracts of land acquired by railroad companies. There is but one single reason for all such conveyances irrespective of whether the deed conveys a fee or an easement. As we stated in *Turner v. Unknown Claimants of Land,* 207 N.W.2d 544, 546 (Iowa 1973), "[o]rdinarily the parties know the tract will be used for a railway; for what other purpose would a railroad purchase a strip of land across a farm."

Lowers v. United States, 663 N.W.2d 408, 410–11 (Iowa 2003) (holding that deed labeled "Rt. of Way Deed" conveying a narrow tract of land to a railroad company conveyed a defeasible fee rather than an easement). Therefore, we conclude that the 1898 Walker/Joyce deed's reference to a "right of way" as the purpose of the conveyance does not necessarily make the conveyance an easement. . . .

Another feature of the 1898 deed that casts light on the intent of the parties is the grantors' apparent release of dower rights. "Dower rights" are an interest that a wife has in the real estate of her husband. *Stitt v. Smith,* 102 Minn. 253, 254, 113 N.W. 632, 633 (1907). An easement, because it is not title to land, does not relinquish dower rights when it is conveyed. *Chicago & S.W. R.R. v. Swinney,* 38 Iowa 182, 182 (Iowa 1874); 28 C.J.S. Dower and Curtesy § 12 (1996). The presence of the release of dower rights in the deed, while not dispositive, and unclear in this case, provides further evidence of intent to convey a fee interest rather than an easement. *See Brewer & Taylor Co. v. Wall,* 299 Ark. 18, 769 S.W.2d 753, 755 (1989).

Further, because the 1898 Walker/Joyce deed is ambiguous as to its intent to convey a fee simple determinable or an easement, we may also look to extrinsic evidence of the surrounding circumstances of the parties in relation to the conveyance, such as the subsequent conduct of the parties. . . . On June 17, 1901, W.T. Joyce and Clotilde G. Joyce, grantors in the 1898 deed, conveyed by deed their interest to land in Hubbard County adjacent to the railway corridor created by the 1898 deed. The Joyces' 1901 deed described the land conveyed and then provided:

> Excepting and reserving there from the land heretobefore conveyed to the Park Rapids and Leech Lake Railway and to the Brainerd and Northern Minnesota Railway for right-of-way.

The term "excepting," when used in a deed, typically indicates that nothing passes. . . . Furthermore, a conveyance that intends to reference a preexisting easement typically indicates that the conveyance is "subject to" the easement. . . . For these reasons, the Joyces' 1901 deed excepting from the conveyance "the land heretobefore conveyed" provides additional support that the parties to the 1898 Walker/Joyce deed intended to convey title in fee simple determinable. By excepting the land conveyed in 1898 from their 1901 conveyance, the Joyces demonstrated an understanding of the 1898 deed a mere three years later that they no longer owned the land conveyed in 1898. . . .

For all of the foregoing reasons, we agree with the district court and conclude that the parties to the 1898 Walker/Joyce deed did not intend to convey a mere easement for use of the land. Rather, we conclude that the parties intended to convey real property in fee simple determinable, subject to the limitation that the conveyance would "cease and terminate if the Railway is removed from the said strips." We believe this conclusion reflects the intent of the parties. We also believe this conclusion best serves many of the policy reasons underlying the Marketable Title Act, which, as we next discuss, should be applied to the interest conveyed in the 1898 Walker/Joyce deed. Accordingly, we reverse the court of appeals and hold that the 1898 deed conveyed title in fee simple determinable.[5]

Having concluded that the interest conveyed by the 1898 Walker/Joyce deed was a fee simple determinable, we next consider, as the district court did, whether the . . . [state] now owns the property in fee simple absolute because of the effect of the Marketable Title Act, Minn. Stat. § 541.023. The Marketable Title Act provides, in relevant part:

> As against a claim of title based upon a source of title,[6] which source has then been of record at least 40 years, no action affecting the possession or title of any real estate shall be commenced by a person, partnership, corporation, other legal entity, state, or any political division thereof, to enforce any right, claim, interest, incumbrance, or lien founded upon any instrument, event or transaction which was executed or occurred more than 40 years prior to the commencement of such action, unless within 40 years after such execution or occurrence there has been recorded in the office of the county recorder in the county in which the real estate affected is situated, a notice sworn to by the claimant or the claimant's agent or attorney setting forth the name of the claimant, a description of the real estate affected and of the instrument, event or transaction on which such claim is founded, and stating whether the right, claim, interest, incumbrance, or lien is mature or immature.

Minn.Stat. § 541.023, subd. 1 (2002). The central tenet of the Marketable Title Act is that a determination of title should be possible from an

---

5. The dissent attempts to distinguish many of the cases we cite to from other jurisdictions which support our decision. The dissent points out specific issues that distinguish those cases, going so far as to call our analysis "troubling." Here, the dissent misses the point. Courts in other jurisdictions consider many factors in ascertaining the intent of the parties as it relates to the nature of the conveyance-whether the conveyance was an easement or a fee simple determinable. We discuss many of those factors here. Our conclusion, based on the numerous factors that point to the conveyance being a fee simple determinable, is that a fee simple determinable more accurately characterizes the intent of the parties to the conveyance at issue.

6. Ed. Note. Thus, this act only affects interests that convey title, not easements]

examination of documents in the chain of title recorded in the 40–year period preceding the title search. *Hersh Properties, LLC,* 588 N.W.2d at 734. An interest is subject to the Marketable Title Act's conclusive presumption of abandonment and cannot be asserted against a claim of title based on a source of title unless the interest is preserved by filing a notice within 40 years of the creation of the interest. *Id.* at 735; Minn. Stat. § 541.023, subds. 1 and 5 (2002).

For the Marketable Title Act to extinguish an interest, two requirements must be met. First, "the party desiring to invoke the statute for his own benefit must have a requisite 'claim of title based upon a source of title, which source has then been of record at least 40 years.' " *Wichelman,* 250 Minn. at 112, 83 N.W.2d at 819. Second, "the person against whom the act is invoked must be one who is 'conclusively presumed to have abandoned all right, claim, interest . . .' in the property." *Id.*

The [state] . . . asserts that it has the requisite "claim of title based upon a source of title" from the 1898 Walker/Joyce deed, recorded in 1900, in which the Brainerd and Northern Minnesota Railway Company conveyed its interest in the property to BNRC. It is undisputed that this source has been of record for at least 40 years and that an estate in fee simple determinable is a source of title under the Marketable Title Act. *Wichelman,* 250 Minn. at 106, 83 N.W.2d at 815–16. Having concluded that the subject property conveyed in 1898 was in fee simple determinable, we conclude that the [state] . . . has the requisite "claim of title based upon a source of title."

The second requirement for extinguishment of the interest is also met. The record before us indicates that no notice of claim based on the possibility of reverter has been filed of record. Therefore, under Minn. Stat. § 541.023, subd. 5, we conclude that a presumption of abandonment arose and the Marketable Title Act extinguished the possibility of reverter created in the 1898 Walker/Joyce deed to the railroad company.

Because the possibility of reverter in the 1898 Walker/Joyce deed was extinguished, we conclude that no genuine issues of material fact exist or remain for decision. Accordingly, we reverse the court of appeals and hold that the district court was correct when it granted summary judgment for the [state because the state] . . . owns the subject property in fee simple absolute as a matter of law.

Reversed.

Dissent omitted.

NOTES AND QUESTIONS

1. The oldest statute that might be called a "marketable title act" was passed in Iowa in 1919. 1919 Iowa Acts, Ch. 270, § 1. It barred any claim that arose prior to 1900, unless the claim was pursued within one year of the date the statute was passed.

2. The application of marketable title acts to roots of title based on wild deeds raises the possibility of a nightmare something like this. In 1940 A buys

a house on Blackacre and lives there. In 1941 B, unknown to A, executes a deed giving the oil and gas rights in Blackacre to C. At the time of this conveyance B has no interest of any kind in Blackacre. C sits quietly for the statutory period, thirty years. In 1972, C sells the oil and gas rights to D, a bona fide purchaser. D immediately claims the rights against A and wins. D's title search found only the wild mineral deed from B. That deed was old enough to qualify as a statutory root of title, so D did not need to search further in order to determine whether B had good title. The only way anyone in a marketable title act state can protect herself is to file a notice of claim at intervals slightly less than the statutory root of title period. See Barnett, Marketable Title Acts—Panacea or Pandemonium?, 53 Cornell L.Rev. 45, 84 (1967). Barnett observes that very few such notices are actually filed in marketable title act states.

In Exchange Nat. Bank of Chicago v. Lawndale Nat. Bank of Chicago, 41 Ill.2d 316, 243 N.E.2d 193 (1968), the court held that the Illinois marketable title act did not permit a "wild" deed to constitute statutory root of title. In justifying its holding, the Illinois Supreme Court cited the possibility of the nightmare described above. Does the Illinois holding mean that the Act becomes useless and the conveyancer must do a title search back to the sovereign anyway? It may mean merely that the searcher must trace the chain of title through the grantee index back to the sovereign in order to insure that the chain is in fact not based on a spurious deed. However, that is generally the easiest part of the title search. Other states have interpreted their marketable title acts the same way as Illinois. See F.A. Requarth Co. v. State, 38 Ohio St.2d 77, 310 N.E.2d 581 (1974); Allen v. Farmers Union Co-operative Royalty Co., 538 P.2d 204 (Okl.1975).

Almost all marketable title acts protect A in the particular example given above by making the statute inapplicable against a person who is in possession of the property at issue. See, e.g., Minn.Stat. § 541.023, subd. 6 (West 2002). As a result, a title search in a marketable title act state should include an inquiry into who is in possession and how long he has been there.

Other acts except mineral rights from their coverage. Still others except easements or payment of taxes on the property. However, as Professor Barnett notes, just one such exception means that the title examiner must do a full title search. The acts do what they are intended to do only if they are subject to no exceptions. 53 Cornell L.Rev. at 91.

3. In Wilson v. Kelley, 226 So.2d 123 (Fla.App.1969) a Florida court held that a "wild" *quitclaim* deed could not be a "root of title" under the Florida marketable title act. Although a wild deed could constitute a root of title, the court reasoned, the deed must purport to create or transfer a specific estate held by the grantor. In this case, the quitclaim deed did not purport to transfer a specific estate, but merely transferred "all the right, title, interest, claim and demand" held by the grantors. In Travick v. Parker, 436 So.2d 957 (Fla.App.1983) another Florida court held that a quitclaim deed *could* constitute a root of title provided that the "deed itself specifically states what interest the grantors intend to convey ...," quoting Wilson v. Kelley, 226 So.2d 123, 128 (Fla.App.1969).

4. A "wild" deed may be effective to convey a real property interest—for example, the grantor may have received title after the conveyance was made and recorded, and thus the deed would be effective under the doctrine of estoppel by deed. However, a *void* deed, such as one bearing a forged signature, conveys no title. Can a void deed constitute a root of title under the marketable title act? Compare Mobbs v. Lehigh, 655 P.2d 547 (Okla.1982) with Wernle v. Bellemead Development Corp., 308 So.2d 97 (Fla.1975) and Damiano v. Weinstein, 355 So.2d 819 (Fla.App.1978). Should it matter whether the defect rendering the deed void is apparent on the face of the deed—for example, the absence of the grantor's signature?

5. Under most Marketable Title Acts any properly placed muniment of title within the statutory period is sufficient to preserve the interest. For example, suppose a searcher does a title search in 2001 in a state with a forty-year statute. Suppose an interest is created outside the chain of title, but is referred to in a document within the chain of title. The interest will be preserved, provided that the subsequent reference contains a "specific identification ... of a record title transaction which creates such ... interest." See Fencl v. City of Harpers Ferry, 620 N.W.2d 808 (Iowa 2000), which held that the city's right to an ally which had been included in a 145 year old plat but never used was preserved because both the plat and the alley were referred to in a 1950 deed constituting the root of title.

§ 16.7 LAND REGISTRATION SYSTEMS:
A SHORT NOTE ON TORRENS

At one time or another about twenty American states have experimented with a land registration system developed in the nineteenth century by South Australian Richard Robert Torrens. Today ten states,[1] Guam and Puerto Rico offer Torrens registration as an alternative to conventional title recordation. Even in those states, however, Torrens is little used, largely because the initial registration cost is very high.

Under the Torrens registration system the owner of property applies for a certificate of registration by going through a proceeding similar to the action to quiet title against all the world. Notice must be given to all persons known to have an interest in the property, and must be published for the benefit of unknown persons. Then an examiner employed by the Torrens system, or perhaps a private attorney working under contract, reports to the relevant county court about the quality of the title. Some systems additionally require that the land in question be surveyed. When this entire process has been completed the court schedules a hearing for anyone who has evidence of ownership in conflict with the evidence offered by the applicant. If no one comes forth, the court orders the preparation of a registration certificate showing title in the applicant and containing a list of exceptions or "memorials" showing any outstanding

---

1. Colorado, Georgia, Hawaii, Massachusetts, Minnesota, New York, North Carolina, Ohio, Virginia, and Washington. The statutes creating the Torrens systems in these states are cited in R. Cunningham, W. Stoebuck, and D. Whitman, The Law of Property § 11.15 (3d ed. 2000). The Illinois system was very largely repealed, effective 1997.

mortgages or liens, easements, covenants, outstanding future interests, leases, etc.

The master copy of the certificate stays with the Torrens registration office and becomes conclusive evidence of ownership in the title holder named on the certificate, as qualified by the described memorials. Each time a memorial is added or removed the Torrens office is notified and a notation is made on the master certificate. When ownership is transferred a new certificate is prepared and the list of memorials is brought up to date.

Theoretically, the Torrens system eliminates the title search. In order to determine the quality of an owner's title one need only examine the master certificate in the Torrens office. Perhaps for this reason, title companies and title insurers have been uniformly hostile toward the Torrens system. In practice, however, the Torrens system offers less protection than the above description suggests, largely because the Torrens statutes create certain exceptions—that is, the systems permit certain interests to survive even though they are not mentioned on a Torrens certificate. For example, many statutes except claims of parties in possession, mechanics liens, public rights-of-way, public tax or assessment liens, or other claims by sovereigns. To the extent these interests are protected even if they are not described on the certificate, a limited title search must be undertaken in addition to the examination of the Torrens certificate.

The most common cause of litigation or loss of title under the Torrens system is error by the registration office. Part of the Torrens registration fees are paid into an assurance fund to compensate people whose interests are lost because they were inadvertently omitted from a certificate. Because the certificate itself is conclusive as to the owner's title, an omitted interest that is not subject to one of the exceptions simply ceases to exist as against a subsequent bona fide purchaser who relied on the certificate. The person whose interest is omitted as a result of the Torrens office's negligence has a claim against the system.

Today the Torrens system is in general decline in the United States and the prospects for its revival are not particularly good. For more on the system see Bostick, Land Title Registration: An English Solution to an American Problem, 63 Ind.L.Rev. 55 (1987).

INDEX

References are to Pages

1317

References are to Pages

†